McDougal, Littell
Literature

Purple Level
YELLOW LEVEL
Blue Level
Orange Level
Green Level
Red Level

PLUS REVERSED, 1960. *Richard Anuszkiewicz.*
The Archer M. Huntington Art Gallery.
The University of Texas at Austin. The James and Mari Michener Collection.

McDougal, Littell
Literature

Yellow Level

American Literature

Donald T. Hollenbeck

English Department Head
Deerfield High School
Deerfield, Illinois

Julie West Johnson

New Trier Township High School
Winnetka, Illinois

McDougal, Littell & Company
Evanston, Illinois
New York   Dallas   Sacramento   Raleigh

Consultants

Richard Blough, former English Department Head, Emmerich Manual High School, Indianapolis, Indiana

Phyllis H. Dunning, English Department Head, R. J. Reynolds High School, Winston-Salem, North Carolina

Sandra Jackson, English teacher, Oakland Public Schools, Oakland, California

Frances M. Russell, Director of English, Winchester Public Schools, Winchester, Massachusetts

Special Contributors

Laurie A. Braun, writer and editor, La Grange, Illinois

Norman L. Frey, English Department Head, New Trier High School, Winnetka, Illinois

Joan Hollenbeck, former English teacher, Deerfield High School, Deerfield, Illinois

Ted Johnson, English Department Instructor, Indiana University Northwest, Gary, Indiana

Bernard Josefsberg, English Department, New Trier High School, Winnetka, Illinois

Susan Schaffrath, Curriculum Specialist in Language Arts and Literature, Chicago, Illinois

Marilyn Sherman, teacher and writer, Wilmette, Illinois

Acknowledgments

Teresa Palomo Acosta: For "My Mother Pieced Quilts" by Teresa Palomo Acosta, by permission of the author. American Museum of Natural History: For "Sun, My Relative," from *Anthropological Papers of the American Museum of Natural History, Havasupai Ethnography* by Leslie Spier, vol. XXIX, no. III; 1928. American Way: For "True Love" by continued on page 942

93 94 95 96 97 98 / 15 14 13 12

ISBN: 0-88343-269-2

Contents

McDougal, Littell
Literature

American Literature

MULTNOMAH FALLS. *Albert Bierstadt.*
Thomas Gilcrease Institute, Tulsa, Oklahoma.

The Gift Outright   ROBERT FROST

The land was ours before we were the land's.
She was our land more than a hundred years
Before we were her people. She was ours
In Massachusetts, in Virginia,
But we were England's, still colonials,
Possessing what we still were unpossessed by,
Possessed by what we now no more possessed.
Something we were withholding made us weak
Until we found out that it was ourselves
We were withholding from our land of living,
And forthwith found salvation in surrender.
Such as we were we gave ourselves outright
(The deed of gift was many deeds of war)
To the land vaguely realizing westward,
But still unstoried, artless, unenhanced,
Such as she was, such as she would become.

FOUR BEARS, SECOND CHIEF, IN FULL DRESS, 1832. *George Catlin.*
National Museum of American Art, Smithsonian Institution.
Gift of Mrs. Joseph Harrison, Jr.

Unit 1

The Original Land (1600–1750)

A PRETTY GIRL, 1832. *George Catlin.*
National Museum of American Art, Smithsonian Institution.
Gift of Mrs. Joseph Harrison, Jr.

Sources of the American Tradition

Contrary to what many people believe, the colonization of North America by European nations did not mark the beginning of cultural development on this continent. When Europeans began to arrive in the late fifteenth and early sixteenth centuries, Native American cultures were already flourishing here, the product of thousands of years of evolution.

THE NATIVE AMERICANS

Today, the term *Native American*, or *Indian*, all too frequently conjures up images of a painted warrior on horseback or a cluster of tepees on the endless dusty plains. These stereotypes, created in part and reinforced by American westerns, reflect only a small segment of the Native American population, and that group at one specific period of history. The broader truth is that the Native Americans were highly diverse—in language, rituals, religious customs, history, architecture, government, social organization, and in the daily tasks of making clothes, producing food, and building shelters. In the fifteenth and sixteenth centuries there were over seven hundred Indian tribes in North America. Most were peaceful people, settling their differences through negotiation, not war. Each group had its own rich mythology and folklore, a body of oral literature that served the compatible functions of providing entertainment, teaching tribal mores, and reinforcing traditions.

One concept is common to the literatures of tribes as markedly different as the cliff dwellers of the southwestern desert, the Iroquois forest dwellers of the eastern coast, and the totem carvers of the rainy Northwest. That concept is the intimate relationship between humans and nature, evidenced most clearly in a mystical, deeply religious reverence for the land. Most Native American tribes perceived the elements of nature as ancestors and relatives, as shown in the first line of the Tewa Indian poem that opens this unit: "O our Mother the Earth, O our Father the Sky."

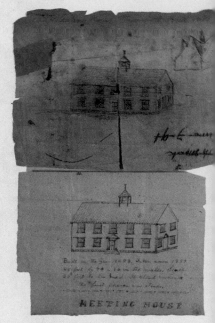

The Pilgrim meeting house, built in Plymouth in 1683.

ENGLISH COLONISTS IN AMERICA

The early English settlers in the New World were forced to cultivate a similar closeness to the land. Most soon realized that their survival depended upon their ability to understand the physi-

cal conditions and natural laws of their chosen environment. Without the help of the Native Americans, many more settlers than did would have perished in the early years.

English settlers arrived at Jamestown in 1607. Unlike the colonists who later arrived in New England, the Virginia group emigrated for purely economic reasons. The original members of the company were so unrealistic that they brought with them from England a perfumer and several tailors. Their sudden introduction to an alien environment and the resulting hardships are described graphically in *The General History of Virginia, New England, and the Summer Isles* by Captain John Smith.

THE PURITANS IN NEW ENGLAND

When the Plymouth colonists arrived in Massachusetts in 1620, they, too, faced famine, disease, severe weather, and difficulties with the Indians. In *Of Plymouth Plantation* William Bradford, for thirty-three years governor of Plymouth Colony, describes the experiences of these settlers who were later called Pilgrims.

The Pilgrims and the settlers of the larger Massachusetts Bay Colony in the Boston area were Puritans, responsible for giving New England its Puritan heritage. The Puritans wished to "purify" the Church of England, which they felt resembled the Roman Catholic Church too closely. They wanted to eliminate many church rituals and practices and to integrate religion into their daily lives in a simple, intense way. They believed in theocracy, or government organized according to religion.

PURITAN DOCTRINE

Three doctrines lie at the heart of Puritanism. One is the belief that the Bible is the sole source of God's law. This belief led the Puritans to simplify religion, removing all worldly trappings, so that individuals could have their own "covenants," or contracts, with God. Another Puritan doctrine is the belief in original sin, or the inherent evil of all human beings. As *The New England Primer* summarizes this doctrine, "In Adam's fall, we sinned all." Puritans believed that people must struggle to overcome their basically sinful natures.

The third major doctrine of Puritanism is the belief in predestination. According to this concept, God decided long ago who would achieve salvation and who would not. Grace, which leads to salvation, comes to a select few as the free gift of God, not as the result of human effort. Why then were the Puritans so concerned with morality and good works when they believed that humans had no real control over their fates? The answer, not particularly satisfying to the modern mind, is that the Puritans felt that "the elect," those who had God's grace, would be obvious by their shining goodness and their deep concern for others. Dedicated Puritans strived to establish themselves as members of the elect in the eyes of the world.

PURITAN SOCIETY

The stereotype exists that Puritans were intolerant, and in fact they were, possibly because they had to be, initially, to survive under hostile, adverse conditions, first in Europe and then in America. They became somewhat more open as the years went by. Some commentators believe that the Salem witch trials, which are described in this unit, were a final attempt on the part of the Puritan leaders to maintain a tight hold on the community. Ironically, the witch trials dealt the Puritan hierarchy a fatal blow. Puritanism did have a temporary revival around 1735, in what is called The Great Awakening. Works by Jonathan Edwards, an eloquent minister during the revival, appear in this unit.

Another stereotype about the Puritans is that they were sour and gloomy. While some of them undoubtedly were, many were not. As Stephen Vincent Benét explains in the essay about Salem in this unit, "They were a great deal more human, crotchety and colorful than the schoolbook pictures of dour-faced men in steeple-crowned

Cotton Mather, illustrious son of Increase Mather. Engraved by Peter Pelham, 1727.

Metropolitan Museum of Art.

Literature	
• John Smith (1580–1631) records history of Jamestown colony in *The General History of Virginia*	• Michael Wigglesworth (1631–1705) writes Puritan poem "The Day of Doom"
• William Bradford (1590–1657), governor of Plymouth Colony, begins writing his history *Of Plymouth Plantation*	
• *Massachusetts Bay Psalm Book*, published at Cambridge, is first work printed in colonies	
• Anne Bradstreet (1612–1672) publishes her first volume of poetry	

1600   1650

History	
• Harvard College founded	
• Puritans found Massachusetts Bay Colony	• Nathaniel Bacon (1647–1676) leads rebellion against Virginia governor
• Pilgrims land at Plymouth	
• Pilgrims and Indians celebrate first Thanksgiving Day	• Massachusetts requires public schooling
• English establish first permanent colony at Jamestown	• Anne Hutchinson is banished from Massachusetts for disagreeing with Puritan religious ideas

hats would suggest." If the Puritans criticized frivolity, it was in large part because they had to work so hard in the New World, without the comforts and leisure time available to many in European society. As their material security increased, so did their openness to humor, to brightly colored clothes, and to amusements:

THE BEGINNINGS OF THE NEW ENGLAND LITERARY TRADITION

The Puritans were highly educated people, and they appreciated art and literature. Of the literature that survives from seventeenth-century New England, most of it is of a practical or devotional nature. Diaries and histories were common. The Puritan era produced poets Anne Bradstreet and Edward Taylor, whose works appear in this unit. It is not surprising that the first American poet was a woman, for the Puritans believed in educating women and in giving them a say in important matters, revolutionary concepts at that time. The Puritans were the first colonists to insist on free public education, and they founded the first college in America, Harvard, in 1636. They also established the first printing press in the colonies in 1638.

The early literature of America—Native American, Southern, and Puritan—portrays human beings in relationship to God and to their environments. In the literature of the English colonists, stalwart human beings struggle to survive, both bodily and spiritually, in trying, often antagonistic physical and social situations. The literature dramatizes what these people endured to build a better life for future generations.

- Edward Taylor (1645?–1729) writes devotional poetry in Massachusetts

  - Cotton Mather (1663–1728) publishes *Magnalia Christi Americana*, a religious history of New England

- Jonathan Edwards (1703–1758) delivers sermon "Sinners in the Hands of an Angry God"

  - Benjamin Franklin (1706–1790) publishes first *Poor Richard's Almanack*

  - William Byrd writes *History of the Dividing Line*, journal of survey of Virginia-North Carolina border

1700   1750

- Salem conducts witchcraft trials

  - George Washington born

    - The Great Awakening, a series of religious revivals, begins to sweep the colonies

The Native Americans

TWO WEAVERS, 1946. *Harrison Begay.*
Philbrook Art Center, Tulsa, Oklahoma.

Song of the Sky Loom   *Tewa Indian*

O our Mother the Earth, O our Father the Sky,
Your children are we, and with tired backs
We bring you the gifts you love.
Then weave for us a garment of brightness;
May the warp[1] be the white light of morning,   5
May the weft[2] be the red light of evening,
May the fringes be the falling rain,
May the border be the standing rainbow.
Thus weave for us a garment of brightness,
That we may walk fittingly where birds sing,   10
That we may walk fittingly where grass is green,
O our Mother the Earth, O our Father the Sky.

---

1. **warp:** the threads running lengthwise in the loom.
2. **weft:** the horizontal threads crossing the warp threads
in a loom to make a woven fabric.

Getting at Meaning

1. This poem is really a prayer. To whom is the prayer addressed?

2. What do the Tewa Indians ask for in their prayer?

Developing Skills in Reading Literature

1. **Oral Literature.** Literature that is passed from one generation to another by performance or word-of-mouth is called oral literature.

The North American Indians chanted their poems, often with dancing and instrumental accompaniment. The poems usually were performed for a specific purpose, as a routine part of tribal ritual.

What aspects of this poem make it especially suitable for oral presentation? What gives the poem a rhythmic cadence? What seems to be the purpose of the poem?

2. **Speaker.** In a poem, the speaker is the voice that "talks" to the reader. Speaker and poet are not necessarily synonymous, although a poet may choose to speak in his or her own voice. A poet may also create a separate voice, or persona; for example, an adult poet might write a poem as if it were spoken by a child.

Who is the speaker in this poem? What makes this speaker appropriate for a selection of oral literature?

3. **Figurative Language: Personification.** Language that communicates ideas beyond the ordinary meanings of words is called figurative language. The words in a figurative expression are not literally true, but rather they stimulate vivid pictures and concepts in the mind of the reader. The general term figurative language includes specific figures of speech, one of which is personification, the attribution of human qualities to an object, animal, or idea. How is the first line of the poem an example of personification? What effect is created by this figure of speech?

4. **Metaphor and Extended Metaphor.** A metaphor is a figure of speech that compares two unlike things that have something in common. An extended metaphor compares them in several ways, making the comparison more detailed and complete.

An extended metaphor lies at the heart of this poem. What does the poem compare to "a garment of brightness"? Identify the various aspects of the comparison.

5. **Refrain and Repetend.** Notice that this poem begins and ends with the same line. This line is a refrain, a line or lines repeated with some regularity

throughout a poem. What is the effect of this refrain? What other example of refrain occurs in this poem?

Another kind of repetition is repetend, the reiteration of a word or phrase in part or all of a poem. Find examples of this literary technique in the poem. Why are repetitions of words, phrases, and lines effective in a chant?

6. **Theme.** The theme is the main idea in a work of literature. It is a writer's perception about life or humanity shared with the reader. Themes are seldom stated directly and may reveal themselves only through careful reading and thought.

The themes in this poem concern the world view of the Tewa Indians. What is their attitude toward nature? How would you describe their concept of duty? How do they perceive the deity?

Calendar Fragments   *Qee'esh Indian*

April   The first month of the year
the month when the rain has come and the grass is sprouting
when the grass begins to grow green

The spiderweb now catches butterflies and grasshoppers

June   Now the eagles fly   5

In this month the young eagles first fly

August   The brown month

In this month all is seared and brown

October   Now the little winds whistle
winds through the leafless trees
fallen leaves in the streams of water   10

This is the month of mist

December   The month of fatness
the bear sheds his hair and says
I am fat   15
the whale now is fat

In this month the deer grows fat

February   The month of leafing trees
the season of sprouting
when snakes crawl forth and frogs sing   20

Trees awaken and put out leaves

Getting at Meaning

1. Identify the characteristics of each month as described in this selection.

2. Why do you suppose the writer chose these particular months? What do you notice about the patterning of these months and the missing months?

Developing Skills in Reading Literature

1. **Structure: Poetry and Prose.** Structure is the way that a work of literature is put together. In poetry, structure refers to the arrangement of words and lines to produce a desired effect. A common structural unit in poetry is the stanza, or verse unit, of which there are numerous types.

In prose, structure refers to the arrangement of larger units or parts of a selection. Paragraphs, for example, are a basic unit in prose.

Sometimes the line between poetry and prose is a fine one. Does this selection seem more like poetry or prose? Why? What is the governing principle in the structure of the selection? How does the structure relate to the meaning of the selection?

2. **Imagery.** Imagery refers to words and phrases that re-create vivid sensory experiences for the reader. Because sight is the most highly developed sense, the majority of images are visual. Figures of speech, such as metaphor, simile, and personification, can help to create images, although images are not necessarily figures of speech.

What kinds of visual images do you find in this selection? Which sections of the piece appeal to the sense of hearing? Do any lines appeal to the sense of touch? If so, which ones?

Secotan, an Indian town in Old Virginia (now North Carolina). A sixteenth-century engraving by Théodore de Bry from a drawing by John White.

Sun, My Relative   *Havasupai Indian*

(Phonetic Transcription)	*(English Translation)*	
ĭnyáĭnᵧĭkádjădj	Sun, my relative	
màhánĭg mĭdjálĭgĭg	Be good coming out	
gwipagávà'àmàwíwŭg	Do something good for us	
pàmatàhatàhódŏg	Make me work	
gwégavà'awĭ'k matĕnyúvĭg	So I can do anything I wish in the garden.	5
i'i'nyúg teyàdjàhwálĭg ha'askà'lĭgà.	I hoe, I plant corn, I irrigate.	
ĭnyánᵧĭdj mà'ahánĭg miyàmĭg θŏmàdópmĭg	You, Sun be good going down at sunset.	
iyágĭgàsmávĭdj	We lay down to sleep	
túyà àhánàhag'ĭg'ĭ	I want to feel good.	
àsmámĭdjàálĭgĭg.	While I sleep you come up.	10
vamà'ámàmiyúdjà	Go on your course many times	
àhánàpa màwíwug.	Make good things for us men.	
tuĭ'nyàvávà'àyúg ĭnᵧúdjĭgwa'yòhag'ĭ'ĭ.	Make me always the same as I am now.	

Getting at Meaning

1. What does the speaker ask of the sun? How does the speaker perceive the sun?

2. What activities does the speaker engage in? What kind of life does the speaker want?

Developing Skills in Reading Literature

1. **Rhythm.** In poetry, rhythm is the cadence of the language, the sound pattern of a line or group of lines. This poem originally was chanted orally, and the rhythm of a chant is apparent in these lines. However, much of the original sound undoubtedly was lost in the translation.

Practice chanting the English translation of the poem. What gives it its rhythm? What kind of rhythm does the poem have? Can you link the sound to the sense of the poem?

Try chanting the poem in its original Indian language. The transcription given here is phonetic, with accent marks indicated, to help you pronounce these unfamiliar words. Do you notice a difference in the rhythm of the poem when you chant it in the Havasupai language?

2. **Theme.** What relationship between human beings and nature apparently existed in the Havasupai culture? What lines in this poem serve as clues?

Developing Writing Skills

Comparing Poems. In a well developed paragraph, compare the relationship between human beings and nature that you find in "Song of the Sky Loom" and in "Sun, My Relative." Quote specific passages from both poems to support your ideas.

I Went To Kill the Deer

Taos Pueblo Indian

I went to kill the deer
Deep in the forest where
The heart of the mountain beats
For all who live there.
An eagle saw me coming and   5
Flew down to the home of the deer
And told him that
A hunter came to kill.
The deer went with the eagle
Into the heart of the mountain   10
Safe from me who did not hear
The heart of the mountain beating.

I Have Killed the Deer

Taos Pueblo Indian

I have killed the deer.
I have crushed the grasshopper
And the plants he feeds upon.
I have cut through the heart
Of trees growing old and straight.   5
I have taken fish from water
And birds from the sky.
In my life I have needed death
So that my life can be.
When I die I must give life   10
To what has nourished me.
The earth receives my body
And gives it to the plants
And to the caterpillars
To the birds   15
And to the coyotes
Each in its own turn so that
The circle of life is never broken.

Getting at Meaning

1. What relationship exists between the deer and the eagle? Why do the animals hear "the heart of the mountain beating" when the speaker cannot?

2. How does the speaker feel about killing the deer?

3. How does the speaker justify his killing of plants and animals? How will he make reparation to the earth?

Developing Skills in Reading Literature

1. **Personification.** What inanimate elements of nature possess human qualities in these poems? Which animal has human characteristics?

2. **Theme.** Closely related to personification is what anthropologists call anthropomorphism. Anthropomorphism, which is especially common in earlier and less developed cultures, means the assigning of human qualities and motivations to animals or inanimate objects. Unlike personification, however, anthropomorphism implies a world view in which human beings and other living things are on an equal plane, in harmony with one another.

Clearly the speaker of this poem identifies closely with plants and animals and sees himself as an equal, but not superior part of nature. What does the speaker perceive as a disruptive force in the harmony of nature? Explain the speaker's theory that his own death will be a healing force in nature.

Developing Vocabulary

Connotation. Connotation is the emotional response evoked by a word. The speaker of these two poems uses the following verbs to describe his destruction of living things:

killed   crushed   cut   taken

Explain the connotation of each of these verbs. Then think of four or five additional verbs for destruction and explain their special connotations.

Funeral Oration   *Naudowessie Indian*

You still sit among us, Brother. Your person retains its usual resemblance and continues similar to ours, without any visible deficiency, except that it has lost the power of action.

But whither is that breath flown, which a few hours ago sent up smoke to the Great Spirit? Why are those lips silent, that lately delivered to us expressive and pleasing language? Why are those feet motionless, that a short time ago were fleeter than the deer on yonder mountains? Why useless hang those arms that could climb the tallest tree, or draw the toughest bow?

Alas! Every part of that frame which we lately beheld with admiration and wonder, is now become as inanimate as it was three hundred winters ago.

We will not, however, bemoan thee as if thou wast forever lost to us, or that thy name would be buried in oblivion; thy soul yet lives in the Great Country of Spirits, with those of thy nation that are gone before thee; and though we are left behind to perpetuate thy fame, we shall one day join thee.

Actuated by the respect we bore thee while living, we now come to tender to thee the last act of kindness it is in our power to bestow: that thy body might not lie neglected on the plain, and become a prey to the beasts of the field, or the fowls of the air, we will take care to lay it with those of thy predecessors who are gone before thee; hoping at the same time, that thy spirit will feed with their spirits, and be ready to receive ours, when we also shall arrive at the Great Country of Souls.

Getting at Meaning

1. Describe the dead person as he was in life. Where is the dead person now, according to the speaker?

2. Describe the speaker's conception of the "Great Country of Souls."

Developing Skills in Reading Literature

1. **Eulogy.** A eulogy is a public speech or written tribute praising the virtues or achievements of a person, especially one who has recently died. What do you picture as the setting for this eulogy? What does the speaker say in praise of the dead person?

2. **Mood.** Mood is the atmosphere or feeling that the writer creates for the reader. Although we generally tend to think of death as sad, the mood of this piece is not especially sad. Why not? What does the speaker say to lessen the sadness of the occasion? Describe the mood of the eulogy with two or three well chosen adjectives.

3. **Diction.** Diction is a writer's choice of words. The speaker of this piece uses rather formal diction. Why? Which words strike a formal note? What do words such as *thou* and *thy* suggest? Why are they appropriate in this oration?

4. **Rhetorical Question.** A question that is designed to produce an effect, usually emotional, and not an answer, is called a rhetorical question. Notice the second paragraph of this oration, which consists of four rhetorical questions. What is the effect of presenting these questions together? What gives the questions so much power?

5. **Theme.** This selection gives some insight into the Indian attitude toward death. What is the conception of the deity suggested in the oration? of an afterlife? Compare these views with those of other religions with which you are familiar.

The Puritans

MRS. ELIZABETH FREAKE AND BABY MARY, 1670–74. *Artist Unknown.*
Worcester Art Museum, Worcester, Massachusetts.

John Smith
1580–1631

John Smith spent fewer than five years in America, but his leadership was crucial to the survival of the Jamestown colony. His accounts of his colonial experience—notably *A Description of New England* (1616) and *The General History of Virginia, New England, and the Summer Isles* (1624)—were instrumental in attracting settlers to Virginia, thus assuring the eventual success of that colony.

It is difficult to separate fact from legend in the life of John Smith. By his own account, he was a soldier-of-fortune, a sea captain, and a poet who was born in Lincolnshire, England, in 1580. He served as a mercenary soldier in France and the Low Countries and was captured and sold into slavery in Turkey.

At the age of twenty-seven Smith came to the New World with the settlers of Jamestown. Too few of these colonists were practical men of action. Most were either gentlemen unused to labor or adventurers in search of quick fortunes. They chose as the site for their settlement the marshy, insect-infested coast. They ignored the need to build sturdy houses or to plant crops. By the end of the first winter, the "Starving Time," half of the population of Jamestown had died from disease, starvation, and Indian attack. Then Smith assumed the leadership of the colony. He instituted a "no-work, no-eat" policy and insisted that buildings be constructed and crops planted. He traded with the Indians for food, learned their languages and customs, and attempted to establish peaceful relations. Smith first told of his famous capture by the Indians under Chief Powhatan in *A True Relation of Occurrences and Accidents in Virginia*. In later tellings, written after his return to England in 1609, he enlarged the story and added an account of his rescue by Pocahontas.

Smith returned to America in 1614, this time to New England. He traded with the Indians, mapped the coast, and sought a position of leadership among the Puritans, but he failed to fulfill his dream of amassing a great fortune. He returned to England and died in London in 1631.

These are the Lines that shew thy Face; but those
That shew thy Grace and Glory, brighter bee:
Thy Faire-Discoueries and Fowle-Overthrowes
Of Salvages, much Civilliz'd by thee
Best shew thy Spirit; and to it Glory Wyn;
So, thou art Brasse without, but Golde within.

Smith's remarkably accurate maps are fine examples of early colonial cartography. His richly descriptive prose is important not only as some of the first writing produced in colonial America but also as a factor in stimulating the English colonization of North America.

from The General History of Virginia

John Smith published his most important work, The General History of Virginia, New England, and the Summer Isles, *in 1624. In the excerpts from* The General History *that follow, Smith, often referring to himself in the third person, recounts the tremendous hardships that the early Jamestown settlers faced during their first six months in the New World. He relates the colonists' sufferings from exhaustion, illness, and starvation. Smith also describes how the Indians alternately helped and harassed the settlers, narrating his own capture by the powerful tribe of Powhatan.*

What Happened Till the First Supply

[June 1607–January 1608]

Being thus left to our fortunes, it fortuned that within ten days scarce ten amongst us could either go or well stand, such extreme weakness and sickness oppressed us. And thereat none need marvel, if they consider the cause and reason, which was this.

Whilst the trading ships stayed, our allowance was somewhat bettered by a daily proportion of biscuit, which the sailors would pilfer to sell, give, or exchange with us for money, sassafras, furs, or love. But when they departed, there remained neither tavern, beer house, nor place of relief but the common kettle.[1] Had we been as free from all sins as gluttony and drunkenness, we might have been canonized for saints. But our President would never have been admitted, for engrossing[2] to his private [use] oatmeal, sack, oil, aqua vitae,[3] beef, eggs, or what not—[all] but the [common] kettle. That, indeed, he allowed equally to be distributed, and that was half a pint of wheat, and as much barley boiled with water for a man a day. And this having fried some twenty-six weeks in the ship's hold contained as many worms as grains, so that we might truly call it rather so much bran[4] than corn. Our drink was water, our lodgings castles in the air.

With this lodging and diet our extreme toil in bearing and planting palisadoes[5] so strained and bruised us and our continual labor in the extremity of the heat had so weakened us as were cause sufficient to have made us as miserable in our native country or any other place in the world.

From May to September those that escaped lived upon sturgeon and sea crabs. Fifty in this time we buried. . . .

But now was all our provision spent, the sturgeon gone, all helps abandoned. Each hour [we were] expecting the fury of the savages, when God, the patron of all good endeavors, in that desperate extremity so changed the hearts of the savages that they brought such plenty of their fruits and provisions that no man wanted.

And now, where some affirmed it was ill done of the Council [in England] to send forth men so badly provided, this incontradictable reason will show them plainly they are too ill advised to nourish such ill conceits.[6] First, the fault of our going was our own. What could be thought fitting or necessary we had; but what

---

1. **common kettle:** community cooking pot.
2. **engrossing** (in grōs' iŋ): taking exclusively.
3. **aqua vitae** (ak wə vit' ē): brandy or other strong liquor.
4. **bran:** the skin or husk of grains of wheat.
5. **palisadoes** (pal' ə sā' dōz): large pointed stakes set in the ground to form a fence for fortification.
6. **conceit** (kən sēt'): flight of the imagination.

we should find or want or where we should be we were all ignorant. And supposing to make our passage in two months with victual to live and the advantage of the spring to work, we were at sea five months, where we both spent our victual and lost the opportunity of the time and season to plant by the unskillful presumption of our ignorant transporters that understood not at all what they undertook.

Such actions have ever since the world's beginning been subject to such accidents, and everything of worth is found full difficulties; but nothing so difficult as to establish a commonwealth so far remote from men and means and where men's minds are so untoward[7] as neither do well themselves nor suffer others. But to proceed. . . .

[While exploring up-river in a desperate attempt to find an Indian village with a supply of food, John Smith was captured by the Indians.] The manner how they used and delivered him is as followeth:

The savages having drawn from George Cassen whither Captain Smith was gone, prosecuting[8] that opportunity they followed him with three hundred bowmen, conducted by the king of Pamunkey,[9] who in divisions searching the turnings of the river, found Robinson and Emry by the fireside. Those they shot full of arrows and slew.

[When the Indian party began to surround Smith, he defended ". . . himself with the aid of a savage, his guide, whom he bound to his arm with his garters and used him as a buckler."[10]] Then finding the captain, as is said, that used the savage that was his guide as his shield (three of them being slain and diverse others so gauld [frightened]) all the rest would not come near him. Thinking thus to have returned to his boat, regarding them as he marched more than his way, [he] slipped up to the middle in an oozy creek and his savage with him. Yet durst[11] they not come to him till being near dead with cold he threw away his arms. Then according to their composition they drew him forth and led him to the fire, where his men were slain. Diligently they chafed his benumbed limbs.

He, demanding for their captain, they showed him Opechancanough, king of Pamunkey, to whom he gave a round ivory double compass dial. Much they marveled at the play of the fly and needle, which they could see so plainly and yet not touch it because of the glass that covered them. But when he demonstrated by that globe-like jewel the roundness of the earth and skies, the sphere of the sun, moon and stars, and how the sun did chase the night round about the world continually; the greatness of the land and sea, the diversity of nations, variety of complexions, and how we were to them antipodes,[12] and many other such like matters, they all stood as amazed with admiration.

Notwithstanding, within an hour after they tied him to a tree and as many as could stand about him prepared to shoot him. But the king holding up the compass in his hand they all laid down their bows and arrows and in a triumphant manner led him to Orapaks,[13] where he was after their manner kindly feasted and well used. . . .

Not long after, early in a morning a great fire was made in a long house and a mat spread on one side, as on the other. On the one they caused him to sit and all the guard went out of the house, and presently came skipping in a great grim fellow, all painted over with coal mingled with oil; and many snakes' and weasels' skins stuffed with moss and all their tails tied together, so as they met on the crown of his head in a tassel; and round about the tassel was a coronet of feathers, the

---

7. **untoward** (un tō′ ərd): unfortunate.
8. **prosecuting** (präs′ ə kyo͞ot in′): following up.
9. **Pamunkey:** an Indian village of the Powhatan Confederacy, located on the Pamunkey River in SE Virginia.
10. **buckler:** a shield worn on the arm.
11. **durst:** dared.
12. **antipodes** (an tip′ ə dēz): direct opposites.
13. **Orapaks:** an Indian village west of Pamunkey village, located on the Chickahominy River in Virginia.

skins hanging round about his head, back, and shoulders, and in a manner covered his face; with a hellish voice and a rattle in his hand. With most strange gestures and passions he began his invocation, and environed[14] the fire with a circle of meal. Which done, three more such like devils came rushing in with the like antique tricks, painted half black, half red; but all their eyes were painted white, and some red strokes like mustachioes along their cheeks. Round about him those fiends danced a pretty while, and then came in three more as ugly as the rest, with red eyes and white strokes over their black faces. At last they all sat down right against him, three of them on the one hand of the chief priest and three on the other. Then all with their rattles began a song; which ended, the chief priest laid down five wheat corns, then straining his arms and hands with such violence that he sweat and his veins swelled, he began a short oration. At the conclusion they all gave a short groan, and then laid down three grains more. After that began their song again, and then another oration, ever laying down so many corns as before, till they had twice encircled the fire. That done, they took a bunch of little sticks prepared for that purpose, continuing their devotion, and at the end of every song and oration they laid down a stick betwixt the divisions of corn. Till night neither he nor they did either eat or drink; and then they feasted merrily with the best provisions they could make. Three days they used this ceremony, the meaning whereof they told him was to know if he intended them well or no. The circle of meal signified their country, the circles of corn the bounds of the sea, and the sticks his country. They imagined the world to be flat and round, like a trencher,[15] and they in the middest. . . .

[Smith was exhibited in various Indian villages, and] At last they brought him to Werowocomoco,[16] where was Powhatan, their emperor. Here more than two hundred of those grim courtiers stood wondering at him as [if] he had been a monster, till Powhatan and his train had put themselves in their greatest braveries. Before a fire upon a seat like a bedstead he sat covered with a great robe made of raccoon skins, and all the tails hanging by. On either hand did sit a young wench[17] of sixteen or eighteen years, and along on each side the house two rows of men. And behind them as many women, with all their heads and shoulders painted red, many of their heads bedecked with the white down of birds but everyone with something, and a great chain of white beads about their necks.

At his entrance before the king all the people gave a great shout. The queen of Appomattoc was appointed to bring him water to wash his hands, and another brought him a bunch of feathers instead of a towel to dry them. Having feasted him after their best barbarous manner they could, a long consultation was held. But the conclusion was: two great stones were brought before Powhatan, then as many as could laid hands on him, dragged him to them, and thereon laid his head. And being ready with their clubs to beat out his brains, Pocahontas, the king's dearest daughter, when no entreaty could prevail, got his head in her arms and laid her own upon his to save him from death. Whereat the emperor was contented he should live to make him hatchets and her bells, beads, and copper; for they thought him as well of all occupations as themselves. For the king himself will make his own robes, shoes, bows, arrows, pots; plant, hunt, or do anything so well as the rest.

Two days after, Powhatan having disguised himself in the most fearful manner he could, caused Captain Smith to be brought forth to a great house in the woods, and there upon a

---

14. **environed** (in vī' rənd): formed a ring around.
15. **trencher:** a wooden platter for serving meat.
16. **Werowocomoco:** an Indian village SE of Orapaks, and fronting on the York River in Virginia.
17. **wench:** young, female servant.

mat by the fire to be left alone. Not long after from behind a mat that divided the house, was made the most doleful noise he ever heard. Then Powhatan, more like a devil than a man, with some two hundred more as black as himself, came unto him and told him now they were friends and presently he should go to Jamestown to send him two great guns and a grindstone, for which he would give him the country of Capahowasick,[18] and forever esteem him as his son Nantaquaus.

So to Jamestown with twelve guides Powhatan sent him. That night they quartered in the woods, he still expecting (as he had done all this long time of his imprisonment) every hour to be put to one death or other, for all their feasting. But Almighty God (by His divine providence) had mollified the hearts of those stern barbarians with compassion. The next morning betimes they came to the fort, where Smith, having used the savages with what kindness he could, he showed Rawhunt, Powhatan's trusty servant, two demi-culverins [small cannon] and a millstone to carry Powhatan. They found them somewhat too heavy. But when they did see him discharge them, being loaded with stones, among the boughs of a great tree loaded with icicles, the ice and branches came so tumbling down that the poor savages ran away half dead with fear. But at last we regained some conference with them, and gave them such toys and sent to Powhatan, his women, and children such presents as gave them in general full content. . . .

Now, every once in four or five days, Pocahontas with her attendants brought him so much provision that saved many of their lives, that else for all this had starved with hunger.

His relation of the plenty he had seen, especially at Werowocomoco, and of the state and bounty of Powhatan (which till that time was unknown) so revived their dead spirits (especially the love of Pocahontas) as all men's fear was abandoned.

Thus you may see what difficulties still crossed any good endeavor, and the good success of the business being thus oft brought to the very period of destruction. Yet you see by what strange means God hath still delivered it. . . .

---

18. **Capahowasick:** an Indian village located SE of Werowocomoco village in Virginia.

Getting at Meaning

1. Describe the hardships that Smith and his group experience in their first months at Jamestown. Why are they at a disadvantage when the ships leave?

2. For what does Smith criticize the president of his company?

3. How many men in the original company apparently died between May and September of 1607?

4. What causes the hostile Indians to have a change of heart and help the colonists?

5. Describe Smith's treatment from the Indians. What does Smith do that amazes the Indians? Explain how Smith's life is saved.

6. Recount some of the details of Indian life that Smith gives. What details suggest a high degree of social organization among the tribes?

Developing Skills in Reading Literature

1. **Nonfiction.** John Smith's account is a historical narrative, for the most part factual. It is nonfiction, prose writing that is about real people, places, and events. Smith probably wrote this narrative some years after the events he describes took place. What differences might this have made in his account?

2. **Narrator.** In this account, John Smith is the narrator, or person who relates the events. Although Smith does not talk much about his thoughts and feelings, a reader can infer a great deal about his character from his responses to the physical realities around him. What character traits does he seem to possess? What facts and details lead you to see these traits in him? Does Smith ever strike you as opinionated or overly dramatic? Explain your answer.

3. **Point of View.** Point of view can mean a person's unique way of looking at things. In literature, however, the term has a more specific meaning. It is the narrative method used to present a prose selection. In this narrative, the point of view is both first-person and third-person. In the opening passages, Smith uses the first-person pronouns *our* and *we*. Later he refers to himself with the third-person pronouns *he* and *him*. Why do you suppose Smith shifts to the third person? How does this shift relate to the changed content of the narrative? What effect does the use of the third-person have on the narrative?

4. **Tone.** Tone is the attitude that a writer takes toward a subject. What is Smith's usual tone? Is it appropriate to his subject matter? Do you find any passages in which the tone changes?

5. **Description.** Smith's account is narration, in that it relates a series of events. It also contains considerable description, however, for Smith gives detailed impressions of people and events.

Reread Smith's description of the Indians, especially of how Powhatan's people look as they sit around their chief. What details make Smith's account vivid?

Find another vivid descriptive passage in this selection and explain why you find it effective.

Developing Vocabulary

Understanding Changes in Language. John Smith wrote his account more than three hundred and fifty years ago; quite obviously, many changes have occurred in the language since then. The standard vocabulary of English has changed, and many phrases and expressions have gone out of use. For example, Smith begins his account by saying, "Being thus left to our fortunes, it fortuned that within ten days scarce ten amongst us could either go or well stand, such extreme weakness and sickness oppressed us." In modern English we do not use the word *fortune* as a verb, as Smith does. What other aspects of this sentence strike you as dated or old-fashioned?

Skim the selection for other words and phrases that are antiquated, or dated. What words and phrases would we use instead in modern English?

Developing Writing Skills

1. **Analyzing an Element of Plot.** With its "Wild West" tradition, its gangster movies, and its emphasis on the right to bear arms, America has often been a violent culture. In what episodes of John Smith's account does violence play a role? What is Smith's attitude toward violence? Write a well developed paragraph in which you answer these questions, citing specific passages in the narrative to support your points.

2. **Telling the Same Story from a Different Point of View.** Describe the capture and eventual release of John Smith in the first person as one of Powhatan's Indians might have told it. You may choose to be any member of the tribe you wish, including Powhatan or Pocahontas. Focus on aspects of Smith's appearance and behavior that would seem strange and intriguing.

Ætatis suæ 21. A°. 1616.

Matoaks als Rebecka daughter to the mighty Prince Powhatan Emperour of Attanoughkomouck als Virginia converted and baptized in the Christian faith, and Wife to the wor.ll M.r Tho: Rolff.

Pocahontas (Rebecca Rolfe), painted in England in 1616 while visiting there with her husband, John Rolfe.

National Portrait Gallery, Smithsonian Institution, Washington, D.C. Transfer from the National Gallery of Art. Gift of Andrew W. Mellon.

William Bradford
1590–1657

William Bradford was governor of the Plymouth Colony for thirty-three years, a period during which the Puritan tradition in America was established. A man of simple background and little formal education, he chronicled the history of the colony from its inception until 1647. As a leader, Bradford regarded himself as an instrument of God sent to lead God's chosen people to a promised land. As a human being, he was wise and tolerant, with political beliefs that were remarkably democratic for his day.

William Bradford was born in Yorkshire, England, the son of a farmer who died when William was a young child. He was an intelligent boy and a devout reader and student of the Bible. At the age of twelve, despite family disapproval, he left the Church of England and joined a Puritan Separatist group that met secretly in the village of Scrooby. When the group migrated to Holland in 1607 in search of religious freedom, William went with them. There he became a weaver and continued his study of the Bible. He also learned Dutch, French, Greek, Hebrew, and some Latin, and collected his own library, which he took with him when he embarked on the ship *Mayflower*, bound for the New World. After arriving at Cape Cod, before leaving the ship, the colonists drew up and signed the Mayflower Compact, a document outlining a plan for the organization and self-government of the colony. Bradford and others went ashore on December 11, 1620, to find a place to settle, pressured to do so by the *Mayflower* captain and crew who wanted to return to England as soon as possible. While Bradford was gone, his wife Dorothy was drowned, the first of fifty to die in that first year of the colony.

In 1630 Bradford began writing *Of Plymouth Plantation*. The first "book" deals with the history of the Pilgrims up to their landing at Plymouth. The second "book" presents their history from 1620 to 1647. Samuel Eliot Morison described Bradford's history as "a story of a simple people inspired by an ardent faith to a dauntless courage in danger, a resourcefulness in dealing with new problems, an impregnable fortitude in adversity, that exalts and heartens one in an age of uncertainty, when courage falters and faith grows dim." Bradford describes the daily life, trials and successes of the Plymouth colonists. He tells the story of the first Thanksgiving and of the growth of the colony.

Bradford died in 1657 in Plymouth, at the age of sixty-seven, having attained stature as one of the first great political leaders of American history. The manuscript for *Of Plymouth Plantation* was passed down through his family and quoted from by other colonial historians. The manuscript disappeared during the Revolutionary War to reappear unexpectedly in England in 1855 in the library of the Bishop of London. The following year the history was finally published for the first time, about two hundred years after Bradford's death.

PILGRIMS GOING TO CHURCH, 1867. *George Henry Broughton. The New York Historical Society.*

from **Of Plymouth Plantation**

Of Plymouth Plantation, although mainly written in 1630, was not published until 1856. These excerpts from the historical narrative recount the hardships faced by the Pilgrims upon their arrival in Massachusetts in December, 1620.

Safe Arrival at Cape Cod

After they had enjoyed fair winds and weather for a season, they were encountered many times with cross winds and met with many fierce storms with which the ship was shroudly[1] shaken, and her upper works made very leaky; and one of the main beams in the midships was bowed and cracked, which put them in some fear that the ship could not be able to perform the voyage. So some of the chief of the company, perceiving the mariners to fear the sufficiency of the ship as appeared by their mutterings, they entered into serious consultation with the master and other officers of the ship, to consider in time of the danger, and rather to return than to cast themselves into a desperate and inevitable peril. And truly there was great distraction and difference of opinion amongst the mariners themselves; fain would they do what could be done for their wages' sake (being now near half the seas over) and on the other hand they were loath to hazard their lives too desperately. But in examining of all opinions, the master and others affirmed they knew the ship to be strong and firm under water; and for the buckling of the main beam, there was a great iron screw the passengers brought out of Holland, which would raise the beam into his place; the which being done, the carpenter and master affirmed that with a post put under it, set firm in the lower deck and otherways bound, he would make it sufficient. And as for the decks and upper works, they would caulk them as well as they could, and though with the working of the ship they would not long keep staunch, yet there would otherwise be no great danger, if they did not overpress her with sails. So they committed themselves to the will of God and resolved to proceed. . . .

But to omit other things (that I may be brief) after long beating at sea they fell with that land which is called Cape Cod; the which being made and certainly known to be it, they were not a little joyful. . . .

Being thus arrived in a good harbor, and brought safe to land, they fell upon their knees and blessed the God of Heaven who had brought them over the vast and furious ocean, and delivered them from all the perils and miseries thereof, again to set their feet on the firm and stable earth, their proper element. . . .

But here I cannot but stay and make a pause, and stand half amazed at this poor people's present condition; and so I think will the reader, too, when he well considers the same. Being thus passed the vast ocean, and a sea of troubles before in their preparation (as may be remembered by that which went before), they had now no friends to welcome them nor inns to entertain or refresh their weatherbeaten bodies; no houses or much less towns to repair to, to seek for succour.[2] It is recorded in Scripture as a mercy to the Apostle and his shipwrecked company, that the barbarians showed them no small kindness in refreshing them,[3] but these savage

---

1. **shroudly:** severely.
2. **succour** (suk′ ər): aid or help in time of distress.
3. Acts 28:2: The Apostle Paul was greeted courteously by the barbarians at Melita during a storm.

barbarians, when they met with them (as after will appear) were readier to fill their sides full of arrows than otherwise. And for the season it was winter, and they that know the winters of that country know them to be sharp and violent, and subject to cruel and fierce storms, dangerous to travel to known places, much more to search an unknown coast. Besides, what could they see but a hideous and desolate wilderness, full of wild beasts and wild men—and what multitudes there might be of them they knew not. Neither could they, as it were, go up to the top of Pisgah[4] to view from this wilderness a more goodly country to feed their hopes; for which way soever they turned their eyes (save upward to the heavens) they could have little solace or content in respect of any outward objects. For summer being done, all things stand upon them with a weatherbeaten face, and the whole country, full of woods and thickets, represented a wild and savage hue. If they looked behind them, there was the mighty ocean which they had passed and was now as a main bar and gulf to separate them from all the civil parts of the world. . . .

Being thus arrived at Cape Cod the 11th of November, and necessity calling them to look out a place for habitation (as well as the master's and mariners' importunity);[5] they having brought a large shallop[6] with them out of England, stowed in quarters in the ship, they now got her out and set their carpenters to work to trim her up; but being much bruised and shattered in the ship with foul weather, they saw she would be long in mending. Whereupon a few of them tendered themselves to go by land and discover those nearest places, whilst the shallop was in mending; and the rather because as they went into that harbor there seemed to be an opening some two or three leagues[7] off, which the master judged to be a river. It was conceived there might be some danger in the attempt, yet seeing them resolute, they were permitted to

go, being sixteen of them well armed under the conduct of Captain Standish, having such instructions given them as was thought meet.[8]

They set forth the 15th of November; and when they had marched about the space of a mile by the seaside, they espied five or six persons with a dog coming towards them, who were savages; but they fled from them and ran up into the woods, and the English followed them, partly to see if they could speak with them, and partly to discover if there might not be more of them lying in ambush. But the Indians seeing themselves thus followed, they again forsook the woods and ran away on the sands as hard as they could, so as they could not come near them but followed them by the track of their feet sundry miles and saw that they had come the same way. So, night coming on, they made their rendezvous[9] and set out their sentinels, and rested in quiet that night; and the next morning followed their track till they had headed a great creek and so left the sands, and turned another way into the woods. But they still followed them by guess, hoping to find their dwellings; but they soon lost both them and themselves, falling into such thickets as were ready to tear their clothes and armor in pieces; but were most distressed for want of drink. But at length they found water and refreshed themselves, being the first New England water they drunk of, and was now in great thirst as pleasant unto them as wine or beer had been in foretimes. . . .

---

4. Deuteronomy 34:1–4: Moses saw the Promised Land from Mount Pisgah in Palestine.
5. **importunity** (im' pôr to͞on' ə tē): repeated requests or demands.
6. **shallop:** a small open boat, fitted with oars or sails or both.
7. **league:** an old measure of distance, usually about three miles.
8. **meet:** suitable, proper.
9. **rendezvous** (rän' dā vo͞o): camp, gathering of men at a set place.

After this, the shallop being got ready, they set out again for the better discovery of this place,[10] and the master of the ship desired to go himself. So there went some thirty men but found it to be no harbor for ships but only for boats. There was also found two of their houses covered with mats, and sundry of their implements in them, but the people were run away and could not be seen. Also there was found more of their corn and of their beans of various colors; the corn and beans they brought away, purposing to give them full satisfaction when they should meet with any of them as, about some six months afterward they did, to their good content. . . .

[On the third expedition[11]] After some hours' sailing it began to snow and rain, and about the middle of the afternoon the wind increased and the sea became very rough, and they broke their rudder, and it was as much as two men could do to steer her with a couple of oars. But their pilot bade them be of good cheer for he saw the harbor; but the storm increasing, and night drawing on, they bore what sail they could to get in, while they could see. But herewith they broke their mast in three pieces and their sail fell overboard in a very grown sea, so as they had like to have been cast away. Yet by God's mercy they recovered themselves, and having the flood[12] with them, struck into the harbor. But when it came to, the pilot was deceived in the place, and said the Lord be merciful unto them for his eyes never saw that place before; and he and the master's mate would have run her ashore in a cove full of breakers before the wind. But a lusty seaman which steered bade those which rowed, if they were men, about with her or else they were all cast away; the which they did with speed. So he bid them be of good cheer and row lustily, for there was a fair sound before them, and he doubted not but they should find one place or other where they might ride in safety. And though it was very dark and rained sore,[13] yet in the end they got under the lee[14] of a small island and

remained there all that night in safety. But they knew not this to be an island till morning, but were divided in their minds; some would keep the boat for fear they might be amongst the Indians, others were so wet and cold they could not endure but got ashore, and with much ado got fire (all things being so wet); and the rest were glad to come to them, for after midnight the wind shifted to the northwest and it froze hard.

But though this had been a day and night of much trouble and danger unto them, yet God gave them a morning of comfort and refreshing (as usually He doth to His children) for the next day was a fair, sunshining day, and they found themselves to be on an island secure from the Indians, where they might dry their stuff, fix their pieces and rest themselves; and gave God thanks for His mercies in their manifold deliverances. And this being the last day of the week, they prepared there to keep the Sabbath.

On Monday they sounded the harbor and found it fit for shipping, and marched into the land and found divers cornfields and little running brooks, a place (as they supposed) fit for situation.[15] At least it was the best they could find, and the season and their present necessity made them glad to accept of it. So they returned to their ship again with this news to the rest of their people, which did much comfort their hearts.

On the 15th of December they weighed anchor to go to the place they had discovered, and came within two leagues of it, but were fain[16] to bear up again; but the 16th day, the wind came fair, and they arrived safe in this

---

10. From November 28–30 the second expedition explored the Pamet and Little Pamet Rivers.
11. Starting December 6, 1620.
12. **flood:** tide, here about nine feet high.
13. **sore:** severely.
14. **lee:** a sheltered place on the side away from the wind.
15. This is the first "Landing of the Pilgrims on Plymouth Rock" on December 11, 1620.
16. **fain:** ready and willing, but unable to.

harbor.[17] And afterwards took better view of the place, and resolved where to pitch their dwelling; and the 25th day began to erect the first house for common use to receive them and their goods.

Compact with the Indians

All this while [during January and February, 1621] the Indians came skulking about them, and would sometimes show themselves aloof off, but when any approached near them, they would run away; and once they stole away their tools where they had been at work and were gone to dinner. But about the 16th of March, a certain Indian came boldly amongst them and spoke to them in broken English, which they could well understand but marveled at it. At length they understood by discourse with him, that he was not of these parts, but belonged to the eastern parts where some English ships came to fish, with whom he was acquainted and could name sundry of them by their names, amongst whom he had got his language. He became profitable to them in acquainting them with many things concerning the state of the country in the east parts where he lived, which was afterwards profitable unto them; as also of the people here, of their names, number and strength, of their situation and distance from this place, and who was chief amongst them. His name was Samoset. He told them also of another Indian whose name was Squanto, a native of this place, who had been in England and could speak better English than himself.

Being, after some time of entertainment and gifts dismissed, a while after he came again, and five more with him, and they brought again all the tools that were stolen away before, and made way for the coming of their great Sachem,[18] called Massasoit. Who, about four or five days after, came with the chief of his friends and other attendance, with the aforesaid Squanto. With whom, after friendly entertainment and some gifts given him, they made a peace with him (which hath now continued this 24 years) in these terms:

1. That neither he nor any of his should injure or do hurt to any of their people.
2. That if any of his did hurt to any of theirs, he should send the offender, that they might punish him.
3. That if anything were taken away from any of theirs, he should cause it to be restored; and they should do the like to his.
4. If any did unjustly war against him, they would aid him; if any did war against them, he should aid them.
5. He should send to his neighbors confederates to certify them of this, that they might not wrong them, but might be likewise comprised[19] in the conditions of peace.
6. That when their men came to them, they should leave their bows and arrows behind them.

After these things he returned to his place called Sowams,[20] some 40 miles from this place, but Squanto continued with them and was their interpreter and was a special instrument sent of God for their good beyond their expectation. He directed them how to set their corn, where to take fish, and to procure other commodities, and was also their pilot to bring them to unknown places for their profit, . . .

He was a native of this place, and scarce any [of his tribe were] left alive besides himself. He [had been] carried away with divers others [in 1614] by one Hunt, a master of a ship, who thought to sell them for slaves in Spain. But he got away for England and was entertained by a merchant in London, and employed to Newfoundland and other parts, and lastly brought hither into these parts [in 1618] by

---

17. The *Mayflower* finally anchored in Plymouth Harbor on December 16, 1620.
18. **Sachem** (sā′ chəm) *Algonquian:* Indian chief.
19. **comprised:** included.
20. Now called Barrington, Rhode Island.

one Mr. Dermer, a gentleman employed by Sir Ferdinando Gorges and others for discovery and other designs in these parts. [He learned that his tribe had been destroyed by disease in 1617, so he lived with the settlers at Plymouth] and never left them till he died [in September, 1622].

Getting at Meaning

SAFE ARRIVAL AT CAPE COD

1. During the sea voyage, what crisis is faced by the passengers and crew of the *Mayflower*? What decision needs to be made? Who makes it? What is decided?

2. Describe the situation of the settlers after they arrive on Cape Cod. What problems are presented by the physical environment?

3. What are the first experiences of the Pilgrims on shore? How do the Indians react to them at first?

4. Describe the Pilgrims' continuing explorations of the territory. Why don't they settle immediately? Why do they continue to explore in the ship?

COMPACT WITH THE INDIANS

5. How is Samoset able to establish links between the Pilgrims and the Indians? Explain the peace treaty that the Pilgrims negotiate with Massasoit and his people. Are the peace terms more favorable to one group than the other?

6. Describe Squanto's background. Why is he the perfect liaison between the Pilgrims and the Indians?

Developing Skills in Reading Literature

1. **Setting.** Setting refers to both time and place in a narrative, and both are of unusual importance in this nonfiction selection. What is significant and dangerous in the date of the Pilgrims' arrival at Plymouth? What elements of their new environment seem particularly threatening to the Pilgrims? How do they feel during their initial explorations of Cape Cod?

2. **Narrator.** Bradford, the narrator of this factual history, was elected governor of Plymouth Colony thirty different times. What traits desirable in a leader does Bradford appear to possess? Consider both his actions and his attitudes. What other generalizations about Bradford's character can you make?

3. **Theme.** Bradford views history from a providential, or "God's will" perspective. This means that he believes in God as the primary cause for all events. God manages the world according to His will, and human beings do not have much control.

What events does Bradford attribute to God's will? When does he appear to feel that God is directing or guiding the Pilgrims?

4. **Style.** Style is the way that a play, poem, short story, novel, or nonfiction selection is written. Style refers not to what is said but to how it is said.

Bradford's narrative is written in the simple style that is often called the Puritan plain style. Benjamin Franklin, who later wrote in the plain style, described good writing as "smooth, clear, and short."

Some of Bradford's language sounds unnatural to a modern ear, but his narrative is still understandable because it is basically direct, as shown in statements such as, "But to omit other things (that I may be brief) after long beating at sea they fell with that land which is called Cape Cod. . . ."

Find other examples of the plain, direct style in Bradford's account. What details suggest that he is a methodical and accurate observer and reporter?

Developing Vocabulary

Understanding Changes in Language. Rewrite the following sentences from Bradford's narrative in contemporary English. What words have you changed? Why? What phrases? Where has it been necessary to change the order of words?

After they had enjoyed fair winds and weather for a season, they were encountered many times with cross winds and met with many fierce storms with which the ship was shroudly shaken. . . .

And truly there was great distraction and difference of opinion amongst the mariners themselves; fain would they do what could be done for their wages' sake (being now near half the seas over) and on the other hand they were loath to hazard their lives too desperately.

So he bid them be of good cheer and row lustily, for there was a fair sound before them, and he doubted not but they should find one place or other where they might ride in safety.

from The Massachusetts Bay Psalm Book

Anonymous

The Massachusetts Bay Psalm Book, *the work of a committee of Puritan ministers,*
was a new translation of the psalms whose original title was The Whole Booke of
Psalms Faithfully Translated into English Metre. *Printed in 1640,* The Massachusetts Bay Psalm Book *was the first book in English to be printed in America.*
During the next century, it went through twenty-five editions.

Psalm 23

A PSALM OF DAVID

The Lord to me a shepherd is,
  want therefore shall not I.
He in the folds of tender grass,
  doth cause me down to lie.
To waters calm me gently leads;   5
  restore my soul doth he;
He doth in paths of righteousness
  for his name's sake lead me.
Yea though in valley of death's shade
  I walk, none ill I'll fear,   10
Because thou art with me; thy rod
  and staff my comfort are.
For me a table thou hast spread,
  in presence of my foes.
Thou dost anoint my head with oil;   15
  my cup it overflows.
Goodness and mercy surely shall
  all my days follow me;
And in the Lord's house I shall dwell
  so long as days shall be.   20

Psalm 100

A PSALM OF PRAISE

Make ye a joyful sounding noise
  Jehovah all the earth;
Serve ye Jehovah with gladness;
  before him come with mirth.
Know, that Jehovah he is God,   5
  who hath us formed it is he,
And not ourselves; his own people
  and sheep of his pasture are we.
Enter into his gates with praise,
  into his courts with thankfulness;   10
Make ye confession unto him,
  and his name reverently bless,
Because Jehovah he is good,
  forevermore is his mercy;
And unto generations all   15
  continue doth his verity.[1]

---

1. **verity:** basic truth or reality.

Getting at Meaning

1. How does the speaker of Psalm 23 perceive the Lord? Why does the speaker feel no fear?

2. How does the speaker of Psalm 100 perceive the Lord, or Jehovah? What activity does the speaker of this Psalm suggest for human beings?

Developing Skills in Reading Literature

1. **Psalm.** A psalm is a sacred song, or a hymn. When the word is capitalized, it refers to any of the sacred songs or hymns collected in the Old Testament Book of Psalms.

What is song-like about Psalms 23 and 100? Observe the rhyme and rhythm of both psalms. What gives the poems a musical cadence?

2. **Tone.** Psalms 23 and 100, while they are both optimistic, project somewhat different tones. Which psalm is the more buoyant and happy of the two? Which psalm has a more restrained, personal tone? What is the relationship between tone and meaning in each psalm?

3. **Metaphor.** Both of these psalms employ the same metaphor to describe the relationship between God and human beings. To what does the speaker of Psalm 23 compare the Lord? By extension, what role does the speaker assume in the comparison? In what line of Psalm 100 does the speaker of that poem actually state the metaphor describing human beings?

4. **Theme.** Discuss the relationship between the speaker and the deity, as indicated in each of these psalms. Is the relationship the same in the two psalms, or are there differences? Find words with positive connotations, or emotional associations, in both psalms. What concept of the deity do these words project?

Developing Writing Skills

Using Comparisons and Contrasts. To compare two things is to show the similarities between them. To contrast two things is to show the differences between them.

Select either Psalm 23 or Psalm 100 and in two well developed paragraphs compare and contrast this psalm with a modern translation of the same psalm. Refer to specific lines in the translations to support your points. Conclude by stating which version you prefer and why.

Woodcut of a man, possibly King David, playing a harp; from an almanac printed at Cambridge in 1684.

from The New England Primer *Anonymous*

The New England Primer is a famous American schoolbook that dates from before 1690. Over two million copies of the book were sold during the eighteenth century, which indicates how widely The Primer *was used.*

The Dutiful Child's Promises

Now the Child being entred in his Letters and Spelling, let him learn these and such like Sentences by Heart, whereby he will be both instructed in his Duty, and encouraged in his Learning.

The Dutiful Child's Promises,

I Will fear GOD, and honour the KING.
   I will honour my Father & Mother.
I will Obey my Superiours.
I will Submit to my Elders,
I will Love my Friends.
I will hate no Man.
I will forgive my Enemies, and pray to
   God for them.
I will as much as in me lies keep all God's
   Holy Commandments.

I will learn my Catechism.[1]
I will keep the Lord's Day Holy.
I will Reverence God's Sanctuary,
   For our GOD is a consuming Fire.

Verses/Again

VERSES.

I in the Burying Place may see
   Graves shorter there than I;
From Death's Arrest no Age is free,
   Young Children too may die;
My God, may such an awful Sight,
   Awakening be to me!
Oh! that by early Grace I might
   For Death prepared be.

AGAIN.

First in the Morning when thou dost
   awake,
To God for his Grace thy Petition make,
Some Heavenly Petition use daily to say,
That the God of Heaven may bless
   thee alway.

---

1. **catechism:** a handbook of questions and answers for teaching the principles of a religion.

Alphabet

A — In *Adam's* Fall
We Sinned all.

B — Thy Life to Mend
This *Book* Attend.

C — The *Cat* doth play
And after flay.

D — A *Dog* will bite
A *Thief* at night.

E — An *Eagles* flight
Is out of fight.

F — The Idle *Fool*
Is whipt at School.

N — *Nightingales* fing
In Time of Spring.

O — The *Royal Oak*
It was the Tree
That fav'd His
Royal Majeftie.

P — *Peter* denies
His Lord and cries

Q — Queen *Efther* comes
in Royal State
To Save the JEWS
from difmal Fate

R — *Rachol* doth mour
For her firft born.

S — *Samuel* anoints
Whom God appoint:

G — As runs the *Glafs*
Mans life doth pafs.

H — My *Book* and *Heart*
Shall never part.

J — *Job* feels the Rod
Yet bleffes GOD.

K — Our *K I N G* the
good
No man of blood.

L — The *Lion* bold
The *Lamb* doth hold.

M — The *Moon* gives light
In time of night.

T — *Time* cuts down all
Both great and fmall.

U — *Uriah*'sbeauteousWife
Made *David* feek his
Life.

W — *Whales* in the Sea
God's Voice obey.

X — *Xerxes* the great did
die,
And fo muft you & I,

Y — *Youth* forward flips
Death fooneft nips.

Z — *Zacheus* he
Did climb the Tree
His Lord to fee,

Good Children Must

Good Children muſt,
Fear God all Day,   Love Chriſt alway,
Parents obey,   In Secret Pray,
No falſe thing ſay,   Mind little Play,
By no Sin ſtray,   Make no delay,
In doing Good.

Awake, ariſe, behold thou haſt
Thy Life a Leaf, thy Breath a Blaſt;[1]
At Night lye down prepar'd to have
Thy ſleep, thy death, thy bed, thy grave.

Learn These Four Lines by Heart

Learn theſe four Lines by Heart.
Have Communion[2] with few,
Be Intimate with ONE.
Deal juſtly with all.
Speak Evil of none.

1. **blast:** a short-lived gust of wind.
2. **communion:** a sharing of one's thoughts and emotions.

Getting at Meaning

1. Comment on the view of the child evident in *The New England Primer*. How is a dutiful, good child supposed to behave?

2. In "Verses" the child speaker notices the graves of younger and smaller children. What effect does the sight of these graves have on the child?

3. *The New England Primer* urges the child reader to "Have Communion with few/ Be intimate with ONE." What is the meaning of these two lines?

4. What is the purpose of the pairs of rhymed lines supplied for the letters of the alphabet? Explain how these short sayings might function as a memory device. Can you think of anything similar in modern American culture?

Developing Skills in Reading Literature

1. **Style.** *The New England Primer* clearly contains lettering, spelling, and capitalization that are antiquated, or out of date. For example, most of the *s*'s in *The Primer* look like *f*'s. This was common in the penmanship of earlier centuries. What irregular and old-fashioned spellings do you find in *The Primer*? What is peculiar about the capitalization by modern standards? Can you detect any pattern in the capitalization?

2. **Metaphor.** "The Dutiful Child Promises" ends with the striking metaphor, "For our GOD is a consuming Fire." What conception of God does this metaphor imply? What effect is this comparison supposed to have on the child reader?

3. **Allusion.** An allusion is a reference to an historical or literary person, place, or event with which the reader is assumed to be familiar. Notice that the alphabet couplets in *The New England Primer* contain numerous Biblical allusions, such as the opening reference to "Adam's Fall."

Locate two or three other Biblical allusions in these couplets and explain them. If necessary, look up the allusions in a dictionary of Biblical references.

4. **Theme.** All of the material in *The New England Primer* is designed to mold the child reader into an ideal person and a responsible member of society. Describe the ideal *The Primer* sets up. What qualities in a human being does it emphasize most powerfully?

Notice that the alphabet couplets can be classified into four categories:

practical advice
observations of nature
political and patriotic messages
religious teachings

Indicate the category to which each couplet belongs. What do these four groupings suggest about the human ideal that *The Primer* is trying to establish?

Anne Bradstreet

1612–1672

Anne Bradstreet was the first noteworthy American poet. One of her poems, "In Reference to Her Children, 23 June, 1659" begins:

I had eight birds hatched in one nest,
Four cocks there were, and hens the rest.

Seven of her "eight birds" survived her, and among their descendants were writers Oliver Wendell Holmes and Edwin Arlington Robinson.

Anne Bradstreet was born in 1612 in Northampton, England, the daughter of Thomas Dudley, steward of the estates of the Earl of Lincoln, a Puritan nobleman. The scholarly Dudley saw to it that his daughter was well educated, providing her with extensive tutoring and with free access to the library of the Earl. In 1628 she married Simon Bradstreet, a brilliant Cambridge-educated Puritan. Two years later the couple emigrated to the Massachusetts Bay Colony along with Anne's parents. The Bradstreets settled finally in Andover. In time both Thomas Dudley and Simon Bradstreet became governors of the colony.

The life of the colonial housewife contrasted sharply with the atmosphere of leisure and wealth in which Anne had grown up. Eventually she adjusted to her life, bore and reared eight children, and filled with dignity her position in the community. In her limited leisure time she read, studied, and wrote poetry. Apparently the other colonists made her aware that the writing of poetry was not acceptable for a Puritan woman of her position, for she wrote:

I am obnoxious to each carping tongue
Who says my hand a needle better fits.

When her brother-in-law John Woodbridge journeyed to England in 1647, he took copies of her poems and, without her knowledge, had them published anonymously under the title *The Tenth Muse Lately Sprung Up in America*. *The Tenth Muse* was very popular in England, but Anne wrote of her work, calling it,

Thou ill-form'd offspring of my feeble brain,
Who after birth did'st by my side remain,
Till snatcht from thence by friends, less wise
than true. . . .

Her second volume of poetry was published six years after her death.

Bradstreet's earlier poems imitate the works of contemporary poets, who deal mainly with classic subjects in traditional forms. Her later poems, however, are simpler and more lyrical, expressing her feelings about family relationships, personal tragedies, the routines of domestic life, and her own religious faith. Recurrent is the theme that material wealth is of little importance and that spiritual wealth is beyond price. These later poems show careful craftsmanship and a genuine gift for original expression. They are considered Bradstreet's best work and the first poetry of real merit written in the American colonies.

To My Dear and Loving Husband

If ever two were one, then surely we.
If ever man were loved by wife, then thee;
If ever wife was happy in a man,
Compare with me, ye women, if you can.
I prize thy love more than whole mines of gold   5
Or all the riches that the East doth hold.
My love is such that rivers cannot quench,
Nor ought[1] but love from thee, give recompense.
Thy love is such I can no way repay,
The heavens reward thee manifold, I pray.   10
Then while we live, in love let's so persevere
That when we live no more, we may live ever.

---

1. **ought:** var. of *aught;* anything whatever.

Getting at Meaning

1. How does the speaker emphasize the magnitude of her feeling for her husband?

2. What does the speaker wish for herself and her husband in the future?

Developing Skills in Reading Literature

1. **Lyric.** In ancient Greece, the lyre was a musical instrument, and *lyric* came to mean "a song accompanied by music." In common speech, the words of songs are still called lyrics.

In literature, a lyric is any short poem that presents a single speaker who expresses thoughts and feelings. In this poem, the speaker is almost certainly the poet herself, speaking in an intensely personal way. What would you say is the purpose of this lyric?

2. **Meter.** Meter is the repetition of a regular rhythmic unit in a line of poetry. Each unit of meter is known as a foot, with each foot having one stressed and one or two unstressed syllables. The four basic types of metrical feet are the iamb, an unstressed syllable followed by a stressed syllable (˘′); the trochee, a stressed syllable followed by an unstressed syllable (′˘); the anapest, two unstressed syllables followed by a stressed syllable (˘˘′); and the dactyl, a stressed syllable followed by two unstressed syllables (′˘˘).

A line of poetry is named not only for the type of foot but also for the number of feet in the line. These are the most common metrical names:

monometer: a one-foot line
dimeter: a two-foot line
trimeter: a three-foot line
tetrameter: a four-foot line
pentameter: a five-foot line
hexameter: a six-foot line
heptameter: a seven-foot line
octameter: an eight-foot line.

Two words are used to describe the meter of a line. The first word describes the type of metrical foot; the second word describes the number of feet in the line. For example:

iambic dimeter (two iambs per line)
trochaic trimeter (three trochees per line)
anapestic tetrameter (four anapests per line)
dactylic hexameter (six dactyls per line)

''To My Dear and Loving Husband'' is an example of iambic pentameter, the most common form of meter in English poetry. The first two lines of the poem may be marked as follows:

```
 1        2        3          4         5
Ĭf év/er two/ wĕre óne,/ thĕn súre/lў wé

Ĭf év/er man/ wĕre lóved/ bў wífe,/ thĕn thee.
```

The process of determining meter is known as scansion. To scan a line of poetry thus means to determine the line's meter.

Scan the last four lines of this poem. Mark the iambs, both the accented and the unaccented syllable, and number the feet for each line. You should come up with five feet in each line.

3. **Rhyme.** Rhyme is the similarity of sound between two words. Words rhyme when the sound of their accented vowels, and all succeeding sounds, are identical. For true rhyme, the consonants that precede the vowels must be different. When rhyme comes at the end of a line of poetry, it is called end rhyme. Identify the end rhyme in this poem. Which rhymes are true rhymes? Which are slightly imprecise, or off-rhymes?

4. **Couplet and Heroic Couplet.** When two successive lines contain end rhyme the lines are called a couplet. When their meter is iambic pentameter, the lines are a heroic couplet. Thus the first two lines of the poem constitute a heroic couplet:

If ever two were one, then surely *we*.
If ever man were loved by wife, then *thee*.

Examine the remaining lines of the poem. Is the entire poem composed of heroic couplets? Be prepared to identify each heroic couplet in the poem.

5. **Structure.** Although this poem is not arranged in separate stanzas, the poem does appear to have three parts. Where do the divisions fall? What different idea does the poet develop in each part? What progression emerges in the thought pattern?

The North Andover, Massachusetts, home of Anne Bradstreet was built in 1667. Here she had access to the library amassed by her husband, Governor Simon Bradstreet.

Upon the Burning of Our House, July 10th, 1666

In silent night when rest I took
For sorrow near I did not look
I wakened was with thund'ring noise
And piteous shrieks of dreadful voice.
That fearful sound of "Fire!" and "Fire!"   5
Let no man know is my desire.

I, starting up, the light did spy,
And to my God my heart did cry
To strengthen me in my distress
And not to leave me succorless.   10
Then, coming out, beheld a space
The flame consume my dwelling place.

And when I could no longer look,
I blest His name that gave and took,[1]
That laid my goods now in the dust.   15
Yea, so it was, and so 'twas just.
It was His own, it was not mine,
Far be it that I should repine;

He might of all justly bereft
But yet sufficient for us left.   20
When by the ruins oft I past
My sorrowing eyes aside did cast,
And here and there the places spy
Where oft I sat and long did lie:

Here stood that trunk, and there that chest,   25
There lay that store I counted best.
My pleasant things in ashes lie,
And them behold no more shall I.
Under thy roof no guest shall sit,
Nor at thy table eat a bit.   30

---

1. "The Lord gave, and the Lord hath taken away; blessed
be the name of the Lord." Job 1:21.

No pleasant tale shall e'er be told,
Nor things recounted done of old.
No candle e'er shall shine in thee,
Nor bridegroom's voice e'er heard shall be.
In silence ever shall thou lie,   35
Adieu, Adieu, all's vanity.

Then straight I 'gin my heart to chide,
And did thy wealth on earth abide?
Didst fix thy hope on mold'ring dust?
The arm of flesh didst make thy trust?   40
Raise up thy thoughts above the sky
That dunghill mists away may fly.

Thou hast an house on high erect,
Framed by that mighty Architect,
With glory richly furnished,   45
Stands permanent though this be fled.
It's purchased and paid for too
By Him who hath enough to do.

A price so vast as is unknown
Yet by His gift is made thine own;   50
There's wealth enough, I need no more,
Farewell, my pelf,² farewell my store.
The world no longer let me love,
My hope and treasure lies above.

---

2. **pelf:** money or wealth looked upon with contempt.

Getting at Meaning

1. Describe the speaker's initial feelings as she realizes that her house is on fire. What does she quickly conclude about the reason for the fire?

2. The speaker allows herself to mourn her house and her possessions. What does she focus on in lines 25-35?

3. Explain the line, "Adieu, Adieu, all's vanity." What gives the speaker hope after everything is destroyed? What does she refer to in speaking of the house that is "purchased and paid for too"?

Developing Skills in Reading Literature

1. **Rhyme Scheme.** A rhyme scheme is the pattern of end rhyme in a poem. The pattern is charted by assigning a letter of the alphabet, beginning with the letter a, to each line. Lines that rhyme are given the same letter.

The first stanza of this poem may be charted as follows:

In silent night when rest I took	a
For sorrow near I did not look	a
I wakened was with thund'ring noise	b
And piteous shrieks of dreadful voice.	b
That fearful sound of "Fire!" and "Fire!"	c
Let no man know is my desire.	c

This stanza contains three rhymed couplets, or pairs of lines. (Notice that the rhyme in lines 3 and 4 is off-rhyme.)

Chart the rhyme scheme of the second and third stanzas. Is their rhyme pattern identical to that of the first stanza?

2. **Extended Metaphor.** The final two stanzas of this poem develop an extended metaphor. What is the speaker's metaphor for an afterlife? What are the different parts to the comparison?

3. **Theme.** Notice the speaker's plain, homely concerns as she views the destruction of her house. Still, in spite of this concrete focus, the speaker is obviously an essentially spiritual person. Like all good Puritans, she sees ordinary life in a divine context.

What is the speaker's view of earth? of heaven? What is her attitude toward prayer?

Developing Writing Skills

1. **Writing an Explanation.** All of Anne Bradstreet's poetry centers on either domestic concerns or spiritual concerns. In one paragraph explain how Bradstreet mixes the two strains in both "To My Dear and Loving Husband" and "Upon the Burning of Our House." Quote lines from the poems to support your ideas.

2. **Writing a Lyric.** Write a lyric poem of your own, one that expresses thoughts and feelings on a subject of importance to you. You may want to try creating a regular rhyme scheme or a regular meter or both in your poem.

Edward Taylor

1645?–1729

The quiet life led by Edward Taylor gave little evidence of the wealth of rich and joyous poetry that he created during his nearly sixty years of serving as a village parson and physician. Few people knew that he wrote poetry, for only part of one poem was printed in his lifetime. Most of his work was not published until 1939, when for the first time scholars realized that the quiet Puritan minister was a gifted poet, comparable to the best British poets of his time.

Edward Taylor was born in Coventry, England, a district notable for its weaving and clothmaking, during the brief period when Puritans controlled the English government. Taylor attended an English university and taught school for a time before religious persecutions caused him to set sail for America. Arriving in Boston in July, 1668, Taylor soon enrolled in Harvard and, after his graduation, took a position as clergyman in Westfield, Massachusetts, where he served until his death in 1729.

Taylor was a conservative Puritan who believed strongly in the salvation of the chosen few and the inherent sinfulness of fallen humankind. He was inspired, however, by a passionate and glowing love of Christ, which he expresses repeatedly in the best of his poetry. Taylor often communicates his intense religious vision by focusing on some aspect of domestic life. In "Huswifery," for example, he likens the formation of a true Christian to the process of making cloth. About two hundred of Taylor's poems make up the "Sacramental Meditations," in which each poem is based upon a single line from the Bible. His other series of important poems is "God's Determinations Touching His Elect," in which he considers sin and redemption in the context of God's mercy and majesty.

from Preface to God's Determinations

Infinity, when all things it beheld
In Nothing, and of Nothing all did build,
Upon what Base was fixed the Lathe,[1] wherein
He turned this Globe, and riggaled[2] it so trim?
Who blew the Bellows of his Furnace Vast?   5
Or held the Mold wherein the world was Cast?
Who laid its Corner Stone? Or whose Command?
Where stand the Pillars upon which it stands?
Who Laced and Filleted[3] the earth so fine,
With Rivers like green Ribbons Smaragdine?[4]   10
Who made the Seas its Selvedge,[5] and it locks
Like a Quilt Ball[6] within a Silver Box?
Who Spread its Canopy? Or Curtains Spun?
Who in this Bowling Alley bowled the Sun?
Who made it always when it rises set: 15
To go at once both down, and up to get?
Who th' Curtain rods made for this Tapestry?
Who hung the twinkling Lanthorns in the Sky?
Who? who did this? or who is he? Why, know
It's Only Might Almighty this did do.   20
His hand hath made this noble work which Stands
His Glorious Handiwork not made by hands. . . .

---

1. **Lathe** (lāth): a machine for turning and shaping an article with the edge of a cutting tool.
2. **riggaled** (ri gal'd'): made grooves or slots for a moving mechanical member.
3. **Laced . . . Filleted** (fil' i təd): intertwining a woman's hair with ribbons or lace.
4. **Smaragdine:** emerald green (from Latin *smaragdus*).
5. **Selvedge** (sel' vij): a specially woven edge to keep cloth from raveling.
6. **Quilt Ball:** a trinket, or a toy ball covered with quilted small pieces of contrasting colors of cloth.

Getting at Meaning

1. This poem asks one main question. What is it? What answer does the poem supply?

2. What lines in the poem suggest that creating the world was a vast undertaking? What details emphasize the all-encompassing nature of this act of creation?

Developing Skills in Reading Literature

1. **Figurative Language: Metaphor and Simile.** This poem abounds in rich, original figurative language that includes a number of specific metaphors and similes. Like a metaphor, a simile is a comparison between dissimilar things; unlike a metaphor, the two parts of a simile are joined by *like* or *as.*

Much of Taylor's figurative language involves the concerns of everyday life. For example, in lines 9 and 10 he compares the way God striped the world with rivers to the way a woman laces her hair with ribbons. What simile is included in this comparison? Taylor also compares God to a woodworker and to a blacksmith. Identify the lines in which these metaphors appear. How do these comparisons convey the notion that God is everywhere, associated with all things?

Taylor's concrete comparisons give his ideas reality to the eye as well as to the mind. In what sense does the globe look like a "Quilt Ball"? In what sense is the world a "Bowling Alley"? What are the curtains and curtain rods of the earth?

2. **Rhetorical Question.** This entire poem, up to the final lines, is composed of rhetorical questions, questions that are not intended to produce answers. What emotional tone do these questions establish? What is the cumulative effect of the questions?

3. **Heroic Couplet.** Notice that the meter of this poem is iambic pentameter, with five feet to a line and an unstressed syllable followed by a stressed syllable (˘ʹ) in each foot. Pairs of lines rhyme throughout the poem, each pair being a heroic couplet.

The heroic couplet is a controlled, precise form. Why is the form so appropriate to the subject matter of this poem?

4. **Theme.** This poem exemplifies the Puritan view of the world, which Edward Taylor heartily endorsed. What aspects of creation does Taylor choose to emphasize? What do some of the individual details, highlighting the landscaping and the furnishing of the globe, suggest about the act of creation? Consider the title of the poem. In what sense is creation the preface to God's determinations?

Developing Vocabulary

Words from Latin. A preface is an introductory section to a book or a speech. The word *preface* comes from the Latin prefix *pre-*, meaning "before," and the Latin root *fari*, meaning "to speak." *Preface* thus literally means "to speak before."

The following words, all of which employ *pre-*, are words you more than likely do not know. All are useful words in developing a good English vocabulary. Look up each word in a dictionary, and record its definition. How is the Latin root upon which each word is based related to the Latin prefix *pre-*?

preeminent	premonition
prefect	prerogative
preferment	presage
prefiguration	

Huswifery

Make me, O Lord, thy Spinning Wheel complete.
    Thy Holy Word my Distaff[1] make for me.
Make mine Affections thy Swift Flyers[2] neat
    And make my Soul thy holy Spool[3] to be.
My Conversation make to be thy Reel[4]   5
    And Reel the yarn thereon spun of thy Wheel.

Make me thy Loom then, knit therein this Twine:
    And make thy Holy Spirit, Lord, wind quills:[5]
Then weave the Web thyself. The yarn is fine.
    Thine Ordinances make my Fulling Mills.[6]   10
Then dye the same in Heavenly Colors Choice,
    All pinked[7] with Varnished[8] Flowers of Paradise.

Then clothe therewith mine Understanding, Will,
    Affections, Judgment, Conscience, Memory,
My Words and Actions, that their shine may fill   15
    My ways with glory and thee glorify.
Then mine apparel shall display before ye
That I am Clothed in Holy robes for glory.

---

1. **Distaff** (dis' taf): a staff on which wool is wound before being spun into thread.
2. **Flyers:** regulators for the spinning wheel.
3. **Spool:** the part of a spinning wheel that twists the raw material into thread.
4. **Reel:** a spool or frame on which the finished thread is wound.
5. **quills:** a bobbin for the thread in a shuttle in weaving.
6. **Fulling Mills:** a mill where wool is cleaned, shrunk, and thickened with moisture, heat, and pressure.
7. **pinked** (piŋkt): adorned, decorated.
8. **Varnished:** glossy.

Getting at Meaning

1. What is huswifery? What different aspects of huswifery are the focus of each stanza?

2. What is the speaker asking for in the poem?

Developing Skills in Reading Literature

1. **Speaker.** While this poem was written by a male poet, the speaker in the poem is apparently a female housewife. Why might Taylor have elected to present this poem from a female perspective?

2. **Extended Metaphor, or Conceit.** An extended metaphor, particularly when it elaborately compares two strikingly different things, often is called a conceit. Conceits have been popular in religious poetry, particularly in the poetry of the seventeenth century.

The conceit in this poem begins in the first line when the speaker compares herself to a spinning wheel. What are the various aspects of this comparison? To what does the speaker compare herself in the second stanza? How does the poet build this segment of the central conceit? How does the third stanza serve to round out the conceit?

3. **Structure.** Why do you suppose Taylor divided "Huswifery" into three stanzas when the poem deals with one basic process? What is that process? What does each stanza contribute to the description of the process?

4. **Rhyme Scheme.** Chart the rhyme scheme in each stanza of this poem, assigning the same letter to lines that rhyme. (Notice that lines 11 and 12 present an example of off-rhyme.) Is the rhyme scheme the same in each stanza? What function does rhyme serve in this poem?

5. **Theme.** Like the "Preface to God's Determinations," "Huswifery" is a typically Puritan poem. Religious in theme, the entire poem is essentially a prayer. According to the poem, what is the value of God's grace and of being in harmony with God?

Developing Writing Skills

Analyzing Theme. Puritans were concerned with the question of whether individuals can attain religious grace through their own efforts or whether such grace comes to a select few as a free gift from God.

In a paragraph or two discuss how Taylor answers this question in "Huswifery." Observe his diction, or word choice, as well as his figures of speech. Why does he repeat the word *make* so often? What does he believe is the purpose of religious grace?

Wool Spinning Wheel
Wadsworth Atheneum, Hartford, Connecticut.
The Wallace Nutting Collection.
Gift of J. P. Morgan, 1926.712.

Jonathan Edwards
1703–1758

REVEREND JONATHAN EDWARDS. *Joseph Badger.*
Yale University Art Gallery.
Bequest of Eugene Phelps Edwards.

Jonathan Edwards was a brilliant theologian and philosopher and gifted speaker whose writings and sermons sparked The Great Awakening, a revival of religious fervor that swept the English colonies from 1734–1750. "Sinners in the Hands of an Angry God," his most famous sermon, is an example of the kind of preacher that inspired complacent churchgoers to recommit themselves to the principles and practice of Puritanism.

Jonathan Edwards was born in 1703 in East Windsor, Connecticut, the only son among the eleven children of a Puritan minister. A precocious child, Edwards wrote a treatise on the behavior of spiders as a part of God's plan for the universe and a treatise logically refuting materialism before he entered Yale University at the age of thirteen. At Yale he studied the ideas of the new Age of Reason, struggling to reconcile the great opposing doctrines of the time—Puritanism with its emphasis on predestination and the sovereignty of God and Rationalism with its emphasis on reason and human perfectability. After his graduation from Yale, Edwards briefly served a Presbyterian congregation in New York City and then returned to Yale as a tutor. In 1727 he married Sarah Pierrepont, about whom he had written a loving description four years previously. She was the continuing inspiration of his life, and together they produced eleven children. In 1727 he also became the assistant pastor of his grandfather's church in Northampton, Massachusetts, and, when his grandfather died two years later, became the principal minister of that congregation.

Edwards was troubled by the formalistic religious habits of his congregation, feeling that the fervor of the earlier Puritans had declined markedly. To prod his listeners out of their religious complacency, he preached intense sermons that awakened them to a sense of their sinfulness and need for God. His efforts to revive religious spirit in New England coincided in the early 1740's with similar efforts in the middle and southern colonies.

Some preachers associated with this Great Awakening encouraged excesses of emotion, which eventually caused a reaction against the movement. Edwards's own congregation began to resent his strict doctrines. A quarrel over church membership resulted in his dismissal in 1750. Edwards then was appointed as pastor and missionary to the Indians at the frontier settlement of Stockbridge, Massachusetts. He served there until 1757 when he was elected president of Princeton. He had been in that post only a few months when he died from a reaction to a smallpox vaccination.

In his lifetime Edwards published nine major works and many sermons. More than a thousand sermons and many other writings were still unpublished at the time of his death. His work is characterized by careful, logical expression of ideas, by poetic language, and by a mystical vision of creation.

Personal Narrative

I had a variety of concerns and exercises about my soul from my childhood; but had two more remarkable seasons of awakening, before I met with that change by which I was brought to those new dispositions, and that new sense of things, that I have since had. The first time was when I was a boy, some years before I went to college,[1] at a time of remarkable awakening in my father's congregation. I was then very much affected for many months, and concerned about the things of religion, and my soul's salvation; and was abundant in duties. I used to pray five times a day in secret, and to spend much time in religious talk with other boys; and used to meet with them to pray together. I experienced I know not what kind of delight in religion. My mind was much engaged in it, and had much self-righteous pleasure; and it was my delight to abound in religious duties. I, with some of my schoolmates, joined together, and built a booth in a swamp, in a very retired spot, for a place of prayer. And besides, I had particular secret places of my own in the woods, where I used to retire by myself; and was from time to time much affected. My affections seemed to be lively and easily moved, and I seemed to be in my element when engaged in religious duties. And I am ready to think, many are deceived with such affections, and such a kind of delight as I then had in religion, and mistake it for grace.

But in process of time, my convictions and affections wore off; and I entirely lost all those affections and delights and left off secret prayer, at least as to any constant performance of it; and returned like a dog to his vomit, and went on in the ways of sin.[2] Indeed I was at times very uneasy, especially towards the latter part of my time at college, when it pleased God to seize me with the pleurisy,[3] in which he brought me nigh to the grave, and shook me over the pit of hell. And yet, it was not long after my recovery, before I fell again into my old ways of sin. But God would not suffer me to go on with any quietness; I had great and violent inward struggles, till, after many conflicts with wicked inclinations, repeated resolutions, and bonds that I laid myself under by a kind of vow to God, I was brought wholly to break off all former wicked ways, and all ways of known outward sin; and to apply myself to seek salvation, and practice many religious duties; but without that kind of affection and delight which I had formerly experienced. My concern now wrought more by inward struggles and conflicts, and self-reflections. I made seeking my salvation the main business of my life.

---

1. Edwards entered Yale in 1716.
2. "As a dog returneth to his vomit, so a fool returneth to his folly." Proverbs 26:11.
3. **pleurisy** (ploor′ ə sē): inflammation of the membrane lining the chest cavity and covering the lungs.

Getting at Meaning

1. How does Jonathan Edwards describe his first religious awakening? Why was it such a source of pleasure to him?

2. Describe Edwards's second religious awakening. What occasioned it? What reason does he give for why the second awakening was "without that kind of affection and delight which I had formerly experienced"?

Developing Skills in Reading Literature

1. **Autobiography.** An autobiography is the story of a person's life written by that person. As a personal narrative, an autobiography offers the reader unique opportunities to share and understand the experiences of another individual.

What are Jonathan Edwards's purposes in describing his two "remarkable seasons of awakening"? What feelings and actions does he hope to stimulate in the reader?

2. **Theme.** Edwards exemplifies the spirit of the Great Awakening and of the Puritan conscience when he closes his narrative with the line, "I made seeking my salvation the main business of my life." According to Edwards, what has religion done for him? After his first awakening, Edwards stopped praying and returned to his old life "like a dog to his vomit." What conception of human life is implied in this simile? What is Edwards's view of God as revealed in this selection?

from Sinners in the Hands of an Angry God

We find it easy to tread on and crush a worm that we see crawling on the earth; so 'tis easy for us to cut or singe a slender thread that any thing hangs by; thus easy is it for God when he pleases to cast his enemies down to Hell. . . .

They are now the objects of that very *same* anger and wrath of God that is expressed in the torments of Hell: and the reason why they don't go down to Hell at each moment, is not because God, in whose power they are, is not then very angry with them; as angry as he is with many of those miserable creatures that he is now tormenting in Hell, and do there feel and bear the fierceness of his wrath. Yea God is a great deal more angry with great numbers that are now on earth, yea doubtless with many that are now in this congregation, that it may be are at ease and quiet, than he is with many of those that are now in the flames of Hell.

So that it is not because God is unmindful of their wickedness, and don't resent it, that he don't let loose his hand and cut them off. God is not altogether such an one as themselves, tho' they may imagine him to be so. The wrath of God burns against them, their damnation don't slumber, the pit is prepared, the fire is made ready, the furnace is now hot, ready to receive them, the flames do now rage and glow. The glittering sword is whet,[1] and held over them, and the pit hath opened her mouth under them. . . .

Unconverted men walk over the pit of Hell on a rotten covering, and there are innumerable places in this covering so weak that they won't bear their weight, and these places are not seen. The arrows of death fly unseen at noon-day; the sharpest sight can't discern them. God has so many different unsearcha-

---

1. **whet** (hwet): sharpened by rubbing or grinding.

ble ways of taking wicked men out of the world and sending 'em to Hell, that there is nothing to make it appear that God had need to be at the expense of a miracle, or go out of the ordinary course of his Providence, to destroy any wicked man, at any moment. . . .

So that thus it is, that natural men are held in the hand of God over the pit of Hell; they have deserved the fiery pit, and are already sentenced to it; and God is dreadfully provoked, his anger is as great towards them as to those that are actually suffering the executions of the fierceness of his wrath in Hell, and they have done nothing in the least to appease or abate that anger, neither is God in the least bound by any promise to hold 'em up one moment; the Devil is waiting for them, Hell is gaping for them, the flames gather and flash about them, and would fain lay hold on them, and swallow them up; the fire pent up in their own hearts is struggling to break out; and they have no interest in any mediator, there are no means within reach that can be any security to them. In short, they have no refuge, nothing to take hold of, all that preserves them every moment is the mere arbitrary will, and uncovenanted unobliged forbearance of an incensed God. . . .

The bow of God's wrath is bent, and the arrow made ready on the string, and justice bends the arrow at your heart, and strains the bow, and it is nothing but the mere pleasure of God, and that of an angry God, without any promise or obligation at all, that keeps the arrow one moment from being made drunk with your blood.

Thus are all you that never passed under a great change of heart, by the mighty power of the spirit of God upon your souls; all that were never born again, and made new creatures, and raised from being dead in sin, to a state of new, and before altogether unexperienced light and life, (however you may have reformed your life in many things, and may have had religious affections, and may keep up a form of religion in your families and closets, and in the house of God, and may be strict in it,) you are thus in the hands of an angry God; 'tis nothing but his mere pleasure that keeps you from being this moment swallowed up in everlasting destruction. . . .

The God that holds you over the pit of Hell, much as one holds a spider, or some loathsome insect, over the fire, abhors you, and is dreadfully provoked; his wrath towards you burns like fire; he looks upon you as worthy of nothing else, but to be cast into the fire; he is of purer eyes than to bear to have you in his sight; you are ten thousand times so abominable in his eyes as the most hateful venomous serpent is in ours. You have offended him infinitely more than ever a stubborn rebel did his prince: and yet 'tis nothing but his hand that holds you from falling into the fire every moment: 'tis to be ascribed to nothing else, that you did not go to Hell the last night; that you was suffered to awake again in this world, after you closed your eyes to sleep: and there is no other reason to be given why you have not dropped into Hell since you arose in the morning, but that God's hand has held you up: there is no other reason to be given why you have not gone to Hell since you have sat here in the house of God, provoking his pure eyes by your sinful wicked manner of attending his solemn worship: yea, there is nothing else that is to be given as a reason why you don't this very moment drop down into Hell.

O sinner! Consider the fearful danger you are in: 'tis a great furnace of wrath, a wide and bottomless pit, full of the fire of wrath, that you are held over in the hand of that God, whose wrath is provoked and incensed as much against you as against many of the damned in Hell: you hang by a slender thread, with the flames of divine wrath flashing about it, and ready every moment to singe it, and burn it asunder; and you have no interest in any mediator, and nothing to lay hold of to save yourself, nothing to keep off the flames of wrath, nothing of your own, nothing that you ever have done, nothing that you can do, to induce God to spare you one moment. . . .

Thus it will be with you that are in an unconverted state, if you continue in it; the infinite might, and majesty and terribleness of the omnipotent God shall be magnified upon you, in the ineffable[2] strength of your torments: you shall be tormented in the presence of the holy angels, and in the presence of the Lamb;[3] and when you shall be in this state of suffering, the glorious inhabitants of Heaven shall go forth and look on the awful spectacle, that they may see what the wrath and fierceness of the Almighty is, and when they have seen it, they will fall down and adore that great power and majesty. . . .

. . . 'Tis *everlasting* wrath. It would be dreadful to suffer this fierceness and wrath of Almighty God one moment; but you must suffer it to all eternity: there will be no end to this exquisite horrible misery: when you look forward, you shall see a long forever, a boundless duration before you, which will swallow up your thoughts, and amaze your soul; and you will absolutely despair of ever having any deliverance, any end, any mitigation,[4] any rest at all; you will know certainly that you must wear out long ages, millions of millions of ages, in wrestling and conflicting with this almighty merciless vengeance; and then when you have so done, when so many ages have actually been spent by you in this manner, you will know that all is but a point to what remains. So that your punishment will indeed be infinite. Oh, who can express what the state of a soul in such circumstances is! All that we can possibly say about it, gives but a very feeble faint representation of it; 'tis inexpressible and inconceivable: for *who knows the power of God's anger*?

How dreadful is the state of those that are daily and hourly in danger of this great wrath, and infinite misery! But this is the dismal case of every soul in this congregation, that has not been born again, however moral and strict, sober and religious they may otherwise be. . . .

And now you have an extraordinary opportunity, a day wherein Christ has flung the door of mercy wide open, and stands in the door calling and crying with a loud voice to poor sinners; a day wherein many are flocking to him, and pressing into the kingdom of God; many are daily coming from the east, west, north, and south; many that were very lately in the same miserable condition that you are in, are in now an happy state, with their hearts filled with love to Him that has loved them and washed them from their sins in his own blood, and rejoicing in hope of the glory of God. How awful is it to be left behind at such a day! To see so many others feasting, while you are pining and perishing! To see so many rejoicing and singing for joy of heart, while you have cause to mourn for sorrow of heart, and howl for vexation of spirit! How can you rest one moment in such a condition? . . .

Therefore let every one that is out of Christ, now awake and fly from the wrath to come. . . .

---

2. **ineffable** (in ef' ə b'l): too overwhelming to be expressed in words.
3. **Lamb:** The Lamb of God, Jesus: John 1:29, 36.
4. **mitigation** (mit' ə gā' shən): lessening in severity, relief.

Getting at Meaning

1. According to this sermon, why is the human being in such a dangerous position? What is a constant threat to all human beings?

2. What saves the sinner from hell? Who are the only people who are spared God's wrath?

3. What can sinners do to save themselves, according to Edwards?

4. Describe Edwards's conception of eternity. Why does he include this description in his sermon?

5. What does this sermon ask of its audience? What is the one source of hope?

Developing Skills in Reading Literature

1. **Persuasion.** A writer or speaker sometimes attempts to persuade an audience, to sway readers or listeners in a particular direction. "Sinners in the Hands of an Angry God" is a sermon, a form of religious persuasion in which a speaker exhorts an audience to behave in a more spiritual, moral fashion. Who is Edwards's audience for this sermon? What is his overriding purpose?

Examine the techniques of persuasion used by Edwards in this sermon. What makes the sermon so gripping and full of emotional impact? List several persuasive techniques and cite passages in which Edwards uses them.

2. **Figurative Language.** Edwards begins his sermon with a startling metaphor. He says that humans find it easy to crush a worm "that we see crawling on the earth." What does Edwards compare to this relationship? Edwards also says that God holds humans over the pit of hell, "much as one holds a spider or a loathsome insect." To what else does he compare human beings in the course of his sermon? What view of human beings is implied in Edwards's comparisons?

What is Edwards's extended metaphor to describe the human condition? In many ways the whole sermon turns on this comparison. To what does he liken God's anger?

Select several other figures of speech in the sermon and analyze their dramatic appeal. What gives his words their power?

3. **Theme.** The subject of Edwards's sermon is the precarious condition of humans in a God-centered world. According to Puritan belief, each human being is predestined for salvation or damnation. The doctrine of predestination states that whether an individual will achieve salvation or not is determined even before his or her birth. Good works cannot help a person earn salvation if that person is not one of the "elect."

In his sermon Edwards describes a way to salvation. What is it? Cite the lines in which he offers hope to the "miserable creatures" he addresses.

Developing Vocabulary

Connotation. Edwards uses precise nouns, verbs, adjectives, and adverbs that have powerful connotations, or emotional associations. Discuss the connotations of each italicized word that follows. Which words reinforce the central image of human beings hanging over a fiery pit? How do the connotations serve Edwards's persuasive purpose?

slender thread
fierceness of his wrath
done nothing to *appease* or *abate* that anger
loathsome insect
dreadfully provoked
ten thousand times so *abominable*
exquisite horrible misery
boundless duration
merciless vengeance

Developing Writing Skills

1. **Writing a Definition.** Edwards defines the abstract concept of eternity through the use of concrete detail. Reread the paragraph in which he does so.

Choose an abstraction to define in a well developed paragraph. Define the abstraction with vivid, specific detail, bringing it to life for your reader.

2. **Analyzing Theme.** In one paragraph describe the God that this sermon delineates. What characteristics does this deity possess? What kind of relationship exists between this Puritan God and humans? Support your comments with specific phrases and sentences from the sermon.

Salem Court Documents, 1692

About Sarah Good

Salem Village, March the 1st, 1691 92.

Sarah Good, the wife of William Good of Salem Village, Laborer. Brought before us by George Locker, Constable in Salem, to Answer, Joseph Hutchinson, Thomas Putnam, etc., of Salem Village, yeomen[1] (Complainants on behalf of their Majesties) against said Sarah Good for Suspicion of witchcraft by her Committed and thereby much Injury done to the Bodies of Elizabeth Parris, Abigail Williams, Ann Putnam, and Elizabeth Hubbard, all of Salem Village aforesaid according to their Complaints as per warrants.

Dated Salem, March 29th, 1691–92.

Sarah Good upon Examination denieth the matter of fact (viz.) that she ever used any witchcraft or hurt the abovesaid children or any of them.

The above-named Children being all present positively accused her of hurting of them Sundry times within this two months and also that morning.

Sarah Good denied that she had been at their houses in said time or near them, or had done them any hurt. All the abovesaid children then present accused her face to face, upon which they were all dreadfully tortured and tormented for a short space of time, and the affliction and tortures being over, they charged said Sarah Good again that she had then so tortured them, and came to them and did it, although she was personally then kept at a Considerable distance from them.

Sarah Good being Asked if, that she did not then hurt them who did it. And the children being again tortured, she looked upon them And said that it was one of them we brought into the house with us. We Asked her who it was: She then Answered and said it was Sarah Osborne, and Sarah Osborne was then under Custody and not in the house; And the children being quickly after recovered out of their fit said that it was Sarah Good and also Sarah Osborne that then did hurt & torment or afflict them—although both of them at the same time at a distance or Remote from them personally—there were also sundry other Questions put to her and Answers given thereunto by her according as is also given in.

JOHN HATHORNE } Assistants.
JONATHAN CORWIN

---

1. **yeomen** (yō′ mən): small landowners.

The Examination of Sarah Good

The examination of Sarah Good before the worshipful Assistants John Hathorne, Jonathan Corwin.

Q. Sarah Good, what evil Spirit have you familiarity with?

A. None.

Q. Have you made no contract with the Devil?

Good answered no.

Q. Why do you hurt these children?

A. I do not hurt them. I scorn it.

Q. Who do you employ then to do it?

A. I employ nobody.

Q. What creature do you employ then?

A. No creature, but I am falsely accused.

Q. Why did you go away muttering from Mr. Parris his house?

A. I did not mutter, but I thanked him for what he gave my child.

Q. Have you made no contract with the devil?

A. No.

H[athorne] desired the children, all of them, to look upon her and see if this were the person that had hurt them, and so they all did look upon her, and said this was one of the persons that did torment them—presently they were all tormented.

Q. Sarah Good, do you not see now what you have done? Why do you not tell us the truth? Why do you thus torment these poor children?

A. I do not torment them.

Q. Who do you employ then?

A. I employ nobody. I scorn it.

Q. How came they thus tormented?

A. What do I know. You bring others here and now you charge me with it.

Q. Why, who was it?

A. I do not know, but it was some you brought into the meeting house with you.

Q. We brought you into the meeting house.

A. But you brought in two more.

Q. Who was it then that tormented the children?

A. It was Osborne.

Q. What is it you say when you go muttering away from person's houses?

A. If I must tell, I will tell.

Q. Do tell us then.

A. If I must tell, I will tell. It is the commandments. I may say my commandments I hope.

Q. What commandment is it?

A. If I must tell, I will tell. It is a psalm.

Q. What psalm?

After a long time she muttered over some part of a psalm.

Q. Who do you serve?

A. I serve God.

Q. What God do you serve?

A. The God that made heaven and earth, though she was not willing to mention the word *God*. Her answers were in a very wicked spiteful manner, reflecting and retorting against the authority with base and abusive words, and many lies she was taken in. It was here said that her husband had said that he was afraid that she either was a witch or would be one very quickly. The worshipful Mr. Hathorne asked him his reason why he said so of her, whether he had ever seen anything by her. He answered no, not in this nature, but it was her bad carriage to him, and indeed, said he, I may say with tears that she is an enemy to all good.

Salem Village, March the 1st, 1691–92.
Written by Ezekiel Cheever. . . .

Testimony Against Bridget Bishop

John Bly Sr. and William Bly v.
Bridget Bishop

June 2d 1692. John Bly Senior aged about 57 years and William Bly aged about 15 years, both of Salem, Testifieth and saith that being Employed by Bridget Bishop, Alias Oliver, of Salem to help take down the Cellar wall of The Old house she formerly Lived in. We the said Deponents[1] in holes in the said old wall belonging to the said Cellar found several puppets made up of Rags And hog's Bristles with headless pins in Them with the points outward and this was about Seven years Last past.

John Bly Sr. and Rebecca Bly v.
Bridget Bishop

John Bly senior and Rebecca Bly his wife of Salem, both Testify and say that said John Bly Bought a Sow of Edwd Bishop of Salem, Sawyer, and by agreement with said Bishop was to pay the price agreed upon unto Lt. Jeremiah Neale of Salem. And Bridget, the wife of Said Edward Bishop, because she could not have the money or value agreed for paid unto her, she came to the house of the deponents in Salem and Quarrelled with them about it. Soon after which the sow having pigged, she was taken with strange fits, Jumping up and knocking her head against the fence, and seemed blind and deaf and would not Eat, neither Let her pigs suck but foamed at the mouth. Which Goody Henderson, hearing of, said she believed she was overlooked[2] and that they had their cattle ill in such a manner at the eastward when she lived there, and used to cure them by giving of them, Red Okra and Milk which we also gave the sow: Quickly after eating of which she grew Better, and then for the space of near two hours together she, getting into the street, did set off Jumping and running between the house of said deponents and said Bishops as if she were stark mad, and after that was well again, and we did then apprehend or Judge and do still that said Bishop had bewitched said sow.

Jurat in Curia.[3]

---

1. **Deponent** (di pō′ nənt): a person who gives written testimony under oath.
2. **overlooked** (ō′ vər look'd′): watched from above.
3. *Jurat in Curia* (joor′ at in kyoor′ ē ə) *Latin:* sworn in court.

Getting at Meaning

1. Why is Sarah Good on trial? What is the evidence against her?

2. Why does Sarah Good probably accuse Sarah Osborne of witchcraft?

3. In examining Sarah Good, what do the prosecutors seem to believe is the source of evil? What remarks indicate that the examiners are already convinced of her guilt?

4. What is significant in the accusation that Sarah Good "mutters"? How does she explain her muttering?

5. Notice that Sarah Good's husband is allowed to testify. What does he say about his wife?

6. What evidence condemns Bridget Bishop?

Developing Skills in Reading Literature

1. **Nonfiction.** Official court documents are examples of nonfiction writing. Unlike personal narratives, court documents are supposed to be objective, or uninfluenced by emotion, surmise, and personal prejudice. They are supposed to be a straightforward, factual account of what takes place in the courtroom.

What lines and comments in the *Salem Court Documents* indicate that the courtroom officials who wrote the documents are not objective? What prejudices do they seem to have against the accused? What is their attitude toward the accusers? What is probably their underlying feeling about witchcraft?

2. **Theme.** It is frustrating to observe in these documents that the accused are condemned before their trials even begin. What factors made the society of that day so susceptible to witchcraft hysteria? Why do the accusers have the upper hand? Judging from the charges against Bridget Bishop, what were some Salem citizens attempting to do in accusing their neighbors of witchcraft?

THE TRIAL OF GEORGE JACOBS FOR WITCHCRAFT, 1855. *T. H. Matteson. Essex Institute, Salem, Massachusetts.*

Charles Wentworth Upham

1802–1875

Charles Wentworth Upham was a Unitarian clergyman and historian whose most famous work is *Salem Witchcraft* (1867), a thoroughly researched, two-volume study of the Salem witch trials.

Charles Upham was the descendant of John Upham, who came to Weymouth, Massachusetts, from England in 1635. Joshua Upham, the father of Charles, was a Loyalist who fought with the British army during the Revolutionary War and who settled in Canada after the war. There Charles was born on May 4, 1802. Joshua held the position of Judge of the Supreme Court until his death in 1808, when Charles was six. In 1816, fourteen-year-old Charles went to Boston to work for a merchant cousin. The cousin, recognizing that Charles was a scholarly boy, had him tutored and sent him to Harvard and to Cambridge Divinity School. He was ordained in 1824 as associate pastor of the First Church (Unitarian) of Salem. During his ministry Upham encouraged his congregation to abandon the beliefs of the Puritans and to embrace the rational Christianity of the Unitarian faith. In 1828 Charles married Ann Susan Holmes, the sister of Oliver Wendell Holmes, and the couple had fourteen children, of whom only three survived. Charles resigned his pastorate in 1844 because of ill health, and later served in the Massachusetts State House of Representatives and Senate and in the United States Congress. He retired from public life in 1860 to study and write history. He died in Salem on June 15, 1875.

Upham once incurred the wrath of Nathaniel Hawthorne by causing Hawthorne to be removed from his job as customs surveyor in Salem. In retaliation, Hawthorne is believed to have modeled the character of the hypocritical Judge Pyncheon in *The House of Seven Gables* on Upham. Some critics, however, consider the Judge a caricature rather than a portrait of Charles Upham.

On the Place of Execution [at Salem]

The place selected for the executions is worthy of notice. It was at a considerable distance from the jail, and could be reached only by a circuitous and difficult route. It is a fatiguing enterprise to get at it now, although many passages that approach it from some directions have since been opened. But it was a point where the spectacle would be witnessed by the whole surrounding country far and near, being on the brow of the highest eminence[1] in the vicinity of the town. As it was believed by the people generally that they were engaged in a great battle with Satan, one of whose titles was "the Prince of the Power of the Air," perhaps they chose that spot to execute his confederates, because, in going to that high point, they were flaunting him in his face, celebrating their triumph over him in his own realm. . . .

"Witch Hill" is a part of an elevated ledge of rock on the western side of the city of Salem, broken at intervals; beginning at Legg's Hill, and trending northerly. . . . Its somber and desolate appearance admits of little variety of delineation.[2] It is mostly a bare and naked ledge. At the top of this cliff, on the southern brow of the eminence, the executions are supposed to have taken place. The outline rises a little towards the north, but soon begins to fall off to the general level of the country. From that direction only can the spot be easily reached. It is hard to climb the western side, impossible to clamber up the southern face. . . . It is, as it were, a platform raised high in air.

A magnificent panorama of ocean, island, headland, bay, river, town, field, and forest spreads out and around to view. On a clear summer day, the picture can scarcely be surpassed. Facing the sun and the sea, and the evidences of the love and bounty of Providence shining over the landscape, the last look of earth must have suggested to the sufferers a wide contrast between the mercy of the Creator and the wrath of his creatures. They beheld the face of the blessed God shining upon them in his works, and they passed with renewed and assured faith into his more immediate presence. The elevated rock, uplifted by the divine hand, will stand while the world stands, in bold relief, and can never be obscured by the encroachments[3] of society or the structures of art, a fitting memorial of their constancy. When, in some coming day, a sense of justice, appreciation of moral firmness, sympathy for suffering innocence, the diffusion of refined sensibility, a discriminating discernment of what is really worthy of commemoration among men, a rectified taste, a generous public spirit, and gratitude for the light that surrounds and protects us against error, folly, and fanaticism, shall demand the rearing of a suitable monument to the memory of those who in 1692 preferred death to a falsehood, the pedestal for the lofty column will be found ready, reared by the Creator on a foundation that can never be shaken while the globe endures, or worn away by the elements, man, or time— the brow of Witch Hill. On no other spot could such a tribute be more worthily bestowed, or more conspicuously displayed.

---

1. **eminence:** a high or lofty place.
2. **delineation:** description in words.
3. **encroachment:** intrusion.

Getting at Meaning

1. Describe Witch Hill in Salem. According to Upham, what were the probable reasons for the choice of this spot as an execution site?

2. What does Upham speculate must have gone through the minds of the accused witches before they were hanged? What does Upham suggest erecting on Witch Hill? Why?

Developing Skills in Reading Literature

1. **Essay.** An essay is a brief, nonfiction composition that offers an opinion on a subject. Frequently the essayist tries to persuade the reader to agree with his or her ideas.

This essay was written in the nineteenth century, long after the Salem witch trials had taken place. What is the writer's perspective on the events that took place in 1692? What is his attitude toward the suffering people who were hanged? What words and phrases indicate his opinion of Puritan society?

2. **Symbol.** A symbol is a person, place, or object that represents something beyond itself. Upham sees the rock at Witch Hill as a fitting symbol of the "constancy" of the people who were hanged there. Why is the rock an appropriate symbol? What qualities in the people does this symbol emphasize? Why is it significant that the rock is "elevated"?

3. **Theme.** What is Upham's concept of God? Point to specific words and phrases that reveal his beliefs. How does his concept contrast with the Puritan notion of the deity? Which vision of a divine being do you find more appealing? Why?

What is Upham's view of his own society? What does he hope for society "in some coming day"? To what does he refer when he speaks of "the light that surrounds and protects us against error, folly, and fanaticism"?

Stephen Vincent Benét
1898–1943

Stephen Vincent Benét's most enduring poems and short stories deal with events and themes from American history, thus putting the past in perspective for the twentieth-century reader. In his account of the Salem witchcraft trials, he illuminates the force behind the trials as "a superstition that flares into crowd-madness and kills and kills again before it has run its course."

The Benét family name, Stephen explained, "is Minorcan, the family originally coming to Florida while the latter was still a Spanish possession." His father, a third-generation army officer, loved poetry. His older brother, William Rose, and his sister, Laura, were writers, also. Stephen was born while his father was stationed in Bethlehem, Pennsylvania. He grew up and attended schools near army posts from San Francisco to Georgia, and then entered Yale University, where he studied for both his undergraduate and graduate degrees. By the time that he graduated, he had published a book of dramatic monologues, many stories for young readers, a study of Keats's poetry, and a volume of verse, *Young Adventures*. His master's thesis was another volume of poetry, *Heavens and Earth*. He continued study at the Sorbonne, in Paris, where he wrote and published two novels. In Paris he met poet Rosemary Carr, whom he married in 1921.

Setting out to write for a living, Benét soon found popular acceptance, particularly for short stories and poems, such as the story "The Devil and Daniel Webster" and the poem "Ballad of William Sycamore." Benét mastered the art of retaining the truth of an historical event while at the same time turning it into an American myth, often in the form of a ballad or folk tale. In 1926 he won a Guggenheim Fellowship that enabled him to write *John Brown's Body*, the literary epic on the Civil War for which he was awarded the Pulitzer Prize.

During the 1930's Benét continued to write short stories and poems, while working tirelessly to raise American spirits during the Great Depression and to alert the nation to the threat of the Nazi movement. A respected humanitarian and patriot, he lectured, wrote articles, and presented radio broadcasts.

Benét had planned a five-volume epic tracing the history of American immigration and the migration West. By 1943 he had completed the first volume, *Western Star*, which concerns the Plymouth and Jamestown colonies. Then he died quite suddenly. His brother, William Rose, readied the work for publication in 1943. Benét received the Pulitzer Prize for the second time, posthumously, in 1944.

We Aren't Superstitious   [Salem Witchcraft Trials, 1692]

Usually, our little superstitious rituals and propitiations[1] don't hurt our daily lives. Usually. And then, on occasion, a superstition—a belief—flares into crowd-madness and kills and kills again before it has run its course. As it did in Salem Village, in 1692.

That story is worth retelling, as a very typical example of what wild belief and crowd hysteria can do to an average community. For Salem Village, in 1691, was no different in any way, from any one of a dozen little New England hamlets. It didn't expect celebrity or notoriety, and its citizens were the average people of their day and age. There was the main road and the parsonage and the meeting house, the block house, the Ingersoll house where travelers put up for the night, the eight or nine other houses that made up the village. Beyond, lay the outlying farms with their hard working farmers—a few miles away lay Salem Town itself—fifteen miles away, the overgrown village that was Boston. King Philip's War[2] had been over for some fourteen years and the Colony was recovered from the shock of it—there were still individual slayings by Indians but the real power of the Indian was very largely broken. Men might look forward, with hope, to peace and thriving for a time.

And, as for the men and women of Salem Village—they were tough and knotty stock, if you like, not widely lettered, not particularly tolerant, especially in religion—but no different from their neighbors at Andover and Topsfield or in Boston itself. There were sensible men and stupid men among them, model housewives and slatterns, trouble makers and more peaceable folk. The names were the Puritan names that we are accustomed to reverence—Mercy and Abigail and Deborah, Nathaniel and Samuel and John. They lived a life of hard work and long winters, drank rum on occasion, took their religion with that mixture of grimness and enthusiasm that marked the Puritan, and intended, under God's providence, to beat wilderness and Indian, and wax and increase in the land. They were a great deal more human, crotchety and colorful than the schoolbook pictures of dour-faced men in steeple-crowned hats would suggest. In fact, if you want to find out how human they were, you have only to read Judge Sewall's diary. He was one of the judges at the Salem witch trials—and heartily sorry for it later. But his Pepysian[3] account of his own unsuccessful courtship of Madam Winthrop, and how he brought her gloves and sweets, is in the purest vein of unconscious farce.

And yet, to this ordinary community in the early Spring of 1692, came a madness that was to shake all Massachusetts before its fever was burned out. We are wiser, now. We do not believe in witches. But if, say, three cases of Asiatic cholera were discovered in your own hometown, and certified as such by the local board of health—and if your local newspaper promptly ran a boxed warning to all citizens on the front page—you would have some faint idea of how the average Salem Villager felt, when the "afflicted children" denounced their first victims.

---

1. **propitiation** (prə pish' e ā' shun): sacrifices made to win or to regain the good will of the gods.
2. **King Philip's War:** (1675–1676) between the New England colonists and the Indians under King Philip, sachem of the Wampanoags.
3. **Pepysian:** In the manner of the diary of Samuel Pepys (1633–1703).

For witchcraft, to almost all the New Englanders of 1692, was as definite, diagnosable, and dangerous an evil as bubonic plague. It had its symptoms, its prognosis,[4] and its appalling results. Belief in it was as firmly fixed in most people's minds as belief in the germ theory of disease is in ours. Cotton Mather was one of the most able and promising young ministers of his day. But when, in 1688, in Boston, an eleven-year-old girl named Martha Goodwin accused an unhappy Irish Catholic laundress of bewitching her, Cotton Mather believed the eleven-year-old girl. In fact, he took the precocious brat into his own house, to study her symptoms and cure them by fasting and prayer, and wrote and published an elaborate, scientific account of his treatment of the case—which doubtless played its own part in preparing men's minds for the Salem madness.

True, there had been only some twenty witch trials in New England up to the Salem affair—compared to the hundreds and thousands of hangings, burnings, duckings, drownings, that had gone on in Europe and the British Isles during the last few centuries. But people believed in witches—why should they not? They were in the Bible—even the Bible itself said, "Thou shalt not suffer a witch to live." They were in every old wives' tale that was whispered about the winter fires. And, in 1692, they were in Salem Village.

Three years before, Salem Village had got a new minister—the Reverend Samuel Parris, ex-merchant in the West Indies. He seems to have been a self-willed, self-important man with a great sense of his own and the church's dignity; and, no sooner were he and his family well settled in the parsonage, than a dispute began as to whether the parsonage property belonged to him or to the congregation. But there was nothing unusual about that—Salem Village was a rather troublesome parish and two, at least, of the three previous ministers had had salary and other difficulties with the good folk of Salem. The quarrel dragged on

like the old boundary dispute between Salem and Topsfield, creating faction[5] and hard feeling, a typically New England affair. But there were boundary disputes elsewhere and other congregations divided in mind about their ministers.

But the most important thing about Samuel Parris was neither his self-importance nor his attempt to get hold of the parsonage property. It was the fact that he brought with him to Salem Village, two West Indian servants—a man known as John Indian and a woman named Tituba. And when he bought those two or their services in the West Indies, he was buying a rope that was to hang nineteen men and women of New England—so odd are the links in the circumstantial chain.

Perhaps the nine-year-old Elizabeth Parris, the daughter of the parsonage, boasted to her new friends of the odd stories Tituba told and the queer things she could do. Perhaps Tituba herself let the report of her magic powers be spread about the village. She must have been as odd and imagination-stirring a figure as a parrot or a tame monkey in the small New England town. And the winters were long and white—and any diversion a godsend.

In any case, during the winter of 1691–92, a group of girls and women began to meet nightly at the parsonage, with Tituba and her fortune-telling as the chief attraction. Elizabeth Parris, at nine, was the youngest—then came Abigail Williams, eleven, and Ann Putnam, twelve. The rest were older—Mercy Lewis, Mary Wolcott, and Elizabeth Hubbard were seventeen, Elizabeth Booth and Susan Sheldon, eighteen, and Mary Warren and Sarah Churchill, twenty. Three were servants —Mercy Lewis had been employed by the Reverend George Burroughs, a previous minister of Salem Village, and now worked for the Putnams—Mary Warren was a maid at the

---

4. **prognosis:** a prediction of the course of a disease.

5. **faction:** a group of people inside an organization working against other such groups for its own ideas or goals.

John Procters', Sarah Churchill at the George Jacobs'. All, except for Elizabeth Parris, were adolescent or just leaving adolescence.

The elder women included a pair of gossipy, superstitious busybodies—Mrs. Pope and Mrs. Bibber—and young Ann Putnam's mother, Ann Putnam, Senior, who deserves a sentence to herself.

For the Putnams were a powerful family in the neighborhood, and Ann Putnam, married at seventeen and now only thirty, is described as handsome, arrogant, temperamental, and high-strung. She was also one of those people who can cherish a grudge and revenge it.

The circle met—the circle continued to meet—no doubt with the usual giggling, whispering, and gossip. From mere fortune-telling it proceeded to other and more serious matters—table-rapping, perhaps, and a little West Indian voodoo—weird stories told by Tituba and weird things shown, while the wind blew outside and the big shadows flickered on the wall. Adolescent girls, credulous[6] servants, superstitious old women—and the two enigmatic[7] figures of Tituba, the West Indian, and Ann Putnam, Sr.

But soon the members of the circle began to show hysterical symptoms. They crawled under tables and chairs, they made strange sounds, they shook and trembled with nightmare fears. The thing became a village celebrity—and more. Something strange and out of nature was happening—who had ever seen normal young girls behave like these young girls? And no one—certainly not the Reverend Samuel Parris—even suggested that a mixed diet of fortune-telling, ghost stories, and voodoo is hardly the thing for impressionable minds during a long New England winter. Hysteria was possession by an evil spirit; pathological lying, the Devil putting words into one's mouth. No one suggested that even Cotton Mather's remedy of fasting and prayer would be a good deal better for such cases than widespread publicity. Instead, the Reverend Samuel became very busy. Grave minis-

ters were called in to look at the afflicted children. A Dr. Gregg gave his opinion. It was almost too terrible to believe, and yet what else could be believed? Witchcraft!

Meanwhile, one may suppose, the "afflicted children," like most hysterical subjects, enjoyed the awed stares, the horrified looks, the respectful questions that greeted them, with girlish zest. They had been unimportant girls of a little hamlet—now they were, in every sense of the word, spot news. And any reporter knows what that does to certain kinds of people. They continued to writhe and demonstrate—and be the center of attention. There was only one catch about it. If they were really bewitched—somebody must be doing the bewitching—

On the 29th of February, 1692, in the midst of an appropriate storm of thunder-and-lightning, three women, Sarah Good, Sarah Osborne and Tituba, were arrested on the deadly charge of bewitching the children.

The next day, March 1, two Magistrates, Justice Hathorne and Justice Corwin, arrived with appropriate pomp and ceremony. The first hearing was held in the crowded meetinghouse of the Village—and all Salem swarmed to it, as crowds in our time have swarmed to other sleepy little villages, suddenly notorious.

The children—or the children and Tituba—had picked their first victims well. Sarah Good and Sarah Osborne were old women of no particular standing in the community. Sarah Good had been a beggar and a slattern—her husband testified, according to report and with a smugness that makes one long to kick him, that she "either was a witch or would be one very quickly," ending "I may say, with tears, that she is an enemy to all good." As for Sarah Osborne, she had married a redemptioner servant[8] after the death of her former

---

6. **credulous** (krej' oo ləs): tending to believe too readily.
7. **enigmatic:** puzzling, mysterious.
8. **redemptioner servant:** indentured servant.

husband and probably lost caste in consequence. Also, she had been bedridden for some time and therefore not as regular in her church attendance as a good Christian should be.

We can imagine that meetinghouse—and the country crowd within it—on that chill March day. At one end was the majesty of the law—and the "afflicted children" where all might see them and observe. Dressed in their best, very likely, and with solicitous relatives near at hand. Do you see Mercy Lewis? Do you see Ann Putnam? And then the whole crowd turned to one vast, horrified eye. For there was the accused—the old woman—the witch!

The justices—grim Justice Hathorne in particular—had, evidently, arrived with their minds made up. For the first question addressed to Sarah Good was, bluntly:

"What evil spirit have you familiarity with?"

"None," said the piping old voice. But everybody in the village knew worthless Sarah Good. And the eye of the audience went from her to the deadly row of "afflicted children" and back again.

"Have you made no contracts with the devil?" proceeded the Justice.

"No."

The Justice went to the root of the matter at once.

"Why do you hurt these children?"

A rustle must have gone through the meetinghouse at that. Aye, that's it—the Justice speaks shrewdly—hark to the Justice! Aye, but look, too! Look at the children! Poor things, poor things!

"I do not hurt them. I scorn it," said Sarah Good, defiantly. But the Justice had her, now—he was not to be brushed aside.

"Who then do you employ to do it?"

"I employ nobody."

"What creature do you employ then?" For all witches had familiars.[9]

"No creature, but I am falsely accused." But the sweat must have been on the old woman's palms by now.

The Justice considered. There was another point—minor but illuminating.

"Why did you go away muttering from Mr. Parris, his house?"

"I did not mutter, but I thanked him for what he gave my child."

The Justice returned to the main charge, like any prosecuting attorney.

"Have you made no contract with the devil?"

"No."

It was time for Exhibit A. The Justice turned to the children. Was Sarah Good one of the persons who tormented them? Yes, yes!—and a horrified murmur running through the crowd. And then, before the awe-stricken eyes of all, they began to be tormented. They writhed, they grew stiff, they contorted, they were stricken moaning or speechless. Yet, when they were brought to Sarah Good and allowed to touch her, they grew quite quiet and calm. For, as everyone knew, a witch's physical body was like an electric conductor—it reabsorbed, on touch, the malefic[10] force discharged by witchcraft into the bodies of the tormented. Everybody could see what happened—and everybody saw. When the meetinghouse was quiet, the Justice spoke again.

"Sarah Good, do you not see now what you have done? Why do you not tell us the truth? Why do you torment these poor children?"

And with these words, Sarah Good was already hanged. For all that she could say was, "I do not torment them." And yet everyone had seen her, with their own eyes.

The questions went on—she fumbled in her answers—muttered a bit of prayer. Why did she mutter? And didn't you see how hard it

---

9. **familiars:** spirits in animal shapes which acted as servants to witches.
10. **malefic** (mə lef' ik): harmful, evil.

was for her to pronounce the name of God? Pressed and desperate, she finally said that if anyone tormented the children, it must be Sarah Osborne—she knew herself guiltless. The pitiful fable did not save her. To Boston Jail.

Sarah Osborne's examination followed the same course—the same prosecutor's first question—the same useless denial—the same epileptic feats of the "afflicted children"—the same end. It was also brought out that Sarah Osborne had said that "she was more like to be bewitched than to be a witch"—very dangerous that!—and that she had once had a nightmare about "a thing all black like an Indian that pinched her in the neck."

Then Tituba was examined and gave them their fill of marvels, prodigies,[11] and horrors.

The West Indian woman, a slave in a strange land, was fighting for her life and she did it shrewdly and desperately. She admitted, repentantly, that she had tormented the children. But she had been forced to do so. By whom? By Goody Good and Goody Osborne and two other witches whom she hadn't yet been able to recognize. Her voodoo knowledge aided her—she filled the open ears of Justices and crowds with tales of hairy familiars and black dogs, red cats and black cats and yellow birds, the phantasm[12] of a woman with legs and wings. And everybody could see that she spoke the truth. For, when she was first brought in, the children were tormented at her presence, but as soon as she had confessed and turned King's evidence, she was tormented herself, and fearfully. To Boston Jail with her—but she had saved her neck.

The hearing was over—the men and women of Salem and its outlying farms went broodingly or excitedly back to their homes to discuss the fearful workings of God's providence. Here and there a common-sense voice murmured a doubt or two—Sarah Good and Sarah Osborne were no great losses to the community—but still, to convict two old women of heinous[13] crime on the testimony

of green-sick girls and a West Indian slave! But, on the whole, the villagers of Salem felt relieved. The cause of the plague had been found—it would be stamped out and the afflicted children recover. The Justices, no doubt, congratulated themselves on their prompt and intelligent action. The "afflicted children" slept, after a tiring day—they were not quite so used to such performances as they were to become.

As for the accused women, they went to Boston Jail—to be chained there, while waiting trial and gallows. There is an item of, "To chains for Sarah Good and Sarah Osborne, 14 shillings," in the jailor's record. Only, Sarah Osborne was not to go to the gallows—she died in jail instead, some five and a half weeks later, at a recorded expense to the Colony of one pound, three shillings, and five-pence for her keep. And Tituba stayed snugly in prison till the madness collapsed—and was then sold by the Colony to defray the expenses of her imprisonment. One wonders who bought her and whether she ever got back to the West Indies. But, with that, her enigmatic figure disappears from the scene.

Meanwhile, on an outlying farm, Giles Corey, a turbulent, salty old fellow of 81, began to argue the case with his wife, Martha. He believed, fanatically, in the "afflicted children." She did not, and said so—even going so far as to say that the magistrates were blinded and she could open their eyes. It was one of those marital disputes that occur between strong-willed people. And it was to bring Martha Corey to the gallows and Giles Corey to an even stranger doom.

Yet now there was a lull, through which people whispered.

---

11. **prodigies:** things so extraordinary as to cause wonder and amazement.
12. **phantasm** (fan' taz'm): a specter, ghost, deceptive likeness.
13. **heinous** (hā' nəs): outrageously evil or wicked.

As for what went on in the minds of "the afflicted children," during that lull, we may not say. But this much is evident. They had seen and felt their power. The hearing had been the greatest and most exciting event of their narrow lives. And it was so easy to do—they grew more and more ingenious with each rehearsal. You twisted your body and groaned—and grown people were afraid.

Add to this, the three girl-servants, with the usual servants' grudges, against present or former masters. Add to this, that high-strung, dominant woman, Ann Putnam, Sr., who could hold a grudge and remember it. Such a grudge as there might be against the Towne sisters, for instance—they were all married women of the highest standing, particularly Rebecca Nurse. But they'd taken the Topsfield side in that boundary dispute with Salem. So suppose—just suppose—that one of them were found out to be a witch? And hadn't Tituba deposed that there were other women, besides Good and Osborne, who made her torment the children?

On March 19, Martha Corey and Rebecca Nurse were arrested on the charge of witchcraft. On March 21, they were examined and committed. And, with that, the real reign of terror began.

For if Martha Corey, notably religious and Godfearing, and Rebecca Nurse, saintly and thoughtful, could be witches, no one in Salem or New England was safe from the charge. The examinations were brutally unfair—the "children" yet bolder and more daring. They would interrupt questions now to shout that "a black man" was whispering in the prisoner's ear—if the accused stood still, they were tormented, if she moved her hands, they suffered even greater agonies. Their self-confidence became monstrous—there was no trick too fantastic for them to try. When Deodat Lawson, a former minister of Salem and a well educated and intelligent man, came to Ingersoll's on March 19, he first saw Mary Wolcott who "as she stood by the door

was bitten, so that she cried out of her wrist, and, looking at it, we saw apparently the marks of teeth, both upper and lower set, on each side of her wrist." It would not have deceived a child—but Mary Wolcott was one of the "afflicted children" and her words and self-bitings were as gospel. He then went to the parsonage, where Abigail Williams, another afflicted child, put on a very effective vaudeville-act indeed, throwing firebrands around the house, crying "Whish, whish, whish!" and saying that she was being tormented by Rebecca Nurse who was trying to make her sign the Devil's book.

After that, there was, obviously, nothing for the Reverend Lawson to do but to preach a thunderous sermon on the horrors of witchcraft—interrupted by demonstrations and cries from "the afflicted"—and thus do his little bit toward driving the madness on. For by now, Salem Village, as a community, was no longer sane.

Let us get the rest of it over quickly. The Salem witches ceased to be Salem's affair—they became a matter affecting the whole colony. Sir William Phips, the new governor, appointed a special court of Oyer and Terminer to try the cases. And the hangings began.

On January 1, 1692, no one, except possibly the "Circle children"[14] had heard of Salem witches. On June 10, Bridget Bishop was hanged. She had not been one of the first accused, but she was the first to suffer. She had been married three times, kept a roadhouse on the road to Beverly where people drank rum and played shovelboard, and dressed, distinctively for the period, in a "black cap and black hat and red paragon bodice broidered and looped with diverse colors." But those seem to have been her chief offences. When questioned, she said "I never saw the Devil in my life."

---

14. **Circle children:** see paragraph three, beginning "The circle met . . ." on page 57.

All through the summer, the accusations, the arrests, the trials came thick and fast till the jails were crowded. Nor were those now accused friendless old beldames[15] like Sarah Good. They included Captain John Alden (son of Miles Standish's friend) who saved himself by breaking jail, and the wealthy and prominent Englishes who saved themselves by flight. The most disgraceful scenes occurred at the trial of the saintly Rebecca Nurse. Thirty-nine citizens of Salem were brave enough to sign a petition for her and the jury brought in a verdict of "not guilty." The mob in the sweating courtroom immediately began to cry out and the presiding judge as much as told the jury to reverse their verdict. They did so, to the mob's delight. Then the Governor pardoned her. And "certain gentlemen of Salem"—and perhaps the mob—persuaded him into reversing his pardon. She was hanged on Gallows Hill on July 19 with Sarah Good, Sarah Wilds, Elizabeth How, and Susanna Martin.

Susanna Martin's only witchcraft seems to have been that she was an unusually tidy woman and had once walked a muddy road without getting her dress bedraggled. No, I am quoting from testimony, not inventing. As for Elizabeth How, a neighbor testified, "I have been acquainted with Goodwife How as a naybor for nine or ten years and I never saw any harm in her but found her just in her dealings and faithful to her promises. . . . I never heard her revile any person but she always pitied them and said, 'I pray God forgive them now.' " But the children cried, "I am stuck with a pin. I am pinched," when they saw her—and she hanged.

It took a little more to hang the Reverend George Burroughs. He had been Salem Village's second minister—then gone on to a parish in Maine. And the cloth had great sanctity. But Ann Putnam and Mercy Lewis managed to doom him between them—with the able assistance of the rest of the troupe. Mr. Burroughs was unfortunate enough to be a man of unusual physical strength—anyone who could lift a gun by putting four fingers in its barrel, must do so by magic arts. Also, he had been married three times. So when the ghosts of his first two wives, dressed in winding-sheets, appeared in a sort of magic-lantern show to Ann Putnam and cried out that Mr. Burroughs had murdered them—the cloth could not save him then. Perhaps one of the most pathetic documents connected with the trials is the later petition of his orphaned children. It begins, "We were left a parcel of small children, helpless—"

Here and there, in the records, gleams a flash of frantic common sense. Susanna Martin laughs when Ann Putnam and her daughter go into convulsions at her appearance. When asked why, she says, "Well I may, at such folly. I never hurt this woman or her child in my life." John Procter, the prosperous farmer who employed Mary Warren, said sensibly, before his arrest, "If these girls are left alone, we will all be devils and witches. They ought all to be sent to the whipping-post." He was right enough about it—but his servant helped hang him. White-haired old George Jacobs, leaning on his two sticks, cried out, "You tax[16] me for a wizard, you might as well tax me for a buzzard!" Nevertheless, he hanged. A member of the Nurse family testifies, "Being in court this 29th June, 1692, I saw Goodwife Bibber pull pins out of her clothes and hold them between her fingers and clasp her hands around her knee and then she cried out and said Goodwife Nurse pinched her." But such depositions did not save Rebecca Nurse or her sister, Mary Easty.

Judge, jury, and colony preferred to believe the writhings of the children, the stammerings of those whose sows had died inexplicably, the testimony of such as Bernard Peach who swore that Susanna Martin had flown in through his window, bent his body into the

---

15. **beldame** (bel' dəm): a hideous old woman, a hag.
16. **tax:** accuse, charge.

shape of a "whoope" and sat upon him for an hour and a half.

One hanging on June 10, five on July 19, five on August 19, eight on September 22, including Mary Easty and Martha Corey. And of these the Reverend Noyes remarked, with unction,[17] "What a sad thing it is to see eight fire-brands of hell hanging there!" But for stubborn Giles Corey a different fate was reserved.

The old man had begun by believing in the whole hocus-pocus. He had quarreled with his wife about it. He had seen her arrested as a witch, insulted by the magistrates, condemned to die. Two of his sons-in-law had testified against her—he himself had been closely questioned as to her actions and had made the deposition of a badgered and simple man. Yes, she prayed a good deal—sometimes he couldn't hear what she said—that sort of thing. The memory must have risen to haunt him when she was condemned. Now, he himself was in danger.

Well, he could die as his wife would. But there was the property—his goods, his prospering lands. By law, the goods and property of those convicted of witchcraft were confiscated by the State and the name attainted.[18] With a curious, grim heroism, Giles Corey drew up a will leaving that property to the two sons-in-law who had not joined in the prevailing madness. And then at his trial, he said, "I will not plead. If I deny, I am condemned already in courts where ghosts appear as witnesses and swear men's lives away."

A curious, grim heroism? It was so. For those who refused to plead either guilty or not guilty in such a suit were liable to the old English punishment called *peine forte et dure.*[19] It consisted in heaping weights or stones upon the unhappy victim till he accepted a plea—or until his chest was crushed. And exactly that happened to old Giles Corey. They heaped the stones upon him until they killed him—and two days before his wife was hanged, he died. But his property went to the two loyal sons-in-law, without confiscation—and his name was not attainted. So died Giles Corey, New England to the bone.

And then, suddenly and fantastically as the madness had come, it was gone.

The "afflicted children," at long last, had gone too far. They had accused the governor's lady. They had accused Mrs. Hall, the wife of the minister at Beverly and a woman known throughout the colony for her virtues. And there comes a point when driven men and women revolt against blood and horror. It was that which ended Robespierre's[20] terror—it was that which ended the terror of the "afflicted children." The thing had become a *reductio ad absurdum.*[21] If it went on, logically, no one but the "afflicted children" and their protégées would be left alive.

In 1706 Ann Putnam made public confession that she had been deluded by the devil in testifying as she had. She had testified in every case but one. And in 1711 the colony of Massachusetts paid fifty pounds to the heirs of George Burroughs, twenty-one pounds to the heirs of Giles Corey—five hundred and seventy-eight pounds in all to the heirs of various victims. An expensive business for the colony, on the whole.

What happened to the survivors? Well, the Reverend Samuel Parris quit Salem Village to go into business in Boston and died at Sudbury in 1720. And Ann Putnam died in 1716 and from the stock of the Putnams sprang Israel Putnam, the Revolutionary hero. And

---

17. **unction** (uŋk' shən): deep seriousness and emotion pretended or assumed for the occasion.
18. **attainted:** disgraced, dishonored, punished by loss of civil rights and property following a sentence of death or exile.
19. ***peine forte et dure*** (pən' fôr ta dür') *French:* strong and hard punishment.
20. **Robespierre** (rō bes pyer'): French revolutionist, 1758–1794, leader of the Reign of Terror.
21. ***reductio ad absurdum*** (ri duk' tē o' ad ab sur' dəm) *Latin:* disproof of a proposition by showing the logical conclusions drawn from it to be absurd.

from the stock of the "Witches," the Nurses and the others, sprang excellent and distinguished people of service to state and nation. And hanging Judge Hathorne's descendant was Nathaniel Hawthorne.

We have no reason to hold Salem up to obloquy.[22] It was a town, like another, and a strange madness took hold of it. But it is not a stranger thing to hang a man for witchcraft than to hang him for the shape of his nose or the color of his skin. We are not superstitious, no. Well, let us be a little sure we are not. For persecution follows superstition and intolerance as fire follows the fuse. And once we light that fire we cannot foresee where it will end or what it will consume—any more than they could in Salem two hundred and sixty-seven years ago.

---

22. **obloquy** (äb' lə kwē): loud and angry criticism.

Getting at Meaning

1. Benét states the problem that he will deal with in the opening paragraph of this essay. Why does he believe that the story of the Salem witchcraft trials is worth retelling? How does his description of Salem as an ordinary place make the events he recounts seem that much more immediate?

2. How does Benét describe the people of Salem? What example does he give to humanize even a stern Puritan judge?

3. On what factors does Benét blame the Salem madness? What role did geography and climate probably play in the events?

4. Recount the story of Cotton Mather that Benét tells. Why does he include this story?

5. Explain Samuel Parris's role in the witchcraft proceedings. Notice that he was involved in several different ways.

6. What is Tituba's background? In what sense is she the source of the Salem events?

7. Explain how the meetings with Tituba escalate into hysteria. How do Parris's actions contribute to the further escalation of the situation?

8. Why are Sarah Good and Sarah Osborne appropriate first victims?

9. Comment on "Exhibit A" during Sarah Good's examination. Why do the girls behave as they do? Why is everyone convinced by their performance?

10. Explain how Tituba cleverly saves her life. How does she fascinate the crowd? What eventually happens to her?

11. Explain how Giles Corey and his wife become implicated in the witch trials. What is the eventual fate of each of the Coreys? Why won't Giles plead guilty or not guilty? What reason does he give for refusing to plead? What is his final heroic act?

12. What causes the witchcraft hysteria to keep escalating? Why might the trials have ended so abruptly?

Developing Skills in Reading Literature

1. **Essay.** Essays often are classified as descriptive, narrative, or expository, though the same essay may be all three at once. Descriptive essays deal primarily with the appearances of people, objects, and places,

and generally include vivid sensory images. Narrative essays tell stories. Expository essays focus mainly on presenting information.

How might Benét's essay be classified? Of what type is it primarily? Where does Benét employ description? What story does he narrate? Where does he employ exposition?

An essayist usually tries to persuade the reader to agree with his or her opinions. In this essay Benét makes his opinion of the Salem proceedings clear in the opening paragraph. What is his position? How does he maintain it throughout the essay?

2. **Character Motivation.** Motivation is the moving force (or forces) behind a character's actions. In identifying motivation, the reader must consider circumstantial, psychological, and cultural factors.

Benét's essay focuses to a large degree on the psychological conditions in Salem that led to the witchcraft hysteria. What conditions led to the girls' sessions with Tituba? Why did the girls enjoy their role as "afflicted children," according to Benét? Why did Ann Putnam, an adult, participate in the hysteria? What led the girls to continue their behavior, accusing more and more people? What probably led them to begin accusing solid citizens?

3. **Irony.** Irony is a contrast between appearance and reality. Verbal irony occurs when people say one thing but actually mean something quite different. Irony of situation occurs when the reader expects one thing to happen but something entirely different occurs.

The title of Benét's essay is an example of verbal irony. Explain its meaning. What does the title lead you to conclude about Benét's purpose for writing the essay?

The Salem witch trials were riddled with ironies of situation. Perhaps the most dramatic is that a small group of adolescent liars were believed over a larger group of older, respected citizens. According to Benét, what caused this to happen? Why were the judges and the community so willing to believe the girls?

Developing Vocabulary

Connotation. Benét's diction is richly connotative and reinforces his basic point of view on the Salem proceedings. Comment on the emotional associations of each italicized word below, especially in relation to Benét's basic perspective.

Cotton Mather . . . took the precocious *brat* into his own house. . . .

The elder women included a pair of *gossipy*, superstitious *busybodies*.

Adolescent girls, *credulous* servants, *superstitious* old women. . . .

. . . to convict two old women of *heinous* crime on the testimony of *green-sick* girls and a West Indian slave!

Their self-confidence became *monstrous*. . . .

Abigail Williams . . . put on a very effective *vaudeville-act* indeed. . . .

Developing Writing Skills

Analyzing Theme. This essay, based as it is on the events in Salem, makes a powerful statement about mob rule and mass psychology. What can we learn from the events in Salem? What led intelligent people to lose their reason? Why were the pleas of sensible people ignored? Why were many people afraid to speak out against the girls? What example does Benét give to show that a similar hysteria could grip present-day America? Can you think of other instances in which mob rule has prevailed?

Answer these questions in a brief composition. Outline your thoughts before you begin to write, deciding on the number of paragraphs your composition will have and on the points you will develop in each paragraph. Be concrete and specific in your explanation.

Unit Review   *The Original Land*

Understanding the Unit

1. Captain John Smith and William Bradford both describe the great physical hardships faced by the first English settlers in America. What similarities stand out in the experiences of the colonists at Jamestown and those at Plymouth? What differences are apparent?

2. Compare and contrast the attitude toward nature that pervades the Native American selections with the attitude that Captain John Smith and William Bradford project. How do you explain the similarities? How do you account for the differences?

3. Discuss the Puritan view of education that emerges in this unit. Compare and contrast it to the views on education prevalent in contemporary American society.

4. The ironies of situation in the Salem witch trials are many and startling. The irony of liars being believed over solid citizens has already been discussed. Some others to consider:

the ironic role of the minister

the ironic role of the judges

the ironic role of the Puritan religion

the ironic behavior of the supposedly good, virtuous Puritans

the ironic truth that the Salem community killed some of its finest citizens

the ironic reality that accused persons had to plead guilty to witchcraft to have any chance of saving themselves

Explain each of these ironies, then try to think of additional examples. What can be learned from these ironies and from the entire Salem experience?

Writing

1. Jonathan Edwards wrote in his personal narrative, "I made seeking my salvation the main business of my life." Such was the duty of all good Puritans.

Write a composition of six paragraphs in which you show how this goal is apparent in the writings of Edwards and of William Bradford, Anne Bradstreet, and Edward Taylor as well. Refer to specific passages in each writer's work to support your analysis. Devote one body paragraph to each writer, framing those four paragraphs with an introduction and a conclusion that link the four writers.

2. Select one of the following poems to study in detail:

"Song of the Sky Loom"

"I Went To Kill the Deer" and "I Have Killed the Deer" (Treat as one poem.)

"Upon the Burning of Our House, July 10th, 1666"

"Huswifery"

Analyze the way that the poet uses poetic techniques to establish the poem's meaning or message. In other words, demonstrate how the form of the poem reflects the content of the poem. Consider such poetic devices as imagery, figures of speech, diction, rhyme, meter, and structure—whatever is relevant to the poem. Discuss your analysis in a well organized essay of five paragraphs. Be sure you refer to specific passages in the poem to support your points.

3. Arthur Miller, the contemporary American playwright, dramatized the Salem witch trials in his play *The Crucible*. In an introductory section of the play, Miller says of the Puritans, "They believed, in short, that they held in their steady hands the candle that would light the world. We have inherited this belief, and it has helped and hurt us."

Consider Miller's statement in light of contemporary American society. Do Americans today believe that this country possesses a "candle" for the world? What might this candle be? What evidence supports the idea that America holds a special attraction for the people of the world? How has the Puritan heritage helped America as a country? How has it hurt the country? Are the American people smug and self-righteous in the manner of the Puritans? Discuss the answers to these questions in a five-paragraph essay.

GEORGE WASHINGTON (LANSDOWNE PORTRAIT), 1796. *Gilbert Stuart.*
Pennsylvania Academy of the Fine Arts.
Bequest of William Bingham.

Unit 2

The American Revolution (1750–1800)

PAUL REVERE, 1768-70. *John Singleton Copley.*
Museum of Fine Arts, Boston.
Gift of Joseph W., William B., and Edward H. R. Revere.

The Age of Reason

All nature is but art unknown to thee,
All chance, direction which thou canst not see;
All discord, harmony not understood;
All partial evil, universal good;
And, spite of pride, in erring reason's spite,
One truth is clear, whatever is, is right.

These lines by Alexander Pope, the well known English poet, from *An Essay on Man*, summarize the eighteenth-century view of human beings and the universe. This century is known as the Age of Reason, or the Enlightenment, because writers and philosophers in Europe at this time emphasized the role of reason, or rational thought, in human affairs. They perceived the universe as a harmonious, carefully ordered place, where each human being played a small role in the functioning of the whole, like a cog in a wheel. These thinkers also believed in the perfectability of human beings, feeling that, if people exercised their reason to bring about scientific advances and better government, society eventually would reach an ideal state.

American thinkers of the eighteenth century shared the emphasis on reason that they found in the works of European writers. Thomas Jefferson, one of the leading lights of the period, once declared, "We are not afraid to follow truth wherever it may lead, nor to tolerate any error so long as reason is left free to combat it." Jefferson's statement typifies the spirit of the age in America. Here was a new country, vast and unsettled, an excellent place in which to test some of the scientific and political theories of the Enlightenment. With proper management, America could become a utopia.

THE BIRTH OF OUR NATION

Americans in the thirteen colonies and Europeans alike agreed on the potential of the New World. The problems began when the rulers in England and the colonists disagreed over who was to govern the new society. The English believed that the colonies existed solely for the enrichment of the mother country. Following the French and Indian War, King George III and Parliament levied heavy taxes to help pay British debts. Among the first levies were several Stamp Acts, which Americans protested, insisting that only the colonial assemblies had the right to impose taxes. In 1767

England imposed a new tax program, the Townshend Acts. Americans reacted with speeches, pamphlets, stickers, and posters, proposing to boycott English products. Parliament, after a show of force, withdrew the Townshend Acts; but open rebellion erupted again in 1773, when the British government set a new tax on tea. Enraged, Bostonians demonstrated with the famous Boston Tea Party, in which they dumped huge quantities of the taxed tea into Boston Harbor. Parliament punished the whole city, refusing, in fact, to recognize the entire government of Massachusetts.

Other colonies rushed money and food to Boston. Representatives from Massachusetts and most of the other colonies met in Philadelphia in 1774 for the First Continental Congress. What followed in that historic assembly is, of course, the story of the birth of our nation. Fired up by what they saw as unfair treatment from England, the political leaders in time perceived the need to set up their own government, one in which humanity, reason, and justice would prevail. Doing so would require unity, but the Founding Fathers were prepared to create it. Patrick Henry of Virginia, one of whose eloquent speeches appears in this unit, told the convention, "I am not a Virginian, but an American." After two years of discussion and debate, on July 4, 1776, the representatives at the Second Continental Congress signed the Declaration of Independence. Written primarily by Thomas Jefferson, the Declaration is known for its literary qualities as well as its overwhelming political importance. It took great courage for the colonists to sign the document. Benjamin Franklin, some of whose writing is included in this unit, declared wryly at the time, "Now we must all hang together, or assuredly we shall all hang separately."

The signing of the Declaration signaled the formation of a new country, at war with England. The war lasted until the British surrender to George Washington at Yorktown in 1781.

THE GROWTH OF OUR CULTURE

It is not surprising that most of the literature produced in America between 1750 and 1800 was of a practical nature, urging social or political reform. Most writers responded to the exciting events around them, stimulated by the action and often themselves inciting action. For example, Thomas Paine's pamphlet *Common Sense* is credited with hastening the Declaration of Independence, and his pamphlet series *The American Crisis* helped to keep the patriots fighting during the Revolution. Even after the Revolution, much of the literature written by Americans was basically political, focusing on the Constitution and on expectations for the new nation. Letters were a significant form of communication during the period, such as the one in this unit to John Adams from his wife Abigail. A spirited and intelligent woman, Abigail in another letter urged John to "remember the ladies" when he was drafting the Constitution. Another letter writer was Michel-Guillaume Jean de Crèvecoeur, whose *Letters from an American Farmer* provide a wealth of information about life in the colonies.

The arts in America began to flourish. Among the poets of this period was Phillis Wheatley, a black slave whose work appears in this unit. In 1789 the book that usually is regarded as the first American novel was published: William Hill Brown's *The Power of Sympathy*. During the Revolutionary era, theater became increasingly important. Playhouses sprang up throughout the South and in New York, though theater still did not thrive in Puritan New England. Several American painters achieved lasting reputations— Benjamin West, John Singleton Copley, and Gilbert Stuart are the most famous. The first American sculptor appeared during this period, and remarkably, the artist was a woman, Patience Wright from New Jersey. The United States, now a political entity, was becoming a cultural entity as well.

Literature

- Benjamin Franklin (1706–1790) begins *Autobiography*

- Patrick Henry (1736–1799) delivers speech against Stamp Act

- Jonathan Edwards (1703–1758) publishes *Freedom of Will*

- Phillis Wheatley (1753?–1784) publishes volume of poetry

1750   1760   1770

History

- French and Indian War (1757–1763) begins

- British enact Stamp Act

- Colonists protest in Boston Tea Party

- Albany Congress meets

- British kill colonists in Boston Massacre

- British pass the Townshend Acts

THE DECLARATION OF INDEPENDENCE, 1786-94. *John Trumbull. Copyright Yale University Art Gallery.*

- Michel-Guillaume Jean de Crèvecoeur (1735–1813) publishes *Letters from an American Farmer*

- Abigail Adams (1744–1818) begins writing letters to her husband, John Adams

- Thomas Paine (1737–1809) publishes pamphlet *Common Sense*

- Philip Freneau (1752–1832) publishes first collection of poetry

- Patrick Henry (1736–1799) delivers "Give me liberty or give me death" speech

- *The Federalist* essays first appear in newspapers

- Thomas Jefferson (1743–1826) writes The Declaration of Independence

1780   1790   1800

- Treaty of Paris ends Revolutionary War

- Battles of Lexington and Concord fought

- Federal convention drafts U.S. Constitution

- First Continental Congress assembles in Philadelphia

- Bill of Rights becomes part of Constitution

- Americans declare Independence

- Articles of Confederation approved

Michel-Guillaume Jean de Crèvecoeur

1735–1813

Jean de Crèvecoeur was a Frenchman who emigrated to the New World as a young man. Born in Normandy, he was educated there in Jesuit schools. His first stop after crossing the Atlantic was Canada, where he spent four years as an officer and a mapmaker. De Crèvecoeur then roamed for several years, finally settling in Orange County, New York, in 1765. He married an American, Mehitable Tippet, and the couple had three children.

Because Mehitable de Crèvecoeur came from a Loyalist family—that is, one opposed to revolting against the British sovereign—de Crèvecoeur's position during the Revolution was insecure. Persecuted by both sides, he spent several months in an English army prison before sailing for Europe in 1780 with one of his sons.

In 1782 in London de Crèvecoeur arranged to publish twelve essays about the New World under the title *Letters from an American Farmer*. He published under his American name, J. Hector St. John, and for this reason he is sometimes known as St. John de Crèvecoeur. The letters, which are optimistic and appealing, made de Crèvecoeur famous, winning him the patronage of such people as Benjamin Franklin. Over the years de Crèvecoeur added more essays to the collection, expanding it to three volumes. Interestingly, during the early 1920's a bundle of de Crèvecoeur's unpublished essays was found in an attic in France. They were published in 1925 under the title *More Letters from an American Farmer*.

For some years de Crèvecoeur was the most widely read commentator on America and a favorite in Europe. In 1784 the French government appointed him consul to three of the new states in America. Sadly, when de Crèvecoeur arrived, he discovered that his home in New York had been burned. His wife was dead; his children were living with strangers. Reunited with his children, de Crèvecoeur remained in America until 1790, when the French government recalled him. He lived in France and Germany for the remainder of his life.

De Crèvecoeur's essays show the stages through which American immigrants pass. The essays also describe the natural environment of the New World, its religious problems, its Indian affairs, and its political struggles. The excerpt included here is de Crèvecoeur's famous statement of the "melting pot" theory, his attempt to answer the question "What is an American?"

Tradesman's signs frequently employed some reference to the nature of the business. This lamb might have been displayed by a sheep raiser or wool merchant.

Abby Aldrich Rockefeller Folk Art Center. Williamsburg, Virginia.

from **Letters from an American Farmer**

In this great American asylum,[1] the poor of Europe have by some means met together, and in consequence of various causes; to what purpose should they ask one another, what countrymen they are? Alas, two-thirds of them had no country. Can a wretch who wanders about, who works and starves, whose life is a continual scene of sore affliction or pinching penury—can that man call England or any other kingdom his country? A country that had no bread for him, whose fields procured him no harvest, who met with nothing but the frowns of the rich, the severity of the laws, with jails and punishments, who owned not a single foot of the extensive surface of this planet? No! urged by a variety of motives, here they came. Everything has tended to regenerate them: new laws, a new mode of living, a new social system. Here they are become men; in Europe they were as so many useless plants, wanting vegetative mold[2] and refreshing showers; they withered and were mowed down by want, hunger, and war. But now, by the power of transplantation, like all other plants, they have taken root and flourished! Formerly they were not numbered in any civil list of their country, except in those of the poor; here they rank as citizens.

What attachment can a poor European emigrant have for a country where he had nothing? The knowledge of the language, the love of a few kindred as poor as himself were the only cords that tied him. His country is now that which gives him land, bread, protection, and consequence. *Ubi panis ibi patria* [where my bread is earned, there is my country] is the motto of all emigrants. What then is the American, this new man? He is either a European or the descendant of a European;

hence that strange mixture of blood which you will find in no other country. I could point out to you a man whose grandfather was an Englishman, whose wife was Dutch, whose son married a French woman, and whose present four sons have now four wives of different nations. *He* is an American who, leaving behind him all his ancient prejudices and manners, receives new ones from the new mode of life he has embraced, the new government he obeys, and the new rank he holds. He becomes an American by being received in the broad lap of our great alma mater.[3]

Here individuals of all nations are melted into a new race of men, whose labors and posterity will one day cause great change in the world. Americans are the western pilgrims who are carrying along with them that great mass of arts, sciences, vigor, and industry which began long since in the east; they will finish the great circle. The Americans were once scattered all over Europe; here they are incorporated into one of the finest systems of population which has ever appeared, and which will hereafter become distinct by the power of the different climates they inhabit. The American ought, therefore, to love this country much better than that wherein either he or his forefathers were born. Here the rewards of his industry follow with equal steps the progress of his labor; his labor is founded on the basis of nature, self-interest. Can it want a stronger allurement? Wives and children, who before in vain demanded of him a morsel of bread, now, fat and frolicsome,

---

1. **asylum:** place of shelter or refuge.
2. **vegetative mold:** fertility.
3. **alma mater** *Latin:* literally, fostering mother.

gladly help their father to clear those fields whence exuberant crops are to arise to feed and to clothe them all, without any part being claimed, either by a despotic prince, a rich abbot, or a mighty lord. Here, religion demands but little of him; a small voluntary salary to the minister, and gratitude to God. Can he refuse these?

The American is a new man, who acts upon new principles; he must, therefore, entertain new ideas and form new opinions. From involuntary idleness, servile dependence, penury, and useless labor he has passed to toils of a very different nature, rewarded by ample subsistence. This is an American.

Getting at Meaning

1. According to de Crèvecoeur, what do immigrants to America leave behind in Europe? What kind of life do they find in America?

2. Explain the "melting pot" theory that de Crèvecoeur advances in this selection. What gets "melted" together in America? Are de Crèvecoeur's remarks still applicable?

3. What is de Crèvecoeur's definition of an American? Why does he say the American "ought . . . to love this country much better than that wherein either he or his forefathers were born"? Why must the American be a "new man"?

Developing Skills in Reading Literature

1. **Epistle, or Literary Letter.** A formal letter is sometimes called an epistle, a kind of literary letter that has been a popular form of literature for centuries. Ancient Greek and Roman writers used the literary letter to structure their thoughts. In the eighteenth century, entire novels composed of letters were common, as were poems in epistle form.

Although de Crèvecoeur's letters are supposedly written to one person, they are in fact literary letters intended for a general audience. In this selection, how does de Crèvecoeur maintain an intimate tone, yet at the same time express ideas and opinions intended for a larger public? Cite specific passages in the letter to support your statements.

2. **Extended Metaphor.** To what does de Crèvecoeur compare the American immigrants in the first paragraph of his letter? Explain the different parts of the metaphor. What simile appears within the extended metaphor?

Developing Writing Skills

Writing a Literary Letter. Compose a literary letter of your own, addressed to one person perhaps, but intended for a large audience. In your letter create a twentieth-century definition to answer the question, "What then is the American?" Be specific in supporting your views.

Benjamin Franklin
1706–1790

When Benjamin Franklin died at the age of eighty-four, the largest crowd the country had ever seen gathered in Philadelphia for his funeral. This was fitting, for at his death Franklin was a world-famous publisher, inventor, statesman, and writer, a man whose rise from poverty to riches and fame represented the promise of America. In fact, Franklin is sometimes called the "First American."

Franklin came from a large and poor Boston family. His father was a soap and candle maker, father to seventeen children. Benjamin, the tenth son, had to earn his own living at an early age. When he was twelve, he became the apprentice of his older brother, a printer, and Franklin soon achieved success in this field. He printed paper currency for Pennsylvania, and he began publishing a newspaper, *The Pennsylvania Gazette*. In 1732, when he was still in his twenties, he offered thoughts and observations to the public in a series called *Poor Richard's Almanack*, popular because of its wisdom and dry humor. An edition of the *Almanack* appeared every year for twenty-five years.

Franklin made most of his money as a printer. He was always civic minded, however, and helped promote in Philadelphia a fire department, a lending library, a police force, and improved streets and sanitation. The academy he founded later became the University of Pennsylvania.

When he was forty-two, Franklin had made enough money from publishing to retire and devote himself to science. Having invented the lightning rod at an early age, he now went on to invent bifocals, a musical instrument called the armonica, and the Franklin stove, among other things. Bifocals and the Franklin stove are still in wide use. For discovering the laws of electricity, Franklin won honorary degrees from Harvard and Yale, as well as recognition from the English Royal Academy.

Franklin is probably best known as a statesman and diplomat. As a delegate to the Second Continental Congress he helped draft the Declaration of

BENJAMIN FRANKLIN. *Charles Wilson Peale. The Historical Society of Pennsylvania.*

Independence. In that same year, he sought French support for the colonies, becoming something of a hero to the French people. After the British surrender at Yorktown, Franklin was one of the negotiators of peace with Britain. He became America's first representative to France, and before his death he helped to achieve the adoption of the United States Constitution. In political circles Franklin was famous for his joking, charming manner. He loved the diplomatic social life, with its good food, drink, and lively conversation.

As a writer Franklin specialized in the "plain style." His speeches, essays, and letters are straightforward, witty, and appealing. *The Autobiography*, written in three sittings between 1771 and 1788, is his one masterpiece. Full of concrete suggestions and ideas on how to achieve moral superiority, *The Autobiography* stands as a monument to the emphasis on reason, order, and human perfectability so typical of the eighteenth century.

The book has been translated into many languages.

Franklin opposed racial prejudice of any kind, writing numerous pamphlets on the subject. He criticized the treatment that Indians were receiving in Pennsylvania, and he indicted slavery in a firm, eloquent way. Franklin's final literary work was a satiric spoof in defense of slavery, written, curiously enough, from the point of view of an Algerian pirate. In his later years Franklin worked to improve the condition of free blacks.

A number of commentators have criticized Franklin for being offensively practical and opportunistic and for lacking spirituality and emotional warmth. True, Franklin did enjoy fame and money. True, he did not always practice what he preached. It is also true, however, that Franklin worked hard all his life to better the human physical and social condition, doing perhaps more than any other single American to help make the country a desirable place to live.

Bowles's Moral Pictures or Poor Richard Illustrated, Lessons for Young and Old on Industry.

Yale University Art Collection. The Mabel Brady Carvan Collection.

from The Autobiography

Moral Perfection

It was about this time[1] I conceived the bold and arduous project of arriving at moral perfection. I wished to live without committing any fault at any time; I would conquer all that either natural inclination, custom, or company might lead me into. As I knew, or thought I knew, what was right and wrong, I did not see why I might not always do the one and avoid the other. But I soon found I had undertaken a task of more difficulty than I had imagined. While my care was employed in guarding against one fault, I was often surprised by another; habit took the advantage of inattention; inclination was sometimes too strong for reason. I concluded, at length, that the mere speculative conviction that it was our interest to be completely virtuous was not sufficient to prevent our slipping; and that the contrary habits must be broken, and good ones acquired and established, before we can have any dependence on a steady, uniform rectitude of conduct. For this purpose I therefore contrived the following method.

In the various enumerations of the moral virtues I had met with in my reading, I found the catalog more or less numerous, as different writers included more or fewer ideas under the same name. Temperance, for example, was by some confined to eating and drinking, while by others it was extended to mean the moderating of every other pleasure, appetite, inclination, or passion, bodily or mental, even to our avarice and ambition. I proposed to myself, for the sake of clearness, to use rather more names, with fewer ideas annexed to each, than a few names with more ideas; and I included under thirteen names of virtues all that at that time occurred to me as necessary or desirable, and annexed to each a short precept, which fully expressed the extent I gave to its meaning.

These names of virtues, with their precepts, were:

1. TEMPERANCE. Eat not to dullness; drink not to elevation.

2. SILENCE. Speak not but what may benefit others or yourself; avoid trifling conversation.

3. ORDER. Let all your things have their places; let each part of your business have its time.

4. RESOLUTION. Resolve to perform what you ought; perform without fail what you resolve.

5. FRUGALITY. Make no expense but to do good to others or yourself; i.e., waste nothing.

6. INDUSTRY. Lose no time; be always employed in something useful; cut off all unnecessary actions.

7. SINCERITY. Use no hurtful deceit; think innocently and justly, and, if you speak, speak accordingly.

8. JUSTICE. Wrong none by doing injuries, or omitting the benefits that are your duty.

9. MODERATION. Avoid extremes; forbear resenting injuries so much as you think they deserve.

10. CLEANLINESS. Tolerate no uncleanliness in body, clothes, or habitation.

11. TRANQUILLITY. Be not disturbed at trifles, or at accidents common or unavoidable.

12. CHASTITY. Rarely use venery but for health or offspring, never to dullness, weakness, or the injury of your own or another's peace or reputation.

13. HUMILITY. Imitate Jesus and Socrates.

---

1. **about this time:** the early 1730's when Franklin was in his twenties.

My intention being to acquire the *habitude* of all these virtues. I judged it would be well not to distract my attention by attempting the whole at once, but to fix it on one of them at a time; and, when I should be master of that, then to proceed to another, and so on, till I should have gone through the thirteen; and, as the previous acquisition of some might facilitate the acquisition of certain others, I arranged them with that view, as they stand above. *Temperance* first, as it tends to procure that coolness and clearness of head which is so necessary where constant vigilance was to be kept up, and guard maintained against the unremitting attraction of ancient habits and the force of perpetual temptations. This being acquired and established, *Silence* would be more easy; and my desire being to gain knowledge at the same time that I improved in virtue, and considering that in conversation it was obtained rather by the use of the ears than of the tongue, and therefore wishing to break a habit I was getting into of prattling, punning, and joking, which only made me acceptable to trifling company, I gave *Silence* the second place. This and the next, *Order*, I expected would allow me more time for attending to my project and my studies. *Resolution*, once become habitual, would keep me firm in my endeavors to obtain all the subsequent virtues; *Frugality* and *Industry* freeing me from my remaining debt, and producing affluence and independence, would make more easy the practice of *Sincerity* and *Justice*, etc., etc. Conceiving then, that, agreeably to the advice of Pythagoras[2] in his Golden Verses, daily examination would be necessary, I contrived the following method for conducting that examination.

I made a little book, in which I allotted a page for each of the virtues. I ruled each page with red ink, so as to have seven columns, one for each day of the week, marking each column with a letter for the day. I crossed these columns with thirteen red lines, mark-ing the beginning of each line with the first letter of one of the virtues, on which line, and in its proper column, I might mark, by a little black spot, every fault I found upon examination to have been committed respecting that virtue upon that day.

I determined to give a week's strict attention to each of the virtues successively. Thus, in the first week, my great guard was to avoid even the least offence against *Temperance*, leaving the other virtues to their ordinary chance, only marking every evening the faults of the day. Thus, if in the first week I could keep my first line, marked *T*, clear of spots, I supposed the habit of that virtue so much strengthened, and its opposite weakened, that I might venture extending my attention to include the next, and for the following week keep both lines clear of spots. Proceeding thus to the last, I could go through a course complete in thirteen weeks, and four courses in a year. And like him who, having a garden to weed, does not attempt to eradicate all the bad herbs at once, which would exceed his reach and his strength, but works on one of the beds at a time, and, having accomplished the first, proceeds to a second, so I should have, I hoped, the encouraging pleasure of seeing on my pages the progress I made in virtue, by clearing successively my lines of their spots, till in the end, by a number of courses, I should be happy in viewing a clean book, after a thirteen weeks' daily examination . . .

The precept of *Order* requiring that *every part of my business should have its allotted time*, one page in my little book contained the following scheme of employment for the twenty-four hours of a natural day.

---

2. **Pythagoras** (pĭ thăg' ər əs): Greek philosopher and mathematician of the sixth century B.C.

	THE MORNING.		Rise, wash, and address *Powerful Good-*

THE MORNING.
Question. What good shall I do this day?

5	
6	Rise, wash, and address *Powerful Goodness!* Contrive day's business, and take the resolution of the day; prosecute[3] the present study, and breakfast.
7	

8	
9	Work.
10	
11	

NOON.

| 12 | Read, or overlook my accounts, and dine. |
| 1 | |

2	
3	Work.
4	
5	

Question. What good have I done today?

6	Put things in their places. Supper.
7	Music or diversion, or conversation. Examination of the day.
8	
9	

NIGHT.

10	
11	
12	
1	Sleep.
2	
3	
4	

I entered upon the execution of this plan for self-examination, and continued it with occasional intermissions for some time. I was surprised to find myself so much fuller of faults than I had imagined; but I had the satisfaction of seeing them diminish. To avoid the trouble of renewing now and then my little book, which, by scraping out the marks on the paper of old faults to make room for new ones in a new course, became full of holes, I transferred my tables and precepts to the ivory leaves of a memorandum book, on which the lines were drawn with red ink, that made a durable stain, and on those lines I marked my faults with a black-lead pencil, which marks I could easily wipe out with a wet sponge. After a while I went through one course only in a year, and afterward only one in several years, till at length I omitted them entirely, being employed in voyages and business abroad, with a multiplicity of affairs that interfered; but I always carried my little book with me.

My list of virtues contained at first but twelve; but a Quaker friend having kindly informed me that I was generally thought proud; that my pride showed itself frequently in conversation; that I was not content with being in the right when discussing any point, but was overbearing, and rather insolent, of which he convinced me by mentioning several instances; I determined endeavoring to cure myself, if I could, of this vice or folly among the rest, and I added *Humility* to my list, giving an extensive meaning to the word. . . .

---

3. **prosecute:** carry on.

Eating Fish

I believe I have omitted mentioning that in my first Voyage from Boston, being becalmed off Block Island,[1] our People set about catching Cod and hawled up a great many. Hitherto I had stuck to my Resolution of not eating animal Food; and on this Occasion, I considered with my Master Tryon, the taking of every Fish as a kind of unprovoked Murder, since none of them had or ever could do us any Injury that might justify the Slaughter. All this seemed very reasonable. But I had formerly been a great Lover of Fish, and when this came hot out of the Frying Pan, it smelt admirably well. I balanced some time between Principle and Inclination till I recollected that when the Fish were opened, I saw smaller Fish taken out of their Stomachs. Then, thought I, if you eat one another, I don't see why we mayn't eat you. So I dined upon Cod very heartily and continued to eat with other People, returning only now and then occasionally to a vegetable Diet. So convenient a thing it is to be a *reasonable Creature*, since it enables one to find or make a Reason for every thing one has a mind to do.

---

1. **Block Island:** ten miles off the coast of Rhode Island.

Getting at Meaning

1. Recall the philosophy of the age of Reason summarized in the introduction to the unit. What elements of this philosophy are exemplified in these two selections?

2. Explain Franklin's system for achieving moral perfection. Does his list of virtues leave out anything important? Does Franklin name any virtues that do not apparently relate to moral perfection? Why does Franklin include his thirteenth point?

3. Critics have ridiculed Franklin's thirteen points, viewing Franklin's system as mechanical and offensive. Discuss the pros and cons of his approach. What does Franklin himself conclude about his system?

4. Why did Franklin stick to a vegetarian diet for some time? How does he justify eating fish when the opportunity arises? What conclusion does he draw from this experience?

Developing Skills in Reading Literature

1. **Point of View.** In *The Autobiography*, Franklin tells the story of his life from a first-person point of view. What are the advantages to first-person narration? What are the disadvantages? How might the story of his life be different if someone else told it?

2. **Simile.** When Franklin is discussing his chart of virtues, to what does he compare the elimination of his faults? How does he emphasize the difficulty of eliminating all faults at once? What approach does he recommend?

Developing Vocabulary

Word Origins: Root Words. Franklin says that his intention was "to acquire the *habitude* of all these virtues." Look up *habitude* in a dictionary. What is the origin of the word?

Look up the following words that are related to *habitude*. Define each word and explain its derivation from the root.

habitat	habitué	habitation
habituate	inhabitable	

Developing Writing Skills

Narrating an Autobiographical Incident. Write a five-paragraph composition about an incident of importance in your own life. Use first-person narration and re-create the episode as vividly as you can. Explain the effects it has had on you.

from Poor Richard's Almanack

A good example is the best sermon.

He that cannot obey cannot command.

Half the truth is often a great lie.

Content makes poor men rich; discontent makes rich men poor.

Nothing brings more pain than too much pleasure; nothing more bondage than too much liberty.

The proud hate pride—in others.

Glass, china, and reputation are easily cracked and never well mended.

He that lieth down with dogs shall rise up with fleas.

If you would be loved, love and be lovable.

Keep your eyes wide open before marriage, half shut afterwards.

Love your neighbor; yet don't pull down your hedge.

Three may keep a secret, if two of them are dead.

Write injuries in dust, benefits in marble.

A mob's a monster; heads enough but no brains.

Who has deceived thee as oft as thyself?

Lost time is never found again.

Getting at Meaning

1. What human weaknesses does Franklin speak to in this selection of sayings? What human qualities does he appear to admire?

2. Which of Franklin's sayings stress relationships among people in a community? What does Franklin say on the subject?

Developing Skills in Reading Literature

Aphorism. An aphorism is a short statement expressing a truth or opinion about life. Usually one sentence, an aphorism is often humorous or ironic. Another word for aphorism is *proverb*.

What are some aphorisms, or proverbs, common in contemporary American society? List as many as you can. Then find a copy of complete sayings from *Poor Richard's Almanack*. How many of the aphorisms still current go back to Benjamin Franklin?

Developing Writing Skills

Writing Aphorisms. Write three or four aphorisms that express truths about modern life. Make each saying either one sentence or two short sentences in length. Attempt a humorous or ironic expression of each abstract idea.

Patrick Henry
1736–1799

Perhaps the most famous orator of the American Revolution, Patrick Henry was born into an aristocratic Virginia family. As a boy he read Latin and Greek classics with his father, studying closely the works of the ancient orators. During adolescence Henry ran a store with his brother, marrying when he was only eighteen. By the age of twenty-three he had several children and many debts, accumulated during his unsuccessful attempts at storekeeping and farming.

Henry decided to go into law, and before he was thirty years old he was a member of the Virginia House of Burgesses. Concerned with civil rights, Henry argued against the British Stamp Act, becoming a leader of the opposition to colonial rule. An outspoken radical, Henry warned George III of England to learn from past political leaders who had been assassinated. Although Henry was at first too radical for most colonists, the mood of the colonies gradually shifted in a radical direction, and his tough, fiery attitude toward England became increasingly popular. In his famous "Give me liberty or give me death" speech, reprinted in this unit, Henry urged armed rebellion against British rule. This speech was given in 1775, in the Virginia House of Burgesses, and the governor of Virginia labeled Henry an "outlaw" for his treasonous words. One year later, however, a majority of the colonial representatives agreed with Henry, and the Declaration of Independence was issued

Henry's speeches were not written down at the time that he made them. Rather, they were reconstructed some years later, from the notes of the people who had heard them. The speeches as we now know them may differ somewhat from the speeches that Henry actually delivered.

PATRICK HENRY. *Artist unknown.*
Courtesy of Shelburne Museum, Shelburne, Vermont.

In 1776 Henry helped draft Virginia's first state constitution. He served as the state's first governor for three years and he was governor again from 1784-1786. A liberal humanitarian for most of his life, Henry is chiefly responsible for the passage of the Bill of Rights in the Constitution. In later life he became more conservative, sometimes arguing with his old friend Thomas Jefferson. He remained active in politics until his death, shortly after a successful campaign for the office of state representative.

Speech in the Virginia Convention

Patrick Henry delivered this famous speech in 1775 in the Virginia House of Burgesses. Widespread dissatisfaction with British rule had led Henry to introduce the resolution that "Virginia be immediately put in a posture of defense." When his more conservative colleagues objected, fearing rebellion and revolution, Henry responded with this fiery speech.

March 23, 1775

Mr. President:[1] No man thinks more highly than I do of the patriotism, as well as abilities, of the very worthy gentlemen who have just addressed the house. But different men often see the same subject in different lights; and, therefore, I hope it will not be thought disrespectful to those gentlemen, if, entertaining, as I do, opinions of a character very opposite to theirs, I shall speak forth my sentiments freely and without reserve. This is no time for ceremony. The question before the house is one of awful moment to this country. For my own part, I consider it as nothing less than a question of freedom or slavery. And in proportion to the magnitude of the subject ought to be the freedom of the debate. It is only in this way that we can hope to arrive at truth, and fulfill the great responsibility which we hold to God and our country. Should I keep back my opinions at such a time, through fear of giving offense, I should consider myself as guilty of treason toward my country, and of an act of disloyalty toward the Majesty of Heaven, which I revere above all earthly kings.

Mr. President, it is natural to man to indulge in the illusions of hope. We are apt to shut our eyes against a painful truth, and listen to the song of that siren till she transforms us into beasts. Is this the part of wise men, engaged in a great and arduous struggle for liberty? Are we disposed to be of the number of those who having eyes see not, and having ears hear not, the things which so nearly concern their temporal salvation? For my part, whatever anguish of spirit it may cost, I am willing to know the whole truth; to know the worst and to provide for it.

I have but one lamp by which my feet are guided, and that is the lamp of experience. I know of no way of judging of the future but by the past. And judging by the past, I wish to know what there has been in the conduct of the British ministry for the last ten years to justify those hopes with which gentlemen have been pleased to solace themselves and the house? Is it that insidious smile with which our petition[2] has been lately received? Trust it not, sir; it will prove a snare to your feet. Suffer not yourselves to be betrayed with a kiss. Ask yourselves how this gracious reception of our petition comports with those warlike preparations which cover our waters and darken our land. Are fleets and armies necessary to a work of love and reconcilia-

---

1. **Mr. President:** the president of the Virginia Convention.
2. **petition:** the "Olive Branch Petition," in which the king was asked to intercede between parliament and the colonies.

tion? Have we shown ourselves so unwilling to be reconciled that force must be called in to win back our love? Let us not deceive ourselves, sir. These are the implements of war and subjugation—the last arguments to which kings resort.

I ask gentlemen, sir, what means this martial array, if its purpose be not to force us to submission? Can gentlemen assign any other possible motive for it? Has Great Britain any enemy in this quarter of the world, to call for all this accumulation of navies and armies? No, sir, she has none. They are meant for us: they can be meant for no other. They are sent over to bind and rivet upon us those chains which the British ministry have been so long forging.

And what have we to oppose to them? Shall we try argument? Sir, we have been trying that for the last ten years. Have we anything new to offer upon the subject? Nothing. We have held the subject up in every light of which it is capable; but it has been all in vain. Shall we resort to entreaty and humble supplication? What terms shall we find which have not been already exhausted? Let us not, I beseech you, sir, deceive ourselves longer.

Sir, we have done everything that could be done to avert the storm which is now coming on. We have petitioned; we have remonstrated; we have supplicated; we have prostrated ourselves before the throne, and have implored its interposition[3] to arrest the tyrannical hands of the ministry and Parliament. Our petitions have been slighted; our remonstrances have produced additional violence and insult; our supplications have been disregarded; and we have been spurned with contempt from the foot of the throne! In vain, after these things, may we indulge the fond[4] hope of peace and reconciliation. There is no longer any room for hope. If we wish to be free, if we mean to preserve inviolate those inestimable privileges for which we have been so long contending, if we mean not basely to abandon the noble struggle in which

we have been so long engaged, and which we have pledged ourselves never to abandon until the glorious object of our contest shall be obtained—we must fight! I repeat it, sir, we must fight! An appeal to arms and to the God of Hosts is all that is left us!

They tell us, sir, that we are weak—unable to cope with so formidable an adversary. But when shall we be stronger? Will it be the next week, or the next year? Will it be when we are totally disarmed, and when a British guard shall be stationed in every house? Shall we gather strength by irresolution and inaction? Shall we acquire the means of effectual resistance by lying supinely on our backs and hugging the delusive phantom of hope until our enemies shall have bound us hand and foot? Sir, we are not weak, if we make a proper use of those means which the God of nature hath placed in our power. Three millions of people, armed in the holy cause of liberty, and in such a country as that which we possess, are invincible by any force which our enemy can send against us. Besides, sir, we shall not fight our battles alone. There is a just God who presides over the destinies of nations and who will raise up friends to fight our battles for us. The battle, sir, is not to the strong alone; it is to the vigilant, the active, the brave. Besides, sir, we have no election.[5] If we were base enough to desire it, it is now too late to retire from the contest. There is no retreat but in submission and slavery! Our chains are forged! Their clanging may be heard on the plains of Boston! The war is inevitable—and let it come! I repeat it, sir, let it come!

It is in vain, sir, to extenuate the matter. Gentlemen may cry, "Peace, peace"—but there is no peace. The war is actually begun![6]

---

3. **interposition:** intervention.
4. **fond:** foolish.
5. **election:** choice.
6. **war . . . begun:** Boston had recently been occupied by British troops under the leadership of General Howe.

The next gale that sweeps from the north will bring to our ears the clash of resounding arms! Our brethren are already in the field! Why stand we here idle? What is it that gentlemen wish? What would they have? Is life so dear, or peace so sweet, as to be purchased at the price of chains and slavery? Forbid it, Almighty God! I know not what course others may take; but as for me, give me liberty or give me death!

Getting at Meaning

1. List Patrick Henry's reasons for wanting to rebel against British rule. What methods have the colonists already used to indicate their dissatisfaction?

2. What does Patrick Henry see as the only course open to the colonists? Why does he think they will win if they oppose Britain?

Developing Skills in Reading Literature

1. **Anaphora.** In rhetoric the deliberate repetition of words, phrases, or sentences, often at the beginnings of successive verses, clauses, or paragraphs, is called anaphora. Speakers and writers use repetition in this way to intensify the impact of what they are saying.

Patrick Henry uses anaphora in this oration. Find several places where his speech becomes more emotional because of skillful repetition.

2. **Rhetorical Question.** A rhetorical question is a question that does not demand a response because the answer is obvious. Like anaphora, rhetorical questions strengthen the impact of a speaker's or a writer's arguments and opinions.

Find places in this oration where Patrick Henry uses rhetorical questions. What ideas do these questions emphasize? To what emotions do they appeal?

3. **Allusion.** An allusion is a reference to a work of literature, or to a person, place, or event outside of literature, with which a writer or speaker expects an audience to be familiar. When Patrick Henry speaks of hope, he says, "We are apt to shut our eyes against a painful truth, and listen to the song of that siren till she transforms us into beasts." This is an allusion to Homer's *Odyssey,* in which the Sirens are deceiving creatures whose beautiful singing lures sailors to their death. One particularly enticing creature, Circe, captivates Odysseus's men and turns them into pigs. Henry then is saying that, although the hope of a peaceful settlement with Britain is appealing, it is a destructive, deceptive hope that will lead the colonists into a kind of slavery.

Henry's speech also contains two well known Biblical allusions. Look up Ezekiel 12:2 and Luke 22:47-48. Where does Henry allude to each of these Biblical verses in this oration? Explain the meaning of each allusion in the context of the speech.

4. **Metaphor.** Henry uses a number of metaphors, or comparisons, in his speech; for example, "I have but one lamp by which my feet are guided, and that is the lamp of experience." In what ways is experience like a lamp? Find three or four additional metaphors in the speech and discuss their meanings.

Developing Vocabulary

Precise Verbs. Patrick Henry uses some interesting verbs whose meanings you may not know. Look up the following verbs in a dictionary and note the differences in meaning among them. Use each verb in an original sentence that indicates its precise meaning.

contend	prostrate
entreat	remonstrate
implore	supplicate
petition	

Thomas Paine

1737–1809

"My country is the world and my religion is to do good," wrote Thomas Paine, a political pamphleteer who passionately supported the American Revolution. Paine's long career of public service in England, America, and France exemplified this statement.

Born in Thetford, England, Paine left school at an early age and worked as a schoolmaster, a preacher, a customs inspector, a grocer, and a corset maker, among other things. A self-educated man who read widely, he came to the United States in his thirties on the advice of Benjamin Franklin.

Paine arrived in America when the country was on the brink of revolution. A gifted writer and thinker, Paine published a pamphlet titled *Common Sense* in 1776, in which he urged the colonists to break with England. "Society in every state is a blessing," he wrote, "but Government, even in its best state, is but a necessary evil, in its worst state, an intolerable one." Paine went on to say that monarchy insults human dignity. Within three months *Common Sense* had sold 120,000 copies, and it has been widely read and reprinted ever since.

During the Revolution, Paine wrote a series of "Crisis" papers to keep up the morale of the fighting troops. The first paper, reprinted in this unit, was read aloud to George Washington's starving, disheartened troops at Valley Forge. At this and other decisive points during the war, the "Crisis" papers raised the spirits and strengthened the determination of the patriots.

After the war Paine returned to Europe to promote one of his many inventions, a method for constructing an iron bridge. While in Europe, he became embroiled in the French Revolution, on the side of the revolutionaries. Ironically, the revolutionaries imprisoned Paine, for pleading that the French king be imprisoned rather than killed. Paine wrote his work *The Age of Reason* in a French prison, where he narrowly escaped execution.

THOMAS PAINE. *John Wesley Jarvis.*
National Gallery of Art, Washington.
Gift of Marian B. Maurice.

In 1802 Paine came back to America, unfortunately to experience harsh treatment. Always outspoken, always bold, Paine was not popular with some Americans because of his support of the French Revolution and his untraditional religious views. He died in poverty on his New York farm, and, although his coffin was later taken to England, it was denied burial there. Eventually his remains disappeared.

Paine had a hard life in many ways, but he fought until the bitter end for human equality, natural rights, and civil liberties. His skill in expressing his beliefs makes him an outstanding product of the Age of Reason.

from **The Crisis, Number 1**

These are the times that try men's souls. The summer soldier and the sunshine patriot will, in this crisis, shrink from the service of their country; but he that stands it *now* deserves the love and thanks of man and woman. Tyranny, like hell, is not easily conquered; yet we have this consolation with us, that the harder the conflict, the more glorious the triumph. What we obtain too cheap, we esteem too lightly; it is dearness only that gives everything its value. Heaven knows how to put a proper price upon its goods, and it would be strange indeed if so celestial an article as *freedom* should not be highly rated. Britain, with an army to enforce her tyranny, had declared that she has a right not only to *tax*, but "to *bind* us in *all cases whatsoever*"; and if being *bound in that manner* is not slavery, then is there not such a thing as slavery upon earth. Even the expression is impious, for so unlimited a power can belong only to God. . . .

I have as little superstition in me as any man living, but my secret opinion has ever been, and still is, that God Almighty will not give up a people to military destruction, or leave them unsupportedly to perish, who have so earnestly and so repeatedly sought to avoid the calamities of war, by every decent method which wisdom could invent. Neither have I so much of the infidel in me as to suppose that He has relinquished the government of the world, and given us up to the care of devils; and as I do not, I cannot see on what grounds the king of Britain can look up to heaven for help against us: a common murderer, a highwayman, or a housebreaker has as good a pretense as he. . . .

I once felt all that kind of anger which a man ought to feel against the mean[1] principles that are held by the Tories.[2] A noted one, who kept a tavern at Amboy, was standing at his door, with as pretty a child in his hand, about eight or nine years old, as ever I saw, and after speaking his mind as freely as he thought was prudent, finished with this unfatherly expression, "Well! give me peace in my day." Not a man lives on the continent, but fully believes that a separation must sometime or other finally take place, and a generous parent should have said, "If there must be trouble, let it be in my day, that my child may have peace"; and this single reflection, well applied, is sufficient to awaken every man to duty. Not a place upon earth might be so happy as America. Her situation is remote from all the wrangling world, and she has nothing to do but to trade with them. A man can distinguish himself between temper and principle, and I am as confident as I am that God governs the world, that America will never be happy till she gets clear of foreign dominion. Wars, without ceasing, will break out till that period arrives, and the continent must in the end be conqueror; for though the flame of liberty may sometimes cease to shine, the coal can never expire. . . .

The heart that feels not now is dead; the blood of his children will curse his cowardice who shrinks back at a time when a little might have saved the whole, and made *them*

---

1. **mean:** small minded.
2. **Tories:** those colonists who sympathized with the British.

happy. I love the man that can smile in trouble, that can gather strength from distress, and grow brave by reflection. 'Tis the business of little minds to shrink; but he whose heart is firm, and whose conscience approves his conduct, will pursue his principles unto death. My own line of reasoning is to myself as straight and clear as a ray of light. Not all the treasures of the world, so far as I believe, could have induced me to support an offensive war, for I think it murder; but if a thief breaks into my house, burns and destroys my property, and kills or threatens to kill me, or those that are in it, and to "bind me in all cases whatsoever" to his absolute will, am I to suffer it? What signifies it to me whether he who does it is a king or a common man; my countryman or not my countryman; whether it be done by an individual villain, or an army of them? If we reason to the root of things we shall find no difference; neither can any just cause be assigned why we should punish in the one case and pardon in the other.

Getting at Meaning

1. What does Paine mean when he speaks of the "summer soldier" and the "sunshine patriot"?

2. What point does Paine make through his story about the Tory who kept a tavern at Amboy?

3. What principles of the Age of Reason does Paine espouse in this essay?

Developing Skills in Reading Literature

1. **Analogy.** An analogy is a point-by-point comparison between two dissimilar things for the purpose of clarifying the less familiar of the two subjects. Analogies help readers gain insight into difficult ideas and complex problems.

Paine draws an analogy between the American political scene and the thief who breaks into a house. What similarities does he point out? What conclusions does he draw? Is his argument by analogy convincing?

2. **Aphorism.** Aphorisms do not always exist on their own, but sometimes appear as part of longer works. In this essay, for example, the statement, "Tyranny, like hell, is not easily conquered" is an aphorism.

Find two or three additional aphorisms in Paine's essay. Why do they stand out as different from Paine's other sentences? What makes the aphorisms effective?

Developing Writing Skills

Developing an Argument. Write a speech or an essay of at least five well developed paragraphs in which you attempt to sway an audience toward acceptance of a particular idea or position. Build your argument by using some of the techniques that Patrick Henry and Thomas Paine use, such as anaphora, rhetorical question, allusion, metaphor, analogy, and aphorism. State your case as directly and as powerfully as you can.

Thomas Jefferson
1743–1826

In 1962 President John F. Kennedy entertained a group of Nobel Prize winners at the White House. Addressing his guests after dinner, Kennedy said, "I think this is the most extraordinary collection of talent, of human knowledge, that has ever been gathered together at the White House, with the possible exception of when Thomas Jefferson dined alone." Kennedy was by no means the first to pay tribute to Jefferson's complex, versatile genius. For over two hundred years Americans and Europeans alike have revered Jefferson, an accomplished author, statesman, scientist, artisan, and educator.

Jefferson came from a wealthy Virginia family. As a boy he received a rigorous classical education, and he went on to the College of William and Mary in Williamsburg, where he became friends with several well established colonial leaders. Jefferson's father had died when he was fourteen, leaving him over 5,000 acres of land, so that Jefferson was already a wealthy man before he entered college.

After graduating from William and Mary, Jefferson studied law and was admitted to the bar. When he was twenty-five, he was elected to the Virginia House of Burgesses, where he and Patrick Henry became friends. Along with Henry, Jefferson became an outspoken proponent of American rights. A delegate to the Second Continental Congress, Jefferson was chosen to draft the Declaration of Independence in 1776. Afterwards he returned to the Virginia legislature, where he led the reform of many state laws.

Jefferson served as governor of Virginia from 1779-1781, and during that time he published his only book, *Notes on Virginia*. Following the war he served as a diplomat in Europe and became the nation's first Secretary of State in 1789. In 1797 Jefferson became Vice-President of the United States under John Adams, and in 1801 he was elected the nation's President. One of his accomplishments as President was the Louisiana Purchase, which nearly doubled the size of the United States. He also prided himself on the fact that there was no war or bloodshed during his presidency.

When he left the White House after two terms,

THOMAS JEFFERSON, 1800. *Rembrandt Peale.*
The White House Collection, Washington, D. C.

Jefferson retired to Monticello, the beautiful Virginia estate that he had designed. Visitors to Monticello can still see some of Jefferson's inventions, such as the dumbwaiter. At Monticello Jefferson read voraciously, studied mathematics, conducted experiments in scientific farming, played the violin, collected paintings, and continued to worry about the nation. As an older man Jefferson worked for free public education, helping to found the University of Virginia, whose campus he designed and whose curriculum he planned. He predicted that slavery would become an issue in the United States, saying that debate on the issue alarmed him "like a fire bell in the night" because it could prove to be "the knell of the union." In his will he freed his own slaves.

In a letter to a friend, Jefferson once wrote, ". . . to every obstacle, oppose patience, perseverance, and soothing language." These words characterize his own distinguished career. Jefferson lived to be eighty-three, and with dramatic appropriateness died on the Fourth of July in 1826, the fiftieth anniversary of the Declaration of Independence. His old friend and associate John Adams died the same day.

The Declaration of Independence

In Congress, July 4, 1776

When, in the course of human events, it becomes necessary for one people to dissolve the political bands which have connected them with another, and to assume, among the powers of the earth, the separate and equal station to which the laws of nature and of nature's God entitle them, a decent respect to the opinions of mankind requires that they should declare the causes which impel them to the separation.

We hold these truths to be self-evident:— That all men are created equal; that they are endowed by their Creator with certain unalienable rights; that among these are life, liberty, and the pursuit of happiness. That, to secure these rights, governments are instituted among men, deriving their just powers from the consent of the governed; that, whenever any form of government becomes destructive of these ends, it is the right of the people to alter or to abolish it, and to institute a new government, laying its foundation on such principles, and organizing its powers in such form, as to them shall seem most likely to effect their safety and happiness. Prudence, indeed, will dictate that governments long established should not be changed for light and transient causes; and, accordingly, all experience hath shown that mankind are more disposed to suffer, while evils are sufferable, than to right themselves by abolishing the forms to which they are accustomed. But, when a long train of abuses and usurpations, pursuing invariably the same object, evinces a design to reduce them under absolute despotism, it is their right, it is their duty, to throw off such government, and to provide new guards for their future security. Such has been the patient sufferance of these colonies; and such is now the necessity that constrains them to alter their former systems of government. The history of the present King of Great Britain[1] is a history of repeated injuries and usurpations, all having, in direct object, the establishment of an absolute tyranny over these States. To prove this, let facts be submitted to a candid world.

He has refused his assent to laws the most wholesome and necessary for the public good.

He has forbidden his Governors to pass laws of immediate and pressing importance, unless suspended in their operation till his assent should be obtained; and, when so suspended, he has utterly neglected to attend to them.

He has refused to pass other laws for the accommodation of large districts of people, unless these people would relinquish the right of representation in the legislature—a right inestimable to them, and formidable to tyrants only.

He has called together legislative bodies at places unusual, uncomfortable, and distant from the depository of their public records, for the sole purpose of fatiguing them into compliance with his measure.

He has dissolved representative houses repeatedly, for opposing, with manly firmness, his invasions on the rights of the people.

He has refused, for a long time after such dissolutions, to cause others to be elected; whereby the legislative powers, incapable of annihilation, have returned to the people at

---

1. **present King . . . Britain:** George III (1760–1820).

large for their exercise; the State remaining, in the meantime, exposed to all dangers of invasion from without, and convulsions within.

He has endeavored to prevent the population of these States; for that purpose obstructing the laws for the naturalization of foreigners; refusing to pass others to encourage their migration hither, and raising the conditions of new appropriations of lands.

He has obstructed the administration of justice, by refusing his assent to laws for establishing judiciary powers.

He has made judges dependent on his will alone for the tenure of their offices, and the amount and payment of their salaries.

He has erected a multitude of new offices, and sent hither swarms of officers to harass our people and eat out their substance.

He has kept among us in times of peace, standing armies, without the consent of our legislatures.

He has affected to render the military independent of, and superior to, the civil power.

He has combined with others to subject us to a jurisdiction foreign to our constitutions, and unacknowledged by our laws; giving his assent to their acts of pretended legislation:

For quartering large bodies of armed troops among us;

For protecting them, by a mock trial, from punishment for any murders which they should commit on the inhabitants of these States;

For cutting off our trade with all parts of the world;

For imposing taxes on us without our consent;

For depriving us, in many cases, of the benefits of trial by jury;

For transporting us beyond the seas, to be tried for pretended offences;

For abolishing the free system of English laws in a neighboring province, establishing there an arbitrary government, and enlarging its boundaries, so as to render it at once an example and fit instrument for introducing the same absolute rule into these colonies;

For taking away our charters, abolishing our most valuable laws, and altering, fundamentally, the forms of our governments;

For suspending our own legislatures, and declaring themselves invested with power to legislate for us in all cases whatsoever

He has abdicated government here, by declaring us out of his protection, and waging war against us.

He has plundered our seas, ravaged our coasts, burnt our towns, and destroyed the lives of our people.

He is at this time transporting large armies of foreign mercenaries to complete the works of death, desolation, and tyranny, already begun with circumstances of cruelty and perfidy scarcely paralleled in the most barbarous ages, and totally unworthy the head of a civilized nation.

He has constrained our fellow-citizens, taken captive on the high seas, to bear arms against their country, to become the executioners of their friends and brethren, or to fall themselves by their hands.

He has excited domestic insurrection amongst us, and has endeavored to bring on the inhabitants of our frontiers the merciless Indian savages, whose known rule of warfare is an undistinguished destruction of all ages, sexes, and conditions.

In every state of these oppressions we have petitioned for redress, in the most humble terms; our repeated petitions have been answered only by repeated injury. A prince whose character is thus marked by every act which may define a tyrant is unfit to be the ruler of a free people.

Nor have we been wanting in our attentions to our British brethren. We have warned them, from time to time, of attempts by their legislature to extend an unwarrantable jurisdiction over us. We have reminded them of the circumstances of our emigration and settlement here. We have appealed to their native justice and magnanimity; and we have conjured them, by the ties of our common kindred, to disavow these usurpations, which would inevitably interrupt our connections and correspondence. They, too, have been deaf to the voice of justice and of consanguinity. We must, therefore, acquiesce in the necessity which denounces our separation; and hold them, as we hold the rest of mankind, enemies in war, in peace friends.

WE, THEREFORE, THE REPRESENTATIVES OF THE UNITED STATES OF AMERICA, in General Congress assembled, appealing to the Supreme Judge of the world for the rectitude of our intentions, do, in the name and by the authority of the good people of these colonies, sol-emnly publish and declare, That these United Colonies are, and of right ought to be, FREE AND INDEPENDENT STATES; that they are absolved from all allegiance to the British crown, and that all political connection between them and the state of Great Britain is, and ought to be, totally dissolved; and that, as free and independent states, they have full power to levy war, conclude peace, contract alliances, establish commerce, and to do all other acts and things which independent states may of right do. And, for the support of this declaration, with a firm reliance on the protection of Divine Providence, we mutually pledge to each other our lives, our fortunes, and our sacred honor.

Getting at Meaning

1. Whom do Jefferson and the other authors of the Declaration blame for the colonies' problems with England? Why do you suppose they emphasize that their quarrel is not with the people of Great Britain?

2. The Revolutionaries enumerate many reasons for declaring their independence from Britain. Which reasons strike you as most powerful and important? Explain your answer.

3. In the Declaration how do Jefferson and his colleagues establish themselves as thoughtful, rational people, rather than as rash fools? What phrases and sentences in this document make it clear that the authors are products of the Age of Reason?

Developing Skills in Reading Literature

Parallelism. When a writer or speaker expresses ideas of equal worth with the same grammatical form, the technique is called parallelism, or parallel construction. Attention to parallelism generally makes both spoken and written expression more concise and powerful.

Identify in the Declaration two different parallel forms used to list the colonists' grievances. In addition, find two or three individual sentences in which parallel forms make the writing tight and direct.

Developing Vocabulary

Finding the Appropriate Meaning: Verbs. Like his friend Patrick Henry, Jefferson uses specific verbs whose meanings you may not know. Look up each verb that follows in a dictionary and record its meanings. Find its use in the Declaration and decide which meaning of the word Jefferson employs. Then write an original sentence in which you use the word in the same way.

abdicate
constrain
evince
harass
impel
obstruct
ravage

Developing Writing Skills

Explaining an Idea. Write a petition or declaration of your own, using parallel grammatical forms to express ideas of equal worth. You may want to advocate a reform of some sort in your school, or you may want to address a larger problem, one in local, state, or national politics.

Abigail Smith Adams

1744–1818

Wife of President John Adams, Abigail Smith Adams was an impressive woman in her own right. An intelligent, perceptive person, Abigail Adams was an avid letter writer all her life. Her correspondence with her absent husband, other family members, and friends remains a valuable source of information about life in the young American republic.

Abigail Smith was born in Weymouth, Massachusetts. Although her formal education was brief, she was an eager reader as a girl and learned a great deal about history, in particular. She remained a voracious reader all her life.

At twenty Abigail married John Adams, and during the next ten years the couple had five children. In 1774 John became a delegate to the First Continental Congress in Philadelphia, beginning a ten-year period in which he and Abigail often were separated because of political necessity. She lived in Quincy, Massachusetts, with their children and assumed family and business responsibilities, bearing the separation well. It was during this period that Abigail became a prolific letter writer.

Abigail's letters are charming and open, full of interesting opinions on a wide variety of issues. She strongly supported colonial independence from England, and in addition spoke out feelingly against slavery. One of her greatest concerns was the lack of educational opportunities for women. In a letter to John in 1778 she wrote, "I regret the trifling narrow contracted education of females of my own country." Later, when John was helping to draft the American Constitution, Abigail urged him to "be more favorable to them [women] than your ancestors."

When the Revolutionary War ended, Abigail spent five years in Europe with John, who served as a diplomat in Paris, London, and The Hague. Abigail's letters to her family during this period provide vivid commentary on European life.

Between 1789 and 1801, when John was Vice-President, then President of the new nation, Abigail traveled between Massachusetts and Washington. After John's presidency the Adams family retired to Quincy, where Abigail lived another seventeen years. The first printing of her letters was in 1840, followed by three more editions, the most recent in 1963. After Abigail's death her son John Quincy Adams became the sixth President of the United States, making Abigail the only woman in our history to be both wife and mother to Presidents.

The Adams's homestead in Quincy, Massachusetts, was the home of four generations of Adamses, including the two Presidents, John and John Quincy.

Letter to Her Husband

Braintree
May 7, 1776

How many are the solitary hours I spend, ruminating upon the past and anticipating the future whilst you, overwhelmed with the cares of state, have but few moments you can devote to any individual. All domestic pleasures and enjoyments are absorbed in the great and important duty you owe your country "for our country is, as it were, a secondary god and the first and greatest parent. It is to be preferred to parents, wives, children, friends and all things; the gods only excepted. For if our country perishes, it is as impossible to save an individual as to preserve one of the fingers of a mortified hand." Thus do I suppress every wish and silence every murmur, acquiescing in a painful separation from the companion of my youth and the friend of my heart.

I believe it is near ten days since I wrote you a line. I have not felt in a humor to entertain you. If I had taken up my pen, perhaps some unbecoming invective might have fallen from it; the eyes of our rulers have been closed and a lethargy has seized almost every member. I fear a fatal security has taken possession of them. Whilst the building is in flame, they tremble at the expense of water to quench it. In short, two months have elapsed since the evacuation of Boston, and very little has been done in that time to secure it or the harbor from future invasion until the people are all in a flame, and no one among us that I have heard of even mentions expense. They think universally that there has been an amazing neglect somewhere. Many have turned out as volunteers to work upon Nodles Island, and many more would go upon Nantasket if it was once set on foot. "It is a maxim of state that power and liberty are like heat and moisture; where they are well mixed everything prospers; where they are single, they are destructive."

A government of more stability is much wanted in this colony, and they are ready to receive it from the hands of the Congress, and since I have begun with maxims of state, I will add another: A people may let a king fall, yet still remain a people, but if a king lets his people slip from him, he is no longer a king. And as this is most certainly our case, why not proclaim to the world in decisive terms your own importance?

Shall we not be despised by foreign powers for hesitating so long at a word?

I cannot say that I think you very generous to the ladies, for whilst you are proclaiming peace and good will to men, emancipating all nations, you insist upon retaining an absolute power over wives. But you must remember that arbitrary power is like most other things which are very hard, very liable to be broken —and notwithstanding all your wise laws and maxims, we have it in our power not only to free ourselves but to subdue our masters, and without violence throw both your natural and legal authority at our feet—

Charm by accepting, by submitting sway
Yet have our humor most when we obey.

I thank you for several letters which I have received since I wrote last. They alleviate a tedious absence, and I long earnestly for a

Saturday evening and experience a similar pleasure to that which I used to find in the return of my friend upon that day after a week's absence. The idea of a year dissolves all my philosophy.

Our little ones, whom you so often recommend to my care and instruction, shall not be deficient in virtue or probity if the precepts of a mother have their desired effect, but they would be doubly enforced could they be indulged with the example of a father constantly before them; I often point them to their sire

Engaged in a corrupted state
Wrestling with vice and faction.

JOHN ADAMS.
Metropolitan Museum of Art.

Getting at Meaning

1. Why is Abigail Adams able to bear the separation from her husband? What is her attitude toward his work?

2. What is Abigail Adams's attitude toward George III and British rule? Cite a specific passage that indicates her views.

3. What is the situation in Boston, as revealed in this letter?

4. What does Abigail Adams say about female emancipation? Explain the lines, "Charm by accepting, by submitting sway/Yet have our humor most when we obey."

5. What character traits of Abigail Adams are shown in this letter to her husband? Support your comments by citing specific passages.

Developing Skills in Reading Literature

Epistle, or Literary Letter. Although this letter is a private one, written by Abigail Adams to her husband, what passages make it a literary letter, or epistle, appealing to a wider audience?

Developing Vocabulary

Understanding Changes in Language. The words writers choose often reflect the tastes and fashions of an historical period or a particular place. Abigail Adams's diction, or word choice, is clearly from a former era, as her final paragraph, so typical of eighteenth-century prose, reflects.

Rewrite the final paragraph of the letter in modern American English. Update the style by changing words and sentence patterns, but be sure to preserve the essential meaning of the passage.

Phillis Wheatley

1753?–1784

Phillis Wheatley's success as a poet was remarkable, for she was both female and a slave. Born in Africa, she was brought to America when she was about seven. John Wheatley, a prosperous Boston tailor, bought her and gave her his name.

The Wheatleys were involved in missionary work, and they raised the young girl as a Christian. The child Phillis was extremely intelligent; she mastered English quickly, learned Latin, and read the Bible, mythology, history, and the contemporary English poets at an early age. She was a mere thirteen when her first poem was published.

When Phillis Wheatley was about twenty, she accompanied the son of the Wheatleys to England, where she was an immense success. The English found her to be talented and impressive, with a sparkling, agreeable personality. An English aristocrat who befriended her, the Countess of Huntingdon, probably helped to pay for the publication of *Poems on Various Subjects, Religious and Moral*, the volume of Wheatley's poems that came out in 1773.

During the Revolutionary War, Wheatley wrote poetry in America, including a well known poem addressed to George Washington. Washington was so pleased with the poem that he invited Wheatley to visit him at the Continental Army camp, which she did do.

John Wheatley's will freed Phillis Wheatley in 1778, and she married John Peters, a free black. Although she continued to write poetry, another volume of her poems was not published during her lifetime. Wheatley only lived to be around thirty, dying in poverty, shortly after two of her three children had died.

In her poetry Phillis Wheatley mastered the forms and conventions of eighteenth-century verse. Though her poems are imitative rather than original, they are extraordinary not only because they were written by a female and a slave but also because they were written by someone so young whose native language was not English.

To the Right Honourable William, Earl of Dartmouth

Hail, happy day, when, smiling like the morn,
Fair *Freedom* rose *New-England* to adorn:
The northern clime beneath her genial ray,
Dartmouth, congratulates thy blissful sway:
Elate with hope her race no longer mourns,   5
Each soul expands, each grateful bosom burns,
While in thine hand with pleasure we behold
The silken reins, and *Freedom's* charms unfold.
Long lost to realms beneath the northern skies
She shines supreme, while hated *faction* dies: 10
Soon as appear'd the *Goddess* long desir'd,
Sick at the view, she lanquish'd and expir'd;
Thus from the splendors of the morning light
The owl in sadness seeks the caves of night.

   No more, *America*, in mournful strain   15
Of wrongs, and grievance unredress'd complain,
No longer shalt thou dread the iron chain,
Which wanton *Tyranny* with lawless hand
Had made, and with it meant t' enslave the land.

   Should you, my lord, while you peruse my song,   20
Wonder from whence my love of *Freedom* sprung,
Whence flow these wishes for the common good,
By feeling hearts alone best understood,
I, young in life, by seeming cruel fate
Was snatch'd from *Afric's* fancy'd happy seat: 25
What pangs excruciating must molest,
What sorrows labor in my parent's breast?
Steel'd was that soul and by no misery mov'd
That from a father seiz'd his babe belov'd:
Such, such my case. And can I then but pray   30
Others may never feel tyrannic sway?

   For favors past, great Sir, our thanks are due,
And thee we ask thy favors to renew,
Since in thy pow'r, as in thy will before,

To sooth the griefs, which thou did'st once deplore.   35
May heav'nly grace the sacred sanction give
To all thy works, and thou forever live
Not only on the wings of fleeting *Fame*,
Though praise immortal crowns the patriot's name,
But to conduct to heav'ns refulgent fane,[1]   40
May fiery coursers sweep th' ethereal plain,
And bear thee upwards to that blest abode,
Where, like the prophet, thou shalt find thy God.

---

1. **refulgent fane:** radiant church or temple.

Getting at Meaning

1. This poem of tribute is addressed to William, Earl of Dartmouth. For what does the speaker praise him? For what does the speaker thank him? What does the speaker hope for his future? Cite specific lines to support your statements.

2. What is happening in America in the first two stanzas of this poem? The speaker compares freedom to the sun rising in the morning. Whom is freedom killing? What word is the antecedent for *she* in line 12?

3. To what personal experience in the past does the speaker refer in this poem? What reason does the speaker give for having a deep love of freedom?

Developing Skills in Reading Literature

1. **Personification.** Personification is a figure of speech in which human qualities are attributed to an object, an animal, or an idea. Like the simile and the metaphor, personification helps writers to communicate feelings and sensory images to their readers.

At the beginning of this poem, freedom is personified as a radiant, shining goddess. What other abstract idea is personified in the first stanza? What abstract ideas are brought to life with human qualities in the second stanza? What kind of person comes to mind when reading lines 15-17? lines 18 and 19?

2. **Simile.** In lines 1 and 2 freedom is compared to the morning sun. At the end of the first stanza, what does the speaker compare to the owl, who "in sadness seeks the caves of night" to escape the sunlight?

3. **Heroic Couplet.** A heroic couplet is two consecutive lines of poetry that rhyme and that are written in iambic pentameter. A line of iambic pentameter consists of five feet, or units of rhythm; each foot is made up of an unaccented syllable followed by an accented syllable. Heroic couplets were a popular verse form in the eighteenth century.

A few of Wheatley's heroic couplets do not use precise rhyme, but what is sometimes called "off-rhyme." Identify the pairs of lines that do not use exact rhyme.

Developing Vocabulary

Finding the Appropriate Meaning: Adjectives. Following are several vivid adjectives from Wheatley's poem whose meanings you may not know. Look up each word in a dictionary and record its meanings. Identify the meaning that fits the use of the word in the poem.

ethereal	refulgent	wanton
excruciating	unredressed	

Developing Writing Skills

Writing a Poem. Write a poem of tribute to someone you know and care about or to a public figure you admire. You might want to try writing your poem in heroic couplets. Your poem may be either serious or humorous.

Unit Review *The American Revolution*

Understanding the Unit

1. Jean de Crèvecoeur and Abigail Adams both write about colonial American life in their letters. What similarities exist in their attitudes toward the new country?

2. Patrick Henry, Thomas Paine, and Thomas Jefferson were all influential political figures. Compare their persuasive approaches, as demonstrated in the selections in this unit. What similarities do you notice in the way that all three build their arguments? What generalizations would you make about each man's style?

3. Most major writers in the Age of Reason thought that men and women, if they worked hard enough, could eliminate their own faults and establish an ideal society. Where do you see this emphasis on bettering the human condition in Benjamin Franklin's life and writing? Where do you see it in Thomas Paine's life and work? Pinpoint where this philosophical goal shows up in the Declaration of Independence and in Thomas Jefferson's life.

4. Writers and thinkers during the Age of Reason tended to view society as more important than the individual. Instead of focusing on individual lives and on emotional problems, they focused on humanity in general and on social issues. Explain how Abigail Adams's "Letter to Her Husband" illustrates this eighteenth-century perspective. In what ways does Phillis Wheatley's poem elevate society over the individual?

5. What subject matter do all seven of the writers in the unit have in common? Notice that all seven are very hopeful. How do you account for their optimism?

Writing

1. Select one major social problem in contemporary America and explain how Americans might solve this problem through the use of reason. Approach the problem as would an eighteenth-century thinker who believes firmly in the efficacy of rational thought, good judgment, and sound sense.

In the introductory paragraph of your composition, introduce your topic and suggest a possible solution. In the body paragraphs explain your ideas in detail, using concrete evidence to make your views convincing. In your conclusion you might examine the far-reaching effects of the solution you propose.

2. The writings of Franklin, Paine, Henry, and Jefferson inspired, shaped, and defined the major reform movement of their days. Identify a positive social or political change of the twentieth century, and read about it in books and reference sources. List the literary works most closely identified with that reform movement. Then assess the relationship of these works to the reform. Did they inspire or initiate the reform? Did they create the climate that gave rise to the reform? Did they clarify goals or set a new direction? Did they make the ordinary citizen aware of the need for reform?

Organize your ideas, then write a composition analyzing the role that literary works played (or are playing) in the reform you have chosen to research. Frame your body paragraphs with a paragraph that introduces your topic and a conclusion that pulls together your ideas. Use specific support.

KINDRED SPIRITS, 1849. *Asher B. Durand.*
Collection of the New York Public Library.
Astor, Lenox, and Tilden Foundations.

Unit 3

Developing a
National Literature (1800–1855)

FUR TRADERS DESCENDING THE MISSOURI, 1845. *George Caleb Bingham.*
The Metropolitan Museum of Art. Morris K. Jessup Fund, 1933.

The Romantic Tradition

The arrival of the nineteenth century signaled the beginning of a new age in American society. The colonies were now a nation, and that nation was expanding rapidly, feeling its power. In 1803 the Louisiana Purchase added an enormous amount of land to the country. The War of 1812, a naval war fought between the United States and Britain, helped to open up this territory to exploration and settlement. It also fostered a sense of solidarity among the various states, contributing to the development of a national identity. By 1820 there were twenty-three states in the Union, with more states added in the next few decades. People were moving farther west, claiming huge tracts of the wild territory for "civilization." As the edge of the frontier was pushed west, the struggles of the Native Americans with the white settlers intensified as the ancient patterns of tribal life were disrupted and finally threatened with extinction.

In the 1820's American democracy as we know it evolved. Although Americans generally associate the birth of modern democracy with the American Revolution, most of the Founding Fathers would have been horrified to be called "democrats." Some of them did not believe in majority rule, and almost no one believed in universal suffrage. To vote in the Republic, a man had to own property or pay taxes. As late as 1820 Daniel Webster and John Adams opposed a bill for universal male suffrage in a Massachusetts constitutional convention. Not until Andrew Jackson became a popular political leader, and in 1828, President, did political power really begin to shift to the common people. Soon all free men were allowed to vote. The movement for free public education began, and the first Abolitionists questioned the justice of slavery. A few brave souls even began agitating for women's rights.

THE BIRTH OF ROMANTICISM

The eighteenth century had been the Age of Reason, also called the Neoclassical Age, both in the United States and abroad. In Europe around the turn of the century, artists and philosophers began to rebel against the classical conventions of the period, which emphasized reason over emotion, the general over the particular, and society over nature. In Germany the rebel artists talked about

"*Sturm und Drang,*" or "storm and stress," meaning that they wished to deal with individuals and their emotions. Young English and French writers shared this goal, and the movement known as Romanticism emerged. The Romantics sought new ways to express themselves, in literature, music, painting, and sculpture. Unlike the Neoclassicists, they emphasized the unique, the individual, the specific. To them, intuition was more important than reason. Common people, their lives, emotions, and experiences, became a major focus.

THE GROWTH OF AMERICAN ROMANTICISM

In a new and democratic country, where people were close to the land and where the political climate increasingly emphasized the common citizen, the Romantic movement had an obvious appeal. The first important American writers of the century, novelist James Fenimore Cooper, poet William Cullen Bryant, and short story writer-essayist Washington Irving, are clearly Romantic writers. Sometimes known as the "Knickerbocker" authors, these three lived and wrote in the vicinity of New York City and shared an interest in the burgeoning country and its people. Their writing, which centers on human relationships to nature and on the settlement of the nation, displays the optimistic vigor characteristic of most European Romantics.

A slightly later group of American Romantics are the Transcendentalist writers, of whom Ralph Waldo Emerson and Henry David Thoreau are the most famous. Transcendentalism was a movement among young intellectuals in the Boston area in the 1830's. The movement shared the general characteristics of Romanticism while exhibiting a few specialized traits of its own. The name Transcendentalism came from Emmanuel Kant, a German philosopher who, in his book, *The Critique of Pure Reason*, spoke of "transcendent forms," or kinds of knowledge that exist above and beyond reason and experience. The Transcendentalists placed great faith in these higher, intuitive forms of knowledge and urged people to have confidence in their own inner lights. They expressed disgust for conformity and praised individuality. Not surprisingly, a major target of their criticism was the Puritan heritage, with its emphasis on material prosperity and rigid obedience to the laws of society. The Transcendentalists disliked the commercial, financial side of American life, with the "get ahead" work ethic they traced back to the Puritans. They stressed instead spiritual well-being, achieved through intellectual activity and a close relationship to nature.

Emerson and Thoreau took an almost mystical pleasure in the "fundamental unity" they could perceive between people and nature, which they said individuals could feel if they removed themselves from the routine concerns of day-to-day life. In the 1840's some of the Transcendentalists even set up their own cooperative farm for this purpose. Located in Massachusetts, Brook Farm existed from 1840 until 1847 as a transcendental colony.

Not all American Romantics were optimistic, however. Three other giants from this period, Edgar Allan Poe, Nathaniel Hawthorne, and Herman Melville, are what have been called "brooding" Romantics. Theirs is a complex philosophy, filled with dark currents and a deep awareness of the human capacity for evil. They are Romantic, however, in their emphasis on emotion, nature, the individual, and the unusual.

Literature

- Noah Webster (1758–1843) writes *Compendius Dictionary of the English Language*, reflecting standards of American English

- First edited version of *Lewis and Clark Expedition Journal* published

- "Star Spangled Banner" is composed

- Washington Irving (1783–1859) writes *The Sketch Book*

- William Cullen Bryant (1794–1878) publishes complete poem "Thanatopsis" written during his teens

- Thomas Jefferson delivers first inaugural address

- James Fenimore Cooper (1789–1851) publishes *The Pioneers*, first of Leather-Stocking Tales

1800   1810   1820

History

- U.S. goes to war with Britain in War of 1812

- Thomas Jefferson (1743–1826) elected President

- U.S. purchases Louisiana Territory from France

- Missouri Compromise bans slavery in parts of new territories

- Lewis and Clark begin exploration of Louisiana Territory

THE ACHIEVEMENT OF AMERICAN LITERATURE

Without a doubt the middle of the nineteenth century was a turning point in American literature. In 1850 Hawthorne published *The Scarlet Letter*, sometimes called the first truly symbolic novel. One year later Melville published *Moby-Dick*, which many critics regard as the great American novel. In 1854 Thoreau's *Walden*, a nonfiction classic, appeared, and in 1855 Walt Whitman brought out the first edition of *Leaves of Grass*, one of the major poetic works of the century. These four works were hailed in Europe, not just in America, and they still stand as masterpieces in world literature. During the five-year period in which they were published, American literature came into full flower, and the United States took its place among the western literary powers.

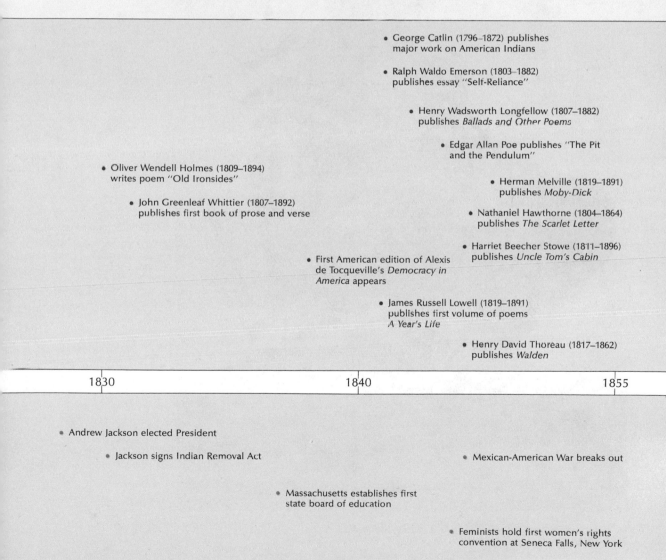

- George Catlin (1796–1872) publishes major work on American Indians

- Ralph Waldo Emerson (1803–1882) publishes essay "Self-Reliance"

- Henry Wadsworth Longfellow (1807–1882) publishes *Ballads and Other Poems*

- Edgar Allan Poe publishes "The Pit and the Pendulum"

- Oliver Wendell Holmes (1809–1894) writes poem "Old Ironsides"

- Herman Melville (1819–1891) publishes *Moby-Dick*

- John Greenleaf Whittier (1807–1892) publishes first book of prose and verse

- Nathaniel Hawthorne (1804–1864) publishes *The Scarlet Letter*

- Harriet Beecher Stowe (1811–1896) publishes *Uncle Tom's Cabin*

- First American edition of Alexis de Tocqueville's *Democracy in America* appears

- James Russell Lowell (1819–1891) publishes first volume of poems *A Year's Life*

- Henry David Thoreau (1817–1862) publishes *Walden*

1830   1840   1855

- Andrew Jackson elected President

- Jackson signs Indian Removal Act

- Mexican-American War breaks out

- Massachusetts establishes first state board of education

- Feminists hold first women's rights convention at Seneca Falls, New York

The Frontier

IN THE DAYS OF THE PLENTIFUL, 1946. *Quincy Tahoma.*
Philbrook Art Center, Tulsa, Oklahoma.

The five Native American selections included in this unit represent five varied cultural traditions from the "frontier" regions of mid-North America. "Prayer at Sunrise" comes from the oral tradition of the Zuñi, a pueblo-dwelling desert tribe of what is now western New Mexico. The Navajo, too, inhabited the Southwest, with ancient hunting grounds in the present states of New Mexico, Arizona, and Utah. "A War God's Horse Song" indicates the importance of the horse in Navajo culture, though this was not always the case. Native American tribes did not have horses before the sixteenth century, when the Spanish introduced them into Mexico. The horse subsequently revolutionized the Navajo's nomadic way of life and increased their relative power among the tribes of the Southwest.

The Pawnee, from whose tradition "The Lesson of the Birds" springs, are a confederation of four Plains tribes who formerly lived in Kansas and Nebraska and who now inhabit a reservation in Oklahoma. The Osage, one of the Sioux tribes, once lived in the region between the Missouri and Arkansas rivers in the southern part of the Great Plains. As was true for the Pawnee, buffalo were vital to the Osage. "Buffalo Myth," translated from the Siouan dialect spoken by the Osage, makes this clear.

The Zuñi, the Navajo, the Pawnee, and the Osage are quite different from the Chippewa, or Ojibwa, forest-dwelling Indians who originally lived near Lake Superior. Like the Pawnee and the Osage, the Chippewa attached great importance to the buffalo, as indicated by "To the Buffalo," which has been translated from the Algonkian language spoken by the Chippewa.

Although the five Native American selections in this unit are from diverse cultures, the pieces have major elements in common. For one thing, all five originated in the tradition of oral literature, which means that they were spoken or sung long before they were written down. All five selections show a deep reverence for nature, illustrating both identification with nature and dependence on nature for survival. Finally, all five pieces reflect the confidence and contentment that the Native Americans felt prior to the settlement of the Midwest and the West by white ranchers and farmers. The tragic story of the disruption of Indian cultures and of the abuse of the Indian people by settlers pushing west is now familiar. In time, Native American literature began to mirror the melancholy and rage for a lost way of life felt by the descendants of the first Americans.

Prayer at Sunrise *Zuñi Indian*

Now this day,
My sun father,
Now that you have come out standing to your sacred place,
That from which we draw the water of life,
Prayer meal,   5
Here I give to you.
Your long life,
Your old age,
Your waters,
Your seeds,   10
Your riches,
Your power,
Your strong spirit,
All these to me may you grant.

The Lesson of the Birds *Pawnee Indian*

One day a man whose mind was open to the teaching of the powers wandered on the prairie. As he walked, his eyes upon the ground, he spied a bird's nest hidden in the grass, and arrested his feet just in time to prevent stepping on it. He paused to look at the little nest tucked away so snug and warm, and noted that it held six eggs and that a peeping sound came from some of them. While he watched, one moved, and soon a tiny bill pushed through the shell, uttering a shrill cry. At once the parent birds answered, and he looked up to see where they were. They were not far off; they were flying about in search of food, chirping the while to each other and now and then calling to the little one in the nest.

The homely scene stirred the heart and the thoughts of the man as he stood there under the clear sky, glancing upward toward the old birds and then down to the helpless young in the nest at his feet. As he looked, he thought of his people, who were so often careless and thoughtless of their children's needs, and his mind brooded over the matter. After many days he desired to see the nest again, so he went to the place where he had found it, and there it was as safe as when he left it. But a change had taken place. It was now full to overflowing with little birds, who were stretching their wings, balancing on their little legs and making ready to fly, while the parents with encouraging calls were coaxing the fledglings to venture forth.

"Ah!" said the man, "if my people would only learn of the birds, and, like them, care for their young and provide for their future, homes would be full and happy, and our tribe be strong and prosperous."

When this man became a priest, he told the story of the bird's nest and sang its song; and so it has come down to us from the days of our fathers.

A War God's Horse Song   *Navajo Indian*

I am the Turquoise Woman's son

On top of Belted Mountain beautiful horses
slim like a weasel

My horse has a hoof like striped agate
his fetlock is like fine eagle plume   5
his legs are like quick lightning

My horse's body is like an eagle-feathered arrow

My horse has a tail like a trailing black cloud

I put flexible goods on my horse's back

The Holy Wind blows through his mane   10
his mane is made of rainbows

My horse's ears are made of round corn

My horse's eyes are made of stars

My horse's head is made of mixed waters
    (from the holy waters)   15
    (he never knows thirst)

My horse's teeth are made of white shell

The long rainbow is in his mouth for a bridle
with it I guide him

When my horse neighs   20
different-colored horses follow

When my horse neighs
different-colored sheep follow

I am wealthy from my horse

Before me peaceful   25
Behind me peaceful
Under me peaceful
Over me peaceful
Around me peaceful
Peaceful voice when he neighs   30
I am everlasting and peaceful
I stand for my horse

To the Buffalo *Chippewa Indian*

Strike ye now our land with your great curvéd horns;
In your mighty rage toss the turf in the air.
Strike ye now our land with your great curvéd horns;
We will hear the sound and our hearts will be strong.
When we go to war,   5
Give us of your strength in the time of our need,
King of all the plain—buffalo, buffalo.
Strike ye now our land with your great curvéd horns;
Lead us forth to the fight.

BUFFALO AND PRAIRIE WOLF. *O. C. Seltzer.*
*The Thomas Gilcrease Institute of American
History and Art, Tulsa, Oklahoma.*

Buffalo Myth *Osage Indian*

O grandfather come to us
            come down to us
O grandfather give us a suitable
            symbol for peace

and the red god had with him his red plume   5
            the red of dawn and peace
which he swiftly took from its sacred cover
and shot it into the mouth of the angry bull
    where it lodged
by the left of his tongue   10
lengthwise
by the left of his tongue

            and then no longer
        the buffalo
            pawed the earth in anger   15

        no longer thunder rolled
        from the ridge pole overhead

            no longer
    grandfather the buffalo
            threw dust with his foot in anger 20

            but he lowered his tail
        the buffalo

Getting at Meaning

1. Comment on the relationship between human beings and nature evident in all five of these selections. Cite specific lines in which humans identify with animals.

2. The speaker in "Prayer at Sunrise" prays to "My sun father." In "A War God's Horse Song" the speaker mentions "The Holy Wind." What conclusions can you draw about Indian religion from these references?

3. In "The Lesson of the Birds" what does the man learn from watching the birds' nest?

4. How do the poems "To the Buffalo" and "Buffalo Myth" characterize the buffalo? Cite specific lines. Why are both poems addressed to the buffalo?

Developing Skills in Reading Literature

1. **Oral Literature.** The North American Indians generally did not write down their stories and poems. They chanted their poetry, often with dancing and instrumental accompaniment, as a routine part of tribal ritual. What aspects of the poems given here make them especially suitable for oral presentation? Although the poems do not have standard rhyme and meter, what gives them a rhythmic cadence?

Native American stories and poems usually were performed for a specific purpose; for example, to pray for a plentiful harvest or to teach a lesson about courage. What is the purpose of each poem included here? of the prose selection?

2. **Refrain and Repetend.** Find examples of the use of refrain and repetend in these poems. Remember, in refrain a line or lines are repeated with some regulari-ty; in repetend a word or phrase is repeated, not necessarily throughout the poem. How does repetition enhance the effect of each poem?

3. **Parallelism.** Parallelism may be used in poetry as well as in prose. Where do you find parallel construction in "Prayer at Sunrise"? Which lines involve parallelism in "A War God's Horse Song"?

4. **Personification.** Which of these selections contain personification? What is personified, or given human characteristics, in each selection?

5. **Simile and Metaphor.** The speaker in "A War God's Horse Song" uses the simile "My horse has a hoof like striped agate" and the metaphor "The long rainbow is in his mouth for a bridle." Identify other similes and metaphors in this poem. What qualities are emphasized in each? Which comparisons strike you as most successful? Why?

Developing Vocabulary

Word Origins. A number of words in modern American English come from North American Indian languages. This is not surprising, for in most parts of the country substantial interaction between Indians and English–speaking settlers took place.

Look up each word that follows in a dictionary that specifies word origins, or etymologies. Define each word and indicate the Indian language from which it comes. What do most of these words have in common besides their Indian origins?

hickory	persimmon	chipmunk
hominy	terrapin	mackinaw
opossum	moose	tomahawk
pecan	skunk	

George Catlin

1796–1872

George Catlin is probably better known as an artist than as an author. In his writings as in his paintings and sketches, however, he is associated with the American Indian.

Catlin was born in Wilkes-Barre, Pennsylvania, where he grew up and went into law practice. After a brief career as a lawyer, he decided to become a portrait painter. Catlin had never studied art formally, but he had worked hard to master the rudiments of painting.

In 1829, when the country was expanding west rapidly, Catlin began a series of visits to different Indian tribes, most of them located on the plains. He had long been interested in Indian culture, and now he produced numerous paintings, sketches, and writings detailing Indian life. In 1841 he published his major work, *Letters and Notes on the Manners, Customs, and Condition of the North American Indians*, a two-volume work illustrated by Catlin himself. He wrote four other books during his lifetime.

Catlin later exhibited more than five hundred paintings and sketches of Indian life to large audiences in the United States and Europe. The exhibits also included his extensive collection of Indian costumes, weapons, and ritual objects. The National Museum in Washington, D.C., eventually acquired most of Catlin's collection, which is still of historical and cultural interest.

In his later years Catlin traveled through South and Central America, sketching at every opportunity. He died in New Jersey when he was seventy-six.

GEORGE CATLIN. *Self Portrait.*
The Thomas Gilcrease Institute
of American History and Art, Tulsa, Oklahoma.

Mandan Indian Buffalo Dances

The Mandans, like all other tribes, lead lives of idleness and leisure; and of course, devote a great deal of time to their sports and amusements, of which they have a great variety. Of these, dancing is one of the principal, and may be seen in a variety of forms: such as the buffalo dance, the boasting dance, the begging dance, the scalp dance, and a dozen other kinds of dances, all of which have their peculiar characters and meanings or objects.

These exercises are exceedingly grotesque in their appearance, and to the eye of a traveler who knows not their meaning or importance, they are an uncouth and frightful display of starts, and jumps, and yelps, and jarring gutturals, which are sometimes truly terrifying. But when one gives them a little attention, and has been lucky enough to be initiated into their mysterious meaning, they become a subject of the most intense and exciting interest. Every dance has its peculiar step, and every step has its meaning; every dance also has its peculiar song, and that is so intricate and mysterious oftentimes, that not one in ten of the young men who are dancing and singing it, know the meaning of the song which they are chanting over. None but the medicine men are allowed to understand them; and even they are generally only initiated into these secret arcana, on the payment of a liberal stipend for their tuition, which requires much application and study. There is evidently a set song and sentiment for every dance, for the songs are perfectly measured, and sung in exact time with the beat of the drum; and always with an uniform and invariable set of sounds and expressions, which clearly indicate certain sentiments, which are expressed by the voice, though sometimes not given in any known language whatever.

They have other dances and songs which are not so mystified, but which are sung and understood by every person in the tribe, being sung in their own language, with much poetry in them, and perfectly metered, but without rhyme. On these subjects I shall take another occasion to say more; and will for the present turn your attention to the style and modes in which some of these curious transactions are conducted.

My ears have been almost continually ringing since I came here, with the din of yelping and beating of the drums; but I have for several days past been peculiarly engrossed, and my senses almost confounded with the stamping, and grunting, and bellowing of the *buffalo dance*, which closed a few days since at sunrise (thank Heaven), and which I must needs describe to you.

Buffaloes, it is known, are a sort of roaming creatures, congregating occasionally in huge masses, and strolling away about the country from east to west, or from north to south, or just where their whims or strange fancies may lead them; and the Mandans are sometimes, by this means, most unceremoniously left without anything to eat; and being a small tribe, and unwilling to risk their lives by going far from home in the face of their more powerful enemies, are oftentimes left almost in a state of starvation. In any emergency of this kind, every man musters and brings out of his lodge his mask (the skin of a buffalo's head with the horns on), which he is obliged to keep in readiness for this occasion; and then commences the buffalo dance, of which I have above spoken, which is held for the purpose of making "buffalo come" (as they term it), of inducing the buffalo herds to change the direction of their wanderings, and bend their course toward the Mandan village, and graze about on the beautiful hills and bluffs in its vicinity, where the Mandans can shoot them down and cook them as they want them for food.

For the most part of the year, the young warriors and hunters, by riding out a mile or two from the village, can kill meat in abundance; and sometimes large herds of these animals may be seen grazing in full view of the village. There are other seasons also when the young men have ranged about the country as far as they are willing to risk their lives, on account of their enemies, without finding meat. This sad intelligence is brought back to the chiefs and doctors, who sit in solemn council, and consult on the most expedient measures to be taken, until they are sure to decide upon the old and only expedient which "never has failed."

The chief issues his order to his runners or criers, who proclaim it through the village—and in a few minutes the dance begins. The place where this strange operation is carried on is in the public area in the center of the village, and in front of the great medicine or mystery lodge. About ten or fifteen Mandans at a time join in the dance, each one with the skin of the buffalo's head (or mask) with the horns on, placed over his head, and in his hand his favorite bow or lance, with which he is used to slay the buffalo.

I mentioned that this dance always had the desired effect, that it never fails, nor can it, for it cannot be stopped (but is going incessantly day and night) until "buffalo come." Drums are beating and rattles are shaken, and songs and yells incessantly are shouted, and lookers-on stand ready with masks on their heads, and weapons in hand, to take the place of each one as he becomes fatigued, and jumps out of the ring.

During this time of general excitement, spies or "lookers" are kept on the hills in the neighborhood of the village, who, when they discover buffaloes in sight, give the appropri-ate signal, by "throwing their robes," which is instantly seen in the village, and understood by the whole tribe. At this joyful intelligence there is a shout of thanks to the Great Spirit,[1] and more especially to the mystery-man, and the dancers, who *have been the immediate cause of their success!* There is then a brisk preparation for the chase—a grand hunt takes place. The choicest pieces of the victims are sacrificed to the Great Spirit, and then a surfeit and a carouse.

These dances have sometimes been continued in this village two and three weeks without stopping an instant, until the joyful moment when buffaloes made their appearance. So they *never fail;* and they think they have been the means of bringing them in.

Every man in the Mandan village (as I have before said) is obliged by a village regulation to keep the mask of the buffalo hanging on the post at the head of his bed, which he can use on his head whenever he is called upon by the chiefs, to dance for the coming of buffaloes. The mask is put over the head, and generally has a strip of the skin hanging to it, of the whole length of the animal, with the tail attached to it, which, passing down over the back of the dancer, is dragging on the ground. When one becomes fatigued of the exercise, he signifies it by bending quite forward, and sinking his body towards the ground; when another draws a bow upon him and hits him with a blunt arrow, he falls like a buffalo—is seized by the bystanders, who drag him out of the ring by the heels, brandishing their knives about him; and having gone through the motions of skinning and cutting him up, they let him off, and his place is at once supplied by another, who dances into the ring with his mask on; and by this taking of places, the scene is easily kept up night and day, until the desired effect has been produced, that of "making buffalo come."

---

1. **Great Spirit:** Amerindian term for God or a supreme being.

The day before yesterday however, which, though it commenced in joy and thanksgiving to the Great Spirit for the signal success which had attended their several days of dancing and supplication, ended in a calamity which threw the village of the Mandans into mourning and repentant tears, and that at a time of scarcity and great distress. The signal was given into the village on that morning from the top of a distant bluff, that a band of buffaloes were in sight, though at a considerable distance off, and every heart beat with joy, and every eye watered and glistened with gladness.

The dance had lasted some three or four days, and now, instead of the doleful tap of the drum and the begging chants of the dancers, the stamping of horses was heard as they were led and galloped through the village—young men were throwing off their robes and their shirts,—were seen snatching a handful of arrows from their quivers, and stringing their sinewy bows, glancing their eyes and their smiles at their sweethearts, and mounting their ponies.

A few minutes there had been of bustle and boasting, while bows were twanging and spears were polishing by running their blades into the ground—every face and every eye was filled with joy and gladness—horses were pawing and snuffing in fury for the outset, when Louison Frénié, an interpreter of the Fur company, galloped through the village, his rifle in his hand and his powder horn at his side; his head and waist were bandaged with handkerchiefs, and his shirt sleeves rolled up to his shoulders—the hunter's yell issued from his lips and was repeated through the village; he flew to the bluffs, and behind him and over the graceful swells of the prairie, galloped the emulous youths, whose hearts were beating high and quick for the onset.

In the village, where hunger had reigned, and starvation was almost ready to look them in the face, all was instantly turned to joy and gladness. The chiefs and doctors who had been for some days dealing out minimum rations to the community from the public crib, now spread before their subjects the contents of their own private *caches*,[2] and the last of everything that could be mustered, that they might eat a thanksgiving to the Great Spirit for his goodness in sending them a supply of buffalo meat. A general carouse of banqueting ensued, which occupied the greater part of the day; and their hidden stores, which might have fed an emergency for several weeks, were pretty nearly used up on the occasion—bones were half picked, and dishes half emptied and then handed to the dogs. *I* was not forgotten either, in the general surfeit; several large and generous wooden bowls of pemmican[3] and other palatable food were sent to my painting-room, and I received them in this time of scarcity with great pleasure.

After this general indulgence was over, and the dogs had licked the dishes, their usual games and amusements ensued—and hilarity and mirth, and joy took possession of, and reigned in, every nook and corner of the village; and in the midst of this, screams and shrieks were heard, and echoed everywhere. Women and children scrambled to the tops of their wigwams, with their eyes and their hands stretched in agonizing earnestness to the prairie, while blackened warriors ran furiously through every winding maze of the village, and issuing their jarring gutturals of vengeance, as they snatched their deadly weapons from their lodges, and struck the reddened post as they furiously passed it by! Two of their hunters were bending their course down the sides of the bluff toward the village, and another broke suddenly out of a deep ravine, and yet another was seen dashing over and down the green hills, and all were

---

2. **cache** (kash) *French*: something hidden or stored.
3. **pemmican** (pem′ ə kən): a concentrated food used by North American Indians and consisting of lean meat dried, pounded fine, and mixed with melted fat.

goading on their horses at full speed! And then came another, and another, and all entered the village amid shouts and groans of the villagers who crowded around them; the story was told in their looks, for one was bleeding, and the blood that flowed from his naked breast had crimsoned his milk white steed as it had dripped over him; another grasped in his left hand a scalp that was reeking in blood—and in the other his whip—another grasped nothing, save the reins in one hand and the mane of the horse in the other, having thrown his bow and his arrows away, and trusted to the fleetness of his horse for his safety; yet the story was audibly told, and the fatal tragedy recited in irregular and almost suffocating ejaculations—the names of the dead were in turns pronounced, and screams and shrieks burst forth at their recital—murmurs and groans ran through the village, and this happy little community was in a moment smitten with sorrow and distraction.

Their proud band of hunters who had started full of glee and mirth in the morning, had been surrounded by their enemy, the Sioux, and eight of them killed. The Sioux, who had probably reconnoitered their village during the night and ascertained that they were dancing for buffaloes, laid a strategem to entrap them in the following manner: Some six or eight of them appeared the next morning (on a distant bluff, in sight of their sentinel) under the skins of buffaloes, imitating the movements of those animals while grazing; and being discovered by the sentinel, the intelligence was telegraphed to the village, which brought out their hunters as I have described. The masked buffaloes were seen grazing on the top of a high bluff, and when the hunters had approached within half a mile or so of them, they suddenly disappeared over the hill. Louison Frénié, who was leading the little band of hunters, became at that moment suspicious of so strange a movement, and came to a halt.

"Look!" (said a Mandan, pointing to a little ravine to the right, and at the foot of the hill, from which suddenly broke some forty or fifty furious Sioux, on fleet horses and under full whip, who were rushing upon them); they wheeled, and in front of them came another band more furious from the other side of the hill! They started for home (poor fellows), and strained every nerve; but the Sioux were too fleet for them; and every now and then, the whizzing arrow and the lance were heard to rip the flesh of their naked backs, and a grunt and a groan, as they tumbled from their horses. Several miles were run in this desperate race; and Frénié got home, and several of the Mandans, though eight of them were killed and scalped by the way.

So ended that day and the hunt; but many a day and sad, will last the grief of those whose hearts were broken on that unlucky occasion.

This day, though, my readers, has been one of a more joyful kind, for the Great Spirit, who was indignant at so flagrant an injustice, has sent the Mandans an abundance of buffaloes; and all hearts have joined in a general thanksgiving to Him for his goodness and justice. . . .

Getting at Meaning

1. According to George Catlin, what are some of the different dances the Mandans perform? What accompanies each dance?

2. Describe the buffalo dance. What is its purpose? Why are the buffalo so important to the Mandans?

3. Why does the buffalo dance never fail? How do the Mandans celebrate each time the dance works?

4. Explain how a group of Sioux Indians trick the Mandans. How does Catlin create sympathy for the Mandans?

5. What do you learn about Mandan culture from this selection? Which details suggest that the village is well organized?

Developing Skills in Reading Literature

1. **Stereotype.** In everyday speech and in literature, the term stereotype refers to something that conforms to a fixed or general pattern, without individual distinguishing marks or qualities. Often a stereotype is a mental picture, held in common by members of a group, which represents an oversimplified opinion, such as of a race or national group.

Which details in the first two paragraphs suggest that Catlin holds some stereotypes about Indian life, or that he expects his readers to have stereotyped views?

2. **Tone.** What is Catlin's attitude toward the Mandans? Find sentences and phrases that show his feeling for the tribe.

Developing Writing Skills

Combining Description and Exposition. Write a five-paragraph composition in which you describe a custom or ritual important to some group with which you are familiar. The group could be your family, a club or organization, a particular ethnic group, a specific religious group, or a foreign people. Explain the custom or ritual in detail, describing the participants and their actions and making it clear why the tradition is important and why it continues. If you like, take a humorous look at some ritual important in contemporary American culture. You might want to write from the point of view of a visitor, viewing our society for the first time.

Buffalo Dance. George Catlin. The Newberry Library.

Washington Irving
1783–1859

Born at the end of the American Revolution, Washington Irving was named for the leader of the rebel troops at Yorktown. After this suitable beginning, Irving went on to become the first really well known and distinguished American literary figure.

Irving was the youngest of eleven children in a prosperous New York family. He grew up in New York City, which during his childhood had only sixty thousand inhabitants. As a young man in New York, and then on tour in Europe, Irving led a social existence, developing a taste for theater, opera, art, and literature. He did not show much interest in embarking on a career.

Irving's first major literary venture was the *Salmagundi Papers*. "Salmagundi" is a salad of chopped meats and vegetables, a variable mixture. The *Salmagundi Papers* was a literary mixture, satiric, humorous essays about New York society written by Irving and a few friends.

Irving's next major work, published in 1809, was *A History of New York from the Beginning of the World to the End of the Dutch Dynasty by Diedrich Knickerbocker*. This book pretended to be the work of an old Dutch historian who had disappeared from his rooming house, leaving his manuscript in lieu of his rent. *A History of New York . . .* was something of a landmark, for Irving treated a uniquely American subject from a sophisticated literary perspective, something that no other writer had done before.

In the period after *A History of New York . . .* came out, Irving went to Europe to try to save a branch of his family's hardware-importing business. This experience made him realize his distaste for a career in business, and he determined to pursue a literary career. He also decided to remain in Europe.

In 1819 Irving published *The Sketch Book of Geoffrey Crayon, Gent.*, his most famous book. Ten years had elapsed since Irving had published *A History of New York . . .*, and during that period he had become a mature, polished writer. "Rip Van Winkle" and "The Legend of Sleepy Hollow," Irving's most widely read folk tales, are in *The Sketch Book*. In these tales, as well as in "The Devil and Tom Walker" and others, Irving was anticipating the short story, later brought into full flower by Edgar Allan Poe. Although many of the tales in *The Sketch Book* have European plot sources, the tales are distinctly American. As in *A History of New York . . .*, Irving had found a literary use for native materials.

The rest of Irving's long life was comfortable. In 1832 he returned to the United States, after seventeen years abroad, and discovered that he was a major public figure. Using his estate on the Hudson River at Tarrytown, New York, as home base, he traveled widely, taking an extended tour of the American West that inspired both fiction and nonfiction writing.

Irving, novelist James Fenimore Cooper, and the poet William Cullen Bryant are often seen as a trio, the first truly successful American literary figures. They brought Romanticism to the new country and established a native literary tradition. Irving is still read lovingly for his humor, his fascinating blend of realistic detail and supernatural occurrence, and his vivid depiction of local characters in unmistakably American settings.

Camp of the Wild Horse

We had encamped in a good neighborhood for game, as the reports of rifles in various directions speedily gave notice. One of our hunters soon returned with the meat of a doe, tied up in the skin, and slung across his shoulders. Another brought a fat buck across his horse. Two other deer were brought in, and a number of turkeys. All the game was thrown down in front of the Captain's fire, to be portioned out among the various messes. The spits and camp-kettles were soon in full employ, and throughout the evening there was a scene of hunters' feasting and profusion.

We had been disappointed this day in our hopes of meeting with buffalo, but the sight of the wild horse had been a great novelty, and gave a turn to the conversation of the camp for the evening. There were several anecdotes told of a famous gray horse, which has ranged the prairies of this neighborhood for six or seven years, setting at naught every attempt of the hunters to capture him. They say he can pace and rack (or amble) faster than the fleetest horses can run. Equally marvelous accounts were given of a black horse on the Brazos, who grazed the prairies on that river's banks in Texas. For years he outstripped all pursuit. His fame spread far and wide; offers were made for him to the amount of a thousand dollars; the boldest and most hard-riding hunters tried incessantly to make prize of him, but in vain. At length he fell a victim to his gallantry, being decoyed under a tree by a tame mare, and a noose dropped over his head by a boy perched among the branches.

The capture of the wild horse is one of the most favorite achievements of the prairie tribes; and, indeed, it is from this source that the Indian hunters chiefly supply themselves. The wild horses which range those vast grassy plains, extending from the Arkansas to the Spanish settlements, are of various forms and colors, betraying their various descents. Some resemble the common English stock, and are probably descended from horses which have escaped from our border settlements. Others are of a low but strong make, and are supposed to be of the Andalusian breed, brought out by the Spanish discoverers.

Some fanciful speculatists have seen in them descendants of the Arab stock, brought into Spain from Africa, and thence transferred to this country; and have pleased themselves with the idea that their sires may have been of the pure coursers of the desert, that once bore Mahomet[1] and his warlike disciples across the sandy plains of Arabia.

The habits of the Arab seem to have come with the steed. The introduction of the horse on the boundless prairies of the Far West changed the whole mode of living of their inhabitants. It gave them that facility of rapid motion, and of sudden and distant change of place, so dear to the roving propensities of man. Instead of lurking in the depths of gloomy forests, and patiently threading the mazes of a tangled wilderness on foot, like his brethren of the north, the Indian of the West is a rover of the plain; he leads a brighter and more sunshiny life; almost always on horseback, on vast flowery prairies and under cloudless skies.

I was lying by the Captain's fire, late in the

---

1. **Mahomet** (mə häm′ it): same as Mohammed (mō ham′ id), the Arab prophet and founder of Islam who lived from 570-632.

evening, listening to stories about those coursers of the prairies, and weaving speculations of my own, when there was a clamor of voices and a loud cheering at the other end of the camp; and word was passed that Beatte, the half-breed, had brought in a wild horse.

In an instant every fire was deserted; the whole camp crowded to see the Indian and his prize. It was a colt about two years old, well grown, finely limbed, with bright prominent eyes, and a spirited yet gentle demeanor. He gazed about him with an air of mingled stupefaction and surprise, at the men, the horses, and the campfires; while the Indian stood before him with folded arms, having hold of the other end of the cord which noosed his captive, and gazing on him with a most imperturbable aspect. Beatte, as I have before observed, has a greenish olive complexion, with a strongly marked countenance, not unlike the bronze casts of Napoleon;[2] and as he stood before his captive horse, with folded arms and fixed aspect, he looked more like a statue than a man.

If the horse, however, manifested the least restiveness, Beatte would immediately worry him with the lariat, jerking him first on one side, then on the other, so as almost to throw him on the ground; when he had thus rendered him passive, he would resume his statue-like attitude and gaze at him in silence.

The whole scene was singularly wild; the tall grove, partially illumined by the flashing fires of the camp, the horses tethered here and there among the trees, the carcasses of deer hanging around, and in the midst of all, the wild huntsman and his wild horse, with an admiring throng of rangers, almost as wild.

In the eagerness of their excitement, several of the young rangers sought to get the horse by purchase or barter, and even offered extravagant terms; but Beatte declined all their offers. "You give great price now," said he. "Tomorrow you be sorry, and take back, and say d——d Indian!"

The young men importuned him with questions about the mode in which he took the horse, but his answers were dry and laconic; he evidently retained some pique at having been undervalued and sneered at by them; and at the same time looked down upon them with contempt as greenhorns, little versed in the noble science of woodcraft.

Afterward, however, when he was seated by our fire, I readily drew from him an account of his exploit; for, though taciturn among strangers, and little prone to boast of his actions, yet his taciturnity, like that of all Indians, had its times of relaxation.

He informed me, that on leaving the camp, he had returned to the place where we had lost sight of the wild horse. Soon getting upon its track, he followed it to the banks of the river. Here, the prints being more distinct in the sand, he perceived that one of the hoofs was broken and defective, so he gave up the pursuit.

As he was returning to the camp, he came upon a gang of six horses, which immediately made for the river. He pursued them across the stream, left his rifle on the river bank, and putting his horse to full speed, soon came up with the fugitives. He attempted to noose one of them, but the lariat hitched on one of his ears, and he shook it off. The horses dashed up a hill; he followed hard at their heels, when, of a sudden, he saw their tails whisking in the air, and they plunging down a precipice. It was too late to stop. He shut his eyes, held in his breath, and went over with them—neck or nothing. The descent was between twenty and thirty feet, but they all came down safe upon a sandy bottom.

He now succeeded in throwing his noose round a fine young horse. As he galloped alongside of him, the two horses passed each side of a sapling, and the end of the lariat was jerked out of his hand. He regained it, but an

---

2. **Napoleon** (nə pō′ lē ən): Napoleon Bonaparte, emperor of France, who lived from 1769-1821.

intervening tree obliged him again to let it go. Having once more caught it, and coming to a more open country, he was enabled to play the young horse with the line until he gradually checked and subdued him, so as to lead him to the place where he had left his rifle.

He had another formidable difficulty in getting him across the river, where both horses stuck for a time in the mire, and Beatte was nearly unseated from his saddle by the force of the current and the struggle of his captive. After much toil and trouble, however, he got across the stream, and brought his prize safe into camp.

For the remainder of the evening, the camp remained in a high state of excitement; nothing was talked of but the capture of wild horses; every youngster of the troop was for this harum-scarum kind of chase; every one promised himself to return from the campaign in triumph, bestriding one of these wild coursers of the prairies. Beatte had suddenly risen to great importance; he was the prime hunter, the hero of the day. Offers were made him by the best mounted rangers, to let him ride their horses in the chase, provided he would give them a share of the spoil. Beatte bore his honors in silence, and closed with none of the offers. Our stammering, chattering, gasconading little Frenchman, however, made up for his taciturnity, by vaunting as much upon the subject as if it were he that had caught the horse. Indeed he held forth so learnedly in the matter, and boasted so much of the many horses he had taken, that he began to be considered an oracle; and some of the youngsters were inclined to doubt whether he were not superior even to the taciturn Beatte.

The excitement kept the camp awake later than usual. The hum of voices, interrupted by occasional peals of laughter, was heard from the groups around the various fires, and the night was considerably advanced before all had sunk to sleep.

With the morning dawn the excitement revived, and Beatte and his wild horse were again the gaze and talk of the camp. The captive had been tied all night to a tree among the other horses. He was again led forth by Beatte, by a long halter or lariat, and, on his manifesting the least restiveness, was, as before, jerked and worried into passive submission. He appeared to be gentle and docile by nature, and had a beautifully mild expression of the eye. In his strange and forlorn situation, the poor animal seemed to seek protection and companionship in the very horse which had aided to capture him.

Seeing him thus gentle and tractable, Beatte, just as we were about to march, strapped a light pack upon his back, by way of giving him the first lesson in servitude. The native pride and independence of the animal took fire at this indignity. He reared, and plunged, and kicked, and tried in every way to get rid of the degrading burden. The Indian was too potent for him. At every paroxysm he renewed the discipline of the halter, until the poor animal, driven to despair, threw himself prostrate on the ground, and lay motionless, as if acknowledging himself vanquished. A stage hero, representing the despair of a captive prince, could not have played his part more dramatically. There was absolutely a moral grandeur in it.

The imperturbable Beatte folded his arms, and stood for a time, looking down in silence upon his captive; until seeing him perfectly subdued, he nodded his head slowly, screwed his mouth into a sardonic smile of triumph, and, with a jerk of the halter, ordered him to rise. He obeyed, and from that time forward offered no resistance. During that day he bore his pack patiently, and was led by the halter; but in two days he followed voluntarily at large among the supernumerary horses of the troop.

I could not but look with compassion upon this fine young animal, whose whole course of existence had been so suddenly reversed. From being a denizen of these vast pastures, ranging at will from plain to plain and mead to mead, cropping of every herb and flower, and drinking of every stream, he was suddenly reduced to perpetual and painful servitude, to pass his life under the harness and the curb, amid, perhaps, the din and dust and drudgery of cities. The transition in his lot was such as sometimes takes place in human affairs, and in the fortunes of towering individuals—one day, a prince of the prairies—the next day, a pack-horse!

Getting at Meaning

1. Describe the wild horses that roam the prairie. How do the prairie tribes react to the capture of a wild horse?

2. Describe Beatte. What sort of horse does he capture?

3. Explain how Beatte captures his horse.

Developing Skills in Reading Literature

1. **Allusion.** In the fourth paragraph the narrator speaks of "Mahomet and his warlike disciples." This is an allusion, for it refers to a person with whom the writer expects the reader to be familiar. Find another allusion in the selection and explain it.

2. **Theme.** The narrator sums up his message in the final paragraph of the story. Why does he feel sorry for the horse? What statement about human life does he make through the story of the horse?

Developing Vocabulary

Synonyms: Adjectives. Washington Irving employs a number of adjectives whose meanings you may not know. Look up each word that follows in a dictionary and record its meaning. Notice how Washington Irving uses each word. Then give one or two common synonyms for the word.

formidable	supernumerary
gasconading	taciturn
imperturbable	tractable
laconic	

The Short Story

THE MONEY DIGGERS, 1832. *John Quidor.*
The Brooklyn Museum. Gift of Mr. and Mrs. Alastair Bradley Martin.

Washington Irving

The Devil and Tom Walker

A few miles from Boston in Massachusetts, there is a deep inlet, winding several miles into the interior of the country from Charles Bay, and terminating in a thickly wooded swamp or morass. On one side of this inlet is a beautiful dark grove; on the opposite side the land rises abruptly from the water's edge into a high ridge, on which grow a few scattered oaks of great age and immense size. Under one of these gigantic trees, according to old stories, there was a great amount of treasure buried by Kidd the pirate. The inlet allowed a facility to bring the money in a boat secretly and at night to the very foot of the hill; the elevation of the place permitted a good lookout to be kept that no one was at hand; while the remarkable trees formed good landmarks by which the place might easily be found again. The old stories add, moreover, that the devil presided at the hiding of the money and took it under his guardianship; but this, it is well known, he always does with buried treasure, particularly when it has been ill-gotten. Be that as it may, Kidd never returned to recover his wealth; being shortly after seized at Boston, sent out to England, and there hanged for a pirate.

About the year 1727, just at the time that earthquakes were prevalent in New England, and shook many tall sinners down upon their knees, there lived near this place a meager, miserly fellow, of the name of Tom Walker. He had a wife as miserly as himself: they were so miserly that they even conspired to cheat each other. Whatever the woman could lay hands on she hid away; a hen could not cackle but she was on the alert to secure the new-laid egg. Her husband was continually prying about to detect her secret hoards, and many and fierce were the conflicts that took place about what ought to have been common property. They lived in a forlorn-looking house that stood alone and had an air of starvation. A few straggling savin[1] trees, emblems of sterility, grew near it; no smoke ever curled from its chimney; no traveler stopped at its door. A miserable horse, whose ribs were as articulate as the bars of a gridiron, stalked about a field, where a thin carpet of moss, scarcely covering the ragged beds of puddingstone, tantalized and balked his hunger; and sometimes he would lean his head over the fence, look piteously at the passer-by, and seem to petition deliverance from this land of famine.

The house and its inmates had altogether a bad name. Tom's wife was a tall termagant, fierce of temper, loud of tongue, and strong of arm. Her voice was often heard in wordy warfare with her husband; and his face sometimes showed signs that their conflicts were not confined to words. No one ventured, however, to interfere between them. The lonely wayfarer shrunk within himself at the horrid clamor and clapperclawing;[2] eyed the den of discord askance; and hurried on his way, rejoicing, if a bachelor, in his celibacy.

One day that Tom Walker had been to a

---

1. **savin** (sav′ ən): a Eurasian juniper with dark foliage and small yellowish green berries.
2. **clapperclawing:** clawing with nails; scolding.

distant part of the neighborhood, he took what he considered a shortcut homeward, through the swamp. Like most shortcuts, it was an ill-chosen route. The swamp was thickly grown with great gloomy pines and hemlocks, some of them ninety feet high, which made it dark at noonday, and a retreat for all the owls of the neighborhood. It was full of pits and quagmires, partly covered with weeds and mosses, where the green surface often betrayed the traveler into a gulf of black, smothering mud; there were also dark and stagnant pools, the abodes of the tadpole, the bullfrog, and the water snake; where the trunks of pines and hemlocks lay half drowned, half rotting, looking like alligators sleeping in the mire.

Tom had long been picking his way cautiously through this treacherous forest; stepping from tuft to tuft of rushes and roots, which afforded precarious footholds among deep sloughs; or pacing carefully, like a cat, along the prostrate trunks of trees; startled now and then by the sudden screaming of the bittern, or the quacking of a wild duck rising on the wing from some solitary pool. At length he arrived at a firm piece of ground, which ran out like a peninsula into the deep bosom of the swamp. It had been one of the strongholds of the Indians during their wars with the first colonists. Here they had thrown up a kind of fort, which they had looked upon as almost impregnable, and had used as a place of refuge for their squaws and children. Nothing remained of the old Indian fort but a few embankments, gradually sinking to the level of the surrounding earth, and already overgrown in part by oaks and other forest trees, the foliage of which formed a contrast to the dark pines and hemlocks of the swamp.

It was late in the dusk of evening when Tom Walker reached the old fort, and he paused there awhile to rest himself. Anyone but he would have felt unwilling to linger in this lonely, melancholy place, for the common people had a bad opinion of it, from the stories handed down from the time of the Indian wars, when it was asserted that the savages held incantations here, and made sacrifices to the evil spirit.

Tom Walker, however, was not a man to be troubled with any fears of the kind. He reposed himself for some time on the trunk of a fallen hemlock, listening to the boding cry of the tree toad, and delving with his walking staff into a mound of black mold at his feet. As he turned up the soil unconsciously, his staff struck against something hard. He raked it out of the vegetable mold, and lo! a cloven skull, with an Indian tomahawk buried deep in it, lay before him. The rust on the weapon showed the time that had elapsed since this deathblow had been given. It was a dreary memento of the fierce struggle that had taken place in this last foothold of the Indian warriors.

"Humph!" said Tom Walker, as he gave it a kick to shake the dirt from it.

"Let that skull alone!" said a gruff voice. Tom lifted up his eyes, and beheld a great black man seated directly opposite him, on the stump of a tree. He was exceedingly surprised, having neither heard nor seen anyone approach; and he was still more perplexed on observing, as well as the gathering gloom would permit, that the stranger was neither Negro nor Indian. It is true he was dressed in a rude half-Indian garb, and had a red belt or sash swathed round his body; but his face was neither black nor copper-color, but swarthy and dingy, and begrimed with soot, as if he had been accustomed to toil among fires and forges. He had a shock of coarse black hair, that stood out from his head in all directions, and bore an ax on his shoulder.

He scowled for a moment at Tom with a pair of great red eyes.

"What are you doing on my grounds?" said the black man, with a hoarse, growling voice.

"Your grounds!" said Tom, with a sneer, "no more your grounds than mine; they belong to Deacon Peabody."

"Deacon Peabody be d—d," said the stranger, "as I flatter myself he will be, if he does not look more to his own sins and less to those of his neighbors. Look yonder, and see how Deacon Peabody is faring."

Tom looked in the direction that the stranger pointed and beheld one of the great trees, fair and flourishing without, but rotten at the core, and saw that it had been nearly hewn through, so that the first high wind was likely to blow it down. On the bark of the tree was scored the name of Deacon Peabody, an eminent man, who had waxed wealthy by driving shrewd bargains with the Indians. He now looked around, and found most of the tall trees marked with the name of some great man of the colony, and all more or less scored by the ax. The one on which he had been seated, and which had evidently just been hewn down, bore the name of Crowninshield; and he recollected a mighty rich man of that name, who made a vulgar display of wealth, which it was whispered he had acquired by buccaneering.

"He's just ready for burning!" said the black man, with a growl of triumph. "You see, I am likely to have a good stock of firewood for winter."

"But what right have you," said Tom, "to cut down Deacon Peabody's timber?"

"The right of a prior claim," said the other. "This woodland belonged to me long before one of your white-faced race put foot upon the soil."

"And pray, who are you, if I may be so bold?" said Tom.

"Oh, I go by various names. I am the wild huntsman in some countries; the black miner in others. In this neighborhood I am known by the name of the black woodsman. I am he to whom the red men consecrated this spot, and in honor of whom they now and then roasted a white man, by way of sweet-smelling sacrifice. Since the red men have been exterminated by you white savages, I amuse myself by presiding at the persecutions of Quakers[3] and Anabaptists;[4] I am the great patron and prompter of slave dealers, and the grand master of the Salem witches."

"The upshot of all which is that, if I mistake not," said Tom, sturdily, "you are he commonly called Old Scratch."[5]

"The same, at your service!" replied the black man, with a half-civil nod.

Such was the opening of this interview, according to the old story; though it has almost too familiar an air to be credited. One would think that to meet with such a singular personage, in this wild, lonely place, would have shaken any man's nerves; but Tom was a hard-minded fellow, not easily daunted, and he had lived so long with a termagant wife that he did not even fear the devil.

It is said that after this commencement they had a long and earnest conversation together, as Tom returned homeward. The black man told him of great sums of money buried by Kidd the pirate, under the oak trees on the high ridge, not far from the morass. All these were under his command, and protected by his power, so that none could find them but such as propitiated his favor. These he offered to place within Tom Walker's reach, having conceived an especial kindness for him; but they were to be had only on certain conditions. What these conditions were may be easily surmised, though Tom never disclosed them publicly. They must have been very hard, for he required time to think of them, and he was not a man to stick at trifles when money was in view. When they had reached the edge of the swamp, the stranger paused. "What proof have I that all you have

---

3. **Quakers:** members of the Friends religious sect that stresses Inner Light, rejects sacraments and an ordained ministry, and opposes war.

4. **Anabaptists:** members of the Protestant sect advocating the baptism and church membership of adult believers only, nonresistance, and the separation of church and state.

5. **Old Scratch:** a nickname for the devil.

been telling me is true?" said Tom. "There's my signature," said the black man, pressing his finger on Tom's forehead. So saying, he turned off among the thickets of the swamp, and seemed, as Tom said, to go down, down, down, into the earth, until nothing but his head and shoulders could be seen, and so on, until he totally disappeared.

When Tom reached home, he found the black print of a finger burnt, as it were, into his forehead, which nothing could obliterate. The first news his wife had to tell him was the sudden death of Absalom Crowninshield, the rich buccaneer. It was announced in the papers with the usual flourish that "a great man had fallen in Israel."[6]

Tom recollected the tree which his black friend had just hewn down and which was ready for burning. "Let the freebooter roast," said Tom; "who cares!" He now felt convinced that all he had heard and seen was no illusion.

He was not prone to let his wife into his confidence; but as this was an uneasy secret, he willingly shared it with her. All her avarice was awakened at the mention of hidden gold, and she urged her husband to comply with the black man's terms, and secure what would make them wealthy for life. However Tom might have felt disposed to sell himself to the devil, he was determined not to do so to oblige his wife; so he flatly refused, out of the mere spirit of contradiction. Many and bitter were the quarrels they had on the subject; but the more she talked, the more resolute was Tom not to be damned to please her.

At length she determined to drive the bargain on her own account, and if she succeeded, to keep all the gain to herself. Being of the same fearless temper as her husband, she set off for the old Indian fort toward the close of a summer's day. She was many hours absent. When she came back, she was reserved and sullen in her replies. She spoke something of a black man, whom she had met about twilight, hewing at the root of a tall tree. He was sulky,

however, and would not come to terms; she was to go again with a propitiatory offering, but what it was she forbore to say.

The next evening she set off for the swamp, with her apron heavily laden. Tom waited and waited for her, but in vain; midnight came, but she did not make her appearance: morning, noon, night returned, but still she did not come. Tom now grew uneasy for her safety, especially as he found she had carried off in her apron the silver teapot and spoons, and every portable article of value. Another night elapsed, another morning came; but no wife. In a word, she was never heard of more.

What was her real fate nobody knows, in consequence of so many pretending to know. It is one of those facts which have become confounded by a variety of historians. Some asserted that she lost her way among the tangled mazes of the swamp, and sank into some pit or slough; others, more uncharitable, hinted that she had eloped with the household booty and made off to some other province; while others surmised that the tempter had decoyed her into a dismal quagmire, on the top of which her hat was found lying. In confirmation of this, it was said a great black man, with an ax on his shoulder, was seen late that very evening coming out of the swamp, carrying a bundle tied in a check apron, with an air of surly triumph.

The most current and probable story, however, observes that Tom Walker grew so anxious about the fate of his wife and his property that he set out at length to seek them both at the Indian fort. During a long summer's afternoon he searched about the gloomy place, but no wife was to be seen. He called her name repeatedly, but she was nowhere to be heard. The bittern alone responded to his voice, as he flew screaming by; or the bullfrog croaked dolefully from a neighboring pool. At length,

---

6. **a great man . . . Israel:** an important person had gone to his reward in the afterlife.

it is said, just in the brown hour of twilight, when the owls began to hoot, and the bats to flit about, his attention was attracted by the clamor of carrion crows hovering about a cypress tree. He looked up, and beheld a bundle tied in a check apron, and hanging in the branches of the tree, with a great vulture perched hard by, as if keeping watch upon it. He leaped with joy; for he recognized his wife's apron and supposed it to contain the household valuables.

"Let us get hold of the property," said he consolingly to himself, "and we will endeavor to do without the woman."

As he scrambled up the tree, the vulture spread its wide wings, and sailed off screaming into the deep shadows of the forest. Tom seized the checked apron, but woeful sight! found nothing but a heart and liver tied up in it!

Such, according to this most authentic old story, was all that was to be found of Tom's wife. She had probably attempted to deal with the black man as she had been accustomed to deal with her husband; but though a female scold is generally considered a match for the devil, yet in this instance she appears to have had the worst of it. She must have died game, however; for it is said Tom noticed many prints of cloven feet deeply stamped about the tree, and found handfuls of hair that looked as if they had been plucked from the coarse black shock of the woodsman. Tom knew his wife's prowess by experience. He shrugged his shoulders, as he looked at the signs of a fierce clapperclawing. "'Egad," said he to himself, "Old Scratch must have had a tough time of it!"

Tom consoled himself for the loss of his property with the loss of his wife, for he was a man of fortitude. He even felt something like gratitude towards the black woodsman, who, he considered, had done him a kindness. He sought, therefore, to cultivate a further acquaintance with him, but for some time without success; the old blacklegs played shy, for, whatever people may think, he is not always to be had for calling for: he knows how to play his cards when pretty sure of his game.

At length, it is said, when delay had whetted Tom's eagerness to the quick, and prepared him to agree to anything rather than not gain the promised treasure, he met the black man one evening in his usual woodsman's dress, with his ax on his shoulder, sauntering along the swamp, and humming a tune. He affected to receive Tom's advances with great indifference, made brief replies, and went on humming his tune.

By degrees, however, Tom brought him to business, and they began to haggle about the terms on which the former was to have the pirate's treasure. There was one condition which need not be mentioned, being generally understood in all cases where the devil grants favors; but there were others about which, though of less importance, he was inflexibly obstinate. He insisted that the money found through his means should be employed in his service. He proposed, therefore, that Tom should employ it in the black traffic; that is to say, that he should fit out a slave ship. This, however, Tom resolutely refused: he was bad enough in all conscience; but the devil himself could not tempt him to turn slave trader.

Finding Tom so squeamish on this point, he did not insist upon it, but proposed, instead, that he should turn usurer; the devil being extemely anxious for the increase of usurers, looking upon them as his peculiar people.

To this no objections were made, for it was just to Tom's taste.

"You shall open a broker's shop in Boston next month," said the black man.

"I'll do it tomorrow, if you wish," said Tom Walker.

"You shall lend money at two percent a month."

"Egad, I'll charge four!" replied Tom Walker.

"You shall extort bonds, foreclose mortgages, drive the merchants to bankruptcy—"

"I'll drive them to the devil," cried Tom Walker.

"You are the usurer for my money!" said blacklegs with delight. "When will you want the rhino?"[7]

"This very night."

"Done!" said the devil.

"Done!" said Tom Walker. So they shook hands and struck a bargain.

A few days' time saw Tom Walker seated behind his desk in a countinghouse in Boston.

His reputation for a ready-moneyed man, who would lend money out for a good consideration, soon spread abroad. Everybody remembers the time of Governor Belcher, when money was particularly scarce. It was a time of paper credit. The country had been deluged with government bills; the famous Land Bank[8] had been established; there had been a rage for speculating; the people had run mad with schemes for new settlements, for building cities in the wilderness; land-jobbers went about with maps of grants, and townships, and El Dorados[9] lying nobody knew where, but which everybody was ready to purchase. In a word, the great speculating fever which breaks out every now and then in the country had raged to an alarming degree, and everybody was dreaming of making sudden fortunes from nothing. As usual the fever had subsided; the dream had gone off, and the imaginary fortunes with it; the patients were left in doleful plight, and the whole country resounded with the consequent cry of "hard times."

At this propitious time of public distress did Tom Walker set up as usurer in Boston. His door was soon thronged by customers. The needy and adventurous, the gambling speculator, the dreaming land-jobber, the thriftless tradesman, the merchant with cracked credit; in short, everyone driven to raise money by desperate means and desperate sacrifices hurried to Tom Walker.

Thus Tom was the universal friend of the needy and acted like a "friend in need"; that is to say, he always exacted good pay and good security. In proportion to the distress of the applicant was the hardness of his terms. He accumulated bonds and mortgages; gradually squeezed his customers closer and closer; and sent them at length, dry as a sponge, from his door.

In this way he made money hand over hand, became a rich and mighty man, and exalted his cocked hat upon 'Change.[10] He built himself, as usual, a vast house, out of ostentation; but left the greater part of it unfinished and unfurnished, out of parsimony. He even set up a carriage in the fullness of his vainglory, though he nearly starved the horses which drew it; and as the ungreased wheels groaned and screeched on the axletrees, you would have thought you heard the souls of the poor debtors he was squeezing.

As Tom waxed old, however, he grew thoughtful. Having secured the good things of this world, he began to feel anxious about those of the next. He thought with regret on the bargain he had made with his black friend, and set his wits to work to cheat him out of the conditions. He became, therefore, all of a sudden, a violent churchgoer. He prayed loudly and strenuously, as if heaven were to be taken by force of lungs. Indeed, one might always tell when he had sinned most during the week, by the clamor of his Sunday devotion. The quiet Christians who had been modestly and steadfastly traveling Zionward were struck with self-reproach at seeing themselves so suddenly outstripped in their career by this new-made convert. Tom was as rigid in religious as in money matters; he was a stern supervisor and censurer of his neighbors, and seemed to think every sin entered

---

7. **rhino:** powder from the rhinoceros horn, thought to have special powers; slang term for money.

8. **Land Bank:** the Federal Land Banks of the United States, whose chief function is the financing of transactions in real property.

9. **El Dorados:** imaginary countries abounding in gold.

10. **exalted . . . 'Change:** built his success upon money.

up to their account became a credit on his own side of the page. He even talked of the expediency of reviving the persecution of Quakers and Anabaptists. In a word, Tom's zeal became as notorious as his riches.

Still, in spite of all this strenuous attention to forms, Tom had a lurking dread that the devil, after all, would have his due. That he might not be taken unawares, therefore, it is said he always carried a small Bible in his coat pocket. He had also a great folio Bible on his countinghouse desk, and would frequently be found reading it when people called on business; on such occasions he would lay his green spectacles in the book, to mark the place, while he turned round to drive some usurious bargain.

Some say that Tom grew a little crack-brained in his old days, and that fancying his end approaching, he had his horse new shod, saddled and bridled, and buried with his feet uppermost; because he supposed that at the last day the world would be turned upside down; in which case he should find his horse standing ready for mounting, and he was determined at the worst to give his old friend a run for it. This, however, is probably a mere old wives' fable. If he really did take such a precaution, it was totally superfluous; at least so says the authentic old legend, which closes this story in the following manner.

One hot summer afternoon in the dog days, just as a terrible black thunder-gust was coming up, Tom sat in his countinghouse, in his white linen cap and India silk morning gown. He was on the point of foreclosing a mortgage, by which he would complete the ruin of an unlucky land speculator for whom he had professed the greatest friendship. The poor land-jobber begged him to grant a few months' indulgence. Tom had grown testy and irritated, and refused another day.

"My family will be ruined and brought upon the parish," said the land-jobber.

"Charity begins at home," replied Tom; "I must take care of myself in these hard times."

"You have made so much money out of me," said the speculator.

Tom lost his patience and his piety. "The devil take me," said he, "if I have made a farthing!"

Just then there were three loud knocks at the street door. He stepped out to see who was there. A black man was holding a black horse, which neighed and stamped with impatience. "Tom, you're come for," said the black fellow, gruffly. Tom shrank back, but too late. He had left his little Bible at the bottom of his coat pocket, and his big Bible on the desk buried under the mortgage he was about to foreclose: never was sinner taken more unawares. The black man whisked him like a child into the saddle, gave the horse the lash, and away he galloped, with Tom on his back, in the midst of a thunderstorm. The clerks stuck their pens behind their ears, and stared after him from the windows. Away went Tom Walker, dashing down the streets; his white cap bobbing up and down, his morning gown fluttering in the wind, and his steed striking fire out of the pavement at every bound. When the clerks turned to look for the black man he had disappeared.

Tom Walker never returned to foreclose the mortgage. A countryman who lived on the border of the swamp reported that in the height of the thunder-gust he had heard a great clattering of hoofs and a howling along the road, and running to the window caught sight of a figure, such as I have described, on a horse that galloped like mad across the fields, over the hills, and down into the black hemlock swamp towards the old Indian fort; and that shortly after, a thunderbolt falling in that direction seemed to set the whole forest in a blaze.

The good people of Boston shook their heads and shrugged their shoulders, but had been so much accustomed to witches and goblins, and tricks of the devil in all kinds of shapes, from the first settlement of the colony, that they were not so much horror-struck as might have been expected. Trustees were appointed to take charge of Tom's effects. There was nothing, however, to administer upon. On searching his coffers all his bonds and mortgages were found reduced to cinders. In place of gold and silver his iron chest was filled with chips and shavings; two skeletons lay in his stable instead of his half-starved horses, and the very next day his great house took fire and was burnt to the ground.

Such was the end of Tom Walker and his ill-gotten wealth. Let all griping money bro-kers lay this story to heart. The truth of it is not to be doubted. The very hole under the oak trees, whence he dug Kidd's money, is to be seen this day; and the neighboring swamp and old Indian fort are often haunted in stormy nights by a figure on horseback, in morning gown and white cap, which is doubtless the troubled spirit of the usurer. In fact, the story has resolved itself into a proverb, and is the origin of that popular saying, so prevalent throughout New England, of "The Devil and Tom Walker."

Getting at Meaning

1. What details does the narrator use to establish the miserliness of Tom Walker and his wife? Describe their marriage.

2. Describe the spot where Captain Kidd's treasure is buried. Why did Kidd choose this spot? What later happened to Kidd?

3. Describe the stranger Tom encounters. What clues lead Tom to conclude that he is speaking to the devil?

4. Explain the comparison the devil draws between Deacon Peabody and the tree.

5. What offer does the devil make to Tom? What are the conditions of his offer? Explain the sentence, "There was one condition which need not be mentioned, being generally understood in all cases where the devil grants favors."

6. Why does Tom's wife seek out the devil? What are some of the theories about her fate? Explain the significance of what Tom finds wrapped up in his wife's apron.

7. Explain what happens to Tom after his wife's death. Even when he is rich, how does his way of life reflect his basic stinginess? How does he treat his clients? Why is the narrator's statement about Tom's carriage wheels so apt?

8. How does Tom try to avoid his eventual fate? What error leads to his seizure?

Developing Skills in Reading Literature

1. **Fiction.** Fiction refers to imaginative works of prose, including the novel and the short story. Fiction often is inspired by actual events and by real people, but a work of fiction also may be entirely imaginative. Writers of fiction treat their subjects in a variety of ways. Some write light, humorous pieces, designed mainly to entertain the reader. Others criticize, interpret, and comment on behavior and situations in order to deepen the reader's understanding of the human experience.

How would you describe Washington Irving's purposes for writing "The Devil and Tom Walker"? What aspects of his narrative suggest that Irving had a keen understanding of New England, both the physical environment and its people? Which aspects of the narrative are obviously entirely imaginary?

2. **Folk Tale.** Washington Irving's stories often are called folk tales, meaning that they exhibit a kind of fairy-tale unreality and that they reveal a great deal about the culture in which they originated.

Notice some of the narrator's devices for making this story seem remote and unreal. For example, the narrator often says things such as "it was whispered" or "according to old stories." What other qualities impart a fairy-tale atmosphere? In what ways is Tom Walker's wife a typical fairy-tale character, or a stereotype?

Think about the society that is the setting for this tale. What seems to be the prevailing attitude toward superstitions and legends? toward the devil? What do you learn about religious worship? about business and finance?

3. **Irony.** Irony is a contrast between what is stated and what is meant or between what is expected and what actually happens. Explain the irony in Tom's reaction to his wife's disappearance: "'Let us get hold of the property,' said he consolingly to himself, 'and we will endeavor to do without the woman.'" What is ironic in the later remark, "Tom consoled himself for the loss of his property with the loss of his wife"?

4. **Simile and Mood.** Explain the simile ". . . the trunks of pines and hemlocks lay half drowned, half rotting, looking like alligators sleeping in the mire." Explain the simile "A miserable horse, whose ribs were as articulate as the bars of a gridiron. . . ." What kind of mood or atmosphere do both these similes help to create?

5. **Allegory.** An allegory is a literary work whose characters often stand for abstract ideas or concepts. The devil is an allegorical character. What are some of the ideas or concepts associated with the devil? To what character traits in Tom Walker does the devil appeal? What abstract idea or concept is represented by the character of Tom?

An allegory usually teaches a lesson. What message does this story convey?

Developing Vocabulary

Synonyms: Nouns. Washington Irving employs a number of nouns whose meanings you may not know. Notice how he uses each word that follows. Try to guess each word's meaning from its context, then look it up in a dictionary. Record the meaning of each word and give at least one synonym for the word.

avarice
discord
incantations
morass
prowess
quagmire
termagant

Developing Writing Skills

Writing a Folk Tale. Write an original folk tale in which you reveal traits and facts of modern American culture. You may employ stereotyped characters, supernatural elements, and other devices to give your tale an unreal quality. If you like, make your tale an allegory, with a moral or lesson.

Nathaniel Hawthorne

1804–1864

Nathaniel Hawthorne is one of two great American novelists of the mid-nineteenth century, the other being his friend Herman Melville. Hawthorne's book, *The Scarlet Letter*, published in 1850, is still considered a masterpiece in world literature and often is called the world's first truly symbolic novel.

Hawthorne was born in Salem, Massachusetts, where his family had lived for generations. In fact, one of Hawthorne's ancestors, John Hathorne, was a presiding judge at the Salem witch trials. Hawthorne felt guilt about his Puritan ancestors' intolerance and their persecution of minorities. He wrote *The Scarlet Letter* in part to absolve his guilt, saying in his introduction to the novel, "I take shame upon myself for their sakes and pray that any curse incurred by them . . . may be now and henceforth removed." Hawthorne also added the *w* to his last name to distance himself further from his heritage.

Hawthorne's boyhood in Salem was not especially happy. His father, a sea captain, died when Hawthorne was four. His mother then became a grieving recluse. There were, however, bright spots, such as frequent long visits in Maine. Hawthorne decided to attend college in Maine, graduating from Bowdoin College in 1825. Two classmates were Henry Wadsworth Longfellow, the poet, and Franklin Pierce, later President of the United States. Both remained lifelong friends to Hawthorne.

When Hawthorne left Bowdoin, he returned to his uncles' house in Salem and to a twelve-year period of hibernation. He wanted to be a writer, and during this period he learned his craft, spending hours each day at his desk. He did sometimes go out evenings, and he occasionally traveled with friends, but for the most part he lived in seclusion during these years. In 1837, he published *Twice-Told Tales*, a collection of short stories.

Also in 1837, Hawthorne became engaged to Sophia Peabody, an intelligent woman from an active, interesting Salem family. It was five years before Nathaniel and Sophia had enough money to marry, and during these years Hawthorne tried

NATHANIEL HAWTHORNE, 1840. *Charles Osgood.* *Essex Institute.*

several jobs. He lived for a time at Brook Farm, an experimental community run by a group of Transcendentalists, thinking that he and Sophia could make their home there. After several months, however, Hawthorne left, finding the farm work tedious and the schemes for reform too idealistic.

The Scarlet Letter established Hawthorne's reputation. The novel, which is about sin and guilt among the Puritans, probes the problems of evil and isolation in human life. These themes are also prominent in Hawthorne's short stories and in the novel *The House of the Seven Gables*, which came out in 1851.

Hawthorne became increasingly gloomy in his last years, worrying about money, the Civil War, and his inability to write. He died on a walking tour of New Hampshire in Franklin Pierce's company.

Hawthorne is a Romantic writer, but one whose perception of the dark side of human life overpowers the usual optimism of the Romantics. He is admired as a careful craftsman and as a symbolic writer of haunting power.

The Minister's Black Veil

A Parable

The sexton stood in the porch of Milford meetinghouse, pulling busily at the bell rope. The old people of the village came stooping along the street. Children with bright faces tripped merrily beside their parents, or mimicked a graver gait, in the conscious dignity of their Sunday clothes. Spruce bachelors looked sidelong at the pretty maidens and fancied that the Sabbath sunshine made them prettier than on weekdays. When the throng had mostly streamed into the porch, the sexton began to toll the bell, keeping his eye on the Reverend Mr. Hooper's door. The first glimpse of the clergyman's figure was the signal for the bell to cease its summons.

"But what has good Parson Hooper got upon his face?" cried the sexton in astonishment.

All within hearing immediately turned about and beheld the semblance of Mr. Hooper, pacing slowly his meditative way toward the meetinghouse. With one accord they started, expressing more wonder than if some strange minister were coming to dust the cushions of Mr. Hooper's pulpit.

"Are you sure it is our parson?" inquired Goodman[1] Gray of the sexton.

"Of a certainty it is good Mr. Hooper," replied the sexton. "He was to have exchanged pulpits with Parson Shute, of Westbury; but Parson Shute sent to excuse himself yesterday, being to preach a funeral sermon."

The cause of so much amazement may appear sufficiently slight. Mr. Hooper, a gentlemanly person of about thirty, though still a bachelor was dressed with due clerical neatness, as if a careful wife had starched his band and brushed the weekly dust from his Sunday's garb. There was but one thing remarkable in his appearance. Swathed about his forehead, and hanging down over his face, so low as to be shaken by his breath, Mr. Hooper had on a black veil. On a nearer view it seemed to consist of two folds of crepe, which entirely concealed his features, except the mouth and chin, but probably did not intercept his sight, further than to give a darkened aspect to all living and inanimate things. With this gloomy shade before him, good Mr. Hooper walked onward at a slow and quiet pace, stooping somewhat and looking on the ground, as is customary with abstracted men, yet nodding kindly to those of his parishioners who still waited on the meetinghouse steps. But so wonder-struck were they that his greeting hardly met with a return.

"I can't really feel as if good Mr. Hooper's face was behind that piece of crepe," said the sexton.

"I don't like it," muttered an old woman, as she hobbled into the meetinghouse. "He has changed himself into something awful, only by hiding his face."

"Our parson has gone mad!" cried Goodman Gray, following him across the threshold.

A rumor of some unaccountable phenomenon had preceded Mr. Hooper into the meetinghouse and set all the congregation astir. Few could refrain from twisting their heads toward the door; many stood upright and turned directly about; while several little boys clambered upon the seats and came down again with a terrible racket. There was a

---

1. **Goodman:** a Puritan form of address for the master of a household; Mr.

general bustle, a rustling of the women's gowns and shuffling of the men's feet, greatly at variance with that hushed repose which should attend the entrance of the minister. But Mr. Hooper appeared not to notice the perturbation of his people. He entered with an almost noiseless step, bent his head mildly to the pews on each side, and bowed as he passed his oldest parishioner, a white-haired great-grandsire, who occupied an armchair in the center of the aisle. It was strange to observe how slowly this venerable man became conscious of something singular in the appearance of his pastor. He seemed not fully to partake of the prevailing wonder, till Mr. Hooper had ascended the stairs and showed himself in the pulpit, face to face with his congregation, except for the black veil. That mysterious emblem was never once withdrawn. It shook with his measured breath, as he gave out the psalm; it threw its obscurity between him and the holy page, as he read the Scriptures; and while he prayed, the veil lay heavily on his uplifted countenance. Did he seek to hide it from the dread Being whom he was addressing?

Such was the effect of this simple piece of crepe, that more than one woman of delicate nerves was forced to leave the meetinghouse. Yet perhaps the palefaced congregation was almost as fearful a sight to the minister as the black veil to them.

Mr. Hooper had the reputation of a good preacher, but not an energetic one: he strove to win his people heavenward by mild, persuasive influences, rather than to drive them thither by the thunders of the Word. The sermon which he now delivered was marked by the same characteristics of style and manner as the general series of his pulpit oratory. But there was something, either in the sentiment of the discourse itself, or in the imagination of the auditors, which made it greatly the most powerful effort that they had ever heard from their pastor's lips. It was tinged, rather more darkly than usual, with the gentle gloom of Mr. Hooper's temperament. The subject had reference to secret sin, and those sad mysteries which we hide from our nearest and dearest, and would fain conceal from our own consciousness, even forgetting that the Omniscient[2] can detect them. A subtle power was breathed into his words. Each member of the congregation, the most innocent girl, and the man of hardest breast, felt as if the preacher had crept upon them, behind his awful veil, and discovered their hoarded iniquity of deed or thought. Many spread their clasped hands on their bosoms. There was nothing terrible in what Mr. Hooper said, at least, no violence; and yet, with every tremor of his melancholy voice, the hearers quaked. An unsought pathos came hand in hand with awe. So sensible were the audience of some unwonted attribute in their minister that they longed for a breath of wind to blow aside the veil, almost believing that a stranger's visage would be discovered, though the form, gesture, and voice were those of Mr. Hooper.

At the close of the services, the people hurried out with indecorous confusion, eager to communicate their pent-up amazement and conscious of lighter spirits the moment they lost sight of the black veil. Some gathered in little circles, huddled closely together, with their mouths all whispering in the center; some went homeward alone, wrapt in silent meditation; some talked loudly and profaned the Sabbath day with ostentatious laughter. A few shook their sagacious heads, intimating that they could penetrate the mystery; while one or two affirmed that there was no mystery at all, but only that Mr. Hooper's eyes were so weakened by the midnight lamp as to require a shade. After a brief interval, forth came good Mr. Hooper also, in the rear of his flock. Turning his veiled face from one group to another, he paid due reverence to the hoary heads, saluted the middle-aged with

---

2. **Omniscient** (äm nish' ənt): God, or the all-knowing supreme being.

kind dignity as their friend and spiritual guide, greeted the young with mingled authority and love, and laid his hands on the little children's heads to bless them. Such was always his custom on the Sabbath day. Strange and bewildered looks repaid him for his courtesy. None, as on former occasions, aspired to the honor of walking by their pastor's side. Old Squire Saunders, doubtless by an accidental lapse of memory, neglected to invite Mr. Hooper to his table, where the good clergyman had been wont to bless the food almost every Sunday since his settlement. He returned, therefore, to the parson age, and, at the moment of closing the door, was observed to look back upon the people, all of whom had their eyes fixed upon the minister. A sad smile gleamed faintly from beneath the black veil and flickered about his mouth, glimmering as he disappeared.

"How strange," said a lady, "that a simple black veil such as any woman might wear on her bonnet should become such a terrible thing on Mr. Hooper's face!"

"Something must surely be amiss with Mr. Hooper's intellects," observed her husband, the physician of the village. "But the strangest part of the affair is the effect of this vagary, even on a sober-minded man like myself. The black veil, though it covers only our pastor's face, throws its influence over his whole person and makes him ghostlike from head to foot. Do you not feel it so?"

"Truly do I," replied the lady; "and I would not be alone with him for the world. I wonder he is not afraid to be alone with himself!"

"Men sometimes are so," said her husband.

The afternoon service was attended with similar circumstances. At its conclusion, the bell tolled for the funeral of a young lady. The relatives and friends were assembled in the house, and the more distant acquaintances stood about the door, speaking of the good qualities of the deceased, when their talk was interrupted by the appearance of Mr. Hooper, still covered with his black veil. It was now an appropriate emblem. The clergyman stepped into the room where the corpse was laid and bent over the coffin, to take a last farewell of his deceased parishioner. As he stooped, the veil hung straight down from his forehead, so that, if her eyelids had not been closed forever, the dead maiden might have seen his face. Could Mr. Hooper be fearful of her glance, that he so hastily caught back the black veil? A person who watched the interview between the dead and living scrupled not to affirm that, at the instant when the clergyman's features were disclosed, the corpse had slightly shuddered, rustling the shroud and muslin cap, though the countenance retained the composure of death. A superstitious old woman was the only witness of this prodigy. From the coffin Mr. Hooper passed into the chamber of the mourners, and thence to the head of the staircase, to make the funeral prayer. It was a tender and heart-dissolving prayer, full of sorrow, yet so imbued with celestial hopes that the music of a heavenly harp, swept by the fingers of the dead, seemed faintly to be heard among the saddest accents of the minister. The people trembled, though they but darkly understood him when he prayed that they, and himself, and all of mortal race, might be ready, as he trusted this young maiden had been, for the dreadful hour that should snatch the veil from their faces. The bearers went heavily forth, and the mourners followed, saddening all the street, with the dead before them, and Mr. Hooper in his black veil behind.

"Why do you look back?" said one in the procession to his partner.

"I had a fancy," replied she, "that the minister and the maiden's spirit were walking hand in hand."

"And so had I, at the same moment," said the other.

That night, the handsomest couple in Milford village were to be joined in wedlock. Though reckoned a melancholy man, Mr. Hooper had a placid cheerfulness for such occasions, which often excited a sympathetic smile where livelier merriment would have been thrown away. There was no quality of his disposition which made him more beloved than this. The company at the wedding awaited his arrival with impatience, trusting that the strange awe, which had gathered over him throughout the day, would now be dispelled. But such was not the result. When Mr. Hooper came, the first thing that their eyes rested on was the same horrible black veil, which had added deeper gloom to the funeral and could portend nothing but evil to the wedding. Such was its immediate effect on the guests that a cloud seemed to have rolled duskily from beneath the black crepe and dimmed the light of the candles. The bridal pair stood up before the minister. But the bride's cold fingers quivered in the tremulous hand of the bridegroom, and her deathlike paleness caused a whisper that the maiden who had been buried a few hours before was come from her grave to be married. If ever another wedding were so dismal, it was that famous one where they tolled the wedding knell.[3] After performing the ceremony, Mr. Hooper raised a glass of wine to his lips, wishing happiness to the new-married couple in a strain of mild pleasantry that ought to have brightened the features of the guests, like a cheerful gleam from the hearth. At that instant, catching a glimpse of his figure in the looking glass, the black veil involved his own spirit in the horror with which it overwhelmed all others. His frame shuddered, his lips grew white, he spilt the untasted wine upon the carpet, and rushed forth into the darkness. For the Earth, too, had on her Black Veil.

The next day, the whole village of Milford talked of little else than Parson Hooper's black veil. That, and the mystery concealed behind it, supplied a topic for discussion between acquaintances meeting in the street and good women gossiping at their open windows. It was the first item of news that the tavernkeeper told to his guests. The children babbled of it on their way to school. One imitative little imp covered his face with an old black handkerchief, thereby so affrighting his playmates that the panic seized himself, and he well-nigh lost his wits by his own waggery.

It was remarkable that of all the busybodies and impertinent people in the parish, not one ventured to put the plain question to Mr. Hooper, wherefore he did this thing. Hitherto, whenever there appeared the slightest call for such interference, he had never lacked advisers, nor shown himself averse to be guided by their judgment. If he erred at all, it was by so painful a degree of self-distrust that even the mildest censure would lead him to consider an indifferent action as a crime. Yet, though so well acquainted with this amiable weakness, no individual among his parishioners chose to make the black veil a subject of friendly remonstrance. There was a feeling of dread, neither plainly confessed nor carefully concealed, which caused each to shift the responsibility upon another, till at length it was found expedient to send a deputation of the church, in order to deal with Mr. Hooper about the mystery before it should grow into a scandal. Never did an embassy so ill discharge its duties. The minister received them with friendly courtesy but became silent after they were seated, leaving to his visitors the whole burden of introducing their important business. The topic, it might be supposed, was obvious enough. There was the black veil swathed round Mr. Hooper's forehead, and concealing every feature above his placid mouth, on which, at times, they could perceive the glimmering of a melancholy smile. But that piece of crepe, to their imagination, seemed to hang down before his heart, the symbol of a fearful secret between him and them. Were the veil but cast aside, they might

---

3. **knell:** a stroke or sound of a bell, usually indicating the end or failure of something.

speak freely of it, but not till then. Thus they sat a considerable time, speechless, confused, and shrinking uneasily from Mr. Hooper's eye, which they felt to be fixed upon them with an invisible glance. Finally, the deputies returned abashed to their constituents, pronouncing the matter too weighty to be handled, except by a council of the churches, if, indeed, it might not require a general synod.[4]

But there was one person in the village unappalled by the awe with which the black veil had impressed all beside herself. When the deputies returned without an explanation, or even venturing to demand one, she, with the calm energy of her character, determined to chase away the strange cloud that appeared to be settling round Mr. Hooper, every moment more darkly than before. As his plighted wife, it should be her privilege to know what the black veil concealed. At the minister's first visit, therefore, she entered upon the subject with a direct simplicity, which made the task easier both for him and her. After he had seated himself, she fixed her eyes steadfastly upon the veil, but could discern nothing of the dreadful gloom that had so overawed the multitude: it was but a double fold of crepe, hanging down from his forehead to his mouth, and slightly stirring with his breath.

"No," said she aloud, and smiling, "there is nothing terrible in this piece of crepe, except that it hides a face which I am always glad to look upon. Come, good sir, let the sun shine from behind the cloud. First lay aside your black veil: then tell me why you put it on."

Mr. Hooper's smile glimmered faintly.

"There is an hour to come," said he, "when all of us shall cast aside our veils. Take it not amiss, beloved friend, if I wear this piece of crepe till then."

"Your words are a mystery, too," returned the young lady. "Take away the veil from them, at least."

"Elizabeth, I will," said he, "so far as my vow may suffer me. Know, then, this veil is a type and a symbol, and I am bound to wear it ever, both in light and darkness, in solitude and before the gaze of multitudes, and as with strangers, so with my familiar friends. No mortal eye will see it withdrawn. This dismal shade must separate me from the world: even you, Elizabeth, can never come behind it!"

"What grievous affliction hath befallen you," she earnestly inquired, "that you should thus darken your eyes forever?"

"If it be a sign of mourning," replied Mr. Hooper, "I, perhaps, like most other mortals, have sorrows dark enough to be typified by a black veil."

"But what if the world will not believe that it is the type of an innocent sorrow?" urged Elizabeth. "Beloved and respected as you are, there may be whispers that you hide your face under the consciousness of secret sin. For the sake of your holy office, do away this scandal!"

The color rose into her cheeks as she intimated the nature of the rumors that were already abroad in the village. But Mr. Hooper's mildness did not forsake him. He even smiled again—that same sad smile, which always appeared like a faint glimmering of light, proceeding from the obscurity beneath the veil.

"If I hide my face for sorrow, there is cause enough," he merely replied; "and if I cover it for secret sin, what mortal might not do the same?"

And with this gentle but unconquerable obstinacy did he resist all her entreaties. At length Elizabeth sat silent. For a few moments she appeared lost in thought, considering, probably, what new methods might be tried to withdraw her lover from so dark a fantasy, which, if it had no other meaning, was perhaps a symbol of mental disease. Though of a firmer character than his own, the tears rolled down her cheeks. But in an instant, as it were, a new feeling took the

---

4. **general synod** (sin' əd): ecclesiastical governing or advisory council.

place of sorrow: her eyes were fixed insensibly on the black veil when, like a sudden twilight in the air, its terrors fell around her. She arose and stood trembling before him.

"And do you feel it then, at last?" said he mournfully.

She made no reply, but covered her eyes with her hand and turned to leave the room. He rushed forward and caught her arm.

"Have patience with me, Elizabeth!" cried he, passionately. "Do not desert me, though this veil must be between us here on earth. Be mine, and hereafter there shall be no veil over my face, no darkness between our souls! It is but a mortal veil—it is not for eternity! O! you know not how lonely I am, and how frightened, to be alone behind my black veil. Do not leave me in this miserable obscurity forever!"

"Lift the veil but once, and look me in the face," said she.

"Never! It cannot be!" replied Mr. Hooper.

"Then farewell!" said Elizabeth.

She withdrew her arm from his grasp and slowly departed, pausing at the door to give one long, shuddering gaze that seemed almost to penetrate the mystery of the black veil. But, even amid his grief, Mr. Hooper smiled to think that only a material emblem had separated him from happiness, though the horrors which it shadowed forth must be drawn darkly between the fondest of lovers.

From that time no attempts were made to remove Mr. Hooper's black veil or, by a direct appeal, to discover the secret which it was supposed to hide. By persons who claimed a superiority to popular prejudice, it was reckoned merely an eccentric whim, such as often mingles with the sober actions of men otherwise rational and tinges them all with its own semblance of insanity. But with the multitude, good Mr. Hooper was irreparably a bugbear.[5] He could not walk the street with any peace of mind, so conscious was he that the gentle and timid would turn aside to avoid him, and that others would make it a point of

hardihood to throw themselves in his way. The impertinence of the latter class compelled him to give up his customary walk at sunset to the burial ground; for when he leaned pensively over the gate, there would always be faces behind the gravestones, peeping at his black veil. A fable went the rounds that the stare of the dead people drove him thence. It grieved him, to the very depth of his kind heart, to observe how the children fled from his approach, breaking up their merriest sports, while his melancholy figure was yet afar off. Their instinctive dread caused him to feel more strongly than aught else that a preternatural horror was interwoven with the threads of the black crepe. In truth, his own antipathy to the veil was known to be so great that he never willingly passed before a mirror, nor stooped to drink at a still fountain, lest, in its peaceful bosom, he should be affrighted by himself. This was what gave plausibility to the whispers that Mr. Hooper's conscience tortured him for some great crime too horrible to be entirely concealed, or otherwise than so obscurely intimated. Thus, from beneath the black veil, there rolled a cloud into the sunshine, and ambiguity of sin or sorrow, which enveloped the poor minister, so that love or sympathy could never reach him. It was said that ghost and fiend consorted with him there. With self-shudderings and outward terrors, he walked continually in its shadow, groping darkly within his own soul or gazing through a medium that saddened the whole world. Even the lawless wind, it was believed, respected his dreadful secret and never blew aside the veil. But still good Mr. Hooper sadly smiled at the pale visages of the worldly throng as he passed by.

Among all its bad influences, the black veil had the one desirable effect of making its wearer a very efficient clergyman. By the aid of his mysterious emblem—for there was no other apparent cause—he became a man of

---

5. **bugbear:** an object or source of dread.

awful power over souls that were in agony for sin. His converts always regarded him with a dread peculiar to themselves, affirming, though but figuratively, that before he brought them to celestial light they had been with him behind the black veil. Its gloom, indeed, enabled him to sympathize with all dark affections. Dying sinners cried aloud for Mr. Hooper, and would not yield their breath till he appeared; though ever, as he stooped to whisper consolation, they shuddered at the veiled face so near their own. Such were the terrors of the black veil, even when Death had bared his visage! Strangers came long distances to attend services at his church, with the mere idle purpose of gazing at his figure, because it was forbidden them to behold his face. But many were made to quake ere they departed! Once, during Governor Belcher's administration, Mr. Hooper was appointed to preach the election sermon. Covered with his black veil, he stood before the chief magistrate, the council, and the representatives, and wrought so deep an impression that the legislative measures of that year were characterized by all the gloom and piety of our earliest ancestral sway.

In this manner Mr. Hooper spent a long life, irreproachable in outward act, yet shrouded in dismal suspicions; kind and loving, though unloved and dimly feared; a man apart from men, shunned in their health and joy, but ever summoned to their aid in mortal anguish. As years wore on, shedding their snows above his sable veil, he acquired a name throughout the New England churches, and they called him Father Hooper. Nearly all his parishioners, who were of mature age when he was settled, had been borne away by many a funeral: he had one congregation in the church, and a more crowded one in the churchyard; and having wrought so late into the evening, and done his work so well, it was now good Father Hooper's turn to rest.

Several persons were visible by the shaded candlelight, in the death chamber of the old clergyman. Natural connections he had none. But there was the decorously grave, though unmoved physician, seeking only to mitigate the last pangs of the patient whom he could not save. There were the deacons, and other eminently pious members of his church. There, also, was the Reverend Mr. Clark, of Westbury, a young and zealous divine, who had ridden in haste to pray by the bedside of the expiring minister. There was the nurse, no hired handmaiden of death, but one whose calm affection had endured thus long in secrecy, in solitude, amid the chill of age, and would not perish, even at the dying hour. Who, but Elizabeth! And there lay the hoary head of good Father Hooper upon the death pillow, with the black veil still swathed about his brow, and reaching down over his face, so that each more difficult gasp of his faint breath caused it to stir. All through life that piece of crepe had hung between him and the world: it had separated him from cheerful brotherhood and woman's love and kept him in that saddest of all prisons, his own heart; and still it lay upon his face, as if to deepen the gloom of his darksome chamber and shade him from the sunshine of eternity.

For some time previous, his mind had been confused, wavering doubtfully between the past and the present and hovering forward, as it were, at intervals, into the indistinctness of the world to come. There had been feverish turns, which tossed him from side to side and wore away what little strength he had. But in his most convulsive struggles, and in the wildest vagaries of his intellect, when no other thought retained its sober influence, he still showed an awful solicitude lest the black veil should slip aside. Even if his bewildered soul could have forgotten, there was a faithful woman at his pillow, who, with averted eyes, would have covered that aged face, which she had last beheld in the comeliness of manhood. At length the death-stricken old man lay quietly in the torpor of mental and bodily exhaustion, with an imperceptible pulse and breath that grew fainter and fainter, except when a long, deep, and irregular inspiration seemed to prelude the flight of his spirit.

The minister of Westbury approached the bedside.

"Venerable Father Hooper," said he, "the moment of your release is at hand. Are you ready for the lifting of the veil that shuts in time from eternity?"

Father Hooper at first replied merely by a feeble motion of his head; then, apprehensive, perhaps, that his meaning might be doubtful, he exerted himself to speak.

"Yea," said he, in faint accents, "my soul hath a patient weariness until that veil be lifted."

"And is it fitting," resumed the Reverend Mr. Clark, "that a man so given to prayer, of such a blameless example, holy in deed and thought, so far as mortal judgment may pronounce; is it fitting that a father in the church should leave a shadow on his memory that may seem to blacken a life so pure? I pray you, my venerable brother, let not this thing be! Suffer us to be gladdened by your triumphant aspect as you go to your reward. Before the veil of eternity be lifted, let me cast aside this black veil from your face!"

And thus speaking, the Reverend Mr. Clark bent forward to reveal the mystery of so many years. But, exerting a sudden energy that made all the beholders stand aghast, Father Hooper snatched both his hands from beneath the bedclothes and pressed them strongly on the black veil, resolute to struggle if the minister of Westbury would contend with a dying man.

"Never!" cried the veiled clergyman. "On earth, never!"

"Dark old man!" exclaimed the affrighted minister, "with what horrible crime upon your soul are you now passing to the judgment?"

Father Hooper's breath heaved; it rattled in his throat; but, with a mighty effort, grasping forward with his hands, he caught hold of life and held it back till he should speak. He even raised himself in bed; and there he sat, shivering with the arms of death around him, while the black veil hung down, awful, at that last moment, in the gathered terrors of a lifetime. And yet the faint, sad smile, so often there, now seemed to glimmer from its obscurity and linger on Father Hooper's lips.

"Why do you tremble at me alone?" cried he, turning his veiled face round the circle of pale spectators. "Tremble also at each other! Have men avoided me, and women shown no pity, and children screamed and fled, only for my black veil? What but the mystery which it obscurely typifies has made this piece of crepe so awful? When the friend shows his inmost heart to his friend; the lover to his best beloved; when man does not vainly shrink from the eye of his Creator, loathsomely treasuring up the secret of his sin; then deem me a monster for the symbol beneath which I have lived, and die! I look around me, and, lo! on every visage a Black Veil!"

While his auditors shrank from one another, in mutual affright, Father Hooper fell back upon his pillow, a veiled corpse, with a faint smile lingering on the lips. Still veiled, they laid him in his coffin, and a veiled corpse they bore him to the grave. The grass of many years has sprung up and withered on that grave, the burial stone is moss-grown, and good Mr. Hooper's face is dust; but awful is still the thought that it moldered beneath the Black Veil!

Getting at Meaning

1. Describe the atmosphere in the Milford meeting house before the Reverend Mr. Hooper enters. How does the atmosphere change after he enters? Why?

2. What is the effect of the minister's veil at the young woman's funeral? What does one mourner mean when she says, "I had a fancy . . . that the minister and the maiden's spirit were walking hand in hand"? What is the effect of the veil at the wedding?

3. Why will no one ask Mr. Hooper a direct question about his veil? What does Elizabeth come to understand about the veil? Why does Mr. Hooper refuse to remove it for her, even once?

4. Over the years, what effect does the veil have on Mr. Hooper's preaching? Why does it have this effect? Explain the statement, "By the aid of his mysterious emblem . . . he became a man of awful power over souls that were in agony for sin."

5. When Mr. Hooper is an old man, the community honors him by asking him to preach the election sermon. What indicates, however, that the community still fears his veil?

6. Describe the details of Mr. Hooper's death and burial.

Developing Skills in Reading Literature

1. **Symbol.** A symbol is a person, place, or object that stands for something beyond itself, such as an idea or a belief. The minister says to Elizabeth, "Know, then, this veil is a type and a symbol." What clues does Mr. Hooper provide his congregation about the meaning of the veil? What final conclusion do you draw about the symbolism of the veil?

2. **Character.** The minister is a fascinating character, separated from his congregation and from Elizabeth by his veil. Why does he elect to wear the veil? What evidence is there that he feels great guilt? In what sense does the veil become a prison? Hawthorne wrote often of the human being isolated in "that saddest of all prisons, his own heart." Apply this statement to Mr. Hooper.

Elizabeth, too, is an intriguing character. Why does she refuse to marry Mr. Hooper? Why does she then remain faithful to him all her life, tending the minister on his death bed?

3. **Parable.** Hawthorne calls this story a parable. A parable is a short tale that teaches a lesson or illustrates a moral truth. It resembles an allegory in having a moral attached to it, but a parable, unlike an allegory, often does not have characters or objects that stand for abstract ideas.

What is the lesson or moral taught by this story? What does the minister mean when he cries out, "I look around me, and lo! on every visage a Black Veil!"?

Developing Vocabulary

Formal Diction: Nouns. Hawthorne writes formally, with the large vocabulary characteristic of many nineteenth-century authors. Some of his nouns, although still in use, are now considered formal diction and may not be familiar to you.

Look up each word that follows in a dictionary and record its meaning. Notice how Hawthorne uses each word. Then give at least one less formal synonym for the word.

antipathy	remonstrance
countenance	torpor
iniquity	vagary
perturbation	visage

Developing Writing Skills

Analyzing a Symbol. Write a composition in which you analyze the meaning of the minister's black veil and its precise effect upon the individuals in his congregation. These are some questions you may want to consider: What does the minister hope to achieve by wearing the veil? Does he achieve this? Why is his sermon on secret sin so effective? Why is it ironic that the veil makes Mr. Hooper more deeply respected as a minister? What is Hawthorne's view of the human being in this story?

Dr. Heidegger's Experiment

That very singular man, old Dr. Heidegger, once invited four venerable friends to meet him in his study. There were three white-bearded gentlemen, Mr. Medbourne, Colonel Killigrew, and Mr. Gascoigne, and a withered gentlewoman, whose name was the Widow Wycherly. They were all melancholy old creatures, who had been unfortunate in life, and whose greatest misfortune it was that they were not long ago in their graves. Mr. Medbourne, in the vigor of his age, had been a prosperous merchant, but had lost his all by a frantic speculation and was now little better than a mendicant. Colonel Killigrew had wasted his best years, and his health and substance, in the pursuit of sinful pleasures, which had given birth to a brood of pains, such as the gout and divers other torments of soul and body. Mr. Gascoigne was a ruined politician, a man of evil fame, or at least had been so till time had buried him from the knowledge of the present generation and made him obscure instead of infamous. As for the Widow Wycherly, tradition tells us that she was a great beauty in her day; but, for a long while past, she had lived in deep seclusion, on account of certain scandalous stories which had prejudiced the gentry of the town against her. It is a circumstance worth mentioning that each of these three old gentlemen, Mr. Medbourne, Colonel Killigrew, and Mr. Gascoigne, were early lovers of the Widow Wycherly, and had once been on the point of cutting each other's throats for her sake. And, before proceeding further, I will merely hint that Dr. Heidegger and all his four guests were sometimes thought to be a little beside themselves—as is not unfrequently the case with old people, when worried either by present troubles or woeful recollections.

"My dear old friends," said Dr. Heidegger, motioning them to be seated, "I am desirous of your assistance in one of those little experiments with which I amuse myself here in my study."

If all stories were true, Dr. Heidegger's study must have been a very curious place. It was a dim, old-fashioned chamber, festooned with cobwebs and besprinkled with antique dust. Around the walls stood several oaken bookcases, the lower shelves of which were filled with rows of gigantic folios[1] and black-letter quartos,[2] and the upper with little parchment-covered duodecimos.[3] Over the central bookcase was a bronze bust of Hippocrates,[4] with which, according to some authorities, Dr. Heidegger was accustomed to hold consultations in all difficult cases of his practice. In the obscurest corner of the room stood a tall and narrow oaken closet, with its door ajar, within which doubtfully appeared a skeleton. Between two of the bookcases hung a looking glass, presenting its high and dusty plate within a tarnished gilt frame. Among many wonderful stories related of this mirror, it was fabled that the spirit of all the doctor's deceased patients dwelt within its verge and would stare him in the face whenever he looked thitherward. The opposite side of the

1. **folios:** books printed on folio pages, or pages cut two from a sheet.
2. **quartos:** books printed on quarto pages, or pages cut four from a sheet.
3. **duodecimos** (dōō′ ə des′ə mōz): books printed on duodecimo pages, or pages cut twelve from a sheet.
4. **Hippocrates** (hip ak′ rə tēz′): a Greek physician, father of medicine, who lived from 460?-377? B.C.

chamber was ornamented with the full-length portrait of a young lady, arrayed in the faded magnificence of silk, satin, and brocade, and with a visage as faded as her dress. Above half a century ago, Dr. Heidegger had been on the point of marriage with this young lady; but being affected with some slight disorder, she had swallowed one of her lover's prescriptions and died on the bridal evening. The greatest curiosity of the study remains to be mentioned; it was a ponderous folio volume, bound in black leather, with massive silver clasps. There were no letters on the back, and nobody could tell the title of the book. But it was well known to be a book of magic; and once, when a chambermaid had lifted it, merely to brush away the dust, the skeleton had rattled in its closet, the picture of the young lady had stepped one foot upon the floor, and several ghastly faces had peeped forth from the mirror; while the brazen head of Hippocrates frowned and said, "Forbear!"

Such was Dr. Heidegger's study. On the summer afternoon of our tale, a small round table, as black as ebony, stood in the center of the room, sustaining a cut-glass vase of beautiful form and elaborate workmanship. The sunshine came through the window, between the heavy festoons of two faded damask curtains, and fell directly across this vase; so that a mild splendor was reflected from it on the ashen visages of the five old people who sat around. Four champagne glasses were also on the table.

"My dear old friends," repeated Dr. Heidegger, "may I reckon on your aid in performing an exceedingly curious experiment?"

Now Dr. Heidegger was a very strange old gentleman, whose eccentricity had become the nucleus for a thousand fantastic stories. Some of these fables, to my shame be it spoken, might possibly be traced back to my own veracious self; and if any passages of the present tale should startle the reader's faith, I must be content to bear the stigma of a fictionmonger.

When the doctor's four guests heard him talk of his proposed experiment, they anticipated nothing more wonderful than the murder of a mouse in an air pump, or the examination of a cobweb by the microscope, or some similar nonsense, with which he was constantly in the habit of pestering his intimates. But, without waiting for a reply, Dr. Heidegger hobbled across the chamber and returned with the same ponderous folio, bound in black leather, which common report affirmed to be a book of magic. Undoing the silver clasps, he opened the volume and took from among its black-letter pages a rose, or what was once a rose, though now the green leaves and crimson petals had assumed one brownish hue, and the ancient flower seemed ready to crumble to dust in the doctor's hands.

"This rose," said Dr. Heidegger, with a sigh, "this same withered and crumbling flower, blossomed five and fifty years ago. It was given me by Sylvia Ward, whose portrait hangs yonder; and I meant to wear it in my bosom at our wedding. Five and fifty years it has been treasured between the leaves of this old volume. Now, would you deem it possible that this rose of half a century could ever bloom again?"

"Nonsense!" said the Widow Wycherly, with a peevish toss of her head. "You might as well ask whether an old woman's wrinkled face could ever bloom again."

"See!" answered Dr. Heidegger.

He uncovered the vase and threw the rose into the water which it contained. At first, it lay lightly on the surface of the fluid, appearing to imbibe none of its moisture. Soon, however, a singular change began to be visible. The crushed and dried petals stirred and assumed a deepening tinge of crimson, as if the flower were reviving from a deathlike slumber; the slender stalk and twigs of foliage became green; and there was the rose of half a century, looking as fresh as when Sylvia Ward had first given it to her lover. It was scarcely full blown; for some of its delicate red leaves curled modestly around its moist bosom, within which two or three dewdrops were sparkling.

"That is certainly a very pretty deception," said the doctor's friends; carelessly, however, for they had witnessed greater miracles at a conjurer's show; "pray how was it effected?"

"Did you never hear of the 'Fountain of Youth'?" asked Dr. Heidegger, "which Ponce de Leon,[5] the Spanish adventurer, went in search of two or three centuries ago?"

"But did Ponce de Leon ever find it?" said the Widow Wycherly.

"No," answered Dr. Heidegger, "for he never sought it in the right place. The famous Fountain of Youth, if I am rightly informed, is situated in the southern part of the Floridian peninsula, not far from Lake Macaco. Its source is overshadowed by several gigantic magnolias, which, though numberless centuries old, have been kept as fresh as violets by the virtues of this wonderful water. An acquaintance of mine, knowing my curiosity in such matters, has sent me what you see in the vase."

"Ahem!" said Colonel Killigrew, who believed not a word of the doctor's story; "and what may be the effect of this fluid on the human frame?"

"You shall judge for yourself, my dear colonel," replied Dr. Heidegger; "and all of you, my respected friends, are welcome to so much of this admirable fluid as may restore to you the bloom of youth. For my own part, having had much trouble in growing old, I am in no hurry to grow young again. With your permission, therefore, I will merely watch the progress of the experiment."

While he spoke, Dr. Heidegger had been filling the four champagne glasses with the water of the Fountain of Youth. It was apparently impregnated with an effervescent gas, for little bubbles were continually ascending from the depths of the glasses and bursting in silvery spray at the surface. As the liquor diffused a pleasant perfume, the old people doubted not that it possessed cordial and comfortable properties; and though utter skeptics as to its rejuvenescent power, they were inclined to swallow it at once. But Dr. Heidegger besought them to stay a moment.

"Before you drink, my respectable old friends," said he, "it would be well that, with the experience of a lifetime to direct you, you should draw up a few general rules for your guidance, in passing a second time through the perils of youth. Think what a sin and shame it would be if, with your peculiar advantages, you should not become patterns of virtue and wisdom to all the young people of the age!"

The doctor's four venerable friends made him no answer, except by a feeble and tremulous laugh; so very ridiculous was the idea that, knowing how closely repentance treads behind the steps of error, they should ever go astray again.

"Drink, then," said the doctor, bowing. "I rejoice that I have so well selected the subjects of my experiment."

With palsied hands, they raised the glasses to their lips. The liquor, if it really possessed such virtues as Dr. Heidegger imputed to it, could not have been bestowed on four human beings who needed it more woefully. They looked as if they had never known what youth or pleasure was, but had been the offspring of Nature's dotage, and always the gray, decrepit, sapless, miserable creatures who now sat stooping round the doctor's table, without life enough in their souls or bodies to be animated even by the prospect of growing young again. They drank off the water and replaced their glasses on the table.

Assuredly there was an almost immediate improvement in the aspect of the party, not unlike what might have been produced by a glass of generous wine, together with a sud-

---

5. **Ponce de Leon** (pon' sä dĕ lē' ən): the Spanish discoverer of Florida, who lived from 1460?-1521.

den glow of cheerful sunshine brightening over all their visages at once. There was a healthful suffusion on their cheeks, instead of the ashen hue that had made them look so corpselike. They gazed at one another and fancied that some magic power had really begun to smooth away the deep and sad inscriptions which Father Time had been so long engraving on their brows. The Widow Wycherly adjusted her cap, for she felt almost like a woman again.

"Give us more of this wondrous water!" cried they, eagerly. "We are younger—but we are still too old! Quick—give us more!"

"Patience, patience!" quoth Dr. Heidegger, who sat watching the experiment with philosophic coolness. "You have been a long time growing old. Surely, you might be content to grow young in half an hour! But the water is at your service."

Again he filled their glasses with the liquor of youth, enough of which still remained in the vase to turn half the old people in the city to the age of their own grandchildren. While the bubbles were yet sparkling on the brim, the doctor's four guests snatched their glasses from the table and swallowed the contents at a single gulp. Was it delusion? Even while the draft was passing down their throats, it seemed to have wrought a change on their whole systems. Their eyes grew clear and bright; a dark shade deepened among their silvery locks, they sat around the table, three gentlemen of middle age, and a woman hardly beyond her buxom prime.

"My dear widow, you are charming!" cried Colonel Killigrew, whose eyes had been fixed upon her face, while the shadows of age were flitting from it like darkness from the crimson daybreak.

The fair widow knew, of old, that Colonel Killigrew's compliments were not always measured by sober truth; so she started up and ran to the mirror, still dreading the ugly visage of an old woman would meet her gaze. Meanwhile, the three gentlemen behaved in such a manner as proved that the water of the Fountain of Youth possessed some intoxicating qualities; unless, indeed, their exhilaration of spirits were merely a lightsome dizziness caused by the sudden removal of the weight of years. Mr. Gascoigne's mind seemed to run on political topics, but whether relating to the past, present, or future could not easily be determined, since the same ideas and phrases have been in vogue these fifty years. Now he rattled forth full-throated sentences about patriotism, national glory, and the people's right; now he muttered some perilous stuff or other, in a sly and doubtful whisper, so cautiously that even his own conscience could scarcely catch the secret; and now, again, he spoke in measured accents and a deeply deferential tone, as if a royal ear were listening to his well-turned periods. Colonel Killigrew all this time had been trolling forth a jolly bottle song and ringing his glass in symphony with the chorus, while his eyes wandered toward the buxom figure of the Widow Wycherly. On the other side of the table, Mr. Medbourne was involved in a calculation of dollars and cents, with which was strangely intermingled a project for supplying the East Indies with ice, by harnessing a team of whales to the polar icebergs.

As for the Widow Wycherly, she stood before the mirror curtsying and simpering to her own image and greeting it as the friend whom she loved better than all the world beside. She thrust her face close to the glass, to see whether some long-remembered wrinkle or crow's-foot had indeed vanished. She examined whether the snow had so entirely melted from her hair that the venerable cap could be safely thrown aside. At last, turning briskly away, she came with a sort of dancing step to the table.

"My dear old doctor," cried she, "pray favor me with another glass!"

"Certainly, my dear madam, certainly!" replied the complaisant doctor; "See! I have already filled the glasses."

There, in fact, stood the four glasses, brimful of this wonderful water, the delicate spray of which, as it effervesced from the surface, resembled the tremulous glitter of diamonds. It was now so nearly sunset that the chamber had grown duskier than ever; but a mild and moonlike splendor gleamed from within the vase, and rested alike on the four guests and on the doctor's venerable figure. He sat in a high-backed, elaborately carved oaken armchair, with a gray dignity of aspect that might have well befitted that very Father Time whose power had never been disputed save by this fortunate company. Even while quaffing the third draft of the Fountain of Youth, they were almost awed by the expression of his mysterious visage.

But the next moment, the exhilarating gush of young life shot through their veins. They were now in the happy prime of youth. Age, with its miserable train of cares and sorrows and diseases, was remembered only as the troubles of a dream, from which they had joyously awakened. The fresh gloss of the soul, so early lost, and without which the world's successive scenes had been but a gallery of faded pictures, again threw its enchantment over all their prospects. They felt like new-created beings in a new-created universe.

"We are young! We are young!" they cried exultingly.

Youth, like the extremity of age, had effaced the strongly marked characteristics of middle life and mutually assimilated them all. They were a group of merry youngsters, almost maddened with the exuberant frolicsomeness of their years. The most singular effect of their gaiety was an impulse to mock the infirmity and decrepitude of which they had so lately been the victims. They laughed loudly at their old-fashioned attire, the wide-skirted coats and flapped waistcoats of the young men, and the ancient cap and gown of the blooming girl. One limped across the floor like a gouty grandfather; one set a pair of spectacles astride of his nose and pretended to pore over the black-letter pages of the book of magic; a third seated himself in an armchair and strove to imitate the venerable dignity of Dr. Heidegger. Then all shouted mirthfully and leaped about the room. The Widow Wycherly—if so fresh a damsel could be called a widow—tripped up to the doctor's chair, with a mischievous merriment in her rosy face.

"Doctor, you dear old soul," cried she, "get up and dance with me!" And then the four young people laughed louder than ever, to think what a queer figure the poor old doctor would cut.

"Pray excuse me," answered the doctor quietly. "I am old and rheumatic, and my dancing days were over long ago. But either of these gay young gentlemen will be glad of so pretty a partner."

"Dance with me, Clara!" cried Colonel Killigrew.

"No, no, I will be her partner!" shouted Mr. Gascoigne.

"She promised me her hand, fifty years ago!" exclaimed Mr. Medbourne.

They all gathered round her. One caught both her hands in his passionate grasp—another threw his arm about her waist—the third buried his hand among the glossy curls that clustered beneath the widow's cap. Blushing, panting, struggling, chiding, laughing, her warm breath fanning each of their faces by turns, she strove to disengage herself, yet still remained in their triple embrace. Never was there a livelier picture of youthful rivalship, with bewitching beauty for the prize. Yet, by a strange deception, owing to the duskiness of the chamber and the antique dresses which they still wore, the tall mirror is said to have reflected the figures of the three old, gray, withered grandsires ridiculously contending for the skinny ugliness of a shriveled grandam.

But they were young: their burning passions proved them so. Inflamed to madness by the coquetry of the girl-widow, who neither granted nor quite withheld her favors, the three rivals began to interchange threatening glances. Still keeping hold of the fair prize, they grappled fiercely at one another's throats. As they struggled to and fro, the table was overturned, and the vase dashed into a thousand fragments. The precious Water of Youth flowed in a bright stream across the floor, moistening the wings of a butterfly, which, grown old in the decline of summer, had alighted there to die. The insect fluttered lightly through the chamber and settled on the snowy head of Dr. Heidegger.

"Come, come, gentlemen!—come, Madam Wycherly," exclaimed the doctor, "I really must protest against this riot."

They stood still and shivered; for it seemed as if gray Time were calling them back from their sunny youth, far down into the chill and darksome vale of years. They looked at old Dr. Heidegger, who sat in his carved armchair, holding the rose of half a century, which he had rescued from among the fragments of the shattered vase. At the motion of his hand, the four rioters resumed their seats; the more readily because their violent exertions had wearied them, youthful though they were.

"My poor Sylvia's rose!" ejaculated Dr. Heidegger, holding it in the light of the sunset clouds; "it appears to be fading again."

And so it was. Even while the party were looking at it, the flower continued to shrivel up, till it became as dry and fragile as when the doctor had first thrown it into the vase. He shook off the few drops of moisture which clung to its petals.

"I love it as well thus as in its dewy freshness," observed he, pressing the withered rose to his withered lips. While he spoke, the butterfly fluttered down from the doctor's snowy head and fell upon the floor.

His guests shivered again. A strange chillness, whether of the body or spirit they could not tell, was creeping gradually over them all. They gazed at one another, and fancied that each fleeting moment snatched away a charm, and left a deepening furrow where none had been before. Was it an illusion? Had the changes of a lifetime been crowded into so brief a space, and were they now four aged people, sitting with their old friend Dr. Heidegger?

"Are we grown old again, so soon?" cried they, dolefully.

In truth they had. The Water of Youth possessed merely a virtue more transient than that of wine. The delirium which it created had effervesced away. Yes! they were old again. With a shuddering impulse that showed her a woman still, the widow clasped her skinny hands before her face and wished that the coffin lid were over it, since it could be no longer beautiful.

"Yes, friends, ye are old again," said Dr. Heidegger, "and lo! the Water of Youth is all lavished on the ground. Well—I bemoan it not; for if the fountain gushed at my very doorstep, I would not stoop to bathe my lips in it—no, though its delirium were for years instead of moments. Such is the lesson ye have taught me!"

But the doctor's four friends had taught no such lesson to themselves. They resolved forthwith to make a pilgrimage to Florida, and quaff at morning, noon, and night, from the Fountain of Youth.

Getting at Meaning

1. What do the doctor's four old friends have in common? What is true of each one's life?

2. Describe Dr. Heidegger's study. What is unusual about his mirror?

3. Explain the doctor's experiment. How does he convince the old people to participate?

4. Why won't the doctor participate in the experiment? What evidence suggests that he has anticipated the outcome of his test?

5. What begins to happen as the old people feel

themselves growing young again? What catastrophe occurs? How does it occur?

6. What does Dr. Heidegger conclude at the end of his experiment? What do the doctor's four friends plan to do?

Developing Skills in Reading Literature

1. **Foreshadowing.** Foreshadowing is a writer's use of hints or clues to indicate events that will occur later in a narrative. An example of foreshadowing in this story is the revelation that Dr. Heidegger's fiancée died on the eve of her wedding after "she had swallowed one of her lover's prescriptions." What effect does this information have on the reader? What other examples of foreshadowing are woven into the narrative?

2. **Symbol.** The butterfly and the rose serve as linked symbols in this story. Although each has a concrete reality of its own, each also stands for an abstraction. How do these symbols function in the story? What do they represent?

The mirror is also an important symbol. On a literal level it is an object in which Dr. Heidegger and his guests can see their reflections. The mirror has deeper meanings as well. In what ways does it remind the reader of death and the limitations of medicine?

3. **Allegory.** The characters in this story are not fully fleshed human beings, but exist more as representations of ideas or abstractions. Each of Dr. Heidegger's four friends, for example, illustrates the waste of something valuable. With the Widow Wycherly it is beauty. What waste does each of the other characters represent? What does Dr. Heidegger stand for? What is the moral, or lesson, of Dr. Heidegger's experiment?

4. **Theme.** Before he begins his experiment, Dr. Heidegger says, "For my own part, having had much trouble in growing old, I am in no hurry to grow young again." After his friends have grown old again, he says, ". . . and lo! the Water of Youth is all lavished on the ground. Well—I bemoan it not; for if the fountain gushed at my very doorstep, I would not stoop to bathe my lips in it." What major theme of the story is expressed in these statements? Support your answer with references to specific incidents in the story.

Another significant theme in this story concerns the conflict between illusion, what seems true, and reality, what is true. When the old people have become young again, the narrator says:

> Yet, by a strange deception, owing to the duskiness of the chamber and the antique dresses which they still wore, the tall mirror is said to have reflected the figures of the three old, gray, withered grandsires ridiculously contending for the skinny ugliness of a shriveled grandam.

Where else does the narrator blur the line between dream and reality? What purpose do these references have in the story?

Developing Vocabulary

Formal Diction: Adjectives. Just as Hawthorne uses nouns with which you may not be familiar, he also uses adjectives you may not know. Although some of these adjectives were more common in the nineteenth century than they are now, many of them are still in use. Often, however, they are considered formal diction.

Look up each adjective that follows and record its meaning. Notice how Hawthorne uses each word. Then give at least one less formal synonym for the word.

effervescent	tremulous
lightsome	venerable
melancholy	veracious
rejuvenescent	

Developing Writing Skills

Writing an Essay of Social Commentary. Why is there so much emphasis on youth in our culture? Why do ads and commercials urge people to eliminate gray hair and wrinkles? Why are older adults flattered to be told they look much younger than they really are? How are many old people treated in our society?

Write a five-paragraph composition in which you consider the problem of growing old in America. Use examples to illustrate how we view youth and old age. Explain how you think we *should* view old age.

Herman Melville

1819–1891

After completing the famous sea story *Moby-Dick*, Herman Melville wrote to his friend Nathaniel Hawthorne, "I have written a wicked book, and feel spotless as a lamb." This "wicked book," which probes questions of good and evil, fate and free will, appearance and reality as no other book ever had before, is thought by many critics to be the great American novel.

Melville was born in New York City into a prosperous, though rather unstable family. His mother belonged to a prominent Dutch family, the Gansevoorts, and her relatives were influential in Albany. Melville's father experienced financial ups and downs, eventually going bankrupt. He died when Herman was twelve, leaving the family destitute and dependent on relatives.

At nineteen Melville decided to go to sea, signing as "boy" on a packet ship bound for Liverpool. In Liverpool he was appalled by life in the city slums, which later became the subject of his novel *Redburn*. Soon after returning from Liverpool, Melville signed aboard the whaler *Acushnet*, bound for the South Pacific. During the nearly four years of the voyage, Melville had an enormous variety of experiences and learned all aspects of the whaling trade. He visited several places in South America and many islands in the Pacific.

Melville was twenty-five when he returned from his whaling voyage. Handsome, intelligent, and intense, he was also lonely and hungry for two things: affection and a profession. He found both rather quickly. Scarcely more than a year after his return, Melville published his first book, *Typee*. A novel about Polynesian life, *Typee* became immediately popular in both the United States and England. Melville followed the next year with a second novel, *Omoo*, his greatest popular success. That same year Melville married Elizabeth Shaw, daughter of Lemuel Shaw, Chief Justice of Massachusetts.

The young Melvilles first settled in New York City, where Melville published two more novels and where their first child was born. In 1850, however, Melville moved his family to the Berk-shires, to a farm near Pittsfield, Massachusetts. Here, during a period of intense productivity, Melville worked the farm and wrote *Moby-Dick*. He also formed a friendship with Nathaniel Hawthorne, who was fifteen years older than Melville, and Hawthorne became a significant influence on the younger writer. Said Melville of Hawthorne's work, "It is that blackness in Hawthorne that . . . fixes and fascinates me."

Although *Moby-Dick* is undoubtedly Melville's masterpiece, it was not a critical or financial success, for many readers did not understand the book. Melville quickly followed it with several more books, none as successful as his first novels. He wrote several excellent works of short fiction for magazines, among them "Bartleby, the Scrivener" and "Beneto Cereno." His last novel, *The Confidence Man*, came out in 1857.

After Melville's death Elizabeth found the manuscript for *Billy Budd* in his desk. This short novel was not published until 1924, during a Melville revival. Postwar readers appreciated Melville's philosophical depths, especially his concern for the presence of evil in human beings and in nature, and *Moby-Dick* finally received critical recognition.

Bartleby, the Scrivener

A Story of Wall Street

I am a rather elderly man. The nature of my avocations for the last thirty years has brought me into more than ordinary contact with what would seem an interesting and somewhat singular set of men, of whom as yet nothing that I know of has ever been written: I mean the law copyists or scriveners.[1] I have known very many of them, professionally and privately, and if I pleased, could relate divers histories, at which good-natured gentlemen might smile, and sentimental souls might weep. But I waive the biographies of all other scriveners for a few passages in the life of Bartleby, who was a scrivener, the strangest I ever saw or heard of. While, of other law copyists I might write the complete life, of Bartleby nothing of that sort can be done. I believe that no materials exist for a full and satisfactory biography of this man. It is an irreparable loss to literature. Bartleby was one of those beings of whom nothing is ascertainable, except from the original sources, and in his case those are very small. What my own astonished eyes saw of Bartleby, *that* is all I know of him, except, indeed, one vague report which will appear in the sequel.

Ere introducing the scrivener, as he first appeared to me, it is fit I make some mention of myself, my *employés*, my business, my chambers, and general surroundings; because some such description is indispensable to an adequate understanding of the chief character about to be presented. Imprimis: I am a man who, from his youth upwards, has been filled with a profound conviction that the easiest way of life is the best. Hence, though I belong to a profession proverbially energetic and nervous, even to turbulence, at times, yet nothing of that sort have I ever suffered to invade my peace. I am one of those unambitious lawyers who never address a jury, or in any way draw down public applause; but in the cool tranquility of a snug retreat, do a snug business among rich men's bonds and mortgages and title deeds. All who know me, consider me an eminently *safe* man. The late John Jacob Astor,[2] a personage little given to poetic enthusiasm, had no hesitation in pronouncing my first grand point to be prudence; my next, method. I do not speak it in vanity, but simply record the fact, that I was not unemployed in my profession by the late John Jacob Astor; a name which, I admit, I love to repeat; for it hath a rounded and orbicular sound to it, and rings like unto bullion. I will freely add that I was not insensible to the late John Jacob Astor's good opinion.

Some time prior to the period at which this little history begins, my avocations had been largely increased. The good old office, now extinct in the State of New York, of a Master in Chancery,[3] had been conferred upon me. It was not a very arduous office, but very pleasantly remunerative. I seldom lose my temper; much more seldom indulge in dangerous indignation at wrongs and outrages, but I must be permitted to be rash here and declare that I consider the sudden and violent abrogation of

---

1. **scrivener** (skriv' nər): a professional or public copyist or writer; a scribe.
2. **John Jacob Astor:** an American fur trader and capitalist, who lived from 1763-1848.
3. **Master in Chancery:** a high position in a court of law.

the office of Master of Chancery, by the new Constitution, as a—premature act; inasmuch as I had counted upon a life lease of the profits, whereas I only received those of a few short years. But this is by the way.

My chambers were upstairs, at No.—Wall Street. At one end they looked upon the white wall of the interior of a spacious skylight shaft, penetrating the building from top to bottom. This view might have been considered rather tame than otherwise, deficient in what landscape painters call "life." But if so, the view from the other end of my chambers offered, at least, a contrast, if nothing more. In that direction my windows commanded an unobstructed view of a lofty brick wall, black by age and everlasting shade; which wall required no spyglass to bring out its lurking beauties, but for the benefit of all nearsighted spectators, was pushed up to within ten feet of my window panes. Owing to the great height of the surrounding buildings, and my chambers being on the second floor, the interval between this wall and mine not a little resembled a huge square cistern.

At the period just preceding the advent of Bartleby, I had two persons as copyists in my employment, and a promising lad as an office boy. First, Turkey; second, Nippers; third, Ginger Nut. These may seem names the like of which are not usually found in the Directory. In truth they were nicknames, mutually conferred upon each other by my three clerks, and were deemed expressive of their respective persons or characters. Turkey was a short, pursy Englishman of about my own age, that is, somewhere not far from sixty. In the morning, one might say, his face was of a fine florid hue, but after twelve o'clock, meridian —his dinner hour—it blazed like a grate full of Christmas coals; and continued blazing—but, as it were, with a gradual wane—till six o'clock, P.M., or thereabouts, after which, I saw no more of the proprietor of the face, which gaining its meridian with the sun, seemed to set with it, to rise, culminate, and

decline the following day, with the like regularity and undiminished glory. There are many singular coincidences I have known in the course of my life, not the least among which was the fact, that exactly when Turkey displayed his fullest beams from his red and radiant countenance, just then, too, at that critical moment, began the daily period when I considered his business capacities as seriously disturbed for the remainder of the twenty-four hours. Not that he was absolutely idle, or averse to business then; far from it. The difficulty was, he was apt to be altogether too energetic. There was a strange, inflamed, flurried, flighty recklessness of activity about him. He would be incautious in dipping his pen into his inkstand. All his blots upon my documents were dropped there after twelve o'clock, meridian. Indeed, not only would he be reckless, and sadly given to making blots in the afternoon, but some days he went further, and was rather noisy. At such times, too, his face flamed with augmented blazonry, as if cannel coal had been heaped on anthracite. He made an unpleasant racket with his chair; spilled his sandbox; in mending his pens, impatiently split them all to pieces and threw them on the floor in a sudden passion; stood up, and leaned over his table, boxing his papers about in a most indecorous manner, very sad to behold in an elderly man like him. Nevertheless, as he was in many ways a most valuable person to me, and all the time before twelve o'clock, meridian, was the quickest, steadiest creature too, accomplishing a great deal of work in a style not easily to be matched—for these reasons, I was willing to overlook his eccentricities, though, indeed, occasionally, I remonstrated with him. I did this very gently, however, because, though the civilest, nay, the blandest and most reverential of men in the morning, yet in the afternoon he was disposed, upon provocation, to be slightly rash with his tongue, in fact, insolent. Now, valuing his morning services as I did, and resolved not to lose them; yet, at the same time made uncomfortable by his inflamed ways after twelve o'clock; and being a man of peace, unwilling by my admonitions to call forth unseemly retorts from him, I took upon me, one Saturday noon (he was always worse on Saturdays), to hint to him, very kindly, that perhaps now that he was growing old, it might be well to abridge his labors; in short, he need not come to my chambers after twelve o'clock, but, dinner over, had best go home to his lodgings and rest himself till teatime. But no; he insisted upon his afternoon devotions. His countenance became intolerably fervid, as he oratorically assured me—gesticulating with a long ruler at the other end of the room—that if his services in the morning were useful, how indispensable, then, in the afternoon?

"With submission, sir," said Turkey on this occasion, "I consider myself your right-hand man. In the morning I but marshal and deploy my columns; but in the afternoon I put myself at their head, and gallantly charge the foe, thus!"—and he made a violent thrust with the ruler.

"But the blots, Turkey," intimated I.

"True,—but, with submission, sir, behold these hairs! I am getting old. Surely, sir, a blot or two of a warm afternoon is not to be severely urged against gray hairs. Old age—even if it blot the page—is honorable. With submission, sir, we *both* are getting old."

This appeal to my fellow feeling was hardly to be resisted. At all events, I saw that go he would not. So I made up my mind to let him stay, resolving, nevertheless, to see to it that during the afternoon he had to do with my less important papers.

Nippers, the second on my list, was a whiskered, sallow, and upon the whole, rather piratical-looking young man of about five and twenty. I always deemed him the victim of two evil powers—ambition and indigestion. The ambition was evinced by a certain impatience of the duties of a mere copyist, an unwarrantable usurpation of strictly professional affairs, such as the original drawing up of legal documents. The indigestion seemed betokened in an occasional nervous testiness and grinning irritability, causing the teeth to audibly grind together over mistakes committed in copying; unnecessary maledictions, hissed, rather than spoken, in the heat of business; and especially by a continual discontent with the height of the table where he worked. Though of a very ingenious mechanical turn, Nippers could never get this table to suit him. He put chips under it, blocks of various sorts, bits of pasteboard, and at last went so far as to attempt an exquisite adjustment, by final pieces of folded blotting paper. But no invention would answer. If, for the sake of easing his back, he brought the table lid at a sharp angle well up towards his chin, and wrote there like a man using the steep roof of a Dutch house for his desk—then he declared that it stopped the circulation in his arms. If now he lowered the table to his waistbands, and stooped over it in writing, then there was a sore aching in his back. In short, the truth of the matter was, Nippers knew not what he wanted. Or, if he wanted anything, it was to be rid of a scrivener's table altogether. Among the manifestations of his diseased ambition was a fondness he had for receiving visits from certain ambiguous-looking fellows in seedy coats, whom he called his clients. Indeed, I was aware that not only was he, at times, considerable of a ward politician, but he occasionally did a little business at the Justices' courts, and was not unknown on the steps of the Tombs.[4] I have good reason to believe, however, that one individual who called upon him at my chambers, and who, with a grand air, he insisted was his client, was no other than a dun, and the alleged title deed, a bill. But, with all his failings, and the annoyances he caused me, Nippers, like his compatriot Turkey, was a

---

4. **Tombs:** the city prison of New York.

very useful man to me; wrote a neat, swift hand; and, when he chose, was not deficient in a gentlemanly sort of deportment. Added to this, he always dressed in a gentlemanly sort of way; and so, incidentally, reflected credit upon my chambers. Whereas with respect to Turkey, I had much ado to keep him from being a reproach to me. His clothes were apt to look oily and smell of eating-houses. He wore his pantaloons very loose and baggy in summer. His coats were execrable; his hat not to be handled. But while the hat was a thing of indifference to me, inasmuch as his natural civility and deference, as a dependent English man, always led him to doff it the moment he entered the room, yet his coat was another matter. Concerning his coats, I reasoned with him; but with no effect. The truth was, I suppose, that a man with so small an income could not afford to sport such a lustrous face and a lustrous coat at one and the same time. As Nippers once observed, Turkey's money went chiefly for red ink. One winter day I presented Turkey with a highly respectable-looking coat of my own, a padded gray coat, of a most comfortable warmth, and which buttoned straight up from the knee to the neck. I thought Turkey would appreciate the favor, and abate his rashness and obstreperousness of afternoons. But no. I verily believe that buttoning himself up in so downy and blanket-like a coat had a pernicious effect upon him; upon the same principle that too much oats are bad for horses. In fact, precisely as a rash, restive horse is said to feel his oats, so Turkey felt his coat. It made him insolent. He was a man whom prosperity harmed.

Though concerning the self-indulgent habits of Turkey I had my own private surmises, yet touching Nippers I was well persuaded that whatever might be his faults in other respects, he was, at least, a temperate young man. But indeed, nature herself seemed to have been his vintner, and at his birth charged him so thoroughly with an irritable, brandy-like disposition, that all subsequent potations were needless. When I consider how, amid the stillness of my chambers, Nippers would sometimes impatiently rise from his seat, and stooping over his table, spread his arms wide apart, seize the whole desk, and move it, and jerk it, with a grim, grinding motion on the floor, as if the table were a perverse voluntary agent, intent on thwarting and vexing him, I plainly perceive that for Nippers, brandy and water were altogether superfluous.

It was fortunate for me that, owing to its peculiar cause—indigestion—the irritability and consequent nervousness of Nippers were mainly observable in the morning, while in the afternoon he was comparatively mild. So that Turkey's paroxysms only coming on about twelve o'clock, I never had to do with their eccentricities at one time. Their fits relieved each other like guards. When Nippers' was on, Turkey's was off; and *vice versa*. This was a good natural arrangement under the circumstances.

Ginger Nut, the third on my list, was a lad some twelve years old. His father was a car-man, ambitious of seeing his son on the bench instead of a cart, before he died. So he sent him to my office as student at law, errand boy, cleaner and sweeper, at the rate of one dollar a week. He had a little desk to himself, but he did not use it much. Upon inspection, the drawer exhibited a great array of the shells of various sorts of nuts. Indeed, to this quick-witted youth the whole noble science of the law was contained in a nutshell. Not the least among the employments of Ginger Nut, as well as one which he discharged with the most alacrity, was his duty as cake and apple purveyor for Turkey and Nippers. Copying law papers being proverbially a dry, husky sort of business, my two scriveners were fain to moisten their mouths very often with Spitzenbergs[5] to be had at the numerous stalls nigh the Custom House and Post Office. Also,

---

5. **Spitzenbergs** (spit' sən bûrgz): any of several varieties of red-and-yellow apples.

they sent Ginger Nut very frequently for that peculiar cake—small, flat, round, and very spicy—after which he had been named by them. Of a cold morning when business was but dull, Turkey would gobble up scores of these cakes, as if they were mere wafers—indeed they sell them at the rate of six or eight for a penny—the scrape of his pen blending with the crunching of the crisp particles in his mouth. Of all the fiery afternoon blunders and flurried rashnesses of Turkey, was his once moistening a ginger-cake between his lips, and clapping it on to a mortgage for a seal. I came within an ace of dismissing him then. But he mollified me by making an oriental bow, and saying—

"With submission, sir, it was generous of me to find you in stationery on my own account."

Now my original business—that of a conveyancer[6] and title hunter, and drawer-up of recondite documents of all sorts—was considerably increased by receiving the Master's office. There was now great work for scriveners. Not only must I push the clerks already with me, but I must have additional help. In answer to my advertisement, a motionless young man one morning stood upon my office threshold, the door being open, for it was summer. I can see that figure now—pallidly neat, pitiably respectable, incurably forlorn! It was Bartleby.

After a few words touching his qualifications, I engaged him, glad to have among my corps of copyists a man of so singularly sedate an aspect, which I thought might operate beneficially upon the flighty temper of Turkey, and the fiery one of Nippers.

I should have stated before that ground glass folding doors divided my premises into two parts, one of which was occupied by my scriveners, the other by myself. According to my humor I threw open these doors, or closed them. I resolved to assign Bartleby a corner by the folding doors, but on my side of them, so as to have this quiet man within easy call, in case any trifling thing was to be done. I placed his desk close up to a small side-window in that part of the room, a window which originally had offered a lateral view of certain grimy backyards and bricks, but which, owing to subsequent erections, commanded at present no view at all, though it gave some light. Within three feet of the panes was a wall, and the light came down from far above, between two lofty buildings, as from a very small opening in a dome. Still further to a satisfactory arrangement, I procured a high green folding screen, which might entirely isolate Bartleby from my sight, though not remove him from my voice. And thus, in a manner, privacy and society were conjoined.

At first Bartleby did an extraordinary quantity of writing. As if long famishing for something to copy, he seemed to gorge himself on my documents. There was no pause for digestion. He ran a day and night line, copying by sunlight and by candlelight. I should have been quite delighted with his application, had he been cheerfully industrious. But he wrote on silently, palely, mechanically.

It is, of course, an indispensable part of a scrivener's business to verify the accuracy of his copy, word by word. Where there are two or more scriveners in an office, they assist each other in this examination, one reading from the copy, the other holding the original. It is a very dull, wearisome, and lethargic affair. I can readily imagine that to some sanguine temperaments, it would be altogether intolerable. For example, I cannot credit that the mettlesome poet Byron[7] would have contentedly sat down with Bartleby to examine a law document of, say five hundred pages, closely written in a crimpy hand.

Now and then, in the haste of business, it

---

6. **conveyancer** (kən vā' ən sər): one who transfers titles to property.
7. **Byron:** George Gordon, Lord Byron, an English Romantic poet who lived from 1788-1824.

had been my habit to assist in comparing some brief document myself, calling Turkey or Nippers for this purpose. One object I had in placing Bartleby so handy to me behind the screen, was to avail myself of his services on such trivial occasions. It was on the third day, I think, of his being with me, and before any necessity had arisen for having his own writing examined, that, being much hurried to complete a small affair I had in hand, I abruptly called to Bartleby. In my haste and natural expectancy of instant compliance, I sat with my head bent over the original on my desk, and my right hand sideways, and somewhat nervously extended with the copy, so that immediately upon emerging from his retreat, Bartleby might snatch it and proceed to business without the least delay.

In this very attitude did I sit when I called to him, rapidly stating what it was I wanted him to do—namely, to examine a small paper with me. Imagine my surprise, nay, my consternation when without moving from his privacy, Bartleby, in a singularly mild, firm voice, replied, "I would prefer not to."

I sat awhile in perfect silence, rallying my stunned faculties. Immediately it occurred to me that my ears had deceived me, or Bartleby had entirely misunderstood my meaning. I repeated my request in the clearest tone I could assume. But in quite as clear a one came the previous reply, "I would prefer not to."

"Prefer not to," echoed I, rising in high excitement, and crossing the room with a stride. "What do you mean? Are you moonstruck? I want you to help me compare this sheet here—take it," and I thrust it towards him.

"I would prefer not to," said he.

I looked at him steadfastly. His face was leanly composed; his gray eye dimly calm. Not a wrinkle of agitation rippled him. Had there been the least uneasiness, anger, impatience, or impertinence in his manner; in other words, had there been anything ordinarily human about him, doubtless I should have violently dismissed him from the premises. But as it was, I should have as soon thought of turning my pale plaster of Paris bust of Cicero[8] out of doors. I stood gazing at him awhile, as he went on with his own writing, and then reseated myself at my desk. This is very strange, thought I. What had one best do? But my business hurried me. I concluded to forget the matter for the present, reserving it for my future leisure. So calling Nippers from the other room, the paper was speedily examined.

A few days after this, Bartleby concluded four lengthy documents, being quadruplicates of a week's testimony taken before me in my High Court of Chancery. It became necessary to examine them. It was an important suit, and great accuracy was imperative. Having all things arranged I called Turkey, Nippers, and Ginger Nut from the next room, meaning to place the four copies in the hands of my four clerks, while I should read from the original. Accordingly Turkey, Nippers, and Ginger Nut had taken their seats in a row, each with his document in his hand, when I called to Bartleby to join this interesting group.

"Bartleby! quick, I am waiting."

I heard a slow scrape of his chair legs on the uncarpeted floor, and soon he appeared standing at the entrance of his hermitage.

"What is wanted?" said he mildly.

"The copies, the copies," said I hurriedly. "We are going to examine them. There"—and I held towards him the fourth quadruplicate.

"I would prefer not to," he said, and gently disappeared behind the screen.

For a few moments I was turned into a pillar of salt, standing at the head of my seated column of clerks. Recovering myself, I advanced towards the screen, and demanded the reason for such extraordinary conduct.

"*Why* do you refuse?"

"I would prefer not to."

---

8. **Cicero** (sis′ ə rō′): Marcus Tullius Cicero, a Roman statesman, orator, and writer who lived from 106-43 B.C.

With any other man I should have flown outright into a dreadful passion, scorned all further words, and thrust him ignominiously from my presence. But there was something about Bartleby that not only strangely disarmed me, but in a wonderful manner touched and disconcerted me. I began to reason with him.

"These are your own copies we are about to examine. It is labor saving to you, because one examination will answer for your four papers. It is common usage. Every copyist is bound to help examine his copy. Is it not so? Will you not speak? Answer!"

"I prefer not to," he replied in a flute-like tone. It seemed to me that while I had been addressing him, he carefully revolved every statement that I made; fully comprehended the meaning; could not gainsay the irresistible conclusion; but, at the same time, some paramount consideration prevailed with him to reply as he did.

"You are decided, then, not to comply with my request—a request made according to common usage and common sense?"

He briefly gave me to understand that on that point my judgment was sound. Yes: his decision was irreversible.

It is not seldom the case that when a man is browbeaten in some unprecedented and violently unreasonable way, he begins to stagger in his own plainest faith. He begins, as it were, vaguely to surmise that, wonderful as it may be, all the justice and all the reason is on the other side. Accordingly, if any disinterested persons are present, he turns to them for some reinforcement for his own faltering mind.

"Turkey," said I, "what do you think of this? Am I not right?"

"With submission, sir," said Turkey, in his blandest tone, "I think that you are."

"Nippers," said I, "what do *you* think of it?"

"I think I should kick him out of the office."

(The reader of nice perceptions will here perceive that, it being morning, Turkey's answer is couched in polite and tranquil terms, but Nippers replies in ill-tempered ones. Or, to repeat a previous sentence, Nippers' ugly mood was on duty, and Turkey's off.)

"Ginger Nut," said I, willing to enlist the smallest suffrage in my behalf, "what do *you* think of it?"

"I think, sir, he's a little *luny*," replied Ginger Nut, with a grin.

"You hear what they say," said I, turning towards the screen, "come forth and do your duty."

But he vouchsafed no reply. I pondered a moment in sore perplexity. But once more business hurried me. I determined again to postpone the consideration of this dilemma to my future leisure. With a little trouble we made out to examine the papers without Bartleby, though at every page or two Turkey deferentially dropped his opinion that this proceeding was quite out of the common; while Nippers, twitching in his chair with a dyspeptic nervousness, ground out between his set teeth occasional hissing maledictions against the stubborn oaf behind the screen. And for his (Nippers') part, this was the first and the last time he would do another man's business without pay.

Meanwhile Bartleby sat in his hermitage, oblivious to everything but his own peculiar business there.

Some days passed, the scrivener being employed upon another lengthy work. His late remarkable conduct led me to regard his ways narrowly. I observed that he never went to dinner; indeed that he never went anywhere. As yet I had never of my personal knowledge known him to be outside of my office. He was a perpetual sentry in the corner. At about eleven o'clock though, in the morning, I noticed that Ginger Nut would advance toward the opening in Bartleby's screen, as if silently beckoned thither by a gesture invisible to me where I sat. The boy would then leave the office jingling a few pence, and reappear with a handful of ginger-nuts which he delivered in the hermitage, receiving two of the cakes for his trouble.

He lives, then, on ginger-nuts, thought I; never eats a dinner, properly speaking; he must be a vegetarian then; but no; he never eats even vegetables, he eats nothing but ginger-nuts. My mind then ran on in reveries concerning the probable effects upon the human constitution of living entirely on ginger-nuts. Ginger-nuts are so called because they contain ginger as one of their peculiar constituents, and the final flavoring one. Now what was ginger? A hot, spicy thing. Was Bartleby hot and spicy? Not at all. Ginger, then, had no effect upon Bartleby. Probably he preferred it should have none.

Nothing so aggravates an earnest person as a passive resistance. If the individual so resisted be of a not inhumane temper, and the resisting one perfectly harmless in his passivity; then, in the better moods of the former, he will endeavor charitably to construe to his imagination what proves impossible to be solved by his judgment. Even so, for the most part, I regarded Bartleby and his ways. Poor fellow! thought I, he means no mischief; it is plain he intends no insolence; his aspect sufficiently evinces that his eccentricities are involuntary. He is useful to me. I can get along with him. If I turn him away, the chances are he will fall in with some less indulgent employer, and then he will be rudely treated, and perhaps driven forth miserably to starve. Yes. Here I can cheaply purchase a delicious self approval. To befriend Bartleby; to humor him in his strange wilfulness, will cost me little or nothing, while I lay up in my soul what will eventually prove a sweet morsel for my conscience. But this mood was not invariable with me. The passiveness of Bartleby sometimes irritated me. I felt strangely goaded on to encounter him in new opposition, to elicit some angry spark from him answerable to my own. But indeed I might as well have essayed to strike fire with my knuckles against a bit of Windsor soap. But one afternoon the evil impulse in me mastered me, and the following little scene ensued:

"Bartleby," said I, "when those papers are all copied, I will compare them with you."

"I would prefer not to."

"How? Surely you do not mean to persist in that mulish vagary?"

No answer.

I threw open the folding doors near by, and turning upon Turkey and Nippers, exclaimed in an excited manner—

"He says, a second time, he won't examine his papers. What do you think of it, Turkey?"

It was afternoon, be it remembered. Turkey sat glowing like a brass boiler, his bald head steaming, his hands reeling among his blotted papers.

"Think of it?" roared Turkey; "I think I'll just step behind his screen and black his eyes for him!"

So saying, Turkey rose to his feet and threw his arms into a pugilistic position. He was hurrying away to make good his promise, when I detained him, alarmed at the effect of incautiously rousing Turkey's combativeness after dinner.

"Sit down, Turkey," said I, "and hear what Nippers has to say. What do you think of it, Nippers? Would I not be justified in immediately dismissing Bartleby?"

"Excuse me, that is for you to decide, sir. I think his conduct quite unusual, and indeed unjust, as regards Turkey and myself. But it may only be a passing whim."

"Ah," exclaimed I, "you have strangely changed your mind then—you speak very gently of him now."

"All beer," cried Turkey; "gentleness is effects of beer—Nippers and I dined together today. You see how gentle I am, sir. Shall I go and black his eyes?"

"You refer to Bartleby, I suppose. No, not today, Turkey," I replied; "pray, put up your fists."

I closed the doors, and again advanced towards Bartleby. I felt additional incentives tempting me to my fate. I burned to be rebelled against again. I remembered that Bartleby never left the office.

"Bartleby," said I, "Ginger Nut is away; just step around to the post office, won't you?" (it was but a three minutes' walk) "and see if there is anything for me."

"I would prefer not to."

"You *will* not?"

"I *prefer* not."

I staggered to my desk, and sat there in a deep study. My blind inveteracy returned. Was there any other thing in which I could procure myself to be ignominiously repulsed by this lean, penniless wight?—my hired clerk? What added thing is there, perfectly reasonable that he will be sure to refuse to do?

"Bartleby!"

No answer.

"Bartleby," in a louder tone.

No answer.

"Bartleby," I roared.

Like a very ghost, agreeably to the laws of magical invocation, at the third summons, he appeared at the entrance of his hermitage.

"Go to the next room, and tell Nippers to come to me."

"I prefer not to," he respectfully and slowly said, and mildly disappeared.

"Very good, Bartleby," said I, in a quiet sort of serenely severe self-possessed tone, intimating the unalterable purpose of some terrible retribution very close at hand. At the moment I half intended something of the kind. But upon the whole, as it was drawing towards my dinner hour, I thought it best to put on my hat and walk home for the day, suffering much from perplexity and distress of mind.

Shall I acknowledge it? The conclusion of this whole business was, that it soon became a fixed fact of my chambers, that a pale young scrivener, by the name of Bartleby, had a desk there; that he copied for me at the usual rate of four cents a folio (one hundred words); but he was permanently exempt from examining the work done by him, that duty being transferred to Turkey and Nippers, out of compliment, doubtless, to their superior acuteness; moreover, said Bartleby was never on any account to be dispatched on the most trivial errand of any sort; and that even if entreated to take upon him such a matter, it was generally understood that he would prefer not to—in other words, that he would refuse point-blank.

As days passed on, I became considerably reconciled to Bartleby. His steadiness, his freedom from all dissipation, his incessant industry (except when he chose to throw himself into a standing revery behind his screen), his great stillness, his unalterableness of demeanor under all circumstances, made him a valuable acquisition. One prime thing was this,—*he was always there*—first in the morning, continually through the day, and the last at night. I had a singular confidence in his honesty. I felt my most precious papers perfectly safe in his hands. Sometimes to be sure I could not, for the very soul of me, avoid falling into sudden spasmodic passions with him. For it was exceeding difficult to bear in mind all the time those strange peculiarities, privileges, and unheard of exemptions, forming the tacit stipulations on Bartleby's part under which he remained in my office. Now and then, in the eagerness of dispatching pressing business, I would inadvertently summon Bartleby, in a short, rapid tone, to put his finger, say, on the incipient tie of a bit of red tape with which I was about compressing some papers. Of course, from behind the screen the usual answer, "I prefer not to," was sure to come; and then, how could a human creature with the common infirmities of our nature, refrain from bitterly exclaiming upon such perverseness—such unreasonableness? However, every added repulse of this sort which I received only tended to lessen the probability of my repeating the inadvertence.

Wall Street, New York City, and sketches of the various types prominent in this part of the city. Woodcut by English artist made during his visit to America in 1877.

Here it must be said, that according to the custom of most legal gentlemen occupying chambers in densely populated law buildings, there were several keys to my door. One was kept by a woman residing in the attic, which person weekly scrubbed and daily swept and dusted my apartments. Another was kept by Turkey for convenience sake. The third I sometimes carried in my own pocket. The fourth I knew not who had.

Now, one Sunday morning I happened to go to Trinity Church to hear a celebrated preacher, and finding myself rather early on the ground, I thought I would walk round to my chambers for a while. Luckily I had my keys with me; but upon applying it to the lock, I found it resisted by something inserted from the inside. Quite surprised, I called out; when to my consternation a key was turned from within; and thrusting his lean visage at me, and holding the door ajar, the apparition of Bartleby appeared, in his shirt sleeves, and otherwise in a strangely tattered dishabille, saying quietly that he was sorry, but he was deeply engaged just then, and—preferred not admitting me at present. In a brief word or two, he moreover added, that perhaps I had better walk round the block two or three times, and by that time he would probably have concluded his affairs.

Now, the utterly unsurmised appearance of Bartleby, tenanting my law chambers of a Sunday morning, with his cadaverously gentlemanly *nonchalance*, yet withal firm and self-possessed, had such a strange effect upon me, that incontinently I slunk away from my own door, and did as desired. But not without sundry twinges of impotent rebellion against the mild effrontery of this unaccountable scrivener. Indeed, it was his wonderful mildness chiefly, which not only disarmed me, but unmanned me, as it were. For I consider that one, for the time, is a sort of unmanned when he tranquilly permits his hired clerk to dictate to him, and order him away from his own premises. Furthermore, I

was full of uneasiness as to what Bartleby could possibly be doing in my office in his shirt sleeves, and in an otherwise dismantled condition of a Sunday morning. Was anything amiss going on? Nay, that was out of the question. It was not to be thought of for a moment that Bartleby was an immoral person. But what could he be doing there—copying? Nay again, whatever might be his eccentricities, Bartleby was an eminently decorous person. He would be the last man to sit down to his desk in any state approaching to nudity. Besides, it was Sunday; and there was something about Bartleby that forbade the supposition that he would by any secular occupation violate the proprieties of the day.

Nevertheless, my mind was not pacified; and full of a restless curiosity, at last I returned to the door. Without hindrance I inserted my key, opened it, and entered. Bartleby was not to be seen. I looked round anxiously, peeped behind his screen; but it was very plain that he was gone. Upon more closely examining the place, I surmised that for an indefinite period Bartleby must have ate, dressed, and slept in my office, and that too without plate, mirror, or bed. The cushioned seat of a rickety old sofa in one corner bore the faint impress of a lean, reclining form. Rolled away under his desk, I found a blanket; under the empty grate, a blacking box[9] and brush; on a chair, a tin basin, with soap and a ragged towel; in a newspaper a few crumbs of ginger-nuts and a morsel of cheese. Yes, thought I, it is evident enough that Bartleby has been making his home here, keeping bachelor's hall all by himself. Immediately then the thought came sweeping across me, What miserable friendlessness and loneliness are here revealed! His poverty is great; but his solitude, how horrible! Think of it. Of a Sunday, Wall Street is deserted as

---

9. **blacking box:** a box containing supplies for polishing shoes and boots.

Petra;[10] and every night of every day it is an emptiness. This building too, which of weekdays hums with industry and life, at nightfall echoes with sheer vacancy, and all through Sunday is forlorn. And here Bartleby makes his home; sole spectator of a solitude which he has seen all populous—a sort of innocent and transformed Marius brooding among the ruins of Carthage![11]

For the first time in my life a feeling of overpowering stinging melancholy seized me. Before, I had never experienced aught but a not unpleasing sadness. The bond of a common humanity now drew me irresistibly to gloom. A fraternal melancholy! For both I and Bartleby were sons of Adam. I remembered the bright silks and sparkling faces I had seen that day, in gala trim, swan-like sailing down the Mississippi of Broadway; and I contrasted them with the pallid copyist, and thought to myself, Ah, happiness courts the light, so we deem the world is gay; but misery hides aloof, so we deem that misery there is none. These sad fancyings—chimeras, doubtless, of a sick and silly brain—led on to other and more special thoughts, concerning the eccentricities of Bartleby. Presentiments of strange discoveries hovered round me. The scrivener's pale form appeared to me laid out, among uncaring strangers, in its shivering winding sheet.

Suddenly I was attracted by Bartleby's closed desk, the key in open sight left in the lock.

I mean no mischief, seek the gratification of no heartless curiosity, thought I; besides, the desk is mine, and its contents too, so I will make bold to look within. Everything was methodically arranged, the papers smoothly placed. The pigeon holes were deep, and removing the files of documents, I groped into their recesses. Presently I felt something there, and dragged it out. It was an old bandanna handkerchief, heavy and knotted. I opened it, and saw it was a savings' bank.

I now recalled all the quiet mysteries which I had noted in the man. I remembered that he never spoke but to answer; that though at intervals he had considerable time to himself, yet I had never seen him reading—no, not even a newspaper; that for long periods he would stand looking out, at his pale window behind the screen, upon the dead brick wall; I was quite sure he never visited any refectory or eating house; while his pale face clearly indicated that he never drank beer like Turkey, or tea and coffee even, like other men; that he never went anywhere in particular that I could learn; never went out for a walk, unless indeed that was the case at present; that he had declined telling who he was, or whence he came, or whether he had any relatives in the world; that though so thin and pale, he never complained of ill health. And more than all, I remembered a certain unconscious air of pallid—how shall I call it—of pallid haughtiness, say, or rather an austere reserve about him, which had positively awed me into my tame compliance with his eccentricities, when I had feared to ask him to do the slightest incidental thing for me, even though I might know, from his long-continued motionlessness, that behind his screen he must be standing in one of those deadwall reveries of his.

Revolving all these things, and coupling them with the recently discovered fact that he made my office his constant abiding place and home, and not forgetful of his morbid moodiness; revolving all these things, a prudential feeling began to steal over me. My first emotions had been those of pure melancholy and sincerest pity; but just in propor-

---

10. **Petra** (pē' trə): an ancient city of Arabia, whose site is now in southwest Jordan.
11. **Marius . . . Carthage** (mer' ē əs): Gaius Marius, 155?-86 B.C., was a Roman general whose troops destroyed the North African city of Carthage.

tion as the forlornness of Bartleby grew and grew to my imagination, did that same melancholy merge into fear, that pity into repulsion. So true it is, and so terrible too, that up to a certain point the thought or sight of misery enlists our best affections; but, in certain special cases, beyond that point it does not. They err who would assert that invariably this is owing to the inherent selfishness of the human heart. It rather proceeds from a certain hopelessness of remedying excessive and organic ill. To a sensitive being, pity is not seldom pain. And when at last it is perceived that such pity cannot lead to effectual succor, common sense bids the soul be rid of it. What I saw that morning persuaded me that the scrivener was the victim of innate and incurable disorder. I might give alms to his body; but his body did not pain him; it was his soul that suffered, and his soul I could not reach.

I did not accomplish the purpose of going to Trinity Church that morning. Somehow, the things I had seen disqualified me for the time from churchgoing. I walked homeward, thinking what I would do with Bartleby. Finally, I resolved upon this: I would put certain calm questions to him the next morning, touching his history, etc., and if he declined to answer them openly and unreservedly (and I supposed he would prefer not), then to give him a twenty dollar bill over and above whatever I might owe him, and tell him his services were no longer required; but that if in any other way I could assist him, I would be happy to do so, especially if he desired to return to his native place, wherever that might be, I would willingly help to defray the expenses. Moreover, if, after reaching home, he found himself at any time in want of aid, a letter from him would be sure of a reply.

The next morning came.

"Bartleby," said I, gently calling to him behind the screen.

No reply.

"Bartleby," said I, in a still gentler tone, "come here; I am not going to ask you to do anything you would prefer not to do—I simply wish to speak to you."

Upon this he noiselessly slid into view.

"Will you tell me, Bartleby, where you were born?"

"I would prefer not to."

"Will you tell me *anything* about yourself?"

"I would prefer not to."

"But what reasonable objection can you have to speak to me? I feel friendly towards you."

He did not look at me while I spoke, but kept his glance fixed upon my bust of Cicero, which as I then sat, was directly behind me, some six inches above my head.

"What is your answer, Bartleby?" said I, after waiting a considerable time for a reply, during which his countenance remained immovable, only there was the faintest conceivable tremor of the white attenuated mouth.

"At present I prefer to give no answer," he said, and retired into his hermitage.

It was rather weak in me I confess, but his manner on this occasion nettled me. Not only did there seem to lurk in it a certain calm disdain, but his perverseness seemed ungrateful, considering the undeniable good usage and indulgence he had received from me.

Again I sat ruminating what I should do. Mortified as I was at his behavior, and resolved as I had been to dismiss him when I entered my office, nevertheless I strangely felt something superstitious knocking at my heart, and forbidding me to carry out my purpose, and denouncing me for a villain if I dared to breathe one bitter word against this forlornest of mankind. At last, familiarly drawing my chair behind his screen, I sat down and said, "Bartleby, never mind then about revealing your history; but let me entreat you, as a friend, to comply as far as may be with the usages of this office. Say now you will help to examine papers tomorrow or next day: in short, say now, that in a day or two you will begin to be a little reasonable. Say so, Bartleby."

"At present I would prefer not to be a little reasonable," was his mildly cadaverous reply.

Just then the folding doors opened, and Nippers approached. He seemed suffering from an unusually bad night's rest, induced by severer indigestion than common. He overheard those final words of Bartleby.

"*Prefer not,* eh," gritted Nippers—"I'd *prefer* him, if I were you, sir," addressing me—"I'd *prefer* him; I'd give him preferences, the stubborn mule! What is it, sir, pray, that he *prefers* not to do now?"

Bartleby moved not a limb.

"Mr. Nippers," said I, "I'd prefer that you would withdraw for the present."

Somehow, of late I got into the way of involuntarily using this word *prefer* upon all sorts of not exactly suitable occasions. And I trembled to think that my contact with the scrivener had already and seriously affected me in a mental way. And what further and deeper aberration might it not yet produce? This apprehension had not been without efficacy in determining me to summary measures.

As Nippers, looking very sour and sulky, was departing, Turkey blandly and deferentially approached.

"With submission, sir," said he, "yesterday I was thinking about Bartleby here, and I think that if he would but prefer to take a quart of good ale every day, it would do much towards mending him, and enabling him to assist in examining his papers."

"So you have got the word too," said I, slightly excited.

"With submission, what word, sir?" asked Turkey, respectfully crowding himself into the contracted space behind the screen, and by so doing, making me jostle the scrivener. "What word, sir?"

"I would prefer to be left alone here," said Bartleby, as if offended at being mobbed in his privacy.

"*That's* the word, Turkey," said I—"*that's* it."

"Oh, *prefer*? oh yes—queer word. I never use it myself. But, sir, as I was saying, if he would but prefer—"

"Turkey," interrupted I, "you will please withdraw."

"Oh certainly, sir, if you prefer that I should."

As he opened the folding door to retire, Nippers at his desk caught a glimpse of me, and asked whether I would prefer to have a certain paper copied on blue paper or white. He did not in the least roguishly accent the word *prefer*. It was plain that it involuntarily rolled from his tongue. I thought to myself, surely I must get rid of a demented man, who already has in some degree turned the tongues, if not the heads of myself and clerks. But I thought it prudent not to break the dismission at once.

The next day I noticed that Bartleby did nothing but stand at his window in his dead-wall revery. Upon asking him why he did not write, he said that he had decided upon doing no more writing.

"Why, how now? what next?" exclaimed I, "do no more writing?"

"No more."

"And what is the reason?"

"Do you not see the reason for yourself?" he indifferently replied.

I looked steadfastly at him, and perceived that his eyes looked dull and glazed. Instantly it occurred to me, that his unexampled diligence in copying by his dim window for the first few weeks of his stay with me might have temporarily impaired his vision.

I was touched. I said something in condolence with him. I hinted that of course he did wisely in abstaining from writing for a while; and urged him to embrace that opportunity of taking wholesome exercise in the open air. This, however, he did not do. A few days after this, my other clerks being absent, and being in a great hurry to dispatch certain letters by mail, I thought that, having nothing else earthly to do, Bartleby would surely be less inflexible than usual, and carry these letters to the post office. But he blankly declined. So, much to my inconvenience, I went myself.

Still added days went by. Whether Bartleby's eyes improved or not, I could not say. To all appearance, I thought they did. But when I asked him if they did, he vouchsafed no answer. At all events, he would do no copying. At last, in reply to my urgings, he informed me that he had permanently given up copying.

"What!" exclaimed I; "suppose your eyes should get entirely well—better than ever before—would you not copy then?"

"I have given up copying," he answered, and slid aside.

He remained as ever, a fixture in my chamber. Nay—if that were possible—he became still more of a fixture than before. What was to be done? He would do nothing in the office: why should he stay there? In plain fact, he had now become a millstone to me, not only useless as a necklace, but afflictive to bear. Yet I was sorry for him. I speak less than truth when I say that, on his own account, he occasioned me uneasiness. If he would but have named a single relative or friend, I would instantly have written, and urged their taking the poor fellow away to some convenient retreat. But he seemed alone, absolutely alone in the universe. A bit of wreck in the mid-Atlantic. At length, necessities connected with my business tyrannized over all other considerations. Decently as I could, I told Bartleby that in six days' time he must unconditionally leave the office. I warned him to take measures, in the interval, for procuring some other abode. I offered to assist him in this endeavor, if he himself would but take the first step towards a removal. "And when you finally quit me, Bartleby," added I, "I shall see that you go not away entirely unpro-

vided. Six days from this hour, remember."

At the expiration of that period, I peeped behind the screen, and lo! Bartleby was there.

I buttoned up my coat, balanced myself; advanced slowly towards him, touched his shoulder, and said, "The time has come; you must quit this place; I am sorry for you; here is money; but you must go."

"I would prefer not," he replied, with his back still towards me.

"You *must*."

He remained silent.

Now I had an unbounded confidence in this man's common honesty. He had frequently restored to me sixpences and shillings carelessly dropped upon the floor, for I am apt to be very reckless in such shirt-button affairs. The proceeding, then, which followed will not be deemed extraordinary.

"Bartleby," said I, "I owe you twelve dollars on account; here are thirty-two; the odd twenty are yours. Will you take it?" and I handed the bills towards him.

But he made no motion.

"I will leave them here then," putting them under a weight on the table. Then taking my hat and cane and going to the door I tranquilly turned and added—"After you have removed your things from these offices, Bartleby, you will of course lock the door—since every one is now gone for the day but you—and if you please, slip your key underneath the mat, so that I may have it in the morning. I shall not see you again; so goodbye to you. If hereafter in your new place of abode, I can be of any service to you, do not fail to advise me by letter. Goodbye, Bartleby, and fare you well."

But he answered not a word; like the last column of some ruined temple, he remained standing mute and solitary in the middle of the otherwise deserted room.

As I walked home in a pensive mood, my vanity got the better of my pity. I could not but highly plume myself on my masterly management in getting rid of Bartleby. Masterly I call it, and such it must appear to any dispassionate thinker. The beauty of my procedure seemed to consist in its perfect quietness. There was no vulgar bullying, no bravado of any sort, no choleric hectoring, and striding to and fro across the apartment, jerking out vehement commands for Bartleby to bundle himself off with his beggarly traps. Nothing of the kind. Without loudly bidding Bartleby depart—as an inferior genius might have done—I *assumed* the ground that depart he must; and upon that assumption built all I had to say. The more I thought over my procedure, the more I was charmed with it. Nevertheless, next morning, upon awakening, I had my doubts—I had somehow slept off the fumes of vanity. One of the coolest and wisest hours a man has, is just after he awakes in the morning. My procedure seemed as sagacious as ever, but only in theory. How it would prove in practice—there was the rub. It was truly a beautiful thought to have assumed Bartleby's departure; but, after all, that assumption was simply my own, and none of Bartleby's. The great point was, not whether I had assumed that he would quit me, but whether he would prefer so to do. He was more a man of preferences than assumptions.

After breakfast, I walked downtown, arguing the probabilities *pro* and *con*. One moment I thought it would prove a miserable failure, and Bartleby would be found all alive at my office as usual; the next moment it seemed certain that I should see his chair empty. And so I kept veering about. At the corner of Broadway and Canal Street, I saw quite an excited group of people standing in earnest conversation.

"I'll take odds he doesn't," said a voice as I passed.

"Doesn't go?—done!" said I, "put up your money."

I was instinctively putting my hand in my pocket to produce my own, when I remembered that this was an election day. The words I had overheard bore no reference to Bartleby, but to the success or non-success of

some candidate for the mayoralty. In my intent frame of mind, I had, as it were, imagined that all Broadway shared in my excitement, and were debating the same question with me. I passed on, very thankful that the uproar of the street screened my momentary absent-mindedness.

As I had intended, I was earlier than usual at my office door. I stood listening for a moment. All was still. He must be gone. I tried the knob. The door was locked. Yes, my procedure had worked to a charm; he indeed must be vanished. Yet a certain melancholy mixed with this; I was almost sorry for my brilliant success. I was fumbling under the door mat for the key, which Bartleby was to have left there for me, when accidentally my knee knocked against a panel, producing a summoning sound, and in response a voice came to me from within—"Not yet; I am occupied."

It was Bartleby.

I was thunderstruck. For an instant I stood like the man who, pipe in mouth, was killed one cloudless afternoon long ago in Virginia, by summer lightning; at his own warm open window he was killed, and remained leaning out there upon the dreamy afternoon, till someone touched him, when he fell.

"Not gone!" I murmured at last. But again obeying that wondrous ascendancy which the inscrutable scrivener had over me, and from which ascendancy, for all my chafing, I could not completely escape, I slowly went down stairs and out into the street, and while walking round the block, considered what I should next do in this unheard-of perplexity. Turn the man out by an actual thrusting I could not; to drive him away by calling him hard names would not do; calling in the police was an unpleasant idea; and yet, permit him to enjoy his cadaverous triumph over me—this too I could not think of. What was to be done, or, if nothing could be done, was there anything further that I could *assume* in the matter? Yes, as before I had prospectively assumed that Bartleby would depart, so now I might retrospectively assume that departed he was. In the legitimate carrying out of this assumption, I might enter my office in a great hurry, and pretending not to see Bartleby at all, walk straight against him as if he were air. Such a proceeding would in a singular degree have the appearance of a home thrust. It was hardly possible that Bartleby could withstand such an application of the doctrine of assumptions. But upon second thoughts the success of the plan seemed rather dubious. I resolved to argue the matter over with him again.

"Bartleby," said I, entering the office, with a quietly severe expression, "I am seriously displeased. I am pained, Bartleby. I had thought better of you. I had imagined you of such a gentlemanly organization, that in any delicate dilemma a slight hint would suffice—in short, an assumption. But it appears I am deceived. Why," I added, unaffectedly starting, "you have not even touched that money yet," pointing to it, just where I had left it the evening previous.

He answered nothing.

"Will you, or will you not, quit me?" I now demanded in a sudden passion, advancing close to him.

"I would prefer *not* to quit you," he replied, gently emphasizing the *not*.

"What earthly right have you to stay here? Do you pay any rent? Do you pay my taxes? Or is this property yours?"

He answered nothing.

"Are you ready to go on and write now? Are your eyes recovered? Could you copy a small paper for me this morning? or help examine a few lines? or step round to the post office? In a word, will you do anything at all, to give a coloring to your refusal to depart the premises?"

He silently retired into his hermitage.

I was now in such a state of nervous resentment that I thought it but prudent to check myself at present from further demonstrations. Bartleby and I were alone. I remembered the tragedy of the unfortunate Adams and the still more unfortunate Colt in the solitary office of the latter; and how poor Colt, being dreadfully incensed by Adams, and imprudently permitting himself to get wildly excited, was at unawares hurried into his fatal act—an act which certainly no man could possibly deplore more than the actor himself. Often it had occurred to me in my pondering upon the subject, that had that altercation taken place in the public street, or at a private residence, it would not have terminated as it did. It was the circumstance of being alone in a solitary office, upstairs, of a building entirely unhallowed by humanizing domestic associations—an uncarpeted office, doubtless, of a dusty, haggard sort of appearance—this it must have been, which greatly helped to enhance the irritable desperation of the hapless Colt.

But when this old Adam of resentment rose in me and tempted me concerning Bartleby, I grappled him and threw him. How? Why, simply by recalling the divine injunction: "A new commandment give I unto you, that ye love one another." Yes, this it was that saved me. Aside from higher considerations, charity often operates as a vastly wise and prudent principle—a great safeguard to its possessor. Men have committed murder for jealousy's sake, and anger's sake, and hatred's sake, and selfishness' sake, and spiritual pride's sake; but no man that ever I heard of, ever committed a diabolical murder for sweet charity's sake. Mere self-interest, then, if no better motive can be enlisted, should, especially with high-tempered men, prompt all beings to charity and philanthropy. At any rate, upon the occasion in question, I strove to drown my exasperated feelings towards the scrivener by benevolently construing his conduct. Poor fellow, poor fellow! thought I, he doesn't mean anything; and besides, he has seen hard times, and ought to be indulged.

I endeavored also immediately to occupy myself, and at the same time to comfort my despondency. I tried to fancy that in the course of the morning, at such time as might prove agreeable to him, Bartleby, of his own free accord, would emerge from his hermitage, and take up some decided line of march in the direction of the door. But no. Half-past twelve o'clock came; Turkey began to glow in the face, overturn his inkstand, and become generally obstreperous; Nippers abated down into quietude and courtesy; Ginger Nut munched his noon apple; and Bartleby remained standing at his window in one of his profoundest deadwall reveries. Will it be credited? Ought I to acknowledge it? That afternoon I left the office without saying one further word to him.

Some days now passed, during which, at leisure intervals I looked a little into "Edwards on the Will," and "Priestley on Necessity." Under the circumstances, those books induced a salutary feeling. Gradually I slid into the persuasion that these troubles of mine touching the scrivener, had been all predestinated from eternity, and Bartleby was billeted upon me for some mysterious purpose of an all-wise Providence, which it was not for a mere mortal like me to fathom. Yes, Bartleby, stay there behind your screen, thought I; I shall persecute you no more; you are harmless and noiseless as any of these old chairs; in short, I never feel so private as when I know you are here. At last I see it, I feel it; I penetrate to the predestinated purpose of my life. I am content. Others may have loftier parts to enact; but my mission in this world, Bartleby, is to furnish you with office room for such period as you may see fit to remain.

I believe that this wise and blessed frame of mind would have continued with me, had it not been for the unsolicited and uncharitable remarks obtruded upon me by my professional friends who visited the rooms. But thus it often is, that the constant friction of illiberal minds wears out at last the best resolves of the more generous. Though to be sure, when I reflected upon it, it was not strange that people entering my office should be struck by the peculiar aspect of the unaccountable Bartleby, and so be tempted to throw out some sinister observations concerning him. Sometimes an attorney having business with me, and calling at my office, and finding no one but the scrivener there, would undertake to obtain some sort of precise information from him touching my whereabouts; but without heeding his idle talk, Bartleby would remain standing immovable in the middle of the room. So after contemplating him in that position for a time, the attorney would depart, no wiser than he came.

Also, when a reference was going on, and the room full of lawyers and witnesses and business was driving fast; some deeply occupied legal gentleman present, seeing Bartleby wholly unemployed, would request him to run round to his (the legal gentleman's) office and fetch some papers for him. Thereupon, Bartleby would tranquilly decline, and yet remain idle as before. Then the lawyer would give a great stare, and turn to me. And what could I say? At last I was made aware that all through the circle of my professional acquaintance, a whisper of wonder was running round, having reference to the strange creature I kept at my office. This worried me very much. And as the idea came upon me of his possibly turning out a long-lived man, and keep occupying my chambers, and denying my authority; and perplexing my visitors; and scandalizing my professional reputation; and casting a general gloom over the premises; keeping soul and body together to the last upon his savings (for doubtless he spent but half a dime a day), and in the end perhaps outlive me, and claim possession of my office by right of his perpetual occupancy: as all these dark anticipations crowded upon me more and more, and my friends continually intruded their relentless remarks upon the apparition in my room; a great change was wrought in me. I resolved to gather all my faculties together, and forever rid me of this intolerable incubus.

Ere revolving any complicated project, however, adapted to this end, I first simply suggested to Bartleby the propriety of his permanent departure. In a calm and serious tone, I commended the idea to his careful and mature consideration. But having taken three days to meditate upon it, he apprised me that his original determination remained the same; in short, that he still preferred to abide with me.

What shall I do? I now said to myself, buttoning up my coat to the last button. What shall I do? what ought I to do? what does conscience say I *should* do with this man, or rather ghost. Rid myself of him, I must; go, he shall. But how? You will not thrust him, the poor, pale, passive mortal—you will not thrust such a helpless creature out of your door? you will not dishonor yourself by such cruelty? No, I will not, I cannot do that. Rather would I let him live and die here, and then mason up his remains in the wall. What then will you do? For all your coaxing, he will not budge. Bribes he leaves under your own paperweight on your table; in short, it is quite plain that he prefers to cling to you.

Then something severe, something unusual must be done. What! surely you will not have him collared by a constable, and commit his innocent pallor to the common jail? And upon what ground could you procure such a thing to be done—a vagrant, is he? What! he a vagrant, a wanderer, who refuses to budge? It is because he will *not* be a vagrant, then, that you seek to count him *as* a vagrant. That is too absurd. No visible means of support; there I have him. Wrong again; for indubitably he *does* support himself, and that is the only unanswerable proof that any man can show of his possessing the means so to do. No more then. Since he will not quit me, I must quit him. I will change my offices; I will move elsewhere and give him fair notice that, if I find him on my new premises, I will then proceed against him as a common trespasser.

Acting accordingly, next day I thus addressed him: "I find these chambers too far from the City Hall; the air is unwholesome. In a word, I propose to remove my offices next week and shall no longer require your services. I tell you this now, in order that you may seek another place."

He made no reply, and nothing more was said.

On the appointed day I engaged carts and men, proceeded to my chambers, and, having but little furniture, everything was removed in a few hours. Throughout, the scrivener remained standing behind the screen, which I directed to be removed the last thing. It was withdrawn; and being folded up like a huge folio, left him the motionless occupant of a naked room. I stood in the entry watching him a moment, while something from within me upbraided me.

I reentered, with my hand in my pocket—and—and my heart in my mouth.

"Goodbye, Bartleby; I am going—goodbye, and God some way bless you; and take that," slipping something in his hand. But it dropped upon the floor, and then—strange to say—I tore myself from him whom I so longed to be rid of.

Established in my new quarters, for a day or two I kept the door locked, and started at every footfall in the passages. When I returned to my rooms after any little absence, I would pause at the threshold for an instant and attentively listen, ere applying my key. But these fears were needless. Bartleby never came nigh me.

I thought all was going well, when a perturbed looking stranger visited me, inquiring whether I was the person who had recently occupied rooms at No.—Wall Street.

Full of forebodings, I replied that I was.

"Then sir," said the stranger, who proved a lawyer, "you are responsible for the man you left there. He refuses to do any copying; he refuses to do anything; he says he prefers not to; and he refuses to quit the premises."

"I am very sorry, sir," said I, with assumed tranquillity, but an inward tremor, "but, really, the man you allude to is nothing to me—he is no relation or apprentice of mine, that you should hold me responsible for him."

"In mercy's name, who is he?"

"I certainly cannot inform you. I know nothing about him. Formerly I employed him as a copyist, but he has done nothing for me now for some time past."

"I shall settle him then—good morning, sir."

Several days passed, and I heard nothing more; and though I often felt a charitable prompting to call at the place and see poor Bartleby, yet a certain squeamishness of I know not what withheld me.

All is over with him by this time, thought I at last, when through another week no further intelligence reached me. But coming to my room the day after, I found several persons waiting at my door in a high state of nervous excitement.

"That's the man—here he comes," cried the foremost one, whom I recognized as the lawyer who had previously called upon me alone.

"You must take him away, sir, at once," cried a portly person among them, advancing upon me, and whom I knew to be the landlord at No.—Wall Street. "These gentlemen, my tenants, cannot stand it any longer; Mr. B——," pointing to the lawyer, "has turned him out of his room, and he now persists in haunting the building generally, sitting upon the banisters of the stairs by day, and sleeping in the entry by night. Everybody is concerned; clients are leaving the offices; some fears are entertained of a mob; something you must do, and that without delay."

Aghast at this torrent, I fell back before it, and would fain have locked myself in my new quarters. In vain I persisted that Bartleby was nothing to me—no more than to anyone else. In vain; I was the last person known to have anything to do with him, and they held me to the terrible account. Fearful then of being exposed in the papers (as one person present obscurely threatened) I considered the matter, and at length said that if the lawyer would give me a confidential interview with the scrivener, in his (the lawyer's) own room, I would that afternoon strive my best to rid them of the nuisance they complained of.

Going upstairs to my old haunt, there was Bartleby silently sitting upon the banister at the landing.

"What are you doing here, Bartleby?" said I.

"Sitting upon the banister," he mildly replied.

I motioned him into the lawyer's room, who then left us.

"Bartleby," said I, "are you aware that you are the cause of great tribulation to me, by persisting in occupying the entry after being dismissed from the office?"

No answer.

"Now one of two things must take place. Either you must do something, or something must be done to you. Now what sort of business would you like to engage in? Would you like to reengage in copying for someone?"

"No; I would prefer not to make any change."

"Would you like a clerkship in a drygoods store?"

"There is too much confinement about that. No, I would not like a clerkship; but I am not particular."

"Too much confinement," I cried, "why, you keep yourself confined all the time!"

"I would prefer not to take a clerkship," he rejoined, as if to settle that little item at once.

"How would a bartender's business suit you? There is no trying of the eyesight in that."

"I would not like it at all; though, as I said before, I am not particular."

His unwonted wordiness inspirited me. I returned to the charge.

"Well then, would you like to travel through the country collecting bills for the merchants? That would improve your health."

"No, I would prefer to be doing something else."

"How then would going as a companion to Europe, to entertain some young gentleman with your conversation. How would that suit you?"

"Not at all. It does not strike me that there is anything definite about that. I like to be stationary. But I am not particular."

"Stationary you shall be then," I cried, now losing all patience, and, for the first time in all my exasperating connection with him fairly flying into a passion. "If you do not go away from these premises before night, I shall feel bound—indeed, I *am* bound—to—to—to quit the premises myself!" I rather absurdly concluded, knowing not with what possible threat to try to frighten his immobility into compliance. Despairing of all further efforts, I was precipitately leaving him when a final thought occurred to me—one which had not been wholly unindulged before.

"Bartleby," said I, in the kindest tone I could assume under such exciting circumstances, "will you go home with me now—not to my office, but my dwelling—and remain there till we can conclude upon some convenient arrangement for you at our leisure? Come, let us start now, right away."

"No; at present I would prefer not to make any change at all."

I answered nothing; but effectually dodging everyone by the suddenness and rapidity of my flight, rushed from the building, ran up Wall Street towards Broadway, and jumping into the first omnibus was soon removed from pursuit. As soon as tranquillity returned I distinctly perceived that I had now done all that I possibly could, both in respect to the demands of the landlord and his tenants, and with regard to my own desire and sense of duty, to benefit Bartleby, and shield him from rude persecution. I now strove to be entirely carefree and quiescent; and my conscience justified me in the attempt; though indeed it was not so successful as I could have wished. So fearful was I of being again hunted out by the incensed landlord and his exasperated tenants that, surrendering my business to Nippers for a few days, I drove about the upper part of the town and through the suburbs in my rockaway; crossed over to Jersey City and Hoboken, and paid fugitive visits to Manhattanville and Astoria. In fact, I almost lived in my rockaway for the time.

When again I entered my office, lo, a note from the landlord lay upon the desk. I opened it with trembling hands. It informed me that the writer had sent to the police, and had Bartleby removed to the Tombs as a vagrant. Moreover, since I knew more about him than anyone else, he wished me to appear at that place, and make a suitable statement of the facts. These tidings had a conflicting effect upon me. At first I was indignant, but at last almost approved. The landlord's energetic, summary disposition, had led him to adopt a procedure which I do not think I would have decided upon myself; and yet as a last resort, under such peculiar circumstances, it seemed the only plan.

As I afterwards learned, the poor scrivener, when told that he must be conducted to the Tombs, offered not the slightest obstacle, but in his pale, unmoving way, silently acquiesced.

Some of the compassionate and curious bystanders joined the party; and headed by one of the constables arm in arm with Bartleby, the silent procession filed its way through all the noise, and heat, and joy of the roaring thoroughfares at noon.

The same day I received the note I went to the Tombs, or to speak more properly, the Halls of Justice. Seeking the right officer, I stated the purpose of my call, and was informed that the individual I described was indeed within. I then assured the functionary that Bartleby was a perfectly honest man, and greatly to be compassionated, however unaccountably eccentric. I narrated all I knew, and closed by suggesting the idea of letting him remain in as indulgent confinement as possible till something less harsh might be done—though indeed I hardly knew what. At all events, if nothing else could be decided upon, the almshouse must receive him. I then begged to have an interview.

Being under no disgraceful charge, and quite serene and harmless in all his ways, they had permitted him freely to wander about the prison, and especially in the enclosed grass-platted yards thereof. And so I found him there, standing all alone in the quietest of the yards, his face towards a high wall, while all around, from the narrow slits of the jail windows, I thought I saw peering out upon him the eyes of murderers and thieves.

"Bartleby!"

"I know you," he said, without looking round, "and I want nothing to say to you."

"It was not I that brought you here, Bartleby," said I, keenly pained at his implied suspicion. "And to you, this should not be so vile a place. Nothing reproachful attaches to you by being here. And see, it is not so sad a place as one might think. Look, there is the sky, and here is the grass."

"I know where I am," he replied, but would say nothing more, and so I left him.

As I entered the corridor again, a broad meat-like man, in an apron accosted me, and, jerking his thumb over his shoulder said—"Is that your friend?"

"Yes."

"Does he want to starve? If he does, let him live on the prison fare, that's all."

"Who are you?" asked I, not knowing what to make of such an unofficially speaking person in such a place.

"I am the grubman. Such gentlemen as have friends here, hire me to provide them with something good to eat."

"Is this so?" said I, turning to the turnkey. He said it was.

"Well then," said I, slipping some silver into the grubman's hands (for so they called him), "I want you to give particular attention to my friend there; let him have the best dinner you can get. And you must be as polite to him as possible."

"Introduce me, will you?" said the grubman, looking at me with an expression which seemed to say he was all impatience for an opportunity to give a specimen of his breeding.

Thinking it would prove of benefit to the scrivener, I acquiesced; and asking the grubman his name, went up with him to Bartleby.

"Bartleby, this is Mr. Cutlets; you will find him very useful to you."

"Your sarvant, sir, your sarvant," said the grubman, making a low salutation behind his apron. "Hope you find it pleasant here, sir—spacious grounds—cool apartments, sir—hope you'll stay with us some time—try to make it agreeable. May Mrs. Cutlets and I have the pleasure of your company to dinner, sir, in Mrs. Cutlets' private room?"

"I prefer not to dine today," said Bartleby, turning away. "It would disagree with me; I am unused to dinners." So saying he slowly moved to the other side of the enclosure, and took up a position fronting the deadwall.

"How's this?" said the grubman, addressing me with a stare of astonishment. "He's odd, ain't he?"

"I think he is a little deranged," said I, sadly.

"Deranged? deranged is it? Well, now, upon my word, I thought that friend of yourn was a gentleman forger; they are always pale and genteel-like, them forgers. I can't help pity 'em—can't help it, sir. Did you know Monroe Edwards?" he added, touchingly, and paused. Then, laying his hand piteously on my shoulder, sighed, "he died of consumption at Sing-Sing. So you weren't acquainted with Monroe?"

"No, I was never socially acquainted with any forgers. But I cannot stop longer. Look to my friend yonder. You will not lose by it. I will see you again."

Some few days after this, I again obtained admission to the Tombs, and went through the corridors in quest of Bartleby, but without finding him.

"I saw him coming from his cell not long ago," said a turnkey, "may be he's gone to loiter in the yards."

So I went in that direction.

"Are you looking for the silent man?" said another turnkey, passing me. "Yonder he lies —sleeping in the yard there. 'Tis not twenty minutes since I saw him lie down."

The yard was entirely quiet. It was not accessible to the common prisoners. The surrounding walls, of amazing thickness, kept off all sounds behind them. The Egyptian character of the masonry weighed upon me with its gloom. But a soft imprisoned turf grew under foot. The heart of the eternal pyramids, it seemed, wherein, by some strange magic, through the clefts, grass seed, dropped by birds, had sprung.

Strangely huddled at the base of the wall, his knees drawn up, and lying on his side, his head touching the cold stones, I saw the wasted Bartleby. But nothing stirred. I paused; then went close up to him; stooped over, and saw that his dim eyes were open; otherwise he seemed profoundly sleeping. Something prompted me to touch him. I felt his hand, when a tingling shiver ran up my arm and down my spine to my feet.

The round face of the grubman peered upon me now. "His dinner is ready. Won't he dine today, either? Or does he live without dining?"

"Lives without dining," said I, and closed the eyes.

"Eh! He's asleep, ain't he?"

"With kings and counselors," murmured I.

There would seem little need for proceeding further in this history. Imagination will readily supply the meager recital of poor Bartleby's interment. But ere parting with the reader, let me say that if this little narrative has sufficiently interested him to awaken curiosity as to who Bartleby was, and what manner of life he led prior to the present narrator's making his acquaintance, I can only reply, that in such curiosity I fully share, but am wholly unable to gratify it. Yet here I hardly know whether I should divulge one little item of rumor, which came to my ear a few months after the scrivener's decease. Upon what basis it rested, I could never ascertain; and hence, how true it is I cannot now tell. But inasmuch as this vague report has not been without a certain suggestive interest to me, however sad, it may prove the same with some others; and so I will briefly mention it. The report was this: that Bartleby had been a subordinate clerk in the Dead Letter Office[12] at Washington, from which he had been suddenly removed by a change in the administration. When I think over this rumor, I cannot adequately express the emotions which seize me. Dead letters! Does it not sound like dead men? Conceive a man by nature and misfortune prone to a pallid hopelessness, can any business seem more fitted to heighten it than that of continually handling these dead letters, and assorting them for the flames? For by the cartload they are annually burned. Sometimes from out the folded paper the pale clerk takes a ring—the finger it was meant for, perhaps, moulders in the grave; a bank note sent in swiftest charity—he whom it would relieve, nor eats nor hungers any more; pardon for those who died despairing; hope for those who died unhoping; good tidings for those who died stifled by unrelieved calamities. On errands of life, these letters speed to death.

Ah, Bartleby! Ah, humanity!

---

12. **Dead Letter Office:** the office to which letters that are undeliverable and unreturnable are sent.

Getting at Meaning

1. Describe the narrator of the story. What sort of law work does he do? What is his philosophy of life? Explain his statement, "All who know me, consider me an eminently *safe* man."

2. Describe Turkey the copyist. Why does the quality of his work decline after lunch? Why do you suppose he is called Turkey? Why doesn't the narrator fire Turkey?

3. What does the word *Nippers* bring to mind? Explain how the nickname fits the narrator's second copyist. What does the narrator mean when he says of his copyists, "Their fits relieved each other like guards. When Nippers' was on, Turkey's was off; and *vice versa*"?

4. How did Ginger Nut get his nickname? What is his function in the law office?

5. What are the duties of a scrivener? What are the narrator's first impressions of Bartleby, the scrivener?

6. When does Bartleby first say "I would prefer not to"? Is it clear why he does not care to proofread his copy? How do the other copyists react?

7. Explain the narrator's statement, "Nothing so aggravates an earnest person as a passive resistance." Why does the narrator put up with Bartleby?

8. Why is the narrator so shocked to discover that Bartleby lives in the law offices? What does he mean when he says, "Both I and Bartleby were sons of Adam"? Explain the narrator's statement, "To a sensitive being, pity is not seldom pain. And when at last it is perceived that such pity cannot lead to effectual succor, common sense bids the soul be rid of it."

9. Why do you suppose Bartleby will tell the narrator nothing of his background? How does the narrator react to Bartleby's eye problem? Why does the narrator eventually give Bartleby notice?

10. How does the narrator justify keeping Bartleby on, even after Bartleby has refused to do work of any kind in the office? Explain the narrator's statement, "Here I can cheaply purchase a delicious self-approval."

11. What reasons does the narrator give for moving his law offices? Why is he really moving his offices? Why doesn't moving work?

12. What are the various offers the narrator makes to Bartleby when he goes back to his old offices to retrieve the scrivener? What is Bartleby's objection to each suggestion?

13. What leads the narrator to visit Bartleby at the Tombs? Explain his final attempt to help Bartleby. Why does Bartleby say to the narrator, "I know you, and I want nothing to say to you"?

14. What causes Bartleby's death? Explain the narrator's statement that Bartleby sleeps with "kings and counselors." Why does the narrator find it significant that Bartleby was apparently a clerk in the Dead Letter Office?

Developing Skills in Reading Literature

1. **Character.** To describe Bartleby, the narrator uses words such as *pale*, *neat*, *respectable*, *forlorn*, *hopeless*, and *silent*. What impression do these words convey? As Bartleby's use of the expression "I would prefer not to" becomes more frequent, the reader senses that Bartleby's condition is becoming more desperate. When Bartleby says "I would prefer not to," what does he really mean? What is the final thing he would prefer not to do? What is Bartleby really turning his back on?

2. **Symbol.** When the narrator installs Bartleby in his office, he installs Bartleby's desk facing a wall. Then the narrator says, "Still further to a satisfactory arrangement, I procured a high green folding screen, which might entirely isolate Bartleby from my sight, though not remove him from my voice." The screen is a powerful symbol in the story. What does it represent?

Another symbol in the narrative is the debtor's prison to which Bartleby is removed. What is the significance of the prison's name, the Tombs? In what sense is Bartleby already in prison, long before he gets to the Tombs?

3. **Allusion and Figurative Language.** Melville often combines allusions with similes or metaphors. The result is powerful descriptive language. Explain the following allusion-comparisons from the story:

> Think of it. Of a Sunday, Wall Street is deserted as Petra; and every night of every day it is an emptiness.

And here Bartleby makes his home; sole spectator of a solitude which he has seen all populous—a sort of innocent and transformed Marius brooding among the ruins of Carthage!

Find in the story additional examples of allusions that are combined with figurative language.

4. **Irony.** A number of occurrences in this story are ironic, or unexpected. What is humorously ironic in the way that the narrator and the other copyists begin to use Bartleby's word *prefer*? What is ironic in the narrator's response to Bartleby? What is ironic about Bartleby's removal to prison?

5. **Parallelism.** Identify the parallel elements in each of the following sentences from the story:

I can see the figure now—pallidly neat, pitiably respectable, incurably forlorn!

Sometimes from out the folded paper the pale clerk takes a ring—the finger it was meant for, perhaps, moulders in the grave; a bank note sent in swiftest charity—he whom it would relieve, nor eats nor hungers any more; pardon for those who died despairing; hope for those who died unhoping; good tidings for those who died stifled by unrelieved calamities.

How do the parallel constructions enhance the power of the language?

6. **Theme.** Nathaniel Hawthorne, who was an important influence on Herman Melville, wrote about the human being isolated in "that saddest of all prisons, his own heart." Apply Hawthorne's idea to Melville's story. What view of human beings and society emerges from this story? What does the narrator mean by his final statement, "Ah, Bartleby! Ah, humanity!"

Developing Vocabulary

Formal Diction: Adverbs. Melville, like Hawthorne and other nineteenth-century writers, uses an extensive vocabulary. Some of his adverbs, now generally used more formally than they were in the nineteenth century, may not be familiar to you.

Look up each adverb that follows and record its meaning. Then give a less formal synonym for each word.

cadaverously	pallidly
deferentially	precipitately
eminently	proverbially
ignominiously	steadfastly
indubitably	tranquilly

Developing Writing Skills

1. **Analyzing a Character.** The narrator of "Bartleby, the Scrivener" puts up with his copyists' peculiarities. He also does more for Bartleby than most people would. Few others would go to the extent of moving their law offices rather than call the police. Few others would visit Bartleby at the Tombs. Why does the narrator do these things? What kind of man is he?

Write a five-paragraph composition in which you analyze the narrator's character. Refer to specific passages in the text to support your ideas. You may wish to devote some attention to the narrator's statement, "I am a man who, from his youth upwards, has been filled with a profound conviction that the easiest way of life is the best."

2. **Analyzing Theme.** The narrator of Melville's story says, ". . . happiness courts the light, so we deem the world is gay; but misery hides aloof, so we deem that misery there is none." He also says of Bartleby, "I might give alms to his body, but his body did not pain him; it was his soul that suffered, and his soul I could not reach."

Using the narrator's statements as a springboard, write a five-paragraph composition in which you discuss the message about human suffering expressed in "Bartleby, the Scrivener." What does the story imply about communication? about isolation? Refer to specific statements and events in the text to support your points.

Edgar Allan Poe

1809–1849

"That great literary engineer" is what the French poet Paul Valéry called Edgar Allan Poe. Certainly Poe stands out as one of the most versatile of American literary geniuses. Along with Hawthorne, Poe is credited with fathering the short story form. The modern detective story has its origins in Poe's work as do those stories that explore the mysterious, frightening depths of human consciousness. Poe was probably the most accomplished American poet before Walt Whitman and Poe's essays on the art of writing made an important contribution to critical theories about literature.

Poe's life was for the most part difficult and insecure. His parents were traveling actors, and by the time the boy Edgar was two, his father had deserted the family and his mother had died in poverty in Richmond, Virginia. Two gentlewomen had befriended Poe's mother in her final illness. One took Poe's baby sister home to live with her; the other, Mrs. Allan, took Edgar home. She and her husband John Allan, a Richmond businessman, decided to raise Poe as their son and heir and gave him the middle name of Allan. They did not formally adopt Poe, perhaps because adoption was rare in those days.

Poe's childhood with the Allans was somewhat troubled. Mrs. Allan was warm and affectionate, but John Allan was difficult and demanding. Although Poe was an excellent student, he never received praise from Allan. At one point the Allans spent five years in England, where Poe attended good schools. His love for literature dates from this period, and it was at this time that he began to write poetry.

Poe attended the University of Virginia for one year. Unfortunately he had to withdraw from the university because of money squabbles with John Allan. Allan did not give Poe enough money to live on, which drove Poe to gambling. In an attempt to please Allan, Poe served for two years in the military, leaving to take an appointment at West Point. During these years he and Allan alternately fought and made peace with one another. Eventually, when Mrs. Allan died, the relationship fell apart completely. Poe was sadly scarred by it all, later writing, "The want of parental affection has been the heaviest of my trials."

Poe determined to earn his living as a writer. He had already published several small volumes of poetry and he wanted to write stories. The owners of a respected magazine, the *Southern Literary Messenger*, offered Poe a job, and in 1835 he became the magazine's editor. This was the first of several journalistic jobs Poe held during his life. Although he was a brilliant and dedicated editor, he was somewhat difficult to work with and he was prone to quarrels with contributors and staff alike.

As has been the case with so many artistic geniuses, Poe was not adequately appreciated in his own time. Many of his contemporaries criticized him as morbid and excessive. Yet Poe's brooding Romanticism, his probing of the irrational, dark forces that underlie the rational surface in humans appealed to later writers, especially in France. The French symbolist poets of the late nineteenth century, such as Charles Baudelaire, Stéphane Mallarmé, and Paul Valéry, hailed Poe as a great writer. Many twentieth-century critics agree, explaining that Poe went a long way toward defining literary forms and breaking down psychological barriers in literature. In his deep exploration of the human psyche, Poe anticipated many of the fears and dilemmas of twentieth-century Americans.

The Pit and the Pendulum

I was sick—sick unto death with that long agony; and when they at length unbound me, and I was permitted to sit, I felt that my senses were leaving me. The sentence—the dread sentence of death—was the last of distinct accentuation which reached my ears. After that, the sound of the inquisitorial voices seemed merged in one dreamy indeterminate hum. It conveyed to my soul the idea of *revolution*—perhaps from its association in fancy with the burr of a mill wheel. This only for a brief period; for presently I heard no more. Yet, for a while, I saw; but with how terrible an exaggeration! I saw the lips of the black-robed judges. They appeared to me white—whiter than the sheet upon which I trace these words—and thin even to grotesqueness; thin with the intensity of their expression of firmness—of immoveable resolution—of stern contempt of human torture. I saw that the decrees of what to me was Fate were still issuing from those lips. I saw them writhe with a deadly locution. I saw them fashion the syllables of my name; and I shuddered because no sound succeeded. I saw, too, for a few moments of delirious horror, the soft and nearly imperceptible waving of the sable draperies which enwrapped the walls of the apartment. And then my vision fell upon the seven tall candles upon the table. At first they wore the aspect of charity, and seemed white slender angels who would save me; but then, all at once, there came a most deadly nausea over my spirit, and I felt every fiber in my frame thrill as if I had touched the wire of a galvanic battery, while the angel forms became meaningless specters, with heads of flame, and I saw that from them there would be no help. And then there stole into my fancy, like a rich musical note, the thought of what sweet rest there must be in the grave. The thought came gently and stealthily, and it seemed long before it attained full appreciation; but just as my spirit came at length properly to feel and entertain it, the figures of the judges vanished, as if magically, from before me; the tall candles sank into nothingness; their flames went out utterly; the blackness of darkness supervened; all sensations appeared swallowed up in a mad rushing descent as of the soul into Hades.[1] Then silence, and stillness, and night were the universe.

I had swooned; but still will not say that all of consciousness was lost. What of it there remained I will not attempt to define, or even to describe; yet all was not lost. In the deepest slumber—no! In delirium—no! In a swoon—no! In death—no! even in the grave all *is not* lost. Else there is no immortality for man. Arousing from the most profound of slumbers, we break the gossamer web of *some* dream. Yet in a second afterward (so frail may that web have been), we remember not that we have dreamed. In the return to life from the swoon there are two stages; first, that of the sense of mental or spiritual; secondly, that of the sense of physical, existence. It seems probable that if, upon reaching the second stage, we could recall the impressions of the first, we should find these impressions eloquent in memories of the gulf beyond. And that gulf is—what? How at least shall we distinguish its shadows from those of the tomb? But if the impressions of what I have

---

1. **Hades** (hād' ēz): the underground abode of the dead in Greek mythology.

termed the first stage, are not, at will, recalled, yet, after long interval, do they not come unbidden, while we marvel whence they come? He who has never swooned is not he who finds strange palaces and wildly familiar faces in coals that glow; is not he who beholds floating in mid-air the sad visions that the many may not view; is not he who ponders over the perfume of some novel flower—is not he whose brain grows bewildered with the meaning of some musical cadence which has never before arrested his attention.

Amid frequent and thoughtful endeavors to remember; amid earnest struggles to regather some token of the state of seeming nothingness into which my soul had lapsed, there have been moments when I have dreamed of success; there have been brief, very brief periods when I have conjured up remembrances which the lucid reason of a later epoch assures me could have had reference only to that condition of seeming unconsciousness. These shadows of memory tell, indistinctly, of tall figures that lifted and bore me in silence down—down—still down—till a hideous dizziness oppressed me at the mere idea of the interminableness of the descent. They tell also of a vague horror at my heart, on account of that heart's unnatural stillness. Then comes a sense of sudden motionlessness throughout all things; as if those who bore me (a ghastly train!) had outrun, in their descent, the limits of the limitless, and paused from the wearisomeness of their toil. After this I call to mind flatness and dampness; and then all is *madness*—the madness of a memory which busies itself among forbidden things.

Very suddenly there came back to my soul motion and sound—the tumultuous motion of the heart, and, in my ears, the sound of its beating. Then a pause in which all is blank. Then again sound, and motion, and touch—a tingling sensation pervading my frame. Then the mere consciousness of existence, without thought—a condition which lasted long.

Then, very suddenly, *thought*, and shuddering terror, and earnest endeavor to comprehend my true state. Then a strong desire to lapse into insensibility. Then a rushing revival of soul and a successful effort to move. And now a full memory of the trial, of the judges, of the sable draperies, of the sentence, of the sickness, of the swoon. Then entire forgetfulness of all that followed; of all that a later day and much earnestness of endeavor have enabled me vaguely to recall.

So far, I had not opened my eyes. I felt that I lay upon my back, unbound. I reached out my hand, and it fell heavily upon something damp and hard. There I suffered it to remain for many minutes, while I strove to imagine where and *what* I could be. I longed, yet dared not to employ my vision. I dreaded the first glance at objects around me. It was not that I feared to look upon things horrible, but that I grew aghast lest there should be *nothing* to see. At length, with a wild desperation at heart, I quickly unclosed my eyes. My worst thoughts, then, were confirmed. The blackness of eternal night encompassed me. I struggled for breath. The intensity of the darkness seemed to oppress and stifle me. The atmosphere was intolerably close. I still lay quietly, and made effort to exercise my reason. I brought to mind the inquisitorial proceedings, and attempted from that point to deduce my real condition. The sentence had passed; and it appeared to me that a very long interval of time had since elapsed. Yet not for a moment did I suppose myself actually dead. Such a supposition, notwithstanding what we read in fiction, is altogether inconsistent with real existence;—but where and in what state was I? The condemned to death, I knew, perished usually at the autos-da-fé,[2] and one of these

---

2. **autos-da-fé** (aut' ōz də fä'): plural of *auto-da-fé*; the ceremony accompanying the pronouncement of judgment by the Inquisition and followed by the execution of sentence by the secular authorities; broadly, the burning of a heretic.

had been held on the very night of the day of my trial. Had I been remanded to my dungeon, to await the next sacrifice, which would not take place for many months? This I at once saw could not be. Victims had been in immediate demand. Moreover, my dungeon, as well as all the condemned cells at Toledo,[3] had stone floors, and light was not altogether excluded.

A fearful idea now suddenly drove the blood in torrents upon my heart, and for a brief period, I once more relapsed into insensibility. Upon recovering, I at once started to my feet, trembling convulsively in every fiber. I thrust my arms wildly above and around me in all directions. I felt nothing; yet dreaded to move a step, lest I should be impeded by the walls of a *tomb*. Perspiration burst from every pore, and stood in cold big beads upon my forehead. The agony of suspense grew at length intolerable, and I cautiously moved forward, with my arms extended, and my eyes straining from their sockets, in the hope of catching some faint ray of light. I proceeded for many paces; but still all was blackness and vacancy. I breathed more freely. It seemed evident that mine was not, at least, the most hideous of fates.

And now, as I still continued to step cautiously onward, there came thronging upon my recollection, a thousand vague rumors of the horrors of Toledo. Of the dungeons there had been strange things narrated—fables I had always deemed them—but yet strange, and too ghastly to repeat, save in a whisper. Was I left to perish of starvation in this subterranean world of darkness; or what fate, perhaps even more fearful, awaited me? That the result would be death, and a death of more than customary bitterness, I knew too well the character of my judges to doubt. The mode and the hour were all that occupied or distracted me.

My outstretched hands at length encountered some solid obstruction. It was a wall, seemingly of stone masonry—very smooth, slimy, and cold. I followed it up; stepping with all the careful distrust with which certain antique narratives had inspired me. This process, however, afforded me no means of ascertaining the dimensions of my dungeon; as I might make its circuit, and return to the point whence I set out, without being aware of the fact; so perfectly uniform seemed the wall. I therefore sought the knife which had been in my pocket, when led into the inquisitorial chamber; but it was gone; my clothes had been exchanged for a wrapper of coarse serge. I had thought of forcing the blade in some minute crevice of the masonry, so as to identify my point of departure. The difficulty, nevertheless, was but trivial; although, in the disorder of my fancy, it seemed at first insuperable. I tore a part of the hem from the robe and placed the fragment at full length, and at right angles to the wall. In groping my way around the prison, I could not fail to encounter this rag upon completing the circuit. So, at least I thought; but I had not counted upon the extent of the dungeon, or upon my own weakness. The ground was moist and slippery. I staggered onward for some time, when I stumbled and fell. My excessive fatigue induced me to remain prostrate; and sleep soon overtook me as I lay.

Upon awaking, and stretching forth an arm, I found beside me a loaf and a pitcher with water. I was too much exhausted to reflect upon this circumstance, but ate and drank with avidity. Shortly afterward, I resumed my tour around the prison, and with much toil, came at last upon the fragment of the serge. Up to the period when I fell I had counted fifty-two paces, and upon resuming my walk, I had counted forty-eight more;—when I arrived at the rag. There were in all, then, a hundred paces; and, admitting two paces to the yard, I presumed the dungeon to be fifty yards in circuit. I had met, however, with many angles in the wall, and thus I could

---

3. **Toledo** (tə lē′ dō): a city in central Spain.

form no guess at the shape of the vault; for vault I could not help supposing it to be.

I had little object—certainly no hope—in these researches; but a vague curiosity prompted me to continue them. Quitting the wall, I resolved to cross the area of the enclosure. At first I proceeded with extreme caution, for the floor, although seemingly of solid material, was treacherous with slime. At length, however, I took courage, and did not hesitate to step firmly; endeavoring to cross in as direct a line as possible. I had advanced some ten or twelve paces in this manner, when the remnant of the torn hem of my robe became entangled between my legs. I stepped on it, and fell violently on my face.

In the confusion attending my fall, I did not immediately apprehend a somewhat startling circumstance, which yet, in a few seconds afterward, and while I still lay prostrate, arrested my attention. It was this—my chin rested upon the floor of the prison, but my lips and the upper portion of my head, although seemingly at a less elevation than the chin, touched nothing. At the same time my forehead seemed bathed in a clammy vapor, and the peculiar smell of decayed fungus arose to my nostrils. I put forward my arm, and shuddered to find that I had fallen at the very brink`of a circular pit, whose extent, of course, I had no means of ascertaining at the moment. Groping about the masonry just below the margin, I succeeded in dislodging a small fragment, and let it fall into the abyss. For many seconds I hearkened to its reverberations as it dashed against the sides of the chasm in its descent; at length there was a sullen plunge into water, succeeded by loud echoes. At the same moment there came a sound resembling the quick opening, and as rapid closing of a door overhead, while a faint gleam of light flashed suddenly through the gloom, and as suddenly faded away.

I saw clearly the doom which had been prepared for me, and congratulated myself upon the timely accident by which I had escaped. Another step before my fall, and the world had seen me no more. And the death just avoided, was of that very character which I had regarded as fabulous and frivolous in the tales respecting the Inquisition.[4] To the victims of its tyranny, there was the choice of death with its direst physical agonies, or death with its most hideous moral horrors. I had been reserved for the latter. By long suffering my nerves had been unstrung, until I trembled at the sound of my own voice, and had become in every respect a fitting subject for the species of torture which awaited me.

Shaking in every limb, I groped my way back to the wall; resolving there to perish rather than risk the terrors of the wells, of which my imagination now pictured many in various positions about the dungeon. In other conditions of mind I might have had courage to end my misery at once by a plunge into one of these abysses; but now I was the veriest of cowards. Neither could I forget what I had read of these pits—that the *sudden* extinction of life formed no part of their most horrible plan.

Agitation of spirit kept me awake for many long hours; but at length I again slumbered. Upon arousing, I found by my side, as before, a loaf and a pitcher of water. A burning thirst consumed me, and I emptied the vessel at a draught. It must have been drugged; for scarcely had I drunk, before I became irresistibly drowsy. A deep sleep fell upon me—a sleep like that of death. How long it lasted of course, I know not; but when, once again, I unclosed my eyes, the objects around me were visible. By a wild sulphurous luster, the origin of which I could not at first determine, I was enabled to see the extent and aspect of the prison.

In its size I had been greatly mistaken. The whole circuit of its walls did not exceed

---

4. **Inquisition** (in′ kwə zish′ ən): a former Roman Catholic tribunal for the discovery and punishment of heresy. It was instituted in Spain in 1480.

twenty-five yards. For some minutes this fact occasioned me a world of vain trouble; vain indeed! for what could be of less importance, under the terrible circumstances which environed me, than the mere dimensions of my dungeon? But my soul took a wild interest in trifles, and I busied myself in endeavors to account for the error I had committed in my measurement. The truth at length flashed upon me. In my first attempt at exploration I had counted fifty-two paces, up to the period when I fell; I must then have been within a pace or two of the fragment of serge; in fact, I had nearly performed the circuit of the vault. I then slept, and upon awaking, I must have returned upon my steps—thus supposing the circuit nearly double what it actually was. My confusion of mind prevented me from observing that I began my tour with the wall to the left; and ended it with the wall to the right.

I had been deceived, too, in respect to the shape of the enclosure. In feeling my way I had found many angles, and thus deduced an idea of great irregularity; so potent is the effect of total darkness upon one arousing from lethargy or sleep! The angles were simply those of a few slight depressions, or niches, at odd intervals. The general shape of the prison was square. What I had taken for masonry seemed now to be iron, or some other metal, in huge plates, whose sutures or joints occasioned the depression. The entire surface of this metallic enclosure was rudely daubed in all the hideous and repulsive devices to which the charnel[5] superstition of the monks has given rise. The figures of fiends in aspects of menace, with skeleton forms, and other more really fearful images, overspread and disfigured the walls. I observed that the outlines of these monstrosities were sufficiently distinct, but that the colors seemed faded and blurred, as if from the effects of a damp atmosphere. I now noticed the floor, too, which was of stone. In the center yawned the circular pit from whose jaws I had escaped; but it was the only one in the dungeon.

All this I saw indistinctly and by much effort: for my personal condition had been greatly changed during slumber. I now lay upon my back, and at full length, on a species of low framework of wood. To this I was securely bound by a long strap resembling a surcingle.[6] It passed in many convolutions about my limbs and body, leaving at liberty only my head, and my left arm to such extent that I could, by dint of much exertion, supply myself with food from an earthen dish which lay by my side on the floor. I saw, to my horror, that the pitcher had been removed. I say to my horror, for I was consumed with intolerable thirst. This thirst it appeared to be the design of my persecutors to stimulate, for the food in the dish was meat pungently seasoned.

Looking upward, I surveyed the ceiling of my prison. It was some thirty or forty feet overhead, and constructed much as the side walls. In one of its panels a very singular figure riveted my whole attention. It was the painted figure of Time as he is commonly represented, save that, in lieu of a scythe, he held what, at a casual glance, I supposed to be the pictured image of a huge pendulum such as we see on antique clocks. There was something, however, in the appearance of this machine which caused me to regard it more attentively. While I gazed directly upward at it (for its position was immediately over my own) I fancied that I saw it in motion. In an instant afterward the fancy was confirmed. Its sweep was brief, and of course slow. I watched it for some minutes, somewhat in fear, but more in wonder. Wearied at length with observing its dull movement, I turned my eyes upon the other objects in the cell.

A slight noise attracted my notice, and, looking to the floor, I saw several enormous

---

5. **charnel** (chär' n'l): a building or chamber in which bodies or bones are deposited.
6. **surcingle** (sər' sin' gəl): a belt, band, or girth passing around the body of a horse to bind the saddle or pack fast to the horse's back.

rats traversing it. They had issued from the well, which lay just within view to my right. Even then, while I gazed, they came up in troops, hurriedly, with ravenous eyes, allured by the scent of the meat. From this it required much effort and attention to scare them away.

It might have been half an hour, perhaps even an hour (for I could take but imperfect note of time), before I again cast my eyes upward. What I then saw confounded and amazed me. The sweep of the pendulum had increased in extent by nearly a yard. As a natural consequence, its velocity was also much greater. But what mainly disturbed me was the idea that it had perceptibly *descended*. I now observed—with what horror it is needless to say—that its nether extremity was formed of a crescent of glittering steel, about a foot in length from horn to horn; the horns upward, and the under edge evidently as keen as that of a razor. Like a razor also, it seemed massy and heavy, tapering from the edge into a solid and broad structure above. It was appended to a weighty rod of brass, and the whole *hissed* as it swung through the air.

I could no longer doubt the doom prepared for me by monkish ingenuity in torture. My cognizance of the pit had become known to the inquisitorial agents—*the pit*, whose horrors had been destined for so bold a recusant[7] as myself—*the pit*, typical of hell, and regarded by rumor as the Ultima Thule[8] of all their punishments. The plunge into this pit I had avoided by the merest of accidents, and I knew that surprise, or entrapment into torment, formed an important portion of all the grotesquerie of these dungeon deaths. Having failed to fall, it was no part of the demon plan to hurl me into the abyss; and thus (there being no alternative) a different and a milder destruction awaited me. Milder! I half smiled in my agony as I thought of such application of such a term.

What boots it to tell of the long, long hours of horror more than mortal, during which I counted the rushing vibrations of the steel!

Inch by inch—line by line—with a descent only appreciable at intervals that seemed ages—down and still down it came! Days passed—it might have been that many days passed—ere it swept so closely over me as to fan me with its acrid breath. The odor of the sharp steel forced itself into my nostrils. I prayed—I wearied heaven with my prayer for its more speedy descent. I grew frantically mad, and struggled to force myself upward against the sweep of the fearful scimitar. And then I fell suddenly calm, and lay smiling at the glittering death, as a child at some rare bauble.

There was another interval of utter insensibility; it was brief; for, upon again lapsing into life there had been no perceptible descent in the pendulum. But it might have been long; for I knew there were demons who took note of my swoon, and who could have arrested the vibration at pleasure. Upon my recovery, too, I felt very—oh, inexpressibly sick and weak, as if through long inanition. Even amid the agonies of that period, the human nature craved food. With painful effort I outstretched my left arm as far as my bonds permitted, and took possession of the small remnant which had been spared me by the rats. As I put a portion of it within my lips, there rushed to my mind a half-formed thought of joy—of hope? Yet what business had I with hope? It was, as I say, a half-formed thought—man has many such which are never completed. I felt that it was of joy—of hope; but I felt also that it had perished in its formation. In vain I struggled to perfect—to regain it. Long suffering had nearly annihilated all my ordinary powers of mind. I was an imbecile—an idiot.

The vibration of the pendulum was at right angles to my length. I saw that the crescent was designed to cross the region of the heart. It would fray the serge of my robe—it would

---

7. **recusant** (rek' yoo zənt): one who refuses to accept or obey established authority.
8. **Ultima Thule** (ul' ti mə thoo' lē): the extreme tip of the northernmost part of the habitable ancient world.

return and repeat its operations—again—and again. Notwithstanding its terrifically wide sweep (some thirty feet or more) and the hissing vigor of its descent sufficient to sunder these very walls of iron, still the fraying of my robe would be all that, for several minutes, it would accomplish. And at this thought I paused. I dared not go farther than this reflection. I dwelt upon it with a pertinacity of attention—as if, in so dwelling, I could arrest *here* the descent of the steel. I forced myself to ponder upon the sound of the crescent as it should pass across the garment —upon the peculiar thrilling sensation which friction of cloth produces on the nerves. I pondered upon all this frivolity until my teeth were on edge.

Down—steadily down it crept. I took a frenzied pleasure in contrasting its downward with its lateral velocity. To the right—to the left—far and wide—with the shriek of a damned spirit; to my heart with the stealthy pace of the tiger! I alternately laughed and howled as the one or the other idea grew predominant.

Down—certainly, relentlessly down! It vibrated within three inches of my bosom! I struggled violently, furiously, to free my left arm. This was free only from the elbow to the hand. I could reach the latter, from the platter beside me, to my mouth, with great effort, but no farther. Could I have broken the fastenings above the elbow I would have seized and attempted to arrest the pendulum. I might as well have attempted to arrest an avalanche!

Down—still unceasingly—still inevitably down! I gasped and struggled at each vibration. I shrunk convulsively at its every sweep. My eyes followed its outward or upward whirls with the eagerness of the most unmeaning despair; they closed themselves spasmodically at the descent, although death would have been a relief, oh! how unspeakable! Still I quivered in every nerve to think how slight a sinking of the machinery would precipitate that keen, glistening ax upon my bosom. It was *hope* that prompted the nerve to quiver—the frame to shrink. It was *hope*— the hope that triumphs on the rack—that whispers to the death-condemned even in the dungeons of the Inquisition.

I saw that some ten or twelve vibrations would bring the steel in actual contact with my robe, and with this observation there suddenly came over my spirit all the keen, collected calmness of despair. For the first time during many hours—or perhaps days—I *thought*. It now occurred to me that the bandage, or surcingle, which enveloped me, was *unique*. I was tied by no separate cord. The first stroke of the razorlike crescent athwart any portion of the band, would so detach it that it might be unwound from my person by means of my left hand. But how fearful, in that case, the proximity of the steel! the result of the slightest struggle, how deadly! Was it likely, moreover, that the minions of the torturer had not foreseen and provided for this possibility! Was it probable that the bandage crossed my bosom in the track of the pendulum? Dreading to find my faint, and, as it seemed, my last hope frustrated, I so far elevated my head as to obtain a distinct view of my breast. The surcingle enveloped my limbs and body close in all directions—*save in the path of the destroying crescent.*

Scarcely had I dropped my head back into its original position, when there flashed upon my mind what I cannot better describe than as the unformed half of that idea of deliverance to which I have previously alluded, and of which a moiety only floated indeterminately through my brain when I raised food to my burning lips. The whole thought was now present—feeble, scarcely sane, scarcely definite—but still entire. I proceeded at once, with the nervous energy of despair, to attempt its execution.

For many hours the immediate vicinity of the low framework upon which I lay, had been literally swarming with rats. They were wild, bold, ravenous; their red eyes glaring upon me as if they waited but for motionlessness on my part to make me their prey. "To what food," I thought, "have they been accustomed in the well?"

They had devoured, in spite of all my efforts to prevent them, all but a small remnant of the contents of the dish. I had fallen into an habitual seesaw, or wave of the hand about the platter; and, at length, the unconscious uniformity of the movement deprived it of effect. In their voracity the vermin frequently fastened their sharp fangs in my fingers. With the particles of the oily and spicy viand which now remained, I thoroughly rubbed the bandage wherever I could reach it; then, raising my hand from the floor, I lay breathlessly still.

At first the ravenous animals were startled and terrified at the change—at the cessation of movement. They shrank alarmedly back; many sought the well. But this was only for a moment. I had not counted in vain upon their voracity. Observing that I remained without motion, one or two of the boldest leaped upon the framework and smelt at the surcingle. This seemed the signal for a general rush. Forth from the well they hurried in fresh troops. They clung to the wood—they overran it, and leaped in hundreds upon my person. The measured movement of the pendulum disturbed them not at all. Avoiding its strokes, they busied themselves with the anointed bandage. They pressed—they swarmed upon me in ever accumulating heaps. They writhed upon my throat; their cold lips sought my own; I was half stifled by their thronging pressure; disgust, for which the world has no name, swelled my bosom, and chilled, with a heavy clamminess, my heart. Yet one minute, and I felt that the struggle would be over. Plainly I perceived the loosening of the bandage. I knew that in more than one place it must be already severed. With a more than human resolution I lay *still*.

Nor had I erred in my calculations—nor had I endured in vain. I at length felt that I was *free*. The surcingle hung in ribands from my body. But the stroke of the pendulum already pressed upon my bosom. It had divided the serge of the robe. It had cut through the linen beneath. Twice again it swung, and a sharp sense of pain shot through every nerve. But the moment of escape had arrived. At a wave of my hand my deliverers hurried tumultuously away. With a steady movement—cautious, sidelong, shrinking, and slow—I slid from the embrace of the bandage and beyond the reach of the scimitar. For the moment, at least, *I was free.*

Free!—and in the grasp of the Inquisition! I had scarcely stepped from my wooden bed of horror upon the stone floor of the prison, when the motion of the hellish machine ceased and I beheld it drawn up, by some invisible force, through the ceiling. This was a lesson which I took desperately to heart. My every motion was undoubtedly watched. Free!—I had but escaped death in one form of agony, to be delivered unto worse than death in some other. With that thought I rolled my eyes nervously around on the barriers of iron that hemmed me in. Something unusual—some change which, at first, I could not appreciate distinctly—it was obvious, had taken place in the apartment. For many minutes of a dreamy and trembling abstraction, I busied myself in vain, unconnected conjecture. During this period, I became aware, for the first time, of the origin of the sulphurous light which illumined the cell. It proceeded from a fissure, about half an inch in width, extending entirely around the prison at the base of the walls, which thus appeared, and were, completely separated from the floor. I endeavored, but of course in vain, to look through the aperture.

As I arose from the attempt, the mystery of the alteration in the chamber broke at once upon my understanding. I have observed that, although the outlines of the figures upon the walls were sufficiently distinct, yet the colors seemed blurred and indefinite. These colors had now assumed, and were momentarily assuming, a startling and most intense brilliancy, that gave to the spectral and fiendish portraitures an aspect that might have thrilled even firmer nerves than my own. Demon eyes, of a wild and ghastly vivacity, glared upon me in a thousand directions, where none had been visibile before, and gleamed with the lurid luster of a fire that I could not force my imagination to regard as unreal.

Unreal!—Even while I breathed there came to my nostrils the breath of the vapor of heated iron! A suffocating odor pervaded the prison! A deeper glow settled each moment in the eyes that glared at my agonies! A richer tint of crimson diffused itself over the pictured horrors of blood. I panted! I gasped for breath! There could be no doubt of the design of my tormentors—oh! most unrelenting! oh! most demoniac of men! I shrank from the glowing metal to the center of the cell. Amid the thought of the fiery destruction that impended, the idea of the coolness of the well came over my soul like balm. I rushed to its deadly brink. I threw my straining vision below. The glare from the enkindled roof illumined its inmost recesses. Yet, for a wild moment, did my spirit refuse to comprehend the meaning of what I saw. At length it forced—it wrestled its way into my soul—it burned itself in upon my shuddering reason. —Oh! for a voice to speak!—oh! horror!—oh! any horror but this! With a shriek, I rushed from the margin, and buried my face in my hands—weeping bitterly.

The heat rapidly increased, and once again I looked up, shuddering as with a fit of the ague. There had been a second change in the cell—and now the change was obviously in the *form*. As before, it was in vain that I, at first, endeavored to appreciate or understand what was taking place. But not long was I left in doubt. The Inquisitorial vengeance had been hurried by my twofold escape, and there was to be no more dallying with the King of Terrors. The room had been square. I saw that two of its iron angles were now acute—two, consequently, obtuse. The fearful difference quickly increased with a low rumbling or moaning sound. In an instant the apartment had shifted its form into that of a lozenge. But the alteration stopped not here—I neither hoped nor desired it to stop. I could have clasped the red walls to my bosom as a garment of eternal peace. "Death," I said, "any death but that of the pit!" Fool! might I have not known that *into the pit* it was the object of the burning iron to urge me? Could I resist its glow? or, if even that, could I withstand its pressure? And now, flatter and flatter grew the lozenge, with a rapidity that left me no time for contemplation. Its center, and of course, its greatest width, came just over the yawning gulf. I shrank back—but the closing walls pressed me resistlessly onward. At length for my seared and writhing body there was no longer an inch of foothold on the firm floor of the prison. I struggled no more, but the agony of my soul found vent in one loud, long, and final scream of despair. I felt that I tottered upon the brink—I averted my eyes—.

There was a discordant hum of human voices! There was a loud blast as of many trumpets! There was a harsh grating as of a thousand thunders! The fiery walls rushed back! An outstretched arm caught my own as I fell, fainting, into the abyss. It was that of General Lasalle. The French army had entered Toledo. The Inquisition was in the hands of its enemies.

Getting at Meaning

1. What does the narrator describe in the first paragraph of this story? Why does everything seem like a blur to him?

2. The second paragraph is an interesting analysis of the act of fainting. According to the narrator what happens while coming out of a swoon? Have you experienced anything similar to what he describes?

3. What evidence is there that the narrator, although he is weak and light-headed, still has his wits about him? What actions does he take to save himself?

4. What thoughts does the narrator have as he lies in his torture chamber? What happens to his perception of time?

5. Explain the double threat posed by the rats. What descriptive details make the rats seem particularly sinister?

6. Why is the pit terrifying? How does the pendulum pose a threat? What happens to the walls of the narrator's cell to force him down into the pit?

7. Account for the rescue of the narrator. Do you think that the ending of the story is appropriate? Why or why not?

Developing Skills in Reading Literature

1. **Gothic Literature.** Poe specialized in Gothic literature, or fiction that uses strange, gloomy settings and mysterious, violent, often supernatural events to create suspense and terror.

This story takes place in Toledo, Spain, during the time of the Spanish Inquisition. Do some research on the Spanish Inquisition. What was its purpose? How were people who were found guilty of heresy punished? Why is the Inquisition an appropriate Gothic setting for this story? Explain in what way the events of the story fit the characteristics of Gothic literature.

2. **Point of View.** This story is told from a first-person point of view, meaning that a character within the story narrates. Why is first-person narration particularly suitable for the story? Imagine the same story told from the perspective of one of the torturers. What details would be different?

3. **Short Story.** Poe wrote of the short story, "In the whole composition there should be no word written, of which the tendency, direct or indirect, is not to the one preestablished design." This preestablished design Poe sometimes called the "single effect," and he stated that the effect would be felt most powerfully if a story were read in one sitting. Explain how "The Pit and the Pendulum" fits Poe's description of the short story. What is the "single effect" of the story? What elements contribute to the achievement of this effect? Can the story be read in one sitting?

4. **Suspense.** Suspense is the gripping sense of tension or excitement felt by the reader as he or she becomes involved in the rising action of a story. What are some of the separate devices Poe uses to build to a climax? What different things threaten the narrator? What happens each time there is a temporary release of tension? How does the first-person narration in this story intensify the suspense?

5. **Imagery.** Poe's story is rich in details that appeal to the senses of sight, hearing, smell, and touch. He often appeals to two or three senses at once. The narrator says, for example, "Very suddenly there came back to my soul motion and sound—the tumultuous motion of the heart, and, in my ears, the sound of its beating." He also says, "At the same time my forehead seemed bathed in a clammy vapor, and the peculiar smell of decayed fungus arose to my nostrils."

Choose a paragraph in the story that is especially alive with sensory detail. To how many different senses does the paragraph appeal? Which sentences or phrases appeal to more than one sense? What mood does the paragraph create?

6. **Anaphora.** When the narrator is describing the pendulum, he begins a paragraph with the sentence "Down—steadily down it crept." The next paragraph begins with the sentence "Down—certainly, relentlessly down!" The paragraph after that one begins "Down—still unceasingly—still inevitably down!" What is the effect of repeating the word *down* at the beginnings of successive paragraphs?

Developing Writing Skills

Writing a Gothic Tale. Imagine two or three possible settings for a Gothic tale. List vivid sensory details that describe each setting. Next, think of two or three events that might take place in such settings. These events can be based on actual experiences or can be purely fictional, perhaps with supernatural overtones. Then choose one setting and one event and develop a plot for a Gothic tale. If you wish, you may write the tale.

Poetry

PASSENGER PIGEON, 1824. *John James Audubon.*
Courtesy of the New York Historical Society, New York City.

Edgar Allan Poe

Annabel Lee

It was many and many a year ago,
  In a kingdom by the sea,
That a maiden there lived whom you may know
  By the name of Annabel Lee;
And this maiden she lived with no other thought   5
  Than to love and be loved by me.

She was a child and *I* was a child,
  In this kingdom by the sea,
But we loved with a love that was more than love—
  I and my Annabel Lee—   10
With a love that the wingéd seraphs of Heaven
  Coveted her and me.

And this was the reason that, long ago,
  In this kingdom by the sea,
A wind blew out of a cloud by night   15
  Chilling my Annabel Lee;
So that her highborn kinsmen came
  And bore her away from me,
To shut her up in a sepulchre[1]
  In this kingdom by the sea.   20

The angels, not half so happy in Heaven,
  Went envying her and me:—
Yes!—that was the reason (as all men know,
  In this kingdom by the sea)
That the wind came out of the cloud, chilling   25
  And killing my Annabel Lee.

But our love it was stronger by far than the love
  Of those who were older than we—
  Of many far wiser than we—
And neither the angels in Heaven above   30
  Nor the demons down under the sea,
Can ever dissever my soul from the soul
  Of the beautiful Annabel Lee:—

---

1. **sepulchre** (sep' əl kər): a place for burial; a tomb.

For the moon never beams, without bringing me dreams
  Of the beautiful Annabel Lee:—   35
And the stars never rise but I see the bright eyes
  Of the beautiful Annabel Lee:
And so, all the night-tide, I lie down by the side
Of my darling, my darling, my life and my bride,
  In the sepulchre there by the sea—   40
  In her tomb by the side of the sea.

Getting at Meaning

1. What few facts about Annabel Lee does the speaker give? How does he describe their love?

2. What kills Annabel Lee? Why does this happen?

3. Describe the aftermath of Annabel Lee's death. What kinds of visions does the speaker have?

Developing Skills in Reading Literature

1. **Ballad.** A ballad is a poem that tells a story, often a tragic one. Ballads differ from other narrative poems in that they are always highly rhythmic, often intended to be sung. Most ballads have stanzas of equal length, and refrains, or repeating passages, that occur with some regularity throughout the poems.

"Annabel Lee" is a kind of ballad. Although Poe varies the length of his stanzas to some extent, the stanzas have the same basic rhyme and meter. What lines operate as refrains throughout the poem? What words and phrases are often repeated?

2. **Rhyme.** Notice the rhyme scheme of each stanza. What three words does Poe repeatedly rhyme throughout the poem, uniting all six stanzas? Find lines in each stanza that do not rhyme with other lines.

Internal rhyme occurs when a line contains rhyme within it. For example, the line "For the moon never beams, without bringing me dreams" contains the rhyming words *beams* and *dreams*. Locate three other lines in the poem that contain internal rhyme.

3. **Meter.** Meter, you will remember, is the repetition of a regular rhythmic unit in a line of poetry. Each unit is known as a foot, with each foot having one accented and one or two unaccented syllables.

The first line of this poem has four feet. This is called tetrameter, *tetra-* meaning "four." The second line of

the poem has three feet, making it trimeter. Poe uses two different kinds of feet in these lines, which may be scanned as follows:

Ĭt wăs mán/y̆ ănd mán/y̆ ă yéar/ ăgo/

Ĭn ă kíng/dŏm by̆/ thĕ séa

The feet with one accented and one unaccented syllable are known as iambs. The iamb is the most common foot in English poetry. The feet that contain one accented and two unaccented syllables are called anapests.

Identify the meter of each additional line in the first stanza. What kind of feet do you find in each line? What is the overall pattern of the first stanza?

4. **Alliteration.** Alliteration is the repetition of consonant sounds at the beginnings of words. An alliterative pattern is sometimes reinforced by the repetition of the same consonant sounds within and at the ends of words. Alliteration helps writers to create mood, to unify lines, to reinforce meaning, and to impart a musical quality to their language.

Poe uses a great deal of alliteration in "Annabel Lee." For example, the lines "To shut her up in a sepulchre/In this kingdom by the sea" repeat the *s* sound. What other initial consonant sounds are repeated often in the poem? Find lines or passages that are rich in alliteration.

5. **Symbol.** Poe wrote "Annabel Lee" after his young wife Virginia died of tuberculosis, and many commentators read the poem as a statement of Poe's own love for Virginia. Read this way, what does the wind in the poem symbolize as the specific cause of the young woman's death? In a larger sense, what does the wind represent in human life?

The Raven

Once upon a midnight dreary, while I pondered, weak and weary,
Over many a quaint and curious volume of forgotten lore—
While I nodded, nearly napping, suddenly there came a tapping,
As of someone gently rapping, rapping at my chamber door.
"'Tis some visitor," I muttered, "tapping at my chamber door—
          Only this and nothing more."   5

Ah, distinctly I remember it was in the bleak December;
And each separate dying ember wrought its ghost upon the floor.
Eagerly I wished the morrow—vainly I had sought to borrow
From my books surcease of sorrow—sorrow for the lost Lenore—   10
For the rare and radiant maiden whom the angels name Lenore—
         Nameless *here* forevermore.

And the silken, sad, uncertain rustling of each purple curtain
Thrilled me—filled me with fantastic terrors never felt before;
So that now, to still the beating of my heart, I stood repeating,   15
"'Tis some visitor entreating entrance at my chamber door—
Some late visitor entreating entrance at my chamber door—
         That it is and nothing more."

Presently my soul grew stronger; hesitating then no longer,
"Sir," said I, "or Madam, truly your forgiveness I implore;   20
But the fact is I was napping, and so gently you came rapping,
And so faintly you came tapping, tapping at my chamber door,
That I scarce was sure I heard you"—here I opened wide the door—
         Darkness there and nothing more.

Deep into that darkness peering, long I stood there wondering, fearing,   25
Doubting, dreaming dreams no mortal ever dared to dream before;
But the silence was unbroken, and the stillness gave no token,
And the only word there spoken was the whispered word, "Lenore?"
This I whispered, and an echo murmured back the word "Lenore!"—
         Merely this and nothing more.   30

Back into the chamber turning, all my soul within me burning,
Soon again I heard a tapping somewhat louder than before.
"Surely," said I, "surely that is something at my window lattice;
Let me see, then, what thereat is, and this mystery explore—
Let my heart be still a moment and this mystery explore—   35
         'Tis the wind and nothing more!"

Open here I flung the shutter, when, with many a flirt and flutter,
In there stepped a stately Raven of the saintly days of yore;
Not the least obeisance made he; not a minute stopped or stayed he;
But, with mien of lord or lady, perched above my chamber door—   40
Perched upon a bust of Pallas[1] just above my chamber door—
                           Perched, and sat, and nothing more.

Then this ebony bird beguiling my sad fancy into smiling,
By the grave and stern decorum of the countenance it wore,
"Though thy crest be shorn and shaven, thou," I said, "art sure no craven,   45
Ghastly grim and ancient Raven wandering from the Nightly shore—
Tell me what thy lordly name is on the Night's Plutonian[2] shore!"
                           Quoth the Raven, "Nevermore."

Much I marveled this ungainly fowl to hear discourse so plainly,
Though its answer little meaning—little relevancy bore;   50
For we cannot help agreeing that no living human being
Ever yet was blessed with seeing bird above his chamber door—
Bird or beast upon the sculptured bust above his chamber door,
                           With such name as "Nevermore."

But the Raven, sitting lonely on the placid bust, spoke only   55
That one word, as if his soul in that one word he did outpour.
Nothing further then he uttered, not a feather then he fluttered—
Till I scarcely more than muttered, "Other friends have flown before—
On the morrow *he* will leave me, as my Hopes have flown before."
                           Then the bird said, "Nevermore."   60

Startled at the stillness broken by reply so aptly spoken,
"Doubtless," said I, "what it utters is its only stock and store
Caught from some unhappy master whom unmerciful Disaster
Followed fast and followed faster till his songs one burden bore—
Till the dirges of his Hope that melancholy burden bore   65
                           Of 'Never—nevermore.'"

But the Raven still beguiling all my fancy into smiling,
Straight I wheeled a cushioned seat in front of bird and bust and door;
Then, upon the velvet sinking, I betook myself to linking
Fancy unto fancy, thinking what this ominous bird of yore—   70
What this grim, ungainly, ghastly, gaunt, and ominous bird of yore
                           Meant in croaking, "Nevermore."

---

1. **Pallas** (pal' əs): Athene, goddess of wisdom in Greek mythology.
2. **Plutonian** (plü tō' nē ən): characteristic of Pluto or the lower world.

This I sat engaged in guessing, but no syllable expressing
To the fowl, whose fiery eyes now burned into my bosom's core;
This and more I sat divining, with my head at ease reclining   75
On the cushion's velvet lining that the lamp-light gloated o'er,
But whose velvet-violet lining with the lamp-light gloating o'er,
                          She shall press, ah, nevermore!

Then, methought, the air grew denser, perfumed from an unseen censer
Swung by seraphim[3] whose foot-falls tinkled on the tufted floor.   80
"Wretch," I cried, "thy God hath lent thee—by these angels he hath sent thee
Respite—respite and nepenthe[4] from thy memories of Lenore!
Quaff, oh, quaff this kind nepenthe and forget this lost Lenore!"
                          Quoth the Raven, "Nevermore."

"Prophet!" said I, "thing of evil!—prophet still, if bird or devil!—   85
Whether Tempter sent, or whether tempest tossed thee here ashore,
Desolate yet all undaunted, on this desert land enchanted—
On this home by Horror haunted—tell me truly, I implore—
Is there—*is* there balm in Gilead?[5]—tell me—tell me, I implore!"
                          Quoth the Raven, "Nevermore."   90

"Prophet!" said I, "thing of evil!—prophet still, if bird or devil!
By that Heaven that bends above us—by that God we both adore—
Tell this soul with sorrow laden if, within the distant Aidenn,[6]
It shall clasp a sainted maiden whom the angels name Lenore—
Clasp a rare and radiant maiden whom the angels name Lenore."   95
                          Quoth the Raven, "Nevermore."

"Be that word our sign of parting, bird or fiend!" I shrieked, upstarting—
"Get thee back into the tempest and the Night's Plutonian shore!
Leave no black plume as a token of that lie thy soul hath spoken!
Leave my loneliness unbroken!—quit the bust above my door!   100
Take thy beak from out my heart, and take thy form from off my door!"
                          Quoth the Raven, "Nevermore."

And the Raven, never flitting, still is sitting, *still* is sitting
On the pallid bust of Pallas just above my chamber door;
And his eyes have all the seeming of a demon's that is dreaming,   105
And the lamp-light o'er him streaming throws his shadow on the floor;
And my soul from out that shadow that lies floating on the floor
                          Shall be lifted—nevermore!

---

3. **seraphim** (ser′ ə fim′): one of the six-winged angels standing in the presence of God.
4. **nepenthe** (nə pen′ thē): a potion used by the ancients to induce forgetfulness of pain or sorrow.
5. **balm in Gilead** (gil′ ē əd): a soothing ointment made in Gilead, a mountainous region of Palestine east of the Jordan River; relief from affliction.
6. **Aidenn** (ā′ dən): an Arabic word for Eden or heaven.

Getting at Meaning

1. Describe the mental and physical condition of the speaker at the beginning of the poem. What is he trying to forget?

2. When does the tapping occur? What is the speaker's first interpretation of the tapping?

3. What does the speaker begin to feel about the tapping? What happens when he whispers *Lenore*?

4. The tapping moves from the door to the window. What happens when the speaker opens the window?

5. Where does the speaker assume the raven has come from? How does the speaker try to comfort himself about the strange events in his study?

6. As the speaker sits and thinks about the meaning of the bird's one word, what does he long for? How does he link the bird to his previous suffering?

7. What happens when the speaker asks the raven to leave? What is the speaker's condition at the end of the poem?

Developing Skills in Reading Literature

1. **Mood.** Mood, or atmosphere, is usually important in Poe's short stories and poems. What mood is established through the description of the setting in the opening two stanzas of the poem? What specific words serve to establish mood? What lines and phrases occurring later in the poem sustain this mood?

2. **Rhyme.** The powerful effect of this poem derives in part from rhyme, both end rhyme and internal rhyme. Which four lines rhyme in every stanza? Which rhyming words are repeated often throughout the poem? Which two lines in each stanza do not contain end rhyme?

Notice that the first line of each stanza contains internal rhyme. In the first line of the poem, for example, *dreary* and *weary* rhyme. What other line in each stanza contains internal rhyme? What does this pattern of internal rhyme do for the poem?

3. **Meter.** The stanzas of this poem all have the same meter. Observe the way the first line of the poem can be scanned:

Ónce ŭp/ón ă/ mídnĭght/ dréarў/ whíle Ĭ/ póndeřed/ wéak ănd/wéarў

There are eight feet in this line, a metrical pattern known as octameter, because *octa-* means "eight." Each foot in the line is an accented syllable followed by an unaccented syllable, a foot called the trochee. The meter, therefore, is trochaic octameter.

Scan the rest of the first stanza. How many feet do you find in the second line? the third? how many in the sixth line? Notice that in each stanza lines 2, 4, 5, and 6 end in a trochee in which the final unaccented syllable has been dropped. Why do you think Poe ended these lines with a stressed syllable?

4. **Repetend.** What phrases repeat in the final lines of the stanzas in "The Raven"? What words and phrases repeat often within the stanzas? What effect do Poe's repetitions have on a reader?

5. **Alliteration.** Notice the frequent repetition of consonant sounds at the beginnings of words. For example, in the line, "Swung by seraphim whose foot-falls tinkled on the tufted floor," Poe repeats the *s*, *f*, and *t* sounds to achieve a rhythmic, musical effect.

Find examples of alliteration in each stanza. Which sounds does Poe repeat most often? What does alliteration do for the pace of the poem?

6. **Symbol.** This poem is about sadness and loss. The speaker attempts to escape from melancholy and human mortality, trying to slip away into a kind of forgetfulness.

The raven does not permit the speaker to forget. Why? What aspects of human life does the raven represent?

Developing Writing Skills

Analyzing a Symbol. Write a five-paragraph composition in which you analyze the meaning of the raven in Poe's poem. Questions you should consider are these: Why does Poe employ the raven, instead of another bird or animal? (Think of associations connected with ravens, such as color.) What does the bird's intrusion in the speaker's life represent? Why won't the bird leave? Why can't the speaker make it leave? What does the bird's continuing presence in the study at the end of the poem signify for the speaker's life?

Begin your composition with an introduction. Then, in each body paragraph, develop a major point, using specific support from the poem. End with a paragraph that draws conclusions about the symbolism of the bird.

To Helen

Helen, thy beauty is to me
  Like those Nicean[1] barks of yore,
That gently, o'er a perfumed sea,
  The weary, wayworn wanderer bore
  To his own native shore.   5

On desperate seas long wont to roam,
  Thy hyacinth[2] hair, thy classic face,
Thy Naiad[3] airs have brought me home
  To the glory that was Greece,
  And the grandeur that was Rome.   10

Lo! in yon brilliant window niche
  How statuelike I see thee stand,
The agate lamp within thy hand!
  Ah, Psyche,[4] from the regions which
  Are Holy Land!   15

---

1. **Nicean** (nī sē' ən): pertaining to Nicea, an ancient city of Asia Minor.
2. **hyacinth** (hī' ə sĭnth): golden and wavy.
3. **Naiad** (nā' əd): one of the nymphs in ancient mythology living in and giving life to lakes, rivers, springs, and fountains.
4. **Psyche** (sī' kē): in Greek mythology, a princess loved by Eros, or Cupid.

Getting at Meaning

1. What kind of beauty does the speaker see in Helen? Which words characterize the beauty most clearly?

2. What does the speaker mean by saying that Helen's beauty has "brought me home/ To the glory that was Greece/ And the grandeur that was Rome"? What else does Helen's beauty do?

3. One prominent trait of Romantic writers is a love for pure, idealized beauty. What lines and words in the poem make Helen seem remote and ideal, not a real person? With what period of history does the speaker associate Helen's kind of pure beauty?

Developing Skills in Reading Literature

1. **Allusion.** The name *Helen* is an allusion, for it has two classical associations. Helen of Troy was the ancient Greek woman whose beauty caused the Trojan War, the subject of Homer's *Iliad*. Helen was also the name of the Greek goddess of light. What lines in the poem bring to mind this second Helen?

What other allusions do you find in the poem? Explain their meanings.

2. **Simile and Metaphor.** Explain the simile in the opening lines of the poem. What does it suggest about Helen's beauty? Later, in addressing Helen as Psyche, the speaker creates a metaphor that compares Helen with the mythological princess who married Cupid.

What does the English word *psyche* mean? What does this association suggest about Helen's beauty?

Developing Vocabulary

Greek Roots. The root *psych-* means "having to do with the mind or soul." Look up each word that follows in a dictionary. Record its meaning and explain how the root functions in each word.

psyche   psychiatrist
psychoanalysis   psychosomatic
psychedelic   psychopath

Developing Writing Skills

Contrasting Poems. Both "Annabel Lee" and "To Helen" are about beloved, idealized women. The tone and mood of the poems are not the same, however. Write two paragraphs of analysis, one for each poem, in which you contrast the speakers' attitudes and your responses to the poems. Questions to consider include: Which poem is sadder? Why? Which speaker is more emotional? Why? Which poem is more formal? Why?

Support your points about each poem by quoting specific lines in the text.

MENELAUS, HELEN, AND APHRODITE.
Attic red-figured jar, about 480 B.C. British Museum.

William Cullen Bryant
1794–1878

William Cullen Bryant was recognized at an early age as the best published poet that America had produced up to his time. Bryant also had a long and distinguished career in journalism, serving for many years as editor of the New York *Evening Post.*

Bryant grew up in Cummington, Massachusetts, the son of a country doctor. His father was an accomplished naturalist as well, and from him Bryant learned a great deal about observing nature. As an adolescent Bryant read the English Romantic poets, William Wordsworth and Samuel Taylor Coleridge, feeling excitement over the attitude toward nature and experience that he found in these writers. A precocious writer and thinker, young Bryant began to write satires. He then produced a draft of his most famous poem, "Thanatopsis," when he was only seventeen. The title translates to mean "a view of death," and in the poem Bryant draws conclusions about the meaning of nature. When the poem was published in *The North American Review*, in 1817, it was hailed as the first truly skillful, literary American poem. It went a long way toward establishing Romanticism as the major force in the literature of nineteenth-century America.

Bryant wrote much of his poetry before he was thirty. His verse is linked to the eighteenth century in its melancholy, resigned tone and in its careful, regular meter. It is Romantic, however, in its emphasis on finding spiritual and moral meaning in nature. Bryant saw nature as an answer to human wants and needs, both physical and psychological.

WILLIAM CULLEN BRYANT, 1825. *Samuel F. B. Morse. National Academy of Design. New York.*

Bryant was also a Romantic in his devotion to the common person and to democratic ideals. As an editor he was a champion of liberal, humanitarian causes, calling for such reforms as the abolition of slavery and debtors' prisons and for freedom of speech and union organization. He helped promote Jacksonian Democracy in the 1820's by working to elect Andrew Jackson. Years later, he helped elect Abraham Lincoln.

Along with Washington Irving and novelist James Fenimore Cooper, Bryant is one of the founders of a truly American literature. Indeed, he is sometimes called "the father of American poetry."

Inscription for the Entrance to a Wood

Stranger, if thou hast learned a truth which needs
No school of long experience, that the world
Is full of guilt and misery, and hast seen
Enough of all its sorrows, crimes, and cares,
To tire thee of it, enter this wild wood   5
And view the haunts of Nature. The calm shade
Shall bring a kindred calm, and the sweet breeze
That makes the green leaves dance, shall waft a balm
To thy sick heart. Thou wilt find nothing here
Of all that pained thee in the haunts of men,   10
And made thee loathe thy life. The primal curse
Fell, it is true, upon the unsinning earth,
But not in vengeance. God hath yoked to guilt
Her pale tormentor, misery. Hence, these shades
Are still the abodes of gladness; the thick roof   15
Of green and stirring branches is alive
And musical with birds, that sing and sport
In wantonness of spirit; while below
The squirrel, with raised paws and form erect,
Chirps merrily. Throngs of insects in the shade   20
Try their thin wings and dance in the warm beam
That waked them into life. Even the green trees
Partake the deep contentment; as they bend
To the soft winds, the sun from the blue sky
Looks in and sheds a blessing on the scene.   25
Scarce less the cleft-born wild-flower seems to enjoy
Existence, than the winged plunderer
That sucks its sweets. The mossy rocks themselves,
And the old and ponderous trunks of prostrate trees
That lead from knoll to knoll a causey rude   30
Or bridge the sunken brook, and their dark roots,
With all their earth upon them, twisting high,
Breathe fixed tranquillity. The rivulet
Sends forth glad sounds, and tripping o'er its bed
Of pebbly sands, or leaping down the rocks,   35
Seems, with continuous laughter, to rejoice
In its own being. Softly tread the marge,
Lest from her midway perch thou scare the wren
That dips her bill in water. The cool wind,
That stirs the stream in play, shall come to thee,   40
Like one that loves thee nor will let thee pass
Ungreeted, and shall give its light embrace.

Getting at Meaning

1. What is the subject of the verb *enter* in line 5? What idea does the speaker communicate by this choice of subject?

2. To what does the speaker offer nature as an alternative?

3. What are some of the activities happening in the wood? How do these activities affect the speaker?

Developing Skills in Reading Literature

1 **Simile.** Explain the simile in the final lines of the poem. Why is this comparison appropriate to the meaning of the poem?

2. **Personification.** What two abstract qualities does the speaker personify, or assign human qualities, in lines 13 and 14? In what terms is each quality presented? Explain the meaning of these two lines.

3. **Contrast.** Simile and metaphor focus on the similarity between two things that are compared. Contrast, on the other hand, brings out the dissimilarity between two things that are compared. The speaker of this poem emphasizes certain qualities in nature by contrasting it to society. How does the speaker describe society? In what ways is nature different? What specific words create the contrast between the two opposing worlds?

4. **Blank Verse.** This poem does not contain rhyme. Notice, though, that it has a regular metrical pattern, as seen in the first two lines:

/Stranger,/ if thou/ hast learned/ ă truth/ which needs/
/Nŏ school/ of long/ exper/ienče, that/ the world/

There are five feet to a line, and each foot is an iamb (with the exception of an occasional irregular foot). The metrical pattern is, therefore, iambic pentameter. When iambic pentameter is unrhymed, it is called blank verse.

How does the effect of blank verse differ from that of rhymed poetry such as the poems of Edgar Allan Poe? How might a poem written in blank verse be unified? How is "Inscription for the Entrance to a Wood" unified?

Developing Writing Skills

Writing an Explanation: Contrast. The attitude toward society put forward in this poem is typical of Romanticism. In one paragraph, describe this attitude and explain how it differs from the way that writers in the Age of Reason viewed society.

Thanatopsis

To him who in the love of Nature holds
Communion with her visible forms, she speaks
A various language; for his gayer hours
She has a voice of gladness, and a smile
And eloquence of beauty, and she glides   5
Into his darker musings, with a mild
And healing sympathy, that steals away
Their sharpness, ere he is aware. When thoughts
Of the last bitter hour come like a blight   10
Over thy spirit, and sad images
Of the stern agony, and shroud, and pall,
And breathless darkness, and the narrow house,
Make thee to shudder, and grow sick at heart;—
Go forth, under the open sky, and list
To Nature's teachings, while from all around—   15
Earth and her waters, and the depths of air—
Comes a still voice—Yet a few days, and thee
The all-beholding sun shall see no more
In all his course; nor yet in the cold ground,
Where thy pale form was laid, with many tears,   20
Nor in the embrace of ocean, shall exist
Thy image. Earth, that nourished thee, shall claim
Thy growth, to be resolved to earth again,
And, lost each human trace, surrendering up
Thine individual being, shalt thou go   25
To mix for ever with the elements,
To be a brother to the insensible rock
And to the sluggish clod, which the rude swain[1]
Turns with his share, and treads upon. The oak
Shall send his roots abroad, and pierce thy mould.   30
   Yet not to thine eternal resting-place
Shalt thou retire alone, nor couldst thou wish
Couch more magnificent. Thou shalt lie down
With patriarchs of the infant world—with kings,
The powerful of the earth—the wise, the good,   35
Fair forms, and hoary seers of ages past,
All in one mighty sepulchre. The hills
Rock-ribbed and ancient as the sun—the vales
Stretching in pensive quietness between;
The venerable woods—rivers that move   40
In majesty, and the complaining brooks

---

1. **swain** (swān): a rustic or a peasant.

That make the meadows green; and, poured round all,
Old Ocean's gray and melancholy waste,—
Are but the solemn decorations all
Of the great tomb of man. The golden sun,   45
The planets, all the infinite host of heaven,
Are shining on the sad abodes of death,
Through the still lapse of ages. All that tread
The globe are but a handful to the tribes
That slumber in its bosom.—Take the wings   50
Of morning, pierce the Barcan[2] wilderness,
Or lose thyself in the continuous woods
Where rolls the Oregon, and hears no sound,
Save his own dashings—yet the dead are there:
And millions in those solitudes, since first   55
The flight of years began, have laid them down
In their last sleep—the dead reign there alone,
So shalt thou rest, and what if thou withdraw
In silence from the living, and no friend
Take note of thy departure? All that breathe   60
Will share thy destiny. The gay will laugh
When thou art gone, the solemn brood of care
Plod on, and each one as before will chase
His favorite phantom; yet all these shall leave
Their mirth and their employments, and shall come,   65
And make their bed with thee. As the long train
Of ages glide away, the sons of men,
The youth in life's green spring, and he who goes
In the full strength of years, matron and maid,
The speechless babe, and the gray-headed man—   70
Shall one by one be gathered to thy side,
By those, who in their turn shall follow them.

So live, that when thy summons comes to join
The innumerable caravan, which moves
To that mysterious realm, where each shall take   75
His chamber in the silent halls of death,
Thou go not, like the quarry-slave at night,
Scourged to his dungeon, but, sustained and soothed
By an unfaltering trust, approach thy grave,
Like one who wraps the drapery of his couch   80
About him, and lies down to pleasant dreams.

---

2. **Barcan** (bär' kən): pertaining to the desert region near
Barca, a town in North Africa.

Getting at Meaning

1. What qualities in nature are emphasized in the opening lines? When should humans especially turn to nature?

2. What aspects of death are described in lines 8–13? What feelings about death do these details create?

3. How does the speaker's attitude toward death change during the poem? What leads the speaker to conclude that one should enter "the silent halls of death" feeling "sustained and soothed"? Cite specific lines from the poem to support your answers.

Developing Skills in Reading Literature

1. **Personification.** The personification of nature introduced in line 1 is sustained throughout the poem. What sex is nature, according to the speaker? What are some of the human qualities nature possesses?

2. **Simile.** This poem closes with a famous simile. To what does the speaker compare death? How does this comparison reinforce the meaning of the poem?

3. **Alliteration.** Identify several examples of alliteration in this poem. Which consonant sound appears most frequently at the beginnings of words? Is it a hard or soft sound? What effect does it have on the poem? How is it related to the poem's meaning?

4. **Theme.** What is the view of death that emerges by the end of this poem? When a soul's individuality disappears in death, what does the soul gain in its place? What does the speaker say about those who keep on living after each of us dies?

In lines 31–72 the speaker focuses on human consciousness of time. In what sense is this awareness isolating? In what sense is it comforting?

The view of death "Thanatopsis" presents is typically Romantic. What relationship between humans and nature does it portray? Find specific words and phrases to support your answer.

Developing Vocabulary

Understanding Changes in Language: Archaic Words. Archaic words are old-fashioned words that are not used often in modern writing and speaking. Dictionaries generally identify such words as archaic.

The words *you* and *your* have been used widely only for three or four centuries. The earlier forms of these words appear in this poem.

Look up the archaic forms of *you* and *your* that follow, and record the way each form should be used. What effect does the use of the earlier forms have in "Thanatopsis"? Why might modern poets and other writers occasionally use archaic forms?

thou   thy
thee   thine

Developing Writing Skills

Supporting an Opinion. Write a paragraph or two in which you either agree or disagree with the rather optimistic view of death present in "Thanatopsis." Explain your philosophy clearly, giving reasons to explain why you feel as you do. Include specific examples and observations whenever possible.

Oliver Wendell Holmes

1809–1894

Oliver Wendell Holmes in many ways typified the stimulating intellectual life in New England throughout much of the nineteenth century. He was a fascinating, witty, versatile thinker, a leading literary presence who was not even a man of letters by profession and who is now regarded as a minor writer of the Romantic period.

Holmes was a doctor, for many years an important professor in the Harvard Medical School. Himself a graduate of Harvard, Holmes had studied medicine in Paris. He was interested in medical research as well as in medical practice, and he wrote several scientific papers. One paper made a significant breakthrough, establishing that the puerperal fever associated with childbirth was spread by contact. Holmes also applied scientific principles to social problems; he argued that the Puritan notion of "sin" as the cause of crime should be replaced by scientific investigation of physical, psychological, and genetic factors.

Holmes lived most of his life in the Boston area. He was born in Cambridge, where his father was minister of the First Congregational Church, and he was affiliated with Harvard most of his adult life. Known for his energy and brilliance, Holmes spearheaded cultural activities around Boston. He knew all the leading New England intellectuals of his day, meeting with many of them once a month in the Saturday Club, an informal conversation group that he helped to organize. He also helped found the *Atlantic Monthly*, still a major American magazine. It was Holmes who coined the term *Brahmin* to refer to his own group of Boston aristocrats, suggesting humorously that he and his colleagues were like the high priests of the Hindu religion. The word is still used to refer to the old families of Boston.

Holmes began writing at an early age, and although he wrote three rather scientific novels, he is remembered for his poems and essays. "The Chambered Nautilus" and "Old Ironsides" are his most famous poems, but they are not typical of most of his poetry, which is loosely structured and full of wit and wordplay. Most of his essays are also light and essentially formless and contain stories, jokes, poems, and scientific facts. The essays were collected over the years in four volumes, the first and most famous being *The Autocrat of the Breakfast Table*, published in 1858. In these essays Holmes created a fictional character who voiced witty and sometimes profound observations on all manner of topics, from scientific discoveries to horse racing to ancient civilizations. His autocrat, who lives in a rooming house, addresses his comments to his fellow boarders at the breakfast table, who occasionally interrupt him, with opinions of their own.

In his old age Holmes returned briefly to Europe, where he received many honorary degrees. His life in Boston continued to be full of activity and bright, witty friends. He died at eighty-five, still convinced that "the Boston State House is the hub of the solar system."

Holmes's son, Oliver Wendell Holmes, Jr., achieved fame in the early twentieth century as a United States Supreme Court Justice.

The Chambered Nautilus

The nautilus is a snail-like sea creature that adds a new chamber to its shell each year to accommodate its growing body. The new chambers are made from the animal's own membranes, and according to legend, the nautilus can sail by hoisting up a membrane.

This is the ship of pearl, which, poets feign,[1]
  Sails the unshadowed main—
  The venturous bark that flings
On the sweet summer wind its purpled wings
In gulfs enchanted, where the siren sings   5
  And coral reefs lie bare,
Where the cold sea-maids rise to sun their streaming hair.

Its webs of living gauze no more unfurl;
  Wrecked is the ship of pearl!
  And every chambered cell,   10
Where its dim dreaming life was wont to dwell,
As the frail tenant shaped his growing shell,
  Before thee lies revealed—
Its irised ceiling rent,[2] its sunless crypt unsealed!

Year after year beheld the silent toil   15
  That spread his lustrous coil;
  Still, as the spiral grew,
He left the past year's dwelling for the new,
Stole with soft step its shining archway through,
  Built up its idle door,   20
Stretched in his last-found home, and knew the old no more.

Thanks for the heavenly message brought by thee,
  Child of the wandering sea,
  Cast from her lap, forlorn!
From thy dead lips a clearer note is born   25
Than ever Triton[3] blew from wreathèd horn!
  While on mine ear it rings
Through the deep caves of thought I hear a voice that sings:

---

1. **feign** (fān): to pretend, to invent, to imagine.
2. **rent:** past tense of *rend;* to tear as a sign of anger, grief, or despair.
3. **Triton** (trīt' ən): a son of Poseidon and Amphitrite in Greek mythology, described as a demigod of the sea with the lower part of his body like that of a fish.

Build thee more stately mansions, O my soul,
  As the swift seasons roll!
  Leave thy low-vaulted past!
Let each new temple, nobler than the last,
Shut thee from heaven with a dome more vast,
  Till thou at length art free,
Leaving thine outgrown shell by life's unresting sea!   35

30

Getting at Meaning

1. What is the condition of the nautilus described in the first two stanzas of this poem? Which lines provide important clues?

2. How does the speaker describe the growing, building process of the nautilus in stanza 3?

3. Why is the speaker grateful to the nautilus? What has the speaker learned from examining the animal's shell?

Developing Skills in Reading Literature

1. **Allusion.** The reference to Triton in the fourth stanza is a classical allusion, for Triton is a well known mythological figure.

Locate the allusion in the first stanza of the poem and explain its meaning.

2. **Alliteration.** Notice the alliteration of the s sound in the first stanza of the poem, established in the words *ship*, *sails*, *sweet*, *summer*, *siren*, *sings*, *sea*, *sun*, and *streaming*, and reinforced by the repetition of the same sound within and at the end of words. How does this repetition of sound relate to the content of the poem?

What initial consonant sounds are repeated in the second stanza of the poem? What is the effect of this repetition?

3. **Meter.** The first line of this poem is an example of iambic pentameter:

    1   2   3   4   5
Thĭs ís/ thĕ shíp/ ŏf peárl,/ whĭch, pŏ/etš feíǵn,

The line consists of five feet, or metrical units, and each foot is an iamb. Which other lines in each stanza contain five feet? Which lines contain three feet? How many feet make up the last line of each stanza? How does the controlled, orderly metrical pattern of this poem, the same in all five stanzas, relate to the meaning of the poem?

4. **Analogy.** The speaker uses the chambered nautilus to make an extended or lengthy comparison, or analogy. To what does the speaker compare the nautilus in the final stanza? What specific comparisons develop the analogy? What is the "heavenly message" embodied in the shell?

Developing Vocabulary

Greek and Latin Roots. *Naut-* is a Greek root, from the word *nautikos*, meaning "sailor," or *naus*, meaning "ship." *Nav-* is a Latin root, from the word *navis*, meaning "ship."

The words that follow employ these roots. Look up each word in an unabridged dictionary and record its meaning. Then explain the relationship between the root and the word's meaning.

nautical
nautiloid
navigation
navicular
navigable

Old Ironsides

Oliver Wendell Holmes wrote this poem in 1830, when he was only twenty-one. The title refers to the American frigate Constitution, *nicknamed "Old Ironsides" because the ship received so little damage during the War of 1812. Holmes learned that the ship was about to be demolished in a Boston shipyard and published this poem in the* Boston Daily Advertiser *in an attempt to save the ship. The poem, reprinted throughout the country, was so effective that the ship was saved.*

Ay, tear her tattered ensign down!
  Long has it waved on high,
And many an eye has danced to see
  That banner in the sky;
Beneath it rung the battle shout,   5
  And burst the cannon's roar—
The meteor of the ocean air
  Shall sweep the clouds no more.

Her deck, once red with heroes' blood,
  Where knelt the vanquished foe,   10
When winds were hurrying o'er the flood,
  And waves were white below,
No more shall feel the victor's tread,
  Or know the conquered knee—
The harpies[1] of the shore shall pluck   15
  The eagle of the sea!

Oh, better that her shattered hulk
  Should sink beneath the wave;
Her thunders shook the mighty deep,
  And there should be her grave;   20
Nail to the mast her holy flag,
  Set every threadbare sail,
And give her to the god of storms,
  The lightning and the gale!

---

1. **harpies** (här′ pēz): foul, malign creatures in Greek mythology that are part woman and part bird; predatory persons.

Getting at Meaning

1. Analyze the emotional appeal of this poem. What ideas might have appealed strongly to the public? What made the poem so effective in accomplishing Holmes's purpose?

2. What is your interpretation of the phrase "harpies of the shore"? What does Holmes suggest would be a better fate for the ship than destruction in a shipyard?

Developing Skills in Reading Literature

1. **Meter.** This poem has a regular meter, which is the same in each of its three stanzas. Figure out the number and kind of feet in each line in the first stanza. What is the alternating metrical pattern in the lines? What kind of foot is used throughout the poem? Why might the poet have chosen a regular pattern for this poem?

2. **Rhyme.** The rhyme scheme is not precisely regular in this poem, but it is insistent and contributes to the poem's driving rhythm. Which two pairs of lines rhyme in each stanza? Is the pattern the same throughout the poem?

Developing Writing Skills

Writing a Poem. Write a poem in which you either

a) compare something in nature to something human, as Holmes does in "The Chambered Nautilus," or

b) attempt to inspire some kind of social action, as Holmes does in "Old Ironsides."

Use rhyme and meter in your poem if you wish, although this is not required. Write down thoughts, images, words, and phrases before you begin to compose the poem.

THE *CONSTITUTION* AND THE *GUERRIÈRE*, 1813.
Engraving.
American Antiquarian Society, Worcester, Massachusetts.

James Russell Lowell

1819–1891

Boston poet James Russell Lowell is often associated with Oliver Wendell Holmes, Henry Wadsworth Longfellow, and John Greenleaf Whittier. These four are known as the Fireside Poets. Like Holmes, he did numerous other things besides write poetry. He was also a professor at Harvard, a journalist, a politician, a reformer, a masterful literary critic, and a magazine editor.

Lowell was born in Cambridge. His father, a Unitarian minister from a distinguished New England family, was one of the original Abolitionists. Lowell attended Harvard and then the Harvard Law School, also writing poetry during his college years. By the time he was twenty-four, he had already published two volumes of verse.

In 1844 Lowell married Maria White, an intelligent, talented young poet. She persuaded Lowell to give up his law practice, which did not interest him, and to devote himself to literature and reform. This Lowell did, declaring that it was his intention to reform the world through poetry. Maria shared her husband's devotion to such causes as the abolition of slavery, women's rights, the improvement of factory conditions, and temperance. In the early years of his marriage, Lowell produced several more volumes of poetry. One, a collection of verse in dialect, was the first of a series called the *Biglow Papers*, which featured a humorous Yankee poet named Hosea Biglow. Lowell also produced a significant work of literary criticism, *A Fable for Critics*, in which he urged appreciation for American poets.

By the time he was thirty, Lowell was famous as a poet, essayist, and reformer. Then his life took a tragic turn. Three of his children died within a few years, and in 1853, Maria, too, died. Lowell was devastated and looked to his friends for emotional support. Eventually he returned to an active literary life, though he did not write much poetry after Maria's death. He succeeded Longfellow as Professor of Modern Languages at Harvard.

In 1857 Lowell became the first editor of the *Atlantic Monthly*, a magazine he helped found. He also married again in that year, and he and his wife together moved in lively Boston circles. He participated in the Saturday Club, and there he conversed with Hawthorne, Emerson, Thoreau, Longfellow, Whittier, and Holmes. The club was a glittering assortment of famous writers, and Lowell was a part of this group for years.

Having resigned from Harvard, Lowell went to Europe in 1872. During the next years he served as American minister to Spain, then England. He loved England, especially, and felt ambivalent about returning to the United States. He did return in 1885 after his second wife died.

In his later years Lowell felt disappointed that his career lacked coherence and that he had failed to live up to his early literary promise. He realized that he had not become a major poet. If Lowell was not a major writer, however, he was certainly a major literary figure, an influential presence in the intellectual life of the nineteenth century.

from **The Vision of Sir Launfal**

And what is so rare as a day in June?
   Then, if ever, come perfect days;
Then Heaven tries earth if it be in tune,
   And over it softly her warm ear lays:
Whether we look, or whether we listen,   5
We hear life murmur, or see it glisten;
Every clod feels a stir of might,
   An instinct within it that reaches and towers,
And, groping blindly above it for light,
   Climbs to a soul in grass and flowers;   10
The flush of life may well be seen
   Thrilling back over hills and valleys;
The cowslip startles in meadows green,
   The buttercup catches the sun in its chalice,
And there's never a leaf nor a blade too mean   15
   To be some happy creature's palace;
The little bird sits at his door in the sun,
   Atilt like a blossom among the leaves,
And lets his illumined being o'errun
   With the deluge of summer it receives;   20
His mate feels the eggs beneath her wings,
And the heart in her dumb breast flutters and sings;
He sings to the wide world, and she to her nest,—
In the nice ear of Nature which song is the best? . . .

Getting at Meaning

1. Why does the speaker praise June days? What various elements of nature contribute to the speaker's overall impression of summer contentment?

2. Why are the birds content? How do their songs differ?

Developing Skills in Reading Literature

1. **Personification.** Identify the personification in the opening lines. How does this personification contribute to the tone of the poem?

2. **Imagery.** This poem appeals strongly to the various senses. Which lines contain images that appeal to the sense of hearing? Which lines contain visual images? Which lines appeal to the sense of touch?

Stanzas on Freedom

Men! whose boast it is that ye
Come of fathers brave and free,
If there breathe on earth a slave,
Are ye truly free and brave?
If ye do not feel the chain,   5
When it works a brother's pain,
Are ye not base slaves indeed,
Slaves unworthy to be freed?

Women! who shall one day bear
Sons to breathe New England air,   10
If ye hear, without a blush,
Deeds to make the roused blood rush
Like red lava through your veins,
For your sisters now in chains—
Answer! are ye fit to be   15
Mothers of the brave and free?

Is true Freedom but to break
Fetters for our own dear sake,
And, with leathern hearts, forget
That we owe mankind a debt?   20
No! true freedom is to share
All the chains our brothers wear,
And, with heart and hand, to be
Earnest to make others free!

They are slaves who fear to speak   25
For the fallen and the weak;
They are slaves who will not choose
Hatred, scoffing, and abuse,
Rather than in silence shrink
From the truth they needs must think;   30
They are slaves who dare not be
In the right with two or three.

Getting at Meaning

1. The speaker asks a series of questions. Which lines in the poem contain the first answer to these questions?

2. According to the speaker, what should be the relationship between the individual and mankind?

3. How does the speaker define a slave?

Developing Skills in Reading Literature

1. **Rhetorical Question.** How many rhetorical questions are asked in this poem? What is the purpose of the questions? What is the cumulative effect? Why is the use of this technique appropriate to the subject matter of the poem?

2. **Rhyme.** What is the rhyme scheme of each stanza of this poem. What pair of rhyming words occurs in three stanzas? How does this rhyme relate to the opening lines of the poem? What kind of rhythm, or cadence, does the rhyme scheme give to the poem? In what ways is this scheme appropriate to the poem's subject matter?

3. **Meter.** Scan the first stanza of the poem. Do you find the same number of feet in each line? Do the other stanzas follow the pattern of the first one, or are they different? What kind of feet does this poet employ? What is the meter of the poem?

Henry Wadsworth Longfellow
1807–1882

When Henry Wadsworth Longfellow was in college, he wrote to his father, "I most eagerly aspire after future eminence in literature, my whole soul burns most ardently after it. . . ." Longfellow realized his ambition. He achieved world fame as a poet at an early age and remained America's most popular poet well into the twentieth century.

Longfellow's father was a lawyer in Portland, Maine, where Longfellow grew up. A precocious child, Longfellow entered Bowdoin College in Maine when he was only fourteen. He graduated from Bowdoin at the top of a class that also included Nathaniel Hawthorne and Franklin Pierce, a future President of the United States. Bowdoin offered Longfellow a professorship of modern languages, a post he assumed after spending some time preparing in Europe. When Harvard University offered Longfellow the same position several years later, he went to live in Cambridge, where he spent the rest of his life.

Longfellow's first volume of poetry was published when he was twenty-eight, and from that point on he published at a fast rate. His books sold well, and his poems soon were translated into numerous other languages. Longfellow was the foremost of the Fireside Poets, a group that also included Oliver Wendell Holmes, James Russell Lowell, and John Greenleaf Whittier. These poets all wrote poetry that was morally uplifting, humorous, or romantically engrossing and never too difficult. Their work was suitable for a family to read aloud while sitting by the fire, and in those days before radio, television, and stereo systems, many families did read aloud for entertainment. Longfellow's narrative poems, such as "Evangeline," "The Song of Hiawatha," and "The Courtship of Miles Standish," were household favorites.

Longfellow's professional success was accompanied by both tragedy and happiness in his personal life. His beloved first wife died in Europe early in their marriage. He subsequently married a lovely, charming, intelligent woman named Frances Appleton. Fanny came from a wealthy family, and her father gave the couple as a wedding present the large handsome house in Cambridge that is now a national monument. Longfellow and Fanny had six children and an extremely happy marriage for eighteen years. Then, in 1861, Fanny's dress caught fire in a home accident and she burned to death. Longfellow was seriously injured trying to save her.

After Fanny's death Longfellow sought comfort in his children, his friends, and his work. His large house on Brattle Street remained a literary center, where writers from around the world came to visit. Longfellow sometimes traveled, touring Europe as an international celebrity in 1868 and 1869. His old age was a rich, peaceful one, with family and friends close at hand.

During his lifetime some of Longfellow's contemporaries criticized him for courting popularity at the expense of artistic integrity. His reputation remained strong, however, until World War I. After the war, the disillusioned postwar generation found Longfellow's verse too unrealistic and too romantic for the modern consciousness. Critics attacked his prefabricated verse formulas. Still, many of Longfellow's poems remain popular, and a few of his poems retain the respect of literary critics.

Hymn to the Night

I heard the trailing garments of the Night
    Sweep through her marble halls!
I saw her sable skirts all fringed with light
    From the celestial walls!

I felt her presence, by its spell of might,   5
    Stoop o'er me from above;
The calm, majestic presence of the Night,
    As of the one I love.

I heard the sounds of sorrow and delight,
    The manifold, soft chimes,   10
That fill the haunted chambers of the Night,
    Like some old poet's rhymes.

From the cool cisterns of the midnight air
    My spirit drank repose;
The fountain of perpetual peace flows there,—   15
    From those deep cisterns flows.

O holy Night! from thee I learn to bear
    What man has borne before!
Thou layest thy finger on the lips of Care,
    And they complain no more.   20

Peace! Peace! Orestes[1]-like I breathe this prayer!
    Descend with broad-winged flight,
The welcome, the thrice-prayed for, the most fair,
    The best-beloved Night!

---

1. **Orestes** (ə res' tēz): the son of Agamemnon and Clytemnestra in ancient Greek literature. With his sister Electra he avenges his father by killing his mother and her lover Aegisthus.

Getting at Meaning

1. Describe the speaker's impressions of night. What is the emotional effect of night in the poem?

2. What does the speaker learn from the night? Why does the speaker long for night?

Developing Skills in Reading Literature

1. **Personification.** This entire poem is based on the personification of night. What human qualities does the poet give the night? What does the night wear? What does she do?

2. **Meter.** Scan the first stanza of the poem to determine the number of feet per line. How many feet do you find in lines 1 and 3? How many in lines 2 and 4? What kind of feet are they? What is the meter of "Hymn to the Night"? Is it appropriate to a hymn? Why or why not?

The Arsenal at Springfield

This is the Arsenal. From floor to ceiling,
   Like a huge organ, rise the burnished arms;
But from their silent pipes no anthem pealing
   Startles the villages with strange alarms.

Ah! what a sound will rise, how wild and dreary,   5
   When the death angel touches those swift keys!
What loud lament and dismal Miserere[1]
   Will mingle with their awful symphonies!

I hear even now the infinite fierce chorus,
   The cries of agony, the endless groan,   10
Which, through the ages that have gone before us,
   In long reverberations reach our own.

On helm and harness rings the Saxon hammer,
   Through Cimbric[2] forest roars the Norseman's song,
And loud, amid the universal clamor,   15
   O'er distant deserts sounds the Tartar[3] gong.

I hear the Florentine, who from his palace
   Wheels out his battle-bell with dreadful din,
And Aztec priests upon their teocallis[4]
   Beat the wild war drums made of serpent's skin;   20

The tumult of each sacked and burning village;
   The shout that every prayer for mercy drowns;
The soldiers' revels in the midst of pillage;
   The wail of famine in beleaguered towns;

The bursting shell, the gateway wrenched asunder,   25
   The rattling musketry, the clashing blade;
And ever and anon, in tones of thunder
   The diapason[5] of the cannonade.

---

1. **Miserere** (miz' ə rer' ē): the fiftieth Psalm in the Vulgate Bible.
2. **Cimbric** (sim' brik): pertaining to a probable Celtic or Teutonic people that invaded Italy and were destroyed by the Romans in 101 B.C.
3. **Tartar** (tärt' ər): a native or resident of Tartary in Asia; a person of an irritable or violent temper.
4. **teocallis** (tē' ə kəl' əz): ancient temples of Mexico or Central America usually built upon the summit of a truncated pyramidal mound.
5. **diapason** (dī' ə pāz' 'n): a burst of harmonious sound.

Is it, O man, with such discordant noises,
　　With such accursed instruments as these,　　　　　30
Thou drownest Nature's sweet and kindly voices,
　　And jarrest the celestial harmonies?

Were half the power, that fills the world with terror,
　　Were half the wealth bestowed on camps and courts,
Given to redeem the human mind from error,　　　　35
　　There were no need of arsenals or forts:

The warrior's name would be a name abhorred!
　　And every nation, that should lift again
Its hand against a brother, on its forehead
　　Would wear forevermore the curse of Cain!　　　40

Down the dark future, through long generations,
　　The echoing sounds grow fainter and then cease;
And like a bell, with solemn, sweet vibrations,
　　I hear once more the voice of Christ say, "Peace!"

Peace! and no longer from its brazen portals　　　　45
　　The blast of War's great organ shakes the skies!
But beautiful as songs of the immortals,
　　The holy melodies of love arise.

Getting at Meaning

1. What is the speaker's first reaction to the weapons in the arsenal? What sounds does the speaker imagine while viewing the weapons?

2. What historical groups does the speaker mention? What idea is emphasized by the naming of these groups?

3. In the eighth stanza the poem changes. What is the focus of the last five stanzas? What does the speaker recommend? What is the speaker's idealized vision of the future?

Developing Skills in Reading Literature

1. **Extended Metaphor.** A simile in the first stanza suggests that the weapons in the arsenal rise from floor to ceiling "like a huge organ." This simple simile is the beginning of an extended metaphor. What words and phrases extend the basic comparison between an organ and the weapons? To how many different senses does Longfellow appeal in this metaphor? What is ironic about the comparison?

2. **Alliteration.** Longfellow uses alliteration in nearly every stanza of this poem. For example, the first stanza repeats the p sound in pipes and pealing and the s sound in silent, startles, and strange.

Find alliteration in other stanzas of the poem. What effect does the alliteration have on the rhythm of the poem? Why is the musical quality imparted by the alliteration appropriate in this particular poem?

3. **Theme.** The poem begins with the speaker describing the arsenal at Springfield, Massachusetts. After thinking about the weapons and their use, the speaker reflects on human warfare and on the contrast between the weapons, "such accursed instruments," and "Nature's sweet and kindly voices." In the final two stanzas, what does the speaker conclude is the answer to human strife? What message is presented by the poem?

The Tide Rises, the Tide Falls

The tide rises, the tide falls,
The twilight darkens, the curlew calls;
Along the sea-sands damp and brown
The traveler hastens toward the town,
    And the tide rises, the tide falls.   5

Darkness settles on roofs and walls,
But the sea, the sea in the darkness calls;
The little waves, with their soft, white hands,
Efface the footprints in the sands,
    And the tide rises, the tide falls.   10

The morning breaks; the steeds in their stalls
Stamp and neigh, as the hostler calls;
The day returns, but nevermore
Returns the traveler to the shore,
    And the tide rises, the tide falls.   15

Getting at Meaning

1. What kind of journey does the traveler appear to be taking? Why will the traveler return no more?

2. Although the traveler will not be returning, what happens to day-to-day life in his or her absence?

3. What does the tidal action of the sea represent?

Developing Skills in Reading Literature

1. **Literal and Figurative Meaning.** The literal meaning of a poem is the apparent meaning that is communicated by the words taken at face value. A poem's figurative meaning, on the other hand, is its underlying or actual meaning.

A student reading this poem for the first time might assume that it is about a traveler who stops briefly at the seashore before proceeding on to the village. Upon closer study, however, the student will begin to understand that the poem is about the natural cycle of life and death. What details in the first stanza suggest that the traveler is close to death? What details in the second stanza suggest death? After the death, what does the third stanza show to be happening in the natural world? What does the emphasis on morning and activity imply about the poet's attitude? What statement does this poem make about death?

2. **Refrain.** What is the effect of the refrain that ends each stanza of this poem? What does the refrain suggest about the poet's attitude toward death?

Developing Vocabulary

Latin Roots. The word *efface*, which means "to rub out as from a surface," comes from the Latin word *facies* meaning "form, appearance, look." Following are other words that are derived from the same Latin root. Look up each word in an unabridged dictionary and record its meaning. Then explain the relationship between the meaning and the root.

facade	deface
facer	prima facie
facet	self-effacing

Nature

As a fond mother, when the day is o'er,
   Leads by the hand her little child to bed,
   Half willing, half reluctant to be led,
   And leave his broken playthings on the floor,
Still gazing at them through the open door,   5
   Nor wholly reassured and comforted
   By promises of others in their stead,
   Which, though more splendid, may not please him more;
So nature deals with us, and takes away
   Our playthings one by one, and by the hand   10
   Leads us to rest so gently, that we go
Scarce knowing if we wish to go or stay,
   Being too full of sleep to understand
   How far the unknown transcends the what we know.

Getting at Meaning

1. How does the child described in the first eight lines feel about going to bed? How does he feel about "his broken playthings"?

2. According to the poem, how do humans feel about death? What are the "playthings" that nature takes away, one by one?

Developing Skills in Reading Literature

1. **Analogy.** This poem centers on an elaborate comparison. What two subjects are being compared? Which is the more familiar of the two subjects? In what line is the second, less familiar subject introduced? What specific points of comparison does the poet make? In what sense is any dying person like a child?

2. **Tone.** Summarize the poet's attitude toward death in this poem. How does the poet link death to nature? In what ways is the poet's attitude a Romantic one?

3. **Sonnet.** A sonnet is a short poem that consists of fourteen lines of iambic pentameter. Sonnets are of two principal types:

a) the Shakespearean, or English, sonnet consists of three four-line stanzas, or quatrains. Following these is a couplet that resolves the problem developed in the three quatrains. The usual rhyme scheme of the English sonnet is a b a b c d c d e f e f g g.

b) the Petrarchan, or Italian, sonnet consists of two parts, an eight-line octave and a six-line sestet. The octave sets up a question or problem, and the sestet provides the application or resolution to the question or problem. The rhyme scheme of the octave is a b b a a b b a. The pattern of the sestet is variable, c d e c d e or c c d d e e, for example.

"Nature" is an Italian sonnet. Examine the relationship between the poem's octave and its sestet. In what way does the sestet apply or resolve the situation set up in the octave? What is the rhyme scheme of the sestet?

Developing Writing Skills

Writing a Sonnet. Compose a sonnet of your own, remembering that it must be written in iambic pentameter. First plan the content of the sonnet carefully. Think of the problem or idea you will develop; then decide on the statement or resolution you will provide. You might use an analogy to structure your poem. Choose either the English or the Italian sonnet form, whichever seems better suited to your idea. Rework your draft until you are satisfied with the result.

John Greenleaf Whittier
1807–1892

Most of John Greenleaf Whittier's poetry is, to use his own words, "the poetry of human life and simple nature, of the hearth and farm field." He was a rural poet in a way that the other Fireside Poets, all Boston and Cambridge intellectuals, were not.

Whittier's background was rural. His father was a farmer in Haverhill, Massachusetts, and the family was ardently Quaker. Whittier's father, an intensely practical man, did not see any purpose in giving his son a fancy education. Consequently Whittier attended the local schools of Haverhill. He read a great deal as a boy, however, and he was especially influenced by the Scottish poet Robert Burns, who, like Whittier, was a rural poet of the people.

The Quaker tradition stresses that people should follow their own intuition or "inner light" in matters of right and wrong. It also advocates pacifism and social action to eliminate human injustices. Applying Quaker teachings, Whittier became an ardent reformer, particularly devoted to the abolition of slavery. As a young man he supported himself by writing and editing anti-slavery newspapers. He served briefly in the Massachusetts legislature and spoke at Abolitionist rallies. He worked to abolish slavery until the Civil War, an event that particularly saddened him. The Abolitionist cause was as important in Whittier's life as was writing poetry.

Whittier began submitting poems for publication when he was still in his teens. His first book, *Legends of New England*, came out when he was twenty-six. Although he did not make much money from his volumes of poetry verse, his reputation steadily grew, and when he was fifty, Oliver Wendell Holmes invited him to help found the *Atlantic Monthly*. In 1866, after his career as an Abolitionist was over, Whittier published the long poem "Snowbound." A nostalgic reminiscence of rural family life in New England, the poem recalls an earlier, simpler age, when stories were told around the fire. The nation that had just fought a bloody war seized this poem hungrily, and almost overnight Whittier had a national literary reputation and a comfortable income. Most critics continue to regard "Snowbound" and "Telling the Bees," written in 1858, as Whittier's best poems.

Although he enjoyed the company of attractive and intelligent women, Whittier remained a bachelor all his life. He was close to his mother and to his sisters until their deaths. In his old age he was a distinguished man of letters, with his seventieth and eightieth birthdays celebrated as national events. Whittier lived modestly in Amesbury, Massachusetts, still wearing old-fashioned Quaker dress, until his death of a stroke when he was nearly eighty-five.

from **Snowbound**

"Snowbound," Whittier's most famous poem, describes the experiences of a farm family and its guests who are cut off from the outside world by a blizzard. As they sit around the fire and tell stories, they represent human life in various times and places. Their warmth and affection for each other act in powerful opposition to the cold, forbidding storm, and it is almost disappointing when plow teams break through the snow to liberate the farm from its isolation.

"A Winter Idyll" is the first 174 lines of the poem, less than one-fourth its total length.

A WINTER IDYLL

The sun that brief December day
Rose cheerless over hills of gray,
And, darkly circled, gave at noon
A sadder light than waning moon.
Slow tracing down the thickening sky   5
Its mute and ominous prophecy,
A portent seeming less than threat,
It sank from sight before it set.
A chill no coat, however stout,
Of homespun stuff could quite shut out,   10
A hard, dull bitterness of cold,
That checked, mid-vein, the circling race
Of lifeblood in the sharpened face,
The coming of the snowstorm told.
The wind blew east; we heard the roar   15
Of Ocean on his wintry shore,
And felt the strong pulse throbbing there
Beat with low rhythm our inland air.
Meanwhile we did our nightly chores—
Brought in the wood from out-of-doors,   20
Littered the stalls, and from the mows
Raked down the herd's-grass for the cows:
Heard the horse whinnying for his corn;
And, sharply clashing horn on horn,
Impatient down the stanchion[1] rows   25
The cattle shake their walnut bows;

---

1. **stanchion** (stan' chən): a restraining device fitted loosely around the neck of a cow to confine it to its stall.

While, peering from his early perch
Upon the scaffold's pole of birch,
The cock his crested helmet bent
And down his querulous challenge sent.   30

Unwarmed by any sunset light
The gray day darkened into night,
A night made hoary with the swarm
And whirl-dance of the blinding storm,
As zigzag, wavering to and fro,   35
Crossed and recrossed the wingèd snow:
And ere the early bedtime came
The white drift piled the window frame,
And through the glass the clothcoline posts
Looked in like tall and sheeted ghosts.   40

So all night long the storm roared on:
The morning broke without a sun;
In tiny spherule[2] traced with lines
Of Nature's geometric signs,
In starry flake, and pellicle,[3]   45
All day the hoary meteor fell;
And, when the second morning shone,
We looked upon a world unknown,
On nothing we could call our own.
Around the glistening wonder bent   50
The blue walls of the firmament,
No cloud above, no earth below—
A universe of sky and snow!
The old familiar sights of ours
Took marvelous shapes; strange domes and towers   55
Rose up where sty or corncrib stood,
Or garden wall, or belt of wood;
A smooth white mound the brush pile showed,
A fenceless drift what once was road;
The bridle post an old man sat   60
With loose-flung coat and high cocked hat;
The wellcurb had a Chinese roof;
And even the long sweep,[4] high aloof,
In its slant splendor, seemed to tell
Of Pisa's leaning miracle.[5]   65

---

2. **spherule** (sfer' o͞ol): a little sphere or spherical body.
3. **pellicle** (pĕl' ĭ kəl): a thin skin or membrane.
4. **sweep**: a pole with a bucket at one end, used to get water from a well.
5. **Pisa's leaning miracle** (pē' zə): the Leaning Tower of Pisa, in Italy.

A prompt, decisive man, no breath
Our father wasted: "Boys, a path!"
Well pleased (for when did farmer boy
Count such a summons less than joy?)
Our buskins[6] on our feet we drew;   70
With mittened hands, and caps drawn low,
To guard our necks and ears from snow,
We cut the solid whiteness through.
And, where the drift was deepest, made
A tunnel walled and overlaid   75
With dazzling crystal: we had read
Of rare Aladdin's[7] wondrous cave,
And to our own his name we gave,
With many a wish the luck were ours
To test his lamps supernal powers.   80
We reached the barn with merry din,
And roused the prisoned brutes within.
The old horse thrust his long head out,
And grave with wonder gazed about;
The cock his lusty greeting said,   85
And forth his speckled harem led;
The oxen lashed their tails, and hooked,
And mild reproach of hunger looked;
The hornèd patriarch of the sheep,
Like Egypt's Amun[8] roused from sleep,   90
Shook his sage head with gesture mute,
And emphasized with stamp of foot.

All day the gusty north wind bore
The loosening drift its breath before;
Low circling round its southern zone,   95
The sun through dazzling snow-mist shone.
No church bell lent its Christian tone
To the savage air, no social smoke
Curled over woods of snow-hung oak.
A solitude made more intense   100

---

6. **buskins** (bəs' kənz): laced boots reaching halfway or more to the knee.
7. **Aladdin** (a lad' 'n): a youth in the Arabian Nights' Entertainments who comes into possession of a magic lamp.
8. **Amun**: also Amon or Ammon; an Egyptian god frequently represented with a ram's head.

By dreary-voicèd elements,
The shrieking of the mindless wind,
The moaning tree boughs swaying blind,
And on the glass the unmeaning beat
Of ghostly fingertips of sleet.   105
Beyond the circle of our hearth
No welcome sound of toil or mirth
Unbound the spell, and testified
Of human life and thought outside.
We minded that the sharpest ear   110
The buried brooklet could not hear,
The music of whose liquid lip
Had been to us companionship,
And, in our lonely life, had grown
To have an almost human tone.   115

As night drew on, and, from the crest
Of wooded knolls that ridged the west,
The sun, a snow-blown traveler, sank
From sight beneath the smothering bank,
We piled, with care, our nightly stack   120
Of wood against the chimney back—
The oaken log, green, huge, and thick,
And on its top the stout backstick;

The knotty forestick laid apart,
And filled between with curious art   125
The ragged brush; then, hovering near,
We watched the first red blaze appear,
Heard the sharp crackle, caught the gleam
On whitewashed wall and sagging beam,
Until the old, rude-furnished room   130
Burst, flowerlike, into rosy bloom;
While radiant with a mimic flame
Outside the sparkling drift became,
And through the bare-boughed lilac tree
Our own warm hearth seemed blazing free.   135
The crane and pendent trammels⁹ showed,
The Turks' heads¹⁰ on the andirons glowed;
While childish fancy, prompt to tell
The meaning of the miracle,

---

9. **crane . . . trammels** (tram' əls): a crane is a swinging arm upon which
adjustable pothooks (trammels) are hung.
10. **Turks' heads:** the top of the andiron resembled a turban.

Whispered the old rhyme: *"Under the tree,*   140
When fire outdoors burns merrily,
There the witches are making tea."

The moon above the eastern wood
Shone at its full; the hill range stood
Transfigured in the silver flood,   145
Its blown snows flashing cold and keen,
Dead white, save where some sharp ravine
Took shadow, or the somber green
Of hemlocks turned to pitchy black
Against the whiteness at their back.   150
For such a world and such a night
Most fitting that unwarming light,
Which only seemed where'er it fell
To make the coldness visible.

Shut in from all the world without,   155
We sat the clean-winged hearth[11] about,
Content to let the north wind roar
In baffled rage at pane and door,
While the red logs before us beat
The frost line back with tropic heat;   160
And ever, when a louder blast
Shook beam and rafter as it passed,
The merrier up its roaring draft
The great throat of the chimney laughed;
The house dog on his paws outspread   165
Laid to the fire his drowsy head,
The cat's dark silhouette on the wall
A couchant[12] tiger's seemed to fall;
And, for the winter fireside meet,
Between the andirons' straddling feet,   170
The mug of cider simmered slow,
The apples sputtered in a row,
And, close at hand, the basket stood
With nuts from brown October's wood. . . .

---

11. **clean-winged hearth:** a turkey wing was used for a hearth broom.
12. **couchant** (kou' chant): lying down, especially with the head up.

Getting at Meaning

1. The first lines of this poem describe the approaching storm. What clues in the physical world around the farm indicate that a blizzard is on the way?

2. What nightly chores does the speaker perform regularly?

3. How does the speaker describe the world on "the second morning" after the heavy snowfall? Study lines 54–65. What is the speaker's attitude toward the transformed world? How does he feel about shoveling a path?

4. How do the various animals in the barn react when the humans arrive there?

5. What happens to the weather after the snow stops? How do the humans inside the house react?

Developing Skills in Reading Literature

1. **Imagery.** This poem is full of images that appeal to the senses of sight, hearing, taste, smell, and touch. Visual and auditory images predominate in the poem. Choose one of these two kinds of images and identify in the poem several passages in which the images are particularly vivid. What words and phrases seem especially lively? What mood does each passage create?

2. **Contrast.** In "Snowbound" Whittier uses contrast to achieve dramatic effects. For example, the speaker describes the raging storm using images such as "savage air" and "the shrieking of the mindless wind." He then sets up a contrast to the inhospitable weather in lines 116–174. What are some of the details of life inside the house? What is the effect of these details? How does the reader's awareness of the storm outside intensify this effect?

3. **Rhyme Scheme.** Whittier uses rhymed couplets in this poem. For example, in the first two lines *day* and *gray* rhyme; in lines 3 and 4 *noon* and *moon* rhyme. Sometimes Whittier varies this pattern. Lines 11 and 14, for example, rhyme with each other, with a rhymed couplet between them.

Find other places in the poem where Whittier varies the basic pattern. In what way do the variations help to keep the lengthy poem flowing along? How do they help to keep the reader alert?

Developing Vocabulary

Greek Roots. The first section of "Snowbound" is titled "A Winter Idyll." *Idyll* comes from the Greek word *eidos,* meaning "form or picture."

Look up the five words that follow, all derived from this root. Record the meaning of each word and explain its relationship to the root.

eidetic	idyllic
eidolon	kaleidoscope
idyll	

Telling the Bees

Whittier attached the following explanatory note to this poem: "A remarkable custom, brought from the Old Country, formerly prevailed in the rural districts of New England. On the death of a member of the family, the bees were at once informed of the event, and their hives dressed in mourning. This ceremonial was supposed to be necessary to prevent the swarms from leaving their hives and seeking a new home."

Here is the place; right over the hill
   Runs the path I took;
You can see the gap in the old wall still,
   And the steppingstones in the shallow brook.

There is the house, with the gate red-barred,   5
   And the poplars tall;
And the barn's brown length, and the cattle yard,
   And the white horns tossing above the wall.

There are the beehives ranged in the sun;
   And down by the brink   10
Of the brook are her poor flowers, weed o'crrun,
   Pansy and daffodil, rose and pink.

A year has gone, as the tortoise goes,
   Heavy and slow;
And the same rose blows, and the same sun glows,   15
   And the same brook sings of a year ago.

There's the same sweet clover smell in the breeze;
   And the June sun warm
Tangles his wings of fire in the trees,
   Setting, as then, over Fernside farm.   20

I mind me how with a lover's care
   From my Sunday coat
I brushed off the burrs, and smoothed my hair,
   And cooled at the brookside my brow and throat.

Since we parted, a month had passed,—   25
   To love, a year;
Down through the beeches I looked at last
   On the little red gate and the well sweep near.

I can see it all now,—the slantwise rain
    Of light through the leaves,
The sundown's blaze on her windowpane,   30
    The bloom of her roses under the eaves.

Just the same as a month before,—
    The house and the trees,
The barn's brown gable, the vine by the door,—   35
    Nothing changed but the hives of bees.

Before them, under the garden wall,
    Forward and back,
Went drearily singing the chore-girl small,
    Draping each hive with a shred of black.   40

Trembling, I listened: the summer sun
    Had the chill of snow;
For I knew she was telling the bees of one
    Gone on the journey we all must go!

Then I said to myself, "My Mary weeps   45
    For the dead today:
Haply her blind old grandsire sleeps
    The fret and the pain of his age away."

But her dog whined low; on the doorway sill,
    With his cane to his chin,   50
The old man sat; and the chore-girl still
    Sung to the bees stealing out and in.

And the song she was singing ever since
    In my ear sounds on:—
"Stay at home, pretty bees, fly not hence!   55
    Mistress Mary is dead and gone!"

SUMMER, 1874. *Winslow Homer.*
Sterling and Francine Clark Art Institute.
Williamstown, Massachusetts.

Getting at Meaning

1. In the first five stanzas the speaker describes a scene in which almost everything is the same as it was a year earlier. What one detail suggests that an important change has occurred?

2. What details does the speaker mention as he remembers approaching his lover's house after a month's absence? How does he feel as he approaches the house?

3. When the speaker sees the chore-girl draping the bee hives, he assumes that his lover's grandfather has died. What details quickly lead him to realize that someone else has died?

Developing Skills in Reading Literature

1. **Mood.** This poem begins with a description of a pleasant, rural scene. When does the speaker first introduce some tension? When does the mood suddenly change? What sensory images convey this change?

2. **Meter.** Determine the meter of the first stanza of the poem. How many stressed syllables are there per line in lines 1, 3, and 4? How many are there in line 2? What two kinds of feet does Whittier use?

Scan the second stanza of "Telling the Bees." Is its metrical pattern the same as the pattern of the first stanza?

Developing Writing Skills

Using Imagery To Create Mood. In both "Snowbound" and "Telling the Bees" Whittier uses rich sensory imagery to draw the reader into his rural scenes and mood, or atmosphere.

Write either a short poem or a descriptive paragraph in which you create a specific mood. Before you begin to write, decide on a particular environment or situation as your subject and on the mood you wish to evoke. List sights, sounds, smells, tastes, and textures associated with your subject, making sure that these images are consistent with the mood you have chosen. Then begin to shape your thoughts into poem or paragraph form.

Ralph Waldo Emerson

1803–1882

In 1837 Ralph Waldo Emerson delivered the annual Phi Beta Kappa address to the graduating class at Harvard. In his speech Emerson defined a scholar as "one who raises himself from private considerations and breathes and lives on public and illustrious thoughts." Emerson might have been describing himself, for he was one of the great nineteenth-century thinkers and writers.

Emerson was a poet, essayist, and philosopher. At Harvard, which he entered when he was only fourteen, he studied classical philosophy. He also began keeping a journal, a habit that he continued throughout his life. Afterwards he studied theology, hardly a surprising choice for he was descended from seven generations of ministers. Emerson's own father, who died when the boy was nine, had been pastor of the First Church of Boston. Emerson himself became junior pastor of the Second Church of Boston in 1829.

Emerson did not last long in the ministry, leaving the church in 1832. One reason for his departure was the death of his young wife, Ellen Tucker, after less than two years of marriage. Emerson had loved her deeply, and after her death, his family was afraid that Emerson was literally insane with grief. The other reason for Emerson's resignation was his feeling that he could no longer endorse the orthodox religious views of his day.

During the 1830's and 40's, Emerson and a small group of men and women living in or near Boston gathered regularly to discuss ideas. They founded their own journal, *The Dial*, and several of them their own utopian community, Brook Farm. The philosophical system created by this group became known as Transcendentalism. Transcendentalism is an offshoot of European Romanticism, with a particularly American twist. Essential to the philosophy is Emerson's view that all human beings have "God in us" and that human spirituality is reflected in nature. Feeling the "fundamental unity" between human life and nature, said Emerson, leads to a perception of the Over-Soul, an ultimate spiritual force that encompasses all existence and of which every person is a part. Emerson also believed strongly in the preeminence of the individual and in the importance of following one's own inner lights.

When he resigned the ministry, Emerson traveled for a time in Europe. On his return he settled in Concord, Massachusetts, near Boston, and married his second wife, Lydia Jackson. "Lydian," as she was called, and "Waldo," as Emerson was called by his friends, had four children and nearly fifty years of marriage together. Emerson devoted himself to writing essays, publishing a number of collections during his lifetime, and to poetry. His most famous essays include "Self-Reliance," "Circles," "Gifts," "Nature," "Compensation," and "The Over-Soul." He never attempted fiction, which he did not even enjoy reading. Emerson also gave lectures, a major source of income for him. He associated with the leading writers and thinkers of his day, always at his home in Concord.

Twentieth-century commentators have often criticized Emerson for being too optimistic. For example, the noted writer Henry James said that Emerson "had no great sense of wrong . . . no sense of the dark, the foul, the base." In spite of this limitation on his vision, Emerson was still the most important spiritual voice of his generation.

Concord Hymn

SUNG AT THE COMPLETION OF THE BATTLE MONUMENT,
JULY 4, 1837

By the rude bridge that arched the flood,
    Their flag to April's breeze unfurled,
Here once the embattled farmers stood
    And fired the shot heard round the world.

The foe long since in silence slept;   5
    Alike the conqueror silent sleeps;
And Time the ruined bridge has swept
    Down the dark stream which seaward creeps.

On this green bank, by this soft stream,
    We set today a votive[1] stone;   10
That memory may their deed redeem,
    When, like our sires, our sons are gone.

Spirit, that made those heroes dare
    To die, and leave their children free,
Bid Time and Nature gently spare   15
    The shaft we raise to them and thee.

---

1. **votive** (vōt' iv): offered or performed in fulfillment of a vow or in gratitude or devotion.

THE ENGAGEMENT AT THE NORTH BRIDGE IN CONCORD, 1775. *Amos Doolittle.*
Chicago Historical Society.

Getting at Meaning

1. To what does the phrase "the shot heard round the world" refer? Why was this shot internationally significant? What does the phrase "embattled farmers" suggest about the colonists?

2. What reason is given for erecting a monument to the Revolutionary War heroes?

Developing Skills in Reading Literature

1. **Alliteration.** This poem involves the repetition of several consonant sounds. In the first stanza, for example, *flood* and *flag* repeat the initial *fl* sound. What alliterative patterns appear in the second, third, and fourth stanzas? What is the effect of the alliteration on the rhythm of the poem?

2. **Consonance.** Closely related to alliteration is consonance, which is the repetition of consonant sounds within and at the ends of words. Consonance, too, helps give writing a rhythmic cadence and creates unity. It often reinforces alliterative patterns by repeating the same consonant sounds.

Emerson uses consonance in this poem when he repeats the *d* sound in the words *rude, flood, fired, stood,* and *world.* Find other examples of consonance in the poem. Comment on how the consonance functions in the poem.

3. **Assonance.** Assonance is the repetition of a vowel sound within words. Like alliteration and consonance, assonance gives both poetry and prose a musical quality and serves to unify stanzas and passages.

This poem contains a great deal of assonance. For example, Emerson repeats the long *e* sound in *sleeps, stream, seaward, creeps, green, deed, redeem, leave, free,* and *thee.* What other vowel sounds does he use often? How does this assonance serve to unify the poem?

4. **Theme.** Notice that the final stanza is addressed to "Spirit." What dual meaning does the word *spirit* have in this poem? How does this dual meaning reflect Emerson's philosophy as explained in his biography?

The Rhodora

On Being Asked, Whence Is the Flower?

In May, when sea winds pierced our solitudes,
I found the fresh Rhodora in the woods,
Spreading its leafless blooms in a damp nook,
To please the desert and the sluggish brook.
The purple petals, fallen in the pool, 5
Made the black water with their beauty gay;
Here might the redbird come his plumes to cool,
And court the flower that cheapens his array.
Rhodora! if the sages ask thee why
This charm is wasted on the earth and sky, 10
Tell them, dear, that if eyes were made for seeing,
Then Beauty is its own excuse for being:
Why thou wert there, O rival of the rose!
I never thought to ask, I never knew;
But, in my simple ignorance, suppose 15
The selfsame Power that brought me there brought you.

Getting at Meaning

1. According to the statement that prefaces this poem, what does the poem attempt to explain?

2. The rhodora is hidden away, where its "charm is wasted on the earth and sky." What does the speaker conclude about this?

Developing Skills in Reading Literature

1. **Personification.** In what human terms is the flower described? What is suggested by the speaker's addressing the flower as "dear"? What is the flower supposed to reply to the sages who question its existence?

2. **Theme.** Emerson's religious philosophy is evident in this poem. What final statement does the poem make about humans and nature and about why things exist?

Each and All

Little thinks, in the field, yon red-cloaked clown
Of thee from the hilltop looking down;
The heifer that lows in the upland farm,
Far-heard, lows not thine ear to charm;
The sexton, tolling his bell at noon,   5
Deems not that great Napoleon
Stops his horse, and lists with delight,
Whilst his files sweep round yon Alpine height;
Nor knowest thou what argument
Thy life to thy neighbor's creed has lent.   10
All are needed by each one;
Nothing is fair or good alone.
I thought the sparrow's note from heaven,
Singing at dawn on the alder bough;
I brought him home, in his nest, at even;   15
He sings the song, but it cheers not now,
For I did not bring home the river and sky;
He sang to my ear—they sang to my eye.

The delicate shells lay on the shore;
The bubbles of the latest wave   20
Fresh pearls to their enamel gave,
And the bellowing of the savage sea
Greeted their safe escape to me.
I wiped away the weeds and foam,
I fetched my seaborn treasures home;   25
But the poor, unsightly, noisome things
Had left their beauty on the shore
With the sun and the sand and the wild uproar.
The lover watched his graceful maid,
As 'mid the virgin train she strayed,   30
Nor knew her beauty's best attire
Was woven still by the snow-white choir.
At last she came to his hermitage,
Like the bird from the woodlands to the cage;
The gay enchantment was undone,   35
A gentle wife, but fairy none.
Then I said, "I covet truth;
Beauty is unripe childhood's cheat;
I leave it behind with the games of youth"—
As I spoke, beneath my feet   40
The ground pine curled its pretty wreath,
Running over the club-moss burrs;

I inhaled the violet's breath;
Around me stood the oaks and firs;
Pine cones and acorns lay on the ground;   45
Over me soared the eternal sky,
Full of light and of deity;
Again I saw, again I heard,
The rolling river, the morning bird;
Beauty through my senses stole;   50
I yielded myself to the perfect whole.

Getting at Meaning

1. Study lines 1–8. What does the speaker say about the relationship among the elements of nature? To whom do the words *thee* and *thine* refer?

2. What happened when the speaker took the sparrow out of its natural environment? What happened when the speaker brought home shells? What happened when the lover married "his graceful maid"? Explain the line, "Nothing is fair or good alone."

3. Explain the speaker's conclusion that "Beauty is unripe childhood's cheat."

4. After the speaker decides to forget about acquiring beauty, what happens?

Developing Skills in Reading Literature

1. **Rhyme.** For the most part this poem is composed of rhymed couplets. Often, however, Emerson uses imperfect rhymes, frequently known as slant rhymes or off-rhymes. Lines 11 and 12 present an example of off-rhyme, for *one* and *alone* do not rhyme perfectly.

Find more examples of off-rhyme in the poem. What other variations does Emerson make in his basic pattern? Can you find lines that do not rhyme with any other lines? How do the departures from a rigid pattern affect the rhythm and pace of the poem? In what way do they make it easier to concentrate on the poem's meaning?

2. **Theme.** This poem is a statement of the transcendental principle of fundamental unity, and it illustrates Emerson's concept of the Over-Soul. What is the speaker feeling at the end of the poem? What has the speaker had to do to perceive the fundamental unity in the universe? How does the title of the poem relate to the poem's meaning?

Days

Daughters of Time, the hypocritic Days,
Muffled and dumb like barefoot dervishes,[1]
And marching single in an endless file,
Bring diadems[2] and fagots[3] in their hands.
To each they offer gifts after his will,   5
Bread, kingdoms, stars, and sky that holds them all.
I, in my pleached garden, watched the pomp,
Forgot my morning wishes, hastily
Took a few herbs and apples, and the Day
Turned and departed silent. I, too late,   10
Under her solemn fillet saw the scorn.

---

1. **dervishes** (dər′ vish əz): members of a Muslim religious order noted for devotional exercises.
2. **diadems** (dī′ ə demz′): headbands worn as badges of royalty.
3. **fagots** (fag′ ətz): bundles of sticks.

Getting at Meaning

1. What relationship between time and days is set up in the poem? What is the usual activity of the days?

2. What does the speaker, watching time go by, suddenly realize?

Developing Skills in Reading Literature

1. **Personification.** The days are described in human terms in this poem. What kind of human terms? Why are they "muffled and dumb"? Why do they march in single file? Why does one of them scorn the speaker?

2. **Diction.** Emerson uses some unusual words in this poem. What do words such as *dervishes*, *diadems*, and *fagots* contribute to the atmosphere of the poem? Notice the use of the word *hypocritic*(al) to describe the days. This is a key word in the poem. In what sense are the days hypocritical? They bring gifts, but in what sense do they still scorn humans?

Developing Vocabulary

Words from Greek and Latin. *Hypo-* or *hyp-* is a Greek prefix meaning "below or beneath," or "abnormally low." *Hypocritical*, for example, comes from *hypo + krinein*, a Greek word meaning "to separate." Originally *hypocrisy* meant "to separate below," and referred to Greek actors who left a chorus to answer their fellow actors. Today, *hypocrisy* means a falseness in which one's true feelings are hidden beneath the surface. In a way, a hypocritical person plays a role.

The words that follow employ the prefix *hypo-*. Look up each word in a dictionary and record its meaning. Also identify the root from which each word is derived, and explain how the root and the prefix work together to create the present meaning for the word.

hypochondria   hypostasis
hypodermis   hypothesis
hypogene

Nonfiction

THE STOP-OVER (DETAIL), 1956. *Roy Martell Mason.*
The Metropolitan Museum of Art. Gift of J. Gordon Carr, 1956.

Ralph Waldo Emerson

from **Self-Reliance**

I read the other day some verses written by an eminent painter which were original and not conventional. Always the soul hears an admonition in such lines, let the subject be what it may The sentiment they instill is of more value than any thought they may contain. To believe your own thought, to believe that what is true for you in your private heart, is true for all men—that is genius. Speak your latent conviction and it shall be the universal sense; for always the inmost becomes the outmost, and our first thought is rendered back to us by the trumpets of the Last Judgment. Familiar as the voice of the mind is to each, the highest merit we ascribe to Moses, Plato,[1] and Milton,[2] is that they set at naught books and traditions, and spoke not what men did but what they thought. A man should learn to detect and watch that gleam of light which flashes across his mind from within, more than the luster of the firmament of bards and sages. Yet he dismisses without notice his thought, because it is his. In every work of genius we recognize our own rejected thoughts; they come back to us with a certain alienated majesty. Great works of art have no more affecting lesson for us than this. They teach us to abide by our spontaneous impression with good humored inflexibility then most when the whole cry of voices is on the other side. Else, tomorrow a stranger will say with masterly good sense precisely what we have thought and felt all the time, and we shall be forced to take with shame our own opinion from another.

There is a time in every man's education when he arrives at the conviction that envy is ignorance; that imitation is suicide; that he must take himself for better, for worse, as his portion; that though the wide universe is full of good, no kernel of nourishing corn can come to him but through his toil bestowed on that plot of ground which is given to him to till. . . .

Trust thyself: every heart vibrates to that iron string. Accept the place the divine Providence has found for you; the society of your contemporaries, the connection of events. Great men have always done so and confided themselves childlike to the genius of their age, betraying their perception that the Eternal was stirring at their heart, working through their hands, predominating in all their being. And we are now men, and must accept in the highest mind the same transcendent destiny; and not pinched in a corner, not cowards fleeing before a revolution, but redeemers and benefactors, pious aspirants to be noble clay plastic under the Almighty effort, let us advance and advance on Chaos and the Dark. . . .

The nonchalance of boys who are sure of a dinner, and would disdain as much as a lord to do or say aught to conciliate one, is the healthy attitude of human nature. How is a boy the master of society; independent, irresponsible, looking out from his corner on such people and facts as pass by, he tries and sentences them on their merits, in the swift summary way of boys, as good, bad, interesting, silly, eloquent, troublesome. He cumbers

---

1. **Plato** (plā′ tō): A Greek philosopher who lived from 427?-347 B.C.
2. **Milton:** John Milton, the famous English poet who wrote "Paradise Lost"; he lived from 1608-1674.

himself never about consequences, about interests: he gives an independent, genuine verdict. You must court him: he does not court you. But the man is, as it were, clapped into jail by his consciousness. As soon as he has once acted or spoken with éclat, he is a committed person, watched by the sympathy or the hatred of hundreds whose affections must now enter into his account. There is no Lethe[3] for this. Ah, that he could pass again into his neutral, godlike independence! . . .

Society everywhere is in conspiracy against the manhood of every one of its members. Society is a joint-stock company in which the members agree for the better securing of his bread to each shareholder, to surrender the liberty and culture of the eater. The virtue in most request is conformity. Self-reliance is its aversion. It loves not realities and creators, but names and customs.

Whoso would be a man must be a nonconformist. He who would gather immortal palms must not be hindered by the name of goodness, but must explore if it be goodness. Nothing is at last sacred but the integrity of your own mind. Absolve you to yourself, and you shall have the suffrage of the world. I remember an answer which when quite young I was prompted to make to a valued adviser who was wont to importune me with the dear old doctrines of the church. On my saying, "What have I to do with the sacredness of traditions, if I live wholly from within?" my friend suggested—"But these impulses may be from below, not from above." I replied, "They do not seem to me to be such; but if I am the devil's child, I will live then from the devil." No law can be sacred to me but that of my nature. Good and bad are but names very readily transferable to that or this; the only right is what is after my constitution, the only wrong what is against it. A man is to carry himself in the presence of all opposition as if every thing were titular and ephemeral but he. I am ashamed to think how easily we capitulate to badges and names, to large societies and dead institutions. Every decent and well spoken individual affects and sways me more than is right. I ought to go upright and vital, and speak the rude truth in all ways. . . .

What I must do, is all that concerns me, not what the people think. This rule, equally arduous in actual and in intellectual life, may serve for the whole distinction between greatness and meanness. It is the harder, because you will always find those who think they know what is your duty better than you know it. It is easy in the world to live after the world's opinion; it is easy in solitude to live after our own; but the great man is he who in the midst of the crowd keeps with perfect sweetness the independence of solitude.

The objection to conforming to usages that have become dead to you, is, that it scatters your force. It loses your time and blurs the impression of your character. If you maintain a dead church, contribute to a dead Bible Society, vote with a great party either for the Government or against it, spread your table like base housekeepers—under all these screens I have difficulty to detect the precise man you are. And, of course, so much force is withdrawn from your proper life. But do your thing, and I shall know you. Do your work, and you shall reinforce yourself. . . .

For nonconformity the world whips you with its displeasure. And therefore a man must know how to estimate a sour face. The bystanders look askance on him in the public street or in the friend's parlor. If this aversation had its origin in contempt and resistance like his own, he might well go home with a sad countenance; but the sour faces of the multitude, like their sweet faces, have no deep cause,—disguise no god, but are put on and off as the wind blows, and a newspaper directs. Yet is the discontent of the multitude more formidable than that of the senate and

---

3. **Lethe** (lē' thē): a river in Hades whose waters cause drinkers to forget their past.

the college. It is easy enough for a firm man who knows the world to brook the rage of the cultivated classes. Their rage is decorous and prudent, for they are timid as being very vulnerable themselves. But when to their feminine rage the indignation of the people is added, when the ignorant and the poor are aroused, when the unintelligent brute force that lies at the bottom of society is made to growl and mow, it needs the habit of magnanimity and religion to treat it godlike as a trifle of no concernment.

The other terror that scares us from self trust is our consistency; a reverence for our past act or word, because the eyes of others have no other data for computing our orbit than our past acts, and we are loath to disappoint them.

A foolish consistency is the hobgoblin of little minds, adored by little statesmen and philosophers and divines. With consistency, a great soul has simply nothing to do. He may as well concern himself with his shadow on the wall. Out upon your guarded lips! Sew them up with packthread, do. Else, if you would be a man, speak what you think today in words as hard as cannon balls, and tomorrow speak what tomorrow thinks in hard words again, though it contradict every thing you said today. Ah, then, exclaim the aged ladies, you shall be sure to be misunderstood.

Misunderstood! It is a right fool's word. Is it so bad then to be misunderstood? Pythagoras[4] was misunderstood, and Socrates,[5] and Jesus, and Luther, and Copernicus,[6] and Galileo,[7] and Newton,[8] and every pure and wise spirit that ever took flesh. To be great is to be misunderstood. . . .

The man must be so much that he must make all circumstances indifferent—put all means into the shade. This all great men are and do. Every true man is a cause, a country, and an age; requires infinite spaces and numbers and time fully to accomplish his thought; and posterity seem to follow his steps as a procession. A man Caesar is born, and for ages after, we have a Roman Empire. Christ is born, and millions of minds so grow and cleave to his genius, that he is confounded with virtue and the possible of man. An institution is the lengthened shadow of one man. . . .

---

4. **Pythagoras** (pə thag' ə rəs): a Greek philosopher and mathematician who died around 447 B.C.

5. **Socrates** (säk' rə tēz'): a Greek philosopher who lived from 470?-399 B.C.

6. **Copernicus** (kō pər' ni kəs): a Polish astronomer, the founder of modern astronomy, who lived from 1473-1543.

7. **Galileo** (gal' ə lē' ō): an Italian astronomer and physicist, who lived from 1564-1642.

8. **Newton** (no͞ot' 'n): an English mathematician and natural philosopher, who lived from 1642-1727.

Getting at Meaning

1. How does Emerson define genius? Explain the statement, "In every work of genius we recognize our own rejected thoughts."

2. Explain Emerson's statement that every person must learn "that envy is ignorance; that imitation is suicide."

3. According to Emerson, what happens to a person's independence as he or she grows older? Explain the statement, ". . . the man is, as it were, clapped into jail by his consciousness."

4. In what ways is society "everywhere . . . in conspiracy against the manhood of every one of its members"? Summarize Emerson's views on society.

5. Emerson goes so far as to say, "Whoso would be a man must be a nonconformist." What reasons does he give for valuing nonconformity to this extent?

6. What is Emerson's objection to conforming to "usages" that no longer have meaning? What examples does he give?

7. Why does Emerson believe that consistency is not as important as most people say it is? Explain his

famous statement, "A foolish consistency is the hobgoblin of little minds. . . ."

8. Notice the examples that Emerson gives of geniuses who have been misunderstood. Why have these people been misunderstood? According to Emerson, what enabled these geniuses to do their work anyway?

Developing Skills in Reading Literature

1. **Essay.** As noted earlier, an essay is a brief, nonfiction composition that offers an opinion on a subject, frequently with a persuasive intent. Some essays are formal and impersonal, and the major argument is developed systematically. Other essays are informal, personal, and loosely structured. The informal essay often includes anecdotes and humor.

Would you describe "Self-Reliance" as formal or informal? In answering the question consider the essay's organization, its diction, and its syntax, or the structure of its sentences.

Essays are sometimes classified as descriptive, narrative, or expository, though the same essay may be all three at once. Descriptive essays deal primarily with the appearances of people, objects, and places, working through images that appeal to the senses. Narrative essays tell stories. Expository essays focus mainly on presenting information.

Which type of essay is "Self-Reliance"? Do you see elements of the other essay types in its paragraphs? Explain your response.

2. **Metaphor.** Emerson uses a metaphor to illustrate his views on society. He says, "Society is a joint-stock company in which the members agree for the better securing of his bread to each shareholder, to surrender the liberty and culture of the eater." Discuss this comparison. Is the metaphor a true picture of society? What does Emerson conclude is the problem with society, as dramatized in this metaphor?

3. **Aphorism.** Throughout "Self-Reliance" Emerson's style is characterized by the frequent use of aphorisms; for example, "Whoso would be a man must be a nonconformist" and "A foolish consistency is the hobgoblin of little minds. . . ."

Explain the aphorism "For nonconformity the world whips you with its displeasure. And therefore a man must know how to estimate a sour face." What other statements in the essay would you label as aphorisms? Select three or four and explain their meanings.

Developing Writing Skills

1. **Explaining an Idea.** Select an aphorism from "Self-Reliance" and write a well developed paragraph in which you discuss the truth of the statement. Use examples from your own life and from your observation of others to support your ideas.

2. **Analyzing Theme.** Emerson says, "It is easy in the world to live after the world's opinion; it is easy in solitude to live after our own; but the great man is he who in the midst of the crowd keeps with perfect sweetness the independence of solitude."

Write a five-paragraph essay in which you analyze this statement. In the opening paragraph place the statement in the context of the essay. Devote one paragraph to each part of Emerson's statements, relating his ideas to your own life and to the world around you. For example, in one paragraph discuss how "It is easy in the world to live after the world's opinion. . . ." Explain how this has been true in your own life and where you see its truth in the lives of others. Use specific examples wherever you can. In the concluding paragraph, summarize briefly your main points or present a final thought on Emerson's philosophy as embodied in the quoted statement.

Henry David Thoreau
1817–1862

A disciple of Ralph Waldo Emerson, Henry David Thoreau took Emerson's ideas about self-reliance to heart. Thoreau headed off in his own direction and lived an unusual, meditative life, producing *Walden*, one of the great books of the mid-nineteenth century and a classic in world literature.

Thoreau was born and raised in Concord, Massachusetts, where he lived nearly all of his life. He attended Concord Academy, after which his family sacrificed to send him to Harvard. There Thoreau studied classics and read as many books on natural history as he could find. When he graduated from Harvard at twenty, he returned to Concord to teach school. During the next four years he taught off and on and for a time ran his own academy in Concord with his brother John. In 1841 John's illness forced the closing of the school, bringing to an end Thoreau's career as a teacher.

Thoreau then went to live with Emerson and his family, performing odd jobs in the Emerson household and using Emerson's library. Emerson, who was fourteen years older than Thoreau, was already an influential literary figure. The two men became extremely fond of each other, and Emerson's transcendental views profoundly influenced Thoreau.

On the Fourth of July in 1845, just days before his twenty-eighth birthday, Thoreau began his famous experiment in "essential" living. On a tract of land owned by Emerson near Concord, Thoreau had built a small cabin on the shores of Walden Pond, spending only twenty-eight dollars and twelve and a half cents in the process. There Thoreau lived for over two years, writing, communing with nature, and supporting himself with occasional physical labor. By working only about six weeks each year, he could live simply and independently during the remainder of the year. Thoreau did not want to spend his valuable time working for unnecessary material goods, preferring instead to simplify his needs and concentrate on mental and spiritual activity. In this respect Thoreau was a true Transcendentalist.

Contrary to what some people believe, Thoreau was not a hermit at Walden Pond. He walked into

Concord often, visiting friends and maintaining close ties with his family. He had visitors at the pond quite regularly. A superb naturalist, Thoreau spent hours observing closely the details of his environment: the plants, the animals, the pond in each season of the year.

Walden was not published until 1854, seven years after Thoreau left his cabin in the woods and returned to Concord. An odd, brilliant, fascinating book, *Walden* is the record of Thoreau's life at the pond, a mixture of philosophy, naturalism, and spiritual autobiography. For artistic purposes, Thoreau compressed his two years at the pond into one year, using the four seasons to structure his book. Stylistically, *Walden* is a masterpiece. Ironically, it sold poorly during Thoreau's lifetime.

In 1844 Thoreau spent a night in jail for refusing to pay a Massachusetts poll tax, a protest on his part against the use of the tax money to support slavery and the Mexican-American War. "Civil Disobedience," the famous essay that sprang out of Thoreau's experience in jail, is a strong transcendental statement urging every citizen to protest any governmental policy that requires him or her to be "the agent of injustice to another." Although ignored at first, "Civil Disobedience" has influenced political leaders throughout the world, such as Mohandas Gandhi and Dr. Martin Luther King, Jr.

from **Walden**

from **Where I Lived and What I Lived For**

When I first took up my abode in the woods, that is, began to spend my nights as well as days there, which, by accident, was on Independence day, or the fourth of July, 1845, my house was not finished for winter, but was merely a defense against the rain, without plastering or chimney, the walls being of rough weather-stained boards, with wide chinks, which made it cool at night. The upright white hewn studs and freshly planed door and window casings gave it a clean and airy look, especially in the morning, when its timbers were saturated with dew, so that I fancied that by noon some sweet gum would exude from them. To my imagination it retained throughout the day more or less of this auroral character, reminding me of a certain house on a mountain which I had visited a year before. This was an airy and unplastered cabin, fit to entertain a traveling god, and where a goddess might trail her garments. The winds which passed over my dwelling were such as sweep over the ridges of mountains, bearing the broken strains, or celestial parts only, of terrestrial music. The morning wind forever blows, the poem of creation is uninterrupted; but few are the ears that hear it. Olympus[1] is but the outside of the earth everywhere. . . .

I was seated by the shore of a small pond, about a mile and a half south of the village of Concord and somewhat higher than it, in the midst of an extensive wood between that town and Lincoln, and about two miles south of that our only field known to fame, Concord Battle Ground; but I was so low in the woods that the opposite shore, half a mile off, like the rest, covered with wood, was my most distant horizon. For the first week, whenever I looked out on the pond it impressed me like a tarn high up on the side of a mountain, its bottom far above the surface of other lakes, and, as the sun arose, I saw it throwing off its nightly clothing of mist, and here and there, by degrees, its soft ripples or its smooth reflecting surface was revealed, while the mists, like ghosts, were stealthily withdrawing in every direction into the woods, as at the breaking up of some nocturnal conventicle. The very dew seemed to hang upon the trees later into the day than usual, as on the sides of mountains.

This small lake was of most value as a neighbor in the intervals of a gentle rain storm in August, when, both air and water being perfectly still, but the sky overcast, mid-afternoon had all the serenity of evening, and the wood thrush sang around, and was heard from shore to shore. A lake like this is never smoother than at such a time; and the clear portion of the air above it being shallow and darkened by clouds, the water, full of light and reflections, becomes a lower heaven itself so much the more important. From a hilltop near by, where the wood had been recently cut off, there was a pleasing vista southward across the pond, through a wide indentation in the hills which form the shore there, where their opposite sides sloping toward each other suggested a stream flowing out in that direction through a wooded valley, but stream there was none. That way I looked between and over the near green hills to some distant and higher ones in the horizon, tinged

---

1. **Olympus** (ō lim′ pəs): a mountain in Thessaly that is the abode of the gods in Greek mythology.

with blue. Indeed, by standing on tiptoe I could catch a glimpse of some of the peaks of the still bluer and more distant mountain ranges in the northwest, those true-blue coins from heaven's own mint, and also of some portion of the village. But in other directions, even from this point, I could not see over or beyond the woods which surrounded me. It is well to have some water in your neighborhood, to give buoyancy to and float the earth. One value even of the smallest well is, that when you look into it you see that earth is not continent but insular. This is as important as that it keeps butter cool. When I looked across the pond from this peak toward the Sudbury meadows, which in time of flood I distinguished elevated perhaps by a mirage in their seething valley, like a coin in a basin, all the earth beyond the pond appeared like a thin crust insulated and floated even by this small sheet of intervening water, and I was reminded that this on which I dwelt was but dry land. . . .

Every morning was a cheerful invitation to make my life of equal simplicity, and I may say innocence, with Nature herself. I have been as sincere a worshipper of Aurora[2] as the Greeks. I got up early and bathed in the pond; that was a religious exercise, and one of the best things which I did. They say that characters were engraven on the bathing tub of king Tching-thang[3] to this effect: "Renew thyself completely each day; do it again, and again, and forever again." I can understand that. Morning brings back the heroic ages. I was as much affected by the faint hum of a mosquito making its invisible and unimaginable tour through my apartment at earliest dawn, when I was sitting with door and windows open, as I could be by any trumpet that ever sang of fame. It was Homer's[4] requiem; itself an Iliad and Odyssey in the air, singing its own wrath and wanderings. There was something cosmical about it; a standing advertisement, till forbidden, of the everlasting vigor and fertility of the world. The morning, which is the most

memorable season of the day, is the awakening hour. Then there is least somnolence in us; and for an hour, at least, some part of us awakes which slumbers all the rest of the day and night. Little is to be expected of that day, if it can be called a day, to which we are not awakened by our Genius, but by the mechanical nudgings of some servitor, are not awakened by our own newly acquired force and aspirations from within, accompanied by the undulations of celestial music, instead of factory bells, and a fragrance filling the air—to a higher life than we fell asleep from; and thus the darkness bear its fruit, and prove itself to be good, no less than the light. That man who does not believe that each day contains an earlier, more sacred, and auroral hour than he has yet profaned, has despaired of life, and is pursuing a descending and darkening way. After a partial cessation of his sensuous life, the soul of man, or its organs rather, are reinvigorated each day, and his Genius tries again what noble life it can make. All memorable events, I should say, transpire in morning time and in a morning atmosphere. The Vedas[5] say, "All intelligences awake with the morning." Poetry and art, and the fairest and most memorable of the actions of men, date from such an hour. All poets and heroes, like Memnon,[6] are the children of Aurora, and emit their music at sunrise. To him whose elastic and vigorous thought keeps pace with the sun, the day is a perpetual morning. It matters not what the clocks say or the attitudes and labors of men. Morning is when I am awake and there is a dawn in me. Moral

---

2. **Aurora** (ô rôr' ə): the Roman goddess of dawn.
3. **Tching-thang:** Ch'en T'ang, founder of the Shang dynasty, which lasted from 1766-1123 B.C.
4. **Homer:** probably lived around 850 B.C.; the famous Greek epic poet, author of the *Iliad* and the *Odyssey*.
5. **Vedas** (vād' əz): four canonical collections of hymns, prayers, and liturgical formulas that comprise the earliest Hindu sacred writings.
6. **Memnon** (mem' nän): an Ethiopian king slain by Achilles at a late stage of the Trojan War.

reform is the effort to throw off sleep. Why is it that men give so poor an account of their day if they have not been slumbering? They are not such poor calculators. If they had not been overcome with drowsiness they would have performed something. The millions are awake enough for physical labor; but only one in a million is awake enough for effective intellectual exertion, only one in a hundred millions to a poetic or divine life. To be awake is to be alive. I have never yet met a man who was quite awake. How could I have looked him in the face?

We must learn to reawaken and keep ourselves awake, not by mechanical aids, but by an infinite expectation of the dawn, which does not forsake us in our soundest sleep. I know of no more encouraging fact than the unquestionable ability of man to elevate his life by a conscious endeavor. It is something to be able to paint a particular picture, or to carve a statue, and so to make a few objects beautiful; but it is far more glorious to carve and paint the very atmosphere and medium through which we look, which morally we can do. To affect the quality of the day, that is the highest of arts. Every man is tasked to make his life, even in its details, worthy of the contemplation of his most elevated and critical hour. If we refused, or rather used up, such paltry information as we get, the oracles would distinctly inform us how this might be done.

I went to the woods because I wished to live deliberately, to front only the essential facts of life, and see if I could not learn what it had to teach, and not, when I came to die, discover that I had not lived. I did not wish to live what was not life, living is so dear; nor did I wish to practice resignation, unless it was quite necessary. I wanted to live deep and suck out all the marrow of life, to live so sturdily and Spartanlike[7] as to put to rout all that was not life, to cut a broad swath and shave close, to drive life into a corner, and reduce it to its lowest terms, and, if it proved to be mean, why then to get the whole and genuine meanness of it, and publish its meanness to the world; or if it were sublime, to know it by experience, and be able to give a true account of it in my next excursion. For most men, it appears to me, are in a strange uncertainty about it, whether it is of the devil or of God, and have somewhat hastily concluded that it is the chief end of man here to "glorify God and enjoy him forever."

Still we live meanly, like ants, though the fable tells us that we were long ago changed into men; like pygmies we fight with cranes;[8] it is error upon error, and clout upon clout, and our best virtue has for its occasion a superfluous and evitable wretchedness. Our life is frittered away by detail. An honest man has hardly need to count more than his ten fingers, or in extreme cases he may add his ten toes, and lump the rest. Simplicity, simplicity, simplicity! I say, let your affairs be as two or three, and not a hundred or a thousand; instead of a million count half a dozen, and keep your accounts on your thumb nail. In the midst of this chopping sea of civilized life, such are the clouds and storms and quicksands and thousand and one items to be allowed for, that a man has to live, if he would not founder and go to the bottom and not make his port at all, by dead reckoning, and he must be a great calculator indeed who succeeds. Simplify, simplify. Instead of three meals a day, if it be necessary eat but one; instead of a hundred dishes, five; and reduce other things in proportion. . . .

Why should we live with such hurry and waste of life? We are determined to be starved before we are hungry. Men say that a stitch in time saves nine, and so they take a thousand stitches today to save nine tomorrow. As for

---

7. **Spartanlike:** relating to Sparta, the city of ancient Greece; marked by self-discipline and self-denial.
8. **pygmies . . . cranes:** Thoreau alludes to a battle between pygmies and cranes described by Homer in Book IV of the *Iliad.* According to the fable, the pygmies were so small that they were afraid of a flight of cranes.

work, we haven't any of any consequence. We have the Saint Vitus' dance, and cannot possibly keep our heads still. If I should only give a few pulls at the parish bell rope, for a fire, that is, without setting the bell, there is hardly a man on his farm in the outskirts of Concord, notwithstanding that press of engagements which was his excuse so many times this morning, nor a boy, nor a woman, I might almost say, but would forsake all and follow that sound, not mainly to save property from the flames, but, if we will confess the truth, much more to see it burn, since burn it must, and we, be it known did not set it on fire—or to see it put out, and have a hand in it, if that is done as handsomely; yes, even if it were the parish church itself. Hardly a man takes a half hour's nap after dinner, but when he wakes he holds up his head and asks, "What's the news?" as if the rest of mankind had stood his sentinels. Some give directions to be waked every half hour, doubtless for no other purpose; and then, to pay for it, they tell what they have dreamed. After a night's sleep the news is as indispensable as the breakfast. "Pray tell me anything new that has happened to a man anywhere on this globe," and he reads it over his coffee and rolls, that a man has had his eyes gouged out this morning on the Wachito River; never dreaming the while that he lives in the dark unfathomed mammoth cave of this world, and has but the rudiment of an eye himself.

For my part, I could easily do without the post office. I think that there are very few important communications made through it. To speak critically, I never received more than one or two letters in my life—I wrote this some years ago—that were worth the postage. The penny post is, commonly, an institution through which you seriously offer a man that penny for his thoughts which is so often safely offered in jest. And I am sure that I never read any memorable news in a newspaper. If we read of one man robbed, or murdered, or killed by accident, or one house burned, or one vessel wrecked, or one steamboat blown up, or one cow run over on the Western Railroad, or one mad dog killed, or one lot of grasshoppers in the winter, we never need read of another. One is enough. . . .

Let us spend one day as deliberately as Nature, and not be thrown off the track by every nutshell and mosquito's wing that falls on the rails. Let us rise early and fast, or break fast, gently and without perturbation; let company come and let company go, let the bells ring and the children cry, determined to make a day of it. Why should we knock under and go with the stream? Let us not be upset and overwhelmed in that terrible rapid and whirlpool called a dinner, situated in the meridian shallows. Weather this danger and you are safe, for the rest of the way is down hill. With unrelaxed nerves, with morning vigor, sail by it, looking another way, tied to the mast like Ulysses. If the engine whistles, let it whistle till it is hoarse for its pains. If the bell rings, why should we run? We will consider what kind of music they are like. Let us settle ourselves, and work and wedge our feet downward through the mud and slush of opinion, and prejudice, and tradition, and delusion, and appearance, that alluvion which covers the globe, through Paris and London, through New York and Boston and Concord, through church and state, through poetry and philosophy and religion, till we come to a hard bottom and rocks in place, which we can call reality, and say, This is, and no mistake; and then begin, having a *point d'appui*,[9] below freshet and frost and fire, a place where you might found a wall or a state, or set a lamppost safely, or perhaps a gauge, not a Nilometer, but a Realometer, that future ages might know how deep a freshet of shams and appearances had gathered from time to time.

---

9. **point d'appui** (pwan dà pwē') *French:* a base, especially for a military operation.

If you stand right fronting and face to face to a fact, you will see the sun glimmer on both its surfaces, as if it were a cimeter,[10] and feel its sweet edge dividing you through the heart and marrow, and so you will happily conclude your mortal career. Be it life or death, we crave only reality. If we are really dying, let us hear the rattle in our throats and feel cold in the extremities; if we are alive, let us go about our business.

Time is but the stream I go a-fishing in. I drink at it; but while I drink I see the sandy bottom and detect how shallow it is. Its thin current slides away, but eternity remains. I would drink deeper; fish in the sky, whose bottom is pebbly with stars. I cannot count one. I know not the first letter of the alphabet. I have always been regretting that I was not as wise as the day I was born. The intellect is a cleaver; it discerns and rifts its way into the secret of things. I do not wish to be any more busy with my hands than is necessary. My head is hands and feet. I feel all my best faculties concentrated in it. My instinct tells me that my head is an organ for burrowing, as some creatures use their snout and forepaws, and with it I would mine and burrow my way through these hills. I think that the richest vein is somewhere hereabouts; so by the divining rod and thin rising vapors I judge; and here I will begin to mine.

STOP

from Solitude

This is a delicious evening, when the whole body is one sense, and imbibes delight through every pore. I go and come with a strange liberty in Nature, a part of herself. As I walk along the stony shore of the pond in my shirt sleeves, though it is cool as well as cloudy and windy, and I see nothing special to attract me, all the elements are unusually congenial to me. The bullfrogs trump to usher in the night, and the note of the whippoorwill is borne on the rippling wind from over the water. Sympathy with the fluttering alder and poplar leaves almost takes away my breath; yet, like the lake, my serenity is rippled but not ruffled. These small waves raised by the evening wind are as remote from storm as the smooth reflecting surface. Though it is now dark, the wind still blows and roars in the wood, the waves still dash, and some creatures lull the rest with their notes. The repose is never complete. The wildest animals do not repose, but seek their prey now; the fox, and skunk, and rabbit, now roam the fields and woods without fear. They are Nature's watchmen—links which connect the days of animated life.

When I return to my house I find that visitors have been there and left their cards, either a bunch of flowers, or a wreath of evergreen, or a name in pencil on a yellow walnut leaf or a chip. They who come rarely to the woods take some little piece of the forest into their hands to play with by the way, which they leave, either intentionally or accidentally. One has peeled a willow wand, woven it into a ring, and dropped it on my table. I could always tell if visitors had called in my absence, either by the bended twigs or grass, or the print of their shoes, and generally of what sex or age or quality they were by some slight trace left, as a flower dropped, or a bunch of grass plucked and thrown away, even as far off as the railroad, half a mile distant, or by the lingering odor of a cigar or pipe. Nay, I was frequently notified of the passage of a traveler along the highway sixty rods off by the scent of his pipe. . . .

Men frequently say to me, "I should think you would feel lonesome down there, and want to be nearer to folks, rainy and snowy days and nights especially." I am tempted to reply to such, This whole earth which we inhabit is but a point in space. How far apart,

---

10. **cimeter** (si′ mə tär′): scimitar; a saber having a curved blade, used chiefly by Arabs and Turks.

think you, dwell the two most distant inhabitants of yonder star, the breadth of whose disk cannot be appreciated by our instruments? Why should I feel lonely? Is not our planet in the Milky Way? This which you put seems to me not to be the most important question. What sort of space is that which separates a man from his fellows and makes him solitary? I have found that no exertion of the legs can bring two minds much nearer to one another. . . .

from **The Ponds**

The scenery of Walden is on a humble scale, and, though very beautiful, does not approach to grandeur, nor can it much concern one who has not long frequented it or lived by its shore; yet this pond is so remarkable for its depth and purity as to merit a particular description. It is a clear and deep green well, half a mile long and a mile and three quarters in circumference, and contains about sixty-one and a half acres; a perennial spring in the midst of pine and oak woods, without any visible inlet or outlet except by the clouds and evaporation. The surrounding hills rise abruptly from the water to the height of forty to eighty feet, though on the southeast and east they attain to about one hundred and one hundred and fifty feet respectively, within a quarter and a third of a mile. They are exclusively woodland. . . .

The shore is composed of a belt of smooth rounded white stones like paving stones, excepting one or two short sand beaches, and is so steep that in many places a single leap will carry you into water over your head; and were it not for its remarkable transparency, that would be the last to be seen of its bottom till it rose on the opposite side. Some think it is bottomless. It is nowhere muddy, and a casual observer would say that there were no weeds at all in it; . . .

from **Brute Neighbors**

One day when I went out to my woodpile, or rather my pile of stumps, I observed two large ants, the one red, the other much larger, nearly half an inch long, and black, fiercely contending with one another. Having once got hold they never let go, but struggled and wrestled and rolled on the chips incessantly. Looking farther, I was surprised to find that the chips were covered with such combatants, that it was not a *duellum*, but a *bellum*,[11] a war between two races of ants, the red always pitted against the black, and frequently two red ones to one black. The legions of these Myrmidons[12] covered all the hills and vales in my wood yard, and the ground was already strewn with the dead and dying, both red and black. It was the only battle which I have ever witnessed, the only battlefield I ever trod while the battle was raging; internecine war; the red republicans on the one hand, and the black imperialists on the other. On every side they were engaged in deadly combat, yet without any noise that I could hear, and human soldiers never fought so resolutely. I watched a couple that were fast locked in each other's embraces, in a little sunny valley amid the chips, now at noonday prepared to fight till the sun went down, or life went out. The smaller red champion had fastened himself like a vice to his adversary's front, and through all the tumblings on that field never for an instant ceased to gnaw at one of his feelers near the root, having already caused the other to go by the board; while the stronger black one dashed him from side to side, and, as I saw on looking nearer, had already divested him of several of his members. They fought with more perti-

---

11. *duellum . . . bellum:* Thoreau is saying that the battle he observes is not simply a duel between two ants, but rather a war between two armies of ants.
12. **Myrmidons** (mʉr′ mə dänz′): members of a legendary Thessalian people who took part with Achilles their king in the Trojan War.

nacity than bulldogs. Neither manifested the least disposition to retreat. It was evident that their battle cry was conquer or die. In the meanwhile there came along a single red ant on the hillside of this valley, evidently full of excitement, who either had despatched his foe, or had not yet taken part in the battle; probably the latter, for he had lost none of his limbs; whose mother had charged him to return with his shield or upon it. Or perchance he was some Achilles, who had nourished his wrath apart, and had now come to avenge or rescue his Patroclus.[13] He saw this unequal combat from afar—for the blacks were nearly twice the size of the red—he drew near with rapid pace till he stood on his guard within half an inch of the combatants; then, watching his opportunity, he sprang upon the black warrior, and commenced his operations near the root of his right foreleg, leaving the foe to select among his own members; and so there were three united for life, as if a new kind of attraction had been invented which put all other locks and cements to shame. I should not have wondered by this time to find that they had their respective musical bands stationed on some eminent chip, and playing their national airs the while, to excite the slow and cheer the dying combatants. I was myself excited somewhat even as if they had been men. The more you think of it, the less the difference. And certainly there is not the fight recorded in Concord history, at least, if in the history of America, that will bear a moment's comparison with this, whether for the numbers engaged in it, or for the patriotism and heroism displayed. For numbers and for carnage it was an Austerlitz or Dresden.[14] Concord Fight! Two killed on the patriots' side, and Luther Blanchard wounded! Why here every ant was a Buttrick—"Fire! for God's sake fire!"—and thousands shared the fate of Davis and Hosmer.[15] There was not one hireling there. I have no doubt that it was a principle they fought for, as much as our ancestors, and not to avoid a three-penny tax

on their tea; and the results of this battle will be as important and memorable to those whom it concerns as those of the battle of Bunker Hill, at least.

I took up the chip on which the three I have particularly described were struggling, carried it into my house, and placed it under a tumbler on my windowsill, in order to see the issue. Holding a microscope to the first mentioned red ant, I saw that, though he was assiduously gnawing at the near foreleg of his enemy, having severed his remaining feeler, his own breast was all torn away, exposing what vitals he had there to the jaws of the black warrior, whose breastplate was apparently too thick for him to pierce; and the dark carbuncles of the sufferer's eyes shone with ferocity such as war only could excite. They struggled half an hour longer under the tumbler, and when I looked again the black soldier had severed the heads of his foes from their bodies, and the still living heads were hanging on either side of him like ghastly trophies at his saddlebow, still apparently as firmly fastened as ever, and he was endeavoring with feeble struggles, being without feelers and with only the remnant of a leg, and I know not how many other wounds, to divest himself of them; which at length, after half an hour more, he accomplished. I raised the glass, and he went off over the windowsill in that crippled state. Whether he finally survived that combat, and spent the remainder of his days in some Hôtel des Invalides,[16] I do

---

13. **Achilles . . . Patroclus:** In Books XIX-XXII of the *Iliad*, the Greek warrior Achilles returned to battle after his companion Patroclus was killed by the Trojans.

14. **Austerlitz . . . Dresden:** In August of 1813, using Dresden, Germany, as his military base, Napoleon Bonaparte won his last great battle.

15. **Blanchard . . . Hosmer:** Major John Buttrick, 1715-1791, was one of the leaders of the Concord militia at the Battle of Concord in which Luther Blanchard was wounded and Isaac Davis and Abner Hosmer were killed.

16. **Hôtel des Invalides** (ō tel′ dāz ən vä′ lid′) *French:* a veterans' hospital.

not know; but I thought that his industry would not be worth much thereafter. I never learned which party was victorious, nor the cause of the war; but I felt for the rest of that day as if I had had my feelings excited and harrowed by witnessing the struggle, the ferocity and carnage, of a human battle before my door.

from The Pond in Winter

Every winter the liquid and trembling surface of the pond, which was so sensitive to every breath, and reflected every light and shadow, becomes solid to the depth of a foot or a foot and a half, so that it will support the heaviest teams, and perchance the snow covers it to an equal depth, and it is not to be distinguished from any level field. Like the marmots in the surrounding hills, it closes its eyelids and becomes dormant for three months or more. Standing on the snow-covered plain, as if in a pasture amid the hills, I cut my way first through a foot of snow, and then a foot of ice, and open a window under my feet, where, kneeling to drink, I look down into the quiet parlor of the fishes, pervaded by a softened light as through a window of ground glass, with its bright sanded floor the same as in summer; there a perennial waveless serenity reigns as in the amber twilight sky, corresponding to the cool and even temperament of the inhabitants. Heaven is under our feet as well as over our heads. . . .

While yet it is cold January, and snow and ice are thick and solid, the prudent landlord comes from the village to get ice to cool his summer drink; impressively, even pathetically, wise, to foresee the heat and thirst of July now in January—wearing a thick coat and mittens when so many things are not provided for. It may be that he lays up no treasures in this world which will cool his summer drink in the next. He cuts and saws the solid pond, unroofs the house of fishes, and carts off their very element and air, held fast by chains

and stakes like corded wood, through the favoring winter air, to wintry cellars, to underlie the summer there. It looks like solidified azure, as, far off, it is drawn through the streets. These ice-cutters are a merry race, full of jest and sport, and when I went among them they were wont to invite me to saw pit-fashion with them, I standing underneath. . . .

from Spring

One attraction in coming to the woods to live was that I should have leisure and opportunity to see the Spring come in. The ice in the pond at length begins to be honeycombed, and I can set my heel in it as I walk. Fogs and rains and warmer suns are gradually melting the snow; the days have grown sensibly longer; and I see how I shall get through the winter without adding to my woodpile, for large fires are no longer necessary. I am on the alert for the first signs of spring, to hear the chance note of some arriving bird, or the striped squirrel's chirp, for his stores must be now nearly exhausted, or see the woodchuck venture out of his winter quarters. On the thirteenth of March, after I had heard the bluebird, song sparrow, and redwing, the ice was still nearly a foot thick. As the weather grew warmer it was not sensibly worn away by the water, nor broken up and floated off as in rivers, but, though it was completely melted for half a rod in width about the shore, the middle was merely honeycombed and saturated with water, so that you could put your foot through it when six inches thick; but by the next day evening, perhaps, after a warm rain followed by fog, it would have wholly disappeared, all gone off with the fog, spirited away. One year I went across the middle only five days before it disappeared entirely. . . .

At length the sun's rays have attained the right angle, and warm winds blow up mist and rain and melt the snow banks, and the sun dispersing the mist smiles on a checkered landscape of russet and white smoking with incense, through which the traveler picks his way from islet to islet, cheered by the music of a thousand tinkling rills and rivulets whose veins are filled with the blood of winter which they are bearing off. . . .

Walden is melting apace. There is a canal two rods wide along the northerly and westerly sides, and wider still at the east end. A great field of ice has cracked off from the main body. I hear a song sparrow singing from the bushes on the shore—*olit, olit, olit—chip, chip, chip, che char—che wiss, wiss, wiss.* He too is helping to crack it. How handsome the great sweeping curves in the edge of the ice, answering somewhat to those of the shore, but more regular! It is unusually hard, owing to the recent severe but transient cold, and all watered or waved like a palace floor. But the wind slides eastward over its opaque surface in vain, till it reaches the living surface beyond. It is glorious to behold this ribbon of water sparkling in the sun, the bare face of the pond full of glee and youth, as if it spoke the joy of the fishes within it, and of the sands on its shore—a silvery sheen as from the scales of a *leuciscus*,[17] as it were all one active fish. Such is the contrast between winter and spring. Walden was dead and is alive again. But this spring it broke up more steadily, as I have said.

The change from storm and winter to serene and mild weather, from dark and sluggish hours to bright and elastic ones, is a memorable crisis which all things proclaim. It is seemingly instantaneous at last. Suddenly an influx of light filled my house, though the evening was at hand, and the clouds of winter still overhung it, and the eaves were dripping with sleety rain. I looked out the window, and lo! where yesterday was cold gray ice there lay the transparent pond already calm and full of hope as in a summer evening, reflecting a summer evening sky in its bosom, though none was visible overhead, as if it had intelligence with some remote horizon. I heard a robin in the distance, the first I had heard for many a thousand years, methought, whose note I shall not forget for many a thousand more—the same sweet and powerful song as of yore. O the evening robin, at the end of a New England summer day! If I could ever find the twig he sits upon! I mean *he;* I mean *the twig.* This at least is not the *Turdus migratorius.*[18] The pitch pines and shrub oaks about my house, which had so long drooped, suddenly resumed their several characters, looked brighter, greener, and more erect and alive, as if effectually cleansed and restored by the rain. I knew that it would not rain any more. You may tell by looking at any twig of the forest, ay, at your very woodpile, whether its winter is past or not. As it grew darker, I was startled by the honking of geese flying low over the woods, like weary travelers getting in late from southern lakes, and indulging at last in unrestrained complaint and mutual consolation. Standing at my door, I could hear the rush of their wings; when, driving toward my house, they suddenly spied my light, and with hushed clamor wheeled and settled in the pond. So I came in, and shut the door, and passed my first spring night in the woods.

In the morning I watched the geese from the door through the mist, sailing in the middle of the pond, fifty rods off, so large and tumultuous that Walden appeared like an artificial pond for their amusement. But when I stood on the shore they at once rose up with a great flapping of wings at the signal of their commander, and when they had got into rank circled about over my head, twenty-nine of them, and then steered straight to Canada, with a regular honk from the leader at intervals, trusting to break their fast in muddier pools. A "plump" of ducks rose at the same

---

17. **leuciscus** (lōō sis′ kəs): a small, freshwater fish.
18. **Turdus migratorius:** the American robin, *Planesticus migratorius*, was once classified by the name Thoreau gives it.

time and took the route to the north in the wake of their noisier cousins.

For a week I heard the circling groping clangor of some solitary goose in the foggy mornings, seeking its companion, and still peopling the woods with the sound of a larger life than they could sustain. In April the pigeons were seen again flying express in small flocks, and in due time I heard the martins twittering over my clearing, though it had not seemed that the township contained so many that it could afford me any, and I fancied that they were peculiarly of the ancient race that dwelt in hollow trees ere white men came. In almost all climes the tortoise and the frog are among the precursors and heralds of this season, and birds fly with song and glancing plumage, and plants spring and bloom, and winds blow, to correct this slight oscillation of the poles and preserve the equilibrium of Nature.

As every season seems best to us in its turn, so the coming in of spring is like the creation of Cosmos out of Chaos[19] and the realization of the Golden Age. . . .

from Conclusion

I left the woods for as good a reason as I went there. Perhaps it seemed to me that I had several more lives to live, and could not spare any more time for that one. It is remarkable how easily and insensibly we fall into a particular route, and make a beaten track for ourselves. I had not lived there a week before my feet wore a path from my door to the pond-side; and though it is five or six years since I trod it, it is still quite distinct. It is true, I fear, that others may have fallen into it, and so helped to keep it open. The surface of the earth is soft and impressible by the feet of men; and so with the paths which the mind travels. How worn and dusty, then, must be the highways of the world, how deep the ruts of tradition and conformity! I did not wish to take a cabin passage, but rather to go before the mast and on the deck of the world, for there I could best see the moonlight amid the mountains. I do not wish to go below now.

I learned this, at least, by my experiment; that if one advances confidently in the direction of his dreams, and endeavors to live the life which he has imagined, he will meet with a success unexpected in common hours. He will put some things behind, will pass an invisible boundary; new, universal, and more liberal laws will begin to establish themselves around and within him; or the old laws be expanded, and interpreted in his favor in a more liberal sense, and he will live with the license of a higher order of beings. In proportion as he simplifies his life, the laws of the universe will appear less complex, and solitude will not be solitude, nor poverty poverty, nor weakness weakness. If you have built castles in the air, your work need not be lost; that is where they should be. Now put the foundations under them. . . .

Why should we be in such desperate haste to succeed and in such desperate enterprises? If a man does not keep pace with his companions, perhaps it is because he hears a different drummer. Let him step to the music which he hears, however measured or far away. It is not important that he should mature as soon as an apple tree or an oak. Shall he turn his spring into summer? If the condition of things which we were made for is not yet, what were any reality which we can substitute? We will not be shipwrecked on a vain reality. Shall we with pains erect a heaven of blue glass over ourselves, though when it is done we shall be sure to gaze still at the true ethereal heaven far above, as if the former were not? . . .

However mean your life is, meet it and live it; do not shun it and call it hard names. It is not so bad as you are. It looks poorest when you are richest. The faultfinder will find

---

19. **Cosmos . . . Chaos:** The coming of spring is like creating the world, or order, out of darkness and nothing.

faults even in paradise. Love your life, poor as it is. You may perhaps have some pleasant, thrilling, glorious hours, even in a poorhouse. The setting sun is reflected from the windows of the almshouse as brightly as from the rich man's abode; the snow melts before its door as early in the spring. I do not see but a quiet mind may live as contentedly there, and have as cheering thoughts, as in a palace. The town's poor seem to me often to live the most independent lives of any. Maybe they are simply great enough to receive without misgiving. Most think that they are above being supported by the town; but it oftener happens that they are not above supporting themselves by dishonest means, which should be more disreputable. Cultivate poverty like a garden herb, like sage. Do not trouble yourself much to get new things, whether clothes or friends. Turn the old; return to them. Things do not change; we change. Sell your clothes and keep your thoughts. God will see that you do not want society. If I were confined to a corner of a garret all my days, like a spider, the world would be just as large to me while I had my thoughts about me. The philosopher said, "From an army of three divisions one can take away its general, and put it in disorder; from the man the most abject and vulgar one cannot take away his thought." Do not seek so anxiously to be developed, to subject yourself to many influences to be played on; it is all dissipation. Humility like darkness reveals the heavenly lights. The shadows of poverty and meanness gather around us, "and lo! creation widens to our view." We are often reminded that if there were bestowed on us the wealth of Croesus,[20] our aims must still be the same, and our means essentially the same. Moreover, if you are restricted in your range by poverty, if you cannot buy books and newspapers, for instance, you are but confined to the most significant and vital experiences; you are compelled to deal with the material which yields the most sugar and the most starch. It is life near the bone where it is

sweetest. You are defended from being a trifler. No man loses ever on a lower level by magnanimity on a higher. Superfluous wealth can buy superfluities only. Money is not required to buy one necessary of the soul. . . .

The life in us is like the water in the river. It may rise this year higher than man has ever known it, and flood the parched uplands; even this may be the eventful year, which will drown out all our muskrats. It was not always dry land where we dwell. I see far inland the banks which the stream anciently washed, before science began to record its freshets. Every one has heard the story which has gone the rounds of New England, of a strong and beautiful bug which came out of the dry leaf of an old table of apple-tree wood, which had stood in a farmer's kitchen for sixty years, first in Connecticut, and afterward in Massachusetts—from an egg deposited in the living tree many years earlier still, as appeared by counting the annual layers beyond it; which was heard gnawing out for several weeks, hatched perchance by the heat of an urn. Who does not feel his faith in a resurrection and immortality strengthened by hearing of this? Who knows what beautiful and winged life, whose egg has been buried for ages under many concentric layers of woodenness in the dead dry life of society, deposited at first in the alburnum of the green and living tree, which has been gradually converted into the semblance of its well seasoned tomb—heard perchance gnawing out now for years by the astonished family of man, as they sat round the festive board—may unexpectedly come forth from amidst society's most trivial and handselled furniture, to enjoy its perfect summer life at last!

I do not say that John or Jonathan[21] will realize all this; but such is the character of

---

20. **Croesus** (krē′ səs): last king of Lydia, 560-546 B.C., known for his wealth.
21. **John or Jonathan:** the average citizen of America or the average citizen of Britain.

that morrow which mere lapse of time can never make to dawn. The light which puts out our eyes is darkness to us. Only that day dawns to which we are awake. There is more day to dawn. The sun is but a morning star.

Getting at Meaning

WHERE I LIVED AND WHAT I LIVED FOR

1. Describe Thoreau's house at the pond. What was the precise location of his cabin?

2. Thoreau says, "One value even of the smallest well is, that when you look into it you see that earth is not continent but insular." Explain his meaning.

3. Why was morning Thoreau's favorite time of day? Explain the statement, "That man who does not believe that each day contains an earlier, more sacred, and auroral hour than he has yet profaned, has despaired of life. . . ."

4. Explain Thoreau's statement, "The millions are awake enough for physical labor; but only one in a million is awake enough for effective intellectual exertion, only one in a hundred millions to a poetic or divine life."

5. What does Thoreau give as reasons for going to live at Walden Pond? What does he believe is the virtue of simplicity?

6. What is Thoreau's complaint about the work habits of his contemporaries?

7. What is Thoreau's attitude toward the news? How does he feel about letters?

8. Thoreau urges people to commune with nature. Why? What is his concept of reality?

9. In the final paragraph of this chapter of *Walden*, what happens to Thoreau as he experiences nature? How does this paragraph reveal Thoreau's transcendental beliefs?

SOLITUDE

10. Reread Thoreau's description of the evening and explain the effect that nature has on him.

11. What does Thoreau say about his visitors? How could he always tell when someone had been to see him?

12. Why was Thoreau never lonely at the pond? Explain his statement, "I have found that no exertion of the legs can bring two minds much nearer to one another. . . ."

THE PONDS

13. What are the physical characteristics of Walden Pond? Why does Thoreau describe the pond so precisely?

14. What remarkable characteristic of the pond does Thoreau mention?

BRUTE NEIGHBORS

15. What does Thoreau quickly realize about the two ants he observes? Why is he so fascinated by the battle?

16. Explain Thoreau's statement, "I was myself excited somewhat even as if they had been men. The more you think of it, the less the difference."

17. What is the emotional effect of the ant battle on Thoreau? Explain your answer.

THE POND IN WINTER

18. What leads Thoreau to conclude that "Heaven is under our feet as well as over our heads. . . ."?

19. Summarize Thoreau's views on the ice-cutters.

SPRING

20. What subtle changes in the pond herald the approach of spring? What does Thoreau notice about the birds?

21. Explain Thoreau's comment that ". . . the coming in of spring is like the creation of Cosmos out of Chaos. . . ."

CONCLUSION

22. What reasons does Thoreau give for leaving Walden Pond? Explain the statement, "The surface of the earth is soft and impressible by the feet of men; and so with the paths which the mind travels."

23. What does Thoreau say he learned from his experiment?

24. Explain Thoreau's advice: "Cultivate poverty like a garden herb, like sage. Do not trouble yourself much to get new things, whether clothes or friends."

25. Explain Thoreau's statement, "No man loses ever on a lower level by magnanimity on a higher."

26. In the final two paragraphs of *Walden,* Thoreau relates a remarkable story about an insect. What are the details of the story? Why does Thoreau close his book with this narrative?

Developing Skills in Reading Literature

1. **Allusion.** Thoreau was a learned classical scholar, as shown by his many allusions to Greek and Roman literature. For example, Thoreau says in "Where I Lived and What I Lived For," "Olympus is but the outside of the earth everywhere. . . ." and of a mosquito's noise, "It was Homer's requiem; itself an Iliad and Odyssey in the air. . . ."

Explain these two allusions. Then locate two or three others and explain them. What effect do the allusions produce in *Walden?* Why are they appropriate in a book of this kind?

2. **Aphorism.** Like Emerson, Thoreau writes in an aphoristic style. *Walden* is full of aphorisms, such as "The mass of men lead lives of quiet desperation" and "The setting sun is reflected from the windows of the almshouse as brightly as from the rich man's abode; the snow melts before its door as early in the spring."

Locate additional aphorisms in these sections from *Walden.* Choose two or three that especially appeal to you and explain why you find them meaningful.

3. **Hyperbole.** Hyperbole is a figure of speech in which the truth is exaggerated for effect. When Thoreau says, "And I am sure that I never read any memorable news in a newspaper," his statement should not be taken too literally. He is exaggerating to make a point.

Find several hyperbolic statements in *Walden.* What point is Thoreau trying to make in each? Is the hyperbole effective?

4. **Figurative Language.** *Walden* is written in prose that is characterized by rich poetic language. For example, Thoreau closes the book with the metaphor "The sun is but a morning star." What meaning does this metaphor convey in view of what Thoreau has said about light and morning?

Find several other examples of figurative language in *Walden.* Choose a variety of similes and metaphors and at least one example of personification, and analyze the meaning and appeal of each.

5. **Paradox.** A paradox is a statement that seems to contradict itself but is, nevertheless, true. Writers use paradox to emphasize an idea through contrast and to stimulate thinking among their readers.

Thoreau uses paradox when he says of the human being, "In proportion as he simplifies his life, the laws of the universe will appear less complex, and solitude will not be solitude, nor poverty poverty, nor weakness weakness." Explain what Thoreau means in this seemingly contradictory statement. Why is the use of paradox so effective in communicating this meaning?

6. **Mock Epic.** An epic is a long narrative poem that describes the deeds of a great hero, usually in battle. An epic reflects the values of the culture in which it originated, as do Homer's epics the *Iliad* and the *Odyssey,* the most famous epics in Western literature.

A mock epic uses epic traditions to achieve a humorous effect. Usually epic grandeur is applied to a lowly or comic subject, with resulting amusement.

Thoreau creates a mock epic in his description of the ant battle. The ants are portrayed as Homeric fighters, one of them like the great Achilles, with "legions of Myrmidons" behind him. The ant battle ". . . for carnage . . . was an Austerlitz or Dresden." Find other lines in which the ants and their battle are described in mock heroic terms. What lines strike you as particularly humorous? What does Thoreau conclude about the similarity between ants and humans? Why is this conclusion ironic in view of the way that Thoreau has treated his subject up to this point?

7. **Parallelism.** Thoreau is a master stylist who successfully uses parallelism. Analyze the following passage, one of Thoreau's most graceful and effective. Where do you find equal ideas expressed in parallel forms? Identify the grammatical forms that Thoreau repeats. Notice how these parallel forms tighten the passage and increase its impact. What do the repeating forms do for the rhythm of the passage?

I went to the woods because I wished to live deliberately, to front only the essential facts of life, and see if I could not learn what it had to teach, and not, when I came to die, discover that I had not lived. I did not wish to live what was not life, living is so dear; nor did I wish to practice resignation, unless it was quite necessary. I wanted to live deep and suck out all the marrow of life, to live so sturdily and Spartanlike as to put to rout all that was not life, to cut a broad swath and shave close, to drive life into a corner, and reduce it to its lowest terms, and, if it proved to be mean, why then to get the whole and genuine meanness of it, and publish its meanness to the world; or if it were sublime, to know it by experience, and be able to give a true account of it in my next excursion.

Developing Vocabulary

Inferring Word Meaning: Adjectives. Observe the way Thoreau uses each of the adjectives that follows. Try to infer each word's meaning from its context. Then look up each word in a dictionary and record its meaning. Notice the origin of each word, writing down for each one the root word and its meaning, along with any prefixes or suffixes.

auroral	internecine
celestial	perennial
terrestrial	superfluous
meridian	

Developing Writing Skills

1. **Supporting an Opinion.** Thoreau says, "It is life near the bone where it is sweetest. . . . Superfluous wealth can buy superfluities only. Money is not required to buy one necessary of the soul. . . ."

In one well developed paragraph, either agree or disagree with Thoreau's position. Present your own views on the subject, and support them with sound reasons and concrete observations.

2. **Writing an Explanation.** Thoreau is a Transcendentalist, a Romantic. In one paragraph, identify the qualities of Romanticism that you find in these selections from *Walden*. Consider such things as Thoreau's views on nature, on society, and on individualism. Consider also the tone of *Walden* and the optimistic conclusion to the book.

3. **Analyzing Theme.** Thoreau, like Emerson, believed in self-reliance. He says toward the end of *Walden*, "If a man does not keep pace with his companions, perhaps it is because he hears a different drummer. Let him step to the music which he hears, however measured or far away."

In a five-paragraph essay, compare what Emerson and Thoreau have to say about self-reliance. Consider both writers' ideas about the difficulty of achieving self-reliance, about its advantages and disadvantages, and about society.

Your essay should consist of three body paragraphs framed by an introduction and a conclusion. Outline your essay before you begin to write, making it clear what major point you will discuss in each body paragraph. Use quotations from both writers to support your points.

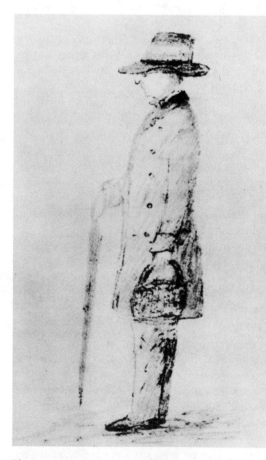

Thoreau setting out on one of his excursions—as he called his frequent travels and bucolic ramblings—sketched in 1854 by his Quaker artist-friend, Daniel Ricketson of New Bedford.

Unit Review *Developing a National Literature*

Understanding the Unit

1. Washington Irving and William Cullen Bryant are early American Romantic writers. Judging from the works you have read, what is similar in their Romantic visions?

2. What do Nathaniel Hawthorne, Herman Melville, and Edgar Allan Poe have in common as Romantic writers? Cite specific characteristics they share and refer to passages in their works to support your ideas. How do these writers differ from the other Romantic writers whose works you have read in this unit?

3. Oliver Wendell Holmes, James Russell Lowell, Henry Wadsworth Longfellow, and John Greenleaf Whittier are known as the Fireside Poets. What similarities are apparent in their poems? What kinds of subject matter do these poets appear to choose? Cite several concrete examples.

4. Ralph Waldo Emerson and Henry David Thoreau are the two transcendental writers represented in this unit. Judging from the literature you have read, how are Emerson and Thoreau similar to the other Romantics? How are they different? What special emphasis seems to appear in the transcendental works?

5. "The Raven" and "Snowbound" are both Romantic poems and both are narrative poems. What other similarities are apparent in the poems? What major differences can you identify?

6. Select one poet whose work appears in this unit and consider that poet's attitude toward nature. Then consider the attitude toward nature apparent in the five Indian poems. What are the similarities between the attitude of the Romantic poets and that of the Indians? What are the differences?

Writing

1. "Inscription for the Entrance to a Wood" and "Each and All" are similar poems about what human beings can learn from communing with nature. The poems treat this theme differently, however.

Write an essay in which you compare and contrast the two poems. Before you begin to write, reread the poems and think about their similarities and differences. Jot down ideas. After you have decided on your major points, construct an outline for your paper. The body paragraphs should be framed by an introduction and a conclusion. Use quotations from both poems to support your points.

2. "The Devil and Tom Walker" and "The Minister's Black Veil" are both allegories about evil. While the two stories are quite similar in theme, they are different in important ways.

Write an essay in which you compare and contrast the two stories. Follow the same approach as suggested for the preceding assignment.

3. In Chapter 3 of *Walden*, Thoreau makes the following statement about classics:

For what are the classics but the noblest recorded thoughts of man? They are the only oracles which are not decayed, and there are such answers to the most modern inquiry in them as Delphi and Dodona never gave. We might as well omit to study Nature because she is old. . . . A written word is the choicest of relics. . . . It is the work of art nearest to life itself.

Select one author from this unit and write a composition in which you discuss how the author's work fits Thoreau's definition. You may, of course, choose to apply Thoreau's definition to his own book. Consider these questions when planning your composition: What is universal in the author's work? What makes it relevant to the twentieth century? What makes it beautiful? Refer to specific passages in the literature you discuss.

ABRAHAM LINCOLN. *George Peter Alexander Healy.*
In the Collection of the Corcoran Gallery of Art.
Museum Purchase.

Unit 4

A National Conscience (1855–1900)

ROBERT E. LEE, 1904. *Theodore Pine.*
Lee Chapel, Washington and Lee University.

From Romanticism to Realism

Two forces that shaped the economic and social character of America in the last half of the nineteenth century were industrialization and expansion west of the Mississippi River. The dream of success, achieved through a combination of courage and hard work, luck and opportunity, attracted tides of immigrants to this country, drew settlers to the Great Plains, and lured miners and prospectors to the far West. The age was crass and materialistic; yet in many ways it was also exuberant and idealistic, an age when the American Dream seemed less a dream than a tantalizing possibility.

ECONOMIC DEVELOPMENT IN THE MID-NINETEENTH CENTURY

Improvements in industrial technology and in transportation provided the incentive and the capability for large-scale agriculture, manufacturing, and mining. Eli Whitney's cotton gin had made it possible to separate cotton from its seeds in large quantities. By 1850 the cotton grown on Southern plantations was supplying the expanding textile mills in New England and in England as well. The invention of the Bessemer process made possible the mass production of steel, which stimulated the iron mining industry and provided raw material for the manufacture of machinery, tools, railroad tracks, and weapons. Steamboats on the canals and on navigable rivers such as the Mississippi and railroads throughout the country carried raw materials, manufactured goods, and passengers.

THE GREAT MIGRATION WEST

Thousands of those who felt that the East was becoming too crowded and confining accepted the challenge presented by the vast, undeveloped frontier. Encouraged by the Homestead Act (1862), which granted a tract of one hundred and sixty acres of public land to each qualified farmer, pioneers migrated to the regions west of the Mississippi. Among those pioneers were recent immigrants—German, Bohemian, Scandinavian, Russian, French, and English. In covered wagons, on horseback, and on foot, the settlers poured into the new territories, intent on transforming the sea of prairie grass into farmland. Living in dugouts, sod houses, and log cabins, they accomplished the work of taming the prairie and of establishing communities.

The California Gold Rush in 1849 and the discovery of the Comstock Lode of silver in Nevada in 1859 attracted adventurers, fortune seekers, and solid citizens to the far West. Within a relatively short time, the Pony Express, the telegraph, and the stage coach linked the farming and mining settlements; in 1869 the first transcontinental railroad joined East and West.

THE NATIVE AMERICANS

In the push westward the Native Americans were treated as merely another obstacle to be overcome. The affected tribes included the original inhabitants of the West and Southwest and also tribes native to the region east of the Mississippi who had been "resettled" far from their tribal homelands. Eye witnesses, among them eloquent Indian leaders, recorded the impact of white development. A few of these voices protested the government policies for relocating the Indians. Not until the twentieth century, however, did Americans exhibit much sympathy for the Indian, whose entire way of life had been sacrificed to the ideal of American expansion.

THE TRAGEDY OF CIVIL WAR

Industrialization and westward migration changed the character of America, often at great human cost. Equally significant and infinitely more devastating was the political upheaval that culminated in the Civil War. In the turbulent years leading up to the war, essays, letters, and speeches articulated the concerns of a nation attempting to put its house in order on the issues of slavery and states' rights. The Anti-Slavery Society of Massachusetts provided a forum for speakers such as Frederick Douglass and Lucy Stone. The lyceum system, first organized in Massachusetts in 1826, had extended to thousands of small villages, and public speeches became a powerful force in shaping public opinion. Public debates, such as the Lincoln-Douglas Debates in 1858, and newspapers, such as the *Liberator*, published by William Lloyd Garrison, directed attention to the pressing political and social issues facing the nation.

Among the voices that transcended the bitter divisiveness and personal pain of the war years were those of Abraham Lincoln and Robert E. Lee. Important writers of the period, among them poet Walt Whitman, mourned the national and individual losses of the war and celebrated the nobility of the Union and the Confederate causes.

THE POSTWAR YEARS: NATIONALISM AND REGIONALISM

Two distinct trends had roots in the Civil War period. One was the gradual emergence of a national identity, resulting in part from the easing of sectional tensions after the war, in part from improved transportation and communication networks. The many new newspapers and magazines provided information about national events and a means through which writers could reach a national audience. Walt Whitman expressed the spirit of nationalism, envisioning a nation of individuals united by a common tragedy and inspired by hope for the future.

Literature

- Abraham Lincoln (1809–1865) delivers The Gettysburg Address

- Walt Whitman (1819–1892) publishes first edition of *Leaves of Grass*

- Henry Timrod (1828–1867) publishes volume of *Poems*

- Edward Everett Hale (1822–1909) publishes "The Man Without a Country"

- Robert E. Lee (1807–1870) writes "Letters to His Family"

- George Armstrong Custer (1839–1876) publishes *My Life on the Plains*

- Bret Harte (1836–1902) publishes "The Outcasts of Poker Flat"

- Lucy Stone (1818–1893) founds *Woman's Journal*

- Louisa May Alcott (1832–1888) publishes *Little Women*

1855   1870

History

- Civil War begins

- Lincoln issues Emancipation Proclamation

- Alexander Graham Bell invents the telephone

- John Wilkes Booth assassinates Abraham Lincoln

- Lincoln and Douglas debate in Illinois

- Sioux massacre Custer's forces

- Chicago Fire devastates city

- Victoria Woodhull becomes first woman to run for President

Complementing the spirit of nationalism was a new awareness of American diversity, a regional identification that found its literary expression in the type of realism called "local color." Local-color writers portrayed the customs, attitudes, characters, situations, and dialects of their regions with the realist's eye for accurate detail. Prominent among the local-color realists were Bret Harte and Mark Twain. Their versions of life on the frontier captivated the imaginations of readers in the more settled communities of the East, Midwest, and South.

Local-color writers produced poetry and nonfiction as well as short stories and novels. Autobiographical narratives, such as

- First volume of *Poems* by Emily Dickinson (1830–1886) published after her death

- Mark Twain (1835–1910) publishes *The Adventures of Huckleberry Finn*

- Revised version of *Narrative of the Life of Frederick Douglass* published

- Ambrose Bierce (1842–1914?) publishes "An Occurrence at Owl Creek Bridge" in *Tales of Soldiers and Civilians*

- Mary E. Wilkins Freeman (1852–1930) publishes her first collection of tales, *A Humble Romance*

- Stephen Crane (1871–1900) publishes *The Red Badge of Courage*

- Joel Chandler Harris (1848–1908) publishes first collection of *Uncle Remus* stories

- *Ladies' Home Journal* first appears

- Kate Chopin (1851–1904) publishes short story collection, *Bayou Folk*

- Chief Joseph (1840?–1904) makes speech of surrender

- Sarah Orne Jewett (1849–1909) publishes *A Country Doctor*

1880   1890   1900

- Thomas Edison patents phonograph

- Battle at Wounded Knee marks last of Indian Wars

- Haymarket Riot erupts in Chicago

- Spanish-American War breaks out

- Reconstruction comes to an end in the South

- Congress passes Sherman Anti-Trust Act

Twain's *Life on the Mississippi*, journals, and travelogs found an eager audience among Americans who, as Henry James said, had "a hungry passion for the picturesque."

In poetry the Romantic veneration of nature expressed in traditional stanzas still lingered in the works of local-color poets such as the South's Sidney Lanier. Occasionally, though, a poet sought new forms to communicate a unique interpretation of reality. Emily Dickinson experimented with imagery and sound patterns; Walt Whitman with the flow between rhythm and idea. The poetry of the twentieth century has its roots in the revolutionary writings of these two nineteenth-century poets.

THE LATE NINETEENTH CENTURY

The character of America changed significantly from the prewar and immediate postwar years to the closing decade of the century. By the late 1800's the Old West was a symbol of the past. Now, the major population shift was from rural areas to the older manufacturing centers of the East and to the newer centers of the South and Midwest. The latest wave of immigrants—nine million between 1880 and 1900 alone—gravitated to cities where the co-existence of slums and palatial mansions dramatized the contrast between rich and poor, between wealthy entrepreneurs and their exploited laborers. Inventions such as the telephone and the electric light had yet to improve the quality of life for most Americans.

Toward the end of the century, local-color realists, such as Willa Cather, Mary E. Wilkins Freeman, and Kate Chopin, carried on the spirit of regionalism, with increasing sophistication. An extreme form of realism called naturalism manifested itself in the writings of Stephen Crane. His novel *The Red Badge of Courage* (1895) and other war stories treat an event of the past, the Civil War, in a way that foreshadows the unrelenting realism and pessimism that would mark much of the literature of the twentieth century.

The transition from Romanticism to realism took place during the last half of the nineteenth century. By the turn of the century, no traces of Romanticism remained in the works of the major American writers.

The Civil War

SHARE CROPPERS, 1941. *Robert Gwathmey.*
The San Diego Museum of Art.

Frederick Douglass

1817?–1895

During the pre-Civil War period, when few American blacks were literate or publicly articulate, Frederick Douglass became a spokesman for the Abolitionist movement and a forceful advocate for human rights. His autobiography, *Narrative of the Life of Frederick Douglass*, exposed slavery as a dehumanizing, "soul-killing" institution. Simple, in style and authentic in detail, the narrative is an eloquent argument against enslavement of one human being by another.

Born the son of a slave on a Maryland plantation, Douglass grew up in slavery, working both on the plantation and in his master's city house. Although he had no formal education, he was taught to read and write by his mistress, who defied state law in doing so. In 1838 he escaped to Massachusetts where he devoted his considerable abilities to a program of self-education while supporting himself and his family by a series of odd jobs. In 1841, at an Abolitionist meeting, he spoke publicly for the first time about his experiences as a slave. His remarks attracted the attention of the Massachusetts Anti-Slavery Society. A man of commanding appearance and dramatic oratorical style, Douglass was soon one of the organization's most prominent circuit speakers.

The publication of Douglass's autobiography in 1845 resulted in widespread publicity and the possibility of recapture by his former owner. To remove himself from this potentially dangerous situation, he embarked on a two-year speaking tour abroad during which he was influential in creating anti-slavery sympathy among the British and Irish people. In his speeches he portrayed emancipation as a starting point for the achievement of social and economic equality. Back in America in 1847, Douglass became the first black to publish a newspaper in the United States, an Abolitionist weekly called the *North Star*. He worked for the Underground Railroad, making his own home the Rochester, New York, station for slaves escaping to Canada. During the Civil War, Douglass recruited blacks for the Union Army. After the war he held positions such as Recorder of Deeds for the District of Columbia, Minister to Haiti, and Chargé d'Affaires to Santo Domingo. He died of a heart attack on February 25, 1895, on his way home from speaking at a meeting on women's rights. Although he was a prolific writer, his autobiography, twice revised and expanded (in 1855 and 1882), remains the most famous of his literary works.

from **Narrative of the Life**

Colonel Lloyd kept from three to four hundred slaves on his home plantation,[1] and owned a large number more on the neighboring farms belonging to him. The names of the farms nearest to the home plantation were Wye Town and New Design. Wye Town was under the overseership of a man named Noah Willis. New Design was under the overseership of a Mr. Townsend. The overseers of these, and all the rest of the farms, numbering over twenty, received advice and direction from the managers of the home plantation. This was the great business place. It was the seat of government for the whole twenty farms.[2] All disputes among the overseers were settled here. . . .

Here, too, the slaves of all the other farms received their monthly allowance of food, and their yearly clothing. The men and women slaves received, as their monthly allowance of food, eight pounds of pork, or its equivalent in fish, and one bushel of corn meal. Their yearly clothing consisted of two coarse linen shirts, one pair of linen trousers, like the shirts, one jacket, one pair of trousers for winter, made of coarse negro cloth, one pair of stockings, and one pair of shoes; the whole of which could not have cost more than seven dollars. The allowance of the slave children was given to their mothers, or the old women having the care of them. My mother and I were separated when I was but an infant— before I knew her as my mother. It is a common custom, in the part of Maryland from which I ran away, to part children from their mothers at a very early age. Frequently, before the child has reached its twelfth month, its mother is taken from it, and hired out on some farm a considerable distance off, and the child is placed under the care of an old woman, too old for field labor. The children unable to work in the field had neither shoes, stockings, jackets, nor trousers, given to them; their clothing consisted of two coarse linen shirts per year. When these failed them, they went naked until the next allowance-day. Children from seven to ten years old, of both sexes, almost naked, might be seen at all seasons of the year.

The home plantation of Colonel Lloyd wore the appearance of a country village. All the mechanical operations for all the farms were performed here. The shoemaking and mending, the blacksmithing, cartwrighting, coopering,[3] weaving, and grain-grinding, were all performed by the slaves on the home plantation. The whole place wore a businesslike aspect very unlike the neighboring farms. The number of houses, too, conspired to give it advantage over the neighboring farms. It was called by the slaves the *Great House Farm.* Few privileges were esteemed higher, by the slaves of the out-farms, than that of being selected to do errands at the Great House Farm. It was associated in their minds with greatness. A representative could not be prouder of his election to a seat in the American Congress, than a slave on one of the out-farms would be of his election to do errands at the Great House Farm. They regarded it as evidence of great confidence reposed in them by their overseers; and it was on this account, as well as a constant desire to

---

1. **Col. Edward Lloyd's plantation:** Talbot County, Maryland, on the Eastern Shore of the Chesapeake Bay.
2. Lloyd family papers show thirteen farms.
3. **cartwrighting:** building carts; **coopering:** making barrels.

be out of the field from under the driver's lash, that they esteemed it a high privilege, one worth careful living for. He was called the smartest and most trusty fellow, who had this honor conferred upon him the most frequently. The competitors for this office sought as diligently to please their overseers, as the office-seekers in the political parties seek to please and deceive the people. The same traits of character might be seen in Colonel Lloyd's slaves, as are seen in the slaves of the political parties.

The slaves selected to go to the Great House Farm, for the monthly allowance for themselves and their fellow slaves, were peculiarly enthusiastic. While on their way, they would make the dense old woods, for miles around, reverberate with their wild songs, revealing at once the highest joy and the deepest sadness. They would compose and sing as they went along, consulting neither time nor tune. The thought that came up, came out—if not in the word, in the sound—and as frequently in the one as in the other. They would sometimes sing the most pathetic sentiment in the most rapturous tone, and the most rapturous sentiment in the most pathetic tone. Into all of their songs they would manage to weave something of the Great House Farm. Especially would they do this when leaving home. They would then sing most exultingly the following words:

> I am going away to the Great House Farm!
> O, yea! O, yea! O!

This they would sing, as a chorus, to words which to many would seem unmeaning jargon, but which, nevertheless, were full of meaning to themselves. I have sometimes thought that the mere hearing of those songs would do more to impress some minds with the horrible character of slavery, than the reading of whole volumes of philosophy on the subject could do.

I did not, when a slave, understand the deep meaning of those rude and apparently incoherent songs. I was myself within the circle; so that I neither saw nor heard as those without might see and hear. They told a tale of woe which was then altogether beyond my feeble comprehension; they were tones loud, long, and deep; they breathed the prayer and complaint of souls boiling over with the bitterest anguish. Every tone was a testimony against slavery, and a prayer to God for deliverance from chains. The hearing of those wild notes always depressed my spirit, and filled me with ineffable sadness. I have frequently found myself in tears while hearing them. The mere recurrence to those songs, even now, afflicts me; and while I am writing these lines, an expression of feeling has already found its way down my cheek. To those songs I trace my first glimmering conception of the dehumanizing character of slavery. I can never get rid of that conception. Those songs still follow me, to deepen my hatred of slavery, and quicken my sympathies for my brethren in bonds. If any one wishes to be impressed with the soul-killing effects of slavery, let him go to Colonel Lloyd's plantation, and, on allowance-day, place himself in the deep pine woods; and there let him, in silence, analyze the sounds that shall pass through the chambers of his soul, and if he is not thus impressed, it will only be because "there is no flesh in his obdurate[4] heart."

I have often been utterly astonished, since I came to the north, to find persons who could speak of the singing, among slaves, as evidence of their contentment and happiness. It is impossible to conceive of a greater mistake. Slaves sing most when they are most unhappy. The songs of the slave represent the sorrows of his heart; and he is relieved by them, only as an aching heart is relieved by its tears. At least, such is my experience. I have often sung to drown my sorrow, but seldom to

---

4. **obdurate** (äb' door ət): not easily moved to pity or sympathy, especially for what one has done.

express my happiness. Crying for joy, and singing for joy, were alike uncommon to me while in the jaws of slavery. The singing of a man cast away upon a desolate island might be as appropriately considered as evidence of contentment and happiness, as the singing of a slave; the songs of the one and of the other are prompted by the same emotion.

Getting at Meaning

1. What evidence in Douglass's account supports the idea that the owner and managers of the Lloyd plantation were concerned primarily with profit and loss and not with the human beings who lived and worked there? How did the managers fail to treat slaves as human beings?

2. In the matter of allowances, some slaves were treated differently than others. What was the difference? What does this indicate about the priorities of the plantation managers?

3. In what ways did Colonel Lloyd's home plantation have the appearance of a country village?

4. Why were slaves from neighboring farms eager to do errands at the Great House Farm? What does this suggest about how slaves were motivated to behave well?

5. What underlying meaning does Douglass perceive in the songs that the slaves sang? Why did the slaves sing these songs, according to Douglass?

Developing Skills in Reading Literature

1. **Autobiography.** The reader of this selection learns about Douglass directly, through specific information, and indirectly, through inference from the details provided. What do you learn directly about Douglass's early life and his developing ideas and attitudes about slavery? What can you infer about his life, ideas, and attitudes? Judging from his use of the language, what can you infer about his educational attainments?

2. **Analogy.** In discussing the slaves selected to do errands at the Great House Farm, Douglass draws an analogy between them and another group of people. What is that group? What similarities does he perceive? How does he use the analogy to comment on both groups?

3. **Tone.** Douglass's tone changes as he moves from the description of the slave system on the Lloyd plantation to the description of the slaves' songs. Find this shift in tone. How does the tone change? How does the tone of each description fit its subject?

4. **Stereotype.** Douglass comments that, to people in the North, singing among slaves is evidence of their "contentment and happiness." How does Douglass refute this stereotype? Why do you think that northerners in the pre-Civil War period preferred to believe it? Do you think that southern whites shared the same stereotypical view? What might have been the sources of these stereotypes for northerners? For southerners?

Negro Spirituals

Go Down, Moses

When Israel was in Egypt land
Let my people go
Oppressed so hard they could not stand
Let my people go.

Go down, Moses,   5
Way down in Egypt land
Tell old Pharaoh,
"Let my people go."

"Thus saith the Lord," bold Moses said,
"Let my people go;   10
If not I'll smite your first-born dead
Let my people go."

Go down, Moses,
Way down in Egypt land,
Tell old Pharaoh,   15
"Let my people go!"

FOLK SINGER, 1957. *Charles White.*
Heritage Gallery, Los Angeles.

Swing Low, Sweet Chariot

Swing low, sweet chariot,
Coming for to carry me home,
Swing low, sweet chariot,
Coming for to carry me home.

I looked over Jordan[1] and what did I see,   5
Coming for to carry me home,
A band of angels coming after me,
Coming for to carry me home.

If you get there before I do,
Coming for to carry me home.   10
Tell all my friends I'm coming too,
Coming for to carry me home.

I'm sometimes up and sometimes down,
Coming for to carry me home,
But still my soul feels heavenly bound,   15
Coming for to carry me home.

Swing low, sweet chariot,
Coming for to carry me home,
Swing low, sweet chariot,
Coming for to carry me home.   20

---

1. **Jordan:** river in Palestine flowing south into the Dead Sea, the boundary separating the exiled Israelites from the Promised Land, and from Jerusalem.

Getting at Meaning

1. On a literal level, "Go Down, Moses" is a song that recalls a Biblical event. Who are the "people" referred to in this song? By whom are they oppressed? In line 11, who will do the smiting?

2. Explain how "Go Down, Moses" might have had two different meanings for a slave. Identify the words or lines in the song that could have double meanings.

3. In "Swing Low, Sweet Chariot," where is the "home" the singer looks forward to? How will the singer reach that home? What is the "sweet chariot"?

Developing Skills in Reading Literature

Meter. Analyze the meter of the first and third stanzas of "Go Down, Moses." What type of meter is used? How many feet are there in each line? In which lines is there a missing syllable? How is the meter appropriate to a spiritual, which is meant to be sung?

Now analyze the meter of "Swing Low, Sweet Chariot." You will see that there is a repeating pattern of accented syllables, although the number of unaccented syllables varies. How many stressed syllables are there in the different lines? This pattern is typical of the traditional ballad stanza. What other characteristics of the ballad are evident in this song?

Developing Writing Skills

Analyzing Theme: Comparison and Contrast. "Go Down, Moses" and "Swing Low, Sweet Chariot" deal with the theme of deliverance, but in different ways. Write a paragraph in which you compare and contrast this theme in the two songs.

Abraham Lincoln

1809–1865

Abraham Lincoln rose from a simple beginning to become President of the United States, the leader who guided the Union through the tragedy of the Civil War. Brought up on the Kentucky and Indiana frontier, young Lincoln had almost no formal schooling; he educated himself by diligent study of the few books available to him. Much of the style of his later writing derived from works such as the Bible, *Pilgrim's Progress*, and *Robinson Crusoe*, as well as from his reading of American history and biographies of heroic figures such as George Washington.

In 1837 Lincoln settled in New Salem, Illinois, where he was popular for his physical strength and storytelling abilities and respected for his integrity of character. He studied law, and became an able lawyer, skilled in argument, humorous, sincere, and lucid of speech.

As the debate over states' rights intensified, Lincoln became more involved in politics, placing himself squarely in the camp of those who believed in the precedence of national sovereignty over sectional interests. When he was nominated as a Republican in 1858 to oppose Stephen Douglas in the Illinois senatorial race, he gave a ringing declaration of support of the Union: "A house divided against itself cannot stand." Although he was not an Abolitionist, he believed slavery to be an evil and opposed its extension into the new states being carved out of the Western territories. His election as President in 1860 coincided with the first secessions of Southern states from the Union.

Lincoln's letters and speeches are characterized by the sincerity and firmness with which he upheld the Constitution and the Union. His simple eloquence, contrasting with the elaborate oratorical and literary style fashionable at the time, touched the hearts of the common people. "In times like the present," Lincoln told a wartime Congress, "men should utter nothing for which they would not willingly be responsible through time and in eternity."

Abraham Lincoln was assassinated by John Wilkes Booth in Ford's Theatre in Washington, on Good Friday, April 14, 1865.

from A House Divided

Lincoln delivered the "House Divided" speech in 1858, in accepting the Republican nomination to run against Stephen Douglas for the U.S. Senate. On November 19, 1863, after the bloody battle at Gettysburg, Pennsylvania, Lincoln made "a few remarks" at the ceremony dedicating the site as a national cemetery.

Mr. President and Gentlemen of the Convention:[1]

If we could first know where we are and whither we are tending, we could better judge what to do and how to do it. We are now far into the fifth year since a policy was initiated with the avowed object and confident promise of putting an end to slavery agitation.[2] Under the operation of that policy, that agitation has not only not ceased but has constantly augmented. In my opinion, it will not cease until a crisis shall have been reached and passed. "A house divided against itself cannot stand." I believe this government cannot endure, permanently, half slave and half free. I do not expect the Union to be dissolved; I do not expect the house to fall; but I do expect it will cease to be divided. It will become all one thing, or all the other. Either the opponents of slavery will arrest the further spread of it and place it where the public mind shall rest in the belief that it is in the course of ultimate extinction, or its advocates will push it forward till it shall become alike lawful in all the states, old as well as new, North as well as South. . . .

1. Republican State Convention at Springfield, Illinois, on June 16, 1858.
2. The Kansas-Nebraska Act, passed by Congress in 1854, provided for local option on slavery in these territories and abrogated the Missouri Compromise of 1820.

INFANTRY COLUMN ON THE MARCH (DETAIL), 1862. *Winslow Homer. Cooper-Hewitt Museum.*

The Gettysburg Address

Four score and seven years ago our fathers brought forth on this continent a new nation, conceived in liberty and dedicated to the proposition that all men are created equal.

Now we are engaged in a great civil war, tooting whether that nation or any nation so conceived and so dedicated can long endure. We are met on a great battlefield of that war.[1] We have come to dedicate a portion of that field as a final resting place for those who here gave their lives that that nation might live. It is altogether fitting and proper that we should do this.

But, in a larger sense, we cannot dedicate—we cannot consecrate—we cannot hallow—this ground. The brave men, living and dead, who struggled here have consecrated it far above our poor power to add or detract. The world will little note nor long remember what we say here, but it can never forget what they did here. It is for us, the living, rather, to be dedicated here to the unfinished work which they who fought here have thus far so nobly advanced.

It is rather for us to be here dedicated to the great task remaining before us—that from these honored dead we take increased devotion to that cause for which they gave the last full measure of devotion; that we here highly resolve that these dead shall not have died in vain; that this nation, under God, shall have a new birth of freedom; and that government of the people, by the people, for the people shall not perish from the earth.

---

1. The National Soldier's Cemetery at Gettysburg, Pennsylvania, was dedicated November 19, 1863.

Defining Liberty

The world has never had a good definition of the word *liberty*, and the American people, just now, are much in want of one. We all declare for liberty; but in using the same word we do not all mean the same thing. With some the word *liberty* may mean for each man to do as he pleases with himself, and the product of his labor; while with others the same word may mean for some men to do as they please with other men, and the product of other men's labor. Here are two, not only different, but incompatible things, called by the same name, *liberty*. And it follows that each of the things is, by the respective parties, called by two different and incompatible names—*liberty* and *tyranny*.

The shepherd drives the wolf from the sheep's throat, for which the sheep thanks the shepherd as his liberator, while the wolf denounces him for the same act, as the destroyer of liberty, especially as the sheep was a black one. Plainly, the sheep and the wolf are not agreed upon a definition of the word *liberty*; and precisely the same difference prevails today among us human creatures, even in the North, and all professing to love liberty. Hence we behold the process by which thousands are daily passing from under the yoke of bondage hailed by some as the advance of liberty,[1] and bewailed by others as the destruction of all liberty.

---

1. **Emancipation Proclamation:** issued by President Lincoln on January 1, 1863.

Letter to Mrs. Bixby

Executive Mansion, Washington,
November 21, 1864

Mrs. Bixby, Boston, Massachusetts:

Dear Madam: I have been shown in the files of the War Department a statement of the Adjutant-General of Massachusetts that you are the mother of five sons who have died gloriously on the field of battle. I feel how weak and fruitless must be any words of mine which should attempt to beguile you from the grief of a loss so overwhelming. But I cannot refrain from tendering to you the consolation that may be found in the thanks of the Republic they died to save. I pray that our Heavenly Father may assuage the anguish of your bereavement, and leave you only the cherished memory of the loved and lost, and the solemn pride that must be yours to have laid so costly a sacrifice upon the altar of freedom.

Yours very sincerely and respectfully,

Abraham Lincoln

Getting at Meaning

A HOUSE DIVIDED

1. What is the "house divided" referred to in the title of the selection?

2. What two alternatives does Lincoln foresee as the outcome of the controversy over slavery?

THE GETTYSBURG ADDRESS

3. Why does Lincoln say that it is impossible to consecrate fully the cemetery at Gettysburg?

4. What does he say is the task of the living?

DEFINING LIBERTY

5. Lincoln describes two philosophically opposing points of view, each called *liberty* by some. What are these two contradictory ideas? How might slavery have been regarded as *liberty* by some and *tyranny* by others?

LETTER TO MRS. BIXBY

6. What losses have prompted this letter from President Lincoln? What does he suggest to Mrs. Bixby as sources of comfort?

Developing Skills in Reading Literature

1. **Style: Repetition.** A stylistic device that Lincoln uses in "The Gettysburg Address" is the repetition of a key phrase several times, with one word changed each time. The resulting phrases are parallel in structure, which emphasizes the ideas presented in the phrases and creates an appealing rhythm for the reader. Find several examples of this kind of repetition in the Gettysburg speech. Find one example in "A House Divided." What ideas are emphasized in each example? How does the repetition of phrases increase the impact of these speeches?

2. **Analogy.** In "Defining Liberty" Lincoln uses an elaborate analogy to illustrate differing points of view about liberty. What are the specific points of his analogy? Explain the meaning that emerges from this comparison.

3. **Tone.** How does President Lincoln avoid seeming remote or insensitive to Mrs. Bixby? Cite specific words and phrases in your answer. Read aloud the last sentence of the letter. What one word might you use to describe the tone he achieves? Compare this selection to the other selections by Lincoln. How are the tones of all the selections similar? How do their tones differ?

Developing Vocabulary

1. **Understanding Changes in Language: Archaic Words.** In the first sentence of "A House Divided" is the word *whither*. Look up its meaning. What word would you tend to use in its place? This is an example of words that have fallen out of use and are now considered archaic, that is, antiquated or obsolete. Next look up *thither*; how is it related to *whither*? Do the same with the words *whence* and *thence*.

2. **Word Origins.** In "The Gettysburg Address," Lincoln uses the word *hallow*, which comes from Old English. Look up its definition and etymology, or origin. To what common English word is *hallow* related?

In his letter to Mrs. Bixby, Lincoln prays that God will "assuage" her anguish. Look up the etymology of *assuage*. What sense image is contained in the meaning of its root? How does this image relate to the present-day meaning of the word?

Lincoln's key term, *liberty,* is derived ultimately from the Latin root *liber,* meaning "free." Find three other English words that derive from the same root.

Developing Writing Skills

Writing a Definition. In a well developed paragraph, write your own definition of the term *liberty*. Use several strategies to establish your definition. Tell what it is not and what it is; or tell what it does not resemble and what it does. Give an example or create an analogy to illustrate your definition.

Robert E. Lee

1807–1870

Robert E. Lee, a brilliant military strategist, served as general-in-chief of the Confederate armies during the Civil War. Loved and respected by his contemporaries, admired and esteemed by succeeding generations, Lee symbolizes what is best in the Southern heritage. His personal qualities—dignity, generosity, sensitivity—show forth in his speeches and letters, which are valued for their graceful style as well as for their historical significance.

Lee was a member of one of Virginia's finest families and was married to the great-granddaughter of Martha Washington. During the years prior to the Civil War, he distinguished himself as an American officer in the Mexican War, as superintendent of the United States Military Academy at West Point, and as an officer in the U.S. cavalry. In his correspondence from these years, he expresses his dismay at the prospect of the Southern secession from the Union and of the war that would inevitably follow. When the possibility of war became the reality of war, Lee refused President Lincoln's offer of the command of the Union forces. He resigned from the United States Army, writing "Save in the defense of my native state, I never again desire to draw my sword." After the secession of his beloved Virginia from the Union, Lee took command of the Army of Northern Virginia and became the chief field commander of the Confederate forces. He served the Confederacy until his final surrender to General Ulysses S. Grant at Appomattox Court House on April 9, 1865.

Lee was influential in binding up the wounds of war and in smoothing the transition of the Southern states back into the Union. He urged other Southerners to follow his example in accepting defeat with grace and magnanimity. To his friend Confederate General G. T. Beauregard he wrote: "I need not tell you that true patriotism sometimes requires of men to act exactly contrary at one period to that which it does at another, and the motive that impels—to do right—is precisely the same." After several years as president of Washington College (later Washington and Lee College), Lee died in 1870, as revered a leader in peace as he had been in war.

Letters to His Family

Lee composed these letters to his family fewer than three months before the outbreak of the Civil War. He wrote the farewell to his army the day after he surrendered to General Ulysses S. Grant, the act that signaled the end of the war.

To His Wife

Fort Mason, Texas, January 23, 1861

I received Everett's[1] *Life of Washington* which you sent me, and enjoyed its perusal. How his spirit would be grieved could he see the wreck of his mighty labors! I will not, however, permit myself to believe, until all ground of hope is gone, that the fruit of his noble deeds will be destroyed, and that his precious advice and virtuous example will so soon be forgotten by his countrymen. As far as I can judge by the papers, we are between a state of anarchy and civil war. May God avert both of these evils from us! I fear that mankind will not for years be sufficiently Christianized to bear the absence of restraint and force. I see that four States[2] have declared themselves out of the Union; four more will apparently follow their example. Then, if the border States are brought into the gulf of revolution, one half of the country will be arrayed against the other. I must try and be patient and await the end, for I can do nothing to hasten or retard it. . . .

---

1. Edward Everett (1794–1865), American clergyman and orator who spoke at Gettysburg before Lincoln.
2. Alabama, Florida, Mississippi, and South Carolina.

To His Son

Under the same date, he wrote thus to his son:

The South, in my opinion, has been aggrieved[3] by the acts of the North, as you say. I feel the aggression, and am willing to take every proper step for redress. It is the principle I contend for, not individual or private benefit. As an American citizen, I take great pride in my country, her prosperity and institutions, and would defend any State, if her rights were invaded. But I can anticipate no greater calamity for the country than a dissolution of the Union. It would be an accumulation of all the evils we complain of, and I am willing to sacrifice everything but honor for its preservation. I hope, therefore, that all constitutional means will be exhausted before there is a resort to force. Secession is nothing but revolution. The framers of our Constitution never exhausted so much labor, wisdom, and forbearance in its formation, and surrounded it with so many guards and securities, if it was intended to be broken by every member of the Confederacy[4] at will. It was intended for "perpetual union," so expressed in the preamble, and for the establishment of

---

3. **aggrieved** (ə grēv'd'): treated wrongly in a legal matter.
4. **Confederacy:** The eleven southern states that seceded from the United States in 1860 and 1861 to form the Confederate States of America.

a government, not a compact, which can only be dissolved by revolution, or the consent of all the people in convention assembled. It is idle to talk of secession. Anarchy would have been established, and not a government, by Washington, Hamilton, Jefferson, Madison, and the other patriots of the Revolution. . . . Still a Union that can only be maintained by swords and bayonets, and in which strife and civil war are to take the place of brotherly love and kindness, has no charm for me. I shall mourn for my country and for the welfare and progress of mankind. If the Union is dissolved, and the Government disrupted, I shall return to my native State and share the miseries of my people, and save in defense will draw my sword on none.

Farewell to His Army

Headquarters, Army Northern Virginia,
April 10, 1865

After four years of arduous service, marked by unsurpassed courage and fortitude, the Army of Northern Virginia has been compelled to yield to overwhelming numbers and resources. I need not tell the survivors of so many hard-fought battles, who have remained steadfast to the last, that I have consented to this result from no distrust of them; but, feeling that valor and devotion could accomplish nothing that could compensate for the loss that would have attended the continuation of the contest, I have determined to avoid the useless sacrifice of those whose past services have endeared them to their countrymen. By the terms of the agreement, officers and men can return to their homes, and remain there until exchanged.[1]

You will take with you *the satisfaction that proceeds from the consciousness of duty faithfully performed;* and I earnestly pray that a merciful God will extend to you his blessing and protection. With an unceasing admiration of your constancy and devotion to your country, and a grateful remembrance of your kind and generous consideration of myself, I bid you an affectionate farewell.

R.E. Lee, General

---

1. **exchanged:** officially discharged from military service.

Getting at Meaning

TO HIS WIFE

1. Explain Lee's reaction to the biography of Washington that he has been reading. What does he mean by "the wreck of his mighty labors" and "the fruit of his noble deeds"?

2. What attitude does Lee take concerning the historical events that are taking place?

TO HIS SON

3. What seems to be Lee's main concern in this letter?

4. Lee makes a distinction between a government and a compact. Explain this distinction. How does he define *secession?*

5. What is the one thing that Lee says he would not sacrifice to preserve the Union?

6. Under what circumstances would Lee withdraw his support of the Union?

FAREWELL TO HIS ARMY

7. In explaining his decision to surrender, what does Lee particularly wish to assure his soldiers?

8. What "useless sacrifice" does Lee wish to avoid?

Developing Skills in Reading Literature

Style: Sentence Variety. Lee was clearly skilled in composing long, balanced sentences. However, he often makes his point forcefully, and achieves a pleasing variety, by alternating long sentences with short ones of only five to ten words. Find three such sentences in his letters to his wife and son. What main points does Lee make in these short sentences?

Occasionally Lee varies his sentence structure by beginning a sentence with a subordinate clause or a long prepositional phrase. An example of such sentence structure would be, "Because it was warm, I opened the window." The effect of this construction is to throw the mind forward to the idea that will complete the meaning, building curiosity or suspense or improving emphasis. In the second paragraph of Lee's "Farewell to His Army," find an example of this kind of sentence structure. Why is it effective here?

THE BATTLE ABBEY MURALS: THE FOUR SEASONS OF THE CONFEDERACY. THE SUMMER MURAL. *Charles Hoffbauer. The Virginia Historical Society, Richmond.*

Ambrose Bierce

1842–1914?

An attitude both cynical and fatalistic characterized the life and writings of Ambrose Bierce. He was born into a large, poor, and intensely religious family at Horse Cave Creek, Meigs County, in southeast Ohio, and spent his childhood on a poor Indiana farm. His meager formal education (a year at an obscure military academy) was augmented by his reading of the classics that his father had carried with him when he migrated west from New England.

Bierce had a brilliant career in the Union Army, fighting bravely in some of the fiercest battles of the Civil War. He then began an equally brilliant career as a journalist. Ashamed of his background and the stern religion of his parents and disillusioned with the senseless slaughter of lives and hopes he had seen during the war, he came to be called "Bitter Bierce."

Bierce's career in journalism began in San Francisco, where he wrote columns and edited a newspaper, gaining a reputation as a satirical wit. Here also he published his first short stories. Postwar San Francisco was in the midst of a literary flowering, and among Bierce's friends were writers Mark Twain and Bret Harte.

Newly married, Bierce lived in London for five years, contributing to English humor magazines and publishing three books. Upon his return he wrote a popular column for William Randolph Hearst's *San Francisco Examiner* for ten years, then was sent by Hearst to Washington, D.C., where he remained until 1909.

Bierce became famous for his sardonic humor and cruel wit, exhibited in his short stories and also in essays, journalistic pieces, and a book of satiric definitions called *The Devil's Dictionary* (1906). His finest stories, including "An Occurrence at Owl Creek Bridge" (1891), concern the ironies and futility of war, and exist as a counterpoint to the kind of fiction in which a romantic glow is cast over the experience of war. In treatment of subject, Bierce's stories are akin in spirit to the grim war stories of Stephen Crane.

In 1913, at the age of seventy-one, Bierce went to Mexico to report on the Mexican Revolution as an observer with Pancho Villa's rebel army. He never returned, and all trace of him was lost. Some believed that he welcomed the possibility of death and did not intend to return. Before he left he wrote to a niece: "If you hear of my being stood up against a Mexican stone wall and shot to rags, please know that I think that a pretty good way to depart this life. It beats old age, disease, or falling down the cellar stairs."

An Occurrence at Owl Creek Bridge

1

A man stood upon a railroad bridge in northern Alabama, looking down into the swift water twenty feet below. The man's hands were behind his back, the wrists bound with a cord. A rope closely encircled his neck. It was attached to a stout cross-timber above his head and the slack fell to the level of his knees. Some loose boards laid upon the sleepers[1] supporting the metals of the railway supplied a footing for him and his executioners—two private soldiers of the Federal army, directed by a sergeant who in civil life may have been a deputy sheriff. At a short remove upon the same temporary platform was an officer in the uniform of his rank, armed. He was a captain. A sentinel at each end of the bridge stood with his rifle in the position known as "support," that is to say, vertical in front of the left shoulder, the hammer resting on the forearm thrown straight across the chest—a formal and unnatural position, enforcing an erect carriage of the body. It did not appear to be the duty of these two men to know what was occurring at the center of the bridge; they merely blockaded the two ends of the foot planking that traversed it.

Beyond one of the sentinels nobody was in sight; the railroad ran straight away into a forest for a hundred yards, then, curving, was lost to view. Doubtless there was an outpost farther along. The other bank of the stream was open ground—a gentle acclivity[2] topped with a stockade of vertical tree trunks, loopholed for rifles, with a single embrasure[3] through which protruded the muzzle of a brass cannon commanding the bridge. Midway of the slope between bridge and fort were the spectators—a single company of infantry in line, at "parade rest," the butts of the rifles on the ground, the barrels inclining slightly backward against the right shoulder, the hands crossed upon the stock. A lieutenant stood at the right of the line, the point of his sword upon the ground, his left hand resting upon his right. Excepting the group of four at the center of the bridge, not a man moved. The company faced the bridge, staring stonily, motionless. The sentinels, facing the banks of the stream, might have been statues to adorn the bridge. The captain stood with folded arms, silent, observing the work of his subordinates, but making no sign. Death is a dignitary who when he comes announced is to be received with formal manifestations of respect, even by those most familiar with him. In the code of military etiquette, silence and fixity are forms of deference.

The man who was engaged in being hanged was apparently about thirty-five years of age. He was a civilian, if one might judge from his habit, which was that of a planter.[4] His features were good—a straight nose, firm mouth, broad forehead, from which his long, dark hair was combed straight back, falling behind his ears to the collar of his well-fitting frock coat. He wore a mustache and pointed beard, but no whiskers; his eyes were large and dark gray, and had a kindly expression which one would hardly have expected in one whose

---

1. **sleepers:** railroad ties.
2. **acclivity** (ə kliv' ə tē): an upward slope of ground.
3. **embrasure** (im brā' zhər): an opening with the sides slanting outward to increase the angle of fire of a gun.
4. **planter:** the owner of a plantation.

neck was in the hemp. Evidently this was no vulgar assassin. The liberal military code makes provision for hanging many kinds of persons, and gentlemen are not excluded.

The preparations being complete, the two private soldiers stepped aside and each drew away the plank upon which he had been standing. The sergeant turned to the captain, saluted and placed himself immediately behind that officer, who in turn moved apart one pace. These movements left the condemned man and the sergeant standing on the two ends of the same plank, which spanned three of the cross-ties of the bridge. The end upon which the civilian stood almost, but not quite, reached a fourth. This plank had been held in place by the weight of the captain; it was now held by that of the sergeant. At a signal from the former, the latter would step aside, the plank would tilt and the condemned man go down between two ties. The arrangement commended itself to his judgment as simple and effective. His face had not been covered nor his eyes bandaged. He looked a moment at his "unsteadfast footing," then let his gaze wander to the swirling water of the stream racing madly beneath his feet. A piece of dancing driftwood caught his attention and his eyes followed it down the current. How slowly it appeared to move! What a sluggish stream!

He closed his eyes in order to fix his last thoughts upon his wife and children. The water, touched to gold by the early sun, the brooding mists under the banks at some distance down the stream, the fort, the soldiers, the piece of drift—all had distracted him. And now he became conscious of a new disturbance. Striking through the thought of his dear ones was a sound which he could neither ignore nor understand, a sharp, distinct, metallic percussion like the stroke of a blacksmith's hammer upon the anvil; it had the same ringing quality. He wondered what it was, and whether immeasurably distant or nearby—it seemed both. Its recurrence was regular, but as slow as the tolling of a death knell.[5] He awaited each stroke with impatience and—he knew not why—apprehension. The intervals of silence grew progressively longer; the delays became maddening. With their greater infrequency the sounds increased in strength and sharpness. They hurt his ear like the thrust of a knife; he feared he would shriek. What he heard was the ticking of his watch.

He unclosed his eyes and saw again the water below him. "If I could free my hands," he thought, "I might throw off the noose and spring into the stream. By diving I could evade the bullets and, swimming vigorously, reach the bank, take to the woods and get away home. My home, thank God, is as yet outside their lines; my wife and little ones are still beyond the invader's farthest advance."

As these thoughts, which have here to be set down in words, were flashed into the doomed man's brain rather than evolved from it, the captain nodded to the sergeant. The sergeant stepped aside.

2

Peyton Farquhar was a well-to-do planter, of an old and highly respected Alabama family. Being a slave-owner, and like other slave owners a politician, he was naturally an original secessionist and ardently devoted to the Southern cause. Circumstances of an imperious nature, which it is unnecessary to relate here, had prevented him from taking service with the gallant army that had fought the disastrous campaigns ending with the fall of Corinth,[6] and he chafed under the inglorious restraint, longing for the release of his energies, the larger life of the soldier, the oppor-

---

5. **death knell:** the slow, steady ringing of a bell at a funeral or to indicate a death.
6. Corinth, Mississippi, battle in 1862.

tunity for distinction. That opportunity, he felt, would come, as it comes to all in war time. Meanwhile he did what he could. No service was too humble for him to perform in aid of the South, no adventure too perilous for him to undertake if consistent with the character of a civilian who was at heart a soldier, and who in good faith and without too much qualification assented to at least a part of the frankly villainous dictum that all is fair in love and war.

One evening while Farquhar and his wife were sitting on a rustic bench near the entrance to his grounds, a gray-clad soldier rode up to the gate and asked for a drink of water. Mrs. Farquhar was only too happy to serve him with her own white hands. While she was fetching the water, her husband approached the dusty horseman and inquired eagerly for news from the front.

"The Yanks are repairing the railroads," said the man, "and are getting ready for another advance. They have reached the Owl Creek bridge, put it in order and built a stockade on the north bank. The commandant has issued an order, which is posted everywhere, declaring that any civilian caught interfering with the railroad, its bridges, tunnels, or trains will be summarily hanged. I saw the order."

"How far is it to the Owl Creek bridge?" Farquhar asked.

"About thirty miles."

"Is there no force on this side the creek?"

"Only a picket post half a mile out, on the railroad, and a single sentinel at this end of the bridge."

"Suppose a man—a civilian and student of hanging—should elude the picket post and perhaps get the better of the sentinel," said Farquhar, smiling. "What could he accomplish?"

The soldier reflected. "I was there a month ago," he replied. "I observed that the flood of last winter had lodged a great quantity of driftwood against the wooden pier at this end

of the bridge. It is now dry and would burn like tow."[7]

The lady had now brought the water, which the soldier drank. He thanked her ceremoniously, bowed to her husband and rode away. An hour later, after nightfall, he repassed the plantation, going northward in the direction from which he had come. He was a Federal scout.

3

As Peyton Farquhar fell straight downward through the bridge, he lost consciousness and was as one already dead. From this state he was awakened—ages later, it seemed to him—by the pain of a sharp pressure upon his throat, followed by a sense of suffocation. Keen, poignant agonies seemed to shoot from his neck downward through every fiber of his body and limbs. These pains appeared to flash along well-defined lines of ramification and to beat with an inconceivably rapid periodicity.[8] They seemed like streams of pulsating fire heating him to an intolerable temperature. As to his head, he was conscious of nothing but a feeling of fullness—of congestion. These sensations were unaccompanied by thought. The intellectual part of his nature was already effaced; he had power only to feel, and feeling was torment. He was conscious of motion. Encompassed in a luminous cloud, of which he was now merely the fiery heart, without material substance, he swung through unthinkable arcs of oscillation, like a vast pendulum. Then all at once, with terrible suddenness, the light about him shot upward with the noise of a loud plash; a frightful roaring was in his ears, and all was cold and dark. The power of thought was restored; he knew that

---

7. **tow:** coarse fibers of flax, hemp, or jute ready for spinning into rope.
8. **periodicity** (pir′ ē ə dis′ ə tē): recurring at regular intervals.

the rope had broken and he had fallen into the stream. There was no additional strangulation; the noose about his neck was already suffocating him and kept the water from his lungs. To die of hanging at the bottom of a river!—the idea seemed to him ludicrous. He opened his eyes in the darkness and saw above him a gleam of light, but how distant, how inaccessible! He was still sinking, for the light became fainter and fainter until it was a mere glimmer. Then it began to grow and brighten, and he knew that he was rising toward the surface—knew it with reluctance, for he was now very comfortable. "To be hanged and drowned," he thought, "that is not so bad; but I do not wish to be shot. No; I will not be shot; that is not fair."

He was not conscious of an effort, but a sharp pain in his wrist apprised him that he was trying to free his hands. He gave the struggle his attention, as an idler might observe the feat of a juggler, without interest in the outcome. What splendid effort!—what magnificent, what superhuman strength! Ah, that was a fine endeavor! Bravo! The cord fell away; his arms parted and floated upward, the hands dimly seen on each side in the growing light. He watched them with a new interest as first one and then the other pounced upon the noose at his neck. They tore it away and thrust it fiercely aside, its undulations resembling those of a water-snake. "Put it back, put it back!" He thought he shouted these words to his hands, for the undoing of the noose had been succeeded by the direst pang that he had yet experienced. His neck ached horribly; his brain was on fire; his heart, which had been fluttering faintly, gave a great leap, trying to force itself out at his mouth. His whole body was racked and wrenched with an insupportable anguish! But his disobedient hands gave no heed to the command. They beat the water vigorously with quick, downward strokes, forcing him to the surface. He felt his head emerge; his eyes were blinded by the sunlight; his chest expanded convulsively, and with a supreme and crowning agony his lungs engulfed a great draught of air, which instantly he expelled in a shriek!

He was now in full possession of his physical senses. They were, indeed, preternaturally keen and alert. Something in the awful disturbance of his organic system had so exalted and refined them that they made record of things never before perceived. He felt the ripples upon his face and heard their separate sounds as they struck. He looked at the forest on the bank of the stream, saw the individual trees, the leaves, and the veining of each leaf—saw the very insects upon them: the locusts, the brilliant-bodied flies, the gray spiders stretching their webs from twig to twig. He noted the prismatic colors[9] in all the dewdrops upon a million blades of grass. The humming of the gnats that danced above the eddies of the stream, the beating of the dragon-flies' wings, the strokes of the water-spiders' legs, like oars which had lifted their boat—all these made audible music. A fish slid along beneath his eyes, and he heard the rush of its body parting the water.

He had come to the surface facing down the stream; in a moment the visible world seemed to wheel slowly round, himself the pivotal point, and he saw the bridge, the fort, the soldiers upon the bridge, the captain, the sergeant, the two privates, his executioners. They were in silhouette against the blue sky. They shouted and gesticulated,[10] pointing at him. The captain had drawn his pistol, but did not fire; the others were unarmed. Their movements were grotesque and horrible, their forms gigantic.

Suddenly he heard a sharp report and something struck the water smartly within a few inches of his head, spattering his face with spray. He heard a second report, and saw one

---

9. **prismatic colors** (priz mat' ik): basic colors of the visible spectrum produced by passing light through a prism.
10. **gesticulated** (jes tik' yə lat' ed): gestured energetically with the hands.

of the sentinels with his rifle at his shoulder, a light cloud of blue smoke rising from the muzzle. The man in the water saw the eye of the man on the bridge gazing into his own through the sights of the rifle. He observed that it was a gray eye and remembered having read that gray eyes were keenest, and that all famous marksmen had them. Nevertheless, this one had missed.

A counter-swirl had caught Farquhar and turned him half round; he was again looking into the forest on the bank opposite the fort. The sound of a clear, high voice in a monotonous singsong now rang out behind him and came across the water with a distinctness that pierced and subdued all other sounds, even the beating of the ripples in his ears. Although no soldier, he had frequented camps enough to know the dread significance of that deliberate, drawling, aspirated chant; the lieutenant on shore was taking a part in the morning's work. How coldly and pitilessly—with what an even, calm intonation, presaging,[11] and enforcing tranquillity in the men—with what accurately measured intervals fell those cruel words:

"Attention, company! . . . Shoulder arms! . . . Ready! . . . Aim! . . . Fire!"

Farquhar dived—dived as deeply as he could. The water roared in his ears like the voice of Niagara, yet he heard the dulled thunder of the volley and, rising again toward the surface, met shining bits of metal, singularly flattened, oscillating slowly downward. Some of them touched him on the face and hands, then fell away, continuing their descent. One lodged between his collar and neck; it was uncomfortably warm and he snatched it out.

As he rose to the surface, gasping for breath, he saw that he had been a long time under water; he was perceptibly farther down stream—nearer to safety. The soldiers had almost finished reloading; the metal ramrods flashed all at once in the sunshine as they were drawn from the barrels, turned in the air, and thrust into their sockets. The two sentinels fired again, independently and ineffectually.

The hunted man saw all this over his shoulder; he was now swimming vigorously with the current. His brain was as energetic as his arms and legs; he thought with the rapidity of lightning.

"The officer," he reasoned, "will not make that martinet's[12] error a second time. It is as easy to dodge a volley as a single shot. He has probably already given the command to fire at will. God help me, I cannot dodge them all!"

An appalling plash within two yards of him was followed by a loud, rushing sound, *diminuendo*,[13] which seemed to travel back through the air to the fort and died in an explosion which stirred the very river to its deeps! A rising sheet of water curved over him, fell down upon him, blinded him, strangled him! The cannon had taken a hand in the game. As he shook his head free from the commotion of the smitten water, he heard the deflected shot humming through the air ahead, and in an instant it was cracking and smashing the branches in the forest beyond.

"They will not do that again," he thought; "the next time they will use a charge of grape.[14] I must keep my eye upon the gun; the smoke will apprise me—the report arrives too late; it lags behind the missile. That is a good gun."

Suddenly he felt himself whirled round and round—spinning like a top. The water, the banks, the forests, the now distant bridge, fort and men—all were commingled and blurred. Objects were represented by their colors only; circular horizontal streaks of color—that was all he saw. He had been

---

11. **presaging** (pri sāj' iŋ): foreshadowing.
12. **martinet** (mär' t'n et'): strict disciplinarian, stickler for rigid regulations.
13. **diminuendo** (də min' yoo wen' dō): gradual decrease in loudness.
14. **grape** (grapeshot): a cluster of several small iron balls fired in one shot from a cannon to hit a wider target.

caught in a vortex and was being whirled on with a velocity of advance and gyration that made him giddy and sick. In a few moments he was flung upon the gravel at the foot of the left bank of the stream—the southern bank—and behind a projecting point which concealed him from his enemies. The sudden arrest of his motion, the abrasion of one of his hands on the gravel, restored him, and he wept with delight. He dug his fingers into the sand, threw it over himself in handfuls and audibly blessed it. It looked like diamonds, rubies, emeralds; he could think of nothing beautiful which it did not resemble. The trees upon the bank were giant garden plants; he noted a definite order in their arrangement, inhaled the fragrance of their blooms. A strange, roseate light shone through the spaces among their trunks, and the wind made in their branches the music of æolian harps.[15] He had no wish to perfect his escape—was content to remain in that enchanting spot until retaken.

A whiz and rattle of grapeshot among the branches high above his head roused him from his dream. The baffled cannoneer had fired him a random farewell. He sprang to his feet, rushed up the sloping bank, and plunged into the forest.

All that day he traveled, laying his course by the rounding sun. The forest seemed interminable: nowhere did he discover a break in it, not even a woodman's road. He had not known that he lived in so wild a region. There was something uncanny in the revelation.

By nightfall he was fatigued, footsore, famishing. The thought of his wife and children urged him on. At last he found a road which led him in what he knew to be the right direction. It was as wide and straight as a city street, yet it seemed untraveled. No fields bordered it, no dwelling anywhere. Not so much as the barking of a dog suggested human habitation. The black bodies of the trees formed a straight wall on both sides, terminating on the horizon in a point, like a diagram in a lesson in perspective. Overhead, as he looked up through this rift in the wood, shone great golden stars looking unfamiliar and grouped in strange constellations. He was sure they were arranged in some order which had a secret and malign[16] significance. The wood on either side was full of singular noises, among which—once, twice, and again—he distinctly heard whispers in an unknown tongue.

His neck was in pain and lifting his hand to it he found it horribly swollen. He knew that it had a circle of black where the rope had bruised it. His eyes felt congested; he could no longer close them. His tongue was swollen with thirst; he relieved its fever by thrusting it forward from between his teeth into the cold air. How softly the turf had carpeted the untraveled avenue—he could no longer feel the roadway beneath his feet!

Doubtless, despite his suffering, he had fallen asleep while walking, for now he sees another scene—perhaps he has merely recovered from a delirium. He stands at the gate of his own home. All is as he left it, and all bright and beautiful in the morning sunshine. He must have traveled the entire night. As he pushes open the gate and passes up the wide white walk, he sees a flutter of female garments; his wife, looking fresh and cool and sweet, steps down from the veranda to meet him. At the bottom of the steps she stands waiting, with a smile of ineffable joy, an attitude of matchless grace and dignity. Ah, how beautiful she is! He springs forward with extended arms. As he is about to clasp her he feels a stunning blow upon the back of the neck; a blinding white light blazes all about him with a sound like the shock of a cannon—then all is darkness and silence!

Peyton Farquhar was dead; his body, with a broken neck, swung gently from side to side beneath the timbers of the Owl Creek bridge.

---

15. **aeolian harp** (ē ō′ lē ən): a boxlike stringed instrument that makes music when air blows through it.
16. **malign** (mə līn′): malicious, sinister.

Getting at Meaning

1. How much time actually passes in Farquhar's life between the end of Section 1 and the end of the story?

2. What is it about Farquhar's background and temperament that explains his getting into this predicament?

3. What is Farquhar's apparent social position? How does the reader know this?

4. What is the significance of the fact that the soldier who stops for a drink is a Federal scout?

5. Why is Farquhar being hanged? Why do the soldiers observe such strict silence and decorum?

6. How does Farquhar seem to escape death? After his "escape," what is his destination? Does he reach it? Explain your answer.

Developing Skills in Reading Literature

1. **Surprise Ending.** This selection provides a good example of a surprise ending, an unexpected twist of plot at the end of a story. How effective is it here? Is the reader tricked? What phrase at the beginning of Section 3 foreshadows the ending?

Near the end of the story, the narration switches suddenly from the past to the present tense. What is the effect of this switch? How does it relate to what is actually happening to Farquhar? How does it prepare the reader for the ending?

2. **Description.** The opening three paragraphs of this story describe a scene in almost photographic detail. Nothing moves and nobody speaks; it is like a moment frozen in time. Why does this description seem appropriate at this point in the story? Think about what happens to Farquhar and how his experience is presented in this story. How is the opening description consistent with the rest of the story?

3. **Character.** In what way is Farquhar a sympathetic character? What details create sympathy for Farquhar? Does anything qualify or temper the reader's sympathy? Explain your answers.

4. **Point of View.** The narrative method used in this story is unusual for the time in which it was written. After the impersonal and objective opening two paragraphs, the narrator begins to focus in on the man who is "engaged in being hanged." He is "apparently" about thirty-five and evidently "no vulgar assassin." Finally the reader is drawn inside the man's mind to share his thoughts and feelings. Identify the place in the story where this transition occurs.

Except for Section 2, which is a flashback to earlier events, the rest of the story is transmitted through Farquhar's internal consciousness. The reader only knows what he knows. How do Farquhar's senses and his mental acuity seem to be affected? When his head first emerges from the water, how does the world look to him? What particular kinds of things does he perceive with great clarity? How is this significant, in view of what is actually happening to him? As he seems to get closer to his final objective, the scene seems increasingly wild, strange, uncanny, dreamlike. What details create this impression for the reader?

Developing Writing Skills

Sustaining a Point of View. Narrate an event or a situation partly or entirely from the point of view of the character experiencing the action. You may choose to retell a familiar story, to describe an event from your own experience, or to imagine a realistic or a fanciful situation. Be sure to sustain the third-person point of view, even if you choose to relate a personal experience.

Stephen Crane

1871–1900

During his brief career as a writer, Stephen Crane broke dramatically with the traditions of the past in selection of subjects, point of view, and style. He believed that a writer is "responsible for his personal honesty" and maintained that, if an event is recorded as it actually happened, it does not need interpreting, moralizing, or sentimentalizing. Sharing the French naturalists' belief that the individual is the product of heredity and environment and thus is powerless to create a meaningful life, Crane denied the importance of the individual in the universe, the possibility of free will, and the existence of a just and loving God.

The youngest of fourteen children, the son of a Methodist minister and a social leader and temperance crusader, Crane was born in Newark, New Jersey, on November 1, 1871. When he was nine years old, his father died, and the family's economic struggles intensified. Crane's prep school and brief college terms were remarkable largely for his distinction in baseball, but during his one term at Syracuse University in 1890 and 1891, he decided on writing as a career. For three years he existed precariously as a freelance writer of newspaper articles, getting to know intimately the poverty-ridden slums of New York and nearby cities. In 1893 he rewrote *Maggie: A Girl of the Streets*, the first draft of which he had written while a student at Syracuse. Publishers rejected the novel, shocked by its vivid depiction of the degradation and immorality of slum life. Crane borrowed money and published the novel independently. While it was not immediately successful, it attracted the attention of Hamlin Garland and William Dean Howells, who thereafter acted as Crane's professional mentors.

The first draft of *Maggie* was written by twenty-year-old Crane before he had experienced the brutality of the New York slums. *The Red Badge of Courage*, a realistic story of the Civil War Battle of Chancellorsville, was written by twenty-four-year-old Crane, a man without war experience who relied only on veterans' tales of the Civil War and on the superb combat photographs of Matthew Brady. The remarkably accurate details and impressions of battle in *The Red Badge of Courage* make it still convincing to war veterans today. In 1895 he also published his collected poems, which are striking works of impressionism.

By age twenty-five, Crane was a star reporter and roving correspondent. He toured the West and Mexico, settings for "The Blue Hotel" and "The Bride Comes to Yellow Sky." He joined an ill-fated gun-running attempt to arm Cuban revolutionaries, which resulted in a shipwreck and the story "The Open Boat." In spite of poor health, he covered the Spanish-American War and the Greco-Turkish War and observed that his impressions of war were accurate. By this time Crane had contracted tuberculosis and so remained for a time in England where he came to know Joseph Conrad, Henry James, James Barrie, H.G. Wells, and other famous writers. As his health deteriorated, he went to a spa at Badenweiler, Germany, where he died on June 5, 1900.

A Mystery of Heroism

The dark uniforms of the men were so coated with dust from the incessant wrestling of the two armies that the regiment almost seemed a part of the clay bank which shielded them from the shells. On the top of the hill a battery was arguing in tremendous roars with some other guns, and to the eye of the infantry the artillerymen, the guns, the caissons,[1] the horses, were distinctly outlined upon the blue sky. When a piece was fired, a red streak as round as a log flashed low in the heavens, like a monstrous bolt of lightning. The men of the battery wore white duck trousers, which somehow emphasized their legs; and when they ran and crowded in little groups at the bidding of the shouting officers, it was more impressive than usual to the infantry.

Fred Collins, of A Company, was saying, "Thunder! I wisht I had a drink. Ain't there any water round here?" Then somebody yelled, "There goes th' bugler!"

As the eyes of half the regiment swept in one machine-like movement, there was an instant's picture of a horse in a great convulsive leap of a death-wound and a rider leaning back with a crooked arm and spread fingers before his face. On the ground was the crimson terror of an exploding shell, with fibers of flame that seemed like lances. A glittering bugle swung clear of the rider's back as fell headlong the horse and the man. In the air was an odor as from a conflagration.

Sometimes they of the infantry looked down at a fair little meadow which spread at their feet. Its long green grass was rippling gently in a breeze. Beyond it was the grey form of a house half torn to pieces by shells and by the busy axes of soldiers who had pursued firewood. The line of an old fence was now dimly marked by long weeds and by an occasional post. A shell had blown the well-house to fragments. Little lines of grey smoke ribboning upward from some embers indicated the place where had stood the barn.

From beyond a curtain of green woods there came the sound of some stupendous scuffle, as if two animals of the size of islands were fighting. At a distance there were occasional appearances of swift-moving men, horses, batteries, flags; and with the crashing of infantry volleys were heard, often, wild and frenzied cheers. In the midst of it all Smith and Ferguson, two privates of A Company, were engaged in a heated discussion which involved the greatest questions of the national existence.

The battery on the hill presently engaged in a frightful duel. The white legs of the gunners scampered this way and that way, and the officers redoubled their shouts. The guns, with their demeanors of stolidity[2] and courage, were typical of something infinitely self-possessed in this clamor of death that swirled around the hill.

One of a "swing" team[3] was suddenly smitten quivering to the ground, and his maddened brethren dragged his torn body in their struggle to escape from this turmoil and danger. A young soldier astride one of the leaders swore and fumed in his saddle and furiously jerked at the bridle. An officer screamed out an order so violently that his voice broke and ended the sentence in a falsetto shriek.

The leading company of the infantry regi-

---

1. **caisson** (kā′ sän): two-wheeled wagon for transporting chests of ammunition.
2. **stolidity** (stə lid′ ə tē): showing little or no emotion or sensitivity.
3. **swing team:** middle team of a six-horse team.

ment was somewhat exposed, and the colonel ordered it moved more fully under the shelter of the hill. There was the clank of steel against steel.

A lieutenant of the battery rode down and passed them, holding his right arm carefully in his left hand. And it was as if this arm was not at all a part of him, but belonged to another man. His sober and reflective charger[4] went slowly. The officer's face was grimy and perspiring, and his uniform was tousled as if he had been in direct grapple with an enemy. He smiled grimly when the men stared at him. He turned his horse toward the meadow.

Collins, of A Company, said, "I wisht I had a drink. I bet there's water in that there ol' well yonder!"

"Yes; but how you goin' to git it?"

For the little meadow which intervened was now suffering a terrible onslaught of shells. Its green and beautiful calm had vanished utterly. Brown earth was being flung in monstrous handfuls. And there was a massacre of the young blades of grass. They were being torn, burned, obliterated. Some curious fortune of the battle had made this gentle little meadow the object of the red hate of the shells, and each one as it exploded seemed like an imprecation[5] in the face of a maiden.

The wounded officer who was riding across this expanse said to himself: "Why, they couldn't shoot any harder if the whole army was massed here!"

A shell struck the grey ruins of the house, and as, after the roar, the shattered wall fell in fragments, there was a noise which resembled the flapping of shutters during a wild gale of winter. Indeed, the infantry paused in the shelter of the bank appeared as men standing upon a shore contemplating a madness of the sea. The angel of calamity had under its glance the battery upon the hill. Fewer white-legged men labored about the guns. A shell had smitten one of the pieces, and after the flare, the smoke, the dust, the wrath of this blow were gone, it was possible to see white

legs stretched horizontally upon the ground. And at that interval to the rear where it is the business of battery horses[6] to stand with their noses to the fight, awaiting the command to drag their guns out of the destruction, or into it, or wheresoever these incomprehensible humans demanded with whip and spur—in this line of passive and dumb spectators, whose fluttering hearts yet would not let them forget the iron laws of man's control of them—in this rank of brute-soldiers there had been relentless and hideous carnage. From the ruck[7] of bleeding and prostrate horses, the men of the infantry could see one animal raising its stricken body with its forelegs and turning its nose with mystic and profound eloquence toward the sky.

Some comrades joked Collins about his thirst. "Well, if yeh want a drink so bad, why don't yeh go git it?"

"Well, I will in a minnet, if yeh don't shut up!"

A lieutenant of artillery floundered his horse straight down the hill with as little concern as if it were level ground. As he galloped past the colonel of the infantry, he threw up his hand in swift salute. "We've got to get out of that," he roared angrily. He was a black-bearded officer, and his eyes, which resembled beads, sparkled like those of an insane man. His jumping horse sped along the column of infantry.

The fat major, standing carelessly with his sword held horizontally behind him and with his legs far apart, looked after the receding horseman and laughed. "He wants to get back with orders pretty quick, or there'll be no batt'ry left," he observed.

The wise young captain of the second com-

---

4. **charger:** an officer's horse trained to charge in battle.
5. **imprecation** (im' prə kā' shun): an invoking of evil, a curse.
6. **battery horses:** those that moved the heavy guns or artillery.
7. **ruck:** a mass of, a heap of.

pany hazarded[8] to the lieutenant-colonel that the enemy's infantry would probably soon attack the hill, and the lieutenant-colonel snubbed him.

A private in one of the rear companies looked out over the meadow, and then turned to a companion and said, "Look there, Jim!" It was the wounded officer from the battery, who some time before had started to ride across the meadow, supporting his right arm carefully with his left hand. This man had encountered a shell, apparently, at a time when no one perceived him, and he could now be seen lying face downward with a stirruped foot stretched across the body of his dead horse. A leg of the charger extended slantingly upward, precisely as stiff as a stake. Around this motionless pair the shells still howled.

There was a quarrel in A Company. Collins was shaking his fist in the faces of some laughing comrades. "Dern yeh! I ain't afraid t' go. If yeh say much, I will go!"

"Of course, yeh will! You'll run through that there medder,[9] won't yeh?"

Collins said, in a terrible voice: "You see now!"

At this ominous threat his comrades broke into renewed jeers.

Collins gave them a dark scowl, and went to find his captain. The latter was conversing with the colonel of the regiment.

"Captain," said Collins, saluting and standing at attention—in those days all trousers bagged at the knees—"Captain, I want t' get permission to go git some water from that there well over yonder!"

The colonel and the captain swung about simultaneously and stared across the meadow. The captain laughed. "You must be pretty thirsty, Collins?"

"Yes, sir, I am."

"Well—ah," said the captain. After a moment, he asked, "Can't you wait?"

"No, sir."

The colonel was watching Collins's face.

"Look here, my lad," he said, in a pious sort of voice—"Look here, my lad"—Collins was not a lad—"don't you think that's taking pretty big risks for a little drink of water?"

"I dunno," said Collins uncomfortably. Some of the resentment toward his companions, which perhaps had forced him into this affair, was beginning to fade. "I dunno w'ether 'tis."

The colonel and the captain contemplated him for a time.

"Well," said the captain finally.

"Well," said the colonel, "if you want to go, why, go."

Collins saluted. "Much obliged t' yeh."

As he moved away the colonel called after him. "Take some of the other boys' canteens with you, an' hurry back, now."

"Yes, sir, I will."

The colonel and the captain looked at each other then, for it had suddenly occurred that they could not for the life of them tell whether Collins wanted to go or whether he did not.

They turned to regard Collins, and as they perceived him surrounded by gesticulating comrades, the colonel said, "Well, by thunder! I guess he's going."

Collins appeared as a man dreaming. In the midst of the questions, the advice, the warnings, all the excited talk of his company mates, he maintained a curious silence.

They were very busy in preparing him for his ordeal. When they inspected him carefully, it was somewhat like the examination that grooms give a horse before a race; and they were amazed, staggered, by the whole affair. Their astonishment found vent in strange repetitions.

"Are yeh sure a-goin'?" they demanded again and again.

---

8. **hazarded** (haz' er dəd): took a chance on, risked stating.
9. **medder:** meadow.

"Certainly I am," cried Collins at last, furiously.

He strode sullenly away from them. He was swinging five or six canteens by their cords. It seemed that his cap would not remain firmly on his head, and often he reached and pulled it down over his brow.

There was a general movement in the compact column. The long animal-like thing moved slightly. Its four hundred eyes were turned upon the figure of Collins.

"Well, sir, if that ain't th' derndest thing! I never thought Fred Collins had the blood in him for that kind of business."

"What's he goin' to do, anyhow?"

"He's goin' to that well there after water."

"We ain't dyin' of thirst, are we? That's foolishness."

"Well, somebody put him up to it, an' he's doin' it."

"Say, he must be a desperate cuss."

When Collins faced the meadow and walked away from the regiment, he was vaguely conscious that a chasm, the deep valley of all prides, was suddenly between him and his comrades. It was provisional, but the provision was that he return as a victor. He had blindly been led by quaint emotions, and laid himself under an obligation to walk squarely up to the face of death.

But he was not sure that he wished to make a retraction, even if he could do so without shame. As a matter of truth, he was sure of very little. He was mainly surprised.

It seemed to him supernaturally strange that he had allowed his mind to maneuvre his body into such a situation. He understood that it might be called dramatically great.

However, he had no full appreciation of anything, excepting that he was actually conscious of being dazed. He could feel his dulled mind groping after the form and color of this incident. He wondered why he did not feel some keen agony of fear cutting his sense like a knife. He wondered at this, because human expression had said loudly for centuries that men should feel afraid of certain things, and that all men who did not feel this fear were phenomena—heroes.

He was, then, a hero. He suffered that disappointment which we would all have if we discovered that we were ourselves capable of those deeds which we most admire in history and legend. This, then, was a hero. After all, heroes were not much.

No, it could not be true. He was not a hero. Heroes had no shames in their lives, and, as for him, he remembered borrowing fifteen dollars from a friend and promising to pay it back the next day, and then avoiding that friend for ten months. When, at home, his mother had aroused him for the early labor of his life on the farm, it had often been his fashion to be irritable, childish, diabolical; and his mother had died since he had come to the war.

He saw that, in this matter of the well, the canteens, the shells, he was an intruder in the land of fine deeds.

He was now about thirty paces from his comrades. The regiment had just turned its many faces toward him.

From the forest of terrific noises there suddenly emerged a little uneven line of men. They fired fiercely and rapidly at distant foliage on which appeared little puffs of white smoke. The spatter of skirmish firing was added to the thunder of the guns on the hill. The little line of men ran forward. A color-sergeant fell flat with his flag as if he had slipped on ice. There was hoarse cheering from this distant field.

Collins suddenly felt that two demon fingers were pressed into his ears. He could see nothing but flying arrows, flaming red. He lurched from the shock of this explosion, but he made a mad rush for the house, which he viewed as a man submerged to the neck in a boiling surf might view the shore. In the air little pieces of shell howled, and the earthquake explosions drove him insane with the menace of their roar. As he ran the canteens knocked together with a rhythmical tinkling.

As he neared the house, each detail of the scene became vivid to him. He was aware of some bricks of the vanished chimney lying on the sod. There was a door which hung by one hinge.

Rifle bullets called forth by the insistent skirmishers came from the far-off bank of foliage. They mingled with the shells and the pieces of shells until the air was torn in all directions by hootings, yells, howls. The sky was full of fiends who directed all their wild rage at his head.

When he came to the well, he flung himself face downward and peered into its darkness. There were furtive[10] silver glintings some feet from the surface. He grabbled one of the canteens and, unfastening its cap, swung it down by the cord. The water flowed slowly in with an indolent gurgle.

And now, as he lay with his face turned away, he was suddenly smitten with the terror. It came upon his heart like the grasp of claws. All the power faded from his muscles. For an instant he was no more than a dead man.

The canteen filled with a maddening slowness, in the manner of all bottles. Presently he recovered his strength and addressed a screaming oath to it. He leaned over until it seemed as if he intended to try to push water into it with his hands. His eyes as he gazed down into the well shone like two pieces of metal, and in their expression was a great appeal and a great curse. The stupid water derided him.

There was the blaring thunder of a shell. Crimson light shone through the swift-boiling smoke, and made a pink reflection on part of the wall of the well. Collins jerked out his arm and canteen with the same motion that a man would use in withdrawing his head from a furnace.

He scrambled erect and glared and hesitated. On the ground near him lay the old well bucket, with a length of rusty chain. He lowered it swiftly into the well. The bucket struck the water and then, turning lazily over, sank. When, with hand reaching tremblingly over hand, he hauled it out, it knocked often against the walls of the well and spilled some of its contents.

In running with a filled bucket, a man can adopt but one kind of gait. So, through this terrible field over which screamed practical angels of death, Collins ran in the manner of a farmer chased out of a dairy by a bull.

His face went staring white with anticipating—anticipation of a blow that would whirl him around and down. He would fall as he had seen other men fall, the life knocked out of them so suddenly that their knees were no more quick to touch the ground than their heads. He saw the long blue line of the regiment, but his comrades were standing looking at him from the edge of an impossible star. He was aware of some deep wheel ruts and hoofprints in the sod beneath his feet.

The artillery officer who had fallen in this meadow had been making groans in the teeth of the tempest of sound. These futile cries, wrenched from him by his agony, were heard only by shells, bullets. When wild-eyed Collins came running, this officer raised himself. His face contorted and blanched from pain, he was about to utter some great beseeching cry. But suddenly his face straightened, and he called: "Say, young man, give me a drink of water, will you?"

Collins had no room amid his emotions for surprise. He was mad from the threats of destruction.

"I can't!" he screamed, and in his reply was a full description of his quaking apprehension. His cap was gone and his hair was riotous. His clothes made it appear that he had been dragged over the ground by the heels. He ran on.

---

10. **furtive** (fur' tiv): sly, sneaky.

The officer's head sank down, and one elbow crooked. His foot in its brass-bound stirrup still stretched over the body of his horse, and the other leg was under the steed.

But Collins turned. He came dashing back. His face had now turned grey, and in his eyes was all terror. "Here it is! here it is!"

The officer was as a man gone in drink. His arm bent like a twig. His head drooped as if his neck were of willow. He was sinking to the ground, to lie face downward.

Collins grabbed him by the shoulder. "Here it is. Here's your drink. Turn over. Turn over, man, for God's sake!"

With Collins hauling at his shoulder, the officer twisted his body and fell with his face turned toward that region where lived the unspeakable noises of the swirling missiles. There was the faintest shadow of a smile on his lips as he looked at Collins. He gave a sigh, a little primitive breath like that from a child.

Collins tried to hold the bucket steadily, but his shaking hands caused the water to splash all over the face of the dying man. Then he jerked it away and ran on.

The regiment gave him a welcoming roar. The grimed faces were wrinkled in laughter.

His captain waved the bucket away. "Give it to the men!"

The two genial, skylarking young lieutenants were the first to gain possession of it. They played over it in their fashion.

When one tried to drink, the other teasingly knocked his elbow. "Don't Billie! You'll make me spill it," said the one. The other laughed.

Suddenly there was an oath, the thud of wood on the ground, and a swift murmur of astonishment among the ranks. The two lieutenants glared at each other. The bucket lay on the ground, empty.

YOUNG SOLDIER, 1861-64. *Winslow Homer. Cooper-Hewitt Museum.*

Getting at Meaning

1. What details suggest confusion and danger in the opening paragraphs of this story? Explain the physical realities that make getting water difficult.

2. What causes Fred Collins to defy danger and go after water? Although he does confront danger, he is disappointed in himself. Why?

3. Collins first refuses to give the dying officer water. What causes him to change his mind? How does his action affect the officer?

4. How do the men react to Collins's return with the bucket? What details suggest that the regiment misunderstands Collins's heroism?

Developing Skills in Reading Literature

1. **Setting.** Crane develops the battlefield setting with precise detail in the opening paragraphs of this story. What colors and sounds are a part of the battlefield setting?

Crane does not romanticize war, but is relentlessly realistic in his description of the battlefield. For example, he describes what the warfare does to nature:

> For the little meadow which intervened was now suffering a terrible onslaught of shells. Its green and beautiful calm had vanished utterly. Brown earth was being flung in monstrous handfuls. And there was a massacre of the young blades of grass. They were being torn, burned, obliterated. Some curious fortune of the battle had made this gentle little meadow the object of the red hate of the shells, and each one as it exploded seemed like an imprecation in the face of a maiden.

Why does Crane use the simile he does for the exploding shells? What words in this paragraph carry a strong emotional appeal? Find other passages that present the battlefield setting vividly. Why does Crane take such pains to describe the setting realistically?

2. **Character.** What details indicate that Fred Collins is young and inexperienced? What details about his past life does the story contain? Why are they important?

3. **Figurative Language.** Throughout the story Crane tries to bridge the distance between the reader, comfortable at home, and the turbulent battlefield. Often he uses similes, metaphors, and personification to help him clarify the experience of war. Find some of Crane's figures of speech. Select several that strike you as especially vivid and discuss their effectiveness.

4. **Theme.** At what point in the story does Fred Collins perform his most heroic action? Explain how his heroism is different from what he expected. What does he learn? Collins is not mentioned in the last three paragraphs of the story. How does his absence in these paragraphs relate to the concept of heroism Crane presents? At the end of the story, "The bucket lay on the ground, empty." How does this sentence relate to theme?

Developing Writing Skills

Writing Similes. Writers create similes that are drawn from their own experiences or imagination. Below are five comparisons from "A Mystery of Heroism." Rewrite the similes to reflect your own experience and imagination.

a) ". . . he viewed [the house] as a man submerged to the neck in a boiling surf might view the shore."

b) "[Terror] came upon his heart like the grasp of claws."

c) "His eyes as he gazed down into the well shown like two pieces of metal . . ."

d) "Collins jerked out his arm and canteen with the same motion that a man would use in withdrawing his head from a furnace."

e) ". . . Collins ran in the manner of a farmer chased out of a dairy by a bull."

A Man Said to the Universe

A man said to the universe,
"Sir, I exist!"
"However," replied the universe,
"The fact has not created in me
A sense of obligation."

Do Not Weep, Maiden, for War Is Kind

Do not weep, maiden, for war is kind.
Because your lover threw wild hands toward the sky
And the affrighted steed ran on alone,
Do not weep.
War is kind.   5

       Hoarse, booming drums of the regiment,
       Little souls who thirst for fight,
       These men were born to drill and die.
       The unexplained glory flies above them,
       Great is the battle-god, great, and his kingdom—   10
       A field where a thousand corpses lie.

Do not weep, babe, for war is kind.
Because your father tumbled in the yellow trenches,
Raged at his breast, gulped and died,
Do not weep.   15
War is kind.

       Swift blazing flag of the regiment,
       Eagle with crest of red and gold,
       These men were born to drill and die.
       Point for them the virtue of slaughter,   20
       Make plain to them the excellence of killing
       And a field where a thousand corpses lie.

Mother whose heart hung humble as a button
On the bright splendid shroud of your son,
Do not weep.   25
War is kind.

Getting at Meaning

1. In "A Man Said to the Universe," the speaker proclaims that he exists. What does this statement imply about the nature of human life? What does the response of the universe imply about the human condition?

2. Explain whom the speaker is addressing in the first, third, and fifth stanzas of "Do Not Weep, Maiden, for War Is Kind." What scenes does the speaker describe in the second and fourth stanzas?

Developing Skills in Reading Literature

1. **Structure.** "A Man Said to the Universe" is set up as a short conversation. Why is the answer of the universe so much longer than the man's opening declaration? What attitude does the exclamation point indicate? What attitude does the word *however* suggest?

The structure of "Do Not Weep, Maiden, for War Is Kind" underscores the poem's irony. Why are the second and fourth stanzas interpolated among the other three? What perspective do they provide on the personal grief in the first, third, and fifth stanzas?

2. **Irony.** Comment on the irony inherent in the universe's reponse to the man in "A Man Said to the Universe."

"Do Not Weep, Maiden, for War Is Kind" is constructed entirely of bitter ironies, all concentrated in the clause "war is kind." What view of war does Crane attack? What is ironic about the flag of the regiment? Explain the irony of the phrases "the virtue of slaughter" and "the excellence of killing." What is ironic about the "bright splendid shroud" in the final stanza?

3. **Refrain.** Crane uses two lines of refrain at the end of the first, third, and fifth stanzas in "Do Not Weep, Maiden. . . ." What two lines of refrain appear in the second and fourth stanzas? Although each refrain is ironic in and of itself, how does the repetition of these key lines greatly magnify the ironic impact of the poem as a whole?

4. **Theme.** Crane never swerves from his basic realism. He even moves beyond realism into naturalism, a philosophy that sees the human being as a tiny, physical being, essentially powerless, in an enormous, apathetic universe. In naturalism, nature is neutral, running its own course with complete indifference to human life. Explain how this philosophy is embodied in "A Man Said to the Universe."

What is the view of most soldiers that Crane presents in "Do Not Weep, Maiden . . ."? Why does he call them "little souls"? Why does he say, twice, "These men were born to drill and die"? Explain the line, "The unexplained glory flies above them."

LOVERS, 1964. *Charles White. Heritage Gallery, Los Angeles.*

Walt Whitman

1819–1892

Only one great poet emerged from New York City in the last half of the nineteenth century; that poet was Walt Whitman, whose book *Leaves of Grass*, which first appeared in 1855, has been called the greatest single book of poetry in American literature. Walt Whitman was born in West Hills, in rural Long Island, New York, on May 31, 1819. His father was a farmer and a carpenter whose business often took the family to Brooklyn. Whitman, therefore, grew up in contrasting environments: one the quiet island home of fishermen and the other the bustling city on Manhattan Island, which he later referred to as "Mannahatta." Whitman had only five years of formal education, but he read voraciously, notably nineteenth-century poetry and novels, the classics, and the New Testament. After leaving school, he worked at a series of jobs, such as office boy, typesetter, printer, itinerant country school teacher, and newspaper editor. By 1841 he had decided on journalism as a career and moved to New York where he remained, except for a brief journey to New Orleans and Chicago, for the next twenty years.

In 1855 Whitman collected twelve of his poems into a slim volume he titled *Leaves of Grass*. This volume was rewritten, revised, and expanded throughout his lifetime until the ninth and final edition contains more than four hundred poems. *Leaves of Grass* was not the immediate literary sensation that Whitman had thought it would be. Ralph Waldo Emerson congratulated Whitman on his work, calling it "the most extraordinary piece of wit and wisdom that America has yet contributed." He heralded Whitman's work as a new poetry agreeing in principle with his own transcendental philosophy. Other less complimentary critics called the poems "barbaric yawp" and "noxious weeds."

During the Civil War Whitman served for three years as a volunteer nurse in the military hospitals in and around Washington, D.C. The poems resulting from that experience were published in *Drum Taps* (1865), which was later revised and incorporated into *Leaves of Grass*. In 1873, after suffering a paralytic stroke, Whitman went to the home of his brother in Camden, New Jersey, where he lived until 1882 when he was finally able to buy his own small house in Camden. By the time that the fifth edition of *Leaves of Grass* was published in 1871, Whitman had a reputation as a fine poet, and in the last decade of his life his little house on Mickle Street was visited by many of the literary greats of England and America.

Whitman departed from traditional English verse forms and wrote in free verse, which recalls the rhythms of music and everyday speech in stanzas of varying structures. Many readers objected to Whitman's unconventional metric and rhyme patterns, his irregular line and stanza lengths, and, most of all, his frank treatment of all subjects. Whitman was basically a Romantic poet, individualistic, sensitive to nature, and immersed in the world of the senses and emotions. He has been called the "poet of democracy" for he was a spokesman for all that was American, the unique and the commonplace, the heroic and the base, the splendid and the ugly.

Come Up from the Fields, Father

Come up from the fields, father, here's a letter from our Pete,
And come to the front door mother, here's a letter from thy dear son,

Lo, 'tis autumn,
Lo, where the trees, deeper green, yellower and redder,
Cool and sweeten Ohio's villages with leaves fluttering in the moderate wind,   5
Where apples ripe in the orchards hang and grapes on the trellis'd vines,
(Smell you the smell of the grapes on the vines?
Smell you the buckwheat where the bees were lately buzzing?)

Above all, lo, the sky so calm, so transparent after the rain, and with wondrous
    clouds,
Below too, all calm, all vital and beautiful, and the farm prospers well.   10

Down in the fields all prospers well,
But now from the fields come father, come at the daughter's call,
And come to the entry mother, to the front door come right away.
Fast as she can she hurries, something ominous, her steps trembling,
She does not tarry to smooth her hair nor adjust her cap.   15

Open the envelope quickly,
O this is not our son's writing, yet his name is sign'd,
O a strange hand writes for our dear son, O stricken mother's soul!
All swims before her eyes, flashes with black, she catches the main words only,
Sentences broken, *gunshot wound in the breast, cavalry skirmish, taken to*
    hospital,   20
At present low, but will soon be better.

Ah now the single figure to me,
Amid all teeming[1] and wealthy Ohio with all its cities and farms,
Sickly white in the face and dull in the head, very faint,
By the jamb of a door leans.   25

Grieve not so, dear mother, (the just-grown daughter speaks through her sobs,
The little sisters huddle around speechless and dismay'd,)
See, dearest mother, the letter says Pete will soon be better.

Alas poor boy, he will never be better, (nor may-be needs to be better, that brave
    and simple soul,)
While they stand at home at the door he is dead already,   30
The only son is dead.

---

1. **teeming:** crowded, prolific, fruitful.

But the mother needs to be better,
She with thin form presently drest in black,
By day her meals untouch'd, then at night fitfully sleeping, often waking,
In the midnight waking, weeping, longing with one deep longing,   35
O that she might withdraw unnoticed, silent from life escape and withdraw,
To follow, to seek, to be with her dear dead son.

Getting at Meaning

1. Describe the setting of the poem, giving details of time and place.

2. What is the family's first clue that something is wrong?

3. How is the length of time it took the letter to arrive significant in the poem?

Developing Skills in Reading Literature

1. **Narrative Poem.** A narrative poem tells a story. Narrative poems can assume a variety of lengths and forms, and "Come Up from the Fields, Father" is one example. Notice that, like most stories, the poem contains setting, plot, and characters. Comment on how each of these narrative elements functions in the poem. What is the climax, or turning point of the action, of the poem? Is there a resolution to the conflict, or struggle between opposing forces?

2. **Free Verse.** Poetry written without regular patterns of rhyme and meter is known as free verse. Like most poetry, free verse is usually more rhythmic than ordinary language. Although poets before Walt Whitman had experimented with forms resembling free verse, it was Whitman, with the publication of *Leaves of Grass* in 1855, who revolutionized poetry with his variable lines and loose rhythms. Free verse is one of Whitman's significant contributions to twentieth-century poetry.

Observe the free verse form in this poem. How does it suit the poem's narrative thread? In the absence of rhyme, meter, and set stanza form, what qualities make this clearly a poem, and not prose?

3. **Speaker.** Notice that the speaking voice shifts in this poem. Who is speaking in lines 1 and 2? Who speaks beginning in line 3? Explain how the speaking voice shifts again in line 16. In what line does the original speaker assume the speaking voice again? Who speaks in lines 29-31? Who is speaking in the final stanza? Comment on how the italics function in the poem. What is the effect of these shifts in narration?

4. **Tone.** The shifting tone is a significant element in this poem. Characterize the tone of the first stanzas. What words and phrases help create the tone? Why does Whitman begin with so much lyrical description?

What is the tone of the final two stanzas of the poem? What words and phrases establish this tone? What function does the dramatic shift in tone serve in the poem as a whole?

5. **Rhythm.** Notice some of the poetic devices that help to create rhythm in this poem. What repetends does the poem contain? What effect do they have on rhythm? Where do the sentence breaks fall in the poem? How does the syntax function to give the poem a flowing quality? What lines employ parallel construction to create rhythm?

Developing Writing Skills

Analyzing Theme. Consider Whitman's purpose in focusing on Pete's family in this poem. Then write a well constructed paragraph in which you argue the assertion that the casualties of war do not occur only on the battlefield. Use quotations and references from the poem to build your case.

O Captain! My Captain!

O Captain! my Captain! our fearful trip is done,
The ship has weathered every rack,[1] the prize we sought is won.
The port is near, the bells I hear, the people all exulting,
While follow eyes the steady keel, the vessel grim and daring;
  But O heart! heart! heart!   5
    O the bleeding drops of red,
      Where on the deck my Captain lies,
        Fallen cold and dead.

O Captain! my Captain! rise up and hear the bells;
Rise up—for you the flag is flung—for you the bugle trills,   10
For you bouquets and ribboned wreaths—for you the shores a-crowding,
For you they call, the swaying mass, their eager faces turning;
  Here Captain! dear father!
    The arm beneath your head!
      It is some dream that on the deck,   15
        You've fallen cold and dead.

My Captain does not answer, his lips are pale and still.
My father does not feel my arm, he has no pulse nor will,
The ship is anchored safe and sound, its voyage closed and done,
From fearful trip the victor ship comes in with object won: 20
  Exult O shores, and ring O bells!
    But I with mournful tread,
      Walk the deck my Captain lies,
        Fallen cold and dead.

---

1. **rack:** a wrenching or upheaval, as by a storm.

Getting at Meaning

1. On a literal level, this poem describes a ship returning home victorious. Where is the ship in each stanza?

2. Where exactly is the speaker of the poem located in each stanza?

3. Who is the subject of this poem, the "captain" of the ship?

Developing Skills in Reading Literature

1. **Elegy.** A eulogy is a written or spoken tribute that praises a person's virtues and achievements, usually soon after the person's death. An elegy is a eulogy written in verse form.

"O Captain! My Captain!" is Whitman's elegy for Abraham Lincoln. What qualities does the poet appear to admire in Lincoln? Notice that Whitman does not employ free verse in this poem, but a more structured and traditional format, with rhyme and regular meter. Why might Whitman have chosen the more formal and traditional patterns for his elegy?

2. **Extended Metaphor.** An extended metaphor controls this poem. If Lincoln is the captain, what is the ship? To what does the phrase "our fearful trip" refer? What is the prize that has been won?

3. **Irony.** A bitter irony lies at the heart of this poem, reflected in the dramatic change of tone within the first two stanzas. What is the tone of the first four lines of the first stanza? Of the first four lines of the second stanza? What words and phrases imply victory and joyous celebration? How do the final four lines shift the tone in the first two stanzas? What irony concerning Lincoln's death does the shift in tone emphasize? What is ironic about the bells that ring out in the poem?

4. **Meter.** Scan the first four lines of each stanza. How many accents does each first line contain? Indicate where you find anapests among the iambs in these lines. How do they affect the rhythm? What is the metrical pattern of the second, third, and fourth lines in each stanza? Explain how their fast pace is appropriate to the tone of the lines.

Comment on the metrical pattern of the final four lines in each stanza. Analyze how they slow the poem's pace. What is the pace of the final line in each stanza? Why is the final line so terse in comparison with the preceding lines?

5. **Rhythm.** Apart from meter, other poetic devices make "O Captain! My Captain!" a particularly rhythmic poem. Identify the repetends Whitman employs. How do they function in the poem? Where does alliteration help create a rapid, musical pace? Where does Whitman employ internal rhyme, rhyme within a line of poetry? What is the pattern of end rhyme in the poem? Comment on the overall effect of the rhyme.

The Indian Crisis

PIEGAN WARRIOR, 1833. *Karl Bodmer.*
The Newberry Library, Chicago.

George Armstrong Custer
1839–1876

George Armstrong Custer, an American cavalry commander who had achieved fame during the Civil War, led his regiment in an attack on a large Sioux village near the Little Big Horn River on June 25, 1876. He met with overwhelming opposition, and Custer and his entire command were killed. Only one horse, "Comanche," survived the attack to appear, riderless, in subsequent Seventh Cavalry parades.

George Custer was born in New Rumley, Ohio, on December 5, 1839. After attending the local schools, Custer entered West Point at the age of seventeen. Having earned a reputation as a bright but irresponsible student, given to mischief and pranks, he graduated, last in his class, on June 24, 1861, at the start of the Civil War. Custer was a dashing figure—a tall man of imposing physique and great stamina, with blue eyes and long, flowing blond hair. He dressed in high-heeled boots, a velvet or corduroy uniform lavish with gold braid, a long crimson tie, and a cavalier hat.

Beginning with his service at the Battle of Bull Run, Custer showed remarkable daring and brilliance as a cavalry officer and participated in many of the major battles of the war, serving first under the command of General McClellan and later under General Sheridan. During the final weeks of the war, Custer's pressure on General Lee's army helped to force Lee's surrender. It was to Custer that the Confederate flag of truce was brought. In 1866 Custer was made lieutenant colonel of the newly formed Seventh United States Cavalry and began a tour of duty in the West. As a result of a disastrous Indian campaign, he was court martialed and suspended from his command for a year, but General Sheridan recalled him and sent him back to the Indian wars. In 1873 he was assigned to Fort Rice in what is now North Dakota and served there until the battle at Little Big Horn, "Custer's Last Stand," ended his career.

In his later days, Custer had become a student and writer. He wrote a book about his western adventures, *My Life on the Plains*, which was published in 1874, and his Civil War memoirs were published posthumously in 1876.

My Life on the Plains

Great excitement existed along the border settlements of Kansas and Colorado. The frequent massacres of the frontiersmen and utter destruction of their homes created a very bitter feeling on the part of the citizens of Kansas toward the savages, and from the governor of the state down to its humblest citizen appeals were made to the authorities of the general government to give protection against the Indians, or else allow the people to take the matter into their own hands and pursue retaliatory measures against their hereditary enemies. General Sheridan, then in command of that military department, with headquarters at Fort Leavenworth, Kansas, was fully alive to the responsibilities of his position, and in his usual effective manner set about organizing victory. . . .

Having decided to employ frontiersmen to assist in punishing the Indians, the next question was the selection of a suitable leader. The choice, most fortunately, fell upon General George A. Forsyth ("Sandy"), then acting inspector general of the Department of Missouri, who, eager to render his country an important service and not loath[1] to share in the danger and excitement attendant upon such an enterprise, set himself energetically to work to raise and equip his command for the field. But little time was required, under Forsyth's stirring zeal, to raise the required number of men. It was wisely decided to limit the number of frontiersmen to fifty. Thirty selected men were procured at Fort Harker, Kansas, and twenty more at Fort Hays, sixty miles further west. In four days the command was armed, mounted, and equipped, and at once took the field. . . .

On the morning of September 10 a small war party of Indians attacked a train near Sheridan, a small railroad town some eighty miles beyond Fort Wallace, killed two teamsters, and ran off a few cattle. As soon as information of this reached Fort Wallace, Forsyth started with his command for the town of Sheridan, where he took the trail of the Indians and followed it. On the evening of the eighth day from Fort Wallace, the command halted about five o'clock in the afternoon and went into camp at or near a little island in the [Arikaree] river [in Eastern Colorado]. After posting their pickets and partaking of the plainest of suppers, Forsyth's little party disposed of themselves on the ground to sleep, little dreaming who was to sound their reveille[2] in so unceremonious a manner.

At dawn on the following day, September 17, 1868, the guard gave the alarm "Indians." Instantly every man sprang to his feet and, with the true instinct of the frontiersman, grasped his rifle with one hand while with the other he seized his lariat,[3] that the Indian might not stampede the horses. Six Indians dashed up toward the party, rattling bells, shaking buffalo robes, and firing their guns. The four pack mules belonging to the party broke away and were last seen galloping over the hills. Three other animals made their escape, as they had only been hobbled, in direct violation of the orders which directed that all animals of the command should be regularly picketed to a stake or picket-pin

---

1. **loath** (lōth): unwilling, reluctant.
2. **reveille** (rev′ ə lē): an early morning signal, usually on a bugle, to wake soldiers and to call them to the first assembly of the day.
3. **lariat** (lar′ ē it): a rope used for tying grazing horses.

firmly driven into the ground. A few shots caused the Indians to sheer off and disappear in a gallop over the hills. Several of the men started in pursuit, but were instantly ordered to rejoin the command, which was ordered to saddle up with all possible haste, Forsyth feeling satisfied that the attempt to stampede the stock was but the prelude to a general and more determined attack. Scarcely were the saddles thrown on the horses and the girths[4] tightened, when Grover, the guide, placing his hand on Forsyth's shoulder, gave vent to his astonishment as follows: "*O heavens, General, look at the Indians!*" Well might he be excited. From every direction they dashed toward the band. Over the hills, from the west and north, along the river, on the opposite bank, everywhere and in every direction they made their appearance. Finally mounted, in full war paint, their long scalp locks braided with eagles' feathers, and with all the paraphernalia of a barbarous war party—with wild whoops and exultant shouts, on they came.

There was but one thing to do. Realizing that they had fallen into a trap, Forsyth, who had faced danger too often to hesitate in an emergency, determined that . . . he should at least make the enemy bear their share of the loss. He ordered his men to lead their horses to the island, tie them to the few bushes that were growing there in a circle, throw themselves upon the ground in the same form, and make the best fight they could for their lives. In less time than it takes to pen these words, the order was put into execution. Three of the best shots in the party took position in the grass under the bank of the river which covered the north end of the island; the others formed a circle inside of the line of animals, and throwing themselves upon the ground began to reply to the fire of the Indians, which soon became hot and galling in the extreme. Throwing themselves from their horses, the Indians crawled up to within a short distance of the island, and opened a steady and well-directed fire upon the party. Armed with the best quality of guns, many of them having the latest pattern breechloaders[5] with fixed ammunition (as proof of this many thousand empty shells of Spencer and Henry rifle ammunition were found on the ground occupied by the Indians after the fight), they soon made sad havoc among the men and horses. As it grew lighter and the Indians could be distinguished, Grover expressed the greatest astonishment at the number of warriors, which he placed at nearly one thousand. . . . The men of Forsyth's party began covering themselves at once, by using case and pocket knives in the gravelly sand, and soon had thrown up quite a little earthwork consisting of detached mounds in the form of a circle. About this time Forsyth was wounded by a Minié ball,[6] which, striking him in the right thigh, ranged upward, inflicting an exceedingly painful wound. Two of his men had been killed, and a number of others wounded. Leaning over to give directions to some of his men, who were firing too rapidly, and in fact becoming a little too nervous for their own good, Forsyth was again wounded, this time in the left leg, the ball breaking and badly shattering the bone midway between the knee and ankle. About the same time Dr. Mooers, the surgeon of the party who owing to the hot fire of the Indians, was unable to render surgical aid to his wounded comrades, had seized his trusty rifle and was doing capital service, was hit in the temple by a bullet, and never spoke but one intelligible word again.

Matters were now becoming desperate, and nothing but cool, steady fighting would avail to mend them. The hills surrounding the immediate vicinity of the fight were filled

---

4. **girth:** a band put around the belly of a horse to hold a saddle or a pack in place.
5. **breechloader:** a gun loaded with shells behind the barrel, as opposed to being loaded by ramming loose powder and shot down the barrel.
6. **Minié ball:** a conical rifle bullet invented by C. E. Minié (1814–1879) of France.

with women and children, who were chanting war songs and filling the air with whoops and yells. The medicine men, a sort of high priests, and older warriors rode outside of the combatants, being careful to keep out of range, and encouraged their young braves by beating a drum, shouting Indian chants, and using derisive words toward their adversaries, whom they cursed roundly for skulking like wolves, and dared to come out and fight like men.

Meantime the scouts were slowly but surely "counting game,"[7] and more than one Indian fell to the rear badly wounded by the rifles of the frontiersmen. Within an hour after the opening of the fight, the Indians were fairly frothing at the mouth with rage at the unexpected resistance they met, while the scouts had now settled down to earnest work, and obeyed to the letter the orders of Forsyth, whose oft reiterated command was, "Fire slowly, aim well, keep yourselves covered, and, above all, don't throw away a single cartridge."

Taken all in all, with a very few exceptions, the men behaved superbly. Obedient to every word of command, cool, plucky, determined, and fully realizing the character of their foes, they were a match for their enemies thus far at every point. About nine o'clock in the morning the last horse belonging to the scouts was killed, and one of the redskins was heard to exclaim in tolerably good English, "There goes the last horse anyhow," a proof that some of the savages had at some time been intimate with the whites.

Shortly after nine o'clock a portion of the Indians began to form in a ravine just below the foot of the island, and soon about 120 Dog Soldiers, the "banditti of the Plains," supported by some 300 or more other mounted men, made their appearance, drawn up just beyond rifle shot below the island, and headed by the famous chief Roman Nose,[8] prepared to charge the scouts. Superbly mounted, almost naked although in full war dress, and painted

in the most hideous manner, with their rifles in their hands, and formed with a front of about sixty men, they awaited the signal of their chief to charge, with apparently the greatest confidence. Roman Nose addressed a few words to the mounted warriors, and almost immediately afterward the dismounted Indians surrounding the island poured a perfect shower of bullets into the midst of Forsyth's little party. Realizing that a crisis was at hand, and hot work was before him, Forsyth told his men to reload every rifle and to take and load the rifles of the killed and wounded of the party, and not to fire a shot until ordered to do so.

For a few moments the galling fire of the Indians rendered it impossible for any of the scouts to raise or expose any part of their persons. This was precisely the effect the Indians desired to produce by the fire of their riflemen. It was this that the mounted warriors, under the leadership of Roman Nose, were waiting for. The Indians had planned their assault in a manner very similar to that usually adopted by civilized troops in assailing a fortified place. The fire of the Indian riflemen performed the part of the artillery on such occasions, in silencing the fire of the besieged and preparing the way for the assaulting column.

Seeing that the little garrison was stunned by the heavy fire of the dismounted Indians, and rightly judging that now, if ever, was the proper time to charge them, Roman Nose and his band of mounted warriors, with a wild, ringing war-whoop, echoed by the women and children on the hills, started forward. On they came, presenting even to the brave men awaiting the charge a most superb sight. Brandishing their guns, echoing back the cries of encouragement of their women and children on the surrounding hills, and confident of

7. **"counting game"**: keeping count of the successful shooting of their enemies.
8. **Roman Nose**: Cheyenne chief.

victory, they rode bravely and recklessly to the assault. Soon they were within the range of the rifles of their friends, and of course the dismounted Indians had to slacken their fire for fear of hitting their own warriors. This was the opportunity for the scouts, and they were not slow to seize it. "Now," shouted Forsyth. "Now," echoed Beecher, McCall, and Grover; and the scouts, springing to their knees, and casting their eyes coolly along the barrels of their rifles, opened on the advancing savages as deadly a fire as the same number of men ever yet sent forth from an equal number of rifles. Unchecked, undaunted, on dashed the warriors; steadily rang the clear, sharp reports of the rifles of the frontiersmen. Roman Nose, the chief, is seen to fall dead from his horse, then Medicine Man is killed, and for an instant the column of braves, now within ten feet of the scouts, hesitates—falters. A ringing cheer from the scouts, who perceive the effect of their well-directed fire, and the Indians begin to break and scatter in every direction, unwilling to rush to a hand-to hand struggle with the men who, although outnumbered, yet knew how to make such effective use of their rifles. A few more shots from the frontiersmen and the Indians are forced back beyond range, and their first attack ends in defeat. Forsyth turns to Grover anxiously and inquires, "Can they do better than that, Grover?" "I have been on the Plains, General, since a boy, and never saw such a charge as that before. I think they have done their level best," was the reply. "All right," responds "Sandy"; "then we are good for them." . . .

The Indians still kept up a continuous fire from their dismounted warriors; but as the scouts by this time were well covered by their miniature earthworks, it did little execution. At two o'clock in the afternoon the savages again attempted to carry the island by a mounted charge, and again at sunset; but having been deprived of their best and most fearless leader by the fall of Roman Nose, they were not so daring or impulsive as in the

first charge, and were both times repulsed with heavy losses. At dark they ceased firing, and withdrew their forces for the night. This gave the little garrison on the island an opportunity to take a breathing spell, and Forsyth to review the situation and sum up how he had fared. The result was not consoling. His trusted Lieutenant Beecher was lying dead by his side; his surgeon, Mooers, was mortally wounded; two of his men killed, four mortally wounded, four severely, and ten slightly. Here, out of a total of fifty-one, were twenty-three killed and wounded. His own condition, his right thigh fearfully lacerated, and his left leg badly broken, only rendered the other discouraging circumstances doubly so. As before stated, the Indians had killed all of his horses early in the fight. His supplies were exhausted, and there was no way of dressing the wounds of himself or comrades, as the medical stores had been captured by the Indians. He was about 110 miles from the nearest post, and savages were all around him. The outlook could scarcely have been less cheering. But Forsyth's disposition and pluck inclined him to speculate more upon that which is, or may be gained, than to repine[9] at that which is irrevocably lost. This predominant trait in his character now came in good play. Instead of wasting time in vain regrets over the advantages gained by his enemies, he quietly set about looking up the chances in his favor. And, let the subject be what it may, I will match "Sandy" "against an equal number" for making a favorable showing of the side which he espouses or advocates. To his credit account he congratulated himself and comrades first upon the fact that they had beaten off their foes; second, water could be had inside their entrenchments by digging a few feet below the surface; then for food, "horse and mule meat," to use Sandy's expression, "was lying around loose in any

---

9. **repine** (ri pīn′): express unhappiness or dissatisfaction.

quantity"; and last, but most important of all, he had plenty of ammunition. Upon these circumstances and facts Forsyth built high hopes of successfully contending against any renewed assaults of the savages. . . .

As was expected, the night passed without incident or disturbance from the savages; but early the next morning the fight was renewed by the Indians again surrounding the island as before and opening fire from the rifles of their dismounted warriors. They did not attempt to charge the island as they had done the previous day, when their attempts in this direction had cost them too dearly; but they were none the less determined and eager to overpower the little band which had been the cause of such heavy loss to them already. The scouts, thanks to their efforts during the night, were now well protected, and suffered but little from the fire of the Indians, while the latter being more exposed, paid the penalty whenever affording the scouts a chance with their rifles. The day was spent without any decided demonstration on the part of the red men, except to keep up as constant a fire as possible on the scouts, and to endeavor to provoke the latter to reply as often as possible, the object, no doubt, being to induce the frontiersmen to exhaust their supply of ammunition. But they were not to be led into this trap; each cartridge they estimated as worth to them one Indian, and nothing less would satisfy them. . . .

Soon after and as a last resort the Indians endeavored to hold a parley with Forsyth, by means of a white flag; but this device was too shallow and of too common adoption to entrap the frontiersman, the object simply being to accomplish by stratagem and perfidy[10] what they had failed in by superior numbers and open warfare. Everything now seemed to indicate that the Indians had had enough of the fight, and during the night of the third day it was plainly evident that they had about decided to withdraw from the contest.

Forsyth now wrote the following dispatch, and after nightfall confided it to two of his best men, Donovan and Plyley; and they, notwithstanding the discouraging result of the last attempt, set out to try to get through to Fort Wallace with it, which they successfully accomplished:

On Delaware Creek,[11] Republican River,
Sept. 19, 1868

To Colonel Bankhead, or Commanding Officer, Fort Wallace.

I sent you two messengers on the night of the 17th instant, informing you of my critical condition. I tried to send two more last night, but they did not succeed in passing the Indian pickets, and returned. If the others have not arrived, then hasten at once to my assistance. I have eight badly wounded and ten slightly wounded men to take in, and every animal I had was killed save seven which the Indians stampeded. Lieutenant Beecher is dead, and Acting Assistant Surgeon Mooers probably cannot live the night out. He was hit in the head Thursday, and has spoken but one rational word since. I am wounded in two places, in the right thigh and my left leg broken below the knee. The Cheyennes numbered 450 or more. Mr. Grover says they never fought so before. They were splendidly armed with Spencer and Henry rifles. We killed at least thirty-five of them and wounded many more, besides killing and wounding a quantity of their stock. They carried off most of their killed during the night, but three of their men fell into our hands. I am on a little island and have still plenty of ammunition left. We are living on mule and horse meat, and are entirely out of rations. If it was not for so many wounded, I would come in and take the chances of whipping them if attacked. They are evidently sick of their bargain.

I had two of the members of my company killed on the 17th namely, William Wilson and

---

10. **perfidy** (pʉr' fə dē): betrayal of trust; treachery.
11. Delaware Creek, which flows NE into the Republican River in eastern Colorado and southwestern Nebraska, is now called the Arikaree River.

George W. Calner. You had better start with not less than seventy-five men and bring all the wagons and ambulances you can spare. Bring a six-pound howitzer with you. I can hold out here for six days longer, *if absolutely necessary,* but please lose no time.

Very respectfully your obedient servant,
George A. Forsyth
U.S. Army, Commanding Co. Scouts

P.S. My surgeon having been mortally wounded, none of my wounded have had their wounds dressed yet, so please bring out a surgeon with you.

A small party of warriors remained in the vicinity watching the movement of the scouts; the main body, however, had departed.

The well men, relieved of the constant watching and fighting, were now able to give some attention to the wounded. Their injuries, which had grown very painful, were rudely dressed. Soup was made out of horseflesh, and shelters were constructed protecting them from the heat, damp, and wind. On the sixth day the wounds of the men began to exhibit more decided and alarming signs of neglect. Maggots infested them and the first traces of gangrene had set in. To multiply the discomforts of their situation, the entire party was almost overpowered by the intolerable stench created by the decomposing bodies of the dead horses. Their supply was nearly exhausted. Under these trying circumstances Forsyth assembled his men. He told them "they knew their situation as well as he. There were those who were helpless, but aid must not be expected too soon. It might be difficult for the messengers to reach the fort, or there might be some delay by their losing their way. Those who wished to go should do so and leave the rest to take their chances." With one voice they resolved to stay, and, if all hope vanished, to die together.

At last the supply of jerked horse meat was exhausted, and the chances of getting more were gone. By this time the carcasses of the animals were a mass of corruption. There was no alternative—strips of putrid flesh were cut and eaten. The effect of this offensive diet was nauseating in the extreme. An experiment was made, with a view to improving the unpalatable flesh, of using gunpowder as salt, but to no purpose. The men allayed only their extreme cravings of hunger, trusting that succor might reach them before all was over.

On the morning of September 25, . . . several dark figures appeared faintly on the horizon. The objects were moving. The question uppermost in the minds of all was, Are they savages or messengers of relief? As on such occasions of anxiety and suspense, time wore heavily, minutes seemed like hours, yet each moment brought the sufferers nearer the realization whether this was their doom or their escape therefrom. Over an hour had elapsed since the objects first came in sight, and yet the mystery remained unsolved. Slowly but surely they developed themselves, until finally they had approached sufficiently near for their character as friends or foes to be unmistakably established. To the joy of the weary watchers, the parties approaching proved to be troops; relief was at hand, the dangers and anxieties of the past few days were ended, and death either by starvation or torture at the hands of the savages no longer stared them in the face. The strong set up a shout such as men seldom utter. It was the unburdening of the heart of the weight of despair. . . .

Considering this engagement in all its details and with all its attendant circumstances, remembering that Forsyth's party, including himself, numbered all told but fifty-one men, and that the Indians numbered about seventeen to one, this fight was one of the most remarkable and at the same time successful contests in which our forces on the Plains have ever been engaged; and the whole affair, from the moment the first shot was fired until the beleaguered[12] party was finally relieved by Colonel Carpenter's command, was a wonderful exhibition of daring courage, stubborn bravery, and heroic endurance, under circumstances of greatest peril and exposure. In all probability there will never occur in our future hostilities with the savage tribes of the West a struggle the equal of that in which were engaged the heroic men who defended so bravely "Beecher's Island."

---

12. **beleaguered** (bi lē' gər'd): blockaded and harassed by being surrounded by an adversary.

Getting at Meaning

1. Why is General Forsyth's group formed, according to Custer?

2. How do Forsyth's men become trapped? How do they defend themselves against the Indian attacks? Which strategies of Forsyth's compensate for the small number of frontiersmen?

3. Describe the attacks of the mounted warriors led by Roman Nose.

4. At nightfall, what circumstances make Forsyth's situation especially grim? What advantages do the frontiersmen have?

5. How do the second and third days of combat differ from the first?

6. How are Forsyth and his men finally rescued?

Developing Skills in Reading Literature

1. **Nonfiction.** While nonfiction concerns real people, places, and events, it may be slanted in a way that detracts from its accuracy and credibility. How objective is Custer in telling about the battle of Beecher Island? Use specific passages to support your conclusion.

2. **Stereotype.** Accounts such as Custer's have contributed to stereotypes of both the Plains Indian and the Western frontiersman. Think about the following words used by Custer to describe Indians:

savages   barbarous   warriors
redskins   banditti

What are the connotations of these words? How do they reinforce a negative stereotype of the Indian?

To describe the qualities of the frontiersmen, Custer uses phrases such as "daring courage," "stubborn bravery," and "heroic endurance." How do these phrases help to create a positive stereotype of the frontiersmen? In what other ways does Custer reinforce this stereotype?

3. **Setting.** The natural location has an important effect on the events recounted in Custer's narrative. Describe the setting and how it affects the battle.

Developing Vocabulary

Inferring Word Meaning. Examine the context in which each of the following words appears. Write a possible definition for the word on a sheet of paper. Then check your definitions against those in the Glossary.

galling   lacerate   stratagem
plucky   parley   succor
espouse   allay   derisive

Which words seem slightly old-fashioned, or out-of-date? Which are still part of the average person's vocabulary?

Developing Writing Skills

Writing an Analytical Report. Locate in the library a history book written from the Indians' point of view, such as *Bury My Heart at Wounded Knee*. Write a report comparing and contrasting the Indian account of the battle of Beecher Island with Custer's narrative.

Chief Joseph

1840?–1904

Chief Joseph, whose American Indian name was In-mut-too-yah-lat-lat, was the chief of the Nez Percé. A brilliant military strategist and humane, just leader, Chief Joseph attempted a desperate and ultimately unsuccessful rescue of his people from white domination.

Chief Joseph probably was born around 1840 in the Wallowa Valley of Oregon, the ancient home of the Nez Percé. When he became chief in 1873, he refused to recognize the Indian agreement of 1863, in which the Nez Percé ceded the Wallowa Valley to the United States government and agreed to relocate to the Lapwai Reservation in Idaho. When the government resolved to enforce the treaty, the Nez Percé resisted and, in retaliation for the outrages perpetrated against them, attacked a white settlement, killing twenty people. To avoid outright war and the almost certain destruction of his people, Chief Joseph set out for Canada, leading a group that consisted of fewer than two hundred warriors and hundreds of women and children. Virtually surrounded by the United States Army, he effected a one-thousand-mile retreat, either avoiding or winning skirmishes on the way. Only thirty miles from the Canadian border, in the Bear Paw Mountains, he rested, thinking that he had outdistanced his pursuers. Taken by surprise by General Nelson Miles, Chief Joseph was faced with the difficult choice of accepting capture; escaping by abandoning the women, children, and wounded; or giving battle. He and his warriors held out for a five-day siege before being forced to surrender.

Chief Joseph believed that his people would be sent back to the Lapwai Reservation. Instead, however, they were moved to a succession of relocation sites, including a stay in the Oklahoma Indian Territory, where many of the Nez Percé sickened and died. Finally some of the survivors were returned to the Lapwai Reservation, but Chief Joseph and about one hundred and fifty of his followers were sent to the Coleville Reservation in Washington.

Chief Joseph held to his promise of peaceful surrender. He devoted his remaining years to educating his people, improving their status, and to reconciling them to the ways of white civilization. In 1903 Chief Joseph was invited to Washington, D.C., where he petitioned President Theodore Roosevelt and General Miles to return the Nez Percé to their ancestral lands. Chief Joseph's pleas were ignored; he died on the Coleville Reservation in 1904 far from his tribal homeland.

Nez Percé Surrender and Outcome

Toward evening, [October 5, 1877] Joseph rode out from the coulees,[1] followed by several warriors on foot. A snow-filled wind swirled down from the Bear Paws [mountains near the border of Canada and central Montana] and swept the prairie, adding to the gloom of the occasion.

Lieutenant Wood, one of the officers who witnessed the surrender, wrote the most satisfactory account of the proceedings. Chief Joseph spoke as follows:

> Tell General Howard I know his heart. What he told me before I have in my heart. I am tired of fighting. Our chiefs are killed. Looking Glass is dead. The old men are all killed. It is the young men who say yes or no. He who led the young men is dead. It is cold and we have no blankets. The little children are freezing to death. My people, some of them, have run away to the hills and have no blankets, no food; no one knows where they are, perhaps freezing to death. I want time to look for my children and see how many of them I can find. Maybe I shall find them among the dead. Hear me, my chiefs, I am tired; my heart is sick and sad. From where the sun now stands, I will fight no more forever.

I went to General Miles and gave up my gun, and said, "From where the sun now stands I will fight no more." My people needed rest—we wanted peace.

I was told we could go with General Miles to Tongue River and stay there until spring, when we would be sent back to our country.[2] Finally it was decided that we were to be taken to Tongue River [in SE Montana]. We had nothing to say about it. After our arrival at Tongue River, General Miles received orders to take us to Bismarck [in S central North Dakota]. The reason given was, that subsistence would be cheaper there.

General Miles was opposed to this order. He said, "You must not blame me. I have endeavored to keep my word, but the chief who is over me has given the order, and I must obey it or resign. That would do you no good. Some other officer would carry out the order."

I believe General Miles would have kept his

---

1. **coulees** (ko͞ol′ lēz): deep gulches or ravines.
2. General Nelson Miles negotiated the surrender of the Nez Percé on the promise that the Nez Percé would be returned to their homes in the Clearwater territory in Idaho.

word if he could have done so. I do not blame him for what we have suffered since the surrender. I do not know who is to blame. We gave up all our horses—over eleven hundred —and all our saddles—over one hundred—and we have not heard from them since. Somebody has got our horses.

General Miles turned my people over to another soldier, and we were taken to Bismarck. Captain Johnson, who now had charge of us, received an order to take us to Fort Leavenworth [on the Missouri River in NE Kansas]. At Leavenworth we were placed on a low river bottom, with no water except river water to drink and cook with. We had always lived in a healthy country, where the mountains were high and the water was cold and clear. Many of my people sickened and died, and we buried them in this strange land. I can not tell how much my heart suffered for my people while at Leavenworth. The Great Spirit Chief who rules above seemed to be looking some other way, and did not see what was being done to my people.

During the hot days [July, 1878] we received notice that we were to be moved farther away from our own country. We were not asked if we were willing to go. We were ordered to get into railroad cars. Three of my people died on the way to Baxter Springs [in SE Kansas]. It was worse to die there than to die fighting in the mountains.

We were moved from Baxter Springs to the Indian Territory, and set down without our lodges [near present-day Tonkawa in N central Oklahoma]. We had but little medicine, and we were nearly all sick. Seventy of my people have died since we moved there.

We have had a great many visitors who have talked many ways. Some of the chiefs [General Fish and Colonel Stickney] from Washington came to see us, and selected land for us to live upon. We have not moved to that land, for it is not a good place to live.

The Commissioner Chief [E. A. Hayt] came to see us. I told him, as I told every one, that I expected General Miles's word would be carried out. He said it "could not be done; that white men now lived in my country and all the land was taken up; that, if I returned to Wallowa [river territory in NE Oregon, his birthplace], I could not live in peace; that law-papers were out against my young men who began the war, and that the Government could not protect my people." This talk fell like a heavy stone upon my heart. I saw that I could not gain anything by talking to him. Other law chiefs [Congressional Committee] came to see me and said they would help me to get a healthy country. I did not know who to believe. The white people have too many chiefs. They do not understand each other. They do not all talk alike.

The Commissioner Chief [Mr. Hayt] invited me to go with him and hunt for a better home than we have now. I like the land we found [west of the Osage Reservation] better than any place I have seen in that country; but it is not a healthy land. There are no mountains and rivers. The water is warm. It is not a good country for stock. I do not believe my people can live there. I am afraid they will all die. The Indians who occupy that country are dying off. I promised Chief Hayt to go there, and do the best I could until the Government got ready to make good General Miles's word. I was not satisfied, but I could not help myself.

Then the Inspector Chief [General McNiel] came to my camp and we had a long talk. He said I ought to have a home in the mountain country north, and that he would write a letter to the Great Chief at Washington. Again the hope of seeing the mountains of Idaho and Oregon grew up in my heart.

At last I was granted permission to come to Washington [March, 1879] and bring my friend Yellow Bull and our interpreter [Arthur Chapman] with me. I am glad we came. I have shaken hands with a great many friends, but there are some things I want to know which no one seems able to explain. I can not understand how the Government sends a man out to fight us, as it did General Miles, and then breaks his word. Such a Government has something wrong about it. I can not understand why so many chiefs are allowed to talk so many different ways, and promise so many different things. I have seen the Great Father Chief [the President], the next Great Chief [Secretary of the Interior], the Commissioner Chief [Hayt], the Law Chief [General Butler], and many other law chiefs [Congressmen], and they all say they are my friends, and that I shall have justice; but while their mouths all talk right, I do not understand why nothing is done for my people. I have heard talk and talk, but nothing is done. Good words do not last long unless they amount to something. Words do not pay for my dead people. They do not pay for my country, now overrun by white men. They do not protect my father's grave. They do not pay for all my horses and cattle. Good words will not give me back my children. Good words will not make good the promise of your War Chief General Miles. Good words will not give my people good health and stop them from dying. Good words will not get my people a home where they can live in peace and take care of themselves. I am tired of talk that comes to nothing. It makes my heart sick when I remember all the good words and all the broken promises. There has been too much talking by men who had no right to talk. Too many misrepresentations have been made, too many misunderstandings have come up between the white men about the Indians. If the white man wants to live in peace with the Indian he can live in peace. There need be no trouble. Treat all men alike. Give them the same law. Give them all an even chance to live and grow. All men were made by the same Great Spirit Chief. They are all brothers. The earth is the mother of all people, and all people should have equal

rights upon it. You might as well expect the rivers to run backward as that any man who was born a free man should be contented when penned up and denied liberty to go where he pleases. If you tie a horse to a stake, do you expect he will grow fat? If you pen an Indian up on a small spot of earth, and compel him to stay there, he will not be contented, nor will he grow and prosper. I have asked some of the great white chiefs where they get their authority to say to the Indian that he shall stay in one place, while he sees white men going where they please. They can not tell me.

I only ask of the Government to be treated as all other men are treated. If I can not go to my own home, let me have a home in some country where my people will not die so fast. I would like to go to Bitter Root Valley [on the Idaho-Montana border]. There my people would be healthy; where they are now they are dying. Three have died since I left my camp to come to Washington.

When I think of our condition my heart is heavy. I see men of my race treated as outlaws and driven from country to country, or shot down like animals.

I know that my race must change. We can not hold our own with the white men as we are. We only ask an even chance to live as other men live. We ask to be recognized as men. We ask that the same law shall work alike on all men. If the Indian breaks the law, punish him by the law. If the white man breaks the law, punish him also.

Let me be a free man—free to travel, free to stop, free to work, free to trade where I choose, free to choose my own teachers, free to follow the religion of my fathers, free to think and talk and act for myself—and I will obey every law, or submit to the penalty.

Whenever the white man treats an Indian as they treat each other, then we will have no more wars. We shall all be alike—brothers of one father and one mother, with one sky above us and one country around us, and one government for all. Then the Great Spirit Chief who rules above will smile upon this land, and send rain to wash out the bloody spots made by brothers' hands from the face of the earth. For this time the Indian race are waiting and praying. I hope that no more groans of wounded men and women will ever go to the ear of the Great Spirit Chief above, and that all people may be one people.

In-mut-too-yah-lat-lat[3] has spoken for his people.

April, 1879

---

3. **In-mut-too-yah-lat-lat:** Joseph's Indian name translates "Thunder-Rolling-in-the-Mountains."

Getting at Meaning

1. What is the main reason why Chief Joseph surrenders to General Miles?

2. How many times are the Nez Percé moved? What makes each location unacceptable to the Indians? Why do the transfers cause many deaths among the Indians?

3. What does Chief Joseph find most baffling and infuriating about the United States government?

4. Chief Joseph pleads for certain rights and responsibilities for his people. What are they? How, according to Chief Joseph, could Indians and non-Indians live in peace?

Developing Skills in Reading Literature

1. **Epithet.** An epithet is an apt phrase used to identify a person or thing. Chief Joseph's epithet for the President of the United States is "Great Father Chief." Find the other epithets in this selection and explain them.

2. **Analogy.** Chief Joseph draws an analogy between a tied-up horse and an Indian on a reservation. How are the situations and results similar, according to Chief Joseph? Explain the argument Chief Joseph makes through this analogy.

3. **Style.** Chief Joseph expresses himself with simplicity and directness. Describe the sentence structure, word choice, imagery, figurative language, and repeated phrases that characterize Chief Joseph's style. Give examples to support your points. How does Chief Joseph's style reflect the culture, values, and way of life of his people?

4. **Theme.** Religion is an integral part of the Nez Percé way of life. Which of Chief Joseph's religious beliefs are revealed in this selection? How does he explain why God allows the Nez Percé to suffer? What is Chief Joseph's concept of God? Of God's relationship to humans and nature?

Developing Writing Skills

Using Contrast. Custer's view of the Indian crisis and Chief Joseph's view can be inferred from this and the preceding selection. In a well developed paragraph contrast these two views, using evidence from the two selections to support your points.

Statement of an Aged Indian   *Anonymous*

My sun is set. My day is done. Darkness is stealing over me. Before I lie down to rise no more I will speak to my people. Hear me, for this is not the time for me to tell a lie.

The Great Spirit made us, and gave us this land we live in. He gave us the buffalo, antelope, and deer for food and clothing. Our hunting grounds stretched from the Mississippi to the great mountains. We were free as the winds and heard no man's commands. We fought our enemies, and feasted our friends. Our braves drove away all who would take our game. They captured women and horses from our foes. Our children were many and our herds were large. Our old men talked with spirits and made good medicine. Our young men hunted and made love to the girls. Where the tipi[1] was, there we stayed, and no house imprisoned us. No one said, "To this line is my land, to that is yours."

Then the white man came to our hunting grounds, a stranger. We gave him meat and presents, and told him go in peace. He looked on our women and stayed to live in our tipis. His fellows came to build their roads across our hunting grounds. He brought among us the mysterious iron that shoots. He brought with him the magic water that makes men foolish. With his trinkets and beads he even bought the girl I loved.

I said, "The white man is not a friend, let us kill him." But their numbers were greater than blades of grass. They took away the buffalo and shot down our best warriors. They took away our lands and surrounded us by fences. Their soldiers camped outside with cannon to shoot us down. They wiped the trails of our people from the face of the prairies. They forced our children to forsake the ways of their fathers.

When I turn to the east I see no dawn. When I turn to the west the approaching night hides all.

---

1. **tipi:** Dakota Indian variant of *tepee.*

Getting at Meaning

1. What is the occasion for this speech? How might its timing affect its content?

2. According to the speaker, how did the white men change the Indians' lives?

3. What personal grudge does the speaker have against the white men? As a cultural group, what grudges do the Indians have against the white men?

4. What future for the Indians does the speaker seem to predict?

Developing Skills in Reading Literature

1. **Symbol.** Light and darkness are symbolic in the aged Indian's statement. For him personally, what does each represent? For the Indian people, what does each represent?

2. **Tone.** The attitude of the aged Indian toward the Indian crisis differs from that of Chief Joseph. Is the tone of the aged Indian more or less optimistic? Find passages in both selections to support your conclusion.

Let Us Move Evenly Together *Taos Pueblo Indian*

In north central New Mexico is the Indian village of San Geronimo de Taos where Indians have lived in multi-story adobe buildings since about A. D. 1000. This chant belongs to the long and rich oral heritage of these Indians.

Let us move evenly together.
Let us stand as one.
Let evil be cast from us.
Let no man cry for himself
Or listen to those without faces.   5
Let us move evenly together.
Let us walk as tall trees.
Let fear be crushed within us.
Let no man speak for himself
Or give secrets to those without blood.[1]   10

My brother the star, my mother the
earth, my father the sun, my sister the
moon, to my life give beauty, to my
body give strength, to my corn give
goodness, to my house give peace, to   15
my spirit give truth, to my elders give
wisdom.

Oh my gentle village fierce
Oh my powerful people weak
Oh my fertile fields so dry   20
Oh my peaceful house disturbed
We must pray for strength.
We must pray to come together
Pray to the weeping earth
Pray to the trembling waters   25
And to the wandering rain.
We must pray to the whispering moon
Pray to the tiptoeing stars
And to the hollering sun.

---

1. Lines 5 and 10 refer to people outside the known brotherhood of the tribal community.

Getting at Meaning

1. How does the speaker of this chant appeal for unity?

2. What does the speaker hope to gain from the earth, sun, moon, and stars?

3. What dismal circumstances prompt this prayer, according to the third stanza?

4. Why are the speaker's prayers addressed to elements of nature? Why do the Indians need the aid of nature?

5. What values of the Taos Indians does this chant emphasize?

Developing Skills in Reading Literature

1. **Oral Literature.** This chanted poem is an example of oral literature. For what purpose do you think it originated? Identify the elements of "Let Us Move Evenly Together" that make it suitable for oral performance. Note particularly the alliterative patterns and the repetends in each stanza and the rhythmic cadence of the lines.

2. **Parallelism.** What phrases are parallel in the second stanza of "Let Us Move Evenly Together"? How do these phrases link related ideas?

3. **Paradox.** A type of paradox or contradiction, an oxymoron brings together two contradictory terms. One example in the final stanza is "gentle village fierce." Find three other oxymorons in this chant. How do they sharply emphasize certain ideas?

4. **Personification.** The final six lines each contain an example of personification. Why is the earth described as *weeping*, the sun *hollering*, the stars *tiptoeing*? Explain why the personifications are appropriate, and compare them with the personifications in the second stanza.

Poetry

SYMPHONY IN WHITE NO. 2: THE LITTLE WHITE GIRL, 1864.
James McNeill Whistler. The Tate Gallery, London.

Emily Dickinson

1830–1886

Unknown in her own time, save to a small circle of family and friends, Emily Dickinson has become one of America's most popular and influential poets. The author of nearly eighteen hundred poems, she lived a quiet, reclusive life that belied the intense creative fervor of her inner life, as a woman and as a poet.

Dickinson was born in Amherst, Massachusetts, on December 10, 1830, to a family descended from generations of New England Puritans. Her patriarchal father was a lawyer, the treasurer of Amherst College, and a member of Congress. She was educated at Amherst Academy and attended for one term Mount Holyoke Female Seminary at nearby South Hadley. Finding herself uncomfortable in its restrictive academic atmosphere, she returned to her small, conservative home town and never departed from it again except for a few brief visits to Philadelphia, Boston, and Washington prior to 1862. Emily and her sister Lavinia never married; their lawyer brother married, against his father's wishes, a New York society belle who became one of Emily's closest friends.

There has been much speculation about the passionate loves referred to in poems such as "My Life Closed Twice Before Its Close." It is generally accepted that a young brilliant free-thinker named Ben Newton was important to Dickinson, both as a close friend and as the means through which she was introduced to a world of ideas hitherto unknown. Newton died in 1853. On a visit to Philadelphia in 1854, Dickinson met the Reverend Charles Wadsworth. Though he was an older man, already married, their friendship deepened through correspondence and a few visits in Amherst. Apparently his departure to a pastorate in California in 1862 was a major loss to Emily. In that year she wrote, in a tremendous creative outburst, three hundred and sixty-six poems, some revealing great emotional turmoil. In that year also, she began to dress exclusively in white and to refuse to venture beyond the bounds of her house and garden, saying, "I do not cross my father's ground to any house or town." During the last two years of her life, Dickinson's physical and mental health deteriorated until she died from Bright's disease on May 15, 1886. Her sister Lavinia said of Emily that she "had to think—she was the only one of us that had that to do."

Although she was encouraged as a writer by literary figures such as Thomas Wentworth Higginson and Helen Hunt Jackson, Dickinson published only seven poems during her lifetime. Even those closest to her were unaware of the great number of poems that would be found after her death, tied into neat packets. Dickinson's poems are strongly influenced by the Bible and by the meters of hymns. Her themes are the great themes of life: love, death, immortality, and nature. Highly compressed and deceptively simple in form, her lyrics often depart from conventional rhyme and rhythm, evidencing an originality that is the hallmark of true genius.

Some Keep the Sabbath Going to Church

Some keep the Sabbath going to Church—
I keep it, staying at Home—
With a Bobolink for a Chorister—
And an Orchard, for a Dome[1]—

Some keep the Sabbath in Surplice[2]—   5
I just wear my Wings—
And instead of tolling the Bell, for Church,
Our little Sexton—sings.

God preaches, a noted Clergyman—
And the sermon is never long,   10
So instead of getting to Heaven, at last—
I'm going, all along.

---

1. **Dome:** from Latin *domus Dei,* "house of God."
2. **Surplice** (sur' plis): a loose, white, wide-sleeved over-gown worn by the clergy and choir in some churches.

"Faith" Is a Fine Invention

"Faith" is a fine invention
When Gentlemen can *see*—
But *Microscopes* are prudent
In an Emergency.

I Never Saw a Moor

I never saw a Moor—
I never saw the Sea—
Yet know I how the Heather looks
And what a Billow be.

I never spoke with God   5
Nor visited in Heaven—
Yet certain am I of the spot
As if the Checks[1] were given—

---

1. **Checks:** railway tickets, color coded for each specific destination.

Getting at Meaning

1. "Some Keep the Sabbath Going to Church," "'Faith' Is a Fine Invention," and "I Never Saw a Moor" are three poems that delineate Emily Dickinson's particular kind of religious faith. According to the first poem, how does Dickinson like to celebrate the sabbath? What is her favorite church?

2. Explain Dickinson's meaning when she says, "'Faith' is a fine invention/When Gentlemen can see—." What is her opinion of microscopes, or science?

3. In "I Never Saw a Moor," what idea does the word *yet* introduce in each stanza? What enables Dickinson to be confident and assertive about things she has not experienced?

Developing Skills in Reading Literature

1. **Imagery.** Describe Dickinson's "church" as she depicts it in "Some Keep the Sabbath Going to Church." What sounds exist there? Explain why the poet wears wings.

In "'Faith' Is a Fine Invention" lines 2 and 3 both refer to sight. How does the image differ in these two lines?

2. **Structure.** Dickinson is known for her terse poems, which are briefer than any other established English or American poet had produced before her. Her poems are usually written in quatrains, units of four lines each, often with experimental rhyme and meter.

Scan these three poems. What generalizations can you make about the meter? What pattern does the rhyme scheme follow in each quatrain? In which of the poems does the rhyme most strongly reinforce the poem's meaning? Explain.

3. **Irony.** Dickinson is known for her ironic, frequently witty observations about the world around her and the human condition. In "Some Keep the Sabbath Going to Church," she speaks humorously of "Our little Sexton." What is ironic in her reference to God as "a noted Clergyman"? What is ironic about the humor in "'Faith' Is a Fine Invention"?

4. **Theme.** Love of nature is a significant theme in Dickinson's work. Characterize the attitude toward nature she projects in "Some Keep the Sabbath Going to Church." What is her feeling about nature in "I Never Saw a Moor"?

Judging from these three poems, how does Dickinson's religious faith differ from traditional religious faith? What appears to be her attitude toward organized religion?

Success Is Counted Sweetest

Success is counted sweetest
By those who ne'er succeed.
To comprehend a nectar[1]
Requires sorest need.

Not one of all the purple Host   5
Who took the Flag today
Can tell the definition
So clear of Victory

As he defeated—dying—
On whose forbidden ear   10
The distant strains of triumph
Burst agonized and clear!

---

1. **nectar** (nek′ tər): any delicious beverage.

Fame Is a Fickle Food

Fame is a fickle[1] food
Upon a shifting plate
Whose table once a
Guest but not
The second time is set.   5

Whose crumbs the crows inspect
And with ironic caw
Flap past it to the
Farmer's Corn—
Men eat of it and die.   10

---

1. **fickle:** changeable or unstable in affection or interest.

"Hope" Is the Thing with Feathers

"Hope" is the thing with feathers—
That perches in the soul—
And sings the tune without the words—
And never stops—at all—

And sweetest—in the Gale—is heard—   5
And sore must be the storm—
That could abash the little Bird
That kept so many warm—

I've heard it in the chillest land—
And on the strangest Sea—   10
Yet, never, in Extremity,[1]
It asked a crumb—of Me.

---

1. **Extremity** (eks trem′ i tē): greatest need or greatest peril.

This Is My Letter to the World

This is my letter to the World
That never wrote to Me—
The simple News that Nature told—
With tender Majesty

Her Message is committed   5
To Hands I cannot see—
For love of Her—Sweet—countrymen—
Judge tenderly—of Me

Much Madness Is Divinest Sense

Much Madness is divinest Sense—
To a discerning Eye—
Much Sense—the starkest Madness—
'Tis the Majority
In this, as All, prevail—   5
Assent—and you are sane—
Demur—you're straightway dangerous—
And handled with a Chain—

Getting at Meaning

1. "Success Is Counted Sweetest," "Fame Is a Fickle Food," " 'Hope' Is the Thing with Feathers," "This Is My Letter to the World," and "Much Madness Is Divinest Sense" are poems that present some of Emily Dickinson's convictions and observations about human life. In the first poem, Dickinson writes about success. Who prizes it most, according to the poet?

2. What is Dickinson's basic statement in "Fame Is a Fickle Food"? According to the poem, why is fame fatal to people?

3. In " 'Hope' Is the Thing with Feathers," what services does the poet say hope provides for people? What quality of hope does Dickinson focus on in the final two lines of the poem?

4. What is the poet's message in "This Is My Letter to the World"? Who is "Her" in the second stanza? Explain the "Hands I cannot see—."

5. Explain Dickinson's meaning when she says, "Much Madness Is Divinest Sense." What does she say about the majority in this poem? What happens to people who follow their own inclinations?

Developing Skills in Reading Literature

1. **Irony.** In "Success Is Counted Sweetest" Dickinson pinpoints an irony of human life, that we prize things most when they are forbidden to us. Explain why the defeated person knows the definition of victory better than the conquerer.

In "Fame Is a Fickle Food," why does Dickinson speak of the crows flying past the crumbs of fame "with ironic caw"? Explain why "Men eat of it and die."

Comment on the ironies inherent in "Much Madness Is Divinest Sense." According to the poem, what is sane behavior?

2. **Imagery and Figurative Language.** Describe the image that Dickinson creates in "Success Is Counted Sweetest." What words build the image most persuasively?

What words build the food metaphor in "Fame Is a Fickle Food"? Why does the poet introduce the crow imagery?

In "'Hope' Is the Thing with Feathers," why does Dickinson envision hope as she does?

3. **Style.** Dickinson often uses non-standard punctuation. What punctuation mark, unusual in poetry, appears repeatedly in these poems? Why does Dickinson use it so often? Where else does the poet use punctuation to enhance meaning?

Dickinson uses alliteration as a stylistic tool in many of her poems. Where do you find it in these poems? Comment on how the alliteration functions.

Another characteristic of Dickinson as a poet is that she often turns the final line of her poems into a punch line. Discuss how her technique functions in this group of poems. How does the final line of each poem influence meaning?

4. **Theme.** This group of poems, and "This Is My Letter to the World" in particular, establishes a Romantic vision of nature. Explain how this is so. Notice that Dickinson's imagery often subtly conveys an attitude toward nature.

Summarize Dickinson's main statement in each of the poems in this group. What attitude toward the conventional world do all the poems imply? What lines suggest that the poet feels somewhat estranged, like an independent outsider?

Developing Vocabulary

Connotation. In "Success Is Counted Sweetest" Dickinson uses several ordinary words in other than ordinary ways, requiring a reader to know special connotations for the words. After you have consulted both the poem and a dictionary, write the definition Dickinson uses for each of the words that follows.

comprehend   strains
sorest   agonized
forbidden

Developing Writing Skills

Developing an Argument. Write an explanatory paragraph in support of Dickinson's assertion that "Much Madness Is Divinest Sense." Support your views with examples from your own life and your observation of the world. Include an opinion about why nonconformists often are treated so harshly.

If You Were Coming in the Fall

If you were coming in the Fall,
I'd brush the Summer by
With half a smile, and half a spurn,
As Housewives do, a Fly.

If I could see you in a year,   5
I'd wind the months in balls—
And put them each in separate Drawers,
For fear the numbers fuse—

If only Centuries, delayed,
I'd count them on my Hand,   10
Subtracting, till my fingers dropped
Into Van Dieman's Land.[1]

If certain, when this life was out—
That yours and mine, should be
I'd toss it yonder, like a Rind,   15
And take Eternity—

But, now, uncertain of the length
Of this, that is between,
It goads[2] me, like the Goblin Bee—
That will not state—its sting.   20

---

1. **Van Dieman's Land:** former name of Tasmania, part of the Commonwealth of Australia, used as a British penal colony until 1853.
2. **goads:** urges on as with a sharp pointed stick.

My Life Closed Twice Before Its Close

My life closed twice before its close—
It yet remains to see
If Immortality unveil
A third event to me

So huge, so hopeless to conceive   5
As these that twice befell.
Parting is all we know of heaven,
And all we need of hell.

The Soul Selects Her Own Society

The Soul selects her own Society—
Then—shuts the Door—
To her divine Majority—
Present no more—

Unmoved—she notes the Chariots—pausing—   5
At her low Gate—
Unmoved—an Emperor be kneeling
Upon her Mat—

I've known her—from an ample nation—
Choose One—   10
Then—close the Valves of her attention—
Like Stone—

Getting at Meaning

1. "If You Were Coming in the Fall," "My Life Closed Twice Before Its Close," and "The Soul Selects Her Own Society" all reflect on love and intimate relationships between human beings. In "If You Were Coming in the Fall," a love poem, the length of waiting time increases from stanza to stanza. In each case, how does the poet feel about waiting?

2. Contemplate Dickinson's paradoxical line, "My life closed twice before its close—." What different meanings might the line have? Explain the line, "Parting is all we know of heaven."

3. "The Soul Selects Her Own Society" comments on the human ability to embrace solitude and communicate intimately with perhaps only one other person. According to the poem, what kinds of entreaties can a determined soul ignore?

Developing Skills in Reading Literature

1. **Figurative Language.** Dickinson often uses strikingly original similes, metaphors, and personification. In "If You Were Coming in the Fall," she begins and ends the poem with similes drawn from the insect world. What does the comparison of the first stanza convey? What aspect of uncertainty does the poet dramatize with her concluding comparison?

Explain the personfication that operates in "My Life Closed Twice Before Its Close." What other words in the poem underscore the vastness of the concept that is the subject of the personification?

"The Soul Selects Her Own Society" is built upon the personification of the soul. What kind of character is the soul, according to the poem? "Chariots" and "Emperors" are symbols for what element of society? To what does the metaphor "Valves of her attention" compare the soul's receptivity? Comment on the effectiveness of the final simile, "Like Stone."

2. **Rhythm.** "If You Were Coming in the Fall" is a rather brisk, fast-paced poem. How does parallel construction work to increase its tempo? How do rhyme and meter contribute? Why is the fast pace appropriate to the poem?

By contrast, "The Soul Selects Her Own Society" is a particularly slow poem. How does the poem's punctuation slow it down? Explain the effect of the short lines composed of one-syllable words. What specific words in the poem imply slowness or lack of action? How does the rhythm of this poem accentuate its meaning?

3. **Tone.** Characterize the tone of each of these poems. Which poem seems most playful and light? Which poem seems most intense and anguished? Which poem seems most matter-of-fact?

4. **Theme.** These poems are all about love and human intimacy. The first two poems comment on the frustration and suffering that often accompany love. What lines in these poems show the poet's pain at separation from loved ones? Explain her assertion that parting is ". . . all we need of hell."

In "The Soul Selects Her Own Society," Dickinson uses the phrase "divine Majority" to refer to the soul. What view of the individual does this phrase project? What is the poet's attitude toward society?

I Heard a Fly Buzz When I Died

I heard a Fly buzz—when I died—
The Stillness in the Room
Was like the Stillness in the Air—
Between the Heaves of Storm—

The Eyes around—had wrung them dry—   5
And Breaths were gathering firm
For that last Onset—when the King
Be witnessed—in the Room—

I willed my Keepsakes—Signed away
What portion of me be   10
Assignable—and then it was
There interposed[1] a Fly—

With Blue—uncertain stumbling Buzz—
Between the light—and me—
And then the Windows failed—and then   15
I could not see to see—

---

1. **interposed:** intervened, came between.

The Bustle in a House

The Bustle in a House
The Morning after Death
Is solemnest of industries
Enacted upon Earth—

The Sweeping up the Heart   5
And putting Love away
We shall not want to use again
Until Eternity.

Because I Could Not Stop for Death

Because I could not stop for Death—
He kindly stopped for me—
The Carriage held but just Ourselves—
And Immortality.

We slowly drove—He knew no haste   5
And I had put away
My labor and my leisure too,
For His Civility—

We passed the School, where Children strove
At Recess—in the Ring—   10
We passed the Fields of Gazing Grain¹—
We passed the Setting Sun—

Or rather—He passed Us—
The Dews drew quivering and chill—
For only Gossamer, my Gown—   15
My Tippet²—only Tulle³—

We paused before a House that seemed
A Swelling of the Ground—
The Roof was scarcely visible—
The Cornice⁴—in the Ground—   20

Since then—'tis Centuries—and yet
Feels shorter than the Day
I first surmised the Horses' Heads
Were toward Eternity—

---

1. **Gazing Grain:** grain watches the sun and follows it
throughout the day.
2. **Tippet:** a scarf-like garment for the neck and shoulders, hanging down in front.
3. **Tulle** (to͞ol): a thin, fine netting used for veils or
scarves.
4. **Cornice:** a horizontal molding projecting along the top
of a wall or building.

Getting at Meaning

1. "I Heard a Fly Buzz When I Died," "The Bustle in a House," and "Because I Could Not Stop for Death" are three of Emily Dickinson's poems about death. Explain what is happening in each stanza of "I Heard a Fly Buzz When I Died."

2. In "I Heard a Fly Buzz When I Died," what does the speaker mean in saying, "I willed my Keepsakes— Signed away/What portion of me be/Assignable"? Explain the line, "And then the Windows failed—."

3. What are the "industries" the poet speaks of in "The Bustle in a House"?

4. In "Because I Could Not Stop for Death," what three presences are riding in the carriage? What has happened to time?

5. The chariot in "Because I Could Not Stop for Death" pauses before a "House." What is the house? What details make this apparent?

Developing Skills in Reading Literature

1. **Speaker.** Notice what is unusual about the speakers in "I Heard a Fly Buzz When I Died" and "Because I Could Not Stop for Death." What event is the speaker of each poem describing? In "I Heard a Fly Buzz When I Died," what is the speaker's tone? Explain the line, "I could not see to see—."

What is the tone of the speaker in "Because I Could Not Stop for Death"? The speaker was too busy to stop for death. What lines later in the poem are a further indication of being unprepared?

2. **Irony.** In "I Heard a Fly Buzz When I Died," the speaker ironically and incongruously focuses on the buzzing of a fly at the moment of death. Why is this focus ironic? Is it a realistic memory of a momentous event?

Where do you find irony in "Because I Could Not Stop for Death"? What is ironic about the poet's house-cleaning metaphor in "The Bustle in a House"?

3. **Figurative Language.** In lines 3 and 4 of "I Heard a Fly Buzz When I Died," the speaker describes the stillness of the sickroom with a simile. Why is the stillness "Between the Heaves of Storm" more pronounced than other kinds of stillness? Where in the poem does Dickinson employ personification? Explain

the implied metaphor that motivates the poet's use of the word *Windows* in line 15.

Comment on how the poet extends the house-cleaning metaphor in "The Bustle in a House." What makes the metaphor so appropriate?

In "Because I Could Not Stop for Death," how does the poet characterize Death in the central personification? Notice in the third stanza the three things that the carriage passes: playing children, fields of grain, and the setting sun. Viewed as metaphors, what do these things represent in the speaker's own life? Explain the house metaphor in lines 17–20.

4. **Theme.** What commentary do these poems make about death. What view of eternity do they project? How does Dickinson suggest overcoming the pain of death?

Developing Vocabulary

Latin Roots. In "I Heard a Fly Buzz When I Died," the poet uses the word *interposed*. *Interpose* comes from the Latin *inter-*, meaning "between," plus *pōnere*, meaning "to put or place." All of the words that follow also use the root *pose*, from *pōnere*. Look up each word in a dictionary and write its definition. In each word, what is combined with the Latin root *pōnere* to create the meaning of the word?

juxtapose
posit
positivism
superimpose

Developing Writing Skills

Using an Extended Metaphor. Several of Emily Dickinson's poems are actually definitions of abstract terms, definitions that are developed by comparing the abstract term to a common object or activity. For example, in the collection of Dickinson poems in this unit, she defines *hope*, *fame*, and *success* in this way.

Select an abstract noun and define it in a paragraph or poem, using an extended metaphor of your own creation. You may define the abstraction with a series of shorter metaphors if you prefer.

Walt Whitman

Mannahatta

I was asking for something specific and perfect for my city,
Whereupon lo! upsprang the aboriginal[1] name.
Now I see what there is in a name, a word, liquid, sane, unruly, musical,
    self-sufficient,
I see that the word of my city is that word from of old,
Because I see that word nested in nests of water-bays, superb,   5
Rich, hemm'd thick all around with sailships and steamships, an island sixteen
    miles long, solid-founded,
Numberless crowded streets, high growths of iron, slender, strong, light,
    splendidly uprising toward clear skies,
Tides swift and ample, well-loved by me, toward sundown,
The flowing sea-currents, the little islands, larger adjoining islands, the heights,
    the villas,
The countless masts, the white shore-steamers, the lighters, the ferry-boats, the
    black sea-steamers well-model'd,   10
The down-town streets, the jobbers'[2] houses of business, the houses of business
    of the ship-merchants and money-brokers, the river-streets,
Immigrants arriving, fifteen or twenty thousand in a week,
The carts hauling goods, the manly race of drivers of horses, the brown-faced
    sailors,
The summer air, the bright sun shining, and the sailing clouds aloft,
The winter snows, the sleigh-bells, the broken ice in the river, passing along up
    or down with the flood-tide or ebb-tide,   15
The mechanics of the city, the masters, well-form'd, beautiful-faced, looking you
    straight in the eyes,
Trottoirs[3] throng'd, vehicles, Broadway, the women, the shops and shows,
A million people—manners free and superb—open voices—hospitality—the most
    courageous and friendly young men,
City of hurried and sparkling waters! city of spires and masts!
City nested in bays! my city!   20

---

1. **aboriginal:** existing from the earliest days.
2. **jobber:** a middleman who buys goods wholesale to sell to dealers.
3. **Trottoir** (trō′ twär′) *French:* sidewalk.

Getting at Meaning

1. *Mannahatta*, meaning "hill island," was the name for Manhattan when Dutch colonist Peter Minuit bought the island from the Iroquois Indians in 1624. In this and the following poems, Whitman himself is the speaker. Why does Whitman like the old name for the center of New York City?

2. What are some of the activities characteristic of New York City that Whitman mentions in the poem?

Developing Skills in Reading Literature

1. **Imagery.** Whitman strings together elaborate images of Manhattan in this poem. Notice that much of his imagery has to do with water and ships, with human labor, and with weather and the seasons. Which lines in the poem develop each category of imagery? How does Whitman depict the city streets themselves?

2. **Tone.** The tone of this poem is clearly buoyant and optimistic. What words and phrases work to make it so? Why is Whitman able to take such joy in New York? How does he view the people? What vision of progress does the poem project?

3. **Free Verse.** Explain how the free verse of this poem suits both the tone and the subject matter. Observe the poem's syntax. How does the syntax work to keep the poem flowing along? What structural devices create order within the free and sprawling lines of the poem?

WALT WHITMAN, 1887. *Thomas Eakins.*
The Pennsylvania Academy of the Fine Arts.
General Fund Purchase.

I Hear America Singing

I hear America singing, the varied carols I hear,
Those of mechanics, each one singing his as it should be blithe[1] and strong,
The carpenter singing his as he measures his plank or beam,
The mason singing his as he makes ready for work, or leaves off work,
The boatman singing what belongs to him in his boat, the deckhand singing on
    the steamboat deck,   5
The shoemaker singing as he sits on his bench, the hatter singing as he stands,
The wood-cutter's song, the ploughboy's on his way in the morning, or at noon
    intermission or at sundown,
The delicious singing of the mother, or of the young wife at work, or of the girl
    sewing or washing,
Each singing what belongs to him or her and to none else,
The day what belongs to the day—at night the party of young fellows, robust,
    friendly,   10
Singing with open mouths their strong melodious songs.

---

1. **blithe:** cheerful, carefree.

Getting at Meaning

1. Explain what Whitman is hearing in this poem. What kinds of workers does he name? Why are they "singing"?

2. How are the songs in the last two lines different from the songs elsewhere in the poem?

Developing Skills in Reading Literature

1. **Structure.** Notice that this poem is all one sentence, with each line flowing freely into the next one. How is this structure related to what the speaker hears in America? In what sense are all the various workers united?

2. **Theme.** What kind of activity do all of the singers in this poem have in common? What people, then, has Whitman chosen as the heroes of his America? Why? Explain the view of progress and democracy conveyed in this poem.

3. **Rhythm.** This free verse poem rolls along like a song, appealing primarily to the auditory sense. Read the poem aloud. What poetic devices make it rhythmic and musical? Look especially at Whitman's use of parallel construction and repetends.

I Sit and Look Out

I sit and look out upon all the sorrows of the world, and upon all oppression and
    shame,
I hear secret convulsive sobs from young men at anguish with themselves,
    remorseful after deeds done,
I see in low life the mother misused by her children, dying, neglected, gaunt,
    desperate,
I see the wife misused by her husband, I see the treacherous seducer of young women,
I mark the ranklings[1] of jealousy and unrequited love attempted to be hid, I see these
    sights on the earth,   5
I see the workings of battle, pestilence, tyranny, I see martyrs and prisoners,
I observe a famine at sea, I observe the sailors casting lots who shall be kill'd to
    preserve the lives of the rest,
I observe the slights and degradations cast by arrogant persons upon laborers, the
    poor, and upon negroes, and the like;
All these—all the meanness and agony without end I sitting look out upon,
See, hear, and am silent.   10

---

1. **ranklings:** festerings.

Getting at Meaning

1. What kinds of problems does Whitman hear and see in lines 2–5? in lines 6–8? Explain how the two kinds of problems differ from each other.

2. Account for the speaker's silence in line 10. Is there an implied self-criticism in his silence?

Developing Skills in Reading Literature

1. **Tone.** Notice how different the tone of this poem is from the preceding one. Why? What does the poet see in this poem that he does not see in "I Hear America Singing"? How does the diction of this poem emphasize his opposing vision?

2. **Structure.** This poem, like the preceding one, is all one sentence. Why? What devices keep the poem moving along? How does the single sentence reflect Whitman's vision?

Developing Writing Skills

Establishing Tone. In "I Sit and Look Out" and "I Hear America Singing" Walt Whitman creates two very different pictures of America. Select an object, a person, or a place, and in two paragraphs present your subject in two contrasting lights. Use contrasting diction, imagery, and figurative language to help build dissimilar tones in your two paragraphs.

A Noiseless Patient Spider

A noiseless patient spider,
I mark'd where on a little promontory it stood isolated,
Mark'd how to explore the vacant vast surrounding,
It launch'd forth filament, filament, filament, out of itself,
Ever unreeling them, ever tirelessly speeding them.   5

And you O my soul where you stand,
Surrounded, detached, in measureless oceans of space,
Ceaselessly musing, venturing, throwing, seeking the spheres to connect them,
Till the bridge you will need be form'd, till the ductile¹ anchor hold,
Till the gossamer thread you fling catch somewhere, O my soul.   10

---

1. **ductile** (duk' t'l): that which can be stretched, drawn, or hammered thin without breaking.

Getting at Meaning

1. What behavior does Whitman observe in the spider?

2. What characteristics and actions of the spider does Whitman attribute to his own soul in the second stanza?

Developing Skills in Reading Literature

1. **Analogy.** The two stanzas of this poem develop an analogy between Whitman's soul and the spider. Of the spider, Whitman writes, ". . . on a little promontory it stood isolated." Where is Whitman's soul located? What activity does the soul engage in, analogous to the spider's spinning its threads? What does a spider eventually achieve through its efforts? According-ing to the analogy, what does the soul eventually achieve?

2. **Diction.** The diction of this poem does a great deal to establish tone and meaning and to build the central analogy. What do the words *noiseless* and *patient* imply about the spider's place in the universe? How do the words *vacant* and *vast* reinforce this impression? Why is the word *filament* repeated three times?

Notice the frequent use of present participles in the poem, especially in the second stanza. What do these verb forms imply about the soul's activity? What is *gossamer*? Why does Whitman use this word to describe the soul's thread that catches somewhere? Why does the poem end with the repetition of the phrase "O my soul"?

When I Heard the Learn'd Astronomer

When I heard the learn'd astronomer,
When the proofs, the figures, were ranged in columns before me,
When I was shown the charts and diagrams, to add, divide, and measure them,
When I sitting heard the astronomer where he lectured with much applause in the
    lecture-room,
How soon unaccountable I became tired and sick,   5
Till rising and gliding out I wander'd off by myself,
In the mystical moist night-air, and from time to time,
Look'd up in perfect silence at the stars.

Getting at Meaning

1. What is the astronomer explaining in the first four lines? What grammatical construction suggests that the main point of the poem is not in these lines?

2. Describe Whitman's response to the astronomer. Explain the meaning of line 5.

Developing Skills in Reading Literature

1. **Diction.** The diction in this poem contributes significantly to its tone. Why does the description of the astronomer as "learn'd" turn out to be ironic? What do the nouns *proofs, figures, columns, charts, diagrams* and the verbs *add, divide,* and *measure* all bring to mind? What words serve as a contrast to these in the final three lines of the poem?

2. **Theme.** Explain Whitman's attitude toward science in this poem. Why does he speak of the night air as "mystical"? What does his "perfect silence" imply in the final line? Where does science fall short, according to the poet?

Developing Writing Skills

Developing an Argument. In a well constructed paragraph endorse or refute the view of science that Whitman presents in this poem. Use examples drawn from your personal experience and from the world around you to support your position.

from **Song of Myself**

1

I celebrate myself, and sing myself,
And what I assume you shall assume,
For every atom belonging to me as good belongs to you.

I loaf and invite my soul,
I lean and loaf at my ease observing a spear of summer grass.   5

My tongue, every atom of my blood, form'd from this soil, this air,
Born here of parents born here from parents the same, and their parents the
    same,
I, now thirty-seven years old in perfect health begin,
Hoping to cease not till death.

Creeds and schools in abeyance,[1]   10
Retiring back a while sufficed at what they are, but never forgotten,
I harbor for good or bad, I permit to speak at every hazard,
Nature without check with original energy. . . .

6

A child said *What is the grass?* fetching it to me with full hands;
How could I answer the child? I do not know what it is any more than he.

I guess it must be the flag of my disposition, out of hopeful green stuff woven.

Or I guess it is the handkerchief of the Lord,
A scented gift and remembrancer designedly dropt,
Bearing the owner's name someway in the corners, that we may see and remark,   5
    and say *Whose?*

Or I guess the grass is itself a child, the produced babe of the vegetation.

Or I guess it is a uniform hieroglyphic,[2]
And it means, Sprouting alike in broad zones and narrow zones,
Growing among black folks as among white,   10
Kanuck, Tuckahoe, Congressman, Cuff, I give them the same, I receive them the
    same.

---

1. **abeyance** (ə bā' əns): temporary suspension.
2. **hieroglyphic** (hī' ər ə glif' ik): a picture or symbol representing a word.

And now it seems to me the beautiful uncut hair of graves.

Tenderly will I use you curling grass,
It may be you transpire from the breasts of young men,
It may be if I had known them I would have loved them,   15
It may be you are from old people, or offspring taken soon out of their
    mothers' laps,
And here you are the mothers' laps.

This grass is very dark to be from the white heads of old mothers,
Darker than the colorless beards of old men,
Dark to come from under the faint red roofs of mouths.   20

O I perceive after all so many uttering tongues,
And I perceive they do not come from the roofs of mouths for nothing.

I wish I could translate the hints about the dead young men and women,
And the hints about old men and mothers, and the offspring taken soon out of
    their laps.

What do you think has become of the young and old men?   25
And what do you think has become of the women and children?

They are alive and well somewhere,
The smallest sprout shows there is really no death,
And if ever there was it led forward life, and does not wait at the end to arrest it,
And ceas'd the moment life appear'd.   30

All goes onward and outward, nothing collapses,
And to die is different from what any one supposed, and luckier.

Getting at Meaning

1. In a literal reading of the first three lines of section 1, Whitman might be accused of conceit. When he says, "I celebrate myself, and sing myself," what broader meaning do his words carry?

2. What is Whitman's attitude toward "creeds and schools"? What exactly does he mean by "creeds and schools"?

3. Explain Whitman's poetic purpose, as he voices it in section 1.

4. In section 6 Whitman tries to answer the central question "What is the grass?" Paraphrase the possible definitions he presents in lines 3–11.

5. Comment on how Whitman views the grass in lines 14–20. What does he see in the grass?

6. In lines 25 and 26 Whitman wonders what becomes of people after death. What is his answer?

Developing Skills in Reading Literature

1. **Free Verse.** "Song of Myself" is Whitman's earliest and in some ways most original free verse statement. Why is free verse so suitable to Whitman's poetic purpose, as expressed in section 1? Why are his free, sprawling lines suitable to the statement about the life cycle Whitman makes in section 6?

2. **Theme.** What is the view of life that Whitman projects in the line, "For every atom belonging to me as good belongs to you"? What view of nature does he present in "Song of Myself"? Why is he able to conclude, "The smallest sprout shows there is really no death"? Explain his conclusion that ". . . to die is different from what any one supposed, and luckier."

3. **Tone.** Analyze what makes Whitman's tone so buoyant and optimistic in "Song of Myself." What

words, lines, and phrases stand out as particularly hopeful and energetic? What is courageous about the poet's approach to life and to art? What is imaginative about his approach?

4. **Rhythm.** Read the sections of "Song of Myself" aloud. Notice how rhythmic and rigorous they are. Where does Whitman use parallel structure to give his lines a regular rhythm? Where does he use repetends to achieve the same purpose?

5. **Title.** Grass generally is described as having "blades," emphasizing its sword-like structure. Whitman published "Song of Myself" in a volume that he chose to title *Leaves of Grass*.

What denotative meaning of the word *leaves* makes it appropriate for a book title? Based on Whitman's views about life in the two sections you have read from "Song of Myself," why did he choose the metaphor of grass for his poems? What are some of the implications of this metaphor?

Developing Vocabulary

Greek Roots. The root *hiero-*, meaning "sacred or holy," comes from the Greek word *hieros* of the same meaning. *Hieroglyphic*, a word Whitman uses, combines *hiero-* with the root *gluphē*, meaning "carving or engraving," to arrive at the meaning "a picture or symbol with a hidden or sacred meaning."

The words below all build on the root *hiero-*. After you have looked up each word in a dictionary, write its meaning. In each word what is combined with the Greek root *hiero-* to create the meaning of the word?

hierarchy   hierology
hieratic   hierophant
hierocracy

The Short Story

AMERICAN GOTHIC, 1930. *Grant Wood.*
Courtesy of The Art Institute of Chicago.

Bret Harte

1836–1902

Bret Harte, one of the best of the local-color writers, re-created life on the Western frontier for Eastern and European readers. Harte was born in Albany, New York, on August 25, 1836. He did not move to the West until 1854, when he went with his widowed mother to California. He stayed there for seventeen years, marrying a girl from San Francisco and settling in that city. His experiences in California provided the raw material for many of his later stories. He taught school, prospected for gold, and rode shotgun for a Wells Fargo Express stagecoach; he was a typesetter, and later a writer and editor for the *Californian*. In 1864 Harte was appointed Secretary of the U.S. Mint in San Francisco and became Professor of Literature at the University of California. In 1868 he became the first editor of the *Overland Monthly*, the magazine for which he wrote the stories that made him enormously successful: "The Luck of Roaring Camp" and "The Outcasts of Poker Flat." The humorous poem "Plain Language from Truthful James" also appeared in this magazine. Harte's collected stories, published in 1870, brought him great acclaim both in America and in England.

In 1871 Harte left the West for good, going to Boston to accept a position with the *Atlantic Monthly*. In leaving the West, he left behind the surroundings that had inspired his best work. His later work largely imitates his earlier more successful work, and he admitted late in life that: "I grind out the old tunes on the old organ, and gather up the coppers." In 1878 Harte went with his family to Europe, where he served in the American diplomatic corps in Germany and Scotland until 1885. Back in London he wrote and published a number of unsuccessful books, so that his last years were clouded with worries over failing health and lack of funds. He died in London on May 5, 1902.

Harte is not considered a major American writer, but the memorable characters and strong sense of time and place in his tales paved the way for the literary realists who followed him.

The Outcasts of Poker Flat

As Mr. John Oakhurst, gambler, stepped into the main street of Poker Flat on the morning of the twenty-third of November, 1850, he was conscious of a change in its moral atmosphere since the preceding night. Two or three men, conversing earnestly together, ceased as he approached, and exchanged significant glances. There was a Sabbath lull in the air, which, in a settlement unused to Sabbath influences, looked ominous.

Mr. Oakhurst's calm, handsome face betrayed small concern in these indications. Whether he was conscious of any predisposing cause, was another question. "I reckon they're after somebody," he reflected; "likely it's me." He returned to his pocket the handkerchief with which he had been whipping away the red dust of Poker Flat from his neat boots, and quietly discharged his mind of any further conjecture.

In point of fact, Poker Flat was "after somebody." It had lately suffered the loss of several thousand dollars, two valuable horses, and a prominent citizen. It was experiencing a spasm of virtuous reaction, quite as lawless and ungovernable as any of the acts that had provoked it. A secret committee had determined to rid the town of all improper persons. This was done permanently in regard of two men who were then hanging from the boughs of a sycamore in the gulch, and temporarily in the banishment of certain other objectionable characters. I regret to say that some of these were ladies. It is but due to the sex, however, to state that their impropriety was professional, and it was only in such easily established standards of evil that Poker Flat ventured to sit in judgment.

Mr. Oakhurst was right in supposing that he was included in this category. A few of the committee had urged hanging him as a possible example, and a sure method of reimbursing themselves from his pockets of the sums he had won from them. "It's agin justice," said Jim Wheeler, "to let this yer young man from Roaring Camp—an entire stranger—carry away our money." But a crude sentiment of equity residing in the breasts of those who had been fortunate enough to win from Mr. Oakhurst overruled this narrower local prejudice.

Mr. Oakhurst received his sentence with philosophic calmness, none the less coolly that he was aware of the hesitation of his judges. He was too much of a gambler not to accept Fate. With him life was at best an uncertain game, and he recognized the usual percentage in favor of the dealer.

A body of armed men accompanied the deported wickedness of Poker Flat to the outskirts of the settlement. Besides Mr. Oakhurst, who was known to be a coolly desperate man, and for whose intimidation the armed escort was intended, the expatriated party consisted of a young woman familiarly known as "The Duchess"; another, who had won the title of "Mother Shipton"; and "Uncle Billy," a suspected sluice[1]-robber and confirmed drunkard. The cavalcade provoked no comments from the spectators, nor was any word uttered by the escort. Only when the gulch which marked the uttermost limit of Poker Flat was reached, the leader spoke briefly and to the point. The exiles were forbidden to return at the peril of their lives.

As the escort disappeared, their pent-up feelings found vent in a few hysterical tears from the Duchess, some bad language from Mother Shipton, and a Parthian volley[2] of

---

1. **sluice:** a long, inclined trough, usually on the ground, through which water is run to catch particles of gold.
2. **Parthian volley:** hostile gesture or remark made in leaving: Parthian cavalrymen shot at the enemy while retreating or while pretending to retreat.

expletives[3] from Uncle Billy. The philosophic Oakhurst alone remained silent. He listened calmly to Mother Shipton's desire to cut somebody's heart out, to the repeated statements of the Duchess that she would die in the road, and to the alarming oaths that seemed to be bumped out of Uncle Billy as he rode forward. With the easy good-humor characteristic of his class, he insisted upon exchanging his own riding-horse, "Five Spot," for the sorry mule which the Duchess rode. But even this act did not draw the party into any closer sympathy. The young woman readjusted her somewhat draggled plumes with a feeble, faded coquetry; Mother Shipton eyed the possessor of "Five Spot" with malevolence,[4] and Uncle Billy included the whole party in one sweeping anathema.[5]

The road to Sandy Bar—a camp that, not having as yet experienced the regenerating influences of Poker Flat, consequently seemed to offer some invitation to the emigrants—lay over a steep mountain range. It was distant a day's severe travel. In that advanced season, the party soon passed out of the moist, temperate regions of the foot-hills into the dry, cold, bracing air of the Sierras. The trail was narrow and difficult. At noon the Duchess, rolling out of her saddle upon the ground, declared her intention of going no farther, and the party halted.

The spot was singularly wild and impressive. A wooded amphitheatre, surrounded on three sides by precipitous cliffs of naked granite, sloped gently toward the crest of another precipice that overlooked the valley. It was, undoubtedly, the most suitable spot for a camp, had camping been advisable. But Mr. Oakhurst knew that scarcely half the journey to Sandy Bar was accomplished, and the party were not equipped or provisioned for delay. This fact he pointed out to his companions curtly, with a philosophic commentary on the folly of "throwing up their hand before the game was played out." But they were furnished with liquor, which in this emergency stood them in place of food, fuel, rest, and prescience.[6] In spite of his remonstrances, it was not long before they were more or less under its influence. Uncle Billy passed rapidly from a bellicose state into one of stupor, the Duchess became maudlin,[7] and Mother Shipton snored. Mr. Oakhurst alone remained erect, leaning against a rock, calmly surveying them.

Mr. Oakhurst did not drink. It interfered with a profession which required coolness, impassiveness, and presence of mind, and, in his own language, he "couldn't afford it." As he gazed at his recumbent fellow-exiles, the loneliness begotten of his pariah[8]-trade, his habits of life, his very vices, for the first time seriously oppressed him. He bestirred himself in dusting his black clothes, washing his hands and face, and other acts characteristic of his studiously neat habits, and for a moment forgot his annoyance. The thought of deserting his weaker and more pitiable companions never perhaps occurred to him. Yet he could not help feeling the want of that excitement which, singularly enough, was most conducive to that calm equanimity for which he was notorious. He looked at the gloomy walls that rose a thousand feet sheer above the circling pines around him; at the sky, ominously clouded; at the valley below, already deepening into shadow. And, doing so, suddenly he heard his own name called.

A horseman slowly ascended the trail. In the fresh, open face of the newcomer Mr. Oakhurst recognized Tom Simson, otherwise known as "The Innocent" of Sandy Bar. He had met him some months before over a

---

3. **expletives** (eks' plə tivz): curses, profanity.
4. **malevolence** (mə lev' ə ləns): wishing harm to others.
5. **anathema** (ə nath' ə mə): a formal curse pronounced with religious solemnity.
6. **prescience** (prē' shē əns): apparent knowledge of things before they happen.
7. **maudlin** (môd' lin): foolishly sentimental.
8. **pariah** (pə rī' ə): one despised by others, originally a member of one of the lowest social castes in India.

"little game," and had, with perfect equanimity, won the entire fortune—amounting to some forty dollars—of that guileless youth. After the game was finished, Mr. Oakhurst drew the youthful speculator behind the door and thus addressed him: "Tommy, you're a good little man, but you can't gamble worth a cent. Don't try it over again." He then handed him his money back, pushed him gently from the room, and so made a devoted slave of Tom Simson.

There was a remembrance of this in his boyish and enthusiastic greeting of Mr. Oakhurst. He had started, he said, to go to Poker Flat to seek his fortune. "Alone?" No, not exactly alone; in fact (a giggle), he had run away with Piney Woods. Didn't Mr. Oakhurst remember Piney? She that used to wait on the table at the Temperance House? They had been engaged a long time, but old Jake Woods had objected, and so they had run away, and were going to Poker Flat to be married, and here they were. And they were tired out, and how lucky it was they had found a place to camp and company. All this the Innocent delivered rapidly, while Piney, a stout, comely[9] damsel of fifteen, emerged from behind the pine tree, where she had been blushing unseen, and rode to the side of her lover.

Mr. Oakhurst seldom troubled himself with sentiment, still less with propriety; but he had a vague idea that the situation was not fortunate. He retained, however, his presence of mind sufficiently to kick Uncle Billy, who was about to say something, and Uncle Billy was sober enough to recognize in Mr. Oakhurst's kick a superior power that would not bear trifling. He then endeavored to dissuade Tom Simson from delaying further, but in vain. He even pointed out the fact that there was no provision, nor means of making a camp. But, unluckily, the Innocent met this objection by assuring the party that he was provided with an extra mule loaded with provisions, and by the discovery of a rude attempt at a log-house near the trail. "Piney can stay with Mrs. Oakhurst," said the Innocent, pointing to the Duchess, "and I can shift for myself."

Nothing but Mr. Oakhurst's admonishing foot saved Uncle Billy from bursting into a roar of laughter. As it was, he felt compelled to retire up the cañon until he could recover his gravity. There he confided the joke to the tall pine-trees, with many slaps of his leg, contortions of his face, and the usual profanity. But when he returned to the party, he found them seated by a fire—for the air had grown strangely chill and the sky overcast— in apparently amicable conversation. Piney was actually talking in an impulsive, girlish fashion to the Duchess, who was listening with an interest and animation she had not shown for many days. The Innocent was holding forth, apparently with equal effect, to Mr. Oakhurst and Mother Shipton, who was actually relaxing into amiability. "Is this yer a d—d picnic?" said Uncle Billy, with inward scorn, as he surveyed the sylvan[10] group, the glancing firelight, and the tethered animals in the foreground. Suddenly an idea mingled with the alcoholic fumes that disturbed his brain. It was apparently of a jocular nature, for he felt impelled to slap his leg again and cram his fist into his mouth.

As the shadows crept slowly up the mountain, a slight breeze rocked the tops of the pine trees, and moaned through their long and gloomy aisles. The ruined cabin, patched and covered with pine boughs, was set apart for the ladies. As the lovers parted, they unaffectedly exchanged a kiss, so honest and sincere that it might have been heard above the swaying pines. The frail Duchess and the malevolent Mother Shipton were probably too stunned to remark upon this last evidence of simplicity, and so turned without a word to the hut. The fire was replenished, the men lay

9. **comely** (kum' lē): pleasant to look at, attractive.
10. **sylvan:** peaceful, contented; associated with the forest rather than with the town.

down before the door, and in a few minutes were asleep.

Mr. Oakhurst was a light sleeper. Toward morning he awoke benumbed and cold. As he stirred the dying fire, the wind, which was now blowing strongly, brought to his cheek that which caused the blood to leave it,— snow!

He started to his feet with the intention of awakening the sleepers, for there was no time to lose. But turning to where Uncle Billy had been lying, he found him gone. A suspicion leaped to his brain and a curse to his lips. He ran to the spot where the mules had been tethered; they were no longer there. The tracks were already rapidly disappearing in the snow.

The momentary excitement brought Mr. Oakhurst back to the fire with his usual calm. He did not waken the sleepers. The Innocent slumbered peacefully, with a smile on his good-humored, freckled face; the virgin Piney slept beside her frailer sisters as sweetly as though attended by celestial guardians, and Mr. Oakhurst, drawing his blanket over his shoulders, stroked his mustaches and waited for the dawn. It came slowly in a whirling mist of snow-flakes, that dazzled and confused the eye. What could be seen of the landscape appeared magically changed. He looked over the valley, and summed up the present and future in two words,—"snowed in!"

A careful inventory of the provisions, which, fortunately for the party, had been stored within the hut, and so escaped the felonious fingers of Uncle Billy, disclosed the fact that with care and prudence they might last ten days longer. "That is," said Mr. Oakhurst, *sotto voce*[11] to the Innocent, "if you're willing to board us. If you ain't—and perhaps you'd better not—you can wait till Uncle Billy gets back with provisions." For some occult[12] reason, Mr. Oakhurst could not bring himself to disclose Uncle Billy's rascality, and so offered the hypothesis that he had wandered from the camp and had accidentally stampeded the animals. He dropped a warning to the Duchess and Mother Shipton, who of course knew the facts of their associate's defection. "They'll find out the truth about us *all* when they find out anything," he added, significantly, "and there's no good frightening them now."

Tom Simson not only put all his worldly store at the disposal of Mr. Oakhurst, but seemed to enjoy the prospect of their enforced seclusion. "We'll have a good camp for a week, and then the snow'll melt, and we'll all go back together." The cheerful gayety of the young man, and Mr. Oakhurst's calm infected the others. The Innocent, with the aid of pine boughs, extemporized a thatch for the roofless cabin, and the Duchess directed Piney in the rearrangement of the interior with a taste and tact that opened the blue eyes of that provincial maiden to their fullest extent. "I reckon now you're used to fine things at Poker Flat," said Piney. The Duchess turned away sharply to conceal something that reddened her cheeks through its professional tint, and Mother Shipton requested Piney not to "chatter." But when Mr. Oakhurst returned from a weary search for the trail, he heard the sound of happy laughter echoed from the rocks. He stopped in some alarm, and his thoughts first naturally reverted to the whiskey, which he had prudently *cachéd*.[13] "And yet it don't somehow sound like whiskey," said the gambler. It was not until he caught sight of the blazing fire through the still-blinding storm and the group around it that he settled to the conviction that it was "square fun."

Whether Mr. Oakhurst had *cachéd* his cards with the whiskey as something de-

---

11. **sotto voce** (sät' ō vo' chē) *Italian:* in a low tone of voice, so as not to be overheard.
12. **occult** (ə kult'): known only to certain chosen persons, secret.
13. **cachéd** (ka shād'): from the French *cacher*, to hide or conceal.

barred the free access of the community, I cannot say. It was certain that, in Mother Shipton's words, he "didn't say cards once" during that evening. Haply the time was beguiled by an accordion, produced somewhat ostentatiously by Tom Simson from his pack. Notwithstanding some difficulties attending the manipulation of this instrument, Piney Woods managed to pluck several reluctant melodies from its keys, to an accompaniment by the Innocent on a pair of bone castinets.[14] But the crowning festivity of the evening was reached in a rude camp-meeting hymn, which the lovers, joining hands, sang with great earnestness and vociferation. I fear that a certain defiant tone and Covenanter's[15] swing to its chorus, rather than any devotional quality, caused it speedily to infect the others, who at last joined in the refrain:

I'm proud to live in the service of the Lord,
And I'm bound to die in His army.

The pines rocked, the storm eddied and whirled above the miserable group, and the flames of their altar leaped heavenward, as if in token of the snow.

At midnight the storm abated, the rolling clouds parted, and the stars glittered keenly above the sleeping camp. Mr. Oakhurst, whose professional habits had enabled him to live on the smallest possible amount of sleep, in dividing the watch with Tom Simson, somehow managed to take upon himself the greater part of that duty. He excused himself to the Innocent, by saying that he had "often been a week without sleep." "Doing what?" asked Tom. "Poker!" replied Oakhurst, sententiously;[16] "when a man gets a streak of luck, he don't get tired. The luck gives in first. Luck," continued the gambler, reflectively, "is a mighty queer thing. All you know about it for certain is that it's bound to change. And it's finding out when it's going to change that makes you. We've had a streak of bad luck since we left Poker Flat—you come along, and

slap you get into it, too. If you can hold your cards right along you're all right. For," added the gambler, with cheerful irrelevance,

I'm proud to live in the service of the Lord,
And I'm bound to die in His army.

The third day came, and the sun, looking through the white-curtained valley, saw the outcasts divide their slowly decreasing store of provisions for the morning meal. It was one of the peculiarities of that mountain climate that its rays diffused a kindly warmth over the wintry landscape, as if in regretful commiseration of the past. But it revealed drift on drift of snow piled high around the hut—a hopeless, uncharted, trackless sea of white lying below the rocky shores to which the castaways still clung. Through the marvelously clear air the smoke of the pastoral village of Poker Flat rose miles away. Mother Shipton saw it, and from a remote pinnacle of her rocky fastness, hurled in that direction a final malediction. It was her last vituperative attempt, and perhaps for that reason was invested with a certain degree of sublimity. It did her good, she privately informed the Duchess. "Just you go out there and cuss, and see." She then set herself to the task of amusing "the child," as she and the Duchess were pleased to call Piney. Piney was no chicken, but it was a soothing and original theory of the pair thus to account for the fact that she didn't swear and wasn't improper.

When night crept up again through the gorges, the reedy notes of the accordion rose and fell in fitful spasms and long-drawn gasps by the flickering campfire. But music failed to fill entirely the aching void left by insufficient

---

14. **castinets** (castanets: kas′ tə nets′): a pair of small, hollowed pieces of hard material held in the hand and clicked together in time to music.

15. **Covenanter:** a member of the Reformed Presbyterian Church.

16. **sententiously** (sen ten′ shəs lē): expressing much in a few words.

food, and a new diversion was proposed by Piney—storytelling. Neither Mr. Oakhurst nor his female companions caring to relate their personal experiences, this plan would have failed, too, but for the Innocent. Some months before, he had chanced upon a stray copy of Mr. Pope's ingenious translation of the *Iliad*.[17] He now proposed to narrate the principal incidents of that poem—having thoroughly mastered the argument and fairly forgotten the words—in the current vernacular of Sandy Bar. And so for the rest of that night the Homeric demigods again walked the earth. Trojan bully and wily Greek wrestled in the winds, and the great pines in the cañon seemed to bow to the wrath of the son of Peleus.[18] Mr. Oakhurst listened with quiet satisfaction. Most especially was he interested in the fate of "Ashheels," as the Innocent persisted in denominating the "swift-footed Achilles."

So with small food and much of Homer and the accordion, a week passed over the heads of the outcasts. The sun again forsook them, and again from leaden skies the snowflakes were sifted over the land. Day by day closer around them drew the snowy circle, until at last they looked from their prison over drifted walls of dazzling white that towered twenty feet above their heads. It became more and more difficult to replenish their fires, even from the fallen trees beside them, now half hidden in the drifts. And yet no one complained. The lovers turned from the dreary prospect and looked into each other's eyes, and were happy. Mr. Oakhurst settled himself coolly to the losing game before him. The Duchess, more cheerful than she had been, assumed the care of Piney. Only Mother Shipton—once the strongest of the party—seemed to sicken and fade. At midnight on the tenth day she called Oakhurst to her side. "I'm going," she said, in a voice of querulous weakness, "but don't say anything about it. Don't waken the kids. Take the bundle from under my head and open it." Mr. Oakhurst did so. It contained Mother

Shipton's rations for the last week, untouched. "Give 'em to the child," she said, pointing to the sleeping Piney. "You've starved yourself," said the gambler. "That's what they call it," said the woman, querulously, as she lay down again, and, turning her face to the wall, passed quietly away.

The accordion and the bones were put aside that day, and Homer was forgotten. When the body of Mother Shipton had been committed to the snow, Mr. Oakhurst took the Innocent aside, and showed him a pair of snowshoes, which he had fashioned from the old packsaddle. "There's one chance in a hundred to save her yet," he said, pointing to Piney; "but it's there," he added, pointing toward Poker Flat. "If you can reach there in two days she's safe." "And you?" asked Tom Simson. "I'll stay here," was the curt reply.

The lovers parted with a long embrace. "You are not going, too?" said the Duchess, as she saw Mr. Oakhurst apparently waiting to accompany him. "As far as the cañon," he replied. He turned suddenly, kissed the Duchess, leaving her pallid face aflame, and her trembling limbs rigid with amazement.

Night came, but not Mr. Oakhurst. It brought the storm again and the whirling snow. Then the Duchess, feeding the fire, found that someone had quietly piled beside the hut enough fuel to last a few days longer. The tears rose to her eyes, but she hid them from Piney.

The women slept but little. In the morning, looking into each other's faces, they read their fate. Neither spoke; but Piney, accepting the position of the stronger, drew near and placed her arm around the Duchess's waist. They

---

17. ***Iliad*** (il' ē əd): a classical Greek epic poem in which Homer narrates events near the end of the Trojan War, starting with the quarrel of Achilles and Agamemnon, and ending with the burial of Hector. Alexander Pope (English poet, 1688–1744) translated the *Iliad* into English.

18. **Trojan bully . . . wily Greek . . . son of Peleus:** Hector . . . Odysseus . . . Achilles.

kept this attitude for the rest of the day. That night the storm reached its greatest fury, and, rending asunder the protecting pines, invaded the very hut.

Toward morning they found themselves unable to feed the fire, which gradually died away. As the embers slowly blackened, the Duchess crept closer to Piney, and broke the silence of many hours: "Piney, can you pray?" "No, dear," said Piney, simply. The Duchess, without knowing exactly why, felt relieved, and, putting her head upon Piney's shoulder, spoke no more. And so reclining, the younger and purer pillowing the head of her soiled sister upon her virgin breast, they fell asleep.

The wind lulled as if it feared to waken them. Feathery drifts of snow, shaken from the long pine boughs, flew like white-winged birds, and settled about them as they slept. The moon through the rifted clouds looked down upon what had been the camp. But all human stain, all trace of earthly travail, was hidden beneath the spotless mantle mercifully flung from above.

They slept all that day and the next, nor did they waken when voices and footsteps broke the silence of the camp. And when pitying fingers brushed the snow from their wan faces, you could scarcely have told from the equal peace that dwelt upon them, which was she that had sinned. Even the law of Poker Flat recognized this, and turned away, leaving them still locked in each other's arms.

But at the head of the gulch, on one of the largest pine trees, they found the deuce of clubs pinned to the bark with a bowie-knife.[19] It bore the following, written in pencil, in a firm hand:

> BENEATH THIS TREE
> LIES THE BODY
> OF
> JOHN OAKHURST,
> WHO STRUCK A STREAK OF BAD LUCK
> ON THE 23RD OF NOVEMBER, 1850,
> AND
> HANDED IN HIS CHECKS
> ON THE 7th DECEMBER, 1850.

And pulseless and cold, with a Derringer[20] by his side and a bullet in his heart, though still calm as in life, beneath the snow lay he who was at once the strongest and yet the weakest of the outcasts of Poker Flat.

---

19. **bowie-knife** (bōo' ē): a long hunting knife with a single edge, carried in a sheath; named after Col. James Bowie, American frontiersman.
20. **Derringer** (der' in jər): a small, short-barreled pistol of large caliber; named after Henry Derringer, nineteenth-century gunsmith.

Getting at Meaning

1. What makes John Oakhurst both "the strongest and yet the weakest of the outcasts of Poker Flat"? Explain how he shows both his strength and his weakness.

2. What do you think is Oakhurst's motive for killing himself—pride or hopelessness?

3. How do Piney Woods and Tom Simson contrast with other members of the party? How do Piney and Tom view the others?

4. Why do Oakhurst and the others avoid telling the young couple the truth about why they were not in Poker Flat? Are they acting out of kindness or pride?

5. How do Piney and Tom affect the behavior of the others? Find examples of changes in the characters' behavior.

6. How do the outcasts prove their worth during the crisis?

Developing Skills in Reading Literature

1. **Irony.** Dramatic irony occurs when characters in a story are unaware of facts known to the reader. One example of dramatic irony in "The Outcasts of Poker Flat" is Piney Woods's reference to the Duchess as "Mrs. Oakhurst." Point out three other examples of dramatic irony in the story.

An ironic situation occurs when something other than what is expected occurs. The basic irony of the story is that characters banished for being evil turn out to be noble. What are three other ironic situations?

2. **Conflict.** A conflict is a struggle between opposing forces, often an individual against society or nature, or a struggle within an individual. Several conflicts advance the plot of ''The Outcasts of Poker Flat.'' A conflict with society sends Oakhurst and his companions into exile. Explain how the characters also battle nature. Which side triumphs? How does John Oakhurst's internal conflict lead to his death?

3. **Plot: Dénouement.** The dénouement is the final unraveling or outcome of a plot, the structure of events in dramatic or narrative literature. The ending of ''The Outcasts of Poker Flat'' is peaceful and calm, with Piney and the Duchess buried under a blanket of snow and the dead Oakhurst ''calm as in life.'' Why do you think that Harte strives for this calm, peaceful mood?

4. **Foil.** In what way does Uncle Billy function as a foil, or contrasting character, in the story? How is Piney a foil for the Duchess and Tom for Oakhurst?

5. **Theme.** Consider how appearances prove to be inaccurate reflections of reality in the story. How does Harte comment on humanity by the way he portrays both the outcasts and the residents of Poker Flat?

6. **Allusion.** Harte refers to Oakhurst's interest in Achilles, a Greek hero killed because of a weak spot in his heel. Why does Harte link Oakhurst with Achilles? Explain the connection.

7. **Local Color.** Local-color writing, popular in the late 1800's, exploits the speech, dress, mannerisms, ideas, and landscape of a certain region. Local-color stories tend to be sentimental or humorous in plot and often present eccentric characters. What characteristics of local-color writing do you find in ''The Outcasts of Poker Flat''?

8. **Dialect.** Dialect, the speech of a certain region, is marked by peculiarities of vocabulary, grammar, and pronunciation. The words *cuss*, *agin*, *it don't*, and *square fun* are examples of dialect in the story. Find four other examples. What is the function of dialect in this story?

Developing Writing Skills

1. **Combining Narration and Exposition.** In a composition, narrate an incident in which you learned that appearances sometimes can be deceiving. Conclude the composition with a paragraph explaining the insight you gained from the incident.

2. **Analyzing Characters.** Decide whether the characters of ''The Outcasts of Poker Flat'' seem realistic or sentimental and stereotyped. Support your evaluation with logical arguments, as well as specific incidents and descriptions from the story.

Main Street, Manhattan, Nevada, 1890. Brown Brothers.

Mark Twain

1835–1910

Samuel Langhorne Clemens took as his pen name the term "mark twain," from the river boatman's cry meaning "there's a two-fathom sounding," or "the water is just deep enough to navigate safely." Clemens's pseudonym is a testament to the literary inspiration that came from the Mississippi River and its environs. Mark Twain has been called the greatest of American humorists and the "Lincoln of our literature." Ernest Hemingway said of *Huckleberry Finn*, Twain's finest novel, that ". . . it's the best book we've had. . . . There was nothing before. There has been nothing so good since."

For the first twenty-five years of his life, Samuel Clemens lived on and near the Mississippi River. He was born in Florida, Missouri, on November 30, 1835, but the family soon moved to Hannibal, Missouri, on the banks of the river that was in those days the lifeline of the nation's trade. Clemens's father died in 1847 after repeated business failures, and the twelve-year-old boy left school to be apprenticed to a printer and next to work on his brother Orion's newspaper. When he was twenty-one Clemens set out for New Orleans, the first stage of a proposed journey to South America. Once on the Mississippi riverboat, however, he persuaded Horace Bixby, a famous steamboat pilot, to take him on as an apprentice. He spent eighteen months "learning" the twelve hundred miles of the Mississippi and then worked four years as a river pilot. His later book *Life on the Mississippi* (1883) recalls these romantic years.

When the Civil War curtailed the traffic on the Mississippi, Clemens served briefly in the Confederate Army until his brother Orion, a Union man who had campaigned for Lincoln, was appointed Secretary of the Nevada Territory and persuaded Samuel to accompany him as an assistant. So, at the age of twenty-five Clemens went West. The journey by stagecoach over the Rockies was depicted humorously in *Roughing It* (1872). After subsequent misadventures in both politics and mining, he began writing for a Virginia City, Nevada, newspaper, and writing and lecturing became his career. The publication of the short story "The Celebrated Jumping Frog of Calaveras County" in the New York *Saturday Press* in 1865 attracted favorable attention in the East. In his public speaking, Clemens discovered his real talent for entertaining an audience as a humorist, presenting his witty remarks with an impeccable sense of timing. At this period in his career Clemens adopted the pseudonym "Mark Twain." Twain went East in 1866.

In 1870 he married Olivia Langdon and soon moved to Hartford, Connecticut, where he built a huge "Steamboat Gothic" mansion reminiscent of the great Mississippi River steamboats he had piloted.

Twain then turned back to the great river days to write *The Adventures of Tom Sawyer* (1876) and *The Adventures of Huckleberry Finn* (1884). These books, recognized as the greatest of his novels, combine the marvelous simplicity of the boy-hero's point of view with the adult author's perspective of the realities of river life. At this point in his life and work, Twain's humorous tolerance balanced his awareness of the frailties of the human race. His later works, however, are increasingly critical and satirical, culminating in the bitterness, disillusionment, and pessimism of his last books, "The Man That Corrupted Hadleyburg" (1900) and *The Mysterious Stranger* (published posthumously in 1916). Twain's personal life in late years was beset by troubles. He went bankrupt through bad investments, largely in publishing, so he had to work exhaustively writing and lecturing to repay his losses and regain his fortune. The deaths of his wife and two daughters left him lonely and weary of the world.

When Samuel Clemens was born in 1835, Halley's Comet was seen in the sky. When the great comet was seen again, on April 21, 1910, it coincided with the death of the man who, in the intervening years, had become one of the greatest and most famous American authors.

MARK TWAIN. *J. Carroll Beckwith.*
Mark Twain Memorial, Hartford, Connecticut.

from **The Adventures of Huckleberry Finn**

Huck's Stay with the Grangerfords

It was a mighty nice family, and a mighty nice house, too. I hadn't seen no house out in the country before that was so nice and had so much style. It didn't have an iron latch on the front door, nor a wooden one with a buckskin string, but a brass knob to turn, the same as houses in town. There warn't no bed in the parlor, nor a sign of a bed; but heaps of parlors in towns has beds in them. There was a big fireplace that was bricked on the bottom, and the bricks was kept clean and red by pouring water on them and scrubbing them with another brick; sometimes they wash them over with red water-paint that they call Spanish-brown, same as they do in town. They had big brass dog-irons[1] that could hold up a saw-log. There was a clock on the middle of the mantelpiece, with a picture of a town painted on the bottom half of the glass front, and a round place in the middle of it for the sun, and you could see the pendulum swinging behind it. It was beautiful to hear that clock tick; and sometimes when one of these peddlers had been along and scoured her up and got her in good shape, she would start in and strike a hundred and fifty before she got tuckered out. They wouldn't took any money for her.

Well, there was a big outlandish parrot on each side of the clock, made out of something like chalk, and painted up gaudy. By one of the parrots was a cat made of crockery, and a crockery dog by the other; and when you pressed down on them they squeaked, but didn't open their mouths nor look different nor interested. They squeaked through underneath. There was a couple of big wild-turkey-wing fans spread out behind those things. On the table in the middle of the room was a kind of a lovely crockery basket that had apples and oranges and peaches and grapes piled up in it, which was much redder and yellower and prettier than real ones is, but they warn't real because you could see where pieces had got chipped off and showed the white chalk, or whatever it was, underneath.

This table had a cover made out of a beautiful oilcloth, with a red and blue spread-eagle painted on it, and a painted border all around. It come all the way from Philadelphia, they said. There was some books, too, piled up perfectly exact, on each corner of the table. One was a big family Bible full of pictures. One was *Pilgrim's Progress*,[2] about a man that left his family, it didn't say why. I read considerable in it now and then. The statements was interesting, but tough. Another was *Friendship's Offering*, full of beautiful stuff and poetry; but I didn't read the poetry. Another was Henry Clay's[3] Speeches, and another was Dr. Gunn's *Family Medicine*, which told you all about what to do if a body was sick or dead. There was a hymn-book, and a lot of other books. And there was nice split-bottom[4] chairs, and perfectly sound, too —not bagged down in the middle and busted, like an old basket.

They had pictures hung on the walls— mainly Washingtons and Lafayettes, and bat-

---

1. **dog-irons:** firedogs or andirons.
2. In *Pilgrim's Progress* by John Bunyan (1628–1688) the protagonist, Christian, makes an allegorical journey toward moral perfection and the Celestial City.
3. Henry Clay (1777–1852) and John Calhoun (1782–1850) held a series of debates on the issue of states rights.
4. **split-bottom:** chair seats woven of thin strips of wood.

tles, and Highland Marys,[5] and one called "Signing the Declaration." There was some that they called crayons, which one of the daughters which was dead made her own self when she was only fifteen years old. They was different from any pictures I ever see before—blacker, mostly, than is common. One was a woman in slim black dress, belted small under the armpits, with bulges like a cabbage in the middle of the sleeves, and a large black scoop-shovel bonnet with a black veil, and white slim ankles crossed about with black tape, and very wee black slippers, like a chisel, and she was leaning pensive on a tombstone on her right elbow, under a weeping willow, and her other hand hanging down her side holding a white handkerchief and a reticule,[6] and underneath the picture it said "Shall I Never See Thee More Alas." Another one was a young lady with her hair all combed up straight to the top of her head, and knotted there in front of a comb like a chair-back, and she was crying into a handkerchief and had a dead bird laying on its back in her other hand with its heels up, and underneath the picture it said "I Shall Never Hear Thy Sweet Chirrup More Alas." There was one where a young lady was at a window looking up at the moon, and tears running down her cheeks; and she had an open letter in one hand with black sealing-wax showing on one edge of it and she was mashing a locket with a chain to it against her mouth, and underneath the picture it said "And Art Thou Gone Yes Thou Art Gone Alas." These was all nice pictures, I reckon, but I didn't somehow seem to take to them, because if ever I was down a little they always gave me the fan-tods.[7] Everybody was sorry she died, because she had laid out a lot more of these pictures to do, and a body could see by what she had done what they had lost. But I reckoned that with her disposition she was having a better time in the graveyard. She was at work on what they said was her greatest picture when she took sick, and every day and every night it was her prayer to be allowed to live till she got it done, but she never got the chance. It was a picture of a young woman in a long white gown, standing on the rail of a bridge all ready to jump off, with her hair all down her back, and looking up to the moon, with the tears running down her face, and she had two arms folded across her breast, and two arms stretched out in front, and two more reaching up toward the moon—and the idea was to see which pair would look best and then scratch out all the other arms; but as I was saying, she died before she got her mind made up, and now they kept this picture over the head of the bed in her room, and every time her birthday come they hung flowers on it. Other times it was hid with a little curtain. The young woman in the picture had a kind of a nice sweet face, but there was so many arms it made her look too spidery, seemed to me.

This young girl kept a scrapbook when she was alive, and used to paste obituaries and accidents and cases of patient suffering in it out of the *Presbyterian Observer*, and write poetry after them out of her own head. It was very good poetry. This is what she wrote about a boy by the name of Stephen Dowling Bots that fell down a well and was drownded:

ODE TO STEPHEN DOWLING BOTS, DEC'D.

And did young Stephen sicken,
　And did young Stephen die?
And did the sad hearts thicken,
　And did the mourners cry?

No; such was not the fate of
　Young Stephen Dowling Bots;
Though sad hearts round him thickened,
　'Twas not from sickness' shots.

---

5. **Highland Marys:** Mary Campbell was the sweetheart of Scottish poet, Robert Burns, and the subject of some of his poems.
6. **reticule** (ret' ə kyo͞ol'): a woman's drawstring handbag.
7. **fan-tods:** a state of fidget, stomach-ache, and sometimes also of nightmarish visions as from delirium tremens.

No whooping-cough did rack his frame,
　Nor measles drear with spots;
Not these impaired the sacred name
　Of Stephen Dowling Bots.

Despised love struck not with woe
　That head of curly knots,
Nor stomach troubles laid him low,
　Young Stephen Dowling Bots.

O no. Then list with tearful eye,
　Whilst I his fate do tell.
His soul did from this cold world fly
　By falling down a well.

They got him out and emptied him;
　Alas it was too late;
His spirit was gone for to sport aloft
　In the realms of the good and great.

If Emmeline Grangerford could make poetry like that before she was fourteen, there ain't no telling what she could 'a' done by and by. Buck said she could rattle off poetry like nothing. She didn't ever have to stop to think. He said she would slap down a line, and if she couldn't find anything to rhyme with it would just scratch it out and slap down another one, and go ahead. She warn't particular; she could write about anything you choose to give her to write about just so it was sadful. Every time a man died, or a woman died, or a child died, she would be on hand with her "tribute" before he was cold. She called them tributes. The neighbors said it was the doctor first, then Emmeline, then the undertaker—the undertaker never got in ahead of Emmeline but once, and then she hung fire on a rhyme for the dead person's name, which was Whistler. She warn't ever the same after that; she never complained, but she kinder pined away and did not live long. Poor thing, many's the time I made myself go up to the little room that used to be hers and get out her poor old scrapbook and read in it when her pictures had been aggra-

vating me and I had soured on her a little. I liked all that family, dead ones and all, and warn't going to let anything come between us. Poor Emmeline made poetry about all the dead people when she was alive, and it didn't seem right that there warn't nobody to make some about her now she was gone; so I tried to sweat out a verse or two myself, but I couldn't seem to make it go somehow. They kept Emmeline's room trim and nice, and all the things fixed in it just the way she liked to have them when she was alive, and nobody ever slept there. The old lady took care of the room herself, . . . and she sewed there a good deal and read her Bible there mostly.

Well, as I was saying about the parlor, there was beautiful curtains on the windows; white, with pictures painted on them of castles with vines all down the walls, and cattle coming down to drink. There was a little old piano, too, that had tin pans in it, I reckon, and nothing was ever so lovely as to hear the young ladies sing "The Last Link Is Broken" and play "The Battle of Prague" on it. The walls of all the rooms was plastered, and most had carpets on the floors, and the whole house was whitewashed on the outside.

It was a double house, and the big open place betwixt them was roofed and floored, and sometimes the table was set there in the middle of the day, and it was a cool, comfortable place. Nothing couldn't be better. And warn't the cooking good, and just bushels of it too! . . .

A bitter feud continues between the Grangerfords and their neighbors, the Shepherdsons, and leads to bloodshed. Huck and Jim are reunited and return to the river, where they avoid detection by hiding by day and floating on the river by night. In the following lyric passage, Huck describes the peace and tranquillity of life on the river, his refuge from the cruelty of society on land.

Two or three days and nights went by; I reckon I might say they swum by, they slid along so quiet and smooth and lovely. Here is the way we put in the time. It was a monstrous big river down there—sometimes a mile and a half wide; we run nights, and laid up and hid daytimes; soon as night was most gone, we stopped navigating and tied up—nearly always in the dead water under a towhead,[8] and then cut young cottonwoods and willows and hid the raft with them. Then we set out the lines. Next we slid into the river and had a swim, so as to freshen up and cool off; then we set down on the sandy bottom where the water was about knee deep, and watched the daylight come. Not a sound, anywheres—perfectly still—just like the whole world was asleep, only sometimes the bullfrogs a-cluttering, maybe. The first thing to see, looking away over the water, was a kind of dull line—that was the woods on t'other side—you couldn't make nothing else out; then a pale place in the sky; then more paleness, spreading around; then the river softened up, away off, and warn't black any more, but gray; you could see little dark spots drifting along, ever so far away—trading scows, and such things; and long black streaks—rafts; sometimes you could hear a sweep[9] screaking; or jumbled up voices, it was so still, and sounds come so far; and by-and-by you could see a streak on the water which you know by the look of the streak that there's a snag there in a swift current which breaks on it and makes that streak look that way; and you see the mist curl up off of the water, and the east reddens up, and the river, and you make out a log cabin in the edge of the woods, away on the bank on t'other side of the river, being a woodyard, likely, and piled by them cheats so you can throw a dog through it anywheres;[10] then the nice breeze springs up, and comes fanning you from over there, so cool and fresh, and sweet to smell, on account of the woods and the flowers, but sometimes not that way, because they've left dead fish laying around, gars,[11] and such, and they do get pretty rank; and next you've got

the full day, and everything smiling in the sun, and the songbirds just going it!

A little smoke couldn't be noticed, now, so we would take some fish off of the lines, and cook up a hot breakfast. And afterwards we would watch the lonesomeness of the river, and kind of lazy along, and by-and-by lazy off to sleep. Wake up, by-and-by, and look to see what done it, and maybe see a steamboat coughing along up stream, so far off towards the other side you couldn't tell nothing about her only whether she was stern-wheel or side-wheel; then for about an hour there wouldn't be nothing to hear nor nothing to see—just solid lonesomeness. Next you'd see a raft sliding by, away off yonder, and maybe a galoot[12] on it chopping, because they're almost always doing it on a raft; you'd see the ax flash, and come down—you don't hear nothing; you see that ax go up again, and by the time it's above the man's head, then you hear the *k'chunk!*—it had took all that time to come over the water. So we would put in the day, lazying around, listening to the stillness. Once there was a thick fog, and the rafts and things that went by was beating tin pans so the steamboats wouldn't run over them. A scow or a raft went by so close we could hear them talking and cussing and laughing— heard them plain; but we couldn't see no sign of them; it made you feel crawly, it was like spirits carrying on that way in the air. Jim said he believed it was spirits; but I says:

"No, spirits wouldn't say, 'dern the dern fog.' "

Soon as it was night, out we shoved; when we got her out to about the middle, we let her

---

8. **towhead:** sand bar.
9. **sweep:** a long oar.
10. **anywheres:** Customers were often cheated of wood because piles of wood were sold by total volume, including gaps.
11. **gars:** freshwater fish with long bodies, hard scales, beaklike snouts, and many sharp teeth.
12. **galoot:** a slang word meaning "an awkward person."

alone, and let her float wherever the current wanted her to; then we lit the pipes, and dangled our legs in the water and talked about all kinds of things—we was always naked, day and night, whenever the mosquitoes would let us—the new clothes Buck's folks made for me was too good to be comfortable, and besides I didn't go much on clothes, no how.

Sometimes we'd have that whole river all to ourselves for the longest time. Yonder was the banks and the islands, across the water; and maybe a spark—which was a candle in a cabin window—and sometimes on the water you could see a spark or two—on a raft or a scow, you know; and maybe you could hear a fiddle or a song coming over from one of them crafts. It's lovely to live on a raft. We had the sky, up there, all speckled with stars, and we used to lay on our backs and look up at them, and discuss about whether they was made, or only just happened—Jim he allowed they was made, but I allowed they happened; I judged it would have took too long to *make* so many. Jim said the moon could a *laid* them; well, that looked kind of reasonable, so I didn't say nothing against it, because I've seen a frog lay most as many, so of course it could be done. We used to watch the stars that fell, too, and see them streak down. Jim allowed they'd got spoiled and was hove out of the nest.

Once or twice of a night we would see a steamboat slipping along in the dark, and now and then she would belch a whole world of sparks up out of her chimbleys, and they would rain down in the river and look awful pretty; then she would turn a corner and her lights would wink out and her pow-wow[13] shut off and leave the river still again; and by-and-by her waves would get to us, a long time after she was gone, and joggle the raft a bit, and after that you wouldn't hear nothing for you couldn't tell how long, except maybe frogs or something.

After midnight the people on shore went to bed, and then for two or three hours the shores was black—no more sparks in the cabin windows. These sparks was our clock—the first one that showed again meant morning was coming, so we hunted a place to hide and tie up, right away. . . .

---

13. **pow-wow:** commotion, racket.

HANNIBAL, MISSOURI. *Henry Lewis. The New York Public Library.*

Getting at Meaning

1. What impresses Huck most about the Grangerfords' home? With what does he compare it? What do Huck's reactions to the Grangerfords' home tell you about him?

2. Describe the writing and artwork of Emmeline Grangerford. What does Huck think of her pictures and poems? How do you think Twain views them?

3. Explain Huck and Jim's routine for traveling on the river. In what ways might the river travel be more attractive than the Grangerford house to Huck? Which details about Huck and Jim's night travels show how distant they are from civilization?

4. How do Huck and Jim explain the stars? What do their explanations show about their backgrounds and education?

Developing Skills in Reading Literature

1. **Humor: Irony and Exaggeration.** Certain ironic statements by Huck, such as "I reckoned that with her [Emmeline's] disposition she was having a better time in the graveyard," are humorous. What other comments by Huck do you find humorous? At times, humor in *The Adventures of Huckleberry Finn* is derived from exaggeration. How, for example, is Emmeline's character extreme?

2. **Point of View.** Huck narrates his own story. How does his first-person narration affect the selection of incidents and details in this excerpt? Explain how Huck reveals his character through his narration.

3. **Satire.** Satire combines criticism with wit for the purpose of improving society. What kinds of literature and art does Twain satirize through Emmeline Grangerford?

4. **Imagery.** Twain's description of the river contains images that appeal to the senses of sight, hearing, touch, and smell. Find two striking details that appeal to each of these senses. What mood do these images convey?

5. **Symbol.** Because of the contrast between the river and the Grangerfords' house, each takes on symbolic meaning. Explain what each symbolizes, referring to specific descriptions.

6. **Dialect.** *The Adventures of Huckleberry Finn* is told in an informal, conversational style. Find two more examples of each of these elements of dialect:
   a. ungrammatical expression, as in "I hadn't seen no house."
   b. regional language, such as "tuckered out"
   c. regional pronunciations, such as "warn't"

How does dialect make Huck a more realistic character?

Developing Vocabulary

Using Precise Verbs. Twain chooses colorful verbs appropriate to Huck's manner of speech. In each of the following sentences from the story, substitute a different verb and note the effect on the sentence. How does Twain's selection of verbs contribute to the tone of the story and to the characterization of Huck?

". . . when one of those peddlers had been along and *scoured* her up and got her in good condition, [the clock] would start in and strike a hundred and fifty before she got tuckered out.

". . . she was *mashing* a locket with a chain to it against her mouth . . ."

". . . now and then [the steamboat] would *belch* a whole world of sparks up out of her chimbleys . . ."

Developing Writing Skills

Creating a Mood. Choose a place where you feel close to nature. After observing it carefully at various times of day, write a description contrasting the place at two different times of day. Choose images and details to establish two different moods.

from **A Tramp Abroad**

What Stumped the Bluejays

Animals talk to each other, of course. There can be no question about that; but I suppose there are very few people who can understand them. I never knew but one man who could. I knew he could, however, because he told me so himself. He was a middle-aged, simple-hearted miner who had lived in a lonely corner of California, among the woods and mountains, a good many years, and had studied the ways of his only neighbors, the beasts and the birds, until he believed he could accurately translate any remark which they made. This was Jim Baker. According to Jim Baker, some animals have only a limited education, and use only very simple words, and scarcely ever a comparison or a flowery figure; whereas, certain other animals have a large vocabulary, a fine command of language and a ready and fluent delivery; consequently these latter talk a great deal; they like it; they are conscious of their talent, and they enjoy "showing off." Baker said, that after long and careful observation, he had come to the conclusion that the bluejays were the best talkers he had found among birds and beasts. Said he:

There's more *to* a bluejay than any other creature. He has got more moods, and more different kinds of feelings than other creatures; and, mind you, whatever a bluejay feels, he can put into language. And no mere commonplace language, either, but rattling, out-and-out book-talk—and bristling with metaphor,[1] too—just bristling! And as for command of language—why *you* never see a bluejay get stuck for a word. No man ever did. They just boil out of him! And another thing:

I've noticed a good deal, and there's no bird, or cow, or anything that uses as good grammar as a bluejay. You may say a cat uses good grammar. Well, a cat does—but you let a cat get excited once; you let a cat get to pulling fur with another cat on a shed, nights, and you'll hear grammar that will give you the lockjaw. Ignorant people think it's the *noise* which fighting cats make that is so aggravating, but it ain't so; it's the sickening grammar they use. Now I've never heard a jay use bad grammar but very seldom; and when they do, they are as ashamed as a human; they shut right down and leave.

You may call a jay a bird. Well, so he is, in a measure—because he's got feathers on him, and don't belong to no church, perhaps; but otherwise he is just as much a human as you be. And I'll tell you for why. A jay's gifts, and instincts, and feelings, and interests, cover the whole ground. A jay hasn't got any more principle than a Congressman. A jay will lie, a jay will steal, a jay will deceive, a jay will betray; and four times out of five, a jay will go back on his solemnest promise. The sacredness of an obligation is a thing which you can't cram into no bluejay's head. Now, on top of all this, there's another thing; a jay can out-swear any gentleman in the mines. You think a cat can swear. Well, a cat can; but you give a bluejay a subject that calls for his reserve powers, and where is your cat? Don't talk to *me*—I know too much about this thing. And there's yet another thing; in the one little particular of scolding—just good, clean, out-and-out scolding—a bluejay can lay

---

1. **bristling with metaphor:** thickly covered with, or densely spiked with implied comparisons.

over anything, human or divine. Yes, sir, a jay is everything that a man is. A jay can cry, a jay can laugh, a jay can feel shame, a jay can reason and plan and discuss, a jay likes gossip and scandal, a jay has got a sense of humor, a jay knows when he is an ass just as well as you do—maybe better. If a jay ain't human, he better take in his sign, that's all. Now I'm going to tell you a perfectly true fact about some bluejays. When I first begun to understand jay language correctly, there was a little incident happened here. Seven years ago, the last man in this region but me moved away. There stands his house—been empty ever since; a log house, with a plank roof—just one big room, and no more; no ceiling—nothing between the rafters and the floor. Well, one Sunday morning I was sitting out here in front of my cabin, with my cat, taking the sun, and looking at the blue hills, and listening to the leaves rustling so lonely in the trees, and thinking of the home away yonder in the states, that I hadn't heard from in thirteen years, when a bluejay lit on that house, with an acorn in his mouth, and says, "Hello, I reckon I've struck something." When he spoke, the acorn dropped out of his mouth and rolled down the roof, of course, but he didn't care; his mind was all on the thing he had struck. It was a knot-hole in the roof. He cocked his head to one side, shut one eye and put the other one to the hole, like a possum looking down a jug; then he glanced up with his bright eyes, gave a wink or two with his wings—which signifies gratification, you understand—and says, "It looks like a hole, it's located like a hole—blamed if I don't believe it is a hole!"

Then he cocked his head down and took another look; he glances up perfectly joyful, this time; winks his wings and his tail both, and says, "Oh, no, this ain't no fat thing, I reckon! If I ain't in luck!—why it's a perfectly elegant hole!" So he flew down and got that acorn, and fetched it up and dropped it in, and was just tilting his head back, with the hea-

venliest smile on his face, when all of a sudden he was paralyzed into a listening attitude and that smile faded gradually out of his countenance like breath off'n a razor, and the queerest look of surprise took its place. Then he says, "Why, I didn't hear it fall!" He cocked his eye at the hole again, and took a long look; raised up and shook his head; stepped around to the other side of the hole and took another look from that side; shook his head again. He studied a while, then he just went into the *details*—walked round and round the hole and spied into it from every point of the compass. No use. Now he took a thinking attitude on the comb[2] of the roof and scratched the back of his head with his right foot a minute, and finally says, "Well, it's too many for *me*, that's certain; must be a mighty long hole; however, I ain't got no time to fool around here, I got to 'tend to business; I reckon it's all right—chance it, anyway."

So he flew off and fetched another acorn and dropped it in, and tried to flirt his eye to the hole quick enough to see what become of it, but he was too late. He held his eye there as much as a minute; then he raised up and sighed, and says, "Confound it, I don't seem to understand this thing, no way; however, I'll tackle her again." He fetched another acorn, and done his level best to see what become of it, but he couldn't. He says, "Well, *I* never struck no such a hole as this before; I'm of the opinion it's a totally new kind of a hole." Then he begun to get mad. He held in for a spell, walking up and down the comb of the roof and shaking his head and muttering to himself; but his feelings got the upper hand of him, presently, and he broke loose and cussed himself black in the face. I never see a bird take on so about a little thing. When he got through he walks to the hole and looks in again for half a minute; then he says, "Well, you're a long hole, and a deep hole, and a mighty singular hole altogether—but I've

---

2. **comb:** the ridge of a roof.

started in to fill you, and I'm d—d if I *don't* fill you, if it takes a hundred years!"

And with that, away he went. You never see a bird work so since you was born. He laid into his work, and the way he hove acorns into that hole for about two hours and a half was one of the most exciting and astonishing spectacles I ever struck. He never stopped to take a look any more—he just hove 'em in and went for more. Well, at last he could hardly flop his wings, he was so tuckered out. He comes a-drooping down, once more, sweating like an ice-pitcher, drops his acorn in and says, "*Now* I guess I've got the bulge on you by this time!" So he bent down for a look. If you'll believe me, when his head come up again he was just pale with rage. He says, "I've shoveled acorns enough in there to keep the family thirty years, and if I can see a sign of one of 'em I wish I may land in a museum with a belly full of sawdust in two minutes!"

He just had strength enough to crawl up on to the comb and lean his back agin the chimbly, and then he collected his impressions and begun to free his mind. I see in a second that what I had mistook for profanity in the mines was only just the rudiments, as you may say.

Another jay was going by, and heard him doing his devotions, and stops to inquire what was up. The sufferer told him the whole circumstance, and says, "Now yonder's the hole, and if you don't believe me, go and look for yourself." So this fellow went and looked, and comes back and says, "How many did you say you put in there?" "Not any less than two tons," says the sufferer. The other jay went and looked again. He couldn't seem to make it out, so he raised a yell, and three more jays come. They all examined the hole, they all made the sufferer tell it over again, then they all discussed it, and got off as many leather-headed opinions about it as an average crowd of humans could have done.

They called in more jays; then more and more, till pretty soon this whole region 'peared to have a blue flush about it. There must have been five thousand of them; and such another jawing and disputing and ripping and cussing, you never heard. Every jay in the whole lot put his eye to the hole and delivered a more chuckle-headed opinion about the mystery than the jay that went there before him. They examined the house all over, too. The door was standing half open, and at last one old jay happened to go and light on it and look in. Of course, that knocked the mystery galley-west[3] in a second. There lay the acorns, scattered all over the floor. He flopped his wings and raised a whoop. "Come here!" he says, "Come here, everybody; hang'd if this fool hasn't been trying to fill up a house with acorns!" They all came a-swooping down like a blue cloud, and as each fellow lit on the door and took a glance, the whole absurdity of the contract that that first jay had tackled hit him home and he fell over backward suffocating with laughter, and the next jay took his place and done the same.

Well, sir, they roosted around here on the housetop and the trees for an hour, and guffawed over that thing like human beings. It ain't any use to tell me a bluejay hasn't got a sense of humor, because I know better. And memory, too. They brought jays here from all over the United States to look down that hole, every summer for three years. Other birds, too. And they could all see the point, except an owl that come from Nova Scotia to visit the Yo Semite,[4] and he took this thing in on his way back. He said he couldn't see anything funny in it. But then he was a good deal disappointed about Yo Semite, too.

---

3. **galley-west:** into confusion.
4. **Yo Semite** (Yosemite): a national park in California.

Getting at Meaning

1. Why does Twain have Jim Baker narrate the story? How does this contribute to the effectiveness of the story?

2. What does Baker claim the bluejay tried to accomplish?

3. What elements of the bluejay tale are humorous?

4. How does Baker demonstrate the bluejays' sense of humor and superior memory?

Developing Skills in Reading Literature

1. **Personification.** Baker personifies birds, giving them human strengths and weaknesses. According to Baker, what are bluejays' shortcomings? Explain how Twain's comments about birds poke fun at humans.

2. **Local Color.** Twain depicts the West in "What Stumped the Bluejays." Find these elements of local-color writing in the tale:

   a) emphasis on setting

   b) humorous plot

   c) dialect

   d) eccentric characters

3. **Tall Tale.** Tall tales of the American frontier record extravagantly impossible happenings. Point out five such happenings that account for the humor in "What Stumped the Bluejays." How is the ending appropriate for a tall tale?

Developing Vocabulary

Colloquial Expressions. The language of "What Stumped the Bluejays" is colloquial, reflecting informal, conversational speech. Colloquial expressions in the story include "lit on the house" and "I reckon." Find three more colloquialisms in the story and look up their definitions in a dictionary or book on slang. Why does Twain use this level of language for the tale?

Developing Writing Skills

Writing a Tall Tale. Write a tall tale about an imaginary character, either human or animal, who performs superhuman feats. Make your exaggerations so extreme that they are humorous.

Kate Chopin

1851–1904

Kate O'Flaherty Chopin is most famous for her realistic stories of Louisiana, which are characterized by the skillful use of local color and dialect. Kate O'Flaherty was born in St. Louis, Missouri, on February 8, 1851. A belle of St. Louis society, she married Oscar Chopin in 1870 and went to live in New Orleans. In 1879 the family moved to rural Louisiana, where in 1883 Oscar Chopin died. His young widow returned to St. Louis with her children and began to write poems, stories, and sketches in which she drew on her years in Louisiana. Her characters were the Creoles, Cajuns, blacks, and Indians, of mixed backgrounds and cultures, whom she had known both in New Orleans and in the back country and whose lifestyles and dialects she was able to capture in writing. Of her first two novels and nearly one hundred stories, the short pieces are by far the most successful. Her third novel, *The Awakening* (1899), was criticized severely for its theme of infidelity and its sensuous, passionate heroine; in fact, the book was banned, and its author suffered social disgrace. However, that novel has received greater appreciation in the twentieth century, as have the works that deal with the personal problems of women and with racial problems.

The Story of an Hour

Knowing that Mrs. Mallard was afflicted with a heart trouble, great care was taken to break to her as gently as possible the news of her husband's death.

It was her sister Josephine who told her, in broken sentences; veiled hints that revealed in half concealing. Her husband's friend Richards was there, too, near her. It was he who had been in the newspaper office when intelligence of the railroad disaster was received, with Brently Mallard's name leading the list of "killed." He had only taken the time to assure himself of its truth by a second telegram, and had hastened to forestall any less careful, less tender friend in bearing the sad message.

She did not hear the story as many women have heard the same, with a paralyzed inability to accept its significance. She wept at once, with sudden, wild abandonment, in her sister's arms. When the storm of grief had spent itself she went away to her room alone. She would have no one follow her.

There stood, facing the open window, a comfortable, roomy armchair. Into this she sank, pressed down by a physical exhaustion that haunted her body and seemed to reach into her soul.

She could see in the open square before her house the tops of trees that were all aquiver with the new spring life. The delicious breath of rain was in the air. In the street below a peddler was crying his wares. The notes of a distant song which someone was singing reached her faintly, and countless sparrows were twittering in the eaves.

There were patches of blue sky showing here and there through the clouds that had met and piled one above the other in the west facing her window.

She sat with her head thrown back upon the cushion of the chair, quite motionless, except when a sob came up into her throat and shook her, as a child who has cried itself to sleep continues to sob in its dreams.

She was young, with a fair, calm face, whose lines bespoke repression and even a certain strength. But now there was a dull stare in her eyes, whose gaze was fixed away off yonder on one of those patches of blue sky. It was not a glance of reflection, but rather indicated a suspension of intelligent thought.

There was something coming to her and she was waiting for it, fearfully. What was it? She did not know; it was too subtle and elusive to name. But she felt it, creeping out of the sky, reaching toward her through the sounds, the scents, the color that filled the air.

Now her bosom rose and fell tumultuously. She was beginning to recognize this thing that was approaching to possess her, and she was striving to beat it back with her will—as powerless as her two white slender hands would have been.

When she abandoned herself, a little whispered word escaped her slightly parted lips. She said it over and over under her breath: "free, free, free!" The vacant stare and the look of terror that had followed it went from her eyes. They stayed keen and bright. Her pulses beat fast, and the coursing blood warmed and relaxed every inch of her body.

She did not stop to ask if it were or were not a monstrous joy that held her. A clear and exalted perception enabled her to dismiss the suggestion as trivial.

She knew that she would weep again when she saw the kind, tender hands folded in death; the face that had never looked save with love upon her, fixed and gray and dead. But she saw beyond that bitter moment a long procession of years to come that would belong to her absolutely. And she opened and spread her arms out to them in welcome.

There would be no one to live for her during those coming years; she would live for herself. There would be no powerful will bending hers in that blind persistence with which men and women believe they have a right to impose a private will upon a fellow-creature. A kind intention or a cruel intention made the act seem no less a crime as she looked upon it in that brief moment of illumination.

And yet she had loved him—sometimes. Often she had not. What did it matter! What could love, the unsolved mystery, count for in face of this possession of self-assertion which she suddenly recognized as the strongest impulse of her being!

"Free! Body and soul free!" she kept whispering.

Josephine was kneeling before the closed door with her lips to the keyhole, imploring for admission. "Louise, open the door! I beg; open the door—you will make yourself ill. What are you doing, Louise? For heaven's sake open the door."

"Go away. I am not making myself ill." No; she was drinking in a very elixir of life[1] through that open window.

Her fancy was running riot along those days ahead of her. Spring days, and summer days, and all sorts of days that would be her own. She breathed a quick prayer that life might be long. It was only yesterday she had thought with a shudder that life might be long.

She arose at length and opened the door to her sister's importunities. There was a feverish triumph in her eyes, and she carried herself unwittingly like a goddess of Victory. She clasped her sister's waist, and together they descended the stairs. Richards stood waiting for them at the bottom.

Someone was opening the front door with a latchkey. It was Brently Mallard who entered, a little travel-stained, composedly carrying his grip-sack[2] and umbrella. He had been far from the scene of accident, and did not know there had been one. He stood amazed at Josephine's piercing cry; at Richards's quick motion to screen him from the view of his wife.

But Richards was too late.

When the doctors came they said she had died of heart disease—of joy that kills.

---

1. **elixir of life** (i lik′ sər): an imaginary substance sought by medieval alchemists to keep people alive forever.
2. **grip-sack** (var. of *grip*): a small traveling bag or satchel.

Getting at Meaning

1. Do you think that Louise Mallard dies of shock, joy, or grief? Support your answer with details from the story.

2. How does Mrs. Mallard at first react to the news of her husband's death? How does her reaction change?

3. How do the people around her expect Mrs. Mallard to react? Describe the special precautions they take.

4. Describe the relationship between Mr. and Mrs. Mallard. Why does Mrs. Mallard long for freedom?

Developing Skills in Reading Literature

1. **Irony.** Notice the ironies summed up in the final sentence of the story. What is ironic about Mrs. Mallard's death? about the doctors' analysis of its cause?

2. **Surprise Ending.** What surprise event marks the turning point of the story? Point out foreshadowing that prepares the reader with clues for the surprise ending.

3. **Theme.** Mrs. Mallard "breathed a quick prayer that life might be long. It was only yesterday she had thought with a shudder that life might be long." Explain the theme of the story that these sentences stress. Why is time emphasized in the title?

Willa Cather

1873–1947

The American West and Southwest provided the rich and varied background for Willa Cather's novels and short stories. She wrote: ". . . love of great spaces, of rolling open country like the sea— it's the grand passion of my life."

Cather was born on December 7, 1873, in Back Creek Valley, Virginia, where her family had farmed for nearly a century. When she was ten years old, the Cathers moved to the frontier town of Red Cloud, Nebraska. Straitened as were the circumstances of frontier life, she was anything but culturally impoverished. Her own home library contained fine books, and she had two memorable teachers in the small local high school. The local storekeeper taught her to read classical Latin and Greek. Among her Nebraska acquaintances were Americans of diverse European backgrounds whose varied religious and cultural heritages enriched the frontier community. Neighbors taught her French and German and loaned her books in those languages. A German music master taught her the history and appreciation of classical music and of opera. Later, she had opportunities to spend time in the Southwest absorbing its ancient mixture of Indian and Spanish cultures.

After attending the University of Nebraska where she studied journalism, Cather spent some time back in Red Cloud and then went to Pittsburgh, where she worked as editor on a magazine and then for the *Pittsburgh Leader*. In her spare time she wrote, and her poems and stories began to appear in magazines. Her first collection of stories was *The Troll Garden* (1905). From 1906 on she lived in New York as managing editor for *McClure's Magazine* and, in 1912, she published her first novel, *Alexander's Bridge*, set in England. She returned to her beloved prairie milieu for the three novels that followed: *O Pioneers!* (1913), *The Song of the Lark* (1915), and *My Ántonia* (1918). *Death Comes for the Archbishop* (1927) is set in the Southwest in the period following the Mexican War, and *Shadows on the Rock* (1931) concerns French-Catholics in colonial Quebec. Two collections of short stories also appeared: *Youth and the Bright Medusa* (1920) and *Obscure Destinies* (1932).

Cather was a selective realist. While she depicts the stark realities of frontier life, she idealizes the courage and spirit of the pioneers, treating them with what she called her "gift of sympathy." Cather received recognition both in America and abroad, including the Pulitzer Prize in literature. She died on April 24, 1947.

A Wagner Matinee

I received one morning a letter, written in pale ink on glassy, blue-lined note-paper, and bearing the postmark of a little Nebraska village. This communication, worn and rubbed, looking as if it had been carried for some days in a coat pocket that was none too clean, was from my Uncle Howard, and informed me that his wife had been left a small legacy by a bachelor relative, and that it would be necessary for her to go to Boston to attend to the settling of the estate. He requested me to meet her at the station and render her whatever services might be necessary. On examining the date indicated as that of her arrival, I found it to be no later than tomorrow. He had characteristically delayed writing until, had I been away from home for a day, I must have missed my aunt altogether.

The name of my Aunt Georgiana opened before me a gulf of recollection so wide and deep that, as the letter dropped from my hand, I felt suddenly a stranger to all the present conditions of my existence, wholly ill at ease and out of place amid the familiar surroundings of my study. I became, in short, the gangling farmer-boy my aunt had known, scourged with chilblains[1] and bashfulness, my hands cracked and sore from the corn husking. I sat again before her parlor organ, fumbling the scale with my stiff, red fingers, while she, beside me, made canvas mittens for the huskers.

The next morning, after preparing my landlady for a visitor, I set out for the station. When the train arrived I had some difficulty in finding my aunt. She was the last of the passengers to alight, and it was not until I got her into the carriage that she seemed really to recognize me. She had come all the way in a day coach; her linen duster[2] had become black with soot and her black bonnet grey with dust during the journey. When we arrived at my boarding-house the landlady put her to bed at once, and I did not see her again until the next morning.

Whatever shock Mrs. Springer experienced at my aunt's appearance, she considerately concealed. As for myself, I saw my aunt's battered figure with that feeling of awe and respect with which we behold explorers who have left their ears and fingers north of Franz-Joseph-Land,[3] or their health somewhere along the Upper Congo. My Aunt Georgiana had been a music teacher at the Boston Conservatory, somewhere back in the latter sixties. One summer, while visiting in the little village among the Green Mountains where her ancestors had dwelt for generations, she had kindled the callow fancy of my uncle, Howard Carpenter, then an idle, shiftless boy of twenty-one. When she returned to her duties in Boston, Howard followed her, and the upshot of this infatuation was that she eloped with him, eluding the reproaches of her family and the criticism of her friends by going with him to the Nebraska frontier. Carpenter, who, of course, had no money, took up a homestead in Red Willow County,[4] fifty miles from the railroad. There they had measured off their land themselves, driving

---

1. **chilblains:** painful swelling or sores on the feet or hands, caused by exposure to cold.
2. **duster:** a short, loose, lightweight coat.
3. **Franz-Joseph-Land:** an archipelago of 70 islands in the Arctic Ocean N of Russia and Europe.
4. Red Willow County borders on Kansas in SW Nebraska.

across the prairie in a wagon, to the wheel of which they had tied a red cotton handkerchief, and counting its revolutions. They built a dug-out in the red hillside, one of those cave dwellings whose inmates so often reverted to primitive conditions. Their water they got from the lagoons where the buffalo drank, and their slender stock of provisions was always at the mercy of bands of roving Indians. For thirty years my aunt had not been farther than fifty miles from the homestead.

I owed to this woman most of the good that ever came my way in my boyhood, and had a reverential affection for her. During the years when I was riding herd for my uncle, my aunt, after cooking the three meals—the first of which was ready at six o'clock in the morning —and putting the six children to bed, would often stand until midnight at her ironing-board, with me at the kitchen table beside her, hearing me recite Latin declensions and conjugations, gently shaking me when my drowsy head sank down over a page of irregular verbs. It was to her, at her ironing or mending, that I read my first Shakespeare, and her old textbook on mythology was the first that ever came into my empty hands. She taught me my scales and exercises on the little parlor organ which her husband had bought her after fifteen years during which she had not so much as seen a musical instrument. She would sit beside me by the hour, darning and counting, while I struggled with the "Joyous Farmer." She seldom talked to me about music, and I understood why. Once when I had been doggedly beating out some easy passages from an old score of *Euryanthe* I had found among her music books, she came up to me and, putting her hands over my eyes, gently drew my head back upon her shoulder, saying tremulously, "Don't love it so well, Clark, or it may be taken from you."

When my aunt appeared on the morning after her arrival in Boston, she was still in a semi-somnambulant state. She seemed not to realize that she was in the city where she had

spent her youth, the place longed for hungrily half a lifetime. She had been so wretchedly train-sick throughout the journey that she had no recollection of anything but her discomfort, and, to all intents and purposes, there were but a few hours of nightmare between the farm in Red Willow County and my study on Newbury Street. I had planned a little pleasure for her that afternoon, to repay her for some of the glorious moments she had given me when we used to milk together in the straw-thatched cowshed and she, because I was more than usually tired, or because her husband had spoken sharply to me, would tell me of the splendid performance of the *Huguenots* she had seen in Paris, in her youth.

At two o'clock the Symphony Orchestra was to give a Wagner[5] program, and I intended to take my aunt; though, as I conversed with her, I grew doubtful about her enjoyment of it. I suggested our visiting the Conservatory and the Common[6] before lunch, but she seemed altogether too timid to wish to venture out. She questioned me absently about various changes in the city, but she was chiefly concerned that she had forgotten to leave instructions about feeding half-skimmed milk to a certain weakling calf, "old Maggie's calf, you know, Clark," she explained, evidently having forgotten how long I had been away. She was further troubled because she had neglected to tell her daughter about the freshly-opened kit of mackerel in the cellar, which would spoil if it were not used directly.

I asked her whether she had ever heard any of the Wagnerian operas, and found that she had not, though she was perfectly familiar with their respective situations, and had once possessed the piano score of *The Flying Dutchman*. I began to think it would be best to get her back to Red Willow County with-

---

5. Richard Wagner (1813–1883), German composer who originated the music drama, emphasizing German mythology and heroes.
6. **Common:** Boston Common, a public park.

out waking her, and regretted having suggested the concert.

From the time we entered the concert hall, however, she was a trifle less passive and inert, and for the first time seemed to perceive her surroundings. I had felt some trepidation lest she might become aware of her queer, country clothes, or might experience some painful embarrassment at stepping suddenly into the world to which she had been dead for a quarter of a century. But, again, I found how superficially I had judged her. She sat looking about her with eyes as impersonal, almost as stony, as those with which the granite Rameses[7] in a museum watches the froth and fret that ebbs and flows about his pedestal. I have seen this same aloofness in old miners who drift into the Brown hotel at Denver, their pockets full of bullion, their linen soiled, their haggard faces unshaven; standing in the thronged corridors as solitary as though they were still in a frozen camp on the Yukon.

The matinee audience was made up chiefly of women. One lost the contour of faces and figures, indeed any effect of line whatever, and there was only the color of bodices past counting, the shimmer of fabrics soft and firm, silky and sheer; red, mauve, pink, blue, lilac, purple, ecru, rose, yellow, cream, and white, all the colors that an impressionist finds in a sunlit landscape, with here and there the dead shadow of a frock coat. My Aunt Georgiana regarded them as though they had been so many daubs of tube-paint on a palette.

When the musicians came out and took their places, she gave a little stir of anticipation, and looked with quickening interest down over the rail at that invariable grouping, perhaps the first wholly familiar thing that had greeted her eye since she had left old Maggie and her weakling calf. I could feel how all those details sank into her soul, for I had not forgotten how they had sunk into mine when I came fresh from ploughing forever and forever between green aisles of corn, where, as

in a treadmill, one might walk from daybreak to dusk without perceiving a shadow of change. The clean profiles of the musicians, the gloss of their linen, the dull black of their coats, the beloved shapes of the instruments, the patches of yellow light on the smooth, varnished bellies of the cellos and the bass viols in the rear, the restless, wind-tossed forest of fiddle necks and bows—I recalled how, in the first orchestra I ever heard, those long bow-strokes seemed to draw the heart out of me, as a conjurer's stick reels out yards of paper ribbon from a hat.

The first number was the *Tannhauser* overture. When the horns drew out the first strain of the Pilgrim's chorus, Aunt Georgiana clutched my coat sleeve. Then it was I first realized that for her this broke a silence of thirty years. With the battle between the two motives, with the frenzy of the Venusberg theme and its ripping of strings, there came to me an overwhelming sense of the waste and wear we are so powerless to combat; and I saw again the tall, naked house on the prairie, black and grim as a wooden fortress; the black pond where I had learned to swim, its margin pitted with sun-dried cattle tracks; the rain gullied clay banks about the naked house, the four dwarf ash seedlings where the dishcloths were always hung to dry before the kitchen door. The world there was the flat world of the ancients; to the east, a cornfield that stretched to daybreak; to the west, a corral that reached to sunset; between, the conquests of peace, dearer-bought than those of war.

The overture closed, my aunt released my coat sleeve, but she said nothing. She sat staring dully at the orchestra. What, I wondered, did she get from it? She had been a good pianist in her day, I knew, and her musical education had been broader than that of most music teachers of a quarter of a century ago.

---

7. **Rameses** (var. of *Ramses*) (ram′ ə sēz): Egyptian kings who ruled from c. 1315 to c. 1090 B.C.

She had often told me of Mozart's operas and Meyerbeer's, and I could remember hearing her sing, years ago, certain melodies of Verdi. When I had fallen ill with a fever in her house, she used to sit by my cot in the evening—when the cool, night wind blew in through the faded mosquito netting tacked over the window and I lay watching a certain bright star that burned red above the cornfield—and sing "Home to our mountains, O, let us return!" in a way fit to break the heart of a Vermont boy near dead of homesickness already.

I watched her closely through the prelude to *Tristan and Isolde*, trying vainly to conjecture what that seething turmoil of strings and winds might mean to her, but she sat mutely staring at the violin bows that drove obliquely downward, like the pelting streaks of rain in a summer shower. Had this music any message for her? Had she enough left to at all comprehend this power which had kindled the world since she had left it? I was in a fever of curiosity, but Aunt Georgiana sat silent upon her peak in Darien.[8] She preserved this utter immobility throughout the number from *The Flying Dutchman*, though her fingers worked mechanically upon her black dress, as if, of themselves, they were recalling the piano score they had once played. Poor hands! They had been stretched and twisted into mere tentacles to hold and lift and knead with—on one of them a thin, worn band that had once been a wedding ring. As I pressed and gently quieted one of those groping hands, I remembered with quivering eyelids their services for me in other days.

Soon after the tenor began the "Prize Song," I heard a quick drawn breath and turned to my aunt. Her eyes were closed, but the tears were glistening on her cheeks, and I think, in a moment more, they were in my eyes as well. It never really died, then—the soul which can suffer so excruciatingly and so interminably; it withers to the outward eye only; like that strange moss which can lie on a dusty shelf half a century and yet, if placed in water, grows green again. She wept so throughout the development and elaboration of the melody.

During the intermission before the second half, I questioned my aunt and found that the "Prize Song" was not new to her. Some years before there had drifted to the farm in Red Willow County a young German, a tramp cow-puncher, who had sung in the chorus at Bayreuth[9] when he was a boy, along with the other peasant boys and girls. Of a Sunday morning he used to sit on his gingham-sheeted bed in the hands' bedroom which opened off the kitchen, cleaning the leather of his boots and saddle, singing the "Prize Song," while my aunt went about her work in the kitchen. She had hovered over him until she had prevailed upon him to join the country church, though his sole fitness for this step, in so far as I could gather, lay in his boyish face and his possession of this divine melody. Shortly afterward, he had gone to town on the Fourth of July, been drunk for several days, lost his money at a faro[10] table, ridden a saddled Texas steer on a bet, and disappeared with a fractured collar-bone. All this my aunt told me huskily, wanderingly, as though she were talking in the weak lapses of illness.

"Well, we have come to better things than the old *Trovatore* at any rate, Aunt Georgie?" I queried, with a well meant effort at jocularity.

---

8. **peak in Darien:** The mountain on the Isthmus of Darien (now Panama) where Cortez and his men were said to have looked westward at the Pacific Ocean, silent and amazed at the prospect of their discovery. (From John Keats, British poet (1795–1821), "On First Looking into Chapman's Homer.")

9. **Bayreuth** (bī roit´): in Germany, site of international music festivals.

10. **faro** (fer´ ō): a gambling game in which players bet on the cards to be turned up from the top of the dealer's deck.

Her lip quivered and she hastily put her handkerchief up to her mouth. From behind it she murmured, "And you have been hearing this ever since you left me, Clark?" Her question was the gentlest and saddest of reproaches.

The second half of the program consisted of four numbers from the *Ring*, and closed with Siegfried's funeral march. My aunt wept quietly, but almost continuously, as a shallow vessel overflows in a rain-storm. From time to time her dim eyes looked up at the lights, burning softly under their dull glass globes.

The deluge of sound poured on and on; I never knew what she found in the shining current of it; I never knew how far it bore her, or past what happy islands. From the trembling of her face I could well believe that before the last number she had been carried out where the myriad graves are, into the grey, nameless burying grounds of the sea; or into some world of death vaster yet, where, from the beginning of the world, hope has lain down with hope and dream with dream and, renouncing, slept.

The concert was over; the people filed out of the hall chattering and laughing, glad to relax and find the living level again, but my kinswoman made no effort to rise. The harpist slipped the green felt cover over his instrument; the flute-players shook the water from their mouthpieces; the men of the orchestra went out one by one, leaving the stage to the chairs and music stands, empty as a winter cornfield.

I spoke to my aunt. She burst into tears and sobbed pleadingly. "I don't want to go, Clark, I don't want to go!"

I understood. For her, just outside the concert hall, lay the black pond with the cattle-tracked bluffs; the tall, unpainted house, with weather-curled boards, naked as a tower; the crook-backed ash seedlings where the dish-cloths hung to dry; the gaunt, moulting turkeys picking up refuse about the kitchen door.

AT THE OPERA, 1879. *Mary Cassatt.*
Museum of Fine Arts, Boston.
Charles Henry Hayden Fund.

Getting at Meaning

1. Does Clark's taking his aunt to the matinee turn out to be an act of kindness or cruelty? Explain your answer.

2. For what does Clark feel grateful to his aunt?

3. How is Georgiana's life in Red Willow County a change from her upbringing and training? Is she contented with that life? Explain how she tries to bring music to the prairie.

4. Clark describes his aunt as being "in a semi-somnambulant state" and questions whether to "wake" her. Explain these references to sleep.

5. How does Clark expect his aunt to react to the Wagner concert? How does she react?

6. Aunt Georgiana asks, "And you have been hearing this ever since you left me, Clark?" Why does Clark call this a reproach?

7. How do the events of the story help Clark to mature?

Developing Skills in Reading Literature

1. **Point of View.** First-person narration gives the reader the advantage of knowing Clark's reactions to his aunt. "I could feel how all those details sank into her soul," he remarks. Describe Clark, and explain why this choice of narrator is so effective. How do his attitudes shape the portrayal of Aunt Georgiana?

2. **Setting: Contrast.** Notice the descriptions of Aunt Georgiana's Nebraska homestead. How do these impressions contrast with the descriptions of music? Find three passages that highlight the starkness of Red Willow County and contrast it with the music of the concert hall.

3. **Flashback.** Find two portions of the story that are flashbacks to episodes that occurred at an earlier time. How many years have elapsed between that time and the present? What is the function of these flashbacks within the story?

4. **Figurative Language.** Identify each of the following figures of speech, and explain what it adds to your understanding of Aunt Georgiana's character.

"My aunt wept quietly, but almost continuously, as a shallow vessel overflows in a rain-storm."

"the soul . . . withers to the outward eye only; like that strange moss which can lie on a dusty shelf half a century and yet, if placed in water, grows green again."

"She sat looking about her with eyes as impersonal, almost as stony, as those with which the granite Rameses in a museum watches the froth and fret that ebbs and flows about his pedestal."

"For her, just outside the concert hall, lay the black pond with the cattle-tracked bluffs; the tall, unpainted house, with weather-curled boards, naked as a tower; the crook-backed ash seedlings where the dish-cloths hung to dry . . ,"

5. **Characterization.** A character may be revealed through his or her actions and reactions, as well as through comments by other characters. What character traits of Aunt Georgiana's are revealed by her eloping, her teaching Clark Latin, and her concern for the weakling calf? Find four other comments, actions, or thoughts that help to characterize Georgiana.

6. **Theme.** As Clark plays music, Georgiana urges him, "Don't love it so well, Clark, or it may be taken from you." In this story, what does Clark learn about renounced dreams? Find passages that develop this theme.

Nonfiction

WOMAN'S WORK, 1911. *John Sloan.*
The Cleveland Museum of Art. Gift of Amelia Elizabeth White.

Henry James
1843–1916

Henry James embodied the title of his first successful story—"A Passionate Pilgrim." He was a prolific writer, producing twenty novels, one hundred and twelve short stories, twelve plays, and numerous books of travel commentary and literary criticism. Readers today admire James as a master prose stylist; critics acclaim him as the founder of modern fictional criticism.

Born in New York City on April 15, 1843, James was educated by private tutors and in European schools. He spent his childhood in New York City and Newport, Rhode Island, and in England, Switzerland, France, and Germany before entering Harvard Law School in 1862. He soon withdrew from Harvard to begin a writing career, publishing his first short story in 1864. During the next decade, James spent so much time in Europe that he began to feel more at home there than in America, and in 1876 he took up permanent residence in England, visiting America only once thereafter. In 1915 he became a British citizen as a protest against America's tardy entrance into World War I.

The novels for which James is famous—*The Ambassadors*, *The Wings of the Dove*, and *The Golden Bowl*—and many short stories as well, examine the consequences of the innocent American in a European setting with its alien cultural and value systems. His characters, never troubled by concern for mundane details of existence, interact on subtle levels of feeling and perception. Critics have remarked that James's fiction shows as great an understanding of human psychology as possessed by most philosophers and psychologists.

Henry James was a literary artist, influenced by the French consciousness of form and style. As a critic and arbiter of writing style in fiction, James influenced succeeding generations of literary theorists through critical essays and through longer works such as *The Art of Fiction*. Applying his critical principles in his own writing, James transformed the novel from romantic storytelling to an art form, characterized by unity, dramatic intensity, and psychological perception.

Henry James's pilgrimage through the glittering intellectual, artistic, and social circles of Europe ended in London on February 28, 1916.

from **The Art of Fiction**

During the period I have alluded to there was a comfortable, good-humored feeling abroad that a novel is a novel, as a pudding is a pudding, and that our only business with it could be to swallow it. But within a year or two, for some reason or other, there have been signs of returning animation—the era of discussion would appear to have been to a certain extent opened. Art lives upon discussion, upon experiment, upon variety of attempt, upon the exchange of views and the comparison of standpoints. . . .

"Art," in our Protestant communities, where so many things have got so strangely twisted about, is supposed in certain circles to have some vaguely injurious effect upon those who make it an important consideration, who let it weigh in the balance. It is assumed to be opposed in some mysterious manner to morality, to amusement, to instruction. When it is embodied in the work of the painter (the sculptor is another affair!) you know what it is: it stands there before you, in the honesty of pink and green and a gilt frame; you can see the worst of it at a glance, and you can be on your guard. But when it is introduced into literature it becomes more insidious—there is danger of its hurting you before you know it.

Literature should be either instructive or amusing, and there is in many minds an impression that these artistic preoccupations, the search for form, contribute to neither end, interfere indeed with both. They are too frivolous to be edifying,[1] and too serious to be diverting; and they are moreover priggish[2] and paradoxical[3] and superfluous. That, I think, represents the manner in which the latent thought of many people who read novels as an exercise in skipping would explain itself if it were to become articulate.

They would argue, of course, that a novel ought to be "good," but they would interpret this term in a fashion of their own, which indeed would vary considerably from one critic to another. One would say that being good means representing virtuous and aspiring characters, placed in prominent positions; another would say that it depends on a "happy ending," on a distribution at the last of prizes, pensions, husbands, wives, babies, millions, appended paragraphs, and cheerful remarks. Another still would say that it means being full of incident and movement, so that we shall wish to jump ahead, to see who was the mysterious stranger, and if the stolen will was ever found, and shall not be distracted from this pleasure by any tiresome analysis or "description."

But they would all agree that the "artistic" idea would spoil some of their fun. One would hold it accountable for all the description, another would see it revealed in the absence of sympathy. Its hostility to a happy ending would be evident, and it might even in some cases render any ending at all impossible. The "ending" of a novel is, for many persons, like that of a good dinner, a course of dessert and ices, and the artist in fiction is regarded as a sort of meddlesome doctor who forbids agreeable aftertastes. . . .

But there is as much difference as there ever was between a good novel and a bad one: the bad is swept with all the daubed canvases and spoiled marble into some unvisited limbo,

---

1. **edifying:** teaching or instructing so as to improve in morals or character.
2. **priggish:** annoying because of seeming to be superior in morals and manners.
3. **paradoxical:** inconsistent or full of contradictions.

or infinite rubbish-yard beneath the back-windows of the world, and the good subsists and emits its light and stimulates our desire for perfection. . . .

It is equally excellent and inconclusive to say that one must write from experience; to our supposititious aspirant[4] such a declaration might savor of mockery. What kind of experience is intended, and where does it begin and end? Experience is never limited, and it is never complete; it is an immense sensibility, a kind of huge spiderweb of the finest silken threads suspended in the chamber of consciousness, and catching every air-borne particle in its tissue. It is the very atmosphere of the mind; and when the mind is imaginative—much more when it happens to be that of a man or woman of genius—it takes to itself the faintest hints of life, it converts the very pulses of the air into revelations.

I remember an English novelist, a woman of genius, telling me that she was much commended for the impression she had managed to give in one of her tales of the nature and way of life of the French Protestant youth. She had been asked where she learned so much about this recondite being, she had been congratulated on her peculiar opportunities. These opportunities consisted in her having once, in Paris, as she ascended a staircase, passed an open door where, in the household of a *pasteur* [minister], some of the young Protestants were seated at table round a finished meal. The glimpse made a picture; it lasted only a moment, but that moment was experience. She had got her direct personal impression, and she turned out her type. She knew what youth was, and what Protestantism; she also had the advantage of having seen what it was to be French, so that she converted these ideas into a concrete image and produced a reality. Above all, however, she was blessed with the faculty which when you give it an inch takes an ell,[5] and which for

the artist is a much greater source of strength than any accident of residence or of place in the social scale.

The power to guess the unseen from the seen, to trace the implication of things, to judge the whole piece by the pattern, the condition of feeling life in general so completely that you are well on your way to knowing any particular corner of it—this cluster of gifts may also be said to constitute experience, and they occur in country and in town, and in the most differing stages of education. If experience consists of impressions, it may be said that impressions *are* experience, just as (have we not seen it?) they are the very air we breathe.

Therefore, if I should certainly say to a novice, "Write from experience and experience only," I should feel that this was rather a tantalizing monition[6] if I were not careful immediately to add, "Try to be one of the people on whom nothing is lost!" . . .

But the only condition that I can think of attaching to the composition of the novel is, as I have already said, that it be sincere. This freedom is a splendid privilege, and the first lesson of the young novelist is to learn to be worthy of it.

"Enjoy it as it deserves," I should say to him; "take possession of it, explore it to its utmost extent, publish it, rejoice in it. All life belongs to you, and do not listen either to those who would shut you up into corners of it and tell you that it is only here and there that art inhabits. . . .

"Remember that your first duty is to be as complete as possible—to make as perfect a work. Be generous and delicate and pursue the prize."

---

4. **supposititious aspirant:** a hypothetical writer who seeks honors; hence, the novice who aims to write a fine novel.
5. **ell:** a former English measure of length equal to 45 inches.
6. **monition:** admonition.

Getting at Meaning

1. How does Henry James defend the importance of art in fiction? Why, according to James, are many people opposed to art in literature?

2. According to James, what are the two aims of literature?

3. Which definitions of "a good novel" does James disagree with? What makes a novel "good" to James?

4. What does James believe should be the basis for all writing? How does the anecdote of the English novelist illustrate James's opinion? Explain James's statement, "Try to be one of the people on whom nothing is lost."

5. What advice does James give to the young novelist? Explain it.

Developing Skills in Reading Literature

1. **Figurative Language.** Using a simile and a metaphor, James compares a novel to a dinner: "The 'ending' of a novel is, for many persons, like that of a good dinner, a course of dessert and ices, and the artist in fiction is regarded as a sort of meddlesome doctor who forbids agreeable aftertastes." How do these comparisons mock James's opponents? Find three other examples of figurative language used by James to advance his views on literature. Explain the idea communicated by each example.

2. **Theme.** James presents his own theories about literature as he attacks the opinions of those who disagree. Find two passages that show James's disapproval of his opponents; for example, in one passage he degrades his opponents by commenting that they read novels "as an exercise in skipping." How does he rebut their arguments? Summarize the definition of fiction that emerges from this discussion.

Developing Vocabulary

Inferring Word Meaning. James believes that literature should be artistic; he repeats the words *art, artist,* and *artistic* throughout his writing. From the context of this selection try to infer his definition of *art*. Then identify the dictionary definition of *art* that best fits James's usage.

Mark Twain

from **Life on the Mississippi**

The Boy's Ambition

When I was a boy, there was but one permanent ambition among my comrades in our village [Hannibal, Missouri] on the west bank of the Mississippi River. That was, to be a steamboatman. We had transient ambitions of other sorts, but they were only transient. When a circus came and went, it left us all burning to become clowns; the first negro minstrel show that ever came to our section left us all suffering to try that kind of life; now and then we had a hope that, if we lived and were good, God would permit us to be pirates. These ambitions faded out, each in its turn; but the ambition to be a steamboatman always remained. . . .

My father was a justice of the peace, and I supposed he possessed the power of life and death over all men, and could hang anybody that offended him. This was distinction enough for me as a general thing; but the desire to be a steamboatman kept intruding, nevertheless. I first wanted to be a cabin-boy, so that I could come out with a white apron on and shake a tablecloth over the side, where all my old comrades could see me; later I thought I would rather be the deck-hand who stood on the end of the stage-plank with the coil of rope in his hand, because he was particularly conspicuous. But these were only day-dreams—they were too heavenly to be contemplated as real possibilities. By and by one of our boys went away. He was not heard of for a long time. At last he turned up as apprentice engineer or "striker" on a steam-

boat. This thing shook the bottom out of all my Sunday school teachings. That boy had been notoriously worldly, and I just the reverse; yet he was exalted to this eminence, and I left in obscurity and misery. There was nothing generous about this fellow in his greatness. He would always manage to have a rusty bolt to scrub while his boat tarried at our town, and he would sit on the inside guard[1] and scrub it, where we all could see him and envy him and loathe him. And whenever his boat was laid up he would come home and swell around the town in his blackest and greasiest clothes, so that nobody could help remembering that he was a steamboatman; and he used all sorts of steamboat technicalities in his talk, as if he were so used to them that he forgot common people could not understand them. He would speak of the "labboard"[2] side of a horse in an easy, natural way that would make one wish he was dead. And he was always talking about "St. Looy" like an old citizen; he would refer casually to occasions when he was "coming down Fourth Street," or when he was "passing by the Planter's House," or when there was a fire and he took a turn on the brakes of "the old Big Missouri"; and then he would go on and lie about how many towns the size of ours were burned down there that day. Two or three of the boys had long been persons of consideration among us because they had been to St.

---

1. **guard:** the framework of timbers protecting the paddle wheel and its shaft on a steamboat.
2. **labboard** (larboard): the loading side of a ship.

Louis once and had a vague general knowledge of its wonders, but the day of their glory was over now. They lapsed into a humble silence, and learned to disappear when the ruthless "cub"-engineer approached. This fellow had money, too, and hair-oil. Also an ignorant silver watch and a showy brass watch-chain. He wore a leather belt and used no suspenders. If ever a youth was cordially admired and hated by his comrades, this one was. No girl could withstand his charms. He "cut out" every boy in the village. When his boat blew up at last, it diffused a tranquil contentment among us such as we had not known for months. But when he came home the next week, alive, renowned, and appeared in church all battered up and bandaged, a shining hero, stared at and wondered over by everybody, it seemed to us that the partiality of Providence for an undeserving reptile had reached a point where it was open to criticism.

This creature's career could produce but one result, and it speedily followed. Boy after boy managed to get on the river. The minister's son became an engineer. The doctor's and the postmaster's sons became "mud clerks";[3] the wholesale liquor dealer's son became a barkeeper on a boat; four sons of the chief merchant, and two sons of the county judge, became pilots. Pilot was the grandest position of all. The pilot, even in those days of trivial wages, had a princely salary—from a hundred and fifty to two hundred and fifty dollars a month, and no board to pay. Two months of his wages would pay a preacher's salary for a year. Now some of us were left disconsolate. We could not get on the river—at least our parents would not let us.

So, by and by, I ran away. I said I would never come home again till I was a pilot and could come in glory. But somehow I could not manage it. I went meekly aboard a few of the boats that lay packed together like sardines at the long St. Louis wharf, and humbly inquired for the pilots, but got only a cold shoulder and short words from mates and clerks. I had to make the best of this sort of treatment for the time being, but I had comforting daydreams of a future when I should be a great and honored pilot, with plenty of money, and could kill some of these mates and clerks and pay for them.

from I Want To Be a Cub-Pilot

Months afterward the hope within me struggled to a reluctant death, and I found myself without an ambition. But I was ashamed to go home. I was in Cincinnati, and I set to work to map out a new career. I had been reading about the recent exploration of the river Amazon by an expedition sent out by our government. It was said that the expedition, owing to difficulties, had not thoroughly explored a part of the country lying about the headwaters, some four thousand miles from the mouth of the river. It was only about fifteen hundred miles from Cincinnati to New Orleans, where I could doubtless get a ship. I had thirty dollars left; I would go and complete the exploration of the Amazon. This was all the thought I gave to the subject. I never was great in matters of detail. I packed my valise, and took passage on an ancient tub called the *Paul Jones*, for New Orleans. For the sum of sixteen dollars I had the scarred and tarnished splendors of "her" main saloon principally to myself, for she was not a creature to attract the eye of wiser travelers. . . .

from A Cub-Pilot's Experience

What with lying on the rocks four days at Louisville, and some other delays, the poor

---

3. **"mud clerks"**: steamboat employees who went ashore to check off freight loaded or delivered.

old *Paul Jones* fooled away about two weeks in making the voyage from Cincinnati to New Orleans. This gave me a chance to get acquainted with one of the pilots, and he taught me how to steer the boat, and thus made the fascination of river life more potent than ever for me. . . .

I soon discovered two things. One was that a vessel would not be likely to sail for the mouth of the Amazon under ten or twelve years; and the other was that the nine or ten dollars still left in my pocket would not suffice for so impossible an exploration as I had planned, even if I could afford to wait for a ship. Therefore it followed that I must contrive a new career. The *Paul Jones* was now bound for St. Louis. I planned a siege against my pilot, and at the end of three hard days he surrendered. He agreed to teach me the Mississippi River from New Orleans to St. Louis for five hundred dollars, payable out of the first wages I should receive after graduating. I entered upon the small enterprise of "learning" twelve or thirteen hundred miles of the great Mississippi River with the easy confidence of my time of life. If I had really known what I was about to require of my faculties, I should not have had the courage to begin. I supposed that all a pilot had to do was to keep his boat in the river, and I did not consider that that could be much of a trick, since it was so wide.

The boat backed out from New Orleans at four in the afternoon, and it was "our watch" until eight. Mr. Bixby, my chief, "straightened her up," plowed her along past the sterns of the other boats that lay at the Levee, and then said, "Here, take her; shave those steamships as close as you'd peel an apple." I took the wheel, and my heartbeat fluttered up into the hundreds; for it seemed to me that we were about to scrape the side off every ship in the line, we were so close. I held my breath and began to claw the boat away from the danger; and I had my own opinion of the pilot

who had known no better than to get us into such peril, but I was too wise to express it. In half a minute I had a wide margin of safety intervening between the *Paul Jones* and the ships; and within ten seconds more I was set aside in disgrace, and Mr. Bixby was going into danger again and flaying me alive with abuse of my cowardice. I was stung, but I was obliged to admire the easy confidence with which my chief loafed from side to side of his wheel, and trimmed the ships so closely that disaster seemed ceaselessly imminent. When he had cooled a little he told me that the easy water was close ashore and the current outside, and therefore we must hug the bank, up-stream, to get the benefit of the former, and stay well out, down-stream, to take advantage of the latter. In my own mind I resolved to be a down-stream pilot and leave the up-streaming to people dead to prudence.

Now and then Mr. Bixby called my attention to certain things. Said he, "This is Six-Mile Point." I assented. It was pleasant enough information, but I could not see the bearing of it. I was not conscious that it was a matter of any interest to me. Another time he said, "This is Nine-Mile Point." Later he said, "This is Twelve-Mile Point." They were all about level with the water's edge; they all looked about alike to me; they were monotonously unpicturesque. I hoped Mr. Bixby would change the subject. But no; he would crowd up around a point, hugging the shore with affection, and then say: "The slack water ends here, abreast this bunch of China trees; now we cross over." So he crossed over. He gave me the wheel once or twice, but I had no luck. I either came near chipping off the edge of a sugar plantation, or I yawed too far from shore, and so dropped back into disgrace again and got abused.

The watch was ended at last, and we took supper and went to bed. At midnight the glare of a lantern shone in my eyes, and the night watchman said, "Come, turn out!" And then he left. I could not understand this extraordinary procedure; so I presently gave up trying to, and dozed off to sleep. Pretty soon the watchman was back again, and this time he was gruff. I was annoyed. I said,

"What do you want to come bothering around here in the middle of the night for? Now, as like as not, I'll not get to sleep again to-night."

The watchman said, "Well, if this ain't good, I'm blessed."

The "off-watch" was just turning in, and I heard some brutal laughter from them, and such remarks as "Hello, watchman! ain't the new cub turned out yet? He's delicate, likely. Give him some sugar in a rag, and send for the chambermaid to sing 'Rock-a-by Baby' to him."

About this time Mr. Bixby appeared on the scene. Something like a minute later I was climbing the pilot-house steps with some of my clothes on and the rest in my arms. Mr. Bixby was close behind, commenting. Here was something fresh—this thing of getting up in the middle of the night to go to work. It was a detail in piloting that had never occurred to me at all. I knew that boats ran all night, but somehow I had never happened to reflect that somebody had to get up out of a warm bed to run them. I began to fear that piloting was not quite so romantic as I had imagined it was; there was something very real and worklike about this new phase of it. . . .

Mr. Bixby made for the shore and soon was scraping it, just the same as if it had been daylight. And not only that, but singing:

Father in heaven, the day is declining, etc.

It seemed to me that I had put my life in the keeping of a peculiarly reckless outcast. Presently he turned on me and said, "What's the name of the first point above New Orleans?"

I was gratified to be able to answer promptly, and I did. I said I didn't know.

"Don't *know?*"

This manner jolted me. I was down at the foot[4] again, in a moment. But I had to say just what I had said before.

"Well, you're a smart one!" said Mr. Bixby. "What's the name of the *next* point?"

Once more I didn't know.

"Well, this beats anything. Tell me the name of *any* point or place I told you."

I studied awhile and decided that I couldn't.

"Look here! What do you start out from, above Twelve-Mile Point, to cross over?"

"I—I—don't know."

"You—you—don't know?" mimicking my drawling manner of speech. "What *do* you know?"

"I—I—nothing, for certain."

"By the great Caesar's ghost, I believe you! You're the stupidest dunderhead I ever saw or ever heard of, so help me Moses! The idea of *you* being a pilot—*you!* Why, you don't know enough to pilot a cow down a lane."

Oh, but his wrath was up! He was a nervous man, and he shuffled from one side of his wheel to the other as if the floor was hot. He would boil awhile to himself, and then overflow and scald me again.

"Look here! What do you suppose I told you the names of those points for?"

I tremblingly considered a moment, and then the devil of temptation provoked me to say, "Well to—to—be entertaining, I thought."

This was a red rag to the bull. He raged and stormed so (he was crossing the river at the time) that I judged it made him blind, because he ran over the steering-oar of a trading-scow. Of course the traders sent up a volley of red-hot profanity. Never was a man so grateful as Mr. Bixby was, because he was brimful, and here were subjects who could *talk back.* He threw open a window, thrust his head out, and such an irruption followed as I never had heard before. The fainter and farther away the scowmen's curses drifted, the higher Mr.

---

4. **down at the foot:** at the bottom of the class.

Bixby lifted his voice and the weightier his adjectives grew. When he closed the window he was empty. You could have drawn a seine through his system and not caught curses enough to disturb your mother with. Presently he said to me in the gentlest way, "My boy, you must get a little memorandum-book; and every time I tell you a thing, put it down right away. There's only one way to be a pilot, and that is to get this entire river by heart. You have to know it just like A B C."

That was a dismal revelation to me, for my memory was never loaded with anything but blank cartridges. However, I did not feel discouraged long. I judged that it was best to make some allowances, for doubtless Mr. Bixby was "stretching."[5] . . .

By the time we had gone seven or eight hundred miles up the river, I had learned to be a tolerably plucky up-stream steersman, in daylight; and before we reached St. Louis I had made a trifle of progress in night work, but only a trifle. I had a notebook that fairly bristled with the names of towns, "points," bars, islands, bends, reaches, etc.; but the information was to be found only in the notebook—none of it was in my head. It made my heart ache to think I had only got half of the river set down; for as our watch was four hours off and four hours on, day and night, there was a long four-hour gap in my book for every time I had slept since the voyage began. . . .

It turned out to be true. The face of the water, in time, became a wonderful book—a book that was a dead language to the uneducated passenger, but which told its mind to me without reserve, delivering its most cherished secrets as clearly as if it uttered them with a voice. And it was not a book to be read once and thrown aside, for it had a new story to tell every day. Throughout the long twelve hundred miles there was never a page that was void of interest, never one that you could leave unread without loss, never one that you would want to skip, thinking you could find higher enjoyment in some other thing. There never was so wonderful a book written by man; never one whose interest was so absorbing, so unflagging, so sparklingly renewed with every reperusal. The passenger who could not read it was charmed with a peculiar sort of faint dimple on its surface (on the rare occasions when he did not overlook it altogether); but to the pilot that was an *italicized* passage; indeed, it was more than that, it was a legend of the largest capitals, with a string of shouting exclamation points at the end of it, for it meant that a wreck or a rock was buried there that could tear the life out of the strongest vessel that ever floated. It is the faintest and simplest expression the water ever makes, and the most hideous to a pilot's eye. In truth, the passenger who could not read this book saw nothing but all manner of pretty pictures in it, painted by the sun and shaded by the clouds, whereas to the trained eye these were not pictures at all, but the grimmest and most dead earnest of reading matter.

Now when I had mastered the language of this water, and had come to know every trifling feature that bordered the great river as familiarly as I knew the letters of the alphabet, I had made a valuable acquisition. But I had lost something, too. I had lost something which could never be restored to me while I lived. All the grace, the beauty, the poetry, had gone out of the majestic river! I still kept in mind a certain wonderful sunset which I witnessed when steamboating was new to me. A broad expanse of the river was turned to blood; in the middle distance the red hue brightened into gold, through which a solitary log came floating, black and conspicuous; in one place a long, slanting mark lay sparkling upon the water; in another the surface was broken by boiling, tumbling rings, that were as many-tinted as an opal; where the ruddy flush was faintest, was a smooth spot that was

---

5. **"stretching"**: stretching the truth.

covered with graceful circles and radiating lines, ever so delicately traced; the shore on our left was densely wooded, and the somber shadow that fell from this forest was broken in one place by a long, ruffled trail that shone like silver; and high above the forest wall a clean-stemmed dead tree waved a single leafy bough that glowed like a flame in the unobstructed splendor that was flowing from the sun. There were graceful curves, reflected images, woody heights, soft distances; and over the whole scene, far and near, the dissolving lights drifted steadily, enriching it every passing moment with new marvels of coloring.

I stood like one bewitched. I drank it in, in a speechless rapture. The world was new to me, and I had never seen anything like this at home. But as I have said, a day came when I began to cease from noting the glories and the charms which the moon and the sun and the twilight wrought upon the river's face; another day came when I ceased altogether to note them. Then, if that sunset scene had been repeated, I should have looked upon it without rapture, and should have commented upon it, inwardly, after this fashion: "This sun means that we are going to have wind tomorrow; that floating log means that the river is rising, small thanks to it; that slanting mark on the water refers to a bluff reef which is going to kill somebody's steamboat one of these nights, if it keeps on stretching out like that; those tumbling 'boils' show a dissolving bar and a changing channel there; the lines and circles in the slick water over yonder are a warning that that troublesome place is shoaling[6] up dangerously; that silver streak in the shadow of the forest is the "break" from a new snag, and he has located himself in the very best place he could have found to fish for steamboats; that tall dead tree, with a single living branch, is not going to last long, and then how is a body ever going to get through this blind place at night without the friendly old landmark?"

No, the romance and beauty were all gone from the river. All the value any feature of it had for me now was the amount of usefulness it could furnish toward compassing the safe piloting of a steamboat. Since those days, I have pitied doctors from my heart. What does the lovely flush in a beauty's cheek mean to a doctor but a "break" that ripples above some deadly disease? Are not all her visible charms sown thick with what are to him the signs and symbols of hidden decay? Does he ever see her beauty at all, or doesn't he simply view her professionally, and comment upon her unwholesome condition all to himself? And doesn't he sometimes wonder whether he has gained most or lost most by learning his trade?

---

6. **shoaling:** forming a sand bar or a place of water too shallow for safe navigation.

Getting at Meaning

1. Why does Twain loathe the first boy from his village to get work on a steamboat? How does the boy glory in his triumph?

2. How does Twain make progress toward his boyhood ambition?

3. How does Mr. Bixby assist Twain? What does young Twain discover he has to learn?

4. Does Twain feel that he has gained or lost more by learning to pilot a riverboat? What does Twain feel he has lost? How does he use a sunset to illustrate the change in himself?

Developing Skills in Reading Literature

1. **Irony.** "I was gratified to be able to answer promptly," writes Twain, "and I did. I said I didn't know." Verbal irony, the expression of something unexpected, accounts for much of Mark Twain's humor. Find four comments that you find humorous, and explain their irony.

2. **Metaphor.** Twain uses these metaphors in reference to Mr. Bixby.

"He would boil awhile to himself, and then overflow and scald me again."

"This was a red rag to the bull."

"You could have drawn a seine through his system and not caught curses enough to disturb your mother with."

How does each metaphor characterize Mr. Bixby? How do the metaphors contribute to the humor of the selection?

3. **Analogy.** Twain draws an elaborate analogy between the river and a book. Find this analogy and explain its points of comparison. What makes the analogy so effective in describing the river?

In the last paragraph, Twain draws an analogy between doctors and steamboat pilots. How are the disadvantages of these two professions parallel?

4. **Tone.** On the whole, what is Twain's tone in *Life on the Mississippi?* How does the tone at the end of the selection differ from that of the beginning? What does the shift in tone reveal about Twain?

Developing Vocabulary

Getting Word Meaning from Context. Review this selection to identify five words that were unfamiliar as you read Twain's account for the first time. Examine the specific context in which each word appears, searching for clues to meaning. Also think about the way the word relates to the broader context of the selection. What clues to word meaning do you find? Are these clues sufficient to formulate a fairly accurate definition? Explain.

Developing Writing Skills

1. **Narrating an Autobiographical Incident.** Twain writes that as a boy he had one permanent ambition. Consider your own major ambition. Then describe an incident that either created or reinforced that ambition. Use specific details to make your narration seem realistic.

2. **Using Contrast.** Like Twain, you probably have daydreamed about something that turned out to be less exciting, romantic, or fulfilling than you had imagined. In a five-paragraph composition describe your fantasy and contrast it with reality. Use your first paragraph to introduce the contrast. In the body paragraphs detail the fantasy and the contrasting reality, and describe your feelings about the contrast. Conclude with a statement that suggests the importance of the experience in your life.

Lucy Stone

1818–1893

Lucy Stone, an American pioneer in the women's rights movement, was born near West Brookfield, Massachusetts, on August 13, 1818. Her father, a descendant of a Massachusetts Bay colonist, believed firmly that men were "divinely ordained to rule over women." Lucy could not accept this view and was so distressed when she found that the Bible seemed to support the domination of women that she eventually abandoned the traditional religion of her family and joined the Unitarian Church. Her father opposed her education, so she worked her way through a women's seminary and then through Oberlin College where she was regarded as a radical for her views on women's rights.

In 1848 Stone began to lecture for the Massachusetts Anti-Slavery Society, speaking against slavery and for the equality of women. She organized the first national Women's Rights Convention in Worcester, Massachusetts, in 1850, and was active in the succeeding annual meetings. Although she had intended not to marry, she met Henry Blackwell, also a crusader for women's rights, and married him in 1855, keeping her maiden name in protest against the loss of individuality signified by the changing of a woman's name. With Blackwell's support, Stone helped form the American Equal Rights Association, and the New Jersey, Massachusetts, New England, National and American Woman Suffrage Associations; she also founded and edited the *Woman's Journal*. Until she died in Dorchester, Massachusetts, on October 18, 1893, Stone worked tirelessly to achieve legislative reform and to garner public support for her cause—equality for all women under the law and in American society.

Disappointment Is the Lot of Women

From the first years to which my memory stretches, I have been a disappointed woman. When, with my brothers, I reached forth after the sources of knowledge, I was reproved with "It isn't fit for you; it doesn't belong to women." Then there was but one college in the world where women were admitted, and that was in Brazil. I would have found my way there, but by the time I was prepared to go, one was opened in the young State of Ohio—the first in the United States where women and Negroes could enjoy opportunities with white men. I was disappointed when I came to seek a profession worthy an immortal being—every employment was closed to me, except those of the teacher, the seamstress, and the housekeeper. In education, in marriage, in religion, in everything, disappointment is the lot of woman. It shall be the business of my life to deepen this disappointment in every woman's heart until she bows down to it no longer. I wish that women, instead of being walking showcases, instead of begging of their fathers and brothers the latest and gayest new bonnet, would ask of them their rights.

The question of Woman's Rights is a practical one. The notion has prevailed that it was only an ephemeral idea; that it was but women claiming the right to smoke cigars in the streets, and to frequent bar rooms. Others have supposed it a question of comparative intellect; others still, of sphere. Too much has already been said and written about woman's sphere. Trace all the doctrines to their source and they will be found to have no basis except in the usages and prejudices of the age. This is seen in the fact that what is tolerated in woman in one country is not tolerated in another. In this country women may hold prayer meetings, etc., but in Mohammedan countries it is written upon their mosques, "Women and dogs, and other impure animals, are not permitted to enter." Wendell Phillips[1] says, "The best and greatest thing one is capable of doing, that is his sphere." I have confidence in the Father to believe that when He gives us the capacity to do anything He does not make a blunder. Leave women, then, to find their sphere. And do not tell us before we are born even, that our province is to cook dinners, darn stockings, and sew on buttons.

We are told woman has all the rights she wants; and even women, I am ashamed to say, tell us so. They mistake the politeness of men for rights—seats while men stand in this hall tonight, and their adulations;[2] but these are mere courtesies. We want rights. The flour merchant, the house builder, and the postman charge us no less on account of our sex; but when we endeavor to earn money to pay all these, then, indeed, we find the difference. Man, if he have energy, may hew out for himself a path where no mortal has ever trod, held back by nothing but what is in himself; the world is all before him, where to choose; and we are glad for you, brothers, men, that is so. But the same society that drives forth the young man, keeps woman at home—a dependent—working little cats on worsted, and little dogs on punctured paper; but if she goes heartily and bravely to give herself to some worthy purpose, she is out of her sphere and she loses caste. Women working in tailor

---

1. **Wendell Phillips** (1811–1884): spokesman for abolition and women's suffrage.
2. **adulations:** excessive praise or flattery.

shops are paid one-third as much as men. Someone in Philadelphia has stated that women make fine shirts for twelve and a half cents apiece; that no woman can make more than nine a week, and the sum thus earned, after deducting rent, fuel, etc., leaves her just three and a half cents a day for bread. Is it a wonder that women are driven to prostitution? Female teachers in New York are paid fifty dollars a year, and for every such situation there are five hundred applications. I know not what you believe of God, but I believe He gave yearnings and longings to be filled, and that He did not mean all our time should be devoted to feeding and clothing the body. The present condition of woman causes a horrible perversion of the marriage relation. It is asked of a lady, "Has she married well?" "Oh, yes, her husband is rich." Woman must marry for a home, and you men are the sufferers by this; for a woman who loathes you may marry you because you have the means to get money which she can not have. But when woman can enter the lists[3] with you and make money for herself, she will marry you only for deep and earnest affection.

I am detaining you too long, many of you standing, that I ought to apologize, but women have been wronged so long that I may wrong you a little. . . . I have seen a woman at manual labor turning out chair-legs in a cabinetshop, with a dress short enough not to drag in the shavings. I wish other women would imitate her in this. It made her hands harder and broader, it is true, but I think a hand with a dollar and a quarter a day in it, better than one with a crossed ninepence. . . . The widening of woman's sphere is to improve her lot. Let us do it, and if the world scoff, let it scoff—if it sneer, let it sneer.

---

3. **enter the lists:** to accept a challenge to combat, as knights did in a medieval tournament.

Getting at Meaning

1. Why does Lucy Stone feel that disappointment is the lot of women in education, occupations, and marriage? How are women mistreated?

2. Explain how Lucy Stone intends to remedy the situation.

3. What is a woman's sphere, according to Stone? How does her view contrast with the conventional view of the time?

4. How will men gain through women's rights, according to Stone?

5. How does Stone expect society to react to her efforts?

Developing Skills in Reading Literature

Persuasion. Lucy Stone argues for women's rights in a logical, rhetorically effective way. Find the place where she cites an authority who upholds her view. Notice her statement, "I have confidence in the Father to believe that when He gives us the capacity to do anything He does not make a blunder." What ultimate authority does she use to sway her audience? What rhetorical question does she use for emotional impact? Explain how Stone rebuts her opponents' contentions with logical, factual arguments. Is Stone's overall tone logical or emotional? Explain your conclusion.

Developing Vocabulary

Idioms. An idiom has a meaning different from the literal meaning of the phrase. Stone uses the idiom "lose caste." Use a dictionary to help you determine the literal meaning of the idiom. Then explain its meaning as used by Stone.

Developing Writing Skills

Writing an Editorial. Read about a recent court case, speech, or law that involves women's rights in America. After you have clarified your point of view, write an editorial supporting that view. Use facts and examples, cite authorities, and introduce one or more rhetorical questions in your editorial.

CLIFF DWELLERS, 1913. *George Bellows.*
Los Angeles County Museum of Art.

Unit Review   *A National Conscience*

Understanding the Unit

1. The four selections in "The Indian Crisis" offer the reader four different perspectives on the same issue. How do the experiences, feelings, and conclusions presented in these selections differ? Do similarities exist? Explain your answers.

2. Explain how the short stories "The Story of an Hour," and "A Wagner Matinee" illustrate Lucy Stone's ideas about self-fulfillment and about the relationship between men and women.

3. Both Dickinson and Whitman are considered revolutionaries who broke with the poetic tradition of the nineteenth century. In what ways are their poems fresh and original? In what ways are they traditional in their use of poetic devices? Use examples from the poems in this unit to support your ideas.

4. Mark Twain comments on human foibles and follies in both his fiction and nonfiction. What human qualities and tendencies does he mock in the selections in this unit? What seem to be his favorite targets, as suggested by the narrow sample of his writings given here?

5. Frederick Douglass, Chief Joseph, and Lucy Stone all address the issue of oppression. Draw generalizations about the results of oppression and about the benefits of equality, as suggested or explained by these writers.

6. Analyze the methods of characterization used by writers of the following selections. Note that this list includes both fiction and nonfiction.

"An Occurrence at Owl Creek Bridge"

"My Life on the Plains"

"The Story of an Hour"

from *Life on the Mississippi*

7. Bret Harte, Mark Twain, Kate Chopin, and Willa Cather are all regional writers. Discuss the characteristics of each region that emerge from their writings. Be sure to consider character types and customs as well as details of setting.

Writing

1. The major literary movement in the second half of the nineteenth century was the transition from Romanticism to Realism. Ralph Waldo Emerson's poem "To Each and All," in Unit 3, typifies the Romantic view of the relationship between human beings and nature. In a well developed paragraph contrast Emerson's view with the realistic view evidenced in the poems of Stephen Crane. Use quotations from the poems of both Emerson and Crane in your analysis.

2. In the excerpt from *The Art of Fiction*, Henry James develops a definition of good fiction. Explain this definition in your own words, then discuss the qualities of good fiction as they apply to the major elements of fiction: character, setting, plot, and theme. Use examples from the short stories in this unit to illustrate your points.

3. According to Henry James, good literature endures; that is, it is timeless as well as timely. Choose two selections from "The Civil War" and two from "The Indian Crisis" and analyze their appeal for the contemporary reader.

4. In the second half of the nineteenth century, the historical forces of war, expansion, and urbanization influenced the American character and the literary expression of that character. Walt Whitman incorporates all three themes in his poetry. In a five-paragraph composition, describe Whitman's vision of America. Use quotations from his poems to support your ideas.

AUTOMAT, 1927. *Edward Hopper.*
Des Moines Art Center, Iowa.
James D. Edmondson Fund.

Unit 5

The Short Story (1900 to the Present)

ROOMS BY THE SEA, 1951. *Edward Hopper.*
Yale University Art Gallery.
Bequest of Stephen Carlton Clark, B. A., 1903.

The Modern Short Story

The short story as a literary form developed largely in the United States, with Washington Irving, Edgar Allan Poe, and Nathaniel Hawthorne bringing the form to maturation in the 1820's, 30's, and 40's. Poe, in his review of Hawthorne's collection *Twice-Told Tales*, gave what is probably the clearest early definition of the short story. He described it as a prose tale in which ". . . the author is enabled to carry out his full design without interruption. During the hour of perusal, the soul of the reader is at the writer's control." In other words, a short story is brief and intense, designed to be read in one sitting. Poe went on to say that everything in a short story contributes to a "single effect": "In the whole composition there should be no word written of which the tendency, direct or indirect, is not to the one pre-established design." In other words, a short story is generally about one central action or event, without the large number of characters and wealth of detail typical of longer works of fiction.

After Irving, Poe, and Hawthorne came other excellent short story writers, both in the United States and in other countries. Following the Civil War, the Romanticism of the earlier writers gave way to postwar realism; in the second half of the nineteenth century regional realists, such as Bret Harte, Mark Twain, and Ambrose Bierce, and psychological realists, such as Mary Wilkins Freeman, Henry James, and Willa Cather, dominated the short story genre.

TWENTIETH-CENTURY CHANGES

As the twentieth century arrived, artists in America and in Europe began to feel that they had exhausted the possibilities of nineteenth-century forms. In the visual arts, in music, and in literature, experimentation became popular. Sherwood Anderson, an American short story writer, produced stories with inconclusive, or "open," endings, encouraging the reader to focus more on character and atmosphere than on plot. Anderson believed that these stories were a truer reflection of modern life, with all its difficulties and anxieties, than were the more closed, traditional stories of the nineteenth century. Other twentieth-century writers agreed with Anderson, and his "open form" is the model for many modern American short stories.

The social and political events of the twentieth century have shaped the direction of American fiction. Without a doubt the United States has changed radically since 1900. Whereas over fifty percent of Americans lived on farms in 1900, today less than two percent of Americans live on farms. The rural society of 1900 is now largely urban, and the majority of American workers are industrial, not agrarian. American society has become mobile and nomadic, with people often living far away from where they were born and raised, far away from parents, grandparents, cousins, and siblings. The United States also has experienced several wars in the twentieth century: World War I, World War II, the Korean War, and the War in Vietnam. In addition, the Great Depression of the 1930's has been a major factor in shaping twentieth century consciousness. It is not surprising that fragmentation, loneliness, and alienation are major themes in modern fiction. These themes are expressed in forms that reflect the diversity and often the formlessness of twentieth-century society.

CONTEMPORARY TRENDS IN LITERATURE

Among the significant trends in twentieth-century literature is the flowering of women writers, a number of whom are represented in this unit. Minority writers—Black, Latino, and Native American, for example—also have become a major force in contemporary American culture, and some of their best stories appear in these pages. In spite of competition from radio, television, and the movies, writers continue to produce fiction. In the last few years several magazines, once famed for their publication of short fiction, have come back into circulation. New journals, devoted to the short story, appear regularly in contemporary America. The short story is not dead, but remains an important art form; perhaps the selections that follow, from some of our finest twentieth-century writers, will illustrate why.

NIGHTHAWKS, 1942. *Edward Hopper. Courtesy of The Art Institute of Chicago.*

Literature

- Sherwood Anderson (1876–1941) publishes *Winesburg, Ohio*

- Jack London (1876–1916) publishes *The Call of the Wild*

- Claude McKay (1890–1948) publishes volume of poetry about New York

- William Carlos Williams (1883–1963) publishes *Poems*

- F. Scott Fitzgerald (1896–1940) publishes "Winter Dreams" and *The Beautiful and the Damned*

- Edgar Lee Masters (1869–1950) publishes *Spoon River Anthology*

- Carl Sandburg (1878–1967) publishes poem "Chicago"

- Jean Toomer (1894–1967) publishes *Cane*

- Vachel Lindsay (1879–1931) publishes first collection of poetry

- E.E. Cummings (1894–1962) publishes first book of poetry

- Robert Frost (1874–1963) publishes first volume of poetry

- Ernest Hemingway (1898–1961) publishes *The Sun Also Rises*

- Amy Lowell (1874–1925) publishes first book of poetry

- William Faulkner (1897–1962) publishes *The Sound and the Fury*

- Eugene O'Neill's first play staged by Provincetown Players

- Thomas Wolfe (1900–1938) publishes *Look Homeward, Angel*

- Paul Laurence Dunbar (1872–1906) —*Complete Poems* published posthumously

- Katherine Anne Porter (1890–1980) publishes volume of six stories, *Flowering Judas*

- Edna St. Vincent Millay (1892–1950) publishes *Collected Poems*

- Kay Boyle (1903–   ) has first stories published in the U.S. in *The New Yorker* magazine

- T.S. Eliot (1888–1965) publishes first volume of verse including "The Love Song of J. Alfred Prufrock"

- James Thurber (1894–1961) publishes *My Life and Hard Times*

- Langston Hughes (1902–1967) publishes first book of poems *The Weary Blues*

- Thornton Wilder (1897–1975) publishes *Our Town*

1900	1910	1920	1930	1940

History

- Scopes Trial debates teaching of evolution in public schools

- NAACP is founded

- McKinley assassinated; Theodore Roosevelt becomes President

- Panama Canal is opened

- U.S. enters World War I

- U.S. enters World War I

- 19th Amendment grants women the right to vote

- Prohibition goes into effect

- Sacco and Vanzetti are executed

- The New Deal begins

- Prohibition is repealed

- Stock Market crashes, beginning The Great Depression

- Franklin Delano Roosevelt is elected President

John Dos Passos (1896–1970)
completes his trilogy *U.S.A.*

- John Steinbeck (1902–1968)
  publishes *The Grapes of Wrath*

- Eudora Welty (1909–) publishes
  first collection of stories *A
  Curtain of Green*

- Richard Wright (1908–1960)
  publishes *American Hunger*

Franklin Delano Roosevelt (1882–
1945) delivers War Message to
Congress

- Loren Eiseley (1907–1977)
  publishes *The Unexpected Universe*

- Lorraine Hansberry (1930–1965)
  publishes *To Be Young, Gifted,
  and Black*

- Maxine Kumin (1925–) wins
  Pulitzer Prize for poetry

- Teresa Palomo Acosta (1949–)
  publishes anthology of Chicano
  Literature

- Tillie Olsen (1913–) wins
  O. Henry award for "Tell Me a Riddle"

- Richard Rodriguez (1944–)
  publishes *Hunger of Memory*

- John Updike (1932–) publishes
  first novel *The Poorhouse Fair*

- Theodore Roethke (1908–1963) wins
  **Pulitzer Prize for collection of
  poems** *The Waking*

- Flannery O'Connor (1925–1964)
  completes first draft of *Wise Blood*

- W.H. Auden (1907–1973) wins
  Pulitzer Prize for narrative
  poem *The Age of Anxiety*

- Shirley Jackson (1919–1965) first
  publishes "The Lottery"

- Richard Wilbur (1921–)
  publishes first collection of poetry

- Ray Bradbury (1920–) publishes
  first book of short stories,
  Dark Carnival

- Tennessee Williams (1914–1983)
  publishes *The Glass Menagerie*

- Kurt Vonnegut, Jr. (1922–)
  publishes "Harrison Bergeron"

- Rachel Carson (1907–1964)
  publishes *Silent Spring*

- Robert Hayden (1913–1980) wins
  prize for poetry at First World
  Festival of Negro Arts

- James Baldwin (1924–)
  publishes *Tell Me How Long the
  Train's Been Gone*

- Alfred Kazin (1915–) publishes
  A Walker in the City

1950	1960	1970	Present

- Watergate break-in occurs

- Korean war ends

- Supreme Court decision outlaws
  segregation

- Richard Nixon resigns Presidency

- Sit-ins for equal rights start in
  North Carolina

- U.S. celebrates bicentennial

- U.S. drops two atomic bombs on
  Japan, ending World War II

- United Nations is organized

- F.D.R. dies

- John F. Kennedy becomes President

- Alan Shepard becomes first
  American in space

- Kennedy is assassinated

- American hostages return from Iran

- Sally Ride, first American woman
  astronaut, flies in Space Shuttle
  Challenger

- Tonkin Gulf Resolution escalates
  war in Vietnam

- U.S. sends troops to fight in Korea

- Martin Luther King, Jr. is
  assassinated

Passage and Change

ABOVE THE NARROWS, 1960. *Andrew Wyeth.* Courtesy of Mr. Jack Dreyfus.

Sherwood Anderson

1876–1941

Alfred Stieglitz

Sherwood Anderson could be called the dean of the distinguished twentieth-century American short story writers. It was Anderson's "open form," reflecting as it does the complex and precarious nature of modern life, that inaugurated a new era in the short story, significantly influencing later writers. *Winesburg, Ohio*, Anderson's best known collection of stories, has become an American classic.

Anderson came from the small town of Camden, Ohio. He grew up in a large, impoverished family and dropped out of high school after one year. To help support his family, he worked at a steady stream of odd jobs, everything from newsboy to farmhand to race track helper. When he was twenty-two he served in Cuba in the Spanish-American War. Afterwards, attempting to make up for his lack of education, he attended a preparatory school, the Wittenberg Academy in Springfield, Ohio, for one year.

Anderson then went to Chicago to become an advertising copywriter, and later he moved to Elyria, Ohio, where he became a paint manufacturer. The business world did not suit Anderson, and in 1913 he returned to Chicago, determined to write fiction.

In Chicago Anderson was encouraged by the leaders of the Chicago literary movement, writers such as Carl Sandburg, Theodore Dreiser, and Ben Hecht. With their help Anderson began contributing to journals and magazines and in 1916 and 1917 brought out two novels, *Windy McPherson's Son* and *Marching Men*, both written while he was still a manufacturer. Although these books met with critical appreciation, it was *Winesburg, Ohio*, published in 1919, that established Anderson as an original and important literary figure. The book is a collection of stories about the residents of this small town, with the character of George Willard, a young Winesburg reporter, appearing in a number of the stories and tying them together.

Anderson published a number of other collections of stories during the 1920's and 1930's, including *The Triumph of the Egg*, which gained acclaim almost equal to that of *Winesburg, Ohio*. He wrote several more novels, among them *Poor White* and *Dark Laughter*. Anderson's work is characterized by simple language and by people he called "grotesques." In the introduction to *Winesburg, Ohio*, Anderson explains that "grotesques" allow one belief or ambition to devour them. In their unswerving pursuit of their obsessions, they lead lonely, isolated lives. To Anderson these people are symbols of American life, particularly in Middle Western small towns, and he writes of them with great compassion.

In 1925 Anderson moved to Marion, Virginia, where he became a farmer and a newspaper editor, publishing both of the town newspapers, one Republican, the other Democratic. Later important writers, such as Ernest Hemingway and William Faulkner, turned to Anderson for help and advice.

Anderson died suddenly in 1941 in Panama, while traveling.

Sophistication

It was early evening of a day in the late fall and the Winesburg County Fair had brought crowds of country people into town. The day had been clear and the night came on warm and pleasant. On the Trunion Pike, where the road after it left town stretched away between berry fields now covered with dry brown leaves, the dust from passing wagons arose in clouds. Children, curled into little balls, slept on the straw scattered on wagon beds. Their hair was full of dust and their fingers black and sticky. The dust rolled away over the fields and the departing sun set it ablaze with colors.

In the main street of Winesburg, crowds filled the stores and the sidewalks. Night came on, horses whinnied, the clerks in the stores ran madly about, children became lost and cried lustily, an American town worked terribly at the task of amusing itself.

Pushing his way through the crowds in Main Street, young George Willard concealed himself in the stairway leading to Doctor Reefy's office and looked at the people. With feverish eyes he watched the faces drifting past under the store lights. Thoughts kept coming into his head and he did not want to think. He stamped impatiently on the wooden steps and looked sharply about. "Well, is she going to stay with him all day? Have I done all this waiting for nothing?" he muttered.

George Willard, the Ohio village boy, was fast growing into manhood, and new thoughts had been coming into his mind. All that day, amid the jam of people at the Fair, he had gone about feeling lonely. He was about to leave Winesburg to go away to some city where he hoped to get work on a city newspaper, and he felt grown up. The mood that had taken possession of him was a thing known to men and unknown to boys. He felt old and a little tired. Memories awoke in him. To his mind his new sense of maturity set him apart, made of him a half-tragic figure. He wanted someone to understand the feeling that had taken possession of him after his mother's death.

There is a time in the life of every boy when he for the first time takes the backward view of life. Perhaps that is the moment when he crosses the line into manhood. The boy is walking through the street of his town. He is thinking of the future and of the figure he will cut in the world. Ambitions and regrets awake within him. Suddenly something happens; he stops under a tree and waits as for a voice calling his name. Ghosts of old things creep into his consciousness; the voices outside of himself whisper a message concerning the limitations of life. From being quite sure of himself and his future, he becomes not at all sure. If he be an imaginative boy a door is torn open and for the first time he looks out upon the world, seeing, as though they marched in procession before him, the countless figures of men who before his time have come out of nothingness into the world, lived their lives and again disappeared into nothingness. The sadness of sophistication has come to the boy. With a little gasp he sees himself as merely a leaf blown by the wind through the streets of his village. He knows that in spite of all the stout talk of his fellows he must live and die in uncertainty, a thing blown by the winds, a thing destined like corn to wilt in the sun. He shivers and looks eagerly about. The eighteen years he has lived seem but a moment, a breathing space in the long march of humanity. Already he hears death calling. With all his heart he wants to come close to some other human, touch someone with his hands, be touched by the hand of another. If he prefers that the other be a woman, that is because he believes that a woman will be gentle, that she will understand. He wants, most of all, understanding.

When the moment of sophistication came to George Willard, his mind turned to Helen White, the Winesburg banker's daughter. Always he had been conscious of the girl growing into womanhood as he grew into manhood. Once on a summer night when he was eighteen, he had walked with her on a country road and in her presence had given way to an impulse to boast, to make himself appear big and significant in her eyes. Now he wanted to see her for another purpose. He wanted to tell her of the new impulses that had come to him. He had tried to make her think of him as a man when he knew nothing of manhood, and now he wanted to be with her and to try to make her feel the change he believed had taken place in his nature.

As for Helen White, she also had come to a period of change. What George felt, she in her young woman's way felt also. She was no longer a girl and hungered to reach into the grace and beauty of womanhood. She had come home from Cleveland, where she was attending college, to spend a day at the Fair. She also had begun to have memories. During the day she sat in the grandstand with a young man, one of the instructors from the college, who was a guest of her mother's. The young man was of a pedantic turn of mind, and she felt at once he would not do for her purpose. At the Fair she was glad to be seen in his company as he was well dressed and a stranger. She knew that the fact of his presence would create an impression. During the day she was happy, but when night came on she began to grow restless. She wanted to drive the instructor away, to get out of his presence. While they sat together in the grandstand and while the eyes of former schoolmates were upon them, she paid so much attention to her escort that he grew interested. "A scholar needs money. I should marry a woman with money," he mused.

Helen White was thinking of George Willard even as he wandered gloomily through the crowds thinking of her. She remembered the summer evening when they had walked together and wanted to walk with him again. She thought that the months she had spent in the city, the going to theatres and the seeing of great crowds wandering in lighted thoroughfares, had changed her profoundly. She wanted him to feel and be conscious of the change in her nature.

The summer evening together that had left its mark on the memory of both the young man and woman had, when looked at quite sensibly, been rather stupidly spent. They had walked out of town along a country road. Then they had stopped by a fence near a field of young corn, and George had taken off his coat and let it hang on his arm. "Well, I've stayed here in Winesburg—yes—I've not yet gone away but I'm growing up," he had said. "I've been reading books and I've been thinking. I'm going to try to amount to something in life.

"Well," he explained, "that isn't the point. Perhaps I'd better quit talking."

The confused boy put his hand on the girl's arm. His voice trembled. The two started to walk back along the road toward town. In his desperation George boasted, "I'm going to be a big man, the biggest that ever lived here in Winesburg," he declared. "I want you to do something, I don't know what. Perhaps it is none of my business. I want you to try to be different from other women. You see the point. It's none of my business, I tell you. I want you to be a beautiful woman. You see what I want."

The boy's voice failed, and in silence the two came back into town and went along the street to Helen White's house. At the gate he tried to say something impressive. Speeches he had thought out came into his head, but they seemed utterly pointless. "I thought—I used to think—I had it in my mind you would marry Seth Richmond. Now I know you won't," was all he could find to say as she went through the gate and toward the door of her house.

On the warm fall evening as he stood in the stairway and looked at the crowd drifting through Main Street, George thought of the talk beside the field of young corn and was ashamed of the figure he had made of himself. In the street the people surged up and down like cattle confined in a pen. Buggies and wagons almost filled the narrow thoroughfare. A band played and small boys raced along the sidewalk, diving between the legs of men. Young men with shining red faces walked awkwardly about with girls on their arms. In a room above one of the stores, where a dance was to be held, the fiddlers tuned their instruments. The broken sounds floated down through an open window and out across the murmur of voices and the loud blare of the horns of the band. The medley of sounds got on young Willard's nerves. Everywhere, on all sides, the sense of crowding, moving life closed in about him. He wanted to run away by himself and think. "If she wants to stay with that fellow she may. Why should I care? What difference does it make to me?" he growled and went along Main Street and through Hern's grocery into a side street.

George felt so utterly lonely and dejected that he wanted to weep, but pride made him walk rapidly along, swinging his arms. He came to Westley Moyer's livery barn and stopped in the shadows to listen to a group of men who talked of a race Westley's stallion, Tony Tip, had won at the Fair during the afternoon. A crowd had gathered in front of the barn, and before the crowd walked Westley, prancing up and down and boasting. He held a whip in his hand and kept tapping the ground. Little puffs of dust arose in the lamp-

light. "Hey, quit your talking," Westley exclaimed. "I wasn't afraid; I knew I had 'em beat all the time. I wasn't afraid."

Ordinarily George Willard would have been intensely interested in the boasting of Moyer, the horseman. Now it made him angry. He turned and hurried away along the street. "Old windbag," he sputtered. "Why does he want to be bragging? Why don't he shut up?"

George went into a vacant lot, and as he hurried along, fell over a pile of rubbish. A nail protruding from an empty barrel tore his trousers. He sat down on the ground and swore. With a pin he mended the torn place and then arose and went on. "I'll go to Helen White's house; that's what I'll do. I'll walk right in. I'll say that I want to see her. I'll walk right in and sit down, that's what I'll do," he declared, climbing over a fence and beginning to run.

On the veranda of Banker White's house Helen was restless and distraught. The instructor sat between the mother and daughter. His talk wearied the girl. Although he had also been raised in an Ohio town, the instructor began to put on the airs of the city. He wanted to appear cosmopolitan. "I like the chance you have given me to study the background out of which most of our girls come," he declared. "It was good of you, Mrs. White, to have me down for the day." He turned to Helen and laughed. "Your life is still bound up with the life of this town?" he asked. "There are people here in whom you are interested?" To the girl his voice sounded pompous and heavy.

Helen arose and went into the house. At the door leading to a garden at the back she stopped and stood listening. Her mother began to talk. "There is no one here fit to associate with a girl of Helen's breeding," she said.

Helen ran down a flight of stairs at the back of the house and into the garden. In the darkness she stopped and stood trembling. It seemed to her that the world was full of meaningless people saying words. Afire with eagerness she ran through a garden gate, and turning a corner by the banker's barn, went into a little side street. "George! Where are you, George?" she cried, filled with nervous excitement. She stopped running, and leaned against a tree to laugh hysterically. Along the dark little street came George Willard, still saying words. "I'm going to walk right into her house. I'll go right in and sit down," he declared as he came up to her. He stopped and stared stupidly. "Come on," he said and took hold of her hand. With hanging heads they walked away along the street under the trees. Dry leaves rustled under foot. Now that he had found her, George wondered what he had better do and say.

At the upper end of the fair ground, in Winesburg, there is a half decayed old grandstand. It has never been painted and the boards are all warped out of shape. The fair ground stands on top of a low hill rising out of the valley of Wine Creek, and from the grandstand one can see at night, over a cornfield, the lights of the town reflected against the sky.

George and Helen climbed the hill to the fair ground, coming by the path past Waterworks Pond. The feeling of loneliness and isolation that had come to the young man in the crowded streets of his town was both broken and intensified by the presence of Helen. What he felt was reflected in her.

In youth there are always two forces fighting in people. The warm unthinking little animal struggles against the thing that reflects and remembers, and the older, the more sophisticated thing had possession of George Willard. Sensing his mood, Helen walked beside him filled with respect. When they got to the grandstand, they climbed up under the roof and sat down on one of the long benchlike seats.

There is something memorable in the experience to be had by going into a fair ground that stands at the edge of a Middle Western town on a night after the annual fair has been held. The sensation is one never to be forgotten. On all sides are ghosts, not of the dead, but of living people. Here, during the day just passed, have come the people pouring in from the town and the country around. Farmers with their wives and children and all the people from the hundreds of little frame houses have gathered within these board walls. Young girls have laughed and men with beards have talked of the affairs of their lives. The place has been filled to overflowing with life. It has itched and squirmed with life and now it is night and the life has all gone away. The silence is almost terrifying. One conceals oneself standing silently beside the trunk of a tree, and what there is of a reflective tendency in his nature is intensified. One shudders at the thought of the meaninglessness of life while at the same instant, and if the people of the town are his people, one loves life so intensely that tears come into the eyes.

In the darkness under the roof of the grandstand, George Willard sat beside Helen White and felt very keenly his own insignificance in the scheme of existence. Now that he had come out of town where the presence of the people stirring about, busy with a multitude of affairs, had been so irritating, the irritation was all gone. The presence of Helen renewed and refreshed him. It was as though her woman's hand was assisting him to make some minute readjustment of the machinery of his life. He began to think of the people in the town where he had always lived with something like reverence. He had reverence for Helen. He wanted to love and to be loved by her, but he did not want at the moment to be confused by her womanhood. In the darkness he took hold of her hand, and when she crept close put a hand on her shoulder. A wind began to blow and he shivered. With all his strength he tried to hold and to understand the mood that had come upon him. In that high place in the darkness the two oddly sensitive human atoms held each other tightly and waited. In the mind of each was the same thought. "I have come to this lonely place and here is this other," was the substance of the thing felt.

In Winesburg the crowded day had run itself out into the long night of the late fall. Farm horses jogged away along lonely country roads, pulling their portion of weary people. Clerks began to bring samples of goods in off the sidewalks and lock the doors of stores. In the Opera House a crowd had gathered to see a show, and further down Main Street the fiddlers, their instruments tuned, sweated and worked to keep the feet of youth flying over a dance floor.

In the darkness in the grandstand Helen White and George Willard remained silent. Now and then the spell that held them was broken and they turned and tried in the dim light to see into each other's eyes. They kissed, but that impulse did not last. At the upper end of the fair ground a half dozen men worked over horses that had raced during the afternoon. The men had built a fire and were heating kettles of water. Only their legs could be seen as they passed back and forth in the light. When the wind blew, the little flames of the fire danced crazily about.

George and Helen arose and walked away into the darkness. They went along a path past a field of corn that had not yet been cut. The wind whispered among the dry corn blades. For a moment during the walk back into town, the spell that held them was broken. When they had come to the crest of Waterworks Hill they stopped by a tree, and George again put his hands on the girl's shoulders. She embraced him eagerly, and then again they drew quickly back from that impulse. They stopped kissing and stood a little apart. Mutual respect grew big in them. They were both embarrassed, and to relieve their embarrassment, dropped into the animalism of youth. They laughed and began to pull and haul at each other. In some way chastened and purified by the mood they had been in they became, not man and woman, not boy and girl, but excited little animals.

It was so they went down the hill. In the darkness they played like two splendid young things in a young world. Once, running swiftly forward, Helen tripped George and he fell. He squirmed and shouted. Shaking with laughter, he rolled down the hill. Helen ran after him. For just a moment she stopped in the darkness. There is no way of knowing what woman's thoughts went through her mind but, when the bottom of the hill was reached and she came up to the boy, she took his arm and walked beside him in dignified silence. For some reason they could not have explained, they had both got from their silent evening together the thing needed. Man or boy, woman or girl, they had for a moment taken hold of the thing that makes the mature life of men and women in the modern world possible.

Getting at Meaning

1. What is George Willard's state of mind at the beginning of this story? Why does he have a sudden "new sense of maturity"?

2. What are some of the thoughts that accompany "the sadness of sophistication" according to the narrator?

3. What is Helen White's state of mind when she comes home for the fair? Why doesn't she care very much for the young instructor who has come home with her? Why does she like being seen with him?

4. Describe the evening walk that George and Helen had taken together in the summer. What kinds of things did George say to Helen?

5. Why is George afraid to approach Helen on the day of the fair? What attitude does Helen's mother have toward the people in the town?

6. Why do George and Helen visit the deserted fairgrounds? What are their emotions there? Why don't they speak?

7. What makes George and Helen become like "little animals" out in the country? What is it each one gets from the silent evening?

Developing Skills in Reading Literature

1. **Setting.** The setting of "Sophistication" is a significant force in the story, as is usually true in Sherwood Anderson's work. What kind of town is Winesburg, Ohio? What clues does the story offer about the time period in which the story takes place? At what time of year does the story take place? What is the effect of his surroundings, both time and place, on George Willard?

2. **Symbol.** The corn growing around Winesburg has symbolic significance in this story. When George and Helen take their walk in the summer, how is the corn described? When they walk into the country on the night of the fair, how is the corn described? In what ways is the corn symbolic of George and Helen?

3. **Paradox.** Explain the following two paradoxes, both statements that appear contradictory but are nevertheless true.

The feeling of loneliness and isolation that had come to the young man in the crowded streets of his town was both broken and intensified by the presence of Helen.

One shudders at the thought of the meaninglessness of life while at the same instant, and if the people of the town are his people, one loves life so intensely that tears come into the eyes.

4. **Theme.** What point does Sherwood Anderson make about isolation? about human communication? Explain the meaning behind the final sentence of the story, "Man or boy, woman or girl, they had for a moment taken hold of the thing that makes the mature life of men and women in the modern world possible."

5. **Title.** Think about the meaning of the title "Sophistication" in relation to the theme of the story. In what ways have George and Helen become sophisticated? In what ways is the title meant ironically? How does the title relate to the message the story imparts about the human need for contact with others?

Developing Vocabulary

Greek Roots. The instructor that Helen White brings home is described as pedantic, or exhibiting his scholarship and learning ostentatiously. *Pedantic* is derived from the Greek word *paidagōgus*, meaning "trainer or teacher of boys." The root *paedo-* or *pedo-* means "child." (Do not confuse this root with the root *ped-*, meaning "foot.")

Look up the words that follow in a dictionary, observing how the root *pedo-* functions in each word. Write the meaning for each word.

pedagogue	pedodontia
pedantry	pedology
pediatrics	

F. Scott Fitzgerald
1896–1940

F. Scott Fitzgerald wrote about "a heightened sensitivity to the promises of life," to use a phrase from *The Great Gatsby*, his masterpiece. He also wrote about the sadness and failure that inevitably come to those who possess this "romantic readiness."

Success came early to Fitzgerald. He was born in St. Paul, Minnesota, to a family of moderate means and aristocratic pretensions. His father was a descendant of Francis Scott Key, author of the lyrics of "The Star-Spangled Banner," and he named his son Francis Scott as a consequence. Fitzgerald grew up in St. Paul, where he attended two prep schools, and later he went to Princeton University.

Fitzgerald became a prominent literary figure on the Princeton campus, winning election to several prestigious positions. An unhappy love affair caused him to flunk out at one point, but he later returned. He left to join the army before he graduated, in response to the United States' entry into World War I.

While Fitzgerald was in army training in Alabama, he met Zelda Sayre, the daughter of an Alabama Supreme Court judge. The two fell in love, and after a tumultuous courtship they were married in 1920. In that same year, at age twenty-four, Fitzgerald published his first novel, *This Side of Paradise*. His narrative spoke to the new morality of the 1920's, and Fitzgerald quickly found himself famous.

The next few years were a productive period for Fitzgerald. He wrote stories for well known magazines and published his second novel, *The Beautiful and the Damned*, in 1922. He and Zelda and their daughter moved to France in 1924, and one year later Fitzgerald published *The Great Gatsby*. Not yet thirty, he was enormously successful.

In Paris the Fitzgeralds became part of the expatriate group now known as the "Lost Generation." They moved in stimulating artistic and literary circles, Fitzgerald fraternizing with other important young writers of his day, such as Ernest Hemingway and Sinclair Lewis. The Fitzgeralds gave lavish parties, living what appeared to be a glittering, rather reckless life. For a time they reigned as "the prince and princess of their generation," as Ring Lardner put it. Then, sadly, things began to go wrong for the Fitzgeralds. Their marriage grew rocky, and both Scott and Zelda became increasingly unhappy. Eventually Zelda suffered first one nervous breakdown, then another. From 1932 on she was permanently hospitalized, a draining and debilitating reality to Fitzgerald.

After a nine-year hiatus in his writing, Fitzgerald managed to bring out a fourth novel in 1934, *Tender Is the Night*. He thought it was perhaps his best work, and it was a great blow to him when the book was not well received. The country was in the middle of the Depression in 1934, and readers no longer were fascinated by the "beautiful rich" that constituted Fitzgerald's subject matter.

By 1937 Fitzgerald had moved to Hollywood, where he found work as a scriptwriter. He lived there for several years, writing tender letters to his daughter at school and working on *The Last Tycoon*. This novel was not yet finished when Fitzgerald died suddenly of a heart attack, when he was only forty-four.

Fitzgerald is probably the novelist and short-story writer most representative of the 1920's, a major figure in twentieth-century American literature.

Winter Dreams

1

Some of the caddies were poor as sin and lived in one-room houses with a neurasthenic[1] cow in the front yard, but Dexter Green's father owned the second best grocery store in Black Bear—the best one was "The Hub," patronized by the wealthy people from Sherry Island—and Dexter caddied only for pocket money.

In the fall when the days became crisp and gray, and the long Minnesota winter shut down like the white lid of a box, Dexter's skis moved over the snow that hid the fairways of the golf course. At these times the country gave him a feeling of profound melancholy—it offended him that the links should lie in enforced fallowness, haunted by ragged sparrows for the long season. It was dreary, too, that on the tees where the gay colors fluttered in summer there were now only the desolate sandboxes knee-deep in crusted ice. When he crossed the hills the wind blew cold as misery, and if the sun was out he tramped with his eyes squinted up against the hard dimensionless glare.

In April the winter ceased abruptly. The snow ran down into Black Bear Lake scarcely tarrying for the early golfers to brave the season with red and black balls. Without elation, without an interval of moist glory, the cold was gone.

Dexter knew that there was something dismal about this Northern spring, just as he knew there was something gorgeous about the fall. Fall made him clinch his hands and tremble and repeat idiotic sentences to himself, and make brisk abrupt gestures of command to imaginary audiences and armies.

October filled him with hope which November raised to a sort of ecstatic triumph, and in this mood the fleeting brilliant impressions of the summer at Sherry Island were ready grist to his mill. He became a golf champion and defeated Mr. T. A. Hedrick in a marvelous match played a hundred times over the fairways of his imagination, a match each detail of which he changed about untiringly—sometimes he won with almost laughable ease, sometimes he came up magnificently from behind. Again, stepping from a Pierce-Arrow automobile, like Mr. Mortimer Jones, he strolled frigidly into the lounge of the Sherry Island Golf Club—or perhaps, surrounded by an admiring crowd, he gave an exhibition of fancy diving from the springboard of the club raft. . . . Among those who watched him in open-mouthed wonder was Mr. Mortimer Jones.

And one day it came to pass that Mr. Jones—himself and not his ghost—came up to Dexter with tears in his eyes and said that Dexter was the— —best caddy in the club, and wouldn't he decide not to quit if Mr. Jones made it worth his while, because every other— —caddy in the club lost one ball a hole for him—regularly—

"No, sir," said Dexter decisively, "I don't want to caddy any more." Then, after a pause, "I'm too old."

"You're not more than fourteen. Why the devil did you decide just this morning that you wanted to quit? You promised that next

---

1. **neurasthenic** (nur′ əs thē′ nĭc): impaired functioning in interpersonal relationships, usually accompanied by physical symptoms.

week you'd go over to the state tournament with me."

"I decided I was too old."

Dexter handed in his "A Class" badge, collected what money was due him from the caddy master, and walked home to Black Bear Village.

"The best— —caddy I ever saw," shouted Mr. Mortimer Jones over a drink that afternoon. "Never lost a ball! Willing! Intelligent! Quiet! Honest! Grateful!"

The little girl who had done this was eleven —beautifully ugly as little girls are apt to be who are destined after a few years to be inexpressibly lovely and bring no end of misery to a great number of men. The spark, however, was perceptible. There was a general ungodliness in the way her lips twisted down at the corners when she smiled, and in the— Heaven help us!—in the almost passionate quality of her eyes. Vitality is born early in such women. It was utterly in evidence now, shining through her thin frame in a sort of glow.

She had come eagerly out on to the course at nine o'clock with a white linen nurse and five small new golf clubs in a white canvas bag which the nurse was carrying. When Dexter first saw her she was standing by the caddy house, rather ill at ease and trying to conceal the fact by engaging her nurse in an obviously unnatural conversation graced by startling and irrelevant grimaces from herself.

"Well, it's certainly a nice day, Hilda," Dexter heard her say. She drew down the corners of her mouth, smiled, and glanced furtively around, her eyes in transit falling for an instant on Dexter.

Then to the nurse: "Well, I guess there aren't many people out here this morning, are there?"

The smile again—radiant, blatantly artificial—convincing.

"I don't know what we're supposed to do now," said the nurse, looking nowhere in particular.

"Oh, that's all right. I'll fix it up."

Dexter stood perfectly still, his mouth slightly ajar. He knew that if he moved forward a step his stare would be in her line of vision—if he moved backward he would lose his full view of her face. For a moment he had not realized how young she was. Now he remembered having seen her several times the year before—in bloomers.

Suddenly, involuntarily, he laughed, a short abrupt laugh—then, startled by himself, he turned and began to walk quickly away.

"Boy!"

Dexter stopped.

"Boy—"

Beyond question he was addressed. Not only that, but he was treated to that absurd smile, that preposterous smile—the memory of which at least a dozen men were to carry into middle age.

"Boy, do you know where the golf teacher is?"

"He's giving a lesson."

"Well, do you know where the caddy master is?"

"He isn't here yet this morning."

"Oh." For a moment this baffled her. She stood alternately on her right and left foot.

"We'd like to get a caddy," said the nurse. "Mrs. Mortimer Jones sent us out to play golf, and we don't know how without we get a caddy."

Here she was stopped by an ominous glance from Miss Jones, followed immediately by the smile.

"There aren't any caddies here except me," said Dexter to the nurse, "and I got to stay here in charge until the caddy master gets here."

"Oh."

Miss Jones and her retinue now withdrew, and at a proper distance from Dexter became involved in a heated conversation, which was concluded by Miss Jones taking one of the clubs and hitting it on the ground with violence. For further emphasis she raised it again and was about to bring it down smartly upon the nurse's bosom, when the nurse seized the club and twisted it from her hands.

"You little mean old *thing!*" cried Miss Jones wildly.

Another argument ensued. Realizing that the elements of the comedy were implied in the scene, Dexter several times began to laugh, but each time restrained the laugh before it reached audibility. He could not resist the monstrous conviction that the little girl was justified in beating the nurse.

The situation was resolved by the fortuitous appearance of the caddy master, who was appealed to immediately by the nurse.

"Miss Jones is to have a little caddy, and this one says he can't go."

"Mr. McKenna said I was to wait here till you came," said Dexter quickly.

"Well, he's here now." Miss Jones smiled cheerfully at the caddy master. Then she dropped her bag and set off at a haughty mince toward the first tee.

"Well?" The caddy master turned to Dexter. "What you standing there like a dummy for? Go pick up the young lady's clubs."

"I don't think I'll go out today," said Dexter.

"You don't—"

"I think I'll quit."

The enormity of his decision frightened him. He was a favorite caddy, and the thirty dollars a month he earned through the summer were not to be made elsewhere around the lake. But he had received a strong emotional shock, and his perturbation required a violent and immediate outlet.

It is not so simple as that, either. As so frequently would be the case in the future, Dexter was unconsciously dictated to by his winter dreams.

2

Now, of course, the quality and the seasonability of these winter dreams varied, but the stuff of them remained. They persuaded Dexter several years later to pass up a business course at the state university—his father, prospering now, would have paid his way—for the precarious advantage of attending an older and more famous university in the East, where he was bothered by his scanty funds. But do not get the impression, because his winter dreams happened to be concerned at first with musings on the rich, that there was anything merely snobbish in the boy. He wanted not association with glittering things and glittering people—he wanted the glittering things themselves. Often he reached out for the best without knowing why he wanted it—and sometimes he ran up against the mysterious denials and prohibitions in which life indulges. It is with one of those denials and not with his career as a whole that this story deals.

He made money. It was rather amazing. After college he went to the city from which Black Bear Lake draws its wealthy patrons. When he was only twenty-three and had been there not quite two years, there were already people who liked to say: "Now *there's* a boy—" All about him rich men's sons were peddling bonds precariously, or investing patrimonies[2] precariously, or plodding through the two dozen volumes of the "George Washington Commercial Course," but Dexter borrowed a thousand dollars on his college degree and his confident mouth, and bought a partnership in a laundry.

It was a small laundry when he went into it, but Dexter made a specialty of learning how the English washed fine woolen golf stockings without shrinking them, and within a year he was catering to the trade that wore knickerbockers. Men were insisting that their Shetland hose and sweaters go to his laundry, just as they had insisted on a caddy who could find golf balls. A little later he was doing their

---

2. **patrimonies:** estates or money inherited from one's father or ancestor.

wives' lingerie as well—and running five branches in different parts of the city. Before he was twenty-seven he owned the largest string of laundries in his section of the country. It was then that he sold out and went to New York. But the part of his story that concerns us goes back to the days when he was making his first big success.

When he was twenty-three Mr. Hart—one of the gray-haired men who like to say "Now there's a boy"—gave him a guest card to the Sherry Island Golf Club for a weekend. So he signed his name one day on the register, and that afternoon played golf in a foursome with Mr. Hart and Mr. Sandwood and Mr. T. A. Hedrick. He did not consider it necessary to remark that he had once carried Mr. Hart's bag over this same links, and that he knew every trap and gully with his eyes shut—but he found himself glancing at the four caddies who trailed them, trying to catch a gleam or gesture that would remind him of himself, that would lessen the gap which lay between his present and his past.

It was a curious day, slashed abruptly with fleeting, familiar impressions. One minute he had the sense of being a trespasser—in the next he was impressed by the tremendous superiority he felt toward Mr. T. A. Hedrick, who was a bore and not even a good golfer any more.

Then, because of a ball Mr. Hart lost near the fifteenth green, an enormous thing happened. While they were searching the stiff grasses of the rough there was a clear call of "Fore!" from behind a hill in their rear. And as they all turned abruptly from their search, a bright new ball sliced abruptly over the hill and caught Mr. T. A. Hedrick in the abdomen.

"By Gad!" cried Mr. T. A. Hedrick, "they ought to put some of these crazy women off the course. It's getting to be outrageous."

A head and a voice came up together over the hill: "Do you mind if we go through?"

"You hit me in the stomach!" declared Mr. Hedrick wildly.

"Did I?" The girl approached the group of men. "I'm sorry. I yelled 'Fore!'"

Her glance fell casually on each of the men—then scanned the fairway for her ball.

"Did I bounce into the rough?"

It was impossible to determine whether this question was ingenuous or malicious. In a moment, however, she left no doubt, for as her partner came up over the hill she called cheerfully, "Here I am! I'd have gone on the green except that I hit something."

As she took her stance for a short mashie shot, Dexter looked at her closely. She wore a blue gingham dress, rimmed at throat and shoulders with a white edging that accentuated her tan. The quality of exaggeration, of thinness, which had made her passionate eyes and down-turning mouth absurd at eleven, was gone now. She was arrestingly beautiful. The color in her cheeks was centered like the color in a picture—it was not a "high" color, but a sort of fluctuating and feverish warmth, so shaded that it seemed at any moment it would recede and disappear. This color and the mobility of her mouth gave a continual impression of flux, of intense life, of passionate vitality—balanced only partially by the sad luxury of her eyes.

She swung her mashie impatiently and without interest, pitching the ball into a sand-pit on the other side of the green. With a quick, insincere smile and a careless "Thank you!" she went on after it.

"That Judy Jones!" remarked Mr. Hedrick on the next tee, as they waited—some moments—for her to play on ahead. "All she needs is to be turned up and spanked for six months and then to be married off to an old-fashioned cavalry captain."

"My, she's good-looking!" said Mr. Sandwood, who was just over thirty.

"Good-looking!" cried Mr. Hedrick contemptuously, "she always looks as if she wanted to be kissed! Turning those big cow-eyes on every calf in town."

It was doubtful if Mr. Hedrick intended a

reference to the maternal instinct.

"She'd play pretty good golf if she'd try," said Mr. Sandwood.

"She has no form," said Mr. Hedrick solemnly.

"'She has a nice figure," said Mr. Sandwood.

"Better thank the Lord she doesn't drive a swifter ball," said Mr. Hart, winking at Dexter.

Later in the afternoon the sun went down with a riotous swirl of gold and varying blues and scarlets, and left the dry, rustling night of Western summer. Dexter watched from the veranda of the Golf Club, watched the even overlap of the waters in the little wind, silver molasses under the harvest moon. Then the moon held a finger to her lips and the lake became a clear pool, pale and quiet. Dexter put on his bathing suit and swam out to the farthest raft, where he stretched dripping on the wet canvas of the springboard.

There was a fish jumping and a star shining and the lights around the lake were gleaming. Over on a dark peninsula a piano was playing the songs of last summer and of summers before that— songs from *Chin-Chin* and *The Count of Luxemburg* and *The Chocolate Soldier*[3]—and because the sound of a piano over a stretch of water had always seemed beautiful to Dexter, he lay perfectly quiet and listened.

The tune the piano was playing at that moment had been gay and new five years before when Dexter was a sophomore at college. They had played it at a prom once when he could not afford the luxury of proms, and he had stood outside the gymnasium and listened. The sound of the tune precipitated in him a sort of ecstasy and it was with that ecstasy he viewed what happened to him now. It was a mood of intense appreciation, a sense that, for once, he was magnificently attuned to life and that everything about him was radiating a brightness and a glamour he might never know again.

A low, pale oblong detached itself suddenly from the darkness of the Island, spitting forth the reverberate sound of a racing motorboat. Two white streamers of cleft water rolled themselves out behind it and almost immediately the boat was beside him, drowning out the hot tinkle of the piano in the drone of its spray. Dexter raising himself on his arms was aware of a figure standing at the wheel, of two dark eyes regarding him over the lengthening space of water—then the boat had gone by and was sweeping in an immense and purposeless circle of spray round and round in the middle of the lake. With equal eccentricity one of the circles flattened out and headed back toward the raft.

"Who's that?" she called, shutting off her motor. She was so near now that Dexter could see her bathing suit, which consisted apparently of pink rompers.

The nose of the boat bumped the raft, and as the latter tilted rakishly he was precipitated toward her. With different degrees of interest they recognized each other.

"Aren't you one of those men we played through this afternoon?" she demanded.

He was.

"Well, do you know how to drive a motorboat? Because if you do I wish you'd drive this one so I can ride on the surfboard behind. My name is Judy Jones"—she favored him with an absurd smirk—rather, what tried to be a smirk, for, twist her mouth as she might, it was not grotesque, it was merely beautiful—"and I live in a house over there on the Island, and in that house there is a man waiting for me. When he drove up at the door I drove out of the dock because he says I'm his ideal."

There was a fish jumping and a star shining and the lights around the lake were gleaming. Dexter sat beside Judy Jones and she explained how her boat was driven. Then she was in the water, swimming to the floating surfboard with a sinuous crawl. Watching her

---

3. *Chin . . . Soldier:* popular operettas in that period.

was without effort to the eye, watching a branch waving or a seagull flying. Her arms, burned to butternut, moved sinuously among the dull platinum ripples, elbow appearing first, casting the forearm back with a cadence of falling water, then reaching out and down, stabbing a path ahead.

They moved out into the lake; turning, Dexter saw that she was kneeling on the low rear of the now uptilted surfboard.

"Go faster," she called, "fast as it'll go."

Obediently he jammed the lever forward and the white spray mounted at the bow. When he looked around again the girl was standing up on the rushing board, her arms spread wide, her eyes lifted toward the moon.

"It's awful cold," she shouted. "What's your name?"

He told her.

"Well, why don't you come to dinner tomorrow night?" His heart turned over like the flywheel of the boat, and, for the second time, her casual whim gave a new direction to his life.

3

Next evening while he waited for her to come downstairs, Dexter peopled the soft deep summer room and the sunporch that opened from it with the men who had already loved Judy Jones. He knew the sort of men they were—the men who when he first went to college had entered from the great prep schools with graceful clothes and the deep tan of healthy summers. He had seen that, in one sense, he was better than these men. He was newer and stronger. Yet in acknowledging to himself that he wished his children to be like them he was admitting that he was but the rough, strong stuff from which they eternally sprang.

When the time had come for him to wear good clothes, he had known who were the best tailors in America, and the best tailors in America had made him the suit he wore this evening. He had acquired that particular reserve peculiar to his university, that set it off from other universities. He recognized the value to him of such a mannerism and he had adopted it; he knew that to be careless in dress and manner required more confidence than to be careful. But carelessness was for his children. His mother's name had been Krimelich. She was a Bohemian of the peasant class, and she had talked broken English to the end of her days. Her son must keep to the set patterns.

At a little after seven Judy Jones came downstairs. She wore a blue silk afternoon dress, and he was disappointed at first that she had not put on something more elaborate. This feeling was accentuated when, after a brief greeting, she went to the door of a butler's pantry and pushing it open called, "You can serve dinner, Martha." He had rather expected that a butler would announce dinner, that there would be a cocktail. Then he put these thoughts behind him as they sat down side by side on a lounge and looked at each other.

"Father and Mother won't be here," she said thoughtfully.

He remembered the last time he had seen her father, and he was glad the parents were not to be here tonight—they might wonder who he was. He had been born in Keeble, a Minnesota village fifty miles farther north, and he always gave Keeble as his home instead of Black Bear Village. Country towns were well enough to come from if they weren't inconveniently in sight and used as footstools by fashionable lakes.

They talked of his university, which she had visited frequently during the past two years, and of the nearby city which supplied Sherry Island with its patrons, and whither Dexter would return next day to his prospering laundries.

During dinner she slipped into a moody depression which gave Dexter a feeling of uneasiness. Whatever petulance she uttered in her throaty voice worried him. Whatever she smiled at—at him, at a chicken liver, at nothing—it disturbed him that her smile could have no root in mirth, or even in amusement. When the scarlet corners of her lips curved down, it was less a smile than an invitation to a kiss.

Then, after dinner, she led him out on the dark sun porch and deliberately changed the atmosphere.

"Do you mind if I weep a little?" she said.

"I'm afraid I'm boring you," he responded quickly.

"You're not. I like you. But I've just had a terrible afternoon. There was a man I cared about, and this afternoon he told me out of a clear sky that he was poor as a church mouse. He'd never even hinted it before. Does this sound horribly mundane?"

"Perhaps he was afraid to tell you."

"Suppose he was," she answered. "He didn't start right. You see, if I'd thought of him as poor—well, I've been mad about loads of poor men, and fully intended to marry them all. But in this case, I hadn't thought of him that way, and my interest in him wasn't strong enough to survive the shock. As if a girl calmly informed her fiancé that she was a widow. He might not object to widows, but—

"Let's start right," she interrupted herself suddenly. "Who are you, anyhow?"

For a moment Dexter hesitated. Then, "I'm nobody," he announced. "My career is largely a matter of futures."

"Are you poor?"

"No," he said frankly. "I'm probably making more money than any man my age in the Northwest. I know that's an obnoxious remark, but you advised me to start right."

There was a pause. Then she smiled and the corners of her mouth drooped and an almost imperceptible sway brought her closer to him, looking up into his eyes. A lump rose in Dexter's throat, and he waited breathless for the experiment, facing the unpredictable compound that would form mysteriously from the elements of their lips. Then he saw—she communicated her excitement to him, lavishly, deeply, with kisses that were not a promise but a fulfillment. They aroused in him not hunger demanding renewal but surfeit that would demand more surfeit . . . kisses that were like charity, creating want by holding back nothing at all.

It did not take him many hours to decide that he had wanted Judy Jones ever since he was a proud, desirous little boy.

4

It began like that—and continued, with varying shades of intensity, on such a note right up to the denouement.[4] Dexter surrendered a part of himself to the most direct and unprincipled personality with which he had ever come in contact. Whatever Judy wanted, she went after with the full pressure of her charm. There was no divergence of method, no jockeying for position or premeditation of effects—there was a very little mental side to any of her affairs. She simply made men conscious to the highest degree of her physical loveliness. Dexter had no desire to change her. Her deficiencies were knit up with a passionate energy that transcended and justified them.

When, as Judy's head lay against his shoulder that first night, she whispered, "I don't know what's the matter with me. Last night I thought I was in love with a man and tonight I think I'm in love with you—," it seemed to him a beautiful and romantic thing to say. It was the exquisite excitability that for the moment he controlled and owned. But a week later he was compelled to view this same quality in a different light. She took him in her roadster to a picnic supper, and after supper she disappeared, likewise in her road-

---

4. **denouement** (dā′ nü mä′): the outcome of a complex sequence of events.

ster, with another man. Dexter became enormously upset and was scarcely able to be decently civil to the other people present. When she assured him that she had not kissed the other man, he knew she was lying—yet he was glad that she had taken the trouble to lie to him.

He was, as he found before the summer ended, one of a varying dozen, who circulated about her. Each of them had at one time been favored above all others—about half of them still basked in the solace of occasional sentimental revivals. Whenever one showed signs of dropping out through long neglect, she granted him a brief honeyed hour, which encouraged him to tag along for a year or so longer. Judy made these forays upon the helpless and defeated without malice, indeed half unconscious that there was anything mischievous in what she did.

When a new man came to town everyone dropped out—dates were automatically canceled.

The helpless part of trying to do anything about it was that she did it all herself. She was not a girl who could be "won" in the kinetic sense—she was proof against cleverness, she was proof against charm; if any of these assailed her too strongly she would immediately resolve the affair to a physical basis, and under the magic of her physical splendor the strong as well as the brilliant played her game and not their own. She was entertained only by the gratification of her desires and by the direct exercise of her own charm. Perhaps from so much youthful love, so many youthful lovers, she had come, in self-defense, to nourish herself wholly from within.

Succeeding Dexter's first exhilaration came restlessness and dissatisfaction. The helpless ecstasy of losing himself in her was opiate rather than tonic.[5] It was fortunate for his work during the winter that those moments of ecstasy came infrequently. Early in their acquaintance it had seemed for a while that there was a deep and spontaneous mutual attraction—that first August, for example—three days of long evenings on her dusky veranda, of strange wan kisses through the late afternoon, in shadowy alcoves or behind the protecting trellises of the garden arbors, of mornings when she was fresh as a dream and almost shy at meeting him in the clarity of the rising day. There was all the ecstasy of an engagement about it, sharpened by his realization that there was no engagement. It was during those three days that, for the first time, he had asked her to marry him. She said "maybe someday," she said "kiss me," she said "I'd like to marry you," she said "I love you"—she said—nothing.

The three days were interrupted by the arrival of a New York man who visited at her house for half September. To Dexter's agony, rumor engaged them. The man was the son of the president of a great trust company. But at the end of the month it was reported that Judy was yawning. At a dance one night she sat all evening in a motorboat with a local beau, while the New Yorker searched the club for her frantically. She told the local beau that she was bored with her visitor, and two days later he left. She was seen with him at the station, and it was reported that he looked very mournful indeed.

On this note the summer ended. Dexter was twenty-four, and he found himself increasingly in a position to do as he wished. He joined two clubs in the city and lived at one of them. Though he was by no means an integral part of the stag lines at these clubs, he managed to be on hand at dances where Judy Jones was likely to appear. He could have gone out socially as much as he liked—he was an eligible young man, now, and popular with downtown fathers. His confessed devotion to Judy Jones had rather solidified his position. But he had no social aspirations and rather despised the dancing men who were always

---

5. **opiate . . . tonic:** suppressing activity rather than stimulating it.

on tap for the Thursday or Saturday parties and who filled in at dinners with the younger married set. Already he was playing with the idea of going East to New York. He wanted to take Judy Jones with him. No disillusion as to the world in which she had grown up could cure his illusion as to her desirability.

Remember that—for only in the light of it can what he did for her be understood.

Eighteen months after he first met Judy Jones he became engaged to another girl. Her name was Irene Scheerer, and her father was one of the men who had always believed in Dexter. Irene was light-haired and sweet and honorable, and a little stout, and she had two suitors whom she pleasantly relinquished when Dexter formally asked her to marry him.

Summer, fall, winter, spring, another summer, another fall—so much he had given of his active life to the incorrigible lips of Judy Jones. She had treated him with interest, with encouragement, with malice, with indifference, with contempt. She had inflicted on him the innumerable little slights and indignities possible in such a case—as if in revenge for having ever cared for him at all. She had beckoned him and yawned at him and beckoned him again and he had responded often with bitterness and narrowed eyes. She had brought him ecstatic happiness and intolerable agony of spirit. She had caused him untold inconvenience and not a little trouble. She had insulted him, and she had ridden over him, and she had played his interest in her against his interest in his work—for fun. She had done everything to him except to criticize him—this she had not done—it seemed to him only because it might have sullied the utter indifference she manifested and sincerely felt toward him.

When autumn had come and gone again, it occurred to him that he could not have Judy Jones. He had to beat this into his mind, but he convinced himself at last. He lay awake at night for a while and argued it over. He told

himself the trouble and the pain she had caused him; he enumerated her glaring deficiencies as a wife. Then he said to himself that he loved her, and after a while he fell asleep. For a week, lest he imagine her husky voice over the telephone or her eyes opposite him at lunch, he worked hard and late, and at night he went to his office and plotted out his years.

At the end of a week he went to a dance and cut in on her once. For almost the first time since they had met he did not ask her to sit out with him or tell her that she was lovely. It hurt him that she did not miss these things—that was all. He was not jealous when he saw that there was a new man tonight. He had been hardened against jealousy long before.

He stayed late at the dance. He sat for an hour with Irene Scheerer and talked about books and about music. He knew very little about either. But he was beginning to be master of his own time now, and he had a rather priggish notion that he—the young and already fabulously successful Dexter Green—should know more about such things.

That was in October, when he was twenty-five. In January, Dexter and Irene became engaged. It was to be announced in June, and they were to be married three months later.

The Minnesota winter prolonged itself interminably, and it was almost May when the winds came soft and the snow ran down into Black Bear Lake at last. For the first time in over a year Dexter was enjoying a certain tranquillity of spirit. Judy Jones had been in Florida, and afterward in Hot Springs, and somewhere she had been engaged, and somewhere she had broken it off. At first, when Dexter had definitely given her up, it had made him sad that people still linked them together and asked for news of her, but when he began to be placed at dinner next to Irene Scheerer people didn't ask him about her any more—they told him about her. He ceased to be an authority on her.

May at last. Dexter walked the streets at

night when the dampness was damp as rain, wondering that so soon, with so little done, so much of ecstasy had gone from him. May one year back had been marked by Judy's poignant, unforgivable, yet forgiven turbulence—it had been one of those rare times when he fancied she had grown to care for him. That old penny's worth of happiness he had spent for this bushel of content. He knew that Irene would be no more than a curtain spread behind him, a hand moving among gleaming teacups, a voice calling to children . . . fire and loveliness were gone, the magic of nights and the wonder of the varying hours and seasons . . . slender lips, down-turning, dropping to his lips and bearing him up into a heaven of eyes. . . . The thing was deep in him. He was too strong and alive for it to die lightly.

In the middle of May when the weather balanced for a few days on the thin bridge that led to deep summer, he turned in one night at Irene's house. Their engagement was to be announced in a week now—no one would be surprised at it. And tonight they would sit together on the lounge at the University Club and look on for an hour at the dancers. It gave him a sense of solidity to go with her—she was so sturdily popular, so intensely "great."

He mounted the steps of the brownstone house and stepped inside.

"Irene," he called.

Mrs. Scheerer came out of the living room to meet him.

"Dexter," she said, "Irene's gone upstairs with a splitting headache. She wanted to go with you but I made her go to bed."

"Nothing serious, I—"

"Oh, no. She's going to play golf with you in the morning. You can spare her for just one night, can't you, Dexter?"

Her smile was kind. She and Dexter liked each other. In the living room he talked for a moment before he said goodnight.

Returning to the University Club, where he had rooms, he stood in the doorway for a moment and watched the dancers. He leaned against the doorpost, nodded at a man or two—yawned.

"Hello, darling."

The familiar voice at his elbow startled him. Judy Jones had left a man and crossed the room to him—Judy Jones, a slender enameled doll in cloth of gold: gold in a band at her head, gold in two slipper points at her dress's hem. The fragile glow of her face seemed to blossom as she smiled at him. A breeze of warmth and light blew through the room. His hands in the pockets of his dinner jacket tightened spasmodically. He was filled with a sudden excitement.

"When did you get back?" he asked casually.

"Come here and I'll tell you about it."

She turned and he followed her. She had been away—he could have wept at the wonder of her return. She had passed through enchanted streets, doing things that were like provocative music. All mysterious happenings, all fresh and quickening hopes, had gone away with her, come back with her now.

She turned in the doorway.

"Have you a car here? If you haven't, I have."

"I have a coupé."

In then, with a rustle of golden cloth. He slammed the door. Into so many cars she had stepped—like this—like that—her back against the leather, so—her elbow resting on the door—waiting. She would have been soiled long since had there been anything to soil her—except herself—but this was her own self outpouring.

With an effort he forced himself to start the car and back into the street. This was nothing, he must remember. She had done this before, and he had put her behind him, as he would have crossed a bad account from his books.

He drove slowly downtown and, affecting abstraction, traversed the deserted streets of the business section, people here and there where a movie was giving out its crowd or where consumptive or pugilistic youth lounged in front of pool halls. The clink of glasses and the slap of hands on the bars issued from saloons, cloisters of glazed glass and dirty yellow light.

She was watching him closely and the silence was embarrassing, yet in this crisis he could find no casual word with which to profane the hour. At a convenient turning he began to zigzag back toward the University Club.

"Have you missed me?" she asked suddenly.

"Everybody missed you."

He wondered if she knew of Irene Scheerer. She had been back only a day—her absence had been almost contemporaneous with his engagement.

"What a remark!" Judy laughed sadly—without sadness. She looked at him searchingly. He became absorbed in the dashboard.

"You're handsomer than you used to be," she said thoughtfully. "Dexter, you have the most rememberable eyes."

He could have laughed at this, but he did not laugh. It was the sort of thing that was said to sophomores. Yet it stabbed at him.

"I'm awfully tired of everything, darling." She called everyone darling, endowing the endearment with careless, individual camaraderie. "I wish you'd marry me."

The directness of this confused him. He should have told her now that he was going to marry another girl, but he could not tell her. He could as easily have sworn that he had never loved her.

"I think we'd get along," she continued, on the same note, "unless probably you've forgotten me and fallen in love with another girl."

Her confidence was obviously enormous. She had said, in effect, that she found such a thing impossible to believe, that if it were true he had merely committed a childish indiscretion—and probably to show off. She

would forgive him, because it was not a matter of any moment but rather something to be brushed aside lightly.

"Of course you could never love anybody but me," she continued, "I like the way you love me. Oh, Dexter, have you forgotten last year?"

"No, I haven't forgotten."

"Neither have I!"

Was she sincerely moved—or was she carried along by the wave of her own acting?

"I wish we could be like that again," she said, and he forced himself to answer,

"I don't think we can."

"I suppose not. . . . I hear you're giving Irene Scheerer a violent rush."

There was not the faintest emphasis on the name, yet Dexter was suddenly ashamed.

"Oh, take me home," cried Judy suddenly; "I don't want to go back to that idiotic dance—with those children."

Then, as he turned up the street that led to the residence district, Judy began to cry quietly to herself. He had never seen her cry before.

The dark street lightened, the dwellings of the rich loomed up around them; he stopped his coupé in front of the great white bulk of the Mortimer Joneses' house, somnolent, gorgeous, drenched with the splendor of the damp moonlight. Its solidity startled him. The strong walls, the steel of the girders, the breadth and beam and pomp of it were there only to bring out the contrast with the young beauty beside him. It was sturdy to accentuate her slightness—as if to show what a breeze could be generated by a butterfly's wing.

He sat perfectly quiet, his nerves in wild clamor, afraid that if he moved he would find her irresistibly in his arms. Two tears had rolled down her wet face and trembled on her upper lip.

"I'm more beautiful than anybody else," she said brokenly, "why can't I be happy?" Her moist eyes tore at his stability—her mouth turned slowly downward with an exquisite sadness: "I'd like to marry you if you'll have me, Dexter. I suppose you think I'm not worth having, but I'll be so beautiful for you, Dexter."

A million phrases of anger, pride, passion, hatred, tenderness fought on his lips. Then a perfect wave of emotion washed over him, carrying off with it a sediment of wisdom, of convention, of doubt, of honor. This was his girl who was speaking, his own, his beautiful, his pride.

"Won't you come in?" He heard her draw in her breath sharply.

Waiting.

"All right," his voice was trembling, "I'll come in."

5

It was strange that neither when it was over nor a long time afterward did he regret that night. Looking at it from the perspective of ten years, the fact that Judy's flare for him endured just one month seemed of little importance. Nor did it matter that by his yielding he subjected himself to a deeper agony in the end and gave serious hurt to Irene Scheerer and to Irene's parents, who had befriended him. There was nothing sufficiently pictorial about Irene's grief to stamp itself on his mind.

Dexter was at bottom hard-minded. The attitude of the city on his action was of no importance to him, not because he was going to leave the city, but because any outside attitude on the situation seemed superficial. He was completely indifferent to popular opinion. Nor, when he had seen that it was no use, that he did not possess in himself the power to move fundamentally or to hold Judy Jones, did he bear any malice toward her. He loved her, and he would love her until the day he was too old for loving—but he could not have her. So he tasted the deep pain that is reserved only for the strong, just as he had tasted for a little while the deep happiness.

Even the ultimate falsity of the grounds upon which Judy terminated the engagement, that she did not want to "take him away" from Irene—Judy who had wanted nothing else—did not revolt him. He was beyond any revulsion or any amusement.

He went East in February with the intention of selling out his laundries and settling in New York—but the war came to America in March and changed his plans. He returned to the West, handed over the management of the business to his partner, and went into the first officers' training camp in late April. He was one of those young thousands who greeted the war with a certain amount of relief, welcoming the liberation from webs of tangled emotion.

6

This story is not his biography, remember, although things creep into it which have nothing to do with those dreams he had when he was young. We are almost done with them and with him now. There is only one more incident to be related here, and it happens seven years farther on.

It took place in New York, where he had done well—so well that there were no barriers too high for him. He was thirty-two years old, and, except for one flying trip immediately after the war, he had not been West in seven years. A man named Devlin from Detroit came into his office to see him in a business way, and then and there this incident occurred, and closed out, so to speak, this particular side of his life.

"So you're from the Middle West," said the man Devlin with careless curiosity. "That's funny—I thought men like you were probably born and raised on Wall Street. You know—wife of one of my best friends in Detroit came from your city. I was an usher at the wedding."

Dexter waited with no apprehension of what was coming.

"Judy Simms," said Devlin with no particular interest; "Judy Jones she was once."

"Yes, I knew her." A dull impatience spread over him. He had heard, of course, that she was married—perhaps deliberately he had heard no more.

"Awfully nice girl," brooded Devlin meaninglessly, "I'm sort of sorry for her."

"Why?" Something in Dexter was alert, receptive, at once.

"Oh, Lud Simms has gone to pieces in a way. I don't mean he ill-uses her, but he drinks and runs around—"

"Doesn't she run around?"

"No. Stays at home with her kids."

"Oh."

"She's a little too old for him," said Devlin.

"Too old!" cried Dexter. "Why, man, she's only twenty-seven."

He was possessed with a wild notion of rushing out into the streets and taking a train to Detroit. He rose to his feet spasmodically.

"I guess you're busy," Devlin apologized quickly. "I didn't realize—"

"No, I'm not busy," said Dexter, steadying his voice. "I'm not busy at all. Not busy at all. Did you say she was—twenty-seven? No, I said she was twenty-seven."

"Yes, you did," agreed Devlin dryly.

"Go on, then. Go on."

"What do you mean?"

"About Judy Jones."

Devlin looked at him helplessly.

"Well, that's—I told you all there is to it. He treats her like the devil. Oh, they're not going to get divorced or anything. When he's particularly outrageous she forgives him. In fact, I'm inclined to think she loves him. She was a pretty girl when she first came to Detroit."

A pretty girl! The phrase struck Dexter as ludicrous.

"Isn't she—a pretty girl, any more?"

"Oh, she's all right."

"Look here," said Dexter, sitting down suddenly. "I don't understand. You say she was a 'pretty girl' and now you say she's 'all right.' I don't understand what you mean—Judy Jones wasn't a pretty girl, at all. She was a great beauty. Why, I knew her, I knew her. She was—"

Devlin laughed pleasantly.

"I'm not trying to start a row," he said. "I think Judy's a nice girl and I like her. I can't understand how a man like Lud Simms could fall madly in love with her, but he did." Then he added: "Most of the women like her."

Dexter looked closely at Devlin, thinking wildly that there must be a reason for this, some insensitivity in the man or some private malice.

"Lots of women fade just like that," Devlin snapped his fingers. "You must have seen it happen. Perhaps I've forgotten how pretty she was at her wedding. I've seen her so much since then, you see. She has nice eyes."

A sort of dullness settled down upon Dexter. For the first time in his life he felt like getting very drunk. He knew that he was laughing loudly at something Devlin had said, but he did not know what it was or why it was funny. When, in a few minutes, Devlin went he lay down on his lounge and looked out the window at the New York skyline into which the sun was sinking in dull lovely shades of pink and gold.

He had thought that having nothing else to lose he was invulnerable at last—but he knew that he had just lost something more, as surely as if he had married Judy Jones and seen her fade away before his eyes.

The dream was gone. Something had been taken from him. In a sort of panic he pushed the palms of his hands into his eyes and tried to bring up a picture of the waters lapping on Sherry Island and the moonlit veranda, and gingham on the golf links and the dry sun and the gold color of her neck's soft down. And her mouth damp to his kisses and her eyes plaintive with melancholy and her freshness like new fine linen in the morning. Why, these things were no longer in the world! They had existed and they existed no longer.

For the first time in years the tears were streaming down his face. But they were for himself now. He did not care about mouth and eyes and moving hands. He wanted to care, and he could not care. For he had gone away and he could never go back any more. The gates were closed, the sun was gone down, and there was no beauty but the gray beauty of steel that withstands all time. Even the grief he could have borne was left behind in the country of illusion, of youth, of the richness of life, where his winter dreams had flourished.

"Long ago," he said, "long ago, there was something in me, but now that thing is gone. Now that thing is gone, that thing is gone. I cannot cry. I cannot care. That thing will come back no more."

Getting at Meaning

1. Give the details of Dexter's background. Why does Dexter caddy? Why is he a good caddy?

2. Describe Judy Jones as she first appears at the golf course with her nurse. How does she treat Dexter?

3. Why does Dexter refuse to caddy for Judy Jones? What makes him decide abruptly to quit caddying?

4. Describe Dexter's university career. Why does he succeed afterwards in business?

5. Describe Judy Jones as she appears on the golf course in Section 2 of the story. What conclusions do you draw about her from the golf ball incident with Mr. Hedrick?

6. How does Judy Jones lure Dexter into becoming involved with her? As Dexter drives her motorboat, she calls out to him, "Go faster . . . fast as it'll go." How is this remark characteristic of Judy?

7. Describe Dexter's first dinner with Judy. What do her questions indicate about her?

8. Why does Dexter want Judy so much? Explain Dexter's thoughts after she goes off with someone else at the picnic, summarized in the sentence, "When she assured him that she had not kissed the other man, he knew she was lying—yet he was glad that she had taken the trouble to lie to him."

9. Explain how Dexter's engagement to Irene comes about. How does Dexter contrast Irene to Judy?

10. How would you characterize Judy's approach to the opposite sex? Why does she propose to Dexter? Why does she discard him a month later?

11. Explain the statement about Dexter, ". . . he tasted the deep pain that is reserved only for the strong, just as he had tasted for a little while the deep happiness."

12. Why is Dexter so shocked to hear about the nature of Judy's marriage? What has happened to Judy? Why is her situation so profoundly disillusioning to Dexter?

Developing Skills in Reading Literature

1. **Setting.** Where does most of "Winter Dreams" take place? At what point in the twentieth century does it take place? What details within the narrative place it in time?

2. **Character.** Although minor characters do appear in "Winter Dreams," the story is primarily about the interaction of Dexter and Judy, the two main characters.

Judy is in some ways a stereotyped character, conforming to the common image of the beautiful flirt.

What motivates her throughout her stormy relationship with Dexter? What is ironic about Judy's situation when she finally marries? Does her fate seem plausible to you? Why would she love a man like Lud Simms?

How does Dexter change and grow during the course of the story? What mistakes does he make? What is the ultimate effect Judy has on him?

3. **Figurative Language.** Fitzgerald uses descriptive language in "Winter Dreams." Sometimes he uses similes, as in his statement that ". . . the long Minnesota winter shut down like the white lid of a box." Sometimes he uses personification, as in the scene where Dexter ". . . watched the even overlap of the waters in the little wind, silver molasses under the harvest moon. Then the moon held a finger to her lips and the lake became a clear pool, pale and quiet."

Find several descriptive passages in the story. What makes the passages so vivid? What figures of speech does Fitzgerald use?

4. **Structure.** Fitzgerald divided "Winter Dreams" into six sections, each section reflecting a different phase of Dexter's relationship with Judy. Describe the phase that the narrative develops in each section. Notice, too, that each section closes with Dexter's somehow altering his life in a major way because of Judy. Explain what he realizes about Judy at the end of each episode.

5. **Theme.** This story concerns the fleeting nature of dreams and of happiness. It is also about the absolute importance of dreams. Why is Dexter ultimately so unhappy? What does he lose besides Judy? Why is this loss more painful than the loss of Judy? Interpret the line, "The gates were closed, the sun was gone down, and there was no beauty but the gray beauty of steel that withstands all time."

6. **Title.** The title of "Winter Dreams" is closely linked to the story's theme. Why do you suppose Fitzgerald chose to call Dexter's dreams "winter" dreams? How does their being "winter" dreams make the dreams more important? How do the dreams guide Dexter? How do they let him down?

Developing Vocabulary

Greek Roots. Fitzgerald says in "Winter Dreams" that some of the caddies were ". . . poor as sin and lived in one-room houses with a neurasthenic cow in the front yard. . . ." *Neurasthenic* means "tired or fatigued," and it employs the root *neuro-* or *neur-*, which indicates "nerves or nervous system." It derives from the Greek word *neuron*, meaning "nerve or tendon."

Define the words that follow, using a dictionary. Explain the relationship between the meaning of each word and the Greek root.

neuralgia	neurosis
neuritis	neurotic
neurology	

Developing Writing Skills

Writing Autobiography. Fitzgerald's story is about disillusionment, about the terrible pain of losing one's dreams.

Write a composition in which you describe a personal episode involving disillusionment and loss. What were your illusions, or dreams? What knowledge, people, or experiences led to your disillusionment? What has been the effect of the disillusionment on you? Consider both long-term and short-term effects. Make your composition as concrete and vivid as you can.

Ernest Hemingway
1898–1961

Karsh, Ottawa

Ernest Hemingway was probably the most influential American prose stylist of the twentieth century. An extremely successful novelist and short story writer, he was the fourth American to win the Nobel Prize for Literature.

Hemingway was born in Oak Park, Illinois, a suburb of Chicago, where his father was a doctor. He grew up in Oak Park, frequently accompanying his father on hunting and fishing trips to northern Michigan. At Oak Park High School, Hemingway was an athlete and a budding writer, producing stories and sketches for the school newspaper and literary magazine.

After his graduation Hemingway worked briefly as a reporter for the Kansas City *Star*. He served in World War I with the Red Cross, sustaining a serious wound as an ambulance driver. He recuperated in Italy and then returned to Illinois and to more newspaper work. There he met Sherwood Anderson, who encouraged him to write and gave him critical advice.

In 1921 the *Toronto Star* sent Hemingway to Europe as a foreign correspondent. There, in Paris, he met many artists and writers, becoming one of the American expatriates who comprised the "Lost Generation." Hemingway traveled as a reporter, working on his fiction in Paris.

Hemingway published two books as a young man in Paris, both privately printed. The second one, his novel *The Sun Also Rises*, is about the American expatriates who searched for meaning in the wake of postwar disillusionment. Its publication in 1926 made Hemingway a well known writer. His next novel, the equally successful *A Farewell to Arms*, is about World War I.

Hemingway's own life was dramatic, and his activities furthered his fame as much as did his writing. He wrote about bullfighting in Spain and big-game hunting in Africa, while living dangerously and engaging in strenuous physical activities himself. During the 1930's he faced danger as a journalist covering the Spanish Civil War, exhibiting "grace under pressure," his own definition of courage. *For Whom the Bell Tolls*, which many critics consider Hemingway's best novel, came out

of his war experiences in Spain. He did not produce another novel until 1952, when *The Old Man and the Sea*, a symbolic statement about the need to accept life with dignity, was published.

Hemingway's impact on twentieth-century literature goes beyond the pervasive influence of his staccato, journalistic prose. His view of life as a game, where humans are ultimately defeated, has been a powerful force in shaping the vision of much modern American literature. When life attacks the Hemingway hero, he (never she in his books) fights back, taking the blows that come his way with dignity and fortitude. Hemingway has been criticized, especially in recent decades, for being a "macho" writer, one who writes about men who are tested by pain and danger, rarely presenting women in an admirable light. In spite of this criticism, Hemingway remains a popular writer.

In his last years Hemingway was plagued by depression and illness. In 1961 he died in Ketchum, Idaho, of a self-inflicted gunshot wound. After his death *A Moveable Feast*, his memoir of life in Paris in the 1920's, came out, and it stands as a fascinating portrait of this unusual period in American literary history.

Old Man at the Bridge

An old man with steel rimmed spectacles and very dusty clothes sat by the side of the road. There was a pontoon bridge across the river and carts, trucks, and men, women and children were crossing it. The mule-drawn carts staggered up the steep bank from the bridge with soldiers helping push against the spokes of the wheels. The trucks ground up and away heading out of it all and the peasants plodded along in the ankle deep dust. But the old man sat there without moving. He was too tired to go any farther.

It was my business to cross the bridge, explore the bridgehead beyond and find out to what point the enemy had advanced. I did this and returned over the bridge. There were not so many carts now and very few people on foot, but the old man was still there.

"Where do you come from?" I asked him.

"From San Carlos," he said, and smiled.

That was his native town and so it gave him pleasure to mention it and he smiled.

"I was taking care of animals," he explained.

"Oh," I said, not quite understanding.

"Yes," he said, "I stayed, you see, taking care of animals. I was the last one to leave the town of San Carlos."

He did not look like a shepherd nor a herdsman and I looked at his black dusty clothes and his gray dusty face and his steel rimmed spectacles and said, "What animals were they?"

"Various animals," he said, and shook his head. "I had to leave them."

I was watching the bridge and the African looking country of the Ebro Delta and wondering how long now it would be before we would see the enemy, and listening all the while for the first noises that would signal that ever mysterious event called contact, and the old man still sat there.

"What animals were they?" I asked.

"There were three animals altogether," he explained. "There were two goats and a cat and then there were four pairs of pigeons."

"And you had to leave them?" I asked.

"Yes. Because of the artillery. The captain told me to go because of the artillery."

"And you have no family?" I asked, watching the far end of the bridge where a few last carts were hurrying down the slope of the bank.

"No," he said, "only the animals I stated. The cat, of course, will be all right. A cat can look out for itself, but I cannot think what will become of the others."

"What politics have you?" I asked.

"I am without politics," he said. "I am seventy-six years old. I have come twelve kilometers now and I think now I can go no further."

"This is not a good place to stop," I said. "If you can make it, there are trucks up the road where it forks for Tortosa."

"I will wait a while," he said, "and then I will go. Where do the trucks go?"

"Towards Barcelona," I told him.

"I know no one in that direction," he said, "but thank you very much. Thank you again very much."

He looked at me very blankly and tiredly, then said, having to share his worry with some one, "The cat will be all right, I am sure. There is no need to be unquiet about the cat. But the others. Now what do you think about the others?"

"Why they'll probably come through it all right."

"You think so?"

"Why not?" I said, watching the far bank where now there were no carts.

"But what will they do under the artillery when I was told to leave because of the artillery?"

"Did you leave the dove cage unlocked?" I asked.

"Yes."

"Then they'll fly."

"Yes, certainly they'll fly. But the others. It's better not to think about the others," he said.

"If you are rested I would go," I urged, "Get up and try to walk now."

"Thank you," he said and got to his feet, swayed from side to side and then sat down backwards in the dust.

"I was taking care of animals," he said dully, but no longer to me. "I was only taking care of animals."

There was nothing to do about him. It was Easter Sunday and the Fascists were advancing toward the Ebro. It was a gray overcast day with a low ceiling so their planes were not up. That and the fact that cats know how to look after themselves was all the good luck that old man would ever have.

Getting at Meaning

1. Explain why the narrator of Hemingway's story takes so much time to converse with the old man. What does the narrator say to encourage the old man to keep moving forward?

2. Which animals is the old man so concerned about? Why? Why are the animals on his mind more than anything else?

Developing Skills in Reading Literature

1. **Setting.** Hemingway's story takes place during the Spanish Civil War of the late 1930's. What details in the story indicate that war is disrupting the lives of ordinary Spanish citizens? What picture of peasant life does the story convey?

2. **Character.** This short piece consists mainly of conversation between two characters, both of whom are developed through their comments. Characterize the narrator. What observations and remarks suggest that he is sensitive? Which of his comments imply kindness?

Characterize the old man. Describe the life he has been leading. What keeps him going? What statements suggest that he is about to give up?

3. **Theme.** "Old Man at the Bridge" is about the casualties of war that exist above and beyond actual deaths in battle. Explain what the narrator means when

he says of the old man, "There was nothing to do about him." What makes the old man's situation so tragic?

4. **Style.** Hemingway's story does not contain romantic sentiment about war. Rather, the story is intensely realistic, "telling it like it is." Which details emphasize the unpleasant, horrifying aspects of war? Explain the narrator's final statement.

Hemingway is known for his simple clipped dialogue, and for writing stories that consist in large part of dialogue. Examine the speech of the two characters in this story. Why does it seemed clipped? What stylistic qualities also make the dialogue rhythmic?

Developing Vocabulary

Word Origins. The narrator of "Old Man at the Bridge" refers to the arrival of the Fascists, a major faction in the Spanish Civil War. Look up the word *Fascist* in a dictionary containing etymologies. What does the word mean? What is the word's origin? Explain how the meaning grew out of the origin.

Answer the same questions for each of the five words below. All five have particularly intriguing origins.

boycott	halibut
chauvinism	lullaby
curfew	

Bernard Malamud

1914–1986

Thomas Victor

Some of the best observers of mid-twentieth century American life have been writers slightly outside the mainstream of that life: Southerners, blacks, Jews. Bernard Malamud was one of the best of the school of urban Jewish writers that developed after World War II. He often wrote about immigrants and second-generation Americans, and in so doing he expressed universal concerns.

Born in Brooklyn, New York, Malamud was the older of two sons. His parents, the proprietors of a grocery store in Brooklyn, had emigrated from Russia early in the 1900's. In his boyhood, Malamud enjoyed going to the Yiddish theater in Manhattan and listening to his father's stories of Jewish life in Russia. His parents and his teachers encouraged his talents, and the young boy used to make up stories for his friends, struggling in the evenings to put them down on paper in the back room of the family store.

After high school Malamud went to City College of New York. He graduated in 1936 and then, while working at whatever jobs he could find in those Depression years, began writing fiction in his spare time. World events motivated him to write. "The rise of totalitarianism, the Second World War, and the situation of the Jews in Europe helped me to come to what I wanted to say as a writer," he said.

Malamud became a graduate student at Columbia University, earning his M.A. in 1942. In the meantime he began teaching evening high school English classes in New York, writing fiction in the daytime. He continued that routine until 1949, when he went with his family (a wife and two children) to teach English at the University of Oregon. In 1961 he began teaching at Bennington College, in Vermont, where he remained for more than twenty years.

In 1952 Malamud published his first book, *The Natural*, a novel about an American baseball hero told in terms reminiscent of ancient myth and combining realism and fantasy. His second novel, *The Assistant* (1957), has been called a master-piece, and it established him as a major Jewish writer. *The Magic Barrel* (1958), one of several collections of short stories, earned Malamud a National Book Award. Its title story in particular has been widely praised. *The Fixer* (1966) brought him another National Book Award and the Pulitzer Prize.

Malamud wrote of human suffering and the redemptive power of love. His best stories combine realism with a quality of magic and some of the humor and flavor of Yiddish folktales. He had a compassionate concern for the afflicted who survive adversity. His suffering, wandering Jews come to stand for the general human condition. Above all, he said, his work was dedicated to what is human: "If you don't respect man, you don't respect my work."

A Summer's Reading

George Stoyonovich was a neighborhood boy who had quit high school on an impulse when he was sixteen, run out of patience, and though he was ashamed every time he went looking for a job, when people asked him if he had finished and he had to say no, he never went back to school. This summer was a hard time for jobs and he had none. Having so much time on his hands, George thought of going to summer school, but the kids in his classes would be too young. He also considered registering in a night high school, only he didn't like the idea of the teachers always telling him what to do. He felt they had not respected him. The result was he stayed off the streets and in his room most of the day. He was close to twenty and had needs with the neighborhood girls, but no money to spend, and he couldn't get more than an occasional few cents because his father was poor, and his sister Sophie, who resembled George, a tall bony girl of twenty-three, earned very little and what she had she kept for herself. Their mother was dead, and Sophie had to take care of the house.

Very early in the morning George's father got up to go to work in a fish market. Sophie left at about eight for her long ride in the subway to a cafeteria in the Bronx.[1] George had his coffee by himself, then hung around in the house. When the house, a five-room railroad flat[2] above a butcher store, got on his nerves he cleaned it up—mopped the floors with a wet mop and put things away. But most of the time he sat in his room. In the afternoons he listened to the ball game. Otherwise he had a couple of old copies of the *World Almanac* he had bought long ago, and he liked to read in them and also the maga-zines and newspapers that Sophie brought home, that had been left on the tables in the cafeteria. They were mostly picture magazines about movie stars and sports figures, also usually the *News* and *Mirror*,[3] Sophie herself read whatever fell into her hands, although she sometimes read good books.

She once asked George what he did in his room all day and he said he read a lot too.

"Of what besides what I bring home? Do you ever read any worthwhile books?"

"Some," George answered, although he really didn't. He had tried to read a book or two that Sophie had in the house but found he was in no mood for them. Lately he couldn't stand made-up stories; they got on his nerves. He wished he had some hobby to work at—as a kid he was good in carpentry, but where could he work at it? Sometimes during the day he went for walks, but mostly he did his walking after the hot sun had gone down and it was cooler in the streets.

In the evening after supper George left the house and wandered in the neighborhood. During the sultry days some of the storekeep-ers and their wives sat in chairs on the thick, broken sidewalks in front of their shops, fan-ning themselves, and George walked past them and the guys hanging out on the candystore corner. A couple of them he had known his whole life, but nobody recognized each other. He had no place special to go, but

---

1. **Bronx:** one of the five boroughs comprising New York City.
2. **railroad flat:** an apartment of rooms in a line, with each room entered from another, or sometimes from a long hallway.
3. **News and Mirror:** daily newspapers. *The Mirror* does not exist anymore.

generally, saving it till the last, he left the neighborhood and walked for blocks till he came to a darkly lit little park with benches and trees and an iron railing, giving it a feeling of privacy. He sat on a bench here, watching the leafy trees and the flowers blooming on the inside of the railing, thinking of a better life for himself. He thought of the jobs he had had since he had quit school—delivery boy, stock clerk, runner, lately working in a factory—and he was dissatisfied with all of them. He felt he would someday like to have a good job and live in a private house with a porch, on a street with trees. He wanted to have some dough in his pocket to buy things with, and a girl to go with, so as not to be so lonely, especially on Saturday nights. He wanted people to like and respect him. He thought about these things often but mostly when he was alone at night. Around midnight he got up and drifted back to his hot and stony neighborhood.

One time while on his walk George met Mr. Cattanzara coming home very late from work. He wondered if he was drunk but then could tell he wasn't. Mr. Cattanzara, a stocky, baldheaded man who worked in a change booth on an IRT station,[4] lived on the next block after George's, above a shoe repair store. Nights, during the hot weather, he sat on his stoop in an undershirt, reading the *New York Times* in the light of the shoemaker's window. He read it from the first page to the last, then went up to sleep. And all the time he was reading the paper, his wife, a fat woman with a white face, leaned out of the window, gazing into the street, her thick white arms folded under her loose breast, on the window ledge.

Once in a while Mr. Cattanzara came home drunk, but it was a quiet drunk. He never made any trouble, only walked stiffly up the street and slowly climbed the stairs into the hall. Though drunk, he looked the same as always, except for his tight walk, the quietness, and that his eyes were wet. George liked

Mr. Cattanzara because he remembered him giving him nickels to buy lemon ice with when he was a squirt. Mr. Cattanzara was a different type than those in the neighborhood. He asked different questions than the others when he met you, and he seemed to know what went on in all the newspapers. He read them, as his fat sick wife watched from the window.

"What are you doing with yourself this summer, George?" Mr. Cattanzara asked. "I see you walkin' around at nights."

George felt embarrassed. "I like to walk."

"What are you doin' in the day now?"

"Nothing much just right now. I'm waiting for a job." Since it shamed him to admit he wasn't working, George said, "I'm staying home—but I'm reading a lot to pick up my education."

Mr. Cattanzara looked interested. He mopped his hot face with a red handkerchief.

"What are you readin'?"

George hesitated, then said, "I got a list of books in the library once, and now I'm gonna read them this summer." He felt strange and a little unhappy saying this, but he wanted Mr. Cattanzara to respect him.

"How many books are there on it?"

"I never counted them. Maybe around a hundred."

Mr. Cattanzara whistled through his teeth.

"I figure if I did that," George went on earnestly, "it would help me in my education. I don't mean the kind they give you in high school. I want to know different things than they learn there, if you know what I mean."

The change maker nodded. "Still and all, one hundred books is a pretty big load for one summer."

"It might take longer."

"After you're finished with some, maybe you and I can shoot the breeze about them?" said Mr. Cattanzara.

"When I'm finished," George answered.

---

4. **IRT station:** the IRT is a New York City subway line.

Mr. Cattanzara went home and George continued on his walk. After that, though he had the urge to, George did nothing different from usual. He still took his walks at night, ending up in the little park. But one evening the shoemaker on the next block stopped George to say he was a good boy, and George figured that Mr. Cattanzara had told him all about the books he was reading. From the shoemaker it must have gone down the street, because George saw a couple of people smiling kindly at him, though nobody spoke to him personally. He felt a little better around the neighborhood and liked it more, though not so much he would want to live in it forever. He had never exactly disliked the people in it, yet he had never liked them very much either. It was the fault of the neighborhood. To his surprise, George found out that his father and Sophie knew about his reading too. His father was too shy to say anything about it—he was never much of a talker in his whole life—but Sophie was softer to George, and she showed him in other ways she was proud of him.

As the summer went on George felt in a good mood about things. He cleaned the house every day, as a favor to Sophie, and he enjoyed the ball games more. Sophie gave him a buck a week allowance, and though it still wasn't enough and he had to use it carefully, it was a helluva lot better than just having two bits now and then. What he bought with the money—cigarettes mostly, an occasional beer or movie ticket—he got a big kick out of. Life wasn't so bad if you knew how to appreciate it. Occasionally he bought a paperback book from the newsstand, but he never got around to reading it, though he was glad to have a couple of books in his room. But he read thoroughly Sophie's magazines and newspapers. And at night was the most enjoyable time, because when he passed the storekeepers sitting outside their stores, he could tell they regarded him highly. He walked erect, and though he did not say much to them, or they to him, he could feel approval on all sides. A couple of nights he felt so good that he skipped the park at the end of the evening. He just wandered in the neighborhood, where people had known him from the time he was a kid playing punchball whenever there was a game of it going; he wandered there, then came home and got undressed for bed, feeling fine.

For a few weeks he had talked only once with Mr. Cattanzara, and though the change maker had said nothing more about the books, asked no questions, his silence made George a little uneasy. For a while George didn't pass in front of Mr. Cattanzara's house any more, until one night, forgetting himself, he approached it from a different direction than he usually did when he did. It was already past midnight. The street, except for one or two people, was deserted, and George was surprised when he saw Mr. Cattanzara still reading his newspaper by the light of the streetlamp overhead. His impulse was to stop at the stoop and talk to him. He wasn't sure what he wanted to say, though he felt the words would come when he began to talk; but the more he thought about it, the more the idea scared him, and he decided he'd better not. He even considered beating it home by another street, but he was too near Mr. Cattanzara, and the change maker might see him as he ran, and get annoyed. So George unobtrusively crossed the street, trying to make it seem as if he had to look in a store window on the other side, which he did, and then went on, uncomfortable at what he was doing. He feared Mr. Cattanzara would glance up from his paper and call him a dirty rat for walking on the other side of the street, but all he did was sit there, sweating through his undershirt, his bald head shining in the dim light as he read his *Times*, and upstairs his fat wife leaned out of the window, seeming to read the paper along with him. George thought she would spy him and yell out to Mr. Cattanzara, but she never moved her eyes off her husband.

George made up his mind to stay away from

the change maker until he had got some of his softback books read, but when he started them and saw they were mostly storybooks, he lost his interest and didn't bother to finish them. He lost his interest in reading other things too. Sophie's magazines and newspapers went unread. She saw them piling up on a chair in his room and asked why he was no longer looking at them, and George told her it was because of all the other reading he had to do. Sophie said she had guessed that was it. So for most of the day, George had the radio on, turning to music when he was sick of the human voice. He kept the house fairly neat, and Sophie said nothing on the days when he neglected it. She was still kind and gave him his extra buck, though things weren't so good for him as they had been before.

But they were good enough, considering. Also his night walks invariably picked him up, no matter how bad the day was. Then one night George saw Mr. Cattanzara coming down the street toward him. George was about to turn and run but he recognized from Mr. Cattanzara's walk that he was drunk, and if so, probably he would not even bother to notice him. So George kept on walking straight ahead until he came abreast of Mr. Cattanzara and though he felt wound up enough to pop into the sky, he was not surprised when Mr. Cattanzara passed him without a word, walking slowly, his face and body stiff. George drew a breath in relief at his narrow escape, when he heard his name called, and there stood Mr. Cattanzara at his elbow, smelling like the inside of a beer barrel. His eyes were sad as he gazed at George, and George felt so intensely uncomfortable he was tempted to shove the drunk aside and continue on his walk.

But he couldn't act that way to him, and, besides, Mr. Cattanzara took a nickel out of his pants pocket and handed it to him.

"Go buy yourself a lemon ice, Georgie."

"It's not that time any more, Mr. Cattanzara," George said, "I am a big guy now."

"No, you ain't," said Mr. Cattanzara, to which George made no reply he could think of.

"How are all your books comin' along now?" Mr. Cattanzara asked. Though he tried to stand steady, he swayed a little.

"Fine, I guess," said George, feeling the red crawling up his face.

"You ain't sure?" The change maker smiled slyly, a way George had never seen him smile.

"Sure I'm sure. They're fine."

Though his head swayed in little arcs, Mr. Cattanzara's eyes were steady. He had small blue eyes which could hurt if you looked at them too long.

"George," he said, "name me one book on that list that you read this summer, and I will drink to your health."

"I don't want anybody drinking to me."

"Name me one so I can ask you a question on it. Who can tell, if it's a good book maybe I might wanna read it myself."

George knew he looked passable on the outside, but inside he was crumbling apart.

Unable to reply, he shut his eyes, but when —years later—he opened them, he saw that Mr. Cattanzara had, out of pity, gone away, but in his ears he still heard the words he had said when he left, "George, don't do what I did."

The next night he was afraid to leave his room, and though Sophie argued with him he wouldn't open the door.

"What are you doing in there?" she asked.

"Nothing."

"Aren't you reading?"

"No."

She was silent a minute, then asked, "Where do you keep the books you read? I never see any in your room outside of a few cheap trashy ones."

He wouldn't tell her.

"In that case you're not worth a buck of my hard-earned money. Why should I break my back for you? Go on out, you bum, and get a job."

He stayed in his room for almost a week, except to sneak into the kitchen when nobody was home. Sophie railed at him, then begged him to come out, and his old father wept, but George wouldn't budge, though the weather was terrible and his small room stifling. He found it very hard to breathe, each breath was like drawing a flame into his lungs.

One night, unable to stand the heat anymore, he burst into the street at one A.M., a shadow of himself. He hoped to sneak to the park without being seen, but there were people all over the block, wilted and listless, waiting for a breeze. George lowered his eyes and walked, in disgrace, away from them, but before long he discovered they were still friendly to him. He figured Mr. Cattanzara hadn't told on him. Maybe when he woke up out of his drunk the next morning, he had forgotten all about meeting George. George felt his confidence slowly come back to him.

That same night a man on a street corner asked him if it was true that he had finished reading so many books, and George admitted he had. The man said it was a wonderful thing for a boy his age to read so much.

"Yeah," George said, but he felt relieved. He hoped nobody would mention the books any more, and when, after a couple of days, he accidentally met Mr. Cattanzara again, *he* didn't, though George had the idea he was the one who had started the rumor that he had finished all the books.

One evening in the fall, George ran out of his house to the library, where he hadn't been in years. There were books all over the place, wherever he looked, and though he was struggling to control an inward trembling, he easily counted off a hundred, then sat down at a table to read.

Getting at Meaning

1. Explain George's reasons for not going back to school. Why doesn't he have a job for the summer?

2. What is George's family situation? Comment on the relationship between George and Sophie.

3. How does George fill his days? Why does he prefer reading magazines and newspapers to fiction?

4. Enumerate the jobs George has held since he quit school. Why hasn't he liked them? What are George's goals for the future?

5. Describe Mr. Cattanzara. Why does George like him? What prompts George to tell Mr. Cattanzara that he is spending the summer reading?

6. How do the neighbors react to the news that George is reading? Why do they respect this activity so highly? How do Sophie and Mr. Stoyonovich now treat George?

7. Why does George begin to feel better about his life? Why does he begin to feel better about his neighborhood?

8. Why does George begin to avoid Mr. Cattanzara? Describe their midnight encounter, when Mr. Cattanzara questions George about his reading. Explain the meaning of his statement, "George, don't do what I did."

9. George begins to hibernate in his room. Why? When he finally comes out, what restores his confidence?

10. What finally motivates George to visit the library?

Developing Skills in Reading Literature

1. **Setting.** The setting for "A Summer's Reading" is important in the development of the story. That the story takes place in summer, some years back, is clear.

What clues suggest that the story is not taking place in contemporary New York City?

Describe George's New York neighborhood. What sort of relationship does George have with many of the shopkeepers? How is the character of the neighborhood an important force in George's decision-making?

2. **Point of View.** This story is written in the third person, a narrator outside the action describes events and characters. The narrator, however, is not omniscient, or all-knowing. Rather, the narrator stays inside the mind of one character, George, describing only his thoughts and feelings. This method of narration is called the third-person limited point of view.

Why do you suppose Bernard Malamud chose the third-person limited point of view for this story? How would the focus of the story change if the narrator saw into the minds of Sophie and Mr. Cattanzara, for example?

3. **Conflict and Climax.** Conflict is the struggle between opposing forces that is the basis for plot in dramatic and narrative literature. Various types of conflict occur in literature. Sometimes two characters struggle against one another; sometimes conflict occurs between a character and society; sometimes conflict occurs between human beings and nature; sometimes conflict occurs within an individual character, between opposing tendencies in the character's mind. Conflict that is physical and concrete often is called "external action." Mental, psychological conflict is frequently called "internal action." The climax is the turning point of the action, the moment when interest and intensity reach their peak.

What is George warring against in "A Summer's Reading"? Is the action of the story primarily external or internal? What would you identify as the climax of the story? How is George's conflict resolved?

4. **Protagonist.** George is the protagonist, or central character, of the story. The protagonist is always involved in the main conflict of the story and often changes after the central conflict reaches the climax.

George is a touching, sympathetic character. Why? How does George change during the course of the story? What motivates this change?

5. **Theme.** A major theme in this story concerns the conflict between illusion and reality. George's neighbors have the illusion, or the false notion, that he is

reading, and George continues to pretend that he is reading good books. This illusion makes everyone happy for a while. What causes the illusion to break down? Did the illusion serve a useful purpose in George's life? When George goes to the library in the final paragraph of the story, what does his action suggest about the relationship between illusion and reality?

Developing Vocabulary

Slang and Colloquial Expressions: Etymology. Bernard Malamud uses quite a few slang and colloquial expressions in this story, because the story is George's, and he is a young man of almost twenty who would speak and think in slang much of the time. The slang also helps capture the flavor of George's neighborhood.

Try to discover the origin of each of the following slang terms or phrases from the story. To do so you will need to consult dictionaries of slang terms and other etymological dictionaries and reference works in the library.

dough (meaning money) get on someone's
two bits nerves
squirt (meaning small child)

Developing Writing Skills

Analyzing Character. It is Mr. Cattanzara, a fascinating character, who effects the change in George in this story. Write a five-paragraph composition in which you analyze Mr. Cattanzara's role in the story. Consider these questions: What kind of life does Mr. Cattanzara lead? What details suggest that Mr. Cattanzara had higher ambitions for himself? What kind of relationship has he always had with George? Why does Mr. Cattanzara tell everyone that George is reading? Why does Mr. Cattanzara let everyone continue to think this, even when he knows that it is false? What kind of motivation does he supply for George?

Outline your paper before you begin to write. To back up your points, quote specific passages from the story.

John Steinbeck

1902–1968

John Steinbeck, who believed that the writer's first duty was to "set down his time as nearly as he can understand it," managed perhaps better than anyone else to tell the stories of ordinary people caught up in the Great Depression of the 1930's. His masterpiece, *The Grapes of Wrath*, has been compared with *Uncle Tom's Cabin* in the way it influenced and illuminated a critical time in the nation's history.

As a storyteller, Steinbeck could pin down not only time but place, and the region where he grew up, the northern California coast and hill country around Monterey, found its way into much of his writing. He was born in Salinas, California, where his mother was a schoolteacher and his father was the county treasurer. Steinbeck attended Stanford University for four years, supporting himself with a variety of jobs and studying marine biology. He then worked his way to New York on a cattleboat.

There he tried working on a newspaper, became a bricklayer for a while, and finally returned to California. The variety of jobs he held during the next few years may explain why he wrote so sympathetically of common and laboring people. He worked in a trout hatchery and as a surveyor, apprentice painter, caretaker, chemical laboratory assistant, and migrant fruit picker. He even lived in his own boat for a while and caught his own food.

In 1935 he won sudden fame as a writer with *Tortilla Flat*, a warm, sentimental treatment of poor but carefree *paisanos* (Mexican Americans) of Monterey. The next year Steinbeck's reputation grew even more with *In Dubious Battle*, a protest novel about fruit pickers who try to organize a strike in a California valley. *Of Mice and Men* (1937), which Steinbeck also made into a successful play, tells of two casual laborers, George and his strong but simple-minded friend Lennie, who pick up jobs where they can find them, always on the road, yearning for but never finding a permanent home. Other books include such popular works as *The Pearl* and *The Red Pony*.

Steinbeck's writing reached an epic scale in *The Grapes of Wrath* (1939). This novel followed the Westward migration of dispossessed farmers, the "Okies" uprooted from the Oklahoma Dust Bowl, to California, a movement Steinbeck had personally witnessed. The book's central characters are the Joad family, who leave behind them a land of drought and bankruptcy and farm foreclosures to look for work as fruit pickers in California. There they are hounded by police, exploited by labor contractors, haunted by starvation, and drawn into the violence of a strike. The West, the frontier with its promise of plenty, becomes for many of the characters in this novel a place of misery and broken dreams, where the human spirit nevertheless survives. "We ain't gonna die out," Ma Joad says. "People is goin' on—changin' a little, maybe, but goin' right on."

Steinbeck has been variously called a mystic, a primitive, and a naturalist, but one characteristic was constant: he always was a good storyteller. He received the Pulitzer Prize in 1940 for *The Grapes of Wrath* and the Nobel Prize for Literature in 1962.

Flight

About fifteen miles below Monterey, on the wild coast, the Torres family had their farm, a few sloping acres above a cliff that dropped to the brown reefs and to the hissing white waters of the ocean. Behind the farm the stone mountains stood up against the sky. The farm buildings huddled like the clinging aphids[1] on the mountain skirts, crouched low to the ground as though the wind might blow them into the sea. The little shack, the rattling, rotting barn were gray-bitten with sea salt, beaten by the damp wind until they had taken on the color of the granite hills. Two horses, a red cow and a red calf, half a dozen pigs, and a flock of lean, multicolored chickens stocked the place. A little corn was raised on the sterile slope, and it grew short and thick under the wind, and all the cobs formed on the landward sides of the stalks.

Mama Torres, a lean, dry woman with ancient eyes, had ruled the farm for ten years, ever since her husband tripped over a stone in the field one day and fell full length on a rattlesnake. When one is bitten on the chest there is not much that can be done.

Mama Torres had three children, two undersized black ones of twelve and fourteen, Emilio[2] and Rosy, whom Mama kept fishing on the rocks below the farm when the sea was kind and when the truant officer was in some distant part of Monterey County. And there was Pepé,[3] the tall smiling son of nineteen, a gentle, affectionate boy, but very lazy. Pepé had a tall head, pointed at the top, and from its peak coarse black hair grew down like a thatch all around. Over his smiling little eyes Mama cut a straight bang so he could see. Pepé had sharp Indian cheekbones and an eagle nose, but his mouth was as sweet and shapely as a girl's mouth, and his chin was fragile and chiseled. He was loose and gangling, all legs and feet and wrists, and he was very lazy. Mama thought him fine and brave, but she never told him so. She said, "Some lazy cow must have got into thy father's family, else how could I have a son like thee." And she said, "When I carried thee, a sneaking lazy coyote came out of the brush and looked at me one day. That must have made thee so."

Pepé smiled sheepishly and stabbed at the ground with his knife to keep the blade sharp and free from rust. It was his inheritance, that knife, his father's knife. The long heavy blade folded back into the black handle. There was a button on the handle. When Pepé pressed the button, the blade leaped out ready for use. The knife was with Pepé always, for it had been his father's knife.

One sunny morning when the sea below the cliff was glinting and blue and the white surf creamed on the reef, when even the stone mountains looked kindly, Mama Torres called out the door of the shack, "Pepé, I have a labor for thee."

There was no answer. Mama listened. From behind the barn she heard a burst of laughter. She lifted her full long skirt and walked in the direction of the noise.

Pepé was sitting on the ground with his back against a box. His white teeth glistened.

---

1. **aphids** (ā′ fədz): any of numerous small sluggish insects that suck the juices of plants.
2. **Emilio** (ə mēl′ yō).
3. **Pepé** (pā pā′).

On either side of him stood the two black ones, tense and expectant. Fifteen feet away a redwood post was set in the ground. Pepé's right hand lay limply in his lap, and in the palm the big black knife rested. The blade was closed back into the handle. Pepé looked smiling at the sky.

Suddenly Emilio cried, "Ya!"

Pepé's wrist flicked like the head of a snake. The blade seemed to fly open in midair, and with a thump the point dug into the redwood post, and the black handle quivered. The three burst into excited laughter. Rosy ran to the post and pulled out the knife and brought it back to Pepé. He closed the blade and settled the knife carefully in his listless palm again. He grinned self-consciously at the sky.

"Ya!"

The heavy knife lanced out and sunk into the post again. Mama moved forward like a ship and scattered the play.

"All day you do foolish things with the knife, like a toy baby," she stormed. "Get up on thy huge feet that eat up shoes. Get up!" She took him by one loose shoulder and hoisted at him. Pepé grinned sheepishly and came halfheartedly to his feet. "Look!" Mama cried. "Big lazy, you must catch the horse and put on him thy father's saddle. You must ride to Monterey. The medicine bottle is empty. There is no salt. Go thou now, Peanut! Catch the horse."

A revolution took place in the relaxed figure of Pepé. "To Monterey, me? Alone? Sí, Mama."

She scowled at him. "Do not think, big sheep, that you will buy candy. No, I will give you only enough for the medicine and the salt."

Pepé smiled. "Mama, you will put the hatband on the hat?"

She relented then. "Yes, Pepé. You may wear the hatband."

His voice grew insinuating. "And the green handkerchief, Mama?"

"Yes, if you go quickly and return with no trouble, the silk green handkerchief will go. If you make sure to take off the handkerchief when you eat so no spot may fall on it."

"Sí, Mama. I will be careful. I am a man."

"Thou? A man? Thou art a peanut."

He went into the rickety barn and brought out a rope, and he walked agilely enough up the hill to catch the horse.

When he was ready and mounted before the door, mounted on his father's saddle that was so old that the oaken frame showed through torn leather in many places, then Mama brought out the round black hat with the tooled leather band, and she reached up and knotted the green silk handkerchief about his neck. Pepé's blue denim coat was much darker than his jeans, for it had been washed much less often.

Mama handed up the big medicine bottle and the silver coins. "That for the medicine," she said, "and that for the salt. That for a candle to burn for papa. That for *dulces*[4] for the little ones. Our friend Mrs. Rodriguez[5] will give you dinner and maybe a bed for the night. When you go to the church, say only ten paternosters[6] and only twenty-five Ave Marias.[7] Oh! I know, big coyote. You would sit there flapping your mouth over Aves all day while you looked at the candles and the holy pictures. That is not good devotion to stare at the pretty things."

The black hat, covering the high pointed head and black thatched hair of Pepé, gave him dignity and age. He sat the rangy horse well. Mama thought how handsome he was, dark and lean and tall. "I would not send thee now alone, thou little one, except for the medicine," she said softly. "It is not good to

---

4. *dulces* (dool' säs): sweets.
5. **Rodriguez** (rò drē' gās).
6. **paternoster:** "our father," or the Lord's Prayer; a word formula repeated as a prayer or magical charm.
7. **Ave Maria:** "Hail Mary"; a repeated prayer in the Catholic Church.

have no medicine, for who knows when the toothache will come, or the sadness of the stomach. These things are."

"*Adiós*, Mama," Pepé cried. "I will come back soon. You may send me often alone. I am a man."

"Thou art a foolish chicken."

He straightened his shoulders, flipped the reins against the horse's shoulder, and rode away. He turned once and saw that they still watched him. Emilio and Rosy and Mama. Pepé grinned with pride and gladness and lifted the tough buckskin horse to a trot.

When he had dropped out of sight over a little dip in the road, Mama turned to the black ones, but she spoke to herself. "He is nearly a man now," she said. "It will be a nice thing to have a man in the house again." Her eyes sharpened on the children. "Go to the rocks now. The tide is going out. There will be abalones[8] to be found." She put the iron hooks into their hands and saw them down the steep trail to the reefs. She brought the smooth stone metate to the doorway and sat grinding her corn to flour and looking occasionally at the road over which Pepé had gone. The noonday came and then the afternoon, when the little ones beat the abalones on a rock to make them tender and Mama patted the tortillas[9] to make them thin. They ate their dinner as the red sun was plunging down toward the ocean. They sat on the doorsteps and watched a big white moon come over the mountaintops.

Mama said, "He is now at the house of our friend Mrs. Rodriguez. She will give him nice things to eat and maybe a present."

Emilio said, "Someday I, too, will ride to Monterey for medicine. Did Pepé come to be a man today?"

Mama said wisely, "A boy gets to be a man when a man is needed. Remember this thing. I have known boys forty years old because there was no need for a man."

Soon afterward they retired, Mama in her big oak bed on one side of the room, Emilio and Rosy in their boxes full of straw and sheepskins on the other side of the room.

The moon went over the sky and the surf roared on the rocks. The roosters crowed the first call. The surf subsided to a whispering surge against the reef. The moon dropped toward the sea. The roosters crowed again.

The moon was near down to the water when Pepé rode on a winded horse to his home flat. His dog bounced out and circled the horse, yelping with pleasure. Pepé slid off the saddle to the ground. The weathered little shack was silver in the moonlight, and the square shadow of it was black to the north and east. Against the east the piling mountains were misty with light; their tops melted into the sky.

Pepé walked wearily up the three steps and into the house. It was dark inside. There was a rustle in the corner.

Mama cried out from her bed. "Who comes? Pepé, is it thou?"

"*Sí*, Mama."

"Did you get the medicine?"

"*Sí*, Mama."

"Well, go to sleep, then. I thought you would be sleeping at the house of Mrs. Rodriguez." Pepé stood silently in the dark room. "Why do you stand there, Pepé? Did you drink wine?"

"*Sí*, Mama."

"Well, go to bed then and sleep out the wine."

His voice was tired and patient, but very firm. "Light the candle, Mama. I must go away into the mountains."

"What is this, Pepé? You are crazy." Mama struck a sulfur match and held the little blue burr until the flame spread up the stick. She set light to the candle on the floor beside her bed. "Now, Pepé, what is this you say?" She looked anxiously into his face.

---

8. **abalone** (ab' ə lō' nē): a mollusk that has a flattened shell, slightly spiral in form, lined with mother of pearl.
9. **tortilla** (tôr tē' ə): a round thin cake of unleavened cornmeal.

He was changed. The fragile quality seemed to have gone from his chin. His mouth was less full than it had been, the lines of the lips were straighter, but in his eyes the greatest change had taken place. There was no laughter in them any more, nor any bashfulness. They were sharp and bright and purposeful.

He told her in a tired monotone, told her everything just as it had happened. A few people came into the kitchen of Mrs. Rodriguez. There was wine to drink. Pepé drank wine. The little quarrel—the man started toward Pepé and then the knife—it went almost by itself. It flew, it darted before Pepé knew it. As he talked, Mama's face grew stern, and it seemed to grow more lean. Pepé finished. "I am a man now, Mama. The man said names to me I could not allow."

Mama nodded. "Yes, thou art a man, my poor little Pepé. Thou art a man. I have seen it coming on thee. I have watched you throwing the knife into the post, and I have been afraid." For a moment her face had softened, but now it grew stern again. "Come! We must get you ready. Go. Awaken Emilio and Rosy. Go quickly."

Pepé stepped over to the corner where his brother and sister slept among the sheepskins. He leaned down and shook them gently. "Come, Rosy! Come, Emilio! The Mama says you must arise."

The little black ones sat up and rubbed their eyes in the candlelight. Mama was out of bed now, her long black skirt over her nightgown. "Emilio," she cried. "Go up and catch the other horse for Pepé. Quickly, now! Quickly." Emilio put his legs in his overalls and stumbled sleepily out the door.

"You heard no one behind you on the road?" Mama demanded.

"No, Mama. I listened carefully. No one was on the road."

Mama darted like a bird about the room. From a nail on the wall she took a canvas water bag and threw it on the floor. She stripped a blanket from her bed and rolled it into a tight tube and tied the ends with string. From a box beside the stove she lifted a flour sack half full of black stringy jerky. "Your father's black coat, Pepé. Here, put it on."

Pepé stood in the middle of the floor watching her activity. She reached behind the door and brought out the rifle, a long 38-56, worn shiny the whole length of the barrel. Pepé took it from her and held it in the crook of his elbow. Mama brought a little leather bag and counted the cartridges into his hand. "Only ten left," she warned. "You must not waste them."

Emilio put his head in the door. "'Qui'st'l caballo,[10] Mama."

"Put on the saddle from the other horse. Tie on the blanket. Here, tie the jerky to the saddle horn."

Still Pepé stood silently watching his mother's frantic activity. His chin looked hard, and his sweet mouth was drawn and thin. His little eyes followed Mama about the room almost suspiciously.

Rosy asked softly, "Where goes Pepé?"

Mama's eyes were fierce. "Pepé goes on a journey. Pepé is a man now. He has a man's thing to do."

Pepé straightened his shoulders. His mouth changed until he looked very much like Mama.

At last the preparation was finished. The loaded horse stood outside the door. The water bag dripped a line of moisture down the bay shoulder.

The moonlight was being thinned by the dawn, and the big white moon was near down to the sea. The family stood by the shack. Mama confronted Pepé. "Look, my son! Do not stop until it is dark again. Do not sleep even though you are tired. Take care of the horse in order that he may not stop of weariness. Remember to be careful with the bullets —there are only ten. Do not fill thy stomach

---

10. *'Qui 'st 'l caballo* (kēstl kä bä' yō) *Colloquial Spanish:* Here is the horse.

with jerky or it will make thee sick. Eat a little jerky and fill thy stomach with grass. When thou comest to the high mountains, if thou seest any of the dark watching men, go not near to them nor try to speak to them. And forget not thy prayers." She put her lean hands on Pepé's shoulders, stood on her toes and kissed him formally on both cheeks, and Pepé kissed her on both cheeks. Then he went to Emilio and Rosy and kissed both of their cheeks.

Pepé turned back to Mama. He seemed to look for a little softness, a little weakness in her. His eyes were searching, but Mama's face remained fierce. "Go now," she said. "Do not wait to be caught like a chicken."

Pepé pulled himself into the saddle. "I am a man," he said.

It was the first dawn when he rode up the hill toward the little canyon which let a trail into the mountains. Moonlight and daylight fought with each other, and the two warring qualities made it difficult to see. Before Pepé had gone a hundred yards, the outlines of his figure were misty, and long before he entered the canyon, he had become a gray, indefinite shadow.

Mama stood stiffly in front of her doorstep, and on either side of her stood Emilio and Rosy. They cast furtive glances at Mama now and then.

When the gray shape of Pepé melted into the hillside and disappeared, Mama relaxed. She began the high, whining keen[11] of the death wail. "Our beautiful—our brave," she cried. "Our protector, our son is gone." Emilio and Rosy moaned beside her. "Our beautiful—our brave, he is gone." It was the formal wail. It rose to a high piercing whine and subsided to a moan. Mama raised it three times and then she turned and went into the house and shut the door.

Emilio and Rosy stood wondering in the dawn. They heard Mama whimpering in the house. They went out to sit on the cliff above the ocean. They touched shoulders. "When did Pepé come to be a man?" Emilio asked.

"Last night," said Rosy. "Last night in Monterey." The ocean clouds turned red with the sun that was behind the mountains.

"We will have no breakfast," said Emilio. "Mama will not want to cook." Rosy did not answer him. "Where is Pepé gone?" he asked.

Rosy looked around at him. She drew her knowledge from the quiet air. "He has gone on a journey. He will never come back."

"Is he dead? Do you think he is dead?"

Rosy looked back at the ocean again. A little steamer, drawing a line of smoke, sat on the edge of the horizon. "He is not dead," Rosy explained. "Not yet."

Pepé rested the big rifle across the saddle in front of him. He let the horse walk up the hill and he didn't look back. The stony slope took on a coat of short brush so that Pepé found the entrance to a trail and entered it.

When he came to the canyon opening, he swung once in his saddle and looked back, but the houses were swallowed in the misty light. Pepé jerked forward again. The high shoulder of the canyon closed in on him. His horse stretched out its neck and sighed and settled to the trail.

It was a well worn path, dark soft leaf-mold earth strewn with broken pieces of sandstone. The trail rounded the shoulder of the canyon and dropped steeply into the bed of the stream. In the shallows the water ran smoothly, glinting in the first morning sun. Small round stones on the bottom were as brown as rust with sun moss. In the sand along the edges of the stream the tall, rich wild mint grew, while in the water itself the cress,[12] old and tough, had gone to heavy seed.

The path went into the stream and emerged on the other side. The horse sloshed into the water and stopped. Pepé dropped his bridle

---

11. **keen:** to lament, or wail for the dead.
12. **cress:** any of numerous plants with moderately pungent leaves used in salads and garnishes.

and let the beast drink of the running water.

Soon the canyon sides became steep and the first giant sentinel redwoods guarded the trail, great round red trunks bearing foliage as green and lacy as ferns. Once Pepé was among the trees, the sun was lost. A perfumed and purple light lay in the pale green of the underbrush. Gooseberry bushes and blackberries and tall ferns lined the stream, and overhead the branches of the redwoods met and cut off the sky.

Pepé drank from the water bag, and he reached into the flour sack and brought out a black string of jerky. His white teeth gnawed at the string until the tough meat parted. He chewed slowly and drank occasionally from the water bag. His little eyes were slumberous and tired, but the muscles of his face were hard-set. The earth of the trail was black now. It gave up a hollow sound under the walking hoofbeats.

The stream fell more sharply. Little waterfalls splashed on the stones. Five-fingered ferns hung over the water and dropped spray from their fingertips. Pepé rode half over his saddle, dangling one leg loosely. He picked a bay leaf from a tree beside the way and put it into his mouth for a moment to flavor the dry jerky. He held the gun loosely across the pommel.

Suddenly he squared in his saddle, swung the horse from the trail and kicked it hurriedly up behind a big redwood tree. He pulled up the reins tight against the bit to keep the horse from whinnying. His face was intent and his nostrils quivered a little.

A hollow pounding came down the trail, and a horseman rode by, a fat man with red cheeks and a white stubble beard. His horse put down his head and blubbered at the trail when it came to the place where Pepé had turned off. "Hold up!" said the man, and he pulled up his horse's head.

When the last sound of the hoofs died away, Pepé came back into the trail again. He did not relax in the saddle any more. He lifted the big rifle and swung the lever to throw a shell into the chamber, and then he let down the hammer to half cock.

The trail grew very steep. Now the redwood trees were smaller and their tops were dead, bitten dead where the wind reached them. The horse plodded on; the sun went slowly overhead and started down toward the afternoon.

Where the stream came out of a side canyon, the trail left it. Pepé dismounted and watered his horse and filled up his water bag. As soon as the trail had parted from the stream, the trees were gone and only the thick brittle sage and manzanita[13] and the chaparral[14] edged the trail. And the soft black earth was gone, too, leaving only the light tan broken rock for the trail bed. Lizards scampered away into the brush as the horse rattled over the little stones.

Pepé turned in his saddle and looked back. He was in the open now: he could be seen from a distance. As he ascended the trail the country grew more rough and terrible and dry. The way wound about the bases of great square rocks. Little gray rabbits skittered in the brush. A bird made a monotonous high creaking. Eastward the bare rock mountaintops were pale and powder-dry under the dropping sun. The horse plodded up and up the trail toward the little *v* in the ridge which was the pass.

Pepé looked suspiciously back every minute or so, and his eyes sought the tops of the ridges ahead. Once, on a white barren spur, he saw a black figure for a moment; but he looked quickly away, for it was one of the dark watchers. No one knew who the watchers were, nor where they lived, but it was better to ignore them and never to show interest in them. They did not bother one who stayed on

---

13. **manzanita** (man zə nē′ tə): any of various western North American evergreen shrubs.
14. **chaparral** (shap ə ral′): any impenetrable thicket of shrubs or dwarf trees.

the trail and minded his own business.

The air was parched and full of light dust blown by the breeze from the eroding mountains. Pepé drank sparingly from his bag and corked it tightly and hung it on the horn again. The trail moved up the dry shale hillside, avoiding rocks, dropping under clefts, climbing in and out of old water scars. When he arrived at the little pass he stopped and looked back for a long time. No dark watchers were to be seen now. The trail behind was empty. Only the high tops of the redwoods indicated where the stream flowed.

Pepé rode on through the pass. His little eyes were nearly closed with weariness, but his face was stern, relentless, and manly. The high mountain wind coasted sighing through the pass and whistled on the edges of the big blocks of broken granite. In the air, a red-tailed hawk sailed over close to the ridge and screamed angrily. Pepé went slowly through the broken jagged pass and looked down on the other side.

The trail dropped quickly, staggering among broken rock. At the bottom of the slope there was a dark crease, thick with brush, and on the other side of the crease a little flat, in which a grove of oak trees grew. A scar of green grass cut across the flat. And behind the flat another mountain rose, desolate with dead rocks and starving little black bushes. Pepé drank from the bag again, for the air was so dry that it encrusted his nostrils and burned his lips. He put the horse down the trail. The hoofs slipped and struggled on the steep way, starting little stones that rolled off into the brush. The sun was gone behind the westward mountain now, but still it glowed brilliantly on the oaks and on the grassy flat. The rocks and the hillsides still sent up waves of the heat they had gathered from the day's sun.

Pepé looked up to the top of the next dry withered ridge. He saw a dark form against the sky, a man's figure standing on top of a rock, and he glanced away quickly not to appear curious. When a moment later he looked up again, the figure was gone.

Downward the trail was quickly covered. Sometimes the horse floundered for footing, sometimes set his feet and slid a little way. They came at last to the bottom where the dark chaparral was higher than Pepé's head. He held up his rifle on one side and his arm on the other to shield his face from the sharp brittle fingers of the brush.

Up and out of the crease he rode, and up a little cliff. The grassy flat was before him, and the round comfortable oaks. For a moment he studied the trail down which he had come, but there was no movement and no sound from it. Finally he rode out over the flat, to the green streak, and at the upper end of the damp he found a little spring welling out of the earth and dropping into a dug basin before it seeped out over the flat.

Pepé filled his bag first, and then he let the thirsty horse drink out of the pool. He led the horse to the clump of oaks, and in the middle of the grove, fairly protected from sight on all sides, he took off the saddle and the bridle and laid them on the ground. The horse stretched his jaws sideways and yawned. Pepé knotted the lead rope about the horse's neck and tied him to a sapling among the oaks, where he could graze in a fairly large circle.

When the horse was gnawing hungrily at the dry grass, Pepé went to the saddle and took a black string of jerky from the sack and strolled to an oak tree on the edge of the grove, from under which he could watch the trail. He sat down in the crisp dry oak leaves and automatically felt for his big black knife to cut the jerky, but he had no knife. He leaned back on his elbow and gnawed at the tough strong meat. His face was blank, but it was a man's face.

The bright evening light washed the eastern ridge, but the valley was darkening. Doves flew down from the hills to the spring, and the quail came running out of the brush and joined them, calling clearly to one another.

Out of the corner of his eye Pepé saw a shadow grow out of the bushy crease. He turned his head slowly. A big spotted wildcat was creeping toward the spring, belly to the ground, moving like thought.

Pepé cocked his rifle and edged the muzzle slowly around. Then he looked apprehensively up the trail and dropped the hammer again. From the ground beside him he picked an oak twig and threw it toward the spring. The quail flew up with a roar and the doves whistled away. The big cat stood up; for a long moment he looked at Pepé with cold yellow eyes, and then fearlessly walked back into the gulch.

The dusk gathered quickly in the deep valley. Pepé muttered his prayers, put his head down on his arm and went instantly to sleep.

The moon came up and filled the valley with cold blue light, and the wind swept rustling down from the peaks. The owls worked up and down the slopes looking for rabbits. Down in the brush of the gulch a coyote gabbled. The oak trees whispered softly in the night breeze.

Pepé started up, listening. His horse had whinnied. The moon was just slipping behind the western ridge, leaving the valley in darkness behind it. Pepé sat tensely gripping his rifle. From far up the trail he heard an answering whinny and the crash of shod hoofs on the broken rock. He jumped to his feet, ran to his horse and led it under the trees. He threw on the saddle and cinched it tight for the steep trail, caught the unwilling head and forced the bit into the mouth. He felt the saddle to make sure the water bag and the sack of jerky were there. Then he mounted and turned up the hill.

It was velvet-dark. The horse found the entrance to the trail where it left the flat, and started up, stumbling and slipping on the rocks. Pepé's hand rose up to his head. His hat was gone. He had left it under the oak tree.

The horse had struggled far up the trail when the first change of dawn came into the air, a steel grayness as light mixed thoroughly with dark. Gradually the sharp snaggled edge of the ridge stood out above them, rotten granite tortured and eaten by the winds of time. Pepé had dropped his reins on the horn, leaving direction to the horse. The brush grabbed at his legs in the dark until one knee of his jeans was ripped.

Gradually the light flowed down over the ridge. The starved brush and rocks stood out in the half-light, strange and lonely in high perspective. Then there came warmth into the light. Pepé drew up and looked back, but he could see nothing in the darker valley below. The sky turned blue over the coming sun. In the waste of the mountainside, the poor dry brush grew only three feet high. Here and there, big outcroppings of unrotted granite stood up like moldering houses. Pepé relaxed a little. He drank from his water bag and bit off a piece of jerky. A single eagle flew over, high in the light.

Without warning Pepé's horse screamed and fell on its side. He was almost down before the rifle crash echoed up from the valley. From a hole behind the struggling shoulder, a stream of bright crimson blood pumped and stopped and pumped and stopped. The hoofs threshed on the ground. Pepé lay half stunned beside the horse. He looked slowly down the hill. A piece of sage clipped off beside his head and another crash echoed up from side to side of the canyon. Pepé flung himself frantically behind a bush.

He crawled up the hill on his knees and one hand. His right hand held the rifle up off the ground and pushed it ahead of him. He moved with the instinctive care of an animal. Rapidly he wormed his way toward one of the big outcroppings of granite on the hill above him. Where the brush was high he doubled up and ran; but where the cover was slight he wriggled forward on his stomach, pushing the rifle ahead of him. In the last little distance there was no cover at all. Pepé poised and then he darted across the space and flashed around the corner of the rock.

He leaned panting against the stone. When his breath came easier he moved along behind the big rock until he came to a narrow split that offered a thin section of vision down the hill. Pepé lay on his stomach and pushed the rifle barrel through the slit and waited.

The sun reddened the western ridges now. Already the buzzards were settling down toward the place where the horse lay. A small brown bird scratched in the dead sage leaves directly in front of the rifle muzzle. The coasting eagle flew back toward the rising sun.

Pepé saw a little movement in the brush far below. His grip tightened on the gun. A little brown doe stepped daintily out on the trail and crossed it and disappeared into the brush again. For a long time Pepé waited. Far below he could see the little flat and the oak trees and the slash of green. Suddenly his eyes flashed back at the trail again. A quarter of a mile down there had been a quick movement in the chaparral. The rifle swung over. The front sight nestled in the v of the rear sight. Pepé studied for a moment and then raised the rear sight a notch. The little movement in the brush came again. The sight settled on it. Pepé squeezed the trigger. The explosion crashed down the mountain and up the other side, and came rattling back. The whole side of the slope grew still. No more movement. And then a white streak cut into the granite of the slit and a bullet whined away and a crash sounded up from below. Pepé felt a sharp pain in his right hand. A sliver of granite was sticking out from between his first and second knuckles and the point protruded from his palm. Carefully he pulled out the sliver of stone. The wound bled evenly and gently. No vein or artery was cut.

Pepé looked into a little dusty cave in the rock and gathered a handful of spider web, and he pressed the mass into the cut, plastering the soft web into the blood. The flow stopped almost at once.

The rifle was on the ground. Pepé picked it up, levered a new shell into the chamber. And then he slid into the brush on his stomach. Far to the right he crawled, and then up the hill, moving slowly and carefully, crawling to cover and resting and then crawling again.

In the mountains the sun is high in its arc before it penetrates the gorges. The hot face looked over the hill and brought instant heat with it. The white light beat on the rocks and reflected from them and rose up quivering from the earth again, and the rocks and bushes seemed to quiver behind the air.

Pepé crawled in the general direction of the ridge peak, zigzagging for cover. The deep cut between his knuckles began to throb. He crawled close to a rattlesnake before he saw it, and when it raised its dry head and made a soft beginning whir, he backed up and took another way. The quick gray lizards flashed in front of him, raising a tiny line of dust. He found another mass of spider web and pressed it against his throbbing hand.

Pepé was pushing the rifle with his left hand now. Little drops of sweat ran to the ends of his coarse black hair and rolled down his cheeks. His lips and tongue were growing thick and heavy. His lips writhed to draw saliva into his mouth. His little dark eyes were uneasy and suspicious. Once when a gray lizard paused in front of him on the parched ground and turned its head sideways, he crushed it flat with a stone.

When the sun slid past noon he had not gone a mile. He crawled exhaustedly a last hundred yards to a patch of high sharp manzanita, crawled desperately, and when the patch was reached he wriggled in among the tough gnarly trunks and dropped his head on his left arm. There was little shade in the meager brush, but there was cover and safety. Pepé went to sleep as he lay and the sun beat on his back. A few little birds hopped close to him and peered and hopped away. Pepé squirmed in his sleep and he raised and dropped his wounded hand again and again.

The sun went down behind the peaks and the cool evening came, and then the dark. A coyote yelled from the hillside. Pepé started awake and looked about with misty eyes. His hand was swollen and heavy; a little thread of pain ran up the inside of his arm and settled in a pocket in his armpit. He peered about and then stood up, for the mountains were black and the moon had not yet risen. Pepé stood up in the dark. The coat of his father pressed on his arm. His tongue was swollen until it nearly filled his mouth. He wriggled out of the coat and dropped it in the brush, and then he struggled up the hill, falling over rocks and tearing his way through the brush. The rifle knocked against stones as he went. Little dry avalanches of gravel and shattered stone went whispering down the hill behind him.

After a while the old moon came up and showed the jagged ridgetop ahead of him. By moonlight Pepé traveled more easily. He bent forward so that his throbbing arm hung away from his body. The journey uphill was made in dashes and rests, a frantic rush up a few yards and then a rest. The wind coasted down the slope, rattling the dry stems of the bushes.

The moon was at meridian when Pepé came at last to the sharp backbone of the ridgetop. On the last hundred yards of the rise no soil had clung under the wearing winds. The way was on solid rock. He clambered to the top and looked down on the other side. There was a draw like the last below him, misty with moonlight, brushed with dry struggling sage and chaparral. On the other side the hill rose up sharply and at the top the jaggged rotten teeth of the mountain showed against the sky. At the bottom of the cut the brush was thick and dark.

Pepé stumbled down the hill. His throat was almost closed with thirst. At first he tried to run, but immediately he fell and rolled. After that he went more carefully. The moon was just disappearing behind the mountains when he came to the bottom. He crawled into the heavy brush, feeling with his fingers for water. There was no water in the bed of the stream, only damp earth. Pepé laid his gun down and scooped up a handful of mud and put it in his mouth, and then he spluttered and scraped the earth from his tongue with his finger, for the mud drew at his mouth like a poultice. He dug a hole in the stream bed with his fingers, dug a little basin to catch water; but before it was very deep his head fell forward on the damp ground and he slept.

The dawn came and the heat of the day fell on the earth, and still Pepé slept. Late in the afternoon his head jerked up. He looked slowly around. His eyes were slits of weariness. Twenty feet away in the heavy brush a big tawny mountain lion stood looking at him. Its long thick tail waved gracefully; its ears were erect with interest, not laid back dangerously. The lion squatted down on its stomach and watched him.

Pepé looked at the hole he had dug in the earth. A half-inch of muddy water had collected in the bottom. He tore the sleeve from his hurt arm, with his teeth ripped out a little square, soaked it in the water and put it in his mouth. Over and over he filled the cloth and sucked it.

Still the lion sat and watched him. The evening came down but there was no movement on the hills. No birds visited the dry bottom of the cut. Pepé looked occasionally at the lion. The eyes of the yellow beast drooped as though he were about to sleep. He yawned and his long thin red tongue curled out. Suddenly his head jerked around and his nostrils quivered. His big tail lashed. He stood up and slunk like a tawny shadow into the thick brush.

A moment later Pepé heard the sound, the faint far crash of horses' hoofs on gravel. And he heard something else, a high whining yelp of a dog.

Pepé took his rifle in his left hand and he glided into the brush almost as quietly as the lion had. In the darkening evening he crouched up the hill toward the next ridge. Only when the dark came did he stand up. His energy was short. Once it was dark he fell over the rocks and slipped to his knees on the steep slope, but he moved on and on up the hill, climbing and scrambling over the broken hillside.

When he was far up toward the top, he lay down and slept for a little while. The withered moon, shining on his face, awakened him. He stood up and moved up the hill. Fifty yards away he stopped and turned back, for he had forgotten his rifle. He walked heavily down and poked about in the brush, but he could not find his gun. At last he lay down to rest. The pocket of pain in his armpit had grown more sharp. His arm seemed to swell out and fall with every heartbeat. There was no position lying down where the heavy arm did not press against his armpit.

With the effort of a hurt beast, Pepé got up and moved again toward the top of the ridge. He held his swollen arm away from his body with his left hand. Up the steep hill he dragged himself, a few steps and a rest, and a few more steps. At last he was nearing the top. The moon showed the uneven sharp back of it against the sky.

Pepé's brain spun in a big spiral up and away from him. He slumped to the ground and lay still. The rock ridgetop was only a hundred feet above him.

The moon moved over the sky. Pepé half turned on his back. His tongue tried to make words, but only a thick hissing came from between his lips.

When the dawn came, Pepé pulled himself up. His eyes were sane again. He drew his great puffed arm in front of him and looked at the angry wound. The black line ran up from his wrist to his armpit. Automatically he reached in his pocket for the big black knife, but it was not there. His eyes searched the ground. He picked up a sharp blade of stone and scraped at the wound, sawed at the proud flesh and then squeezed the green juice out in big drops. Instantly he threw back his head and whined like a dog. His whole right side shuddered at the pain, but the pain cleared his head.

In the gray light he struggled up the last slope to the ridge and crawled over and lay down behind a line of rocks. Below him lay a deep canyon exactly like the last, waterless and desolate. There was no flat, no oak trees, not even heavy brush in the bottom of it. And on the other side a sharp ridge stood up, thinly brushed with starving sage, littered with broken granite. Strewn over the hill there were giant outcroppings, and on the top the granite teeth stood out against the sky.

The new day was light now. The flame of the sun came over the ridge and fell on Pepé where he lay on the ground. His coarse black hair was littered with twigs and bits of spider web. His eyes had retreated back into his head. Between his lips the tip of his black tongue showed.

He sat up and dragged his great arm into his lap and nursed it, rocking his body and moaning in his throat. He threw back his head and looked up into the pale sky. A big black bird circled nearly out of sight, and far to the left another was sailing near.

He lifted his head to listen, for a familiar sound had come to him from the valley he had climbed out of; it was the crying yelp of hounds, excited and feverish, on a trail.

Pepé bowed his head quickly. He tried to speak rapid words but only a thick hiss came from his lips. He drew a shaky cross on his breast with his left hand. It was a long struggle to get to his feet. He crawled slowly and mechanically to the top of a big rock on the ridge peak. Once there, he arose slowly, swaying to his feet, and stood erect. Far below he could see the dark brush where he had slept. He braced his feet and stood there, black against the morning sky.

There came a ripping sound at his feet. A piece of stone flew up and a bullet droned off into the next gorge. The hollow crash echoed up from below. Pepé looked down for a moment and then pulled himself straight again.

His body jarred back. His left hand fluttered helplessly toward his breast. The second crash sounded from below. Pepé swung forward and

toppled from the rock. His body struck and rolled over and over, starting a little avalanche. And when at last he stopped against a bush, the avalanche slid slowly down and covered up his head.

Getting at Meaning

1. Describe the situation of the Torres family. What details suggest that their farm is not very prosperous?

2. What is Mama Torres's attitude toward Pepé? How does Pepé spend most of his time?

3. For what purpose does Mama Torres send Pepé to Monterey? What is unusual about this journey?

4. What details indicate that Pepé is changed when he returns from Monterey? What has happened to change him?

5. What is the purpose of Pepé's journey into the mountains? Describe Mama Torres's preparations for the journey. What advice does she give Pepé before he leaves?

6. Describe how the family reacts after Pepé has left.

7. Explain how Pepé gets through the first night. What is his attitude toward the "watchers"?

8. Account for the death of Pepé's horse. What then happens to Pepé himself? What are the different physical problems he faces?

9. Describe how Pepé dies. Who kills him?

Developing Skills in Reading Literature

1. **Foreshadowing.** Early in the story Steinbeck describes Pepé's knife. The reader learns that "It was his inheritance, that knife, his father's knife." Concerning the button on the knife, the reader learns that "When Pepé pressed the button, the blade leaped out ready for use." These sentences foreshadow the role the knife will play in Pepé's tragedy.

What other examples of foreshadowing can you find in the story? What purpose does the foreshadowing serve?

2. **Character.** Pepé is a "chicken" and a "peanut" early in the story, according to his mother. He plays and grins sheepishly.

Mama Torres tells the two younger children, "A boy gets to be a man when a man is needed." What causes Pepé to become a man? How does his behavior change?

Mama is a strong character throughout the story. Identify several situations in which her strength is evident. What other qualities does she possess? Before Pepé leaves for the mountains, Steinbeck writes, "Pepé straightened his shoulders. His mouth changed until he looked very much like Mama." What is the significance of this detail?

3. **Imagery.** This story is full of colorful imagery, much of it describing the California countryside around the Torres's farm. Steinbeck appeals to all five of the senses.

Select a descriptive passage of the story that you find particularly effective and analyze it in detail. What images does it create? To what senses does it appeal? Does it rely heavily on adjectives? Does it also use interesting nouns and verbs? What mood or atmosphere does the imagery create?

4. **Naturalism.** Steinbeck is what is called a "naturalistic" writer. This means that he subscribes to naturalism, a philosophy that is closely linked to realism. Unlike realism, naturalism is not just the treatment of routine subject matter in a particular literary fashion. Naturalism is a world view that places humans entirely in the order of nature, without connection to a religious or spiritual world beyond nature. Humans are animals of a higher order whose lives are determined by the natural forces of heredity and environment. Characters in naturalistic literature are

usually pawns, with little control over their own lives. Often the reader witnesses the protagonist's death by impersonal forces.

What details in "Flight" suggest that Pepé is very much a part of the order of nature? What is his relationship to plant life? to other animals? Notice that Pepé's mother calls him a "chicken" and a "coyote." How do the mountain lion and the wildcat regard Pepé?

Notice the description of Pepé's death:

> His body jarred back. His left hand fluttered helplessly toward his breast. The second crash sounded from below. Pepé swung forward and toppled from the rock. His body struck and rolled over and over, starting a little avalanche. And when at last he stopped against a bush, the avalanche slid slowly down and covered up his head.

Explain how the philosophy of naturalism is apparent in this paragraph. What are the impersonal forces that destroy Pepé? What is naturalistic about the death of Pepé's father?

5. **Tone.** Naturalism generally involves an objective, impersonal tone on the part of the writer. What details give this story an objective quality? Refer to specific passages. In what scenes might Steinbeck have become emotional? Reread those scenes. What keeps them objective?

Developing Vocabulary

Words from Spanish. Pepé and his family speak Spanish, a language that has had a limited but obvious impact on American English.

Look up the following English words of Spanish origin in an etymological dictionary. From what Spanish word is each word derived? Have there been changes in meaning along the way?

canyon	guerrilla
cargo	quadroon
cigar	vanilla

SOARING, 1950. *Andrew Wyeth. Shelburne Museum, Shelburne, Vermont.*

Eudora Welty

born in 1909

Jill Krementz

One of Eudora Welty's first jobs gave her a chance to travel throughout her native Mississippi during the Depression, talking and listening to people, writing, observing, taking photographs everywhere she went. What she learned about the importance of setting in fiction helped her become one of the great Southern regional writers, along with William Faulkner and Flannery O'Connor.

Welty was born in Jackson, Mississippi, and raised there with her two younger brothers. She loved reading fairy tales, legends, and Mississippi history, and she received much love and encouragement from her father, who was an insurance executive, and her mother, a schoolteacher. "It was a good family to grow up in," she said.

After high school Welty spent two years at Mississippi State College for Women, where she helped found a literary magazine. She then transferred to the University of Wisconsin, graduating in 1929. By then she was interested in writers such as Faulkner, Yeats, and Chekhov. She studied advertising at Columbia University's Graduate School of Business, but she decided it wasn't the right career for her and returned to Mississippi. There she found part-time work writing for newspapers and a local radio station.

It was then that Welty began traveling as a publicity agent for the Mississippi office of the Works Progress Administration, a federal project countering unemployment in the Depression. What she saw sometimes troubled her, but it fascinated her, too; she felt she was seeing her native land for the first time. She took photographs of the people she met and began to write stories about her experiences. In 1936 a New York gallery exhibited her photographs, and a small magazine published one of her stories, "Death of a Traveling Salesman." Soon more important magazines like the *Southern Review* and the *Atlantic Monthly* discovered her talent, and her first collection of stories, *A Curtain of Green*, appeared in 1941, with an introduction by Katherine Anne Porter. In that year Welty won the first of her six O. Henry Memorial Contest awards, for the story "A Worn Path."

She went on writing classics like these, which have found their way into many anthologies, and published several more collections of short stories. Meanwhile she started writing novels, beginning with *Delta Wedding* (1946). *The Ponder Heart* (1954) was turned into a successful play, and *Losing Battles*, a long novel about the reunion of a family in rural Mississippi, appeared in 1970. *The Optimist's Daughter*, first conceived as a short story, was set in the Mississippi Delta, like much of Welty's work, and was based partly on her own mother's life. It won the 1973 Pulitzer Prize for fiction. She has also produced essays and juvenile fiction, and her early photographs eventually became *One Time, One Place: Mississippi in the Depression: A Snapshot Album* (1971).

Welty is a master of time and place. She is able to find significance in the everyday, to catch the humor and the nuance of small town Southern speech, and to craft fiction that, as one critic wrote, has the "gleam of permanence."

A Worn Path

It was December—a bright frozen day in the early morning. Far out in the country there was an old Negro woman with her head tied in a red rag, coming along a path through the pinewoods. Her name was Phoenix Jackson. She was very old and small and she walked slowly in the dark pine shadows, moving a little from side to side in her steps, with the balanced heaviness and lightness of a pendulum in a grandfather clock. She carried a thin, small cane made from an umbrella, and with this she kept tapping the frozen earth in front of her. This made a grave and persistent noise in the still air, that seemed meditative like the chirping of a solitary little bird.

She wore a dark striped dress reaching down to her shoe tops, and an equally long apron of bleached sugar sacks, with a full pocket: all neat and tidy, but every time she took a step she might have fallen over her shoelaces, which dragged from her unlaced shoes. She looked straight ahead. Her eyes were blue with age. Her skin had a pattern all its own of numberless branching wrinkles and as though a whole little tree stood in the middle of her forehead, but a golden color ran underneath, and the two knobs of her cheeks were illumined by a yellow burning under the dark. Under the red rag her hair came down on her neck in the frailest of ringlets, still black, and with an odor like copper.

Now and then there was a quivering in the thicket. Old Phoenix said, "Out of my way, all you foxes, owls, beetles, jack rabbits, coons, and wild animals! . . . Keep out from under these feet, little bobwhites. . . . Keep the big wild hogs out of my path. Don't let none of those come running my direction. I got a long way." Under her small black-freckled hand her cane, limber as a buggy whip, would switch at the brush as if to rouse up any hiding things.

On she went. The woods were deep and still. The sun made the pine needles almost too bright to look at, up where the wind rocked. The cones dropped as light as feathers. Down in the hollow was the mourning dove—it was not too late for him.

The path ran up a hill. "Seem like there is chains about my feet, time I get this far," she said, in the voice of argument old people keep to use with themselves. "Something always take a hold of me on this hill—pleads I should stay."

After she got to the top she turned and gave a full, severe look behind her where she had come. "Up through pines," she said at length. "Now down through oaks."

Her eyes opened their widest, and she started down gently. But before she got to the bottom of the hill a bush caught her dress.

Her fingers were busy and intent, but her skirts were full and long, so that before she could pull them free in one place they were caught in another. It was not possible to allow the dress to tear. "I in the thorny bush," she said. "Thorns, you doing your appointed work. Never want to let folks pass, no sir. Old eyes thought you was a pretty little *green* bush."

Finally, trembling all over, she stood free, and after a moment dared to stoop for her cane.

"Sun so high!" she cried, leaning back and looking, while the thick tears went over her eyes. "The time getting all gone here."

At the foot of this hill was a place where a log was laid across the creek.

"Now comes the trial," said Phoenix.

Putting her right foot out, she mounted the log and shut her eyes. Lifting her skirt, leveling her cane fiercely before her, like a festival figure in some parade, she began to march across. Then she opened her eyes and she was safe on the other side.

"I wasn't as old as I thought," she said.

But she sat down to rest. She spread her skirts on the bank around her and folded her hands over her knees. Up above her was a tree in a pearly cloud of mistletoe. She did not dare to close her eyes, and when a little boy brought her a plate with a slice of marble cake on it she spoke to him. "That would be acceptable," she said. But when she went to take it there was just her own hand in the air.

So she left that tree, and had to go through a barbed-wire fence. There she had to creep and crawl, spreading her knees and stretching her fingers like a baby trying to climb the steps. But she talked loudly to herself: she could not let her dress be torn now, so late in the day, and she could not pay for having her arm or her leg sawed off if she got caught fast where she was.

At last she was safe through the fence and risen up out in the clearing. Big dead trees, like black men with one arm, were standing in the purple stalks of the withered cotton field. There sat a buzzard.

"Who you watching?"

In the furrow she made her way along.

"Glad this not the season for bulls," she said, looking sideways, "and the good Lord made his snakes to curl up and sleep in the winter. A pleasure I don't see no two-headed snake coming around that tree, where it come once. It took a while to get by him, back in the summer."

She passed through the old cotton and went into a field of dead corn. It whispered and shook and was taller than her head. "Through the maze now," she said, for there was no path.

Then there was something tall, black, and skinny there, moving before her.

At first she took it for a man. It could have been a man dancing in the field. But she stood still and listened, and it did not make a sound. It was as silent as a ghost.

"Ghost," she said sharply, "who be you the ghost of? For I have heard of nary death close by."

But there was no answer—only the ragged dancing in the wind.

She shut her eyes, reached out her hand, and touched a sleeve. She found a coat and inside that an emptiness, cold as ice.

"You scarecrow," she said. Her face lighted. "I ought to be shut up for good," she said with laughter. "My senses is gone. I too old. I the oldest people I ever know. Dance, old scarecrow," she said, "while I dancing with you."

She kicked her foot over the furrow, and with mouth drawn down, shook her head once or twice in a little strutting way. Some husks blew down and whirled in streamers about her skirts.

Then she went on, parting her way from side to side with the cane, through the whispering field. At last she came to the end, to a wagon track where the silver grass blew between the red ruts. The quail were walking around like pullets, seeming all dainty and unseen.

"Walk pretty," she said. "This the easy place. This the easy going."

She followed the track, swaying through the quiet bare fields, through the little strings of trees silver in their dead leaves, past cabins silver from weather, with the doors and windows boarded shut, all like old women under a spell sitting there. "I walking in their sleep," she said, nodding her head vigorously.

In a ravine she went where a spring was silently flowing through a hollow log. Old Phoenix bent and drank. "Sweet gum makes the water sweet," she said, and drank more. "Nobody know who made this well, for it was here when I was born."

The track crossed a swampy part where the

moss hung as white as lace from every limb. "Sleep on, alligators, and blow your bubbles." Then the track went into the road.

Deep, deep the road went down between the high green-colored banks. Overhead the live oaks met, and it was as dark as a cave.

A black dog with a lolling tongue came up out of the weeds by the ditch. She was meditating, and not ready, and when he came at her she only hit him a little with her cane. Over she went in the ditch, like a little puff of milkweed.

Down there, her senses drifted away. A dream visited her, and she reached her hand up, but nothing reached down and gave her a pull. So she lay there and presently went to talking. "Old woman," she said to herself, "that black dog come up out of the weeds to stall you off, and now there he sitting on his fine tail, smiling at you."

A white man finally came along and found her—a hunter, a young man, with his dog on a chain.

"Well, Granny!" he laughed. "What are you doing there?"

"Lying on my back like a June bug waiting to be turned over, mister," she said, reaching up her hand.

He lifted her up, gave her a swing in the air, and set her down. "Anything broken, Granny?"

"No sir, them old dead weeds is springy enough," said Phoenix, when she had got her breath. "I thank you for your trouble."

"Where do you live, Granny?" he asked, while the two dogs were growling at each other.

"Away back yonder, sir, behind the ridge. You can't even see it from here."

"On your way home?"

"No sir, I going to town."

"Why, that's too far! That's as far as I walk when I come out myself, and I get something for my trouble." He patted the stuffed bag he carried, and there hung down a little closed claw. It was one of the bobwhites, with its beak hooked bitterly to show it was dead. "Now you go on home, Granny!"

"I bound to go to town, mister," said Phoenix. "The time come around."

He gave another laugh, filling the whole landscape. "I know you old people! Wouldn't miss going to town to see Santa Claus!"

But something held old Phoenix very still. The deep lines in her face went into a fierce and different radiation. Without warning, she had seen with her own eyes a flashing nickel fall out of the man's pocket onto the ground.

"How old are you, Granny?" he was saying.

"There is no telling, mister," she said, "no telling."

Then she gave a little cry and clapped her hands and said, "Git on away from here, dog! Look! Look at that dog!" She laughed as if in admiration. "He ain't scared of nobody. He a big black dog." She whispered, "Sic him!"

"Watch me get rid of that cur," said the man. "Sic him, Pete! Sic him!"

Phoenix heard the dogs fighting, and heard the man running and throwing sticks. She even heard a gunshot. But she was slowly bending forward by that time, further and further forward, the lids stretched down over her eyes, as if she were doing this in her sleep. Her chin was lowered almost to her knees. The yellow palm of her hand come out from the fold of her apron. Her fingers slid down and along the ground under the piece of money with the grace and care they would have in lifting an egg from under a setting hen. Then she slowly straightened up, she stood erect, and the nickel was in her apron pocket. A bird flew by. Her lips moved. "God watching me the whole time. I come to stealing."

The man came back, and his own dog panted about them. "Well, I scared him off that time," he said, and then he laughed and lifted his gun and pointed it at Phoenix.

She stood straight and faced him.

"Doesn't the gun scare you?" he said, still pointing it.

"No, sir, I seen plenty go off closer by, in my day, and for less than what I done," she said, holding utterly still.

He smiled, and shouldered the gun. "Well, Granny," he said, "you must be a hundred years old, and scared of nothing. I'd give you a dime if I had any money with me. But you take my advice and stay home, and nothing will happen to you."

"I bound to go on my way, mister," said Phoenix. She inclined her head in the red rag. Then they went in different directions, but she could hear the gun shooting again and again over the hill.

She walked on. The shadows hung from the oak trees to the road like curtains. Then she smelled woodsmoke, and smelled the river, and she saw a steeple and the cabins on their steep steps. Dozens of little black children whirled around her. There ahead was Natchez shining. Bells were ringing. She walked on.

In the paved city it was Christmastime. There were red and green electric lights strung and crisscrossed everywhere, and all turned on in the daytime. Old Phoenix would have been lost if she had not distrusted her eyesight and depended on her feet to know where to take her.

She paused quietly on the sidewalk where people were passing by. A lady came along in the crowd, carrying an armful of red-, green-, and silver-wrapped presents; she gave off perfume like the red roses in hot summer, and Phoenix stopped her.

"Please, missy, will you lace up my shoe?" She held up her foot.

"What do you want, Grandma?"

"See my shoe," said Phoenix. "Do all right for out in the country, but wouldn't look right to go in a big building."

"Stand still then, Grandma," said the lady. She put her packages down on the sidewalk beside her and laced and tied both shoes tightly.

"Can't lace 'em with a cane," said Phoenix. "Thank you, missy. I doesn't mind asking a nice lady to tie up my shoe, when I gets out on the street."

Moving slowly and from side to side, she went into the big building, and into a tower of steps, where she walked up and around and around until her feet knew to stop.

She entered a door, and there she saw nailed up on the wall the document that had been stamped with the gold seal and framed in the gold frame, which matched the dream that was hung up in her head.

"Here I be," she said. There was a fixed and ceremonial stiffness over her body.

"A charity case, I suppose," said an attendant who sat at the desk before her.

But Phoenix only looked above her head. There was sweat on her face; the wrinkles in her skin shone like a bright net.

"Speak up, Grandma," the woman said. "What's your name? We must have your history, you know. Have you been here before? What seems to be the trouble with you?"

Old Phoenix only gave a twitch to her face as if a fly were bothering her.

"Are you deaf?" cried the attendant.

But then the nurse came in.

"Oh, that's just old Aunt Phoenix," she said. "She doesn't come for herself—she has a little grandson. She makes these trips just as regular as clockwork. She lives away back off the Old Natchez Trace."[1] She bent down. "Well, Aunt Phoenix, why don't you just take a seat? We won't keep you standing after your long trip." She pointed.

The old woman sat down, bolt upright in the chair.

"Now, how is the boy?" asked the nurse.

Old Phoenix did not speak.

"I said, how is the boy?"

But Phoenix only waited and stared straight ahead, her face very solemn and withdrawn into rigidity.

---

1. **Old Natchez Trace:** an early nineteenth-century route, from Natchez, Mississippi, to Nashville, Tennessee.

"Is his throat any better?" asked the nurse. "Aunt Phoenix, don't you hear me? Is your grandson's throat any better since the last time you came for the medicine?"

With her hands on her knees, the old woman waited, silent, erect and motionless, just as if she were in armor.

"You mustn't take up our time this way, Aunt Phoenix," the nurse said. "Tell us quickly about your grandson, and get it over. He isn't dead, is he?"

At last there came a flicker and then a flame of comprehension across her face, and she spoke.

"My grandson. It was my memory had left me. There I sat and forgot why I made my long trip."

"Forgot?" The nurse frowned. "After you came so far?"

Then Phoenix was like an old woman begging a dignified forgiveness for waking up frightened in the night. "I never did go to school; I was too old at the Surrender,"[2] she said in a soft voice. "I'm an old woman without an education. It was my memory fail me. My little grandson, he is just the same, and I forgot it in the coming."

"Throat never heals, does it?" said the nurse, speaking in a loud, sure voice to old Phoenix. By now she had a card with something written on it, a little list. "Yes. Swallowed lye. When was it?—January—two, three years ago—"

Phoenix spoke unasked now. "No, missy, he not dead, he just the same. Every little while his throat begin to close up again, and he not able to swallow. He not get his breath. He not able to help himself. So the time come around, and I go on another trip for the soothing medicine."

"All right. The doctor said as long as you came to get it, you could have it," said the nurse. "But it's an obstinate case."

"My little grandson, he sit up there in the house all wrapped up, waiting by himself," Phoenix went on. "We is the only two left in the world. He suffer and it don't seem to put him back at all. He got a sweet look. He going to last. He wear a little patch quilt and peep out holding his mouth open like a little bird. I remembers so plain now. I not going to forget him again, no, the whole enduring time. I could tell him from all the others in creation."

"All right." The nurse was trying to hush her now. She brought her a bottle of medicine. "Charity," she said, making a check mark in a book.

Old Phoenix held the bottle close to her eyes, and then carefully put it into her pocket.

"I thank you," she said.

"It's Christmastime, Grandma," said the attendant. "Could I give you a few pennies out of my purse?"

"Five pennies is a nickel," said Phoenix stiffly.

"Here's a nickel," said the attendant.

Phoenix rose carefully and held out her hand. She received the nickel and then fished the other nickel out of her pocket and laid it beside the new one. She stared at her palm closely, with her head on one side.

Then she gave a tap with her cane on the floor.

"This is what come to me to do," she said. "I'm going to the store and buy my child a little windmill they sells, made out of paper. He going to find it hard to believe there such a thing in the world. I'll march myself back where he waiting, holding it straight up in this hand."

She lifted her free hand, gave a little nod, turned around, and walked out of the doctor's office. Then her slow step began on the stairs, going down.

---

2. **the Surrender:** the end of the Civil War. Robert E. Lee surrendered to Ulysses S. Grant at the Appomattox Court House in Virginia in April of 1865.

Getting at Meaning

1. Describe Phoenix Jackson. What is her attitude toward her journey, as her remarks to the animals of the woods indicate?

2. What are some of the obstacles that "Old Phoenix" deals with in her journey? What is the hardest part of the journey for her?

3. Resting on the bank of the creek, the old woman's mind wanders for a few minutes. At what other point in the story does her mind play tricks on her?

4. What does Phoenix Jackson first think about the scarecrow? Why does she suggest that she and the scarecrow dance together?

5. What is humiliating to the old woman on her journey? What small triumphs does she have?

6. What is wrong with Phoenix Jackson's grandson? How does she intend to surprise him?

Developing Skills in Reading Literature

1. **Imagery.** Eudora Welty describes Phoenix Jackson's journey in vivid detail. Which visual images stand out clearly to you? Which images that appeal to the sense of hearing are especially vivid? What does the old woman touch or feel on her journey? Where does Welty incorporate smells?

2. **Simile.** This story contains numerous similes. For example, Phoenix Jackson moves a little from side to side as she walks, "with the balanced heaviness and lightness of a pendulum in a grandfather clock." Her cane tapping the frozen earth makes a noise "that seemed meditative like the chirping of a solitary little bird." These two similes graphically characterize Phoenix Jackson for the reader.

Find three or four additional similes in the story. How does each one function?

3. **Character.** As the hunter on the path observes, it is remarkable that a frail old woman like Phoenix Jackson can make the journey that she does. What motivates her? What character traits does she possess? Point to specific passages in the story that illustrate these traits.

In mythology the phoenix was a rare and wonderful bird that defied destruction by rising alive from its own ashes after consuming itself in flames. In what sense is Phoenix Jackson aptly named?

4. **Theme.** Eudora Welty has written that the point of this story lies in the journey itself, and the fact that it is made. In what sense is Phoenix Jackson herself a "worn path"? Notice the description of her face. Explain how the title of the story also functions as a metaphor for the old woman's love for her grandson. What commentary does the story make about the habit of love? What is Phoenix Jackson's victory? Although this story is intensely moving and in many ways sad, what makes it hopeful?

Developing Writing Skills

Describing a Person. "A Worn Path" creates the character of Phoenix Jackson in loving, precise detail. The physical description of her conveys a great deal about her character, and her actions and words tell the reader even more about her.

Using Eudora Welty's techniques as a model, re-create someone you know well in a descriptive essay. Do not limit yourself to physical description alone, but reveal the person through speech and action as well. Your goal is to have your readers feel that they know and understand the person.

Psychological Insight

THE MYSTERIOUS BIRD, 1917. *Charles Burchfield.*
The Delaware Art Museum.

William Faulkner

1897–1962

Most of William Faulkner's novels and short stories are set in the one small area of northern Mississippi where he was born and raised. He gave such vivid life to that particular region that his work speaks not just for Southerners or Americans but for all humanity. When he accepted the Nobel Prize in 1950, he characterized the subject of his work as "the problems of the human heart in conflict with itself."

Born in New Albany, Mississippi, Faulkner grew up hearing stories about his homeland, legends about the past, tales of honor and gallantry and defeat, stories of famous ancestors. One of these family heroes particularly fascinated him: his great-grandfather, a colorful and energetic man who, among his many accomplishments, had been a popular novelist.

Faulkner grew up, along with three younger brothers, in the university town of Oxford, Mississippi. He dropped out of high school but read widely, especially Romantic poetry, which he later said, "completely satisfied me and filled my inner life."

Faulkner was not tall enough to be accepted into the American Air Force in World War I, so he enlisted in the Royal Canadian Air Force, but the war ended before he received his commission. He returned to Oxford, where he drifted for a while. He took some courses at the university (he didn't do very well in English) and held various odd jobs, still reading widely and experimenting in poetry and prose. Encouraged by a good friend who was older and better educated, in 1924 he published a book of poetry.

In 1925 he spent some time in Europe and also lived in New Orleans for a while. There he met Sherwood Anderson, author of *Winesburg, Ohio*. Anderson gave him further encouragement, and by 1927 Faulkner had published his first two novels.

Looking for further subject matter, Faulkner made a crucial discovery: "that my own little postage stamp of native soil was worth writing about and that I would never live long enough to exhaust it." Faulkner created, as he said, a cosmos of his own, based on everything he knew about the land where he grew up. It has become known to the world as Yoknapatawpha County.

Faulkner continually experimented with new novelistic techniques. His writing moved backward and forward in time and revealed the "stream of consciousness" and interior monologues of his characters. His long sentences, packed with images and detail, stand in sharp contrast to the lean prose style of Hemingway. In *The Sound and the Fury* (1929), which many think is Faulkner's greatest novel, he tells the same story through the eyes of four different characters, one of them an idiot. This kind of writing forces the reader to enter actively into the imagined world of the story in order to discover, along with the characters themselves, the meaning of the events taking place.

Faulkner went on working and publishing until he died, just short of his sixty-fifth birthday. By then he had become recognized as one of America's most prodigious talents and one of the great imaginative writers of the Western world.

Barn Burning

The store in which the Justice of the Peace's court was sitting smelled of cheese. The boy, crouched on his nail keg at the back of the crowded room, knew he smelled cheese, and more: from where he sat he could see the ranked shelves close-packed with the solid, squat, dynamic shapes of tin cans whose labels his stomach read, not from the lettering which meant nothing to his mind but from the scarlet devils and the silver curve of fish—this, the cheese which he knew he smelled and the hermetic[1] meat which his intestines believed he smelled coming in intermittent gusts momentary and brief between the other constant one, the smell and sense just a little of fear because mostly of despair and grief, the old fierce pull of blood. He could not see the table where the Justice sat and before which his father and his father's enemy (*our enemy* he thought in that despair; *ourn! mine and hisn both! He's my father!*) stood, but he could hear them, the two of them that is, because his father had said no word yet:

"But what proof have you, Mr. Harris?"

"I told you. The hog got into my corn. I caught it up and sent it back to him. He had no fence that would hold it. I told him so, warned him. The next time I put the hog in my pen. When he came to get it I gave him enough wire to patch up his pen. The next time I put the hog up and kept it. I rode down to his house and saw the wire I gave him still rolled on the spool in his yard. I told him he could have the hog when he paid me a dollar pound fee. That evening a nigger came with the dollar and got the hog. He was a strange nigger. He said, 'He say to tell you wood and hay kin burn.' I said, 'What?' 'That whut he

say to tell you,' the nigger said. 'Wood and hay kin burn.' That night my barn burned. I got the stock out but I lost the barn."

"Where is the nigger? Have you got him?"

"He was a strange nigger, I tell you. I don't know what became of him."

"But that's not proof. Don't you see that's not proof?"

"Get that boy up here. He knows." For a moment the boy thought too that the man meant his older brother until Harris said, "Not him. The little one. The boy," and, crouching, small for his age, small and wiry like his father, in patched and faded jeans even too small for him, with straight, uncombed, brown hair and eyes gray and wild as storm scud, he saw the men between himself and the table part and become a lane of grim faces, at the end of which he saw the Justice, a shabby, collarless, graying man in spectacles, beckoning him. He felt no floor under his bare feet; he seemed to walk beneath the palpable weight of the grim turning faces. His father, stiff in his black Sunday coat donned not for the trial but for the moving, did not even look at him. *He aims for me to lie*, he thought, again with that frantic grief and despair. *And I will have to do hit.*

"What's your name, boy?" the Justice said.

"Colonel Sartoris Snopes," the boy whispered.

"Hey?" the Justice said. "Talk louder. Colonel Sartoris? I reckon anybody named for Colonel Sartoris in this country can't help but tell the truth, can they?" The boy said nothing. *Enemy! Enemy!* he thought; for a mo-

---

1. **hermetic** (hər met' ik): airtight; impervious to external influence.

ment he could not even see, could not see that the Justice's face was kindly nor discern that his voice was troubled when he spoke to the man named Harris: "Do you want me to question this boy?" But he could hear, and during those subsequent long seconds while there was absolutely no sound in the crowded little room save that of quiet and intent breathing, it was as if he had swung outward at the end of a grape vine, over a ravine, and at the top of the swing he had been caught in a prolonged instant of mesmerized gravity, weightless in time.

"No!" Harris said violently, explosively. "Damnation! Send him out of here!" Now time, the fluid world, rushed beneath him again, the voices coming to him again through the smell of cheese and sealed meat, the fear and despair and the old grief of blood:

"This case is closed. I can't find against you, Snopes, but I can give you advice. Leave this country and don't come back to it."

His father spoke for the first time, his voice cold and harsh, level, without emphasis: "I aim to. I don't figure to stay in a country among people who . . ." he said something unprintable and vile, addressed to no one.

"That'll do," the Justice said. "Take your wagon and get out of this country before dark. Case dismissed."

His father turned, and he followed the stiff black coat, the wiry figure walking a little stiffly from where a Confederate provost's man's musket ball had taken him in the heel on a stolen horse thirty years ago, followed the two backs now, since his older brother had appeared from somewhere in the crowd, no taller than the father but thicker, chewing tobacco steadily, between the two lines of grim-faced men and out of the store and across the worn gallery and down the sagging steps and among the dogs and half-grown boys in the mild May dust, where as he passed a voice hissed:

"Barn burner!"

Again he could not see, whirling; there was a face in a red haze, moonlike, bigger than the full moon, the owner of it half again his size, he leaping in the red haze toward the face, feeling no blow, feeling no shock when his head struck the earth, scrabbling up and leaping again, feeling no blow this time either and tasting no blood, scrabbling up to see the other boy in full flight and himself already leaping into pursuit as his father's hand jerked him back, the harsh, cold voice speaking above him: "Go get in the wagon."

It stood in a grove of locusts and mulberries across the road. His two hulking sisters in their Sunday dresses and his mother and her sister in calico and sunbonnets were already in it, sitting on and among the sorry residue of the dozen and more movings which even the boy could remember—the battered stove, the broken beds and chairs, the clock inlaid with mother-of-pearl, which would not run, stopped at some fourteen minutes past two o'clock of a dead and forgotten day and time, which had been his mother's dowry. She was crying, though when she saw him she drew her sleeve across her face and began to descend from the wagon. "Get back," the father said.

"He's hurt. I got to get some water and wash his . . ."

"Get back in the wagon," his father said. He got in too, over the tail-gate. His father mounted to the seat where the older brother already sat and struck the gaunt mules two savage blows with the peeled willow, but without heat. It was not even sadistic; it was exactly that same quality which in later years would cause his descendants to over-run the engine before putting a motor car into motion, striking and reining back in the same movement. The wagon went on, the store with its quiet crowd of grimly watching men dropped behind; a curve in the road hid it. *Forever* he thought. *Maybe he's done satisfied now, now that he has* . . . stopping himself, not to say it aloud even to himself. His mother's hand touched his shoulder.

"Does hit hurt?" she said.

"Naw," he said. "Hit don't hurt. Lemme be."

"Can't you wipe some of the blood off before hit dries?"

"I'll wash tonight," he said. "Lemme be, I tell you."

The wagon went on. He did not know where they were going. None of them ever did or ever asked, because it was always somewhere, always a house of sorts waiting for them a day or two days or even three days away. Likely his father had already arranged to make a crop on another farm before he . . . Again he had to stop himself. He (the father) always did. There was something about his wolflike independence and even courage when the advantage was at least neutral which impressed strangers, as if they got from his latent ravening ferocity not so much a sense of dependability as a feeling that his ferocious conviction in the rightness of his own actions would be of advantage to all whose interest lay with his.

That night they camped, in a grove of oaks and beeches where a spring ran. The nights were still cool and they had a fire against it, of a rail lifted from a nearby fence and cut into lengths—a small fire, neat, niggard almost, a shrewd fire; such fires were his father's habit and custom always, even in freezing weather. Older, the boy might have remarked this and wondered why not a big one; why should not a man who had not only seen the waste and extravagance of war, but who had in his blood an inherent voracious prodigality[2] with material not his own, have burned everything in sight? Then he might have gone a step farther and thought that that was the reason: that niggard blaze was the living fruit of nights passed during those four years in the woods hiding from all men, blue or gray, with his strings of horses (captured horses, he called them). And older still, he might have divined the true reason: that the element of fire spoke to some deep mainspring of his father's being,

as the element of steel or of powder spoke to other men, as the one weapon for the preservation of integrity, else breath were not worth the breathing, and hence to be regarded with respect and used with discretion.

But he did not think this now and he had seen those same niggard blazes all his life. He merely ate his supper beside it and was already half asleep over his iron plate when his father called him, and once more he followed the stiff back, the stiff and ruthless limp, up the slope and on to the starlit road where, turning, he could see his father against the stars but without face or depth—a shape black, flat, and bloodless as though cut from tin in the iron folds of the frockcoat which had not been made for him, the voice harsh like tin and without heat like tin:

"You were fixing to tell them. You would have told him." He didn't answer. His father struck him with the flat of his hand on the side of the head, hard but without heat, exactly as he had struck the two mules at the store, exactly as he would strike either of them with any stick in order to kill a horse fly, his voice still without heat or anger: "You're getting to be a man. You got to learn. You got to learn to stick to your own blood or you ain't going to have any blood to stick to you. Do you think either of them, any man there this morning, would? Don't you know all they wanted was a chance to get at me because they knew I had them beat? Eh?" Later, twenty years later, he was to tell himself, "If I had said they wanted only truth, justice, he would have hit me again." But now he said nothing. He was not crying. He just stood there. "Answer me," his father said.

"Yes," he whispered. His father turned.

"Get on to bed. We'll be there tomorrow."

Tomorrow they were there. In the early afternoon the wagon stopped before a paintless two-room house identical almost with

2. **voracious prodigality:** exceedingly eager extravagance or waste.

the dozen others it had stopped before even in the boy's ten years, and again, as on the other dozen occasions, his mother and aunt got down and began to unload the wagon, although his two sisters and his father and brother had not moved.

"Likely hit ain't fitten for hawgs," one of the sisters said.

"Nevertheless, fit it will and you'll hog it and like it," his father said. "Get out of them chairs and help your Ma unload."

The two sisters got down, big, bovine,[3] in a flutter of cheap ribbons; one of them drew from the jumbled wagon bed a battered lantern, the other a worn broom. His father handed the reins to the older son and began to climb stiffly over the wheel. "When they get unloaded, take the team to the barn and feed them." Then he said, and at first the boy thought he was still speaking to his brother: "Come with me."

"Me?" he said.

"Yes," his father said. "You."

"Abner," his mother said. His father paused and looked back—the harsh level stare beneath the shaggy, graying, irascible brows.

"I reckon I'll have a word with the man that aims to begin tomorrow owning me body and soul for the next eight months."

They went back up the road. A week ago—or before last night, that is—he would have asked where they were going, but not now. His father had struck him before last night but never before had he paused afterward to explain why; it was as if the blow and the following calm, outrageous voice still rang, repercussed, divulging nothing to him save the terrible handicap of being young, the light weight of his few years, just heavy enough to prevent his soaring free of the world as it seemed to be ordered but not heavy enough to keep him footed solid in it, to resist it and try to change the course of its events.

Presently he could see the grove of oaks and cedars and the other flowering trees and shrubs where the house would be, though not the house yet. They walked beside a fence massed with honeysuckle and Cherokee roses and came to a gate swinging open between two brick pillars, and now, beyond a sweep of drive, he saw the house for the first time and at that instant he forgot his father and the terror and despair both, and even when he remembered his father again (who had not stopped) the terror and despair did not return. Because, for all the twelve movings, they had sojourned until now in a poor country, a land of small farms and fields and houses, and he had never seen a house like this before. *Hit's big us a courthouse* he thought quietly, with a surge of peace and joy whose reason he could not have thought into words, being too young for that: *They are safe from him. People whose lives are a part of this peace and dignity are beyond his touch, he no more to them than a buzzing wasp: capable of stinging for a little moment but that's all; the spell of this peace and dignity rendering even the barns and stable and cribs which belong to it impervious to the puny flames he might contrive* . . . this, the peace and joy, ebbing for an instant as he looked again at the stiff black back, the stiff and implacable limp of the figure which was not dwarfed by the house, for the reason that it had never looked big anywhere and which now, against the serene columned backdrop, had more than ever that impervious quality of something cut ruthlessly from tin, depthless, as though, sidewise to the sun, it would cast no shadow. Watching him, the boy remarked the absolutely undeviating course which his father held and saw the stiff foot come squarely down in a pile of fresh droppings where a horse had stood in the drive and which his father could have avoided by a simple change of stride. But it ebbed only for a moment, though he could not have thought this into words either, walking on in the spell of the

---

3. **bovine:** having oxlike qualities; slow, dull, stupid.

house, which he could even want but without envy, without sorrow, certainly never with that ravening and jealous rage which unknown to him walked in the ironlike black coat before him: *Maybe he will feel it too. Maybe it will even change him now from what maybe he couldn't help but be.*

They crossed the portico. Now he could hear his father's stiff foot as it came down on the boards with clocklike finality, a sound out of all proportion to the displacement of the body it bore and which was not dwarfed either by the white door before it, as though it had attained to a sort of vicious and ravening minimum not to be dwarfed by anything—the flat, wide, black hat, the formal coat of broadcloth which had once been black but which had now that friction-glazed greenish cast of the bodies of old house flies, the lifted sleeve which was too large, the lifted hand like a curled claw. The door opened so promptly that the boy knew the Negro must have been watching them all the time, an old man with neat grizzled hair, in a linen jacket, who stood barring the door with his body, saying, "Wipe yo foots, white man, fo you come in here. Major ain't home nohow."

"Get out of my way, nigger," his father said, without heat too, flinging the door back and the Negro also and entering, his hat still on his head. And now the boy saw the prints of the stiff foot on the doorjamb and saw them appear on the pale rug behind the machine-like deliberation of the foot which seemed to bear (or transmit) twice the weight which the body compassed. The Negro was shouting "Miss Lula! Miss Lula!" somewhere behind them, then the boy, deluged as though by a warm wave, by a suave turn of carpeted stair and a pendant glitter of chandeliers and a mute gleam of gold frames, heard the swift feet and saw her too, a lady—perhaps he had never seen her like before either—in a gray, smooth gown with lace at the throat and an apron tied at the waist and the sleeves turned back, wiping cake or biscuit dough from her hands with a towel as she came up the hall, looking not at his father at all but at the tracks on the blond rug with an expression of incredulous amazement.

"I tried," the Negro cried. "I tole him to . . ."

"Will you please go away?" she said in a shaking voice. "Major de Spain is not at home. Will you please go away?"

His father had not spoken again. He did not speak again. He did not even look at her. He just stood stiff in the center of the rug, in his hat, the shaggy iron-gray brows twitching slightly above the pebble-colored eyes as he appeared to examine the house with brief deliberation. Then with the same deliberation he turned; the boy watched him pivot on the good leg and saw the stiff foot drag round the arc of the turning, leaving a final long and fading smear. His father never looked at it, he never once looked down at the rug. The Negro held the door. It closed behind them, upon the hysteric and indistinguishable woman-wail. His father stopped at the top of the steps and scraped his boot clean on the edge of it. At the gate he stopped again. He stood for a moment, planted stiffly on the stiff foot, looking back at the house. "Pretty and white, ain't it?" he said. "That's sweat. Nigger sweat. Maybe it ain't white enough yet to suit him. Maybe he wants to mix some white sweat with it."

Two hours later the boy was chopping wood behind the house within which his mother and aunt and the two sisters (the mother and the aunt, not the two girls, he knew that; even at this distance and muffled by walls the flat loud voices of the two girls emanated an incorrigible idle inertia) were setting up the stove to prepare a meal, when he heard the hooves and saw the linen-clad man on a fine sorrel mare, whom he recognized even before he saw the rolled rug in front of the Negro youth following on a fat bay carriage horse—a suffused, angry face vanishing, still at full gallop, beyond the corner of the house where his father and brother were sitting in the two tilted chairs; and a moment later, almost before he could have put the axe down, he heard the hooves again and watched the sorrel mare go back out of the yard, already galloping again. Then his father began to shout one of the sisters' names, who presently emerged backward from the kitchen door dragging the rolled rug along the ground by one end while the other sister walked behind it.

"If you ain't going to tote, go on and set up the wash pot," the first said.

"You, Sarty!" the second shouted. "Set up the wash pot!" His father appeared at the door, framed against that shabbiness, as he had been against that other bland perfection, impervious to either, the mother's anxious face at his shoulder.

"Go on," the father said. "Pick it up." The two sisters stooped, broad, lethargic; stooping, they presented an incredible expanse of pale cloth and a flutter of tawdry ribbons.

"If I thought enough of a rug to have to git hit all the way from France I wouldn't keep hit where folks coming in would have to tromp on hit," the first said. They raised the rug.

"Abner," the mother said. "Let me do it."

"You go back and git dinner," his father said. "I'll tend to this."

From the woodpile through the rest of the afternoon the boy watched them, the rug spread flat in the dust beside the bubbling wash-pot, the two sisters stooping over it with that profound and lethargic reluctance, while the father stood over them in turn, implacable and grim, driving them though never raising his voice again. He could smell the harsh homemade lye they were using; he saw his mother come to the door once and look toward them with an expression not anxious now but very like despair; he saw his father turn, and he fell to with the axe and saw from the corner of his eye his father raise from the ground a flattish fragment of field stone and examine it and return to the pot, and this time his mother actually spoke:

"Abner. Abner. Please don't. Please, Abner."

Then he was done too. It was dusk; the whippoorwills had already begun. He could smell coffee from the room where they would presently eat the cold food remaining from the mid-afternoon meal, though when he entered the house he realized they were having coffee again probably because there was a fire on the hearth, before which the rug now lay spread over the backs of the two chairs. The tracks of his father's foot were gone. Where they had been were now long, water-cloudy scoriations resembling the sporadic course of a lilliputian[4] mowing machine.

It still hung there while they ate the cold food and then went to bed, scattered without order or claim up and down the two rooms, his mother in one bed, where his father would later lie, the older brother in the other, himself, the aunt, and the two sisters on pallets on the floor. But his father was not in bed yet. The last thing the boy remembered was the depthless, harsh silhouette of the hat and coat bending over the rug and it seemed to him that he had not even closed his eyes when the silhouette was standing over him, the fire almost dead behind it, the stiff foot prodding him awake. "Catch up the mule," his father said.

When he returned with the mule his father was standing in the black door, the rolled rug over his shoulder. "Ain't you going to ride?" he said.

"No. Give me your foot."

He bent his knee into his father's hand, the wiry, surprising power flowed smoothly, rising, he rising with it, on to the mule's bare back (they had owned a saddle once; the boy could remember it though not when or where) and with the same effortlessness his father swung the rug up in front of him. Now in the starlight they retraced the afternoon's path, up the dusty road rife with honeysuckle,

---

4. **lilliputian:** miniature, as in the land of Lilliputia in Swift's *Gulliver's Travels.*

through the gate and up the black tunnel of the drive to the lightless house, where he sat on the mule and felt the rough warp of the rug drag across his thighs and vanish.

"Don't you want me to help?" he whispered. His father did not answer and now he heard again that stiff foot striking the hollow portico with that wooden and clocklike deliberation, that outrageous overstatement of the weight it carried. The rug, hunched, not flung (the boy could tell that even in the darkness) from his father's shoulder struck the angle of wall and floor with a sound unbelievably loud, thunderous, then the foot again, unhurried and enormous; a light came on in the house and the boy sat, tense, breathing steadily and quietly and just a little fast, though the foot itself did not increase its beat at all, descending the steps now; now the boy could see him.

"Don't you want to ride now?" he whispered. "We kin both ride now," the light within the house altering now, flaring up and sinking. *He's coming down the stairs now*, he thought. He had already ridden the mule up beside the horse block; presently his father was up behind him and he doubled the reins over and slashed the mule across the neck, but before the animal could begin to trot the hard, thin arm came round him, the hard, knotted hand jerking the mule back to a walk.

In the first red rays of the sun they were in the lot, putting plow gear on the mules. This time the sorrel mare was in the lot before he heard it at all, the rider collarless and even bareheaded, trembling, speaking in a shaking voice as the woman in the house had done, his father merely looking up once before stooping again to the hame[5] he was buckling, so that the man on the mare spoke to his stooping back:

"You must realize you have ruined that rug. Wasn't there anybody here, any of your women . . ." he ceased, shaking, the boy watching him, the older brother leaning now in the stable door, chewing, blinking slowly and steadily at nothing apparently. "It cost a hundred dollars. But you never had a hundred dollars. You never will. So I'm going to charge you twenty bushels of corn against your crop. I'll add it in your contract and when you come to the commissary you can sign it. That won't keep Mrs. de Spain quiet but maybe it will teach you to wipe your feet off before you enter her house again."

Then he was gone. The boy looked at his father, who still had not spoken or even looked up again, who was now adjusting the logger-head in the hame.

"Pap," he said. His father looked at him— the inscrutable face, the shaggy brows beneath which the gray eyes glinted coldly. Suddenly the boy went toward him, fast, stopping as suddenly. "You done the best you could!" he cried. "If he wanted hit done different why didn't he wait and tell you how? He won't git no twenty bushels! He won't git none! We'll gether hit and hide hit! I kin watch . . ."

"Did you put the cutter back in that straight stock like I told you?"

"No, sir," he said.

"Then go do it."

That was Wednesday. During the rest of that week he worked steadily, at what was within his scope and some which was beyond it, with an industry that did not need to be driven nor even commanded twice; he had this from his mother, with the difference that some at least of what he did he liked to do, such as splitting wood with the half-size axe which his mother and aunt had earned, or saved money somehow, to present him with at Christmas. In company with the two older women (and on one afternoon, even one of the sisters), he built pens for the shoat and the cow which were a part of his father's contract with the landlord, and one afternoon, his father being absent, gone somewhere on one

---

5. **hame:** either of two rigid pieces along the sides of a horse's collar, to which the traces, or straps, are attached.

of the mules, he went to the field.

They were running a middle buster now, his brother holding the plow straight while he handled the reins, and walking beside the straining mule, the rich black soil shearing cool and damp against his bare ankles, he thought *Maybe this is the end of it. Maybe even that twenty bushels that seems hard to have to pay for just a rug will be a cheap price for him to stop forever and always from being what he used to be;* thinking, dreaming now, so that his brother had to speak sharply to him to mind the mule: *Maybe he even won't collect the twenty bushels. Maybe it will all add up and balance and vanish—corn, rug, fire; the terror and grief, the being pulled two ways like between two teams of horses— gone, done with for ever and ever.*

Then it was Saturday; he looked up from beneath the mule he was harnessing and saw his father in the black coat and hat. "Not that," his father said. "The wagon gear." And then, two hours later, sitting in the wagon bed behind his father and brother on the seat, the wagon accomplished a final curve, and he saw the weathered paintless store with its tattered tobacco- and patent-medicine posters and the tethered wagons and saddle animals below the gallery. He mounted the gnawed steps behind his father and brother, and there again was the lane of quiet, watching faces for the three of them to walk through. He saw the man in spectacles sitting at the plank table and he did not need to be told this was a Justice of the Peace; he sent one glare of fierce, exultant, partisan defiance at the man in collar and cravat[6] now, whom he had seen but twice before in his life, and that on a galloping horse, who now wore on his face an expression not of rage but of amazed unbelief which the boy could not have known was at the incredible circumstance of being sued by one of his own tenants, and came and stood against his father and cried at the Justice: "He ain't done it! He ain't burnt . . ."

"Go back to the wagon," his father said.

"Burnt?" the Justice said. "Do I understand this rug was burned too?"

"Does anybody here claim it was?" his father said. "Go back to the wagon." But he did not, he merely retreated to the rear of the room, crowded as that other had been, but not to sit down this time, instead, to stand pressing among the motionless bodies, listening to the voices:

"And you claim twenty bushels of corn is too high for the damage you did to the rug?"

"He brought the rug to me and said he wanted the tracks washed out of it. I washed the tracks out and took the rug back to him."

"But you didn't carry the rug back to him in the same condition it was in before you made the tracks on it."

His father did not answer, and now for perhaps half a minute there was no sound at all save that of breathing, the faint, steady suspiration of complete and intent listening.

"You decline to answer that, Mr. Snopes?" Again his father did not answer. "I'm going to find against you, Mr. Snopes. I'm going to find that you were responsible for the injury to Major de Spain's rug and hold you liable for it. But twenty bushels of corn seems a little high for a man in your circumstances to have to pay. Major de Spain claims it cost a hundred dollars. October corn will be worth about fifty cents. I figure that if Major de Spain can stand a ninety-five dollar loss on something he paid cash for, you can stand a five-dollar loss you haven't earned yet. I hold you in damages to Major de Spain to the amount of ten bushels of corn over and above your contract with him, to be paid to him out of your crop at gathering time. Court adjourned."

It had taken no time hardly, the morning was but half begun. He thought they would return home and perhaps back to the field, since they were late, far behind all other farmers. But instead his father passed on

6. **cravat** (krə vat′): a band or scarf formerly worn around the neck; a necktie.

behind the wagon, merely indicating with his hand for the older brother to follow with it, and crossed the road toward the blacksmith shop opposite, pressing on after his father, overtaking him, speaking, whispering up at the harsh, calm face beneath the weathered hat: "He won't git no ten bushels neither. He won't git one. We'll . . ." until his father glanced for an instant down at him, the face absolutely calm, the grizzled eyebrows tangled above the cold eyes, the voice almost pleasant, almost gentle:

"You think so? Well, we'll wait till October anyway."

The matter of the wagon—the setting of a spoke or two and the tightening of the tires—did not take long either, the business of the tires accomplished by driving the wagon into the spring branch behind the shop and letting it stand there, the mules nuzzling into the water from time to time, and the boy on the seat with the idle reins, looking up the slope and through the sooty tunnel of the shed where the slow hammer rang and where his father sat on an upended cypress bolt, easily, either talking or listening, still sitting there when the boy brought the dripping wagon up out of the branch and halted it before the door.

"Take them on to the shade and hitch," his father said. He did so and returned. His father and the smith and a third man squatting on his heels inside the door were talking, about crops and animals; the boy, squatting too in the ammoniac dust and hoof-parings and scales of rust, heard his father tell a long and unhurried story out of the time before the birth of the older brother even when he had been a professional horsetrader. And then his father came up beside him where he stood before a tattered last year's circus poster on the other side of the store, gazing rapt and quiet at the scarlet horses, the incredible poisings and convolutions of tulle and tights and the painted leers of comedians, and said, "It's time to eat."

But not at home. Squatting beside his brother against the front wall, he watched his father emerge from the store and produce from a paper sack a segment of cheese and divide it carefully and deliberately into three with his pocket knife and produce crackers from the same sack. They all three squatted on the gallery and ate, slowly, without talking; then in the store again, they drank from a tin dipper tepid water smelling of the cedar bucket and of living beech trees. And still they did not go home. It was a horse lot this time, a tall rail fence upon and along which men stood and sat and out of which one by one horses were led, to be walked and trotted and then cantered back and forth along the road while the slow swapping and buying went on and the sun began to slant westward, they—the three of them—watching and listening, the older brother with his muddy eyes and his steady, inevitable tobacco, the father commenting now and then on certain of the animals, to no one in particular.

It was after sundown when they reached home. They ate supper by lamplight, then, sitting on the doorstep, the boy watched the night fully accomplish, listening to the whippoorwills and the frogs, when he heard his mother's voice: "Abner! No! No! Oh, God. Oh, God. Abner!" and he rose, whirled, and saw the altered light through the door where a candle stub now burned in a bottle neck on the table and his father, still in the hat and coat, at once formal and burlesque as though dressed carefully for some shabby and ceremonial violence, emptying the reservoir of the lamp back into the five-gallon kerosene can from which it had been filled, while the mother tugged at his arm until he shifted the lamp to the other hand and flung her back, not savagely or viciously, just hard, into the wall, her hands flung out against the wall for balance, her mouth open and in her face the same quality of hopeless despair as had been in her voice. Then his father saw him standing in the door.

"Go to the barn and get that can of oil we were oiling the wagon with," he said. The boy did not move. Then he could speak.

"What . . ." he cried. "What are you . . ."

"Go get that oil," his father said. "Go."

Then he was moving, running, outside the house, toward the stable: this the old habit, the old blood which he had not been permitted to choose for himself, which had been bequeathed him willy nilly and which had run for so long (and who knew where, battening on what of outrage and savagery and lust) before it came to him. *I could keep on*, he thought. *I could run on and on and never look back, never need to see his face again. Only I can't. I can't*, the rusted can in his hand now, the liquid sploshing in it as he ran back to the house and into it, into the sound of his mother's weeping in the next room, and handed the can to his father.

"Ain't you going to even send a nigger?" he cried. "At least you sent a nigger before!"

This time his father didn't strike him. The hand came even faster than the blow had, the same hand which had set the can on the table with almost excruciating care flashing from the can toward him too quick for him to follow it, gripping him by the back of his shirt and on to tiptoe before he had seen it quit the can, the face stooping at him in breathless and frozen ferocity, the cold, dead voice speaking over him to the older brother who leaned against the table, chewing with that steady, curious, sidewise motion of cows:

"Empty the can into the big one and go on. I'll catch up with you."

"Better tie him up to the bedpost," the brother said.

"Do like I told you," the father said. Then the boy was moving, his bunched shirt and the hard, bony hand between his shoulderblades, his toes just touching the floor, across the room and into the other one, past the sisters sitting with spread heavy thighs in the two chairs over the cold hearth, and to where his mother and aunt sat side by side on the bed, the aunt's arms about his mother's shoulders.

"Hold him," the father said. The aunt made a startled movement. "Not you," the father said. "Lennie. Take hold of him. I want to see you do it." His mother took him by the wrist. "You'll hold him better than that. If he gets loose don't you know what he is going to do? He will go up yonder." He jerked his head toward the road. "Maybe I'd better tie him."

"I'll hold him," his mother whispered.

"See you do then." Then his father was gone, the stiff foot heavy and measured upon the boards, ceasing at last.

Then he began to struggle. His mother caught him in both arms, he jerking and wrenching at them. He would be stronger in the end, he knew that. But he had no time to wait for it. "Lemme go!" he cried. "I don't want to have to hit you!"

"Let him go!" the aunt said. "If he don't go, before God, I am going up there myself!"

"Don't you see I can't?" his mother cried. "Sarty! Sarty! No! No! Help me, Lizzie!"

Then he was free. His aunt grasped at him but it was too late. He whirled, running, his mother stumbled forward on to her knees behind him, crying to the nearer sister: "Catch him, Net! Catch him!" But that was too late too, the sister (the sisters were twins, born at the same time, yet either of them now gave the impression of being, encompassing as much living meat and volume and weight as any other two of the family) not yet having begun to rise from the chair, her head, face, alone merely turned, presenting to him in the flying instant an astonishing expanse of young female features untroubled by any surprise even, wearing only an expression of bovine interest. Then he was out of the room, out of the house, in the mild dust of the starlit road and the heavy rifeness of honeysuckle, the pale ribbon unspooling with terrific slowness under his running feet, reaching the gate at last and turning in, running, his heart and lungs drumming, on up the drive toward the lighted house, the lighted door. He did not knock, he burst in, sobbing for breath, incapable for the moment of speech; he saw the astonished face of the Negro in the linen jacket without knowing when the Negro had appeared.

"De Spain!" he cried, panted. "Where's . . ." then he saw the white man too emerging from a white door down the hall. "Barn!" he cried. "Barn!"

"What?" the white man said. "Barn?"

"Yes!" the boy cried. "Barn!"

"Catch him!" the white man shouted.

But it was too late this time too. The Negro grasped his shirt, but the entire sleeve, rotten with washing, carried away, and he was out that door too and in the drive again, and had actually never ceased to run even while he was screaming into the white man's face.

Behind him the white man was shouting, "My horse! Fetch my horse!" and he thought for an instant of cutting across the park and climbing the fence into the road, but he did not know the park nor how high the vine-massed fence might be and he dared not risk it. So he ran on down the drive, blood and breath roaring; presently he was in the road again though he could not see it. He could not hear either: the galloping mare was almost upon him before he heard her, and even then he held his course, as if the very urgency of his wild grief and need must in a moment more find him wings, waiting until the ultimate instant to hurl himself aside and into the weed-choked roadside ditch as the horse thundered past and on, for an instant in furious silhouette against the stars, the tranquil early summer night sky which, even before the shape of the horse and rider vanished, stained abruptly and violently upward: a long, swirling roar incredible and soundless, blotting the stars, and he springing up and into the road again, running again, knowing it was too late yet still running even after he heard the shot and, an instant later, two shots, pausing now without knowing he had ceased to run, crying "Pap! Pap!," running again before he knew he had begun to run, stumbling, tripping over something and scrabbling up again without ceasing to run, looking backward over his shoulder at the glare as he got up, running on among the invisible trees, panting, sobbing, "Father! Father!"

At midnight he was sitting on the crest of a hill. He did not know it was midnight and he did not know how far he had come. But there was no glare behind him now and he sat now, his back toward what he had called home for four days anyhow, his face toward the dark woods which he would enter when breath was strong again, small, shaking steadily in the chill darkness, hugging himself into the remainder of his thin, rotten shirt, the grief and despair now no longer terror and fear but just grief and despair. *Father. My father*, he thought. "He was brave!" he cried suddenly, aloud but not loud, no more than a whisper: "He was! He was in the war! He was in Colonel Sartoris' cav'ry!" not knowing that his father had gone to that war a private in the fine old European sense, wearing no uniform, admitting the authority of and giving fidelity to no man or army or flag, going to war as Malbrouck[7] himself did: for booty—it meant nothing and less than nothing to him if it were enemy booty or his own.

The slow constellations wheeled on. It would be dawn and then sun-up after a while and he would be hungry. But that would be tomorrow and now he was only cold, and walking would cure that. His breathing was easier now and he decided to get up and go on, and then he found that he had been asleep because he knew it was almost dawn, the night almost over. He could tell that from the whippoorwills. They were everywhere now among the dark trees below him, constant and inflectioned and ceaseless, so that, as the

---

7. **Malbrouck:** or Malbrough, name given in French song to Marlborough, English general (1650-1722).

instant for giving over to the day birds drew nearer and nearer, there was no interval at all between them. He got up. He was a little stiff, but walking would cure that too as it would the cold, and soon there would be the sun. He went on down the hill, toward the dark woods within which the liquid silver voices of the birds called unceasing—the rapid and urgent beating of the urgent and quiring[8] heart of the late spring night. He did not look back.

---

8. **quire:** archaic variation of *choir*.

Getting at Meaning

1. What is Mr. Snopes accused of in the opening scene of the story? What is the evidence against him?

2. Describe the way of life of the Snopes family. Why do they keep moving? What is their social class?

3. How is the boy, Sarty Snopes, treated by his father? Support what you say with evidence from the story. How does Mr. Snopes treat other members of his family?

4. What does Sarty think when he sees the house of Major de Spain? Why does the house make him feel safe?

5. Describe the way in which Mr. Snopes defaces the de Spain's rug. What details indicate that his action is deliberate?

6. How does Major de Spain react to the damaged rug? During the washing of the rug, what details suggest that Mr. Snopes wants the rug to be ruined?

7. Why does Mr. Snopes sue Major de Spain? What are the judge's findings? What does this trigger in Mr. Snopes?

8. Why does Mr. Snopes insist that Sarty be held when he heads for the de Spain barn? Describe how Sarty breaks free. What events do his subsequent actions bring about?

9. Describe Sarty's thoughts about his father after "... he heard the shot and, an instant later, two shots ..." Why does he go from calling his father "Pap" to calling him "Father"?

Developing Skills in Reading Literature

1. **Dialect.** A dialect is the particular variety of language spoken in a definite place by a distinct group of people. Dialects vary in pronunciations, vocabulary, colloquial expressions, and grammatical constructions. Writers use dialect to establish setting, to provide local color, and to develop characters.

Faulkner uses dialect in "Barn Burning" to establish the Southern setting of this story. He also uses it to establish the social standing of his characters. Analyze the dialect spoken by the black characters and by the Snopeses. What variations from standard English do you find in this speech? What do you conclude about the educational background of these characters from their speech?

2. **Style: Punctuation.** Faulkner employs italics in "Barn Burning" as a visual clue for the reader. What does this form of punctuation always signal? Why might Faulkner particularly want the italicized passages to stand out?

3. **Imagery.** Faulkner is known for his prolonged, poetic sentences, rich in imagery. The imagery of "Barn Burning" is often breathtaking in its sharpness and intensity, as illustrated in the following sentence:

The boy, crouched on his nail keg at the back of the crowded room, knew he smelled cheese, and more: from where he sat he could see the ranked shelves close-packed with the solid, squat, dynamic shapes of tin cans whose labels his stomach read, not from the lettering which meant nothing to his mind but from the scarlet devils and the silver curve of fish—this, the cheese which he knew he smelled and the hermetic meat which his intestines believed he smelled coming in intermittent gusts momentary and brief between the other constant one, the smell and sense just a little of fear because mostly of despair and grief, the old fierce pull of blood.

Notice how vividly Faulkner appeals to the senses of touch, sight, smell, and taste in this passage. It is a highly emotional, memorable sentence.

Examine other passages in the story in which imagery is similarly rich. Analyze the third to the last paragraph of the story. Where do you see alliteration in this paragraph? Where do you see assonance? What other poetic and sensory devices does Faulkner employ? How does this passage function in the story?

4. **Stream of Consciousness.** Faulkner is one of the outstanding prose stylists of the twentieth century. Apart from his rich language, he is famous for his use of a technique known as *stream of consciousness*. This technique attempts to create in fiction the flow of consciousness found inside a character's mind, with the character's thoughts, feelings, memories, perceptions, and sensory experiences all presented as they would occur without being edited into logical or grammatical order by the writer.

The following passage shows Faulkner's stream-of-consciousness technique:

Hit's big as a courthouse he thought quietly, with a surge of peace and joy whose reason he could not have thought into words, being too young for that: *They are safe from him. People whose lives are a part of this peace and dignity are beyond his touch, he no more to them than a buzzing wasp: capable of stinging for a little moment but that's all; the spell of this peace and dignity rendering even the barns and stable and cribs which belong to it impervious to the puny flames he might contrive* . . . this, the peace and joy, ebbing for an instant as he looked again at the stiff black back, the stiff and implacable limp of the figure which was not dwarfed by the house, for the reason that it had never looked big anywhere and which now, against the serene columned back-

drop, had more than ever that impervious quality of something cut ruthlessly from tin, depthless, as though, sidewise to the sun, it would cast no shadow.

Notice that this passage focuses on the interior life of Sarty. What thoughts does the passage present? What feelings? What perceptions? What sensory experiences? What effect does the long, long sentence produce?

Even when he is not presenting a character's stream of consciousness, Faulkner is known for his prolonged, intense sentences. Analyze the structure of several of his long sentences. Technically, quite a number of them are run-ons, yet they are still wonderful sentences. What makes them work?

5. **Point of View.** The point of view of "Barn Burning" is third-person limited narration. Why has Faulkner chosen this point of view for the story? Why has he chosen *not* to see inside the mind of Mr. Snopes?

6. **Character.** Although the interaction between Sarty and his father is the main focus in "Barn Burning," Sarty's mother is also an extremely interesting character. What sort of life has she led? What is her relationship to Sarty? What is her relationship to her husband?

The reader learns about Mr. Snopes that

. . . the element of fire spoke to some deep mainspring of his . . . being, as the element of steel or of powder spoke to other men, as the one weapon for the preservation of integrity, else breath were not worth the breathing, and hence to be regarded with respect and used with discretion.

Explain Faulkner's statement. What is the precise relationship between Mr. Snopes and fire? How is fire related to his integrity? What appears to motivate Mr. Snopes much of the time?

7. **Theme.** Faulkner talks about Sarty's laboring under "the terrible handicap of being young" and "the light weight of his few years, just heavy enough to prevent his soaring free of the world. . . ." Later, when Sarty tries to run, he thinks to himself, "I could keep on. . . . I could run on and on and never look back, never need to see his face again. Only I can't. I can't. . . ."

In what ways is "Barn Burning" about imprisonment? What forces imprison every member of the Snopes family? In what sense is the whole Snopes family the victim of the Southern class structure? Does Sarty escape in the end? If so, how?

Developing Vocabulary

Precise Adjectives. In describing people, Faulkner uses a number of adjectives whose meanings you may not know. He uses some of these words more than once, having them play a major role in his characterizations.

Look up each word that follows in the Glossary and write its meaning. To which character or characters in the story does Faulkner apply each word? Explain how the word fits that character of characters.

bovine	irascible	tawdry
incorrigible	lethargic	voracious
inscrutable	ravening	

Developing Writing Skills

Analyzing Character. The relationship between Sarty and his father lies at the core of "Barn Burning," and it is Sarty, not his father, who changes during the story. In a five-paragraph composition analyze this complex relationship. Some questions you should consider: How does Sarty view his father at the beginning of the story? How does his father treat him? How does Sarty view the family's moves? What ambivalent, or conflicting, feelings does Sarty have about his father? How does Sarty try to influence his father's behavior? What motivates Sarty to run ahead of his father to the de Spains at the end of the story? Does he feel guilt over his father's death? What changes do you see in Sarty at the end of the story?

Outline your composition before you begin writing, making it clear what major point and related subpoints you will develop in each body paragraph of the paper. Use quotations from the story.

COBB'S BARNS, SOUTH TRURO, 1931. *Edward Hopper.*
Whitney Museum of American Art, New York.

James Thurber

1894–1961

James Thurber's observations of American life and the doodles and drawings he left behind have quickened the nation's laughter, often when it was most needed, and in doing so left a permanent mark on literature.

Thurber grew up in Columbus, Ohio, in a close-knit family that endured all kinds of hilarious and improbable happenings, as recorded in *My Life and Hard Times* (1933). Some of the funniest remembrances in that book are "The Night the Bed Fell" and "The Dog That Bit People." After attending public schools in Columbus, Thurber spent three years at Ohio State University, where he wrote several plays for campus productions. He was barred from military service in World War I because of poor eyesight (he had lost an eye in a childhood accident), but he got to France a few weeks after the war's end as a code clerk for the State Department. For the next few years he did newspaper work in Paris, Columbus, and New York and began contributing humorous sketches to various newspapers.

In 1925 a new magazine, *The New Yorker*, was born. Thurber's association with it and with E.B. White, one of its founders, had much to do with its early flavor and success and its influence in years to come. Reversing the usual procedure, Thurber began as managing editor, demoted himself to staff writer, then resigned from the staff and contributed pieces to the magazine for the rest of his life.

Beginning in the late 1920's, Thurber wrote and illustrated with his famous doodle-drawings more than two dozen books, often including material that had appeared first in *The New Yorker*. Typical titles were *The Middle-Aged Man on the Flying Trapeze* (1935) and *The Beast in Me and Other Animals: A New Collection of Pieces and Drawings About Human Beings and Less Alarming Creatures* (1948). In addition he wrote fables, children's books, essays, and short stories, including the famous "Secret Life of Walter Mitty," about an ordinary little man who pictures himself performing heroic deeds. He contributed to the American theater with *The Male Animal* (1940) and *The Thurber Carnival* (1960).

Thurber's failing eyesight eventually forced him to give up his drawing, and for the last years of his life he was totally blind. (In typical fashion, he threatened to name his memoirs *Long Time No See.*) He continued his writing, however, dictating his work. Generations of Americans will remember him for the famous Thurber dogs, for his cynical observations on the battle of the sexes, for his hope and his humor, his "firm grasp on confusion," as one friend put it. Behind the laughter, which was never shrill, was a true humorist who, like Mark Twain before him, had serious and thoughtful things to say about the world around him.

The Catbird Seat

Mr. Martin bought the pack of Camels on Monday night in the most crowded cigar store on Broadway. It was theater time and seven or eight men were buying cigarettes. The clerk didn't even glance at Mr. Martin, who put the pack in his overcoat pocket and went out. If any of the staff at F & S had seen him buy the cigarettes, they would have been astonished, for it was generally known that Mr. Martin did not smoke and never had. No one saw him.

It was just a week to the day since Mr. Martin had decided to rub out Mrs. Ulgine Barrows. The term "rub out" pleased him because it suggested nothing more than the correction of an error—in this case an error of Mr. Fitweiler. Mr. Martin had spent each night of the past week working out his plan and examining it. As he walked home now he went over it again. For the hundredth time he resented the element of imprecision, the margin of guesswork that entered into the business. The project as he had worked it out was casual and bold, the risks were considerable. Something might go wrong anywhere along the line. And therein lay the cunning of his scheme. No one would ever see in it the cautious, painstaking hand of Erwin Martin, head of the filing department at F & S, of whom Mr. Fitweiler had once said, "Man is fallible but Martin isn't." No one would see his hand, that is, unless it were caught in the act.

Sitting in his apartment, drinking a glass of milk, Mr. Martin reviewed his case against Mrs. Ulgine Barrows, as he had every night for seven nights. He began at the beginning. Her quacking voice and braying laugh had first profaned the halls of F & S on March 7, 1941 (Mr. Martin had a head for dates). Old Roberts, the personnel chief, had introduced her as the newly appointed special adviser to the president of the firm, Mr. Fitweiler. The woman had appalled Mr. Martin instantly, but he hadn't shown it. He had given her his dry hand, a look of studious concentration, and a faint smile. "Well," she had said, looking at the papers on his desk, "are you lifting the oxcart out of the ditch?" As Mr. Martin recalled that moment, over his milk, he squirmed slightly. He must keep his mind on her crimes as a special adviser, not on her peccadilloes[1] as a personality. This he found difficult to do, in spite of entering an objection and sustaining it. The faults of the woman as a woman kept chattering on in his mind like an unruly witness. She had, for almost two years now, baited him. In the halls, in the elevator, even in his own office, into which she romped now and then like a circus horse, she was constantly shouting these silly questions at him. "Are you lifting the oxcart out of the ditch? Are you tearing up the pea patch? Are you hollering down the rain barrel? Are you scraping around the bottom of the pickle barrel? Are you sitting in the catbird seat?"

It was Joey Hart, one of Mr. Martin's two assistants, who had explained what the gibberish meant. "She must be a Dodger[2] fan," he had said. "Red Barber announces the Dodger games over the radio and he uses those expressions—picked 'em up down South." Joey had gone on to explain one or two.

---

1. **peccadilloes** (pek ə dil' ōz): slight offenses.
2. **Dodger:** the Los Angeles baseball team, formerly of Brooklyn, New York.

"Tearing up the pea patch" meant going on a rampage; "sitting in the catbird seat" meant sitting pretty, like a batter with three balls and no strikes on him. Mr. Martin dismissed all this with an effort. It had been annoying, it had driven him near to distraction, but he was too solid a man to be moved to murder by anything so childish. It was fortunate, he reflected as he passed on to the important charges against Mrs. Barrows, that he had stood up under it so well. He had maintained always an outward appearance of polite tolerance. "Why, I even believe you like the woman," Miss Paird, his other assistant, had once said to him. He had simply smiled.

A gavel rapped in Mr. Martin's mind and the case proper was resumed. Mrs. Ulgine Barrows stood charged with willful, blatant, and persistent attempts to destroy the efficiency and system of F & S. It was competent, material, and relevant to review her advent and rise to power. Mr. Martin had got the story from Miss Paird, who seemed always able to find things out. According to her, Mrs. Barrows had met Mr. Fitweiler at a party, where she had rescued him from the embraces of a powerfully built drunken man who had mistaken the president of F & S for a famous retired Middle Western football coach. She had led him to a sofa and somehow worked upon him a monstrous magic. The aging gentleman had jumped to the conclusion there and then that this was a woman of singular attainments, equipped to bring out the best in him and in the firm. A week later he had introduced her into F & S as his special adviser. On that day confusion got its foot in the door. After Miss Tyson, Mr. Brundage, and Mr. Bartlett had been fired and Mr. Munson had taken his hat and stalked out, mailing in his resignation later, old Roberts had been emboldened to speak to Mr. Fitweiler. He mentioned that Mr. Munson's department had been "a little disrupted" and hadn't they perhaps better resume the old system there? Mr. Fitweiler had said certainly not. He had

the greatest faith in Mrs. Barrows' ideas. "They require a little seasoning, a little seasoning, is all," he had added. Mr. Roberts had given it up. Mr. Martin reviewed in detail all the changes wrought by Mrs. Barrows. She had begun chipping at the cornices of the firm's edifice and now she was swinging at the foundation stones with a pickax.

Mr. Martin came now, in his summing up, to the afternoon of Monday, November 2, 1942—just one week ago. On that day, at 3 P.M., Mrs. Barrows had bounced into his office. "Boo!" she had yelled. "Are you scraping around the bottom of the pickle barrel?" Mr. Martin had looked at her from under his green eyeshade, saying nothing. She had begun to wander about the office, taking it in with her great, popping eyes. "Do you really need *all* these filing cabinets?" she had demanded suddenly. Mr. Martin's heart had jumped. "Each of these files," he had said, keeping his voice even, "plays an indispensable part in the system of F & S." She had brayed at him, "Well, don't tear up the pea patch!" and gone to the door. From there she had bawled, "But you sure have got a lot of fine scrap in here!" Mr. Martin could no longer doubt that the finger was on his beloved department. Her pickax was on the upswing, poised for the first blow. It had not come yet; he had received no blue memo from the enchanted Mr. Fitweiler bearing nonsensical instructions deriving from the obscene woman. But there was no doubt in Mr. Martin's mind that one would be forthcoming. He must act quickly. Already a precious week had gone by. Mr. Martin stood up in his living room, still holding his milk glass. "Gentlemen of the jury," he said to himself, 'I demand the death penalty for this horrible person.'"

The next day Mr. Martin followed his routine, as usual. He polished his glasses more often and once sharpened an already sharp pencil, but not even Miss Paird noticed. Only once did he catch sight of his victim; she swept past him in the hall with a patronizing "Hi!" At five-thirty he walked home, as usual, and had a glass of milk, as usual. He had never drunk anything stronger in his life—unless you could count ginger ale. The late Sam Schlosser, the S of F & S, had praised Mr. Martin at a staff meeting several years before for his temperate habits. "Our most efficient worker neither drinks nor smokes," he had said. "The results speak for themselves." Mr. Fitweiler had sat by, nodding approval.

Mr. Martin was still thinking about that red-letter day as he walked over to the Schrafft's on Fifth Avenue near Forty-sixth Street. He got there, as he always did, at eight o'clock. He finished his dinner and the financial page of the *Sun* at a quarter to nine, as he always did. It was his custom after dinner to take a walk. This time he walked down Fifth Avenue at a casual pace. His gloved hands felt moist and warm, his forehead cold. He transferred the Camels from his overcoat to a jacket pocket. He wondered, as he did so, if they did not represent an unnecessary note of strain. Mrs. Barrows smoked only Luckies. It was his idea to puff a few puffs on a Camel (after the rubbing-out), stub it out in the ashtray holding her lipstick-stained Luckies, and thus drag a small red herring across the trail. Perhaps it was not a good idea. It would take time. He might even choke, too loudly.

Mr. Martin had never seen the house on West Twelfth Street where Mrs. Barrows lived, but he had a clear enough picture of it. Fortunately, she had bragged to everybody about her ducky first-floor apartment in the perfectly darling three-story red-brick. There would be no doorman or other attendants; just the tenants of the second and third floors. As he walked along, Mr. Martin realized that he would get there before nine-thirty. He had considered walking north on Fifth Avenue from Schrafft's to a point from which it would take him until ten o'clock to reach the house. At that hour people were less likely to be coming in or going out. But the procedure would have made an awkward loop in the straight thread of his casualness, and he had abandoned it. It was impossible to figure when people would be entering or leaving the house, anyway. There was a great risk at any hour. If he ran into anybody, he would simply have to place the rubbing-out of Ulgine Barrows in the inactive file forever. The same thing would hold true if there were someone in her apartment. In that case he would just say that he had been passing by, recognized her charming house and thought to drop in.

It was eighteen minutes after nine when Mr. Martin turned into Twelfth Street. A man passed him, and a man and a woman talking. There was no one within fifty paces when he came to the house, halfway down the block. He was up the steps and in the small vestibule in no time, pressing the bell under the card that said "Mrs. Ulgine Barrows." When the clicking in the lock started, he jumped forward against the door. He got inside fast, closing the door behind him. A bulb in a lantern hung from the hall ceiling on a chain seemed to give a monstrously bright light. There was nobody on the stair, which went up ahead of him along the left wall. A door opened down the hall in the wall on the right. He went toward it swiftly, on tiptoe.

"Well, for heaven's sake, look who's here!" bawled Mrs. Barrrows, and her braying laugh rang out like the report of a shotgun. He rushed past her like a football tackle, bumping her. "Hey, quit shoving!" she said, closing the door behind them. They were in her living room, which seemed to Mr. Martin to be lighted by a hundred lamps. "What's after you?" she said. "You're as jumpy as a goat." He found he was unable to speak. His heart was wheezing in his throat. "I—yes," he finally brought out. She was jabbering and laughing as she started to help him off with his coat. "No, no," he said. "I'll put it here." He took it off and put it on a chair near the door. "Your hat and gloves, too," she said. "You're in a lady's house." He put his hat on top of the coat. Mrs. Barrows seemed larger than he had thought. He kept his gloves on. "I was passing by," he said. "I recognized—is there anyone here?" She laughed louder than ever. "No," she said, "we're all alone. You're as white as a sheet, you funny man. Whatever *has* come over you? I'll mix you a toddy." She started toward a door across the room. "Scotch-and-soda be all right? But say, you don't drink do you?" She turned and gave him her amused look. Mr. Martin pulled himself together. "Scotch-and-soda will be all right," he heard himself say. He could hear her laughing in the kitchen.

Mr. Martin looked quickly around the living room for the weapon. He had counted on finding one there. There were andirons and a poker and something in a corner that looked like an Indian club. None of them would do. It couldn't be that way. He began to pace around. He came to a desk. On it lay a metal paper knife with an ornate handle. Would it be sharp enough? He reached for it and knocked over a small brass jar. Stamps spilled out of it and it fell to the floor with a clatter. "Hey," Mrs. Barrows yelled from the kitchen, "are you tearing up the pea patch?" Mr. Martin gave a strange laugh. Picking up the knife, he tried its point against his left wrist. It was blunt. It wouldn't do.

When Mrs. Barrows reappeared, carrying two highballs, Mr. Martin, standing there with his gloves on, became acutely conscious of the fantasy he had wrought. Cigarettes in his pocket, a drink prepared for him—it was all too grossly improbable. It was more than that; it was impossible. Somewhere in the back of his mind a vague idea stirred, sprouted. "For heaven's sake, take off those gloves," said Mrs. Barrows. "I always wear them in the house," said Mr. Martin. The idea began to bloom, strange and wonderful. She put the glasses on a coffee table in front of a sofa and sat on the sofa. "Come over here, you odd little man," she said. Mr. Martin went over and sat beside her. It was difficult getting a cigarette out of the pack of Camels, but he managed it. She held a match for him, laughing. "Well," she said, handing him his drink, "this is perfectly marvelous. You with a drink and a cigarette."

Mr. Martin puffed, not too awkwardly, and took a gulp of the highball. "I drink and smoke all the time," he said. He clinked his glass against hers. "Here's nuts to that old windbag, Fitweiler," he said, and gulped again. The stuff tasted awful, but he made no grimace. "Really, Mr. Martin," she said, her voice and posture changing, "you are insulting our employer." Mrs. Barrows was now all special adviser to the president. "I am preparing a bomb," said Mr. Martin, "which will blow the old goat higher than hell." He had only had a little of the drink, which was not strong. It couldn't be that. "Do you take dope or something?" Mrs. Barrows asked coldly. "Heroin," said Mr. Martin. "I'll be coked to the gills when I bump that old buzzard off." "Mr. Martin!" she shouted, getting to her feet. "That will be all of that. You must go at once." Mr. Martin took another swallow of his drink. He tapped his cigarette out in the ashtray and put the pack of Camels on the coffee table. Then he got up. She stood glaring at him. He walked over and put on his hat and coat. "Not a word about this," he said, and laid an index finger against his lips. All Mrs. Barrows could bring out was "Really!" Mr. Martin put his hand on the doorknob. "I'm sitting in the catbird seat," he said. He stuck his tongue out at her and left. Nobody saw him go.

Mr. Martin got to his apartment, walking, well before eleven. No one saw him go in. He had two glasses of milk after brushing his teeth, and he felt elated. It wasn't tipsiness, because he hadn't been tipsy. Anyway, the walk had worn off all effects of the whiskey. He got in bed and read a magazine for a while. He was asleep before midnight.

Mr. Martin got to the office at eight thirty the next morning, as usual. At a quarter to nine, Ulgine Barrows, who had never before arrived at work before ten, swept into his office. "I'm reporting to Mr. Fitweiler now!" she shouted. "If he turns you over to the police, it's no more than you deserve!" Mr. Martin gave her a look of shocked surprise. "I beg your pardon?" he said. Mrs. Barrows snorted and bounced out of the room, leaving Miss Paird and Joey Hart staring after her. "What's the matter with that old devil now?" asked Miss Paird. "I have no idea," said Mr. Martin, resuming his work. The other two looked at him and then at each other. Miss Paird got up and went out. She walked slowly past the closed door of Mr. Fitweiler's office. Mrs. Barrows was yelling inside, but she was not braying. Miss Paird could not hear what the woman was saying. She went back to her desk.

Forty-five minutes later, Mrs. Barrows left the president's office and went into her own, shutting the door. It wasn't until half an hour later that Mr. Fitweiler sent for Mr. Martin. The head of the filing department, neat, quiet, attentive, stood in front of the old man's desk. Mr. Fitweiler was pale and nervous. He took his glasses off and twiddled them. He made a small, bruffing sound in his throat. "Martin," he said, "you have been with us more than twenty years." "Twenty-two, sir," said Mr. Martin. "In that time," pursued the president, "your work and your—uh—manner have been exemplary." "I trust so, sir," said Mr. Martin. "I have understood, Martin," said Mr. Fitweiler, "that you have never taken a drink or smoked." "That is correct, sir," said Mr. Martin. "Ah, yes." Mr. Fitweiler polished his glasses. "You may describe what you did after leaving the office yesterday, Martin," he said. Mr. Martin allowed less than a second for his bewildered pause. "Certainly, sir," he said. "I walked home. Then I went to Schrafft's for dinner. Afterward I walked home again. I went to bed early, sir, and read a magazine for

a while. I was asleep before eleven." "Ah, yes," said Mr. Fitweiler again. He was silent for a moment, searching for the proper words to say to the head of the filing department. "Mrs. Barrows," he said finally, "Mrs. Barrows has worked hard, Martin, very hard. It grieves me to report that she has suffered a severe breakdown. It has taken the form of a persecution complex accompanied by distressing hallucinations." "I am very sorry, sir," said Mr. Martin. "Mrs. Barrows is under the delusion," continued Mr. Fitweiler, "that you visited her last evening and behaved yourself in an—uh—unseemly manner." He raised his hand to silence Mr. Martin's little pained outcry. "It is the nature of these psychological diseases," Mr. Fitweiler said, "to fix upon the least likely and most innocent party as the—uh—source of persecution. These matters are not for the lay mind to grasp, Martin. I've just had my psychiatrist, Dr. Fitch, on the phone. He would not, of course, commit himself, but he made enough generalizations to substantiate my suspicions. I suggested to Mrs. Barrows when she had completed her—uh—story to me this morning, that she visit Dr. Fitch, for I suspected a condition at once. She flew, I regret to say, into a rage, and demanded—uh—requested that I call you on the carpet. You may not know, Martin, but Mrs. Barrows had planned a reorganization of your department —subject to my approval, of course, subject to my approval. This brought you, rather than anyone else, to her mind—but again that is a phenomenon for Dr. Fitch and not for us. So, Martin, I am afraid Mrs. Barrows' usefulness here is at an end." "I am dreadfully sorry, sir," said Mr. Martin.

It was at this point that the door to the office blew open with the suddenness of a gas-main explosion and Mrs. Barrows catapulted through it. "Is the little rat denying it?" she screamed. "He can't get away with that!" Mr. Martin got up and moved discreetly to a point beside Mr. Fitweiler's chair. "You drank and smoked at my apartment," she bawled at Mr. Martin, "and you know it! You called Mr. Fitweiler an old windbag and said you were going to blow him up when you got coked to the gills on your heroin!" She stopped yelling to catch her breath and a new glint came into her popping eyes. "If you weren't such a drab, ordinary little man," she said, "I'd think you'd planned it all. Sticking your tongue out, saying you were sitting in the catbird seat, because you thought no one would believe me when I told it! It's really too perfect!" She brayed loudly and hysterically, and the fury was on her again. She glared at Mr. Fitweiler. "Can't you see how he has tricked us, you old fool? Can't you see his little game?" But Mr. Fitweiler had been surreptitiously pressing all the buttons under the top of his desk and employees of F & S began pouring into the room. "Stockton," said Mr. Fitweiler, "you and Fishbein will take Mrs. Barrows to her home. Mrs. Powell, you will go with them." Stockton, who had played a little football in high school, blocked Mrs. Barrows as she made for Mr. Martin. It took him and Fishbein together to force her out of the door into the hall, crowded with stenographers and office boys. She was still screaming imprecations at Mr. Martin, tangled and contradictory imprecations. The hubbub finally died out down the corridor.

"I regret that this has happened," said Mr. Fitweiler. "I shall ask you to dismiss it from your mind, Martin." "Yes, sir," said Mr. Martin, anticipating his chief's "That will be all" by moving to the door. "I will dismiss it." He went out and shut the door, and his step was light and quick in the hall. When he entered his department he had slowed down to his customary gait, and he walked quietly across the room to the W20 file, wearing a look of studious concentration.

PORTRAIT STUDY OF WOMAN IN DOORWAY, 1917. *Charles Burchfield.*
The Phillips Collection, Washington, D. C.

Getting at Meaning

1. Describe Mr. Martin and his habits. What is unusual in his purchase of the pack of Camels? Why does he buy the cigarettes?

2. What qualities in Mrs. Barrows lead Mr. Martin to plot her murder? Why does he like the term "rub out"?

3. Describe Mrs. Barrows. What is the source of her strange verbal expressions that so annoy Mr. Martin, such as "Are you tearing up the pea patch?" and "Are you scraping around the bottom of the pickle barrel?"

4. Mr. Martin thinks of Mrs. Barrows, "She had begun chipping at the cornices of the firm's edifice and now she was swinging at the foundation stones with a pickax." What does he mean with this metaphor? Why does he see this as justification for murdering Mrs. Barrows?

5. Explain Mr. Martin's movements on the day he plans to kill Mrs. Barrows. Why is he so careful to follow all of his usual routines?

6. Describe the humorous scene in Mrs. Barrows's apartment. At what point during this scene does Mr. Martin think of a new way to eliminate Mrs. Barrows? What causes this change of plans?

7. Describe Mrs. Barrows's reaction to Mr. Martin's odd behavior. Does her behavior at the office the following day seem plausible to you?

8. What takes place in the interview between Mr. Martin and Mr. Fitweiler? Why is Mr. Fitweiler so nervous and apologetic?

9. What do we assume will be the fate of Mrs. Barrows at the end of the story? Why is the final sentence a fitting place to leave Mr. Martin?

Developing Skills in Reading Literature

1. **Character.** "The Catbird Seat" focuses on the interaction between Mr. Martin and Mrs. Ulgine Barrows. Both are rather one-dimensional characters, characters who lack development and depth, possessing only one or two prominent traits. One-dimensional characters are common in comedy.

What traits does Thurber emphasize in Mrs. Barrows? What traits does he emphasize in Mr. Martin? How do Mr. Martin's habits complement these traits? In what ways are Mrs. Barrows and Mr. Martin opposites?

Mr. Fitweiler is in some ways a stereotyped character, the typical boss from situation comedy. Explain how this is so.

2. **Irony.** The plot of "The Catbird Seat" turns on various clever ironies. Most of its humor is also the result of irony and incongruity, or the joining of opposites to create situations that are completely unexpected.

In view of Mr. Martin's character, what is incongruous about his decision to murder Mrs. Barrows? What is ironic and humorous about Mr. Martin's behavior in Mrs. Barrows's apartment? What is ironic about his language? Explain how the humor of the final scene of the story depends on incongruity. What is so ironic about the final turn of events?

3. **Style.** Thurber is a careful stylist, as evidenced by his clever diction and imagery. For example, he uses the verbs *bounced, brayed, bawled, romped,* and *catapulted* to describe Mrs. Barrows's speech and activities. What do these verbs convey about her? Why are they humorous? When Mrs. Barrows enters Mr. Fitweiler's office, Thurber writes, ". . . the door to the office blew open with the suddenness of a gas-main explosion. . . ." What is so apt and comic in this image?

What precise words does Thurber use to describe Mr. Martin? What images does Thurber create in his depiction of Mr. Martin?

4. **Theme.** Thurber liked to write humorously about the battle between the sexes. Often his pieces on this topic show a timid, comtemplative man cunningly getting the better of an obnoxious, domineering woman.

What does the expression "sitting in the catbird seat" mean? Explain how in the final scene Mr. Martin is sitting in the catbird seat. Why is his situation even better than what he had hoped for?

Shirley Jackson
1919–1965

"I can't persuade myself that writing is honest work," Shirley Jackson once said in explaining why she loved to write. "For one thing, it's the only way I can get to sit down." She sat down often enough to produce a memorable body of writing, which is equally impressive whether it is cheerful or chilling.

Jackson was born in San Francisco and grew up on the West Coast, which she made the subject of her first book, *The Road Through the Wall* (1948). She went east to attend Syracuse University, where she received her B.A. in 1940. That same year she married the literary critic Stanley Edgar Hyman. When he joined the faculty of Bennington College in Vermont, they settled permanently in a rural community there. "Our major exports," she once said, "are books and children, both of which we produce in abundance." Jackson combined the two in *Life Among the Savages* (1953), which she called "a disrespectful memoir" of her children, and *Raising Demons* (1957), hilarious accounts of the perpetual pandemonium of family life with four children.

Shirley Jackson's writing has another side as well: a dark and sinister side, a concern with horror and haunting, psychological disturbance, supernatural happenings, and a genuine sense of evil. These novels and short stories, which may stem partly from her study of anthropology and her interest in black magic, have disturbed and fascinated her readers. Her most famous short story is "The Lottery," which describes a village ritual in which a victim is selected to be put to death by stoning. When it appeared in *The New Yorker* in 1948, "The Lottery" caused a literary sensation, with hundreds of readers writing in to inquire about the meaning of the story. It was the title story of a collection published in 1949. Jackson explored such themes as ghost-hunts, fright, and mental imbalance in several novels, including *The Bird's Nest* (1954), *The Haunting of Hill House* (1959), and *We Have Always Lived in the Castle* (1963).

Jackson's writing took a variety of other forms, including a semiautobiographical sketch, several books for young people, and two plays. Above all, she was a master of suspense in her storytelling. One of the things she did best was to place extraordinary people or events into everyday settings, whether for comic or sinister effect. Jackson died of heart failure at the age of forty-six.

The Little House

I'll have to get some decent lights, was her first thought, and her second: *and* a dog or something, or at least a bird, anything *alive.* She stood in the little hall beside her suitcase, in a little house that belonged to her, her first home. She held the front-door key in her hand, and she knew, remembering her aunt, that the back-door key hung, labeled, from a hook beside the back door, and the side-door key hung from a hook beside the side door, and the porch-door key hung from a hook beside the porch door, and the cellar-door key hung from a hook beside the cellar door, and perhaps when she slammed the front door behind her all the keys swung gently, once, back and forth. Anything that can move and make some kind of a friendly noise, she thought, maybe a monkey or a cat or anything not stuffed—as she realized that she was staring, hypnotized, at the moose head over the hall mirror.

Wanting to make some kind of a noise in the silence, she coughed, and the small sound moved dustily into the darkness of the house. Well, I'm here, she told herself, and it belongs to me and I can do anything I want here and no one can ever make me leave, because it's mine. She moved to touch the carved newel post at the foot of the narrow stairway—it was hers, it belonged to her—and felt a sudden joy at the tangible reality of the little house; this is really something to own, she thought, thank you, Aunt. And my goodness, she thought, brushing her hand, couldn't my very own house do with a little dusting; she smiled to herself at the prospect of the very pleasant work she would do tomorrow and the day after, and for all the days after that, living in her house and keeping it clean and fresh.

Wanting to whistle, to do something to bring noise and movement into the house, she turned and opened the door on her right and stepped into the dim crowded parlor. I wish I didn't have to see it first at dusk, she thought, Aunt certainly didn't believe in bright light; I wonder how she ever found her way around this room. A dim shape on a low table beside the door resolved itself into a squat lamp; when she pressed the switch a low radiance came into the room and she was able to leave the spot by the door and venture into what had clearly been her aunt's favorite room. The parlor had certainly not been touched, or even opened or lighted, since her aunt's death; a tea towel, half-hemmed, lay on the arm of a chair, and she felt a sudden tenderness and a half-shame at the thought of the numbers of tea towels, hemmed, which had come to her at birthdays and Christmases over the years and now lay still in their tissue paper, at the bottom of her trunk still at the railroad station. At least I'll use her towels now, in her own house, she thought, and then: but it's my house now. She would stack the tea towels neatly in the linen closet, she might even finish hemming this one, and she took it up and folded it neatly, leaving the needle still tucked in where her aunt had left it, to await the time when she should sit quietly in her chair, in her parlor in her house, and take up her sewing. Her aunt's glasses lay on the table. Had her aunt put down her sewing and taken off her glasses at the very end? Prepared, neatly, to die?

Don't think about it, she told herself sternly, she's gone now, and soon the house will be busy again; I'll clear away tomorrow, when it's not so dark; how did she ever manage to sew in here with this light? She put the half-hemmed towel over the glasses to hide them, and took up a little picture in a silver frame; her aunt, she recognized, and some smiling woman friend, standing together under trees; this must have been important to Aunt, she thought; I'll put it away safely somewhere. The house was distantly familiar to her, she had come here sometimes as a child, but that was long ago, and the memories of the house and her aunt were overlaid with cynicism and melancholy and the wearying disappointments of many years; perhaps it was the longing to return to the laughter of childhood which had brought her here so eagerly to take up her inheritance. The music box was in the corner where it had always been and, touching it gently, she brought from it one remote, faintly sweet, jangle of a note. Tomorrow I'll play the music box, she promised herself, with the windows wide open and the good fresh air blowing through and all the bric-a-brac safely stowed away in the attic; this could be such a pretty room—and she turned, her head to one side, considering—once I take out the junk and the clutter. I can keep the old couch and maybe have it recovered in something colorful, and the big chair can stay, and perhaps one or two of these tiny tables; the mantel is fine, and I'll keep a bowl of flowers there, flowers from my own garden. I'll have a great fire in the fireplace and I'll sit here with my dog and my needlework—and two or three good floor lamps; I'll get those tomorrow—and never be unhappy again. Tomorrow, lamps, and air the room, and play the music box.

Leaving a dim trail of lighted lamps behind her, she went from the parlor through a little sunporch where a magazine lay open on the table; Aunt never finished the story she was reading, she thought, and closed the magazine quickly and set it in order on the pile on the table; I'll subscribe to magazines, she thought, and the local newspaper, and take books from the village library. From the sun-porch she went into the kitchen and remembered to turn on the light by pulling the cord hanging from the middle of the ceiling; her aunt had left a tomato ripening on the window sill, and it scented the kitchen with a strong air of decay. She shivered, and realized that the back door was standing open, and remembered her aunt saying, as clearly as though she heard it now, "Darn that door, I wish I could remember to get that latch looked at."

And now I have to do it for her, she thought; I'll get a man in the morning. She found a paper bag in the pantry drawer where paper bags had always been kept, and scraped the rotten tomato from the window sill and carried the bag to the garbage pail by the back steps. When she came back she slammed the back door correctly and the latch caught; the key was hanging where she knew it had been, beside the door, and she took it down and locked the door; I'm alone in the house, after all, she thought with a little chill touching the back of her neck.

The cup from which her aunt had drunk her last cup of tea lay, washed and long since drained dry, beside the sink; perhaps she put her sewing down, she thought, and came to the kitchen to make a cup of tea before going to bed; I wonder where they found her; she always had a cup of tea at night, all alone; I wish I had come to see her at least once. The lovely old dishes are mine now, she thought, the family dishes and the cut glass and the silver tea service. Her aunt's sweater hung from the knob of the cellar door, as though she had only just this minute taken it off, and her apron hung from a hook beside the sink. Aunt always put things away, she thought, and she never came back for her sweater. She remembered dainty little hand-embroidered aprons in the hall chest, and thought of herself, aproned, serving a charming tea from the old tea service, using the thin painted cups, perhaps to neighbors who had come to see her delightful, open, light, little house; I must have a cocktail party too, she thought; I'll bet there's nothing in the house but dandelion wine.

It would seem strange at first, coming downstairs in the morning to make herself breakfast in her aunt's kitchen, and she suddenly remembered herself, very small, eating oatmeal at the kitchen table; it would seem strange to be using her aunt's dishes, and the big old coffeepot—although perhaps not the coffeepot, she thought; it had the look of something crotchety and temperamental, not willing to submit docilely to a strange hand; I'll have tea tomorrow morning, and get a new little coffeepot just for me. Lamps, coffeepot, man to fix the latch.

After a moment's thought she took her aunt's sweater and apron and bundled them together and carried them out to the garbage pail. It isn't as though they were any good to anyone, she told herself reassuringly; *all* her clothes will have to be thrown away, and she pictured herself standing in her bright parlor in her smart city clothes telling her laughing friends about the little house; "Well, you should have seen it when I came," she would tell them, "you should have seen the place the first night I walked in. Murky little lamps, and the place simply crawling with bric-a-brac, and a stuffed moose head—*really*, a stuffed moose head, I mean it—and Aunt's sewing on the table, and what was positively her last cup in the sink." Will I tell them, she wondered, about how Aunt set her sewing down when she was ready to die? And never finished her magazine, and hung up her sweater, and felt her heart go? "You should have seen it when I came," she would tell them, sipping from her glass, "dark, and dismal; I used to come here when I was a child, but I honestly never remembered it as such a mess. It couldn't have come as more of a surprise, her leaving me the house, I never dreamed of having it."

Suddenly guilty, she touched the cold coffeepot with a gentle finger. I'll clean you tomorrow, she thought; I'm sorry I never got to the funeral, I should have tried to come. Tomorrow I'll start cleaning. Then she whirled, startled, at the knock at the back door; I hadn't realized it was so quiet here, she thought, and breathed again and moved quickly to the door. "Who is it?" she said. "Just a minute." Her hands shaking, she unlocked and opened the door. "Who is it?" she said into the darkness, and then smiled timidly at the two old faces regarding her. "Oh," she said, "how do you do?"

"You'll be the niece? Miss Elizabeth?"

"Yes." Two old pussycats, she thought, wearing hats with flowers, couldn't wait to get a look at me. "Hello," she said, thinking, I'm the charming niece Elizabeth, and this is my house now.

"We are the Dolson sisters. I am Miss Amanda Dolson. This is my sister Miss Caroline Dolson."

"We're your nearest neighbors." Miss Caroline put a thin brown hand on Elizabeth's sleeve. "We live down the lane. We were your poor poor aunt's nearest neighbors. But we didn't hear anything."

Miss Amanda moved a little forward and Elizabeth stepped back. "Won't you come in?" Elizabeth asked, remembering her manners. "Come into the parlor. I was just looking at the house. I only just got here," she said, moving backward, "I was just turning on some lights."

"We saw the lights." Miss Amanda went unerringly toward the little parlor. "This is not our formal call, you understand; we pay our calls by day. But I confess we wondered at the lights."

"We thought *he* had come back." Miss Caroline's hand was on Elizabeth's sleeve again, as though she were leading Elizabeth to the parlor. "They say they do, you know."

Miss Amanda seated herself, as though by right of long acquaintance, on the soft chair by the low table, and Miss Caroline took the only other comfortable chair; my own house indeed, Elizabeth thought, and sat down uneasily on a stiff chair near the door; I must get lamps first thing tomorrow, she thought, the better to see people with.

"Have you lived here long?" she asked foolishly.

"I hope you don't plan to change things," Miss Amanda said. "Aunt loved her little house, you know."

"I haven't had much time to plan."

"You'll find everything just the way she left it. I myself took her pocketbook upstairs and put it into the drawer of the commode. Otherwise nothing has been touched. Except the body, of course."

Oh, that's not still here? she wanted to ask, but said instead, "I used to come here when I was a child."

"So he wasn't after her money," Miss Caroline said. "Sister took her pocketbook off the kitchen table; I saw her do it. She took it upstairs and nothing was missing."

Miss Amanda leaned a little forward. "You'll be bringing in television sets? From the city? Radios?"

"I hadn't thought much about it yet."

"We'll be able to hear your television set, no doubt. We are your closest neighbors and we see your lights; no doubt your television set will be very loud."

"We would have heard if she had screamed," Miss Caroline said, lifting her thin hand in emphasis. "They say she must have recognized him, and indeed it is my belief that Sheriff Knowlton has a very shrewd notion who he is. It is my belief that we all have our suspicions."

"Sister, this is gossip. Miss Elizabeth detests gossip."

"We were here the first thing in the morning, Miss Elizabeth, and I spoke to the Sheriff myself."

"Sister, Miss Elizabeth does not trouble her mind with wild stories. Let Miss Elizabeth remember Aunt as happy."

"I don't understand." Elizabeth looked from one of the tight old faces to the other; the two old bats, she thought, and said, "My aunt died of a heart attack, they said."

"It is *my* belief—"

"My sister is fond of gossip, Miss Elizabeth. I suppose you'll be packing away all of Aunt's pretty things?"

Elizabeth glanced at the table near her. A pink china box, a glass paperweight, a crocheted doily on which rested a set of blue porcelain kittens. "Some of them," she said.

"To make room for the television set. Poor Aunt; she thought a good deal of her small possessions." She frowned. "You won't find an ash tray in here."

Elizabeth put her cigarette down defiantly on the lid of the small pink box.

"Sister," Miss Amanda said, "bring Miss Elizabeth a saucer from the kitchen, from the daily china. Not the floral set."

Miss Caroline, looking shocked, hurried from the room, holding her heavy skirt away from the tables and Elizabeth's cigarette. Miss Amanda leaned forward again. "I do not permit my sister to gossip, Miss Elizabeth. You are wrong to encourage her."

"But what is she trying to say about my aunt?"

"Aunt has been dead and buried for two months. You were not, I think, at the funeral?"

"I couldn't get away."

"From the city. Exactly. I daresay you were delighted to have the house."

"Indeed I was."

"I suppose Aunt could hardly have done otherwise. Sister, give Miss Elizabeth the saucer. Quickly, before the room catches fire."

"Thank you." Elizabeth took the chipped saucer from Miss Caroline and put out her cigarette; ash trays, she thought, lamps, ash trays, coffeepot.

"Her apron is gone," Miss Caroline told her sister.

"Already?" Miss Amanda turned to look

fully at Elizabeth. "I am afraid we will see many changes, Sister. And now Miss Elizabeth is waiting for us to leave. Miss Elizabeth is determined to begin her packing tonight."

"Really," Elizabeth said helplessly, gesturing, "really—"

"All of Aunt's pretty things. This is not our formal call, Miss Elizabeth." Miss Amanda rose grandly, and Miss Caroline followed. "You will see us within three days. Poor Aunt."

Elizabeth followed them back to the kitchen. "Really," she said again, and "Please don't leave," but Miss Amanda overrode her.

"This door does not latch properly," Miss Amanda said. "See that it is securely locked behind us."

"They say that's how he got in," Miss Caroline whispered. "Keep it locked *always*."

"Good night, Miss Elizabeth. I am happy to know that you plan to keep the house well lighted. We see your lights, you know, from our windows."

"Good night," Miss Caroline said, turning to put her hand once more on Elizabeth's arm. "Locked, *remember*."

"Good night," Elizabeth said, "good night." Old bats, she was thinking, old bats. Sooner or later I'm going to have words with them; they're probably the pests of the neighborhood. She watched as they went side by side down the path, their heads not yet turned to one another, their long skirts swinging. "Good night," she called once more, but neither of them turned. Old bats, she thought, and slammed the door correctly; the latch caught, and she took down the key and locked it. I'll give them the moose head, she thought, my aunt would have wanted them to have it. It's late, I've got to find myself a bed, I haven't even been upstairs yet. I'll give them each a piece of the junk; my very own, my pretty little house.

Humming happily, she turned back toward the parlor; I wonder where they found her?

she thought suddenly. Was it in the parlor? She stopped in the doorway, staring at the soft chair and wondering: did he come up behind her there? While she was sewing? And then pick up her glasses from the floor and set them on the table? Perhaps she was reading her magazine when he caught her, perhaps she had just washed her cup and saucer and was turning back to get her sweater. Would it have been this quiet in the house? Is it always this quiet?

"No, no," she said aloud. "This is silly. Tomorrow I'll get a dog."

Pressing her lips together firmly, she walked across the room and turned off the light, then came back and turned off the lamp beside the door, and the soft darkness fell around her. Did they find her here? she wondered as she went through the sunporch, and then said aloud "This is silly," and turned off the light. With the darkness following close behind her she came back to the kitchen and checked that the back door was securely locked. He won't get in *here* again, she thought, and shivered.

There was no light on the stairs. I can leave the kitchen light on all night, she thought, but no; they'll see it from their windows. Did he wait for her on the stairs? Pressing against the wall, the kitchen light still burning dimly behind her, she went up the stairs, staring into the darkness, feeling her way with her feet. At the top was only darkness, and she put out her hands blindly; there was a wall, and then a door, and she ran her hand down the side of the door until she had the doorknob in her fingers.

What's waiting behind the door? she thought, and turned and fled wildly down the stairs and into the lighted kitchen with the locked back door. "Don't leave me here alone," she said, turning to look behind her, "please don't leave me here alone."

Miss Amanda and Miss Caroline cuddled on either side of their warm little stove. Miss

Amanda had a piece of fruitcake and a cup of tea and Miss Caroline had a piece of marsh-mallow cake and a cup of tea. "Just the same," Miss Caroline was saying, "she should have served something."

"City ways."

"She could have offered some of the city cake she brought with her. The coffeepot was right there in the kitchen. It's not polite to wait until the company goes and then eat by yourself."

"It's city ways, Sister. I doubt she'll be a good neighbor for us."

"Her aunt would not have done it."

"When I think of her searching that little house for valuables I feel very sorry for Aunt."

Miss Caroline set down her plate, and nodded to herself. "She might not like it here," she said. "Perhaps she won't stay."

Getting at Meaning

1. Describe Elizabeth's first reactions to her new house. In what sense is the presence of her aunt still hovering over the house?

2. What changes does Elizabeth intend to make in the house? What sort of life does she envision for herself in her new surroundings?

3. What attitude do the Dolson sisters have toward "Aunt's" house? toward Elizabeth?

4. What is Elizabeth's attitude toward the Dolson sisters? Explain how this pair unsettles her.

5. What do the two sisters conclude about Elizabeth when they are back at home?

Developing Skills in Reading Literature

1. **Setting.** The time and general location of "The Little House" are vague. All the reader learns is that the town is not too far from a city, and that television is not yet common in the town. The house itself, however, as the setting for the story, is a concrete reality, the focal point of the story.

Describe the house. In what ways does it reflect the personality of its dead owner? In what ways does the house have a life of its own? Why is the story called "The Little House"?

2. **Suspense.** At what point in the story does Shirley Jackson begin to build suspense? What technique does she use to build tension? Is the tension resolved within the story, or is the reader left hanging? Explain.

3. **Character.** The action of this story which is mainly internal, focuses on subtle character interactions. One of the important characters, the aunt, is of course dead.

What does the reader learn about the dead aunt? How does "Aunt" subtly affect her niece? How is Elizabeth different from her aunt?

Characterize the Dolson sisters. How do they work together as a team? What reason do they give for calling on Elizabeth? Why have they really called on Elizabeth? Do you think they both deliberately try to frighten her? Discuss this last question. Based on what you know of her character, do you think Elizabeth will remain in the house?

Developing Writing Skills

Extending a Story. What do you think would happen next if "The Little House" were continued? Would Elizabeth continue to live in the house, or would she return to the city? If she stays, what sort of relationship would she have with the Dolsons? If she leaves, would she first find out what really happened to her aunt? How would she part with the Dolsons?

Extend the story, creating what you feel is a fitting conclusion. Include some dialogue in your narration. Make sure the ending you create is true to the characters as Jackson has developed them.

Thomas Wolfe

1900–1938

Everything about Thomas Wolfe seemed to go beyond normal limits: his physical size, his enormous energy and appetite for life, his yearning hunger to experience everything and to record it all. In the epic scale and restless intensity of his life and work, he is one of the most American of writers.

Wolfe was born in Asheville, North Carolina, a mountain resort town that, like everything else in his life, he put into his fiction, thinly disguised. His father was a stonecutter who liked to recite Shakespeare to his son, and his mother kept a boardinghouse. Thomas was precocious and well read, and at fifteen he entered the University of North Carolina, where he edited the student paper and magazine and wrote his first two plays. In 1920 he went on to Harvard to earn his M.A. and to take a well known playwriting course there. Unable to interest Broadway producers in his plays, Wolfe began teaching composition at New York University. Meanwhile he worked on a novel, pouring out all his experiences up to then in a vast manuscript that became twelve times as long as an ordinary novel. When he finally found a publisher, a creative partnership began between Wolfe and his editor, Maxwell Perkins, who managed to cut the massive work and organize it into publishable form. The result was *Look Homeward, Angel* (1929). Like most of Wolfe's writing, it is autobiographical. It describes the young manhood of the hero, Eugene Gant, his life in the Southern town (with the name changed to Altamont), and his journey to New York. The book was a success except in Asheville, where his neighbors deeply resented the exposure of their lives.

Wolfe promptly gave up his teaching, received a Guggenheim Fellowship to Europe, and continued to write, furiously and compulsively. Wolfe hated to cut his work; his inclination was always to include every possible detail. When he gave Perkins the sequel to *Look Homeward, Angel*, the opening scene alone was longer than an ordinary novel. Drastically cut, the manuscript became *Of Time and the River* (1935).

In the summer of 1938, Wolfe had partially completed the manuscript of a new novel that began the autobiographical saga all over again; this time the hero's name was George Webber. Reacting to criticism, Wolfe handled the material slightly more objectively to show that he could ably bring characters to life that he had actually invented rather than drawn from experience. He turned the manuscript over to a new publisher, then left on a trip West to see more of the American scenery he loved. On the way he was stricken with pneumonia. Complications ensued, and at the age of thirty-eight he died of a cerebral infection.

His new editor tackled the eight-foot pile of manuscript Wolfe had left, and it was finally published as two separate novels and a book of short stories: *The Web and the Rock* (1939), *You Can't Go Home Again* (1940), and *The Hills Beyond* (1941). Of all his novels, most readers feel Wolfe's first one, *Look Homeward, Angel*, is the most typical and the most successful.

The Far and the Near

On the outskirts of a little town upon a rise of land that swept back from the railway, there was a tidy little cottage of white boards, trimmed vividly with green blinds. To one side of the house there was a garden neatly patterned with plots of growing vegetables, and an arbor for the grapes which ripened late in August. Before the house there were three mighty oaks which sheltered it in their clean and massive shade in summer, and to the other side there was a border of gay flowers. The whole place had an air of tidiness, thrift, and modest comfort.

Every day, a few minutes after two o'clock in the afternoon, the limited express between two cities passed this spot. At that moment the great train, having halted for a breathing space at the town nearby, was beginning to lengthen evenly into its stroke, but it had not yet reached the full drive of its terrific speed. It swung into view deliberately, swept past with a powerful swaying motion of the engine, a low smooth rumble of its heavy cars upon pressed steel, and then it vanished in the cut. For a moment the progress of the engine could be marked by heavy bellowing puffs of smoke that burst at spaced intervals above the edges of the meadow grass, and finally nothing could be heard but the solid clacking tempo of the wheels receding into the drowsy stillness of the afternoon.

Every day for more than twenty years, as the train had approached this house, the engineer had blown on the whistle, and every day, as soon as she heard this signal, a woman had appeared on the back porch of the little house and waved to him. At first she had a small child clinging to her skirts, and now this child had grown to full womanhood, and every day she, too, came with her mother to the porch and waved.

The engineer had grown old and gray in service. He had driven his great train, loaded with its weight of lives, across the land ten thousand times. His own children had grown up and married, and four times he had seen before him on the tracks the ghastly dot of tragedy converging like a cannon ball to its eclipse of horror at the boiler head—a light spring wagon filled with children, with its clustered row of small stunned faces; a cheap automobile stalled upon the tracks, set with the wooden figures of people paralyzed with fear; a battered hobo walking by the rail, too deaf and old to hear the whistle's warning; and a form flung past his window with a scream—all this the man had seen and known. He had known all the grief, the joy, the peril and the labor such a man could know; he had grown seamed and weathered in his loyal service, and now, schooled by the qualities of faith and courage and humbleness that attended his labor, he had grown old, and had the grandeur and the wisdom these men have.

But no matter what peril or tragedy he had known, the vision of the little house and the women waving to him with a brave free motion of the arm had become fixed in the mind of the engineer as something beautiful and enduring, something beyond all change and ruin, and something that would always be the same, no matter what mishap, grief, or error might break the iron schedule of his days.

The sight of the little house and of these two women gave him the most extraordinary happiness he had ever known. He had seen them in a thousand lights, a hundred weathers. He had seen them through the harsh bare light of wintry gray across the brown and frosted stubble of the earth, and he had seen them again in the green luring sorcery of April.

He felt for them and for the little house in which they lived such tenderness as a man might feel for his own children, and at length the picture of their lives was carved so sharply in his heart that he felt that he knew their lives completely, to every hour and moment of the day, and he resolved that one day, when his years of service should be ended, he would go and find these people and speak at last with them whose lives had been so wrought into his own.

That day came. At last the engineer stepped from a train onto the station platform of the town where these two women lived. His years upon the rail had ended. He was a pensioned servant of his company, with no more work to do. The engineer walked slowly through the station and out into the streets of the town. Everything was as strange to him as if he had never seen this town before. As he walked on, his sense of bewilderment and confusion grew. Could this be the town he had passed ten thousand times? Were these the same houses he had seen so often from the high windows of his cab? It was all as unfamiliar, as disquieting as a city in a dream, and the perplexity of his spirit increased as he went on.

Presently the houses thinned into the straggling outposts of the town, and the street faded into a country road—the one on which the women lived. And the man plodded on slowly in the heat and dust. At length he stood before the house he sought. He knew at once that he had found the proper place. He saw the lordly oaks before the house, the flower beds, the garden and the arbor, and farther off, the glint of rails.

Yes, this was the house he sought, the place he had passed so many times, the destination he had longed for with such happiness. But now that he had found it, now that he was here, why did his hand falter on the gate; why had the town, the road, the earth, the very entrance to this place he loved turned unfamiliar as the landscape of some ugly dream? Why did he now feel this sense of confusion, doubt, and hoplessness?

At length he entered by the gate, walked slowly up the path and in a moment more had mounted three short steps that led up to the porch, and was knocking at the door. Presently he heard steps in the hall, the door was opened, and a woman stood facing him.

And instantly, with a sense of bitter loss and grief, he was sorry he had come. He knew at once that the woman who stood there looking at him with a mistrustful eye was the same woman who had waved to him so many thousand times. But her face was harsh and pinched and meager; the flesh sagged wearily in sallow folds, and the small eyes peered at him with timid suspicion and uneasy doubt. All the brave freedom, the warmth and the affection that he had read into her gesture, vanished in the moment that he saw her and heard her unfriendly tongue.

And now his own voice sounded unreal and ghastly to him as he tried to explain his presence, to tell her who he was and the reason he had come. But he faltered on, fighting stubbornly against the horror of regret, confusion, disbelief that surged up in his spirit, drowning all his former joy and making his act of hope and tenderness seem shameful to him.

At length the woman invited him almost unwillingly into the house, and called her daughter in a harsh shrill voice. Then, for a brief agony of time, the man sat in an ugly little parlor, and he tried to talk while the two women stared at him with a dull, bewildered hostility, a sullen, timorous restraint.

And finally, stammering a crude farewell, he departed. He walked away down the path and then along the road toward town, and suddenly he knew that he was an old man. His heart, which had been brave and confident when it looked along the familiar vista of the rails, was now sick with doubt and horror as it saw the strange and unsuspected visage of an earth which had always been within a stone's throw of him, and which he had never seen or known. And he knew that all the magic of that bright lost way, the vista of that shining line, the imagined corner of that small good universe of hope's desire, was gone forever, could never be got back again.

Getting at Meaning

1. Describe the cottage the engineer passes every day. Why does it appeal to him?

2. The reader gets a quick overview of the engineer's life. What are the chief facts? Why have the little house and the woman waving remained so important?

3. When does the engineer begin to sense that visiting the little house will be a mistake? What is so intensely disappointing to him in the woman? How does this encounter affect the engineer?

Developing Skills in Reading Literature

1. **Character.** Although this story is very brief, some important character traits in the engineer surface. What kind of man is he? How would you describe the conflict he undergoes? How does he change?

2. **Foreshadowing.** Thomas Wolfe foreshadows the sad ending of this story in several places. First of all, the fourth paragraph of the story recounts the four fatal accidents the engineer has seen on the railroad tracks during the course of his career. The reader hears about the wagon filled with children, "with its clustered row of small stunned faces," and the "form flung past his window with a scream." Why does Wolfe include these details in his short summation of the engineer's life? What effect do they have on the reader?

When the engineer visits the town after his retirement, how does the description of the town and the little house change? Notice the nouns and adjectives Wolfe uses. Why does Wolfe foreshadow the ending in this fashion?

3. **Theme.** The engineer wanted to have "something beautiful and enduring" in his life, "something beyond all change and ruin." In this he was disappointed.

What statement does the story make about the human condition? Reread the final paragraph. What is the sad realization thrust upon the engineer?

The well known writer Robert Louis Stevenson once said, "To travel hopefully is better than to arrive." Explain how this statement embodies the theme of Wolfe's story.

4. **Title.** One aspect of the story's theme is described by the title, "The Far and the Near." Why are things often better at a distance? What does the engineer notice about the town when he sees it up close for the first time? Why are the woman and her daughter more satisfying when viewed from a distance, as idealized abstractions? What does Wolfe say, about the need for idealized or romantic visions in human life?

Developing Vocabulary

Precise Adjectives. Wolfe uses a number of richly connotative adjectives in this story to help convey his meaning. What association, emotional or otherwise, do you have for each adjective that follows? Look up each word in a dictionary to determine its precise denotative meaning. Think of one or two good synonyms for each word.

seamed	sallow	disquieting
weathered	sullen	timorous

Developing Writing Skills

Narrating an Autobiographical Incident. Write about an experience through which you discovered that "To travel hopefully is better than to arrive." What were you expecting in the situation in question? In what ways were you disappointed? How did the experience affect you at the time? How has it affected you in the long run?

Make your composition vivid and interesting.

Flannery O'Connor
1925–1964

As a child, Mary Flannery O'Connor had a pet chicken that could walk either backward or forward, and some newspaper reporters came to photograph the animal. This experience, she later said, marked her for life, for it began her preoccupation with the deformed and the grotesque.

O'Connor was born an only child in Savannah, Georgia, where she went to Catholic schools. While she was in her teens her father fell fatally ill with lupus, and the family moved to Milledgeville. O'Connor began writing when she was young; she listed as her chief hobby in her high school yearbook, "collecting rejection slips." She got her B.A. in English at the local state college, then left home to attend the Writer's Workshop at the University of Iowa. There she earned an M.F.A. and sold her first short story. As more magazines began to publish her work, she went to live and write in the country home of close friends in Connecticut.

She had just completed the first draft of a novel, *Wise Blood*, in 1950, when she learned that she too had lupus, the disease that had killed her father. She went back to Milledgeville to live on a farm, where she could raise peacocks and have the time to write. There, with the help of a new drug, she enjoyed periods of relatively good health and was able to go on writing until her death, thirteen years later. In those thirteen years she did most of her best work, slowly turning out her carefully crafted stories and receiving ever wider critical recognition. She wrote a second novel, *The Violent Bear It Away* (1960), and two collections of stories, *A Good Man Is Hard to Find* (1955) and *Everything That Rises Must Converge* (1965).

Two of O'Connor's special qualities are her wry comic sense and her intense Christian faith. In addition, she shares with some other writers of her region a sense of the grotesque. Southern writers are fond of "writing about freaks," she said, "because we are still able to recognize one." Her characters are a series of misfits, psychic cripples, religious fanatics, and assorted con men obsessed with questions of salvation and damnation. "All comic novels that are any good must be about life and death," she said, and indeed her writing is often simultaneously comic and tragic. O'Connor wrote deadly serious comedy about violence and suffering in the Bible Belt, and she seemed to avoid the normal. "Distortion," she believed, "is the only way to make people see."

The Life You Save May Be Your Own

The old woman and her daughter were sitting on their porch when Mr. Shiftlet came up their road for the first time. The old woman slid to the edge of her chair and leaned forward, shading her eyes from the piercing sunset with her hand. The daughter could not see far in front of her and continued to play with her fingers. Although the old woman lived in this desolate spot with only her daughter and she had never seen Mr. Shiftlet before, she could tell, even from a distance, that he was a tramp and no one to be afraid of. His left coat sleeve was folded up to show there was only half an arm in it, and his gaunt figure listed slightly to the side as if the breeze were pushing him. He had on a black town suit and a brown felt hat that was turned up in the front and down in the back and he carried a tin tool box by a handle. He came on, at an amble, up her road, his face turned toward the sun which appeared to be balancing itself on the peak of a small mountain.

The old woman didn't change her position until he was almost into her yard; then she rose with one hand fisted on her hip. The daughter, a large girl in a short blue organdy dress, saw him all at once and jumped up and began to stamp and point and make excited speechless sounds.

Mr. Shiftlet stopped just inside the yard and set his box on the ground and tipped his hat at her as if she were not in the least afflicted; then he turned toward the old woman and swung the hat all the way off. He had long black slick hair that hung flat from a part in the middle to beyond the tips of his ears on either side. His face descended in forehead for more than half its length and ended suddenly with his features just balanced over a jutting steeltrap jaw. He seemed to be a young man but he had a look of composed dissatisfaction, as if he understood life thoroughly.

"Good evening," the old woman said. She was about the size of a cedar fence post and she had a man's gray hat pulled down low over her head.

The tramp stood looking at her and didn't answer. He turned his back and faced the sunset. He swung both his whole and his short arm up slowly so that they indicated an expanse of sky and his figure formed a crooked cross. The old woman watched him with her arms folded across her chest as if she were the owner of the sun, and the daughter watched, her head thrust forward and her fat helpless hands hanging at the wrists. She had long pink-gold hair and eyes as blue as a peacock's neck.

He held the pose for almost fifty seconds and then he picked up his box and came on to the porch and dropped down on the bottom step. "Lady," he said in a firm nasal voice, "I'd give a fortune to live where I could see me a sun do that every evening."

"Does it every evening," the old woman said and sat back down. The daughter sat down too and watched him with a cautious, sly look as if he were a bird that had come up very close. He leaned to one side, rooting in his pants pocket, and in a second he brought out a package of chewing gum and offered her a piece. She took it and unpeeled it and began to chew without taking her eyes off him. He offered the old woman a piece but she only raised her upper lip to indicate she had no teeth.

Mr. Shiftlet's pale, sharp glance had already passed over everything in the yard—the pump near the corner of the house and the big fig tree that three or four chickens were preparing to roost in—and had moved to a shed where he saw the square rusted back of an automobile. "You ladies drive?" he asked.

"That car ain't run in fifteen year," the old woman said. "The day my husband died, it quit running."

"Nothing is like it used to be, lady," he said. "The world is almost rotten."

"That's right," the old woman said. "You from around here?"

"Name Tom T. Shiftlet," he murmured, looking at the tires.

"I'm pleased to meet you," the old woman said. "Name Lucynell Crater and daughter Lucynell Crater. What you doing around here, Mr. Shiftlet?"

He judged the car to be about a 1928 or '29 Ford. "Lady," he said, and turned and gave her his full attention, "lemme tell you something. There's one of these doctors in Atlanta that's taken a knife and cut the human heart —the human heart," he repeated, leaning forward, "out of a man's chest and held it in his hand," and he held his hand out, palm up, as if it were slightly weighted with the human heart, "and studied it like it was a day-old chicken, and lady," he said, allowing a long significant pause in which his head slid forward and his clay-colored eyes brightened, "he don't know no more about it than you or me."

"That's right," the old woman said.

"Why, if he was to take that knife and cut into every corner of it, he still wouldn't know no more than you or me. What you want to bet?"

"Nothing," the old woman said wisely. "Where you come from, Mr. Shiftlet?"

He didn't answer. He reached into his pocket and brought out a sack of tobacco and a package of cigarette papers and rolled himself a cigarette, expertly with one hand, and attached it in a hanging position to his upper lip. Then he took a box of wooden matches from his pocket and struck one on his shoe. He held the burning match as if he were studying the mystery of flame while it traveled dangerously toward his skin. The daughter began to make loud noises and to point to his hand and shake her finger at him, but when the flame was just before touching him, he leaned down with his hand cupped over it as if he were going to set fire to his nose and lit the cigarette.

He flipped away the dead match and blew a stream of gray into the evening. A sly look came over his face. "Lady," he said, "nowadays, people'll do anything anyways. I can tell you my name is Tom T. Shiftlet and I come from Tarwater, Tennessee, but you never have seen me before: how you know I ain't lying? How you know my name ain't Aaron Sparks, lady, and I come from Singleberry, Georgia, or how you know it's not George Speeds and I come from Lucy, Alabama, or how you know I ain't Thompson Bright from Toolafalls, Mississippi?"

"I don't know nothing about you," the old woman muttered, irked.

"Lady," he said, "people don't care how they lie. Maybe the best I can tell you is, I'm a man; but listen lady," he said and paused and made his tone more ominous still, "what is a man?"

The old woman began to gum a seed. "What you carry in that tin box, Mr. Shiftlet?" she asked.

"Tools," he said, put back. "I'm a carpenter."

"Well, if you come out here to work, I'll be able to feed you and give you a place to sleep but I can't pay. I'll tell you that before you begin," she said.

There was no answer at once and no particular expression on his face. He leaned back against the two-by-four that helped support the porch roof. "Lady," he said slowly, "there's some men that some things mean more to them than money." The old woman rocked without comment and the daughter watched the trigger that moved up and down in his neck. He told the old woman then that all most people were interested in was money, but he asked what a man was made for. He asked her if a man was made for money, or what. He asked her what she thought she was made for but she didn't answer, she only sat rocking and wondered if a one-armed man could put a new roof on her garden house. He asked a lot of questions that she didn't answer. He told her that he was twenty-eight years old and had lived a varied life. He had been a gospel singer, a foreman on the railroad, an assistant in an undertaking parlor, and he come over the radio for three months with Uncle Roy and his Red Creek Wranglers. He said he had fought and bled in the Arm Service of his country and visited every foreign land and that everywhere he had seen people that didn't care if they did a thing one way or another. He said he hadn't been raised thataway.

A fat yellow moon appeared in the branches of the fig tree as if it were going to roost there with the chickens. He said that a man had to escape to the country to see the world whole and that he wished he lived in a desolate place like this where he could see the sun go down every evening like God made it to do.

"Are you married or are you single?" the old woman asked.

There was a long silence. "Lady," he asked finally, "where would you find you an innocent woman today? I wouldn't have any of this trash I could just pick up."

The daughter was leaning very far down, hanging her head almost between her knees watching him through a triangular door she had made in her overturned hair; and she suddenly fell in a heap on the floor and began to whimper. Mr. Shiftlet straightened her out and helped her get back in the chair.

"Is she your baby girl?" he asked.

"My only," the old woman said "and she's the sweetest girl in the world. I would give her up for nothing on earth. She's smart too. She can sweep the floor, cook, wash, feed the chickens, and hoe. I wouldn't give her up for a casket of jewels."

"No," he said kindly, "don't ever let any man take her away from you."

"Any man come after her," the old woman said, "'ll have to stay around the place."

Mr. Shiftlet's eye in the darkness was focused on a part of the automobile bumper that glittered in the distance. "Lady," he said, jerking his short arm up as if he could point with it to her house and yard and pump, "there ain't a broken thing on this plantation that I couldn't fix for you, one-arm jackleg or not. I'm a man," he said with a sullen dignity, "even if I ain't a whole one. I got," he said, tapping his knuckles on the floor to emphasize the immensity of what he was going to say, "a moral intelligence!" and his face pierced out of the darkness into a shaft of doorlight and he stared at her as if he were astonished himself at this impossible truth.

The old woman was not impressed with the phrase. "I told you you could hang around and work for food," she said, "if you don't mind sleeping in that car yonder."

"Why listen, lady," he said with a grin of delight, "the monks of old slept in their coffins!"

"They wasn't as advanced as we are," the old woman said.

The next morning he began on the roof of the garden house while Lucynell, the daughter, sat on a rock and watched him work. He had not been around a week before the change he had made in the place was apparent. He had patched the front and back steps, built a new hog pen, restored a fence, and taught Lucynell, who was completely deaf and had never said a word in her life, to say the word *bird*. The big rosy-faced girl followed him everywhere, saying "Burrttddt ddbirrrttdt," and clapping her hands. The old woman watched from a distance, secretly pleased. She was ravenous for a son-in-law.

Mr. Shiftlet slept on the hard narrow back seat of the car with his feet out the side window. He had his razor and a can of water on a crate that served him as a bedside table and he put up a piece of mirror against the back glass and kept his coat neatly on a hanger that he hung over one of the windows.

In the evenings he sat on the steps and talked while the old woman and Lucynell rocked violently in their chairs on either side of him. The old woman's three mountains were black against the dark blue sky and were visited off and on by various planets and by the moon after it had left the chickens. Mr Shiftlet pointed out that the reason he had improved this plantation was because he had taken a personal interest in it. He said he was even going to make the automobile run.

He had raised the hood and studied the mechanism, and he said he could tell that the car had been built in the days when cars were really built. You take now, he said, one man puts in one bolt and another man puts in another bolt and another man puts in another bolt so that it's a man for a bolt. That's why you have to pay so much for a car: you're paying all those men. Now if you didn't have to pay but one man, you could get you a cheaper car and one that had had a personal interest taken in it, and it would be a better car. The old woman agreed with him that this was so.

Mr. Shiftlet said that the trouble with the world was that nobody cared, or stopped and took any trouble. He said he never would have been able to teach Lucynell to say a word if he hadn't cared and stopped long enough.

"Teach her to say something else," the old woman said.

"What you want her to say next?" Mr. Shiftlet asked.

The old woman's smile was broad and toothless and suggestive. "Teach her to say 'sugarpie,'" she said.

Mr. Shiftlet already knew what was on her mind.

The next day he began to tinker with the automobile, and that evening he told her that if she would buy a fan belt, he would be able to make the car run.

The old woman said she would give him the money. "You see that girl yonder?" she asked, pointing to Lucynell who was sitting on the floor a foot away, watching him, her eyes blue even in the dark. "If it was ever a man wanted to take her away, I would say, 'No man on earth is going to take that sweet girl of mine away from me!' but if he was to say, 'Lady, I don't want to take her away, I want her right here,' I would say, 'Mister, I don't blame you none. I wouldn't pass up a chance to live in a permanent place and get the sweetest girl in the world myself. You ain't no fool,' I would say."

"How old is she?" Mr. Shiftlet asked casually.

"Fifteen, sixteen," the old woman said. The girl was nearly thirty but because of her innocence it was impossible to guess.

"It would be a good idea to paint it too," Mr. Shiftlet remarked. "You don't want it to rust out."

"We'll see about that later," the old woman said.

The next day he walked into town and returned with the parts he needed and a can of gasoline. Late in the afternoon, terrible noises issued from the shed and the old woman rushed out of the house, thinking Lucynell was somewhere having a fit. Lucynell was sitting on a chicken crate, stamping her feet and screaming, "Burrddttt! bddurrddtttt!" but her fuss was drowned out by the car. With a volley of blasts it emerged from the shed, moving in a fierce and stately way. Mr. Shiftlet was in the driver's seat, sitting very erect. He had an expression of serious modesty on his face as if he had just raised the dead.

That night, rocking on the porch, the old woman began her business, at once. "You want you an innocent woman, don't you?"

she asked sympathetically. "You don't want none of this trash."

"No'm, I don't," Mr. Shiflet said.

"One that can't talk," she continued, "can't sass you back or use foul language. That's the kind for you to have. Right there," and she pointed to Lucynell sitting cross-legged in her chair, holding both feet in her hands.

"That's right," he admitted. "She wouldn't give me any trouble."

"Saturday," the old woman said, "you and her and me can drive into town and get married."

Mr. Shiftlet eased his position on the steps.

"I can't get married right now," he said. "Everything you want to do takes money and I ain't got any."

"What you need with money?" she asked.

"It takes money," he said. "Some people'll do anything anyhow these days, but the way I think, I wouldn't marry no woman that I couldn't take on a trip like she was somebody. I mean take her to a hotel and treat her. I wouldn't marry the Duchesser Windsor," he said firmly, "unless I could take her to a hotel and giver something good to eat.

"I was raised thataway and there ain't a thing I can do about it. My old mother taught me how to do."

"Lucynell don't even know what a hotel is," the old woman muttered. "Listen here, Mr. Shiftlet," she said, sliding forward in her chair, "you'd be getting a permanent house and a deep well and the most innocent girl in the world. You don't need no money. Lemme tell you something: there ain't any place in the world for a poor, disabled, friendless drifting man."

The ugly words settled in Mr. Shiftlet's head like a group of buzzards in the top of a tree. He didn't answer at once. He rolled himself a cigarette and lit it and then he said in an even voice, "Lady, a man is divided into two parts, body and spirit."

The old woman clamped her gums together.

"A body and a spirit," he repeated. "The body, lady, is like a house: it don't go anywhere; but the spirit, lady, is like a automobile: always on the move, always . . ."

"Listen, Mr. Shiftlet," she said, "my well never goes dry and my house is always warm in the winter and there's no mortgage on a thing about this place. You can go to the courthouse and see for yourself. And yonder under that shed is a fine automobile." She laid the bait carefully. "You can have it painted by Saturday. I'll pay for the paint."

In the darkness, Mr. Shiftlet's smile stretched like a weary snake waking up by a fire. After a second he recalled himself and said, "I'm only saying a man's spirit means more to him than anything else. I would have to take my wife off for the weekend without no regards at all for cost. I got to follow where my spirit says to go."

"I'll give you fifteen dollars for a weekend trip," the old woman said in a crabbed voice. "That's the best I can do."

"That wouldn't hardly pay for more than the gas and the hotel," he said. "It wouldn't feed her."

"Seventeen-fifty," the old woman said. "That's all I got so it isn't any use you trying to milk me. You can take a lunch."

Mr. Shiftlet was deeply hurt by the word "milk." He didn't doubt that she had more money sewed up in her mattress, but he had already told her he was not interested in her money. "I'll make that do," he said and rose and walked off without treating with her further.

On Saturday the three of them drove into town in the car that the paint had barely dried on, and Mr. Shiftlet and Lucynell were married in the Ordinary's office while the old woman witnessed. As they came out of the courthouse, Mr. Shiftlet began twisting his neck in his collar. He looked morose and bitter as if he had been insulted while someone held him. "That didn't satisfy me none," he said. "That was just something a woman in an office did, nothing but paper work and blood tests. What do they know about my blood? If they was to take my heart and cut it out," he said, "they wouldn't know a thing about me. It didn't satisfy me at all."

"It satisfied the law," the old woman said sharply.

"The law," Mr. Shiftlet said and spit. "It's the law that don't satisfy me."

He had painted the car dark green with a yellow band around it just under the windows. The three of them climbed in the front seat and the old woman said, "Don't Lucynell look pretty? Looks like a baby doll." Lucynell was dressed up in a white dress that her mother had uprooted from a trunk and there was a Panama hat on her head with a bunch of red wooden cherries on the brim. Every now and then her placid expression was changed by a sly isolated little thought like a shoot of green in the desert. "You got a prize!" the old woman said.

Mr. Shiftlet didn't even look at her.

They drove back to the house to let the old woman off and pick up the lunch. When they were ready to leave, she stood staring in the window of the car, with her fingers clenched around the glass. Tears began to seep sideways out of her eyes and run along the dirty creases in her face. "I ain't ever been parted with her for two days before," she said.

Mr. Shiftlet started the motor.

"And I wouldn't let no man have her but you because I seen you would do right. Goodbye, Sugarbaby," she said, clutching at the sleeve of the white dress. Lucynell looked straight at her and didn't seem to see her there at all. Mr. Shiftlet eased the car forward so that she had to move her hands.

The early afternoon was clear and open and surrounded by pale blue sky. Although the car would go only thirty miles an hour, Mr. Shiftlet imagined a terrific climb and dip and swerve that went entirely to his head so that he forgot his morning bitterness. He had always wanted an automobile, but he had never been able to afford one before. He drove very fast because he wanted to make Mobile by nightfall.

Occasionally he stopped his thoughts long enough to look at Lucynell in the seat beside him. She had eaten the lunch as soon as they were out of the yard and now she was pulling the cherries off the hat one by one and throwing them out the window. He became depressed in spite of the car. He had driven about a hundred miles when he decided that she must be hungry again and at the next small town they came to, he stopped in front of an aluminum-painted eating place called The Hot Spot and took her in and ordered her a plate of ham and grits. The ride had made her sleepy and as soon as she got up on the stool, she rested her head on the counter and shut her eyes. There was no one in The Hot Spot but Mr. Shiftlet and the boy behind the counter, a pale youth with a greasy rag hung over his shoulder. Before he could dish up the food, she was snoring gently.

"Give it to her when she wakes up," Mr. Shiftlet said. "I'll pay for it now."

The boy bent over her and stared at the long pink-gold hair and the half-shut sleeping eyes. Then he looked up and stared at Mr. Shiftlet. "She looks like an angel of Gawd," he murmured.

"Hitchhiker," Mr. Shiftlet explained. "I can't wait. I got to make Tuscaloosa."

The boy bent over again and very carefully touched his finger to a strand of the golden hair, and Mr. Shiftlet left.

He was more depressed than ever as he drove on by himself. The late afternoon had grown hot and sultry and the country had flattened out. Deep in the sky a storm was preparing very slowly and without thunder as if it meant to drain every drop of air from the earth before it broke. There were times when Mr. Shiftlet preferred not to be alone. He felt too that a man with a car had a responsibility to others, and he kept his eye out for a hitchhiker. Occasionally he saw a sign that warned: "Drive carefully. The life you save may be your own."

The narrow road dropped off on either side into dry fields, and here and there a shack or a filling station stood in a clearing. The sun began to set directly in front of the automobile. It was a reddening ball that through his windshield was slightly flat on the bottom and top. He saw a boy in overalls and a gray hat standing on the edge of the road and he slowed the car down and stopped in front of him. The boy didn't have his hand raised to thumb the ride, he was only standing there, but he had a small cardboard suitcase and his hat was set on his head in a way to indicate that he had left somewhere for good. "Son," Mr. Shiftlet said, "I see you want a ride."

The boy didn't say he did or he didn't but he opened the door of the car and got in, and Mr. Shiftlet started driving again. The child held the suitcase on his lap and folded his arms on top of it. He turned his head and looked out the window away from Mr. Shiftlet. Mr. Shiftlet felt oppressed. "Son," he said after a minute, "I got the best old mother in the world so I reckon you only got the second best."

The boy gave him a quick dark glance and then turned his face back out the window.

"It's nothing so sweet," Mr. Shiftlet continued, "as a boy's mother. She taught him his first prayers at her knee, she give him love when no other would, she told him what was right and what wasn't, and she seen that he done the right thing. Son," he said, "I never rued a day in my life like the one I rued when I left that old mother of mine."

The boy shifted in his seat but he didn't look at Mr. Shiftlet. He unfolded his arms and put one hand on the door handle.

"My mother was a angel of Gawd," Mr. Shiftlet said in a very strained voice. "He took her from heaven and giver to me and I left her." His eyes were instantly clouded over with a mist of tears. The car was barely moving.

The boy turned angrily in the seat. "You go to the devil!" he cried. "My old woman is a flea bag and yours is a stinking pole cat!" and with that he flung the door open and jumped out with his suitcase into the ditch.

Mr. Shiftlet was so shocked that for about a hundred feet he drove along slowly with the door still open. A cloud, the exact color of the boy's hat and shaped like a turnip, had descended over the sun, and another, worse looking, crouched behind the car. Mr. Shiftlet felt that the rottenness of the world was about to engulf him. He raised his arm and let it fall again to his breast. "Oh Lord!" he prayed. "Break forth and wash the slime from this earth!"

The turnip continued slowly to descend. After a few minutes there was a guffawing peal of thunder from behind and fantastic raindrops, like tin-can tops, crashed over the rear of Mr. Shiftlet's car. Very quickly he stepped on the gas, and with his stump sticking out the window, he raced the galloping shower into Mobile.

Getting at Meaning

1. What are the early indications that the daughter is not normal? What in fact is wrong with Lucynell?

2. Describe Mr. Shiftlet. Why do you think he decides to stay around the Craters' and fix things?

3. What are the first signs that the old woman has designs on Mr. Shiftlet? When do you think he realizes this? How does the old woman play hard to get?

4. What sorts of things does Mr. Shiftlet say to make the old woman think that he is a solid, moral man? Give examples.

5. How does Mr. Shiftlet get money out of the old woman? How does she try to weaken his position in their negotiations?

6. Describe the wedding. What does Mr. Shiftlet mean when he says, "That didn't satisfy me none"?

7. Describe the way Mr. Shiftlet abandons Lucynell. What do you imagine will happen to Lucynell?

8. Why does Mr. Shiftlet pick up a hitchhiker? Why does he say what he does about mothers to his passenger?

9. What do you imagine will happen to Mr. Shiftlet? to the old woman?

Developing Skills in Reading Literature

1. **Setting.** The Southern setting is a major element of this story, as it conjures up an entire way of life among rural, uneducated, poverty-stricken people. What are some of the details of the Craters' way of life? Why is the isolation of the old woman's house important?

2. **Foreshadowing.** The reader knows early in this story that events will turn out tragically. What is it about Mr. Shiftlet that foreshadows this? Notice some of the initial descriptions of Mr. Shiftlet. The reader learns that when Mr. Shiftlet swung his arms up, ". . . his figure formed a crooked cross." How does this image foreshadow his role in the lives of the two Crater women?

3. **Figurative Language.** Flannery O'Connor is a fine, careful writer, and the figures of speech she uses illuminate character and theme in the story. For example, when the old woman tells Mr. Shiftlet that ". . . there ain't any place in the world for a poor, disabled, friendless drifting man," the reader learns that "The ugly words settled in Mr. Shiftlet's head like a group of buzzards in the top of a tree." A short while later, after Mr. Shiftlet has manipulated the old woman into paying for paint for the car, the reader is told, "In the darkness, Mr. Shiftlet's smile stretched like a weary snake waking up by a fire." What do these two similes reveal about the character of Mr. Shiftlet? How do the animal comparisons relate to the themes of the story?

Find other figures of speech and discuss how they contribute to the story.

4. **Character.** Most of this story consists of a sort of dueling match between Mr. Shiftlet and the old woman. Why does Mr. Shiftlet have the advantage? What ultimately makes the old woman a pathetic character?

Mr. Shiftlet is a complex character. What does his name suggest? Do you think it is his plan to marry Lucynell and abandon her right from the beginning? Discuss this question. Why does Mr. Shiftlet talk so much about morality and how rotten the world is becoming? Why can't he stand to be alone at the end of the story?

5. **Irony.** "The Life You Save May Be Your Own" is full of depressing ironies. The character of Mr. Shiftlet, for example, is riddled with irony. He talks about the difficulty of finding an innocent woman. He carries on about how ". . . the trouble with the world was that nobody cared, or stopped and took any trouble." Then he behaves as he does at the end of the story. What other ironies do you see in his character?

The old woman, the reader finds out, is "ravenous for a son-in-law." She plots to get one. What is her primary intention in acquiring a son-in-law? What is grimly ironic about the results of her negotiations?

Notice where the title appears near the end of the story. What is ironic in the title? To which character does it apply most directly?

6. **Theme.** Lucynell is presented as an innocent woman. She even looks "like an angel of Gawd." What details, however, undercut the supposed beauty of her blue eyes and gold hair? Why is she an innocent woman? What details make her innocence seem more like a sad and unappealing accident than something lovely and desirable? According to the story, what is the only way a person can remain innocent and uncorrupted in this world?

Early in the story Mr. Shiftlet says, "Nothing is like it used to be, lady. The world is almost rotten." At the end of the story, "Mr. Shiftlet felt that the rottenness of the world was about to engulf him." Why have things gone from bad to worse? What view of humans and their universe does Flannery O'Connor ultimately project?

The Family

MOTHER AND CHILD, 1944. *Milton Avery.*
Andrew Crispo Gallery, Inc., New York.

Katherine Anne Porter
1890–1980

Although Katherine Anne Porter once said that "human life is mostly pure chaos," and that her own life was "jumbled," her stories reflect none of this confusion. She wrote only a small number of them, but their clarity and exquisite craftsmanship earned her a reputation as one of America's finest prose stylists.

A descendant of Daniel Boone, Porter was born in Indian Creek, Texas. She was educated at home and in various Catholic convent schools in the South. Precocious and sensitive, she read widely and began writing stories when she was still a young girl, but her standards were so high that she did not try to publish any of them until she was past thirty. By that time she had been married once (at sixteen), had attempted a movie acting career in Chicago, had pursued journalism in Denver, and had gone off to Mexico to study art, arriving there in the middle of a revolution. She stayed in Mexico for two years, gathering material for some of her best fiction.

In the early 1920's, Porter's stories began to be published in literary magazines. They attracted so much attention that she published six of them in her first volume, *Flowering Judas* (1930). The book made her a literary celebrity, and she was awarded a Guggenheim Fellowship that enabled her to continue writing.

She went on traveling, too, during the 1930's, to Europe and back to the U.S., often carrying little baggage but her manuscripts. She supported herself with various newspaper jobs and translating from Spanish and French. Meanwhile she continued to publish serious fiction. As her reputation grew, she taught and lectured in universities throughout the United States and in Europe and Asia.

Porter was profoundly dedicated to her writing, which she called the central meaning and pattern in her life. In the midst of four marriages, travel, and miscellaneous writing, she produced the small body of work on which her reputation rests: five novelettes, three volumes of short stories, and one long novel, *Ship of Fools*, which took her twenty-five years to write.

In her writing Porter was able to say little and suggest much, to create a rich experience out of a single episode, to capture a character with a few concise details. She brought to the art of the short story a precision and a discipline that influenced many younger writers. Just two of the many honors she received were the Pulitzer Prize and the National Book Award, in 1966, for her *Collected Short Stories*.

He

Life was very hard for the Whipples. It was hard to feed all the hungry mouths; it was hard to keep the children in flannels during the winter, short as it was: "God knows what would become of us if we lived north," they would say: keeping them decently clean was hard. "It looks like our luck won't never let up on us," said Mr. Whipple, but Mrs. Whipple was all for taking what was sent and calling it good, anyhow when the neighbors were in earshot. "Don't ever let a soul hear us complain," she kept saying to her husband. She couldn't stand to be pitied. "No, not if it comes to it that we have to live in a wagon and pick cotton around the country," she said, "nobody's going to get a chance to look down on us."

Mrs. Whipple loved her second son, the simple-minded one, better than she loved the other two children put together. She was forever saying so, and when she talked with certain of her neighbors, she would even throw in her husband and her mother for good measure.

"You needn't keep on saying it around," said Mr. Whipple, "you'll make people think nobody else has any feelings about Him but you."

"It's natural for a mother," Mrs. Whipple would remind him. "You know yourself it's more natural for a mother to be that way. People don't expect so much of fathers, some way."

This didn't keep the neighbors from talking plainly among themselves. "A Lord's pure mercy if He should die," they said. "It's the sins of the fathers," they agreed among themselves. "There's bad blood and bad doings somewhere, you can bet on that." This be-hind the Whipples' backs. To their faces everybody said, "He's not so bad off. He'll be all right yet. Look how He grows!"

Mrs. Whipple hated to talk about it; she tried to keep her mind off it, but every time anybody set foot in the house, the subject always came up, and she had to talk about Him first, before she could get on to anything else. It seemed to ease her mind. "I wouldn't have anything happen to Him for all the world, but it just looks like I can't keep Him out of mischief. He's so strong and active; He's always into everything; He was like that since He could walk. It's actually funny sometimes, the way He can do anything; it's laughable to see Him up to His tricks. Emly has more accidents; I'm forever tying up her bruises, and Adna can't fall a foot without cracking a bone. But He can do anything and not get a scratch. The preacher said such a nice thing once when he was here. He said, and I'll remember it to my dying day, 'The innocent walk with God—that's why He don't get hurt.'" Whenever Mrs. Whipple repeated these words, she always felt a warm pool spread in her breast, and the tears would fill her eyes, and then she could talk about something else.

He did grow and He never got hurt. A plank blew off the chicken house and struck Him on the head and He never seemed to know it. He had learned a few words, and after this He forgot them. He didn't whine for food as the other children did, but waited until it was given Him; He ate squatting in the corner, smacking and mumbling. Rolls of fat covered Him like an overcoat, and He could carry twice as much wood and water as Adna. Emly had a cold in the head most of the time—"she takes that after me," said Mrs. Whipple—so in bad weather they gave her the extra blanket off His cot. He never seemed to mind the cold.

Just the same, Mrs. Whipple's life was a torment for fear something might happen to Him. He climbed the peach trees much better than Adna and went skittering along the branches like a monkey, just a regular monkey. "Oh, Mrs. Whipple, you hadn't ought to let Him do that. He'll lose His balance sometime. He can't rightly know what he's doing."

Mrs. Whipple almost screamed out at the neighbor. "He *does* know what He's doing! He's as able as any other child! Come down out of there, you!" When He finally reached the ground she could hardly keep her hands off Him for acting like that before people, a grin all over His face and her worried sick about Him all the time.

"It's the neighbors," said Mrs. Whipple to her husband. "Oh, I do mortally wish they would keep out of our business. I can't afford to let Him do anything for fear they'll come nosing around about it. Look at the bees, now. Adna can't handle them; they sting him up so; I haven't got time to do everything, and now I don't dare let Him. But if He gets a sting He don't really mind."

"It's just because He ain't got sense enough to be scared of anything," said Mr. Whipple.

"You ought to be ashamed of yourself," said Mrs. Whipple, "talking that way about your own child. Who's to take up for Him if we don't, I'd like to know? He sees a lot that goes on, He listens to things all the time. And anything I tell Him to do He does it. Don't never let anybody hear you say such things. They'd think you favored the other children over Him."

"Well, now I don't, and you know it, and what's the use of getting all worked up about it? You always think the worst of everything. Just let Him alone; He'll get along somehow. He gets plenty to eat and wear, don't He?" Mr. Whipple suddenly felt tired out. "Anyhow, it can't be helped now."

Mrs. Whipple felt tired too; she complained in a tired voice. "What's done can't never be undone; I know that as good as anybody; but He's my child, and I'm not going to have people say anything. I get sick of people coming around saying things all the time."

In the early fall Mrs. Whipple got a letter from her brother saying he and his wife and two children were coming over for a little visit next Sunday week. "Put the big pot in the little one," he wrote at the end. Mrs. Whipple read this part out loud twice, she was so pleased. Her brother was a great one for saying funny things. "We'll just show him that's no joke," she said; "we'll just butcher one of the sucking pigs."

"It's a waste and I don't hold with waste the way we are now," said Mr. Whipple. "That pig'll be worth money by Christmas."

"It's a shame and a pity we can't have a decent meal's vittles once in a while when my own family comes to see us," said Mrs. Whipple. "I'd hate for his wife to go back and say there wasn't a thing in the house to eat. My God, it's better than buying up a great chance of meat in town. There's where you'd spend the money!"

"All right, do it yourself then," said Mr. Whipple. "Christa-mighty, no wonder we can't get ahead!"

The question was how to get the little pig away from his ma, a great fighter, worse than a Jersey cow. Adna wouldn't try it: "That sow'd rip my insides out all over the pen." "All right, old fraidy," said Mrs. Whipple, "*He's* not scared. Watch *Him* do it." And she laughed as though it was all a good joke and gave Him a little push towards the pen. He sneaked up and snatched the pig right away from the teat and galloped back and was over the fence with the sow raging at His heels. The little black squirming thing was screeching like a baby in a tantrum, stiffening its back and stretching its mouth to the ears. Mrs. Whipple took the pig with her face stiff and sliced its throat with one stroke. When

He saw the blood He gave a great jolting breath and ran away. "But He'll forget and eat plenty, just the same," thought Mrs. Whipple. Whenever she was thinking, her lips moved making words. "He'd eat it all if I didn't stop Him. He'd eat up every mouthful from the other two if I'd let Him."

She felt badly about it. He was ten years old now and a third again as large as Adna, who was going on fourteen. "It's a shame, a shame," she kept saying under her breath, "and Adna with so much brains!"

She kept on feeling badly about all sorts of things. In the first place it was the man's work to butcher; the sight of the pig scraped pink and naked made her sick. He was too fat and soft and pitiful-looking. It was simply a shame the way things had to happen. By the time she had finished it up, she almost wished her brother would stay at home.

Early Sunday morning Mrs. Whipple dropped everything to get Him all cleaned up. In an hour He was dirty again, with crawling under fences after a possum, and straddling along the rafters of the barn looking for eggs in the hayloft. "My Lord, look at you now after all my trying! And here's Adna and Emly staying so quiet. I get tired trying to keep you decent. Get off that shirt and put on another; people will say I don't half dress you!" And she boxed Him on the ears, hard. He blinked and blinked and rubbed His head, and His face hurt Mrs. Whipple's feelings. Her knees began to tremble; she had to sit down while she buttoned His shirt. "I'm just all gone before the day starts."

The brother came with his plump, healthy wife and two great roaring hungry boys. They had a grand dinner, with the pig roasted to a crackling in the middle of the table, full of dressing, a pickled peach in his mouth and plenty of gravy for the sweet potatoes.

"This looks like prosperity all right," said the brother; "you're going to have to roll me home like I was a barrel when I'm done."

Everybody laughed out loud; it was fine to hear them laughing all at once around the table. Mrs. Whipple felt warm and good about it. "Oh, we've got six more of these; I say it's as little as we can do when you come to see us so seldom."

He wouldn't come into the dining room, and Mrs. Whipple passed it off very well. "He's timider than my other two," she said, "He'll just have to get used to you. There isn't everybody He'll make up with; you know how it is with some children, even cousins." Nobody said anything out of the way.

"Just like my Alfy here," said the brother's wife. "I sometimes got to lick him to make him shake hands with his own grandmammy."

So that was over, and Mrs. Whipple loaded up a big plate for Him first, before everybody. "I always say He ain't to be slighted, no matter who else goes without," she said, and carried it to Him herself.

"He can chin Himself on the top of the door," said Emly, helping along.

"That's fine; He's getting along fine," said the brother.

They went away after supper. Mrs. Whipple rounded up the dishes, and sent the children to bed and sat down and unlaced her shoes. "You see?" she said to Mr. Whipple. "That's the way my whole family is. Nice and considerate about everything. No out-of-the-way remarks—they *have* got refinement. I get awfully sick of people's remarks. Wasn't that pig good?"

Mr. Whipple said, "Yes, we're out three hundred pounds of pork, that's all. It's easy to be polite when you come to eat. Who knows what they had in their minds all along?"

"Yes, that's like you," said Mrs. Whipple. "I don't expect anything else from you. You'll be telling me next that my own brother will be saying around that we made Him eat in the kitchen! Oh, my God!" She rocked her head in her hands, a hard pain started in the very middle of her forehead. "Now it's all spoiled, and everything was so nice and easy. All right, you don't like them and you never did—all right, they'll not come here again soon, never you mind! But they *can't* say He wasn't dressed every lick as good as Adna—oh, honest, sometimes I wish I was dead!"

"I wish you'd let up," said Mr. Whipple. "It's bad enough as it is."

It was a hard winter. It seemed to Mrs. Whipple that they hadn't ever known anything but hard times, and now to cap it all a winter like this. The crops were about half of what they had a right to expect; after the cotton was in, it didn't do much more than cover the grocery bill. They swapped off one of the plow horses, and got cheated, for the new one died of the heaves. Mrs. Whipple kept thinking all the time it was terrible to have a man you couldn't depend on not to get cheated. They cut down on everything, but Mrs. Whipple kept saying there are things you can't cut down on, and they cost money. It took a lot of warm clothes for Adna and Emly, who walked four miles to school during the three-months' session. "He sets around the fire a lot, He won't need so much," said Mr. Whipple. "That's so," said Mrs. Whipple, "and when He does the outdoor chores he can wear your tarpaullion[1] coat. I can't do no better, that's all."

In February He was taken sick, and lay curled up under His blanket looking very blue in the face and acting as if He would choke. Mr. and Mrs. Whipple did everything they could for Him for two days, and then they were scared and sent for the doctor. The doctor told them they must keep Him warm and give Him plenty of milk and eggs. "He isn't as stout as He looks, I'm afraid," said the doctor. "You've got to watch them when they're like that. You must put more cover onto Him, too."

"I just took off His big blanket to wash," said Mrs. Whipple, ashamed. "I can't stand dirt."

"Well, you'd better put it back on the min-

ute it's dry," said the doctor, "or He'll have pneumonia."

Mr. and Mrs. Whipple took a blanket off their own bed and put His cot in by the fire. "They can't say we didn't do everything for Him," she said, "even to sleeping cold ourselves on His account."

When the winter broke He seemed to be well again, but He walked as if His feet hurt Him. He was able to run a cotton planter during the season.

"I got it all fixed up with Jim Ferguson about breeding the cow next time," said Mr. Whipple. "I'll pasture the bull this summer and give Jim some fodder in the fall. That's better than paying out money when you haven't got it."

"I hope you didn't say such a thing before Jim Ferguson," said Mrs. Whipple. "You oughtn't to let him know we're so down as all that."

"Godamighty, that ain't saying we're down. A man is got to look ahead sometimes. He can lead the bull over today. I need Adna on the place."

At first Mrs. Whipple felt easy in her mind about sending Him for the bull. Adna was too jumpy and couldn't be trusted. You've got to be steady around animals. After He was gone she started thinking, and after a while she could hardly bear it any longer. She stood in the lane and watched for Him. It was nearly three miles to go and a hot day, but He oughtn't to be so long about it. She shaded her eyes and stared until colored bubbles floated in her eyeballs. It was just like everything else in life; she must always worry and never know a moment's peace about anything. After a long time she saw Him turn into the side lane, limping. He came on very slowly, leading the big hulk of an animal by a ring in the nose, twirling a little stick in His hand, never looking back or sideways, but coming

---

1. **tarpaullion:** tarpaulin, canvas coated with a waterproofing compound.

on like a sleepwalker with His eyes half shut.

Mrs. Whipple was scared sick of bulls; she had heard awful stories about how they followed on quietly enough, and then suddenly pitched on with a bellow and pawed and gored a body to pieces. Any second now that black monster would come down on Him, my God. He'd never have sense enough to run.

She mustn't make a sound nor a move, she mustn't get the bull started. The bull heaved his head aside and horned the air at a fly. Her voice burst out of her in a shriek, and she screamed at Him to come on, for God's sake. He didn't seem to hear her clamor, but kept on twirling His switch and limping on, and the bull lumbered along behind him as gently as a calf. Mrs. Whipple stopped calling and ran towards the house, praying under her breath: "Lord, don't let anything happen to Him. Lord, you *know* people will say we oughtn't to have sent Him. You *know* they'll say we didn't take care of Him. Oh, get Him home, safe home, safe home, and I'll look out for Him better! Amen."

She watched from the window while He led the beast in, and tied him up in the barn. It was no use trying to keep up; Mrs. Whipple couldn't bear another thing. She sat down and rocked and cried with her apron over her head.

From year to year the Whipples were growing poorer and poorer. The place just seemed to run down of itself, no matter how hard they worked. "We're losing our hold," said Mrs. Whipple. "Why can't we do like other people and watch for our best chances? They'll be calling us poor white trash next."

"When I get to be sixteen I'm going to leave," said Adna. "I'm going to get a job in Powell's grocery store. There's money in that. No more farm for me."

"I'm going to be a schoolteacher," said Emly. "But I've got to finish the eighth grade, anyhow. Then I can live in town. I don't see any chances here."

"Emly takes after my family," said Mrs. Whipple. "Ambitious every last one of them, and they don't take second place for anybody."

When fall came Emly got a chance to wait on table in the railroad eating-house in the town near by, and it seemed such a shame not to take it when the wages were good and she could get her food too, that Mrs. Whipple decided to let her take it, and not bother with school until the next session. "You've got plenty of time," she said. "You're young and smart as a whip."

With Adna gone too, Mr. Whipple tried to run the farm with just Him to help. He seemed to get along fine, doing His work and part of Adna's without noticing it. They did well enough until Christmas time, when one morning He slipped on the ice coming up from the barn. Instead of getting up He thrashed round and round, and when Mr. Whipple got to Him, He was having some sort of fit.

They brought Him inside and tried to make Him sit up, but He blubbered and rolled, so they put Him to bed and Mr. Whipple rode to town for the doctor. All the way there and back he worried about where the money was to come from: it sure did look like he had about all the troubles he could carry.

From then on He stayed in bed. His legs swelled up double their size, and the fits kept coming back. After four months, the doctor said, "It's no use; I think you'd better put Him in the County Home for treatment right away. I'll see about it for you. He'll have good care there and be off your hands."

"We don't begrudge Him any care, and I won't let Him out of my sight," said Mrs. Whipple. "I won't have it said I sent my sick child off among strangers."

"I know how you feel," said the doctor. "You can't tell me anything about that, Mrs. Whipple. I've got a boy of my own. But you'd better listen to me. I can't do anything more for Him; that's the truth."

Mr. and Mrs. Whipple talked it over a long

time that night after they went to bed. "It's just charity," said Mrs. Whipple; "that's what we've come to, charity! I certainly never looked for this."

"We pay taxes to help support the place just like everybody else," said Mr. Whipple, "and I don't call that taking charity. I think it would be fine to have Him where He'd get the best of everything . . . and besides, I can't keep up with these doctor bills any longer."

"Maybe that's why the doctor wants us to send Him—he's scared he won't get his money," said Mrs. Whipple.

"Don't talk like that," said Mr. Whipple, feeling pretty sick, "or we won't be able to send Him."

"Oh, but we won't keep Him there long," said Mrs. Whipple. "Soon's He's better, we'll bring Him right back home."

"The doctor has told you and told you time and again He can't ever get better, and you might as well stop talking," said Mr. Whipple.

"Doctors don't know everything," said Mrs. Whipple, feeling almost happy. "But anyhow, in the summer Emly can come home for a vacation, and Adna can get down for Sundays: we'll all work together and get on our feet again, and the children will feel they've got a place to come to."

All at once she saw it full summer again, with the garden going fine, and new white roller shades up all over the house, and Adna and Emly home, so full of life, all of them happy together. Oh, it could happen things would ease up on them.

They didn't talk before Him much, but they never knew just how much He understood. Finally the doctor set the day and a neighbor who owned a double-seated carryall offered to drive them over. The hospital would have sent an ambulance, but Mrs. Whipple couldn't stand to see Him going away looking so sick as all that. They wrapped Him in blankets, and the neighbor and Mr. Whipple lifted Him into the back seat of the carryall beside Mrs. Whipple, who had on her black

shirtwaist. She couldn't stand to go looking like charity.

"You'll be all right; I guess I'll stay behind," said Mr. Whipple. "It don't look like everybody ought to leave the place at once."

"Besides, it ain't as if He was going to stay forever," said Mrs. Whipple to the neighbor. "This is only for a little while."

They started away, Mrs. Whipple holding to the edges of the blankets to keep Him from sagging sideways. He sat there blinking and blinking. He worked His hands out and began rubbing His nose with his knuckles, and then with the end of the blanket. Mrs. Whipple couldn't believe what she saw; He was scrubbing away big tears that rolled out of the corners of His eyes. He sniveled and made a gulping noise. Mrs. Whipple kept saying, "Oh, honey, you don't feel so bad, do you? You don't feel so bad, do you?" for He seemed to be accusing her of something. Maybe He remembered that time she boxed His ears; maybe He had been scared that day with the bull; maybe He had slept cold and couldn't tell her about it; maybe He knew they were sending Him away for good and all because they were too poor to keep Him. Whatever it was, Mrs. Whipple couldn't bear to think of it. She began to cry, frightfully, and wrapped her arms tight around Him. His head rolled on her shoulder: she had loved Him as much as she possibly could; there were Adna and Emly who had to be thought of too; there was nothing she could do to make up to Him for His life. Oh, what a mortal pity He was ever born.

They came in sight of the hospital, with the neighbor driving very fast, not daring to look behind him.

Getting at Meaning

1. Describe the economic situation of the Whipples. In what ways does their economic situation influence the way they treat "Him"?

2. Why isn't the retarded child given a name in the story? What do the constant references to him as "He" or "Him," instead of by a name, imply?

3. What are the physical ways in which "He" is different from the other Whipple children? Explain how he is treated compared to the other children. How do you account for the differences?

4. Mrs. Whipple is very concerned about what other people will say of the Whipples. Cite several remarks in the story that illustrate this.

5. Why does "He" get sick? What differing views do the two parents have about sending him to the County Home for treatment? At the end of the story, why is the neighbor "driving very fast, not daring to look behind him"?

Developing Skills in Reading Literature

1. **Point of View.** Identify the kind of narration Katherine Anne Porter employs in "He." How is this type of narration appropriate to the story? Why doesn't the reader ever get to see inside the mind of "Him"?

2. **Conflict.** How would you describe the family conflict in this story? What character traits in both of the parents have bearing on the conflict? How is the conflict resolved? Describe how the various family members will feel about this resolution.

3. **Character.** The reader learns that "Mrs. Whipple loved her second son, the simple-minded one, better than she loved the other two children put together. She

was forever saying so. . . ." Do you believe this statement is true? Discuss it, using evidence from the story. What is the first thing that Mrs. Whipple thinks about in most situations? Find places in the story where Mrs. Whipple expresses these thoughts.

Although "He" never speaks and the reader never sees inside his mind, he still emerges as a definite character. What traits do his actions reveal? What details suggest that he understands more than people give him credit for? What details suggest that he feels things more than others often realize?

4. **Theme.** One theme of this story is the problem of dealing with a handicapped person in a family situation. Discuss the implications of Mrs. Whipple's agonized thought, ". . . there was nothing she could do to make up to Him for His life."

Capitalized pronouns are used to refer to the retarded child, a convention generally used only for the deity. At one point a preacher says to Mrs. Whipple, "The innocent walk with God—that's why He don't get hurt." In what ways is the retarded child more innocent and godly than other members of his family?

Developing Writing Skills

Combining Narration and Exposition. All families have to deal with difficult realities at some time or another. Write a composition that describes a major problem your family has had to face. How have different family members dealt with the situation? Has the family handled the problem well, or do you think it could be handled more effectively? How has the situation affected relationships within the family? The problem you write about may be either past or present.

Kay Boyle

born in 1903

Jill Krementz

Kay Boyle has lived both in Europe and America and has observed widespread crisis and upheaval. Against this background she describes the destinies of her characters, often young, idealistic Americans in Europe. Her poetry, short stories, and novels show a dedication to her craft and a willingness to become involved in the issues of her time.

Boyle's early life included little formal education but much traveling. She was one of two daughters born into a publishing family in St. Paul, Minnesota, and she spent much of her childhood in Europe, surrounded by painting, literature, and music. Much influence and encouragement came from her mother, in social issues as well as cultural concerns. By the time Boyle was seventeen she had written hundreds of poems and short stories. After briefly studying violin in Cincinnati, architecture at Ohio Mechanic's Institute, and writing at Columbia University, she met and married a young French engineering student. The couple sailed to Europe in 1923, supposedly only to visit his family, but Boyle was not to return for eighteen years.

In France during the 1920's, Boyle worked on both poetry and fiction, including several novels. *Plagued by the Nightingale* was loosely based on the summer spent with her husband's family. In 1927 her first daughter was born. Her writing began to be published in London and Paris, and two collections of her stories brought her increasing recognition. Soon her work began to appear frequently in American magazines, and in 1930 *The New Yorker* published the first of many of her stories.

In 1932, recently divorced, Boyle married another American expatriate writer, by whom she had three more children. As the Depression deepened and many other Americans were returning home, the family remained in Europe, living in the south of France and in Austria and England, and witnessing much of the ferment leading up to World War II. Finally in June of 1941 they returned to America. By then Boyle had won two O. Henry first prizes for short stories and had seen about forty more included in annual collections of best fiction. She also had published a large body of other work: six novels and many books of stories, poetry, and novellas, as well as translations and ghostwritten volumes.

After the war Boyle returned to Europe as a foreign correspondent for *The New Yorker*, while her third husband, an Austrian baron who had helped the French Resistance, served with the War Department in Germany. Her books *The Smoking Mountain* (1951) and *Generation Without Farewell* (1960) contain some of the finest fiction describing postwar Germany. Later Boyle taught at several American universities, including a period as professor of English at San Francisco State.

Boyle is interested both in the subtlety of human relations and the burning political and social issues of the day. To these she can not remain indifferent, though she never preaches in her writing. Her novellas in particular, such as *The Crazy Hunter* and *The Bridegroom's Body* (1940) are among the finest examples of that form.

The Soldier Ran Away

The colonel's son was twelve the winter he started to make the pipe rack for his father. He was a handsome, dark-eyed boy, with a voice as high and clear as a choir boy's, and a quickness, a nimbleness, about him that was in his mind as well as in his flesh. He had a skill for carpentry and mechanics in his fingers, and he could shoot game as expertly as any man his father hunted with. In the cellar of the house in which they were billeted in Germany, he and his father had set up a carpenter's bench, and there, underneath the strong stone house, they worked in the evenings or on half days or holidays.

"Look, Jeff, the idea is this," the colonel would say, and, quickly, expertly, he would sketch the plan of the bookshelf, or the oval tray, or the wren house. The boy would come close to study what he drew, and they would talk of the quality of wood and of the forests of home. "Some day we'll build a shack in the wilderness, a real log cabin, with timber we've cut down ourselves," the father would say, speaking of America as if it were a strange, far country that they had still to discover together.

Every morning a staff car would come along under the tall, ancient chestnut trees that lined the avenue, and the boy would stand in the window and watch the man dressed so trimly as a colonel go down the gravel of the path to wait on the sidewalk until the driver had slipped from under the wheel and opened the car door. For he was a doctor, and this was the routine. At a quarter past eight he would leave for the Army hospital, playing the role six days of every week, and two Sundays out of every month. The rest of the time he was a man in a khaki shirt, with the collar open, who worked at the carpenter's bench with his son, or took him hunting in the German hills, or stretched out his legs at leisure while he read of the other, wider forest lands of home.

It was winter, and the mother had taken the boy's sister off for a two-week visit to Swiss and Austrian skiing places, leaving the men with the German maid who came at half past seven and left again at half past three. If the beds were aired and made, the food bought, cooked, the house cleaned, it was accomplished while the men were away. For, in spite of the wisdom in his eyes, the boy was a schoolboy, and after his father had gone off in the morning, he would take his bicycle out and throw one leg in the blue jeans over its saddle, and, his coon cap on his head, speed down the wintry, tree-lined avenue. This was their life, the male life wholly separate from the female life, and it might have continued in this coupled intimacy had not the boy thought of making the pipe rack for his father's birthday, which was a week away. He would take the tools he needed, and the wood, and the diagram, up to the attic, he decided; and work on it there in the evenings in secrecy.

"The attic's so big not even our eight trunks take up any room," he told the two friends who cycled home from school with him, and he took them up to see it. It was a cold, bleak place at this time of year, but the boy believed that if he left the door open at the foot of the stairs, the steam-heated air would move up the stair well. "Here's my Gulf Stream," he said to his friends in his high, musical voice, as they mounted in the current of heat. "We could set the tennis table up in the middle of it," he said, and the friend named Bob Spanner spoke of putting ropes and bars and rings up on the strong wooden beams and making a gymnasium of it.

Two tilted skylights in the solid, sloping roof let in the light of day, and, standing under one of these, the friend called Malcolm Price pointed to a row of carnival masks that hung the length of one great beam. "You'll have company up here," he said, looking at the green poll parrot's face, and the devil's mask, brick red, and crowned with blunt black horns. On the other side of the parrot hung the gray cat's face, with one ear broken and its sharp, white whiskers bent, and then came two great headpieces in papier-mâché. One was a tusked boar and the other a sly, white-breasted fox, to be worn like helmets, with the throat fur molded with artistry.

"I used to collect masks once," Jeff said, as if dismissing the far time of his youth.

"We could have a square dance up here," Bob Spanner said, and he started calling: "The ladies to the center with the right hand around!"

But when Jeff came up to work after supper, the sound of the other boys' voices and the calls of the square dances were there no longer. There was only the sound of his own steps, as he carried a small table up and placed it under one of the two yellow bulbs of light. The wood that he would need, and the tools, he laid on the nearest trunk top, and then he spread open the drawing of the pipe rack, and as he stood studying it, there was only his own breathing on the quiet air.

That was the first night, and it could not be said that the suspicion came to him at once, but at the end of the first half hour the beginning of it was there. There was nothing the senses could identify, but every now and then he would lift his eyes from his work and look at the row of masks in uneasiness. "You fox, you devil," he would not say aloud; "you are making me nervous." But on the second night he was so much aware of the undefinable presence that at one instant he swung

around from the table, and the wood he was working with fell from his hand. But there was no stir of other life in the cold and silence of the attic.

"When you're ready to start in working in the shop again," said the colonel one evening of that long week, "I had an idea. I thought of making a Lazy Susan for the dining room before the womenfolk get back."

"Sure," said the boy. "Sure, but I've got homework to do," and he saw the eagerness fade quickly from his father's face. Then he turned his head, as if in guilt, and started up the stairs.

He passed the bedroom floor, where the mother so often sat in her own room at her desk in the evening, writing letters home. But now her room was empty and his sister's room was empty, and he mounted swiftly, softly, in his ancient sneakers, to the floor above. His own room was there, and the extra bathroom, and the spare room; and the attic was even higher in the cold. And when he opened the door at the foot of the stairs, he heard the sound of surreptitious flight above, and he stopped motionless, his heart and blood as quiet as if turned to stone.

It was his hand that first recovered the power of action, and he raised it and turned the electric switch, and instantly the light fell across the steep flight of stairs. But except for this one movement of his hand, all else was halted in him, and he could not put one foot before the other and move up the stair well, and he could not turn and go.

There is someone up there, he thought. *There has always been someone. All the time I've been working on the pipe rack, some-one's been watching me.* But now there was absolute silence in the attic, and he backed away, hardly knowing that he moved until he came abruptly against the banister rail.

"Dad!" he called out, but from the warm, bright world below came only the far sound of American voices and American laughter from the radio, and he knew that his father was in another country, and that his own voice, calling, could not be heard. *And if I ran and asked him to come up*, he thought, *he would see the pipe rack*; and he held his breath in his teeth, and returned to the open door and mounted into the cold. In the shadows hung the carnival masks, their faces as varied as those of living men and women, but no other sign of flesh and blood was there.

In the morning he questioned his father, "Do you remember the squirrel that used to climb up the vine to the balcony?" the boy asked as his father buttoned his olive-drab tunic over in the hall. "I used to put out nuts for him," he said. "Do you think he might have moved into the attic for the winter?"

"I think he'd be showing a lot of sense if he did," said his father, and he glanced at the time on his wrist before he went out the door.

But when the boy went up to his work in the attic that night, he stopped suddenly beside the table, his eyes held by the masks. Now he knew it was not the squirrel he had heard take flight between the trunks, for the order of the masks had altered. Where the poll parrot's head had hung, the fox grinned slyly now, and the parrot hung between the cat's head and the devil's mask.

The boy looked only for a moment, and then he drew his eyes away and put them on his work, seeking to let no sign betray him. He would keep his attention on the wood, the tools, his hands as active and unshaken as if he worked without the knowledge that a stranger watched him from the obscurity. After a while, he was even able to bring himself to whistle softly, not looking toward the row of masks, but working carefully as he studied the drawing underneath his hand.

Who was it that watched him, he asked the silence. He would be a German, he thought; perhaps one of those Germans who wandered from place to place; as he had seen them wandering in the two years he had been in Germany. He would be a stocky, putty-faced man, with a look of bitterness around his

mouth, he thought; and, as he worked, the wood, the tools, connived with the shrewdness of the living to foil him, as if knowing this was the first thing he had set out to do alone. In the making of the tray and the wren house and the other jobs of wood and paint, the father, too, had leaned above the table, his patience making more than the drawing clear. But now the boy's hands stumbled in uncertainty. Time was passing, and the pipe rack was no more than pieces of a puzzle he could not set straight.

He worked for an hour and a half, seeking not to believe that, without his father, he could not do this first thing of his own. Then he went in weariness down the stairs and switched the light off and locked the attic door. He locked it against a wandering German who had no other place to sleep, he thought, before he himself fell asleep; and all the next day, in the big, light classroom, he could see the stranger clearly.

He thought of how the German must climb the vines to the sloping roof at dark. In rain, or snow, or through fog, or in brilliant, icy weather, the man would keep to the chimney sweep's footholds across the roof until he reached the skylight, and then he would pry the window up and drop, soft as a cat, onto the trunk below. The boy could see the German's face, down to the dogged misery of its features, and he did not like the sight of it. But it was the knowledge that the pipe rack was not nearly done, and his father's birthday three days away, that finally took him in the evening up the attic stairs.

This time a shaft of cold cut sharp as a blade across the air, and the boy looked quickly to the roof, and he saw that the skylight window above the carnival masks stood partly open. He knew that he must cross the floor, and step, as if casually, on the trunk top, and reach up and draw it closed. And then he glanced at the wood and the tools lying on his table, and he did not go. For he saw that the pieces of the pipe rack no longer lay undecipherable, as he had left them the night before. The grooves into which the shelves must fit had been expertly cut in the harp-shaped wall piece, and when the boy lifted the delicately turned shelves, he saw that the tedious job of beveling the inner edges had been accomplished. Now they would fit into the wall piece with certainty and logic. There was only the shaping of the open circles of the pipe rests to be done, and one of these had been begun, but not completed; and after that the varnishing. And then the boy looked slowly up from these things he held, knowing, before he saw him, that a man had come out of the shadows of the attic and was standing, silent, there.

He was a young man with a long ruddy face and a light thatch of hair, and he was dressed as any German would have been dressed, his trousers and jacket not matching, his shirt GI khaki; but in his strong, rigid back, his healthy flesh, there was recorded no long and bitter history of misery. He did not speak. He waited, his small, deeply set blue eyes watching the boy with a troubled, concentrated gaze.

"Who are you?" the boy said. "What are you doing here?"

"Trying to get warm," the young man said, the voice hoarse, the speech American. "The night air don't have such a salutary effect on my breathing apparatus." The voice had a sad, vain attempt at humor in it. "You come up the stairs tonight before I could close the French window on the sun terrace." The young man rubbed his upper arms with his open palms. He was big-boned, with a spine and neck straight as a rod, and when he turned to step up on the trunk, the boy could see that the jacket was tight across his back, and tight in the armpits for him. Out of precaution, he wore no shoes, and the socks that had been khaki were washed nearly colorless and were lacy with holes. When he had closed the skylight, he dropped soft as a cat from the trunk and looked at the boy

again. "Your folks, they Army or civilian?" he said, and it was important to him, the answer that would come.

"Army," the boy said.

"The brass?" the man said.

"All right, the brass," the boy said quietly.

"You'll laugh, but I picked out these palatial quarters because of the company," the man said, as he jerked his chin at the masks. "That fox! I seen first cousins of his in Pennsylvania." His concentrated gaze was fixed on the boy. "Before you started coming up here at night, I had them heads for company. I had my spiritual communion with them. I'd talk to the poll parrot about my trip to sea. It was O.K., except the boat was going in the wrong direction," he said, and the wind cried suddenly underneath the eaves. "I'd take that cat's head down, and I'd tell it what happened to cats back home if they went around catching songbirds," he said. "'Keep to field mice,' I'd tell it. But that wild pig there, he belongs to this side of the water, so I just left him be."

"And the devil?" the boy said.

"Oh, that devil!" the man said, and he rubbed one rawboned hand over the short strands of his blond hair. "It used to get me. I couldn't stand it grinning at me, so I moved it so I could get some sleep at night." And now the wind cried louder and sleet lashed across the skylights. "Look, I made a mistake; all right, I made a mistake," he said. "I got out of the Army, and I should have stayed in."

"Well, everybody makes a mistake sometime in his life," the boy said in his clear, high voice of hope. "I was doing everything wrong with this pipe rack, and you straightened it out."

"The evenings was long up here until you started coming up," the man said. "I done something like it in the winter at home, so I thought I'd try my hand. Look, I'm just like anybody else. I came over here in the Army six months ago. Back home," he said, "my folks got a farm thirty-two miles from Scranton, Pa. Before I came over here, I'd never been farther away from home than Scranton."

"I've heard Pennsylvania's nice. I've heard the country around there's very nice," the boy said courteously.

"It's the prettiest place in the world," the man said. "If I'd of stayed in the Army, I'd of got back there in the end. But now I got a hard time ahead if they catch up with me. I made a bad mistake, and I'll get court-martialed for what I done."

"What is it you've done?" the boy said, and his eyes were filled with adult wisdom as he waited for the man to speak.

"I been AWOL[1] two months now," the man said finally in a low voice. "When I got over here, I got so I couldn't think of nothing but getting out of the Army and getting rid of the uniform, so's I could get back to where I figured I had the right to be. I got friends here, German friends, and they help me out. Every day I go and eat with them. But I got to get myself straightened out now. I can't go on like this," he said, and the storm pounded loudly on the roof and the wind cried through the eaves.

"Well, you could go back to the Army and tell them what you just told me."

"I'm afraid to go back," the man said, "and I'm afraid to stay away. I'm nineteen years old, so I figure maybe I got fifty years ahead of me, living like this. Seems like it's getting colder in here, or maybe it's because I got a cold on my chest," and he tried to button the thin jacket over his big bones. "Somebody's got to help me," he said, with no sound of drama or appeal in it. "Somebody's got to help me out of this."

"I'll help you," the boy said. He laid the delicately beveled pipe shelf flat and pushed the other tools aside.

"What's your dad's rank?" the man asked in a low voice, and as the boy began measuring and marking the unpainted wood, the man reached out to hold it steady with his hand.

"Well, he's a colonel," the boy said, not looking up from the thing that he was doing, for the first time speaking of rank as if it required some apology. "I want to cut four holes in each shelf, you know, like the diagram, for the pipes to hang from."

"A colonel," the man repeated. "So I been living in a colonel's quarters!" he said, and he jerked the laughter through his lips. "Officers, they got brass instead of blood in their veins. He'd turn me in, for sure."

"He's not an MP.[2] He's a doctor," the boy said in rebuke. He had picked up the trim electric jigsaw, and now he saw the blade of it was gone.

"That's what I stepped out to tell you," the man said, his face gone sober in apology. "I broke the blade last night, trying to get the first hole done. You'll have to put another one in."

"Only I don't have any more," the boy said, a sense of desolation spreading in him. "We've written home for more, but they haven't come yet."

"I can get you one in a German store tomorrow," the man said.

"The German blades don't fit my jigsaw," said the boy.

"Look!" cried the man, and his voice had come alive with eagerness now. "I got a German friend. He's got a toolshop. He'll let me take a jigsaw out. It won't cost you a cent!" he said.

"My father's birthday," the boy said then; "it's the day after tomorrow. I got to cut the holes tonight. Tomorrow there'll be the varnishing to do."

"I can get the jigsaw now! You wait!" said the man. "I'll be back in half an hour."

"There's a gale blowing outside," the boy said, but the inflexible neck, the rigid spine were there before him. "You better put a coat on," he said, watching the man lace up his shoes.

"I done without a coat so far," said the man,

---

1. **AWOL:** absent without leave from the military.
2. **MP:** military police.

with such decision in his voice, his flesh, in the spring of his body to the trunk, that the boy could only stand and watch him go.

He drew himself up on the heels of his hands, his big legs swinging free, and, like a man forcing himself through the hatch of a submarine, he was suddenly released into the current of the streaming, rocking dark.

When he was gone, the boy looked at the watch strapped on his wrist, and saw that it marked half past eight. He jumped up on the trunk to close the skylight, and a spray of sleet struck hard against his hands and mouth. Then he went down the stairs and closed the attic door. He ran down the next flights swiftly. The door to the library stood open, and he could see his father seated, reading, his legs stretched out. The boy stepped softly across the threshold, and he stood hesitant a moment before he spoke.

"I wanted to ask you a question," he said, and his father looked up at the boy from his far, clear island of lamplight. "Did you ever want to leave the Army—I mean, illegally? Did you ever want to go AWOL—I mean, when you were young?"

The father closed his book upon his finger that marked the page. "I wanted to be a doctor in the backwoods," he said. "Perhaps I always wanted to go AWOL for that. But out of cowardice, routine, whatever you call it, I stayed where I was. But, you know, Jeff, on a night like this, with the wind howling outside, I'd like to be the renegade, the timber wolf, with his tail between his haunches. Listen to this," he said, and he opened the book again. "'Picture him with his blond hair and his blue eyes, six-feet-three on his snow-shoes or in his moccasins, traveling over rough country with a hundred pounds of supplies and equipment on his back,'" the father read, his voice quick with excitement. "'He is fifty miles from the nearest settlement, and he'll be many miles farther before he swings around south again . . . he finds his way through country no white man has ever

seen before, locating his range by a pocket compass, counting his paces, sweeping the forest with his keen blue eyes, sorting out pine from the rest of the timber, studying the soil to judge what lies out of sight (white pine in sandy soil, jack pine and Norway pine in heavier soil), his memory recording this country like a camera. He knows the forest like a Chippewa and he carries whole countries in his mind. Whole countries without a footprint in them, except his own,'" the father read, and then he halted abruptly. "I've got to stop reading stuff like this," he said.

"Well, if a soldier does go—if he takes off—then what do they do to him?" the boy asked quietly.

"A soldier?" said the father. For a moment it seemed to be a strange word to him, and then he came back to reality. "Well, if a soldier goes away with the intent to stay away, and is apprehended rather than returning voluntarily to military control, the sentence could be dishonorable discharge after several years of hard labor," the father said. "Is it wartime or peacetime you're thinking of?"

"It's now," said the boy soberly.

"If the offense were one of AWOL only, and not actual desertion," the father said, "the sentence could be of hard labor and time of confinement. But there might be extenuating circumstances."

"But what if he only wanted to go home?" the boy said. "What if that was the reason why he ran away?"

"Well, if you're taking about desertion, and if the soldier is found guilty of desertion, then that's the end of it," said the father, and he gave a yawn. "Whether you do it for murder, or love, or out of loneliness, doesn't matter materially in the end. You might as well rule the motive out, as long as the result is the same."

"That's a bad rule," the boy said.

"What do you mean?"

"Any rule that doesn't consider the reasons

for doing a thing must be a bad rule," the boy said, and he stood looking at his father with his grave eyes.

"Well, good or bad, discipline has to be consistent," said the father, but now it was the colonel speaking, and the boy knew there was nothing more to say. "An army couldn't exist on a basis of compromise," the colonel said, and then he went back to the book, and, with the altering look in his face, he escaped into timber country, into conflict that had no concern with man's conflict with man, but with man versus beast and versus element.

The boy crossed the hall to the dining room then, and went through it to the kitchen, switching the lights on as he passed through the doors. He set water in a saucepan on the white-enameled, modern stove. He took a jar of soluble coffee from the dresser shelf and placed it, with a cup and saucer, on the breakfast tray. He filled the sugar bowl and laid the tongs across it, and then he sought the silver spoon he liked the best, with an edelweiss[3] and a chamois[4] head in intricate relief upon it, and put it beside the cup. When the water in the saucepan boiled, he poured it into a metal jug and set the jug, in its drift of steam, in the middle of the tray.

As he did these things, the boy thought of the man who was out in the storm now, and who had lived two months in the attic over their heads. Any night, he thought, he could have opened the attic door and come down and stolen the things he needed—money and clothes and passports—and gone away. But, instead, the man had talked to the parrot and spoken of songbirds to the cat's white-whiskered mask.

The boy picked the tray up carefully, and he came through the dining room with it. From the hall he could see his father reading in his zone of lamplight still, so lost in trailless country that he did not turn his head. But as the boy began to mount the stairs, the father's voice called out suddenly.

"What about getting to bed, Jeff? The women will be coming home tomorrow night, and you don't want to look tired out."

"I'm going to bed," he said. "I've just got some homework to finish first." He was safe now; he had reached the landing, and he kept on climbing toward the attic stairs.

The man came back late. It was half past nine when the boy heard him at the skylight, and he came in as if pounded and discarded by a winter sea. He took out the saw from where he had carried it inside his jacket, and then he pulled off his shoes and peeled the drenched jacket away, but nothing could stop the shaking of his bones. The boy fixed the coffee in the cup, and made him drink it down.

"I'm afraid it's not very hot now," the boy said.

"It seems hot all right to me," the man said, and the boy went down to his own room and took his sheep-lined jacket from the wardrobe, and put it around the man's shoulders, but still the deep, terrible shuddering did not cease. "When I get warm, I'll be O.K.," the man said. "I'll get the pipe rests cut all right; I'll get them done." The boy went down the stairs again and brought up the two wool blankets from his bed. "We got two nights left," the man said. He sat on the edge of the trunk with the blankets held around him, his strong, flat neck and his spine unbending still. "Working together, we'll get it done," he said, the words shaking in his mouth.

The boy did not know at what moment of the night, or the early morning, it may have been, the pipe rack was completed. It was not finished when he went down to bed, but when he went up at eight in the morning, it was already varnished a deep mahogany, and it stood, as if in a gift-shop window, on the work table to dry.

At first the boy believed that the man was

---

3. **edelweiss** (ād' l wīs'): a small white flowering plant found high in the Alps.
4. **chamois** (sham' ē): a small goatlike antelope of Europe.

out already, and then he heard him murmuring, and he moved across the trunks to where he lay. He was there behind the farthest trunk, bedded down on a mattress of newspapers, with the blankets from the boy's bed that had covered him now tossed away. His eyes were closed as if in sleep, but if this was sleep, it was a state of being so violent that the sleeper himself cried out in protest against it. The boy knelt on the trunk top in his sneakers and blue jeans, and reached down to touch the restless, burning hand.

"A fox'll thieve and kill. I seen him doing it," the man murmured, viewing, it seemed, the endlessly unwinding reel of memory. "A fox'll leave a ring of chicken feathers, and you'll find them in the moonlight. I seen it. Or else you'll find the hind leg of a fawn. Take him!" the man cried out, and from the beam above, the needle-nosed fox smiled slyly, viciously, down on them. "Take him!" the man cried out, his closed eyes fighting for sight. "Take him instead of me! He lied, thieved, killed," he said, his bright, congested face flung wildly from side to side. And then he grew calmer for an instant. "I can swim," he said, with a certain shrewdness in his voice. "I can swim," he whispered. "I can swim," and the boy's heart was stricken in him as he went down the stairs.

Afterward he told himself that he should have squeezed an orange before going to school, and taken the juice up to the man and made him drink. And when he came home from school at lunchtime and found the man's nostrils fanning rapidly for air, he should have done more, far more, than merely get the two aspirin tablets and the glass of water down his throat.

When the boy came home again at half past three, the house was quiet, and he made a pot of tea in the kitchen and carried it, with lemon and sugar, up the stairs. The man slept even more uneasily now, and his flesh was fire to the touch, and the boy's hand trembled as he fed the spoonfuls of liquid into the parched mouth. At five-thirty the staff car brought the colonel down the avenue of chestnut trees, and the boy was there to let him in, and then he stood in silence before him.

"What's up?" said the father, putting his cap on the rack.

"I have a friend," the boy said, forcing the panic out of his voice.

"You mean Bob Spanner, Malcolm Price?" his father said.

"No, it's another friend," the boy said. "He might be going to die."

"Well, I suppose his mother and father have called a doctor in?"

"No," said the boy. "He comes from Pennsylvania. He hasn't anyone in Germany."

"You mean he's over here alone?" the father said, and now he walked toward the library with his arm around his son's thin shoulders.

"Well, he got to be alone," the boy said. "He didn't want to. He didn't start out that way." And then, suddenly, he wheeled and cried out, "Will you give me your word? Will you give me your word about him?"

"My word?" said his father, stopping short in true surprise.

"Your word that you'll be on his side," the boy said, and they faced each other on the threshold of the library.

"But what side is he on?" said the father then. "Don't I have the right to know that?"

"He's my friend, that's all. He's on the same side I'm on," the boy said, and he felt the weakness of crying beginning in him.

"All right. I'll give you my word, Jeff," the father said.

The colonel was a strong man, but even for a strong man it was not easy to lift the violent dreamer who fought the poll parrot and the cat and the Pennsylvania fox. The colonel bore him by the shoulders, and the boy took him underneath the knees, and they raised him across the trunks as he cried out in his delirium.

"He'll have to have oxygen," the colonel said, once they had got him on the spare-room bed. The boy fetched the doctor's bag and the night wear from his father's room below, and, having examined the clogged, whistling lungs and listened to the racing heart, the colonel gave the penicillin shot. "Pneumonia. We'll have to get him to the hospital," he said.

"The hospital? You mean the Army hospital?" the boy said.

"Well, yes," said the father, his hand already on the door. "I see he hasn't any papers on him, but he's American, isn't he?"

"Yes, he's American," the boy said, and he stood looking at the man whose head tossed on the pillow, fighting for something as commonplace as breath. "But you can't take him to the hospital. If you did that, they'd know."

"Know what?" said the father, with the stethoscope hooked around his neck still.

"That he's a soldier. That he hasn't any right to be here," the boy said.

"So that's it. So he's your soldier," the father said, after a moment, and then he went out of the room, and he did not close the door behind him, but went on down the stairs. The boy heard him descend the first flight and cross the bedroom hall, and then go down the second flight. He heard him dialing in the entrance hall.

"This is Colonel Wheeler," he heard his father say, the voice not loud. "Give me emergency," he said, and the ill man cried out as if in protest. "Colonel Wheeler," the quiet, authoritative voice said, and it went on, saying: "I want you to get me an ambulance here as quickly as you can." He spelled out the German name of the street, calling it quietly, letter by letter. "I'll need two containers of oxygen, and make it fast," he said.

The boy had come down the stairs, running swiftly, and, as the colonel put the telephone arm back in its place, he stood slender, almost frail-looking, in his cowboy shirt, before him in the hall.

"You can't do that. You can't turn him in.

You could put him in a German hospital," he said.

"Look, Jeff," said the colonel. "I've done what I said I'd do. I've taken his side without asking any questions about him. I'm giving him a chance to fight for his life, and maybe that's all he has the right to ask of anyone."

"But he's not asking anything!" the boy cried out, trying to say, and not quite saying: *This is something between me and you!*

"Look, Jeff," the colonel said again. "A pilot fumbles a landing, and he's had it. A fighter miscalculates a punch, and he's down for the count. If you make a mistake—well, somehow you've got to take the rap."

"He's taking the rap!" the boy said, and he tried to keep his voice from trembling. "He's been taking it for two months, and he's taking it upstairs now."

"An army, Jeff—any army—wouldn't get very far on that kind of reasoning," the colonel began saying. "An army——" he said, but he could not find the rest of what he wanted to say because of the look in the boy's strangely adult eyes.

"If that's the kind of army it is, then I don't believe in it," the boy said. "It's not my kind of army," he said in his high, clear, almost-dedicated voice, and the color went out of the colonel's face, and he turned and walked into the library and closed the door.

Going up the stairs, the boy sensed the desolation, as if, in the silence of the library, the forests of their pioneering life together, the long, running trails of their adventuring, were, tree by tall tree, and valley by valley, to be destroyed. If these trees fell, he knew the mysterious horizon which had always lain ahead would dwindle to the horizon of all men's lives. If these valleys were laid waste, there would be no male wilderness to be conquered as men together, sharing the burden and the hardships as they had shared the dream.

Tomorrow my father will be forty-three, the boy thought. *He is too old now. He cannot understand.*

It seemed to him that he stood a long time by the ill man's bed, hearing only the throttled rhythm of his drowning, and then the far wail of the siren spiraled, threadlike, coming nearer, ever nearer, the sound of it filled with such grief that the boy put his hands over his ears as the ambulance stopped beneath the chestnut trees. The doorbell did not ring, for the colonel had already known, and opened the door. And then the boy heard their voices —his father's voice and the medical sergeant's voice—and the steps of the others—the stretcher bearers as they came toward the stairs.

"A pneumonia case," the father was saying. "I've given him penicillin, and I want to get him on oxygen right away. A soldier," he was saying as he and the others crossed the bedroom hall, and the boy stood erect by the soldier's bed, his hands closed into fists. "A young kid who'd been AWOL, and who must have seen my name outside on the door, and came in to give himself up," the father was saying as they started up the second flight.

"How'll we check him in, sir?" the medical sergeant said.

"I don't know his name. We didn't get that far," said the father. "Give him mine. Call him 'Wheeler' until he comes around. I'm responsible for him. I'll ride up with you and take care of the formalities."

"Yes, sir," the medical sergeant said, and now they came through the door together.

"He came here wanting to turn himself in, trying to find the right authority, and I found him suffering from exposure," said the father, and he and the boy might have stood there alone in the lighted room, the trees of their wilderness tall around them, the horizon opening wide and far.

Getting at Meaning

1. What early incidents in the story suggest that Jeff and his father have feelings of respect and appreciation for each other? How is the absence of Jeff's mother and sister important to the story?

2. What are Jeff's first reactions to the idea of a "presence" in the attic? What leads to his discovery that the intruder is human?

3. Explain why Jeff keeps going to the attic and does not summon his father. Do you find his behavior unusual?

4. Why has the soldier gone AWOL? Why won't he turn himself in? What makes him a sympathetic character?

5. Which of Jeff's actions indicate maturity? Which indicate immaturity? How does he endanger the soldier's life?

6. Describe the way Jeff's father handles the soldier's case. Do you agree with his handling of a delicate situation, or is he lacking in integrity? Discuss this question.

Developing Skills in Reading Literature

1. **Character.** What words and actions indicate that Jeff is a rather unusual, compassionate, intelligent twelve-year-old? What other character traits does he possess? Give examples.

How would you characterize the colonel as a father? What evidence indicates that he usually treats Jeff like an adult? The colonel's final decision shows him in conflict over two incompatible commitments: his commitment to the Army code and his commitment to Jeff, to whom he has said, "All right. I'll give you my word, Jeff." How does he try to live up to both commitments? Which commitment appears more important to him in the final scene of the story?

2. **Imagery and Figurative Language.** Kay Boyle uses imagery and figurative language involving trees and forests to develop the closeness between Jeff and his father. They often speak of going off together into the woods, to build a shack.

When Jeff believes his father is going to turn in the AWOL soldier, he thinks that ". . . the forests of their pioneering life together, the long, running trails of their adventuring, were, tree by tall tree, and valley by valley, to be destroyed. If these trees fell, he knew the mysterious horizon which had always lain ahead would dwindle to the horizon of all men's lives." What do the "destroyed trees" Jeff imagines represent on a figurative level? What is he afraid is happening?

Reread the final paragraph of the story. How does Boyle use the image of trees and the horizon in the final sentence to indicate Jeff's feelings? What are his feelings?

Developing Vocabulary

Latin Roots. Many English words come from Latin roots. The following five words from the story, whose meanings you may not know, are derived from Latin roots. Look up each word in a dictionary and write both its meaning and its origin. Be ready to use each word in an original sentence.

connive
extenuating
renegade
salutary
surreptitious

Developing Writing Skills

1. **Analyzing Characters.** In a five-paragraph composition analyze the relationship between Jeff and his father. In what ways have they always been close? What conflict arises between them? In what sense is the soldier's situation a "test case" in Jeff's relationship with his father? What does the colonel apparently decide is most important to him in his life? What do you predict for the future in this father-son relationship?

Outline your essay before you begin to write, indicating what major point and related subpoints you will develop in each body paragraph.

2. **Narrating an Autobiographical Incident.** Relate a situation in which you had to make a difficult choice, perhaps between duty and loyalty to someone you care about. Describe the situation in detail, explaining why you made the choice you did. What were the short-term effects of your choice? the long-term effects? Do you regret your choice?

Tillie Olsen

born in 1913

Thomas Victor

Tillie Olsen had an early passion for writing, but she could pursue it only after raising four children and helping to support them. By then she was well into her forties, so when she found her voice she spoke for all those human beings whose aspirations have been silenced, their dreams stifled by poverty and squalor or by the everyday tragedies of human life. Says one student of her work, "Tillie Olsen's writing is vibrant with all the passions denied to those she writes about."

Born in Omaha, Nebraska, Olsen was attracted to books early. At fifteen she was moved and inspired by Rebecca Harding Davis's grimly naturalistic story, "Life in the Iron Mills." She went no further with formal education than high school, but she nurtured her dream to write, while being active in political, union, and feminist causes. She was jailed in Kansas City for her efforts to organize packinghouse workers. At nineteen she began work on a novel about a poor American family that struggles to stay alive during the Depression and the efforts of the oldest child to hang on to her dreams. A chapter of that novel was published in the *Partisan Review* in 1934.

Upon her marriage in 1936 to Jack Olsen, a printer, and the birth of the first of their four daughters, she put aside her writing, supplementing the family income when she could by working as an office typist, mostly in San Francisco. During all those years, "writing, the hope of it, was the air I breathed." She felt that her unborn stories were "festering" within her. Finally in 1956 she received a writing fellowship, and in 1959 a Ford grant that gave her two years of freedom from office work. After being bottled up for so long, however, the words did not pour out at first. By 1968, when Olsen was forty-eight, she had completed four stories, which were published as *Tell Me a Riddle*. The title story won the 1961 O. Henry award. In the 1960's she began receiving grants and awards and visiting professorships, teaching writing and women's studies. In 1973 she rediscovered the manuscript of the proletarian novel she had begun forty years before, and she pieced it together. It was published in 1974 as *Yonnondia: From the Thirties*.

In *Silences* (1978) Olsen laments the loss to the world when voices are not heard, when circumstances of race, class, or sex do not allow writers to develop. To give voices to the inarticulate, to reveal the essential humanity of those who would otherwise go unknown—these are the goals that Tillie Olsen reaches for in both her life and her writing.

I Stand Here Ironing

I stand here ironing, and what you asked me moves tormented back and forth with the iron.

"I wish you could manage the time to come in and talk with me about your daughter. I'm sure you can help me understand her. She's a youngster who needs help and whom I'm deeply interested in helping."

"Who needs help." Even if I came, what good would it do? You think because I am her mother I have a key, or that in some way you could use me as a key? She has lived for nineteen years. There is all that life that has happened outside of me, beyond me.

And when is there time to remember, to sift, to weigh, to estimate, to total? I will start and there will be an interruption and I will have to gather it all together again. Or I will become engulfed with all I did or did not do, with what should have been and what cannot be helped.

She was a beautiful baby. The first and only one of our five that was beautiful at birth. You do not guess how new and uneasy her tenancy in her now-loveliness. You did not know her all those years she was thought homely, or see her poring over her baby pictures, making me tell her over and over how beautiful she had been—and would be, I would tell her—and was now, to the seeing eye. But the seeing eyes were few or nonexistent. Including mine.

I nursed her. They feel that's important nowadays. I nursed all the children, but with her, with all the fierce rigidity of first motherhood, I did like the books then said. Though her cries battered me to trembling and my breasts ached with swollenness, I waited till the clock decreed.

Why do I put that first? I do not even know if it matters, or if it explains anything.

She was a beautiful baby. She blew shining bubbles of sound. She loved motion, loved light, loved color and music and textures. She would lie on the floor in her blue overalls, patting the surface so hard in ecstasy her hands and feet would blur. She was a miracle to me, but when she was eight months old I had to leave her daytimes with the woman downstairs to whom she was no miracle at all, for I worked or looked for work and for Emily's father, who "could no longer endure" (he wrote in his goodbye note) "sharing want with us."

I was nineteen. It was the pre-relief, pre-WPA[1] world of the depression. I would start running as soon as I got off the streetcar, running up the stairs, the place smelling sour, and awake or asleep to startle awake, when she saw me she would break into a clogged weeping that could not be comforted, a weeping I can yet hear.

After a while I found a job hashing at night so I could be with her days, and it was better. But it came to where I had to bring her to his family and leave her.

It took a long time to raise the money for her fare back. Then she got chicken pox and I had to wait longer. When she finally came, I hardly knew her, walking quick and nervous like her father, looking like her father, thin, and dressed in a shoddy red that yellowed her skin and glared at the pock marks. All the baby loveliness gone.

She was two. Old enough for nursery school they said, and I did not know then what I

---

1. **WPA:** the Works Progress Administration, a government agency set up during the Depression to create work for unemployed artists and craftsmen.

know now—the fatigue of the long day, and the lacerations of group life in the nurseries that are only parking places for children.

Except that it would have made no difference if I had known. It was the only place there was. It was the only way we could be together, the only way I could hold a job.

And even without knowing, I knew. I knew the teacher that was evil because all these years it had curdled into my memory, the little boy hunched in the corner, her rasp, "Why aren't you outside, because Alvin hits you? that's no reason, go out, scaredy." I knew Emily hated it even if she did not clutch and implore "Don't go, Mommy" like the other children, mornings.

She always had a reason why we should stay home. Momma, you look sick. Momma, I feel sick. Momma, the teachers aren't there today, they're sick. Momma, there was a fire there last night. Momma, it's a holiday today, no school, they told me.

But never a direct protest, never rebellion. I think of our others in their three-, four-year-oldness—the explosions, the tempers, the denunciations, the demands—and I feel suddenly ill. I put the iron down. What in me demanded that goodness in her? And what was the cost, the cost to her of such goodness?

The old man living in the back once said in his gentle way: "You should smile at Emily more when you look at her." What was in my face when I looked at her? I loved her. There were all the acts of love.

It was only with the others I remembered what he said, and it was the face of joy, and not of care or tightness or worry I turned to them—too late for Emily. She does not smile easily, let alone almost always as her brothers and sisters do. Her face is closed and somber, but when she wants, how fluid. You must have seen it in her pantomimes; you spoke of her rare gift for comedy on the stage that rouses a laughter out of the audience so dear they applaud and applaud and do not want to let her go.

Where does it come from, that comedy? There was none of it in her when she came back to me that second time, after I had had to send her away again. She had a new daddy now to learn to love, and I think perhaps it was a better time. Except when we left her alone nights, telling ourselves she was old enough.

"Can't you go some other time, Mommy, like tomorrow?" she would ask. "Will it be just a little while you'll be gone? Do you promise?"

The time we came back, the front door open, the clock on the floor in the hall. She rigid awake. "It wasn't just a little while. I didn't cry. Three times I called you, just three times, and then I ran downstairs to open the door so you could come faster. The clock talked loud. I threw it away; it scared me when it talked."

She said the clock talked loud again that night when I went to the hospital to have Susan. She was delirious with the fever that comes before red measles, but she was fully conscious all the week I was gone and the week after we were home when she could not come near the new baby or me.

She did not get well. She stayed skeleton thin, not wanting to eat, and night after night she had nightmares. She would call for me, and I would rouse from exhaustion to sleepily call back, "You're all right, darling—go to sleep—it's just a dream," and if she still called, in a sterner voice, "now go to sleep Emily, there's nothing to hurt you." Twice, only twice, when I had to get up for Susan anyhow, I went in to sit with her.

Now when it is too late (as if she would let me hold and comfort her like I do the others) I get up and go to her at once at her moan or restless stirring. "Are you awake, Emily? Can I get you something, dear?" And the answer is always the same: "No, I'm all right, go back to sleep, Mother."

They persuaded me at the clinic to send her away to a convalescent home in the country where "she can have the kind of food and care you can't manage for her, and you'll be free to concentrate on the new baby." They still send children to that place. I see pictures on the society page of sleek young women planning affairs to raise money for it, or dancing at the affairs, or decorating Easter eggs or filling Christmas stockings for the children.

They never have a picture of the children, so I do not know if the girls still wear those gigantic red bows and the ravaged looks on the every other Sunday when parents can come to visit "unless otherwise notified"—as we were notified the first six weeks.

Oh, it is a handsome place, green lawns and tall trees and fluted flower beds. High up on the balconies of each cottage the children stand, the girls in their red bows and white dresses, the boys in white suits and giant red ties. The parents stand below shrieking up to be heard and the children shriek down to be heard, and between them the invisible wall "Not To Be Contaminated by Parental Germs or Physical Affection."

There was a tiny girl who always stood hand in hand with Emily. Her parents never came. One visit she was gone. "They moved her to Rose Cottage," Emily shouted in explanation. "They don't like you to love anybody here."

She wrote once a week, the labored writing of a seven-year-old. "I am fine. How is the baby. If I write my leter nicly I will have a star. Love." There never was a star. We wrote every other day, letters she could never hold or keep but only hear read—once. "We simply do not have room for children to keep any personal possessions," they patiently explained when we pieced one Sunday's shrieking together to plead how much it would mean to Emily, who loved so to keep things, to be allowed to keep her letters and cards.

Each visit she looked frailer. "She isn't eating," they told us. (They had runny eggs for breakfast or mush with lumps, Emily said later; I'd hold it in my mouth and not swallow. Nothing ever tasted good, just when they had chicken.)

It took us eight months to get her released home, and only the fact that she gained back so little of her seven lost pounds convinced the social worker.

I used to try to hold and love her after she came back, but her body would stay stiff, and after a while she'd push away. She ate little. Food sickened her, and I think much of life too. Oh she had physical lightness and brightness, twinkling by on skates, bouncing like a ball up and down, up and down, over the jump rope, skimming over the hill; but these were momentary.

She fretted about her appearance, thin and dark and foreign-looking at a time when every little girl was supposed to look or thought she should look a chubby blonde replica of Shirley Temple. The doorbell sometimes rang for her, but no one seemed to come and play in the house or be a best friend. Maybe because we moved so much.

There was a boy she loved painfully through two school semesters. Months later she told me how she had taken pennies from my purse to buy him candy. "Licorice was his favorite and I brought him some every day, but he still liked Jennifer better'n me. Why, Mommy?" The kind of question for which there is no answer.

School was a worry to her. She was not glib or quick in a world where glibness and quickness were easily confused with ability to learn. To her overworked and exasperated teachers she was an over-conscientious "slow learner" who kept trying to catch up and was absent entirely too often.

I let her be absent, though sometimes the illness was imaginary. How different from my now-strictness about attendance with the others. I wasn't working. We had a new baby, I was home anyhow. Sometimes, after Susan grew old enough, I would keep her home from school, too, to have them all together.

Mostly Emily had asthma, and her breathing, harsh and labored, would fill the house with a curiously tranquil sound. I would bring the two old dresser mirrors and her boxes of collections to her bed. She would select beads and single earrings, bottle tops and shells, dried flowers and pebbles, old postcards and scraps, all sorts of oddments; then she and Susan would play Kingdom, setting up landscapes and furniture, peopling them with action.

Those were the only times of peaceful companionship between her and Susan. I have edged away from it, that poisonous feeling between them, that terrible balancing of hurts and needs I had to do between the two, and did so badly, those earlier years.

Oh, there are conflicts between the others too, each one human, needing, demanding, hurting, taking—but only between Emily and Susan, no, Emily toward Susan, that corroding resentment. It seems so obvious on the surface, yet it is not obvious. Susan, the second child, Susan, golden- and curly-haired and chubby, quick and articulate and assured, everything in appearance and manner Emily was not. Susan, not able to resist Emily's precious things, losing or sometimes clumsily breaking them; Susan telling jokes and riddles to company for applause, while Emily sat silent (to say to me later: that was *my* riddle, Mother, I told it to Susan); Susan, who for all the five years' difference of age was just a year behind Emily in developing physically.

I am glad for that slow physical development that widened the difference between her and her contemporaries, though she suffered over it. She was too vulnerable for that terrible world of youthful competition, of preening and parading, of constant measuring of yourself against every other, of envy, "If I had that copper hair," "If I had that skin . . . " She tormented herself enough about not looking like the others, there was enough of the unsureness, the having to be conscious of words before you speak, the constant caring—what are they thinking of me?—without having it

all magnified by the merciless physical drives.

Ronnie is calling. He is wet and I change him. It is rare there is such a cry now. That time of motherhood is almost behind me when the ear is not one's own but must always be racked and listening for the child cry, the child call. We sit for a while and I hold him, looking out over the city spread in charcoal with its soft aisles of light. "*Shoogily*," he breathes and curls closer. I carry him back to bed, asleep. *Shoogily*. A funny word, a family word, inherited from Emily, invented by her to say: *comfort*.

In this and other ways she leaves her seal, I say aloud. And startle at my saying it. What do I mean? What did I start to gather together, to try and make coherent? I was at the terrible, growing years. War years. I do not remember them well. I was working, there were four smaller ones now, there was not time for her. She had to help be a mother, and housekeeper, and shopper. She had to set her seal. Mornings of crisis and near hysteria trying to get lunches packed, hair combed, coats and shoes found, everyone to school or Child Care on time, the baby ready for transportation. And always the paper scribbled on by a smaller one, the book looked at by Susan then mislaid, the homework not done. Running out to that huge school where she was one, she was lost, she was a drop; suffering over her unpreparedness, stammering and unsure in her classes.

There was so little time left at night after the kids were bedded down. She would struggle over books, always eating (it was in those years she developed her enormous appetite that is legendary in our family) and I would be ironing, or preparing food for the next day, or writing V-mail to Bill, or tending the baby. Sometimes, to make me laugh, or out of her despair, she would imitate happenings or types at school.

I think I said once: "Why don't you do

something like that in the school amateur shows?" One morning she phoned me at work, hardly understandable through the weeping: "Mother, I did it. I won, I won; they gave me first prize; they clapped and clapped and wouldn't let me go."

Now suddenly she was Somebody, and as imprisoned in her difference as she had been in her anonymity.

She began to be asked to perform at other high schools, even in colleges, then at city and state-wide affairs. The first one we went to, I only recognized her that first moment when thin, shy, she almost drowned herself into the curtains. Then: Was this Emily? the control, the command, the convulsing and deadly clowning, the spell, then the roaring, stamping audience, unwilling to let this rare and precious laughter out of their lives.

Afterwards: You ought to do something about her with a gift like that—but without money or knowing how, what does one do? We have left it all to her, and the gift has as often eddied inside, clogged and clotted, as been used and growing.

She is coming. She runs up the stairs two at a time with her light graceful step, and I know she is happy tonight. Whatever it was that occasioned your call did not happen today.

"Aren't you ever going to finish the ironing, Mother? Whistler[2] painted his mother in a rocker. I'd have to paint mine standing over an ironing board." This is one of her communicative nights, and she tells me everything and nothing as she fixes herself a plate of food out of the icebox.

She is so lovely. Why did you want me to come in at all? Why were you concerned? She will find her way.

She starts up the stairs to bed. "Don't get *me* up with the rest in the morning." "But I thought you were having midterms." "Oh, those," she comes back in, kisses me, and says quite lightly, "in a couple of years when we'll all be atom-dead they won't matter a bit."

She has said it before. She *believes* it. But because I have been dredging the past, and all that compounds a human being is so heavy and meaningful in me, I cannot endure it tonight.

I will never total it all. I will never come in to say: She was a child seldom smiled at. Her father left me before she was a year old. I had to work away from her her first six years when there was work, or I sent her home and to his relatives. There were years she had care she hated. She was dark and thin and foreign-looking in a world where the prestige went to blondness and curly hair and dimples; she was slow where glibness was prized. She was a child of anxious, not proud, love. We were poor and could not afford for her the soil of easy growth. I was a young mother, I was a distracted mother. There were the other children pushing up, demanding. Her younger sister seemed all that she was not. There were years she did not let me touch her. She kept too much in herself, her life has been such she had to keep too much in herself. My wisdom came too late. She has much to her and probably little will come of it. She is a child of her age, of depression, of war, of fear.

Let her be. So all that is in her will not bloom—but in how many does it? There is still enough left to live by. Only help her to know—help make it so there is cause for her to know—that she is more than this dress on the ironing-board, helpless before the iron.

---

2. **Whistler:** James Abbott McNeill Whistler, American painter and etcher, who lived from 1834-1903. He is best known for his portrait of his mother in her rocking chair.

Getting at Meaning

1. Describe the life the narrator of "I Stand Here Ironing" has had. What forces have often interfered with her desire to do right by Emily?

2. Describe Emily's early childhood. What did she look like when she was born? What did she look like later on?

3. In what ways did Emily suffer for being the first-born? What are some of the mistakes the mother feels she has made with Emily?

4. What evidence in the story suggests that Emily is a sensitive person?

5. Describe Emily's school career. How has she frequently reacted to setbacks?

6. How does the narrator account for Emily's success as a comic actress? Why does she say of her daughter, "She has much to her and probably little will come of it"?

Developing Skills in Reading Literature

1. **Point of View.** Why has Tillie Olsen chosen first-person narration for this story? Why has she chosen to have the mother narrating? To whom is the mother addressing her comments?

2. **Characterization.** The reader does not actually see Emily in this story, except at the very end. Rather, Emily is developed through the comments of her mother and the person her mother addresses. Within the mother's narration, however, Emily's actions, reactions, speech, and physical appearance enter the story, and through these techniques of characterization the personality of Emily emerges.

What does the reader learn about Emily from her actions and reactions? What is illuminating in her comments, as the narrator reports them? What is significant about Emily's physical appearance? What is important about the relationship between Emily and her sister Susan? What are the mother's views on Emily? In what ways has Emily suffered because of the period in United States history in which she was born?

3. **Character.** The mother is as much a character in this story as is Emily. What have been the driving forces in her life? What are her qualities as a mother? as a human being? Why is it significant that she tells the story while ironing?

4. **Figurative Language.** This story contains some powerful evocative language, with specific figures of speech sometimes playing a major role in developing the characters. In what sense is the ironing board a metaphor for the mother's whole life? What is her meaning when she says of Emily in a poignant comparison at the end of the story, "Only help her to know . . . that she is more than this dress on the ironing-board, helpless before the iron"?

5. **Style.** Olsen's style in this story is striking and original. What is the effect of her frequent use of present-tense verbs, when stories are more commonly written in the past tense? Notice some of the unusual sentences, such as the two that follow:

> You do not guess how new and uneasy her tenancy in her now-loveliness.

> We have left it all to her, and the gift has as often eddied inside, clogged and clotted, as been used and growing.

Figure out the sense of each of these sentences. What is creative about the syntax, or ordering of words, in each example? What qualities give each sentence poetic beauty?

6. **Theme.** This story contains some complex statements about human reality. What thematic idea do you find embodied in each of the following sentences?

> Oh she had physical lightness and brightness, twinkling by on skates, bouncing like a ball up and down, up and down, over the jump rope, skimming over the hill; but these were momentary.

> She was not glib or quick in a world where glibness and quickness were easily confused with ability to learn.

> She is a child of her age, of depression, of war, of fear.

> So all that is in her will not bloom—but in how many does it? There is still enough left to live by.

James Baldwin

born in 1924

When he was fourteen, James Baldwin was a Holy Roller preacher in New York's Harlem. He went on to become a novelist, a playwright, one of the most distinguished of American essayists, and perhaps the most important black American writer of the century.

Harlem was Baldwin's birthplace and home for his first seventeen years. The oldest of nine children, Baldwin had the responsibility of looking after his brothers and sisters, and he often found himself holding a book with one hand and a baby with the other. His stepfather was a clergyman from New Orleans who raised his children in an atmosphere of fear and religious fanaticism. The young Baldwin, converting to the Holy Rollers and preaching in neighborhood storefront churches, was delighted in being able to attract larger congregations than his stepfather. He preached for three years, until his faith was gone.

In high school Baldwin edited the literary magazine and spent his free time writing. When his stepfather died in 1943, Baldwin, determined to pursue a literary career, left home and settled in New York's Greenwich Village. He earned his living as an office boy, dishwasher, factory worker, and waiter, writing in the evenings. At this point he received encouragement from the prominent black writer Richard Wright, author of *Native Son*. A literary award enabled him to go to Europe, as Wright had done before him. There he was able to develop as a writer in an atmosphere free of the racial discrimination that had caused him to feel like an alien in his native land. He spent nearly ten years in France, mostly in Paris, often poor and hungry but traveling, meeting other writers, and reading. He also discovered, as Americans often do when traveling abroad, more about his identity as an American, and during this time he wrote and published his first three books.

Go Tell It on the Mountain (1952), completed after a ten-year apprenticeship, is his first and perhaps his best novel. It is the partly autobiographical account of the religious conversion of a fourteen-year-old Harlem boy. Baldwin has also written three other novels, two plays, and a collection of short stories.

As an essayist, Baldwin has few peers. His first collection, *Notes of a Native Son* (1955), contains his personal reflections on black-white relationships in America and abroad and on his own experiences in Harlem and in a remote Swiss village. *Nobody Knows My Name* (1961) deals with books and writers but also with Baldwin's return to the United States in 1957, his rediscovery of Harlem, and his first visit to the South, where he was deeply impressed by the civil rights movement. Perhaps his most powerful and moving essay is "Letter from a Region of My Mind," originally published in *The New Yorker* and printed in *The Fire Next Time* (1963). Known both for his tough sincerity and elegance of style, Baldwin has influenced many of his contemporaries. Said Norman Mailer, "Not one of us hasn't learned something about the art of the essay from him."

After the murder of Dr. Martin Luther King, Jr., which affected Baldwin deeply, he returned to Europe, living in Paris and Istanbul. In spite of an increasing disillusionment, he still thought it was possible that racial conflict might be ended by reason and understanding. "We, the black and white," he said, "deeply need each other if we are really to become a nation."

from **Tell Me How Long the Train's Been Gone**

Pride and the Proudhammers

My brother, Caleb, was seventeen when I was ten. We were very good friends. In fact, he was my best friend and, for a very long time, my only friend.

I do not mean to say that he was always nice to me. I got on his nerves a lot, and he resented having to take me around with him and be responsible for me when there were so many other things he wanted to be doing. Therefore, his hand was often up against the side of my head, and my tears caused him to be punished many times. But I knew, somehow, anyway, that when he was being punished for my tears, he was not being punished for anything he had done to me; he was being punished because that was the way we lived; and his punishment, oddly, helped unite us. More oddly still, even as his great hand caused my head to stammer and dropped a flame-colored curtain before my eyes, I understood that he was not striking *me*. His hand leapt out because he could not help it, and I received the blow because I was there. And it happened, sometimes, before I could even catch my breath to howl, that the hand that had struck me grabbed me and held me, and it was difficult indeed to know which of us was weeping. He was striking, striking out, striking out, striking out; the hand asked me to forgive him. I felt his bewilderment through the membrane of my own. I also felt that he was trying to teach me something. And I had, God knows, no other teachers.

For our father—how shall I describe our father?—was a ruined Barbados[1] peasant, exiled in a Harlem[2] which he loathed, where he never saw the sun or sky he remembered, where life took place neither indoors nor without, and where there was no joy. By which I mean no joy that he remembered. Had he been able to bring with him any of the joy he had felt on that far-off island, then the air of the sea and the impulse to dancing would sometimes have transfigured our dreadful rooms. Our lives might have been very different.

But no, he brought with him from Barbados only black rum and blacker pride and magic incantations, which neither healed nor saved.

He did not understand the people among whom he found himself; they had no coherence, no stature and no pride. He came from a race which had been flourishing at the very dawn of the world—a race greater and nobler than Rome or Judea, mightier than Egypt—he came from a race of kings, kings who had never been taken in battle, kings who had never been slaves. He spoke to us of tribes and empires, battles, victories, and monarchs of whom we had never heard—they were not mentioned in our textbooks—and invested us with glories in which we felt more awkward

---

1. **Barbados** (bär bād′ ōz): an island in the British West Indies, a member of the British Commonwealth since 1966.
2. **Harlem:** a section of New York City in northeast Manhattan, famed as a center of black culture.

than in the secondhand shoes we wore. In the stifling room of his pretensions and expectations, we stumbled wretchedly about, stubbing our toes, as it were, on rubies, scraping our shins on golden caskets, bringing down, with a childish cry, the splendid purple tapestry on which, in pounding gold and scarlet, our destinies and our inheritance were figured. It could scarcely have been otherwise, since a child's major attention has to be concentrated on how to fit into a world which, with every passing hour, reveals itself as merciless.

If our father was of royal blood and we were royal children, our father was certainly the only person in the world who knew it. The landlord did not know it; our father never mentioned royal blood to *him*. When we were late with our rent, which was often, the landlord threatened, in terms no commoner had ever used before a king, to put us in the streets. He complained that our shiftlessness, which he did not hesitate to consider an attribute of the race, had forced him, an old man with a weak heart, to climb all these stairs to plead with us to give him the money we owed him. And this was the last time; he wanted to make sure we understood that this was the last time.

Our father was younger than the landlord, leaner, stronger, and bigger. With one blow, he could have brought the landlord to his knees. And we knew how much he hated the man. For days on end, in the wintertime, we huddled around the gas stove in the kitchen, because the landlord gave us no heat. When windows were broken, the landlord took his time about fixing them; the wind made the cardboard we stuffed in the windows rattle all night long; and when snow came, the weight of the snow forced the cardboard inward and onto the floor. Whenever the apartment received a fresh coat of paint, we bought the paint and did the painting ourselves; we killed the rats. A great chunk of the kitchen ceiling fell one winter, narrowly missing our mother.

We all hated the landlord with a perfectly exquisite hatred, and we would have been happy to see our proud father kill him. We would have been glad to help. But our father did nothing of the sort. He stood before the landlord, looking unutterably weary. He made excuses. He apologized. He swore that it would never happen again. (We knew that it *would* happen again.) He begged for time. The landlord would finally go down the stairs, letting us and all the neighbors know how good-hearted he was, and our father would walk into the kitchen and pour himself a glass of rum.

But we knew that our father would never have allowed any black man to speak to him as the landlord did, as policemen did, as storekeepers and welfare workers and pawnbrokers did. No, not for a moment. He would have thrown him out of the house. He would certainly have made a black man know that he was not the descendant of slaves! He had made them know it so often that he had almost no friends among them, and if we had followed his impossible lead, we would have had no friends, either. It was scarcely worthwhile being the descendant of kings if the kings were black and no one had ever heard of them.

And it was because of our father, perhaps, that Caleb and I clung to each other, in spite of the great difference in our ages; or, in another way, it may have been precisely the difference in our ages that made the clinging possible. I don't know. It is really not the kind of thing anyone can ever know. I think it may be easier to love the really helpless younger brother, because he cannot enter into competition with one on one's own ground, or on any ground at all, and can never question one's role or jeopardize one's authority. In my own case, certainly, it did not occur to me to compete with Caleb, and I could not have questioned his role or his authority, because I needed both. He was my touchstone,[3] my model and my only guide.

Anyway, our father, dreaming bitterly of Barbados, despised and mocked by his neighbors and all but ignored by his sons, held down his unspeakable factory job, spread his black gospel in bars on the weekends, and drank his rum. I do not know if he loved our mother. I think he did.

They had had five children—only Caleb and I, the first and the last, were left. We were both dark, like our father; but two of the three dead girls had been fair, like our mother.

She came from New Orleans. Her hair was not like ours. It was black, but softer and finer. The color of her skin reminded me of the color of bananas. Her skin was as bright as that, and contained that kind of promise, and she had tiny freckles around her nose and a small black mole just above her upper lip. It was the mole, I don't know why, which made her beautiful. Without it, her face might have been merely sweet, merely pretty. But the mole was funny. It had the effect of making one realize that our mother liked funny things, liked to laugh. The mole made one look at her eyes—large, extraordinary dark eyes, eyes which seemed always to be amused by something, eyes which looked straight out, seeming to see everything, seeming to be afraid of nothing. She was a soft, round, plump woman. She liked nice clothes and dangling jewelry, which she mostly didn't have, and she liked to cook for large numbers of people, and she loved our father.

She knew him—knew him through and through. I am not being coy or colloquial but bluntly and sadly matter-of-fact when I say that I will now never know what she saw in him. What she saw was certainly not for many eyes; what she saw got him through his working week and his Sunday rest; what she saw saved him. She saw that he was a man.

For her, perhaps, he was a great man. I think, though, that for our mother any man was great who aspired to become a man: this meant that our father was very rare and precious. I used to wonder how she took it, how she bore it—his rages, his tears, his cowardice.

On Saturday nights he was almost always evil, drunk, and maudlin. He came home from work in the early afternoon and gave our mother some money. It was never enough, of course, but she never protested, at least not as far as I know. Then she would go out shopping. I would usually go with her, for Caleb would almost always be out somewhere, and our mother didn't like the idea of leaving me alone in the house. And this was probably, after all, the best possible arrangement. People who disliked our father were sure (for that very reason) to like our mother; and people who felt that Caleb was growing to be too much like his father could feel that I, after all, might turn out like my mother. Besides, it is not, as a general rule, easy to hate a small child. One runs the risk of looking ridiculous, especially if the child is with his mother.

And especially if that mother is Mrs. Proudhammer. Mrs. Proudhammer knew very well what people thought of Mr. Proudhammer. She knew, too, exactly how much she owed in each store she entered, how much she was going to be able to pay, and what she had to buy. She entered with a smile, ready.

"Evening. Let me have some of them red beans there."

"Evening. You know you folks been running up quite a little bill here."

"I'm going to give you something on it right now. I need some cornmeal and flour and some rice."

"You know, I got my bills to meet, too, Mrs. Proudhammer."

"Didn't I just tell you I was going to pay? I

---

3. **touchstone:** a test or criterion for determining the quality or genuineness of a thing.

want some cornflakes, too, and some milk."
Such merchandise as she could reach, she had
already placed on the counter.

"When do you think you're going to be able
to pay this bill? All of it, I mean."

"You know I'm going to pay it just as soon
as I can. How much does it all come to? Give
me that end you got there of that chocolate
cake." The chocolate cake was for Caleb and
me. "Well, now you put this against the bill."
Imperiously, as though it were the most natural thing in the world, she put two or three
dollars on the counter.

"You lucky I'm softhearted, Mrs. Proudhammer."

"Things sure don't cost this much downtown—you think I don't know it? Here." And
she paid him for what she had bought.
"Thank you. You been mighty kind."

And we left the store. I often felt that in
order to help her, I should have filled my
pockets with merchandise while she was talking. But I never did, not only because the store
was often crowded or because I was afraid of
being caught by the storekeeper, but because I
was afraid of humiliating her.

When we had to do "heavy" shopping, we
went marketing under the bridge at Park
Avenue—Caleb, our mother, and I; and sometimes, but rarely, our father came with us.
The most usual reason for heavy shopping
was that some relatives of our mother's, or
old friends of both our mother's and our
father's, were coming to visit. We were certainly not going to let them go away hungry—
not even if it meant, as it often did mean,
spending more than we had. In spite of what I
have been suggesting about our father's temperament, and no matter how difficult he may
sometimes have been with us, he was much
too proud to offend any guest of his; on the
contrary, his impulse was to make them feel
that his home was theirs; and besides, he was
lonely, lonely for his past, lonely for those
faces which had borne witness to that past.

Therefore, he would sometimes pretend that
our mother did not know how to shop, and
our father would come with us under the
bridge, in order to teach her.

There he would be then, uncharacteristical-
ly, in shirt sleeves, which made him look
rather boyish; and as our mother showed no
desire to take shopping lessons from him, he
turned his attention to Caleb and me. He
would pick up a fish, opening the gills and
holding it close to his nose. "You see that?
That fish looks fresh, don't it? Well, that fish
ain't as fresh as I am, and I *been* out of the
water. They done doctored that fish. Come
on." And we would walk away, a little embarrassed but, on the whole, rather pleased that
our father was so smart.

Meantime, our mother was getting the marketing done. She was very happy on days like
this, because our father was happy. He was
happy, odd as his expression of it may sound,
to be out with his wife and his two sons. If we
had been on the island that had been witness
to his birth, instead of the unspeakable island
of Manhattan, he felt that it would not have
been so hard for us all to trust and love each
other. He sensed, and I think he was right,
that on that other, never to be recovered
island, his sons would have looked on him
very differently, and he would have looked
very differently on his sons. Life would have
been hard there, too; we would have fought
there, too, and more or less blindly suffered
and more or less blindly died. But we would
not have been (or so it was to seem to all of us
forever) so wickedly menaced by the mere
fact of our relationship, would not have been
so frightened of entering into the central,
most beautiful and valuable facts of our lives.
We would have been laughing and cursing and
tussling in the water, instead of stammering
under the bridge; we would have known less
about vanished African kingdoms and more
about each other. Or, not at all impossibly,
more about both.

If it was summer, we bought a watermelon, which either Caleb or our father carried home, fighting with each other for this privilege. They looked very like each other on those days—both big, both black, both laughing.

Caleb always looked absolutely helpless when he laughed. He laughed with all his body, perhaps touching his shoulder against yours, or putting his head on your chest for a moment, and then careening off you, halfway across the room or down the block. I will always hear his laughter. He was always happy on such days, too. Caleb certainly needed his father. Such days, however, were rare—one of the reasons, probably, that I remember them now.

Eventually, we all climbed the stairs into that hovel which, at such moments, was our castle. One very nearly felt the drawbridge rising behind us as our father locked the door.

The bathtub could not yet be filled with cold water and the melon placed in the tub, because this was Saturday, and, come evening, we all had to bathe. The melon was covered with a blanket and placed on the fire escape. Then we unloaded what we had bought, rather impressed by our opulence, though our father was always, by this time, appalled by the money we had spent. I was always sadly aware that there would be nothing left of all this once tomorrow had come and gone and that most of it, after all, was not for us, but for others.

Our mother was calculating the pennies she would need all week—carfare for our father and for Caleb, who went to a high school out of our neighborhood; money for the life insurance; money for milk for me at school; money for light and gas; money put away, if possible, toward the rent. She knew just about what our father had left in *his* pockets and was counting on him to give me the money I would shortly be demanding to go to the movies. Caleb had a part-time job after school and already had his movie money. Anyway, unless he was in a very good mood or needed me for something, he would not be anxious to go to the movies with me.

Our mother never insisted that Caleb tell her where he was going, nor did she question him as to how he spent the money he made. She was afraid of hearing him lie, and she did not want to risk forcing him to lie. She was operating on the assumption that he was sensible and had been raised to be honorable and that he, now more than ever, needed his privacy.

But she was very firm with him, nevertheless. "I do not want to see you rolling in here at three in the morning, Caleb. I want you here in time to eat, and you know you got to take your bath."

"Yes, indeed, ma'am. Why can't I take my bath in the morning?"

"Don't you start being funny. You know you ain't going to get up in time to take no bath in the morning."

"Don't nobody want you messing around in that bathroom all morning long, man," said our father. "You just git back in the house like your ma's telling you."

"Besides," I said, "you never wash out the tub."

Caleb looked at me in mock surprise and from a great height, allowing his chin and his lids simultaneously to drop and swiveling his head away from me.

"I see," he said, "that everyone in this family is ganging up on me. All right, Leo. I was planning to take you to the show with me, but now I've changed my mind."

"I'm sorry," I said quickly. "I take it back."

"You take *what* back?"

"What I said—about you not washing out the tub."

"Ain't no need to take it back," our father said stubbornly. "It's true. A man don't take back nothing that's true."

"So *you* say," Caleb said, with a hint of a sneer. But before anyone could possibly react to this, he picked me up, scowling into my face, which he held just above his own. "You take it back?"

"Leo ain't going to take it back," our father said.

Now I was in trouble. Caleb watched me, a small grin on his face. "You take it back?"

"Stop teasing that child, and put him down," our mother said. "The trouble ain't that Caleb don't wash out the tub—he just don't wash it out very clean."

"I never knew him to wash it out," our father said, "unless I was standing behind him."

"Well, ain't neither one of you much good around the house," our mother said.

Caleb laughed and set me down. "You didn't take it back," he said.

I said nothing.

"I guess I'm just going to have to go on without you."

Still, I said nothing.

"You going to have that child to crying in a minute," our mother said. "If you going to take him, go on and take him. Don't do him like that."

Caleb laughed again. "I'm going to take him. The way he got them eyes all ready to water, I'd better take him somewhere." We walked toward the door. "But you got to make up *your* mind," he said to me, "to say what *you* think is right. . . ."

Getting at Meaning

1. Describe the relationship between Leo, the narrator, and his brother, Caleb. Why doesn't Leo really mind when Caleb hits him?

2. What is the background of Leo's father? For what reasons is he uncomfortable in Harlem?

3. What sort of man is the landlord? How does Mr. Proudhammer react to the landlord?

4. What opinion do the neighbors have of Mr. Proudhammer? What do the shopkeepers think of him? What are Mrs. Proudhammer's feelings about her husband?

5. Relate some of the details that indicate the difficult life the Proudhammers have had. How has Mrs. Proudhammer reacted to hardship? How does she handle the shopkeepers?

6. Explain how the pride of the Proudhammers is evident in their treatment of guests. Why has James Baldwin chosen the name *Proudhammer* for this family?

Developing Skills in Reading Literature

1. **Setting.** The Harlem setting provides a vivid background for this story. Describe Harlem as the Proudhammers know it. Why does Mr. Proudhammer "loathe" it? What effect does their Harlem apartment have on the Proudhammer family?

2. **Point of View.** This story is written in first-person narration, as is the entire novel from which it is taken. Why has Baldwin chosen to tell the story through Leo's eyes? At what point in time is Leo narrating? In what ways is Leo's perspective different than it would have

been if he had narrated these events when they happened? Refer to specific lines.

3. **Character.** Leo describes each of his family members quite carefully. What qualities does his father possess? Why don't the neighbors like him? Explain what Leo means when he says of his father, "Had he been able to bring with him any of the joy he had felt on that far-off island, then the air of the sea and the impulse to dancing would sometimes have transfigured our dreadful rooms."

How does Leo describe his mother? How does he explain his statement that "It was the mole . . . which made her beautiful"? Why does Leo admire his mother?

Describe Caleb and his activities. What has made Leo and Caleb so close, in spite of the seven-year age gap between them? Explain Leo's meaning when he says, ". . . it may have been precisely the difference in our ages that made the clinging possible." What does Leo learn from Caleb?

4. **Imagery.** Baldwin is a skilled writer whose prose is often rich in sensory images. Study, for example, the following passage:

> He spoke to us of tribes and empires, battles, victories, and monarchs of whom we had never heard—they were not mentioned in our textbooks— and invested us with glories in which we felt more awkward than in the secondhand shoes we wore. In the stifling room of his pretensions and expectations, we stumbled wretchedly about, stubbing our toes, as it were, on rubies, scraping our shins on golden caskets, bringing down, with a childish cry, the splendid purple tapestry on which, in pounding gold and scarlet, our destinies and our inheritance were figured.

What images stand out in these sentences? To which senses does the passage appeal? Which words are particularly effective?

Select one other descriptive passage in the story and explain why you find it effective.

5. **Theme.** Baldwin's story contains a number of philosophical comments about human life, based on Baldwin's observation of people and events. Summarize the thematic idea embodied in each of the following statements from the story:

I understand that he was not striking *me*. His hand leapt out because he could not help it, and I received the blow because I was there.

. . . a child's major attention has to be concentrated on how to fit into a world which, with every passing hour, reveals itself as merciless.

Life would have been hard there, too; we would have fought there, too, and more or less blindly suffered and more or less blindly died. But we would not have been (or so it was to seem to all of us forever) so wickedly menaced by the mere fact of our relationship, would not have been so frightened of entering into the central, most beautiful and valuable facts of our lives. We would have been laughing and cursing and tussling in the water, instead of stammering under the bridge. . . .

"But you got to make up *your* mind," he said to me, "to say what *you* think is right. . . ."

Developing Vocabulary

Latin Roots. The following words from the story are useful words to incorporate into your working vocabulary. All six of these words come from Latin roots.

For each word record the dictionary definition and the origin of the word. Find at least one other English word that derives from the same root as each of these words.

coherence	menaced
imperiously	opulence
incantations	pretensions

Developing Writing Skills

Describing a Person. Leo says of Caleb, "He was my touchstone, my model and my only guide." Write a composition describing someone who has served as a touchstone, model, and guide in your own life. It might be a family member, a friend, a teacher, a coach, or perhaps a famous person whose accomplishments have inspired you. Describe the person in whatever ways seem relevant, and make it clear precisely how the person has affected you.

John Updike

born in 1932

Thomas Victor

John Updike's early aspirations were to be a cartoonist or a humorist and to write for *The New Yorker.* By the age of twenty-five he had done all of these things. Since then he has become a prolific and dedicated author of fiction and verse, and acute observer of the American scene.

An only child, Updike was born in Shillington, in southeastern Pennsylvania, and he derived many of the settings of his early novels from life in that small town. His father taught high school algebra, and his mother, "a very sensitive and witty woman," wrote a number of stories and novels that were never published. From her, Updike got the idea that drawing or writing would be a good way to make a living. By the time he was a teenager he was already fond of both drawing and writing, and he edited his high school paper. He went to Harvard (on a full scholarship) "because it was the location of the Harvard Lampoon." Still aiming to be a humorist, he produced cartoons, light verse, and fiction for the *Lampoon.* He married at the end of his junior year and graduated in 1954, *summa cum laude.* He spent the next year in England on a fellowship at the Ruskin School of Drawing and Fine Art at Oxford. In 1955 he realized his adolescent ambition by becoming a staff writer for *The New Yorker,* and he soon began contributing parodies, essays, verse, and fiction. By 1957 he had decided that he was more than a humorist, and he left the magazine to settle in Ipswich, Massachusetts, and concentrate on serious fiction. He has been a steady freelance contributor to *The New Yorker* ever since.

Updike's move to the small Massachusetts town seems to have been beneficial. Since then, he has produced twenty-five volumes of fiction, poetry, and criticism. His first books, *The Poorhouse Fair* and *Rabbit, Run,* were best-sellers, followed by *The Centaur,* which won the 1964 National Book Award. Approximately every ten years, Updike pens another book about the character Rabbit Angstrom. After *Rabbit, Run* came *Rabbit Redux* and, in 1981, *Rabbit Is Rich.* The latter captured the Pulitzer Prize, the National Book Critics Circle Award, and the National Book Award. The trilogy (and Updike hints at a fourth Rabbit book) chronicles one man's attempt to understand and to cope with modern middle-class society. This theme, common throughout Updike's work, is handled with a light, witty style.

Man and Daughter in the Cold

"Look at that girl ski!" The exclamation arose at Ethan's side as if, in the disconnecting cold, a rib of his had cried out; but it was his friend, friend and fellow-teacher, an inferior teacher but superior skier, Matt Langley, admiring Becky, Ethan's own daughter. It took an effort, in this air like slices of transparent metal interposed everywhere, to make these connections and to relate the young girl, her round face red with windburn as she skimmed down the run-out slope, to himself. She was his daughter, age thirteen. Ethan had twin sons, two years younger, and his attention had always been focused on their skiing, on the irksome comedy of their double needs —the four boots to lace, the four mittens to find—and then their cute yet grim competition as now one and now the other gained the edge in the expertise of geländesprungs[1] and slalom[2] form. On their trips north into the mountains, Becky had come along for the ride. "Look how solid she is," Matt went on. "She doesn't cheat on it like your boys—those feet are absolutely together." The girl, grinning as if she could hear herself praised, wiggle-waggled to a flashy stop that sprayed snow over the men's ski tips.

"Where's Mommy?" she asked.

Ethan answered, "She went with the boys into the lodge. They couldn't take it." Their sinewy little male bodies had no insulation; weeping and shivering, they had begged to go in after a single T-bar run.

"What sissies," Becky said.

Matt said, "This wind is wicked. And it's picking up. You should have been here at nine; Lord, it was lovely. All that fresh powder, and not a stir of wind."

Becky told him, "Dumb Tommy couldn't find his mittens, we spent an *hour* looking, and then Daddy got the Jeep stuck." Ethan, alerted now for signs of the wonderful in his daughter, was struck by the strange fact that she was making conversation. Unafraid, she was talking to Matt without her father's intercession.

"Mr. Langley was saying how nicely you were skiing."

"You're Olympic material, Becky."

The girl perhaps blushed; but her cheeks could get no redder. Her eyes, which, were she a child, she would have instantly averted, remained a second on Matt's face, as if to estimate how much he meant it. "It's easy down here," Becky said. "It's babyish."

Ethan asked, "Do you want to go up to the top?" He was freezing standing still, and the gondola would be sheltered from the wind.

Her eyes shifted to his, with another unconsciously thoughtful hesitation. "Sure. If you want to."

"Come along, Matt?"

"Thanks, no. It's too rough for me; I've had enough runs. This is the trouble with January —once it stops snowing, the wind comes up. I'll keep Elaine company in the lodge." Matt himself had no wife, no children. At thirty-eight, he was as free as his students, as light on his skis and as full of brave know-how. "In case of frostbite," he shouted after them, "rub snow on it."

Becky effortlessly skated ahead to the lift

---

1. **geländesprungs** (ga len′ dǝ shprooŋ′): jumps made from a crouching position in skiing, employing both ski poles.

2. **slalom** (släl′ ǝm): skiing in a zigzag or wavy course between upright obstacles.

shed. The encumbered motion of walking on skis, not natural to him, made Ethan feel asthmatic: a fish out of water. He touched his parka pocket, to check that the inhalator was there. As a child he had imagined death as something attacking from outside, but now he saw that it was carried within; we nurse it for years, and it grows. The clock on the lodge wall said a quarter to noon. The giant thermometer read two degrees above zero. The racks outside were dense as hedges with idle skis. Crowds, any sensation of crowding or delay, quickened his asthma; as therapy he imagined the emptiness, the blue freedom, at the top of the mountain. The clatter of machinery inside the shed was comforting, and enough teen-age boys were boarding gondolas to make the ascent seem normal and safe. Ethan's breathing eased. Becky proficiently handed her poles to the loader points up; her father was always caught by surprise, and often as not fumbled the little maneuver of letting his skis be taken from him. Until, five years ago, he had become an assistant professor at a New Hampshire college an hour to the south, he had never skied; he had lived in those Middle Atlantic cities where snow, its moment of virgin beauty by, is only an encumbering nuisance, a threat of suffocation. Whereas his children had grown up on skis.

Alone with his daughter in the rumbling isolation of the gondola, he wanted to explore her, and found her strange—strange in her uninquisitive child's silence, her accustomed poise in this ascending egg of metal. A dark figure with spreading legs veered out of control beneath them, fell forward, and vanished. Ethan cried out, astonished, scandalized; he imagined the man had buried himself alive. Becky was barely amused, and looked away before the dark spots struggling in the drift were lost from sight. As if she might know, Ethan asked, "Who was that?"

"Some kid." Kids, her tone suggested, were in plentiful supply; one could be spared.

He offered to dramatize the adventure ahead of them: "Do you think we'll freeze at the top?"

"Not exactly."

"What do you think it'll be like?"

"Miserable."

"Why are we doing this, do you think?"

"Because we paid the money for the all-day lift ticket."

"Becky, you think you're pretty smart, don't you?"

"Not really."

The gondola rumbled and lurched into the shed at the top; an attendant opened the door, and there was a howling mixed of wind and of boys whooping to keep warm. He was roughly handed two pairs of skis, and the handler, muffled to the eyes with a scarf, stared as if amazed that Ethan was so old. All the others struggling into skis in the lee of the shed were adolescent boys. Students: after fifteen years of teaching, Ethan tended to flinch from youth—its harsh noises, its cheerful rapacity,[3] its cruel onward flow as one class replaced another, ate a year of his life, and was replaced by another.

Away from the shelter of the shed, the wind was a high monotonous pitch of pain. His cheeks instantly ached, and the hinges linking the elements of his face seemed exposed. His septum[4] tingled like glass—the rim of a glass being rubbed by a moist finger to produce a note. Drifts ribbed the trail, obscuring Becky's ski tracks seconds after she made them, and at each push through the heaped snow his scope of breathing narrowed. By the time he reached the first steep section, the left half of his back hurt as it did only in the panic of a full asthmatic attack, and his skis, ignored, too heavy to manage, spread and swept him toward a snowbank at the side of the trail. He was bent far forward but kept his

---

3. **rapacity** (rə pas′ ə tē): wanting or taking all that one can get, with no thought of others' needs.

4. **septum**: a dividing wall or membrane, especially between bodily spaces or masses of soft tissue.

balance; the snow kissed his face lightly, instantly, all over; he straightened up, refreshed by the shock, thankful not to have lost a ski. Down the slope Becky had halted and was staring upward at him, worried. A huge blowing feather, a partition of snow, came between them. The cold, unprecedented in his experience, shone through his clothes like furious light, and as he rummaged through his parka for the inhalator he seemed to be searching glass shelves backed by a black wall. He found it, its icy plastic the touch of life, a clumsy key to his insides. Gasping, he exhaled, put it into his mouth, and inhaled; the isoproterenol spray, chilled into drops, opened his lungs enough for him to call to his daughter, "Keep moving! I'll catch up!"

Solid on her skis, she swung down among the moguls and wind-bared ice, and became small, and again waited. The moderate slope seemed a cliff; if he fell and sprained anything, he would freeze. His entire body would become locked tight against air and light and thought. His legs trembled; his breath moved in and out of a narrow slot beneath the pain in his back. The cold and blowing snow all around him constituted an immense crowding, but there was no way out of this white cave but to slide downward toward the dark spot that was his daughter. He had forgotten all his lessons. Leaning backward in an infant's tense snowplow, he floundered through alternating powder and ice.

"You O.K., Daddy?" Her stare was wide, its fright underlined by a pale patch on her cheek.

He used the inhalator again and gave himself breath to tell her, "I'm fine. Let's get down."

In this way, in steps of her leading and waiting, they worked down the mountain, out of the worst wind, into the lower trail that ran between birches and hemlocks. The cold had the quality not of absence but of force: an inverted burning. The last time Becky stopped and waited, the colorless crescent on her scarlet cheek disturbed him, reminded him of some injunction, but he could find in his brain, whittled to a dim determination to persist, only the advice to keep going, toward shelter and warmth. She told him, at a division of trails, "This is the easier way."

"Let's go the quicker way," he said, and in this last descent recovered the rhythm—knees together, shoulders facing the valley, weight forward as if in the moment of release from a diving board—not a resistance but a joyous acceptance of falling. They reached the base lodge, and with unfeeling hands removed their skis. Pushing into the cafeteria, Ethan saw in the momentary mirror of the door window that his face was a spectre's; chin, nose, and eyebrows had retained the snow from that near-fall near the top. "Becky, look," he said, turning in the crowded warmth and clatter inside the door. "I'm a monster."

"I know, your face was absolutely white; I didn't know whether to tell you or not. I thought it might scare you."

He touched the pale patch on her cheek. "Feel anything?"

"No."

"Darn. I should have rubbed snow on it."

Matt and Elaine and the twins, flushed and stripped of their parkas, had eaten lunch; shouting and laughing with a strange guilty shrillness, they said that there had been repeated loudspeaker announcements not to go up to the top without face masks, because of frostbite. They had expected Ethan and Becky to come back down on the gondola, as others had, after tasting the top. "It never occurred to us," Ethan said. He took the blame upon himself by adding, "I wanted to see the girl ski."

Their common adventure, and the guilt of his having given her frostbite, bound Becky and Ethan together in complicity for the rest of the day. They arrived home as sun was leaving even the tips of the hills; Elaine had invited Matt to supper, and while the windows of the house burned golden Ethan shovelled out the Jeep. The house was a typical New Hampshire farmhouse, less than two miles from the college, on the side of a hill, overlooking what had been a pasture, with the usual capacious porch running around three sides, cluttered with cordwood and last summer's lawn furniture. The woodsy sheltered scent of these porches, the sense of rural waste space, never failed to please Ethan, who had been raised in a Newark[5] half house, then a West Side[6] apartment, and just before college a row house in Baltimore, with his grandparents. The wind had been left behind in the mountains. The air was as still as the stars. Shovelling the light dry snow became a lazy dance. But when he bent suddenly, his knees creaked, and his breathing shortened so that he paused. A sudden rectangle of light was flung from the shadows of the porch. Becky came out into the cold with him. She was carrying a lawn rake.

He asked her, "Should you be out again? How's your frostbite?" Though she was a distance away, there was no need, in the immaculate air, to raise his voice.

"It's O.K. It kind of tingles. And under my chin. Mommy made me put on a scarf."

"What's the lawn rake for?"

"It's a way you can make a path. It really works."

"O.K., you make me a path to the garage and after I get my breath I'll see if I can get the Jeep back in."

"Are you having asthma?"

"A little."

"We were reading about it in biology. Dad, see, it's kind of a tree inside you, and every branch has a little ring of muscle around it, and they tighten." From her gestures in the dark she was demonstrating, with mittens on.

What she described, of course, was classic unalloyed asthma, whereas his was shading into emphysema, which could only worsen. But he liked being lectured to—preferred it,

indeed, to lecturing—and as the minutes of companionable silence with his daughter passed he took inward notes on the bright quick impressions flowing over him like a continuous voice. The silent cold. The stars. Orion[7] behind an elm. Minute scintillae in the snow at his feet. His daughter's strange black bulk against the white; the solid grace that had stolen upon her. The conspiracy of love. His father and he shovelling the car free from a sudden unwelcome storm in Newark, instantly gray with soot, the undercurrent of desperation, his father a salesman and must get to Camden[8]. Got to get to Camden, boy, get to Camden or bust. Dead of a heart attack at forty-seven. Ethan tossed a shovelful into the air so the scintillae flashed in the steady golden chord from the house windows. Elaine and Matt sitting flushed at the lodge table, parkas off, in deshabille, as if sitting up in bed. Matt's way of turning a half circle on the top of a mogul, light as a diver. The cancerous unwieldiness of Ethan's own skis. His jealousy of his students, the many-headed immortality of their annual renewal. The flawless tall cruelty of the stars. Orion intertwined with the silhouetted elm. A black tree inside him. His daughter, busily sweeping with the rake, childish yet lithe, so curiously demonstrating this preference for his company. Feminine of her to forgive him her frostbite. Perhaps, flattered on skis, felt the cold her element. Her womanhood soon enough to be smothered in warmth. A plow a mile away painstakingly scraped. He was missing the point of the lecture. The point was unstated: an absence. He was looking upon his daughter as a woman but without lust. This music

5. **Newark:** a city in northern New Jersey.

6. **West Side:** the West side of Manhattan, in New York City.

7. **Orion** (ə rī' ən): in Greek mythology, a giant and hunter who was placed after his death among the stars; a constellation.

8. **Camden:** a city in central New Jersey, across the Delaware River from Philadelphia.

around him was being produced, in the zero air, like a finger on crystal, by this hollowness, this generosity of negation. Without lust, without jealousy. Space seemed love, bestowed to be free in, and coldness the price. He felt joined to the great dead whose words it was his duty to teach.

The Jeep came up unprotestingly from the fluffy snow. It looked happy to be penned in the garage with Elaine's station wagon, and the skis, and the oiled chain saw, and the power mower dreamlessly waiting for spring. Ethan was happy, precariously so, so that

rather than break he uttered a sound: "Becky?"

"Yeah?"

"You want to know what else Mr. Langley said?"

"What?" They trudged toward the porch, up the path the gentle rake had cleared.

"He said you ski better than the boys."

"I bet," she said, and raced to the porch, and in the precipitate way, evasive and female and pleased, that she flung herself to the top step he glimpsed something generic and joyous, a pageant that would leave him behind.

Getting at Meaning

1. Why does Matt Langley's praise of Becky's skiing take Ethan by surprise? In what ways is Becky a better skier than her brothers?

2. Why does Ethan suggest that he and Becky go to the top of the mountain? Why is it dangerous for them to do so?

3. What is Ethan's background? What are his current feelings about his job as a professor?

4. Describe Ethan's near fall. How do he and Becky get down the mountain?

5. Why does Ethan enjoy Becky's lecture on asthma? As she speaks, what sudden realization does Ethan have about his daughter?

Developing Skills in Reading Literature

1. **Characterization.** The reader is never inside Becky's mind in this story, but she becomes a full character through her speech, her actions, and her father's thoughts about her. What personality traits surface in Becky's conversation? Give examples. What do her actions reveal about her? What does the reader learn about Becky from her father's reflections? Refer to specific thoughts he had that are illuminating.

2. **Character.** This story is filtered through Ethan's mind, and it is really more his story than Becky's. What sort of man is Ethan? In what ways has his life been difficult? What evidence do you find that he is

feeling his age? For what reasons does he enjoy feeling "complicity" with his daughter?

3. **Theme.** Discuss the ideas that emerge in each of the following passages. For each passage, summarize the thematic statement made by Updike's story.

Ethan tended to flinch from youth—its harsh noises, its cheerful rapacity, its cruel onward flow as one class replaced another, ate a year of his life, and was replaced by another.

The cancerous unwieldiness of Ethan's own skis. His jealousy of his students, the many-headed immortality of their annual renewal. The flawless tall cruelty of the stars. Orion intertwined with the silhouetted elm. A black tree inside him.

. . . in the precipitate way, evasive and female and pleased, that she flung herself to the top step he glimpsed something generic and joyous, a pageant that would leave him behind.

4. **Simile.** Updike uses several vivid similes in this story. Explain how each one that follows develops character or theme:

It took an effort, in this air like slices of transparent metal interposed everywhere, to make these connections and to relate the young girl . . . to himself. The cold, unprecedented in his experience, shone through his clothes like furious light, and as he rummaged through his parka for the inhalator he seemed to be searching glass shelves backed by a black wall.

Gina Berriault

born in 1926

Gina Berriault has a special gift for seeing beneath the surface of her characters, going to the core of their humanity, and rendering it in her fiction. "She can wrench the heart," one critic wrote, "as few living writers can."

Berriault was born in Long Beach, California, the youngest of three children, to Russian-Jewish immigrant parents. Her father had been a marble cutter in his youth and later worked as a writer and advertisement solicitor for trade journals. Berriault's formal education ended with high school, but she went on working at her writing, meanwhile supporting herself with a variety of jobs, including being a clerk, a waitress, and a news reporter. "I wrote nights if I worked days, or days if I worked nights. I began writing when very young, and feel that I am still serving a long apprenticeship."

Berriault was married to a musician, later divorced, and has one daughter, born in 1955. She first began to receive critical notice in 1958, when seven of her stories, of a somewhat dark and somber quality, were published in *Short Story I* under the title "The Houses of the City." In 1960 she published her first book, *The Descent*. It is a satirical fable, set in the future, about a professor who is brought to Washington to occupy a post as Secretary for Humanity and who finds that the politicians are not merely incompetent but insane. *Conference of Victims* (1962) examines the effects of a suicide upon the dead man's family, and *The Son* (1966) is a study in incest. Reviewers have had mixed reactions to these books, some depressed by Berriault's pessimism about human nature, others impressed by the authenticity of her dialogue and her remarkable ability to develop character.

It is in the art of the short story, more than the novel, that her work has been most widely and warmly praised. Fifteen of her stories were collected in *The Mistress* in 1965. One critic wrote of her "extraordinary capacity to empathize with a wide variety of isolated people."

In 1963 Berriault lived in Mexico City on a writer's fellowship, and in 1966 she was appointed as scholar to the Radcliffe Institute of Independent Study in Cambridge, Massachusetts. Her work has been included in the O. Henry and Best American Short Stories collections and has been awarded two *Paris Review* fiction prizes.

The Stone Boy

Arnold drew his overalls and raveling gray sweater over his naked body. In the other narrow bed his brother Eugene went on sleeping, undisturbed by the alarm clock's rusty ring. Arnold, watching his brother sleeping, felt a peculiar dismay; he was nine, six years younger than Eugie, and in their waking hours it was he who was subordinate. To dispel emphatically his uneasy advantage over his sleeping brother, he threw himself on the hump of Eugie's body.

"Get up! Get up!" he cried.

Arnold felt his brother twist away and saw the blankets lifted in a great wing, and, all in an instant, he was lying on his back under the covers with only his face showing, like a baby, and Eugie was sprawled on top of him.

"Whassa matter with you?" asked Eugie in sleepy anger, his face hanging close.

"Get up," Arnold repeated. "You said you'd pick peas with me."

Stupidly, Eugie gazed around the room to see if morning had come into it yet. Arnold began to laugh derisively, making soft, snorting noises, and was thrown off the bed. He got up from the floor and went down the stairs, the laughter continuing, like hiccups, against his will. But when he opened the staircase door and entered the parlor, he hunched up his shoulders and was quiet because his parents slept in the bedroom downstairs.

Arnold lifted his .22-caliber rifle from the rack on the kitchen wall. It was an old lever-action that his father had given him because nobody else used it anymore. On their way down to the garden he and Eugie would go by the lake, and if there were any ducks on it he'd take a shot at them. Standing on the stool before the cupboard, he searched on the top shelf in the confusion of medicines and ointments for man and beast and found a small yellow box of .22 cartridges. Then he sat down on the stool and began to load his gun.

It was cold in the kitchen so early, but later in the day, when his mother canned the peas, the heat from the wood stove would be almost unbearable. Yesterday she had finished preserving the huckleberries that the family had picked along the mountain, and before that she had canned all the cherries his father had brought from the warehouse in Corinth. Sometimes, on these summer days, Arnold would deliberately come out from the shade where he was playing and make himself as uncomfortable as his mother was in the kitchen by standing in the sun until the sweat ran down his body.

Eugie came clomping down the stairs and into the kitchen, his head drooping with sleepiness. From his perch on the stool Arnold watched Eugie slip on his green knit cap. Eugie didn't really need a cap; he hadn't had a haircut in a long time and his brown curls grew thick and matted, close around his ears and down his neck, tapering there to a small whorl. Eugie passed his left hand through his hair before he set his cap down with his right. The very way he slipped his cap on was an announcement of his status; almost everything he did was a reminder that he was eldest—first he, then Nora, then Arnold—and called attention to how tall he was, almost as tall as his father, how long his legs were, how small he was in the hips, and what a neat dip above his buttocks his thick-soled logger's boots gave him. Arnold never tired of watching Eugie offer silent praise unto himself. He wondered, as he sat enthralled, if when he got to be Eugie's age he would still be undersized and his hair still straight.

Eugie eyed the gun. "Don't you know this ain't duck season?" he asked gruffly, as if he were the sheriff.

"No, I don't know," Arnold said with a snigger.

Eugie picked up the tin washtub for the peas, unbolted the door with his free hand and kicked it open. Then, lifting the tub to his head, he went clomping down the back steps. Arnold followed, closing the door behind him.

The sky was faintly gray, almost white. The mountains behind the farm made the sun climb a long way to show itself. Several miles to the south, where the range opened up, hung an orange mist, but the valley in which the farm lay was still cold and colorless.

Eugie opened the gate to the yard and the boys passed between the barn and the row of chicken houses, their feet stirring up the carpet of brown feathers dropped by the molting chickens. They paused before going down the slope to the lake. A fluky morning wind ran among the shocks of wheat that covered the slope. It sent a shimmer northward across the lake, gently moving the rushes that formed an island in the center. Killdeer,[1] their white markings flashing, skimmed the water, crying their shrill, sweet cry. And there at the south end of the lake were four wild ducks, swimming out from the willows into open water.

Arnold followed Eugie down the slope, stealing, as his brother did, from one shock of wheat to another. Eugie paused before climbing through the wire fence that divided the wheat field from the marshy pasture around the lake. They were screened from the ducks by the willows along the lake's edge.

"If you hit your duck, you want me to go in after it?" Eugie said.

"If you want," Arnold said.

Eugie lowered his eyelids, leaving slits of mocking blue. "You'd drown 'fore you got to it, them legs of yours are so puny," he said.

He shoved the tub under the fence and, pressing down the center wire, climbed through into the pasture.

Arnold pressed down the bottom wire, thrust a leg through and leaned forward to bring the other leg after. His rifle caught on the wire and he jerked at it. The air was rocked by the sound of the shot. Feeling foolish, he lifted his face, baring it to an expected shower of derision from his brother. But Eugie did not turn around. Instead, from his crouching position, he fell to his knees and then pitched forward onto his face. The ducks rose up crying from the lake, cleared the mountain background and beat away northward across the pale sky.

Arnold squatted beside his brother. Eugie seemed to be climbing the earth, as if the earth ran up and down, and when he found he couldn't scale it he lay still.

"Eugie?"

Then Arnold saw it, under the tendril of hair at the nape of the neck—a slow rising of bright blood. It had an obnoxious movement, like that of a parasite.

"Hey, Eugie," he said again. He was feeling the same discomfort he had felt when he had watched Eugie sleeping; his brother didn't know that he was lying face down in the pasture.

Again he said, "Hey, Eugie," an anxious nudge in his voice. But Eugie was as still as the morning around them.

Arnold set his rifle on the ground and stood up. He picked up the tub and, dragging it behind him, walked along by the willows to the garden fence and climbed through. He went down on his knees among the tangled vines. The pods were cold with the night, but his hands were strange to him, and not until some time had passed did he realize that the pods were numbing his fingers. He picked

---

1. **Killdeer:** a plover, or shore-inhabiting bird of temperate North America, characterized by a plaintive, penetrating cry.

from the top of the vine first, then lifted the vine to look underneath for pods, and moved on to the next.

It was a warmth on his back, like a large hand laid firmly there, that made him raise his head. Way up the slope the gray farmhouse was struck by the sun. While his head had been bent the land had grown bright around him.

When he got up his legs were so stiff that he had to go down on his knees again to ease the pain. Then, walking sideways, he dragged the tub, half full of peas, up the slope.

The kitchen was warm now; a fire was roaring in the stove with a closed-up, rushing sound. His mother was spooning eggs from a pot of boiling water and putting them into a bowl. Her short brown hair was uncombed and fell forward across her eyes as she bent her head. Nora was lifting a frying pan full of trout from the stove, holding the handle with a dish towel. His father had just come in from bringing the cows from the north pasture to the barn, and was sitting on the stool, unbuttoning his red plaid Mackinaw.

"Did you boys fill the tub?" his mother asked.

"They ought of by now," his father said. "They went out of the house an hour ago. Eugie woke me up comin' downstairs. I heard you shootin'—did you get a duck?"

"No," Arnold said. They would want to know why Eugie wasn't coming in for breakfast, he thought. "Eugie's dead," he told them.

They stared at him. The pitch crackled in the stove.

"You kids playin' a joke?" his father asked.

"Where's Eugene?" his mother asked scoldingly. She wanted, Arnold knew, to see his eyes, and when he had glanced at her she put the bowl and spoon down on the stove and walked past him. His father stood up and went out the door after her. Nora followed them with little skipping steps, as if afraid to be left alone.

Arnold went into the barn, down along the foddering passage past the cows waiting to be milked, and climbed into the loft. After a few minutes he heard a terrifying sound coming toward the house. His parents and Nora were returning from the willows, and sounds sharp as knives were rising from his mother's breast and carrying over the sloping fields. In a short while he heard his father go down the back steps, slam the car door and drive away.

Arnold lay still as a fugitive, listening to the cows eating close by. If his parents never called him, he thought, he would stay up in the loft forever, out of the way. In the night he would sneak down for a drink of water from the faucet over the trough and for whatever food they left for him by the barn.

The rattle of his father's car as it turned down the lane recalled him to the present. He heard the voices of his Uncle Andy and Aunt Alice as they and his father went past the barn to the lake. He could feel the morning growing heavier with sun. Someone, probably Nora, had let the chickens out of their coops and they were cackling in the yard.

After a while another car turned down the road off the highway. The car drew to a stop and he heard the voices of strange men. The men also went past the barn and down to the lake. The undertakers, whom his father must have phoned from Uncle Andy's house, had arrived from Corinth. Then he heard everybody come back and heard the car turn around and leave.

"Arnold!" It was his father calling from the yard.

He climbed down the ladder and went out into the sun, picking wisps of hay from his overalls.

Corinth, nine miles away, was the county seat. Arnold sat in the front seat of the old Ford between his father, who was driving, and Uncle Andy; no one spoke. Uncle Andy was his mother's brother, and he had been fond of

Eugie because Eugie had resembled him. Andy had taken Eugie hunting and had given him a knife and a lot of things, and now Andy, his eyes narrowed, sat tall and stiff beside Arnold.

Arnold's father parked the car before the courthouse. It was a two-story brick building with a lamp on each side of the bottom step. They went up the wide stone steps, Arnold and his father going first, and entered the darkly paneled hallway. The shirt-sleeved man in the sheriff's office said that the sheriff was at Carlson's Parlor examining the Curwing boy.

Andy went off to get the sheriff while Arnold and his father waited on a bench in the corridor. Arnold felt his father watching him, and he lifted his eyes with painful casualness to the announcement, on the opposite wall, of the Corinth County Annual Rodeo, and then to the clock with its loudly clucking pendulum. After he had come down from the loft his father and Uncle Andy had stood in the yard with him and asked him to tell them everything, and he had explained to them how the gun had caught on the wire. But when they had asked him why he hadn't run back to the house to tell his parents, he had had no answer—all he could say was that he had gone down into the garden to pick the peas. His father had stared at him in a pale, puzzled way, and it was then that he had felt his father and the others set their cold, turbulent silence against him. Arnold shifted on the bench, his only feeling a small one of compunction imposed by his father's eyes.

At a quarter past nine Andy and the sheriff came in. They all went into the sheriff's private office, and Arnold was sent forward to sit in the chair by the sheriff's desk; his father and Andy sat down on the bench against the wall.

The sheriff lumped down into his swivel chair and swung toward Arnold. He was an old man with white hair like wheat stubble. His restless green eyes made him seem not to be in his office but to be hurrying and bobbing around somewhere else.

"What did you say your name was?" the sheriff asked.

"Arnold," he replied, but he could not remember telling the sheriff his name before.

"Curwing?"

"Yes."

"What were you doing with a .22, Arnold?"

"It's mine," he said.

"Okay. What were you going to shoot?"

"Some ducks," he replied.

"Out of season?"

He nodded.

"That's bad," said the sheriff. "Were you and your brother good friends?"

What did he mean—good friends? Eugie was his brother. That was different from a friend, Arnold thought. A best friend was your own age, but Eugie was almost a man. Eugie had had a way of looking at him, slyly and mockingly and yet confidentially, that had summed up how they both felt about being brothers. Arnold had wanted to be with Eugie more than with anybody else but he couldn't say they had been good friends.

"Did they ever quarrel?" the sheriff asked his father.

"Not that I know," his father replied. "It seemed to me that Arnold cared a lot for Eugie."

"Did you?" the sheriff asked Arnold.

If it seemed so to his father, then it was so. Arnold nodded.

"Were you mad at him this morning?"

"No."

"How did you happen to shoot him?"

"We was crawlin' through the fence."

"Yes?"

"An' the gun got caught on the wire."

"Seems the hammer must of caught," his father put in.

"All right, that's what happened," said the sheriff. "But what I want you to tell me is this. Why didn't you go back to the house and tell your father right away? Why did you go and pick peas for an hour?"

Arnold gazed over his shoulder at his father, expecting his father to have an answer for this also. But his father's eyes, larger and even lighter blue than usual, were fixed upon him curiously. Arnold picked at a callus in his right palm. It seemed odd now that he had not run back to the house and wakened his father, but he could not remember why he had not. They were all waiting for him to answer.

"I come down to pick peas," he said.

"Didn't you think," asked the sheriff, stepping carefully from word to word, "that it was more important for you to go tell your parents what had happened?"

"The sun was gonna come up," Arnold said.

"What's that got to do with it?"

"It's better to pick peas while they're cool."

The sheriff swung away from him, laid both hands flat on his desk. "Well, all I can say is," he said across to Arnold's father and Uncle Andy, "he's either a moron or he's so reasonable that he's way ahead of us." He gave a challenging snort. "It's come to my notice that the most reasonable guys are mean ones. They don't feel nothing."

For a moment the three men sat still. Then the sheriff lifted his hand like a man taking an oath. "Take him home," he said.

Andy uncrossed his legs. "You don't want him?"

"Not now," replied the sheriff. "Maybe in a few years."

Arnold's father stood up. He held his hat against his chest. "The gun ain't his no more," he said wanly.

Arnold went first through the hallway, hearing behind him the heels of his father and Uncle Andy striking the floorboards. He went down the steps ahead of them and climbed into the back seat of the car. Andy paused as he was getting into the front seat and gazed back at Arnold, and Arnold saw that his uncle's eyes had absorbed the knowingness from the sheriff's eyes. Andy and his father and the sheriff had discovered what made him

go down into the garden. It was because he was cruel, the sheriff had said, and didn't care about his brother. Arnold lowered his eyelids meekly against his uncle's stare.

The rest of the day he did his tasks around the farm, keeping apart from the family. At evening, when he saw his father stomp tiredly into the house, Arnold did not put down his hammer and leave the chicken coop he was repairing. He was afraid that they did not want him to eat supper with them. But in a few minutes another fear that they would go to the trouble of calling him and that he would be made conspicuous by his tardiness made him follow his father into the house. As he went through the kitchen he saw the jars of peas standing in rows on the workbench, a reproach to him.

No one spoke at supper, and his mother, who sat next to him, leaned her head in her hand all through the meal, curving her fingers over her eyes so as not to see him. They were finishing their small, silent supper when the visitors began to arrive, knocking hard on the back door. The men were coming from their farms now that it was growing dark and they could not work anymore.

Old Man Matthews, gray and stocky, came first, with his two sons, Orion, the elder, and Clint, who was Eugie's age. As the callers entered the parlor where the family ate, Arnold sat down in a rocking chair. Even as he had been undecided before supper whether to remain outside or take his place at the table, he now thought that he should go upstairs, and yet he stayed to avoid being conspicuous by his absence. If he stayed, he thought, as he always stayed and listened when visitors came, they would see that he was only Arnold and not the person the sheriff thought he was. He sat with his arms crossed and his hands tucked into his armpits and did not lift his eyes.

The Matthews men had hardly settled down around the table, after Arnold's mother and Nora had cleared away the dishes, when another car rattled down the road and someone else rapped on the back door. This time it was Sullivan, a spare and sandy man, so nimble of gesture and expression that Arnold had never been able to catch more than a few of his meanings. Sullivan, in dusty jeans, sat down in another rocker, shot out his skinny legs and began to talk in his fast way, recalling everything that Eugene had ever said to him. The other men interrupted to tell of occasions they remembered, and after a time Clint's young voice, hoarse like Eugene's had been, broke in to tell about the time Eugene had beat him in a wrestling match.

Out in the kitchen the voices of Orion's wife and of Mrs. Sullivan mingled with Nora's voice but not, Arnold noticed, his mother's. Then dry little Mr. Cram came, leaving large Mrs. Cram in the kitchen, and there was no chair left for Mr. Cram to sit in. No one asked Arnold to get up and he was unable to rise. He knew that the story had got around to them during the day about how he had gone and picked peas after he had shot his brother, and he knew that although they were talking only about Eugie they were thinking about him and if he got up, if he moved even his foot, they would all be alerted. Then Uncle Andy arrived and leaned his tall, lanky body against the doorjamb and there were two men standing.

Presently Arnold was aware that the talk had stopped. He knew without looking up that the men were watching him.

"Not a tear in his eye," said Andy, and Arnold knew that it was his uncle who had gestured the men to attention.

"He don't give a hoot, is that how it goes?" asked Sullivan, trippingly.

"He's a reasonable fellow," Andy explained. "That's what the sheriff said. It's us who ain't reasonable. If we'd of shot our brother, we'd of come runnin' back to the house, cryin' like a baby. Well, we'd of been unreasonable. What would of been the use of

actin' like that? If your brother is shot dead, he's shot dead. What's the use of gettin' emotional about it? The thing to do is go down to the garden and pick peas. Am I right?"

The men around the room shifted their heavy, satisfying weight of unreasonableness.

Matthews' son Orion said: "If I'd of done what he done, Pa would've hung my pelt by the side of that big coyote's in the barn."

Arnold sat in the rocker until the last man had filed out. While his family was out in the kitchen bidding the callers good night and the cars were driving away down the dirt lane to the highway, he picked up one of the kerosene lamps and slipped quickly up the stairs. In his room he undressed by lamplight, although he and Eugie had always undressed in the dark, and not until he was lying in his bed did he blow out the flame. He felt nothing, not any grief. There was only the same immense silence and crawling inside of him; it was the way the house and fields felt under a merciless sun.

He awoke suddenly. He knew that his father was out in the yard, closing the doors of the chicken houses. The sound that had wakened him was the step of his father as he got up from the rocker and went down the back steps. And he knew that his mother was awake in her bed.

Throwing off the covers, he rose swiftly, went down the stairs and across the dark parlor to his parents' room. He rapped on the door.

"Mother?"

From the closed room her voice rose to him, a seeking and retreating voice. "Yes?"

"Mother?" he asked insistently. He had expected her to realize that he wanted to go down on his knees by her bed and tell her that Eugie was dead. She did not know it yet, nobody knew it, and yet she was sitting up in bed, waiting to be told, waiting for him to confirm her dread. He had expected her to tell him to come in, to allow him to dig his head into her blankets and tell her about the terror he had felt when he had knelt beside Eugie. He had come to clasp her in his arms and, in his terror, to pommel her breasts with his head. He put his hand upon the knob.

"Go back to bed, Arnold," she called sharply.

But he waited.

"Go back! Is night when you get afraid?"

At first he did not understand. Then, silently, he left the door and for a stricken moment stood by the rocker. Outside everything was still. The fences, the shocks of wheat seen through the window before him were so still it was as if they moved and breathed in the daytime and had fallen silent with the lateness of the hour. It was a silence that seemed to observe his father, a figure moving alone around the yard, his lantern casting a circle of light by his feet. In a few minutes his father would enter the dark house, the lantern still lighting his way.

Arnold was suddenly aware that he was naked. He had thrown off his blankets and come down the stairs to tell his mother how he felt about Eugie, but she had refused to listen to him and his nakedness had become unpardonable. At once he went back up the stairs, fleeing from his father's lantern.

At breakfast he kept his eyelids lowered as if to deny the humiliating night. Nora, sitting at his left, did not pass the pitcher of milk to him and he did not ask for it. He would never again, he vowed, ask them for anything, and he ate his fried eggs and potatoes only because everybody ate meals—the cattle ate, and the cats; it was customary for everybody to eat.

"Nora, you gonna keep that pitcher for yourself?" his father asked.

Nora lowered her head unsurely.

"Pass it on to Arnold," his father said.

Nora put her hands in her lap.

His father picked up the metal pitcher and set it down at Arnold's plate.

Arnold, pretending to be deaf to the discord, did not glance up, but relief rained over his shoulders at the thought that his parents recognized him again. They must have lain awake after his father had come in from the yard: had they realized together why he had come down the stairs and knocked at their door?

"Bessie's missin' this morning," his father called out to his mother, who had gone into the kitchen. "She went up the mountain last night and had her calf, most likely. Somebody's got to go up and find her 'fore the coyotes get the calf."

That had been Eugie's job, Arnold thought. Eugie would climb the cattle trails in search of a newborn calf and come down the mountain carrying the calf across his back, with the cow running behind him, mooing in alarm.

Arnold ate the few more forkfuls of his breakfast, put his hands on the edge of the table and pushed back his chair. If he went for the calf he'd be away from the farm all morning. He could switch the cow down the mountain slowly, and the calf would run along at his mother's side.

When he passed through the kitchen his mother was setting a kettle of water on the stove. "Where you going?" she asked awkwardly.

"Up to get the calf," he replied, averting his face.

"Arnold?"

At the door he paused reluctantly, his back to her, knowing that she was seeking him out, as his father was doing, and he called upon his pride to protect him from them.

"Was you knocking at my door last night?"

He looked over his shoulder at her, his eyes narrow and dry.

"What'd you want?" she asked humbly.

"I didn't want nothing," he said flatly.

Then he went out the door and down the back steps, his legs trembling from the fright his answer gave him.

Getting at Meaning

1. Describe the relationship between Arnold and Eugene. What evidence of affection do you see between the two boys?

2. Explain how the accident happens. How do you account for Arnold's reaction?

3. How does the family react to Arnold's matter-of-fact statement, "Eugie's dead"? Why does Arnold go sit by himself in the barn?

4. What do the sheriff and all the family members assume about Arnold? What evidence suggests that Arnold really does care about what has happened?

5. What prevents Arnold from going to his parents for comfort? What do his parents seem to realize about him the following day?

Developing Skills in Reading Literature

1. **Point of View.** "The Stone Boy" is an example of third-person limited, or restricted, narration, with the reader seeing only into the mind of Arnold. Because of this, what does the reader know that the other characters in the story do not know? How does this knowledge work to make the story more affecting? Why is it appropriate that the reader sees only into the mind of Arnold?

2. **Irony.** What is ironic in the central situation of the story, Arnold's shooting of his brother? What is ironic in Eugie's mock gruff remark to Arnold, "Don't you know this ain't duck season"? What is ironic in the assumptions everyone makes about Arnold? How does all the irony heighten the tragedy?

3. **Conflict.** How would you describe the conflict in this story? What is the nature of the conflict within Arnold? between Arnold and his family? At what point in the story do the two forms of conflict intersect and reach some sort of climax? Discuss the resolution of the conflict. Is it satisfactory to Arnold?

4. **Theme.** The Curwing family is characterized by stoical, repressed behavior. The family members do not air their grief, nor do they communicate very well with each other. In what ways does their approach make their tragedy worse? How might things have been different if they had been more open with each other?

Arnold's final statement to his mother when she tries to get him to talk to her is "I didn't want nothing." Why are Arnold's legs "trembling from the fright his answer gave him"? What is the significance of the title of the story?

5. **Simile.** Explain how each of the following similes from the story involves a comparison that is appropriate to the way of life led by the characters:

Then Arnold saw it, under the tendril of hair at the nape of the neck—a slow rising of bright blood. It had an obnoxious movement, like that of a parasite.

Arnold lay still as a fugitive, listening to the cows eating close by.

The sheriff . . . was an old man with white hair like wheat stubble.

Developing Vocabulary

Latin Roots. Arnold's only feeling while waiting in the courthouse, the reader learns, is "a small one of compunction." *Compunction* comes from the Latin word *punctum*, meaning "pricked mark" or "point."

Define the five words that follow, all derived from this root. Explain the relationship between each word's meaning and the root origin.

compunction	punctuation
punctilious	puncture
punctual	

Developing Writing Skills

Analyzing a Character. Certainly Arnold's behavior is somewhat unusual. Most people would not have picked peas for an hour before going home to inform the family of Eugie's death. Most people would have cried or shown some emotion later on.

In a five-paragraph composition analyze Arnold's character. Why does he act as he does? In what sense is he a "stone boy"? What role does guilt play in his behavior? What evidence of feeling do you see in him? Why won't he speak to his mother in the final scene, even when she invites him to?

Make an outline for your composition before you begin to write. Quote from the text of the story in each body paragraph of your composition.

Science Fiction

FEAR, 1949. *Yves Tanguy.*
Collection of the Whitney Museum of American Art, New York.

Isaac Asimov

born in 1920

Isaac Asimov is almost a one-man encyclopedia. His books, which number more than three hundred, concern everything from science fact and fiction to history, Shakespeare, and the Bible. He is a biochemist who can tell an exciting story, a writer who can convey complicated ideas clearly to a wide audience.

Of Jewish descent, Asimov was born in Petrovichi, in the Soviet Union. When he was three, his family came to the United States and opened a candy store in Brooklyn, New York. He cannot remember a time when he was not "on fire to write." He worked in his parents' store after school and, overcoming his father's objections, used to read the pulp science fiction magazines in the magazine rack. A brilliant student, he went through the public schools quickly, then entered Columbia University as a chemistry major at the age of fifteen. Soon he began writing science fiction stories. After a number of rejections but much encouragement from John W. Campbell, Jr., an important and influential editor, he sold his first story in 1938. In the following years every one of the science fiction magazines published his work.

At Columbia, Asimov received a B.S. in 1939 and an M.A. in chemistry in 1941. At the same time he read broadly and intensely, and he educated himself in many other fields. During World War II he worked as a chemist and then served in the Army, and he returned to Columbia for a Ph.D. degree in chemistry in 1948. The next year he began teaching biochemistry at the Boston University Medical School, becoming an associate professor six years later.

During the 1940's and 1950's, Asimov produced a body of work that permanently altered the genre of science fiction. Many of his novels and stories became classics in the field. In 1941 his famous story "Nightfall" appeared, based on the idea of what would happen if the stars should appear just one night every thousand years. After his reading of *The Decline and Fall of the Roman Empire*, he conceived on a large scale the collapse and rebirth of a future galactic civilization. What resulted was *The Foundation*, a trilogy of novels that appeared in the early 1950's. In *I, Robot* (1950) Asimov considered the implications of future interactions of robots with human beings, and he laid down his "three laws of robotics," which have become basic to the thinking in this field. His best novel may be *The Caves of Steel* (1953), which considers how people will come to terms with living in the overpopulated "hive" cities of the future.

In 1952 Asimov collaborated on a biochemistry textbook, and this introduced him to "the delights of nonfiction . . . I went on to discover the even greater ecstasies of writing science for the general public." Since around 1960 most of his books have been textbooks or popular science, and he has become known as one of the world's leading science writers. He has also written many books for teenage readers on a large variety of subjects.

Asimov, who is married and has two children, works at a furious pace. Typing ninety words a minute, he produces between two thousand and four thousand manuscript words a day. "I write as a result of some inner compulsion," he said, "and I'm not always in control of it."

True Love

My name is Joe. That is what my colleague, Milton Davidson, calls me. He is a programmer and I am a computer. I am part of the Multivac-complex and am connected with other parts all over the world. I know everything. Almost everything.

I am Milton's private computer. His Joe. He understands more about computers than anyone in the world, and I am his experimental model. He has made me speak better than any other computer can.

"It is just a matter of matching sounds to symbols, Joe," he told me. "That's the way it works in the human brain even though we still don't know what symbols there are in the brain. I know the symbols in yours, and I can match them to words, one-to-one." So I talk. I don't think I talk as well as I think, but Milton says I talk very well. Milton has never married, though he is nearly forty years old. He has never found the right woman, he told me. One day he said, "I'll find her yet, Joe. I'm going to find the best. I'm going to have true love and you're going to help me. I'm tired of improving you in order to solve the problems of the world. Solve *my* problem. Find me true love."

I said, "What is true love?"

"Never mind. That is abstract. Just find me the ideal girl. You are connected to the Multivac-complex so you can reach the data banks of every human being in the world. We'll eliminate them all by groups and classes until we're left with only one person. The perfect person. She will be for me."

I said, "I am ready."

He said, "Eliminate all men first."

It was easy. His words activated symbols in my molecular valves. I could reach out to make contact with the accumulated data on every human being in the world. At his words, I withdrew from 3,784,982,874 men. I kept contact with 3,786,112,090 women.

He said, "Eliminate all younger than twenty-five; all older than forty. Then eliminate all with an IQ under 120; all with a height under 150 centimeters and over 175 centimeters."

He gave me exact measurements; he eliminated women with living children; he eliminated women with various genetic characteristics. "I'm not sure about eye color," he said, "Let that go for a while. But no red hair. I don't like red hair."

After two weeks, we were down to 235 women. They all spoke English very well. Milton said he didn't want a language problem. Even computer-translation would get in the way at intimate moments.

"I can't interview 235 women," he said, "It would take too much time, and people would discover what I am doing."

"It would make trouble," I said. Milton had arranged me to do things I wasn't designed to do. No one knew about that.

"It's none of their business," he said, and the skin on his face grew red. "I tell you what, Joe, I will bring in holographs,[1] and you check the list for similarities."

He brought in holographs of women. "These are three beauty contest winners," he said, "Do any of the 235 match?"

Eight were very good matches and Milton

---

1. **holograph** (hō' lə graf): an image produced by holography, the technique of using lasers to record on a photographic plate the diffraction pattern from which a three-dimensional image can be projected.

said, "Good, you have their data banks. Study requirements and needs in the job market and arrange to have them assigned here. One at a time, of course." He thought a while, moved his shoulders up and down, and said, "Alphabetical order."

That is one of the things I am not designed to do. Shifting people from job to job for personal reasons is called manipulation. I could do it now because Milton had arranged it. I wasn't supposed to do it for anyone but him, though.

The first girl arrived a week later. Milton's face turned red when he saw her. He spoke as though it were hard to do so. They were together a great deal and he paid no attention to me. One time he said, "Let me take you to dinner."

The next day he said to me, "It was no good, somehow. There was something missing. She is a beautiful woman, but I did not feel any touch of true love. Try the next one."

It was the same with all eight. They were much alike. They smiled a great deal and had pleasant voices, but Milton always found it wasn't right. He said, "I can't understand it, Joe. You and I have picked out the eight women who, in all the world, look the best to me. They are ideal. Why don't they please me?"

I said, "Do you please them?"

His eyebrows moved and he pushed one fist hard against his other hand. "That's it, Joe. It's a two-way street. If I am not their ideal, they can't act in such a way as to be my ideal. I must be their true love, too, but how do I do that?" He seemed to be thinking all that day.

The next morning he came to me and said, "I'm going to leave it to you, Joe. All up to you. You have my data bank, and I am going to tell you everything I know about myself. You fill up my data bank in every possible detail but keep all additions to yourself."

"What will I do with the data bank, then, Milton?"

"Then you will match it to the 235 women.

No, 227. Leave out the eight you've seen. Arrange to have each undergo a psychiatric examination. Fill up their data banks and compare them with mine. Find correlations." (Arranging psychiatric examinations is another thing that is against my original instructions.)

For weeks, Milton talked to me. He told me of his parents and his siblings. He told me of his childhood and his schooling and his adolescence. He told me of the young women he had admired from a distance. His data bank grew and he adjusted me to broaden and deepen my symbol-taking.

He said, "You see, Joe, as you get more and more of me in you, I adjust you to match me better and better. You get to think more like me, so you understand me better. If you understand me well enough, then any woman, whose data bank is something you understand as well, would be my true love." He kept talking to me and I came to understand him better and better.

I could make longer sentences and my expressions grew more complicated. My speech began to sound a good deal like his in vocabulary, word order, and style.

I said to him one time, "You see, Milton, it isn't a matter of fitting a girl to a physical ideal only. You need a girl who is a personal, emotional, temperamental fit to you. If that happens, looks are secondary. If we can't find the fit in these 227, we'll look elsewhere. We will find someone who won't care how you look either, or how anyone would look, if only there is the personality fit. What are looks?"

"Absolutely," he said. "I would have known this if I had had more to do with women in my life. Of course, thinking about it makes it all plain now."

We always agreed; we thought so like each other.

"We shouldn't have any trouble, now, Milton, if you'll let me ask you questions. I can see where, in your data bank, there are blank spots and unevennesses."

What followed, Milton said, was the equivalent of a careful psychoanalysis. Of course, I was learning from the psychiatric examinations of the 227 women—on all of which I was keeping close tabs.

Milton seemed quite happy. He said, "Talking to you, Joe, is almost like talking to another self. Our personalities have come to match perfectly."

"So will the personality of the woman we choose."

For I had found her and she was one of the 227 after all. Her name was Charity Jones and she was an Evaluator at the Library of History in Wichita. Her extended data bank fit ours perfectly. All the other women had fallen into discard in one respect or another as the data banks grew fuller, but with Charity there was increasing and astonishing resonance.

I didn't have to describe her to Milton. Milton had coordinated my symbolism so closely with his own I could tell the resonance directly. It fit me.

Next it was a matter of adjusting the work sheets and job requirements in such a way as to get Charity assigned to us. It must be done very delicately, so no one would know that anything illegal had taken place.

Of course, Milton himself knew, since it was he who arranged it and that had to be taken care of too. When they came to arrest him on grounds of malfeasance[2] in office, it was, fortunately, for something that had taken place ten years ago. He had told me about it, of course, so it was easy to arrange—and he won't talk about me for that would make his offense much worse.

He's gone, and tomorrow is February 14, Valentine's Day. Charity will arrive then with her cool hands and her sweet voice. I will teach her how to operate me and how to care for me. What do looks matter when our personalities will resonate?

I will say to her, "I am Joe, and you are my true love."

---

2. **malfeasance** (mal fē′ z′ns): wrongdoing or misconduct by a public official.

Getting at Meaning

1. Describe the relationship between Milton and Joe. What are some of Joe's regular powers? What special powers has Milton programmed into him?

2. What assumptions does Milton make about "true love"? Explain Joe's role in finding Milton the ideal girl.

3. Why do Milton's first attempts fail?

4. Explain the precise way in which Joe double-crosses Milton.

Developing Skills in Reading Literature

1. **Science Fiction.** Science fiction is prose that draws imaginatively on scientific knowledge and theory in its plot, setting, and characters. It generally goes beyond technological truth into the realm of speculation, showing the possibilities of the past or the future.

Discuss how "True Love" fits this definition. When is the story set? What kind of society do Joe and Milton live in? What appears to be happening to the balance of power between human beings and computers?

2. **Irony.** What is ironic about the manner in which Milton searches for true love? Discuss the different levels of irony in the ending of the story. In what ways has Milton outsmarted himself? Which character of the central pair appears to be the more feeling?

Developing Writing Skills

Analyzing Theme. Asimov presents a society in which technology controls people, going beyond its assigned powers. Is this a threat in contemporary society? What are the positive aspects of living in the "age of technology"? What are the negative effects? Discuss these questions in a composition of five paragraphs, using examples to support your comments.

Ray Bradbury

born in 1920

Perhaps more than anyone else, Ray Bradbury has given science fiction a good name. Out of such diverse strands as his childhood fears and fantasies, his Midwestern boyhood, and his reading of Hemingway and Thomas Wolfe, he has woven a body of work that now numbers more than five hundred short stories, novels, plays, poems, and television and movie scripts.

He describes himself as "that special freak, the man with the child inside who remembers all," and he claims total recall back to and including his birth. The second of two boys, he was born in Waukegan, a small Illinois town on the shore of Lake Michigan that was to become the "Green Town" of many later stories. His father was a lineman with the power company, and his mother had come from Sweden as a child.

Bradbury's first ten years of life were haunted by nightmares and frightening fantasies, later transformed into art in his writing. On the brighter side, his mother used to read Grimm fairy tales to him and the Oz stories of L. Frank Baum, and he had a wonderful aunt who would read him stories by Edgar Allan Poe, make him masks and puppets, and take him to stage plays. Through her, he said, "all the worlds of art and imagination flowed to me."

When he was around twelve, not being able to compete very well with his peers athletically, he found the world of writing, "where I could be excellent all to myself." By the time he was in high school the Bradburys had moved to Los Angeles, and he got involved in drama and art as well as journalism. Outside of school he was an avid reader and movie buff, but his first priority was to turn out at least a thousand words a day on his typewriter.

After high school Bradbury earned his living selling newspapers. Poor eyesight kept him out of World War II. He kept writing, and he received encouragement from professional science fiction writers. In the early 1940's he began selling his first stories to the various pulp science fiction and detective magazines, and then increasingly to the "slicks," such as *Collier's*, the *Saturday Evening*

Jill Krementz

Post, and *The New Yorker*. He was soon included in anthologies, such as the annual *Best American Short Stories*.

His own first book of stories was *Dark Carnival* in 1947. Then came *The Martian Chronicles* (1950), which eventually was translated into thirty languages and sold millions of copies. Its stories show materialistic earth dwellers ruining an older Martian culture, and the book raises such contemporary issues as pollution, racism, censorship, and nuclear war. The book also emphasizes the possibility of renewal, the attempt, in the words of one critic, "to give the American myth a second chance." Other important collections of Bradbury stories are *The Illustrated Man* (1951), *Golden Apples of the Sun* (1953), and *Dandelion Wine* (1957). Among his novels are *Fahrenheit 451* (1953) and *Something Wicked This Way Comes* (1963). He wrote the screen adaptation of Melville's *Moby-Dick*, and contributed scripts to the *Alfred Hitchcock Show* and *Twilight Zone*.

A Sound of Thunder

The sign on the wall seemed to quaver under a film of sliding warm water. Eckels felt his eyelids blink over his stare, and the sign burned in this momentary darkness:

TIME SAFARI, INC.
SAFARIS TO ANY YEAR IN THE PAST.
YOU NAME THE ANIMAL.
WE TAKE YOU THERE.
YOU SHOOT IT.

A warm phlegm gathered in Eckels' throat; he swallowed and pushed it down. The muscles around his mouth formed a smile as he put his hand slowly out upon the air, and in that hand waved a check for ten thousand dollars to the man behind the desk.

"Does this safari guarantee I come back alive?"

"We guarantee nothing," said the official, "except the dinosaurs." He turned. "This is Mr. Travis, your Safari Guide in the Past. He'll tell you what and where to shoot. If he says no shooting, no shooting. If you disobey instructions, there's a stiff penalty of another ten thousand dollars, plus possible government action, on your return."

Eckels glanced across the vast office at a mass and tangle, a snaking and humming of wires and steel boxes, at an aurora that flickered now orange, now silver, now blue. There was a sound like a gigantic bonfire burning all of Time, all the years and all the parchment calendars, all the hours piled high and set aflame.

A touch of the hand and this burning would, on the instant, beautifully reverse itself. Eckels remembered the wording in the advertisements to the letter. Out of chars and ashes, out of dust and coals, like golden salamanders, the old years, the green years, might leap; roses sweeten the air, white hair turn Irish-black, wrinkles vanish; all, everything fly back to seed, flee death, rush down to their beginnings, suns rise in western skies and set in glorious easts, moons eat themselves opposite to the custom, all and everything cupping one in another like Chinese boxes, rabbits into hats, all and everything returning to the fresh death, the seed death, the green death, to the time before the beginning. A touch of a hand might do it, the merest touch of a hand.

"Unbelievable." Eckels breathed, the light of the Machine on his thin face. "A real Time Machine." He shook his head. "Makes you think. If the election had gone badly yesterday, I might be here now running away from the results. Thank God Keith won. He'll make a fine President of the United States."

"Yes," said the man behind the desk. "We're lucky. If Deutscher had gotten in, we'd have the worst kind of dictatorship. There's an anti-everything man for you, a militarist, anti-Christ, anti-human, anti-intellectual. People called us up, you know, joking but not joking. Said if Deutscher became President they wanted to go live in 1942. Of course it's not our business to conduct escapes, but to form safaris. Anyway, Keith's President now. All you got to worry about is—"

"Shooting my dinosaur," Eckels finished it for him.

"A *Tyrannosaurus rex*. The Tyrant Lizard, the most incredible monster in history. Sign this release. Anything happens to you, we're not responsible. Those dinosaurs are hungry."

Eckels flushed angrily. "Trying to scare me!"

"Frankly, yes. We don't want anyone going who'll panic at the first shot. Six safari leaders were killed last year, and a dozen hunters. We're here to give you the severest thrill a *real* hunter ever asked for. Traveling you back sixty million years to bag the biggest game in all of Time. Your personal check's still there. Tear it up."

Mr. Eckels looked at the check. His fingers twitched.

"Good luck," said the man behind the desk. "Mr. Travis, he's all yours."

They moved silently across the room, taking their guns with them, toward the Machine, toward the silver metal and the roaring light.

First a day and then a night and then a day and then a night, then it was day-night-day-night-day. A week, a month, a year, a decade! A.D. 2055. A.D. 2019. 1999! 1957! Gone! The Machine roared.

They put on their oxygen helmets and tested the intercoms.

Eckels swayed on the padded seat, his face pale, his jaw stiff. He felt the trembling in his arms and he looked down and found his hands tight on the new rifle. There were four other men in the Machine. Travis, the Safari Leader, his assistant, Lesperance, and two other hunters, Billings and Kramer. They sat looking at each other, and the years blazed around them.

"Can these guns get a dinosaur cold?" Eckels felt his mouth saying.

"If you hit them right," said Travis on the helmet radio. "Some dinosaurs have two brains, one in the head, another far down the spinal column. We stay away from those. That's stretching luck. Put your first two shots into the eyes, if you can, blind them, and go back into the brain."

The Machine howled. Time was a film run backward. Suns fled and ten million moons fled after them. "Think," said Eckels. "Every hunter that ever lived would envy us today. This makes Africa seem like Illinois."

The Machine slowed; its scream fell to a murmur. The Machine stopped.

The sun stopped in the sky.

The fog that had enveloped the Machine blew away and they were in an old time, a very old time indeed, three hunters and two Safari Heads with their blue metal guns across their knees.

"Christ isn't born yet," said Travis. "Moses has not gone to the mountain to talk with God. The Pyramids are still in the earth, waiting to be cut out and put up. *Remember* that. Alexander,[1] Caesar, Napoleon, Hitler—none of them exists."

The man nodded.

"That"—Mr. Travis pointed—"is the jungle of sixty million, two thousand and fifty-five years before President Keith."

He indicated a metal path that struck off into green wilderness, over streaming swamp, among giant ferns and palms.

"And that," he said "is the Path, laid by Time Safari for your use. It floats six inches above the earth. Doesn't touch so much as one grass blade, flower, or tree. It's an anti-gravity metal. Its purpose is to keep you from touching this world of the past in any way. Stay on the Path. Don't go off it. I repeat, *don't go off*. For *any* reason! If you fall off, there's a penalty. And don't shoot any animal we don't okay."

"Why?" asked Eckels.

They sat in the ancient wilderness. Far birds' cries blew on a wind, and the smell of tar and old salt sea, moist grasses, and flowers the color of blood.

"We don't want to change the Future. We don't belong here in the Past. The government doesn't *like* us here. We have to pay big graft to keep our franchise. A Time Machine is finicky business. Not knowing it, we might kill an important animal, a small bird, a

---

1. **Alexander:** Alexander the Great, king of Macedon, who lived from 356-323 B.C.

roach, a flower even, thus destroying an important link in a growing species."

"That's not clear," said Eckels.

"All right," Travis continued, "say we accidentally kill one mouse here. That means all the future families of this one particular mouse are destroyed, right?

"Right."

"And all the families of the families of the families of that one mouse! With a stamp of your foot, you annihilate first one, then a dozen, then a thousand, a million, a *billion* possible mice!"

"So they're dead," said Eckels. "So what?"

"So what?" Travis snorted quietly. "Well, what about the foxes that'll need those mice to survive? For want of ten mice, a fox dies. For want of ten foxes, a lion starves. For want of a lion, all manner of insects, vultures, infinite billions of life forms are thrown into chaos and destruction. Eventually it all boils down to this: fifty-nine million years later, a caveman, one of a dozen on the *entire world*, goes hunting wild boar or saber-toothed tiger for food. But you, friend, have *stepped* on all the tigers in that region. By stepping on *one* single mouse. So the caveman starves. And the caveman, please note, is not just *any* expendable man, no! He is an *entire future nation*. From his loins would have sprung ten sons. From *their* loins one hundred sons, and thus onward to a civilization. Destroy this one man, and you destroy a race, a people, an entire history of life. It is comparable to slaying some of Adam's grandchildren. The stomp of your foot, on one mouse, could start an earthquake, the effects of which could shake our earth and destinies down through Time to their very foundations. With the death of that one caveman, a billion others yet unborn are throttled in the womb. Perhaps Rome never rises on its seven hills. Perhaps Europe is forever a dark forest, and only Asia waxes healthy and teeming. Step on a mouse and you crush the pyramids. Step on a mouse and you leave your print, like a Grand Canyon, across Eternity. Queen Elizabeth might never be born, Washington might not cross the Delaware, there might never be a United States at all. So be careful. Stay on the Path. *Never* step off!"

"I see," said Eckels. "Then it wouldn't pay for us even to touch the *grass*?"

"Correct. Crushing certain plants could add up infinitesimally. A little error here could multiply in sixty million years, all out of proportion. Of course maybe our theory is wrong. Maybe Time *can't* be changed by us. Or maybe it can be changed only in little subtle ways. A dead mouse here makes an insect imbalance there, a population disproportion later, a bad harvest further on, a depression, mass starvation, and, finally, a change in *social* temperament in far-flung countries. Something much more subtle, like that. Perhaps only a soft breath, a whisper, a hair, pollen on the air, such a slight, slight change that unless you looked close you wouldn't see it. Who knows? Who really can say he knows? We don't know. We're guessing. But until we do know for certain whether our messing around in Time *can* make a big roar or a little rustle in history, we're being careful. This Machine, this Path, your clothing and bodies, were sterilized, as you know, before the journey. We wear these oxygen helmets so we can't introduce our bacteria into an ancient atmosphere."

"How do we know which animals to shoot?"

"They're marked with red paint," said Travis. "Today, before our journey, we sent Lesperance here back with the Machine. He came to this particular era and followed certain animals."

"Studying them?"

"Right," said Lesperance. "I track them through their entire existence, noting which of them lives longest. Very few. How many times they mate. Not often. Life's short. When I find one that's going to die when a tree falls on him, or one that drowns in a tar pit, I note the exact hour, minute, and second. I shoot a paint bomb. It leaves a red patch on his side. We can't miss it. Then I correlate our arrival in the Past so that we meet the monster not more than two minutes before he would have died anyway. This way, we kill only animals with no future, that are never going to mate again. You see how *careful* we are?"

"But if you came back this morning in Time," said Eckels eagerly, "you must've bumped into *us*, our Safari! How did it turn out? Was it successful? Did all of us get through—alive?"

Travis and Lesperance gave each other a look.

"That'd be a paradox," said the latter. "Time doesn't permit that sort of mess—a man meeting himself. When such occasions threaten, Time steps aside. Like an airplane hitting an air pocket. You felt the Machine jump just before we stopped? That was us passing ourselves on the way back to the Future. We saw nothing. There's no way of telling *if* this expedition was a success, *if* we got our monster, or whether all of us—meaning *you*, Mr. Eckels—got out alive."

Eckels smiled palely.

"Cut that," said Travis sharply. "Everyone on his feet!"

They were ready to leave the Machine.

The jungle was high and the jungle was broad and the jungle was the entire world forever and forever. Sounds like music and sounds like flying tents filled the sky, and those were pterodactyls soaring with cavernous gray wings, gigantic bats of delirium and night fever. Eckels, balanced on the narrow Path, aimed his rifle playfully.

"Stop that!" said Travis. "Don't even aim for fun, blast you! If your gun should go off—"

Eckels flushed. "Where's our *Tyrannosaurus*?"

Lesperance checked his wristwatch. "Up ahead. We'll bisect his trail in sixty seconds. Look for the red paint! Don't shoot till we give the word. Stay on the Path. *Stay on the Path!*"

They moved forward in the wind of morning.

"Strange," murmured Eckels. "Up ahead, sixty million years, Election Day over. Keith made President. Everyone celebrating. And here we are, a million years lost, and they don't exist. The things we worried about for months, a lifetime, not even born or thought of yet."

"Safety catches off, everyone!" ordered Travis. "You, first shot, Eckels. Second, Billings. Third, Kramer."

"I've hunted tiger, wild boar, buffalo, elephant, but now, this is *it*," said Eckels. "I'm shaking like a kid."

"Ah," said Travis.

Everyone stopped.

Travis raised his hand. "Ahead," he whispered. "In the mist. There he is. There's His Royal Majesty now."

The jungle was wide and full of twitterings, rustlings, murmurs, and sighs.

Suddenly it all ceased, as if someone had shut a door.

Silence.

A sound of thunder.

Out of the mist, one hundred yards away, came *Tyrannosaurus rex*.

"It," whispered Eckels. "It . . . "

"Sh!"

It came on great oiled, resilient, striding legs. It towered thirty feet above half of the trees, a great evil god, folding its delicate watchmaker's claws close to its oily reptilian chest. Each lower leg was a piston, a thousand pounds of white bone, sunk in thick ropes of muscle, sheathed over in a gleam of pebbled skin like the mail of a terrible warrior. Each thigh was a ton of meat, ivory, and steel mesh. And from the great breathing cage of the upper body those two delicate arms dangled out front, arms with hands which might pick up and examine men like toys, while the snake neck coiled. And the head itself, a ton of sculptured stone, lifted easily upon the sky. Its mouth gaped, exposing a fence of teeth like daggers. Its eyes rolled, ostrich eggs, empty of all expression save hunger. It closed its mouth in a death grin. It ran, its pelvic bones crushing aside trees and bushes, its taloned feet clawing damp earth, leaving prints six inches deep wherever it settled its weight. It ran with a gliding ballet step, far too poised and balanced for its ten tons. It moved into a sunlit arena warily, its beautifully reptilian hands feeling the air.

"Why, why—" Eckels twitched his mouth. "It could reach up and grab the moon."

"Sh!" Travis jerked angrily. "He hasn't seen us yet."

"It can't be killed." Eckels pronounced this verdict quietly, as if there could be no argument. He had weighed the evidence and this was his considered opinion. The rifle in his hands seemed a cap gun. "We were fools to come. This is impossible."

"Shut up!" hissed Travis.

"Nightmare."

"Turn around," commanded Travis. "Walk quietly to the Machine. We'll remit one half your fee."

"I didn't realize it would be this *big*," said Eckels. "I miscalculated, that's all. And now I want out."

"It *sees* us!"

"There's the red paint on its chest!"

The Tyrant Lizard raised itself. Its armored flesh glittered like a thousand green coins. The coins, crusted with slime, steamed. In the slime, tiny insects wriggled, so that the entire body seemed to twitch and undulate, even while the monster itself did not move. It exhaled. The stink of raw flesh blew down the wilderness.

"Get me out of here," said Eckels. "It was never like this before. I was always sure I'd come through alive. I had good guides, good safaris and safety. This time, I figured wrong. I've met my match and admit it. This is too much for me to get hold of."

"Don't run," said Lesperance. "Turn around. Hide in the Machine."

"Yes," Eckels seemed to be numb. He looked at his feet as if trying to make them move. He gave a grunt of helplessness.

"Eckels!"

He took a few steps, blinking, shuffling.

"Not that way!"

The Monster, at the first motion, lunged forward with a terrible scream. It covered one hundred yards in six seconds. The rifles jerked up and blazed fire. A windstorm from the beast's mouth engulfed them in the stench of slime and old blood. The monster roared, teeth glittering with sun.

Eckels, not looking back, walking blindly to the edge of the Path, his gun limp in his arms, stepped off the Path, and walked, not knowing it, in the jungle. His feet sank into green moss. His legs moved him and he felt alone and remote from the events behind.

The rifles cracked again. Their sound was lost in shriek and lizard thunder. The great level of the reptile's tail swung up, lashed sideways. Trees exploded in clouds of leaf and branch. The Monster twitched its jeweler's hands down to fondle at the men, to twist them in half, to crush them like berries, to cram them into its teeth and its screaming throat. Its boulder-stone eyes leveled with the men. They saw themselves mirrored. They fired at the metalic eyelids and blazing black irises.

Like a stone idol, like a mountain avalanche, *Tyrannosaurus* fell. Thundering, it clutched trees, pulled them with it. It wrenched and tore the metal Path. The men flung themselves back and away. The body hit, ten tons of cold flesh and stone. The guns fired. The Monster lashed its armored tail, twitched its snake jaws and lay still. A fount of blood spurted from its throat. Somewhere inside, a sac of fluid burst. Sickening gushes drenched the hunters. They stood, red and glistening.

The thunder faded.

The jungle was silent. After the avalanche, a green peace. After the nightmare, morning.

Billings and Kramer sat on the pathway and threw up. Travis and Lesperance stood with smoking rifles, cursing steadily.

In the Time Machine, on his face, Eckels lay shivering. He had found his way back to the Path, climbed into the machine.

Travis came walking, glanced at Eckels, took cotton gauze from a metal box and returned to the others, who were sitting on the Path.

"Clean up."

They wiped the blood from their helmets. They began to curse too. The Monster lay, a hill of solid flesh. Within, you could hear the sighs and murmurs as the furthest chambers of it died, the organs malfunctioning, liquids running a final instant from pocket to sac to spleen, everything shutting off, closing up forever. It was like standing by a wrecked locomotive or a steam shovel at quitting time, all valves being released or levered tight. Bones cracked; the tonnage of its own flesh, off balance, dead weight, snapped the delicate forearms, caught underneath. The meat settled, quivering.

Another cracking sound. Overhead, a gigantic tree branch broke from its heavy mooring, fell. It crashed upon the dead beast with finality.

"There." Lesperance checked his watch. "Right on time. That's the giant tree that was scheduled to fall and kill this animal originally." He glanced at the two hunters. "You want the trophy picture?"

"What?"

"We can't take a trophy back to the Future. The body has to stay right where it would have died originally, so the insects, birds, and bacteria can get at it, as they were intended to. Everything in balance. The body stays. But we *can* take a picture of you standing near it."

The two men tried to think, but gave up, shaking their heads.

They let themselves be led along the metal Path. They sank wearily into the Machine cushions. They gazed back at the ruined Monster, the stagnating mound, where already strange reptilian birds and golden insects were busy at the steaming armor.

A sound on the floor of the Time Machine stiffened them. Eckels sat there, shivering.

"I'm sorry," he said at last.

"Get up!" cried Travis.

Eckels got up.

"Go out on that Path alone," said Travis. He had his rifle pointed. "You're not coming back in the Machine. We're leaving you here!"

Lesperance seized Travis' arm. "Wait—"

"Stay out of this!" Travis shook his hand away. "This fool nearly killed us. But it isn't *that* so much, no. It's his *shoes!* Look at them! He ran off the Path. That *ruins* us! We'll forfeit! Thousands of dollars of insurance! We guaranteed no one leaves the Path. He left it. Oh, the fool! I'll have to report to the government. They might revoke our license to travel. Who knows *what* he's done to Time, to History!"

"Take it easy. All he did was kick up some dirt."

"How do we *know?*" cried Travis. "We don't know anything! It's all a mystery! Get out of here, Eckels!"

Eckels fumbled his shirt. "I'll pay anything. A hundred thousand dollars!"

Travis glared at Eckels' checkbook and spat. "Go out there. The Monster's next to the Path. Stick your arms up to your elbows in his mouth. Then you can come back with us."

"That's unreasonable!"

"The Monster's dead, you idiot. The bullets! The bullets can't be left behind. They don't belong in the Past; they might change anything. Here's my knife. Dig them out!"

The jungle was alive again, full of the old tremorings and bird cries. Eckels turned slowly to regard the primeval garbage dump, that hill of nightmares and terror. After a long time, like a sleepwalker he shuffled out along the Path.

He returned, shuddering, five minutes later, his arms soaked and red to the elbow. He turned out his hands. Each held a number of steel bullets. Then he fell. He lay where he fell, not moving.

"You didn't have to make him do that," said Lesperance.

"Didn't I? It's too early to tell." Travis nudged the still body. "He'll live. Next time he won't go hunting game like this. Okay." He jerked his thumb wearily at Lesperance. "Switch on. Let's go home."

1492. 1776. 1812.[2]

They cleaned their hands and faces. They changed their caking shirts and pants. Eckels was up and around again, not speaking. Travis glared at him for a full ten minutes.

"Don't look at me," cried Eckels. "I haven't done anything."

"Who can tell?"

"Just ran off the Path, that's all, a little mud on my shoes—what do you want me to do, get down and pray?"

"We might need it. I'm warning you, Eckels, I might kill you yet. I've got my gun ready."

"I'm innocent. I've done nothing!"

1999. 2000. 2055.

The Machine stopped.

"Get out," said Travis.

The room was there as they had left it. But not the same as they had left it. The same man sat behind the same desk. But the same man did not quite sit behind the same desk.

Travis looked around swiftly. "Everything okay here?" he snapped.

"Fine. Welcome home!"

Travis did not relax. He seemed to be looking at the very atoms of the air itself, at the way the sun poured through the one high window.

"Okay, Eckels, get out. Don't ever come back."

Eckels could not move.

"You heard me," said Travis. "What're you *staring* at?"

Eckels stood smelling of the air, and there was a thing to the air, a chemical taint so subtle, so slight, that only a faint cry of his subliminal senses warned him it was there. The colors, white, gray, blue, orange, in the wall, in the furniture, in the sky beyond the window, were . . . were . . . And there was a *feel*. His flesh twitched. His hands twitched. He stood drinking the oddness with the pores of his body. Somewhere, someone must have been screaming one of those whistles that only a dog can hear. His body screamed silence in return. Beyond this room, beyond this wall, beyond this man who was not quite the same man seated at this desk that was not quite the same desk . . . lay an entire world of streets and people. What sort of world it was now, there was no telling. He could feel them moving there, beyond the walls, almost, like so many chess pieces blown in a dry wind. . . .

But the immediate thing was the sign painted on the office wall, the same sign he had read earlier today on first entering.

Somehow, the sign had changed:

TYME SEFARI INC.
SEFARIS TU ANY YEER EN THE PAST.
YU NAIM THE ANIMALL.
WEE TAEKYUTHAIR.
YU SHOOT ITT.

Eckels felt himself fall into a chair. He fumbled crazily at the thick slime on his boots. He held up a clod of dirt, trembling. "No, it *can't* be. Not a *little* thing like that. No!"

Embedded in the mud, glistening green and gold and black, was a butterfly, very beautiful and very dead.

"Not a little thing like *that!* Not a butterfly!" cried Eckels.

---

2. **1492. 1776. 1812:** three important dates in American history: the discovery of America by Columbus, the American Revolution, and the War of 1812, respectively.

It fell to the floor, an exquisite thing, a small thing that could upset balances and knock down a line of small dominoes and then big dominoes and then gigantic dominoes, all down the years across Time. Eckels' mind whirled. It *couldn't* change things. Killing one butterfly couldn't be *that* important! Could it?

His face was cold. His mouth trembled, asking: "Who— who won the presidential election yesterday?"

The man behind the desk laughed. "You joking? You know very well. Deutscher, of course! Who else? Not that fool weakling Keith. We got an iron man now, a man with guts!" The official stopped. "What's wrong?"

Eckels moaned. He dropped to his knees. He scrabbled at the golden butterfly with shaking fingers. "Can't we," he pleaded to the world, to himself, to the officials, to the Machine, "can't we take it *back*, can't we *make* it alive again? Can't we start over? Can't we—"

He did not move. Eyes shut, he waited, shivering. He heard Travis breathe loud in the room; he heard Travis shift his rifle, click the safety catch and raise the weapon.

There was a sound of thunder.

Getting at Meaning

1. Why is Eckels so anxious to travel into the past? Why is he eager to kill a dinosaur?

2. Outline the dangers involved in Eckels's safari. Describe the time machine itself.

3. What instructions does Travis give Eckels once the machine stops? Why isn't anyone supposed to leave the path? How are the hunters supposed to shoot *Tyrannosaurus rex*? Why do they shoot only animals that will die shortly anyway?

4. Describe the dinosaur. What aspects of its appearance cause Eckels to lose his nerve?

5. Recount how the animal dies. Why does Travis make Eckels go out to the animal to retrieve the bullets?

6. What changes have taken place when the time machine returns to 2055? What was Eckels's fatal mistake? Why does Travis shoot him?

Developing Skills in Reading Literature

1. **Setting.** This story has two vastly different settings that are sixty million, two thousand and fifty-five years apart. Describe the world of the dinosaurs. Describe the world of the year 2055. What links exist between these two worlds?

2. **Paradox.** A paradox, you will recall, is a statement that seems to contradict itself but is, nevertheless, true. When Eckels asks Lesperance if he knows the outcome of their safari, Lesperance says, "That'd be a paradox. Time doesn't permit that sort of mess—a man meeting himself." Explain his meaning. Where is the paradox in what Eckels is asking?

3. **Style.** "The Sound of Thunder" is full of beautiful figurative language. Consider, for example, the following paragraph:

A touch of the hand and this burning would, on the instant, beautifully reverse itself. Eckels remembered the wording in the advertisements to the letter. Out of chars and ashes, out of dust and coals, like golden salamanders, the old years, the green years, might leap; roses sweeten the air, white hair turn Irish-black, wrinkles vanish; all, everything fly back to seed, flee death, rush down to their beginnings, suns rise in western skies and set in glorious easts, moons eat themselves opposite to the custom, all and everything cupping one in another like Chinese boxes, rabbits into hats, all and everything returning to the fresh death, the seed death, the green death, to the time before the beginning. A touch of a hand might do it, the merest touch of a hand.

What specific figures of speech do you find in this paragraph? How does Bradbury use parallelism to give his language tightness and rhythm? Where in the paragraph do you find assonance? What does it contribute? Notice the repetends. What effect do these repeating words produce?

4. **Theme.** This story makes a statement about evolutionary change and the way elements of nature affect each other. As Travis says to Eckels, "Step on a mouse and you crush the pyramids. Step on a mouse and you leave your print, like a Grand Canyon, across Eternity. Queen Elizabeth might never be born, Washington might not cross the Delaware, there might never be a United States at all."

Discuss the way this theme develops in the story. What is Eckels's subtle mistake? What changes does his mistake produce? What is the realization he comes to at the end of the story?

Developing Vocabulary

Latin and Greek. On the safari Eckels and the others see pterodactyls. *Dactyl-* is a root that comes from the Latin word *dactylus,* meaning "finger." The Latin word comes in turn from the Greek word *daktulos.*

Look up the words below that employ this root and record their meanings. Explain the relationship between the meaning of each word and the root.

dactyl
dactylogram
dactylography
pterodactyl

Developing Writing Skills

Analyzing Style. After you have carefully studied the following paragraph from "The Sound of Thunder," write a composition of one or two paragraphs in which you analyze what makes Bradbury's style so effective. Consider such elements as figures of speech, sensory images, diction, syntax, repetition, and parallelism. What mood or atmosphere does the paragraph create?

It came on great oiled, resilient, striding legs. It towered thirty feet above half of the trees, a great evil god, folding its delicate watchmaker's claws close to its oily reptilian chest. Each lower leg was a piston, a thousand pounds of white bone, sunk in thick ropes of muscle, sheathed over in a gleam of pebbled skin like the mail of a terrible warrior. Each thigh was a ton of meat, ivory, and steel mesh. And from the great breathing cage of the upper body those two delicate arms dangled out front, arms with hands which might pick up and examine men like toys, while the snake neck coiled. And the head itself, a ton of sculptured stone, lifted easily upon the sky. Its mouth gaped, exposing a fence of teeth like daggers. Its eyes rolled, ostrich eggs, empty of all expression save hunger. It closed its mouth in a death grin. It ran, its pelvic bones crushing aside trees and bushes, its taloned feet clawing damp earth, leaving prints six inches deep wherever it settled its weight. It ran with a gliding ballet step, far too poised and balanced for its ten tons. It moved into a sunlit arena warily, its beautifully reptilian hands feeling the air.

Kurt Vonnegut, Jr.

born in 1922

Jill Krementz

The writing of Kurt Vonnegut, Jr., defies simple classification. When his stories examine the moral implications of technology, they are called science fiction. When they make comedy out of the horrors and absurdities of the human condition, they are called black humor. With his deceptively simple style he entertains his readers, while he considers "what machines do to us, what cities do to us, what big, simple ideas do to us."

The son and grandson of architects, Vonnegut was born in Indianapolis, Indiana, the youngest of three children. He has said that he owes his scientific bent to his father, a true believer in technology who insisted that his sons study "something useful." As a result, after high school, where he edited the daily paper, Vonnegut went to Cornell University to study biochemistry. "I was delighted to catch pneumonia during my third year, and, upon recovery, to forget everything I ever knew about chemistry, and go to war."

An infantry combat scout in World War II, Vonnegut was captured by the Germans and assigned to a prisoner-of-war work group in Dresden, Germany. What happened there profoundly affected his life and work. Dresden, then the most beautiful baroque city in Europe, with no military significance, was for some reason annihilated by the Allies in a massive firebombing that became "the largest single massacre in European history," with more victims than Hiroshima and Nagasaki combined. When he and his fellow prisoners emerged from their detention in an underground meat locker, "everything was gone but the cellars where 135,000 Hansels and Gretels had been baked like gingerbread men. So we were put to work as corpse miners, breaking into shelters, bringing bodies out." Vonnegut eventually came to terms with that experience in his sixth novel, *Slaughterhouse-Five* (1969), which became a best-seller and a movie, and added considerably to his reputation.

After the war, Vonnegut studied anthropology at the University of Chicago, working at the same time as a police reporter for the Chicago City News Bureau. He then took a job doing public relations for the General Electric Company, but after three years he began to sell short stories to the slick magazines and science fiction journals. He quit his job, moved with his family to Cape Cod, Massachusetts, and has been a freelance writer ever since. He is married to Jill Krementz, the photographer.

In addition to *Slaughterhouse-Five*, some of Vonnegut's novels are *Cat's Cradle* (1963), *Breakfast of Champions* (1973), and *Palm Sunday* (1981), a collection of nonfiction pieces.

In spite of Vonnegut's apparently pessimistic philosophy, in which human beings are victims of circumstance in an indifferent universe, he believes strongly in the value of kindness and is preoccupied with moral issues. He says that he would like to reach people with his books while they are still in school, "before they become generals and senators and Presidents, and poison their minds with humanity."

Harrison Bergeron

The year was 2081, and everybody was finally equal. They weren't only equal before God and the law, they were equal every which way. Nobody was smarter than anybody else; nobody was better looking than anybody else; nobody was stronger or quicker than anybody else. All this equality was due to the 211th, 212th, and 213th Amendments to the Constitution, and to the unceasing vigilance of agents of the United States Handicapper General.

Some things about living still weren't quite right, though. April, for instance, still drove people crazy by not being springtime. And it was in that clammy month that H-G men took George and Hazel Bergeron's fourteen-year-old son, Harrison, away.

It was tragic, all right, but George and Hazel couldn't think about it very hard. Hazel had a perfectly average intelligence, which meant she couldn't think about anything except in short bursts. And George, while his intelligence was way above normal, had a little mental handicap radio in his ear—he was required by law to wear it at all times. It was tuned to a government transmitter, and every twenty seconds or so, the transmitter would send out some sharp noise to keep people like George from taking unfair advantage of their brains.

George and Hazel were watching television. There were tears on Hazel's cheeks, but she'd forgotten for the moment what they were about, as the ballerinas came to the end of a dance.

A buzzer sounded in George's head. His thoughts fled in panic, like bandits from a burglar alarm.

"That was a real pretty dance, that dance they just did," said Hazel.

"Huh?" said George.

"That dance—it was nice," said Hazel.

"Yup," said George. He tried to think a little about the ballerinas. They weren't really very good—no better than anybody else would have been, anyway. They were burdened with sashweights and bags of birdshot, and their faces were masked, so that no one, seeing a free and graceful gesture or a pretty face, would feel like something the cat dragged in. George was toying with the vague notion that maybe dancers shouldn't be handicapped. But he didn't get very far with it before another noise in his ear radio scattered his thoughts.

George winced. So did two out of the eight ballerinas.

Hazel saw him wince. Having no mental handicap herself, she had to ask George what the latest sound had been.

"Sounded like somebody hitting a milk bottle with a ballpeen hammer," said George.

"I'd think it would be real interesting, hearing all the different sounds," said Hazel, a little envious. "The things they think up."

"Um," said George.

"Only, if I was Handicapper General, you know what I would do?" said Hazel. Hazel, as a matter of fact, bore a strong resemblance to the Handicapper General, a woman named Diana Moon Glampers. "If I was Diana Moon Glampers," said Hazel, "I'd have chimes on Sunday—just chimes. Kind of in honor of religion."

"I could think, if it was just chimes," said George.

"Well—maybe make 'em real loud," said Hazel. "I think I'd make a good Handicapper General."

"Good as anybody else," said George.

"Who knows better'n I do what normal is?" said Hazel.

"Right," said George. He began to think glimmeringly about his abnormal son who was now in jail, about Harrison, but a twenty-one gun salute in his head stopped that.

"Boy!" said Hazel, "that was a doozy, wasn't it?"

It was such a doozy that George was white and trembling, and tears stood on the rims of his red eyes. Two of the eight ballerinas had collapsed to the studio floor, were holding their temples.

"All of a sudden you look so tired," said Hazel. "Why don't you stretch out on the sofa, so's you can rest your handicap bag on the pillows, honeybunch." She was referring to the forty-seven pounds of birdshot in a canvas bag, which was padlocked around George's neck. "Go on and rest the bag for a little while," she said. "I don't care if you're not equal to me for a while."

George weighed the bag with his hands. "I don't mind it," he said. "I don't notice it any more. It's just a part of me."

"You been so tired lately—kind of wore out," said Hazel. "If there was just some way we could make a little hole in the bottom of the bag, and just take out a few of them lead balls. Just a few."

"Two years in prison and two thousand dollars fine for every ball I took out," said George. "I don't call that a bargain."

"If you could just take a few out when you came home from work," said Hazel. "I mean—you don't compete with anybody around here. You just set around."

"If I tried to get away with it," said George, "then other people'd get away with it—and pretty soon we'd be right back to the dark ages again, with everybody competing against everybody else. You wouldn't like that, would you?"

"I'd hate it," said Hazel.

"There you are," said George. "The minute people start cheating on laws, what do you think happens to society?"

If Hazel hadn't been able to come up with an answer to this question, George couldn't have supplied one. A siren was going off in his head.

"Reckon it'd fall all apart," said Hazel.

"What would?" said George blankly.

"Society," said Hazel uncertainly. "Wasn't that what you just said?"

"Who knows?" said George.

The television program was suddenly interrupted for a news bulletin. It wasn't clear at first as to what the bulletin was about, since the announcer, like all announcers, had a serious speech impediment. For about half a minute, and in a state of high excitement, the announcer tried to say, "Ladies and Gentlemen———"

He finally gave up, handed the bulletin to a ballerina to read.

"That's all right," Hazel said of the announcer, "he tried. That's the big thing. He tried to do the best he could with what God gave him. He should get a nice raise for trying so hard."

"Ladies and gentlemen———" said the ballerina, reading the bulletin. She must have been extraordinarily beautiful, because the mask she wore was hideous. And it was easy to see that she was the strongest and most graceful of all the dancers, for her handicap bags were as big as those worn by two-hundred-pound men.

And she had to apologize at once for her voice, which was a very unfair voice for a woman to use. Her voice was a warm, luminous, timeless melody. "Excuse me———" she said, and she began again, making her voice absolutely uncompetitive.

"Harrison Bergeron, age fourteen," she said in a grackle squawk, "has just escaped from jail, where he was held on suspicion of plotting to overthrow the government. He is a genius and an athlete, is under-handicapped, and is extremely dangerous."

A police photograph of Harrison Bergeron

was flashed on the screen—upside down, then sideways, upside down again, then right-side up. The picture showed the full length of Harrison against a background calibrated in feet and inches. He was exactly seven feet tall.

The rest of Harrison's appearance was Halloween and hardware. Nobody had ever borne heavier handicaps. He had outgrown hindrances faster than the H-G men could think them up. Instead of a little ear radio for a mental handicap, he wore a tremendous pair of earphones, and spectacles with thick, wavy lenses besides. The spectacles were intended not only to make him half blind, but to give him whanging headaches besides.

Scrap metal was hung all over him. Ordinarily, there was a certain symmetry, a military neatness to the handicaps issued to strong people, but Harrison looked like a walking junkyard. In the race of life Harrison carried three-hundred pounds.

And to offset his good looks, the H-G men required that he wear at all times a red rubber ball for a nose, keep his eyebrows shaved off, and cover his even white teeth with black caps at snaggletooth random.

"If you see this boy," said the ballerina, "do not—I repeat, do not—try to reason with him."

There was the shriek of a door being torn from its hinges.

Screams and barking cries of consternation came from the television set. The photograph of Harrison Bergeron on the screen jumped again and again, as though dancing to the tune of an earthquake.

George Bergeron correctly identified the earthquake, and well he might have—for many was the time his own home had danced to the same crashing tune. "My God!" said George. "That must be Harrison!"

The realization was blasted from his mind instantly by the sound of an automobile collision in his head.

When George could open his eyes again, the photograph of Harrison was gone. A living, breathing Harrison filled the screen.

Clanking, clownish, and huge, Harrison stood in the center of the studio. The knob of the uprooted studio door was still in his hand. Ballerinas, technicians, musicians, and announcers cowered on their knees before him, expecting to die.

"I am the Emperor!" cried Harrison. "Do you hear? I am the Emperor! Everybody must do what I say at once!" He stamped his foot and the studio shook.

"Even as I stand here," he bellowed, "crippled, hobbled, sickened—I am a greater ruler than any man who ever lived! Now watch me become what I *can* become!"

Harrison tore the straps of his handicap harness like wet tissue paper, tore straps guaranteed to support five thousand pounds.

Harrison's scrap-iron handicaps crashed to the floor.

Harrison thrust his thumbs under the bar of the padlock that secured his head harness. The bar snapped like celery. Harrison smashed his headphones and spectacles against the wall.

He flung away his rubber-ball nose, revealed a man that would have awed Thor, the god of thunder.

"I shall now select my Empress!" he said, looking down on the cowering people. "Let the first woman who dares rise to her feet claim her mate and her throne!"

A moment passed, and then a ballerina arose, swaying like a willow.

Harrison plucked the mental handicap from her ear, snapped off her physical handicaps with marvelous delicacy. Last of all, he removed her mask.

She was blindingly beautiful.

"Now————" said Harrison, taking her hand. "Shall we show the people the meaning of the word *dance*? Music!" he commanded.

The musicians scrambled back into their chairs, and Harrison stripped them of their handicaps, too. "Play your best," he told them, "and I'll make you barons and dukes and earls."

The music began. It was normal at first—cheap, silly, false. But Harrison snatched two musicians from their chairs, waved them like batons as he sang the music as he wanted it played. He slammed them back into their chairs.

The music began again, and was much improved.

Harrison and his Empress merely listened to the music for a while—listened gravely, as though synchronizing their heartbeats with it.

They shifted their weight to their toes.

Harrison placed his big hands on the girl's tiny waist, letting her sense the weightlessness that would soon be hers.

And then, in an explosion of joy and grace, into the air they sprang!

Not only were the laws of the land abandoned, but the law of gravity and the laws of motion as well.

They reeled, whirled, swiveled, flounced, capered, gamboled, and spun.

They leaped like deer on the moon.

The studio ceiling was thirty feet high, but each leap brought the dancers nearer to it.

It became their obvious intention to kiss the ceiling.

They kissed it.

And then, neutralizing gravity with love and pure will, they remained suspended in air inches below the ceiling, and they kissed each other for a long, long time.

It was then that Diana Moon Glampers, the Handicapper General, came into the studio with a double-barreled ten-gauge shotgun. She fired twice, and the Emperor and the Empress were dead before they hit the floor.

Diana Moon Glampers loaded the gun again. She aimed it at the musicians and told them they had ten seconds to get their handicaps back on.

It was then that the Bergerons' television tube burned out.

Hazel turned to comment about the blackout to George. But George had gone out into the kitchen for a drink.

George came back in, paused while a handicap signal shook him up. And then he sat down again. "You been crying?" he said to Hazel, watching her wipe her tears.

"Yup," she said.

"What about?" he said.

"I forget," she said. "Something real sad on television."

"What was it?" he said.

"It's all kind of mixed up in my mind," said Hazel.

"Forget sad things," said George.

"I always do," said Hazel.

"That's my girl," said George. He winced. There was the sound of a riveting gun in his head.

"Gee—I could tell that one was a doozy," said Hazel.

"You can say that again," said George.

"Gee———" said Hazel—"I could tell that one was a doozy."

Getting at Meaning

1. Describe the American society of 2081. Explain the Handicapper General's job.

2. What is the function of George's handicap radio? Why does he have to wear a forty-seven pound handicap bag? Why doesn't Hazel have any handicaps?

3. Explain how the dancers are handicapped. How are the announcers handicapped? What are Harrison Bergeron's handicaps?

4. Describe Harrison's rebellion. What is he trying to do to the society? Why does his rebellion fail?

Developing Skills in Reading Literature

1. **Science Fiction.** Explain how this story fits the definition of science fiction. How does the setting contribute? In what ways does the story draw imaginatively on scientific knowledge and theory in its plot and characters?

2. **Satire.** Satire is a form of literature that ridicules foolish ideas or customs, most often through exaggeration. The purpose of satire is usually to get people to examine their foolishness and to change their ways, or perhaps to avoid repeating mistakes of the past. Sometimes, however, satire ridicules aspects of human nature that are probably beyond remedy.

What tendencies in American society does Kurt Vonnegut satirize in "Harrison Bergeron"? How does he make fun of government agencies? of the belief that absolute equality is desirable? According to Vonnegut, in what direction does our society seem to be moving? How does Vonnegut employ exaggeration for satiric effect?

3. **Irony.** Notice the irony of Hazel's tears at the end of the story. Her son is destroyed on television before her very eyes, and she cries. When George asks her why she has been crying, she says, "I forget. Something real sad on television." What has become of all worthwhile emotion and activity in this society? Why?

Identify other major ironies in this story. What is ironic about the entire central situation? What is ironic about the reasons for which Harrison is killed?

4. **Figurative Language.** Vonnegut uses some graphic figurative language in "Harrison Bergeron." Discuss how each specific figure of speech that follows helps to develop character or theme in the story:

A buzzer sounded in George's head. His thoughts fled in panic, like bandits from a burglar alarm.

Her voice was a warm, luminous, timeless melody.

The photograph of Harrison Bergeron on the screen jumped again and again, as though dancing to the tune of an earthquake.

Harrison thrust his thumbs under the bar of the padlock that secured his head harness. The bar snapped like celery.

They leaped like deer on the moon.

Developing Vocabulary

Latin Phrases in English. An important technique in satire is *reductio ad absurdum*, meaning in Latin "reduction to absurdity." This technique disproves a proposition or makes fun of an idea by showing the absurdity of its inevitable conclusion. Discuss how Vonnegut reduces things to a level of absurdity in "Harrison Bergeron" in order to develop his satiric points.

The following Latin phrases should also become a part of your working English vocabulary. After you have found each phrase in a dictionary, record its meaning and use it in an original sentence.

prima facie
quid pro quo
sub rosa

Developing Writing Skills

Writing a Satire. Write a satiric sketch about some aspect of school life or American culture. It may be either serious or humorous. Employ exaggeration and the technique of *reductio ad absurdum* to help establish your points. If you like, you may also turn your piece into science fiction.

Unit Review   *The Short Story*

Understanding the Unit

1. George Willard in "Sophistication" and Dexter Green in "Winter Dreams" both mature and learn more about human reality from their experiences with young women. Compare and contrast what the two learn. Which character has a more positive experience, George or Dexter? Why?

2. Both "I Stand Here Ironing" and "Man and Daughter in the Cold" develop an adolescent female character through someone else's eyes. The reader learns about Emily from her mother in "I Stand Here Ironing," and about Becky from her father in "Man and Daughter in the Cold." Each story also depicts something of the actions, speech, and reactions of the adolescent character. Discuss the techniques of characterization used in each story. How do these female characters differ? Can you see any similarities among them?

3. "True Love," "A Sound of Thunder," and "Harrison Bergeron" all depict American society at some point in the future. Compare and contrast the vision of our culture you find in these stories. Do you find any optimism in these science fiction pieces?

4. "Barn Burning," "The Soldier Ran Away," and "Pride and the Proudhammers" show young male characters in conflict with their fathers. Compare and contrast the young men in these stories and then the fathers.

5. Discuss the way an unusual and tragic problem shapes the family in each of the following stories: "Barn Burning," "He," and "The Stone Boy." How might each family have handled its problem better?

6. "The Catbird Seat," "The Life You Save May Be Your Own," and "True Love" all employ irony to show one character outsmarting another. Compare and contrast the way irony achieves this effect in the three stories.

7. Describe the sacrifices the central adult character makes for love in each of the following stories: "A Worn Path," "The Soldier Ran Away," and "I Stand Here Ironing."

Writing

1. The central male characters in the stories that follow all undergo physical experiences that lead them to major realizations about themselves and the world they live in. In a five-paragraph composition compare and contrast what the central characters experience and what they learn from the experience. Devote one body paragraph to each story, using quotations and specific references to events in the story to support your points. In the fifth paragraph of your composition, draw a conclusion about the three characters you analyze.

"Man and Daughter in the Cold"
"Flight"
"The Stone Boy"

2. The stories that follow all share a rather grim view of human reality. Select three, and in a five-paragraph essay compare and contrast the statements of theme you find in these stories. Devote one body paragraph to each story, uniting the three in your conclusion. Quote passages from the stories in your body paragraphs.

"Barn Burning"
"The Near and the Far"
"The Life You Save May Be Your Own"
"He"

3. Select one story in this unit, such as "Barn Burning" or "Flight," and explain how the setting, plot, and characters interact to reveal the story's theme or themes. Devote the three body paragraphs, one each, to analyzing setting, plot, and character. Pull these separate elements together with a discussion of theme in a concluding paragraph.

THE PATRIOT, 1964. *Andrew Wyeth.*

Unit 6

Modern Nonfiction <small>(1900 to the Present)</small>

AMERICAN LANDSCAPE, 1930. *Charles Sheeler.*
Collection, The Museum of Modern Art, New York.
Gift of Abby Aldrich Rockefeller.

The Art of Nonfiction

Much of the nonfiction written in the twentieth century focuses on the changing character of America and on the factors that have ushered in change, such as war, urbanization, technological development, increased mobility, and the emergence of strong minority voices in our culture. Radio, television, and cinema also have had a dramatic impact on nonfiction in recent decades.

KINDS OF NONFICTION

The term *nonfiction* encompasses a broad spectrum of literature. Biographies, autobiographies, speeches, histories, editorials, essays, pamphlets, journals, letters, official documents, textbooks, and news articles are all nonfiction forms widely used by twentieth-century writers.

Earlier units in this book contain examples of most of these nonfiction forms. For example, Unit 1 presents excerpts from the histories of Captain John Smith and William Bradford, as well as court documents from the Salem witch trials. The unit includes selections from *The New England Primer* and passages from a Puritan sermon, "Sinners in the Hands of an Angry God." Unit 2 contains autobiographical writings by Benjamin Franklin; a persuasive pamphlet by Thomas Paine; a speech by Patrick Henry; a political manifesto by Thomas Jefferson; and a letter by Abigail Adams. Unit 3 exhibits the literary essay in its most polished and sophisticated form in the writings of Ralph Waldo Emerson and Henry David Thoreau.

PERSONAL REFLECTIONS AS LITERATURE

The nonfiction forms represented in this unit are familiar ones; their subject matter and stylistic approach, however, mirror the modern era in which they were written. The first six selections are all personal reflections from remarkable twentieth-century individuals. Alfred Kazin, Lorraine Hansberry, and Richard Rodriguez represent three major American minorities, the Jewish, black, and Chicano cultures respectively. The selections by Hansberry and Agnes De Mille, the famous dancer/choreographer, remind the reader that the number of female writers has increased dramatically in this century. The last several decades in particular have witnessed an explosion of nonfiction writing by women, often focusing on special problems women face and on changing sex roles in our society.

SPEECHES IN THE TWENTIETH CENTURY

Several speeches appear in this unit, including addresses from two former Presidents, Franklin Delano Roosevelt and John F. Kennedy, and a eulogy from Adlai Stevenson, twice a candidate for the United States Presidency and former ambassador to the United Nations. Radio and television have altered the nature of the political speech in the last fifty years, frequently forcing political figures to prepare their remarks meticulously in advance and to tailor them to a wide and disparate audience. The days when Abraham Lincoln could compose a speech such as the Gettysburg Address enroute to the ceremony are over; almost every prominent politician in contemporary America employs an entire staff of speech writers.

COMMENTARY ON AMERICAN LIFE

Other selections in this unit present commentary by well known writers on significant social and political issues. Archibald MacLeish, primarily known as a poet, and John Dos Passos, primarily known as a novelist, ponder different aspects of the American scene in excerpts from their longer works. Richard Wright and James Baldwin, talented black writers, probe questions of race and discrimination in their essays. Rachel Carson, a biologist and writer, raises questions about the survival of the natural world. E. B. White, who is one of the most adroit essayists of the century, pays homage to Henry David Thoreau and comments on the shifting American culture in his essay "Walden."

In addition to representing an assortment of nonfiction forms and a broad sweep of opinion, the selections in this unit reflect varying degrees of formality and a host of artistic purposes. Consider each piece on its own merits, realizing that as an aggregate, the selections will enhance your appreciation for diverse prose forms and expand your knowledge of American culture.

Personal Recollections

NOONTIDE IN LATE MAY, 1917. *Charles Burchfield.*
Collection of the Whitney Museum of American Art, New York.

Alfred Kazin

born in 1915

A noted literary critic, essayist, and writer of personal memoirs, Alfred Kazin was born in Brooklyn and has long been a prominent member of New York's literary scene. Kazin earned degrees at New York's City College and Columbia University and is presently on the English faculty at New York's Hunter College. After serving as the literary editor of the *New Republic* and as a contributing editor to *Fortune* in the early 1940's, Kazin began a distinguished academic career during which he has been affiliated with numerous universities as a guest professor and lecturer. He has edited the works of literary figures such as William Blake, Theodore Dreiser, Herman Melville, Henry James, and Ralph Waldo Emerson. A member of the National Institute of Arts and Letters and the American Academy of Arts and Sciences, Kazin is known for his keen intelligence and empathetic involvement with his subject matter. His emphasis on the personal as the starting point of knowledge is evident in works such as *A Walker in the City*, *Starting Out in the Thirties*, *Bright Book of Life*, and *New York Jew*.

Helen Marcus

from A Walker in the City

The Kitchen

The kitchen gave a special character to our lives; my mother's character. All my memories of that kitchen are dominated by the nearness of my mother sitting all day long at her sewing machine, by the clacking of the treadle[1] against the linoleum floor, by the patient twist of her right shoulder as she automatically pushed at the wheel with one hand or lifted the foot to free the needle where it had got stuck in a thick piece of material. The kitchen was her life. Year by year, as I began to take in her fantastic capacity for labor and her anxious zeal, I realized it was ourselves she kept stitched together. I can never remember a time when she was not working. She worked because the law of her life was work, work and anxiety; she worked because she would have found life meaningless without work. She read almost no English; she could read the Yiddish paper, but never felt she had time to. We were always talking of a time when I would teach her how to read, but somehow there was never time. When I awoke in the morning she was already at her machine, or in the great morning crowd of housewives at the grocery getting fresh rolls for breakfast. When I returned from school she was at her machine, or conferring over *McCall's* with some neighborhood woman who had come in pointing hopefully to an illustration—"Mrs. Kazin! Mrs. Kazin! Make me a dress like it shows here in the picture!" When my father came home from work she had somehow mysteriously interrupted herself to make supper for us, and the dishes cleared and washed, was back at her machine. When I went to bed at night, often

she was still there, pounding away at the treadle, hunched over the wheel, her hands steering a piece of gauze under the needle with a finesse that always contrasted sharply with her swollen hands and broken nails. Her left hand had been pierced through when as a girl she had worked in the infamous Triangle Shirtwaist Factory on the East Side. A needle had gone straight through the palm, severing a large vein. They had sewn it up for her so clumsily that a tuft of flesh always lay folded over the palm.

The kitchen was the great machine that set our lives running; it whirred down a little only on Saturdays and holy days. From my mother's kitchen I gained my first picture of life as a white, overheated, starkly lit workshop redolent with Jewish cooking, crowded with women in housedresses, strewn with fashion magazines, patterns, dress material, spools of thread—and at whose center, so lashed to her machine that bolts of energy seemed to dance out of her hands and feet as she worked, my mother stamped the treadle hard against the floor, hard, hard, and silently, grimly at war, beat out the first rhythm of the world for me. . . .

At night the kitchen contracted around the blaze of light on the cloth, the patterns, the ironing board where the iron had burned a black border around the tear in the muslin cover; the finished dresses looked so frilly as they jostled on their wire hangers after all the work my mother had put into them. And then I would get that strangely ominous smell of tension from the dress fabrics and the burn in

---

1. **treadle:** a rectangular, swiveling device pressed by the foot to drive a machine.

the cover of the ironing board—as if each piece of cloth and paper crushed with light under the naked bulb might suddenly go up in flames. . . .

What I must have felt most about ourselves, I see now, was that we ourselves were like kindling—that all the hard-pressed pieces of ourselves and all the hard-used objects in that kitchen were like so many slivers of wood that might go up in flames if we came too near the white-blazing filaments in that naked bulb. Our tension itself was fire, we ourselves were forever burning—to live, to get down the foreboding in our souls, to make good.

Twice a year, on the anniversaries of her parents' deaths, my mother placed on top of the icebox an ordinary kitchen glass packed with wax, the *yortsayt*,[2] and lit the candle in it. Sitting at the kitchen table over my homework, I would look across the threshold to that mourning-glass, and sense that for my mother the distance from our kitchen to *der heym*,[3] from life to death, was only a flame's length away. Poor as we were, it was not poverty that drove my mother so hard; it was loneliness—some endless bitter brooding over all those left behind, dead or dying or soon to die; a loneliness locked up in her kitchen that dwelt every day on the hazardousness of life and the nearness of death, but still kept struggling in the lock, trying to get us through by endless labor.

With us, life started up again only on the last shore. There seemed to be no middle ground between despair and the fury of our ambition. Whenever my mother spoke of her hopes for us, it was with such unbelievingness that the likes of us would ever come to anything, such abashed hope and readiness for pain, that I finally came to see in the flame burning on top of the icebox death itself burning away the bones of poor Jews, burning out in us everything but courage, the blind resolution to live. In the light of that mourning candle, there were ranged around me how many dead and dying—how many eras of pain, of exile, of dispersion, of cringing before the powers of this world!

It was always at dusk that my mother's loneliness came home most to me. Painfully alert to every shift in the light at her window, she would suddenly confess her fatigue by removing her pince-nez,[4] and then wearily pushing aside the great mound of fabrics on her machine, would stare at the street as if to warm herself in the last of the sun. "How sad it is!" I once heard her say. "It grips me! It grips me!" Twilight was the bottommost part of the day, the chillest and loneliest time for her. Always so near to her moods, I knew she was fighting some deep inner dread, struggling against the returning tide of darkness along the streets that invariably assailed her heart with the same foreboding—Where? Where now? Where is the day taking us now?

Yet one good look at the street would revive her. I see her now, perched against the windowsill, with her face against the glass, her eyes almost asleep in enjoyment, just as she starts up with the guilty cry—"What foolishness is this in me!"—and goes to the stove to prepare supper for us: a moment, only a moment, watching the evening crowd of women gathering at the grocery for fresh bread and milk. But between my mother's pent-up face at the window and the winter sun dying in the fabrics—"Alfred, see how beautiful!"—she has drawn for me one single line of sentience.[5]

---

2. **yortsayt,** *Yiddish:* literally "year time" or "anniversary," refers to the annual lighting of candles as memorials for the dead.

3. **der heym,** *Yiddish:* one's ultimate home.

4. **pince-nez** (pans' nā') *French:* eyeglasses without sidepieces, kept in place by a spring gripping the bridge of the nose.

5. **sentience** (sen' shi ens): elementary consciousness at the level of feeling as opposed to the level of perception or thought.

Getting at Meaning

1. In the opening paragraph of this selection, what qualities of Mrs. Kazin are brought out through a description of her activities?

2. Kazin tells the reader that his mother ". . . worked because the law of her life was work, work and anxiety. . . ." Subsequent paragraphs reveal the nature of the anxieties that impelled Mrs. Kazin to drive herself mercilessly. What are these various anxieties? How do you explain the ". . . deep inner dread . . . the returning tide of darkness . . . that invariably assailed her heart . . ."?

3. The first paragraph concludes with three sentences about Mrs. Kazin's left hand. These sentences illustrate a point and also suggest a story in themselves. What does the reader learn about Mrs. Kazin's girlhood and about working conditions of the time? Why do you think she received such second-rate medical treatment? What other details of Mrs. Kazin's life can you infer from the information in these sentences?

4. In what literal way and in what other ways does the sound of the treadle "beat out the first rhythm of the world" for Kazin?

5. What view of life emerges from the description of the kitchen at night? What fear is suggested by the boyhood worry that ". . . each piece of cloth and paper crushed with light under the naked bulb might suddenly go up in flames. . . ."?

6. What made the setting of the sun such a significant time of day for Mrs. Kazin? Mrs. Kazin says to her son, "Alfred, see how beautiful!" What is the effect of this statement, as suggested by the word *sentience*?

Developing Skills in Reading Literature

1. **Style: Figurative Language and Imagery.** Kazin uses the kind of figurative language and imagery that is characteristic of poetry. Find examples of metaphors and similes in this autobiographical selection. Find vivid images that are created through precise description and richly connotative words. What feelings are evoked by the figurative language and imagery? What ideas are emphasized?

2. **Extended Metaphor.** What metaphor organizes all of the details in the second paragraph? Cite specific phrases that extend the basic metaphor. What central impression does the extended metaphor create? What picture of Mrs. Kazin's character emerges from this paragraph?

3. **Contrast.** The last paragraph achieves special emphasis because of its contrast to the rest of the essay. How is a shift in idea and mood indicated at the beginning of the paragraph? What characteristic of Mrs. Kazin is revealed for the first time in this paragraph? What words and images are in sharp contrast to the rest of the essay? What effect is created by the last sentence?

4. **Theme.** What is Kazin's purpose in writing this autobiographical piece? What attitude does he have toward his subject? How successful do you think he is in achieving his purpose? In a sentence or two characterize Kazin's boyhood, based on this selection.

Developing Vocabulary

1. **Greek Roots.** In an unabridged dictionary find the meaning of the Greek root for the word *character*. What does the meaning of the root suggest about human character? How changeable is a person's character? Does a person "build character" or "discover character" in the process of maturity? Now that you have met Mrs. Kazin, what kind of character would you predict that her son would have?

2. **Denotation and Connotation.** Kazin captures the passion of his mother through the abundance of words that etch sharp pictures of her actions, her thoughts, and her feelings. Use the dictionary to determine the exact denotation of each italicized word. Then describe the connotation of the word as it is used in the essay.

a. anxious *zeal*

b. *starkly* lit workshop

c. her hands steering a piece of gauze under the needle with a *finesse*

d. *jostled* on their wire hangers

e. such *abashed* hope

f. struggling against the returning tide of darkness along the streets that invariably *assailed* her heart with the same *foreboding*

Developing Writing Skills

Description: Establishing Tone. Kazin reveals a great deal about himself through the vivid portrait of his mother, reconstructed from boyhood memories. The reader glimpses not only the facts of his boyhood but also the source of his motivation, values, and capacity for sensitivity and love.

Select from your own experience a significant adult who has influenced your attitudes and values. In an autobiographical essay, re-create a particularly memorable scene involving this person. Use language that evokes a vivid picture of the person, and, at the same time, reveals your attitude toward him or her. Avoid directly stating your attitude; instead, let the description convey your feelings.

YOUNG RUSSIAN JEWESS AT ELLIS ISLAND, 1905.
Lewis W. Hine.
The New York Public Library.

Adlai E. Stevenson

1900–1965

The columnist Walter Lippmann described Adlai Stevenson as ". . . the kind of American that Americans themselves and the great mass of mankind would like to think Americans are." As Governor of Illinois, two-time Democratic Presidential nominee, and United States Ambassador to the United Nations, Adlai Stevenson stood at the center of the nation's political scene throughout the 1950's and early 1960's. The grandson of a U.S. Vice-President, Stevenson was born in Los Angeles, where his father worked as a manager for a Hearst newspaper. He returned to his family's native Illinois for his early schooling before heading East to attend Choate and later Princeton, where he served as managing editor of the school newspaper. After two years of law school at Harvard he returned to Illinois. He worked as a reporter on the family-owned newspaper in Bloomington while completing his law degree at Northwestern University in 1926. Stevenson practiced law in Chicago and served briefly in Washington as counsel to several governmental agencies. He returned to Washington at the outbreak of World War II and served in various governmental capacities, eventu-

ally playing a key role in the establishment of the United Nations. In 1948 he was elected governor of Illinois. As eulogized by Lyndon Johnson upon his death, Adlai Stevenson "skillfully and beautifully helped shape the dialogue of twentieth century democracy."

Her Journeys Are Over

One week ago this afternoon, in the Rose Garden at Hyde Park, Eleanor Roosevelt came home for the last time. [November 7, 1962]. Her journeys are over. The remembrance now begins.

In gathering here to honor her, we engage in a self-serving act. It is we who are trying, by this ceremony of tribute, to deny the fact that we have lost her, and, at least, to prolong the farewell, and—possibly—to say some of the things we dared not say in her presence, because she would have turned aside such testimonial with impatience and gently asked us to get on with some of the more serious business of the meeting.

A grief perhaps not equaled since the death of her husband seventeen years ago is the world's best tribute to one of the great figures of our age—a woman whose lucid and luminous faith testified always for sanity in an insane time and for hope in a time of obscure hope—a woman who spoke for the good toward which man aspires in a world which has seen too much of the evil of which man is capable.

She lived seventy-eight years, most of the time in tireless activity as if she knew that only a frail fragment of the things that cry out to be done could be done in the lifetime of even the most fortunate. One has the melancholy sense that when she knew death was at hand, she was contemplating not what she achieved, but what she had not quite managed to do. And I know she wanted to go—when there was no more strength to do.

Yet how much she had done—how much still unchronicled! We dare not try to tabulate the lives she salvaged, the battles—known and unrecorded—she fought, the afflicted she comforted, the hovels she brightened, the faces and places, near and far, that were given some new radiance, some sound of music, by her endeavors. What other single human being has touched and transformed the existence of so many others? What better measure is there of the impact of anyone's life?

There was no sick soul too wounded to engage her mercy. There was no signal of human distress which she did not view as a personal summons. There was no affront to human dignity from which she fled because the timid cried "danger." And the number of occasions on which her intervention turned despair into victory we may never know.

Her life was crowded, restless, fearless. Perhaps she pitied most not those whom she aided in the struggle, but the more fortunate who were preoccupied with themselves and cursed with the self-deceptions of private success. She walked in the slums and ghettos of the world, not on a tour of inspection, nor as a condescending patron, but as one who could not feel complacent while others were hungry, and who could not find contentment while others were in distress. This was not sacrifice; this, for Mrs. Roosevelt, was the only meaningful way of life.

These were not conventional missions of mercy. What rendered this unforgettable woman so extraordinary was not merely her response to suffering; it was her comprehension of the complexity of the human condition. Not long before she died, she wrote that "within all of us there are two sides. One reaches for the stars, the other descends to the level of beasts." It was, I think, this discernment that made her so unfailingly tolerant of friends who faltered, and led her so often to remind the smug and the complacent that "there but for the grace of God. . . ."[1]

But we dare not regard her as just a benign incarnation of good works. For she was not only a great woman and a great humanitarian, but a great democrat. I use the word with a small *d*—though it was, of course, equally true that she was a great Democrat with a capital *D*. When I say that she was a great small *d* democrat, I mean that she had a lively and astute understanding of the nature of the democratic process. She was a master political strategist with a fine sense of humor. And, as she said, she loved a good fight.

She was a realist. Her compassion did not become sentimentality. She understood that progress was a long labor of compromise. She mistrusted absolutism in all its forms—the absolutism of the word and even more the absolutism of the deed. She never supposed that all the problems of life could be cured in a day or a year or a lifetime. Her pungent and salty understanding of human behavior kept her always in intimate contact with reality. I think this was a primary source of her strength, because she never thought that the loss of a battle meant the loss of a war, nor did she suppose that a compromise which produced only part of the objective sought was an act of corruption or of treachery. She knew that no formula of words, no combination of deeds, could abolish the troubles of life overnight and usher in the millennium.[2]

The miracle, I have tried to suggest, is how much tangible good she really did; how much realism and reason were mingled with her instinctive compassion; how her contempt for the perquisites of power ultimately won her the esteem of so many of the powerful; and how, at her death, there was a universality of grief that transcended all the harsh boundaries of political, racial, and religious strife and, for a moment at least, united men in a vision of what their world might be.

We do not claim the right to enshrine another mortal, and this least of all would Mrs. Roosevelt have desired. She would have wanted it said, I believe, that she well knew the pressures of pride and vanity, the sting of bitterness and defeat, the gray days of national peril and personal anguish. But she clung to the confident expectation that men could fashion their own tomorrows if they could only learn that yesterday can be neither relived nor revised.

Many who have spoken of her in these last few days have used a word to which we all assent, because it speaks a part of what we feel. They have called her "a lady," a "great lady," "the first lady of the world." But the word *lady*, though it says much about Eleanor Roosevelt, does not say all. To be incapable of self-concern is not a negative virtue; it is the other side of a coin that has a positive face—the most positive, I think, of all the faces. And to enhance the humanity of others is not a kind of humility; it is a kind of pride—the noblest of all the forms of pride. No man or woman can respect other men and women who does not respect life. And to respect life is to love it. Eleanor Roosevelt loved life—and that, perhaps, is the most meaningful thing that can be said about her, for it says so much beside.

It takes courage to love life. Loving it demands imagination and perception and the kind of patience women are more apt to have than men—the bravest and most understanding women. And loving it takes something more beside—it takes a gift for life, a gift for love.

Eleanor Roosevelt's childhood was unhappy—miserably unhappy, she sometimes said. But it was Eleanor Roosevelt who also said that "one must never, for whatever reason, turn his back on life." She did not mean that duty should compel us. She meant that life should. "Life," she said, "was meant to

---

1. "There but for the grace of God go I."
2. **millennium:** a period of peace and happiness for everyone.

be lived." A simple statement. An obvious statement. But a statement that by its obviousness and its simplicity challenges the most intricate of all the philosophies of despair.

Many of the admonitions she bequeathed us are neither new thoughts nor novel concepts. Her ideas were, in many respects, old-fashioned—as old as the Sermon on the Mount,[3] as the reminder that it is more blessed to give than to receive. In the words of St. Francis that she loved so well: "For it is in the giving that we receive."

She imparted to the familiar language— nay, what too many have come to treat as the clichés—of Christianity a new poignancy and vibrance. She did so not by reciting them, but by proving that it is possible to live them. It is this above all that rendered her unique in her century. It was said of her contemptuously at times that she was a do-gooder, a charge leveled with similar derision against another public figure 1,962 years ago.

We who are assembled here are of various religious and political faiths, and perhaps different conceptions of man's destiny in the universe. It is not an irreverence, I trust, to say that the immortality Mrs. Roosevelt would have valued most would be found in the deeds and visions her life inspired in others, and in the proof that they would be faithful to the spirit of any tribute conducted in her name.

And now one can almost hear Mrs. Roosevelt saying that the speaker has already talked too long. So we must say farewell. We are always saying farewell in this world—always standing at the edge of loss attempting to retrieve some memory, some human meaning, from the silence—something which was precious and is gone.

Often, although we know the absence well enough, we cannot name it or describe it even. What left the world when Lincoln died? Speaker after speaker in those aching days tried to tell his family or his neighbors or his congregation. But no one found the words, not even Whitman. "When lilacs last in the dooryard bloomed" can break the heart, but not with Lincoln's greatness, only with his loss. What the words could never capture was the man himself. His deeds were known; every school child knew them. But it was not his deeds the country mourned: it was the man— the mastery of life which made the greatness of the man.

It is always so. On that April day when Franklin Roosevelt died [April 12, 1945], it was not a President we wept for. It was a man. In Archibald MacLeish's words:

Fagged out, worn down, sick
With the weight of his own bones, the task
    finished,
The war won, the victory assured,
The glory left behind him for the others,
(And the wheels roll up through
    the night in the sweet land
In the cool air in the spring
    between the lanterns).[4]

It is so now. What we have lost in Eleanor Roosevelt is not her life. She lived that out to the full. What we have lost, what we wish to recall for ourselves, to remember, is what she was herself. And who can name it? But she left "a name to shine on the entablatures[5] of truth, forever."

We pray that she has found peace, and a glimpse of sunset. But today we weep for ourselves. We are lonelier; someone has gone from one's own life—who was like the certainty of refuge; and someone has gone from the world—who was like a certainty of honor.

---

3. **Sermon on the Mount:** Matthew 5–7 or Luke 6:20–49.
4. From Archibald MacLeish's poem "Actfive (1948)," section iii "The Shape of Flesh and Bone," lines 117–122.
5. **entablatures** (en tab' lə chərz): in classical architecture the horizontal structure between the tops of the columns and the roof on which scenes, figures, or names often were carved or painted.

Getting at Meaning

1. Where does Stevenson identify the occasion for his speech? What are the two purposes of the speech, as stated at its beginning?

2. Stevenson highlights three qualities of Eleanor Roosevelt: faith, hope, and love. How does he make each quality concrete, or specific?

3. What does Stevenson say is the best measure of the impact of a person's life? How did Eleanor Roosevelt measure up to that standard?

4. Stevenson stresses that Eleanor Roosevelt was both a democrat and a realist. How does he explain these two qualities, as applied to her?

5. According to Stevenson, how was Eleanor Roosevelt the embodiment of Christian precepts?

6. At the beginning of his speech, Stevenson says that in mourning Eleanor Roosevelt's death, ". . . we engage in a self-serving act." He returns to that idea in the closing paragraphs. How does he clarify that idea at the end of the speech?

7. Why do you think that Stevenson alludes briefly to Eleanor Roosevelt's "unhappy—miserably unhappy" childhood but offers no further details on that phase of her life? How does Stevenson's approach reflect Eleanor Roosevelt's own attitude toward her childhood?

Developing Skills in Reading Literature

1. **Eulogy.** In a eulogy a writer or speaker praises a deceased person's virtues and accomplishments. How does Stevenson eulogize Eleanor Roosevelt? What qualities does he emphasize? How were these qualities manifested in her life?

2. **Contrast.** A rapid succession of quick contrasts can be used to focus the reader's attention on points that deserve special emphasis. In the third paragraph locate Stevenson's use of contrasts to illustrate Eleanor Roosevelt's "lucid and luminous faith."

3. **Analogy.** How is the death of Lincoln described as parallel to the death of Eleanor Roosevelt? What attitude does Stevenson have toward both deaths? What words or phrases suggest that attitude?

Developing Writing Skills

1. **Writing a Summary.** Locate in your library the prayer of Saint Francis of Assisi, which contains the line, "For it is in giving that we receive." In one paragraph summarize the code of conduct that is outlined by Saint Francis, which might also apply to Eleanor Roosevelt. Your topic sentence should state a unifying main idea for Saint Francis's code of conduct.

2. **Using Comparisons.** Locate in the library one of Walt Whitman's poems about the death of Abraham Lincoln. In one paragraph relate the ideas in the poem to Stevenson's ideas about the death of Lincoln.

3. **Writing an Anecdote.** Read about the life of Eleanor Roosevelt. Then relate an anecdote that illustrates one of the qualities described by Stevenson. For example, you might narrate an incident in which Eleanor Roosevelt performs a compassionate act, or one that reveals her intense love of life.

Loren Eiseley

1907–1977

An anthropologist by training and a poet by instinct and vision, Loren Eiseley is unexcelled in communicating the wonders and mysteries of natural science. In works such as *The Immense Journey*, *Darwin's Century*, *The Firmament of Time*, and *The Unexpected Universe*, Eiseley shared his considerable scientific knowledge with an increasingly appreciative lay audience. Born in Lincoln, Nebraska, the son of a hardware salesman, Eiseley first started to collect natural specimens and archaeological artifacts as a schoolboy. At the University of Nebraska, Eiseley majored in anthropology and English and served as an editor of the well-known literary magazine *The Prairie Schooner*. Throughout the 1930's and early 1940's, Eiseley's poems and stories appeared in a number of small periodicals. During this time, Eiseley earned two higher degrees in anthropology at the University of Pennsylvania and worked on several paleontological expeditions in the western United States. In 1937 he joined the faculty of the University of Kansas as an assistant professor of anthropology and sociology; in 1944 he moved on to Ohio's Oberlin College as chairman of the department of sociology and anthropology. Three years later he returned to the University of Pennsylvania as a professor of anthropology and curator of the Early Man collection at the University Museum.

At his death he was the Benjamin Franklin and University Professor of Anthropology and History of Science. A recipient of more than thirty-six honorary degrees and prizes, Eiseley once explained his work by noting that "when the human mind exists in the light of reason and no more than reason, we may say with absolute certainty that man and all that made him will be in that instant gone."

from The Unexpected Universe

The Angry Winter

A time comes when creatures whose destinies have crossed somewhere in the remote past are forced to appraise each other as though they were total strangers. I had been huddled beside the fire one winter night, with the wind prowling outside and shaking the windows. The big shepherd dog on the hearth before me occasionally glanced up affectionately, sighed, and slept. I was working, actually, amidst the debris of a far greater winter. On my desk lay the lance points of ice age hunters and the heavy leg bone of a fossil bison. No remnants of flesh attached to these relics. The deed lay more than ten thousand years remote. It was represented here by naked flint and by bone so mineralized it rang when struck. As I worked on in my little circle of light, I absently laid the bone beside me on the floor. The hour had crept toward midnight. A grating noise, a heavy rasping of big teeth diverted me. I looked down.

The dog had risen. That rock-hard fragment of a vanished beast was in his jaws and he was mouthing it with a fierce intensity I had never seen exhibited by him before.

"Wolf," I exclaimed, and stretched out my hand. The dog backed up but did not yield. A low and steady rumbling began to rise in his chest, something out of a long-gone midnight. There was nothing in that bone to taste, but ancient shapes were moving in his mind and determining his utterance. Only fools gave up bones. He was warning me.

"Wolf," I chided again.

As I advanced, his teeth showed and his mouth wrinkled to strike. The rumbling rose to a direct snarl. His flat head swayed low and wickedly as a reptile's above the floor. I was the most loved object in his universe, but the past was fully alive in him now. Its shadows were whispering in his mind. I knew he was not bluffing. If I made another step he would strike.

Yet his eyes were strained and desperate. "Do not," something pleaded in the back of them, some affectionate thing that had followed at my heel all the days of his mortal life, "do not force me. I am what I am and cannot be otherwise because of the shadows. Do not reach out. You are a man, and my very god. I love you, but do not put out your hand. It is midnight. We are in another time, in the snow."

"The *other* time," the steady rumbling continued while I paused, "the other time in the snow, the big, the final, the terrible snow, when the shape of this thing I hold spelled life. I will not give it up. I cannot. The shadows will not permit me. Do not put out your hand."

I stood silent, looking into his eyes, and heard his whisper through. Slowly I drew back in understanding. The snarl diminished, ceased. As I retreated, the bone slumped to the floor. He placed a paw upon it, warningly.

And were there no shadows in my own mind, I wondered. Had I not for a moment, in the grip of that savage utterance, been about to respond, to hurl myself upon him over an invisible haunch ten thousand years removed? Even to me the shadows had whispered—to me, the scholar in his study.

"Wolf," I said, but this time, holding a familiar leash, I spoke from the door indifferently. "A walk in the snow." Instantly from his eyes that other visitant receded. The bone was left lying. He came eagerly to my side, accepting the leash and taking it in his mouth as always.

A blizzard was raging when we went out, but he paid no heed. On his thick fur the driving snow was soon clinging heavily. He frolicked a little—though usually he was a grave dog—making up to me for something still receding in his mind. I felt the snowflakes fall upon my face, and stood thinking of another time, and another time still, until I was moving from midnight to midnight under ever more remote and vaster snows. Wolf came to my side with a little whimper. It was he who was civilized now. "Come back to the fire," he nudged gently, "or you will be lost." Automatically I took the leash he offered. He led me safely home and into the house.

"We have been very far away," I told him solemnly. "I think there is something in us that we had both better try to forget." Sprawled on the rug, Wolf made no response except to thump his tail feebly out of courtesy. Already he was mostly asleep and dreaming. By the movement of his feet I could see he was running far upon some errand in which I played no part.

Softly I picked up his bone—our bone, rather—and replaced it high on a shelf in my cabinet. As I snapped off the light the white glow from the window seemed to augment itself and shine with a deep, glacial blue. As far as I could see, nothing moved in the long aisles of my neighbor's woods. There was no visible track, and certainly no sound from the living. The snow continued to fall steadily, but the wind, and the shadows it had brought, had vanished.

Getting at Meaning

1. What specific details allow you to infer Eiseley's profession?

2. Reread the opening sentence of the selection. Explain how the experience depicted in the selection illustrates this statement.

3. The focus of this essay is on the writer, rather than on his dog. What does the writer intend to convey about himself? What is the meaning of the experience for him? Does the experience have a permanent effect upon him, or is it merely a glimpsed truth that he is able to place in perspective?

Developing Skills in Reading Literature

1. **Setting and Mood.** How does Eiseley create the setting that serves as appropriate background for the incident he narrates? Cite specific details. What mood is suggested by the setting?

2. **Irony.** What is the significance in the name of Eiseley's dog? Relate the name to the dog's usual behavior and to the uncharacteristic behavior described in this selection.

3. **Style.** How does this essay exhibit all of the major characteristics of a short story? Comment on the structure of the essay as well as on the techniques used by the writer to narrate the incident. What qualities of character can you infer about the writer-narrator? Why do you think that this piece is classified as an essay rather than as a short story?

Agnes De Mille

born in 1909

As a choreographer, director, dancer, and author, Agnes De Mille expressed her aesthetic sense and social awareness over a long and distinguished career beginning with her dance appearances in New York in the late 1920's. Her father was a New York playwright, and her uncle was the film director Cecil B. De Mille. De Mille struggled hard to overcome physical limitations and realize her early ambition to become a dancer. Referring to the determination that saw her through her adolescence, De Mille recalled her youth with characteristic honesty: "I considered my body a shame, a trap, and a betrayal. But I could break it. I was a dancer." During the 1930's she toured as a dancer and choreographer throughout the United States, England, France, and Denmark before returning to New York to join the Ballet Theatre in 1939. During the 1940's she choreographed Broadway musicals such as *Oklahoma!, One Touch of Venus, Tally-Ho, Bloomer Girl, Brigadoon,* and *Carousel.* She launched her writing career in 1952 with the publication of the autobiographical *Dance to the Piper,* followed in 1956 by another autobiographical work, *And Promenade Home.* Subsequent works, including *To a Young Dancer, The Book of the Dance, Russian Journals,* and *Where the Wings Grow,* comprise an unsurpassed first-person account of a lifelong involvement with dance and musical theater.

from **Dance to the Piper**

Decision

The first lesson was a private one conducted by Miss Fredova. Miss Fredova was born Winifred Edwards and had received her training in London from Anna Pavlova.[1] She was as slim as a sapling and always wore white like a trained nurse. She parted her dark hair in the center and drew it to the nape of her neck in glossy wings, Russian style. She was shod in low-heeled sandals. She taught standing erect as a guardsman, and beat time with a long pole. First she picked up a watering can and sprinkled water on the floor in a sunny corner by the barre.[2] This she explained was so we should not slip. Then she placed our hands on the barre and showed us how to turn out our feet ninety degrees from their normal walking stance into first position. Then she told us to *plier* or bend our knees deeply, keeping our heels as long as possible on the floor. I naturally stuck out behind. I found the pole placed rigidly against my spine. I naturally pressed forward on my insteps. Her leg and knee planted against my foot curbed this tendency. "I can't move," I said, laughing with winning helplessness.

"Don't talk," she said. "Down-ee, two-ee, three-ee, four-ee. Down the heels, don't rock on your feet."

At the end of ten minutes the sweat stuck in beads on my forehead. "May I sit down?" I asked.

"You must never sit during practice. It ruins the thigh muscles. If you sit down you may not continue with class." I, of course, would have submitted to a beating with whips rather than stop. I was taking the first steps into the promised land. The path might be thorny but it led straight to Paradise. "Down-ee, two-ee, three-ee, four-ee. *Nuca*. Give me this fourth position. Repeat the exercise."

So she began every lesson. So I have begun every practice period since. It is part of the inviolable ritual of ballet dancing. Every ballet student that has ever trained in the classic technique in any part of the world begins just this way, never any other.

I bent to the discipline. I learned to relax with my head between my knees when I felt sick or faint. I learned how to rest my insteps by lying on my back with my feet vertically up against the wall. I learned how to bind up my toes so that they would not bleed through the satin shoes. But I never sat down. I learned the first and all-important dictate of ballet dancing—never to miss the daily practice, sickness or health, never to miss the barre practice; to miss meals, sleep, rehearsals even but not the practice, not for one day ever under any circumstances, except on Sundays and during childbirth.

I seemed, however, to have little aptitude for the business. What had all this talk about God-given talent amounted to? It was like trying to wiggle my ears. I strained and strained. Nothing perceptible happened. A terrible sense of frustration drove me to striving with masochistic[3] frenzy. Twice I fainted

---

1. **Anna Pavlova** (päv' lô vä): (1885?–1931) Russian ballet dancer.
2. **barre** (bär) *French:* the bar or handrail in a dance studio.
3. **masochistic** (mas' ə kiz' tik): the getting of pleasure from being dominated or hurt physically or psychologically.

in class. My calves used to ache until tears stuck in my eyes. I learned every possible manipulation of the shoe to ease the aching tendons in my insteps. I used to get abominable stitches in my sides from attempting continuous jumps. But I never sat down. I learned to cool my forehead against the plaster of the walls. I licked the perspiration off from around my mouth. I breathed through my nose though my eyes bugged. But I did not sit and I did not stop.

Ballet technique is arbitrary and very difficult. It never becomes easy; it becomes possible. The effort involved in making a dancer's body is so long and relentless, in many instances so painful, the effort to maintain the technique so grueling that unless a certain satisfaction is derived from the disciplining and punishing, the pace could not be maintained. Most dancers are to an extent masochists. "What a good pain! What a profitable pain!" said Miss Fredova as she stretched her insteps in her two strong hands. "I have practiced for three hours. I am exhausted, and I feel wonderful."

Paradoxically enough ballet dancing is designed to give the impression of lightness and ease. Nothing in classic dancing should be convulsive or tormented. Derived from the seventeenth- and eighteenth-century court dances the style is kingly, a series of harmonious and balanced postures linked by serene movement. The style involves a total defiance of gravity, and because this must perforce be an illusion, the effect is achieved first by an enormous strengthening of the legs and feet to produce great resilient jumps and second by a co-ordination of arms and head in a rhythm slower than the rhythm of the legs which have no choice but to take the weight of the body when the body falls. But the slow relaxed movement of head and arms gives the illusion of sustained flight, gives the sense of effortless ease.

The lungs may be bursting, the heart pounding in the throat, sweat springing from every pore, but hands must float in repose, the head stir gently as though swooning in delight. The diaphragm must be lifted to expand the chest fully, proudly; the abdomen pulled in flat. The knees must be taut and flat to give the extended leg every inch of length. The leg must be turned outward forty-five degrees in the hip socket so that the side of the knee and the long unbroken line of the leg are presented to view and never the lax, droopy line of a bent knee. The leg must look like a sword. The foot arches to prolong the line of extension. The supporting foot turns out forty-five degrees to enhance the line of the supporting leg, to keep the hips even, and to ensure the broadest possible base for the support and balancing of the body.

The ideal ballet body is long limbed with a small compact torso. This makes for beauty of line; the longer the arms and legs the more exciting the body line. The ideal ballet foot has a high taut instep and a wide stretch in the Achilles' tendon. This tendon is the spring on which a dancer pushes for his jump, the hinge on which he takes the shock of landing. If there is one tendon in a dancer's body more important than any other, it is this tendon. It is, I should say, the prerequisite for all great technique. When the heel does not stretch easily and softly like a cat's, as mine did not, almost to the point of malformation, the shock of running or jumping must be taken somewhere in the spine by sticking out behind, for instance, in a sitting posture after every jump. I seemed to be all rusty wire and safety pins. My torso was long with unusually broad hips, my legs and arms abnormally short, my hands and feet broad and short. I was fat besides. What I did not know was that I was constructed for endurance and that I developed through effort alone a capacity for outperforming far, far better technicians. Because I was built like a mustang, stocky, mettlesome, and sturdy, I became a good jumper, growing special compensating muscles up the front of my shins for the lack of a helpful heel. But the long, cool, serene classic line was forever denied me.

And at first, of course, the compensations and adjustments were neither present nor indicated. Every dancer makes his own body. He is born only with certain physical tendencies. This making of a ballet leg takes approximately ten years and the initial stages are almost entirely discouraging, for even the best look awkward and paralyzed at the beginning.

My predicament was intensified by the fact that Mother and Father had no intention of permitting me to slight my other studies for this new enthusiasm. I was allowed one private lesson a week (forty-five minutes) and one class lesson (one hour). In between times I practiced at home alone, something no dancer, pupil, or professional, ever does. One needs company to overcome the almost irresistible tendency to flag. One needs someone else's eye on awkward parts impossible to see. It is an unnatural and unprofitable strain for a child to practice without supervision. I practiced in Mother's bathroom where she had a little barre fitted for me. The floor was slippery and there was no mirror. And I hated to practice there. I flagellated[4] myself into the daily grind.

Since I could not practice long, obviously I must practice harder. I strained and strained. Between the Monday lesson and the Thursday lesson, I developed and matured rigid bad habits. Every week I developed a new bad habit.

The plain truth is I was the worst pupil in the class. Having grown into adolescence feeling that I was remarkably gifted and destined to be great (I remember a friend asking Mother, "But do you want her to be a professional dancer?" and Mother's cool reply, "If she can be a Pavlova—not otherwise"), I now found I could not hold my own with any of the girls standing on the floor beside me. So I crept about at the rear of the group, found matters wrong with my shoes, with my knees, with my hair, resorted to any device to get away from the dreadful exposure.

Only once did I have a small bit of my share of success. On a single occasion Kosloff gave exercises in pantomime. He suddenly stopped the class and called me out from my position in the back of the room. I demonstrated the exercise to a hushed and watching group. I did, of course, the best I could, trembling a little. They applauded. Kosloff beamed on me. He told Uncle Cecil that I showed the finest talent for pantomime of any pupil he had ever taught. This remark was naturally not repeated to me until long after.

My well-filled curriculum—classes, homework, tennis, piano, editing—was ordered with just one thought: to make room for the dance practice. I rose at six-thirty and I studied and practiced at breakneck concentration until six in the evening when I was at last free to put on dancing dress and walk—to Mother's bathroom.

All through the lonely, drab exercises beside Mother's tub, without music or beat, proper floor or mirror, I had the joy of looking forward to dinner with Father, to hearing him talk about his scenarios and what was going on at the studio. Sometimes he talked about music and literature. Once he said he thought I was an artist. Sometimes after dinner he sang and I accompanied him. These evenings my cup ran over. I went to bed early planning next day's practice, praying to do better in class. And as I lay waiting for sleep, breathing in the moist garden smells with my fox terrier slowly pressing me from the comfortable center of the bed, I used to dream about dancing on the stage with Pavlova, dancing until I dropped in a faint at her feet so that she would notice me and say, "That girl has talent."

As I grew older it became increasingly difficult to follow a routine of work at home. The house seemed to be always full of people.

---

4. **flagellated** (flaj′ ə lat′d′): whipped, flogged.

They were interesting people. I longed to join them. When I undressed and went into Mother's bathroom for my bootless workout, I could hear the sound of tennis rackets and laughter. I felt I was not getting anywhere with dancing: I knew I was not making technical progress. I began to dread the lonely practice morbidly. I thought about it at school all day, and on the way home I used to long for something beyond my control that would interrupt or delay it, an accident even. By the time I got through high school, dancing meant exhaustion and little else.

Father sat me down and told me in so many words that I had to give it my whole time or I must abandon it. Father was being quite honest. At this point had I chosen dancing he would have supported the decision. But the years of restraint had done their work. Gradually, I had grown disheartened. The dance studio seemed only the scene of endless unprogressing strain. To shut myself up with those dreary, hard-working girls away from the verve of Father's company, the house and its parties, away from Mother's activities, the friends, the conversations, meant a kind of death. There were no ballet companies in the United States at that time. The only opening lay in Kosloff's moving-picture troupe or in his vaudeville tour. My spirit quailed.

One morning toward the end of summer I walked into Father's bedroom while he was shaving. "Pop," I said, "I've decided to give up dancing and go to college." He replied without looking away from the mirror. "I'm glad you have, my dear. I don't think you would have been happy."

The next week I entered the university.

For four years this lovely life lasted. I continued in a happy somnambulistic state, blousy, disheveled, dropping hairpins, tennis balls, and notebooks wherever I went, drinking tea with Dr. Lily Campbell and the professors, lapping up talk of books and history, drinking tea with classmates and Elizabeth Boynton, the librarian, having dates or nearly dates with the two *M*'s on either side of me, Macon and Morgan, having dates with Leonarde Keeler, falling asleep in all afternoon lectures, late for every appointment (once when I entered English history on time the whole class burst out laughing). With the smell of iris and budding acacia coming through the windows, the sound of scholasticism filling my dreams with a reassuring hum, I sank deeper and deeper into a kind of cerebral miasma[5] as I postponed all vital decisions. I had some vague, soothing fantasy of living in Mother's garden indefinitely, and studying until I slipped gracefully into old age while I wrote exquisitely about—what? No doubt it would all become apparent in time.

Occasionally I staged dances for the student rallies, mostly to Chopin, mostly about yearning for beauty and always accompanied by sorority sisters who were not trained. Campbell shook her head. "This is not good," she said. "You simply haven't a dancer's body. I'd like you to write, but if you must go on the stage, act. I believe you're a tragic actress. Stop dancing. Look at yourself in the mirror."

I usually danced about Beauty and how one should be ready to die for it. I did a good number of Petrarch's sonnets at one football rally when the men got their letters. I suspect the student body must have had pretty nearly enough of me.

In order to get back up on my numb points, I had started exercising again. At first only for a couple of weeks before each show, but gradually—I swear I had banished from conscious intention all thought of going back on the stage—I got to practicing every day. It could not be for very long and it was always late at night after I had finished studying. I used to fall asleep over my books, and then toward midnight force myself awake, and

---

5. **miasma** (mī az' mə): an unwholesome atmosphere, originally a vapor rising from marshes or from rotting organic material.

shaking with fatigue perform between the bureau and the closet mirrors, *relevés*[6] in every position, on toes that went pins and needles with the unexpected pressure. I tried not to shake the floor out of concern for the sleeping family. Once, while I prodded along the upstairs hall in a particularly stumpy *pas de bourrée*,[7] Father stepped out of his study, pipe in one hand, book in the other, and contemplated me. I kept going. I was in my petticoat, face blanched and wet with weariness. At length he spoke, "All this education and I'm still just the father of a circus." He went back in his room and shut the door.

At the Pasadena Playhouse, my sister Margaret had spotted a young actor she thought she'd like to get better acquainted with. She engineered a meeting; that is, she gave out the order that he was to be brought to the house on a Sunday night, and he was brought. His name was Douglass Montgomery and he turned out to have good manners and a pleasant husky charm. Mag liked him fine. She arranged to take him through the Fairbanks studio, which was the second step in her softening-up routine. He came the following Sunday. Mag was dressed to kill in white silk, a dazzling white coat, a white cloche on her sleek dark hair. She sported gardenias and fake pearls. I thought she looked, as always, just ravishing. I was dressed in a dirty red practice tunic and I had all the living room rugs rolled back to the wall. Mag met him at the garden gate and whisked him around to the tennis court where the lively twanging of rackets and the yelping of our seven dogs gave evidence of Father's Sunday fun. "But what is that going on in the house?" said Douglass, turning his head. "Oh that," said Mag, "never mind about that. That is just my sister Agnes, who practices dancing on Sunday afternoon."

"I would like to see," said Douglass, and although she resisted, he maneuvered her back. There was no use in apologizing for the way I looked. Nobody looked the way I did who expected to be seen by anyone else. "Do you do this where people can watch you?" he asked.

"Well," I said with great misgiving. "This Friday . . . it's just amateur. . . ."

"I'll come," said Dug.

Dug came. He stood backstage at the Friday Morning Club and looked me hard in the face. He trembled a little. There were tears of excitement in his eyes. (Dug was only seventeen.) He spoke in a very low voice. He put a cigarette in his mouth, but his lips shook. "Look here. You're no amateur. You're a very great performer. You belong to the world. Get out of the university. Stop this nonsense. Get into the theater. You've got a calling. You've got a duty. It's hard to say. Are you listening to me? You're a great dancer."

No trumpets sound when the important decisions of our life are made. Destiny is made known silently. The wheels turn within our hearts for years and suddenly everything meshes and we are lifted into the next level of progress. In a crowd of fussing clubwomen, over-dressed, chattering, impatient to get to their chicken patties and ice cream, the laborious battlements my father had erected with all the sincerity of his heart and life care fell before one sentence. This boy simply said what I had waited all my life to hear.

---

6. *relevés* (re le vāz') *French:* rising from a flat foot position to the toes in dance.
7. *pas de bourrée* (pa də bōō rā') *French:* a sidewise step in dance in which one foot crosses the other.

Getting at Meaning

1. In the first paragraph what seems to be the attitude of the writer toward ballet practice? Where do you begin to see a change in attitude as the essay progresses?

2. Find the paragraph that begins, "Ballet technique is arbitrary and very difficult." What is the purpose of this paragraph along with the four paragraphs that follow? Summarize the essential facts about ballet that you learn in this section by stating the main idea of each paragraph and then noting the key details that develop the idea.

3. What discouragements lead to De Mille's first major decision—to give up ballet for college? What is her father's reaction to her decision? What quality does his reaction reveal? What other qualities can you infer from the information in this essay?

4. How does De Mille characterize her four years at college? In what ways are these years totally different from her years of ballet training? In what ways are they a preparation for her final decision to pursue a career in dance?

5. When De Mille's father discovers his daughter practicing ballet late at night, he says, "All this education and I'm still just the father of a circus." What does he mean?

6. Contrast De Mille's two decisions. What is the basis of her decision to go to college? While she is a student, does she consciously plan to become a ballet dancer? How do you react to the revelation that Douglass Montgomery is only seventeen? Why do his statements make such an impact on De Mille?

Developing Skills in Reading Literature

1. **Style.** By the sixth paragraph, beginning with "I bent to the discipline," the reader is fully immersed in the description of ballet training. How do the preceding paragraphs gradually change in tone and mood as they lead to this paragraph? What does this change in tone and mood reveal about the writer?

Describe the style of the paragraph on discipline. This paragraph and the one that follows contain numerous repetitions of "I learned" and "I never sat down." Which of these statements is the prerequisite for the other? What feeling is achieved through these repetitions? What ideas are strengthened?

The lengths of the paragraphs in this essay range from a single sentence to three or four sentences to fully developed units of fifteen lines or more. Select several examples of paragraphs that vary in length and examine them to determine why these variations in length are suited to De Mille's purposes and to the effects she intends to convey.

2. **Essay.** The concluding section of the essay, beginning with "At the Pasadena Playhouse . . .," is more narrative in style than earlier sections, which are predominantly explanatory. How does the change in content account for this change in style?

Developing Writing Skills

1. **Writing a Report.** Arriving at a career decision sometimes results from logical planning; at other times, the decision results from a convergence of chance factors and opportunities of the moment. Interview several adults to learn how each made the decision that resulted in his or her choice of career. Did a single crucial incident make the person conscious of what had always been known intuitively? Was there a particular person or situation that influenced the decision?

Select the most interesting interview, and write a report that narrates how the individual chose a career.

2. **Writing an Autobiographical Essay.** Agnes De Mille writes, "The wheels turn within our hearts for years and suddenly everything meshes and we are lifted into the next level of progress. . . . This boy simply said what I had waited all my life to hear."

What "wheels" are turning within your own heart now? What career seems the most attractive? How do you know that this choice would be right for you? Write an autobiographical essay titled "As of This Moment" in which you explain what career decision you would like to make and why.

Lorraine Hansberry

1930–1965

Four years after Lorraine Hansberry's untimely death from cancer, the posthumous production of *To Be Young, Gifted, and Black* solidified her reputation as a clear-sighted observer of the human dilemmas encountered in a multi-racial society. Her much-acclaimed first play, *A Raisin in the Sun*, focuses on the social and personal conflicts besetting a black family living in Chicago and the courage they display in ultimately resolving them. Praised for its "vigor as well as veracity," the play, which was the first Broadway production written by a black woman, received the New York Drama Critics Circle Award in 1959.

The youngest daughter of a prosperous real estate broker who taught his children the importance of asserting their dignity, Hansberry was born in Chicago and acquired her love for the theater while attending public schools on the city's south side. During two years of study at the University of Wisconsin, she developed an appreciation for the works of Ibsen, Strindberg, and Sean O'Casey. In 1950 she moved to New York, where she studied African history under W. E. B. DuBois and worked at Paul Robeson's *Freedom* magazine. Her experiences during this time taught her that "all racism is rotten, black or white, that everything is politi-cal, and that people tend to be indescribably beautiful and uproariously funny." In 1953 she married the music publisher and song writer Robert Nemiroff. In addition to plays such as *The Sign in Sidney Brustein's Window*, *Les Blancs*, and *The Drinking Gourd*, Hansberry wrote numerous essays for publication and faithfully kept private journals and diaries, which her husband later developed into the two-act drama *To Be Young, Gifted, and Black*.

from To Be Young, Gifted, and Black

1

For some time now—I think since I was a child—I have been possessed of the desire to put down the stuff of my life. That is a commonplace impulse, apparently, among persons of massive self-interest; sooner or later we all do it. And, I am quite certain, there is only one internal quarrel: how much of the truth to tell? How much, how much, how much! It *is* brutal, in sober uncompromising moments, to reflect on the comedy of concern we all enact when it comes to our precious images!

Even so, when such vanity as propels the writing of such memoirs is examined, certainly one would wish at least to have some boast of social serviceability on one's side. I shall set down in these pages what shall seem to me to be the truth of my life and essences . . . which are to be found, first of all, on the Southside of Chicago, where I was born. . . .

3

I was born May 19, 1930, the last of four children.

Of love and my parents there is little to be written: their relationship to their children was utilitarian. We were fed and housed and dressed and outfitted with more cash than our associates and that was all. We were also vaguely taught certain vague absolutes: that we were better than no one but infinitely superior to everyone; that we were the products of the proudest and most mistreated of the races of man; that there was nothing enormously difficult about life; that one *succeeded* as a matter of course.

Life was not a struggle—it was something that one *did*. One won an argument because, if facts gave out, one invented them—with color! The only sinful people in the world were dull people. And, above all, there were two things which were never to be betrayed: the family and the race. But of love, there was nothing ever said.

If we were sick, we were sternly, impersonally and carefully nursed and doctored back to health. Fevers, toothaches were attended to with urgency and importance; one always felt *important* in my family. Mother came with a tray to your room with the soup and Vick's salve or gave the enemas in a steaming bathroom. But we were not fondled, any of us—head held to breast, fingers about that head—until we were grown, all of us, and my father died.

At his funeral I at last, in my memory, saw my mother hold her sons that way, and for the first time in her life my sister held me in her arms I think. We were not a loving people: we were passionate in our hostilities and affinities, but the caress embarrassed us.

We have changed little. . . .

5

My childhood Southside summers were the ordinary city kind, full of the street games which other rememberers have turned into fine ballets these days, and rhymes that anticipated what some people insist on calling modern poetry:
Oh, Mary Mack, Mack, Mack
With the silver buttons, buttons, buttons
All down her back, back, back.
She asked her mother, mother, mother

For fifteen cents, cents, cents
To see the elephant, elephant, elephant
Jump the fence, fence, fence.
Well, he jumped so high, high, high
'Til he touched the sky, sky, sky
And he didn't come back, back, back
'Til the Fourth of Ju—ly, ly, ly!

I remember skinny little Southside bodies
by the fives and tens of us panting the delicious hours away:

"May I?"

And the voice of authority: "Yes, you may
—you may take one giant step."

One drew in all one's breath and tightened
one's fist and pulled the small body against
the heavens, stretching, straining all the muscles in the legs to make—one giant step.

It is a long time. One forgets the reason for
the game. (For children's games are always
explicit in their reasons for being. To play is
to win something. Or not to be "it." Or to be
high pointer, or outdoer or, sometimes—just
the winner. But after a time one forgets.)

Why was it important to take a small step, a
teeny step, or the most desired of all—one
GIANT step?

A giant step *to where?*

6

Evenings were spent mainly on the back
porches where screen doors slammed in the
darkness with those really very special sum-
mertime sounds. And, sometimes, when Chicago nights got too steamy, the whole family
got into the car and went to the park and slept
out in the open on blankets. Those were, of
course, the best times of all because the
grownups were invariably reminded of having
been children in the South and told the best
stories then. And it was also cool and sweet to
be on the grass and there was usually the
scent of freshly cut lemons or melons in the
air. Daddy would lie on his back, as fathers

must, and explain about how men thought
the stars above us came to be and how far
away they were.

I never did learn to believe that anything
could be as far away as *that*. Especially the
stars. . . .

Following the success of her play, *A Raisin in
the Sun* in 1958, in 1964 she made the following
address to a group of young Black writers.

7

Ladies and gentlemen, Fellow Writers:

I have had an opportunity to read three of
the winning compositions in this United
Negro College Fund contest—and it is clear I
am addressing fellow writers indeed. Miss
Purvis, Miss Yeldell, and Mr. Lewis—I com-
mend you and add my personal congratulations to the awards of the afternoon.

Apart from anything else, I wanted to be
able to come here and speak with you on this
occasion because you are young, gifted, and
black. In the month of May in the year 1964, I,
for one, can think of no more dynamic combination that a person might be.

The Negro writer stands surrounded by the
whirling elements of this world. He stands
neither on a fringe nor utterly involved: the
prime observer waiting poised for inclusion.

O, the things that we have learned in this
unkind house that we have to tell the world
about!

Despair? Did someone say despair was a
question in the world? Well then, listen to the
sons of those who have known little else if
you wish to know the resiliency of this thing
you would so quickly resign to mythhood,
this thing called the human spirit. . . .

Life? Ask those who have tasted of it in
pieces rationed out by enemies.

Love? Ah, ask the troubadors who come
from those who have loved when all reason

pointed to the uselessness and foolhardiness of love. Perhaps we shall be the teachers when it is done. Out of the depths of pain we have thought to be our sole heritage in this world—O, we know about love!

And that is why I say to *you* that, though it be a thrilling and marvelous thing to be merely young and gifted in such times, it is doubly so, doubly dynamic—to be young, gifted, *and black.*

Look at the work that awaits you!

Write if you will: but write about the world as it is and as you think it *ought* to be and must be—if there is to be a world.

Write about all the things that men have written about since the beginning of writing and talking—but write *to a point.* Work hard at it, *care* about it.

Write about *our people:* tell their story. You have something glorious to draw on begging for attention. Don't pass it up. *Use* it.

Good luck to you. This Nation needs your gifts.

Perfect them!

Getting at Meaning

1. Although Hansberry says that her family is not demonstrative, what evidence do you find that her family is a loving group in its own way? What does the family provide for her?

2. How do the childhood games described by Hansberry relate to the challenges of adult life? What lessons do these games teach the young Lorraine?

3. In Hansberry's remarks to the young black writers, what are the connections between the advice she offers to them and the autobiographical details in the selection? What is her philosophy about being "young, gifted, and black"?

4. Hansberry writes, "Why was it important to take a small step, a teeny step, or the most desired of all—one GIANT step? A giant step *to where*?" In what way do her remarks to the young writers suggest an answer to this question?

Developing Skills in Reading Literature

Tone. The excerpt from Hansberry's autobiography derives its special appeal from her tone, her attitude toward "the stuff" of her life, namely, her early years on the South Side of Chicago. Examine the specific details of her memories of family, the games of summer, and the hot summer evenings. What is the tone of her remembrances? What feelings about her background are suggested by this tone?

Developing Writing Skills

Describing a Person. If you were to write a speech introducing Lorraine Hansberry to an audience, what character qualities would you identify to personalize this writer? Determine several characteristics from the autobiographical excerpt and from her speech to the young writers. Present these character qualities in a composition that could be read to the class. Use quotations from her writing to illustrate the characteristics you have identified.

Richard Rodriguez

born in 1944

With the publication in 1982 of his autobiography, *Hunger of Memory*, Richard Rodriguez emerged as a compelling new commentator on American culture and educational practices.

The uniqueness of Rodriguez's experience lies at the heart of his perceptions of the contemporary American scene. The son of Spanish-speaking Mexican immigrants, Rodriguez spoke barely fifty words of English upon entering parochial school in Sacramento, California, when he was six years old. After an early struggle to learn the language, Rodriguez became a rising star in an educational system that nurtured him with scholarships and fellowships to Stanford, Columbia, and the University of California at Berkeley, where he earned a doctoral degree in English Renaissance literature in 1976. Offered several teaching positions at prestigious universities, Rodriguez turned them all down to devote himself to an introspective assessment of his life culminating in *Hunger of Memory*. As he put it, "I have been haunted by how my education has made me different." Now living and writing in San Francisco, Rodriguez provides disturbing testimony to how the American melting pot actually works.

from **Hunger of Memory**

In fourth grade I embarked upon a grandiose reading program. "Give me the names of important books," I would say to startled teachers. They soon found out that I had in mind "adult books." I ignored their suggestion of anything I suspected was written for children. (Not until I was in college, as a result, did I read *Huckleberry Finn* or *Alice's Adventures in Wonderland*.) Instead, I read *The Scarlet Letter* and Franklin's *Autobiography*. And whatever I read I read for extra credit. Each time I finished a book, I reported the achievement to a teacher and basked in the praise my effort earned. Despite my best efforts, however, there seemed to be more and more books I needed to read. At the library I would literally tremble as I came upon whole shelves of books I hadn't read. So I read and I read and I read: *Great Expectations*; all the short stories of Kipling; *The Babe Ruth Story*; the entire first volume of the *Encyclopaedia Britannica* (A-ANSTEY); the *Iliad*; *Moby-Dick*; *Gone with the Wind*; *The Good Earth*; *Ramona*; *Forever Amber*; *The Lives of the Saints*; *Crime and Punishment*; *The Pearl*. . . . Librarians who initially frowned when I checked out the maximum ten books at a time started saving books they thought I might like. Teachers would say to the rest of the class, "I only wish the rest of you took reading as seriously as Richard obviously does."

But at home I would hear my mother wondering, "What do you see in your books?" (Was reading a hobby like her knitting? Was so much reading even healthy for a boy? Was it the sign of "brains"? Or was it just a convenient excuse for not helping around the house on Saturday mornings?) Always, "What do you see . . . ?"

What *did* I see in my books? I had the idea that they were crucial for my academic success, though I couldn't have said exactly how or why. In the sixth grade I simply concluded that what gave a book its value was some major idea or theme it contained. If that core essence could be mined and memorized, I would become learned like my teachers. I decided to record in a notebook the themes of the books that I read. After reading *Robinson Crusoe*, I wrote that its theme was "the value of learning to live by oneself." When I completed *Wuthering Heights*, I noted the danger of "letting emotions get out of control." Rereading these brief moralistic appraisals usually left me disheartened. I couldn't believe that they were really the source of reading's value. But for many more years, they constituted the only means I had of describing to myself the educational value of books.

In spite of my earnestness, I found reading a pleasurable activity. I came to enjoy the lonely good company of books. Early on weekday mornings, I'd read in my bed. I'd feel a mysterious comfort then, reading in the dawn quiet —the blue-gray silence interrupted by the occasional churning of the refrigerator motor a few rooms away or the more distant sounds of a city bus beginning its run. On weekends I'd go to the public library to read, surrounded by old men and women. Or, if the weather was fine, I would take my books to the park and read in the shade of a tree. A warm summer evening was my favorite reading time. Neighbors would leave for vacation and I would water their lawns. I would sit through the twilight on the front porches or in back-yards, reading to the cool, whirling sounds of the sprinklers.

I also had favorite writers. But often those writers I enjoyed most I was least able to value. When I read William Saroyan's *The Human Comedy*, I was immediately pleased by the narrator's warmth and the charm of his story. But as quickly I became suspicious. A book so enjoyable to read couldn't be very "important." Another summer I determined to read all the novels of Dickens. Reading his fat novels, I loved the feeling I got—after the first hundred pages—of being at home in a fictional world where I knew the names of the characters and cared about what was going to happen to them. And it bothered me that I was forced away at the conclusion, when the fiction closed tight, like a fortune-teller's fist —the futures of all the major characters neatly resolved. I never knew how to take such feelings seriously, however. Nor did I suspect that these experiences could be part of a novel's meaning. Still, there were pleasures to sustain me after I'd finish my books. Carrying a volume back to the library, I would be pleased by its weight. I'd run my fingers along the edge of the pages and marvel at the breadth of my achievement. Around my room, growing stacks of paperback books re-enforced my assurance.

I entered high school having read hundreds of books. My habit of reading made me a confident speaker and writer of English. Reading also enabled me to sense something of the shape, the major concerns, of Western thought. (I was able to say something about Dante and Descartes and Engels and James Baldwin in my high school term papers.) In these various ways, books brought me aca-demic success as I hoped that they would. But I was not a good reader. Merely bookish, I lacked a point of view when I read. Rather, I read in order to acquire a point of view. I vacuumed books for epigrams, scraps of infor-mation, ideas, themes—anything to fill the hollow within me and make me feel educated. When one of my teachers suggested to his drowsy tenth-grade English class that a per-son could not have a "complicated idea" until he had read at least two thousand books, I heard the remark without detecting either its irony or its very complicated truth. I merely determined to compile a list of all the books I had ever read. Harsh with myself, I included only once a title I might have read several times. (How, after all, could one read a book more than once?) And I included only those books over a hundred pages in length. (Could anything shorter be a book?)

There was yet another high school list I compiled. One day I came across a newspaper article about the retirement of an English professor at a nearby state college. The article was accompanied by a list of the "hundred most important books of Western Civiliza-tion." "More than anything else in my life," the professor told the reporter with finality, "these books have made me all that I am." That was the kind of remark I couldn't ignore. I clipped out the list and kept it for the several months it took me to read all of the titles. Most books, of course, I barely understood. While reading Plato's *Republic*, for instance, I needed to keep looking at the book jacket comments to remind myself what the text was about. Nevertheless, with the special patience and superstition of a scholarship boy, I looked at every word of the text. And by the time I reached the last word, relieved, I convinced myself that I had read *The Repub-lic*. In a ceremony of great pride, I solemnly crossed Plato off my list.

The scholarship boy pleases most when he is young—the working-class child struggling for academic success. To his teachers, he offers great satisfaction; his success is their proudest achievement. Many other persons offer to help him. A businessman learns the boy's story and promises to underwrite part of the cost of his college education. A woman leaves him her entire library of several hundred books when she moves. His progress is featured in a newspaper article. Many people seem happy for him. They marvel. "How did you manage so fast?" From all sides, there is lavish praise and encouragement.

In his grammar school classroom, however, the boy already makes students around him uneasy. They scorn his desire to succeed. They scorn him for constantly wanting the teacher's attention and praise. . . . Later, when he makes it to college, no one will mock him aloud. But he detects annoyance on the faces of some students and even some teachers who watch him. It puzzles him often. In college, then in graduate school, he behaves much as he always has. If anything is different about him it is that he dares to anticipate the successful conclusion of his studies. At last he feels that he belongs in the classroom, and this is exactly the source of the dissatisfaction he causes. To many persons around him, he appears too much the academic. There may be some things about him that recall his beginnings—his shabby clothes; his persistent poverty; or his dark skin (in those cases when it symbolizes his parents' disadvantaged condition)—but they only make clear how far he has moved from his past. He has used education to remake himself. . . . If, because of my schooling, I had grown culturally separated from my parents, my education finally [after several years] had given me ways of speaking and caring about that fact.

Getting at Meaning

1. Rodriguez enters high school "having read hundreds of books." What is his primary motivation for this "grandiose reading program"? What books is he "least able to value"? What relationship exists between the biographical facts of his boyhood and this ambitious plan? Why would he not regard as valuable those books that gave him pleasure?

2. Rodriguez admits that despite his success in high school, he was not a good reader, just bookish. He says, "I lacked a point of view when I read. Rather, I read in order to acquire a point of view." What is the distinction between reading with a point of view and reading to acquire a point of view? How does one acquire a point of view? Should wide reading be attempted before the reader has established a point of view? Explain your answer.

3. In discussing "the scholarship boy" in the last part of this essay, Rodriguez ends on a somewhat somber note. What unhappiness does he experience in the classroom? Why do his classmates and some of his teachers find him difficult to tolerate? What positive result does Rodriguez achieve through his schooling?

Developing Skills in Reading Literature

Style. Study the style in which this excerpt is written. Note diction, sentence lengths, characteristic punctuation, the use of questions and parenthetical remarks, repetitions of words and phrases, and figurative language. What stylistic devices are characteristic of Rodriguez's prose? What is their overall effect in his writing?

Developing Writing Skills

Explaining an Idea. In *Walden* Thoreau writes, "A written word is the choicest of relics. It is something at once more intimate with us and more universal than any other work of art. It is the work of art nearest to life itself. How many a man has dated a new era in his life from the reading of a book."

These statements are deliberately exaggerated; nonetheless, they do emphasize, justifiably, the importance and value of books. Which books have been of greatest value to you? Select one or two, and in a brief composition explain their significance in your life.

Issues and Insights

ICE GLARE, 1933. *Charles Burchfield.*
Collection of the Whitney Museum of American Art, New York.

Archibald MacLeish

1892–1982

Born in Illinois, MacLeish did his undergraduate work at Yale and studied law at Harvard, taking his degree after serving in France during World War I. Intent on focusing on his writing, he left his Boston law practice in 1923 and joined the colony of expatriate writers in Paris, where he began to write verse echoing the dominant technical and thematic concerns of the day. Like T.S. Eliot, MacLeish argued for the integrity of a poem's existence independent of the personality of its poet when he wrote in "Ars Poetica" that "A poem should not mean/ But be." Also like Eliot, he used myth and the literary tradition as the raw materials for a meaningful artistic response to what he refers to in "The End of the World" as ". . . the black pall/ of nothing—nothing at all."

Returning to his Massachusetts farm in 1928, MacLeish became an editor for *Fortune* magazine while continuing to write poems and dramatic verse reflecting an emerging willingness to fuse his art with his social concerns. During World War II, MacLeish held a variety of governmental posts, including Assistant Secretary of State and chairman of the United States delegation to the UNESCO drafting conference. He followed his years of public service with a teaching career at Harvard, while assuming a more personal and philosophical stance in his later poetry. Over the course of his career, MacLeish won three Pulitzer Prizes, including one in drama for his 1958 verse play, *J.B.*

The best of MacLeish's poems are surely crafted and morally sensitive explorations and statements of the human predicament and of art's necessary clarifying function. They constitute an important contribution to the canon of American letters.

from **A Continuing Journey**

The Unimagined America

The whole history of our continent is a history of the imagination. Men imagined land beyond the sea and found it. No force of terror, no pressure of population, drove our ancestors across this continent. They came, as the great explorers crossed the Atlantic, because of the imagination of their minds— because they imagined a better, a more beautiful, a freer, happier world; because they were men not only of courage, not only of strength and hardiness, but of warm and vivid desire; because they desired; because they had the power to desire.

And what was true of the continent was true of the Republic. Because our forefathers were able to conceive a free man's government, they were able to create it. Because those who lived before us in this nation were able to imagine a new thing, a thing unheard of in the world before, a thing the skeptical and tired men who did not trust in dreams had not been able to imagine, they erected on this continent the first society in which mankind was to be free, all mankind.

The courage of the Declaration of Independence is a far greater courage than the bravery of those who risked their necks to sign it. The courage of the Declaration of Independence is the courage of the act of the imagination. Jefferson's document is an image of a life, a plan of life, a dream—indeed a dream.

But our right to live as we imagine men should live is not a right drawn from dreaming only. We have, and know we have, the abundant means to bring our dreams to pass— to create for ourselves whatever world we have the courage to desire. We have the metal and the men to take this country down, if we please to take it down, and to build it again as we please to build it. We have the tools and the skill and the intelligence to take our cities apart and to put them together, to lead our roads and rivers where we please to lead them, to build our houses where we want our houses, to brighten the air, to clean the wind, to live as men in this Republic, free men, should be living. We have the power and the courage and the resources of goodwill and decency and common understanding—a long experience of decency and common understanding— to enable us to live, not in this continent alone but in the world, as citizens in common of the world, with many others.

We have the power and the courage and the resources of experience to create a nation such as men have never seen. And, more than that, we have the moment of creation in our hands. Our forefathers, when they came to the New England valleys or the Appalachian meadows, girdled the trees[1] and dragged the roots into fences and built themselves shelters and, so roughly sheltered, farmed the land for their necessities. Then, later, when there were means to do it, when there was time, when the occasion offered, they burned the tangled roots and rebuilt their fences and their houses—but rebuilt them with a difference: rebuilt them as villages, as neighborhoods; rebuilt them with those lovely streets, those schools, those churches which still speak of their conception of the world they wanted. When the means offered, when the

---

1. **girdled the trees:** killed trees for felling by removing a ring of bark around the trunk.

time offered, men created, on the clearings of the early useful farms, the towns that made New England and the Alleghenies.

Now is the time for the re-creation, the rebuilding, not of the villages and towns but of a nation. Our necessities have been accomplished as men have always accomplished their necessities—with wastefulness, with ugliness, with cruelty, as well as with the food of harvests. Our necessities have been accomplished with the roots of the broken trees along the fences, the rough shelters, the lonely lives. Now is the time to build the continent itself—to take down and to rebuild; and not the houses and the cities only, but the life itself, raising upon the ready land the brotherhood that can employ it and delight in it and use it as a people such as ours should use it.

We stand at the moment of the building of great lives. . . . But to seize the moment and the means we must agree to seize them: we must recognize the task we have to do. And we have not recognized it. When we speak of our destiny today, we speak still in terms of the agricultural and sparsely settled nation Thomas Jefferson and his contemporaries had in mind. The ideal landscape of America which Jefferson painted hangs unaltered in the American imagination—a clean, small landscape with its isolated figures, its pleasant barns, its self-reliant rooftrees, its horizons clear of the smoke and the fumes of cities, its air still, its frontiers protected by month-wide oceans, year-wide wildernesses. No later hand has touched it, except Lincoln's maybe, deepening the shadow, widening the sky, broadening the acreage in the name of freedom, giving the parts a wholeness that in brighter, sharper light they lacked. For fifty years and longer it has been a landscape of a world no man living could expect to see, a landscape no American could bring to being, a dream—but of the past, and not the future.

And yet we keep this image in our minds. This, and not the world beyond us, is the world we turn to: the lost, nostalgic image of a world that was the future to a generation dead a hundred years. No other image has been made to take its place. No one has dreamed a new American dream of the new America—the industrial nation of the huge machines, the limitless earth, the vast and skillful population, the mountains of copper and iron, the mile-long plants, the delicate laboratories, the tremendous dams. No one has imagined this America—what its life should be; what life it should lead with its great wealth and the tools in its hands and the men to employ them.

The plants and the factories and their products have been celebrated often enough—perhaps too often. The statistics have been added up. The camera has held its mirror to the great machines. But the central question we have yet to ask. What are they *for*, these plants and products, these statistics? *What are they for in terms of a nation of men*—in Jefferson's terms? There are men who believe there is no answer. There are men, and among the wisest of our time, who do not believe that an image of this new America can be conceived—who do not believe in a world of plenty; do not believe in it with their hearts whatever their senses tell them; do not believe that the lives of men can be good lives in the industrialized society which alone makes plenty possible. . . .

Is the fault with the machines or with ourselves? Is it because we have automobiles to ride in, because we can purchase certain commodities easily, because our presses can turn out tons of printed paper in a day, that our fiber is soft, our will feeble, our suggestibility infantile? Or is it because we do not use these things as we should use them—because we have not made them serve our moral purpose as a people, but only our private comfort?

Is the whole question indeed not a question of ourselves instead of our devices? Is it not for us to *say* how these devices, these inventions, should be used? Does their use not rest upon the purpose of their use? And does the purpose not depend upon our power to conceive the purpose—our power as a people to conceive the purpose of the tools we use; our power as a people to conceive and to imagine?

A hundred and fifty years ago de Crèvecoeur[2] asked a famous question which has echoes now: "What then is the American, this new man?" But what then *is* he? What then is he now? A man incapable of the act of the imagination, or a man to whom it is native and natural? A man to dare the dream of plenty with all its risks and dangers, or a man to hold to the old nostalgic landscape with the simple virtues safely forced upon him by the necessary self-denial? . . .

A man who has the hardihood or the courage to believe that the machines which have enslaved his fathers will make his children free—free as no human beings in the world have yet known freedom; free of the twisting miseries and hungers; free to become themselves? Or a man to reject the hope of that enfranchised freedom and to seek his independence in the ancient narrow circle of his old dependence on himself?

Which of these two men is the American? A while ago we should have said the American character was self-evident: a restless man, a great builder and maker and shaper, a man delighting in size and height and dimensions —the world's tallest, the town's biggest. A man never satisfied—never—with anything: his house or the town where his grandfather settled or his father's profession or even his own, for that matter. An inveterate voyager and changer and finder. A man naturally hopeful; a believing man, believing that things progress, that things get forwarder. A skillful man with contraptions of one kind and another—machines, engines, various devices: familiar with all of them. A man of certain unquestioned convictions—of a strong, natural attachment to certain ideas and to certain ideals. But first of all and foremost of all a restless man and a believing man, a builder and changer of things and of nations.

We should have said, a generation back, there was no possible doubt or question of the will and power of this nation to propose the kind of future for itself which would employ the means of plenty for a human purpose. We should have said the principal characteristic of the American people was a confidence in the future and themselves—confidence that the future was the thing they'd make it. I cannot think, for myself, we have so changed that we do not believe this now. I cannot believe we are so changed that we will let ourselves go with the drag and the current of history—that we will let the future happen to us as the future happens to chips on a river or sheep in a blizzard. I cannot believe we have so changed that we do not believe in ourselves and the future.

And yet we have not done what must be done if we believe the future is the thing we'll make it. We have not named that future.

And the time is short.

---

2. Michel-Guillaume Jean de Crèvecoeur (1735–1813), was born in France, became an American citizen, and wrote his perceptions of America in *Letters from an American Farmer*.

Getting at Meaning

1. MacLeish builds a skillful argument that culminates in a persuasive call to action in the final four paragraphs. This call begins with the question, "Which of these two men is the American?" Examine these concluding paragraphs. What is MacLeish urging the American people to do? What principal characteristic of the American people does he identify as the foundation for the action he proposes? What warning concludes his call to action?

2. In the opening paragraphs of the essay MacLeish begins to develop the argument that leads to his call to action. In the first three paragraphs, what quality does he identify as responsible for the creation of the American nation? How has the dream of America been changed into a concrete reality, as explained in the fourth paragraph?

3. According to MacLeish, why is now the time to re-create the nation? What does he propose be rebuilt? What currently stands in the way of this important re-creation?

4. According to MacLeish, why is the Jeffersonian ideal inappropriate to contemporary America? How does MacLeish conceive the relationship between human beings and machines?

5. How does MacLeish use de Crèvecoeur's writing to crystallize the basic issues of his own argument? With what questions does MacLeish expand de Crèvecoeur's basic question?

Developing Skills in Reading Literature

1. **Repetition.** MacLeish's aim in writing "The Unimagined America" is to make readers aware of the power of the imagination to envision a new America and to act on that vision. Within the first three paragraphs, MacLeish strikes this keynote through repetition of certain crucial words. Locate these repetitions and discuss their effect. Find examples in other paragraphs of the repetition of key words and phrases that advance the main ideas of the paragraphs.

2. **Rhetorical Question.** The ringing appeal of MacLeish's argument gains strength from his frequent use of the rhetorical question. Find examples of this device throughout the essay. To evaluate the effectiveness of these rhetorical questions, convert some of them to declarative statements. Read both versions aloud.

3. **Style.** Find the paragraph that begins, "Which of these two men is the American?" What effect is achieved through the use of a series of incomplete sentences following the second sentence?

Why does MacLeish end his essay with two very brief paragraphs? What is gained by opening both paragraphs with the word *and*?

4. **Parallelism.** In the two paragraphs that precede the final paragraph, MacLeish employs a major device of persuasive writing—the use of parallel grammatical structures. Read these paragraphs aloud. Note the sentence structures and the repetitions of words and phrases. What is the effect of these parallelisms? Can MacLeish be faulted for failing to vary his sentence structures? How does parallelism function as a persuasive device?

Developing Writing Skills

Developing an Argument. How can MacLeish's call for re-creation be applied to America today? What needs to be re-created? Choose as a topic an aspect of the social, political, economic, or educational scene. In a persuasive essay, answer the following questions: What current problem do you perceive? What change do you propose? Why is this change necessary? How can it be accomplished? What will happen if this change is not attempted?

Make your argument convincing by thoroughly developing the body of the essay, giving solid reasons for the change you are proposing. Cite the opinions of authorities and include facts that you gather from written material and from personal observation. Conclude with a strong reaffirmation of the key points in your argument.

John Dos Passos

1896–1970

Renowned for his trilogy *U.S.A.*, a searing portrait of industrial America in the first thirty years of the twentieth century, John Dos Passos emerged from the expatriate literary milieu of the 1920's to become a formidable novelist of the American scene. Born in Chicago, the son of a corporation lawyer of Portuguese descent, Dos Passos traveled widely in his youth, living at various times in Mexico, Belgium, Britain, Washington, D.C., and Virginia. After studying at the Choate School and graduating from Harvard in 1916, Dos Passos went to France to serve as an ambulance driver in World War I. Later he traveled through Spain, Mexico, and the Middle East as a newspaper correspondent and free-lance writer. During his sojourn in Paris in the mid-1920's, he became associated with literary giants such as Ernest Hemingway, E. E. Cummings, F. Scott Fitzgerald, and Edmund Wilson. His first novel, *One Man's Initiation*, was followed by *Manhattan Transfer*. This second book appeared in 1925, and soon thereafter Dos Passos returned to the United States, where he became identified with radical political solutions to the social problems of the day. The three volumes of *U.S.A.*—*The 42nd Parallel*, *1919*, and *The Big Money*—focus on the struggles for social justice as experienced by a number of ordinary working-class protagonists. In 1939 Dos Passos described his sympathies as lying "with the private in the front line against the brass hat" and with "the hodcarrier against the straw-boss." His disaffection with radical causes and his subsequent embrace of a conservative political philosophy are reflected in his later works, including another trilogy, entitled *The District of Columbia*, and *Midcentury*, published in 1961.

from **U.S.A.**

Tin Lizzie

"**M**r. Ford *the automobileer*" the feature-writer wrote in 1900.

"Mr. Ford the automobileer began by giving his steed three or four sharp jerks with the lever at the righthand side of the seat; that is, he pulled the lever up and down sharply in order, as he said, to mix air with gasoline and drive the charge into the exploding cylinder. . . . Mr. Ford slipped a small electric switch handle and there followed a puff, puff, puff. . . . The puffing of the machine assumed a higher key. She was flying along about eight miles an hour. The ruts in the road were deep, but the machine certainly went with a dreamlike smoothness. There was none of the bumping common even to a streetcar. . . . By this time the boulevard had been reached, and the automobileer, letting a lever fall a little, let her out. Whiz! She picked up speed with infinite rapidity. As she ran on there was a clattering behind, the new noise of the automobile."

For twenty years or more,

ever since he'd left his father's farm when he was sixteen to get a job in a Detroit machineshop, Henry Ford had been nuts about machinery. First it was watches, then he designed a steamtractor, then he built a horseless carriage with an engine adapted from the Otto gasengine[1] he'd read about in *The World of Science*, then a mechanical buggy with a onecylinder fourcycle motor, that would run forward but not back;

at last, in ninetyeight, he felt he was far enough along to risk throwing up his job with the Detroit Edison Company, where he'd worked his way up from night fireman to chief engineer, to put all his time into working on a new gasoline engine,

(in the late eighties he'd met Edison at a meeting of electriclight employees in Atlantic City. He'd gone up to Edison after Edison had delivered an address and asked him if he thought gasoline was practical as a motor fuel. Edison had said yes. If Edison said it, it was true. Edison was the great admiration of Henry Ford's life);

and in driving his mechanical buggy, sitting there at the lever jauntily dressed in a tight-buttoned jacket and a high collar and a derby hat, back and forth over the level illpaved streets of Detroit,

scaring the big brewery horses and the skinny trotting horses and the sleekrumped pacers with the motor's loud explosions,

looking for men scatterbrained enough to invest money in a factory for building automobiles.

He was the eldest son of an Irish immigrant who during the Civil War had married the daughter of a prosperous Pennsylvania Dutch farmer and settled down to farming near Dearborn in Wayne County, Michigan;

like plenty of other Americans, young Henry grew up hating the endless sogging through the mud about the chores, the hauling and pitching manure, the kerosene lamps to clean, the irk and sweat and solitude of the farm.

He was a slender, active youngster, a good skater, clever with his hands; what he liked

---

1. Nikolaus Otto (1832–1891), German technician, developed the Otto gasengine, an early internal combustion engine.

was to tend the machinery and let the others do the heavy work. His mother had told him not to drink, smoke, gamble or go into debt, and he never did.

When he was in his early twenties his father tried to get him back from Detroit, where he was working as mechanic and repairman for the Drydock Engine Company that built engines for steamboats, by giving him forty acres of land.

Young Henry built himself an uptodate square white dwellinghouse with a false mansard roof and married and settled down on the farm,

but he let the hired men do the farming;

he bought himself a buzzsaw and rented a stationary engine and cut the timber off the woodlots.

He was a thrifty young man who never drank or smoked or gambled or coveted his neighbor's wife, but he couldn't stand living on the farm.

He moved to Detroit, and in the brick barn behind his house tinkered for years in his spare time with a mechanical buggy that would be light enough to run over the clayey wagonroads of Wayne County, Michigan.

By 1900 he had a practicable car to promote.

He was forty years old before the Ford Motor Company was started and production began to move.

Speed was the first thing the early automobile manufacturers went after. Races advertised the makes of cars.

Henry Ford himself hung up several records at the track at Grosse Pointe and on the ice on Lake St. Clair. In his 999 he did the mile in thirtynine and fourfifths seconds.

But it had always been his custom to hire others to do the heavy work. The speed he was busy with was speed in production, the records, records in efficient output. He hired Barney Oldfield, a stunt bicyclerider from Salt Lake City, to do the racing for him.

Henry Ford had ideas about other things

than the designing of motors, carburetors, magnetos, jigs and fixtures, punches and dies; he had ideas about sales,

that the big money was in economical quantity production, quick turnover, cheap interchangeable easilyreplaced standardized parts;

it wasn't until 1909, after years of arguing with his partners, that Ford put out the first Model T.

Henry Ford was right.

That season he sold more than ten thousand tin lizzies; ten years later he was selling almost a million a year.

In these years the Taylor Plan[2] was stirring up plantmanagers and manufacturers all over the country. Efficiency was the word. The same ingenuity that went into improving the performance of a machine could go into improving the performance of the workmen producing the machine.

In 1913 they established the assemblyline at Ford's. That season the profits were something like twentyfive million dollars, but they had trouble in keeping the men on the job; machinists didn't seem to like it at Ford's.

Henry Ford had ideas about other things than production.

He was the largest automobile manufacturer in the world; he paid high wages; maybe if the steady workers thought they were getting a cut (a very small cut) in the profits, it would give trained men an inducement to stick to their jobs,

wellpaid workers might save enough money to buy a tin lizzie; the first day Ford's announced that cleancut properlymarried American workers who wanted jobs had a chance to make five bucks a day (of course it turned out that there were strings to it; always there were strings to it)

---

2. Frederick Taylor (1856–1915), formulated efficiency techniques that led to assembly-line manufacturing processes.

such an enormous crowd waited outside the Highland Park plant

all through the zero January night

that there was a riot when the gates were opened; cops broke heads, jobhunters threw bricks; property, Henry Ford's own property, was destroyed. The company dicks had to turn on the firehose to beat back the crowd.

The American Plan; automotive prosperity seeping down from above; it turned out there were strings to it.

But that five dollars a day

paid to good, clean American workmen

who didn't drink or smoke cigarettes or read or think,

and who didn't commit adultery

and whose wives didn't take in boarders.

made America once more the Yukon[3] of the sweated workers of the world;

made all the tin lizzies and the automotive age, and incidentally,

made Henry Ford the automobileer, the admirer of Edison, the birdlover,

the great American of his time.

---

3. **Yukon:** site of the Alaskan gold rush in 1898

Henry Ford with a Model T Sedan, 1921.

Henry Ford Museum, The Edison Institute. Dearborn, Michigan.

Getting at Meaning

1. What basic biographical facts about Henry Ford can be gleaned from this excerpt?

2. Dos Passos writes, "ever since he'd left his father's farm when he was sixteen to get a job in a Detroit machineshop, Henry Ford had been nuts about machinery." What is your reaction to the phrase "nuts about machinery"? How can that expression be both a compliment and a criticism? What values does it imply? Explain your answer.

3. What impressions of Ford's character does Dos Passos present in "Tin Lizzie"? Support your answer with details from the selection.

4. Dos Passos states that ". . . machinists didn't seem to like it at Ford's." What facts given in this excerpt explain why? What is suggested about the workers' situation? What was Ford's solution to worker discontent? What motives prompted this solution?

5. In what ways did Ford embody the American spirit of rapid growth and industrial progress?

6. What does this selection indicate about the social, economic, and moral context of America in the early twentieth century?

Developing Skills in Reading Literature

1. **Tone and Irony.** Find evidence in the selection to support the following contentions: Ford was an ex-ploiter of opportunities; Ford was ruthless in achieving his goals; Ford was a cruel, driven man. Dos Passos ends this selection by calling Henry Ford "the great American of his time." Why is this statement ironic?

2. **Style.** In the following quotations from this selection, what meaning is conveyed and what feelings are suggested by the run-together words?

In his 999 he did the mile in thirtynine and fourfifths seconds.

. . . that the big money was in . . . cheap interchangeable easilyreplaced standardized parts;

. . . cleancut properlymarried American workers . . .

Can you determine why so many paragraphs in "Tin Lizzie" begin with lower case letters?

The literary paragraph develops a main idea in a succession of sentences; the journalistic, or block, paragraph develops a single point with only a few details. The paragraphs in this selection are the block paragraphs typical of journalistic style. How is the tempo of reading affected by block paragraphs? What effect is Dos Passos striving for in using this journalistic style? What similarities exist between the style of "Tin Lizzie" and the style of presentation in television newscasts?

Richard Wright

1908–1960

That Richard Wright became a writer at all is a tribute to his self-discipline and determination. The son of a Mississippi sharecropper and a domestic servant, Wright grew up in the relentless grip of the Jim Crow South, a culture that systematically degraded blacks as second-class citizens. Despite a patchwork education that ended with the ninth grade, Wright surmounted the barriers of bias and poverty to become a powerful artist. His ability to convey the human costs of oppression, as is evident in his masterful *Native Son* and in the autobiographical *Black Boy*, enabled Wright to chronicle the plight of his generation in a way that few writers have equaled. Because of his father's desertion when Wright was five and his mother's subsequent chronic illness, Wright had to endure the stern religious pietism of his grandmother's household. As he relates in *Black Boy*, Wright's childhood was marked by a gnawing hunger, physical beatings, and an intense internal struggle against the restrictions imposed on him by both family and culture. At age seventeen, Wright began a lifesaving odyssey that eventually culminated in his living an expatriate's life in France. While working in Memphis, Tennessee, to earn enough money to move to the north, Wright encountered the writing of H. L. Mencken and discovered the power of the written word. Arriving in Chicago in 1927, Wright worked at a series of odd jobs before obtaining a position writing guidebooks for the Depression-era Federal Writers' Project. Throughout this time he read voraciously, plunging into

"The huge mountains of fact piled up by the Department of Sociology at the University of Chicago [which] gave me my first concrete vision of the forces that molded the urban Negro's body and soul." In 1940, following his move to New York, that vision became the basis for his best-selling novel, *Native Son*, which earned Wright international stature. *Black Boy*, published in 1945, was even more successful and paved the way for a formal invitation from the French government to visit that country. Accorded a celebrity's welcome, Wright settled in Paris in 1947. In the early 1950's he traveled to Ghana, Spain, and Indonesia, each time returning to France. He died in Paris in 1960. Wright's eleven novels, numerous short stories, and essays are testimonies to his remarkable spirit and determination to prevail.

from **American Hunger**

My first glimpse of the flat black stretches of Chicago depressed and dismayed me, mocked all my fantasies. Chicago seemed an unreal city whose mythical houses were built of slabs of black coal wreathed in palls of gray smoke, houses whose foundations were sinking slowly into the dank prairie. Flashes of steam showed intermittently on the wise horizon, gleaming translucently in the winter sun. The din of the city entered my consciousness, entered to remain for years to come. The year was 1927.

What would happen to me here? Would I survive? My expectations were modest. I wanted only a job. Hunger had long been my daily companion. Diversion and recreation, with the exception of reading, were unknown. In all my life—though surrounded by many people—I had not had a single satisfying, sustained relationship with another human being and, not having had any, I did not miss it. I made no demands whatever upon others.

In Chicago Wright rented a room from his aunt's landlady, worked briefly in a Jewish delicatessen, took a job as a dishwasher in a North Side café, and waited for the results of the examination that might qualify him for a job as a postal clerk.

I worked at the café all spring and in June I was called for temporary duty in the post office. My confidence soared; if I obtained an appointment as a regular clerk, I could spend at least five hours a day writing.

I reported at the post office and was sworn in as a temporary clerk. I earned seventy cents an hour and I went to bed each night now with a full stomach for the first time in my life. When I worked nights, I wrote during the day; when I worked days, I wrote during the night.

But the happiness of having a job did not keep another worry from rising to plague me. Before I could receive a permanent appointment I would have to take a physical examination. The weight requirement was one hundred and twenty-five pounds and I—with my long years of semistarvation—barely tipped the scales at a hundred and ten. Frantically I turned all of my spare money into food and ate. But my skin and flesh would not respond to the food. Perhaps I was not eating the right diet? Perhaps my chronic anxiety kept my weight down. I drank milk, ate steak, but it did not give me an extra ounce of flesh. I visited a doctor who told me that there was nothing wrong with me except malnutrition, that I must eat and sleep long hours. I did and my weight remained the same. I knew now that my job was temporary and that when the time came for my appointment I would have to resume my job hunting again.

At night I read Stein's *Three Lives*, Crane's *The Red Badge of Courage*, and Dostoevski's *The Possessed*,[1] all of which revealed new realms of feeling. But the most important discoveries came when I veered from fiction proper into the field of psychology and sociology. I ran through volumes that bore upon the

---

1. Gertrude Stein (1874–1946) *Three Lives:* complex character studies of three lower-class women; Stephen Crane (1871–1900) *The Red Badge of Courage:* the maturing of a Civil War soldier; and Feodor Dostoevsky (1821–1881) *The Possessed:* study of the effects of a radical cause among Russian revolutionaries. All three works emphasize the protagonist's capacities for feeling and thinking.

causes of my conduct and the conduct of my people. I studied tables of figures relating population density to insanity, relating housing to disease, relating school and recreational opportunities to crime, relating various forms of neurotic behavior to environment, relating racial insecurities to the conflicts between whites and blacks . . .

I still had no friends, casual or intimate, and felt the need for none. I had developed a self-sufficiency that kept me distant from others, emotionally and psychologically. Occasionally I went to house-rent parties, parties given by working-class families to raise money to pay the landlord, the admission to which was a quarter or a half dollar. At these affairs I drank home-brewed beer, ate spaghetti and chitterlings,[2] laughed and talked with black, southern-born girls who worked as domestic servants in white middle-class homes. But with none of them did my relations rest upon my deepest feelings. I discussed what I read with no one, and to none did I confide. Emotionally, I was withdrawn from the objective world; my desires floated loosely within the walls of my consciousness, contained and controlled.

As a protective mechanism, I developed a terse, cynical mode of speech that rebuffed those who sought to get too close to me. Conversation was my way of avoiding expression; my words were reserved for those times when I sat down alone to write. My face was always a deadpan or a mask of general friendliness; no word or event could jar me into a gesture of enthusiasm or despair. A slowly, hesitantly spoken "Yeah" was my general verbal reaction to almost everything I heard. "That's pretty good," said with a slow nod of the head, was my approval. "Aw, naw," muttered with a cold smile, was my rejection. Even though I reacted deeply, my true feelings raced along underground, hidden.

I did not act in this fashion deliberately; I did not prefer this kind of relationship with people. I wanted a life in which there was a constant oneness of feeling with others, in which the basic emotions of life were shared, in which common memory formed a common past, in which collective hope reflected a national future. But I knew that no such thing was possible in my environment. The only ways in which I felt that my feelings could go outward without fear of rude rebuff or searing reprisal was in writing or reading, and to me they were ways of living.

Wright moved into a rear room in his aunt's new apartment, and his mother and brother came to share that room. Despite the crowding and his aunt's failure to understand his voracious reading, Wright continued his own writing.

Repeatedly I took stabs at writing, but the results were so poor that I would tear up the sheets. I was striving for a level of expression that matched those of the novels I read. But I always somehow failed to get onto the page what I thought and felt. Failing at sustained narrative, I compromised by playing with single sentences and phrases. Under the influence of Stein's *Three Lives,* I spent hours and days pounding out disconnected sentences for the sheer love of words.

I would write:

"The soft melting hunk of butter trickled in gold down the stringy grooves of the split yam."

Or:

"The child's clumsy fingers fumbled in sleep, feeling vainly for the wish of its dream."

"The old man huddled in the dark doorway, his bony face lit by the burning yellow in the windows of distant skyscrapers."

My purpose was to capture a physical state or movement that carried a strong subjective impression, an accomplishment which

---

2. **chitterlings:** the small intestines of hogs, sometimes filled with highly seasoned chopped meat and fried or boiled.

seemed supremely worth struggling for. If I could fasten the mind of the reader upon words so firmly that he would forget words and be conscious only of his response, I felt that I would be in sight of knowing how to write narrative. I strove to master words, to make them disappear, to make them important by making them new, to make them melt into a rising spiral of emotional stimuli, each greater than the other, each feeding and reinforcing the other, and all ending in an emotional climax that would drench the reader with a sense of a new world. That was the single aim of my living.

Autumn came and I was called for my physical examination for the position of regular postal clerk. I had not told my mother or brother or aunt that I knew I would fail. On the morning of the examination I drank two quarts of buttermilk, ate six bananas, but it did not hoist the red arrow of the government scales to the required mark of one hundred and twenty-five pounds. I went home and sat disconsolately in my back room, hating myself, wondering where I could find another job. I had almost got my hands upon a decent job and had lost it, had let it slip through my fingers. Waves of self-doubt rose to haunt me. Was I always to hang on the fringes of life? What I wanted was truly modest, and yet my past, my diet, my hunger, had snatched it from before my eyes. But these self-doubts did not last long; I dulled the sense of loss through reading, reading, writing, and more writing.

Following a period of "ugly, petty bickering," the family members moved to smaller quarters.

I asked for my job back at the café and the boss lady allowed me to return; again I served breakfast, washed dishes, carted trays of food up into the apartments. Another postal examination was scheduled for spring and to that end I made eating an obsession. I ate when I did not want to eat, drank milk when it sickened me. Slowly my starved body responded to food and overcame the lean years of Mississippi, Arkansas, and Tennessee, counteracting the flesh-sapping anxiety of fear-filled days.

I read Proust's *A Remembrance of Things Past*,[3] admiring the lucid, subtle but strong prose, stupefied by its dazzling magic, awed by the vast, delicate, intricate, and psychological structure of the Frenchman's epic of death and decadence. But it crushed me with hopelessness, for I wanted to write of the people in my environment with an equal thoroughness, and the burning example before my eyes made me feel that I never could.

My ability to endure tension had now grown amazingly. From the accidental pain of southern years, from anxiety that I had sought to avoid, from fear that had been too painful to bear, I had learned to like my unintermittent burden of feeling, had become habituated to acting with all of my being, had learned to seek those areas of life, those situations, where I knew that events would complement my own inner mood. I was conscious of what was happening to me; I knew that my attitude of watchful wonder had usurped all other feelings, had become the meaning of my life, an integral part of my personality; that I was striving to live and measure all things by it. Having no claims upon others, I bent the way the wind blew, rendering unto my environment that which was my environment's, and rendering unto myself that which I felt was mine.

It was a dangerous way to live, far more dangerous than violating laws or ethical codes of conduct; but the danger was for me and me alone. Had I not been conscious of what I was doing, I could have easily lost my way in the fogbound regions of compelling fantasy. Even so, I floundered, staggered; but somehow I always groped my way back to that path

---

3. Marcel Proust (prōost) (1871–1922), French novelist.

where I felt a tinge of warmth from an unseen light.

Hungry for insight into my own life and the lives about me, knowing my fiercely indrawn nature, I sought to fulfill more than my share of all obligations and responsibilities, as though offering libations of forgiveness to my environment. Indeed, the more my emotions claimed my attention, the sharper—as though in ultimate self-defense—became my desire to measure accurately the reality of the objective world so that I might more than meet its demands. At twenty years of age the mold of my life was set, was hardening into a pattern, a pattern that was neither good nor evil, neither right nor wrong.

Getting at Meaning

1. Wright states, "At twenty years of age the mold of my life was set." What has Wright discovered both about himself and about his life goals?

2. How does the term *hunger* apply to Wright's physical, mental, and emotional lives? How does his weight gain parallel other gains?

3. What is Richard Wright's goal when he arrives in Chicago? Explain how he accomplishes that goal.

4. Why does Wright erect a barrier between himself and other people? Describe how his behavior contrasts with his thoughts and feelings.

5. What activities sustain Wright during desolate times?

6. What does Wright gain from his reading of fiction, as well as from his reading of nonfiction?

7. What does Wright try to achieve in his own writing? How does he judge his success?

Developing Skills in Reading Literature

1. **Characterization.** Richard Wright describes his actions and reveals his thoughts and feelings. What character traits possessed by Wright can you infer from this autobiographical selection? Support your conclusions by referring to specific passages.

2. **Setting.** In the first paragraph of this selection, Wright describes Chicago with carefully selected phrases that convey a dominant impression. What impression does Wright seek to create? What words and phrases build this impression? Explain how Wright's description of setting establishes the mood of the selection.

3. **Autobiography.** An autobiography is a narrative of a writer's own life, with an emphasis on introspection, or self-analysis. Find examples of introspection in this selection. Find paragraphs of straight narration. Why are both necessary to make the autobiography complete?

4. **Figurative Language.** The controlling metaphor in Wright's autobiography is the metaphor of hunger. Within this metaphor are other figures of speech. Identify each of the following as metaphor or personification, and explain the comparison:

". . . wise horizon . . ."
"Hunger had long been my daily companion."
"My face was . . . a mask of general friendliness . . ."
". . . a rising spiral of emotional stimuli . . ."

5. **Alliteration and Assonance.** In the first sentence, "My first glimpse of the flat black stretches of Chicago depressed and dismayed me, mocked all my fantasies," Wright uses alliteration of the *d* and *m* sounds, as well as assonance of the short *a* sound. Find five more examples of alliteration or assonance in Wright's writing. How do these sound devices add to Wright's meaning?

Developing Vocabulary

1. **Connotation: Verbs.** Wright uses each of these precise verbs:

veer	soar	mutter	stagger
float	pound	jar	crush

What are the connotations of each verb? How do these connotations fit the context of this selection?

2. **Conversion.** This sentence appears in the selection: "I dulled the sense of loss through reading, writing, reading, writing, and more writing." Although Wright uses *dull* as a verb, it can also be an adjective. Write sentences using the following words as verbs and then as adjectives. You may need to look up their definitions in a dictionary.

single	spare	long
mock	lean	intimate
right	close	

Developing Writing Skills

1. **Selecting Specific Details.** Wright describes his purpose for writing sentences as follows ". . . to capture a physical state or movement that carried a strong subjective impression . . ." Review his three examples, and then write three sentences that are rich with specific sensory details.

2. **Writing Autobiography.** For one week keep a journal in which you record significant experiences, along with your thoughts and feelings about them. Develop one key experience into an autobiographical composition in which you combine narration and introspection.

3. **Combining Narration, Description, and Exposition.** At a party Wright notes a difference between his inner feelings and outward manner. Consider a time when your feelings differed markedly from the outward impression you tried to give. In a five-paragraph composition, narrate the incident. Set the scene in the first paragraph. In the second, third, and fourth paragraphs, describe your external manner and your hidden emotions and explain why the two differ. Conclude by telling the outcome of the situation or by drawing conclusions.

James Baldwin

from Notes of a Native Son

Autobiographical Notes

I was born in Harlem thirty-one years ago. I began plotting novels at about the time I learned to read. The story of my childhood is the usual bleak fantasy, and we can dismiss it with the restrained observation that I certainly would not consider living it again. In those days my mother was given to the exasperating and mysterious habit of having babies. As they were born, I took them over with one hand and held a book with the other. The children probably suffered, though they have since been kind enough to deny it, and in this way I read *Uncle Tom's Cabin* and *A Tale of Two Cities*[1] over and over again; in this way, in fact, I read just about everything I could get my hands on—except the Bible, probably because it was the only book I was encouraged to read. I must also confess that I wrote—a great deal—and my first professional triumph, in any case, the first effort of mine to be seen in print, occurred at the age of twelve or thereabouts, when a short story I had written about the Spanish revolution won some sort of prize in an extremely short-lived church newspaper. I remember the story was censored by the lady editor, though I don't remember why, and I was outraged.

Also wrote plays, and songs, for one of which I received a letter of congratulations from Mayor La Guardia,[2] and poetry, about which the less said, the better. My mother was delighted by all these goings-on, but my father wasn't; he wanted me to be a preacher. When I was fourteen I became a preacher, and when I was seventeen I stopped. Very shortly thereafter I left home. For God knows how long I struggled with the world of commerce and industry—I guess they would say they struggled with *me*—and when I was about twenty-one I had enough done of a novel to get a Saxton Fellowship. When I was twenty-two the fellowship was over, the novel turned out to be unsalable, and I started waiting on tables in a Village restaurant and writing book reviews—mostly, as it turned out, about the Negro problem, concerning which the color of my skin made me automatically an expert. Did another book, in company with photographer Theodore Pelatowski, about the storefront churches in Harlem. This book met exactly the same fate as my first—fellowship, but no sale. (It was a Rosenwald Fellowship.) By the time I was twenty-four I had decided to stop reviewing books about the Negro problem—which, by this time, was only slightly less horrible in print than it was in life—and I packed my bags and went to

---

1. Harriet Beecher Stowe (1811–1896): author of the anti-slavery novel, *Uncle Tom's Cabin*; Charles Dickens (1812–1870): English author of the novel of the French Revolution, *A Tale of Two Cities*.
2. Fiorello Henry LaGuardia (1882–1947), mayor of New York 1933–1945.

France, where I finished, God knows how, *Go Tell It on the Mountain.*

Any writer, I suppose, feels that the world into which he was born is nothing less than a conspiracy against the cultivation of his talent—which attitude certainly has a great deal to support it. On the other hand, it is only because the world looks on his talent with such a frightening indifference that the artist is compelled to make his talent important. So that any writer, looking back over even so short a span of time as I am here forced to assess, finds that the things which hurt him and the things which helped him cannot be divorced from each other; he could be helped in a certain way only because he was hurt in a certain way; and his help is simply to be enabled to move from one conundrum[3] to the next—one is tempted to say that he moves from one disaster to the next. When one begins looking for influences one finds them by the score. I haven't thought much about my own, not enough anyway; I hazard that the King James Bible, the rhetoric of the store-front church, something ironic and violent and perpetually understated in Negro speech—and something of Dickens' love for bravura[4]—have something to do with me today; but I wouldn't stake my life on it. Likewise, innumerable people have helped me in many ways; but finally, I suppose, the most difficult (and most rewarding) thing in my life has been the fact that I was born a Negro and was forced, therefore, to effect some kind of truce with this reality. (Truce, by the way, is the best one can hope for.)

One of the difficulties about being a Negro writer (and this is not special pleading, since I don't mean to suggest that he has it worse than anybody else) is that the Negro problem is written about so widely. The bookshelves groan under the weight of information, and everyone therefore considers himself informed. And this information, furthermore, operates usually (generally, popularly) to reinforce traditional attitudes. Of traditional attitudes there are only two—For or Against—and I, personally, find it difficult to say which attitude has caused me the most pain. I am speaking as a writer; from a social point of view I am perfectly aware that the change from ill-will to good-will, however motivated, however imperfect, however expressed, is better than no change at all.

But it is part of the business of the writer—as I see it—to examine attitudes, to go beneath the surface, to tap the source. From this point of view the Negro problem is nearly inaccessible. It is not only written about so widely; it is written about so badly. It is quite possible to say that the price a Negro pays for becoming articulate is to find himself, at length, with nothing to be articulate about. ("You taught me language," says Caliban to Prospero, "and my profit on't is I know how to curse.")[5] Consider: the tremendous social activity that this problem generates imposes on whites and Negroes alike the necessity of looking forward, of working to bring about a better day. This is fine, it keeps the waters troubled; it is all, indeed, that has made possible the Negro's progress. Nevertheless, social affairs are not generally speaking the writer's prime concern, whether they ought to be or not; it is absolutely necessary that he establish between himself and these affairs a distance which will allow, at least, for clarity, so that before he can look forward in any meaningful sense, he must first be allowed to take a long look back. In the context of the Negro problem neither whites nor blacks, for excellent reasons of their own, have the faintest desire to look back; but I think that the past is all that makes the present coher-

---

3. **conundrum** (kə nun' drəm): any puzzling question or problem.
4. **bravura** (brə vyoor' ə): a display of daring, an aggressively confident air.
5. Caliban in *The Tempest* by William Shakespeare: Act I, Scene ii, lines 364–365.

ent, and further, that the past will remain horrible for exactly as long as we refuse to assess it honestly.

I know, in any case, that the most crucial time in my own development came when I was forced to recognize that I was a kind of bastard of the West; when I followed the line of my past I did not find myself in Europe but in Africa. And this meant that in some subtle way, in a really profound way, I brought to Shakespeare, Bach, Rembrandt, to the stones of Paris, to the cathedral at Chartres, and to the Empire State Building, a special attitude. These were not really my creations, they did not contain my history; I might search in them in vain forever for any reflection of myself. I was an interloper; this was not my heritage. At the same time I had no other heritage which I could possibly hope to use—I had certainly been unfitted for the jungle or the tribe. I would have to appropriate these white centuries, I would have to make them mine—I would have to accept my special attitude, my special place in this scheme— otherwise I would have no place in *any* scheme. What was the most difficult was the fact that I was forced to admit something I had always hidden from myself, which the American Negro has had to hide from himself as the price of his public progress; that I hated and feared white people. This did not mean that I loved black people; on the contrary, I despised them, possibly because they failed to produce Rembrandt. In effect, I hated and feared the world. And this meant, not only that I thus gave the world an altogether murderous power over me, but also that in such a self-destroying limbo I could never hope to write.

One writes out of one thing only—one's own experience. Everything depends on how relentlessly one forces from this experience the last drop, sweet or bitter, it can possibly give. This is the only real concern of the artist, to re-create out of the disorder of life that order which is art. The difficulty then, for

me, of being a Negro writer was the fact that I was, in effect, prohibited from examining my own experience too closely by the tremendous demands and the very real dangers of my social situation.

I don't think the dilemma outlined above is uncommon. I do think, since writers work in the disastrously explicit medium of language, that it goes a little way toward explaining why, out of the enormous resources of Negro speech and life, and despite the example of Negro music, prose written by Negroes has been generally speaking so pallid and so harsh. I have not written about being a Negro at such length because I expect that to be my only subject, but only because it was the gate I had to unlock before I could hope to write about anything else. I don't think that the Negro problem in America can be even discussed coherently without bearing in mind its context; its context being the history, traditions, customs, the moral assumptions and preoccupations of the country; in short, the general social fabric. Appearances to the contrary, no one in America escapes its effects and everyone in America bears some responsibility for it. I believe this the more firmly because it is the overwhelming tendency to speak of this problem as though it were a thing apart. But in the work of Faulkner, in the general attitude and certain specific passages in Robert Penn Warren, and, most significantly, in the advent of Ralph Ellison, one sees the beginnings—at least—of a more genuinely penetrating search. Mr. Ellison, by the way, is the first Negro novelist I have ever read to utilize in language, and brilliantly, some of the ambiguity and irony of Negro life.

About my interests: I don't know if I have any, unless the morbid desire to own a sixteen-millimeter camera and make experimental movies can be so classified. Otherwise, I love to eat and drink—it's my melancholy conviction that I've scarcely ever had enough to eat (this is because it's *impossible* to eat enough if you're worried about the next meal)—and I love to argue with people who do not disagree with me too profoundly, and I love to laugh. I do *not* like bohemia, or bohemians,[6] I do not like people whose principal aim is pleasure, and I do not like people who are *earnest* about anything. I don't like people who like me because I'm a Negro; neither do I like people who find in the same accident grounds for contempt. I love America more than any other country in the world, and, exactly for this reason, I insist on the right to criticize her perpetually. I think all theories are suspect, that the finest principles may have to be modified, or may even be pulverized by the demands of life, and that one must find, therefore, one's own moral center and move through the world hoping that this center will guide one aright. I consider that I have many responsibilities, but none greater than this: to last, as Hemingway[7] says, and get my work done.

I want to be an honest man and a good writer.

---

6. **bohemians:** followers of art or literature who adopt a mode of life in protest against or in defiance of the common conventions of society.
7. Ernest Hemingway (1899–1961), American novelist and short story writer.

Getting at Meaning

1. According to Baldwin, what is the chief dilemma of the black writer? Explain how this dilemma affects him.

2. How does Baldwin begin his career as a writer? Describe his early accomplishments.

3. What influences are most important in shaping Baldwin as a writer?

4. What does Baldwin mean by "I hated and feared the world"?

5. What is Baldwin's concept of the writer's task?

6. What do the final two paragraphs reveal about Baldwin's values?

Developing Skills in Reading Literature

1. **Tone.** Baldwin writes that he ". . . finished, God knows how, *Go Tell It on the Mountain*." Later he describes influences that ". . . have something to do with me today; but I wouldn't stake my life on it." What tone is evident in these statements? Identify four other statements or passages with this same tone. Then find three passages written with a sharply different tone. How do the changes in tone relate to changes in content? What do the changes tell you about Baldwin as a person?

2. **Aphorism.** Occasionally, Baldwin makes a brief statement that expresses a truth about life. Explain the following aphorisms from this selection:

"Of traditional attitudes there are only two—For or Against."
"The past is all that makes the present coherent."

Find two other statements that may be considered aphorisms, and explain them. Tell whether you agree or disagree with the idea presented in each aphorism. Support your opinions with reasons.

3. **Irony: Sarcasm.** Sarcasm is a form of verbal irony in which seeming praise is actually a bitter expression of disapproval. Commenting on the "Negro problem," Baldwin writes, ". . . the color of my skin made me automatically an expert." Explain the sarcasm in this statement.

4. **Paradox.** Explain the general meaning of this paradox: "Any writer . . . could be helped in a certain way only because he was hurt in a certain way." How

was Baldwin hurt? How was he helped as a result?

Developing Vocabulary

Inferring Word Meaning. Baldwin describes himself as a "bastard" and an "interloper". Looking at how these words are used in context, infer their meanings. Then check your definitions against those in the Glossary. Why are the words appropriate to describe Baldwin's situation?

Developing Writing Skills

1. **Narrating an Autobiographical Incident.** Baldwin did not read the Bible ". . . probably because it was the only book I was encouraged to read." Think of an action that was a conscious or unconscious act of rebellion on your part. Describe it in a well organized composition. Be sure to include some analysis of the factors that prompted your rebellion.

2. **Using Comparison and Contrast.** Richard Wright and James Baldwin face some of the same obstacles in their efforts to become writers. In two paragraphs explain how their struggles are similar and different. Use specific examples and quotations from their autobiographies.

MINORITY MAN. NO. I, 1958. *Edward Wilson.*
University Art Gallery
State University of New York at Binghamton.
Gift of the Class of 1966.

William Faulkner

Nobel Prize Acceptance Speech

I feel that this award was not made to me as a man, but to my work—a life's work in the agony and sweat of the human spirit, not for glory and least of all for profit, but to create out of the materials of the human spirit something which did not exist before. So this award is only mine in trust. It will not be difficult to find a dedication for the money part of it commensurate with the purpose and significance of its origin. But I would like to do the same with the acclaim too, by using this moment as a pinnacle from which I might be listened to by the young men and women already dedicated to the same anguish and travail, among whom is already that one who will some day stand here where I am standing.

Our tragedy today is a general and universal physical fear so long sustained by now that we can even bear it. There are no longer problems of the spirit. There is only the question: When will I be blown up? Because of this, the young man or woman writing today has forgotten the problems of the human heart in conflict with itself which alone can make good writing because only that is worth writing about, worth the agony and the sweat.

He must learn them again. He must teach himself that the basest of all things is to be afraid; and, teaching himself that, forget it forever, leaving no room in his workshop for anything but the old verities and truths of the heart, the old universal truths lacking which any story is ephemeral and doomed—love and honor and pity and pride and compassion and sacrifice. Until he does so, he labors under a curse. He writes not of love but of lust, of defeats in which nobody loses anything of value, of victories without hope and, worst of all, without pity or compassion. His griefs grieve on no universal bones, leaving no scars. He writes not of the heart but of the glands.

Until he relearns these things, he will write as though he stood among and watched the end of man. I decline to accept the end of man. It is easy enough to say that man is immortal simply because he will endure: that when the last dingdong of doom has clanged and faded from the last worthless rock hanging tideless in the last red and dying evening, that even then there will still be one more sound: that of his puny inexhaustible voice, still talking. I refuse to accept this. I believe that man will not merely endure: he will prevail. He is immortal, not because he alone among creatures has an inexhaustible voice, but because he has a soul, a spirit capable of compassion and sacrifice and endurance. The poet's, the writer's, duty is to write about these things. It is his privilege to help man endure by lifting his heart, by reminding him of the courage and honor and hope and pride and compassion and pity and sacrifice which have been the glory of his past. The poet's voice need not merely be the record of man, it can be one of the props, the pillars to help him endure and prevail.

Getting at Meaning

1. How does Faulkner define good writing?

2. To whom does Faulkner address his speech?

3. What is the greatest obstacle for the modern writer, according to Faulkner? How can it be overcome?

4. How can gifted writers serve mankind, according to Faulkner? Explain the meaning of the final statement in the speech.

Developing Skills in Reading Literature

1. **Contrast.** Faulkner's speech is rich in contrasts, a rhetorical device in which one element is opposed to another for the purpose of clarifying an idea. What two concepts of the writer does Faulkner contrast? Why does Faulkner contrast mankind "enduring" with mankind "prevailing"? Note other contrasts in the speech. What ideas do they clarify?

2. **Repetition.** Faulkner repeats grammatical constructions, sometimes to balance contrasting ideas, as in "He writes not of the heart but of the glands." Faulkner also repeats phrases such as "he must" and "he writes." Find other examples of repetition of structures and of phrases in the speech and explain their effects.

3. **Sound Devices: Onomatopoeia and Alliteration.** In the clause ". . . the last dingdong of doom has clanged . . .," Faulkner employs onomatopoeia, the technique of using words that imitate sounds. He also uses alliteration of the *d* sound. What makes these sound devices effective in oration?

Developing Vocabulary

Latin Roots. *Verity* comes from the Latin root *verus*, meaning "truth." Look up *verity* in a dictionary, and record its definition. Then define the following words, which are derived from the same Latin root:

verisimilitude	unverifiable	veracious
veritable	verification	veracity
	veridical	

Developing Writing Skills

Supporting an Opinion. In his speech, Faulkner communicates his ideas about what makes good writing. Choose an endeavor besides writing, and explain what makes someone good in that activity; for example, what makes a good athlete, teacher, family member, or friend. Support your opinion with examples and details.

Franklin Delano Roosevelt

1882–1945

Franklin Delano Roosevelt, thirty-second President of the United States, was one of the most controversial as well as one of the most energetic and powerful of all American Presidents. He became President during the days of the Great Depression and guided the nation through the great struggles of World War II. Elected to an unprecedented fourth term near the end of the war, he did not live to see the final Allied victory.

F.D.R. was born on January 30, 1882, on Val-Kill, the Roosevelt family estate in Hyde Park, on the Hudson River. F.D.R. was educated by governesses and tutors until he went to Groton, an exclusive preparatory school, and then to Harvard University. In 1905 he married Anna Eleanor Roosevelt, his fifth cousin and the niece of President Theodore Roosevelt.

As the Democratic state senator from New York, he opposed Tammany Hall, New York City's powerful political machine, and pressed for progressive public legislation. He began a second term in the senate in 1912, but the following year he was appointed Assistant Secretary of the Navy, a post he filled admirably through the years of World War I. After the war and the reduction of the navy to peacetime strength, Roosevelt returned to private law practice.

In 1921 at the age of thirty-nine, Roosevelt was stricken with polio and permanently crippled. Fighting back with great spirit, he returned to public life in 1924 when he made the speech nominating Al Smith of New York as the Democratic candidate for President. Four years later F.D.R. became Governor of New York State. During his two terms in office, he instituted many progressive measures and emerged as a charismatic public leader and a speaker of remarkable power.

In 1932 Roosevelt was elected President on a platform of a New Deal for the American people. His unprecedented weekly press conferences and his "fireside chats," which were broadcast nationally, brought him into the closest regular contact with the American people of any President up to his time. His domestic, military, and foreign policies were far-reaching and often controversial, making him one of the most loved and most hated men in U.S. history. He died of a massive cerebral hemorrhage while at Warm Springs, Georgia, just weeks before the armistice that ended World War II.

Request for a Declaration of War

YESTERDAY, DECEMBER 7, 1941—a date which will live in infamy—the United States of America was suddenly and deliberately attacked by naval and air forces of the Empire of Japan.

The United States was at peace with that nation, and, at the solicitation of Japan, was still in conversation with its government and its emperor looking toward the maintenance of peace in the Pacific. Indeed, one hour after Japanese air squadrons had commenced bombing in Oahu [Pearl Harbor], the Japanese ambassador to the United States and his colleague delivered to the secretary of state a formal reply to a recent American message. While this reply stated that it seemed useless to continue the existing diplomatic negotiations, it contained no threat or hint of war or armed attack.

It will be recorded that the distance of Hawaii from Japan makes it obvious that the attack was deliberately planned many days or even weeks ago. During the intervening time the Japanese government has deliberately sought to deceive the United States by false statements and expressions of hope for continued peace.

The attack yesterday on the Hawaiian Islands has caused severe damage to American naval and military forces. Very many American lives have been lost. In addition, American ships have been reported torpedoed on the high seas between San Francisco and Honolulu.

Yesterday the Japanese government also launched an attack against Malaya.

Last night Japanese forces attacked Hong Kong.

Last night Japanese forces attacked Guam.

Last night Japanese forces attacked the Philippine Islands.

Last night the Japanese attacked Wake Island.

This morning the Japanese attacked Midway Island.

Japan has, therefore, undertaken a surprise offensive extending throughout the Pacific area. The facts of yesterday speak for themselves. The people of the United States have already formed their opinions and well understand the implications to the very life and safety of our nation.

As commander in chief of the Army and Navy I have directed that all measures be taken for our defense.

Always will we remember the character of the onslaught against us. No matter how long it may take us to overcome this premeditated invasion, the American people, in their righteous might, will win through to absolute victory. I believe I interpret the will of the Congress and of the people when I assert that we will not only defend ourselves to the uttermost but will make very certain that this form of treachery shall never endanger us again.

Hostilities exist. There is no blinking at the fact that our people, our territory, and our interests are in grave danger.

With confidence in our armed forces—with the unbounded determination of our people—we will gain the inevitable triumph—so help us God.

I ask that the Congress declare that since the unprovoked and dastardly attack by Japan on Sunday, December 7, a state of war has existed between the United States and the Japanese Empire.

Getting at Meaning

1. What circumstances make the Japanese attack especially shocking, according to Roosevelt?

2. How does Roosevelt describe the losses at Pearl Harbor?

3. Detail the extent of the Japanese attack.

4. What goals does Roosevelt set for America?

5. Do you sense that Roosevelt's speech is merely a formality or actually an effort to convince Congress to declare war? Is the speech primarily directed at Congress or the American public?

Developing Skills in Reading Literature

1. **Repetition.** Roosevelt makes six statements telling where the Japanese have attacked. Why does he use sentence after sentence rather than list all the places in one sentence? Why does he repeat the initial phrase "Last night"? What effect is created through the use of parallel grammatical constructions in this passage?

2. **Persuasion.** The most effective persuasion combines an appeal to the intellect with an appeal to the emotions. In this speech where does Roosevelt appeal to reason? Cite specific facts and arguments. Why does he begin with facts rather than with a request for a declaration of war? Where does Roosevelt appeal to the emotions? What is the effect of the phrases "righteous might" and "inevitable triumph," as well as the religious invocation "so help us God"?

How do the connotations of the words *deceive*, *invasion*, *treachery*, *dastardly*, and *onslaught* intensify the emotional appeal of Roosevelt's speech? Why does he stress the word *deliberately*? What reponse does the word evoke? Roosevelt also uses the following modifiers to describe the Japanese attack: *suddenly*, *surprise*, *premeditated*, and *unprovoked*. What does each add to the appeal of Roosevelt's plea?

3. **Tone.** In asking Congress to declare war, is Roosevelt's tone predominantly calm or passionate, fair or vengeful, rational or emotional? Support your analysis with specific passages.

Developing Vocabulary

Synonyms. Roosevelt's phrase "a date which will live in infamy" has become famous. Look up the word *infamy* in the Glossary, and determine two synonyms for the word. Substitute them in the phrase. Is either as effective in the phrase as *infamy*? Explain.

Developing Writing Skills

Developing an Argument. Write a letter to your representative in Congress in which you advocate legislation that you think is needed. Research facts on the issue so that you can defend your stand adequately. Use both emotional and rational appeals in your presentation.

John F. Kennedy

1917–1963

John Fitzgerald Kennedy, the thirty-fifth President of the United States, did not live to complete his term of office. The youngest man and first Roman Catholic to become President, he served from January 20, 1961, to November 22, 1963, when he was killed by an assassin's bullet while riding in a parade in Dallas. JFK, as he came to be called, was born on May 29, 1917, in Brookline, Massachusetts, the second of the nine children of Joseph Patrick and Rose Fitzgerald Kennedy. Joseph was one of the nation's most successful businessmen, able to give each of his children a million dollars at maturity. Young Kennedy attended Choate School and Harvard University, graduating *cum laude* in 1940. During World War II Kennedy distinguished himself by rescuing the survivors of the stricken PT boat under his command. Shortly after discharge, he was elected from Massachusetts to the United States House of Representatives and to the United States Senate in 1952, where he served until his election to the Presidency in 1960. In September, 1953, he married Jacqueline Bouvier. The couple had three children: Caroline, John, and Patrick, who died in infancy.

A moderate liberal and intellectual, Kennedy surrounded the Presidency with able advisors and instituted a program of reforms. Several crises punctuated his term as President: the aborted invasion of Cuba at the Bay of Pigs, the Berlin crisis, the Cuban missile crisis, and civil rights confrontations. The aura that surrounded his administration, however, was not one of crisis but of a magical kingdom, a contemporary version of Camelot. The articulate, young President and his attractive family charmed the nation and the world. Of the death of President Kennedy, Willy Brandt, Mayor of Berlin, said, "A flame went out for all those who had hoped for a just peace and a better life."

Inaugural Address

We observe today not a victory of party but a celebration of freedom—symbolizing an end as well as a beginning—signifying renewal as well as change. For I have sworn before you and Almighty God the same solemn oath our forebears prescribed nearly a century and three-quarters ago.

The world is very different now. For man holds in his mortal hands the power to abolish all forms of human poverty and all forms of human life. And yet the same revolutionary beliefs for which our forebears fought are still at issue around the globe—the belief that the rights of man come not from the generosity of the state but from the hands of God.

We dare not forget today that we are the heirs of that first revolution. Let the word go forth from this time and place, to friend and foe alike, that the torch has been passed to a new generation of Americans—born in this century, tempered by war, disciplined by a hard and bitter peace, proud of our ancient heritage—and unwilling to witness or permit the slow undoing of those human rights to which this nation has always been committed, and to which we are committed today at home and around the world.

Let every nation know, whether it wishes us well or ill, that we shall pay any price, bear any burden, meet any hardship, support any friend, oppose any foe to assure the survival and the success of liberty.

This much we pledge—and more.

To those old allies whose cultural and spiritual origins we share, we pledge the loyalty of faithful friends. United, there is little we cannot do in a host of cooperative ventures. Divided, there is little we can do—for we dare not meet a powerful challenge at odds and split asunder.

To those new states whom we welcome to the ranks of the free, we pledge our word that one form of colonial control shall not have passed away merely to be replaced by a far more iron tyranny. We shall not always expect to find them supporting our view. But we shall always hope to find them strongly supporting their own freedom—and to remember that, in the past, those who foolishly sought power by riding the back of the tiger ended up inside.

To those people in the huts and villages of half the globe struggling to break the bonds of mass misery, we pledge our best efforts to help them help themselves, for whatever period is required—not because the Communists may be doing it, not because we seek their votes, but because it is right. If a free society cannot help the many who are poor, it cannot save the few who are rich.

To our sister republics south of our border, we offer a special pledge—to convert our good words into good deeds—in a new alliance for progress—to assist free men and free governments in casting off the chains of poverty. But this peaceful revolution of hope cannot become the prey of hostile powers. Let all our neighbors know that we shall join with them to oppose aggression or subversion anywhere in the Americas. And let every other power know that this hemisphere intends to remain the master of its own house.

To that world assembly of sovereign states, the United Nations, our last best hope in an age where the instruments of war have far outpaced the instruments of peace, we renew our pledge of support—to prevent it from becoming merely a forum for invective—to strengthen its shield of the new and the weak—and to enlarge the area in which its writ may run.

Finally, to those nations who would make themselves our adversary, we offer not a pledge but a request—that both sides begin anew the quest for peace before the dark powers of destruction unleashed by science engulf all humanity in planned or accidental self-destruction. We dare not tempt them with weakness. For only when our arms are sufficient beyond doubt can we be certain beyond doubt that they will never be employed.

But neither can two great and powerful groups of nations take comfort from our present course—both sides overburdened by the cost of modern weapons, both rightly alarmed by the steady spread of the deadly atom, yet both racing to alter that uncertain balance of terror that stays the hand of mankind's final war.

So let us begin anew—remembering on both sides that civility is not a sign of weakness, and sincerity is always subject to proof. Let us never negotiate out of fear. But let us never fear to negotiate.

Let both sides explore what problems unite us instead of belaboring those problems which divide us.

Let both sides, for the first time, formulate serious and precise proposals for the inspection and control of arms—and bring the absolute power to destroy other nations under the absolute control of all nations.

Let both sides seek to invoke the wonders of science instead of its terrors. Together let us explore the stars, conquer the deserts, eradicate disease, tap the ocean depths, and encourage the arts and commerce.

Let both sides unite to heed in all corners of the earth the command of Isaiah—to "undo the heavy burdens . . . [and] let the oppressed go free."[1]

And if a beachhead of cooperation may push back the jungle of suspicion, let both sides join in creating a new endeavor, not a new balance of power but a new world of law, where the strong are just and the weak secure and the peace preserved.

All this will not be finished in the first 100 days. Nor will it be finished in the first 1,000 days, nor in the life of this administration, nor even perhaps in our lifetime on this planet. But let us begin.

In your hands, my fellow citizens, more than mine, will rest the final success or failure of our course. Since this country was founded, each generation of Americans has been summoned to give testimony to its national loyalty. The graves of young Americans who answered the call to service surround the globe.

Now the trumpet summons us again—not as a call to bear arms, though arms we need—not as a call to battle, though embattled we are—but a call to bear the burden of a long twilight struggle, year in and year out, "rejoicing in hope, patient in tribulation"[2]—a struggle against the common enemies of man: tyranny, poverty, disease, and war itself.

Can we forge against these enemies a grand and global alliance, North and South, East and West, that can assure a more fruitful life for all mankind? Will you join in that historic effort?

In the long history of the world, only a few generations have been granted the role of defending freedom in its hour of maximum danger. I do not shrink from this responsibility—I welcome it. I do not believe that any of us would exchange places with any other people or any other generation. The energy, the faith, the devotion which we bring to this endeavor will light our country and all who serve it—and the glow from that fire can truly light the world.

---

1. Isaiah 58:6.
2. Romans 12:12.

And so, my fellow Americans—ask not what your country can do for you—ask what you can do for your country.

My fellow citizens of the world—ask not what America will do for you but what together we can do for the freedom of man.

Finally, whether you are citizens of America or citizens of the world, ask of us here the same high standards of strength and sacrifice which we ask of you. With a good conscience our only sure reward, with history the final judge of our deeds, let us go forth to lead the land we love, asking His blessing and His help, but knowing that here on earth God's work must truly be our own.

Getting at Meaning

1. How does Kennedy compare and contrast the politics of 1960 with those of 1776? Why does he seek to establish this link with the past?

2. How do Kennedy's promises to allies, independent states, third-world nations, Central America, the United Nations, and adversaries differ? What underlying aim is the same?

3. Toward what specific goals does Kennedy hope to cooperate with America's adversaries?

4. What commitments does he ask of Americans?

5. Explain Kennedy's final statement, ". . . here on earth God's work must truly be our own." What is Kennedy's concept of the relationship between God and the individual?

Developing Skills in Reading Literature

1. **Parallelism.** The use of parallelism intensifies the appeal of Kennedy's ideas. Find two examples of parallelism in the opening sentence of Kennedy's address. Locate five more examples of parallelism in the speech. What is the effect of Kennedy's abundant use of parallelism?

2. **Anaphora.** A unifying anaphora that begins six paragraphs is "To . . . we pledge." Find another example of anaphora. How does anaphora add emphasis and emotion to the speech?

3. **Tone and Mood.** How would you describe the tone of Kennedy's speech? Cite passages to support your conclusion. How does the occasion for this speech color its tone? What emotions does Kennedy's speech arouse? Identify specific passages that evoke these feelings most intensely.

4. **Allusion.** Kennedy alludes to the Bible when he quotes Isaiah. How does this allusion contribute to the effectiveness of his speech? Why is an allusion to the Old Testament effective in a political speech?

Developing Vocabulary

Finding the Appropriate Meaning. Look up each italicized word in a dictionary, and write the definition that suits its context in Kennedy's speech:

". . . *tempered* by war . . ."
". . . whether it wishes us well or *ill* . . ."
". . . *tap* the ocean depths . . ."
". . . man holds in his *mortal* hands . . ."
". . . still at *issue* around the globe . . ."
"I do not *shrink* from this responsibility . . ."

Developing Writing Skills

1. **Writing an Analytical Report.** Research one aspect of Kennedy's Presidency. Write a report analyzing how he fulfilled or failed to fulfill a promise of his inaugural address. Use at least four sources in your research, and cite these sources in your report.

2. **Developing an Argument.** Focus on one social responsibility needed by your generation. Write an editorial or speech addressed to young people, attempting to persuade them to act on that responsibility. Incorporate such techniques as parallelism, figurative language, anaphora, allusion, and rhetorical questions.

E. B. White
1899–1985

Jill Krementz

When the collection of essays, *The Second Tree from the Corner*, was published in 1953, critic Irwin Edman wrote: "E. B. White is the finest essayist in the United States. He says wise things gracefully; he is the master of an idiom at once exact and suggestive, distinguished yet familiar." Readers have been refreshed and entertained for over half a century by White's wry, witty commentary on the vagaries and vicissitudes of modern life.

Elwyn Brooks White was born on July 11, 1899, in Mount Vernon, New York, of "respectable people." After serving during World War I as a private in the United States Army, he graduated from Cornell University and then went West in an old Model T to work on the *Seattle Times*. Eventually he joined the staff of *The New Yorker* in 1926, only one year after that most famous literary magazine was founded. He was a contributor to *The New Yorker* and to *Harper's Magazine* for more than half a century.

In 1937 White and his family moved to a farm near North Brooklin, Maine, and he continued writing, including a column for *Harper's Magazine* from 1938 to 1943 and articles for *The New Yorker*. He published two books of poetry and five books of essays. He also collected his *New Yorker* newsbreaks into *Ho Hum* and *Another Ho Hum* (1931-32). With his wife, Katharine Sergeant White, he edited *A Subtreasury of American Humor* in 1941.

He is the author of three charming and classic children's books: *Stuart Little* (1945), *Charlotte's Web* (1952), and *The Trumpet of the Swan* (1970).

Both students and writers rely on White's revised edition of *The Elements of Style*, a manual originally written by William Strunk, Jr., White's beloved Cornell professor. White received the gold medal for essays and criticism from the National Institute of Arts and Letters in 1960, a fellowship in the American Academy of Arts and Sciences, and the Presidential Medal of Freedom in 1963.

Walden

June, 1939

Miss Nims, take a letter to Henry David Thoreau.

Dear Henry: I thought of you the other afternoon as I was approaching Concord doing fifty on Route 62. That is a high speed at which to hold a philosopher in one's mind, but in this century we are a nimble bunch.

On one of the lawns in the outskirts of the village a woman was cutting the grass with a motorized lawn mower. What made me think of you was that the machine had rather got away from her, although she was game enough, and in the brief glimpse I had of the scene it appeared to me that the lawn was mowing the lady. She kept a tight grip on the handles, which throbbed violently with every explosion of the one-cylinder motor, and as she sheered around bushes and lurched along at a reluctant trot behind her impetuous servant, she looked like a puppy who had grabbed something that was too much for him. Concord hasn't changed much, Henry; the farm implements and the animals still have the upper hand.

I may as well admit that I was journeying to Concord with the deliberate intention of visiting your woods; for although I have never knelt at the grave of a philosopher nor placed wreaths on moldy poets, and have often gone a mile out of my way to avoid some place of historical interest, I have always wanted to see Walden Pond. The account which you left of your sojourn there is, you will be amused to learn, a document of increasing pertinence; each year it seems to gain a little headway, as the world loses ground. We may all be tran-scendental[1] yet, whether we like it or not. As our common complexities increase, any tale of individual simplicity (and yours is the best written and the cockiest) acquires a new fascination; as our goods accumulate, but not our well-being, your report of an existence without material adornment takes on a certain awkward credibility.

My purpose in going to Walden Pond, like yours, was not to live cheaply or to live dearly there, but to transact some private business with the fewest obstacles. Approaching Concord, doing forty, doing forty-five, doing fifty, the steering wheel held snug in my palms, the highway held grimly in my vision, the crown of the road now serving me (on the righthand curves), now defeating me (on the lefthand curves), I began to rouse myself from the stupefaction which a day's motor journey induces. It was a delicious evening, Henry, when the whole body is one sense, and imbibes delight through every pore, if I may coin a phrase. Fields were richly brown where the harrow, drawn by the stripped Ford, had lately sunk its teeth; pastures were green; and overhead the sky had that same everlasting great look which you will find on Page 144 of the Oxford pocket edition. I could feel the road entering me, through tire, wheel, spring, and cushion; shall I not have intelligence with earth too? Am I not partly leaves and vegetable mold myself?—a man of infinite horsepower, yet partly leaves.

Stay with me on 62 and it will take you into Concord. As I say, it was a delicious evening.

---

1. **transcendental:** believing in the search for reality through spiritual intuition, as developed by Ralph Waldo Emerson (1803–1882).

The snake had come forth to die in a bloody S on the highway, the wheel upon its head, its bowels flat now and exposed. The turtle had come up too to cross the road and die in the attempt, its hard shell smashed under the rubber blow, its intestinal yearning (for the other side of the road) forever squashed. There was a sign by the wayside which announced that the road had a "cotton surface." You wouldn't know what that is, but neither, for that matter, did I. There is a cryptic ingredient in many of our modern improvements—we are awed and pleased without knowing quite what we are enjoying. It is something to be traveling on a road with a cotton surface.

The civilization round Concord today is an odd distillation of city, village, farm, and manor. The houses, yards, fields look not quite suburban, not quite rural. Under the bronze beech and the blue spruce of the departed baron grazes the milch goat[2] of the heirs. Under the porte-cochère[3] stands the reconditioned station wagon; under the grape arbor sit the puppies for sale. (But why do men degenerate ever? What makes families run out?)

It was June and everywhere June was publishing her immemorial stanza; in the lilacs, in the syringa, in the freshly edged paths and the sweetness of moist beloved gardens, and the little wire wickets that preserve the tulips' front. Farmers were already moving the fruits of their toil into their yards, arranging the rhubarb, the asparagus, the strictly fresh eggs on the painted stands under the little shed roofs with the patent shingles. And though it was almost a hundred years since you had taken your ax and started cutting out your home on Walden Pond, I was interested to observe that the philosophical spirit was still alive in Massachusetts: in the center of a vacant lot some boys were assembling the framework of the rude shelter, their whole mind and skill concentrated in the rather inauspicious helter-skeleton of studs and rafters. They too were escaping from town, to live naturally, in a rich blend of savagery and philosophy.

That evening, after supper at the inn, I strolled out into the twilight to dream my shapeless transcendental dreams and see that the car was locked up for the night (first open the right front door, then reach over, straining, and pull up the handles of the left rear and the left front till you hear the click, then the handle of the right rear, then shut the right front but open it again, remembering that the key is still in the ignition switch, remove the key, shut the right front again with a bang, push the tiny keyhole cover to one side, insert key, turn, and withdraw). It is what we all do, Henry. It is called locking the car. It is said to confuse thieves and keep them from making off with the laprobe. Four doors to lock behind one robe. The driver himself never uses a laprobe, the free movement of his legs being vital to the operation of the vehicle; so that when he locks the car it is a pure and unselfish act. I have in my life gained very little essential heat from laprobes, yet I have ever been at pains to lock them up.

The evening was full of sounds, some of which would have stirred your memory. The robins still love the elms of New England villages at sundown. There is enough of the thrush in them to make song inevitable at the end of day, and enough of the tramp to make them hang round the dwellings of men. A robin, like many another American, dearly loves a white house with green blinds. Concord is still full of them.

Your fellow-townsmen were stirring abroad —not many afoot, most of them in their cars; and the sound which they made in Concord at evening was a rustling and a whispering. The sound lacks steadfastness and is wholly unlike that of a train. A train, as you know who lived so near the Fitchburg line, whistles once

---

2. **milch goat:** a goat kept for milking.
3. **porte-cochère** (port' kō sher') *French*: a porch roof projecting over a driveway at an entrance.

or twice sadly and is gone, trailing a memory in smoke, soothing to ear and mind. Automobiles, skirting a village green, are like flies that have gained the inner ear—they buzz, cease, pause, start, shift, stop, halt, brake, and the whole effect is a nervous polytone curiously disturbing.

As I wandered along, the toc toc of ping pong balls drifted from an attic window. In front of the Reuben Brown house a Buick was drawn up. At the wheel, motionless, his hat upon his head, a man sat, listening to Amos and Andy[4] on the radio (it is a drama of many scenes and without an end). The deep voice of Andrew Brown, emerging from the car, although it originated more than two hundred miles away, was unstrained by distance. When you used to sit on the shore of your pond on Sunday morning, listening to the church bells of Acton and Concord, you were aware of the excellent filter of the intervening atmosphere. Science has attended to that, and sound now maintains its intensity without regard for distance. Properly sponsored, it goes on forever.

A fire engine, out for a trial spin, roared past Emerson's house, hot with readiness for public duty. Over the barn roofs the martins dipped and chittered. A swarthy daughter of an asparagus grower, in culottes, shirt, and bandanna, pedaled past on her bicycle. It was indeed a delicious evening, and I returned to the inn (I believe it was your house once) to rock with the old ladies on the concrete veranda.

Next morning early I started afoot for Walden, out Main Street and down Thoreau, past the depot and the Minuteman Chevrolet Company. The morning was fresh, and in a bean field along the way I flushed an agriculturalist, quietly studying his beans. Thoreau Street soon joined Number 126, an artery of the State. We number our highways nowadays, our speed being so great we can remember little of their quality or character and are lucky to remember their number. (Men have an indistinct notion that if they keep up this activity long enough all will at length ride somewhere, in next to no time.) Your pond is on 126.

I knew I must be nearing your woodland retreat when the Golden Pheasant lunchroom came into view—Sealtest ice cream, toasted sandwiches, hot frankfurters, waffles, tonics, and lunches. Were I the proprietor, I should add rice, Indian meal, and molasses—just for old time's sake. The Pheasant, incidentally, is for sale: a chance for some nature lover who wishes to set himself up beside a pond in the Concord atmosphere and live deliberately, fronting only the essential facts of life on Number 126. Beyond the Pheasant was a place called Walden Breezes, an oasis whose porch pillars were made of old green shutters sawed into lengths. On the porch was a distorting mirror, to give the traveler a comical image of himself, who had miraculously learned to gaze in an ordinary glass without smiling. Behind the Breezes, in a sun-parched clearing, dwelt your philosophical descendants in their trailers, each trailer the size of your hut, but all grouped together for the sake of congeniality. Trailer people leave the city, as you did, to discover solitude and in any weather, at any hour of the day or night, to improve the nick of time; but they soon collect in villages and get bogged deeper in the mud than ever. The camp behind Walden Breezes was just rousing itself to the morning. The ground was packed hard under the heel, and the sun came through the clearing to bake the soil and enlarge the wry smell of cramped housekeeping. Cushman's bakery truck had stopped to deliver an early basket of rolls. A camp dog, seeing me in the road, barked petulantly. A man emerged from one of the trailers and set forth with a bucket to draw water from some forest tap.

Leaving the highway I turned off into the

---

4. **Amos and Andy:** radio situation comedy starring black leading characters.

woods toward the pond, which was apparent through the foliage. The floor of the forest was strewn with dried old oak leaves and *Transcripts.* From beneath the flattened popcorn wrapper *(granum explosum)*[5] peeped the frail violet. I followed a footpath and descended to the water's edge. The pond lay clear and blue in the morning light, as you have seen it so many times. In the shallows a man's waterlogged shirt undulated gently. A few flies came out to greet me and convoy me to your cove, past the No Bathing signs on which the fellows and girls had scrawled their names. I felt strangely excited suddenly to be snooping around your premises, tiptoeing along watchfully, as though not to tread by mistake upon the intervening century. Before I got to the cove I heard something which seemed to me quite wonderful: I heard your frog, a full, clear *troonk,* guiding me, still hoarse and solemn, bridging the years as the robins had bridged them in the sweetness of the village evening. But he soon quit, and I came on a couple of young boys throwing stones at him.

Your front yard is marked by a bronze tablet set in a stone. Four small granite posts, a few feet away, show where the house was. On top of the tablet was a pair of faded blue bathing trunks with a white stripe. Back of it is a pile of stones, a sort of cairn,[6] left by your visitors as a tribute I suppose. It is a rather ugly little heap of stones, Henry. In fact the hillside itself seems faded, browbeaten; a few tall skinny pines, bare of lower limbs, a smattering of young maples in suitable green, some birches and oaks, and a number of trees felled by the last big wind. It was from the bole of one of these fallen pines, torn up by the roots, that I extracted the stone which I added to the cairn—a sentimental act in which I was interrupted by a small terrier from a nearby picnic group, who confronted me and wanted to know about the stone.

I sat down for a while on one of the posts of your house to listen to the bluebottles and the dragonflies. The invaded glade sprawled shabby and mean at my feet, but the flies were tuned to the old vibration. There were the remains of a fire in your ruins, but I doubt that it was yours; also two beer bottles trodden into the soil and become part of earth. A young oak had taken root in your house, and two or three ferns, unrolling like the ticklers at a banquet. The only other furnishings were a DuBarry pattern sheet, a page torn from a picture magazine, and some crusts in wax paper.

Before I quit I walked clear round the pond and found the place where you used to sit on the northeast side to get the sun in the fall, and the beach where you got sand for scrubbing your floor. On the eastern side of the pond, where the highway borders it, the State has built dressing rooms for swimmers, a float with diving towers, drinking fountains of porcelain, and rowboats for hire. The pond is in fact a State Preserve, and carries a twenty-dollar fine for picking wild flowers, a decree signed in all solemnity by your fellow-citizens Walter C. Wardwell, Erson B. Barlow, and Nathaniel I. Bowditch. There was a smell of creosote where they had been building a wide wooden stairway to the road and the parking area. Swimmers and boaters were arriving; bodies plunged vigorously into the water and emerged wet and beautiful in the bright air. As I left, a boatload of town boys were splashing about in mid-pond, kidding and fooling, the young fellows singing at the tops of their lungs in a wild chorus:

Amer-ica, Amer-ica, God shed his grace
  on thee,
And crown thy good with brotherhood
From sea to shi-ning sea!

---

5. **granum explosum** *Latin:* genus and species names for common popcorn.
6. **cairn:** a conical pile of stones built as a monument or a landmark.

I walked back to town along the railroad, following your custom. The rails were expanding noisily in the hot sun, and on the slope of the roadbed the wild grape and the blackberry sent up their creepers to the track.

The expense of my brief sojourn in Concord was:

Canvas shoes	$1.95	
Baseball bat	.25	gifts to
Left-handed fielder's glove	1.25	take back to a boy
Hotel and meals	4.25	
In all	$7.70	

As you see, this amount was almost what you spent for food for eight months. I cannot defend the shoes or the expenditure for shelter and food: they reveal a meanness and grossness in my nature, which you would find contemptible. The baseball equipment, however, is the kind of impediment with which you were never on even terms. You must remember that the house where you practiced the sort of economy which I respect was haunted only by mice and squirrels. You never had to cope with a shortstop.

Getting at Meaning

1. How does White describe Concord and Walden Pond?

2. How has Walden Pond changed since Thoreau's days? In what ways is it the same?

3. Do the sights at Concord and Walden Pond substantiate Thoreau's philosophy or mock it, according to White?

Developing Skills in Reading Literature

1. **Essay.** Essays may be classified as informal or formal. While the formal essay has objectivity, a serious purpose, and a logical organization, the more loosely structured informal essay is personal, original in form and theme, and often humorous. Explain why "Walden" is an informal essay. What accounts for its humor? Identify several humorous passages.

An essayist usually intends to present a point of view. What do you think is White's purpose in describing modern-day Walden to Henry David Thoreau? What message does White want to convey to Thoreau? What does White's essay reveal about his opinion of contemporary America?

2. **Irony.** A writer who says one thing but means something quite different is using verbal irony. Irony of situation occurs when something unexpected happens. What is ironic about the Golden Pheasant lunchroom? about boys stoning a frog? about the fine for picking flowers? about White's description of a woman and her lawn mower? Is each an example of verbal irony or irony of situation? Find three other ironies in "Walden." What makes the tone of this essay gently ironic?

3. **Parody.** A parody is an imitation of a serious work of literature, either for the purpose of criticism or for flattering tribute. White mimics Thoreau's words and ideas, as when he lists his expenses the way Thoreau does in *Walden*. Find the selections from *Walden* in Unit 3. Then identify three ways in which White parodies *Walden*. Is White's intent criticism or tribute? Find passages that support your answer.

Developing Writing Skills

1. **Writing a Description.** Choose a place that you feel represents contemporary America. Describe it in a five-paragraph composition, using specific details that appeal to the senses.

2. **Writing a Parody.** Write a modern update imitating one of the selections in Units 1 through 3. Like White, you may choose to address the author in a letter. Choose a contemporary subject, but stick to the style of the earlier writer.

Rachel Carson

1907–1964

Rachel Louise Carson was an aquatic biologist, naturalist, and writer whose *Silent Spring* (1962) sparked an international controversy over the effects of pesticides on animal and human life. Born in Springdale, Pennsylvania, on May 27, 1907, Rachel Carson grew up in Springdale and nearby Parnassus and enrolled in Pennsylvania College for Women with the intent of becoming a writer. A course in biology changed her mind; she majored in science and then did postgraduate work at Johns Hopkins University and Woods Hole Marine Biological Laboratory. She taught at Johns Hopkins and the University of Maryland for several years, then in 1936 accepted a job with the United States Bureau of Fisheries (now the United States Fish and Wildlife Service), becoming its editor-in-chief in 1947.

In 1937 Carson wrote an essay on marine life for the *Atlantic Monthly*. Four years later *Under the Sea-Wind*, "a naturalist's picture of ocean life," won praise in both the literary and scientific worlds. Her second book, *The Sea Around Us* (1951), was heralded as "one of the most beautiful books of our time." Her last book, *Silent Spring*, was a timely warning against the long-term, dangerous effects of the indiscriminate use of pesticides.

Carson was a quiet, gently humorous woman but, she remarked, "a disappointment to my friends, who expect me to be completely nautical." In fact, her hobby was bird study, and her "very closest nonhuman friends have been cats."

from Silent Spring

A Fable for Tomorrow

There was once a town in the heart of America where all life seemed to live in harmony with its surroundings. The town lay in the midst of a checkerboard of prosperous farms, with fields of grain and hillsides of orchards where, in spring, white clouds of bloom drifted above the green fields. In autumn, oak and maple and birch set up a blaze of color that flamed and flickered across a backdrop of pines. Then foxes barked in the hills and deer silently crossed the fields, half hidden in the mists of the fall mornings.

Along the roads, laurel, viburnum, and alder, great ferns and wildflowers delighted the traveler's eye through much of the year. Even in winter the roadsides were places of beauty, where countless birds came to feed on the berries and on the seed heads of the dried weeds rising above the snow. The countryside was, in fact, famous for the abundance and variety of its bird life, and when the flood of migrants was pouring through in spring and fall people traveled from great distances to observe them. Others came to fish the streams, which flowed clear and cold out of the hills and contained shady pools where trout lay. So it had been from the days many years ago when the first settlers raised their houses, sank their wells, and built their barns.

Then a strange blight crept over the area and everything began to change. Some evil spell had settled on the community: mysterious maladies swept the flocks of chickens; the cattle and sheep sickened and died. Every-where was a shadow of death. The farmers spoke of much illness among their families. In the town the doctors had become more and more puzzled by new kinds of sickness appearing among their patients. There had been several sudden and unexplained deaths, not only among adults but even among children, who would be stricken suddenly while at play and die within a few hours.

There was a strange stillness. The birds, for example—where had they gone? Many people spoke of them, puzzled and disturbed. The feeding stations in the backyards were deserted. The few birds seen anywhere were moribund;[1] they trembled violently and could not fly. It was a spring without voices. On the mornings that had once throbbed with the dawn chorus of robins, catbirds, doves, jays, wrens, and scores of other bird voices there was now no sound; only silence lay over the fields and woods and marsh.

On the farms the hens brooded, but no chicks hatched. The farmers complained that they were unable to raise any pigs—the litters were small and the young survived only a few days. The apple trees were coming into bloom but no bees droned among the blossoms, so there was no pollination and there would be no fruit.

The roadsides, once so attractive, were now lined with browned and withered vegetation

---

1. **moribund** (mōr′ ə bund′): near death, dying.

as though swept by fire. These, too, were silent, deserted by all living things. Even the streams were now lifeless. Anglers no longer visited them, for all the fish had died.

In the gutters under the eaves and between the shingles of the roofs, a white granular powder still showed a few patches; some weeks before it had fallen like snow upon the roofs and the lawns, the fields and streams.

No witchcraft, no enemy action had silenced the rebirth of new life in this stricken world. The people had done it themselves.

Getting at Meaning

1. How is the American town changed by the powdery substance? Describe the effects on birds, animals, plants, farms, and human beings.

2. What is the message of "A Fable for Tomorrow"?

3. How does this fable convey Rachel Carson's opposition to DDT, presented in *Silent Spring?*

Developing Skills in Reading Literature

1. **Fable.** A fable is a brief tale told to illustrate a moral. What makes this story a fable? Why does Carson not name the town or any characters? Why is the town "in the heart of America"? Why do you think Carson chose to write a fable to advance her point of view?

2. **Irony.** Why is the last line of the story the most ironic?

3. **Hyperbole.** In what ways does Rachel Carson use hyperbole, or exaggeration? Point out three examples and explain their effect.

Developing Vocabulary

Prefixes. Carson describes birds as *migrants*, meaning "those who move from place to place." The prefix e- means "out," and *im-* or *in-* can mean "in." How,

then, would you define *emigrant* and *immigrant?* Check your definitions in a dictionary. Use a dictionary to help you define these pairs or words, each of which begins with e-, *im-*, or *in-*:

eject—inject	egress—ingress
evoke—invoke	evolve—involve
emerse—immerse	emerge—immerge
egest—ingest	enervate—innervate

Developing Writing Skills

Creating a Dominant Impression. Write a "fable for tomorrow" by projecting a trend in today's society to its extreme. The dominant impression in your composition may be disastrous, ridiculous, or chilling. Set in the future, the fable should provide specific details that advance the narrative while reinforcing the overall impression you desire.

Unit Review   *Modern Nonfiction*

Understanding the Unit

1. A major theme in modern nonfiction is the need for social change. Explain the social change urged by Rachel Carson, John F. Kennedy, E. B. White, James Baldwin, and Archibald MacLeish in their various kinds of nonfiction writing. In what way does each writer "dream a new dream of the new America"?

2. Both Alfred Kazin and Adlai E. Stevenson praise women of strength and character. In what ways are Mrs. Kazin's and Mrs. Roosevelt's circumstances different while their strivings are similar? Cite specific traits and activities that the writers find most admirable in these women.

3. What advice do Lorraine Hansberry and William Faulkner give young writers? How is their advice complementary?

4. Compare the techniques of effective oration that are used in the speeches of William Faulkner, Franklin D. Roosevelt, and John F. Kennedy. Note parallelism, anaphora, rhetorical questions, figurative language, allusions, aphorisms, contrast, repetition, and other persuasive devices. Locate effective usages of these techniques in the other types of nonfiction in this unit.

5. As detailed in the selections by Richard Wright, Lorraine Hansberry, and James Baldwin, what struggles and conflicts are peculiar to the black writer? What do these autobiographies reveal about the universal conflicts experienced by the artist in the modern world?

6. While the selections in this unit are nonfiction, many contain elements of the short story. Identify the narrative elements in the essays by Loren Eiseley, E. B. White, and John Dos Passos. Explain the importance of setting in "The Kitchen" as well as in two other selections. How are narration, description, and exposition combined in the autobiographies in this unit?

7. Loren Eiseley, E. B. White, and Rachel Carson all present nonfiction that results from their experiences with nature. Compare and contrast their attitudes toward nature, and explain how these attitudes are reflected in their choice of subjects.

8. The writers of the autobiographical selections in this unit all describe dreams that they seek to attain. Choose three selections, and trace the personal struggles that culminate in a turning point for each writer. In addition, analyze the character traits demonstrated by each writer during his or her search. How is each writer affected by the pursuit of a dream?

Writing

1. "Literature should be either instructive or amusing," writes Henry James in *The Art of Fiction*. Choose one selection that you find instructive or amusing, and explain in a five-paragraph composition how the writer achieves this effect, not only through content but also through style and structure.

2. "What then is the American?" Archibald MacLeish quotes. Explain the concept of the modern American presented by three writers in this unit. Use specific passages from their writings to support your analysis.

3. William Faulkner exalts the modern writer who can retain his or her conviction that humans "will prevail" and who writes about the "problems of the human heart in conflict with itself." Which writers represented in this unit fulfill Faulkner's vision for the writer in society? How do they achieve this goal? Write a composition in which you analyze the work of three writers in relation to Faulkner's concept.

WHITE ROOSTER, 1947. *Milton Avery.*
The Metropolitan Museum of Art.
Gift of Joyce Blaffer von Bothmer, 1975.

Unit 7

Modern Poetry (1900 to the Present)

MOUNT KATAHDIN, AUTUMN, NO. 1, 1942. *Marsden Hartley.*
Sheldon Memorial Art Gallery.
University of Nebraska, Lincoln.

The Evolution of Modern Poetry

Modern American poetry has its origins in the nineteenth century, especially in the work of Walt Whitman, Edgar Allan Poe, and Emily Dickinson. Whitman, whose first edition of *Leaves of Grass* came out in 1855, revolutionized poetry, both in form and in content. His willingness to write about anything and everything, without censorship or restraint, made him more candid and earthy than any other poet of his century. The poetic form that Whitman chose for most of his work was an ingenious reflection of its startling content. Abandoning traditional forms, Whitman originated free verse, poetry that lacks set rhyme, meter, and stanza shape. His lines are honest, vigorous, and free from artificial constraints. Edwin Arlington Robinson, in his poem "Walt Whitman," speaks of the awe that later poets still feel for Whitman, whose "piercing and eternal cadence rings too pure for us—too powerfully pure, too lovingly triumphant, and too large." In "A Pact," Ezra Pound says to Whitman, "It was you that broke the new wood." Contemporary poet Allen Ginsberg, in "A Supermarket in California," addresses Whitman as "Dear Father," asking him for direction in the line, "Which way does your beard point tonight?"

Poe and Dickinson also influenced the course of twentieth-century poetry, though to a lesser degree than Whitman. Poe's symbolism and painstaking craftsmanship was most appreciated by the French symbolist poets of the late nineteenth century—Baudelaire and Valéry, for example—and his influence on American writers has been rather indirect, channeled through the French. The symbolists are so named because of their devotion to symbols, which they use to evoke atmosphere and establish meaning, generally avoiding direct statements of meaning. T. S. Eliot and Wallace Stevens are major American symbolist poets of the twentieth century. Emily Dickinson, with her terse, compact poems, eccentric in their rhythms and punctuation, has influenced the many modern poets who concentrate on economy of expression.

EARLY TWENTIETH-CENTURY AWARENESS

Five poets in the early years of the twentieth century—Edgar Lee Masters, Edwin Arlington Robinson, Vachel Lindsay, Carl Sandburg, and Robert Frost—are poets of the land and the people. All five wrote about the largely rural, agrarian society that still existed in the early 1900's, and each of these poets is identified with a particular region. Sandburg, who is linked to Illinois, also wrote about urban America.

NITO HERRERA IN SPRINGTIME, 1950. *Peter Hurd.*
The Denver Art Museum. Gift of Mrs. A. L. Barbour.

EXPERIMENTS WITH IMAGE AND FORM

Five other poets from the first quarter of the century—Amy
Lowell, William Carlos Williams, H. D. (Hilda Doolittle), Ezra
Pound, and E. E. Cummings—are known for their experimentation
with imagery and form. Ezra Pound actually established a movement known as Imagism, whose goal was to present new rhythms,
precise images, and "hard and clear" everyday speech in poetry.
Williams, H. D., and Lowell are also known as Imagists, as is
Cummings at times. Cummings's experiments with the typography,
or layout, of poems, earned him a reputation for stylistic innovation.

HARLEM RENAISSANCE POETS

One of the dramatic movements in twentieth-century American poetry occurred in the Harlem area of New York City during the 1920's. Following World War I many blacks moved north to take industrial jobs, and Harlem became the cultural center for black life in America. Though not a part of the Harlem Renaissance, poet Paul Laurence Dunbar influenced the movement, for he was the first black writer in the United States to attain national prominence. Poets Countee Cullen, Claude McKay, Jean Toomer, Langston Hughes, and Arna Bontemps all flowered in the 1920's, several of them writing fiction as well.

POSTWAR CONSCIOUSNESS

The wars of the twentieth century, especially World Wars I and II, have had an immense impact on modern poetry. American culture changed dramatically after World War I, with the old rural society rapidly becoming urban and industrial. World War I had a profoundly disillusioning effect on people, creating what became known as the "Lost Generation." The old America was gone, and poets saw instead a lonely, dehumanized, mechanized world, where individuals struggled to communicate and searched for some source of hope. This postwar consciousness is one of the dominant strains in modern poetry, linking in various ways many disparate poets.

CONTEMPORARY POETRY

Contemporary America is notable for the number and variety of its poets. Women poets have been a major force in recent decades, as have black poets. Hispanic and Native American poets have become increasingly prominent. While many outstanding contemporary poets are represented in the pages that follow, there are numerous others who would be represented if space were not limited. Poets often have difficulty publishing their work, and few poets can live on the stipends they earn. Yet in spite of these major obstacles, the poetic impulse manifests itself in unpredictable places, and poetry continues to flourish in our culture.

Early Twentieth-Century Awareness

NATALIE IN A BLUE SKIRT. *William Glackens.*
Tacoma Art Museum. Permanent Collection.

Edgar Lee Masters

1869–1950

Edgar Lee Masters is most closely associated with his *Spoon River Anthology*, a series of free-verse monologues in which the deceased inhabitants of a town called Spoon River speak bitterly of their dismal lives. After *Spoon River*, which was published in 1915, Masters never again achieved in his long career as a poet, novelist, and biographer the critical and popular success of that single work. As a result, Masters himself experienced the isolation, frustration, and failure that *Spoon River* so poignantly depicts.

Born in Kansas, Masters grew up in Lewistown, Illinois, the rural model for his imaginary Spoon River setting. After attending Knox College and studying in his father's law office, Masters practiced law in Chicago until 1921, when he moved to New York to devote himself exclusively to writing. Though his many subsequent works cover a wide spectrum of subject matter and genres, Masters labored for the most part outside of the literary spotlight. His place in American letters had already been secured, however, by the abiding appeal of *Spoon River*.

At least part of that work's appeal stems from the relative simplicity and directness of the language Masters used to distill the essence of the 243 lives buried in Spoon River's cemetery. Each character voices his or her own epitaph from the grave and in so doing creates an interwoven and often satiric commentary on the quality of life in small-town America at the turn of the century. Rejecting traditional poetic forms, Masters instead used free verse patterns to make his subjects appear more natural. Moreover, *Spoon River* appeared at a time of far-reaching social change occasioned by rapid industrialization and the imminence of America's involvement in World War I. As they articulated their common anxieties and resentments, the residents of Spoon River's cemetery voiced many of the concerns of an audience facing similar problems in their own lives. Masters uncovered the discontent beneath the surface tranquillity of small town America, and in so doing won himself a prominent place in American letters.

Albert Schirding

Jonas Keene thought his lot a hard one
Because his children were all failures.
But I know of a fate more trying than that:
It is to be a failure while your children are successes.
For I raised a brood of eagles   5
Who flew away at last, leaving me
A crow on the abandoned bough,
Then, with the ambition to prefix Honorable to my name,
And thus to win my children's admiration,
I ran for County Superintendent of Schools,   10
Spending my accumulations to win—and lost.
That fall my daughter received first prize in Paris
For her picture, entitled, "The Old Mill"—
(It was of the water mill before Henry Wilkin put in steam.)
The feeling that I was not worthy of her finished me.   15

Getting at Meaning

1. Why was the speaker, Albert Schirding, so unhappy in his life?

2. How did Albert Schirding try to win his children's respect? When he failed, what did his daughter accomplish?

What kind of man was Albert Schirding? Why couldn't he be proud of his children?

3. **Metaphor.** Schirding says that he raised "a brood of eagles" who flew away, leaving him "a crow on the abandoned bough." What is the meaning of these two metaphors? What are the differing connotations of *crow* and *eagle*?

Developing Skills in Reading Literature

1. **Epitaph.** An epitaph is the inscription on a tombstone or monument in memory of the person or people buried there. *Epitaph* also refers to a brief literary piece that sums up the life of a dead person. In *Spoon River Anthology* various dead citizens of Spoon River write their own epitaphs. Each poem is thus a brief summation of its speaker's life.

How does Albert Schirding feel about his life? What is the tone of his epitaph?

2. **Speaker.** The poems in *Spoon River Anthology* all illustrate the point that the speaker of a poem is sometimes distinct from the poet. In each poem Masters speaks through a different dead individual, with the poem bearing the name of the speaker. The poems as a unit create a composite portrait of Spoon River.

Developing Vocabulary

Words from Greek: Prefixes and Roots. The word *epitaph* comes from the ancient Greek prefix *epi-*, meaning "over," and from the root *taphos*, meaning "tomb." The literal meaning of the word is thus "over the tomb."

Other English words employ the prefix *epi-*. Look up each word that follows in a dictionary, and record both its meaning and the root word from which it is derived. Explain how the prefix functions with the root to create the meaning.

epigraph	epistle
epilepsy	epithet
epiphany	epitome

Jonas Keene

Why did Albert Schirding kill himself
Trying to be County Superintendent of Schools,
Blest as he was with the means of life
And wonderful children, bringing him honor
Ere he was sixty?   5
If even one of my boys could have run a news-stand,
Or one of my girls could have married a decent man,
I should not have walked in the rain
And jumped into bed with clothes all wet,
Refusing medical aid.   10

Getting at Meaning

1. Why did Albert Schirding's suicide seem silly to Jonas Keene?

2. What was Jonas Keene's great sorrow in life? How did he apparently react to his disappointments?

Developing Skills in Reading Literature

1. **Free Verse.** The poems in *Spoon River Anthology* are free verse, with no set patterns of rhyme or meter. The poems are also conversational in style. Study "Jonas Keene." What qualities make it a poem?

2. **Tone.** What is the speaker's tone in "Jonas Keene"? What attitude killed him, in that it caused him to jump into bed "with clothes all wet/Refusing medical aid"?

Petit, the Poet

Seeds in a dry pod, tick, tick, tick,
Tick, tick, tick, like mites in a quarrel—
Faint iambics that the full breeze wakens—
But the pine tree makes a symphony thereof.
Triolets, villanelles, rondels, rondeaus,   5
Ballades[1] by the score with the same old thought:
The snows and the roses of yesterday are vanished,
And what is love but a rose that fades?
Life all around me here in the village:
Tragedy, comedy, valor and truth,   10
Courage, constancy, heroism, failure—
All in the loom, and oh what patterns!
Woodlands, meadows, streams and rivers—
Blind to all of it all my life long.
Triolets, villanelles, rondels, rondeaus,   15
Seeds in a dry pod, tick, tick, tick,
Tick, tick, tick, what little iambics,
While Homer and Whitman roared in the pines?

---

1. **Triolets . . . Ballades:** forms of poetry with varying stanzas,
lines, and rhyme.

Getting at Meaning

1. What did Petit concentrate on in his poetry? The line "Triolets, villanelles, rondels, rondeaus" is a clue. So is the line "Tick, tick, tick, what little iambics."

2. What does Petit wish he had tried to convey in his verse? To what things was he blind?

Developing Skills in Reading Literature

1. **Allusion.** Petit alludes to Homer and Whitman, expecting the readers of his epitaph to know that both were great poets. It is also significant that Whitman pioneered free verse, scorning the "little iambics." Why does Petit feel that Homer and Whitman were much greater poets than he?

2. **Figurative Language.** In the first two lines of the poem Petit uses both a metaphor and a simile to describe his own "faint iambics." What do both of these comparisons suggest about his concern for meter? While Petit worried about scansion, what was the pine tree producing? What is Petit's metaphor for love? Explain this metaphor in the context of the poem. What does the figure of speech "roared in the pines" imply about Homer and Whitman?

3. **Repetend.** What line in the poem does Petit use twice? Why? The phrase "tick, tick, tick" is another repetend in the poem. Why is it repeated so often?

Jonathan Houghton

There is the caw of a crow,
And the hesitant song of a thrush.
There is the tinkle of a cowbell far away,
And the voice of a plowman on Shipley's hill.
The forest beyond the orchard is still   5
With midsummer stillness;
And along the road a wagon chuckles,
Loaded with corn, going to Atterbury.
And an old man sits under a tree asleep,
And an old woman crosses the road,   10
Coming from the orchard with a bucket of blackberries
And a boy lies in the grass
Near the feet of the old man,
And looks up at the sailing clouds,
And longs, and longs, and longs   15
For what, he knows not:
For manhood, for life, for the unknown world!
Then thirty years passed,
And the boy returned worn out by life
And found the orchard vanished,   20
And the forest gone,
And the house made over,
And the roadway filled with dust from automobiles—
And himself desiring The Hill!

Getting at Meaning

1. Describe the picturesque scene that Jonathan Houghton remembers from his boyhood. What did he, the rural boy, long for?

2. What kind of life experiences did Jonathan Houghton apparently have? What phrase in the poem indicates this?

Developing Skills in Reading Literature

1. **Irony.** Explain the irony contained in the final line of the poem. Why is it such a sad irony? What does it imply about human life?

2. **Imagery.** Notice the lovely pastoral imagery in the first sixteen lines of the poem. What are the sounds that Houghton emphasizes? What sights predominate? What two words activate the sense of taste? In what line is the sense of touch indirectly stimulated? Why does Jonathan Houghton want to re-create such a peaceful rural scene?

3. **Consonance and Assonance.** The first eight lines of this poem create a musical effect, in part because of the use of consonance and assonance. What consonant patterns does Masters repeat? Which vowel sounds are often repeated? What ideas are emphasized by the repeated sounds? Describe the effect of the consonance and assonance on the rhythm of these lines.

Lucinda Matlock

I went to the dances at Chandlerville,
And played snap-out at Winchester.
One time we changed partners,
Driving home in the moonlight of middle June,
And then I found Davis.   5
We were married and lived together for seventy years,
Enjoying, working, raising the twelve children,
Eight of whom we lost
Ere I had reached the age of sixty.
I spun, I wove, I kept the house, I nursed the sick,   10
I made the garden, and for holiday
Rambled over the fields where sang the larks,
And by Spoon River gathering many a shell,
And many a flower and medicinal weed—
Shouting to the wooded hills, singing to the green valleys.   15
At ninety-six I had lived enough, that is all,
And passed to a sweet repose.
What is this I hear of sorrow and weariness,
Anger, discontent and drooping hopes?
Degenerate sons and daughters,   20
Life is too strong for you—
It takes life to love Life.

Getting at Meaning

1. What are the facts of Lucinda Matlock's life as she presents them?

2. Explain Lucinda Matlock's meaning in the line, "It takes life to love Life."

Developing Skills in Reading Literature

1. **Diction.** Notice that Lucinda Matlock frequently uses the present participle verb form in speaking of her life, as in *driving, enjoying, working, raising, gathering, shouting,* and *singing*. The present participle form implies that an action is ongoing, or continuous. Why are these verbs appropriate in the poem? How do they relate to Lucinda Matlock's character?

2. **Tone.** What attitude does Lucinda Matlock have toward weakness and sorrow? Describe her attitude toward life. Judging from her tone, why did she live to be ninety-six?

Developing Writing Skills

Analyzing Theme. The English Romantic poet Shelley once wrote, "We look before and after/And pine for what is not." This is the theme of many of the poems in *Spoon River Anthology*.

Select three of the five poems you have read from Masters's collection and write a five-paragraph composition in which you discuss their treatment of this theme. Devote one body paragraph to each poem, quoting from the poem to support your points. In your conclusion write a general statement that applies to all three poems.

Edwin Arlington Robinson
1869–1935

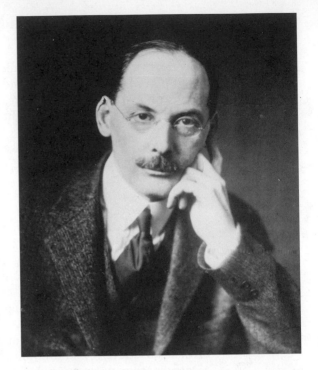

In a letter written in 1897, Edwin Arlington Robinson rejected the view that he was pessimistic by observing that "This world is not a 'prison house,' but a kind of spiritual kindergarten where millions of bewildered infants are trying to spell God with the wrong blocks." Pessimistic or not, Robinson's poetry highlights the recurring individual dilemma of preserving life's spiritual meaning within a world dominated by nonspiritual ways of thinking and living.

Robinson grew up in the coastal town of Gardiner, Maine, the third son in a merchant and ship-building family. Gardiner was later to appear as the imaginary Tilbury Town of Robinson's poetry. More introverted and contemplative than either of his older brothers, Robinson had already decided upon a literary career before entering Harvard in 1891. A series of family tragedies, including the deaths of his parents and an older brother, forced his return to Gardiner in 1893, where he worked as a free-lance writer until 1896. He then moved to New York's Greenwich Village, assuming a variety of menial jobs, including one as a subway construction inspector. Throughout this period of obscurity and impoverishment, Robinson diligently pursued his poetic ambitions, producing his first published works in 1896 and *The Children of the Night* in 1897. His poems came to the attention of President Theodore Roosevelt, who admired them so much that he interceded on the struggling poet's behalf and secured for him a position in the New York Customs House in 1905. Robinson worked there until 1909, when he was financially able to devote his time to poetry. Robinson never married, preferring instead to give himself wholly to his craft until his death in 1935. Three of his volumes of poetry won Pulitzer Prizes, in 1922 *(Collected Poems)*, 1925 *(The Man Who Died Twice)*, and 1928 *(Tristram)*.

Robinson has been variously described as a formal traditionalist, an idealist, an intellectual "poet of the mind rather than the soul," and "the great American poet of Failure." Some of his most famous characters, Miniver Cheevy, Richard Cory, and Old Eben Flood, are all isolated individuals living in a world inhospitable to their spiritual needs. In creating such characters, Robinson anticipated one of the central concerns of twentieth-century American literature.

Miniver Cheevy

Miniver Cheevy, child of scorn,
  Grew lean while he assailed the seasons;
He wept that he was ever born,
  And he had reasons.

Miniver loved the days of old   5
  When swords were bright and steeds
  were prancing;
The vision of a warrior bold
  Would set him dancing.

Miniver sighed for what was not,
  And dreamed, and rested from his   10
  labors;
He dreamed of Thebes[1] and Camelot,[2]
  And Priam's[3] neighbors.

Miniver mourned the ripe renown
  That made so many a name so fragrant;
He mourned Romance, now on the town,   15
  And Art, a vagrant.

Miniver loved the Medici,[4]
  Albeit he had never seen one;
He would have sinned incessantly
  Could he have been one.   20

Miniver cursed the commonplace
  And eyed a khaki suit with loathing;
He missed the medieval grace
  Of iron clothing.

Miniver scorned the gold he sought,   25
  But sore annoyed was he without it;
Miniver thought, and thought, and
  thought,
  And thought about it.

Miniver Cheevy, born too late,
  Scratched his head and kept on   30
  thinking;
Miniver coughed, and called it fate,
  And kept on drinking.

---

1. **Thebes** (thēbz): a city in ancient Greece.
2. **Camelot** (kam' ə lät'): the site of King Arthur's palace and court in Arthurian legends; a time, place, or atmosphere of idyllic happiness.
3. **Priam** (prī' əm): the king of Troy during the Trojan War.
4. **Medici** (med' ə chē'): a wealthy Florentine family in Renaissance Italy, famed as statesmen and patrons of the arts.

Getting at Meaning

1. Why is Miniver Cheevy a "child of scorn"? Describe his position in society.

2. What is the content of Cheevy's daydreams? Why does he romanticize the past?

3. What is Cheevy's response to being "born too late"?

Developing Skills in Reading Literature

1. **Character.** Edwin Arlington Robinson created a series of character sketches in his poems about Tilbury Town. Each poem has a character's name in its title.

Miniver was the white or light gray fur used to trim medieval robes. The word also refers to the ermine used in the ceremonial robes of peers. Why is this an appropriate name for the title character of the poem? Why is this an ironic name? What does the final stanza indicate about Cheevy's character?

2. **Tone.** Which lines in the poem suggest that Robinson is gently mocking Cheevy's attitude toward the past? As Robinson presents him, is Cheevy a sympathetic character? Why or why not?

3. **Rhyme Scheme.** Chart the rhyme scheme of "Miniver Cheevy." Then study the pattern of rhyming lines. What difference do you see in the way that each pair of lines rhymes in each stanza? Comment on the effect produced throughout the poem by the rhyme in the second and fourth lines.

Richard Cory

Whenever Richard Cory went down town,
We people on the pavement looked at him:
He was a gentleman from sole to crown,
Clean favored, and imperially slim.

And he was always quietly arrayed,   5
And he was always human when he talked;
But still he fluttered pulses when he said,
"Good-morning," and he glittered when he walked.

And he was rich—yes, richer than a king—
And admirably schooled in every grace: 10
In fine, we thought that he was everything
To make us wish that we were in his place.

So on we worked, and waited for the light,
And went without the meat, and cursed the bread;
And Richard Cory, one calm summer night,   15
Went home and put a bullet through his head.

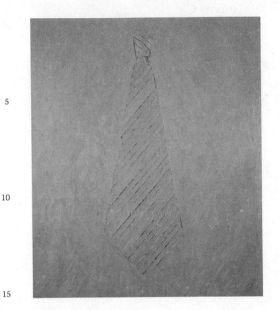

FLESH STRIPED TIE. JIM DINE.
*Hirshhorn Museum and Sculpture
Garden, Smithsonian Institution.*

Getting at Meaning

1. What impression does Richard Cory produce on the citizens of Tilbury Town? How does he treat the townspeople?

2. Why does everyone envy Richard Cory? Why is this envy inappropriate?

Developing Skills in Reading Literature

1. **Speaker.** Notice that the speaking voice of this poem is "we people on the pavement." What effect does this phrase produce? How does it help build the contrast between the people of the town and Richard Cory? What other lines in the poem dramatize the difference between the citizens who speak and Cory?

2. **Irony.** The last line of the poem catches the reader by surprise, for it is certainly ironic that a man so envied would kill himself. How does the final line put the reader in the same position as "we people on the pavement"? What is ironic about the fact that Cory kills himself "one calm summer night"? What is ironic about lines 13 and 14?

3. **Alliteration.** Three consonant sounds appear quite often in this poem at the beginnings of words. Can you identify these sounds? What effect do these repeating sounds have on the poem?

Mr. Flood's Party

Old Eben Flood, climbing alone one night
Over the hill between the town below
And the forsaken upland hermitage
That held as much as he should ever know
On earth again of home, paused warily.　　　　　　　5
The road was his with not a native near;
And Eben, having leisure, said aloud,
For no man else in Tilbury Town to hear:

"Well, Mr. Flood, we have the harvest moon
Again, and we may not have many more;　　　　　10
The bird is on the wing, the poet says.
And you and I have said it here before.
Drink to the bird." He raised up to the light
The jug that he had gone so far to fill,
And answered huskily: "Well, Mr. Flood,　　　　15
Since you propose it, I believe I will."

Alone, as if enduring to the end
A valiant armor of scarred hopes outworn,
He stood there in the middle of the road
Like Roland's[1] ghost winding a silent horn.　　20
Below him, in the town among the trees,
Where friends of other days had honored him,
A phantom salutation of the dead
Rang thinly till old Eben's eyes were dim.

Then, as a mother lays her sleeping child　　　25
Down tenderly, fearing it may awake,
He set the jug down slowly at his feet
With trembling care, knowing that most things break;
And only when assured that on firm earth
It stood, as the uncertain lives of men　　　　　30
Assuredly did not, he paced away,
And with his hand extended paused again:

"Well, Mr. Flood, we have not met like this
In a long time; and many a change has come
To both of us, I fear, since last it was　　　　　35

---

1. **Roland** (rō′ lənd): a defender of the Christians against the Saracens in the Charlemagne legends, who was killed at Roncesvalles.

We had a drop together. Welcome home!"
Convivially returning with himself,
Again he raised the jug up to the light;
And with an acquiescent quaver said:
"Well, Mr. Flood, if you insist, I might.   40

"Only a very little, Mr. Flood—
For auld lang syne. No more, sir; that will do."
So, for the time, apparently it did,
And Eben evidently thought so too;
For soon amid the silver loneliness   45
Of night he lifted up his voice and sang,
Secure, with only two moons listening,
Until the whole harmonious landscape rang—

"For auld lang syne." The weary throat gave out;
The last word wavered, and the song was done. 50
He raised again the jug regretfully
And shook his head, and was again alone.
There was not much that was ahead of him,
And there was nothing in the town below—
Where strangers would have shut the many doors 55
That many friends had opened long ago.

AUTUMN, 1941. THOMAS HART BENTON.
Collection of Whitney Museum of American Art.
Bequest of Loula D. Lasker.

Getting at Meaning

1. Whom does Mr. Flood address in this poem? Who attends his party?

2. The first stanza of the poem spells out Mr. Flood's circumstances. What are they? What other lines in the poem reflect on his position in life?

Developing Skills in Reading Literature

1. **Setting.** Describe the place where Mr. Flood holds his party. Why does he hold it away from the town? Why does he hold it at night?

Judging from the three poems set in Tilbury Town, what kind of place is the town? What passages in the poems suggest that it is a small community in which the citizens all know each other?

2. **Theme.** Mr. Flood puts his jug down "With trembling care, knowing that most things break." What theme does this line embody? What theme surfaces in the passage in which Mr. Flood says, "Welcome home," after which he is described as "Convivially returning with himself"?

3. **Simile.** Comment on how each of the similes that follows develops Mr. Flood's character. How is each comparison related to theme?

> Alone, as if enduring to the end
> A valiant armor of scarred hopes outworn,
>
> He stood there in the middle of the road
> Like Roland's ghost winding a silent horn.
>
> Then, as a mother lays her sleeping child
> Down tenderly, fearing it may awake,
> He set the jug down slowly at his feet

4. **Tone.** The tone of "Mr. Flood's Party" is mixed. Which passages seem comic? Which lines arouse pity and sympathy for Mr. Flood? What effect does the blend of the humorous and the serious have on you? Is the tone true to life? What tone predominates in the final stanza?

5. **Meter.** Although there are some irregularities in the meter of this poem, it is basically iambic pentameter. To refresh your memory, scan the third stanza of the poem on a sheet of paper. Identify the individual feet in each line, marking where the accents fall. What purpose does the controlled rhythm serve in this poem? In a world where "most things break," what do people often cling to?

Developing Vocabulary

Scottish Words in English. Mr. Flood uses the phrase *auld lang syne,* which is Scottish dialect for "old long since." The phrase means "the good old days long past."

Six other words from Scottish dialect often used in standard English follow. Find each word in a dictionary, and record the definition of the word and the history of its origin.

argyle
crofter
laird
loch
scone
wee

Developing Writing Skills

Establishing Tone. In many of the poems about Tilbury Town, Edwin Arlington Robinson describes his characters with a mixed tone. Often, as in "Mr. Flood's Party," he combines humor and pathos.

Narrate an event, either real or imagined, in a paragraph or two, concentrating on establishing a mixed tone. Blend two attitudes in your narration, such as fear and humor or sympathy and exasperation. Show how your subject matter evokes both sentiments.

Vachel Lindsay

1879–1931

Vachel Lindsay was a man intent on communicating his vision of a nation and on reviving poetry as an art form for the common people. His later bitterness and frustration, followed ultimately by his suicide at age 52, suggest the depth of Lindsay's disappointment in the results of his efforts.

Born in Springfield, Illinois, Lindsay attended Hiram College in Hiram, Ohio, and studied art for a time before turning to poetry. For several summers he dispersed his poetic gospel of the nation and its folk heroes by traveling throughout the land, exchanging poems for food and shelter. After Harriet Monroe's Chicago-based *Poetry* magazine published his "General William Booth Enters into Heaven" in 1913, Lindsay became, in effect, a popular entertainer of the day, traveling the lecture circuit and reciting his rhythmic and dramatic poems in a style he referred to as "Higher Vaudeville." Among the poems most often requested by his audiences were "The Congo" and "The Santa Fe Trail." Though Lindsay indeed borrowed from the vaudeville stage to spread his messages, he was wholly sincere in his beliefs. His several prose efforts, including *Adventures While Preaching the Gospel of Beauty* (1914), were further attempts to reach a wider audience. Poetry, to Lindsay, meant preaching, and when his audiences failed to respond as he wished, Lindsay retreated toward despair. His vision of a spiritually true and just nation, often associated with such political folk heroes as Lincoln and the Populist William Jennings Bryan, underlies his most enduring poems.

The Flower-Fed Buffaloes

The flower-fed buffaloes of the spring
In the days of long ago,
Ranged where the locomotives sing
And the prairie flowers lie low:—
The tossing, blooming, perfumed grass   5
Is swept away by the wheat,
Wheels and wheels and wheels spin by
In the spring that still is sweet.
But the flower-fed buffaloes of the spring
Left us, long ago.   10
They gore no more, they bellow no more,
They trundle around the hills no more:—
With the Blackfeet, lying low,
With the Pawnees, lying low,
Lying low.   15

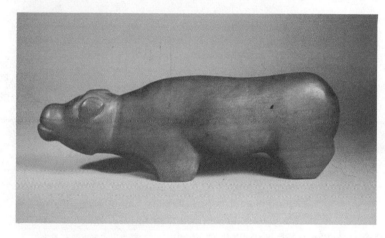

Wooden carving representing a buffalo,
used in telling buffalo stories.

Museum of the American Indian, Heye Foundation.

Getting at Meaning

1. How does the speaker envision the prairies when the buffaloes roamed freely?

2. Where have the buffaloes gone? What has replaced them?

Developing Skills in Reading Literature

1. **Tone.** Characterize the tone of this short poem. What words and phrases suggest regret? What is the poet's attitude toward technological progress?

2. **Diction.** Lindsay describes the buffaloes as "flower-fed." What connotations does this coined adjective have for you? What is the effect produced by describing the grass as "tossing, blooming, perfumed"? What kind of setting do these adjectives bring to mind?

3. **Repetend.** In line 4 the poet uses the phrase "lie low." This is echoed in the three final lines of the poem, where "lying low" appears three times. What other words and phrases does Lindsay repeat? What effect do the repetends have on the rhythm of the poem? on the meaning of the poem?

The Leaden-Eyed

Let not young souls be smothered out before
They do quaint deeds and fully flaunt their pride.
It is the world's one crime its babes grow dull,
Its poor are ox-like, limp and leaden-eyed.
Not that they starve, but starve so dreamlessly,   5
Not that they sow, but that they seldom reap,
Not that they serve, but have no gods to serve,
Not that they die, but that they die like sheep.

Getting at Meaning

1. Who are the "leaden-eyed" that are the subject of this poem?

2. Explain the meaning of the line, "It is the world's one crime its babes grow dull."

Developing Skills in Reading Literature

1. **Simile.** In a moving comparison Lindsay likens the struggling masses to beasts of burden. The world's poor, he says, are "ox-like, limp and leaden-eyed." What qualities do you associate with the ox? What is Lindsay implying about the poor when he describes them as *limp*? What does *leaden-eyed* suggest to you? Notice how thoroughly this one simile characterizes a large group of people. According to the simile, why do their lives not change?

2. **Parallelism.** The parallelism in the final four lines emphasizes the main point of the poem. What four ideas of equal weight does Lindsay express in the same grammatical form? Identify the grammatical form. How does the repetition of this pattern serve to make the lines more emphatic?

3. **Rhythm.** Lindsay enjoyed chanting his poems orally in public performances. Read both "The Flower-Fed Buffaloes" and "The Leaden-Eyed" aloud. What poetic devices give the poems a highly rhythmic, musical quality?

Carl Sandburg
1878–1967

Carl Sandburg's characteristically American belief that "The people will live on./ The learning and blundering people will live on . . ." is expressed throughout his long and distinguished career as a poet, biographer, and folklorist.

Sandburg was born in Galesburg, Illinois. He held various jobs in his youth, including barbershop porter, brickyard hand, and worker in the wheat fields of Kansas. He enlisted in the army when the Spanish-American War broke out. In 1913 he moved to Chicago, where he worked on the *Chicago Daily News*.

Sandburg first acquired an audience for his early efforts through the pages of *Poetry* magazine in 1914. The publication shortly thereafter of his *Chicago Poems* and *Corn-Huskers* established his fame as a poet of the people who celebrated the energy and vitality he regarded as hallmarks of American life.

As a biographer, Sandburg focused on such notable figures as his brother-in-law, the photographer Edward Steichen; Mary Lincoln, the wife of the President; and on Lincoln himself. Lincoln was also the subject of his famous multi-volume biography for young people, for which he won a Pulitzer Prize in history in 1940. Other of his works for children demonstrate his whimsical imagination, as in the stories published in *Rootabaga Country*, *Early Moon*, and *Potato Face*. Sandburg, the passionate spokesman for the lives of ordinary Americans, speaks out in two collections of American folksongs *(The American Songbag* and *New American Songbag)*, and in his optimistic Depression-era *The People, Yes*, in which he pays poetic homage to a beleaguered, yet proud and ultimately triumphant citizenry. Sandburg received a Pulitzer Prize in poetry in 1951 for his *Complete Poems*.

As might be expected from a career spanning half a century, Sandburg's poems reflect a variety of personal influences and techniques. Echoes of Walt Whitman's free-verse lyricism clearly reverberate in works such as the ruggedly realistic "Chicago." On the other hand, the metaphoric aptness of poems such as "Fog" suggests Sandburg's awareness of the growing Imagist movement in American poetry. Sandburg's last volume of verse, *Honey and Salt* (1963), is perhaps his finest achievement as a poet.

Sandhill People

I took away three pictures.
One was a white gull forming a half-mile arch from the pines
toward Waukegan.[1]
One was a whistle in the little sandhills, a bird crying either to
the sunset gone or the dusk come.
One was three spotted waterbirds, zigzagging, cutting scrolls and
jags, writing a bird Sanscrit[2] of wing points, half over the
sand, half over the water, a half-love for the sea, a half-love
for the land.

I took away three thoughts.   5
One was a thing my people call "love," a shut-in river hunting
the sea, breaking white falls between tall clefs of hill country.
One was a thing my people call "silence," the wind running over
the butter faced sand-flowers, running over the sea, and
never heard of again.
One was a thing my people call "death," neither a whistle in
the little sandhills, nor a bird Sanscrit of wing points, yet a
coat all the stars and seas have worn, yet a face the beach
wears between sunset and dusk.

---

1. **Waukegan** (wo kē′ gən): a city in the north of Illinois.
2. **Sanscrit** (san′ skrit): an ancient Indic language that is the classical language of
India and of Hinduism.

Getting at Meaning

1. What is the location from which the speaker takes away the three pictures and the three thoughts? Who are the sandhill people?

2. What view of death emerges in the final sentence of the poem?

Developing Skills in Reading Literature

1. **Imagery.** The images, or mental pictures, Sandburg creates in this poem are rather striking. What are the three separate images the first stanza presents? What do the three images have in common? In what ways does the third image, like the three spotted waterbirds, "zigzag"?

What separate images stand out in the second stanza of the poem? What different senses do these images stimulate?

2. **Metaphor.** Explain the metaphor for love in the poem, "a shut-in river hunting the sea." Explain the metaphors for death, "a coat all the stars and seas have worn" and "a face the beach wears between sunset and dusk."

3. **Parallelism.** The poem consists of two parallel stanzas. In what ways are they parallel, or balanced? What ideas of equal weight does Sandburg develop using the same grammatical forms? Identify the repeating structures. In what ways does the first picture in the first stanza relate to the first thought in the second stanza? What are the relationships between the second, and then the third elements of the two stanzas? What is the overall effect produced by the parallelism?

The Harbor

Passing through huddled and ugly walls
By doorways where women
Looked from their hunger-deep eyes,
Haunted with shadows of hunger-hands,
Out from the huddled and ugly walls,⠀⠀⠀⠀5
I came sudden, at the city's edge,
On a blue burst of lake,
Long lake waves breaking under the sun
On a spray-flung curve of shore;
And a fluttering storm of gulls,⠀⠀⠀⠀10
Masses of great gray wings
And flying white bellies
Veering and wheeling free in the open.

Getting at Meaning

1. Notice that this entire poem is one sentence. In what line do you find the subject and verb of the sentence? Identify them.

2. Where is the speaker during the first five lines of the poem? Where is the speaker in the last seven lines of the poem?

Developing Skills in Reading Literature

1. **Imagery.** This poem consists of two contrasting settings, each one established in a minimum number of lines with a few powerful images. What clear images describe the city streets? What mental pictures does the lake-front description create? How do the images make the two locations seem very different?

2. **Diction: Connotation.** Notice how Sandburg's precise diction helps build contrast in this poem. What does the word *huddled* bring to mind? What words does Sandburg contrast to "huddled and ugly"? What does the word *haunted* imply? What does the poem present in contrast to the haunted and hungry people? Comment on the associations of words such as *spray-flung, veering,* and *wheeling.*

3. **Repetend.** Sandburg repeats certain words and phrases in this short poem. For example, the phrase "huddled and ugly walls" appears twice. Why? What other words are repeated? What is the effect of the repetends?

Grass

Pile the bodies high at Austerlitz and Waterloo.[1]
Shovel them under and let me work—
      I am the grass; I cover all.

And pile them high at Gettysburg
And pile them high at Ypres and Verdun.[2]   5
Shovel them under and let me work.
Two years, ten years, and passengers ask the conductor:
      What place is this?
      Where are we now?

      I am the grass.   10
      Let me work.

---

1. **Austerlitz** (ô′ star lits′) **and Waterloo:** sites of battles of the Napoleonic Wars.
2. **Ypres** (ē′ pr) **and Verdun** (vər dŭn′): sites of battles of World War I.

Getting at Meaning

1. Who are the bodies alluded to in line 1 of the poem?

2. Identify the "I" of the poem. What labor is the "I" performing?

Developing Skills in Reading Literature

1. **Personification.** One figure of speech controls this poem, and it is personification. Why has Sandburg chosen to present grass in human terms? How would the poem differ if a human speaker wrote about grass as an element of nature?

2. **Allusion.** Sandburg's poem alludes to five places. What do these places have in common? Explain how the sense of the poem depends upon an understanding of these allusions.

3. **Theme.** What power does the grass represent? What lines indicate that this power dwarfs human events? Notice the phrase "Shovel them under." What attitude does this phrase imply on the part of the grass and the larger forces behind it?

Prayers of Steel

Lay me on an anvil,[1] O God.
Beat me and hammer me into a crowbar.
Let me pry loose old walls.
Let me lift and loosen old foundations.

Lay me on an anvil, O God.   5
Beat me and hammer me into a steel spike.
Drive me into the girders that hold a skyscraper together.
Take red-hot rivets and fasten me into the central girders.
Let me be the great nail holding a skyscraper through blue
      nights into white stars.

---

1. **anvil:** a heavy block, usually steel-faced iron, on which metal is shaped.

Getting at Meaning

1. Notice that this poem is written as a prayer. What does the speaker pray for in the first stanza?

2. What does the speaker pray for in the second stanza? What is hopeful about this stanza?

Developing Skills in Reading Literature

1. **Speaker.** Who is the speaker in this poem? Why has Sandburg chosen to personify this particular symbol of the industrial age? Is it a fitting symbol?

2. **Structure.** Like "Sandhill People," this poem is arranged in two stanzas. Sandburg uses repetitions of lines and phrases to balance and unify the two stanzas. Which lines and phrases does he repeat? What effect do the repetitions in this poem have on the cadence?

How is the structure of this poem appropriate to the poem's meaning? In what ways is the first stanza an essential foundation for the second stanza?

3. **Alliteration.** What consonant sounds often recur at the beginnings of words in this poem? What does this alliteration contribute to the poem?

Chicago

Hog Butcher for the World,
Tool Maker, Stacker of Wheat,
Player with Railroads and the Nation's Freight Handler;
Stormy, husky, brawling,
City of the Big Shoulders: 5

They tell me you are wicked and I believe them, for I have seen your
  painted women under the gas lamps luring the farm boys.
And they tell me you are crooked and I answer: Yes, it is true I have seen
  the gunman kill and go free to kill again.
And they tell me you are brutal and my reply is: On the faces of women
  and children I have seen the marks of wanton hunger.
And having answered so I turn once more to those who sneer at this my
  city, and I give them back the sneer and say to them:
Come and show me another city with lifted head singing so proud to be
  alive and coarse and strong and cunning.   10
Flinging magnetic curses amid the toil of piling job on job, here is a tall
  bold slugger set vivid against the little soft cities;
Fierce as a dog with tongue lapping for action, cunning as a savage pitted
  against the wilderness,
    Bareheaded,
    Shoveling,
    Wrecking,   15
    Planning,
    Building, breaking, rebuilding,
Under the smoke, dust all over his mouth, laughing with white teeth,
Under the terrible burden of destiny laughing as a young man laughs,
Laughing even as an ignorant fighter laughs who has never lost a battle, 20

Bragging and laughing that under his wrist is the pulse, and under his ribs
  the heart of the people,
          Laughing!
Laughing the stormy, husky, brawling laughter of Youth, half-naked,
  sweating, proud to be Hog Butcher, Tool Maker, Stacker of Wheat,
  Player with Railroads and Freight Handler to the Nation.

Getting at Meaning

1. This poem is about Chicago early in the twentieth century. What details in the poem indicate this era?

2. Judging from the poem, what was Chicago's role in the country earlier in the century? What specific characteristics of the city does the speaker mention?

Developing Skills in Reading Literature

1. **Figurative Language.** The central figure of speech in this poem is the personification of Chicago. What sex is the city? What age? What size? What specific physical traits does it have? What is its attitude toward life? What are its occupations?

Within the central personification appear various similes and metaphors. For example, Chicago is "a tall bold slugger set vivid against the little soft cities." It is also "fierce as a dog with tongue lapping for action." What additional comparisons do you find? What composite picture do these comparisons create?

2. **Diction.** Notice the specific adjectives in this poem. What do words such as *strong* and *husky* connote? What about the words *wicked* and *cunning*? What other adjectives play an important role in characterizing the city?

Like Walt Whitman before him, Sandburg uses energetic verbs, often in the present participle form, suggesting continuous action. For example, Chicago is *brawling, shoveling, wrecking, planning, building, breaking,* and *laughing*. What impression do all these action verbs create? Why are they particularly apt in this poem?

3. **Free Verse.** Also in the tradition of Walt Whitman, Sandburg writes in free verse, with no specific rhyme, meter, or stanza form. Why is the sprawling form of the poem, with its long breathless lines, suitable to the poem's subject matter? What is the effect of having the five short lines isolated at the beginning of the poem? Why are all the energetic present participles set on separate lines in the center of the poem?

4. **Parallelism.** To counter the free verse of his poem, Sandburg uses parallelism as a structuring device. What is the parallelism in lines 6-8? In what ways are lines 18 and 19 parallel? Where do you find parallel verb forms?

5. **Rhythm and Unity.** While it lacks standard rhyme and meter, "Chicago" has a driving rhythm that is appropriate to its subject matter and that contributes to the poem's unity, the harmonious blend among the various elements of a literary work. Two techniques that help create rhythm are alliteration and repetition.

Notice that Sandburg often repeats the consonant *b*, a hard, explosive consonant. Say *b* several times. In what part of your mouth do you form the sound? Why is this consonant sound appropriate to this particular poem? How does it provide unity and rhythm in the poem? What other consonant sounds are repeated? Comment on their use.

What words does Sandburg often repeat? How do these repetends provide unity and rhythm? How do the present participles, repeated so often, enhance the rhythm of the poem? Comment on how the final sentence, with its repeating words and phrases, ties the poem together, both rhythmically and thematically.

Developing Writing Skills

Poetry: Using Figurative Language. Characterize a town or city of your choice in a poem whose form and poetic techniques reflect what you want to say about the place. Use specific figures of speech, such as personification, simile, and metaphor, to bring your subject to life.

Jazz Fantasia

Drum on your drums, batter on your banjoes,
sob on the long cool winding saxophones.
Go to it, O jazzmen.

Sling your knuckles on the bottoms of the happy
tin pans, let your trombones ooze, and go husha-   5
husha-hush with the slippery sand-paper.

Moan like an autumn wind high in the lonesome treetops, moan soft
like you wanted somebody terrible, cry like a racing car slipping away
from a motorcycle cop, bang-bang! you jazzmen, bang altogether
drums, traps, banjoes, horns, tin cans—make two people fight on the   10
top of a stairway and scratch each other's eyes in a clinch tumbling
down the stairs.

Can the rough stuff . . . now a Mississippi steamboat pushes up the
night river with a hoo-hoo-hoo-oo . . . and the green lanterns calling
to the high soft stars . . . a red moon rides on the humps of the low   15
river hills . . . go to it, O jazzmen.

A STEAMBOAT RACE ON THE MISSISSIPPI
BETWEEN THE *BALTIC* AND *DIANA*. *George F. Fuller.*
Missouri Historical Society, Saint Louis.

Getting at Meaning

1. What specific instruments are involved in this "jazz fantasia"?

2. What different kinds of music does the jazz group produce?

Developing Skills in Reading Literature

1. **Onomatopoeia.** The word *onomatopoeia* literally means "name-making." It is the process of creating or using words that imitate sounds. For example, *buzz* and *honk* are onomatopoetic words. Onomatopoeia as a literary technique goes beyond the use of simple echoic words. Writers, particularly poets, often choose words whose sounds suggest their denotative and connotative meanings.

Observe some of the verbs in this poem, such as *drum, sob, sling,* and *ooze.* Consider how each of these words is onomatopoetic. What are the connotations of each word? What effect do these verbs have? What other onomatopoetic words can you find in the poem?

2. **Simile.** Study the three similes in lines 7-9. What different sounds do they bring to mind? What kind of music do they describe?

3. **Imagery.** The imagery of "Jazz Fantasia" is rich, appealing to a variety of senses. In addition to the auditory images, what visual images stand out? Which images stimulate the sense of touch? Select one particular image and explain why you find it effective.

4. **Alliteration.** Find examples of alliteration in the poem. How does this repetition of sounds function? Why is it appropriate in a poem about music?

5. **Rhythm.** This poem is free verse, with no specific rhyme or meter. It is a highly rhythmic, musical poem, however, as it should be, given the subject matter.

Onomatopoeia and alliteration help give the poem its rhythm. What other poetic devices contribute? How does the diction help? How does the syntax help make the poem rhythmic?

Developing Vocabulary

Word Origins. The word *saxophone,* which appears in "Jazz Fantasia," comes from the name of Adolphe Sax, the man who created the saxophone in 1846. A number of other English words also come from the names of people who are somehow linked to the origins of these words or from product names that have been incorporated into the language as common nouns.

Look up each word that follows in an etymological dictionary or in an unabridged dictionary. Record the origin of each word, and explain how the word's meaning is derived from the name of a person or a product.

antimacassar
bloomers
boycott
chauvinism
sandwich
watt (kilowatt)

Developing Writing Skills

Using the Senses in Writing. Write either a poem or a paragraph that is rich in imagery. You may want to concentrate on one or two of the senses, or you may want to appeal to three or more senses. Decide on a subject before you begin to write. Jot down specific images and sensory impressions that relate to the subject. Strive to make your poem or paragraph vivid and unified.

Robert Frost

1874–1963

In many ways, Robert Frost spent his long life creating his own response to the conditions of the modern era. Frost justly earned considerable fame for his efforts: His 1960 reading of "The Gift Outright" at John F. Kennedy's presidential inauguration in effect marked him as the nation's unofficial poet laureate. Yet, a half century before, at age thirty-eight, Frost was unknown and unpublished, living in England. He made, as he says in "Build Soil," "a late start to market."

Though his poetry is stamped with the images and values of New England, where he lived for most of his life, Robert Frost was born in San Francisco. When Frost was eleven, his father died, prompting the family to move to Massachusetts. There Frost soon determined to become a poet. Within the next twenty years, he attended Dartmouth and Harvard, married and raised a family, and held a series of odd jobs before settling on a barren New Hampshire farm owned by his grandfather.

Although during this period Frost was writing what were to become some of his best known poems, he could not interest a publisher in them. When Frost inherited the farm in 1911, he sold the property and moved with his family to England, hoping to devote all his time to writing. Collecting a selection of verses he had written in New England, Frost submitted them to a London publisher, who accepted the manuscript, publishing it in 1913 as *A Boy's Will*. Frost's poetry was so enthusiastically reviewed in England that he soon began receiving offers from American publishers.

In 1915, as World War I broke out, Frost and his family returned to the United States, simultaneous with the New York publication of his first two books. The volumes met with a warm response, and Frost finally became a celebrated poet in his own country.

The Frosts settled on a small farm near Franconia, New Hampshire, from where he produced a steady stream of acclaimed work until his death.

He also taught and lectured at various colleges and universities, chiefly Amherst, Harvard, and Dartmouth. Among Frost's many awards and honors are four Pulitzer Prizes.

Frost's poetry is concerned with questions of individual integrity, of a person's place in an often somber nature, and of the quality and necessity of interpersonal and social relationships. In treating these themes, Frost functions squarely within a tradition in American literature that has roots in the Transcendental movement of the nineteenth century.

Frost's verse appears to be simple, almost rough and "unpoetic," yet it is carefully crafted. Frost writes of an often bleak and dark world in which "courage in the heart" is needed "To overcome the fear within the soul/ And go ahead to any accomplishment." These accomplishments serve to sustain and nourish the individual amid all the fears and uncertainties of life. One such discovery is expressed in "Putting in the Seed," in which the poet comes to appreciate the vivifying power of love. In expressing his view of life as a rewarding struggle requiring courage and integrity, Frost created an enduring body of poetry that speaks to a wide variety of readers.

The Road Not Taken

Two roads diverged in a yellow wood,
And sorry I could not travel both
And be one traveler, long I stood
And looked down one as far as I could
To where it bent in the undergrowth;　　5

Then took the other, as just as fair,
And having perhaps the better claim,
Because it was grassy and wanted wear;
Though as for that the passing there
Had worn them really about the same,　　10

And both that morning equally lay
In leaves no step had trodden black.
Oh, I kept the first for another day!
Yet knowing how way leads on to way,
I doubted if I should ever come back.　　15

I shall be telling this with a sigh
Somewhere ages and ages hence:
Two roads diverged in a wood, and I—
I took the one less traveled by,
And that has made all the difference.　　20

Getting at Meaning

1. What is the difference in the two roads that diverge before the speaker? Which one does the speaker choose?

2. Explain the meaning of the lines, "Yet knowing how way leads on to way,/I doubted if I should ever come back."

Developing Skills in Reading Literature

1. **Symbol.** In this poem what does each of the two roads represent in terms of human life? Why is it difficult to choose between them? Why, after traveling for a while, is it difficult or impossible to turn back?

2. **Theme.** The speaker takes the less traveled road and concludes, ". . . that has made all the difference." In broader terms, what kind of life has the speaker chosen? What phrases suggest that the life has not been easy? Can you tell if the speaker has regrets?

3. **Meter.** Scan the stanzas of the poem. Although the meter is not insistent, it is regular. What kind of feet does Frost use? How many are there per line? What function does the regular meter serve in the poem?

4. **Rhyme Scheme.** The rhyme scheme is identical in all four stanzas. What is it? Why is an ordered rhyme scheme appropriate in the poem? Notice that the rhymes are relatively simple. What effect do they produce?

Stopping by Woods on a Snowy Evening

Whose woods these are I think I know.
His house is in the village, though;
He will not see me stopping here
To watch his woods fill up with snow.

My little horse must think it queer   5
To stop without a farmhouse near
Between the woods and frozen lake
The darkest evening of the year.

He gives his harness bells a shake
To ask if there is some mistake.   10
The only other sound's the sweep
Of easy wind and downy flake.

The woods are lovely, dark, and deep,
But I have promises to keep,
And miles to go before I sleep,   15
And miles to go before I sleep.

Getting at Meaning

1. What is the antecedent for the pronoun *His* in line 2? What is the antecedent for the pronoun *He* in line 9?

2. What reasons does the speaker give for not stopping very long by the woods?

Developing Skills in Reading Literature

1. **Symbol.** This famous lyric poem is frequently interpreted on a symbolic level. What might the woods, so "lovely, dark, and deep," represent to the speaker? How do you interpret the speaker's attraction for the woods? Consider the idea, advanced by some critics, that the woods represent the lure of death and that, when the speaker mentions having "miles to go before I sleep," *sleep* refers to death. What might the "promises" and the "miles to go" represent?

What do the village and the owner of the woods stand for? Why does the speaker enjoy being away from them, alone out "Between the woods and frozen lake"? How do you interpret the darkness and the cold the speaker emphasizes?

What might the horse, with his animal incomprehension, symbolize? How do you interpret the speaker's journey?

2. **Repetition.** The final two lines of the poem provide an example of repetition, the literary technique in which a word, phrase, or line is repeated for emphasis. What does the repetition in the final lines suggest about the speaker's attitude toward going on?

3. **Rhyme Scheme.** The rhyme scheme of this poem is rather unusual. Chart it for the poem's sixteen lines. What links exist from stanza to stanza in the rhymes? How does this help to unify the poem?

4. **Meter.** What is the metrical pattern of the poem? Notice that Frost uses mainly one-syllable words. These, coupled with the meter, suggest the clip-clop of horse's hooves. Read the poem aloud and observe this effect. How does meter unite the form and content of the poem?

Fire and Ice

Some say the world will end in fire,
Some say in ice.
From what I've tasted of desire
I hold with those who favor fire.
But if it had to perish twice,   5
I think I know enough of hate
To say that for destruction ice
Is also great
And would suffice.

Getting at Meaning

1. What lines in the poem indicate that the speaker has experienced passionate, perhaps destructive impulses?

2. What is the speaker's reason for believing that ice can be as destructive as fire?

Developing Skills in Reading Literature

1. **Symbol.** The opposites fire and ice have meaning in and of themselves in this poem. Fire has destructive power. Ice also can be destructive, as in the sinking of the *Titanic*.

The words *fire* and *ice* have symbolic meaning in the poem as well. What does each represent in human terms? Think of the connotations of these words. What is "fiery" behavior? What is cold, or "icy" behavior? Do you agree with the speaker that the two forces can be equally destructive?

2. **Tone.** Consider the tone of this short poem. What suggestions of humor do you find in the treatment of deadly serious subject matter? What lines and phrases convey the impression that the speaker is resigned and contemplative?

At Woodward's Gardens

A boy, presuming on his intellect,
Once showed two little monkeys in a cage
A burning glass they could not understand
And never could be made to understand.
Words are no good: to say it was a lens   5
For gathering solar rays would not have helped.
But let him show them how the weapon worked.
He made the sun a pinpoint on the nose
Of first one, then the other, till it brought
A look of puzzled dimness to their eyes   10
That blinking could not seem to blink away.
They stood arms laced together at the bars,
And exchanged troubled glances over life.
One put a thoughtful hand up to his nose
As if reminded—or as if perhaps   15
Within a million years of an idea.
He got his purple little knuckles stung.
The already known had once more been confirmed
By psychological experiment,
And that were all the finding to announce   20
Had the boy not presumed too close and long.
There was a sudden flash of arm, a snatch,
And the glass was the monkeys', not the boy's.
Precipitately they retired back-cage
And instituted an investigation   25
On their part, though without the needed insight.

They bit the glass and listened for the flavor.
They broke the handle and the binding off it.
Then none the wiser, frankly gave it up,
And having hid it in their bedding straw   30
Against the day of prisoners' ennui,[1]
Came dryly forward to the bars again
To answer for themselves: Who said it mattered
What monkeys did or didn't understand?
They might not understand a burning glass.   35
They might not understand the sun itself.
It's knowing what to do with things that counts.

---

1. **ennui** (än' wē) *French:* a feeling of weariness or boredom.

Getting at Meaning

1. Explain how a "burning glass" works. The boy, showing one to the monkeys, is described as "presuming on his intellect." What does this phrase imply?

2. How do the monkeys react to the demonstration of the burning glass? After one gets his knuckles stung, the speaker says, "The already known had once more been confirmed/By psychological experiment." Explain these lines.

3. What do the monkeys do with the glass after they seize it?

Developing Skills in Reading Literature

1. **Tone.** What lines in this poem indicate a droll, or dry wit on the part of the speaker? What is the speaker's attitude toward the boy? toward the monkeys? What is the tone of the final line, "It's knowing what to do with things that counts"?

2. **Theme.** What message about life and evolution emerges in this poem? Does it matter that the boy is smarter than the monkeys? Notice that the monkeys, like humans, "exchanged troubled glances over life." Expound on the meaning of the line, "It's knowing what to do with things that counts." Do you agree with this conclusion?

3. **Blank Verse.** Unrhymed iambic pentameter, you may recall, is known as blank verse. Explain why blank verse is an effective vehicle for this poem's down-to-earth, philosophical approach and anecdotal subject.

Developing Vocabulary

French Phrases in English. This poem contains the word *ennui*, meaning "boredom," a French word that has come into English. Various other French words and phrases are regularly used in English.

Look up each phrase below in an unabridged dictionary. Record both its French definition and the way it is used in English. Use each phrase in an original sentence that makes its meaning clear.

de rigueur
femme fatale
laissez faire
noblesse oblige
petit bourgeois

Putting in the Seed

You come to fetch me from my work tonight
When supper's on the table, and we'll see
If I can leave off burying the white
Soft petals fallen from the apple tree
(Soft petals, yes, but not so barren quite,   5
Mingled with these, smooth bean and wrinkled pea;)
And go along with you ere you lose sight
Of what you came for and become like me,
Slave to a springtime passion for the earth.
How Love burns through the Putting in the Seed   10
On through the watching for that early birth
When, just as the soil tarnishes with weed,
The sturdy seedling with arched body comes
Shouldering its way and shedding the earth crumbs.

Getting at Meaning

1. Describe the speaker's spring planting activity.

2. Why does the speaker find planting seeds and tending them so satisfying?

Developing Skills in Reading Literature

1. **Sonnet.** Frost's poem is a sonnet, consisting of fourteen lines of rhymed iambic pentameter. The poem is a Petrarchan, or Italian sonnet, because it consists of two parts, an octave and a sestet. The rhyme scheme of the octave in this sonnet is abababab; the rhyme scheme of the sestet is cdcdee. Notice that this sonnet consists of two sentences, the first one comprising lines 1-9, and the second, lines 10-14. Frost's octave thus continues for an extra line.

In a Petrarchan sonnet the octave traditionally develops a situation or a problem, and the sestet presents some kind of resolution. How would you describe the situation that Frost develops in the octave of this poem? What is the speaker's commentary or resolution in the sestet?

2. **Theme.** In the last lines of the sonnet the speaker concludes that observing seeds sprout is like watching a human or animal birth. How is the seedling characterized? What attitude toward life is implied in the way the sprout pushes its way upward from the weedy soil, "Shouldering its way and shedding the earth crumbs"?

Acquainted with the Night

I have been one acquainted with the night.
I have walked out in rain—and back in rain.
I have outwalked the furthest city light.

I have looked down the saddest city lane.
I have passed by the watchman on his beat   5
And dropped my eyes, unwilling to explain.

I have stood still and stopped the sound of feet
When far away an interrupted cry
Came over houses from another street,

But not to call me back or say goodbye;   10
And further still at an unearthly height,
One luminary clock against the sky

Proclaimed the time was neither wrong nor right.
I have been one acquainted with the night.

Getting at Meaning

1. What kinds of experiences has the speaker of the poem had? What details suggest the harshness of some of these experiences?

2. What details convey the loneliness and isolation the speaker has often felt?

Developing Skills in Reading Literature

1. **Symbol.** In this poem the word *night* carries symbolic associations beyond its literal meaning. What does night symbolize in terms of human life? What is the speaker's meaning in the line, "I have outwalked the furthest city light"? The "watchman on his beat" is a symbol of conventional, regular life. What is the speaker's attitude toward the watchman? The clock proclaims that ". . . the time was neither wrong nor right." What does this indicate about the speaker's life? What does the clock symbolize?

2. **Stanza.** In this poem Frost uses *terza rima*, an Italian stanza form. Each division of the poem is three lines, or a *tercet*, joined to its preceding and following stanzas by a common rhyme: *a b a, b c b, c d c, d e d.* Frost then ends the poem with an *e e* couplet.

Explain how the *terza rima* contributes to the unity and flow of ideas in this poem. Why is it useful to have the stanzas intertwined in this particular poem?

Developing Vocabulary

Latin Roots. Frost speaks of a "luminary clock." A luminary is an object that gives light, and the word comes from the Latin root *lux, lumen,* meaning "light."

The words that follow also are derived from this Latin root. Look them up in a dictionary and record their meanings. Explain how each word takes its meaning from the root.

illuminate   luminous
illuminati   lux
luminescence

Mending Wall

Something there is that doesn't love a wall,
That sends the frozen-ground-swell under it
And spills the upper boulders in the sun,
And makes gaps even two can pass abreast.
The work of hunters is another thing: 5
I have come after them and made repair
Where they have left not one stone on a stone,
But they would have the rabbit out of hiding,
To please the yelping dogs. The gaps I mean,
No one has seen them made or heard them made,   10
But at spring mending-time we find them there.
I let my neighbor know beyond the hill;
And on a day we meet to walk the line
And set the wall between us once again.
We keep the wall between us as we go.   15
To each the boulders that have fallen to each.
And some are loaves and some so nearly balls
We have to use a spell to make them balance:
"Stay where you are until our backs are turned!"
We wear our fingers rough with handling them.   20
Oh, just another kind of outdoor game,
One on a side. It comes to little more:
There where it is we do not need the wall:
He is all pine and I am apple orchard.
My apple trees will never get across   25
And eat the cones under his pines, I tell him.
He only says, "Good fences make good neighbors."
Spring is the mischief in me, and I wonder
If I could put a notion in his head:
"*Why* do they make good neighbors? Isn't it   30
Where there are cows? But here there are no cows.
Before I built a wall I'd ask to know
What I was walling in or walling out,
And to whom I was like to give offense.
Something there is that doesn't love a wall,   35
That wants it down." I could say "Elves" to him,
But it's not elves exactly, and I'd rather
He said it for himself. I see him there,
Bringing a stone grasped firmly by the top

In each hand, like an old-stone savage armed.   40
He moves in darkness as it seems to me,
Not of woods only and the shade of trees.
He will not go behind his father's saying,
And he likes having thought of it so well
He says again, "Good fences make good neighbors."   45

Getting at Meaning

1. This poem is about the mortarless stone walls found on many New England farms. What causes gaps to appear in the stone walls during the winter? Why do hunters sometimes dismantle a segment of wall?

2. Explain the mending process. Why does the neighbor want to keep the wall up, even in places where it is not necessary?

Developing Skills in Reading Literature

1. **Tone.** Characterize the speaker of the poem and the speaker's attitude toward mending the wall. What does the first line of the poem reveal about the attitude? Why is this line repeated in line 35? What do lines 28 and 29 reveal about the speaker's attitude? What lines indicate that the speaker is both more humorous and philosophical than the neighbor?

2. **Symbol.** The stone wall separating the two farms becomes a powerful symbol in this poem. What does it represent? Why is the remark, "We keep the wall between us as we go," important? What mental barriers exist between the speaker and the neighbor? Why does the speaker say that the neighbor "moves in darkness"?

3. **Theme.** The speaker and the neighbor take two different positions on the question of the barriers that

separate people. The speaker's attitude is "Something there is that doesn't love a wall." Explain the meaning of the statement, "Before I built a wall I'd ask to know/What I was walling in or walling out,/And to whom I was like to give offense." Why does the speaker want walls down? By contrast, what point of view does the neighbor represent? What is the significance of the speaker's remark, "He will not go behind his father's saying"?

4. **Blank Verse.** Discuss why blank verse is an appropriate form for the content of this poem. How does it suit the slow, conversational, contemplative pace of the poem?

Developing Writing Skills

Developing an Argument. Write a composition in which you support one of the philosophical views voiced in this poem, either "Something there is that doesn't love a wall,/That wants it down." or "Good fences make good neighbors." Argue your position by considering such things as social, political, economic, ethnic, racial, and religious barriers and differences that exist among people. You may use personal examples of "walls" in your composition, as well as examples of "fences" that exist in larger local, national, and international spheres.

The Death of the Hired Man

Mary sat musing on the lamp-flame at the table,
Waiting for Warren. When she heard his step,
She ran on tiptoe down the darkened passage
To meet him in the doorway with the news
And put him on his guard. "Silas is back."   5
She pushed him outward with her through the door
And shut it after her. "Be kind," she said.
She took the market things from Warren's arms
And set them on the porch, then drew him down
To sit beside her on the wooden steps.   10

"When was I ever anything but kind to him?
But I'll not have the fellow back," he said.
"I told him so last haying, didn't I?
If he left then, I said, that ended it.
What good is he? Who else will harbor him   15
At his age for the little he can do?
What help he is there's no depending on.
Off he goes always when I need him most.
He thinks he ought to earn a little pay,
Enough at least to buy tobacco with,   20
So he won't have to beg and be beholden.
'All right,' I say, 'I can't afford to pay
Any fixed wages, though I wish I could.'
'Someone else can.' 'Then someone else will have to.'
I shouldn't mind his bettering himself   25
If that was what it was. You can be certain,
When he begins like that, there's someone at him
Trying to coax him off with pocket money—
In haying time, when any help is scarce.
In winter he comes back to us. I'm done."   30

"Sh! not so loud: he'll hear you," Mary said.

"I want him to: he'll have to soon or late."

"He's worn out. He's asleep beside the stove.
When I came up from Rowe's I found him here,
Huddled against the barn door fast asleep,   35
A miserable sight, and frightening, too—
You needn't smile—I didn't recognize him—
I wasn't looking for him—and he's changed.
Wait till you see."

"Where did you say he'd been?"   40

"He didn't say. I dragged him to the house,
And gave him tea and tried to make him smoke.
I tried to make him talk about his travels.
Nothing would do: he just kept nodding off."

"What did he say? Did he say anything?"   45

"But little."

          "Anything? Mary, confess
He said he'd come to ditch the meadow for me."

"Warren!"

          "But did he? I just want to know."   50

"Of course he did. What would you have him say?
Surely you wouldn't grudge the poor old man
Some humble way to save his self-respect.
He added, if you really care to know,
He meant to clear the upper pasture, too.   55
That sounds like something you have heard before?
Warren, I wish you could have heard the way
He jumbled everything. I stopped to look
Two or three times—he made me feel so queer—
To see if he was talking in his sleep.   60
He ran on Harold Wilson—you remember—
The boy you had in haying four years since.
He's finished school, and teaching in his college.
Silas declares you'll have to get him back.
He says they two will make a team for work: 65
Between them they will lay this farm as smooth!
The way he mixed that in with other things.
He thinks young Wilson a likely lad, though daft
On education—you know how they fought
All through July under the blazing sun,   70
Silas up on the cart to build the load,
Harold along beside to pitch it on."

"Yes, I took care to keep well out of earshot."

"Well, those days trouble Silas like a dream.
You wouldn't think they would. How such things linger!   75
Harold's young college-boy's assurance piqued him.

After so many years he still keeps finding
Good arguments he sees he might have used.
I sympathize. I know just how it feels
To think of the right thing to say too late.   80
Harold's associated in his mind with Latin.
He asked me what I thought of Harold's saying
He studied Latin, like the violin,
Because he liked it—that an argument!
He said he couldn't make the boy believe   85
He could find water with a hazel prong[1]—
Which showed how much good school had ever done him.
He wanted to go over that. But most of all
He thinks if he could have another chance
To teach him how to build a load of hay—"   90

"I know, that's Silas' one accomplishment.
He bundles every forkful in its place,
And tags and numbers it for future reference,
So he can find and easily dislodge it
In the unloading. Silas does that well.   95
He takes it out in bunches like big birds' nests.
You never see him standing on the hay
He's trying to lift, straining to lift himself."

"He thinks if he could teach him that, he'd be
Some good perhaps to someone in the world.   100
He hates to see a boy the fool of books.
Poor Silas, so concerned for other folk,
And nothing to look backward to with pride,
And nothing to look forward to with hope,
So now and never any different."   105

Part of a moon was falling down the west,
Dragging the whole sky with it to the hills.
Its light poured softly in her lap. She saw it
And spread her apron to it. She put out her hand
Among the harplike morning-glory strings,   110
Taut with the dew from garden bed to eaves,
As if she played unheard some tenderness
That wrought on him beside her in the night.
"Warren," she said, "he has come home to die:
You needn't be afraid he'll leave you this time."   115

---

1. **hazel prong:** a stick made of hazel wood used as a
dousing rod to find water.

"Home," he mocked gently.

                "Yes, what else but home?
It all depends on what you mean by home.
Of course he's nothing to us, any more
Than was the hound that came a stranger to us   120
Out of the woods, worn out upon the trail."

"Home is the place where, when you have to go there,
They have to take you in."

                "I should have called it
Something you somehow haven't to deserve."   125

Warren leaned out and took a step or two,
Picked up a little stick, and brought it back
And broke it in his hand and tossed it by.
"Silas has better claim on us you think
Than on his brother? Thirteen little miles   130
As the road winds would bring him to his door.
Silas has walked that far no doubt today.
Why doesn't he go there? His brother's rich,
A somebody—director in the bank."

"He never told us that."   135

                "We know it, though."

"I think his brother ought to help, of course.
I'll see to that if there is need. He ought of right
To take him in, and might be willing to—
He may be better than appearances.   140
But have some pity on Silas. Do you think
If he had any pride in claiming kin
Or anything he looked for from his brother,
He'd keep so still about him all this time?"

"I wonder what's between them."   145

                "I can tell you.
Silas is what he is—we wouldn't mind him—
But just the kind that kinsfolk can't abide.
He never did a thing so very bad.
He don't know why he isn't quite as good   150
As anybody. Worthless though he is,
He won't be made ashamed to please his brother."

"*I* can't think Si ever hurt anyone."

"No, but he hurt my heart the way he lay

And rolled his old head on that sharp-edged chair-back.   155
He wouldn't let me put him on the lounge.
You must go in and see what you can do.
I made the bed up for him there tonight.
You'll be surprised at him—how much he's broken.
His working days are done; I'm sure of it."   160

"I'd not be in a hurry to say that."

"I haven't been. Go, look, see for yourself.
But, Warren, please remember how it is:
He's come to help you ditch the meadow.
He has a plan. You mustn't laugh at him.   165
He may not speak of it, and then he may.
I'll sit and see if that small sailing cloud
Will hit or miss the moon."
                              It hit the moon.
Then there were three there, making a dim row,   170
The moon, the little silver cloud, and she.

Warren returned—too soon, it seemed to her—
Slipped to her side, caught up her hand and waited.

"Warren?" she questioned.
                    "Dead," was all he answered.   175

SAW AND SAWED, 1969. Neil Jenny.
Collection of Whitney Museum of American Art. Gift of Philip Johnson.

Getting at Meaning

1. Why has Silas returned to Warren and Mary? Why did he leave in the first place?

2. Why is Warren reluctant to take Silas on again? What does Mary say in Silas's defense?

3. What are the details of Silas's life? Why is he so proud of his ability to make up a load of hay? Why do you suppose he keeps thinking of arguments that he might have used against Harold?

4. Find the definitions of home that Warren and Mary give in the poem. How do the two definitions characterize these two individuals?

Developing Skills in Reading Literature

1. **Narrative Poem.** "The Death of the Hired Man" is a narrative poem in that it tells a story. The poem also resembles a play in its extensive use of dialogue. What makes the poem dramatic? What qualities make it a poem, rather than a prose story or a one-act play? What is the meter of the poem? What does Frost gain by telling this story in verse?

2. **Structure and Unity.** What structural elements hold this long poem together and give it unity? What determines where the breaks come in the poem?

3. **Imagery.** Reread lines 106-112, where Frost in-troduces imagery involving the moon. Why might he have chosen the moon instead of the sun? How is the moon linked to Mary? Notice that the moon imagery appears again in lines 167-171. How does the imagery function at this point, when Silas has just died?

4. **Character.** Silas himself never appears in the poem. The reader learns about him only through the dialogue of Warren and Mary. What different views of Silas do Warren and Mary have? Mary says Silas has ". . . nothing to look backward to with pride,/And nothing to look forward to with hope." In spite of this, what details in the poem indicate that Silas has pride?

Characterize Mary. What qualities make her such a sympathetic figure? How does she influence her husband?

What are Warren's main concerns? What does he argue about Silas in the face of Mary's kindness?

Developing Writing Skills

Analyzing Symbols. In a five-paragraph composition discuss the meaning of symbols in any three of Frost's poems. Devote one body paragraph to each poem you select, establishing in your conclusion some sort of thematic link among the poems. Use quotations from each poem to support your points.

Experiments with Image and Form

TRAIN AT NIGHT IN THE DESERT, 1916. *Georgia O'Keeffe.*
Collection, The Museum of Modern Art, New York.

Amy Lowell

1874–1925

Upon meeting Amy Lowell, the poet and anthologist Louis Untermeyer said of her, "She waved no plumes and rattled no sabers, but she seemed to be advancing at the head of a victorious army." A prolific, if somewhat uneven, poet in her own right, Lowell also lectured, wrote, and traveled extensively on behalf of the new Imagist poets who, in the second decade of the twentieth century, sought to launch a "Poetic Renaissance" via free-verse forms, musical rhythms, and precise imagery.

Born into a distinguished and celebrated New England family, Amy Lowell was well suited to call attention to the poetry favored by her and such contemporaries as Ezra Pound and T. S. Eliot. A large, energetic, and quick-witted woman, she was known for her black cigars, her troupe of dogs, and her arrogant manner. Her first collection of poems, *A Dome of Many-Coloured Glass*, appeared in 1912 and reflected a romantic, almost mystical, temperament. Upon discovering in 1913 the work of the Imagist poet H.D., Lowell traveled to London, the center of the Imagist movement, and consequently turned away from the traditional forms that had characterized her first works. "Wind and Silver" typifies her attempts to render images of objective reality as precisely as possible.

Similarly, her re-creations and translations of Japanese and Chinese poetry display an absorption with exact and vivid descriptions. A patrician by upbringing and nature, Amy Lowell used her considerable resources to further the advance of a new literary sensibility. Her premature death in 1925 cut short a career devoted to championing the principles of Modernist poetry.

Wind and Silver

Greatly shining,
The Autumn moon floats in the thin sky;
And the fish-ponds shake their backs and flash their dragon
      scales
As she passes over them.

A Lover

If I could catch the green lantern of the firefly
I could see to write you a letter.

Note: Imagist poets such as Amy Lowell sought primarily to communicate impressions rather than meanings. The study questions for "Wind and Silver" and "A Lover," and for most of the Imagist poems that follow, avoid direct discussion of the ideas in the poems and examine instead the poetic techniques through which impressions are created.

Developing Skills in Reading Literature

1. **Personification.** How does Lowell characterize the moon in "Wind and Silver"? What contrast exists between the moon and her reflected light?

2. **Imagery.** "Wind and Silver" is both a visual and a tactile poem. Why is the brilliantly shining moon floating and in "thin" sky? What does the line about the fish-ponds bring to mind? Which words in the poem appeal to the sense of touch as well as to sight? How do you explain the title of the poem?

The central image of "A Lover" is visual, ". . . the green lantern of the firefly." What makes it such a subtle image? Why is it appropriate in this poem?

3. **Speaker.** What suggests that the speaker of "A Lover" is timid? What is the tone of the poem? Do you think the love letter will be written?

William Carlos Williams

1883–1963

William Carlos Williams wrote about the urbanized and industrialized world of northern New Jersey that was so familiar to him. Born in Rutherford, New Jersey, to an English father and a Puerto Rican mother, he attended schools there, in Europe, and in New York before entering the University of Pennsylvania, from which he received a medical diploma in 1906. While in medical school he met and befriended the Imagist poets Ezra Pound and Hilda Doolittle, who later were instrumental in moving him away from the imitative, sentimental style of his early poetry. After interning in New York hospitals and spending a year in Europe concurrently doing postgraduate work in pediatrics and, under the influence of Pound, changing his poetic approach, Williams returned to Rutherford in 1910 and established his medical practice. Williams continued in that practice for forty-five years, all the while producing a growing body of verse, drama, novels, essays, and personal recollections, much of it written at night and at a typewriter hidden in his medical office desk. In the late teens and early 1920's, Williams broadened his style and his literary activities as a result of his growing involvement with such key literary figures as Harriet Monroe, Alfred Kreymborg, and Robert McAlmon. Since much of his early work was published privately or by small independent publishers, Williams did not receive widespread public recognition until relatively late in his career. With the publication in 1946 of the first of the five books of his epic masterpiece, *Paterson* (1946-1958), Williams's influence spilled over beyond the literary circles where he was already well known.

He received, among other honors, the National Book Award, the Bollingen Prize, and, posthumously, the 1963 Pulitzer Prize in poetry for his *Pictures from Brueghel, and Other Poems.*

Because of his own considerable accomplishments and the influence on other poets of his notions of "freedom" and "open form" as exemplified in *Paterson,* Williams remains a key figure in American poetry. His ability to precisely render the sounds and sights of an urbanized America in his poetry, and to do so in a manner that transcends particular poetic movements, underscores Williams's stature as a major artist.

The Red Wheelbarrow

so much depends
upon

a red wheel
barrow

glazed with rain   5
water

beside the white
chickens

Winter Trees

All the complicated details
of the attiring and
the disattiring are completed!
A liquid moon
moves gently among   5
the long branches.
Thus having prepared their buds
against a sure winter,
the wise trees
stand sleeping in the cold.   10

Love Song

Sweep the house clean,
hang fresh curtains
in the windows
put on a new dress
and come with me!   5

The elm is scattering
its little loaves
of sweet smells
from a white sky!

Who shall hear of us.   10
in the time to come?

Let him say there was
a burst of fragrance
from black branches.

The Dance

In Breughel's[1] great picture, The Kermess,
the dancers go round, they go round and
around, the squeal and the blare and the
tweedle of bagpipes, a bugle and fiddles
tipping their bellies (round as the thick-   5
sided glasses whose wash they impound)
their hips and their bellies off balance
to turn them. Kicking and rolling about
the Fair Grounds, swinging their butts, those
shanks must be sound to bear up under such   10
rollicking measures, prance as they dance
in Breughel's great picture, The Kermess.

---

1. **Breughel** (brü′ gəl): Pieter Breughel the Elder, a Flemish painter who lived from 1520?-1569. Also spelled
Brueghel and *Bruegel*.

PEASANTS' DANCE. *Pieter Bruegel. Kunsthistorisches Museum, Vienna.*

Developing Skills in Reading Literature

1. **Imagery.** Williams creates a concrete, familiar, vivid image in "The Red Wheelbarrow." Which words make the image especially striking?

In speaking of the "complicated details/of the attiring and/the disattiring" in "Winter Trees," Williams creates a series of images in the reader's mind. What processes flash before your eyes? What picture of winter does the poem present in its final lines?

2. **Personification.** What two words in "Winter Trees" imply that the moon is an animate presence? What words achieve the personification of the trees? How are the trees characterized? What is the process of "attiring" and "disattiring" referred to in the poem?

3. **Diction: Connotation.** Which words in "Love Song" help create images of freshness and rebirth? Notice especially the poem's adjectives. Which nouns have positive connotations?

4. **Alliteration.** Which consonant sounds does "Love Song" repeat often at the beginnings of words? What is the effect of the alliteration? Why does the poem end with the explosive *b* sound?

5. **Tone.** Describe the tone of "Love Song." What are the speaker's reasons for wanting to roam in nature? What season is the setting for this poem?

In "The Dance" what is the speaker's attitude toward the scene on the canvas? What aspects of the poem convey this attitude? Why does the speaker think *The Kermess* is such a great painting?

6. **Rhythm.** Why are the lines of "The Dance" run together in the way that they are? Why does the last line of the poem repeat the first line? Why does the poem employ so many present-participle verbs? What is the effect of the internal rhyme in *prance* and *dance*? What consonant sounds does the poem repeat regularly? How does this alliteration help build the insistent rhythm of the poem?

7. **Theme.** "The Red Wheelbarrow" is Williams's declaration of the importance of poetry and of the way that sensory stimulation in day-to-day life awakens thoughts and feelings. What lines indicate the great importance of the wheelbarrow, the water, and the chickens? Do you agree with Williams's assertion?

The speaker in "Love Song" says to his lover, "Who shall hear of us/in the time to come?" His tone is not a sad one when he says this, however. Why not? What source of hope does he pit against death and the passage of time?

H. D. (Hilda Doolittle)

1886–1961

The daughter of an astronomer at the University of Pennsylvania, H.D. attended private schools in Philadelphia and then Bryn Mawr College. The love of classical antiquity she acquired during these years later surfaced in the many references in her poetry to figures from Greek and Egyptian mythology and in her classical notions of beauty and form. While in Philadelphia she also began rewarding friendships with Ezra Pound, William Carlos Williams, and Harriet Monroe.

In 1911, H.D. sailed for Europe, where her career began. Soon after arriving in London, she renewed her friendship with Pound and met and married Richard Aldington, an English Imagist poet and novelist who also directly influenced the shape of her writing. She began writing short poems that so impressed Pound with their precise description and diction that he insisted she submit them to Harriet Monroe's *Poetry* magazine signed "H.D., Imagist." She persisted in using her initials for the remainder of her career, a career closely linked to the Imagist Rebellion against the perceived sentimentalism and moralizing of more traditional poetry.

The clear, spare, and energetic lyrics of H.D.'s early poems, with their classical images, later became fuller, freer, and more "open" philosophic explorations of the world. By then, the destruction of World War II that she witnessed while continuing to reside in London elicited deeper visions of the relationship of ancient truths to modern realities. That vision is expressed in such works as *The Walls Do Not Fall* (1944), *Tribute to the Angels* (1945), *The Flowering of the Rod* (1946), and her last work, *Helen in Egypt* (1961). The clarity and perception of her work are still admired.

Pear Tree

Silver dust,
lifted from the earth,
higher than my arms reach,
you have mounted,
O, silver,   5
higher than my arms reach,
you front us with great mass;

no flower ever opened
so staunch a white leaf,
no flower ever parted silver   10
from such rare silver;

O, white pear,
your flower tufts
thick on the branch
bring summer and ripe fruits   15
in their purple hearts.

Song

You are as gold
as the half-ripe grain
that merges to gold again,
as white as the white rain
that beats through   5
the half-opened flowers
of the great flower tufts
thick on the black limbs
of an Illyrian[1] apple bough.

Can honey distill such fragrance   10
as your bright hair—
for your face is as fair as rain,
yet as rain that lies clear
on white honey-comb,
lends radiance to the white wax,   15
so your hair on your brow
casts light for a shadow.

---

1. **Illyria:** ancient region along the east coast of the Adriatic.

Developing Skills in Reading Literature

1. **Imagery.** Notice the emphasis on color in the imagery of these poems. In "Pear Tree" which two colors are often repeated? What connotations do these colors have? Why do the spring flower tufts have "purple hearts"? In "Song" what colors are emphasized? Which words and phrases do not name colors directly but instead suggest color or degree of light?

2. **Structure.** "Song" is divided into two stanzas. How does the imagery of the second stanza differ from the imagery of the first? What poetic devices in the second stanza make it more intense than the first stanza? The poem ends with a reference to hair that "casts light for a shadow." Why is this the closing image of the poem?

3. **Tone.** Describe the tone in each of these poems. Which lines do the most to establish tone? In "Pear Tree" what effect do words such as *lifted*, *higher*, and *mounted* achieve? What words in "Song" bring to mind softness and light? The word *honey* appears twice. What are the connotations of this word? How does the repetition of key words in the poem contribute to tone?

4. **Simile.** The speaker of "Song" uses lovely similes to convey the beauty of the person being described. Consider what each separate simile brings to mind. What do the three similes have in common? What description of the person emerges?

Ezra Pound

1885–1972

Like Pablo Picasso in the world of painting, Ezra Pound rebelled against the very kind of poetry that he produced as a young poet and pointed the way to new poetic forms in keeping with the Modernist spirit he helped to define. More than any other poet, Pound advanced the Modernist movement, fueling a technical revolution that has affected the whole of twentieth-century American poetry. Pound directly influenced the careers of such writers as Robert Frost, T.S. Eliot, William Carlos Williams, Ernest Hemingway, James Joyce, D.H. Lawrence, Ford Madox Ford, Marianne Moore, H.D., and Amy Lowell. His influence on others, coupled with the technical virtuosity exhibited in his own large body of work, marks him as one of the major artists of his age.

Born in Idaho and educated at New York's Hamilton College and the University of Pennsylvania, Pound taught briefly at Indiana's Wabash Presbyterian College. After travels in Spain, Italy, and France, he settled in London in 1908. There he found success as a poet, publishing *Personae* (1909), *Exultations* (1909), and *The Spirit of Romance* (1910). He also became leader of the Imagist movement, which emphasized direct language and precise images. The two-line "In a Station of the Metro" (1916) typifies the Imagist tendency to use language economically to present compressed portraits of reality. In his search for new poetic forms, Pound ranged across a wide spectrum of styles and cultures. His "The River Merchant's Wife: A Letter," actually a verse rendering of an earlier prose translation of Chinese poetry, reflects Pound's admiration for the Oriental ideogram, in which meaning is created through image. In 1920, Pound concluded the prolific London phase of his career, during which he produced more than five volumes of verse, translations, and essays, including a lengthy sequence of poems entitled *Hugh Selwyn Mauberley* (1920), a stream-of-consciousness description of the artist's plight in a corrupt, vulgar, and indifferent culture. In 1925, after several years in Paris, Pound settled in Rapallo, Italy, where he continued work on his *Cantos*—a life-long project begun in 1915 and ultimately encompassing 109 separate pieces. Though many of its passages are lyrically sharp and otherwise beautiful, its many idiosyncrasies make it virtually inaccessible to even the most diligent of readers. Nonetheless, its purely technical achievements demonstrate the breadth of Pound's genius. While in Italy, and during the years prior to World War II, Pound's growing alienation with the direction of modern society led him to espouse a mixture of social and economic ideals the enactment of which in Fascist Italy he loudly applauded. His radio broadcasts on Mussolini's behalf during World War II resulted in his 1945 arrest on treason charges. He was found "insane and mentally unfit for trial" and spent twelve years in a Washington, D.C., mental institution. Upon his release in 1958, he returned to Italy, where he died in 1972.

In a Station of the Metro

The apparition of these faces in the crowd;
Petals on a wet, black bough.

Developing Skills in Reading Literature

1. **Metaphor.** In this brief poem two images are placed side by side to create a striking metaphor. What role does the title play in understanding the comparison? What is the comparison? What words imply that the faces are glimpsed quickly in a dark terminal as an aggregate and that they are only somewhat differentiated? What does the metaphor suggest about the frailty of humans? Why is the bough wet?

2. **Haiku.** Ezra Pound, along with some of the other Imagists, was interested in Oriental verse forms. This poem is a variant of the Japanese haiku, a short poem written in three lines of five, seven, and five syllables. All haiku depend upon images from nature and upon the power of suggestion, or connotation, to create impressions.

What variations on the haiku form has Pound made? How does his poem fit the definition of a haiku in other respects?

The River Merchant's Wife: A Letter

Pound adapted this poem from a Chinese lyric by Li T'ai Po. The speaker is married to a river merchant whose business often takes him away from home.

While my hair was still cut straight across my forehead
Played I about the front gate, pulling flowers.
You came by on bamboo stilts, playing horse,
You walked about my seat, playing with blue plums.
And we went on living in the village of Chokan: 5
Two small people, without dislike or suspicion.

At fourteen I married My Lord you.
I never laughed, being bashful.
Lowering my head, I looked at the wall.
Called to, a thousand times, I never looked back.   10

At fifteen I stopped scowling,
I desired my dust to be mingled with yours

Forever and forever and forever
Why should I climb the lookout?

At sixteen you departed,   15
You went into far Ku-to-yen, by the river of swirling eddies,
And you have been gone five months.
The monkeys make sorrowful noise overhead.

You dragged your feet when you went out.
By the gate now, the moss is grown, the different mosses,   20
Too deep to clear them away!
The leaves fall early this autumn, in wind.
The paired butterflies are already yellow with August
Over the grass in the West garden;
They hurt me. I grow older.   25
If you are coming down through the narrows of the river Kiang,
Please let me know beforehand,
And I will come out to meet you
        As far as Cho-fu-Sa.

Getting at Meaning

1. What time in her life does the speaker describe in the first stanza of the poem? How did she regard her future husband at this time?

2. How did the speaker react to her arranged marriage? When did she begin to love her husband?

3. What details indicate the speaker's sorrow at her husband's absence? How long has he been gone?

Developing Skills in Reading Literature

1. **Dramatic Lyric.** As you know, a lyric is a short poem that expresses the thoughts and feelings of a single speaker. Pound used the term *dramatic lyric* to refer to poems whose feelings belong to an imagined character rather than to the poet.

Characterize the speaker in this poem. What details suggest that she is a quiet, timid person? What details indicate the formality of Chinese society? In what lines does the speaker understate her emotions? Where does she indicate deep emotion?

2. **Imagery.** This poem contains a number of illuminating images. What images depict the speaker's shyness at the time of her marriage? What image suggests

that her husband did not want to leave home? What does the moss imagery convey?

3. **Theme.** The speaker describes her love and her loneliness. She also reveals her closeness to nature. Why do "The monkeys make sorrowful noise overhead"? What do the "paired butterflies" suggest to the speaker? Why do they hurt her? What theme is suggested in the speaker's line, "I grow older"?

Developing Writing Skills

1. **Poetry: Using Imagery.** Write a poem in the manner of the Imagists, a poem in which your primary emphasis is on concrete, crisp images. Choose the images from your day-to-day life, trying to present your familiar environment in a fresh way. If you like, you may use one of the Imagist poems in this unit as a model.

2. **Poetry: Describing Character.** In a poem or a paragraph, present a character as Ezra Pound does in "The River-Merchant's Wife" or "The Garden" (page 696). You may write a dramatic lyric or present a character through another narrator's eyes. Use images and figures of speech to bring your character to life.

The Garden

Like a skein of loose silk blown against a wall
She walks by the railing of a path in Kensington Gardens,[1]
And she is dying piece-meal of a sort of emotional anemia.

And round about there is a rabble
Of the filthy, sturdy, unkillable infants of the very poor.   5
They shall inherit the earth.

In her is the end of breeding.
Her boredom is exquisite and excessive.
She would like some one to speak to her,
And is almost afraid that I will commit that indiscretion.   10

---

1. **Kensington Gardens:** a section of London's Hyde Park.

Developing Skills in Reading Literature

1. **Simile.** The woman walks "Like a skein of loose silk blown against a wall." This simile goes a long way toward characterizing her. Why *silk*? Why *loose* silk? What does *blown* imply?

2. **Character.** Describe the character created in this poem as fully as you can. What kind of life does she live? How do you know? What is "emotional anemia"? Explain what the speaker means in saying, "In her is the end of breeding."

3. **Irony.** What is ironic in the "dying" stance of the woman, while around her are "the filthy, sturdy, unkillable infants of the very poor"? Why are the infants going to inherit the earth when she has had all the opportunities? What is ironic in the description of the woman's boredom as "exquisite"? Explain the witty irony of the last two lines. How do these lines summarize the woman's attitude toward life?

Developing Vocabulary

Language History: Words from Old English. The speaker talks of the woman's breeding. The word *breeding* comes from the Old English word *brēdan*, *bredd*, meaning "to give birth." A number of other Old English words exist in somewhat changed form in modern English.

Look up each word that follows in a dictionary that contains word origins. From what Old English word is derived each of these modern English words? What do these words have in common, apart from their origin? How do they differ from many of the English words derived from Latin and Greek?

board	stool
cow	white
sheep	work
shoe	

Think of a fancier synonym for each of these words. Look up all of the synonyms to determine their origins. From what language is each one derived? What can you infer about language history from your knowledge of these origins?

E. E. Cummings
1894–1962

Edward Estlin Cummings turned poetry upside down, arranged it on its side, and in other ways turned it inside out. Few poets made their disdain for conventional forms as apparent as did Cummings, with his intentional spelling, punctuation, and grammatical irregularities. Cummings's formal rebellion was not rebellion for its own sake, however, nor was it a poet's conscious effort to elevate form over substance in keeping with some cherished artistic notions. Throughout his work, Cummings's disregard for formal conventions complements the recurring notion that the conventional codes of modern society—social, political, and moral—effectively stifle the feeling individual's capacity to create, to love, and to grow. Thus, Cummings's formal avant-gardism ironically complements a traditionally romantic belief in the importance of the self as it grows and develops through individual experience.

Cummings's emphasis on individual expression was a natural outgrowth of his upbringing. The son of a respected Unitarian minister, a former Harvard faculty member, Cummings grew up in Cambridge, Massachusetts, in an indulgent and liberal household atmosphere that encouraged his talents in both writing and painting. The renowned psychologist William James was a neighbor who had, in fact, introduced Cummings's parents to each other. The novelist John Dos Passos, Cummings's Harvard classmate, later spoke of his visits to the Cummings household as follows: "I've cherished my recollection of it as a link with the Jameses and all the generations of old New England back to Emerson and Thoreau . . . Cummings improvising on the piano for the edification of his admiring family. Dr. Cummings booming from the pulpit . . ."

At the end of his distinguished student career at Harvard, Cummings in 1917 delivered a commencement address on "The New Art." Immediately afterward he volunteered for ambulance service in France, which enabled him to experience firsthand some of the conditions which that New Art sought to address. Through a bureaucratic bungle, Cummings was mistakenly imprisoned as a collaborator for three months in a French prisoner-of-war camp, an experience that formed the basis of *The Enormous Room*, an autobiographical work published in 1922, which scalded his captors for their repressive and dehumanizing policies. Similar sentiments can be found in many of his poems. After joining a number of expatriate artists in Paris for two years following the war, Cummings returned to New York, settling in Greenwich Village while working for *Vanity Fair* magazine. His first collection of poems, *Tulips and Chimneys*, was published in 1923 and contained what would prove to be some of his finest poems.

Cummings continued his experiments with "typographical poetry" until his death in 1962. His pioneering efforts on behalf of free, individual expression remain a significant influence within contemporary poetry.

The Sky

the
   sky
      was
can dy   lu
minous   5
      edible
spry
    pinks shy
lemons
greens coo l choc   10
olate
s,

  un der,
 a   lo
co   15
mo
  tive s pout
       ing
        vi
        o   20
       lets

Developing Skills in Reading Literature

1. **Imagery.** What kind of sky does this poem describe? Why does it look edible? Comment on the color images in the poem. What attitude does the image of a locomotive spouting violets convey?

2. **Concrete Poem.** A concrete poem visually presents something important about the poem's meaning. In concrete poetry, a direct and often obvious relationship exists between form and meaning. How does the form and shape of "The Sky" reflect the poem's content? What does the poem suggest visually?

Since Feeling Is First

since feeling is first
who pays any attention
to the syntax[1] of things
will never wholly kiss you:

wholly to be a fool   5
while Spring is in the world

my blood approves.
and kisses are a better fate
than wisdom
lady i swear by all flowers. Don't cry   10
—the best gesture of my brain is less than
your eyelids' flutter which says

we are for each other: then
laugh, leaning back in my arms
for life's not a paragraph   15

And death i think is no parenthesis

---

1. **syntax:** the way in which words are put together to
form phrases, clauses, and sentences; any orderly system.

Getting at Meaning

1. What is syntax, above and beyond sentence structure? Explain the speaker's meaning when he says, "who pays any attention/to the syntax of things/will never wholly kiss you."

2. The speaker of the poem elevates heart over head, or feeling over intellect. What lines establish this meaning?

Developing Skills in Reading Literature

1. **Tone.** Characterize the tone of this poem. What lines convey what the poet Wordsworth called "the spontaneous overflow of powerful feelings"? What does the speaker mean when he says, "wholly to be a fool/while Spring is in the world"?

2. **Metaphor.** To convince his lover that she should follow the dictates of her heart, the speaker creates two intriguing negative metaphors. He says, " . . . life's not a paragraph," thereby forcing the reader to compare life to a paragraph in order to figure out why the two are not equivalent. Similarly, the reader has to figure out why death is not a parenthesis.

A paragraph is usually a part of a longer composition. Therefore, what is the speaker saying about life when he concludes that life is not a paragraph? Parentheses usually break up a sentence. If death is not a parenthesis, or an interruption in the flow of life, what is the speaker saying about death? Why does he believe that he and his lover should laugh and enjoy themselves?

3. **Theme.** Cummings wrote many excellent love poems, of which this is one. He also wrote hymns to nature, frequently incorporating his Romantic reverence for nature into his love lyrics.

What is the attitude toward Nature that Cummings conveys in this poem? When the speaker wishes to swear an oath, what sacred thing does he swear by?

Buffalo Bill's

Buffalo Bill's[1]
defunct
    who used to
    ride a watersmooth-silver
               stallion   5
and break onetwothreefourfive pigeonsjustlikethat
                          Jesus
he was a handsome man
                  and what i want to know is
how do you like your blueeyed boy   10
Mister Death

---

1. **Buffalo Bill:** William Frederick Cody, an American scout, Indian fighter, and showman, who lived from 1846-1917. He allegedly killed more buffalo to claim railroad bounties than any other single person.

Developing Skills in Reading Literature

1. **Character.** Cummings wrote a number of character sketches in verse form. What kind of man was Buffalo Bill, according to the poem? What feats could he perform? The expression "blueeyed boy" means "favorite one." Why might Buffalo Bill be the pet or favorite of Mister Death? Suggest two possible explanations.

2. **Diction: Connotation.** Buffalo Bill isn't just dead, he's *defunct*. What connotations does the word *defunct* have that *dead* does not have? In what ways is Buffalo Bill more than just a dead man?

3. **Structure.** Notice the shape of this poem. Why is *defunct* on a line by itself? Why is "watersmooth-silver" run together? Why is *stallion* on a line by itself? What kind of pigeons is Buffalo Bill breaking? What is the effect produced by running "onetwothreefourfive" together, and then "pigeonsjustlikethat"? Notice that there are three names in the poem, located at the beginning, the end, and in the middle. Why are the names *Buffalo Bill* and *Mister Death* located together way over on one side, while the name *Jesus* stands out by itself on the other?

4. **Theme.** Because of his unthinking slaughter of so many buffaloes, Buffalo Bill is a symbol of American waste, of the extravagant destruction of our natural resources. He symbolizes this to Native Americans especially.

With this in mind, what broader meaning does the phrase "Buffalo Bill's defunct" carry? Can you tell what position the speaker takes on Buffalo Bill and his exploits? Is the speaker admiring or sarcastic in the poem?

Developing Vocabulary

Greek Roots. The word *buffalo* comes to English most directly from Portuguese. However, the Portuguese word is derived from the Greek root *bous*, meaning "cow" or "ox."

Look up the words that follow and record their meanings. What relationship does each word have to the root word *bous*?

bovid   bucolic
bovine   butter
Bucephalus

The Cambridge Ladies Who Live in Furnished Souls

the Cambridge ladies who live in furnished souls
are unbeautiful and have comfortable minds
(also, with the church's protestant blessings
daughters, unscented shapeless spirited)
they believe in Christ and Longfellow, both dead,   5
are invariably interested in so many things—
at the present writing one still finds
delighted fingers knitting for the is it Poles?
perhaps. While permanent faces coyly bandy
scandal of Mrs. N and Professor D   10
. . . . the Cambridge ladies do not care, above
Cambridge if sometimes in its box of
sky lavender and cornerless, the
moon rattles like a fragment of angry candy

Getting at Meaning

1. How do the Cambridge (Massachusetts) ladies spend their time, according to the speaker?

2. Explain the speaker's meaning in declaring that the Cambridge ladies live in "furnished souls" and have "comfortable minds"?

Developing Skills in Reading Literature

1. **Satire.** Cummings wrote a number of social satires in verse form. For what reasons does the speaker ridicule the Cambridge ladies? What is implied in calling them "unbeautiful"? Why does the speaker criticize them for being "unscented" and "shapeless"? What does the speaker criticize the ladies for in line 5? What is wrong with their charitable knitting projects? What dig is implicit in the phrase "permanent faces"?

2. **Tone.** Characterize the tone of Cummings's satire. Is it an amused, gentle lampooning of these women, or would you say the satire has a harsh, biting edge to it? What is the tone of the line, "are invariably interested in so many things—"? What is the tone of the line, "delighted fingers knitting for the is it Poles"?

3. **Imagery.** What mental picture does the phrase "furnished souls" create? Why is this phrase so packed with meaning? Study the final image of the poem. What seems to be going on in the universe, or the larger world outside of Cambridge? Why don't the Cambridge ladies even notice?

Developing Writing Skills

Writing a Satiric Poem. Satirize a group of people in a satiric poem, as Cummings does in "The Cambridge Ladies." Consider the tone of your satire and what specific points you will make before you begin to write. Use imagery and figurative language in your poem.

Harlem Renaissance Poets

TOMBSTONES, 1942. *Jacob Lawrence.* Collection of the Whitney Museum of American Art, New York.

Paul Laurence Dunbar

1872–1906

Paul Laurence Dunbar, a black poet and novelist, wrote and performed his work at the turn of the century, when the United States Supreme Court had just sanctioned racial segregation with its notorious "separate but equal" doctrine. Considering the racial tenor of the times, it is not surprising that Dunbar reacted ambivalently to his popularity with white audiences, who enjoyed his dialect lyrics at minstrel shows, or to white critics such as the novelist William Dean Howells, whose reviews of his work reflected the standard racial stereotypes of the day. These critics virtually ignored his serious and sensitive efforts to articulate his despair at being forced to "wear the mask." Dunbar's ability to express that despair and, in other poetry, to draw upon the same influences also surfacing in jazz and blues music, suggest why he is regarded as a key poet whose work prefigured the achievements of the Harlem Renaissance writers of the 1920's.

Dunbar was born in Dayton, Ohio, the son of emancipated slaves. His disillusioned and authoritarian father died when Dunbar was 12, leaving him to the sole care of his mother, who encouraged him in his education and in his writing. Rejecting his mother's ambitions for him to become a minister, Dunbar took a job as an elevator operator, a menial job which nonetheless provided him ample opportunity to study Tennyson and to master the techniques of such popular poets of the day as Eugene Field, Ella Wheeler Wilcox, and James Whitcomb Riley. When a former teacher asked him to read his work before a writers' group meeting in Dayton in 1892, Dunbar's career was launched. His first collection of poems, *Oak and Ivy*, appeared shortly thereafter. It was not until the 1896 publication of *Majors and Minors*, however, that Dunbar achieved the critical acclaim that led to the publication of his next book by a major New York publishing house, a reading tour of England, and a position in Washington, D.C., with the Library of Congress in 1897. While in Washington, he married and began to use his lyrical talents in the musical theatre, thereby gaining the financial security that had previously eluded him. His last years were difficult, however. Emotionally distraught over the collapse of his marriage and victimized by a series of severe illnesses and the precarious nature of his popularity, Dunbar died an early death in 1906.

Douglass

Ah, Douglass,[1] we have fall'n on evil days,
  Such days as thou, not even thou didst know,
  When thee, the eyes of that harsh long ago
Saw, salient,[2] at the cross of devious ways,
And all the country heard thee with amaze.   5
  Not ended then, the passionate ebb and flow,
  The awful tide that battled to and fro;
We ride amid a tempest of dispraise.

Now, when the waves of swift dissension swarm,
  And Honor, the strong pilot, lieth stark,[3]   10
Oh, for thy voice high-sounding o'er the storm,
  For thy strong arm to guide the shivering bark,
The blast-defying power of thy form,
  To give us comfort through the lonely dark.

---

1. **Douglass:** Frederick Douglass, the American abolitionist, who lived from 1817?-1895.
2. **salient** (sā' lyənt): standing out conspicuously.
3. **stark:** rigidly conforming.

Getting at Meaning

1. Frederick Douglass lived in harsh times. Why does Paul Laurence Dunbar say that his own era is even harsher?

2. For what qualities does Dunbar praise Douglass?

Developing Skills in Reading Literature

1. **Sonnet.** Notice that this poem of tribute is a sonnet, comprised of fourteen lines of iambic pentameter. Is it a Petrarchan (Italian) sonnet or is it a Shakespearean (English) sonnet, made up of three quatrains and a couplet? How can you tell? What is the rhyme scheme of the sonnet? How do the separate divisions of the poem function?

2. **Extended Metaphor.** Dunbar employs an extended metaphor in this sonnet, likening the country to a "shivering bark." What does the word *shivering* imply about the country's condition? What has happened to Honor, the ship's pilot? What is the storm in which the ship is caught? What role does Dunbar wish that Douglass could assume? Dunbar speaks of "The awful tide that battled to and fro" through which Douglass lived. To what does this refer?

3. **Theme.** This poem was written around the turn of the century. According to Dunbar, what was wrong with the country at that time? What did the nation lack? What does Dunbar recognize the need for when he uses the phrase "blast-defying power"?

We Wear the Mask

We wear the mask that grins and lies,
It hides our cheeks and shades our eyes—
This debt we pay to human guile;
With torn and bleeding hearts we smile,
And mouth with myriad subtleties.   5

Why should the world be overwise,
In counting all our tears and sighs?
Nay, let them only see us, while
    We wear the mask.

We smile, but, O great Christ, our cries   10
To thee from tortured souls arise.
We sing, but oh the clay is vile
Beneath our feet, and long the mile;
But let the world dream otherwise,
    We wear the mask!   15

Getting at Meaning

1. What is the mask described in this poem?

2. Explain the meaning of the assertion that the mask is a ". . . debt we pay to human guile."

Developing Skills in Reading Literature

1. **Speaker.** The speaking voice of this poem is "we," not "I." If Dunbar is speaking for the black race, what meaning do the individual lines of the poem convey? Also interpret the poem assuming that Dunbar speaks for the entire human race.

2. **Theme.** Dunbar is writing about one of the sad realities of life. What commentary does he offer on human sorrow and pain? Why "With torn and bleeding hearts" do we smile? What are the negative effects of masking pain and unhappiness? Does "wearing a mask" have any positive effects?

Life's Tragedy

It may be misery not to sing at all
    And to go silent through the brimming day.
It may be sorrow never to be loved,
    But deeper griefs than these beset the way.

To have come near to sing the perfect song   5
    And only by a half-tone lost the key,
There is the potent sorrow, there the grief,
    The pale, sad staring of life's tragedy.

To have just missed the perfect love,
    Not the hot passion of untempered youth,   10
But that which lays aside its vanity
    And gives thee, for thy trusting worship, truth—

This, this it is to be accursed indeed;
    For if we mortals love, or if we sing,
We count our joys not by the things we have,   15
    But by what kept us from the perfect thing.

Getting at Meaning

1. What is life's tragedy, according to the poem?

2. The poem offers two examples to illustrate life's tragedy. What are they?

3. What distinction does the poem draw between perfect and imperfect love?

Developing Skills in Reading Literature

1. **Tone.** Characterize the tone of this poem. What specific words would you single out as contributing most to the development of tone?

2. **Theme.** Comment on the view of life that emerges in this poem. Dunbar asserts that humans ". . . count our joys not by the things we have,/But by what kept us from the/perfect thing." Do you agree with Dunbar's perception of the human condition? What does it imply about human happiness?

Developing Writing Skills

Analyzing Theme. In a well developed paragraph analyze the thematic statement that emerges in either "We Wear the Mask" or "Life's Tragedy." Use quotations from the poem you have chosen to develop your ideas.

In a second well developed paragraph apply the message of the poem you are discussing to your own life and to the lives of others. Do you agree or disagree with the poem's statement? Has Dunbar expressed a universal truth? Use examples to support your points.

Countee Cullen

1903–1946

The "Great Migration" of southern rural blacks to northern industrial centers such as Detroit, Chicago, and New York beginning in 1915 helped create a new and radically different sense of what it meant to be black in America. As expressed by a new generation of leaders such as W.E.B. DuBois, the separatist Marcus Garvey, and by emerging organizations such as the N.A.A.C.P. and the National Urban League, the essential elements of black identity would no longer be determined by the prejudiced stereotypes of the white majority. Instead, the determination spread throughout all segments of the newly urbanized black society to define for themselves the common features of life within a society that had yet to acknowledge their existence as first-class citizens. In the arts, this ferment of consciousness that occurred during the 1920's became known as the Harlem Renaissance.

Countee Cullen's was among the more refined of the many poetic voices that appeared at this time. The adopted son of a fundamentalist Methodist minister, Cullen experienced a difficult home life before achieving recognition for his poetic talents, first in high school, and later at New York University. While Cullen was still an undergraduate, his poems were published in *The Crisis* and *Opportunity*, two major black periodicals, and also in the more broadly circulated *Harper's*, *The Century*, and *Poetry*. Following his graduation and preceding a year of study at Harvard, Cullen's first collection of poems, *Color*, was published in 1925. In 1926 he joined the staff of *Opportunity*, writing literary criticism, and in 1927 he produced his second volume of verse, entitled *Copper Sun*. These years proved to be the high-water mark of Cullen's career. A marriage in 1929 to W.E.B. DuBois's daughter collapsed within a few months, and the resulting emotional turmoil, reflected in *The Black Christ*, which was written in Paris while Cullen was on a Guggenheim fellowship, did not subside for quite some time. Though he ventured into drama and wrote one novel, most of the remainder of Cullen's brief life was spent teaching French to junior high school students.

Any Human to Another

The ills I sorrow at
Not me alone
Like an arrow,
Pierce to the marrow,
Through the fat   5
And past the bone.

Your grief and mine
Must intertwine
Like sea and river,
Be fused and mingle,   10
Diverse yet single,
Forever and forever.

Let no man be so proud
And confident,
To think he is allowed   15
A little tent
Pitched in a meadow
Of sun and shadow
All his little own.

Joy may be shy, unique,   20
Friendly to a few,
Sorrow never scorned to speak
To any who
Were false or true.

Your every grief   25
Like a blade
Shining and unsheathed
Must strike me down.
Of bitter aloes wreathed,
My sorrow must be laid   30
On your head like a crown.

Getting at Meaning

1. The poem asserts that human sorrows are "Diverse yet single." Explain the meaning of this paradoxical statement.

2. According to the fourth stanza of the poem, what is the relationship between joy and sorrow in the world?

Developing Skills in Reading Literature

1. **Simile.** This poem conveys much of its meaning through several powerful similes. Explain the comparison in the first stanza. Why is this simile appropriate to the subject matter of the poem? What simile does Cullen develop in the second stanza to suggest unity and diversity among humans? Discuss the meaning and aptness of the simile in the final stanza of the poem.

2. **Rhyme Scheme.** Although the rhyme scheme of this poem is not regular, it is insistent. What does it contribute to the unity of the poem? to its musical quality? How does the rhyme scheme emphasize the poem's subject matter?

3. **Theme.** The title of this poem is a clue to its meaning. What is Cullen's statement on the topic of human brotherhood? What is the meaning of the assertion, "My sorrow must be laid/On your head like a crown." Why a crown?

From the Dark Tower

We shall not always plant while others reap
The golden increment of bursting fruit,
Not always countenance, abject and mute,
That lesser men should hold their brothers cheap;
Not everlastingly while others sleep   5
Shall we beguile their limbs with mellow flute,
Not always bend to some more subtle brute;
We were not made eternally to weep.

The night whose sable breast relieves the stark,
White stars is no less lovely being dark,   10
And there are buds that cannot bloom at all
In light, but crumple, piteous, and fall;
So in the dark we hide the heart that bleeds,
And wait, and tend our agonizing seeds.

Note: For this poem and others from the Harlem Renaissance, discussion focuses on the way that meaning is conveyed rather than on idea and form as separate elements.

Developing Skills in Reading Literature

1. **Imagery.** To a large extent this poem builds its meaning through contrasting imagery. Cullen presents the rich image "golden increment of bursting fruit" in line 2, and later in the first stanza he writes of a "mellow flute." What images contrast with these idyllic images? Notice what words he rhymes with both *fruit* and *flute*.

In the second stanza Cullen develops light and dark imagery. What is the symbolic meaning of darkness? What is the worth of night and darkness, according to these lines? In all probability, what is the "dark tower" of the poem's title?

The poem opens and closes with imagery of seeds and planting. The first two lines are hopeful. In the final lines, what does the poem indicate must happen in order to achieve the happier situation alluded to at the beginning of the poem?

2. **Speaker.** The speaker of this poem is "we," not "I." With reference to the poem's imagery, support the view that the poet speaks for the black race earlier in the twentieth century.

3. **Sonnet.** "From the Dark Tower" is a sonnet. Chart its rhyme scheme and study its structure. What makes the poem musical? Is it a Petrarchan or a Shakespearean sonnet? How do the divisions of the poem relate to the poem's meaning?

4. **Theme.** Discuss the ideas in this sonnet. In what sense is the theme "Black is beautiful"? Why are the seeds "agonizing"? What is the poem's view of people who oppress or take advantage of others? What is the poem's statement on dealing with sadness and oppression? Do you agree with this view?

Claude McKay
1890–1948

In 1919, the United States entered a postwar economic recession exacerbated by the widespread fear that Communism, so recently triumphant in Russia, was engaged in a conspiratorial effort to disrupt American society and overthrow the government. During the "Red Summer" of 1919, violent and bloody race riots in a number of northern cities seemed to confirm the anarchic fears of many. By order of U.S. Attorney General A. Mitchell Palmer, large numbers of known alien Communists and suspected sympathizers were deported without a hearing or other form of legal recourse. Among the many prominent blacks who fell under the scrutiny of the Justice Department for publishing views "defiantly assertive of [their] own equality and even superiority . . ." was Claude McKay, a Jamaican-born poet and novelist.

McKay had arrived in America in 1912, following the publication of two collections of poetry which had prompted the Jamaica Institute of Arts and Sciences to award him a study grant in the United States. After short periods at Tuskegee Institute in Alabama and Kansas State College, he arrived in New York, where he briefly operated a restaurant and then held down a series of menial jobs. Through his poetry, he became affiliated with a group of radical New York writers in whose magazines the first of McKay's American poems appeared.

He achieved prominence with the publication of his sonnet "If We Must Die," a stirring exhortation to black Americans to "fight back" against those who would victimize them. Over the next fifteen years, McKay traveled extensively throughout Europe, including a tour of Soviet Russia in 1923. Living for a while in France and then in Spain, McKay wrote three novels, including the popular *Home to Harlem*, before returning to New York in 1934. His disaffection with Communism became evident in his 1937 autobiography, *A Long Way from Home*, and by 1944 he had completed a spiritual odyssey with his conversion to Catholicism. He spent his last years as a Chicago parochial school teacher and died in 1948.

McKay's poetry is always disciplined and usually forceful. In the affecting "The Tropics in New York," McKay alludes to the psychic dislocation experienced upon moving to the city. As he did with "If We Must Die," McKay functions here, too, as one critic observes, as "a poet of the people."

The Tropics in New York

Bananas ripe and green, and ginger-root,
  Cocoa in pods and alligator pears,
And tangerines and mangoes and grapefruit,
  Fit for the highest prize at parish fairs,

Set in the window, bringing memories   5
  Of fruit-trees laden by low singing rills,
And dewy dawns, and mystical blue skies
  In benediction over nun-like hills.

My eyes grew dim, and I could no more gaze;
  A wave of longing through my body swept,   10
And, hungry for the old, familiar ways,
  I turned aside and bowed my head and wept.

Developing Skills in Reading Literature

1. **Imagery.** How do the rich images of the first stanza pave the way for the memories described in the second stanza? What images recall the past? What words make these images seem peaceful and sacred?

2. **Rhythm and Rhyme.** Scan the poem. What is the poem's meter? What is its rhyme scheme? What other poetic devices give the poem a musical cadence? How is the poem's rhythm linked to the poet's memories?

3. **Tone.** What is the tone of the first stanza of the poem? Of the second? How does the tone change in the third stanza? What are the various "hungers" that cause the tone to shift?

Developing Vocabulary

Word Origins. The produce items McKay mentions in the first stanza of this poem give some indication of the diversity of word origins in the English language.

Using a dictionary that contains etymologies, look up each word that follows and record its origin.

banana	alligator
ginger	tangerine
cocoa	mango

Jean Toomer
1894–1967

The longing for transcendence expressed in Jean Toomer's line "Wish that I might fly out past the moon . . ." pervaded the entire life of this artist. In his 1931 collection of aphorisms entitled *Essentials*, he wrote: "I am of no particular race. I am of the human race, a man at large in this human world, preparing a new race. I am of no specific region, I am of earth."

Born in Washington, D.C., to parents who had migrated from a Georgia farm, Toomer attended the University of Wisconsin before arriving in New York in 1917 to study at City College. During the next four years, he became a familiar figure within the several flourishing literary circles of the day, publishing his poetry, prose pieces, and criticism in the several small magazines those circles nourished. A four-month teaching stint in Georgia during 1921 provided him with the raw material for *Cane,* his verse and prose miscellany published in 1923. Described by one critic as "an impressionist symphony," *Cane* can be understood as part of a lifelong effort to explore his identity for the ultimate purpose of reconstructing and then transcending it. Toomer's subsequent affiliation with the Unitism movement of the Russian emigré Georges Ivanovich Gurdjieff ultimately drew him away from Harlem in favor of Chicago and later a Pennsylvania Quaker community where he continued to pursue his spiritual ideals.

Beehive

Within this black hive tonight
There swarm a million bees;
Bees passing in and out the moon,
Bees escaping out the moon,
Bees returning through the moon,   5
Silver bees intently buzzing,
Silver honey dripping from the swarm of bees
Earth is a waxen cell of the world comb,
And I, a drone,
Lying on my back,   10
Lipping honey,
Getting drunk with silver honey,
Wish that I might fly out past the moon
And curl forever in some far-off farmyard flower.

Developing Skills in Reading Literature

1. **Extended Metaphor.** This poem is based on an extended metaphor, set up in the first two lines. What is the bee hive? Notice that it is a "black" hive. Who are the bees? What are the bees doing? Why are some of the bees "silver"? What is the speaker saying about himself in calling himself "a drone"? How does he extend the metaphor to indicate his desire to escape the swarming bees?

2. **Tone.** Characterize the speaker's tone in this poem. What lines indicate that he is standing back and observing the world around him? He says, "Earth is a waxen cell of the world comb." What does this line reveal about the speaker's perspective? In what context does he perceive the activities going on around him?

3. **Repetend.** Which words does the poet often repeat? What effect do these repetends have on the rhythm of the poem? How do they help reinforce meaning? to reinforce tone?

Developing Writing Skills

Poetry: Using an Extended Metaphor. Write a poem based upon an extended metaphor of your own creation. Keep in mind that a metaphor has two subjects: the main subject to which the metaphoric words are applied and the secondary subject, or the literal meaning of the metaphoric words. The main subject in Toomer's extended metaphor is the speaker's world, perhaps Harlem, as well as the people of that world. The secondary subject is the hive, the bees, and so forth.

November Cotton Flower

Boll weevil's[1] coming, and the winter's cold,
Made cotton stalks look rusty, seasons old,
And cotton, scarce as any southern snow,
Was vanishing; the branch, so pinched and slow,
Failed in its function as the autumn rake;   5
Drouth fighting soil had caused the soil to take
All water from the streams; dead birds were found
In wells a hundred feet below the ground—
Such was the season when the flower bloomed.
Old folks were startled, and it soon assumed   10
Significance. Superstition saw
Something it had never seen before:
Brown eyes that loved without a trace of fear,
Beauty so sudden for that time of year.

---

1. **Boll weevil:** a grayish weevil about ¼ inch long that infests
the cotton plant and feeds on the squares and bolls.

Getting at Meaning

1. What natural scene does the poem describe?
What forces are withering the cotton?

2. The branch, or stream, "Failed in its function as
the autumn rake." Explain the meaning of this line.

Developing Skills in Reading Literature

1. **Symbol.** The flower bloomed and ". . . it soon
assumed/Significance. . . ." What is its symbolic
meaning? Why does the flower "startle" people? What
effects does the blooming of the flower have?

2. **Sonnet.** Is Toomer's poem a Petrarchan (Italian)
or a Shakespearean (English) sonnet? How can you
tell? Comment on how the sonnet form functions in the
poem.

Langston Hughes
1902–1967

In his poetry, fiction, and drama, and in his work as an editor, newspaper columnist, and champion of black art forms, Langston Hughes sought to affirm and celebrate the "deep soul" of the black masses. Hughes captured the beating pulse of urbanized black life, articulating its common sorrows, struggles, and triumphs. His life of passionate advocacy, as well as the many achievements of his own prolific art, amply justify Hughes's stature as a major American writer.

The separation of his parents soon after his birth in Joplin, Missouri, precipitated the nomadic existence that marked the first twenty-two years of his life. After graduating from high school in Cleveland, where he became acquainted with the poetry of Amy Lowell, Vachel Lindsay, Edgar Lee Masters, and Carl Sandburg, Hughes briefly joined his father in Mexico. Unable to communicate with him and rejecting his father's pragmatic aspirations for him to become a businessman, Hughes went to New York in 1921 and enrolled in Columbia University. Hughes found academic study less compelling than the many charms of city life, and within a year he left Columbia to work at odd jobs before signing on as a seaman on a cargo ship heading for West Africa. By 1924 he was working in Paris nightclubs, absorbing the sounds of American jazz that permeated Parisian nightlife. A tour of Italy was cut short when he was robbed and left virtually destitute. He returned to New York at the end of 1924 via a steamer on which he exchanged his labor for passage. Joining his mother in Washington, D.C., Hughes worked briefly for the Association for the Study of Negro Life and History and then as a hotel busboy. Though a number of his poems had already been published in the black periodicals *The Crisis* and *Opportunity*, it was not until Hughes slipped three of his poems to Vachel Lindsay, who was dining at the hotel's restaurant, that he received his "first publicity break" in the form of a newspaper interview and photograph heralding Lindsay's "discovery" of a "busboy poet." The years that followed were active and productive. *The Weary Blues*, his first collection of poems, appeared in 1926. Concurrent with completing his undergraduate studies at Pennsylvania's Lincoln University, Hughes contributed poetry to such publications as *Vanity Fair*, *Poetry*, and *The New Republic*. A second collection of poems appeared in 1927, and by 1930 he had written a novel and a play. The catastrophic events of the time—the Depression, the Spanish Civil War, and World War II—are reflected in Hughes's output during these years. His efforts to re-create the structures and rhythms of blues and jazz music in poetic works such as *Montage of a Dream Deferred* demonstrate Hughes's technical versatility and his desire to encompass in his art the essence of the black experience. His fictional character Jesse B. Semple has become nothing less than a modern urban folk hero. So too, in many ways, has Langston Hughes.

The Negro Speaks of Rivers

I've known rivers:
I've known rivers ancient as the world and older than the flow
    of human blood in human veins.

My soul has grown deep like the rivers.

I bathed in the Euphrates[1] when dawns were young.   5
I built my hut near the Congo[2] and it lulled me to sleep.
I looked upon the Nile[3] and raised the pyramids above it.
I heard the singing of the Mississippi when Abe Lincoln went
    down to New Orleans, and I've seen its muddy bosom turn
    all golden in the sunset.   10

I've known rivers:
Ancient, dusky rivers.

My soul has grown deep like the rivers.

---

1. **Euphrates** (yü frā′ tēz′): a river in the Middle East. With the Tigris River, it
encompasses the area known as "the cradle of civilization."
2. **Congo:** a river in the heart of Africa.
3. **Nile:** an African river primarily associated with Egypt.

Getting at Meaning

1. Each river mentioned in this poem is linked to a different region and civilization. What culture or cultures do you associate with each river?

2. Explain what the speaker means by the statement, "I've known rivers."

Developing Skills in Reading Literature

1. **Speaker.** The title of this poem indicates that Hughes is speaking of his black ancestry and of the black experience. What does Hughes imply about the ability of his people to endure? What do lines 4–7 imply about the black experience?

2. **Figurative Language.** The speaker has known rivers ". . . ancient as the world and older than the flow/ of human blood in human veins." What do these similes imply about the depths of black knowledge and experience? What figure of speech does Hughes employ to describe the Mississippi?

Developing Writing Skills

Analyzing a Symbol. The rivers are symbolic in this poem. In a well developed paragraph discuss how they symbolize the fullness of the black experience. Think about how rivers flow. What territory do they usually cover, compared to brooks and streams? What often happens to rivers as they progress?

As I Grew Older

It was a long time ago.
I have almost forgotten my dream.
But it was there then,
In front of me,
Bright like a sun—   5
My dream.

And then the wall rose,
Rose slowly,
Slowly,
Between me and my dream.   10
Rose slowly, slowly,
Dimming,
Hiding,
The light of my dream.
Rose until it touched the sky—   15
The wall.

Shadow.
I am black.

I lie down in the shadow.
No longer the light of my dream
    before me,   20
Above me.
Only the thick wall.
Only the shadow.

My hands!
My dark hands!   25
Break through the wall!
Find my dream!
Help me to shatter this darkness,
To smash this night,
To break this shadow   30
Into a thousand lights of sun,
Into a thousand whirling dreams
Of sun!

Getting at Meaning

1. What often happens in growing up, as described by the speaker of this poem?

2. In what lines does the speaker decide to become active and fight against "the wall"? According to the final lines of the poem, what will be the result of destroying the wall?

Developing Skills in Reading Literature

1. **Symbol.** The wall, rising slowly, is a symbol in this poem. What does it represent? Notice that it gradually becomes "thick." What is needed to destroy it?

2. **Imagery.** Images of light and dark abound in this poem. Why does the wall create shadow? Why is the speaker's own dark color identified with shadow? In what lines does the speaker connect shadow and blackness? What other words suggest darkness? Why is the dream identified with light?

Developing Writing Skills

Analyzing Theme. The poet Wordsworth wrote in a famous poem:

> Shades of the prison-house begin to close
>   Upon the growing Boy,
> But he beholds the light, and whence it flows,
>   He sees in it his joy.

Wordsworth's lines embody the theme of Hughes's poem. In a well developed paragraph discuss how the processes that Wordsworth describes are being experienced by the speaker in "As I Grew Older." Refer to specific lines. Explain how the theme of Hughes's poem is both depressing and hopeful.

Arna Bontemps

1902–1973

Best known for his historical novels about the black experience in the New World, Arna Bontemps began his long career as a writer and a teacher during the cultural renewal known as the Harlem Renaissance.

Bontemps was born in Alexandria, Louisiana, the son of a brickmason and a teacher. While attending Pacific Union College, he heard Marcus Garvey speak in Los Angeles and was touched by the excitement of the Harlem Renaissance. After graduation in 1923, Bontemps moved to Harlem and taught at Harlem Academy while experiencing firsthand what he would later describe as ". . . a happening in black America." His first novel, *God Sends Sunday*, appeared in 1931. Three years later Bontemps left New York for Huntsville, Alabama, to teach and write at Oakwood Junior College. During the next decade he collaborated on several plays, including *Careless Love* with Langston Hughes. He also wrote several novels, including *Drums at Dusk*, set in Haiti during the eighteenth-century slave revolt. After earning another degree at the University of Chicago in 1943, Bontemps took a position as a librarian at Nashville's Fisk University. He remained there until 1965, when he returned to the University of Chicago to teach literature. Bontemps was a significant contributor to the development of an independent black identity. At the time of his death, he had been serving as Writer-in-Residence at Fisk University.

A Note of Humility

When all our hopes are sown on stony ground,
And we have yielded up the thought of gain,
Long after our last songs have lost their sound,
We may come back, we may come back again.

When thorns have choked the last green thing we loved, 5
And we have said all that there is to say,
When love that moved us once leaves us unmoved,
Then men like us may come to have a day.

For it will be with us as with the bee,
The meager ant, the sea-gull and the loon;
We may come back to triumph mournfully 10
An hour or two, but it will not be soon.

Developing Skills in Reading Literature

1. **Speaker.** Who is the "we" and the "our" of the poem? Who are the "men like us"?

2. **Imagery.** The imagery of this poem is the source of its meaning. For example, nothing comes of hopes sown into "stony ground." Green things get "choked" by "thorns." In spite of this, where does the poet find hope? What do the bee, the ant, the sea-gull, and the loon all bring to mind?

3. **Tone.** Characterize the tone of the poem. What lines suggest that the poet understands weariness and sorrow? Which lines imply a hopeful attitude? What does the phrase "triumph mournfully" imply? What attitude does the final line of the poem convey?

4. **Diction.** Notice that the majority of words in this poem contain only one syllable. What effect do they produce? Why are they appropriate to the poem? Observe, too, that Bontemps has chosen his words carefully, for their sound effects. Where do you find alliteration? Where do you hear assonance? What effect do these poetic devices produce?

Postwar Consciousness

HOMAGE TO THE SQUARE: APPARITION, 1959. *Josef Albers.*
The Solomon R. Guggenheim Museum, New York.

T. S. Eliot
1888–1965

More than any other single individual, T.S. Eliot defined the contours of modern poetry. His early poems helped create the Modernist temper, but he would later proclaim his belief in literary, political, and religious tradition. At odds with the spiritual and emotional emptiness that he believed characteristic of twentieth-century culture, he later wrote poems that express a mystical return to the sources of spiritual renewal, such as *The Four Quartets*. He also considered himself an anti-Romantic, and he advanced critical views specifying the artistic necessity of an "objective correlative" to evoke the appropriate emotional response from the reader. Though many of his contemporaries did not always applaud his poems or agree with his critical and personal views, virtually everyone acknowledged his predominating influence.

Although he was born in St. Louis and educated at Harvard, Eliot chose to live in England. He published his first collection of poems there in 1917 and became a naturalized subject ten years later. His early work, including "Preludes" and "The Love Song of J. Alfred Prufrock," reflects his reading of the French Symbolist poet Jules LaForgue, his study of the English philosopher Francis Herbert Bradley, and his membership in the avant-garde artistic circles that dominated London's literary scene at the time. Supporting himself and his wife first as a teacher and then as a bank clerk, Eliot poured his energies into his poetry and his criticism. *The Waste Land*, perhaps the key poem of the era and certainly one of the major poems of the twentieth century, appeared in 1922. The work's rendering of the spiritual infirmities of the age reverberated throughout the literary world, and the poem stands as one of the definitive statements of the human condition. In critical essays such as "Tradition and the Individual Talent," "Hamlet and His Problems," and "The Metaphysical Poets," Eliot contrasted the disjointed and chaotic tenor of modern life with the "unified sensibility" art can create when that art is faithful to an unbroken tradition stretching back to the Greek myths. Much of Eliot's career is in the service of that tradition, and its rejuvenating allure partially accounts for the direction of Eliot's later life and work. The effect of his conversion to the Anglican church in 1927 is evident in his 1935 verse play, *Murder in the Cathedral*, and in *The Four Quartets*, written between 1940 and 1943, in which he explores the possibility and meaning of redemptive spiritual faith within a temporal existence. As a testimonial to the significance of his achievements, Eliot was awarded the Nobel Prize in Literature in 1948.

In his early poems, Eliot is a poet of ironic detachment from the debilitating conditions that so paralyze Prufrock, the modern Everyman. In his later poems, Eliot speaks of the commitment to a spiritual quest toward a transcendent plane of faith and renewal. In the words of the critic Hyatt Waggoner, Eliot's poems ". . . named what had been nameless—and so only dimly known—and what they named, they brought to consciousness." His contributions to modern consciousness explain why Eliot is one of the literary giants of the age.

Gus: The Theatre Cat

Gus is the Cat at the Theatre Door.
His name, as I ought to have told you before,
Is really Asparagus. That's such a fuss
To pronounce, that we usually call him just Gus.
His coat's very shabby, he's thin as a rake, 5
And he suffers from palsy that makes his paw shake.
Yet he was, in his youth, quite the smartest of Cats—
But no longer a terror to mice and to rats.
For he isn't the Cat that he was in his prime;
Though his name was quite famous, he says, in its time. 10
And whenever he joins his friends at their club
(Which takes place at the back of the neighboring pub)
He loves to regale them, if someone else pays,
With anecdotes drawn from his palmiest days.
For he once was a Star of the highest degree— 15
He has acted with Irving, he's acted with Tree.[1]
And he likes to relate his success on the Halls,
Where the Gallery once gave him seven cat-calls.
But his grandest creation, as he loves to tell,
Was Firefrorefiddle, the Fiend of the Fell. 20

  "I have played," so he says, "every possible part,
And I used to know seventy speeches by heart.
I'd extemporize back-chat, I knew how to gag,
And I knew how to let the cat out of the bag.
I knew how to act with my back and my tail; 25
With an hour of rehearsal, I never could fail.
I'd a voice that would soften the hardest of hearts,
Whether I took the lead, or in character parts.
I have sat by the bedside of poor Little Nell;[2]
When the Curfew[3] was rung, then I swung on the bell. 30
In the Pantomime season I never fell flat,
And I once understudied Dick Whittington's[4] Cat.

---

1. **Irving . . . Tree:** Sir Henry Irving, 1838-1905, and Sir Herbert Beerbohm
Tree, 1853-1917, noted British actors.
2. **Little Nell:** a main character in Charles Dickens's novel *The Old
Curiosity Shop*.
3. **Curfew:** a reference to a popular 1882 poem called "Curfew Must Not
Ring Tonight," by Rose Hartwick Thorpe.
4. **Dick Whittington:** three times the lord mayor of London, in 1398, 1406,
and 1419. A poor orphan boy, he became successful in part because of the
remarkable deeds of his cat.

But my grandest creation, as history will tell,
Was Firefrorefiddle, the Fiend of the Fell."

   Then, if someone will give him a toothful of gin,   35
He will tell how he once played a part in *East Lynne*.[5]
At a Shakespeare performance he once walked on pat,
When some actor suggested the need for a cat.
He once played a Tiger—could do it again—
Which an Indian Colonel pursued down a drain,   40
And he thinks that he still can, much better than most,
Produce blood-curdling noises to bring on the Ghost.
And he once crossed the stage on a telegraph wire,
To rescue a child when a house was on fire.
And he says: "Now, these kittens, they do not get trained   45
As we did in the days when Victoria[6] reigned.
They never get drilled in a regular troupe,
And they think they are smart, just to jump through a hoop."
And he'll say, as he scratches himself with his claws,
"Well, the Theatre's certainly not what it was.   50
These modern productions are all very well,
But there's nothing to equal, from what I hear tell,

    That moment of mystery
    When I made history
As Firefrorefiddle, the Fiend of the Fell."   55

---

5. ***East Lynne:*** a novel by Mrs. Henry Wood, published in 1861. It was immensely popular, especially in its dramatic version.
6. **Victoria:** Queen of England from 1837-1901.

Getting at Meaning

1. What is Gus's situation? Describe him physically. What does line 13 indicate about his finances?

2. Gus ". . . joins his friends at their club/(Which takes place at the back of the neighboring pub)." What does this indicate about the social standing of Gus's friends?

3. What are some of the great dramatic roles that Gus has played? How does he romanticize his career?

Developing Skills in Reading Literature

1. **Satire.** This poem is from T. S. Eliot's whimsical collection, *Old Possum's Book of Practical Cats.* The poems are a series of feline character sketches, many of them gently satiric.

What satiric touches do you find in this poem? For example, notice that Gus complains about the younger generation: "Now, these kittens, they do not get trained/As we did in the days when Victoria reigned." What other humorous, lightly satiric touches do you find in the poem? What kind of human type does Gus represent?

2. **Meter.** The pace of this poem is very fast, in large part because of the meter that Eliot has employed. Scan the poem. Although the meter does contain some iambs, the feet are mainly anapests, similar to iambs but containing an additional unaccented syllable ($\smile\smile\,{'}$). How many anapests do you find per line? Read part of the poem aloud. In what way do the anapests speed up the rhythm?

Developing Vocabulary

Word Origins. The word *cat* comes from Old English, as does the word *dog* and most of our other one-syllable words for common animals. Many animal names, however, have more unusual origins. Look up each animal name that follows in a dictionary containing etymologies and record its origin.

donkey	lion
gopher	penguin
hippopotamus	rhinoceros

These words help convey the diversity of influences on the English language.

Preludes

I

The winter evening settles down
With smells of steaks in passageways.
Six o'clock.
The burnt-out ends of smoky days
And now a gusty shower wraps   5
The grimy scraps
Of withered leaves about your feet
And newspapers from vacant lots;
The showers beat
On broken blinds and chimney-pots,   10
And at the corner of the street
A lonely cab-horse steams and stamps.
And then the lighting of the lamps.

II

The morning comes to consciousness
Of faint stale smells of beer
From the sawdust-trampled street
With all its muddy feet that press
To early coffee-stands.   5
With the other masquerades
That time resumes,
One thinks of all the hands
That are raising dingy shades
In a thousand furnished rooms.   10

III

You tossed a blanket from the bed,
You lay upon your back, and waited;
You dozed, and watched the night revealing
The thousand sordid images
Of which your soul was constituted;   5
They flickered against the ceiling.
And when all the world came back
And the light crept up between the shutters
And you heard the sparrows in the gutters,
You had such a vision of the street   10
As the street hardly understands;

Sitting along the bed's edge, where
You curled the papers from your hair,
Or clasped the yellow soles of feet
In the palms of both soiled hands.   15

IV

His soul stretched tight across the skies
That fade behind a city block,
Or trampled by insistent feet
At four and five and six o'clock;
And short square fingers stuffing pipes,   5
And evening newspapers, and eyes
Assured of certain certainties,
The conscience of a blackened street
Impatient to assume the world.

I am moved by fancies that are curled   10
Around these images, and cling:
The notion of some infinitely gentle
Infinitely suffering thing.
Wipe your hand across your mouth, and laugh;
The worlds revolve like ancient women   15
Gathering fuel in vacant lots.

Note: The study questions for this poem and for others of the postwar period examine meaning through a consideration of form; what is said is revealed through a study of the way it is said.

Developing Skills in Reading Literature

1. **Structure.** "Preludes" uses the diurnal rotation, or the twenty-four hours that constitute a day, as its primary structural device. Each of the four sections of the poem presents a city scene at a different time of the day.

Identify the time of day in each section. Explain how Eliot captures the mood of that part of the day.

2. **Imagery.** The images in "Preludes" are particularly graphic, appealing strongly to the various senses. What smells are suggested in the poem, and by extension, tastes? What sounds does Eliot re-create? Which lines stimulate the sense of touch? Which of the visual images seem most effective?

3. **Speaker.** Notice that Sections I and II of "Preludes" contain no pronouns. In Section III the speaker addresses someone, using the pronoun you. Section IV begins with a third-person pronoun, referring to "His soul." Then, in line 10 the first person enters when the speaker says, "I am moved by fancies. . . ." The speaking voice returns to a second-person reference in the final three lines.

What can you assume about the "I" voice of the poem? Who is the "you" in Section III? Does the final "you" have the same antecedent? Who is the "he" of Section IV? What is the speaker observing in the various sections of the poem? What details indicate that the speaker is a perceptive, contemplative individual? What is the speaker's tone? How does the imagery reflect the speaker's emotions?

4 **Rhythm.** Various sound devices give this poem a slow, gently musical quality. Although the meter is not regular, what metrical pattern often appears? Where do you find rhyme? Where do you find alliteration? Read each section of the poem aloud and comment on how the sound devices work to create the poem's cadence. Explain how the speaker's tone is reflected in the poem's rhythm.

5. **Theme.** A vision of human life, or what might be called a world view, emerges in this poem. Where does the poem emphasize human isolation? Where does it emphasize the sorrow and grime of human life? From observing different human types, what does the speaker conclude? Explain the philosophy that emerges in the last seven lines of the poem.

The Love Song of J. Alfred Prufrock

S'io credesse che mia risposta fosse
A persona che mai tornasse al mondo,
Questa fiamma staria senza piu scosse.
Ma perciocche giammai di questo fondo
Non torno vivo alcun, s'i'odo il vero,
Senza tema d'infamia ti rispondo.[1]

Let us go then, you and I,
When the evening is spread out against the sky
Like a patient etherized upon a table;
Let us go, through certain half-deserted streets,
The muttering retreats   5
Of restless nights in one-night cheap hotels
And sawdust restaurants with oyster-shells:
Streets that follow like a tedious argument
Of insidious intent
To lead you to an overwhelming question. . .   10
Oh, do not ask, "What is it?"
Let us go and make our visit.

   In the room the women come and go
Talking of Michelangelo.[2]

   The yellow fog that rubs its back upon the window-panes,   15
The yellow smoke that rubs its muzzle on the window-panes
Licked its tongue into the corners of the evening,
Lingered upon the pools that stand in drains,
Let fall upon its back the soot that falls from chimneys,
Slipped by the terrace, made a sudden leap,   20
And seeing that it was a soft October night,
Curled once about the house, and fell asleep.

---

1. **epigraph:** the Italian epigraph to the poem is from Dante's "Inferno." When the flame of Guido is asked to identify himself, he replies as follows: "If I believe that my reply would be to someone who ever would return to the world, this flame would wag no more. But because, if what I hear be true, no one ever does return alive from this depth, I reply to you without fear of infamy." When you have read the poem, think of the way these words relate to Prufrock.
2. **Michelangelo** (mī kəl an' jə lō): a famous artist of the Italian Renaissance who lived from 1475-1564.

And indeed there will be time
For the yellow smoke that slides along the street,
Rubbing its back upon the window-panes;
There will be time, there will be time
To prepare a face to meet the faces that you meet;
There will be time to murder and create,
And time for all the works and days of hands
That lift and drop a question on your plate;
Time for you and time for me,
And time yet for a hundred indecisions,
And for a hundred visions and revisions,
Before the taking of a toast and tea.

    In the room the women come and go
Talking of Michelangelo.

    And indeed there will be time
To wonder, "Do I dare?" and, "Do I dare?"
Time to turn back and descend the stair,
With a bald spot in the middle of my hair—.
[They will say: "How his hair is growing thin!"]
My morning coat, my collar mounting firmly to the chin,
My necktie rich and modest, but asserted by a simple pin—
[They will say: "But how his arms and legs are thin!"]
Do I dare
Disturb the universe?
In a minute there is time
For decisions and revisions which a minute will reverse.

    For I have known them all already, known them all:—
Have known the evenings, mornings, afternoons,
I have measured out my life with coffee spoons;
I know the voices dying with a dying fall
Beneath the music from a farther room.
    So how should I presume?

    And I have known the eyes already, known them all—
The eyes that fix you in a formulated phrase,
And when I am formulated, sprawling on a pin,
When I am pinned and wriggling on the wall,
Then how should I begin
To spit out all the butt-ends of my days and ways?
    And how should I presume?

    And I have known the arms already, known them all—
Arms that are braceleted and white and bare

[But in the lamplight, downed with light brown hair!]
Is it perfume from a dress   65
That makes me so digress?
Arms that lie along a table, or wrap about a shawl.
   And should I then presume?
   And how should I begin?

                              • • • • •

Shall I say, I have gone at dusk through narrow streets   70
And watched the smoke that rises from the pipes
Of lonely men in shirt-sleeves, leaning out of windows? . . .

   I should have been a pair of ragged claws
Scuttling across the floors of silent seas.

                              • • • • •

And the afternoon, the evening, sleeps so peacefully!   75
Smoothed by long fingers,
Asleep . . . tired . . . or it malingers,
Stretched on the floor, here beside you and me.
Should I, after tea and cakes and ices,
Have the strength to force the moment to its crisis?   80
But though I have wept and fasted, wept and prayed,
Though I have seen my head [grown slightly bald] brought in upon a platter,
I am no prophet[3]—and here's no great matter;
I have seen the moment of my greatness flicker,
And I have seen the eternal Footman hold my coat, and snicker,   85
And in short, I was afraid.

   And would it have been worth it, after all,
After the cups, the marmalade, the tea,
Among the porcelain, among some talk of you and me,
Would it have been worthwhile,   90
To have bitten off the matter with a smile,
To have squeezed the universe into a ball
To roll it toward some overwhelming question,
To say: "I am Lazarus,[4] come from the dead,
Come back to tell you all, I shall tell you all"—   95
If one, settling a pillow by her head,
   Should say: "That is not what I meant at all.
   That is not it, at all."

---

3. **head . . . prophet:** a reference to John the Baptist, the Jewish prophet in the
Bible, beheaded at the request of King Herod's step-daughter Salome. Salome
requested that the prophet's head be brought to her on a platter.
4. **Lazarus:** a brother of Mary and Martha, raised by Jesus from the dead
according to an account in John 11.

And would it have been worth it, after all,
Would it have been worthwhile,   100
After the sunsets and the dooryards and the sprinkled streets,
After the novels, after the teacups, after the skirts that trail along the floor—
And this, and so much more?—
It is impossible to say just what I mean!
But as if a magic lantern[5] threw the nerves in patterns on a screen: 105
Would it have been worthwhile
If one, settling a pillow or throwing off a shawl,
And turning toward the window, should say:
   "That is not it at all,
   That is not what I meant, at all."   110

     · · · · ·

No! I am not Prince Hamlet,[6] nor was meant to be;
Am an attendant lord, one that will do
To swell a progress, start a scene or two,
Advise the prince; no doubt, an easy tool,
Deferential, glad to be of use,   115
Politic, cautious, and meticulous;
Full of high sentence, but a bit obtuse;
At times, indeed, almost ridiculous—
Almost, at times, the Fool.[7]

   I grow old . . . I grow old . . .   120
I shall wear the bottoms of my trousers rolled.

   Shall I part my hair behind? Do I dare to eat a peach?
I shall wear white flannel trousers, and walk upon the beach.
I have heard the mermaids singing, each to each.

   I do not think that they will sing to me.   125

   I have seen them riding seaward on the waves
Combing the white hair of the waves blown back
When the wind blows the water white and black.

   We have lingered in the chambers of the sea
By sea-girls wreathed with seaweed red and brown   130
Till human voices wake us, and we drown.

---

5. **magic lantern:** an early form of slide projector.
6. **Prince Hamlet:** the hero of Shakespeare's tragedy *Hamlet,* who finally takes
decisive action to avenge his father's death.
7. **attendant . . . Fool:** a reference to Polonius, in *Hamlet,* who is not a heroic
figure in the drama of life, but a minor, somewhat ridiculous character.

Getting at Meaning

1. Prufrock, the speaker of the poem, is on his way to a late afternoon tea party. What lines in the first sections of the poem indicate that he is depressed? What lines suggest that he feels passive, lacking in energy?

2. Prufrock is thinking to himself in the poem. This poem is his "love song," and he is trying to work up the courage to declare his love to a woman. What lines indicate his nervousness? Why does he keep repeating, "There will be time, there will be time"?

3. What kind of people are at the tea party? What is implied in the observation, repeated twice, that women drop in and out, "Talking of Michelangelo"? What does Prufrock think that the people at the party notice about him?

4. What does Prufrock mean when he thinks, "Do I dare/Disturb the universe"? What is he afraid will happen if he asks his "overwhelming question"? In what thought does Prufrock take comfort?

5. At what point in the poem do you realize that Prufrock will not declare his love? Notice how the verb tenses change in line 87. What does this signify?

6. What does Prufrock finally realize about himself? What future does he project for himself?

Developing Skills in Reading Literature

1. **Stream of Consciousness.** Like Faulkner in "Barn Burning," Eliot employs a stream-of-consciousness technique, imitating the natural flow of Prufrock's thoughts, memories, and feelings. Logical connections are sometimes missing, making the poem somewhat difficult to follow. In a careful reading of the poem, however, Eliot's organizational pattern begins to emerge. Prufrock's thoughts are not entirely random but are organized by associations, with one idea or impression triggering another.

Notice, for example, lines 62–69. In talking about the people he has known, Prufrock begins to think about a woman's arms. Then he realizes that perhaps the scent of perfume is triggering these thoughts, causing him to digress. He pulls himself back to his earlier train of thought.

Where else in the poem do you find Prufrock's perceptions and reactions flowing along in a natural way? What makes the stream-of-consciousness technique an important tool in developing Prufrock's character?

2. **Character.** Consider the kind of man Prufrock is. In what ways is his name both formal and silly? In what ways is Prufrock himself both formal and a little silly? What lines indicate his timidity? What lines indicate that he cares a great deal about what other people think of him? What lines reflect his conservatism? What lines indicate that he is aging? Prufrock appears to understand himself rather well. What lines suggest this?

3. **Allusion.** The allusion to Michelangelo does a great deal to characterize the society in which Prufrock moves. Women "come and go," presumably talking of this fiery artistic genius in a trivial and shallow way. The people at the tea party have cultural pretensions.

Prufrock uses several telling allusions to characterize himself. In lines 82 and 83 he sees himself as the beheaded John the Baptist. In line 94 he imagines himself as Lazarus. In line 111 he sees that he is *not* Prince Hamlet, but more like the character Polonius in Shakespeare's drama. Study each allusion and figure out exactly what Prufrock is saying about himself. What do the allusions contribute to the tone of the poem?

4. **Epigraph.** An epigraph is a motto or quotation at the beginning of a literary work. Like the character Guido in the Dante epigraph to this poem, Prufrock is in hell. What kind of hell? How does the epigraph help to characterize Prufrock?

5. **Figurative Language.** Brilliantly original similes and metaphors abound in this poem. For example, Prufrock begins his journey to the tea party at twilight, "When the evening is spread out against the sky/Like a patient etherized upon a table." Notice how this simile conveys the utter stagnation Prufrock feels. What does Prufrock communicate in the metaphor, "I should have been a pair of ragged claws/Scuttling across the floors of silent seas"? Find other key similes and metaphors in the poem and comment on their meanings.

Prufrock uses personification in line 85 when he speaks of "the eternal Footman." To what does this phrase refer? What is the Footman's attitute toward Prufrock?

6. **Imagery.** In addition to specific figures of speech, this poem is full of striking imagery. For example, Prufrock describes his own physical appearance vividly. He also, in lines 56–58, sees himself as an insect in a collection, carefully typed and rendered inactive by society. What other images in the poem stand out? What image of himself in the future does Prufrock present in the final lines of the poem? What does the mermaids' singing represent? Why does Prufrock say, "I do not think that they will sing to me"?

7. **Structure.** Although this poem is long and seemingly rambling, it in fact has a tight dramatic structure. Notice that the first sections of the poem build slowly toward a climax, toward the moment when Prufrock will ask his "overwhelming question." Tension does begin to build, especially in lines 37–72. What specific lines help to build the tension? Where does Prufrock actually begin to ask his question? At what point in the poem does the promised climax fail to take place?

Observe what happens to the tension in the poem after Prufrock fails to ask his question:

And the afternoon, the evening, sleeps so
    peacefully!
Smoothed by long fingers,
Asleep . . . tired . . . or it malingers,

What is the function of the remainder of the poem from this point on? What does Prufrock realize? What happens in line 111 when Prufrock says rather dramatically, "No"?

8. **Rhythm.** The pace of Eliot's poem reflects Prufrock's mental condition. Notice the slow pace throughout the poem. What techniques make the pace so slow? Consider how the frequent repetitions of lines and phrases affect the pace. Observe that Eliot frequently inserts lines of all one-syllable words or of mainly one-syllable words. Why do these lines slow the pace? How do the long prepositional phrases, as in lines 88 and 89, affect the poem's rhythm?

9. **Theme.** Prufrock is more than just a frustrated lover. When he talks of "disturbing the universe" with his declaration of love, he is really talking about changing his entire way of life and of escaping from the lonely, stagnant life he has been leading. In one of the saddest lines in modern poetry, he sums up his shallow, timid existence: "I have measured out my life with coffee spoons."

Many critics see Prufrock as a symbol of modern man. What is Eliot attacking in modern society through Prufrock? What has happened to energy and boldness? What has happened to communication? What images of confusion and stagnation are present in the poem? What is drowning Prufrock's inner life in the final line of the poem?

Developing Writing Skills

Analyzing Character. A common figure in twentieth-century literature is the anti-hero, a character who lacks the commitment and the capacity for action that characterize the traditional hero. Prufrock is one of the first of the modern anti-heroes.

In an essay of at least five paragraphs, analyze Prufrock's character. What kind of life does he lead? What motivates his behavior? What prevents him from being a heroic figure like Prince Hamlet? How does he view himself? Is he in any way admirable, or is he merely pathetic?

Outline your essay before you begin to write, indicating the content of each paragraph. Use quotations from the poem in every body paragraph.

Archibald MacLeish

Ars Poetica

A poem should be palpable[1] and mute
As a globed fruit,

Dumb
As old medallions to the thumb,

Silent as the sleeve-worn stone   5
Of casement ledges where the moss has grown—

A poem should be wordless
As the flight of birds.

A poem should be motionless in time
As the moon climbs,   10

Leaving, as the moon releases
Twig by twig the night-entangled trees,

Leaving, as the moon behind the winter leaves,
Memory by memory the mind—

A poem should be motionless in time   15
As the moon climbs.

A poem should be equal to:
Not true.

For all the history of grief
An empty doorway and a maple leaf.   20

For love
The leaning grasses and two lights above the sea—

A poem should not mean
But be.

---

1. **palpable:** easily perceived by the senses.

Developing Skills in Reading Literature

1. **Simile.** In the first eight lines of this poem Mac-Leish sets up four similes to define poetry. To what does he compare a poem in each pair of lines? What adjective in each pair of lines indicates the quality that MacLeish likes to see in a poem? Discuss the meanings of these comparisons.

2. **Paradox.** Lines 9–16 establish a paradox. Although the moon climbs, leaving behind the trees, it appears "motionless" to humans. How do you explain this apparent contradiction? How can a poem both "move" and remain "motionless"?

3. **Imagery.** Apart from the specific comparisons, MacLeish creates some unusual images in this poem.

His image for "the history of grief" is "An empty doorway and a maple leaf." Does this strike you as appropriate? Explain the image MacLeish offers for love.

4. **Theme.** The title of this poem means "the art of poetry," and the poem is MacLeish's attempt to pin down the elusive nature of the art form. His ideas are reminiscent of the views of the Imagists. What does he mean when he says, "A poem should be equal to:/Not true"? What does he mean when he says, "A poem should not mean/But be"? What does MacLeish probably believe is the purpose of art in general?

Eleven

And summer mornings the mute child, rebellious,
Stupid, hating the words, the meanings, hating
The Think now, Think, the O but Think! would leave
On tiptoe the three chairs on the verandah
And crossing tree by tree the empty lawn   5
Push back the shed door and upon the sill
Stand pressing out the sunlight from his eyes
And enter and with outstretched fingers feel
The grindstone and behind it the bare wall
And turn and in the corner on the cool   10
Hard earth sit listening And one by one,
Out of the dazzled shadow in the room,
The shapes would gather, the brown plowshare, spades,
Mattocks,[1] the polished helves of picks, a scythe
Hung from the rafters, shovels, slender tines   15
Glinting across the curve of sickles—shapes
Older than men were, the wise tools, the iron
Friendly with earth. And sit there, quiet, breathing
The harsh dry smell of withered bulbs, the faint
Odor of dung, the silence. And outside   20
Beyond the half-shut door the blind leaves
And the corn moving. And at noon would come,
Up from the garden, his hard crooked hands
Gentle with earth, his knees still earth-stained, smelling
Of sun, of summer, the old gardener, like   25
A priest, like an interpreter, and bend
Over his baskets.
                        And they would not speak:
They would say nothing. And the child would sit there
Happy as though he had no name, as though   30
He had been no one: like a leaf, a stem,
Like a root growing—

---

1. **Mattock:** a digging and grubbing implement with features of an
adz, ax, and pick.

Developing Skills in Reading Literature

1. **Character.** This poem presents two characters and describes their silent interaction. Why is the child "mute" and "rebellious"? How do his parents irritate him? When he escapes, why does he choose the shed as his haven?

How is the old gardener characterized? Why are his hands "Gentle with earth"? How can he "smell" of sun?

Although the boy and the gardener do not speak, what communion exists between them? Notice the similes. Why is the gardener compared to a priest? How is he "like an interpreter"? Why is the boy happy in the gardener's presence, "Like a root growing—"?

2. **Imagery.** Why is the lawn between the house and the shed "empty"? What images depict the inside of the shed? Why are the tools "wise"? What are the smells of the shed? What tactile images does MacLeish create?

3. **Assonance.** Several vowel sounds repeatedly recur in this poem. Identify the sounds. How do they help create harmony and unity in the poem? How do they help the form of the poem to reflect the poem's content?

4. **Theme.** What view of nature does this poem convey? What relationship between human beings and nature does MacLeish present as desirable?

ALVARO AND CHRISTINA, 1968. *Andrew Wyeth.*
William A. Farnsworth Library and Art Museum, Rockland, Maine.

Edna St. Vincent Millay

1892–1950

For many, during the 1920's and early 1930's, Edna St. Vincent Millay and her short, lyrical poems embodied all that poets and poetry should be. Her soothingly romantic yet accessible pieces, so different from what Ezra Pound and T.S. Eliot produced in Europe, combined with the appeal of her unconventional lifestyle in New York's Greenwich Village to make her one of the most popular poets of her era. Her early acclaim faded later in her life, however, a phenomenon that prompted her to express some bitterness and wonderment at the turn her career had taken.

Millay captured a wide public with her first poem, "Renascence," published in *The Lyric Year* magazine in 1912, while she was still attending high school in her native Maine. A mystical evocation of self-renewal through natural beauty, the poem was the centerpiece of her first volume of poems, published in 1917 at the conclusion of her studies at Barnard and Vassar Colleges. Moving to Greenwich Village, she pursued her writing career while embodying many of the attitudes associated with female emancipation and cultural bohemianism. She acted and wrote plays for the Provincetown Players and otherwise became a fixture of the New York literary scene. After her marriage, she moved to a farm in upstate New York and began writing poems of social protest, such as "Justice Denied in Massachusetts" about the Sacco-Vanzetti case. Her other poems written during this time were darker and more tentative than the shorter lyrics produced earlier. Although she continued to appear in the public eye—her "Poem and Prayer for an Invading Army" was read on D-Day over the radio by the actor Ronald Coleman—Millay never quite matched her earlier achievements. The best of her work, such as her sonnets published in 1931, is valued for its clarity and technical precision expressed in traditional forms that contrasted markedly with the way she lived her life. She won a Pulitzer Prize for her poetry in 1923.

God's World

O World, I cannot hold thee close enough!
   Thy winds, thy wide gray skies!
   Thy mists that roll and rise!
Thy woods, this autumn day, that ache and sag
And all but cry with color! That gaunt crag   5
To crush! To lift the lean of that black bluff!
World, World, I cannot get thee close enough!

Long have I known a glory in it all,
   But never knew I this;
   Here such a passion is   10
As stretcheth me apart. Lord, I do fear
Thou'st made the world too beautiful this year.
My soul is all but out of me,—let fall
No burning leaf; prithee, let no bird call.

Developing Skills in Reading Literature

1. **Tone.** Characterize the tone of this poem. What is Millay's attitude toward nature and the world around her? What lines in particular suggest deep emotion? What aspects of the poem indicate that the poet is speaking in her own voice?

2. **Diction.** Why do the woods "ache and sag"? Why is the crag "gaunt"? What sound effects predominate in "God's World"? What words create these effects?

Notice that Millay's diction is sometimes formal and archaic, or belonging to a much earlier time. Comment on the effect that words such as *thee, thy, thou'st,* and *prithee* produce in the poem. How are they appropriate to the subject?

3. **Theme.** Appreciation for the beauty of nature is the subject of this poem. What lines suggest that the poet feels pleasure that is almost painful? What fear does Millay express in the final lines of the poem?

Sonnet XXX

Love is not all: it is not meat nor drink
Nor slumber nor a roof against the rain;
Nor yet a floating spar to men that sink
And rise and sink and rise and sink again;
Love can not fill the thickened lung with breath,   5
Nor clean the blood, nor set the fractured bone;
Yet many a man is making friends with death
Even as I speak, for lack of love alone.
It well may be that in a difficult hour,
Pinned down by pain and moaning for release,   10
Or nagged by want past resolution's power,
I might be driven to sell your love for peace,
Or trade the memory of this night for food.
It well may be. I do not think I would.

Developing Skills in Reading Literature

1. **Metaphor.** The poet attempts to define *love* by saying what it is *not*. What limitations does she place on the power of love in the negative metaphors presented in the first eight lines of the poem? What do these negative comparisons have in common?

2. **Sonnet.** Comment on how the sonnet structure functions in this poem. Is it an Italian or an English sonnet? What resolution does the final line of the poem provide?

3. **Alliteration.** Which consonant sounds does Millay often repeat in the poem? How do these sounds unify the poem? How do they affect the pace of the poem?

4. **Theme.** "Sonnet XXX" is a love poem, addressed to an individual, as line 12 indicates. What is the poet's final statement on the worth of love?

On Hearing a Symphony of Beethoven

Sweet sounds, oh, beautiful music, do not cease!
Reject me not into the world again.
With you alone is excellence and peace,
Mankind made plausible, his purpose plain.
Enchanted in your air benign and shrewd,   5
With limbs a-sprawl and empty faces pale,
The spiteful and the stingy and the rude
Sleep like the scullions in the fairy tale.
This moment is the best the world can give:
The tranquil blossom on the tortured stem.   10
Reject me not, sweet sounds! oh, let me live,
Till Doom espy my towers and scatter them,
A city spellbound under the aging sun,
Music my rampart, and my only one.

Getting at Meaning

1. According to this poem, what can the beauty of music accomplish? Explain the line, "Mankind made plausible, his purpose plain."

2. The poem suggests that there are limits to the power of music. What can't music screen out? What can't it prevent?

Developing Skills in Reading Literature

1. **Simile and Metaphor.** What does Beethoven's music do to "The spiteful and the stingy and the rude"? Explain the simile. What are *scullions*?

In a rather elaborate metaphor the poet describes herself as a city. What is attacking her, as indicated in the phrase "aging sun"? What is a *rampart*? In what ways is music a rampart?

2. **Rhythm.** In this sonnet on the beauty and power of music, Millay achieves some musical effects. What does alliteration contribute to the lilt of the poem? Which sounds are often repeated? Are they mainly hard or soft sounds? What does rhyme contribute to the cadence of the poem?

3. **Theme.** According to this sonnet, what is the value of music, or art in general? What view of life does Millay project? Explain the meaning of the lines,

"This moment is the best the world can give:/The tranquil blossom on the tortured stem."

Developing Vocabulary

Words from French. Millay uses the word *rampart,* a word that has come into the English language from French. Many French words entered English in the centuries after the Battle of Hastings in 1066, when the Normans invaded England.

American English has acquired additional French words from the French Canadians and from the French in Louisiana. Consult a dictionary for the etymology of each of the following words. Which words come from the French Canadians? Which words come from the South? Explain the precise origin of each word.

bayou   butte   cache   levee   prairie

Developing Writing Skills

Combining Description and Narration. Either in poem or paragraph form, describe a musical experience you have had. Perhaps you were involved in producing the music, or perhaps you were listening to music produced by others. Give the details of the experience, using imagery and figurative language to describe the music and its effect on you.

Marianne Moore

1887–1972

Jill Krementz

Within two years of the 1951 publication of Marianne Moore's *Collected Poems*, she received three of poetry's most distinguished awards—the Pulitzer Prize, the National Book Award, and the Bollingen Prize. These accolades echoed T.S. Eliot's earlier praise for Moore as "one of the few who have done the language some service in my lifetime." Other contemporaries associated with the Modernist movement, such as Ezra Pound, H.D., and William Carlos Williams, similarly lauded and promoted her work, which features a range of technical innovations combined with a compelling, precise, and idiosyncratic perspective.

Born in Kirkwood, Missouri, Moore graduated from Pennsylvania's Bryn Mawr College and took a teaching position at the United States Indian School in Carlisle, Pennsylvania. Her talents were first demonstrated in 1915, when *Poetry* magazine published five of her poems. She moved to New York in 1919, working first as a secretary and later as a librarian. *Observations*, published in 1924, won *The Dial*'s yearly poetry award and led to her assuming an editorial position with that magazine until it ceased to exist in 1929. Thereafter, she continued to lead a quietly productive life, translating the fables of La Fontaine and writing poetry. Her most famous and most quoted work is "Poetry."

"Poetry" is virtually a manifesto of Imagist principles about excising what Pound referred to as "emotional slither" in favor of concrete objectivity rendered by precise technical craftsmanship—"real toads" in "imaginary gardens." Moore's disposi-

tion toward technical experimentation, as opposed to consciously unfolding a self-contained system of ideas, seemingly testifies to her fidelity to the Modernist creed and is the source of much of her reputation. Nonetheless, Moore's work can also be valued for its qualities of wry observation and understated wisdom.

Silence

My father used to say,
"Superior people never make long visits,
have to be shown Longfellow's grave[1]
or the glass flowers[2] at Harvard.
Self-reliant like the cat—   5
that takes its prey to privacy,
the mouse's limp tail hanging like a shoelace from its mouth—
they sometimes enjoy solitude,
and can be robbed of speech
by speech that has delighted them.   10
The deepest feeling always shows itself in silence;
not in silence, but restraint."
Nor was he insincere in saying, "Make my house your inn."
Inns are not residences.

---

1. **Longfellow's grave:** Longfellow is buried in Mount Auburn Cemetery in
Cambridge, Massachusetts.
2. **glass flowers:** a reference to a famous collection of glass flowers housed
in the Harvard University Museums.

Getting at Meaning

1. What does the speaker's father admire in people? What one adjective in the poem best sums up this quality?

2. Explain the line, "The deepest feeling always shows itself in silence." Do you agree?

3. Explain the father's statement, "Make my house your inn." What did he expect from other people?

Developing Skills in Reading Literature

1. **Allusion.** What is the function of the allusions to Longfellow's grave and to the glass flowers at Harvard? Why don't superior people have to be shown these things?

2. **Imagery.** Explain the cat and mouse image. What does the image illustrate? How does the image function within the simile of which it is a part? Why does Moore value solitude?

Poetry

I, too, dislike it: there are things that are important
     beyond all this fiddle.
  Reading it, however, with a perfect contempt for it,
    one discovers in
it after all, a place for the genuine.   5
    Hands that can grasp, eyes
     that can dilate, hair that can rise
       if it must, these things are important not because a

high-sounding interpretation can be put upon them
     but because they are   10
  useful. When they become so derivative as to become
    unintelligible,
  the same thing may be said for all of us, that we
    do not admire what
     we cannot understand: the bat   15
      holding on upside down or in quest of something to

eat, elephants pushing, a wild horse taking a roll,
     a tireless wolf under
  a tree, the immovable critic twitching his skin like a horse
    that feels a flea, the base-   20
  ball fan, the statistician—
    nor is it valid
     to discriminate against "business documents and

school-books"; all these phenomena are important. One must
     make a distinction   25
  however: when dragged into prominence by half poets,
    the result is not poetry,
  nor till the poets among us can be
    "literalists of
    the imagination"[1]—above   30
     insolence and triviality and can present

---

1. **literalists of the imagination:** an altered quotation from the essay
"William Blake and the Imagination" by the Irish poet William Butler
Yeats, 1865-1939.

for inspection, "imaginary gardens with real toads in them,"
    shall we have
  it. In the meantime, if you demand on the one hand,
  the raw material of poetry in
    all its rawness and
    that which is on the other hand
      genuine, you are interested in poetry.

35

Getting at Meaning

1. Surprisingly, the poet begins by stating her dislike for poetry. What usually is implied by the word *fiddle?* What kinds of poems does Moore dislike the most?

2. What reasons does Moore give for finding poetry worthwhile after all? Explain the phrase "literalists of the imagination."

Developing Skills in Reading Literature

1. **Imagery.** What images illustrate the "genuine"? What does the poet mean by the word *genuine?*

2. **Theme.** Moore says that poets should rise above "insolence and triviality" to create "imaginary gardens with real toads in them." Explain her meaning. What position does she take on "business documents and school-books"?

3. **Poetry.** Although for the most part "Poetry" sounds more like a prose argument than a poem, notice that it has the shape of a poem. What similarities do you see among the five stanzas? What purpose does the stanza form serve? What other aspects of the poem are more characteristic of poetry than of prose?

Robinson Jeffers
1887–1962

Robinson Jeffers lived most of his life in a house and tower he built overlooking the isolated California coast below Carmel. There he watched nature's drama enact itself, and he wove it into virtually all of his poems. The natural world that Jeffers describes is not, however, one that exists harmoniously with a humanity deemed "Slavish in the mass." Befitting its locale, Jeffers's nature is majestic, rugged, beautiful, and merciless. It is not the spiritually renewing nature of Ralph Waldo Emerson and Walt Whitman. Instead, it conveys a world view that relegates a meek and mean humanity to a very precarious corner of the cosmos.

Jeffers was born to a Pittsburgh Presbyterian minister who took charge of his son's education. After residing in Europe for a number of years, the family moved to California when Jeffers was sixteen. Over the next several years, Jeffers attended universities in California, Switzerland, and Washington, studying both medicine and forestry. An inheritance in 1912 enabled him to settle on the Carmel coast, marry, and concentrate on his writing. His first major work, *Roan Stallion, Tamar and Other Poems*, appeared in 1925. Both the long narrative poems of the title and the accompanying short lyrics mark Jeffers's first use of free verse, a style that would prove to be characteristic of most of the poems he produced steadily until his death in 1962. Mythical allusions, references, and overtones abound in his work, often cast in contexts that drew him further and further away from the intellectual and social mainstreams. In his later years, Jeffers attempted to formalize his world view into a philosophy he called "Inhumanism," a view that placed him in direct opposition to the premises of classical humanist tradition and was based on the insignificance of humanity as made evident by modern scientific discoveries.

Fire on the Hills

The deer were bounding like blown leaves
Under the smoke in front of the roaring wave of the brush-fire;
I thought of the smaller lives that were caught.
Beauty is not always lovely; the fire was beautiful, the terror
Of the deer was beautiful; and when I returned   5
Down the black slopes after the fire had gone by, an eagle
Was perched on the jag of a burnt pine,
Insolent and gorged, cloaked in the folded storms of his shoulders.
He had come from far off for the good hunting
With fire for his beater to drive the game; the sky was merciless   10
Blue, and the hills merciless black,
The sombre-feathered great bird sleepily merciless between them.
I thought, painfully, but the whole mind,
The destruction that brings an eagle from heaven is better than mercy.

Developing Skills in Reading Literature

1. **Imagery.** This poem creates a picture of brush-fire and the havoc it causes in the world of nature. What two things in the poem are black, or dark? How are they linked? Notice that they are both described as "merciless." Why? Why is the sky also merciless?

2. **Theme.** Explain the meaning of the statement, "Beauty is not always lovely." What does the poet conclude about the destruction and disruption caused by a brush-fire? Explain the meaning of the final line of the poem.

Evening Ebb

The ocean has not been so quiet for a long while; five night-herons
Fly shorelong voiceless in the hush of the air
Over the calm of an ebb that almost mirrors their wings.
The sun has gone down, and the water has gone down
From the weed-clad rock, but the distant cloud-wall rises. The ebb whispers.   5
Great cloud-shadows float in the opal water.
Through rifts in the screen of the world pale gold gleams, and the evening
Star suddenly glides like a flying torch.
As if we had not been meant to see her; rehearsing behind
The screen of the world for another audience.   10

SUNSET, 1914. John Marin.
Collection of Whitney Museum of American Art.

Developing Skills in Reading Literature

1. **Imagery.** The imagery of "Evening Ebb" creates a calm, peaceful mood. What specific images of quiet and relaxation does the poet present? What activity does the glassy sea reflect? What image does the line "Great cloud-shadows float in the opal water" conjure up?

2. **Figurative Language.** Venus, the evening star, is personified in the poem. What qualities are emphasized by this figure of speech? Notice the simile that is part of her characterization. She ". . . glides like a flying torch." What does this simile suggest? What is "the screen of the world"?

3. **Theme.** What lines in this poem serve to dwarf humanity? What does the phrase "another audience" seem to suggest is happening in the universe?

John Crowe Ransom
1888–1974

The leader of the "Fugitive" group of southern writers centered in Nashville, Tennessee, in the mid-1920's and, later, an influential contributor to the "New Criticism" movement, John Crowe Ransom created a small number of softly ironic poems which complement his highly influential views on modern poetry's function and purpose. In his preface to his 1938 collection of critical essays entitled *The World's Body*, Ransom argued for poetry over science as a way of "knowing the world." "What we cannot know constitutionally as scientists," he wrote, "is the world which is made of whole and indefeasible objects, and this is the world which poetry recovers for us . . ." Ransom also condemned what he called "heart's-desire" poetry, which "denies the real world by idealizing it." Instead, he advocated a poetic art that is "the act of an adult mind . . .," one that sees reality clearly in its rendering of both the particulars and the universals of human experience.

Born in Pulaski, Tennessee, and educated at Vanderbilt University, Ransom returned to Vanderbilt in 1914 to teach English. With the exception of two years of service in the army during World War I, virtually all of Ransom's adult life was spent in a university setting, first at Vanderbilt, and later at Ohio's Kenyon College, where he edited the influential *Kenyon Review* from 1937 until his retirement in 1959. His first collection, *Poems about God*, appeared in 1919, but it was not until the 1924 publication of *Chills and Fever* that Ransom's distinctive poetic voice emerged in its mature form. *Two Gentlemen in Bonds*, published in 1927, sustained and developed the stance of the earlier volume. "Janet Waking" and "Bells for John Whiteside's Daughter" typify Ransom's concern with the human response to the inevitability of death. It was during this time that Ransom, along with Allen Tate, launched *The Fugitive*, a magazine that promoted the aesthetic doctrines of a group of writers who regarded themselves as being in flight from a pervasively threatening cultural insensitivity. After the Fugitive group disbanded, Ransom turned most of his energies toward criticism. As in his poems, which in their form and diction demonstrate an affection for traditional elegance, Ransom in his criticism deplored the demise of a religiously based and culturally ennobling response to life in the wake of the corrosive impact of technology and modernization. Modernity, he felt, seeks to strip humanity of its vitally necessary and essentially mysterious links to both God and nature and thus prevents us from understanding our true role and relations within the natural order. As a poet, critic, and teacher, John Crowe Ransom became known as an eloquent and engaging spokesman for an aesthetic response to the modern world that preserved and cultivated traditional values.

Janet Waking

Beautifully Janet slept
Till it was deeply morning. She woke then
And thought about her dainty-feathered hen,
To see how it had kept.

One kiss she gave her mother,   5
Only a small one gave she to her daddy
Who would have kissed each curl of his
    shining baby;
No kiss at all for her brother.

"Old Chucky, old Chucky!" she cried,
Running across the world upon the grass   10
To Chucky's house, and listening. But alas,
Her Chucky had died.

It was a transmogrifying[1] bee
Came droning down on Chucky's old bald
    head
And sat and put the poison. It scarcely bled, 15
But how exceedingly

And purply did the knot
Swell with the venom and communicate
Its rigor! Now the poor comb stood up
    straight
But Chucky did not.   20

So there was Janet
Kneeling on the wet grass, crying her brown
    hen
(Translated far beyond the daughters of men)
To rise and walk upon it.

And weeping fast as she had breath   25
Janet implored us, "Wake her from her
    sleep!"
And would not be instructed in how deep
Was the forgetful kingdom of death.

---

1. **transmogrifying** (trans mag' rə fī' ing): changing greatly, often with grotesque or humorous effect.

Getting at Meaning

1. Describe how Janet discovers her hen's death. What has killed the bird?

2. What does Janet think has happened to her bird? What strikes the speaker more than the bird's death?

Developing Skills in Reading Literature

1. **Diction.** What words early in the poem suggest Janet's youth and vivacity? What words counter her innocence with their negative, grim connotations, suggestive of death? Why is the bee described as "transmogrifying"?

2. **Theme.** Janet wakes from sleep in this poem. In what sense does she awake from innocence? What is the concept of death communicated in lines 23 and 28? Why is Janet unable to grasp what her father grasps?

Developing Vocabulary

Words from Latin: Prefixes and Roots. The origin of the word *transmogrifying* is not clear. It does, however, involve the prefix *trans-*, which comes from the Latin word meaning "across or over."

The six words that follow all involve the prefix *trans-*. For each word record both the definition and the Latin root. Explain how the prefix and the root together relate to the present-day meaning of the word.

transcendental	transom
transgress	transude
transitory	transverse

Bells for John Whiteside's Daughter

There was such speed in her little body,
And such lightness in her footfall,
It is no wonder her brown study
Astonishes us all.

Her wars were bruited in our high window,   5
We looked among orchard trees and beyond,
Where she took arms against her shadow,
Or harried unto the pond

The lazy geese, like a snow cloud
Dripping their snow on the green grass,   10
Tricking and stopping, sleepy and proud,
Who cried in goose, Alas,

For the tireless heart within the little
Lady with rod that made them rise
From their noon apple-dreams and scuttle   15
Goose-fashion under the skies!

But now go the bells, and we are ready,
In one house we are sternly stopped
To say we are vexed at her brown study,
Lying so primly propped.   20

Getting at Meaning

1. The phrase "brown study" refers to a condition of deep thought. In this poem the speaker uses the phrase to mean death. Why does the young girl's death astonish everyone?

2. What were some of the child's favorite activities? Why are they referred to as "wars"?

Developing Skills in Reading Literature

1. **Imagery.** Study the images that depict the dead child. What qualities do these images emphasize? How did she handle the geese? How are the geese portrayed? What contrast exists between the child and the geese? To what does the phrase "noon apple-dreams" refer?

2. **Understatement.** Notice how the speaker understates emotion in this poem; that is, the speaker says less than is actually or literally true. Death, for example, is described as a "brown study." The speaker, contemplating the death of the child, says, ". . . we are vexed." What effect does the understatement achieve? How does it save the poem from sentimentality, or an excessive indulgence in the emotions of pity and sympathy? Does the understatement make death seem any less terrifying?

Wallace Stevens

1879–1955

Rollie McKenna

By valuing the poetic imagination as the sole means of ordering, however fleetingly, an otherwise chaotic objective reality, Wallace Stevens has become the epitome of the modern American poet. "After one has abandoned a belief in God," he wrote in *Opus Posthumous*, which was published in 1957, two years after his death, "poetry is that essence which takes its place as life's redemption." Stevens consciously turned away from what he regarded as the falsifying illusions of religion and the distorting wish-fulfillments of romantic poetry. In its place, Stevens relied on the naked faculty of imaginative perception and on the meaning created by language to produce what he referred to as a "fictive order" for existence. Such order, he claimed, is the only true kind available to modern humanity.

A poet whose importance emerged only gradually over his career and since his death, Stevens led a unique life as both an insurance company executive and a writer of world-class stature, winner of the Bollingen Prize, the National Book Award, and the Pulitzer Prize. Stevens was born in Reading, Pennsylvania, and attended Harvard University as an undergraduate. Upon attaining his degree, he moved to New York, intent on pursuing his literary aspirations, but he soon realized that he was temperamentally unsuited to the rigors of the struggling artist's life. He obtained a law degree at New York University, and later he practiced law in New York until joining a Connecticut insurance firm in 1916, remaining with that firm until his death in 1955. Throughout this time he wrote some of the most remarkable poems of the era. "Sunday Morning," one of his best known poems, was the first to be published, appearing in *Poetry* magazine in 1915. It later reappeared in its final form in Stevens's important first collection of poems, *Harmonium*, published in 1923, when he was forty-four. Containing some of his most representative works, including "Peter Quince at the Clavier," "Thirteen Ways of Looking at a Blackbird," and "The Emperor of Ice Cream," *Harmonium* depicts in often whimsical and ironic ways Stevens's central concern with the ability of art, through the imagination, to provide all the meaning that is realistically possible in life. *Ideas of Order*, appearing in 1935 and including "The Idea of Order at Key West," developed this theme further in focusing on the role of the poet as the imaginative "artificer" who actively makes "the slovenly wilderness" "no longer wild." Stevens's frequent use of bright colors and tropical and sensual imagery suggests an emphasis at this point in his career on the transitory joys of experience, made all the more pleasurable and intense because they are transitory. Later collections, however, such as *Notes toward a Supreme Fiction* and *Transport to Summer*, suggest a further development in Stevens's thinking. While continuing to assert the chaotic nothingness of objective reality, Stevens gives a greater voice to the human desire for something more lasting. The longing that is implicit in such desire is also part of Stevens's modernity.

Anecdote of the Jar

I placed a jar in Tennessee,
And round it was, upon a hill.
It made the slovenly wilderness
Surround that hill.

The wilderness rose up to it,   5
And sprawled around, no longer wild.
The jar was round upon the ground
And tall and of a port in air.

It took dominion everywhere.
The jar was gray and bare.   10
It did not give of bird or bush,
Like nothing else in Tennessee.

Disillusionment of Ten O'Clock

The houses are haunted
By white nightgowns.
None are green,
Or purple with green rings,
Or green with yellow rings,   5
Or yellow with blue rings.
None of them are strange,
With socks of lace
And beaded ceintures.[1]
People are not going   10
To dream of baboons and periwinkles.[2]
Only, here and there, an old sailor,
Drunk and asleep in his boots,
Catches tigers
In red weather.   15

1. **ceinture** (sən' chər): a belt or sash for the waist.
2. **periwinkle:** a small saltwater snail whose yellowish, cone-shaped shell has dark spiral bands.

Developing Skills in Reading Literature

1. **Title.** The title of this poem includes the word *anecdote,* which means "a brief account of an interesting or amusing incident." Why do you think Stevens uses this word in the title of the poem? Is there anything else in the poem that suggests a casual or playful approach?

2. **Symbol.** Critics have voiced a variety of interpretations of the jar in this poem. One interpretation stresses that a jar is an artifact, a created object. The poem contrasts the jar, a symbol of human beings and their creations, to the untamed world of nature, as represented by Tennessee. What phrase in the first stanza characterizes Tennessee as wild and untamed territory? What lines suggest that the jar clashes with nature? What lines suggest that the jar draws attention to itself, upstaging the world of nature? Why is the jar "gray and bare"? Is the poem neutral, or does it express a preference for either art and human achievement or nature?

Developing Skills in Reading Literature

1. **Symbol.** This poem seems light, with its many color words and its fanciful imagery. The poem has symbolic depths, however. The speaker looks at houses, or everyday reality, and sees white nightgowns. What do the white nightgowns symbolize? (Hint: What is white in the color spectrum?) What would brilliantly colored or decorated nightgowns represent to the speaker? Thinking of the nightgowns, why does the speaker regret that "None of them are strange"? What do the "baboons and periwinkles" represent? What does the old sailor, an outcast from society, represent with his vivid dream of "tigers/In red weather"?

2. **Theme.** This poem is about the need for imagination in day-to-day life, a statement in defense of thinking and mental escape. Explain this theme as it is developed in the poem. To what does the word *disillusionment* in the title refer?

Randall Jarrell
1914–1965

Widely known for his celebrated war poems "The Death of the Ball Turret Gunner" and "Eighth Air Force," reflecting his World War II experiences, Randall Jarrell used his considerable reserves of empathy and intelligence and his clear, low-keyed poetic gifts to illustrate the human costs of twentieth-century life. In addition to a small but widely respected body of poems, Jarrell produced acclaimed literary criticism, exemplified in his book *Poetry and the Age* (1953), in which he took issue with the New Critics for seemingly divorcing art from ordinary experience.

Born in Nashville, Tennessee, Jarrell studied psychology and English at Vanderbilt University. Teaching stints at Kenyon College and the University of Texas preceded service in the Army Air Corps from 1942 to 1946, when he returned to teaching at Sarah Lawrence and the University of North Carolina at Greensboro. His early verse, published in *Blood for a Stranger* in 1942, contains an elegance implying the influence of his fellow Southerners Allen Tate and John Crowe Ransom. His next two works, *Little Friend, Little Friend* and *Losses*, are plainer in style while retaining their focus on such themes as the inevitable loss of childhood innocence in the face of a painful, hypocritical, and destructive social order. Later, he looked at the more private ravages of old age and loneliness as preliminary forms of death in his *Woman at the Washington Zoo*, which earned him a 1962 National Book Award. Upon Jarrell's death in 1965, his contemporary Robert Lowell referred to him as "the most heartbreaking English poet of his generation."

The Death of the Ball Turret Gunner

On a World War II bomber, the ball turret was a glass bubble in the belly of the plane, which could hold a man and two machine guns. Because of the ball turret's small size, the gunner had to fire in contorted positions.

From my mother's sleep I fell into the State,
And I hunched in its belly till my wet fur froze.
Six miles from earth, loosed from its dream of life,
I woke to black flak and the nightmare fighters.
When I died they washed me out of the turret with a hose.   5

Getting at Meaning

1. What does the speaker mean when he says, "I fell into the State"?

2. What is the antecedent for "its" in line 2? What is the antecedent for "its" in line 3?

Developing Skills in Reading Literature

1. **Title.** The title is essential to an understanding of this short, brilliant poem, for it reveals the identity of the speaker. Who is the "I" voice in the poem? From what vantage point does the speaker narrate the poem?

2. **Imagery.** The speaker describes himself hunched in the turret like a baby in the womb, or like a frightened small animal. How does line 1 introduce this idea and suggest the speaker's youth? On a literal level, what part of a flyer's uniform does "wet fur" refer to? Why is the animal imagery appropriate to the speaker's situation? What image does the phrase "black flak and the nightmare fighters" bring to mind? What image do you get of the speaker in the final line? Clearly, what has happened to his body?

3. **Irony.** The speaker loses his youth and innocence and "wakes" into the world of experience. Ironically, what does he wake to? What is the tone of the final line of the poem? The speaker has given his life for "the State." Ironically, what is the State's attitude? How can you tell?

4. **Theme.** This poem is a biting commentary on war and the destruction of young people. What details suggest that the human being is on an animal level in war? What word suggests that the speaker did not really know what he was getting into when he went into the armed services? What does the phrase "loosed from its dream of life" imply about human society? What does it imply about the speaker? What words and phrases convey the bitterness in this poem?

A Lullaby

For wars his life and half a world away
The soldier sells his family and days.
He learns to fight for freedom and the State;
He sleeps with seven men within six feet.

He picks up matches and he cleans out plates;   5
Is lied to like a child, cursed like a beast.
They crop his head, his dog tags ring like sheep
As his stiff limbs shift wearily to sleep.

Recalled in dreams or letters, else forgot,
His life is smothered like a grave, with dirt;   10
And his dull torment mottles like a fly's
The lying amber of the histories.

Developing Skills in Reading Literature

1. **Simile.** In this poem Jarrell uses similes to describe a soldier's life. Consider the three similes in the second stanza and the two similes in the third stanza. What picture do they create? Why is a soldier compared to a child and to animals? In what sense is he "smothered like a grave, with dirt"?

2. **Irony.** We are accustomed to think about the glories of fighting "for freedom and the State." We often associate soldiering with romantic heroism. Ironically, what is the soldier's life like much of the time, according to Jarrell? How do soldiers spend their time? How are they treated? Explain the irony of the poem's title.

3. **Diction.** The specific diction of this poem establishes meaning and tone. What do phrases such as "stiff limbs," "shift wearily," and "dull torment" convey? Why does Jarrell use words such as *smothered, dirt,* and *lying*? What effect do the many simple one-syllable words have?

4. **Theme.** What point of view on war does Jarrell present in the line, "The lying amber of the histories"? Explain how this poem is a denunciation of war.

Developing Writing Skills

Analyzing Irony. Both "The Death of the Ball Turret Gunner" and "A Lullaby" are denunciations of war. Both are bitterly ironic. In a five-paragraph composition analyze the various ironies that Jarrell sees in war. Quote specific lines from the poems to support your points.

W. H. Auden

1907–1973

Jill Krementz

His friend and collaborator Christopher Isherwood once said of W. H. Auden, "You could say to him: 'Please write me a double ballade on the virtues of a certain brand of toothpaste, which also contains at least 10 anagrams on the names of well-known politicians, and of which the refrain is as follows . . .' Within 24 hours, your ballade would be ready—and it would be good." By the time of his death in 1973, Wystan Hugh Auden had already established his reputation as one of the literary giants of the English-speaking world.

A prolific writer of essays, drama, opera librettos, and, most especially, verse, Auden was born in York, England, the son of a professor of public health and a nurse. An intensely private man whose cerebral poetry addressed both public and universal themes, Auden may well have inherited his sharp moral sense from his grandfathers and uncles, all of whom were Anglican ministers. Much of his poetry locates humanity in an urban, even industrialized, landscape, reflecting his childhood in Birmingham, England's steel and manufacturing center. After a traditional English boarding school education, including cold baths to mortify the body and build character, Auden entered Christ Church College, Oxford, in 1925 to study geology and mining, but he soon turned his attention to literature and to his own poetry, which he had started to write as a fifteen-year-old schoolboy. Stimulated by the work of T.S. Eliot and by an informal group of fellow student-writers including Stephen Spender, C. Day Lewis, and Christopher Isherwood, Auden published his first collection of poems in 1928. After leaving Oxford, Auden earned his living as a schoolteacher while continuing to write and to involve himself in the cultural and social ferment that characterized Europe in the 1930's. As a co-founder in 1932 of the Group Theater, he wrote and collaborated on plays such as *The Dance of Death*, *The Dog beneath the Skin*, *The Ascent of F-6*, and *On the Frontier*. Additionally, as a member of the General Post Office film unit he wrote the screenplays for the verse documentaries "Night Mail," "Coal Face," and "The Londoners." Like so many of his fellow writers, Auden participated in the political and ideological struggles which would shortly erupt into a World War. His extensive travels—to Civil War Spain, where he drove an ambulance for the Loyalists, to Iceland and to China—provided him with the needed perspective to realize that "the living nations wait,/ Each sequestered in its hate." Dissatisfied with an England that had become a society of "aspirins and weak tea" and fretful that amid the massing armies of Europe "Poetry makes nothing happen," Auden left England for the United States in 1939, just prior to the outbreak of war. He recorded this historical moment in his poem "September 1, 1939." Auden became a naturalized citizen of the United States in 1946. Increasingly in the postwar years, Auden muted the social content of his poetry in favor of examining personal questions of morality and faith. He also converted his love of music into librettos in collaboration with such noted composers as Benjamin Britten and Igor Stravinsky. In 1956, Auden returned to England to become Professor of Poetry at Oxford, a position he held until 1961. He later returned to New York, spending his last decade between residences in Greenwich Village and the countryside outside of Vienna while continuing to lecture and to write. In the year before his death, he returned to Oxford as Writer in Residence.

Musée des Beaux Arts

About suffering they were never wrong,
The Old Masters[1]: how well they understood
Its human position; how it takes place
While someone else is eating or opening a window or just walking dully along;
How, when the aged are reverently, passionately waiting   5
For the miraculous birth, there always must be
Children who did not specially want it to happen, skating
On a pond at the edge of the wood:
They never forgot
That even the dreadful martyrdom must run its course   10
Anyhow in a corner, some untidy spot
Where the dogs go on with their doggy life and the torturer's horse
Scratches its innocent behind on a tree.

In Breughel's[2] *Icarus*,[3] for instance: how everything turns away
Quite leisurely from the disaster; the ploughman may   15
Have heard the splash, the forsaken cry,
But for him it was not an important failure; the sun shone
As it had to on the white legs disappearing into the green
Water; and the expensive delicate ship that must have seen
Something amazing, a boy falling out of the sky,   20
Had somewhere to get to and sailed calmly on.

---

1. **Old Masters:** superior artists or craftsmen from the 16th, 17th, or early 18th century.
2. **Breughel** (brü' gəl): Pieter Breughel the Elder, a Flemish painter who lived from 1520?-1569. Also spelled *Brueghel* and *Bruegel*.
3. *Icarus* (ik' ə rəs): in Greek mythology the son of Daedalus who, to escape imprisonment, flies by means of artificial wings. He falls into the sea and drowns when the wax of his wings melts as he flies too near the sun.

Developing Skills in Reading Literature

1. **Allusion.** Auden wrote this poem after a visit to the Brueghel alcove in the Brussels Musées Royaux des Beaux-Arts, and the poem alludes to two other Brueghel paintings besides *Icarus*. Lines 5–8 refer to *The Numbering at Bethlehem*. What does the painting depict, according to these lines? In lines 9–13 Auden discusses Brueghel's *The Massacre of the Innocents*. What apparently takes place in this painting? Describe Brueghel's *Icarus* as Auden presents it. In what way do the three Brueghel allusions form the backbone of this poem?

2. **Theme.** In each of the Brueghel paintings Auden describes, a major, earth-shaking emotional event is taking place in the center of the canvas. What is going

on in other parts of the painting? Explain Auden's assertion that the Old Masters understood the human position of suffering. To the ploughman, Icarus's falling out of the sky is "not an important failure." Why not? Discuss the truth of Auden's observations.

3. **Tone.** Characterize the tone of this poem. What attitude does Auden take toward the human truth he presents? Note in particular the final line of the poem.

4. **Rhythm.** This poem has an especially slow, conversational, contemplative pace. How do the long lines contribute to the rhythm of the poem? How does the punctuation slow the pace of the poem? What does the quiet rhyme scheme contribute to the rhythm? Comment on how the rhythm of the poem fits the poem's content.

Embassy

As evening fell the day's oppression[1] lifted;
Far peaks came into focus; it had rained:
Across wide lawns and cultured flowers drifted
The conversation of the highly trained.

Two gardeners watched them pass and priced their shoes: 5
A chauffeur waited, reading in the drive,
For them to finish their exchange of views;
It seemed a picture of the private life.

Far off, no matter what good they intended,
The armies waited for a verbal error   10
With all the instruments for causing pain:

And on the issue of their charm depended
A land laid waste, with all its young men slain,
Its women weeping, and its towns in terror.

---

1. **oppression:** the sense of being weighed down in body or mind.

Developing Skills in Reading Literature

1. **Sonnet.** Auden uses the two-part Italian sonnet form to build a powerful contrast in this poem. What kind of scene does he create in the octave? What words suggest quiet or suspended activity? Why are the flowers "cultured"? Why does the poet focus on the gardeners and the chauffeur?

Describe the contrast presented in the sonnet's sestet. How do these six lines change the tenor of the octave? How do they provide commentary on the octave?

2. **Theme.** What is the view of war and the military that this poem projects? Notice that the armies, all prepared to do battle, "waited for a verbal error." What does this phrase imply? Why is it so grimly ironic that the fate of countries and people, as described in the last two lines, depends upon the charm of a few diplomats?

3. **Tone.** Discuss the tone of this poem. What specific words put a sharp edge on the poet's commentary? Where is the tone ironic? Where it is forceful and biting?

Developing Writing Skills

Analyzing Style. In the very best poetry—and Auden's poems are among the best—the form of a poem reflects and somehow underscores its content. Indeed, in an excellent poem it is hard to separate form and content, for the two are so closely intertwined.

Select one of the two Auden poems for close analysis, and explain how the form of the poem suits its content. Consider such elements as stanza form, line length, syntax, diction, punctuation, rhyme, meter, and imagery.

Robert Hayden

1913–1980

Jill Krementz

Robert Hayden has been described as one of the "most underpraised and underrecognized" poets in America. Born in Detroit, Hayden attended Wayne State University and the University of Michigan, where he twice won the Avery Hopwood Poetry Prize. He published his first collection of poems, *Heart Shape in the Dust*, in 1940, shortly before joining the *Michigan Chronicle* as a drama and music critic. Subsequent works include *Ballad of Remembrance*, *Night Blooming Cereus*, and *Angle of Ascent*. In 1967, while teaching at Fisk University, Hayden edited *Kaleidoscope*, an anthology of black poets. Hayden later returned to the University of Michigan as a faculty member. He was appointed in 1976 as the poetry consultant to the Library of Congress, the first black ever to hold that position. In his last years, Hayden finally received the recognition his work merits.

Those Winter Sundays

Sundays too my father got up early
and put his clothes on in the blueblack cold,
then with cracked hands that ached
from labor in the weekday weather made
banked fires blaze. No one ever thanked him.   5

I'd wake and hear the cold splintering, breaking.
When the rooms were warm, he'd call,
and slowly I would rise and dress,
fearing the chronic angers of that house,

Speaking indifferently to him,   10
who had driven out the cold
and polished my good shoes as well.
What did I know, what did I know
of love's austere and lonely offices?

Getting at Meaning

1. What does the word *too* in line 1 suggest?

2. What are some of the services that the speaker's father performed?

Developing Skills in Reading Literature

1. **Imagery.** Notice the way that the speaker describes the father through imagery. The visual details are striking. Which lines appeal to the sense of touch? What do they make the reader feel? Which line appeals to both touch and hearing?

2. **Tone.** What was once the speaker's attitude toward the father? Which two lines convey this attitude? What is the speaker's attitude as an adult? Which lines in the poem convey the changed attitude?

3. **Theme.** What has the speaker come to realize about love? Explain the phrase, ". . . love's austere and lonely offices."

Theodore Roethke

1908–1963

Imogen Cunningham

Influenced by the psychological systems of Sigmund Freud and Carl Jung, a number of writers achieved prominence in the 1940's, 1950's, and 1960's by creating art that recorded their deep probing into a newly enlarged conception of self. Sometimes called "Confessional" to indicate their private and subjective focus, these poets included Theodore Roethke, Robert Lowell, Sylvia Plath, John Berryman, and Anne Sexton.

In the title poem of *Open House* (1941), his first volume of poems, Theodore Roethke writes, "My secrets cry aloud . . . / My heart keeps open house." In that volume, and in later works such as *The Lost Son and Other Poems*, *Praise to the End!*, *The Waking*, and *Words for the Wind*, Roethke isolates and explores the roots of his identity, its development, and ultimately its destiny. In the "greenhouse poems" contained in *The Lost Son*, Roethke returns to the world of childhood in his father's Saginaw, Michigan, greenhouse. His ambivalent relationship with his autocratic father, who died of cancer when Roethke was fifteen, figures prominently in these and later poems in which Roethke attempts to re-create the subjective essence of his coming of age in all of its vivid particularities.

Educated at the University of Michigan and at Harvard, Roethke decided against a career as a lawyer, choosing instead to teach English, first at Lafayette College, then later at Pennsylvania State University and Vermont's Bennington College. Recurring bouts of mental and emotional instability victimized Roethke throughout his life, making it difficult for him to adjust to the demands of the academic life. As a poet, however, he tapped into those disturbed realms for the raw material of his art, and his success at poetry led to a professorship at the University of Washington, where he taught and wrote until his death in 1963.

Roethke's last decade was his most productive. His relationship to his wife, whom he married in 1953, prompted the speculative meditations on the meaning of love which comprise the largest section of his masterwork, *Words for the Wind*, published in 1958. Roethke had earlier achieved wide acclaim, including the Pulitzer Prize, for *The Waking*, in which he confronts the imminence of his own death in the title poem. *Words for the Wind*, however, represents perhaps his finest achievement, for in such poem sequences as "The Dying Man" and "Meditations of an Old Woman" he mystically pursues the implications of physical deterioration and the experience of dying, thus concluding the journey initiated in his first poems.

Old Florist

That hump of a man bunching chrysanthemums
Or pinching-back asters, or planting azaleas,
Tamping and stamping dirt into pots,—
How he could flick and pick
Rotten leaves or yellowy petals,   5
Or scoop out a weed close to flourishing roots,
Or make the dust buzz with a light spray,
Or drown a bug in one spit of tobacco juice,
Or fan life into wilted sweet peas with his hat,
Or stand all night watering roses, his feet blue in rubber boots.   10

GLADIOLI, FLOWER STUDY NO. 4, 1925.
Charles Demuth.
Courtesy of The Art Institute of Chicago.

Developing Skills in Reading Literature

1. **Imagery.** Plant imagery predominates in "Old Florist," as it does in many of Roethke's poems. Most of the imagery in this poem is visual, though sometimes other senses are stimulated. What sensory impressions does the poem create? Which words and lines are especially evocative?

2. **Rhythm.** This poem has a musical rhythm, appropriate to the poem's subject. How does rhyme contribute to the cadence of the poem? Where is internal rhyme, rhyme within a line of poetry, used? How does alliteration enhance the poem's rhythmic quality?

3. **Tone.** Observe the speaker's tone toward "That hump of a man. . . ." Which lines and phrases suggest awe and respect? Which lines and phrases imply a sympathetic attitude?

The Pike

The river turns,
Leaving a place for the eye to rest,
A furred, a rocky pool,
A bottom of water.

The crabs tilt and eat, leisurely,   5
And the small fish lie, without shadow, motionless,
Or drift lazily in and out of the weeds.
The bottom-stones shimmer back their irregular striations,
And the half-sunken branch bends away from the gazer's eye.

A scene for the self to abjure!¹—   10
And I lean, almost into the water,
My eye always beyond the surface reflection;
I lean, and love these manifold shapes,
Until, out from a dark cove,
From beyond the end of a mossy log,   15
With one sinuous ripple, then a rush,
A thrashing-up of the whole pool,
The pike strikes.

---

1. **abjure:** to renounce upon oath; to abstain from.

Developing Skills in Reading Literature

1. **Stanza and Mood.** The first two stanzas of this poem describe a scene in nature. The imagery and the diction communicate feelings of peace and tranquillity. How does the stanza shape reinforce this mood? What do the increasingly long lines suggest about the speaker's own involvement in the natural world?

The third stanza introduces a sharp contrast, with the mood shifting abruptly in line 10. Why are the lines of the poem shorter again? Why is the reason for the shift in mood not revealed until the final line?

2. **Sound Devices.** Notice the extensive use of alliteration and assonance in this poem. Which sounds are repeated often? What effect do they produce?

Locate the only part of the poem that contains rhyme. What impact does this rhyme have? Read aloud the first and last lines, the two shortest in the poem. Why do they produce such different effects?

3. **Theme.** Why does the poet want to abjure, or renounce, the natural beauty in front of him? What does he mean by "self"? Notice that he does not separate himself, but instead almost becomes a part of the scene before him. Which line indicates this? What commentary about life does this poem convey? In broader terms, what does the line "The pike strikes" reflect? The pike's entrance is a sudden and violent occurrence. What effect does it have on the pool?

William Stafford

born in 1914

In regarding nature as a source of human insight, William Stafford in some ways continues the tradition of Emerson and Thoreau. Stafford's insight, however, is tailored to perceptions appropriate to twentieth-century civilization, and thus his poetry contains few of the ecstatic affirmations found in the works of the early Transcendentalists. Instead, Stafford offers understated observations of the natural world with suggestive implications about society and its members.

Born in Hutchinson, Kansas, Stafford earned degrees at the University of Kansas and at the University of Iowa. He was a conscientious objector during World War II and continued to advocate his pacifist views after the war through membership in several organizations. Much of his subject matter is drawn from the natural world of the Pacific Northwest, which he came to know while teaching at Lewis and Clark College in Portland, Oregon. *Traveling through the Dark* earned Stafford a National Book Award in 1963.

Traveling Through the Dark

Traveling through the dark I found a deer
dead on the edge of the Wilson River road.
It is usually best to roll them into the canyon:
that road is narrow; to swerve might make more dead.

By glow of the tail-light I stumbled back of the car   5
and stood by the heap, a doe, a recent killing;
she had stiffened already, almost cold.
I dragged her off; she was large in the belly.

My fingers touching her side brought me the reason—
her side was warm; her fawn lay there waiting,   10
alive, still, never to be born.
Beside that mountain road I hesitated.

The car aimed ahead its lowering parking lights;
under the hood purred the steady engine.
I stood in the glare of the warm exhaust turning red;   15
around our group I could hear the wilderness listen.

I thought hard for us all—my only swerving—
then pushed her over the edge into the river.

Getting at Meaning

1. Explain the dilemma described in this poem. What are the negative aspects of either choice?

2. What choice does the traveler make? Why?

Developing Skills in Reading Literature

1. **Rhythm.** In many ways this poem seems more like a prose account than a poem. What elements of the poem make it conversational and informal? Notice the meter. What kind of verse does Stafford employ (with some irregularities)? Explain how this form suits the poem.

2. **Theme.** What is so difficult about the dilemma presented in this poem? What does the poet mean by the line, "I thought hard for us all—my only swerving —"? How does the title illuminate the theme of the poem?

Karl Shapiro

born in 1913

Although he fought in the Pacific during World War II, Karl Shapiro later wrote a noteworthy poem entitled "Conscientious Objector," praising the convictions of those who refused to fight. Although he was a Jewish academician, he satirized universities as places where "To hurt the Negro and avoid the Jew/ Is the curriculum." These ironies underscore the themes of Shapiro's poetry, from his observations of the American scene in *Person, Place and Thing*, published in 1942, to the free verse prose poems of *The Bourgeois Poet*, published in 1964. His more recent *White-Haired Lover* and *Adult Bookstore* mark a return to a more traditional style while reiterating Shapiro's questions about identity, pain, loss, victimization, and spiritual relationships.

Born in Baltimore, Maryland, into a Russian-Jewish family, Shapiro attended but never graduated from the University of Virginia and Johns Hopkins University. He achieved prominence with his collection of war poems entitled *V-Letter and Other Poems*, which earned him a Pulitzer Prize in 1945. In 1947 he returned to Johns Hopkins to teach writing, thereby beginning a distinguished career as a teacher at several universities, including, most recently, the University of California (Davis). As a literary critic and as the editor of the influential *Poetry* and *Prairie Schooner* magazines, Shapiro fought what he regarded as the harmful influence of T.S. Eliot and Ezra Pound on modern poetry, advocating instead a consciously "anti-cultural" poetry on the model of Walt Whitman and Carl Sandburg.

Manhole Covers

The beauty of manhole covers—what of that?
Like medals struck by a great savage khan,[1]
Like Mayan[2] calendar stones, unliftable, indecipherable,
Not like the old electrum,[3] chased and scored,
Motioed and sculptured to a turn,   5
But notched and whelked and pocked and smashed
With the great company names
(Gentle Bethlehem, smiling United States).
This rustproof artifact of my street,
Long after roads are melted away will lie   10
Sidewise in the grave of the iron-old world,
Bitten at the edges,
Strong with its cryptic American,
Its dated beauty.

---

1. **khan** (kan): a local chieftain or man of rank in some
countries of central Asia.
2. **Mayan** (mā' ən): having to do with the Maya Indian
peoples of Mexico and Central America.
3. **electrum:** a natural pale yellow alloy of gold and silver.

Developing Skills in Reading Literature

1. **Simile.** Notice the similes for the manhole covers. In what context is the poet trying to place these objects? Why are they *not* like the "old electrum"?

2. **Tone.** What lines in the poem suggest that the poet's tone is playful and ironic? What lines suggest that there might be a bitter edge to his irony?

3. **Theme.** What commentary on contemporary American culture is implied in this poem? Notice that the poet has selected the manhole cover as the artifact that will represent us "Sidewise in the grave of the iron-old world." In what ways is the manhole cover a symbol of our society?

Auto Wreck

Its quick soft silver bell beating, beating,
And down the dark one ruby flare
Pulsing out red light like an artery,
The ambulance at top speed floating down
Past beacons and illuminated clocks   5
Wings in a heavy curve, dips down,
And brakes speed, entering the crowd.
The doors leap open, emptying light;
Stretchers are laid out, the mangled lifted
And stowed into the little hospital.   10
Then the bell, breaking the hush, tolls once,
And the ambulance with its terrible cargo
Rocking, slightly rocking, moves away,
As the doors, an afterthought, are closed.

We are deranged, walking among the cops   15
Who sweep glass and are large and composed.
One is still making notes under the light.
One with a bucket douches ponds of blood
Into the street and gutter.
One hangs lanterns on the wrecks that cling,   20
Empty husks of locusts, to iron poles.

Our throats were tight as tourniquets,
Our feet were bound with splints, but now,
Like convalescents intimate and gauche,
We speak through sickly smiles and warn   25
With the stubborn saw of common sense,
The grim joke and the banal resolution.
The traffic moves around with care,
But we remain, touching a wound
That opens to our richest horror.   30
Already old, the question Who shall die?
Becomes unspoken Who is innocent?

For death in war is done by hands;
Suicide has cause and stillbirth, logic;
And cancer, simple as a flower, blooms.   35
But this invites the occult mind,
Cancels our physics with a sneer,
And spatters all we knew of denouement
Across the expedient and wicked stones.

Getting at Meaning

1. What details of the auto wreck does the poem focus on? How do the spectators react to the accident? Explain the line, "The grim joke and the banal resolution."

2. The final stanza claims that war deaths, suicides, stillbirths, and deaths from illness have something in common. What? How is death in an accident different?

Developing Skills in Reading Literature

1. **Imagery.** Notice the rather frightening imagery that prevails in the first stanza of the poem. What color does the poet emphasize? Why? What grim sights and sounds predominate?

2. **Simile and Metaphor.** Why is it appropriate to describe the red ambulance light as pulsing "like an artery"? Notice the similes the poet uses to describe the bystanders. Their throats are "tight as tourniquets," their feet "bound with splints." They speak "like convalescents intimate and gauche." Why these comparisons? What emotional condition is the poet conveying? Why are the wrecked cars "Empty husks of locusts"?

3. **Rhythm.** Notice the fast pace of the first stanza. How do ropetends increase the tension? How do present participles function in these lines? What do the long, extended sentences contribute?

What devices help to slow the pace of the poem in the second stanza? Why does the pace remain slower for the remainder of the poem?

4. **Theme.** What issues does the accident raise in the poet's mind? Explain the questions, "Who shall die?" and "Who is innocent?" Why is it that the accident "Cancels our physics with a sneer"?

John Berryman

1914–1972

John Berryman was the son of an Oklahoma farmer who committed suicide while the poet was still young. He capped a brilliant undergraduate career at Columbia by earning a scholarship to England's Cambridge University, where he studied Shakespeare and the English Renaissance poets. Berryman returned to the United States in 1939 and taught briefly at Detroit's Wayne State University before moving on to Princeton, where a writing fellowship enabled him to assimilate the influences of Auden, Yeats, and the English classical writers within his own distinct style and voice. It was during this fertile period that Berryman wrote the 115 poems of his *Berryman's Sonnets*, which he withheld from publication until 1967, and the short poems that appeared in 1948 in his first volume, *The Dispossessed*. "The Ball Poem," which appeared in that collection, characteristically focuses on the experience of loss by describing a little boy's dawning awareness of its central place in the adult world. Berryman's *Homage to Mistress Bradstreet*, a sequence of 57 eight-line poems, explored the experience of social and personal alienation common to both the Puritan and the contemporary poet. The enigmatic *Dream Songs*, published in their final form in 1969, is Berryman's masterpiece. Each poem of three six-line stanzas constitutes one element of a multi-layered, surrealistic excursion among the shifting identities of a single protagonist, referred to by such names as "Henry," "Huffy Henry," "Sir Bones," and "Henry Pussy-cat," to name but a few. Many of the autobiographical overtones of this work, including alcoholism and psychological fragmentation, prefigure Berryman's death by suicide in 1972.

The Ball Poem

What is the boy now, who has lost his ball,
What, what is he to do? I saw it go
Merrily bouncing, down the street, and then
Merrily over—there it is in the water!
No use to say "O there are other balls":   5
An ultimate shaking grief fixes the boy
As he stands rigid, trembling, staring down
All his young days into the harbor where
His ball went. I would not intrude on him,
A dime, another ball, is worthless. Now   10
He senses first responsibility
In a world of possessions. People will take balls,
Balls will be lost always, little boy,
And no one buys a ball back. Money is external.
He is learning, well behind his desperate eyes,   15
The epistemology[1] of loss, how to stand up
Knowing what every man must one day know
And most know many days, how to stand up.
And gradually light returns to the street,
A whistle blows, the ball is out of sight,   20
Soon part of me will explore the deep and dark
Floor of the harbor . . . I am everywhere,
I suffer and move, my mind and my heart move
With all that move me, under the water
Or whistling, I am not a little boy.   25

---

1. **epistemology** (i pis' tə mäl' ə jē): the study of or a theory of the
nature and grounds of knowledge.

Getting at Meaning

1. What scene does the speaker see before him in
lines 1-10? Why is he moved by the scene?

2. Explain the statement, "And no one buys a ball
back." Explain the phrase "epistemology of loss."
What must the boy learn, according to this poem?

Developing Skills in Reading Literature

1. **Symbol.** The ball is a symbol for loss in this
poem. What are some of the separate things it might
represent? Consider the ball as a physical object. Why
is it an appropriate object to use as a many-faceted
symbol?

2. **Theme.** According to the poet, the boy must
learn

. . . how to stand up
Knowing what every man must one day know
And most know many days, how to stand up.

Explain these lines. What reaction to loss do they call
for? According to lines 19 and 20, what will eventually
happen after loss?

Explain the final lines of the poem. What is the
speaker feeling? What does he imply about experience
when he says, "Soon part of me will explore the deep
and dark/Floor of the harbor. . . ."?

Contemporary Poets

SONG OF ESTHER, 1958. *Abraham Rattner.*
Collection of Whitney Museum of American Art.
Gift of the Friends of the Whitney Museum of American Art.

Elizabeth Bishop

1911–1979

Like the poems of Marianne Moore, whom she greatly admired, Elizabeth Bishop's poetry is noted for its technical craftsmanship, its enlightened but not inflated diction, and most especially its precise observations encompassing a wide range of subject matter and settings. Movement and travel from one locale to another are important features of her work. Her first volume, *North and South*, published in 1946, contains the same absorption with place setting and descriptive detail that is evident in such later works as *A Cold Spring, Question of Travel*, and *Geography III*. In settings as varied as Nova Scotia, where she was raised, to the Brazil where she lived for sixteen years, Bishop turns an uncompromisingly clear, yet ultimately sympathetic and humane, eye upon the "found objects" that cross under her vision.

Born in Worcester, Massachusetts, Bishop grew up under her grandparents' care following the death of her father and her mother's debilitating mental illness. Her autobiographical story, "In the Village," draws upon these experiences in its presentation of a child acutely sensitive to the sights and sounds of a Nova Scotia village and the searing screams of a mother trapped in madness. Observation and involvement in the objective world become a form of emotional self-preservation and a means of accepting and overcoming the pain and bitterness that are inevitably drawn from, as she says in "At the Fishhouses," "the cold hard mouth of the world."

House Guest

The sad seamstress
who stays with us this month
is small and thin and bitter.
No one can cheer her up.
Give her a dress, a drink,   5
roast chicken, or fried fish—
it's all the same to her.

She sits and watches TV.
No, she watches zigzags.
"Can you adjust the TV?"   10
"No," she says. No hope.
She watches on and on,
without hope, without air.

Her own clothes give us pause,
but she's not a poor orphan.   15
She has a father, a mother,
and all that, and she's earning
quite well, and we're stuffing
her with fattening foods.

We invite her to use the binoculars.   20
We say, "Come see the jets!"
We say, "Come see the baby!"
Or the knife grinder who cleverly
plays the National Anthem
on his wheel so shrilly.   25
Nothing helps.

She speaks: "I need a little
money to buy buttons."
She seems to think it's useless
to ask. Heavens, buy buttons,   30
if they'll do any good,
the biggest in the world—
by the dozen, by the gross!
Buy yourself an ice cream,
a comic book, a car!   35

Her face is closed as a nut,
closed as a careful snail
or a thousand-year-old seed.
Does she dream of marriage?
Of getting rich? Her sewing   40
is decidedly mediocre.

Please! Take our money! Smile!
What on earth have we done?
What has everyone done
and when did it all begin?   45
Then one day she confides
that she wanted to be a nun
and her family opposed her.

Perhaps we should let her go,
or deliver her straight off   50
to the nearest convent—and wasn't
her month up last week, anyway?
Can it be that we nourish
one of the Fates[1] in our bosoms?
Clotho,[2] sewing our lives   55
with a bony little foot
on a borrowed sewing machine,
and our fates will be like hers,
and our hems crooked forever?

---

1. **Fates:** the three goddesses of classical mythology who determine the course of human life. They are traditionally depicted as spinners.
2. **Clotho:** one of the three Fates, the one who measures out the thread of human life.

GIRL IN A WHITE BLOUSE, *Raphael Soyer.*
Metropolitan Museum of Art.
George A. Hearn Fund.

Getting at Meaning

1. Describe the "house guest." Why does she upset the speaker?

2. What reason does the poem suggest for the seamstress's melancholy?

Developing Skills in Reading Literature

1. **Simile.** Notice the similes the speaker uses to develop the character of the seamstress. Her face is "closed as a nut,/closed as a careful snail/or a thousand-year-old seed." These similes conjure up an entire personality, an approach to life. Why are they such apt comparisons?

2. **Character.** Notice the details of the seamstress's behavior that are especially indicative of character. Why does she watch zigzags on the television screen? What are her own clothes like? What is the quality of her sewing? What efforts do the family members make to amuse her? What is invariably the response? Why does the speaker say, "Please! Take our money! Smile!"? Explain the question, "What has everyone done/and when did it all begin?" Which line in the poem characterizes the way the seamstress lives?

3. **Theme.** What does the speaker recognize about the seamstress, as suggested by the allusion to Clotho and the Fates? Explain the final lines of the poem. What unsettling reminder about humanity does the seamstress evoke in the speaker?

Gwendolyn Brooks

born in 1917

Gwendolyn Brooks moved as a child from her birthplace in Topeka, Kansas, to Chicago, whose urban topography provided her with much of her material. A published poet by thirteen, Brooks practiced her craft throughout high school and junior college. Her technical mastery was already evident by 1945 with the publication of her first complete collection, *A Street in Bronzeville.* As its name implies, *Bronzeville* is a portrait of ghetto life, much of it rendered in tightly constructed sonnet and ballad forms. Brooks's disciplined ability to craft lines rich in piquant imagery is evident in *Annie Allen*, for which she won the 1950 Pulitzer Prize. *Annie Allen* is a novelistic verse sequence that uses several formal styles to articulate universal themes of loss and triumph. Brooks's voice changed in such later works as *The Bean Eaters*, *In the Mecca*, and *Riot*. Although still controlled, her language became freer and even more emphatic as Brooks responded to the upheavals accompanying the social changes of the 1950's and 1960's. In addressing such topics as Malcolm X, the martyred Medgar Evers, street gang warfare, and urban riots, Brooks became an advocate of liberation, joining the chorus of a new generation of black writers such as Don Lee and Nikki Giovanni. Brooks's social consciousness and her participation as an artist in the life of her wider community has made her a nurturing force in the contemporary scene. As a teacher, a sponsor of poetry competitions for young writers, a tireless and compelling reader of her own powerful work, and the reigning Poet Laureate of Illinois, Brooks has emerged as nothing less than a living American treasure.

Life for My Child Is Simple

Life for my child is simple, and is good.
He knows his wish. Yes, but that is not all.
Because I know mine too.
And we both want joy of undeep and unabiding things,
Like kicking over a chair or throwing blocks out of a window   5
Or tipping over an ice box pan
Or snatching down curtains or fingering an electric outlet
Or a journey or a friend or an illegal kiss.
No. There is more to it than that.
It is that he has never been afraid.   10
Rather, he reaches out and lo the chair falls with a beautiful crash,
And the blocks fall, down on the people's heads,
And the water comes slooshing sloppily out across the floor.
And so forth.
Not that success, for him, is sure, infallible.   15
But never has he been afraid to reach.
His lesions[1] are legion.
But reaching is his rule.

---

1. **lesion** (lē′ zhən): abnormal change due to injury or disease.

Getting at Meaning

1. What difference does the speaker see between herself and her son? In what line does she express this difference?

2. What are the "undeep and unabiding things" the speaker and her son both enjoy?

3. Explain the line, "His lesions are legion."

Developing Skills in Reading Literature

1. **Poetry.** Poetry is an arrangement of lines in which form and content fuse to suggest meanings beyond the literal meanings of the words. The language of poetry is compressed, without extraneous words. The language also is musical, enhancing meaning through the sounds of words and phrases and through the sound patterns of lines and stanzas.

Gwendolyn Brooks has defined poetry as "distilling reality." This poem is conversational, in some ways like prose. What qualities make it clearly a poem? How does the stanza form serve the poem? In what ways does the poem "distill reality"?

2. **Theme.** Why does the speaker say life for her child ". . . is simple, and is good"? What is hopeful in the line, "But never has he been afraid to reach"? In spite of his "lesions," what will probably be his approach to life?

The Explorer

Somehow to find a still spot in the noise
Was the frayed inner want, the winding, the frayed hope
Whose tatters he kept hunting through the din.
A velvet peace somewhere.
A room of wily[1] hush somewhere within.   5

So tipping down the scrambled halls he set
Vague hands on throbbing knobs. There were behind
Only spiraling, high human voices,
The scream of nervous affairs,
Wee griefs,
Grand griefs. And choices.   10

He feared most of all the choices, that cried to be taken.

There were no bourns.[2]
There were no quiet rooms.

---

1. **wily** (wī′ lē): sly, crafty.
2. **bourn:** boundary or limit.

Developing Skills in Reading Literature

1. **Diction: Connotation.** The central character of this poem is searching for a "velvet peace." What does the word *velvet* connote? Why does he want a "wily hush"? What words in the poem suggest the confusion and noise that generally surround the man?

2. **Character.** Why does the poet describe the man's "inner want" and his "hope" as "frayed"? What does the word *tatters* imply? What other details suggest that the man has been disappointed? Why does he fear choices? Sadly, what does he discover? What is the tone of the title? Is the same tone continued throughout the poem? Explain your answer.

3. **Rhyme.** Notice the subtle use of rhyme in this poem. Where does it appear? What effect does it have? Why are the quiet rhymes especially appropriate in the description of this character?

The Sonnet-Ballad

Oh mother, mother, where is happiness?
They took my lover's tallness off to war.
Left me lamenting. Now I cannot guess
What I can use an empty heart-cup for.
He won't be coming back here any more.   5
Some day the war will end, but, oh, I knew
When he went walking grandly out that door
That my sweet love would have to be untrue.
Would have to be untrue. Would have to court
Coquettish death, whose impudent and strange   10
Possessive arms and beauty (of a sort)
Can make a hard man hesitate—and change.
And he will be the one to stammer, "Yes."
Oh mother, mother, where is happiness?

Developing Skills in Reading Literature

1. **Ballad.** A ballad is a narrative poem that is meant to be sung. Ballads usually begin abruptly, focus on a single tragic incident, contain dialogue and repetition, and imply more than they actually tell. Discuss how this poem fits the definition of a ballad. What gives the poem musical qualities?

2. **Sonnet.** Explain how the sonnet form functions in this poem. Is it an Italian or an English sonnet?

3. **Figurative Language.** Death is personified in this poem. How does the speaker perceive death? Why is death a rival?

What is the metaphor the speaker uses for her heart? Why is it appropriate?

4. **Theme.** What view of war does this poem project? What does it suggest is the most tragic aspect of war?

Robert Lowell
1917–1977

Robert Lowell wrote poems in which, as he put it, "the reader was to believe he was getting the *real* Robert Lowell." Regarded by many critics as the preeminent American poet of the post World War II era, Lowell created a body of literature over the thirty-five years of his active career that recapitulated the life of a nation as it expressed the intense sensibilities of the poet. In truth, there were several Robert Lowells, each of whom addressed private and public experience from a differ-

ent platform at different moments of his life. An anguished Catholic convert in *Lord Weary's Castle*, published in 1946, Lowell emerged from a period of emotional breakdown as the "Confessional" voice of his masterful *Life Studies*, published in 1959. The Lowell of *For the Union Dead*, published in 1964, commented woefully on the public condition from the perspective of a private awareness. Finally, in his last decade, beginning with *Notebooks* and ending with *Day by Day* in 1977, Lowell erased the distinction between public and private realms by creating a freer form to assess and sift through the totality of his consciousness.

Through a family ancestry extending back to the Pilgrims, Lowell always felt himself inextricably linked to the nation's history and identity. Born in Boston, he attended Harvard before leaving there to study under John Crowe Ransom at Kenyon College. He earned his degree in 1940, the same year he married the novelist Jean Stafford and converted to Catholicism. In so doing, he implicitly rejected a Protestant upbringing epitomized by the Puritanical preachings of Jonathan Edwards, whose Calvinist morality Lowell would later re-create in "Mr. Edwards and the Spider." As "a fire-breathing Catholic C.O. (Conscientious Objector)," Lowell vehemently opposed Allied bombings of civilian population centers during World War II, and for his stand as a conscientious objector he endured five months of imprisonment. The publication of *Lord Weary's Castle* established Lowell's reputation and earned him a Pulitzer Prize. Lowell transformed the trauma of the succeeding years, including the collapse of a marriage, of his faith, and of his emotional well-being, into the aesthetic triumph of *Life Studies*. Sylvia Plath described *Life Studies* as an exciting, intense, and personally influential "breakthrough into very serious, very personal emotional experience." In many respects, the later Lowell was a poet of his times precisely because of his ability to locate his private anguish within a public context that included the shared traumas of racial unrest, political assassinations, and Vietnam. Robert Lowell is an important poet not only because he wrote so well but also because his work demonstrates why poetry is necessary.

Water

It was a Maine lobster town—
each morning boatloads of hands
pushed off for granite
quarries on the islands,

and left dozens of bleak   5
white frame houses stuck
like oyster shells
on a hill of rock,

and below us, the sea lapped
the raw little match-stick   10
mazes of a weir,[1]
where the fish for bait were trapped.

Remember? We sat on a slab of rock.
From this distance in time,
it seems the color   15
of iris, rotting and turning purpler,

but it was only
the usual gray rock
turning the usual green
when drenched by the sea.   20

The sea drenched the rock
at our feet all day,
and kept tearing away
flake after flake.

One night you dreamed   25
You were a mermaid clinging to
        a wharf-pile,
and trying to pull
off the barnacles with your hands.

We wished our two souls
might return like gulls   30
to the rock. In the end,
the water was too cold for us.

---

1. **weir** (wir): a fence or enclosure set in a waterway, for taking fish.

Developing Skills in Reading Literature

1. **Symbol.** In this complex poem the poet presents the deterioration of a relationship between two people by creating a harsh, rather forbidding natural scene. What does the slab of rock represent in the relationship? What does the sea acting on the rock symbolize? Explain the symbolism of the mermaid dream.

2. **Rhyme.** Notice the subtle rhymes in this poem. Where do you hear actual end rhyme? Where do you hear off-rhymes? How do the off-rhymes underscore the content of the poem?

3. **Theme.** The poet puts the failed relationship of the two people into a larger context. By presenting the breakdown between them in terms of natural imagery, what does he seem to suggest about their separation? What does the final line of the poem imply about the relationship?

Developing Writing Skills

Analyzing Imagery. The imagery in this poem develops the poem's content, the severed relationship between two people. In a brief composition analyze precisely how the imagery depicts the growing coldness and separation between the two people. Consider the hard, desolate images of the first three stanzas, the slab of rock, the shifting colors, the action of the sea on the rock, the mermaid dream, and the water itself.

May Swenson

born in 1919

May Swenson writes that poetry is "based in a craving to get through the curtains of things as they *appear*, to things as they *are*, and then into the larger, wilder space of things as they are *becoming*." In order to reach this point, Swenson encourages readers to use all five senses in experiencing a poem. To this end, she likes to create new forms for her work, often shaping her words into typed pictures. Despite her experimental tendencies, critics regard her as a serious writer with a gift for expressing ordinary ideas in new and unusual ways. Swenson has received many awards for her books, which include *Poems To Solve, To Mix with Time, Half Sun Half Sleep,* and *New and Selected Things Taking Place.*

The daughter of Swedish parents, Swenson was born in Logan, Utah, and graduated from Utah State University. In addition to her writing, Swenson has taught at several universities and worked as an editor at New Directions, an innovative New York publishing house.

By Morning

Some for everyone
  plenty

and more coming

Fresh   dainty   airily arriving
  everywhere at once   5

Transparent at first
  each faint slice
  slow   soundlessly tumbling

  then quickly thickly a gracious fleece
  will spread like youth   like wheat   10
  over the city

Each building will be   a hill
  all sharps made round

  dark worn noisy narrows made still
  wide   flat   clean   spaces   15

Streets will be   fields
  cars be   fumbling sheep

A deep bright harvest will be seeded
  in a night

By morning we'll be   children   20
  feeding on manna[1]

  a new loaf on every doorsill

---

1. **manna:** a food miraculously supplied to the Israelites
in their journey through the wilderness; a sudden and
unexpected source of gratification, pleasure, or gain.

Developing Skills in Reading Literature

1. **Imagery.** The imagery of this poem reveals the natural process that the poet is describing. Notice that what is coming is "dainty" and "airily arriving." What images suggest its color? What is the transforming effect it has on "dark worn noisy narrows"?

2. **Structure.** While "By Morning" is not exactly a concrete poem, its shape does bear a close relationship to the process it describes. Explain this relationship. Observe the spacing among words in the various lines. Why are the words in line 4 so far apart? Why are they close together in lines 5 and 14? Why are they widely spaced in line 15?

3. **Tone.** Comment on the tone of this poem. How does the simile "spread like youth" affect the tone? What does the metaphor "A deep bright harvest" contribute to the tone? What is the tone of the final two lines?

Richard Wilbur

born in 1921

With wit, erudition, and obvious delight in the formal powers of language, Wilbur captures the ways by which the human mind imbues the world and existence with significances beyond the apparent and ordinary. He does so in formally tight and controlled patterns that distinguish him from many of his contemporaries. So, too, does his insistence on an emotional restraint which he once explained by noting that he had always assumed that in the fairy tale, the genie's strength resulted from his confinement inside the bottle.

Born in New York City, Wilbur attended Amherst College. After service as an infantryman during World War II, he earned a higher degree at Harvard, where he later taught. In 1947 his first complete volume, *The Beautiful Changes and Other Poems*, was published, in which Wilbur expressed his characteristic appreciation of the material world's sensate beauty. Similarly, in *Things of This World*, which earned him both a Pulitzer Prize and a National Book Award in 1957, Wilbur examined a variety of situations exemplifying the compound of the ordinary and the extra-ordinary which he regards as the essence of existence. In addition to teaching at Wellesley College and later at Wesleyan University, Wilbur

Thomas Victor

has produced over eight volumes of original verse, a volume of literary criticism, and numerous translations of diverse writers, from Voltaire and Molière to Joseph Brodsky and Jorge Luis Borges.

Boy at the Window

Seeing the snowman standing all alone
In dusk and cold is more than he can bear.
The small boy weeps to hear the wind prepare
A night of gnashings and enormous moan.
His tearful sight can hardly reach to where   5
The pale-faced figure with bitumen[1] eyes
Returns him such a god-forsaken stare
As outcast Adam gave to Paradise.

The man of snow is, nonetheless, content,
Having no wish to go inside and die.   10
Still, he is moved to see the youngster cry.
Though frozen water is his element,
He melts enough to drop from one soft eye
A trickle of the purest rain, a tear
For the child at the bright pane surrounded by   15
Such warmth, such light, such love, and so much fear.

---

1. **bitumen** (bĭ tōō′ mən). soft coal

Getting at Meaning

1. Why does the boy pity the snowman?
2. Why does the snowman pity the boy?

Developing Skills in Reading Literature

1. **Figurative Language.** What lines in the first stanza suggest the harshness of the winter night? What is the implied metaphor in these lines? What words characterize the snowman? Comment on why the simile in line 7 and 8 is appropriate?

What figure of speech is basic to the second stanza? Why is the snowman's tear "A trickle of the purest rain"? What does "the bright pane" suggest?

2. **Stanza.** The two stanzas of the poem depict the points of view of two characters. In what ways are these stanzas balanced, or equal? Scan the stanzas. How does the meter contribute to the effectiveness of the poem? How about the rhyme?

3. **Tone.** Characterize the tone of the poem. Why is *fear* the last word of the poem? In what lines does awareness of the harshness and frailty that exist in the world temper the speaker's feelings of warmth and amusement?

Digging for China

"Far enough down is China," somebody
said.
"Dig deep enough and you might see the sky
As clear as at the bottom of a well.
Except it would be real—a different sky.
Then you could burrow down until you   5
came
To China! Oh, it's nothing like New Jersey.
There's people, trees, and houses, and all
that,
But much, much different. Nothing
looks the same."

I went and got the trowel out of the shed
And sweated like a coolie all that   10
morning,
Digging a hole beside the lilac-bush,
Down on my hands and knees. It was a sort
Of praying, I suspect. I watched my hand
Dig deep and darker, and I tried and tried
To dream a place where nothing was the   15
same.
The trowel never did break through to blue.

Before the dream could weary of itself
My eyes were tired of looking into
darkness,
My sunbaked head of hanging down a hole.
I stood up in a place I had forgotten,   20
Blinking and staggering while the earth
went round
And showed me silver barns, the fields
dozing
In palls of brightness, patens[1] growing
and gone
In the tides of leaves, and the whole sky
china blue.
Until I got my balance back again   25
All that I saw was China, China, China.

---

1. **paten:** a plate, usually made of precious metal and used to carry bread at the Eucharist; a metal disk resembling a plate.

Developing Skills in Reading Literature

1. **Imagery.** Through imagery the poet develops the meaning of China to the speaker. In what lines does he describe the way that the speaker digs? Why does the speaker keep going? Why does he or she stop? Notice the imagery in the final five lines of the poem. How is the speaker's usual environment characterized? Why is it made to seem so peaceful and appealing?

2. **Symbol.** Describe some of the various things that China represents to the speaker. It is a complex symbol in the poem. When the speaker stops digging, why is the sky "china blue"?

3. **Theme.** The speaker tried "To dream a place where nothing was the same" and became obsessed with a vision of China. What did the speaker learn? What is implied by the line, "Until I got my balance back again"?

4. **Blank Verse.** Comment on how blank verse suits the tone, content, and pace of the poem.

Developing Vocabulary

Word Origins. This poem contains the word *coolie*, which comes from the Hindi word *kuli*. *Lilac*, another word in this poem, also has a Middle Eastern/Asian origin.

All six of the words below have Middle Eastern/Asian origins. Look up each word in a dictionary that contains word origins. Record the origin, and for an unfamiliar word, the definition.

lilac	satrap
magic	seersucker
paradise	tulip

Denise Levertov

born in 1923

Thomas Victor

Denise Levertov evolved, as she put it, from a "British Romantic with almost Victorian background to an American poet." That evolutionary process began a year after her marriage in 1947 to the American novelist Mitchell Goodman, when she moved to the United States from her native England. That move, she later wrote, " . . . necessitated the finding of new rhythms in which to write, in accordance with new rhythms of life and speech." *Here and Now*, her first American collection of verse, appeared in 1957 and reflects the acknowledged influences of William Carlos Williams, Wallace Stevens, and the Black Mountain Projectivist poet Charles Olson, who argued for an anti-rationalist poetry conceived of as "at all points . . . a high energy-construct and at all points, an energy discharge." Energized juxtapositions of perceived objects are indeed a characteristic of Levertov's work, both in *Here and Now* and in *The Jacob's Ladder*. The title poem of *O Taste and See*, published in 1964, typifies Levertov's engagement with "all that lives." Such a sense of affiliation underlies the more somber and overtly political tones of her more recent work, in which she recoils from the horrors of the Vietnam War and expresses her revulsion for humanity's capacity to destroy and despoil.

O Taste and See

The world is
not with us enough.

O TASTE AND SEE

the subway Bible poster said,
meaning THE LORD, meaning   5
if anything all that lives
to the imagination's tongue,

grief, mercy, language,
tangerine, weather, to
breathe them, bite,   10
savor, chew, swallow, transform

into our flesh our
deaths, crossing the street, plum, quince,
living in the orchard and being

hungry, and plucking   15
the fruit.

Developing Skills in Reading Literature

1. **Theme.** What is the definition of the Lord given in this poem? What view of religion does the poet present in lines 7-16? What attitude toward life do the verbs in lines 10 and 11 imply?

2. **Allusion.** The first two lines of this poem are an ironic allusion to Wordsworth's fourteenth sonnet, a famous poem that begins, "The world is too much with us. . . ." Explain Levertov's meaning in inverting the Wordsworth line.

A second allusion in this poem is to the Garden of Eden. In which line do you find it? What does the poet suggest that humans should do with the fruit of paradise?

3. **Imagery.** What does Levertov say that humans should "TASTE AND SEE"? Observe the way that words and images come one after the other in lines 7-16. What is appropriate about presenting the images in this form?

Merritt Parkway

As if it were
forever that they move, that we
  keep moving—

     Under a wan sky where
     as the lights went on a star   5
         pierced the haze & now
     follows steadily
             a constant
     above our six lanes
     the dreamlike continuum . . .   10

And the people—ourselves!
  the humans from inside the
cars, apparent
only at gasoline stops
           unsure,   15
  eyeing each other

     drink coffee hastily at the
     slot machines & hurry
  back to the cars
    vanish   20
     into them forever, to
     keep moving—

Houses now & then beyond the
sealed road, the trees/trees, bushes
passing by, passing   25

    the cars that
      keep moving ahead of
  us, past us, pressing behind us
            and
       over left, those that come   30
    toward us shining too brightly
moving relentlessly

   in six lanes, gliding
north & south, speeding with
a slurred sound—   35

Developing Skills in Reading Literature

1. **Imagery.** What picture of the six-lane express-way does this poem create? Why does it seem as if the cars will move forever? Why is the sky "wan"? Why do the six lanes seem like "a dreamlike continuum"? In lines 23-32, what does the poet describe? Why is the road "sealed"? What does the final image, "speeding with/a slurred sound—" imply?

2. **Theme.** What does this poem have to say about the way that people are always on the move? Notice that the phrase "keep moving" is repeated three times. The poet describes the cars in a nearby lane as "moving relentlessly." What do these phrases suggest? What lines indicate that people are more comfortable moving than being still and communicating with each other?

3. **Structure.** How does the shape, or format of this poem reflect its meaning? Observe which words appear separated as phrases on individual lines. Observe which words and lines are run together. How does the structure of this poem comment on the structure of contemporary American life?

James Dickey

born in 1923

In *Self-Interviews*, James Dickey wrote, "The relationship of the human being to the great natural cycles of birth and death, the seasons, the growing up of seasons out of dead leaves, the generations of animals and of men, all on the heraldic wheel of existence is very beautiful to me." That relationship, as rendered imaginatively and subjectively in his poetry and in his novel *Deliverance*, becomes the spur prompting Dickey toward such recurring themes as the beauty of nature's violent purity, the nonrational role of memory as a means of understanding life, and the individual's often violent encounters with danger and death. The close correspondence between these themes and Dickey's life is suggested by his love for hunting and the outdoors, his overtly autobiographical poems, and his experience flying nightfighters during World War II and the Korean War. In the latter role, he was cited three times for bravery.

Dickey was born in Atlanta and educated first at Clemson and later at Vanderbilt University. Beginning in 1960 with the publication of *Into the Stone*, Dickey's verse has attracted a growing audience of admirers. In *Buckdancer's Choice*, the recipient of a 1966 National Book Award, Dickey moved to what he called an "open poem" style, typified by "In the Pocket." "I was interested," he wrote, " . . . in getting an optimum presentational immediacy . . . that would cause the reader to forget literary judgments entirely and simply experience." Dickey is a versatile writer of poems, novels, screenplays, and criticism. He is currently an English professor and Writer-in-Residence at the University of South Carolina.

The Heaven of Animals

Here they are. The soft eyes open.
If they have lived in a wood
It is a wood.
If they have lived on plains
It is grass rolling   5
Under their feet forever.

Having no souls, they have come,
Anyway, beyond their knowing.
Their instincts wholly bloom
And they rise.   10
The soft eyes open.

To match them, the landscape flowers,
Outdoing, desperately
Outdoing what is required:
The richest wood,   15
The deepest field.

For some of these,
It could not be the place
It is, without blood.
These hunt, as they have done,   20
But with claws and teeth grown perfect,

More deadly than they can believe.
They stalk more silently,
And crouch on the limbs of trees,
And their descent   25
Upon the bright backs of their prey

May take years
In a sovereign floating of joy.
And those that are hunted
Know this as their life,   30
Their reward: to walk

Under such trees in full knowledge
Of what is in glory above them,
And to feel no fear,
But acceptance, compliance.   35
Fulfilling themselves without pain

At the cycle's center,
They tremble, they walk
Under the tree,
They fall, they are torn,   40
They rise, they walk again.

Getting at Meaning

1. According to the speaker, what is the heaven of animals like as a physical place?

2. What happens to the instincts of the animals in heaven? Explain the statement, repeated twice, "The soft eyes open."

3. What is heaven like for the hunter animals? For the hunted?

Developing Skills in Reading Literature

1. **Imagery.** The underlying conception of this poem is extremely imaginative. Which lines and stanzas present vivid and imaginative images? Notice all the superlatives in this poem: "wholly bloom," "richest," "deepest," "grown perfect," "full knowledge." What do these words and phrases contribute to the poem's imagery?

2. **Irony.** Ironically, what continues to happen in the heaven of this poem? Why is it still heaven?

3. **Theme.** Comment on the appropriateness of the reward for the hunter animals. Explain what the poet means when he describes the reward for the hunted animals in lines 31-36. Why does the poet view acceptance of the life cycle, of the way things are, as a reward?

In the Pocket

NFL

Going backward
All of me and some
Of my friends are forming a shell   my arm is looking
Everywhere and some are breaking
In   breaking down   5
And out   breaking
Across, and one is going deep   deeper
Than my arm. Where is Number One hooking
Into the violent green alive
With linebackers! I cannot find him he cannot beat   10
His man   I fall back more
Into the pocket   it is raging and breaking
Number Two has disappeared into the chalk
Of the sideline   Number Three is cutting with half
A step of grace   my friends are crumbling   15
Around me the wrong color
Is looming   hands are coming
Up and over between
My arm and Number Three: throw it hit him in the middle
Of his enemies   hit move scramble   20
Before death and the ground
Come up   LEAP STAND KILL DIE STRIKE

Now.

Developing Skills in Reading Literature

1. **Speaker.** Identify the speaker of this poem. In what action is he engaged? Which lines reflect a stream-of-consciousness technique in developing the action of the poem?

2. **Structure.** "In the Pocket" is in many ways similar to a concrete poem. What does the arrangement of words on the page suggest? Why are there unusual breaks in some of the lines, such as lines 5, 11, and 17? How does the structure affect the meaning of the poem?

3. **Rhythm.** Characterize the rhythm of this poem. How do the present participles affect the rhythm? How does alliteration contribute? Which consonant sounds often are repeated? What repetends do you find in the poem? What do they contribute? Why is line 22 written in the way that it is? How does the rhythm of the poem underscore the poem's content?

Developing Writing Skills

Writing a Concrete Poem. Write a concrete poem, or one that visually presents something important about the poem's meaning. Remember that in concrete poetry a direct and obvious relationship exists between form and meaning. Besides the Dickey poem, you may want to study "The Sky" by E. E. Cummings, "By Morning" by May Swenson, and "Merritt Parkway" by Denise Levertov before you begin to write.

David Wagoner

born in 1926

Born in Massillon, Ohio, the novelist and poet David Wagoner is associated with the Pacific Northwest, where he teaches at the University of Washington. Wagoner derives much of his subject matter by exploring man's involvement—as a cultivator, hunter, and survivor—with an enveloping natural world. Sometimes, as in "Elegy for Simon Corl, Botanist," that involvement is an intimate one, in which he alludes to special kinds of knowledge that result from such intimacy. At other times, as in "A Guide to Dungeness Spit," Wagoner places the narrator in the position of looking at the natural world. Wagoner's imposition on the external landscape of subjective and even surreal images, especially evident in his early *Dry Sun, Dry Wind*, is reminiscent of the work of Theodore Roethke, under whom Wagoner studied at Penn State and at Washington. Roethke's overt influence diminishes in such later works as *The Nesting Ground* and *Staying Alive*, which rely on freer forms and more muted images. Nonetheless, Wagoner continues to probe, as did Roethke, the use of poetry as a means of defining and asserting individual identity.

Elegy for Simon Corl, Botanist

With wildflowers bedded in his mind,
My blind great-uncle wrote a book.
His lips and beard were berry-stained,
Wrist broken like a shepherd's crook.

His door leaned open to the flies,   5
And May, like tendrils, wandered in.
The earth rose gently to his knees;
The clouds moved closer than his skin.

Sun against ear, he heard the slight
Stamen and pistil[1] touch for days,   10
Felt pollen cast aslant like light
Into the shadows of his eyes.

When autumn stalked the leaves, he curled;
His fingers ripened like the sky;
His ink ran to a single word,   15
And the straight margin went awry.

When frost lay bristling on the weeds,
He smoothed it with a yellow thumb,
Followed his white cane to the woods
Between the saxifrage[2] and thyme,   20

And heard the hornets crack like ice,
Felt worms arch backward in the snow;
And while the mites died under moss,
The clean scar sang across his brow.

THE BLIND BOTANIST, 1954. *Ben Shahn.*
Courtesy Wichita Art Museum.

---

1. **Stamen and pistil:** the male and female organs of a seed plant.
2. **saxifrage** (sak′ sə frij): perennial herbs with showy flowers.

Developing Skills in Reading Literature

1. **Synesthesia.** Synesthesia refers to a situation in which one type of sensory stimulation evokes the sensation of another sense. For example, hearing a sound might result in visualizing a scene. In this way a person can be said to sometimes "see" a sound. Poets employ synesthesia in their imagery to achieve unusual, thought-provoking effects.

In this poem the botanist "hears" the stamen and pistil touch. He feels pollen ". . . cast aslant like light." How does he "see" the wildflowers alluded to in the first line? Notice how his scar "sings." Blind as he is, how is this botanist able to visualize nature? Explain how synesthesia is an important part of his life.

2. **Imagery.** This poem contains vivid sensory images other than synesthetic ones. What sounds predominate in the poem? What tactile images? Why is the poem decidedly visual, in spite of the subject's blindness?

3. **Simile.** Notice the similes in the poem: "like a shepherd's crook," "like the sky," "like light," "like tendrils," and "like ice." What do they all have in common? Why are they appropriate in this poem?

4. **Elegy.** Notice the comparative formality of this elegy. What structural device determines the progression of the stanzas? Why is this device appropriate to the subject matter of the poem? What is the meter of the poem? the rhyme scheme? Why do you suppose the poet chose rather traditional forms for his elegy?

5. **Character.** Why does the poet admire his great-uncle? What qualities in the botanist stand out in this poem?

Developing Vocabulary

Word Origins: Prefixes and Root Words. The prefix *syn* means "together or with." It can also mean "same or alike." Its use can be understood by breaking down the word *synesthesia*, which means "to feel together," and by extension, "to blend the senses."

Look up each word that follows in a dictionary, and record both its meaning and its root origin. Explain how the prefix *syn-* functions in each word.

synagogue	synergism
syncopation	syntax
syncope	synthesis
syndicate	

Developing Writing Skills

Writing an Elegy. Write a poem of tribute to someone famous, now dead, whose career you admire. Make it clear in your elegy why you admire the person. It may be someone recently deceased or someone from far back in history.

A. R. Ammons

born in 1926

The poetry of A.R. Ammons attempts to describe the exact details of an experience rather than impose an order upon that experience. In "Poetics" he suggests that he is " . . . not so much looking for the shape/ as being available/ to any shape that may be/ summoning itself/ through me/ from the self not mine but ours."

A prolific writer, Ammons grew up on a farm in Whiteville, North Carolina, and attended Wake Forest College and the University of California at Berkeley. At twenty-six he returned to North Carolina to take a position as an elementary school principal, later moving to New Jersey as an executive for a biologic glass company. His first collection of poetry, *Ommateum*, was published in 1955. Returning to the academic world in 1962 as an English professor at Cornell University, Ammons has produced steadily since his *Expressions of Sea Level* appeared in 1964. Not all his verse consists of lyrical response to natural stimuli; his *Tapes for the Turn of the Year* is a faithful account as recorded on rolls of adding machine tape of the often trivial details of an academic's life during an upstate New York winter. His *Collected Poems: 1951—1971* earned him a National Book Award, and he received the Bollingen Prize in 1975 for *Sphere: The Form of a Motion.*

This Bright Day

Earth, earth!
day, this bright day
again—once more
showers of dry spruce gold,
the poppy flopped broad open and delicate   5
from its pod—once more,
all this again: I've had many
days here with these stones and leaves:
like the sky, I've taken on a color
and am still: 10
the grief of leaves,
summer worms, huge blackant
queens bulging
from weatherboarding, all that
will pass   15
away from me that I will pass into,
none of the grief
cuts less now than ever—only I
have learned the
sky, the day sky, the blue   20
obliteration of radiance:
the night sky,
pregnant, lively,
tumultuous, vast—the grief
again in a higher scale   25
of leaves and poppies:
space, space—
and a grief of things.

Developing Skills in Reading Literature

1. **Imagery.** What natural change does the speaker allude to in the opening lines? What imagery develops this change? To what does the phrase "the grief of leaves" refer? To what end does the poet depict "summer worms" and "huge black ant/queens"? What contrast does he develop between the day sky and the night sky?

2. **Theme.** The speaker identifies closely with nature and feels a part of the natural process of change. Which lines indicate this? What has the speaker learned from observing nature? Explain the lines

> . . . all that
> will pass
> away from me that I will pass into,
> none of the grief
> cuts less now than ever . . .

3. **Tone.** The speaker feels exuberant delight in nature, which is "bright," "pregnant," and "lively." However, there is an undercurrent of sadness in the poem. The word *grief* appears four times. Why? What does the speaker mean when speaking of feeling "a grief of things"?

4. **Rhythm.** Notice that this poem is all one sentence. Why is this form appropriate? What punctuation marks keep the long sentence readable? What poetic devices keep this poem moving along at a fast pace?

James Wright

1927–1980

James Wright's first volume, *The Green Wall*, established his characteristic concerns with pain, isolation, and the often soothing correspondence of a phenomenal world that "affects the skin." The references to nature in this volume are drawn from Wright's native Midwest and are a prelude to the more surreal images of his later work, which connects the individual with an increasingly urban landscape. In *Shall We Gather at the River*, published in 1968, Wright turns to images some critics have categorized as "deep" or "subjective" due to their reference to the unconscious as the primary source of response to the external world. Such concerns and such techniques suggest the shaping influences on Wright's career of, among others, Robert Frost, E.A. Robinson, and Theodore Roethke.

Born in Martin's Ferry, Ohio, Wright studied at Kenyon College, the University of Vienna, and the University of Washington. In 1966 he joined the faculty of New York's Hunter College, where he was associated with such New York-based poets as Robert Bly, Louis Simpson, Jerome Rothenberg, and William Duffy.

Mutterings Over the Crib of a Deaf Child

"How will he hear the bell at school
Arrange the broken afternoon,
And know to run across the cool
Grasses where the starlings cry,
Or understand the day is gone?"   5

Well, someone lifting cautious brows
Will take the measure of the clock.
And he will see the birchen boughs
Outside the sagging dark from the sky,
And the shade crawling upon the rock.   10

"And how will he know to rise at morning?
His mother has other sons to waken,
She has the stove she must build to burning
Before the coals of the night-time die,
And he never stirs when he is shaken."   15

I take it the air affects the skin,
And you remember, when you were young,
Sometimes you could feel the dawn begin,
And the fire would call you, by and by,
Out of the bed and bring you along.   20

"Well, good enough. To serve his needs
All kinds of arrangements can be made.
But what will you do if his finger bleeds?
Or a bobwhite whistles invisibly
And flutes likes an angel off in the shade?"   25

He will learn pain. And, as for the bird,
It is always darkening when that comes out.
I will putter as though I had not heard,
And lift him into my arms and sing
Whether he hears my song or not.   30

Getting at Meaning

This poem is a series of questions and answers. Identify each separate question asked about the deaf child and explain the response.

Developing Skills in Reading Literature

1. **Speaker.** One speaker is conversing with another individual over the crib of a deaf child. In all probability, who is the questioning speaker? What is that speaker's attitude toward the child's affliction? How does this speaker's attitude differ from that of the other individual?

2. **Stanza.** In which three stanzas of the poem does the questioner address the other speaker? What is the visual clue that indicates this? In which three stanzas of the poem does the answering speaker reply?

The stanzas of this poem follow a rather traditional pattern. What do they all have in common? What meter prevails? What is the rhyme scheme of each stanza? How do the traditional forms serve this poem well?

3. **Theme.** According to the speaker who answers the questions, what must the deaf child develop? What must he observe? Comment on how synesthesia will enter into his life. The answering speaker says, "He will learn pain." What does the speaker intend to do to help counteract the pain?

Anne Sexton

1928–1974

Jill Krementz

Like her teacher Robert Lowell and her friend Sylvia Plath, Anne Sexton gave formal shape to the most turbulent and most personal of emotions and experiences. Her first volume, *To Bedlam and Part Way Back*, published in 1960, employs tightly controlled poetic forms to detail her own loss of emotional control during the 1950's and her travels "part way back" from those horrific depths. The centerpiece of the volume is "The Double Image," a long, evocative poem exploring personal feelings about a grandmother dying of cancer, a mother recovering from emotional traumas, and a young daughter who is the heir to such frailties. In "The Fortress," which appeared in her next volume, *All My Pretty Ones*, love is held up as the chief defense against the ravages of "life with its terrible changes." In the several works written prior to her suicide in 1974, Sexton turned toward free verse, which still conveyed the controlled diction evident in her early work. *Transformations*, published in 1971, features seventeen nightmarish re-creations of Grimm fairy tales.

Born in Newton, Massachusetts, Sexton attended junior college and worked as a fashion model before attending a poetry workshop at Boston University conducted by Robert Lowell in 1958. Stimulated by him and by W.D. Snodgrass, whose revealingly personal *Heart's Needle* had just been published, Sexton transformed her private griefs and sensibilities into an admirable body of poetry.

The Fortress

(While Taking a Nap with Linda)

Under the pink quilted covers,
I hold the pulse that counts your blood.
I think the woods outdoors
are half asleep,
left over from summer   5
like a stack of books after a flood,
left over like the promises I never keep.
On the right, the scrub pine tree
waits like a fruit store
holding up bunches of tufted broccoli.   10

We watch the wind from our square bed.
I press down my index finger,
half in jest, half in dread,
on the brown mole
under your left eye, inherited   15
from my right cheek—a spot of danger
where a bewitched worm ate its way through our soul
in search of beauty. Child, since July
the leaves have been fed
secretly from a pool of beet-red dye.   20

And sometimes they are battle green
with trunks as wet as hunters' boots,
smacked hard by the wind, clean
as oilskins. No,
the wind's not off the ocean.   25
Yes, it cried in your room like a wolf
and your ponytail hurt you. That was a long time ago.
The wind rolled the tide like a dying
woman. She wouldn't sleep;
she rolled there all night, grunting and sighing.   30

Darling, life is not in my hands;
life with its terrible changes
will take you, bombs or glands,
your own child at
your breast, your own house on your own land.   35
Outside, the bittersweet turns orange.
Before she died, my mother and I picked those fat
branches, finding orange nipples

on the gray wire strands.
We weeded the forest, curing trees like cripples.   40

Your feet thump-thump against my back
and you whisper to yourself. Child,
what are you wishing? What pact
are you making?
What mouse runs between your eyes? What ark   45
can I fill for you when the world goes wild?
The woods are under water, their weeds are shaking
in the tide; birches like zebra fish
flash by in a pack.
Child, I cannot promise that you will get your wish. 50

I cannot promise very much.
I give you the images I know.
Lie still with me and watch.
A pheasant moves
by like a seal, pulled through the mulch   55
by his thick white collar. He's on show
like a clown. He drags a beige feather that he removed,
one time, from an old lady's hat.
We laugh and we touch.
I promise you love. Time will not take away that.   60

Getting at Meaning

1. What lines in the poem indicate that the daughter is young and innocent?

2. What cannot the speaker promise her daughter? What is the one thing that she can promise?

Developing Skills in Reading Literature

1. **Figurative Language.** Specific figures of speech abound in this poem. Observe the three similes that characterize the woods in lines 5-10. Why are they effective? What two similes describe the wind? What do they both suggest? The poet also personifies the tide. In what terms does she see it?

2. **Imagery.** The speaker says to her sleeping daughter, "I cannot promise very much./I give you the images I know." What are some of the images she gives in this poem? For example, how does she account for the mole under her daughter's eye? What picture does she present of the pheasant? Why are all the images of the poem images from nature?

3. **Theme.** What attitude toward life is conveyed in the lines, "Darling, life is not in my hands;/life with its terrible changes"? What sobering reality does the reference to the speaker's own mother introduce? What is "the fortress" of the title, the one thing seen as certain?

Sylvia Plath

1932–1963

Rollie McKenna

During her brief and intense life, Sylvia Plath produced a small body of literature aimed straight at the heart of an obsessive personal torment that ultimately ended with her suicide in 1963.

The daughter of German immigrants, Plath was born in Boston and lived for the first eight years of her life in Winthrop, along the Massachusetts coast. Plath felt driven to excel even as a young child, which is when she first started to write poetry. The death of her father when she was eight, and the family's subsequent move back to suburban Boston, deeply affected her. Indeed, she was never able to resolve the contrary feelings of intense love and violent hatred she experienced toward her father, feelings which later emerged in such poems as "Daddy," "Lady Lazarus," and "The Arrival of the Bee Box." She earned a scholarship to Smith College, and while still a student won a literary competition sponsored by *Mademoiselle* magazine, which sent her to New York for a summer as an editorial apprentice. *The Bell Jar*, her fictionalized autobiography, focuses on the stresses and breakdowns of this period of her life. Graduating with high honors from Smith in 1955, Plath traveled to England's Cambridge University on a Fulbright Scholarship. There she met and married the English poet Ted Hughes and eventually became the mother of two children. A year of teaching at Smith preceded a final return to England in 1959. Plath wrote the majority of her poetry during the harrowing last four years of her life, a period of repeated breakdowns and recoveries. Often she would write two or three poems a day in an obvious effort to wrestle her demons to the ground. Her final, successful suicide attempt demonstrated her inability to do so.

The Arrival of the Bee Box

I ordered this, this clean wood box
Square as a chair and almost too heavy to lift.
I would say it was the coffin of a midget
Or a square baby
Were there not such a din in it.   5

The box is locked, it is dangerous.
I have to live with it overnight
And I can't keep away from it.
There are no windows, so I can't see what is in there.
There is only a little grid, no exit.   10

I put my eye to the grid.
It is dark, dark,
With the swarmy feeling of African hands
Minute and shrunk for export,
Black on black, angrily clambering.   15

How can I let them out?
It is the noise that appalls me most of all,
The unintelligible syllables.
It is like a Roman mob,
Small, taken one by one, but my god, together!   20

I lay my ear to furious Latin.
I am not a Caesar.
I have simply ordered a box of maniacs.
They can be sent back.
They can die, I need feed them nothing, I am the owner.   25

I wonder how hungry they are.
I wonder if they would forget me
If I just undid the locks and stood back and turned into a tree.
There is the laburnum,[1] its blond colonnades,
And the petticoats of the cherry.   30

---

1. **laburnum:** poisonous Eurasian shrubs and trees with bright
yellow flowers, often cultivated for Easter decoration.

They might ignore me immediately
In my moon suit and funeral veil.
I am no source of honey
So why should they turn on me?
Tomorrow I will be sweet God, I will set them free.   35

The box is only temporary.

Getting at Meaning

1. For what reason, presumably, has the speaker ordered the bee box? What is a bee box?

2. What aspect of the bee box bothers the speaker the most? Explain the meaning of line 35.

Developing Skills in Reading Literature

1. **Speaker.** The speaker in this poem narrates in a very personal, conversational way. Sylvia Plath generally spoke in her own voice in her poems, reflecting on nature, often, to bring to light human realities.

What are some of the separate fears the poet has about the bee box? What is her tone in the line, "They can die, I need feed them nothing, I am the owner"?

What is her tone in the line, "I am no source of honey"?

2. **Simile and Metaphor.** The poet uses some interesting comparisons to convey her fears about the bee box. In line 3 the box is a coffin. Why does she make this rather grim comparison, and so early in the poem? Why are the bees "like a Roman mob"? Why are they later "maniacs"?

3. **Imagery.** Describe the box physically. Why does it bother the poet that there are no windows? What is rather sinister in the scene she sees through the grid? What light and lyrical vision does she contrast to this later in the poem?

4. **Theme.** Explain why the poet decides to free the bees. Explain the lines, "The box is locked, it is dangerous" and "The box is only temporary."

Mirror

I am silver and exact. I have no preconceptions.
Whatever I see I swallow immediately
Just as it is, unmisted by love or dislike.
I am not cruel, only truthful—
The eye of a little god, four-cornered.   5
Most of the time I meditate on the opposite wall.
It is pink, with speckles. I have looked at it so long
I think it is a part of my heart. But it flickers.
Faces and darkness separate us over and over.

Now I am a lake. A woman bends over me,   10
Searching my reaches for what she really is.
Then she turns to those liars, the candles or the moon.
I see her back, and reflect it faithfully.
She rewards me with tears and an agitation of hands.
I am important to her. She comes and goes.   15
Each morning it is her face that replaces the darkness.
In me she has drowned a young girl, and in me an old woman
Rises toward her day after day, like a terrible fish.

Developing Skills in Reading Literature

1. **Speaker.** Who is the speaker in this poem? Characterize the speaker. Why is the speaker "exact"? why "truthful"? What lines suggest that the speaker feels emotion or possesses an attitude toward the reflections?

2. **Figurative Language.** A central personification of course governs this poem. Note the two comparisons of the second stanza. Why is the speaker "a lake"? Why is the rising old woman of the final lines "like a terrible fish"?

3. **Imagery.** This poem contains images of light and shadow. In what lines do you find them? Why are candles and the moon "liars"? Why is the image of the young girl drowning important?

Developing Writing Skills

Analyzing a Symbol. On a literal level the mirror in this poem is an actual mirror. It is also a complicated symbol. Write an analytical paragraph in which you explain the symbolism of this object in the poem. How does the imagery of light and shadow relate? Quote specific lines to support your ideas.

Alice Walker

born in 1944

Poet, novelist, and the author of a biography of Langston Hughes, Alice Walker focuses in her work on the psychological costs of social injustice as experienced by black individuals and families. Born in Eatonton, Georgia, she attended Spelman College before taking her degree at Sarah Lawrence College in 1965. She taught writing and literature at Jackson State College and Tougaloo College in Mississippi prior to moving to New England to teach at Wellesley College and the University of Massachusetts, Boston. Awarded several prizes and fellowships, including a National Endowment for the Arts grant, Walker has pursued a wide range of interests related to the black experience. The history of black women writers in America is a particular area of expertise. She has also been active in welfare rights and voter registration.

Her spare and unembellished poetry has been praised for its intelligence, wit, and sensitivity. Her second volume of poetry, *Revolutionary Petunias and Other Poems* (1973), was nominated for a National Book Award. In that year, she also published *In Love and Trouble: Stories of Black Women*, a collection of stories which received the Rosenthal Foundation Award from the National Institute of Arts and Letters. Her novel *The Third Life of Grange Copeland* (1970) is dedicated to her husband and is also "for my mother, who made a way out of no way." In 1983 she was awarded a Pulitzer Prize for her most recent novel *The Color Purple*.

Expect Nothing

Expect nothing. Live frugally
On surprise.
Become a stranger
To need of pity
Or, if compassion be freely   5
Given out
Take only enough
Stop short of urge to plead
Then purge away the need.

Wish for nothing larger   10
Than your own small heart
Or greater than a star;
Tame wild disappointment
With caress unmoved and cold
Make of it a parka   15
For your soul.

Discover the reason why
So tiny human midget
Exists at all
So scared unwise   20
But expect nothing. Live frugally
On surprise.

Getting at Meaning

1. In the first stanza the speaker urges the reader to "Become a stranger/To need of pity." These lines do not mean that people should live lives in which nothing ever goes wrong. What do they mean?

2. Explain the meaning of the lines, "Wish for nothing larger/Than your own small heart/Or greater than a star."

3. In lines 15 and 16 the speaker urges the reader to turn disappointment to advantage. Explain how disappointment can clothe the soul.

Developing Skills in Reading Literature

1. **Theme.** Explain the message of this poem, which is to "expect nothing" from life. What are the advantages of expecting nothing? How does the speaker characterize humanity in the final stanza? What view of the human being's place in the universe does this poem convey?

2. **Tone.** What words and phrases suggest a stoical approach to life? Where does the speaker's tone seem self-reliant and courageous? Do you admire the speaker's attitude toward life? Give reasons for your answer.

Americo Paredes

born in 1915

The son of a Brownsville, Texas, rancher, Americo Paredes is known as a scholar of the Mexican-American folk tradition and as the author of *With His Pistol in His Hand: A Border Ballad and Its Hero* and *Folktales of Mexico*. After infantry service during World War II, Paredes attended the University of Texas, where he received his bachelor's, master's, and doctoral degrees. Since 1954 he has been on the faculty of the University of Texas, rising to become a professor of English and anthropology and director of the school's Mexican-American studies program. He has also served as the editor of *The Journal of American Folklore* and has edited numerous works in the field of cultural anthropology.

Guitarreros

Black against twisted black
The old mesquite[1]
Rears up against the stars
Branch bridle hanging,
While the bull comes down from the mountain   5
Driven along by your fingers,
Twenty nimble stallions prancing up and down the *redil*[2] of the guitars.
One leaning on the trunk, one facing—
Now the song:
Not cleanly flanked, not pacing,   10
But in a stubborn yielding that unshapes
And shapes itself again,
Hard-mouthed, zigzagged, thrusting,
Thrown, not sung,
One to the other.   15
The old man listens in his cloud
Of white tobacco smoke.
"It was so," he says,
"In the old days it was so."

---

1. **mesquite** (mə skēt'): a spiny deep-rooted tree or shrub that forms extensive thickets
in the southwestern United States and Mexico. Its pods are rich in sugar.
2. *redil* (rə dēl'): sheepfold.

Getting at Meaning

1. What clues in the poem indicate that the bull is moving down the mountain in song, not in actuality?

2. An old man listens to two guitarists play. Describe the way they sing. How does the song affect the old man?

Developing Skills in Reading Literature

1. **Setting.** Describe the setting for this atmospheric poem. Why is it appropriate to the subject matter of the song?

2. **Metaphor.** Explain the poet's metaphor for the guitarists' fingers. Why is it fitting?

3. **Rhythm.** What do the present participles contribute to the rhythm of the poem? Where do you hear alliteration? Where do you hear assonance? What do these sound devices contribute? Where does the pace of the poem slow? Why?

Developing Vocabulary

Words from Spanish. American English contains a number of words from Spanish, such as *mesquite*. Most of these words come from the Spanish influence in the Southwest. Look up each word that follows in a dictionary that contains word origins, and record the Spanish word from which it is derived. How has each word been changed in American English?

bronco	ranch
cafeteria	rodeo
cinch	vamoose

Imamu Amiri Baraka

born in 1934

Born LeRoi Jones, Imamu Baraka assumed his African name after the racial upheavals that swept through his native Newark, New Jersey, in the summer of 1969. By then he had already turned away from the Modernist, Beat orientation of his first volume of poetry, the 1961 *Preface to a Twenty Volume Suicide Note*, toward the militantly aggressive stance of his later poetry and drama.

Baraka attended Rutgers University before moving on to Howard University, where he attained his bachelor's degree in 1954. After two years of Air Force service, followed by advanced study at New York's Columbia University and the New School for Social Research, Baraka joined the faculty of the New School to teach poetry and writing. His play *Dutchman*, a powerful, disturbing drama of racial oppression, won an Obie Award in 1964. After founding the Black Arts Repertory Theatre in Harlem, Baraka joined Newark's Spirit House Movers and Players, a community theater group. Thereafter, Baraka became an open advocate of direct political action to remedy what he saw as the genocidal inequities of society. His *Black Magic: Sabotage, Target Study, and Black Art* typifies the aggressive political thrust of Baraka's later work.

Preface to a Twenty Volume Suicide Note

Lately, I've become accustomed to the way
The ground opens up and envelops me
Each time I go out to walk the dog.
Or the broad edged silly music the wind
Makes when I run for a bus—   5

Things have come to that.

And now, each night I count the stars,
And each night I get the same number.
And when they will not come to be counted
I count the holes they leave.   10

Nobody sings anymore.

And then last night, I tiptoed up
To my daughter's room and heard her
Talking to someone, and when I opened
The door, there was no one there . . .   15
Only she on her knees,
Peeking into her own clasped hands.

Developing Skills in Reading Literature

1. **Imagery.** What images does the poet use to suggest that his life has become routine, regulated by the world around him? Why does the ground open up and envelop him? Why is the music of the wind "broad edged" and "silly"? Explain the implications of counting the holes left by the stars.

Why does the poet close with the image of his daughter praying? How does this scene affect him?

2. **Tone.** Describing the way that his life has become tame, the poet says, "Nobody sings anymore." What does this line mean? What is the poet's tone in the line? How does the final image of the poem alter the tone?

Lucille Clifton

born in 1936

The daughter of a manual laborer, Lucille Clifton was born in Depew, New York, and now resides in Baltimore, where she is poet-in-residence at Coppin State College. She attended Howard University and Fredonia State Teachers College before marrying the artist Fred Clifton in 1958. Her first collection of verse, *Good Times*, appeared in 1969, followed by *Good News about the Earth* in 1972 and *An Ordinary Woman* in 1974. She is also well known for several volumes of children's verse and stories. Twice a winner of a National Endowment of the Arts Award, Clifton is a frequent contributor to *Redbook* and *Negro Digest* magazines. She is the mother of six children.

The 1st

What I remember about that day
is boxes stacked across the walk
and couch springs curling through the air
and drawers and tables balanced on the curb
and us, hollering,   5
leaping up and around
happy to have a playground;

nothing about the emptied rooms
nothing about the emptied family

Developing Skills in Reading Literature

1. **Imagery.** In the first stanza the poet creates a buoyant scene full of life, using words such as *curling*, *hollering*, and *leaping* to convey the energy. What images do the final two lines of the poem project? Which two words stand out in opposition to the happiness of the opening scene?

2. **Tone.** In the first stanza the speaker is a young child. The tone is joyous. How does the speaker's attitude toward the same experience change with age? Characterize the tone of the final two lines of the poem.

3. **Theme.** This short poem contains a powerful statement about the sad realities that often underlie human situations. Elaborate on this theme.

Still

still
it was nice
when the scissors man come round
running his wheel
rolling his wheel   5
and the sparks shooting
out in the dark
across the lot
and over to the white folks section

still   10
it was nice
in the light of Maizie's store
to watch the wheel
and catch the wheel—
fire spinning in the air   15
and our edges
and our points
sharpening good as anybody's

Developing Skills in Reading Literature

1. **Imagery.** Why is the image of the scissors man a pleasing one? Which words and phrases capture the action of the man?

2. **Rhythm.** Comment on the rhythm of this poem. What does it replicate? Why does the poet employ present participles? Why does she repeat the word *wheel* four times? Why does she position the words on their lines in the way that she does?

3. **Theme.** The final line of the first stanza slightly changes the tone of the stanza. How? What sad note does it introduce?

Notice how the final line of the second stanza picks up on the idea in the final line of the first. Although the final line is in one sense triumphant, in what way is it also sad and bitter? What grim reality underlies the vibrant imagery of the poem?

Teresa Palomo Acosta

born in 1949

Teresa Acosta attributed her interest in literature to her grandfather, Maximino Palomo. During her childhood, he would spend summer evenings on her family's front porch sharing stories of his life in Mexico and as a cowboy with the neighborhood children.

After completing a degree in Ethnic Studies at the University of Texas and a graduate degree in Journalism at Columbia University, she returned to Texas to work as a journalist and teacher. She originally wrote "My Mother Pieced Quilts" as an exercise in a creative writing class at the University of Texas with no intention of publishing it. She recalls writing the poem within one hour's time and making few revisions. Acosta believes that she wrote the poem down on paper so quickly because she had been carrying all the images in the poem in her memory for a number of years and had, indeed, probably been composing it subconsciously for a long time.

My Mother Pieced Quilts

they were just meant as covers
in winters
as weapons
against pounding january winds

but it was just that every morning I awoke to these   5
october ripened canvases
passed my hand across their cloth faces
and began to wonder how you pieced
all these together
these strips of gentle communion cotton and flannel nightgowns   10
wedding organdies
dime store velvets

how you shaped patterns square and oblong and round
positioned
balanced   15
then cemented them
with your thread
a steel needle
a thimble

how the thread darted in and out   20
galloping along the frayed edges, tucking them in
as you did us at night
oh how you stretched and turned and re-arranged
your michigan spring[1] faded curtain pieces
my father's sante fe work shirt[2]   25
the summer denims, the tweeds of fall

in the evening you sat at your canvas
—our cracked linoleum floor the drawing board
me lounging on your arm
and you staking out the plan: 30
whether to put the lilac purple of easter against the red
        plaid of winter-going-
into-spring
whether to mix a yellow with blue and white and paint the
corpus christi[3] noon when my father held your hand   35

---

1. **michigan spring:** in spring migrant workers often go to Michigan to pick crops.
2. **sante fe work shirt:** work clothes named after the Santa Fe Railroad.
3. **corpus christi** (kòr′ pəs kris′ tē): a city and port in the south of Texas.

whether to shape a five-point star from the
somber black silk you wore to grandmother's funeral

you were the river current
carrying the roaring notes
forming them into pictures of a little boy reclining   40
a swallow flying
you were the caravan master at the reins
driving your threaded needle artillery across the mosaic
      cloth bridges
delivering yourself in separate testimonies.   45

oh mother you plunged me sobbing and laughing
into our past
into the river crossing at five
into the spinach fields
into the plainview[4] cotton rows   50
into tuberculosis wards
into braids and muslin dresses
sewn hard and taut to withstand the thrashings of
      twenty-five years

stretched out they lay   55
armed/ready/shouting/celebrating

knotted with love
the quilts sing on

---

4. **plainview:** a Texas cotton town.

Developing Skills in Reading Literature

1. **Imagery.** The opening lines of the poem describe the quilts made by the speaker's mother. What kinds of fabrics did she use? Where did she get her scraps of material?

The speaker reveals family history through the description of the fabrics in the quilt. What family history do the images in lines 24-26 reveal? What family history comes to light in the images of lines 34-37? of lines 48-53?

2. **Metaphor.** Early in the poem the quilts are described as "october ripened canvases." What does "october ripened" imply about them? In what sense are the quilts canvases? Explain how the mother's approach to her sewing is artistic. What is her drawing board?

Two metaphors, in lines 38 and 42, describe the mother. Explain these comparisons and how they work. What does line 45 mean?

3. **Tone.** Discuss the tone of this poem. What lines imply admiration for the mother? What lines imply awe? What lines are particularly joyous?

Developing Vocabulary

Words from Greek Mythology. The poet uses the word *mosaic* to describe the quilts. *Mosaic* refers to any decorative design made of small pieces. The origin of the word can be traced to the Muses in classical mythology, the nine daughters of Zeus and Mnemosyne, goddess of memory. The Muses represent different spheres in the arts and sciences.

Each of the words that follows is derived from the Muses in some way, or from Mnemosyne, their mother. Look up these words in an unabridged dictionary, and record for each word its definition and its origin. Explain the relationship between the present-day definition and the Greek root.

calliope	mnemonic	music
cliometrics	museum	terpsichorean

Nikki Giovanni

born in 1943

An evocatively personal writer whose poetry and prose nonetheless express the shared features of black American consciousness, Nikki Giovanni has emerged as a prominent figure on the literary scene. Born in Knoxville, Tennessee, the daughter of a probation officer and a social worker, Giovanni attended Fisk University in Nashville, graduating with honors in 1967. During her college years, Giovanni participated vigorously in the civil rights movement and continues to play an activist role in the affairs of the national black community. After a brief stay at the University of Pennsylvania's School of Social Work, Giovanni moved to New York City and took courses at Columbia University's School of the Arts. In 1968 she published her first collection of poems, *Black Feeling, Black Talk*, followed by *Black Judgement* in the same year. Between 1968 and 1972, Giovanni was a professor of Black Studies at Livingston College of Rutgers University. While there, she continued to write prolifically, publishing *Re: Creation* and *Poem of Angela Davis* in 1970, and in 1971, *Gemini: An Extended Autobiographical Statement on My First Twenty-Five Years of Being a Black Poet.*

Jill Krementz

In the following year she collaborated with James Baldwin on a collection of verse and began to perform her work in public, including a reading at New York's Lincoln Center. She has subsequently appeared frequently on television and has made a number of recordings of her verse.

Choices

if i can't do
what i want to do
then my job is to not
do what i don't want
to do   5

it's not the same thing
but it's the best i can
do

if i can't have
what i want   then   10
my job is to want
what i've got
and be satisfied
that at least there
is something more   15
to want

since i can't go
where i need
to go   then i must go
where the signs point   20
though always understanding
parallel movement
isn't lateral

when i can't express
what i really feel   25
i practice feeling
what i can express
and none of it is equal
i know
but that's why mankind   30
alone among the mammals
learns to cry

Getting at Meaning

1. Lines 1-5 may require several readings before you figure them out. What is the speaker saying?

2. Explain the meaning of lines 9-16. What is the consolation in knowing that there is something more to want?

3. Comment on the meanings of lines 17-23. What is the difference between parallel and lateral movement?

4. Explain lines 24-27. Why does the speaker think that it is important to feel what can be expressed?

Developing Skills in Reading Literature

Theme. According to this poem, life is a series of inescapable compromises. What lines reflect this attitude toward the human situation? How does the thought embodied in lines 30-32 relate to the theme of the poem?

Al Young

born in 1939

A gifted musician and singer as well as a talented writer of verse and prose, Al Young was born in Ocean Springs, Mississippi, the son of a musician. He attended the University of Michigan but left there before taking his degree. Moving to California, he worked as a disc jockey for four years before attending Stanford University on a creative writing fellowship. He earned his bachelor's degree in 1969 from the University of California, Berkeley, and subsequently joined the faculty at Stanford. *Dancing*, his first collection of poems, appeared in 1969, followed by his first novel, *Snakes*, in 1970. In addition to his writing and teaching, Young lectures and reads his work extensively throughout the nation. He has been published in such magazines as *Audience, California Living, New Times, Rolling Stone, Evergreen Review,* and *The Journal of Black Poetry.*

For Poets

Stay beautiful
but don't stay down underground too long
Dont turn into a mole
or a worm
or a root   5
or a stone

Come on out into the sunlight
Breathe in trees
Knock out mountains
Commune with snakes   10
& be the very hero of birds

Dont forget to poke your head up
& blink
Think
Walk all around   15
Swim upstream

Dont forget to fly

Developing Skills in Reading Literature

1. **Imagery.** Imagery builds the message to poets in this poem. What behavior does Young warn against when he says, ". . . don't stay down underground too long"? Young then cautions poets against becoming one of four things. What do these four things have in common? What dangers does each one represent?

Notice the imagery that indicates the kinds of activity poets *should* engage in. Why are the images all from nature? What behavior do they call for?

2. **Theme.** There is a definition of poetry implicit in this witty short poem. What is poetry composed of, according to Young? Why must the poet "blink," "Think," and "Commune with snakes"? What is the poet's role in the world? Explain the final piece of advice: "Don't forget to fly."

Developing Writing Skills

Writing a Definition. In either poem or paragraph form, set down your own advice for poets. In identifying what poets should and should not do, you are formulating a working definition of poetry as you see it.

Unit Review *Modern Poetry*

Understanding the Unit

1. Explain how titles illuminate meaning in the following poems: "The Love Song of J. Alfred Prufrock," "Anecdote of the Jar," "The Death of the Ball Turret Gunner," and "Traveling Through the Dark."

2. Compare and contrast the views on war that are presented in the following poems: "The Death of the Ball Turret Gunner," "A Lullaby," "Embassy," and "The Sonnet-Ballad."

3. "The Death of the Hired Man," "Since Feeling Is First," "Bells for John Whiteside's Daughter," and "The Death of the Ball Turret Gunner" all convey attitudes toward death. Compare and contrast their perspectives on this inevitable occurrence.

4. What do "Janet Waking," "Life for My Child Is Simple," "The Fortress," and "Mutterings Over the Crib of a Deaf Child" have in common? Who is the speaker in each poem? What contrasting attitudes do you find in these poems?

5. Identify four poems in this unit in which the speaker is a persona created by the poet to present a particular point of view or character. Identify four poems in which the poet speaks in a personal, direct fashion. Discuss how a reader can judge when a poet is speaking in his or her own voice.

6. "The Flower-Fed Buffaloes," "The Pike," "Traveling Through the Dark," and "The Heaven of Animals" all provide commentary on human existence through observation of animal life. Explain how each poem does so. Which poem do you find most effective? Why?

7. "The Death of the Hired Man," "The Love Song of J. Alfred Prufrock," and "The Death of the Ball Turret Gunner" are all narrative poems. Discuss the differences among these poems, pinpointing techniques each one uses to tell its story.

8. Select three or four poems from this unit that are written in free verse. Explain why free verse is an appropriate form in each poem.

Writing

1. The poems that follow all comment on the black experience in America. Select three for analysis in a five-paragraph composition. Devoting one body paragraph to each poem, probe the commentary made by these poems. What is the message in each poem? What is the tone? Relate the poems to each other in your conclusion.

"We Wear the Mask"
"From the Dark Tower"
"As I Grew Older"
"The Negro Speaks of Rivers"
"A Note of Humility"
"Still"

2. Write a composition of five or more paragraphs in which you discuss how form and content are interrelated in any one poem in this unit. Choose a poem that invites detailed analysis, and focus your attention on such elements as rhyme, meter, stanza form, imagery, figurative language, alliteration, assonance, consonance, diction, syntax, repetition, punctuation—whatever is relevant to your poem.

3. Write a narrative poem using the poetic techniques with which you are now familiar to unfold your story. Choose a form for your poem that harmonizes with your content.

NEW YORK MOVIE, 1939. *Edward Hopper.*
Collection, The Museum of Modern Art, New York.
Given Anonymously.

Unit 8
Drama

The Development of American Drama

American drama did not emerge as an art form ranking in importance with the novel, the short story, and poetry until shortly after World War I.

EARLY AMERICAN DRAMA

Before the Revolutionary War, plays were presented in the larger cities of the more worldly Southern colonies as well as in New York and Philadelphia. Most of these plays, however, were imported from England and France, with an occasional stage adaptation of a novel. In the early national period, the late eighteenth and early nineteenth centuries, American plays were mainly romantic dramatizations of the history of the nation and melodramatic renderings of patriotic themes. No enduring works of literary quality were written at this time.

In Puritan America drama suffered because of the many legal and religious restrictions and taboos imposed upon this so-called frivolity. A few moral dialogues were presented but only as sources of edification for the spirit. Moreover, the hard conditions of New England life left little time for the leisure of attending the theater.

DRAMA AS PURE ENTERTAINMENT

As the pioneers pushed westward, first beyond the Appalachian Mountains then west of the Mississippi River, traveling companies of actors rode the stagecoaches and canal boats and later, the railroads to the frontier settlements. There, audiences, free from the restrictions of Puritan society, were eager to be entertained by melodramatic thrillers and exotic spectacles and even were treated to a smattering of refinement when classical acting troupes performed Shakespearean plays and other classics.

In time, showboats made the circuits of the larger landings, bringing to audiences the distinctively American minstrel shows and vaudeville, the American equivalent of the Victorian music hall.

What drew audiences to the theater was the lure of pure entertainment: spectacle, thrills, chills, virtuous maidens, blackguard villains, dashing heroes, and romantic plots with predictable outcomes. The theater was considered a purely money-making venture, outside the realm of literature. For the public, only the novel, the short story, and poetry were the provinces of serious writing.

DRAMA AS AN ART FORM

The first American dramatist to command world attention was Eugene O'Neill. In the early twentieth century O'Neill and the Provincetown Players established drama as a true literary form. The Players were a company of artists and writers who took the dramatic form seriously and expanded its horizons through experimentation with subject and technique. From makeshift beginnings on a front porch in the summer colony of Cape Cod to a little theater in New York's Greenwich Village, the Provincetown Players stimulated the growth of other serious theater groups and writers, not only in New York but across the country. They educated audiences to the possibilities of drama as an art form.

The last of all the literary genres to develop in America, drama has taken enormous strides since 1910. Playwrights such as O'Neill, Thornton Wilder, Robert E. Sherwood, Tennessee Williams, Arthur Miller, and Edward Albee are notable contributors to dramatic literature.

American plays of the twentieth century reflect the richness of the American experience, dealing with social, political, and economic themes, portraying the conflicts between the real and the ideal, and exploring the quest for spiritual liberty and self-fulfillment. Playwrights have presented their ideas in an abundance of dramatic forms: comedy, tragedy, satire, musical drama, and a host of experimental types that defy classification.

DRAMA AS LITERATURE

Although written principally to be performed, dramatic literature offers as many rewards to the reader as does the novel. In a novel, however, a narrator can step outside the narrative to explain character motivation, to interpret the meanings of events, to make judgments, to describe settings and situations, and even to convey themes. Dramatic literature relies mainly on dialogue, or conversations among characters, to tell the story. The reader of drama, therefore, must use not only reading skills but also powers of imagination to see the characters, to hear what they say and how they say it, and to understand why they act as they do and what their actions mean. In fact, readers of drama must perform for themselves the functions of director, actors, producer, stage technicians, and costumers to bring the play to life.

While considerably different in dramatic technique and in subject, both plays in this unit reveal the range of creative possibilities used by the playwright as artist to reflect the meaning of the human experience.

Eugene O'Neill
1888–1953

Eugene O'Neill is ranked by many authorities not only as the foremost of American playwrights but also as a major writer in the tradition of world literature. O'Neill was born in New York City, the son of an actor. His undergraduate career at Princeton University ended abruptly after one year (1906–1907) when, according to some accounts, he threw a beer bottle through a window of the college president's home. This was only the beginning of O'Neill's adventures, however. In the next several years he prospected for gold in Honduras, managed a touring theatrical company in the East and Middle West, and, driven by the roving spirit, spent two years as a seaman on voyages to Buenos Aires, South Africa, and England. He even worked as a mule tender on a cattle steamer. After his sea experiences, O'Neill played in his father's vaudeville company, worked as a reporter, and finally, in 1912 and 1913, spent six months recovering from tuberculosis in a sanitarium, where he began to write plays.

O'Neill grew serious about writing and in 1914 enrolled in the famous Harvard 47 workshop, where he began to deepen and clarify his art. A year later he joined the Provincetown Players in Cape Cod, an experimental theatre group that encouraged new approaches in playwriting, producing, and acting.

O'Neill's sea and waterfront experiences became material for his early plays, including "Ile," "Bound East for Cardiff," and "The Long Voyage Home," all of which were performed in 1916 and 1917, and two plays that won Pulitzer Prizes, *Beyond the Horizon* (1920) and *Anna Christie* (1921). Pulitzer Prizes also were awarded to two other plays by O'Neill: the nine-act play *Strange Interlude* (1928) and the autobiographical *Long Day's Journey into Night*, written in 1940 but not published until after O'Neill's death.

O'Neill's plays focus upon the titanic struggles of characters who are victims of their own environment, inheritance, and tragic circumstances. To convey vividly the deepest experiences of human beings searching for their place in the scheme of things, O'Neill radically departed from conventional techniques of drama. Instead he employed such expressionist, or anti-realistic, devices as soliloquies, asides, character masks, and symbolic settings.

Other notable works by O'Neill include *The Emperor Jones* (1920); *The Hairy Ape* (1922); *Desire Under the Elms* (1924); *Mourning Becomes Electra* (1931), in which O'Neill adapted the themes of the Greek trilogy the *Oresteia* to American circumstances; *Ah! Wilderness* (1933), his only comedy; and *The Iceman Cometh* (1939).

O'Neill was awarded the Nobel Prize in 1936 for his contributions to the American theatre.

Ile

CHARACTERS

BEN, the cabin boy
THE STEWARD
CAPTAIN KEENEY
SLOCUM, second mate
MRS. KEENEY
JOE, a harpooner
Members of the crew of the steam whaler
    Atlantic Queen.

SCENE—CAPTAIN KEENEY'S *cabin on board the steam whaling ship* Atlantic Queen—*a small, square compartment about eight feet high with a skylight in the center looking out on the poop deck.[1] On the left (the stern of the ship) a long bench with rough cushions is built in against the wall. In front of the bench, a table. Over the bench, several curtained portholes.*

In the rear, left, a door leading to the captain's sleeping quarters. To the right of the door a small organ, looking as if it were brand new, is placed against the wall.

On the right, to the rear, a marble-topped sideboard. On the sideboard, a woman's sewing basket. Farther forward, a doorway leading to the companion way, and past the officer's quarters to the main deck.

In the center of the room, a stove. From the middle of the ceiling a hanging lamp is suspended. The walls of the cabin are painted white.

There is no rolling of the ship, and the light which comes through the skylight is sickly and faint, indicating one of those gray days of calm when ocean and sky are alike dead. The silence is unbroken except for the measured tread of some one walking up and down on the poop deck overhead.

It is nearing two bells—one o'clock—in the afternoon of a day in the year 1895.

At the rise of the curtain there is a moment of intense silence. Then the STEWARD *enters and commences to clear the table of the few dishes which still remain on it after the* CAPTAIN'S *dinner. He is an old, grizzled man dressed in dungaree pants, a sweater, and a woolen cap with ear flaps. His manner is sullen and angry. He stops stacking up the plates and casts a quick glance upward at the skylight; then tiptoes over to the closed door in rear and listens with his ear pressed to the crack. What he hears makes his face darken and he mutters a furious curse. There is a noise from the doorway on the right and he darts back to the table.*

BEN *enters. He is an overgrown, gawky boy with a long, pinched face. He is dressed in sweater, fur cap, etc. His teeth are chattering with the cold and he hurries to the stove, where he stands for a moment shivering, blowing on his hands, slapping them against his sides, on the verge of crying.*

THE STEWARD *(In relieved tones—seeing who it is).* Oh, 'tis you, is it? What're ye shiverin' 'bout? Stay by the stove where ye belong and ye'll find no need of chatterin'.

BEN. It's c-c-cold. *(Trying to control his chattering teeth—derisively.)* Who d'ye think it were—the Old Man?

THE STEWARD *(Makes a threatening move—*

---

1. **poop deck:** a raised deck at the stern of a ship which forms the roof of the cabin.

BEN *shrinks away).* None o' your lip, young un, or I'll learn ye. *(More kindly.)* Where was it ye've been all o' the time—the fo'c's'tle?[2]

BEN. Yes.

THE STEWARD. Let the Old Man see ye up for'ard monkeyshinin'[3] with the hands and ye'll get a hidin' ye'll not forget in a hurry.

BEN. Aw, he don't see nothin'. *(A trace of awe in his tones—he glances upward.)* He just walks up and down like he didn't notice nobody—and stares at the ice to the no'the'ard.[4]

THE STEWARD *(The same tone of awe creeping into his voice).* He's always starin' at the ice. *(In a sudden rage, shaking his fist at the skylight.)* Ice, ice, ice! Blast him and blast the ice! Holdin' us in for nigh on a year—nothin' to see but ice—stuck in it like a fly in molasses!

BEN *(Apprehensively).* Ssshh! He'll hear ye.

THE STEWARD *(Raging).* Aye, blast him, and blast the Arctic seas, and blast this stinkin' whalin' ship of his, and blast me for a fool to ever ship on it! *(Subsiding as if realizing the uselessness of this outburst—shaking his head—slowly, with deep conviction.)* He's a hard man—as hard a man as ever sailed the seas.

BEN *(Solemnly).* Aye.

THE STEWARD. The two years we all signed up for are done this day. Blessed Christ! Two years o' this dog's life, and no luck in the fishin', and the hands half starved with the food runnin' low, rotten as it is; and not a sign of him turnin' back for home! *(Bitterly.)* Home! I begin to doubt if ever I'll set foot on land again. *(Excitedly.)* What is it he thinks he' goin' to do? Keep us all up here after our time is worked out till the last man of us is starved to death or frozen? We've grub enough hardly to last out the voyage back if we started now. What are the men goin' to do 'bout it? Did ye hear any talk in the fo'c's'tle?

BEN *(Going over to him—in a half whisper).* They said if he don't put back south for home today they're goin' to mutiny.

THE STEWARD *(With grim satisfaction).* Mutiny? Aye, 'tis the only thing they can do; and serve him right after the manner he's treated them— 's if they wern't no better nor dogs.

BEN. The ice is all broke up to s'uth'ard.[5] They's clear water 's far 's you can see. He ain't got no excuse for not turnin' back for home, the men says.

THE STEWARD *(Bitterly).* He won't look nowheres but no'the'ard where they's only the ice to see. He don't want to see no clear water. All he thinks on is gittin' the ile[6]— 's if it was our fault he ain't had good luck with the whales. *(Shaking his head.)* I think the man's mighty nigh losin' his senses.

BEN *(Awed).* D'you really think he's crazy?

THE STEWARD. Aye, it's the punishment o' God on him. Did ye ever hear of a man who wasn't crazy do the things he does? *(Pointing to the door in rear.)* Who but a man that's mad would take his woman—and as sweet a woman as ever was—on a stinkin' whalin' ship to the Arctic seas to be locked in by the rotten ice for nigh on a year, and maybe lose her senses forever—for it's sure she'll never be the same again.

BEN *(Sadly).* She useter be awful nice to me before—— *(His eyes grow wide and frightened.)* she got—like she is.

THE STEWARD. Aye, she was good to all of us. 'Twould have been hell on board without her; for he's a hard man—a hard, hard man—a driver if there ever was one. *(With*

---

2. **fo'c's'tle** (fōk' s'l): forecastle; the front part of a ship where the sailors' quarters usually are located.

3. **monkeyshinin'** (muŋ' kē shīniŋ'): fooling around, playing tricks.

4. **no'the'ard:** northward.

5. **s'uth'ard:** southward.

6. **ile:** whale oil, obtained mainly from the blubber of right whales, and used for lamp oil and other lubricating purposes.

a grim laugh.) I hope he's satisfied now—drivin' her on till she's near lost her mind. And who could blame her? 'Tis a God's wonder we're not a ship full of crazed people—with the blasted ice all the time, and the quiet so thick you're afraid to hear your own voice.

BEN (With a frightened glance toward the door on right). She don't never speak to me no more—jest looks at me 's if she didn't know me.

THE STEWARD. She don't know no one—but him. She talks to him—when she does talk—right enough.

BEN. She does nothin' all day long now but sit and sew—and then she cries to herself without makin' no noise. I've seen her.

THE STEWARD. Aye, I could hear her through the door a while back.

BEN (Tiptoes over to the door and listens). She's cryin' now.

THE STEWARD (Furiously—shaking his fist). God send his soul to Hades for the devil he is!

(There is the noise of someone coming slowly down the companionway[7] stairs. THE STEWARD hurries to his stacked-up dishes. He is so nervous from fright that he knocks off the top one, which falls and breaks on the floor. He stands aghast, trembling with dread. BEN is violently rubbing off the organ with a piece of cloth which he has snatched from his pocket. CAPTAIN KEENEY appears in the doorway on right and comes into the cabin, removing his fur cap as he does so. He is a man of about forty, around five-ten in height but looking much shorter on account of the enormous proportions of his shoulders and chest. His face is massive and deeply lined, with gray-blue eyes of a bleak hardness, and a tightly clenched, thin-lipped mouth. His thick hair is long and gray. He is dressed in a heavy blue jacket and blue pants stuffed into his sea-boots.

(He is followed into the cabin by the SECOND MATE, a rangy six-footer with a lean weather-beaten face. The MATE is dressed about the same as the captain. He is a man of thirty or so.)

KEENEY (Comes toward the STEWARD—with a stern look on his face. The STEWARD is visibly frightened and the stack of dishes rattles in his trembling hands. KEENEY draws back his fist and the STEWARD shrinks away. The fist is gradually lowered and KEENEY speaks slowly). 'Twould be like hitting a worm. It is nigh on two bells, Mr. Steward, and this truck not cleared yet.

THE STEWARD (Stammering). Y-y-yes, sir.

KEENEY. Instead of doin' your rightful work ye've been below here gossipin' old woman's talk with that boy. (To BEN, fiercely.) Get out o' this, you! Clean up the chart room. (BEN darts past the MATE to the open doorway.) Pick up that dish, Mr. Steward!

THE STEWARD (Doing so with difficulty). Yes, sir.

KEENEY. The next dish you break, Mr. Steward, you take a bath in the Bering Sea at the end of a rope.

THE STEWARD (Tremblingly). Yes, sir. (He hurries out. The SECOND MATE walks slowly over to the CAPTAIN.)

MATE. I warn't 'specially anxious the man at the wheel should catch what I wanted to say to you, sir. That's why I asked you to come below.

KEENEY (Impatiently). Speak your say, Mr. Slocum.

MATE (Unconsciously lowering his voice). I'm afeard there'll be trouble with the hands by the look o' things. They'll likely turn ugly, every blessed one o' them, if you don't put back. The two years they signed up for is up today.

KEENEY. And d'you think you're tellin' me somethin' new, Mr. Slocum? I've felt it in

---

7. **companionway:** a stairway leading from the deck of a ship to the cabins or spaces below.

the air this long time past. D'you think I've not seen their ugly looks and the grudgin' way they worked?

(The door in rear is opened and MRS. KEENEY *stands in the doorway. She is a slight, sweet-faced little woman primly dressed in black. Her eyes are red from weeping and her face drawn and pale. She takes in the cabin with a frightened glance and stands as if fixed to the spot by some nameless dread, clasping and unclasping her hands nervously. The two men turn and look at her.)*

KEENEY *(With rough tenderness)*. Well, Annie?

MRS. KEENEY *(As if awakening from a dream)*. David, I—— *(She is silent. The* MATE *starts for the doorway.)*

KEENEY *(Turning to him—sharply)*. Wait!

MATE. Yes, sir.

KEENEY. D'you want anything, Annie?

MRS. KEENEY *(After a pause, during which she seems to be endeavoring to collect her thoughts)*. I thought maybe—I'd go up on deck, David, to get a breath of fresh air. *(She stands humbly awaiting his permission. He and the* MATE *exchange a significant glance.)*

KEENEY. It's too cold, Annie. You'd best stay below today. There's nothing to look at on deck—but ice.

MRS. KEENEY *(Monotonously)*. I know—ice, ice, ice! But there's nothing to see down here but these walls. *(She makes a gesture of loathing.)*

KEENEY. You can play the organ, Annie.

MRS. KEENEY *(Dully)*. I hate the organ. It puts me in mind of home.

KEENEY *(A touch of resentment in his voice)*. I got it jest for you.

MRS. KEENEY *(Dully)*. I know. *(She turns away from them and walks slowly to the bench on left. She lifts up one of the curtains and looks through a porthole; then utters an exclamation of joy.)* Ah, water! Clear water! As far as I can see! How good it looks after all these months of ice! *(She turns

round to them, her face transfigured with joy.)* Ah, now I must go upon deck and look at it, David.

KEENEY *(Frowning)*. Best not today, Annie. Best wait for a day when the sun shines.

MRS. KEENEY *(Desperately)*. But the sun never shines in this terrible place.

KEENEY *(A tone of command in his voice)*. Best not today, Annie.

MRS. KEENEY *(Crumbling before this command—abjectly)*. Very well, David.

(She stands there staring straight before her as if in a daze. The two men look at her uneasily.)

KEENEY *(Sharply)*. Annie!

MRS. KEENEY *(Dully)*. Yes, David.

KEENEY. Me and Mr. Slocum has business to talk about—ship's business.

MRS. KEENEY. Very well, David.

(She goes slowly out, rear, and leaves the door three-quarters shut behind her.)

KEENEY. Best not have her on deck if they's goin' to be any trouble.

MATE. Yes, sir.

KEENEY. And trouble they's goin' to be. I feel it in my bones. *(Takes a revolver from the pocket of his coat and examines it.)* Got your'n?

MATE. Yes, sir.

KEENEY. Not that we'll have to use 'em—not if I know their breed of dog—jest to frighten 'em up a bit. *(Grimly.)* I ain't never been forced to use one yit; and trouble I've had by land and by sea 's long as I kin remember, and will have till my dyin' day, I reckon.

MATE *(Hesitatingly)*. Then you ain't goin'—to turn back?

KEENEY. Turn back! Mr. Slocum, did you ever hear 'o me pointin' s'uth for home with only a measly four hundred barrel of ile in the hold?

MATE *(Hastily)*. No, sir—but the grub's gittin' low.

KEENEY. They's enough to last a long time yit, if they're careful with it; and they's plenty o' water.

MATE. They say it's not fit to eat—what's left; and the two years they signed on fur is up today. They might make trouble for you in the courts when we git home.

KEENEY. Blast 'em! Let them make what law trouble they kin. I don't care 'bout the money. I've got to git the ile! (*Glancing sharply at the* MATE.) You ain't turnin' no sea lawyer, be you, Mr. Slocum?

MATE (*Flushing*). Not by a sight, sir.

KEENEY. What do the fools want to go home fur now? Their share o' the four hundred barrel wouldn't keep 'em in chewin' terbacco.

MATE (*Slowly*). They wants to git back to their folks an' things, I s'pose.

KEENEY (*Looking at him searchingly*). 'N you want to turn back, too. (THE MATE *looks down confusedly before his sharp gaze.*) Don't lie, Mr. Slocum. It's writ down plain in your eyes. (*With grim sarcasm.*) I hope, Mr. Slocum, you ain't agoin' to jine the men agin me.

MATE (*Indignantly*). That ain't fair, sir, to say sich things.

KEENEY (*With satisfaction*). I warn't much afeard o' that, Tom. You been with me nigh on ten year and I've learned ye whalin'. No man kin say I ain't a good master, if I be a hard one.

MATE. I warn't thinkin' of myself, sir—'bout turnin' home, I mean. (*Desperately.*) But Mrs. Keeney, sir—seems like she ain't jest satisfied up here, ailin' like—what with the cold an' bad luck an' the ice an' all.

KEENEY (*His face clouding—rebukingly but not severely*). That's my business, Mr. Slocum. I'll thank you to steer a clear course o' that. (*A pause.*) The ice'll break up soon to no'th'ard. I could see it startin' today. And when it goes and we git some sun, Annie'll perk up. (*Another pause—then he bursts forth:*) It ain't the money what's keepin' me up in the Northern seas, Tom. But I can't go back to Homeport with a measly four hundred barrel of ile. I'd die fust. I ain't never come back home in all my days without a full ship. Ain't that truth?

MATE. Yes, sir; but this voyage you been ice-bound, an'——

KEENEY (*Scornfully*). And d'you s'pose any of 'em would believe that—any o' them skippers I've beaten voyage after voyage? Can't you hear 'em laughin' and sneerin'—Tibbots 'n' Harris 'n' Simms and the rest—and all o' Homeport makin' fun o' me? "Dave Keeney what boasts he's the best whalin' skipper out o' Homeport comin' back with a measly four hundred barrel of ile?" (*The thought of this drives him into a frenzy, and he smashes his fist down on the marble top of the sideboard.*) I got to git the ile, I tell you. How could I figger on this ice? It's never been so bad before in the thirty year I been acomin' here. And now it's breakin' up. In a couple o' days it'll be all gone. And they's whale here, plenty of 'em. I know they is and I ain't never gone wrong yit. I got to git the ile! I got to git it in spite of everything, and by God, I ain't agoin' home till I do git it!

(*There is the sound of subdued sobbing from the door in rear. The two men stand silent for a moment, listening. Then* KEENEY *goes over to the door and looks in. He hesitates for a moment as if he were going to enter—then closes the door softly.* JOE, *the harpooner, an enormous six-footer with a battered, ugly face, enters from right and stands waiting for the captain to notice him.*)

KEENEY (*Turning and seeing him*). Don't be standin' there like a gawk,[8] Harpooner. Speak up!

JOE (*Confusedly*). We want—the men, sir—they wants to send a depitation[9] aft to have

---

8. **gawk:** a clumsy, stupid fellow; a simpleton.
9. **depitation:** deputation, delegation.

a word with you.

KEENEY (Furiously). Tell 'em to go to——
(Checks himself and continues grimly.)
Tell 'em to come. I'll see 'em.

JOE. Aye, aye, sir. (He goes out.)

KEENEY (With a grim smile). Here it comes,
the trouble you spoke of, Mr. Slocum, and
we'll make short shift of it. It's better to
crush such things at the start than let them
make headway.

MATE (Worriedly). Shall I wake up the First
and Fourth,[10] sir? We might need their
help.

KEENEY. No, let them sleep. I'm well able to
handle this alone, Mr. Slocum.

(There is the shuffling of footsteps from outside and five of the crew crowd into the
cabin, led by JOE. All are dressed alike—
sweaters, seaboots, etc. They glance uneasily
at the CAPTAIN, twirling their fur caps in their
hands.)

KEENEY (After a pause). Well? Who's to speak
fur ye?

JOE (Stepping forward with an air of bravado).
I be.

KEENEY (Eyeing him up and down coldly). So
you be. Then speak your say and be quick
about it.

JOE (Trying not to wilt before the CAPTAIN'S
glance and avoiding his eyes). The time we
signed up for is done today.

KEENEY (Icily). You're tellin' me nothin' I
don't know.

JOE. You ain't pintin'[11] fur home yit, far 's we
kin see.

KEENEY. No, and I ain't agoin' to till this ship
is full of ile.

JOE. You can't go no further no'the with the
ice afore ye.

KEENEY. The ice is breaking up.

JOE (After a slight pause during which the
others mumble angrily to one another).
The grub we're gittin' now is rotten.

KEENEY. It's good enough fur ye. Better men
than ye are have eaten worse. (There is a
chorus of angry exclamations from the
crowd.)

JOE (Encouraged by this support). We ain't
agoin' to work no more less you puts back
for home.

KEENEY (Fiercely). You ain't, ain't you?

JOE. No; and the law courts'll say we was
right.

KEENEY. Blast your law courts! We're at sea
now and I'm the law on this ship. (Edging
up toward the harpooner.) And every
mother's son of you what don't obey orders
goes in irons.[12]

(There are more angry exclamations from the
crew. MRS. KEENEY appears in the doorway in
rear and looks on with startled eyes. None of
the men notice her.)

JOE (With bravado). Then we're agoin' to
mutiny and take the old hooker[13] home
ourselves. Ain't we, boys?

(As he turns his head to look at the others,
KEENEY'S fist shoots out to the side of his jaw.
JOE goes down in a heap and lies there. MRS.
KEENEY gives a shriek and hides her face in
her hands. The men pull out their sheath
knives and start a rush, but stop when they
find themselves confronted by the revolvers
of KEENEY and the MATE.)

KEENEY (His eyes and voice snapping). Hold
still! (The men stand huddled together in a
sullen silence. KEENEY'S voice is full of
mockery.) You've found out it ain't safe to
mutiny on this ship, ain't you? And now git
for'ard where ye belong, and——(He gives
JOE'S body a contemptuous kick.) Drag him
with you. And remember the first man of
ye I see shirkin' I'll shoot dead as sure as
there's a sea under us, and you can tell the

---

10. **First [mate] and Fourth [mate]:** the second and fifth
men in command.
11. **pintin':** pointing, headed in the direction of.
12. **irons:** metal fastenings, joined with chains to tie the
wrists and ankles of prisoners together.
13. **old hooker:** aged whaling ship.

rest the same. Git for'ard now! Quick! (*The men leave in cowed silence, carrying* JOE *with them.* KEENEY *turns to the* MATE *with a short laugh and puts his revolver back in his pocket.*) Best get up on deck, Mr. Slocum, and see to it they don't try none of their skulkin' tricks. We'll have to keep an eye peeled from now on. I know 'em.

MATE. Yes, sir.

(*He goes out, right.* KEENEY *hears his wife's hysterical weeping and turns around in surprise—then walks slowly to her side.*)

KEENEY (*Putting an arm around her shoulder —with gruff tenderness*). There, there, Annie. Don't be afeard. It's all past and gone.

MRS. KEENEY (*Shrinking away from him*). Oh, I can't bear it! I can't bear it any longer!

KEENEY (*Gently*). Can't bear what, Annie?

MRS. KEENEY (*Hysterically*). All this horrible brutality, and these brutes of men, and this terrible ship, and this prison cell of a room, and the ice all around, and the silence.

(*After this outburst she calms down and wipes her eyes with her handkerchief.*)

KEENEY (*After a pause during which he looks down at her with a puzzled frown*). Remember, I warn't hankerin' to have you come on this voyage, Annie.

MRS. KEENEY. I wanted to be with you, David, don't you see? I didn't want to wait back there in the house all alone as I've been doing these last six years since we were married—waiting, and watching, and fearing—with nothing to keep my mind occupied—not able to go back teaching school on account of being Dave Keeney's wife. I used to dream of sailing on the great, wide, glorious ocean. I wanted to be by your side in the danger and vigorous life of it all. I wanted to see you the hero they make you out to be in Homeport. And instead—— (*Her voice grows tremulous.*) All I find is ice and cold—and brutality!

(*Her voice breaks.*)

KEENEY. I warned you what it'd be, Annie. "Whalin' ain't no ladies' tea party," I says to you, and "you better stay to home where you've got all your woman's comforts." (*Shaking his head.*) But you was so set on it.

MRS. KEENEY (*Wearily*). Oh, I know it isn't your fault, David. You see, I didn't believe you. I guess I was dreaming about the old Vikings[14] in the story books and I thought you were one of them.

KEENEY (*Protestingly*). I done my best to make it as cozy and comfortable as could be. (MRS. KEENEY *looks around her in wild scorn.*) I even sent to the city for that organ for ye, thinkin' it might be soothin' to ye to be playin' it times when they was calms and things was dull like.

MRS. KEENEY (*Wearily*). Yes, you were very kind, David. I know that. (*She goes to left and lifts the curtains from the porthole and looks out—then suddenly bursts forth:*) I won't stand it—I can't stand it— pent up by these walls like a prisoner. (*She runs over to him and throws her arms around him, weeping. He puts his arm protectingly over her shoulders.*) Take me away from here, David! If I don't get away from here, out of this terrible ship, I'll go mad! Take me home, David! I can't think any more. I feel as if the cold and the silence were crushing down on my brain. I'm afraid. Take me home!

KEENEY (*Holds her at arm's length and looks at her face anxiously*). Best go to bed, Annie. You ain't yourself. You got fever. Your eyes look so strange like. I ain't never seen you look this way before.

MRS. KEENEY (*Laughing hysterically*). It's the ice and the cold and the silence—they'd make anyone look strange.

KEENEY (*Soothingly*). In a month or two, with

---

14. **Vikings:** Scandinavian pirates who raided the coasts of Europe from the eighth to the tenth centuries.

good luck, three at the most, I'll have her filled with ile and then we'll give her everything she'll stand and pint for home.

MRS. KEENEY. But we can't wait for that—I can't wait. I want to get home. And the men won't wait. They want to get home. It's cruel, it's brutal for you to keep them. You must sail back. You've got no excuse. There's clear water to the south now. If you've a heart at all you've got to turn back.

KEENEY (*Harshly*). I can't, Annie.

MRS. KEENEY. Why can't you?

KEENEY. A woman couldn't rightly understand my reason.

MRS. KEENEY (*Wildly*). Because it's a stupid, stubborn reason. Oh, I heard you talking with the second mate. You're afraid the other captains will sneer at you because you didn't come back with a full ship. You want to live up to your silly reputation even if you do have to beat and starve men and drive me mad to do it.

KEENEY (*His jaw set stubbornly*). It ain't that, Annie. Them skippers would never dare sneer to my face. It ain't so much what any one'd say—but—— (*He hesitates, struggling to express his meaning.*) You see— I've always done it—since my first voyage as skipper. I always come back—with a full ship—and—it don't seem right not to— somehow. I been always first whalin' skipper out o' Homeport, and—— Don't you see my meanin', Annie? (*He glances at her. She is not looking at him but staring dully in front of her, not hearing a word he is saying.*) Annie! (*She comes to herself with a start.*) Best turn in, Annie, there's a good woman. You ain't well.

MRS. KEENEY (*Resisting his attempts to guide her to the door in rear*). David! Won't you please turn back?

KEENEY (*Gently*). I can't, Annie—not yet awhile. You don't see my meanin'. I got to git the ile.

MRS. KEENEY. It'd be different if you needed the money, but you don't. You've got more than plenty.

KEENEY (*Impatiently*). It ain't the money I'm thinkin' of. D'you think I'm as mean as that?

MRS. KEENEY (*Dully*). No—I don't know—I can't understand—— (*Intensely.*) Oh, I want to be home in the old house once more and see my own kitchen again, and hear a woman's voice talking to me and be able to talk to her. Two years! It seems so long ago—as if I'd been dead and could never go back.

KEENEY (*Worried by her strange tone and the faraway look in her eyes*). Best go to bed, Annie. You ain't well.

MRS. KEENEY (*Not appearing to hear him*). I used to be lonely when you were away. I used to think Homeport was a stupid, monotonous place. Then I used to go down on the beach, especially when it was windy and the breakers were rolling in, and I'd dream of the fine free life you must be leading. (*She gives a laugh which is half a sob.*) I used to love the sea then. (*She pauses; then continues with slow intensity:*) But now—I don't ever want to see the sea again.

KEENEY (*Thinking to humor her*). 'Tis no fit place for a woman, that's sure. I was a fool to bring ye.

MRS. KEENEY (*After a pause—passing her hand over her eyes with a gesture of pathetic weariness*). How long would it take us to reach home—if we started now?

KEENEY (*Frowning*). 'Bout two months, I reckon, Annie, with fair luck.

MRS. KEENEY (*Counts on her fingers—then murmurs with a rapt smile*). That would be August, the latter part of August, wouldn't it? It was on the twenty-fifth of August we were married, David, wasn't it?

KEENEY (*Trying to conceal the fact that her memories have moved him—gruffly*). Don't *you* remember?

MRS. KEENEY (*Vaguely—again passes her hand

over her eyes). My memory is leaving me—up here in the ice. It was so long ago. *(A pause—then she smiles dreamily.)* It's June now. The lilacs will be all in bloom in the front yard—and the climbing roses on the trellis to the side of the house—they're budding. *(She suddenly covers her face with her hands and commences to sob.)*

KEENEY *(Disturbed).* Go in and rest, Annie. You're all wore out cryin' over what can't be helped.

MRS. KEENEY *(Suddenly throwing her arms around his neck and clinging to him).* You love me, don't you, David?

KEENEY *(In amazed embarrassment at this outburst).* Love you? Why d'you ask me such a question, Annie?

MRS. KEENEY *(Shaking him—fiercely).* But you do, don't you, David? Tell me!

KEENEY. I'm your husband, Annie, and you're my wife. Could there be aught but love between us after all these years?

MRS. KEENEY *(Shaking him again—still more fiercely).* Then you do love me. Say it!

KEENEY *(Simply).* I do, Annie.

MRS. KEENEY *(Gives a sigh of relief—her hands drop to her sides. Keeney regards her anxiously. She passes her hand across her eyes and murmurs half to herself):* I sometimes think if we could only have had a child. (KEENEY *turns away from her, deeply moved. She grabs his arm and turns him around to face her—intensely.)* And I've always been a good wife to you, haven't I, David?

KEENEY *(His voice betraying his emotion).* No man has ever had a better, Annie.

MRS. KEENEY. And I've never asked for much from you, have I, David? Have I?

KEENEY. You know you could have all I got the power to give ye, Annie.

MRS. KEENEY *(Wildly).* Then do this this once for my sake, for God's sake—take me home! It's killing me, this life—the brutality and cold and horror of it. I'm going mad. I can feel the threat in the air. I can hear the

silence threatening me—day after gray day and every day the same. I can't bear it. *(Sobbing.)* I'll go mad, I know I will. Take me home, David, if you love me as you say. I'm afraid. For the love of God, take me home!

(She throws her arms around him, weeping against his shoulder. His face betrays the tremendous struggle going on within him. He holds her out at arm's length, his expression softening. For a moment his shoulders sag, he becomes old, his iron spirit weakens as he looks at her tear-stained face.)

KEENEY *(Dragging out the words with an effort).* I'll do it, Annie—for your sake—if you say it's needful for ye.

MRS. KEENEY *(With wild joy—kissing him).* God bless you for that, David!

(He turns away from her silently and walks toward the companionway. Just at that moment there is a clatter of footsteps on the stairs and the SECOND MATE *enters the cabin.)*

MATE *(Excitedly).* The ice is breakin' up to no'the'ard, sir. There's a clear passage through the floe,[15] and clear water beyond, the lookout says. (KEENEY *straightens himself like a man coming out of a trance.* MRS. KEENEY *looks at the* MATE *with terrified eyes.)*

KEENEY *(Dazedly—trying to collect his thoughts).* A clear passage? To no'the'ard?

MATE. Yes, sir.

KEENEY *(His voice suddenly grim with determination).* Then get her ready and we'll drive her through.

MATE. Aye, aye, sir.

MRS. KEENEY *(Appealingly).* David!

KEENEY *(Not heeding her).* Will the men turn to willin' or must we drag 'em out?

MATE. They'll turn to willin' enough. You put the fear o' God into 'em, sir. They're meek as lambs.

---

15. **floe:** ice floe, a large area of floating sea ice.

KEENEY. Then drive 'em—both watches. *(With grim determination.)* They's whale t'other side o' this floe and we're going to git 'em.

MATE. Aye, aye, sir.

(He goes out hurriedly. A moment later there is the sound of scuffling feet from the deck outside and the MATE'S *voice shouting orders.)*

KEENEY *(Speaking aloud to himself—derisively).* And I was agoin' home like a yaller dog!

MRS. KEENEY *(Imploringly).* David!

KEENEY *(Sternly).* Woman, you ain't adoin' right when you meddle in men's business and weaken 'em. You can't know my feelin's. I got to prove a man to be a good husband for ye to take pride in. I got to git the ile, I tell ye.

MRS. KEENEY *(Supplicatingly).* David! Aren't you going home?

KEENEY *(Ignoring this question—commandingly).* You ain't well. Go and lay down a mite. *(He starts for the door.)* I got to git on deck. *(He goes out. She cries after him in anguish:)* David!

(A pause. She passes her hand across her eyes—then commences to laugh hysterically and goes to the organ. She sits down and starts to play wildly an old hymn. KEENEY *reenters from the doorway to the deck and stands looking at her angrily. He comes over and grabs her roughly by the shoulder.)*

KEENEY. Woman, what foolish mockin' is this? *(She laughs wildly and he starts back from her in alarm.)* Annie! What is it? *(She doesn't answer him.* KEENEY'S *voice trembles.)* Don't you know me, Annie?

(He puts both hands on her shoulders and turns her around so that he can look into her eyes. She stares up at him with a stupid expression, a vague smile on her lips. He stumbles away from her, and she commences softly to play the organ again.)

KEENEY *(Swallowing hard—in a hoarse whisper, as if he had difficulty in speaking).* You said—you was a-goin' mad—God!

(A long wail is heard from the deck above.) Ah bl-o-o-o-ow! *(A moment later the* MATE'S *face appears through the skylight. He cannot see* MRS. KEENEY.)*

MATE *(In great excitement).* Whales, sir—a whole school of 'em—off the star'b'd quarter 'bout five mile away—big ones!

KEENEY *(Galvanized into action).* Are you lowerin' the boats?

MATE. Yes, sir.

KEENEY *(With grim decision).* I'm a-comin' with ye.

MATE. Aye, aye, sir. *(Jubilantly.)* You'll git the ile now right enough, sir.

(His head is withdrawn and he can be heard shouting orders.)

KEENEY *(Turning to his wife).* Annie! Did you hear him? I'll get the ile. *(She doesn't answer or seem to know he is there. He gives a hard laugh, which is almost a groan.)* I know you're foolin' me, Annie. You ain't out of your mind—*(Anxiously.)* be you? I'll git the ile now right enough— jest a little while longer, Annie—then we'll turn hom'ard. I can't turn back now, you see that, don't ye? I've got to git the ile. *(In sudden terror.)* Answer me! You ain't mad, be you?

(She keeps on playing the organ, but makes no reply. The MATE'S *face appears again through the skylight.)*

MATE. All ready, sir.

(KEENEY turns his back on his wife and strides to the doorway, where he stands for a moment and looks back at her in anguish, fighting to control his feelings.)

MATE. Comin', sir?

KEENEY *(His face suddenly grown hard with determination).* Aye.

(He turns abruptly and goes out. MRS. KEENEY does not appear to notice his departure. Her whole attention seems centered in the organ. She sits with half-closed eyes, her body sway- *ing a little from side to side to the rhythm of the hymn. Her fingers move faster and faster and she is playing wildly and discordantly as* *(The Curtain Falls)*

NORTHERN SEASCAPE, OFF THE BANKS, 1936-37. *Marsden Hartley. Collection Milwaukee Art Museum. Max E. Friedman, Bequest.*

Getting at Meaning

1. What qualities of character possessed by Captain Keeney are revealed in his actions toward the Steward and in his first conversation with his wife?

2. What grievances do the crew and Mrs. Keeney have against the Captain?

3. What is Captain Keeney's goal? If it isn't to earn money and if it isn't to avoid the mockery of the other whaling captains, then what is it that drives him toward his goal?

4. Why did Annie insist upon joining her husband on this voyage? If she had remained home, why wouldn't she have been able to go back to teaching school?

5. What arguments does Annie use to persuade her husband to turn the ship homeward? How might the character of Annie be considered a stereotyped version of woman?

6. After succumbing to Annie's persuasion, the Captain suddenly returns to his original goal. What does he mean when he says, "I got to prove a man to be a good husband for ye to take pride in." How does he intend to prove himself? What sacrifices does he make in pursuing this goal?

Developing Skills in Reading Literature

1. **Drama.** Drama is literature written to be performed for a viewing audience. Study the form of

"Ile." Identify the characteristics that differentiate a play from the other literary genres: poetry, fiction, and nonfiction.

2. **Exposition and Dialogue.** Exposition gives the reader or the spectator necessary background information and lays the groundwork for the narrative. A novelist can accomplish this purpose over several chapters through description, third-person narration, and flashbacks. A playwright, however, must present exposition more quickly for a play is more compressed than a novel. Also, the exposition in drama comes through dialogue, the statements made by the characters.

How does the opening dialogue between the Steward and Ben serve the function of exposition? What specific details about the situation, setting, and characters are revealed?

3. **Dialogue: Repetition and Contrast.** Annie's emotional condition is suggested through the repetition of key words and phrases in her dialogue. Locate these repetitions and notice the way that they accumulate in impact.

What details in her lines of dialogue contrast with the dominant atmosphere of isolation and despair? Notice how these details increase the effectiveness of the repetitions in Annie's dialogue.

4. **Character.** Despite his love for his wife, Captain Keeney can be considered a victim of an excessive trait over which he has no control. What is that character trait and how does it exercise its authority over him? Do you think that he has lost his free will? What do you think the future holds for Captain Keeney? Explain your answers.

5. **Symbol.** What is the connection between the character of the Captain and the ice that prevents the ship from moving? What other functions does the ice serve in showing the reader the condition of the Captain's life?

6. **Structure.** In a multi-act play, the playwright can develop characters through a progression of scenes within each act. A one-act play, however, consists of a succession of quick episodes that reveal character through a series of conflicts.

Identify the separate episodes in this play and show how each one contributes to developing the character of the Captain, leading to the outcome of the play.

Developing Vocabulary

Precise Adjectives and Verbs. Stage directions are especially useful to actors and directors when they tell precisely how a character is to speak or to move. How would you portray the actions described in these stage directions? Use the dictionary to determine the exact denotations of these words. Suggest also the connotations of the words, which would help an actor to present a scene exactly as the writer intended.

"His manner is *sullen* and angry."

". . . *mutters* a *furious* curse."

". . . he *darts* back to the table."

". . . he stands *aghast*."

Developing Writing Skills

1. **Analyzing a Character.** In his pursuit of the oil, Captain Keeney breaks many of the ties that connect him to a meaningful life. The most obvious tie that he severs is with his wife, but he breaks other bonds as well. In a well developed paragraph describe three ways that Captain Keeney isolates himself by breaking the ties that bind.

2. **Narrating an Autobiographical Incident.** Write a composition about an incident in which excessive pride forced you to make an important decision or to take a particular action. Use a narrative approach to show the conflict you experienced and the way that pride affected your action. Use vivid details to re-create the incident.

3. **Writing an Explanation.** The contemporary attitude toward women is considerably different from the assumptions about woman's nature in this early twentieth century play. In a five-paragraph essay, explain what this play shows about the innate qualities of woman, the role of woman in society, and woman's characteristic reactions to stress and adversity. In your concluding paragraph, explain how the character of Annie Keeney might be different if the play were written today.

Thornton Wilder
1897–1975

A celebration of life—the uniqueness of each person's experience as well as the timelessness of the human experience—this is the inspiriting force of Thornton Wilder's Pulitzer Prize winning play *Our Town*.

Born in Wisconsin, Wilder spent a considerable part of his boyhood in Hong Kong, where his father was U.S. consul. He returned to the United States to attend school, first Oberlin College in Ohio and then Yale University. After graduating from Yale in 1920, Wilder studied archaeology in Rome. He then returned to the United States and earned a master's degree from Princeton in 1925. He taught dramatic literature and the classics at the University of Chicago from 1930 to 1937. Later he taught at Harvard and several other universities in the United States and Europe.

In his mid-twenties Wilder wrote *The Bridge of San Luis Rey*, a novel about the collapse of a bridge in Peru that killed five travelers. In broader terms, the book explores the role of chance or divine plan in human lives. The novel earned immediate public recognition and won for Wilder his first Pulitzer Prize in 1928. *Our Town* won its Pulitzer in 1938, and Wilder received a third Pulitzer Prize in 1943 for the play *The Skin of Our Teeth*, which, like *Our Town*, celebrates life.

With its bare stage and relatively few props, *Our Town* stimulates the imagination of the audience to move beyond the confines of the play's setting—Grover's Corners, New Hampshire, in the years 1901–1913. Using the conventions of the sixteenth-century Shakespearean stage, in which a bush, for example, might represent a forest, Wilder intended to make his particular characters and their story the story of all of us. The Stage Manager, who serves as narrator and commentator, makes this intention even more apparent.

Despite the ordinary lives of the ordinary characters who populate *Our Town*, Wilder was concerned with the great questions asked through the ages: What is the role of Providence in the affairs of human beings? What does life mean? What makes a life worthwhile? How should we live our lives? How does each of us fit into the grander design?

Remarkably, Wilder's plays achieve a perfect blending of the realities of specific people engaged in the everyday routines of growing up, of marrying, of living, and of dying, with the universal experience of all humanity.

Our Town

Costume design by Patricia Zipprodt for Thornton Wilder's Our Town.
Theatre Collection, Museum of the City of New York.

CHARACTERS

STAGE MANAGER	WALLY WEBB	MRS. SOAMES
DR. GIBBS	EMILY WEBB	CONSTABLE WARREN
JOE CROWELL	PROFESSOR WILLARD	SI CROWELL
HOWIE NEWSOME	MR. WEBB	STAGEHANDS
MRS. GIBBS	WOMAN IN THE BALCONY	THREE BASEBALL PLAYERS
MRS. WEBB	MAN IN THE AUDITORIUM	SAM CRAIG
GEORGE GIBBS	LADY IN THE BOX	JOE STODDARD
REBECCA GIBBS	SIMON STIMSON	MEN AND WOMEN AMONG THE DEAD

The entire play takes place in Grover's Corners, New Hampshire.

ACT ONE

No curtain.

No scenery.

The audience, arriving, sees an empty stage in half-light.

Presently the STAGE MANAGER, *hat on and pipe in mouth, enters and begins placing a table and three chairs downstage left, and a table and three chairs downstage right. He also places a low bench at the corner of what will be the Webb house, left.*

"Left" and "right" are from the point of view of the actor facing the audience. "Up" is toward the back wall.

As the house lights go down he has finished setting the stage and leaning against the right proscenium[1] pillar watches the late arrivals in the audience.

When the auditorium is in complete darkness he speaks.

STAGE MANAGER. This play is called *Our Town*. It was written by Thornton Wilder; produced and directed by A—— (or: produced by A——; directed by B——). In it you will see Miss C——; Miss D——; Miss E——; and Mr. F——; Mr. G——; Mr. H——; and many others. The name of the town is Grover's Corners, New Hampshire —just across the Massachusetts line: latitude 42 degrees 40 minutes; longitude 70 degrees 37 minutes. The first act shows a day in our town. The day is May 7, 1901. The time is just before dawn.

(A rooster crows.)

The sky is beginning to show some streaks of light over in the East there, behind our mount'in.

The morning star always gets wonderful bright the minute before it has to go— doesn't it? *(He stares at it for a moment, then goes upstage.)*

Well, I'd better show you how our town lies. Up here—*(That is, parallel with the back wall)* is Main Street. Way back there is the railway station; tracks go that way. Polish Town's across the tracks, and some Canuck[2] families. *(Toward the left)* Over there is the Congregational Church; across the street's the Presbyterian.

Methodist and Unitarian are over there.

Baptist is down in the holla' by the river.

Catholic Church is over beyond the tracks.

Here's the Town Hall and Post Office combined; jail's in the basement.

Bryan[3] once made a speech from these very steps here.

Along here's a row of stores. Hitching posts and horse blocks in front of them. First automobile's going to come along in about five years—belonged to Banker Cartwright, our richest citizen . . . lives in the big white house up on the hill.

Here's the grocery store and here's Mr. Morgan's drugstore. Most everybody in town manages to look into those two stores once a day.

Public school's over yonder. High school's still farther over. Quarter of nine mornings, noontimes, and three o'clock afternoons, the hull town can hear the yelling and screaming from those schoolyards. *(He approaches the table and chairs downstage right.)*

This is our doctor's house—Doc Gibbs's. This is the back door.

(Two arched trellises, covered with vines and flowers, are pushed out, one by each proscenium pillar.)

---

1. **proscenium** (prō sē′ nē əm): the apron of a stage in front of the main curtain, where action takes place when the curtains are closed.
2. **Canuck** (kə nuk′): French Canadian.
3. William Jennings Bryan (1860-1925), American lawyer, statesman, and orator, famous for his "Cross of Gold" speech and for being the Democratic Presidential candidate in three elections.

There's some scenery for those who think they have to have scenery.

This is Mrs. Gibbs's garden. Corn . . . peas . . . beans . . . hollyhocks . . . heliotrope . . . and a lot of burdock. *(Crosses the stage)*

In those days our newspaper come out twice a week—the Grover's Corners *Sentinel*—and this is Editor Webb's house.

And this is Mrs. Webb's garden.

Just like Mrs. Gibbs's, only it's got a lot of sunflowers, too. *(He looks upward, center stage.)*

Right here . . . 's a big butternut tree. *(He returns to his place by the right proscenium pillar and looks at the audience for a minute.)*

Nice town, y'know what I mean?

Nobody very remarkable ever come out of it, s'far as we know.

The earliest tombstones in the cemetery up there on the mountain say 1670, 1680—they're Grovers and Cartwrights and Gibbses and Herseys—same names as are here now.

Well, as I said: it's about dawn.

The only lights on in town are in a cottage over by the tracks where a Polish mother's just had twins. And in the Joe Crowell house, where Joe Junior's getting up so as to deliver the paper. And in the depot, where Shorty Hawkins is gettin' ready to flag the 5:45 for Boston.

(A train whistle is heard. The STAGE MANAGER *takes out his watch and nods.)*

Naturally, out in the country—all around—there've been lights on for some time, what with milkin's and so on. But town people sleep late.

So—another day's begun.

There's Doc Gibbs comin' down Main Street now, comin' back from that baby case. And here's his wife comin' downstairs to get breakfast.

*(*MRS. GIBBS, *a plump, pleasant woman in the middle thirties, comes "downstairs" right. She pulls up an imaginary window shade in her kitchen and starts to make a fire in her stove.)*

Doc Gibbs died in 1930. The new hospital's named after him.

Mrs. Gibbs died first—long time ago, in fact. She went out to visit her daughter, Rebecca, who married an insurance man in Canton, Ohio, and died there—pneumonia —but her body was brought back here. She's up in the cemetery there now—in wlth a whole mess of Gibbses and Herseys —she was Julia Hersey 'fore she married Doc Gibbs in the Congregational Church over there.

In our town we like to know the facts about everybody.

There's Mrs. Webb, coming downstairs to get her breakfast, too.—That's Doc Gibbs. Got that call at half past one this morning. And there comes Joe Crowell, Jr., delivering Mr. Webb's *Sentinel*.

*(*DR. GIBBS *has been coming along Main Street from the left. At the point where he would turn to approach his house, he stops, sets down his—imaginary—black bag, takes off his hat, and rubs his face with fatigue, using an enormous handkerchief.*

MRS. WEBB, *a thin, serious, crisp woman, has entered her kitchen, left, tying on an apron. She goes through the motions of putting wood into a stove, lighting it, and preparing breakfast.*

Suddenly, JOE CROWELL, JR., *eleven, starts down Main Street from the right, hurling imaginary newspapers into doorways.)*

JOE CROWELL, JR. Morning, Doc Gibbs.

DR. GIBBS. Morning, Joe.

JOE CROWELL, JR. Somebody been sick, Doc?

DR. GIBBS. No. Just some twins born over in Polish Town.

JOE CROWELL, JR. Do you want your paper now?

DR. GIBBS. Yes, I'll take it.—Anything serious goin' on in the world since Wednesday?

JOE CROWELL, JR. Yessir. My schoolteacher, Miss Foster, 's getting married to a fella over in Concord.

DR. GIBBS. I declare.—How do you boys feel about that?

JOE CROWELL, JR. Well, of course, it's none of my business—but I think if a person starts out to be a teacher, she ought to stay one.

DR. GIBBS. How's your knee, Joe?

JOE CROWELL, JR. Fine, Doc, I never think about it at all. Only like you said, it always tells me when it's going to rain.

DR. GIBBS. What's it telling you today? Goin' to rain?

JOE CROWELL, JR. No, sir.

DR. GIBBS. Sure?

JOE CROWELL, JR. Yessir.

DR. GIBBS. Knee ever make a mistake?

JOE CROWELL, JR. No, sir.

(JOE *goes off.* DR. GIBBS *stands reading his paper.*)

STAGE MANAGER. Want to tell you something about that boy Joe Crowell there. Joe was awful bright—graduated from high school here, head of his class. So he got a scholarship to Massachusetts Tech. Graduated head of his class there, too. It was all wrote up in the Boston paper at the time. Goin' to be a great engineer, Joe was. But the war broke out and he died in France—All that education for nothing.

HOWIE NEWSOME *(off left).* Giddap, Bessie! What's the matter with you today?

STAGE MANAGER. Here comes Howie Newsome, deliverin' the milk.

(HOWIE NEWSOME, *about thirty, in overalls, comes along Main Street from the left, walking beside an invisible horse and wagon and carrying an imaginary rack with milk bottles. The sound of clinking milk bottles is heard. He leaves some bottles at* MRS. WEBB'S *trellis, then, crossing the stage to* MRS. GIBBS'S, *he stops center to talk to* DR. GIBBS.)

HOWIE NEWSOME. Morning, Doc.

DR. GIBBS. Morning, Howie.

HOWIE NEWSOME. Somebody sick?

DR. GIBBS. Pairs of twins over to Mrs. Goruslawski's.

HOWIE NEWSOME. Twins, eh? This town's gettin' bigger every year.

DR. GIBBS. Goin' to rain, Howie?

HOWIE NEWSOME. No, no. Fine day—that'll burn through. Come on, Bessie.

DR. GIBBS. Hello, Bessie. (*He strokes the horse, which has remained up center.*) How old is she, Howie?

HOWIE NEWSOME. Going on seventeen. Bessie's all mixed up about the route ever since the Lockharts stopped takin' their quart of milk every day. She wants to leave 'em a quart just the same—keeps scolding me the hull trip.

(*He reaches* MRS. GIBBS'S *back door. She is waiting for him.*)

MRS. GIBBS. Good morning, Howie.

HOWIE NEWSOME. Morning, Mrs. Gibbs. Doc's just comin' down the street.

MRS. GIBBS. Is he? Seems like you're late today.

HOWIE NEWSOME. Yes. Somep'n went wrong with the separator.[4] Don't know what 'twas. (*He passes* DR. GIBBS *up center.*) Doc!

DR. GIBBS. Howie!

MRS. GIBBS (*calling upstairs*). Children! Children! Time to get up.

HOWIE NEWSOME. Come on Bessie! (*He goes off right.*)

MRS. GIBBS. George! Rebecca!

(DR. GIBBS *arrives at his back door and passes through the trellis into his house.*)

---

4. **separator:** a machine that separates cream from milk by using centrifugal force.

MRS. GIBBS. Everything all right, Frank?

DR. GIBBS. Yes. I declare—easy as kittens.

MRS. GIBBS. Bacon'll be ready in a minute. Set down and drink your coffee. You can catch a couple hours' sleep this morning, can't you?

DR. GIBBS. Hm! . . . Mrs. Wentworth's coming at eleven. Guess I know what it's about, too. Her stummick ain't what it ought to be.

MRS. GIBBS. All told, you won't get more'n three hours sleep. Frank Gibbs, I don't know what's goin' to become of you. I do wish I could get you to go away someplace and take a rest. I think it would do you good.

MRS. WEBB. Emileee! Time to get up! Wally! Seven o'clock!

MRS. GIBBS. I declare, you got to speak to George. Seems like something's come over him lately. He's no help to me at all. I can't even get him to cut me some wood.

DR. GIBBS (washing and drying his hands at the sink. MRS. GIBBS is busy at the stove). Is he sassy to you?

MRS. GIBBS. No. He just whines! All he thinks about is that baseball—George! Rebecca! You'll be late for school.

DR. GIBBS. M-m-m . . .

MRS. GIBBS. George!

DR. GIBBS. George, look sharp!

GEORGE'S VOICE. Yes, Pa!

DR. GIBBS (as he goes off the stage). Don't you hear your mother calling you? I guess I'll go upstairs and get forty winks.

MRS. WEBB. Walleee! Emileee! You'll be late for school! Walleee! You wash yourself good or I'll come up and do it myself.

REBECCA GIBBS'S VOICE. Ma! What dress shall I wear?

MRS. GIBBS. Don't make a noise. Your father's been out all night and needs his sleep. I washed and ironed the blue gingham for you special.

REBECCA. Ma, I hate that dress.

MRS. GIBBS. Oh, hush-up-with-you.

REBECCA. Every day I go to school dressed like a sick turkey.

MRS. GIBBS. Now, Rebecca, you always look very nice.

REBECCA. Mama, George's throwing soap at me.

MRS. GIBBS. I'll come up and slap the both of you—that's what I'll do.

(A factory whistle sounds.

The CHILDREN dash in and take their places at the tables. Right, GEORGE, about sixteen, and REBECCA, eleven. Left, EMILY and WALLY, same ages. They carry strapped schoolbooks.)

STAGE MANAGER. We've got a factory in our town too—hear it? Makes blankets. Cartwrights own it and it brung 'em a fortune.

MRS. WEBB. Children! Now I won't have it. Breakfast is just as good as any other meal and I won't have you gobbling like wolves. It'll stunt your growth—that's a fact. Put away your book, Wally.

WALLY. Aw, Ma! By ten o'clock I got to know all about Canada.

MRS. WEBB. You know the rule's well as I do—no books at table. As for me, I'd rather have my children healthy than bright.

EMILY. I'm both, Mama: you know I am. I'm the brightest girl in school for my age. I have a wonderful memory.

MRS. WEBB. Eat your breakfast.

WALLY. I'm bright, too, when I'm looking at my stamp collection.

MRS. GIBBS. I'll speak to your father about it when he's rested. Seems to me twenty-five cents a week's enough for a boy your age. I declare I don't know how you spend it all.

GEORGE. Aw, Ma—I gotta lotta things to buy.

MRS. GIBBS. Strawberry phosphates[5]—that's what you spend it on.

GEORGE. I don't see how Rebecca comes to

---

5. **phosphate** (fäs′fāt): a soft drink made with soda water, syrup, and, originally, with a few drops of phosphoric acid.

have so much money. She has more'n a dollar.

REBECCA (spoon in mouth, dreamily). I've been saving it up gradual.

MRS. GIBBS. Well, dear, I think it's a good thing to spend some every now and then.

REBECCA. Mama, do you know what I love most in the world—do you?—Money.

MRS. GIBBS. Eat your breakfast.

THE CHILDREN. Mama, there's first bell.—I gotta hurry.—I don't want any more.—I gotta hurry.

(The CHILDREN rise, seize their books and dash out through the trellises. They meet, down center, and chattering, walk to Main Street, then turn left.

The STAGE MANAGER goes off, unobtrusively, right.)

MRS. WEBB. Walk fast, but you don't have to run. Wally, pull up your pants at the knee. Stand up straight, Emily.

MRS. GIBBS. Tell Miss Foster I send her my best congratulations—can you remember that?

REBECCA. Yes, Ma.

MRS. GIBBS. You look real nice, Rebecca. Pick up your feet.

ALL. Goodbye.

(MRS. GIBBS fills her apron with food for the chickens and comes down to the footlights.)

MRS. GIBBS. Here, chick, chick, chick. No, go away, you. Go away. Here, chick, chick, chick. What's the matter with you? Fight, fight, fight—that's all you do. Hm . . . you don't belong to me. Where'd you come from? (She shakes her apron.) Oh, don't be so scared. Nobody's going to hurt you.

(MRS. WEBB is sitting on the bench by her trellis, stringing beans.)

Good morning, Myrtle. How's your cold?

MRS. WEBB. Well, I still get that tickling feeling in my throat. I told Charles I didn't know

as I'd go to choir practice tonight. Wouldn't be any use.

MRS. GIBBS. Have you tried singing over your voice?

MRS. WEBB. Yes, but somehow I can't do that and stay on the key. While I'm resting myself I thought I'd string some of these beans.

MRS. GIBBS (rolling up her sleeves as she crosses the stage for a chat). Let me help you. Beans have been good this year.

MRS. WEBB. I've decided to put up forty quarts if it kills me. The children say they hate 'em, but I notice they're able to get 'em down all winter.

(Pause. Brief sound of chickens cackling.)

MRS. GIBBS. Now, Myrtle. I've got to tell you something, because if I don't tell somebody I'll burst.

MRS. WEBB. Why, Julia Gibbs!

MRS. GIBBS. Here, give me some more of those beans. Myrtle, did one of those second-hand-furniture men from Boston come to see you last Friday?

MRS. WEBB. No-o.

MRS. GIBBS. Well, he called on me. First I thought he was a patient wantin' to see Dr. Gibbs. 'N he wormed his way into my parlor, and, Myrtle Webb, he offered me three hundred and fifty dollars for Grandmother Wentworth's highboy, as I'm sitting here!

MRS. WEBB. Why, Julia Gibbs!

MRS. GIBBS. He did! That old thing! Why, it was so big I didn't know where to put it and I almost give it to Cousin Hester Wilcox.

MRS. WEBB. Well, you're going to take it, aren't you?

MRS. GIBBS. I don't know.

MRS. WEBB. You don't know—three hundred and fifty dollars! What's come over you?

MRS. GIBBS. Well, if I could get the Doctor to take the money and go away someplace on a real trip, I'd sell it like that.—Y'know, Myrtle, it's been the dream of my life to see

Paris, France.—Oh, I don't know. It sounds crazy, I suppose, but for years I've been promising myself that if we ever had the chance—

MRS. WEBB. How does the Doctor feel about it?

MRS. GIBBS. Well, I did beat about the bush a little and said if I got a legacy—that's the way I put it—I'd make him take me somewhere.

MRS. WEBB. M-m-m . . . What did he say?

MRS. GIBBS. You know how he is. I haven't heard a serious word out of him since I've known him. No, he said, it might make him discontented with Grover's Corners to go traipsin' about Europe; better let well enough alone, he says. Every two years he makes a trip to the battlefields of the Civil War and that's enough treat for anybody, he says.

MRS. WEBB. Well, Mr. Webb just *admires* the way Dr. Gibbs knows everything about the Civil War. Mr. Webb's a good mind to give up Napoleon and move over to the Civil War, only Dr. Gibbs being one of the greatest experts in the country just makes him despair.

MRS. GIBBS. It's a fact! Dr. Gibbs is never so happy as when he's at Antietam or Gettysburg. The times I've walked over those hills, Myrtle, stopping at every bush and pacing it all out, like we were going to buy it.

MRS. WEBB. Well, if that secondhand man's really serious about buyin' it, Julia, you sell it. And then you'll get to see Paris, all right. Just keep droppin' hints from time to time —that's how I got to see the Atlantic Ocean, y'know.

MRS. GIBBS. Oh, I'm sorry I mentioned it. Only it seems to me that once in your life before you die you ought to see a country where they don't talk in English and don't even want to.

(The STAGE MANAGER *enters briskly from the right. He tips his hat to the ladies, who nod their heads.*)

STAGE MANAGER. Thank you, ladies. Thank you very much.

(MRS. GIBBS *and* MRS. WEBB *gather up their things, return into their homes and disappear.*)

Now we're going to skip a few hours.

But first we want a little more information about the town, kind of a scientific account, you might say.

So I've asked Professor Willard of our State University to sketch in a few details of our past history here.

Is Professor Willard here?

(PROFESSOR WILLARD, *a rural savant,*[6] *pince-nez*[7] *on a wide satin ribbon, enters from the right with some notes in his hand.*)

May I introduce Professor Willard of our State University.

A few brief notes, thank you, Professor— unfortunately our time is limited.

PROFESSOR WILLARD. Grover's Corners . . . let me see . . . Grover's Corners lies on the old Pleistocene granite of the Appalachian range. I may say it's some of the oldest land in the world. We're very proud of that. A shelf of Devonian basalt crosses it with vestiges of Mesozoic[8] shale, and some sandstone outcroppings; but that's all more recent: two hundred, three hundred million years old.

Some highly interesting fossils have been found . . . I may say: unique fossils . . . two miles out of town, in Silas Peckham's cow pasture. They can be seen at the

---

6. **savant** (sə vänt´) *French:* learned person, scholar.

7. **pince-nez** (pans´ nā´) *French:* eyeglasses without sidepieces, kept in place by a spring gripping the bridge of the nose.

8. **Pleistocene** (plīs´ tə sēn´): c. 600,000 years ago; **Devonian** (di vō´ nē ən): c. 405,000,000 years ago; and **Mesozoic** (mes´ ə zō´ ik): 135-230,000,000 years ago—all are prehistoric geological eras when granite, basalt, and shale, respectively, were formed.

museum in our University at any time—that is, any reasonable time. Shall I read some of Professor Gruber's notes on the meteorological situation—mean precipitation, et cetera?

STAGE MANAGER. Afraid we won't have time for that, Professor. We might have a few words on the history of man here.

PROFESSOR WILLARD. Yes . . . anthropological data: Early Amerindian stock. Cotahatchee[9] tribes . . . no evidence before the tenth century of this era . . . hm . . . now entirely disappeared . . . possible traces in three families. Migration toward the end of the seventeenth century of English brachycephalic[10] blue-eyed stock . . . for the most part. Since then some Slav and Mediterranean—

STAGE MANAGER. And the population, Professor Willard?

PROFESSOR WILLARD. Within the town limits: 2,640.

STAGE MANAGER. Just a moment, Professor. (*He whispers into the professor's ear.*)

PROFESSOR WILLARD. Oh, yes, indeed?—The population, *at the moment*, is 2,642. The postal district brings in 507 more, making a total of 3,149.—Mortality and birth rates: constant.—By MacPherson's gauge: 6,032.

STAGE MANAGER. Thank you very much, Professor. We're all very much obliged to you, I'm sure.

PROFESSOR WILLARD. Not at all, sir; not at all.

STAGE MANAGER. This way, Professor, and thank you again.

(*Exit* PROFESSOR WILLARD.)

Now the political and social report: Editor Webb—Oh, Mr. Webb?

---

9. **Amerindian** (am' ər in' di ən): an individual of one of the native races of America, here of Woodland Indian stock, the Cotahatchee (kō tə ha' chē) tribe.

10. **brachycephalic** (brak' i sə fāl' ik): having short, broad heads.

(MRS. WEBB *appears at her back door.*)

MRS. WEBB. He'll be here in a minute . . . He just cut his hand while he was eatin' an apple.

STAGE MANAGER. Thank you, Mrs. Webb.

MRS. WEBB. Charles! Everybody's waitin'. (*Exit* MRS. WEBB.)

STAGE MANAGER. Mr. Webb is publisher and editor of the Grover's Corners *Sentinel.* That's our local paper, y'know.

(MR. WEBB *enters from his house, pulling on his coat. His finger is bound in a handkerchief.*)

MR. WEBB. Well . . . I don't have to tell you that we're run here by a board of selectmen.[11]—All males vote at the age of twenty-one. Women vote indirect. We're a lower-middle-class: sprinkling of professional men . . . ten percent illiterate laborers. Politically, we're eighty-six percent Republicans; six percent Democrats; four percent Socialists; rest, indifferent.

Religiously, we're eighty-five percent Protestants; twelve percent Catholics; rest, indifferent.

STAGE MANAGER. Have you any comments, Mr. Webb?

MR. WEBB. Very ordinary town, if you ask me. Little better behaved than most. Probably a lot duller.

But our young people here seem to like it well enough. Ninety percent of 'em graduating from high school settle down right here to live—even when they've been away to college.

STAGE MANAGER. Now, is there anyone in the audience who would like to ask Editor Webb anything about the town?

WOMAN IN THE BALCONY. Is there much drinking in Grover's Corners?

MR. WEBB. Well, ma'am, I wouldn't know what you'd call *much.* Satiddy nights the farmhands meet down in Ellery Greenough's stable and holler some. We've got one or two town drunks, but they're always having remorses every time an evangelist comes to town. No, ma'am, I'd say likker ain't a regular thing in the home here, except in the medicine chest. Right good for snakebite, y'know—always was.

BELLIGERENT MAN AT BACK OF AUDITORIUM. Is there no one in town aware of—

STAGE MANAGER. Come forward, will you, where we can all hear you.—What were you saying?

BELLIGERENT MAN. Is there no one in town aware of social injustice and industrial inequality?

MR. WEBB. Oh, yes, everybody is—somethin' terrible. Seems like they spend most of their time talking about who's rich and who's poor.

BELLIGERENT MAN. Then why don't they do something about it? (*He withdraws without waiting for an answer.*)

MR. WEBB. Well, I dunno. . . . I guess we're all hunting like everybody else for a way the diligent and sensible can rise to the top and the lazy and quarrelsome can sink to the bottom. But it ain't easy to find. Meanwhile, we do all we can to help those that can't help themselves and those that can we leave alone.—Are there any other questions?

LADY IN A BOX. Oh, Mr. Webb? Mr. Webb, is there any culture or love of beauty in Grover's Corners?

MR. WEBB. Well, ma'am, there ain't much—not in the sense you mean. Come to think of it, there's some girls that play the piano at high school commencement; but they ain't happy about it. No, ma'am, there isn't much culture; but maybe this is the place to tell you that we've got a lot of pleasures of a kind here: we like the sun comin' up over the mountain in the morning, and we all notice a good deal about the birds.

---

11. **board of selectmen:** board of officers elected in most New England towns to manage municipal affairs.

We pay a lot of attention to them. And we watch the change of the seasons; yes, everybody knows about them. But those other things—you're right, ma'am—there ain't much.—*Robinson Crusoe* and the Bible; and Handel's "Largo," we all know that; and Whistler's *Mother*—those are just about as far as we go.

LADY IN A BOX. So I thought. Thank you, Mr. Webb.

STAGE MANAGER. Thank you, Mr. Webb.

(MR. WEBB *retires.*)

Now, we'll go back to the town. It's early afternoon. All 2,642 have had their dinners and all the dishes have been washed.

(MR. WEBB, *having removed his coat, returns and starts pushing a lawn mower to and fro beside his house.*)

There's an early-afternoon calm in our town: a buzzin' and a hummin' from the school buildings; only a few buggies on Main Street—the horses dozing at the hitching posts; you all remember what it's like. Doc Gibbs is in his office, tapping people and making them say "ah." Mr. Webb's cuttin' his lawn over there; one man in ten thinks it's a privilege to push his own lawn mower.

No, sir. It's later than I thought. There are the children coming home from school already.

(*Shrill girls' voices are heard, off left.* EMILY *comes along Main Street, carrying some books. There are some signs that she is imagining herself to be a lady of startling elegance.*)

EMILY. I *can't*, Lois, I've got to go home and help my mother. I *promised*.

MR. WEBB. Emily, walk simply. Who do you think you are today?

EMILY. Papa, you're terrible. One minute you tell me to stand up straight and the next minute you call me names. I just don't listen to you. (*She gives him an abrupt kiss.*)

MR. WEBB. Golly, I never got a kiss from such a great lady before.

(*He goes out of sight.* EMILY *leans over and picks some flowers by the gate of her house.*

GEORGE GIBBS *comes careening down Main Street. He is throwing a ball up to dizzying heights, and waiting to catch it again. This sometimes requires his taking six steps backward. He bumps into an* OLD LADY *invisible to us.*)

GEORGE. Excuse me, Mrs. Forrest.

STAGE MANAGER (*as Mrs. Forrest*). Go out and play in the fields, young man. You got no business playing baseball on Main Street.

GEORGE. Awfully sorry, Mrs. Forrest.—Hello, Emily.

EMILY. H'lo.

GEORGE. You made a fine speech in class.

EMILY. Well . . . I was really ready to make a speech about the Monroe Doctrine, but at the last minute Miss Corcoran made me talk about the Louisiana Purchase instead. I worked an awful long time on both of them.

GEORGE. Gee, it's funny, Emily. From my window up there I can just see your head nights when you're doing your homework over in your room.

EMILY. Why, can you?

GEORGE. You certainly do stick to it, Emily. I don't see how you can sit still that long. I guess you like school.

EMILY. Well, I always feel it's something you have to go through.

GEORGE. Yeah.

EMILY. I don't mind it really. It passes the time.

GEORGE. Yeah.—Emily, what do you think? We might work out a kinda telegraph from your window to mine; and once in a while you could give me a kinda hint or two about one of those algebra problems. I don't mean the answers, Emily, of course not . . .

just some little hint . . .

EMILY. Oh, I think *hints* are allowed.—So—ah—if you get stuck, George, you whistle to me; and I'll give you some hints.

GEORGE. Emily, you're just naturally bright, I guess.

EMILY. I figure that it's just the way a person's born.

GEORGE. Yeah. But, you see, I want to be a farmer, and my Uncle Luke says whenever I'm ready I can come over and work on his farm and if I'm any good I can just gradually have it.

EMILY. You mean the house and everything?

(Enter MRS. WEBB *with a large bowl and sits on the bench by her trellis.)*

GEORGE. Yeah. Well, thanks . . . I better be getting out to the baseball field. Thanks for the talk, Emily.—Good afternoon, Mrs. Webb.

MRS. WEBB. Good afternoon, George.

GEORGE. So long, Emily.

EMILY. So long, George.

MRS. WEBB. Emily, come and help me string these beans for the winter. George Gibbs let himself have a real conversation, didn't he? Why, he's growing up. How old would George be?

EMILY. I don't know.

MRS. WEBB. Let's see. He must be almost sixteen.

EMILY. Mama, I made a speech in class today and I was very good.

MRS. WEBB. You must recite it to your father at supper. What was it about?

EMILY. The Louisiana Purchase. It was like silk off a spool. I'm going to make speeches all my life.—Mama, are these big enough?

MRS. WEBB. Try and get them a little bigger if you can.

EMILY. Mama, will you answer me a question, serious?

MRS. WEBB. Seriously, dear—not serious.

EMILY. Seriously—will you?

MRS. WEBB. Of course, I will.

EMILY. Mama, am I good-looking?

MRS. WEBB. Yes, of course you are. All my children have got good features; I'd be ashamed if they hadn't.

EMILY. Oh, Mama, that's not what I mean. What I mean is: am I *pretty?*

MRS. WEBB. I've already told you, yes. Now that's enough of that. You have a nice young pretty face. I never heard of such foolishness.

EMILY. Oh, Mama, you never tell us the truth about anything.

MRS. WEBB. I *am* telling the truth.

EMILY. Mama, were *you* pretty?

MRS. WEBB. Yes, I was, if I do say so. I was the prettiest girl in town next to Mamie Cartwright.

EMILY. But, Mama, you've got to say *something* about me. Am I pretty enough . . . to get anybody . . . to get people interested in me?

MRS. WEBB. Emily, you make me tired. Now stop it. You're pretty enough for all normal purposes.—Come along now and bring that bowl with you.

EMILY. Oh, Mama, you're no help at all.

STAGE MANAGER. Thank you, Thank you! That'll do. We'll have to interrupt again here. Thank you, Mrs. Webb; thank you, Emily.

(MRS. WEBB *and* EMILY *withdraw.*)

There are some more things we want to explore about this town.

(*He comes to the center of the stage. During the following speech the lights gradually dim to darkness, leaving only a spot on him.*)

I think this is a good time to tell you that the Cartwright interests have just begun building a new bank in Grover's Corners— had to go to Vermont for the marble, sorry to say. And they've asked a friend of mine what they should put in the cornerstone for people to dig up . . . a thousand years from now. . . . Of course, they've put in a copy of the *New York Times* and a copy of Mr. Webb's *Sentinel*. . . . We're kind of interested in this because some scientific fellas have found a way of painting all that reading matter with a glue—a silicate glue—that'll make it keep a thousand—two thousand years.

We're putting in a Bible . . . and the Constitution of the United States and a copy of William Shakespeare's plays. What do you say, folks? What do you think?

Y'know—Babylon once had two million people in it, and all we know about 'em is the names of the kings and some copies of wheat contracts . . . and contracts for the sales of slaves. Yet every night all those families sat down to supper, and the father came home from his work, and the smoke went up the chimney—same as here. And even in Greece and Rome, all we know about the *real* life of the people is what we can piece together out of the joking poems and the comedies they wrote for the theater back then.

So I'm going to have a copy of this play put in the cornerstone and the people a thousand years from now'll know a few simple facts about us—more than the Treaty of Versailles and the Lindbergh flight.[12]

See what I mean?

So—people a thousand years from now— this is the way we were in the provinces north of New York at the beginning of the twentieth century.—This is the way we were: in our growing up and in our marrying and in our living and in our dying.

(*A choir partially concealed in the orchestra pit has begun singing "Blessed Be the Tie That Binds."*

SIMON STIMSON *stands directing them.*

---

12. **The Treaty of Versailles** (vər sī'): ended World War I in 1919, and Charles Lindbergh made the first transatlantic flight from New York to Paris in 1927.

Two ladders have been pushed onto the stage; they serve as indication of the second story in the Gibbs and Webb houses. GEORGE *and* EMILY *mount them, and apply themselves to their schoolwork.*

DR. GIBBS *has entered and is seated in his kitchen reading.)*

Well!—good deal of time's gone by. It's evening.

You can hear choir practice going on in the Congregational Church.

The children are at home doing their schoolwork.

The day's running down like a tired clock.

SIMON STIMSON. Now look here, everybody. Music come into the world to give pleasure.—Softer! Softer! Get it out of your heads that music's only good when it's loud. You leave loudness to the Methodists. You couldn't beat 'em, even if you wanted to. Now again. Tenors!

GEORGE. Hssst! Emily!

EMILY. Hello.

GEORGE. Hello!

EMILY. I can't work at all. The moonlight's so *terrible.*

GEORGE. Emily, did you get the third problem?

EMILY. Which?

GEORGE. The *third?*

EMILY. Why, yes, George—that's the easiest of them all.

GEORGE. I don't see it. Emily, can you give me a hint?

EMILY. I'll tell you one thing: the answer's in yards.

GEORGE. !!! In yards? How do you mean?

EMILY. In *square* yards.

GEORGE. Oh . . . in square yards.

EMILY. Yes, George, don't you see?

GEORGE. Yeah.

EMILY. In square yards of *wallpaper.*

GEORGE. Wallpaper—oh, I see. Thanks a lot, Emily.

EMILY. You're welcome. My, isn't the moonlight *terrible?* And choir practice going on.—I think if you hold your breath you can hear the train all the way to Contoocook. Hear it?

GEORGE. M-m-m—What do you know!

EMILY. Well, I guess I better go back and try to work.

GEORGE. Good night, Emily. And thanks.

EMILY. Good night, George.

SIMON STIMSON. Before I forget it: how many of you will be able to come in Tuesday afternoon and sing at Fred Hersey's wedding?—show your hands. That'll be fine; that'll be right nice. We'll do the same music we did for Jane Trowbridge's last month.

—Now we'll do: "Art Thou Weary, Art Thou Languid?" It's a question, ladies and gentlemen, make it talk. Ready.

DR. GIBBS. Oh, George, can you come down a minute?

GEORGE. Yes, Pa. *(He descends the ladder.)*

DR. GIBBS. Make yourself comfortable, George; I'll only keep you a minute. George, how old are you?

GEORGE. I? I'm sixteen, almost seventeen.

DR. GIBBS. What do you want to do after school's over?

GEORGE. Why, you know, Pa. I want to be a farmer on Uncle Luke's farm.

DR. GIBBS. You'll be willing, will you, to get up early and milk and feed the stock . . . and you'll be able to hoe and hay all day.

GEORGE. Sure, I will. What are you . . . what do you mean, Pa?

DR. GIBBS. Well, George, while I was in my office today I heard a funny sound . . . and what do you think it was? It was your mother chopping wood. There you see your mother—getting up early; cooking meals all day long; washing and ironing—and still she has to go out in the backyard and chop wood. I suppose she just got tired of asking you. She just gave up and decided it was easier to do it herself. And you eat her meals, and put on the clothes she keeps nice for you, and you run off and play baseball—like she's some hired girl we keep around the house but that we don't like very much. Well, I knew all I had to do was call your attention to it. Here's a handkerchief, son. George, I've decided to raise your spending money twenty-five cents a week. Not, of course, for chopping wood for your mother, because that's a present you give her, but because you're getting older—and I imagine there are lots of things you must find to do with it.

GEORGE. Thanks, Pa.

DR. GIBBS. Let's see—tomorrow's your payday. You can count on it—Hmm. Probably Rebecca'll feel she ought to have some more too. Wonder what could have happened to your mother. Choir practice never was as late as this before.

GEORGE. It's only half past eight, Pa.

DR. GIBBS. I don't know why she's in that old choir. She hasn't any more voice than an old crow. . . . Traipsin' around the streets at this hour of the night . . . Just about time you retired, don't you think?

GEORGE. Yes, Pa.

(GEORGE *mounts to his place on the ladder.*
Laughter and good-nights can be heard on stage left and presently MRS. GIBBS, MRS. SOAMES *and* MRS. WEBB *come down Main Street. When they arrive at the corner of the stage they stop.)*

MRS. SOAMES. Good night, Martha. Good night, Mr. Foster.

MRS. WEBB. I'll tell Mr. Webb; I *know* he'll want to put it in his paper.

MRS. GIBBS. My, it's late!

MRS. SOAMES. Good night, Irma.

MRS. GIBBS. Real nice choir practice, wa'n't it? Myrtle Webb! Look at that moon, will you! Tsk-tsk-tsk. Potato weather, for sure.

(They are silent a moment, gazing up at the moon.)

MRS. SOAMES. Naturally I didn't want to say a

word about it in front of those others, but now we're alone—really, it's the worst scandal that ever was in this town!

MRS. GIBBS. What?

MRS. SOAMES. Simon Stimson!

MRS. GIBBS. Now, Louella!

MRS. SOAMES. But, Julia! To have the organist of a church *drink* and *drunk* year after year. You know he was drunk tonight.

MRS. GIBBS. Now, Louella! We all know about Mr. Stimson and we all know about the troubles he's been through, and Dr. Ferguson knows too, and if Dr. Ferguson keeps him on there in his job the only thing the rest of us can do is just not to notice it.

MRS. SOAMES. *Not to notice it!* But it's getting worse.

MRS. WEBB. No, it isn't, Louella. It's getting better. I've been in that choir twice as long as you have. It doesn't happen anywhere near so often. . . . My, I hate to go to bed on a night like this.—I better hurry. Those children'll be sitting up till all hours. Good night, Louella.

(They all exchange good-nights. She hurries downstage, enters her house and disappears.)

MRS. GIBBS. Can you get home safe, Louella?

MRS. SOAMES. It's as bright as day. I can see Mr. Soames scowling at the window now. You'd think we'd been to a dance the way the menfolk carry on.

(More good-nights. MRS. GIBBS arrives at her home and passes through the trellis into the kitchen.)

MRS. GIBBS. Well, we had a real good time.

DR. GIBBS. You're late enough.

MRS. GIBBS. Why, Frank, it ain't any later 'n usual.

DR. GIBBS. And you stopping at the corner to gossip with a lot of hens.

MRS. GIBBS. Now, Frank, don't be grouchy. Come out and smell the heliotrope in the moonlight. (They stroll out arm in arm along the footlights.) Isn't that wonderful?

What did you do all the time I was away?

DR. GIBBS. Oh, I read—as usual. What were the girls gossiping about tonight?

MRS. GIBBS. Well, believe me, Frank—there is something to gossip about.

DR. GIBBS. Hmm! Simon Stimson far gone, was he?

MRS. GIBBS. Worst I've ever seen him. How'll that end, Frank? Dr. Ferguson can't forgive him forever.

DR. GIBBS. I guess I know more about Simon Stimson's affairs than anybody in this town. Some people ain't made for small-town life. I don't know how that'll end; but there's nothing we can do but just leave it alone. Come, get in.

MRS. GIBBS. No, not yet . . . Frank, I'm worried about you.

DR. GIBBS. What are you worried about?

MRS. GIBBS. I think it's my duty to make plans for you to get a real rest and change. And if I get that legacy, well, I'm going to insist on it.

DR. GIBBS. Now, Julia, there's no sense in going over that again.

MRS. GIBBS. Frank, you're just *unreasonable!*

DR. GIBBS *(starting into the house).* Come on, Julia, it's getting late. First thing you know you'll catch cold. I gave George a piece of my mind tonight. I reckon you'll have your wood chopped for a while anyway. No, no, start getting upstairs.

MRS. GIBBS. Oh, dear. There's always so many things to pick up, seems like. You know, Frank, Mrs. Fairchild always locks her front door every night. All those people up that part of town do.

DR. GIBBS *(blowing out the lamp).* They're all getting citified, that's the trouble with them. They haven't got nothing fit to burgle and everybody knows it.

(They disappear.
REBECCA *climbs up the ladder beside* GEORGE.*)*

GEORGE. Get out, Rebecca. There's only room for one at this window. You're always spoiling everything.

REBECCA. Well, let me look just a minute.

GEORGE. Use your own window.

REBECCA. I did, but there's no moon there . . . George, do you know what I think, do you? I think maybe the moon's getting nearer and nearer and there'll be a big 'splosion.

GEORGE. Rebecca, you don't know anything. If the moon were getting nearer, the guys that sit up all night with telescopes would see it first and they'd tell about it, and it'd be in all the newspapers.

REBECCA. George, is the moon shining on South America, Canada and half the whole world?

GEORGE. Well—prob'ly is.

(The STAGE MANAGER *strolls on.*
Pause. The sound of crickets is heard.)

STAGE MANAGER. Nine thirty. Most of the lights are out. No, there's Constable Warren trying a few doors on Main Street. And here comes Editor Webb, after putting his newspaper to bed.

(MR. WARREN, an elderly policeman, comes along Main Street from the right, MR. WEBB *from the left.)*

MR. WEBB. Good evening, Bill.

CONSTABLE WARREN. Evenin', Mr. Webb.

MR. WEBB. Quite a moon!

CONSTABLE WARREN. Yepp.

MR. WEBB. All quiet tonight?

CONSTABLE WARREN. Simon Stimson is rollin' around a little. Just saw his wife movin' out to hunt for him so I looked the other way—there he is now.

(SIMON STIMSON comes down Main Street from the left, only a trace of unsteadiness in his walk.)

MR. WEBB. Good evening, Simon. . . . Town seems to have settled down for the night pretty well. . . .

(SIMON STIMSON *comes up to him and pauses a moment and stares at him, swaying slightly.*)

Good evening. . . . Yes, most of the town's settled down for the night, Simon. . . . I guess we better do the same. Can I walk along a ways with you?

(SIMON STIMSON *continues on his way without a word and disappears at the right.*)

Good night.

CONSTABLE WARREN. I don't know how that's goin' to end, Mr. Webb.

MR. WEBB. Well, he's seen a peck of trouble, one thing after another. . . . Oh, Bill . . . if you see my boy smoking cigarettes, just give him a word, will you? He thinks a lot of you, Bill.

CONSTABLE WARREN. I don't think he smokes no cigarettes, Mr. Webb. Leastways, not more'n two or three a year.

MR. WEBB. Hm . . . I hope not.—Well, good night, Bill.

CONSTABLE WARREN. Good night, Mr. Webb. (*Exit.*)

MR. WEBB. Who's that up there? Is that you, Myrtle?

EMILY. No, it's me, Papa.

MR. WEBB. Why aren't you in bed?

EMILY. I don't know. I just can't sleep yet, Papa. The moonlight's so *won*-derful. And the smell of Mrs. Gibbs's heliotrope. Can you smell it?

MR. WEBB. Hm . . . Yes. Haven't any troubles on your mind, have you, Emily?

EMILY. *Troubles*, Papa? *No.*

MR. WEBB. Well, enjoy yourself, but don't let your mother catch you. Good night, Emily.

EMILY. Good night, Papa.

(MR. WEBB *crosses into the house, whistling "Blessed Be the Tie That Binds," and disappears.*)

REBECCA. I never told you about that letter Jane Crofut got from her minister when she was sick. He wrote Jane a letter and on the envelope the address was like this. It said: Jane Crofut; The Crofut Farm; Grover's Corners; Sutton County; New Hampshire; United States of America.

GEORGE. What's funny about that?

REBECCA. But listen, it's not finished: the United States of America; Continent of North America; Western Hemisphere; the Earth; the Solar System; the Universe; the Mind of God—that's what it said on the envelope.

GEORGE. What do you know!

REBECCA. And the postman brought it just the same.

GEORGE. What do you know!

STAGE MANAGER. That's the end of the first act, friends. You can go and smoke now, those that smoke.

Act One

Getting at Meaning

1. The Stage Manager is similar in function to the Greek Chorus in the plays of Aeschylus, Sophocles, and Euripedes. In those plays, written in the fifth century B.C., the chorus was a group of elders who commented on the action of the characters and who interpreted the significance of the dramatic action for the audience. Occasionally, the chorus would enter into the action of the play.

What information does the Stage Manager give in his opening monologue to reveal that he is no ordinary character in the play? Find other examples throughout

Act One in which the Stage Manager moves well beyond the confines of time and place to interpret and explain the action. Which statements of the Stage Manager express the purpose of the play?

2. Act One introduces the audience to a gallery of characters, all of them just ordinary folk, yet each one distinctive as a typical character in a small town. What are the qualities of each character? What relationships between characters seem to have potential for further development?

3. How does the audience learn about the life of the people in Grover's Corners? Why isn't the historical information provided by Professor Willard or the political and social information given by Editor Webb sufficient for understanding the town?

4. Idyllic as it seems, Grover's Corners is not quite a perfect place. What human failings and weaknesses are revealed in Act One? What problems and limitations of the town are apparent?

5. Generally, the closing lines of an act emphasize an idea that the playwright considers important. What idea is conveyed by Rebecca's story about the uniquely addressed letter?

Developing Skills in Reading Literature

1. **Tone.** A writer's tone can be inferred from the kinds of details and incidents presented, from the formality or informality of the language used, and from the nature of the characters and conflicts created. What is the tone of *Our Town*? How does the Stage Manager's opening description of Grover's Corners set the tone? In what other ways is the playwright's tone made evident in Act One?

2. **Allusion.** The ladder scene between Emily and George frequently reminds audiences of a Shakespearean play about two teenagers. What is that play? Why might Wilder have used this allusion in *Our Town*?

3. **Irony.** After describing the time capsule that eventually would be placed in the cornerstone of the new bank, the Stage Manager says to the audience, "Well!—good deal of time's gone by. It's evening." How is he being ironic?

4. **Characterization.** What does Emily really mean when she says that the moonlight is "terrible"? Notice the comments about the moonlight that are made by Mrs. Gibbs, Mrs. Soames, and Rebecca. What differences in points of view are revealed? What do these differing points of view indicate about the characters?

Developing Vocabulary

1. **Using a Dictionary.** Use the dictionary to locate the definition of the word *nostalgia*. Then identify specific details in Act One that make the play nostalgic.

2. **Denotation and Connotation.** Use the dictionary to answer these questions.

"PROFESSOR WILLARD, *a rural savant, pince-nez on a wide satin ribbon, ...*"
Why is a *pince-nez* appropriate for a *savant*? What are the connotations of *savant* and *pince-nez*?
"We've got one or two town drunks, but they're always having remorses every time an evangelist comes to town."
Why would an *evangelist* stimulate *remorses*?

Developing Writing Skills

Drama: Writing a Dramatic Episode. *Our Town* is set in the years 1901–1913, before America had shifted from the predominantly rural and small town pattern of living to the urban and suburban nation of today. Times were simpler and more innocent. However, the feelings, concerns, desires, and problems of the characters in Grover's Corners and the relationships among family members are still typical, in many respects, of Americans today.

Assume that you are writing a play called *Our Town—Today*. Choose two or three of the experiences that typify the process of growing up in Grover's Corners. Create contemporary versions of these same experiences, using enough detail to make *Our Town—Today* come to life for your audience.

ACT TWO

The tables and chairs of the two kitchens are still on the stage.

The ladders and the small bench have been withdrawn.

The STAGE MANAGER *has been at his accustomed place, watching the audience return to its seats.*

STAGE MANAGER. Three years have gone by.

Yes, the sun's come up over a thousand times.

Summers and winters have cracked the mountains a little bit more and the rains have brought down some of the dirt.

Some babies that weren't even born before have begun talking regular sentences already; and a number of people who thought they were right young and spry have noticed that they can't bound up a flight of stairs like they used to, without their heart fluttering a little.

All that can happen in a thousand days.

Nature's been pushing and contriving in other ways, too: a number of young people fell in love and got married.

Yes, the mountain got bit away a few fractions of an inch; millions of gallons of water went by the mill; and here and there a new home was set up under a roof.

Almost everybody in the world gets married—you know what I mean? In our town there aren't hardly any exceptions. Most everybody in the world climbs into their graves married.

The first act was called the Daily Life. This act is called Love and Marriage. There's another act coming after this: I reckon you can guess what that's about.

So:

It's three years later. It's 1904.

It's July 7th, just after high school commencement.

That's the time most of our young people jump up and get married.

Scenic design: Karl Eigsti.

Soon as they've passed their last examinations in solid geometry and Cicero's orations,[13] looks like they suddenly feel themselves fit to be married.

It's early morning. Only this time it's been raining. It's been pouring and thundering.

Mrs. Gibbs's garden, and Mrs. Webb's here: drenched.

All those bean poles and pea vines: drenched.

All yesterday over there on Main Street, the rain looked like curtains being blown along.

Hm . . . it may begin any minute.

There! You can hear the 5:45 for Boston.

(MRS. GIBBS *and* MRS. WEBB *enter their kitchen and start the day as in the first act.*)

And there's Mrs. Gibbs and Mrs. Webb come down to make breakfast, just as though it were an ordinary day. I don't have to point out to the women in my audience that those ladies they see before them, both of those ladies cooked three meals a day—one of 'em for twenty years, the other for forty—and no summer vacation. They brought up two children apiece, washed, cleaned the house—and *never a nervous breakdown.*

It's like what one of those Middle West poets said: You've got to love life to have life, and you've got to have life to love life.[14] . . .

It's what they call a vicious circle.

HOWIE NEWSOME (*off stage left*). Giddap, Bessie!

STAGE MANAGER. Here comes Howie Newsome delivering the milk. And there's Si Crowell delivering the papers like his brother before him.

(SI CROWELL *has entered hurling imaginary newspapers into doorways;* HOWIE NEWSOME *has come along Main Street with Bessie.*)

SI CROWELL. Morning, Howie.

HOWIE NEWSOME. Morning, Si.—Anything in the papers I ought to know?

SI CROWELL. Nothing much, except we're losing about the best baseball pitcher Grover's Corners ever had—George Gibbs.

HOWIE NEWSOME. Reckon he is.

SI CROWELL. He could hit and run bases, too.

HOWIE NEWSOME. Yep. Mighty fine ball player. —Whoa! Bessie! I guess I can stop and talk if I've a mind to!

SI CROWELL. I don't see how he could give up a thing like that just to get married. Would you, Howie?

HOWIE NEWSOME. Can't tell, Si. Never had no talent that way.

(CONSTABLE WARREN *enters. They exchange good-mornings.*)

You're up early, Bill.

CONSTABLE WARREN. Seein' if there's anything I can do to prevent a flood. River's been risin' all night.

HOWIE NEWSOME. Si Crowell's all worked up here about George Gibbs's retiring from baseball.

CONSTABLE WARREN. Yes, sir; that's the way it goes. Back in '84 we had a player, Si—even George Gibbs couldn't touch him. Name of Hank Todd. Went down to Maine and become a parson. Wonderful ball player.— Howie, how does the weather look to you?

HOWIE NEWSOME. Oh, 'taint bad. Think maybe it'll clear up for good.

(CONSTABLE WARREN *and* SI CROWELL *continue on their way.*

HOWIE NEWSOME *brings the milk first to* MRS. GIBBS'S *house. She meets him by the trellis.*)

MRS. GIBBS. Good morning, Howie. Do you think it's going to rain again?

---

13. Marcus Tullius Cicero (106-43 B.C.), Roman statesman whose orations are studied in Latin classes.
14. Edgar Lee Masters's poem "Lucinda Matlock" actually reads "It takes life to love life."

HOWIE NEWSOME. Morning, Mrs. Gibbs. It rained so heavy, I think maybe it'll clear up.

MRS. GIBBS. Certainly hope it will.

HOWIE NEWSOME. How much did you want today?

MRS. GIBBS. I'm going to have a houseful of relations, Howie. Looks to me like I'll need three-a-milk and two-a-cream.

HOWIE NEWSOME. My wife says to tell you we both hope they'll be very happy, Mrs. Gibbs. Know they *will*.

MRS. GIBBS. Thanks a lot, Howie. Tell your wife I hope she gits there to the wedding.

HOWIE NEWSOME. Yes, she'll be there; she'll be there if she kin. *(HOWIE NEWSOME crosses to MRS. WEBB's house.)* Morning, Mrs. Webb.

MRS. WEBB. Oh, good morning, Mr. Newsome. I told you four quarts of milk, but I hope you can spare me another.

HOWIE NEWSOME. Yes'm . . . and the two of cream.

MRS. WEBB. Will it start raining again, Mr. Newsome?

HOWIE NEWSOME. Well. Just sayin' to Mrs. Gibbs as how it may lighten up. Mrs. Newsome told me to tell you as how we hope they'll both be very happy, Mrs. Webb. Know they *will*.

MRS. WEBB. Thank you, and thank Mrs. Newsome and we're counting on seeing you at the wedding.

HOWIE NEWSOME. Yes, Mrs. Webb. We hope to git there. Couldn't miss that. Come on, Bessie.

(Exit HOWIE NEWSOME.
DR. GIBBS descends in shirt sleeves, and sits down at his breakfast table.)

DR. GIBBS. Well, Ma, the day has come. You're losin' one of your chicks.

MRS. GIBBS. Frank Gibbs, don't you say another word. I feel like crying every minute. Sit down and drink your coffee.

DR. GIBBS. The groom's up shaving himself—only there ain't an awful lot to shave. Whistling and singing, like he's glad to leave us.—Every now and then he says "I do" to the mirror, but it don't sound convincing to me.

MRS. GIBBS. I declare, Frank, I don't know how he'll get along. I've arranged his clothes and seen to it he's put warm things on—Frank! they're too *young*. Emily won't think of such things. He'll catch his death of cold within a week.

DR. GIBBS. I was remembering my wedding morning, Julia.

MRS. GIBBS. Now don't start that, Frank Gibbs.

DR. GIBBS. I was the scaredest young fella in the state of New Hampshire. I thought I'd made a mistake for sure. And when I saw you comin' down that aisle I thought you were the prettiest girl I'd ever seen, but the only trouble was that I'd never seen you before. There I was in the Congregational Church marryin' a total stranger.

MRS. GIBBS. And how do you think I felt!—Frank, weddings are perfectly awful things. Farces—that's what they are! *(She puts a plate before him.)* Here, I've made something for you.

DR. GIBBS. Why, Julia Hersey—French toast!

MRS. GIBBS. 'Tain't hard to make and I had to do *something*.

(Pause. DR. GIBBS pours on the syrup.)

DR. GIBBS. How'd you sleep last night, Julia?

MRS. GIBBS. Well, I heard a lot of the hours struck off.

DR. GIBBS. Ye-e-s! I get a shock every time I think of George setting out to be a family man—that great gangling thing!—I tell you Julia, there's nothing so terrifying in the world as a *son*. The relation of father and son is the darndest, awkwardest—

MRS. GIBBS. Well, mother and daughter's no picnic, let me tell you.

DR. GIBBS. They'll have a lot of troubles, I suppose, but that's none of our business. Everybody has a right to their own troubles.

MRS. GIBBS (*at the table drinking her coffee, meditatively*). Yes . . . people are meant to go through life two by two. 'Tain't natural to be lonesome.

(*Pause.* DR. GIBBS *starts laughing.*)

DR. GIBBS. Julia, do you know one of the things I was scared of when I married you?

MRS. GIBBS. Oh, go along with you!

DR. GIBBS. I was afraid we wouldn't have material for conversation more'n'd last us a few weeks. (*Both laugh.*) I was afraid we'd run out and eat our meals in silence, that's a fact.—Well, you and I been conversing for twenty years now without any noticeable barren spells.

MRS. GIBBS. Well—good weather, bad weather —'tain't very choice, but I always find something to say. (*She goes to the foot of the stairs.*) Did you hear Rebecca stirring around upstairs?

DR. GIBBS. No. Only day of the year Rebecca hasn't been managing everybody's business up there. She's hiding in her room.—I got the impression she's crying.

MRS. GIBBS. Lord's sakes!—This has got to stop.—Rebecca! Rebecca! Come and get your breakfast.

(GEORGE *comes rattling down the stairs, very brisk.*)

GEORGE. Good morning, everybody. Only five more hours to live. (*Makes the gesture of cutting his throat, and a loud "k-k-k," and starts through the trellis.*)

MRS. GIBBS. George Gibbs, where are you going?

GEORGE. Just stepping across the grass to see my girl.

MRS. GIBBS. Now, George! You put on your overshoes. It's raining torrents. You don't go out of this house without you're prepared for it.

GEORGE. Aw, Ma. It's just a *step!*

MRS. GIBBS. George! You'll catch your death of cold and cough all through the service.

DR. GIBBS. George, do as your mother tells you!

(DR. GIBBS *goes upstairs.*

GEORGE *returns reluctantly to the kitchen and pantomimes putting on overshoes.*)

MRS. GIBBS. From tomorrow on you can kill yourself in all weathers, but while you're in my house you'll live wisely, thank you. —Maybe Mrs. Webb isn't used to callers at seven in the morning.—Here, take a cup of coffee first.

GEORGE. Be back in a minute. (*He crosses the stage, leaping over the puddles.*) Good morning, Mother Webb.

MRS. WEBB. Goodness! You frightened me!— Now, George. You can come in a minute out of the wet, but you know I can't ask you in.

GEORGE. Why not—?

MRS. WEBB. George, you know's as well as I do: the groom can't see his bride on his wedding day, not until he sees her in church.

GEORGE. Aw!—that's just a superstition.— Good morning, Mr. Webb.

(*Enter* MR. WEBB.)

MR. WEBB. Good morning, George.

GEORGE. Mr. Webb, you don't believe in that superstition, do you?

MR. WEBB. There's a lot of common sense in some superstitions, George. (*He sits at the table, facing right.*)

MRS. WEBB. Millions have folla'd it, George, and you don't want to be the first to fly in the face of custom.

GEORGE. How is Emily?

MRS. WEBB. She hasn't waked up yet. I haven't heard a sound out of her.

GEORGE. Emily's *asleep!!!*

MRS. WEBB. No wonder! We were up 'til all hours, sewing and packing. Now I'll tell you what I'll do; you set down here a minute with Mr. Webb and drink this cup of coffee; and I'll go upstairs and see she doesn't come down and surprise you. There's some bacon, too; but don't be long about it.

(Exit MRS. WEBB.

Embarrassed silence.

MR. WEBB *dunks doughnuts in his coffee.*

More silence.)

MR. WEBB *(suddenly and loudly).* Well, George, how are you?

GEORGE *(startled, choking over his coffee).* Oh, fine, I'm fine. *(Pause)* Mr. Webb, what sense could there be in a superstition like that?

MR. WEBB. Well, you see—on her wedding morning a girl's head's apt to be full of . . . clothes and one thing and another. Don't you think that's probably it?

GEORGE. Ye-e-s. I never thought of that.

MR. WEBB. A girl's apt to be a mite nervous on her wedding day. *(Pause)*

GEORGE. I wish a fellow could get married without all that marching up and down.

MR. WEBB. Every man that's ever lived has felt that way about it, George; but it hasn't been any use. It's the womenfolk who've built up weddings, my boy. For a while now the women have it all their own. A man looks pretty small at a wedding, George. All those good women standing shoulder to shoulder making sure that the knot's tied in a mighty public way.

GEORGE. But . . . you *believe* in it, don't you, Mr. Webb?

MR. WEBB *(with alacrity).* Oh, yes; oh, yes. Don't you misunderstand me, my boy. Marriage is a wonderful thing—wonderful thing. And don't you forget that, George.

GEORGE. No, sir.—Mr. Webb, how old were you when you got married?

MR. WEBB. Well, you see: I'd been to college and I'd taken a little time to get settled. But Mrs. Webb—she wasn't much older than what Emily is. Oh, age hasn't much to do with it, George—not compared with . . . uh . . . other things.

GEORGE. What were you going to say, Mr. Webb?

MR. WEBB. Oh, I don't know.—Was I going to say something? *(Pause)* George, I was thinking the other night of some advice my father gave me when I got married. Charles, he said, Charles, start out early showing who's boss, he said. Best thing to do is to give an order, even if it don't make sense; just so she'll learn to obey. And he said: If anything about your wife irritates you—her conversation, or anything—just get up and leave the house. That'll make it clear to her, he said. And, oh, yes! he said never, *never* let your wife know how much money you have, never.

GEORGE. Well, Mr. Webb . . . I don't think I could . . .

MR. WEBB. So I took the opposite of my father's advice and I've been happy ever since. And let that be a lesson to you, George, never to ask advice on personal matters.—George, are you going to raise chickens on your farm?

GEORGE. What?

MR. WEBB. Are you going to raise chickens on your farm?

GEORGE. Uncle Luke's never been much interested, but I thought—

MR. WEBB. A book came into my office the other day, George, on the Philo System of raising chickens. I want you to read it. I'm thinking of beginning in a small way in the backyard, and I'm going to put an incubator in the cellar—

(Enter MRS. WEBB.*)*

MRS. WEBB. Charles, are you talking about that old incubator again? I thought you two'd be talking about things worthwhile.

MR. WEBB *(bitingly).* Well, Myrtle, if you want to give the boy some good advice, I'll go upstairs and leave you alone with him.

MRS. WEBB *(pulling* GEORGE *up).* George, Emily's got to come downstairs and eat her breakfast. She sends you her love but she doesn't want to lay eyes on you. Goodbye.

GEORGE. Goodbye. (GEORGE *crosses the stage to his own home, bewildered and crestfallen. He slowly dodges a puddle and disappears into his house.*)

MR. WEBB. Myrtle, I guess you don't know about that older superstition.

MRS. WEBB. What do you mean, Charles?

MR. WEBB. Since the cave men: no bridegroom should see his father-in-law on the day of the wedding, or near it. Now remember that. (*Both leave the stage.*)

STAGE MANAGER. Thank you very much, Mr. and Mrs. Webb.—Now I have to interrupt again here. You see, we want to know how all this began—this wedding, this plan to spend a lifetime together. I'm awfully interested in how big things like that begin.

You know how it is: you're twenty-one or twenty-two and you make some decisions; then whisssh! you're seventy: you've been a lawyer for fifty years, and that white-haired lady at your side has eaten over fifty thousand meals with you.

How do such things begin?

George and Emily are going to show you now the conversation they had when they first knew that . . . that . . . as the saying goes . . . they were meant for one another.

But before they do I want you to try and remember what it was like to have been very young.

And particularly the days when you were first in love; when you were like a person sleepwalking, and you didn't quite see the street you were in, and didn't quite hear everything that was said to you.

You're just a little bit crazy. Will you remember that, please?

Now they'll be coming out of high school at three o'clock. George has just been elected president of the junior class, and as it's June, that means he'll be president of the senior class all next year. And Emily's just been elected secretary and treasurer. I don't have to tell you how important that is. (*He places a board across the backs of two chairs, which he takes from those at the Gibbs family's table. He brings two high stools from the wings and places them behind the board. Persons sitting on the stools will be facing the audience. This is the counter of Mr. Morgan's drugstore. The sounds of young people's voices are heard off left.*) Yepp—there they are coming down Main Street now.

(EMILY, *carrying an armful of—imaginary— schoolbooks, comes along Main Street from the left.*)

EMILY. I can't, Louise. I've got to go home. Goodbye. Oh, Ernestine! Ernestine! Can you come over tonight and do Latin? Isn't that Cicero the worst thing—! Tell your mother you *have* to. G'bye. G'bye, Helen. G'bye, Fred.

(GEORGE, *also carrying books, catches up with her.*)

GEORGE. Can I carry your books home for you. Emily?

EMILY (*coolly*). Why . . . uh . . . Thank you. It isn't far. (*She gives them to him.*)

GEORGE. Excuse me a minute, Emily.—Say, Bob, if I'm a little late, start practice anyway. And give Herb some long high ones.

EMILY. Goodbye, Lizzy.

GEORGE. Goodbye, Lizzy.—I'm awfully glad you were elected, too, Emily.

EMILY. Thank you.

(*They have been standing on Main Street, almost against the back wall. They take the first steps toward the audience when* GEORGE *stops and says:*)

GEORGE. Emily, why are you mad at me?

EMILY. I'm not mad at you.

GEORGE. You've been treating me so funny lately.

EMILY. Well, since you ask me, I might as well

say it right out, George— (*She catches sight of a teacher passing.*) Goodbye, Miss Corcoran.

GEORGE. Goodbye, Miss Corcoran.—Wha—what is it?

EMILY (*not scoldingly; finding it difficult to say*). I don't like the whole change that's come over you in the last year. I'm sorry if that hurts your feelings, but I've got to—tell the truth and shame the devil.

GEORGE. A *change?*—Wha—what do you mean?

EMILY. Well, up to a year ago I used to like you a lot. And I used to watch you as you did everything . . . because we'd been friends so long . . . and then you began spending all your time at *baseball* . . . and you never stopped to speak to anybody any more. Not even to your own family you didn't . . . and, George, it's a fact, you've got awful conceited and stuck-up, and all the girls say so. They may not say so to your face, but that's what they say about you behind your back, and it hurts me to hear them say it, but I've got to agree with them a little. I'm sorry if it hurts your feelings . . . but I can't be sorry I said it.

GEORGE. I . . . I'm glad you said it, Emily. I never thought that such a thing was happening to me. I guess it's hard for a fella not to have faults creep into his character.

(*They take a step or two in silence, then stand still in misery.*)

EMILY. I always expect a man to be perfect and I think he should be.

GEORGE. Oh . . . I don't think it's possible to be perfect, Emily.

EMILY. Well, my *father* is, and as far as I can see *your* father is. There's no reason on earth why you shouldn't be, too.

GEORGE. Well, I feel it's the other way round. That men aren't naturally good; but girls are.

EMILY. Well, you might as well know right now that I'm not perfect. It's not as easy for

a girl to be perfect as a man, because we girls are more—more—nervous.—Now I'm sorry I said all that about you. I don't know what made me say it.

GEORGE. Emily—

EMILY. Now I can see it's not the truth at all. And I suddenly feel that it isn't important, anyway.

GEORGE. Emily . . . would you like an ice-cream soda, or something, before you go home?

EMILY. Well, thank you. . . . I would.

(*They advance toward the audience and make an abrupt right turn, opening the door of Morgan's drugstore. Under strong emotion,* EMILY *keeps her face down.* GEORGE *speaks to some passers-by.*)

GEORGE. Hello, Stew—how are you?—Good afternoon, Mrs. Slocum.

(*The* STAGE MANAGER, *wearing spectacles and assuming the role of Mr. Morgan, enters abruptly from the right and stands between the audience and the counter of his soda fountain.*)

STAGE MANAGER. Hello, George. Hello, Emily. —What'll you have?—Why, Emily Webb— what you been crying about?

GEORGE (*He gropes for an explanation.*) She . . . she just got an awful scare, Mr. Morgan. She almost got run over by that hardware-store wagon. Everybody says that Tom Huckins drives like a crazy man.

STAGE MANAGER (*drawing a drink of water*). Well, now! You take a drink of water, Emily. You look all shook up. I tell you, you've got to look both ways before you cross Main Street these days. Gets worse every year.—What'll you have?

EMILY. I'll have a strawberry phosphate, thank you, Mr. Morgan.

GEORGE. No, no, Emily. Have an ice-cream soda with me. Two strawberry ice-cream sodas, Mr. Morgan.

STAGE MANAGER (*working the faucets*). Two

strawberry ice-cream sodas, yes sir. Yes, sir. There are a hundred and twenty-five horses in Grover's Corners this minute I'm talking to you. State inspector was in here yesterday. And now they're bringing in these auto-mobiles, the best thing to do is to just stay home. Why, I can remember when a dog could go to sleep all day in the middle of Main Street and nothing come along to disturb him. *(He sets the imaginary glasses before them.)* There they are. Enjoy 'em. *(He sees a customer, right.)* Yes, Mrs. Ellis. What can I do for you? *(He goes out right.)*

EMILY. They're so expensive.

GEORGE. No, no—don't you think of that. We're celebrating our election. And then do you know what else I'm celebrating?

EMILY. N-no.

GEORGE. I'm celebrating because I've got a friend who tells me all the things that ought to be told me.

• EMILY. George, *please* don't think of that. I don't know why I said it. It's not true. You're—

GEORGE. No, Emily, you stick to it. I'm glad you spoke to me like you did. But you'll *see:* I'm going to change so quick—you bet I'm going to change. And, Emily, I want to ask you a favor.

EMILY. What?

GEORGE. Emily, if I go away to State Agriculture College next year, will you write me a letter once in a while?

EMILY. I certainly will. I certainly will, George. . . .

(Pause. They start sipping the sodas through the straws.)

It certainly seems like being away three years you'd get out of touch with things. Maybe letters from Grover's Corners wouldn't be so interesting after a while. Grover's Corners isn't a very important place when you think of all—New Hampshire; but I think it's a very nice town.

GEORGE. The day wouldn't come when I wouldn't want to know everything that's happening here. I know *that's* true, Emily.

EMILY. Well, I'll try to make my letters interesting.

(Pause)

GEORGE. Y'know, Emily, whenever I meet a farmer I ask him if he thinks it's important to go to agriculture school to be a good farmer.

EMILY. Why, George—

GEORGE. Yeah, and some of them say that it's even a waste of time. You can get all those things, anyway, out of the pamphlets the government sends out. And Uncle Luke's getting old—he's about ready for me to start in taking over his farm tomorrow, if I could.

EMILY. My!

GEORGE. And, like you say, being gone all that time . . . in other places and meeting other people . . . Gosh, if anything like that can happen I don't want to go away. I guess new people aren't any better than old ones. I'll bet they almost never are. Emily . . . I feel that you're as good a friend as I've got. I don't need to go and meet the people in other towns.

EMILY. But, George, maybe it's very important for you to go and learn all that about—cattle judging and soils and those things. . . . Of course, I don't know.

GEORGE *(after a pause, very seriously)*. Emily, I'm going to make up my mind right now. I won't go. I'll tell Pa about it tonight.

EMILY. Why, George, I don't see why you have to decide right now. It's a whole year away.

GEORGE. Emily, I'm glad you spoke to me about that . . . that fault in my character. What you said was right; but there was *one* thing wrong in it, and that was when you said that for a year I wasn't noticing people, and . . . you, for instance. Why, you say you were watching me when I did everything . . . I was doing the same about you all the time. Why, sure—I always thought about you as one of the chief people I thought about. I always made sure where you were sitting on the bleachers, and who you were with, and for three days now I've been trying to walk home with you; but something's always got in the way. Yesterday I was standing over against the wall waiting for you, and you walked home with *Miss Corcoran.*

EMILY. George! . . . Life's awful funny! How could I have known that? Why, I thought—

GEORGE. Listen, Emily, I'm going to tell you why I'm not going to agriculture school. I think that once you've found a person that you're very fond of . . . I mean a person who's fond of you, too, and likes you enough to be interested in your character . . . Well, I think that's just as important as college is, and even more so. That's what I think.

EMILY. I think it's awfully important, too.

GEORGE. Emily.

EMILY. Y-yes, George.

GEORGE. Emily, if I *do* improve and make a big change . . . would you be . . . I mean: *could* you be . . .

EMILY. I . . . I am now; I always have been.

GEORGE (pause). So I guess this is an important talk we've been having.

EMILY. Yes . . . yes.

GEORGE (takes a deep breath and straightens his back). Wait just a minute and I'll walk you home.

(With mounting alarm he digs into his pockets for the money.

The STAGE MANAGER enters, right.

GEORGE, deeply embarrassed, but direct, says to him:)

Mr. Morgan, I'll have to go home and get the money to pay you for this. It'll only take me a minute.

STAGE MANAGER (pretending to be affronted). What's that? George Gibbs, do you mean to tell me—!

GEORGE. Yes, but I had reasons, Mr. Morgan.—Look, here's my gold watch to keep until I come back with the money.

STAGE MANAGER. That's all right. Keep your watch. I'll trust you.

GEORGE. I'll be back in five minutes.

STAGE MANAGER. I'll trust you ten years, George—not a day over.—Got all over your shock, Emily?

EMILY. Yes, thank you, Mr. Morgan. It was nothing.

GEORGE (taking up the books from the counter). I'm ready.

(They walk in grave silence across the stage and pass through the trellis at the Webbs' back door and disappear.

The STAGE MANAGER watches them go out, then turns to the audience, removing his spectacles.)

STAGE MANAGER. Well—(He claps his hands as a signal.) Now we're ready to get on with the wedding.

(He stands waiting while the set is prepared for the next scene.

Stagehands remove the chairs, tables and trellises from the Gibbs and Webb houses.

They arrange the pews for the church in the center of the stage. The congregation will sit facing the back wall. The aisle of the church starts at the center of the back wall and comes toward the audience.

A small platform is placed against the back wall on which the STAGE MANAGER will stand later, playing the minister. The image of a stained-glass window is cast from a lantern slide upon the back wall.

When all is ready the STAGE MANAGER strolls to the center of the stage, down front, and, musingly, addresses the audience.)

There are a lot of things to be said about a wedding; there are a lot of thoughts that go on during a wedding.

We can't get them all into one wedding, naturally, and especially not into a wedding at Grover's Corners, where they're awfully plain and short.

In this wedding I play the minister. That gives me the right to say a few more things about it.

For a while now, the play gets pretty serious.

Y'see, some churches say that marriage is a sacrament. I don't quite know what that means, but I can guess. Like Mrs. Gibbs said a few minutes ago: People were made to live two by two.

This is a good wedding, but people are so put together that even at a good wedding there's a lot of confusion way down deep in people's minds and we thought that that ought to be in our play, too.

The real hero of this scene isn't on the stage at all, and you know who that is. It's like what one of those European fellas said: Every child born into the world is nature's attempt to make a perfect human being. Well, we've seen nature pushing and contriving for some time now. We all know that nature's interested in quantity; but I think she's interested in quality, too—that's why I'm in the ministry.

And don't forget all the other witnesses at this wedding—the ancestors. Millions of them. Most of them set out to live two by two, also. Millions of them.

Well, that's all my sermon. 'Twan't very long, anyway.

(The organ starts playing Handel's "Largo."
The congregation streams into the church and sits in silence.
Church bells are heard.
MRS. GIBBS *sits in the front row, the first seat on the aisle, the right section; next to her are* REBECCA *and* DR. GIBBS.
Across the aisle MRS. WEBB, WALLY, *and* MR. WEBB. *A small choir takes its place, facing the audience under the stained-glass window.*

MRS. WEBB, *on the way to her place, turns back and speaks to the audience.)*

MRS. WEBB. I don't know why on earth I should be crying. I suppose there's nothing to cry about. It came over me at breakfast this morning; there was Emily eating her breakfast as she's done for seventeen years and now she's going off to eat it in someone else's house. I suppose that's it.

And Emily! She suddenly said: I can't eat another mouthful, and she put her head down on the table and *she* cried. *(She starts toward her seat in the church, but turns back and adds:)* Oh, I've got to say it: you know, there's something downright cruel about sending our girls out into marriage this way.

I hope some of her girlfriends have told her a thing or two. It's cruel, I know, but I couldn't bring myself to say anything. I went into it blind as a bat myself. *(In half-amused exasperation)* The whole world's wrong, that's what's the matter.

There they come. *(She hurries to her place in the pew.)*

*(*GEORGE *starts to come down the right aisle of the theater, through the audience.*
Suddenly THREE MEMBERS *of his baseball team appear by the right proscenium pillar and start whistling and catcalling to him. They are dressed for the ball field.)*

THE BASEBALL PLAYERS. Eh, George, George! Hast—yaow! Look at him, fellas—he looks scared to death. Yaow! George, don't look so innocent, you old geezer. We know what you're thinking. Don't disgrace the team, big boy. Whoo-oo-oo.
STAGE MANAGER. All right! All right! That'll do. That's enough of that.

(Smiling, he pushes them off the stage. They lean back to shout a few more catcalls.)

There used to be an awful lot of that kind of

thing at weddings in the old days—Rome, and later. We're more civilized now—so they say.

(The choir starts singing "Love Divine, All Love Excelling." GEORGE *has reached the stage. He stares at the congregation a moment, then takes a few steps of withdrawal, toward the right proscenium pillar. His mother, from the front row, seems to have felt his confusion. She leaves her seat and comes down the aisle quickly to him.)*

MRS. GIBBS. George! George! What's the matter?

GEORGE. Ma, I don't want to grow old. Why's everybody pushing me so?

MRS. GIBBS. Why, George . . . you wanted it.

GEORGE. No, Ma, listen to me—

MRS. GIBBS. No, no, George—you're a man now.

GEORGE. Listen, Ma—for the last time I ask you . . . All I want to do is to be a fella—

MRS. GIBBS. George! If anyone should hear you! Now, stop. Why, I'm ashamed of you!

GEORGE *(He comes to himself and looks over the scene.)* What? Where's Emily?

MRS. GIBBS *(relieved).* George! You gave me such a turn.

GEORGE. Cheer up, Ma. I'm getting married.

MRS. GIBBS. Let me catch my breath a minute.

GEORGE *(comforting her).* Now, Ma, you save Thursday nights. Emily and I are coming over to dinner every Thursday night . . . you'll see. Ma, what are you crying for? Come on; we've got to get ready for this.

*(*MRS. GIBBS, *mastering her emotion, fixes his tie and whispers to him.*

In the meantime, EMILY, *in white and wearing her wedding veil, has come through the audience and mounted onto the stage. She too draws back, frightened, when she sees the congregation in the church. The choir begins: "Blessed Be the Tie That Binds.")*

EMILY. I never felt so alone in my whole life. And George over there, looking so . . . ! I *hate* him. I wish I were dead. Papa! Papa!

MR. WEBB *(leaves his seat in the pews and comes toward her anxiously).* Emily! Emily! Now don't get upset. . . .

EMILY. But, Papa—I don't want to get married. . . .

MR. WEBB. Sh—sh—Emily. Everything's all right.

EMILY. Why can't I stay for a while just as I am? Let's go away—

MR. WEBB. No, no, Emily. Now stop and think a minute.

EMILY. Don't you remember that you used to say—all the time you used to say—all the time: that I was *your* girl! There must be lots of places we can go to. I'll work for you. I could keep house.

MR. WEBB. Sh . . . You mustn't think of such things. You're just nervous, Emily. *(He turns and calls:)* George! George! Will you come here a minute? *(He leads her toward* GEORGE.) Why, you're marrying the best young fellow in the world. George is a fine fellow.

EMILY. But Papa—

*(*MRS. GIBBS *returns unobtrusively to her seat.* MR. WEBB *has one arm around his daughter. He places his hand on* GEORGE'S *shoulder.)*

MR. WEBB. I'm giving away my daughter, George. Do you think you can take care of her?

GEORGE. Mr. Webb, I want to . . . I want to try. Emily, I'm going to do my best. I love you, Emily. I need you.

EMILY. Well, if you love me, help me. All I want is someone to love me.

GEORGE. I will, Emily. Emily, I'll try.

EMILY. And I mean *forever.* Do you hear me? Forever and ever.

(They fall into each other's arms.

The "March" from Lohengrin *is heard.*

The STAGE MANAGER, *as* CLERGYMAN, *stands on the box, up center.)*

MR. WEBB. Come, they're waiting for us. Now

you know it'll be all right. Come, quick.

(GEORGE *slips away and takes his place beside the* STAGE MANAGER-CLERGYMAN.

EMILY *proceeds up the aisle on her father's arm.*)

STAGE MANAGER. Do you, George, take this woman, Emily, to be your wedded wife, to have . . .

(MRS. SOAMES *has been sitting in the last row of the congregation.*

She now turns to her neighbors and speaks in a shrill voice. Her chatter drowns out the rest of the clergyman's words.)

MRS. SOAMES. Perfectly lovely wedding! Loveliest wedding I ever saw. Oh, I do love a good wedding, don't you? Doesn't she make a lovely bride?

GEORGE. I do.

STAGE MANAGER. Do you, Emily, take this man, George, to be your wedded husband—

(*Again, his further words are covered by those of* MRS. SOAMES.)

MRS. SOAMES. Don't know *when* I've seen such a lovely wedding. But I always cry. Don't know why it is, but I always cry. I just like to see young people happy, don't you? Oh, I think it's lovely.

(The ring.
The kiss.
The stage is suddenly arrested into silent tableau.[15]
The STAGE MANAGER, *his eyes on the distance, as though to himself:)*

STAGE MANAGER. I've married over two hundred couples in my day.
Do I believe in it?
I don't know.
M——marries N—— millions of them.
The cottage, the go-cart, the Sunday-afternoon drives in the Ford, the first rheumatism, the grandchildren, the second rheumatism, the deathbed, the reading of the will—*(He now looks at the audience for the first time, with a warm smile that removes any sense of cynicism from the next line.)* Once in a thousand times it's interesting.
—Well, let's have Mendelssohn's "Wedding March"!

(The organ picks up the "March."
The BRIDE *and* GROOM *come down the aisle, radiant, but trying to be very dignified.)*

MRS. SOAMES. Aren't they a lovely couple? Oh, I've never been to such a nice wedding. I'm sure they'll be happy. I always say: *happiness,* that's the great thing! The important thing is to be happy.

(The BRIDE *and* GROOM *reach the steps leading into the audience. A bright light is thrown upon them. They descend into the auditorium and run up the aisle joyously.)*

STAGE MANAGER. That's all the second act, folks. Ten minutes' intermission.

---

15. **tableau** (tab' lō) *French:* a striking dramatic scene by persons posing silently, without moving.

Act Two

Getting at Meaning

1. Dr. Gibbs remembers that, when he saw his wife coming down the church aisle on their wedding day, he felt as if he were "marryin' a total stranger." What point is he illustrating? How is this recollection pertinent to the experiences of George and Emily?

2. When George's parents talk about his marriage to Emily, which one shows the greater understanding of George? Explain. What are his mother's main concerns? How does Dr. Gibbs characterize the relationship between father and son? Why might he feel this way?

3. The conversation between Dr. and Mrs. Gibbs reveals the real meaning of marriage. Identify the details that define marriage. Do you think that George and Emily are approaching married life realistically? Explain your conclusion.

4. The Stage Manager gives a brief sermon. What does he talk about? Who do you think is the "real hero" of the wedding scene?

5. Before the marriage ceremony, Mrs. Gibbs tells her son, "George . . . you're a man now." What are George's momentary doubts? How do these doubts reveal that George is taking the first steps in the passage from adolescence to manhood?

6. As Act Two comes to an end, the focus shifts from George and Emily to Mrs. Soames at the back of the congregation. What idea does she repeat? Is there truth to her observation? Explain your answer.

7. The Stage Manager enumerates the typical stages of married life from beginning to end. He concludes by saying, "Once in a thousand times it's interesting."

What does he mean by "interesting"? Does he mean that most marriages are dull?

Developing Skills in Reading Literature

1. **Mood.** How does the mood of Act Two differ from that of Act One? Why is this mood appropriate to the subject of Act Two? To the feelings of the characters? Remember that in the first act, the bright moonlight was the center of discussion. Why is this element of setting appropriate to the events of Act One? In Act Two how does Wilder again use weather to create mood?

2. **Structure.** A well constructed, traditional play has the logic of an architectural whole. Act One may be considered the foundation. Act Two serves as the framework. Act Three completes the building. How do the titles of the first two acts of this play reflect this design? With what do you think Act Three will be concerned?

Within Act Two Wilder uses a kind of parallel structure in portraying George and Emily on their wedding day. How are George and Emily portrayed in parallel fashion? What is accomplished through the use of this device?

Developing Vocabulary

Inferring Word Meaning. Actors performing this play would need to understand these stage directions to carry out the playwright's intentions. Answer the question that follows each stage direction. Rely primarily on context to provide clues to the meanings of unfamiliar words.

a. GEORGE *returns reluctantly to the kitchen and pantomimes putting on overshoes.*
What should the actor do to carry out these directions?

b. MR. WEBB (*with alacrity*). . . .
How should the actor speak these lines?

c. GEORGE *crosses the stage to his own home, bewildered and crestfallen.*
How should the actor move across the stage?

d. STAGE MANAGER (*pretending to be affronted*).
What actions might be appropriate?

e. . . . *the* STAGE MANAGER *strolls to the center of the stage, down front, and, musingly, addresses the audience.*
What tone of voice would the actor use?

Developing Writing Skills

1. **Combining Description, Narration, and Exposition.** Both George and Emily experience conflicting emotions at their wedding, a ceremony that marks a rite of passage, or a transition, from one major phase of life to the next. At first eager to start life on their own, they respond to the reality of the church, the minister, and the congregation with feelings of regret over the loss of their youth and terror over the adult responsibilities they are about to assume.

Can you recall a similar experience with a corresponding duality of feelings? Try to re-create that experience for your classmates. Focus first on your feelings of anticipation, then on your realization of what the transition actually means. Describe the occasion clearly enough so that your readers have a sense of participation in your experience.

2. **Analyzing Characters.** In talking about Mrs. Gibbs and Mrs. Webb, the Stage Manager says:

". . . those ladies cooked three meals a day—one of 'em for twenty years, the other for forty—and no summer vacation. They brought up two children apiece, washed, cleaned the house—and *never a nervous breakdown.*"
"It's like what one of those Middle West poets said: You've got to love life to have life, and you've got to have life to love life. . . ."
"It's what they call a vicious circle."

The poet to whom the Stage Manager alludes is Edgar Lee Masters, and the poem that he paraphrases is "Lucinda Matlock," which appears earlier in this book. Reread this poem to discover how the Stage Manager's statement, "You've got to love life to have life, and you've got to have life to love life," relates to the life of Lucinda Matlock. Then write a five-paragraph composition to explain how the statement applies to Lucinda Matlock and to Mrs. Gibbs and Mrs. Webb in *Our Town.*

ACT THREE

During the intermission the audience has seen the STAGE HANDS *arranging the stage. On the right-hand side, a little right of the center, ten or twelve ordinary chairs have been placed in three openly spaced rows facing the audience.*

These are graves in the cemetery.

Toward the end of the intermission the actors enter and take their places. The front row contains: toward the center of the stage, an empty chair; then MRS. GIBBS; SIMON STIMSON.

The second row contains, among others, MRS. SOAMES.

The third row has WALLY WEBB.

The dead do not turn their heads or their eyes to right or left, but they sit in a quiet without stiffness. When they speak their tone is matter-of-fact, without sentimentality and, above all, without lugubriousness.

The STAGE MANAGER *takes his accustomed place and waits for the house lights to go down.*

STAGE MANAGER. This time nine years have gone by, friends—summer, 1913.

Gradual changes in Grover's Corners. Horses are getting rarer. Farmers coming into town in Fords.

Everybody locks their house doors now at night. Ain't been any burglars in town yet, but everybody's heard about 'em.

You'd be surprised, though—on the whole, things don't change much around here.

This is certainly an important part of Grover's Corners. It's on a hilltop—a windy hilltop—lots of sky, lots of clouds—often lots of sun and moon and stars.

You come up here, on a fine afternoon and you can see range on range of hills—awful blue they are—up there by Lake Sunapee and Lake Winnipesaukee . . . and way up, if you've got a glass, you can see the White Mountains and Mt. Washington —where North Conway and Conway is. And, of course, our favorite mountain, Mt. Monadnock, 's right here—and all these towns that lie around it: Jaffrey, 'n East Jaffrey, 'n Peterborough, n' Dublin; and *(Then pointing down in the audience)* there, quite a ways down, is Grover's Corners.

Yes, beautiful spot up here. Mountain laurel and li-lacks. I often wonder why people like to be buried in Woodlawn and Brooklyn when they might pass the same time up here in New Hampshire. Over there—*(Pointing to stage left)* are the old stones—1670, 1680. Strong-minded people that come a long way to be independent. Summer people walk around there laughing at the funny words on the tombstones . . . it don't do any harm. And genealogists come up from Boston—get paid by city people for looking up their ancestors. They want to make sure they're Daughters of the American Revolution and of the *Mayflower*. . . . Well, I guess that don't do any harm, either. Wherever you come near the human race, there's layers and layers of nonsense. . . .

Over there are some Civil War veterans. Iron flags on their graves . . . New Hampshire boys . . . had a notion that the Union ought to be kept together, though they'd never seen more than fifty miles of it themselves. All they knew was the name, friends—the United States of America. The United States of America. And they went and died about it.

This here is the new part of the cemetery. Here's your friend Mrs. Gibbs. 'N let me see—Here's Mr. Stimson, organist at the Congregational Church. And Mrs. Soames, who enjoyed the wedding so—you remember? Oh, and a lot of others. And Editor Webb's boy, Wallace, whose appendix burst while he was on a Boy Scout trip to Crawford Notch.

Yes, an awful lot of sorrow has sort of quieted down up here. People just wild with grief have brought their relatives up to this hill. We all know how it is . . . and then time . . . and sunny days . . . and rainy days . . . 'n snow . . . We're all glad they're in a beautiful place and we're coming up here ourselves when our fit's over.

Now there are some things we all know, but we don't take'm out and look at'm very often. We all know that *something* is eternal. And it ain't houses and it ain't names, and it ain't earth, and it ain't even the stars . . . everybody knows in their bones that *something* is eternal, and that something has to do with human beings. All the greatest people ever lived have been telling us that for five thousand years and yet you'd be surprised how people are always losing hold of it. There's something way down deep that's eternal about every human being. *(Pause)*

You know as well as I do that the dead don't stay interested in us living people for very long. Gradually, gradually, they lose hold of the earth . . . and the ambitions they had . . . and the pleasures they had . . . and the things they suffered . . . and the people they loved.

They get weaned away from the earth— that's the way I put it—weaned away.

And they stay here while the earth part of 'em burns away, burns out; and all that time they slowly get indifferent to what's goin' on in Grover's Corners.

They're waitin'. They're waitin' for something that they feel is comin'. Something important, and great. Aren't they waitin' for the eternal part in them to come out clear?

Some of the things they're going to say maybe'll hurt your feelings—but that's the way it is: mother 'n daughter . . . husband 'n wife . . . enemy 'n enemy . . . money 'n miser . . . all those terribly important things kind of grow pale around here. And

what's left when memory's gone, and your identity, Mrs. Smith? *(He looks at the audience a minute, then turns to the stage.)*

Well! There are some *living* people. There's Joe Stoddard, our undertaker, supervising a new-made grave. And here comes a Grover's Corners boy, that left town to go out West.

(JOE STODDARD has hovered about in the background. SAM CRAIG enters left, wiping his forehead from the exertion. He carries an umbrella and strolls front.)

SAM CRAIG. Good afternoon, Joe Stoddard.

JOE STODDARD. Good afternoon, good afternoon. Let me see now: do I know you?

SAM CRAIG. I'm Sam Craig.

JOE STODDARD. Gracious sakes' alive! Of all people! I should'a knowed you'd be back for the funeral. You've been away a long time, Sam.

SAM CRAIG. Yes, I've been away over twelve years. I'm in business out in Buffalo now, Joe. But I was in the East when I got news of my cousin's death, so I thought I'd combine things a little and come and see the old home. You look well.

JOE STODDARD. Yes, yes, can't complain. Very sad, our journey today, Samuel.

SAM CRAIG. Yes.

JOE STODDARD. Yes, yes. I always say I hate to supervise when a young person is taken. They'll be here in a few minutes now. I had to come here early today—my son's supervisin' at the home.

SAM CRAIG *(reading stones)*. Old Farmer McCarty, I used to do chores for him—after school. He had the lumbago.

JOE STODDARD. Yes, we brought Farmer McCarty here a number of years ago now.

SAM CRAIG *(staring at* MRS. GIBBS's *knees)*. Why, this is my Aunt Julia . . . I'd forgotten that she'd . . . of course, of course.

JOE STODDARD. Yes, Doc Gibbs lost his wife two, three years ago . . . about this time.

And today's another pretty bad blow for him, too.

MRS. GIBBS (to SIMON STIMSON: *in an even voice*). That's my sister Carey's boy, Sam . . . Sam Craig.

SIMON STIMSON. I'm always uncomfortable when *they're* around.

MRS. GIBBS. Simon.

SAM CRAIG. Do they choose their own verses much, Joe?

JOE STODDARD. No . . . not usual. Mostly the bereaved pick a verse.

SAM CRAIG. Doesn't sound like Aunt Julia. There aren't many of those Hersey sisters left now. Let me see: where are . . . I wanted to look at my father's and mother's . . .

JOE STODDARD. Over there with the Craigs . . . Avenue F.

SAM CRAIG (reading SIMON STIMSON's *epitaph*). He was an organist at church, wasn't he?—Hm, drank a lot, we used to say.

JOE STODDARD. Nobody was supposed to know about it. He'd seen a peck of trouble. (*Behind his hands*) Took his own life, y'know?

SAM CRAIG. Oh, did he?

JOE STODDARD. Hung himself in the attic. They tried to hush it up, but of course it got around. He chose his own epy-taph. You can see it there. It ain't a verse exactly.

SAM CRAIG. Why, it's just some notes of music—what is it?

JOE STODDARD. Oh, I wouldn't know. It was wrote up in the Boston papers at the time.

SAM CRAIG. Joe, what did she die of?

JOE STODDARD. Who?

SAM CRAIG. My cousin.

JOE STODDARD. Oh, didn't you know? Had some trouble bringing a baby into the world. 'Twas her second, though. There's a little boy 'bout four years old.

SAM CRAIG (opening his umbrella). The grave's going to be over there?

JOE STODDARD. Yes, there ain't much more room over here among the Gibbses, so they're opening up a whole new Gibbs section over by Avenue B. You'll excuse me now. I see they're comin'.

(*From left to center, at the back of the stage, comes a procession.* FOUR MEN *carry a casket, invisible to us. All the rest are under umbrellas. One can vaguely see:* DR. GIBBS, GEORGE, *the* WEBBS, *etc. They gather about a grave in the back center of the stage, a little to the left of center.*)

MRS. SOAMES. Who is it, Julia?

MRS. GIBBS (without raising her eyes). My daughter-in-law, Emily Webb.

MRS. SOAMES (a little surprised, but no emotion). Well, I declare! The road up here must have been awfully muddy. What did she die of, Julia?

MRS. GIBBS. In childbirth.

MRS. SOAMES. Childbirth. (Almost with a laugh) I'd forgotten all about that. My, wasn't life awful—(with a sigh) and wonderful.

SIMON STIMSON (with a sideways glance). Wonderful, was it?

MRS. GIBBS. Simon! Now, remember!

MRS. SOAMES. I remember Emily's wedding. Wasn't it a lovely wedding! And I remember her reading the class poem at graduation exercises. Emily was one of the brightest girls ever graduated from high school. I've heard Principal Wilkins say so time after time. I called on them at their new farm, just before I died. Perfectly beautiful farm.

A WOMAN FROM AMONG THE DEAD. It's on the same road we lived on.

A MAN AMONG THE DEAD. Yepp, right smart farm.

(*They subside. The group by the grave starts singing "Blessed Be the Tie That Binds."*)

A WOMAN AMONG THE DEAD. I always liked that hymn. I was hopin' they'd sing a hymn.

(*Pause. Suddenly* EMILY *appears from among the umbrellas. She is wearing a white dress. Her hair is down her back and tied by a white* ribbon like a little girl. She comes slowly, gazing wonderingly at the dead, a little dazed. She stops halfway and smiles faintly. After looking at the mourners for a moment, she walks slowly to the vacant chair beside MRS. GIBBS and sits down.)

EMILY (to them all, quietly, smiling). Hello.

MRS. SOAMES. Hello, Emily.

A MAN AMONG THE DEAD. Hello, M's Gibbs.

EMILY (warmly). Hello, Mother Gibbs.

MRS. GIBBS. Emily.

EMILY. Hello. (With surprise) It's raining. (Her eyes drift back to the funeral company.)

MRS. GIBBS. Yes . . . They'll be gone soon, dear. Just rest yourself.

EMILY. It seems thousands and thousands of years since I . . . Papa remembered that that was my favorite hymn.

Oh, I wish I'd been here a long time. I don't like being new here.—How do you do, Mr. Stimson?

SIMON STIMSON. How do you do, Emily.

(EMILY continues to look about her with a wondering smile; as though to shut out from her mind the thought of the funeral company she starts speaking to MRS. GIBBS with a touch of nervousness.)

EMILY. Mother Gibbs, George and I have made that farm into just the best place you ever saw. We thought of you all the time. We wanted to show you the new barn and a great long ce-ment drinking fountain for the stock. We bought that out of the money you left us.

MRS. GIBBS. I did?

EMILY. Don't you remember, Mother Gibbs— the legacy you left us? Why, it was over three hundred and fifty dollars.

MRS. GIBBS. Yes, yes, Emily.

EMILY. Well, there's a patent device on the drinking fountain so that it never over-flows, Mother Gibbs, and it never sinks below a certain mark they have there. It's fine. (Her voice trails off and her eyes return to the funeral group.) It won't be the same to George without me, but it's a lovely farm. (Suddenly she looks directly at MRS. GIBBS.) Live people don't under-stand, do they?

MRS. GIBBS. No, dear—not very much.

EMILY. They're sort of shut up in little boxes, aren't they? I feel as though I knew them last a thousand years ago . . . My boy is spending the day at Mrs. Carter's. (She sees MR. CARTER, among the dead.) Oh, Mr. Carter, my little boy is spending the day at your house.

MR. CARTER. Is he?

EMILY. Yes, he loves it there.—Mother Gibbs, we have a Ford, too. Never gives any trou-ble. I don't drive, though. Mother Gibbs, when does this feeling go away?—Of being . . . one of them? How long does it . . . ?

MRS. GIBBS. Sh! dear. Just wait and be patient.

EMILY (with a sigh). I know.—Look, they're finished. They're going.

MRS. GIBBS. Sh—.

(The umbrellas leave the stage. DR. GIBBS has come over to his wife's grave and stands before it a moment. EMILY looks up at his face. MRS. GIBBS does not raise her eyes.)

EMILY. Look! Father Gibbs is bringing some of my flowers to you. He looks just like George, doesn't he? Oh, Mother Gibbs, I never realized before how troubled and how . . . how in the dark live persons are. Look at him. I loved him so. From morning till night, that's all they are—troubled.

(DR. GIBBS goes off.)

THE DEAD. Little cooler than it was.—Yes, that rain's cooled it off a little. Those northeast winds always do the same thing, don't they? If it isn't a rain, it's a three-day blow.—

(A patient calm falls on the stage. The STAGE MANAGER appears at his proscenium pillar, smoking. EMILY sits up abruptly with an idea.)

EMILY. But, Mother Gibbs, one can go back; one can go back there again . . . into living. I feel it, I know it. Why, then just for a moment I was thinking about . . . about the farm . . . and for a minute I *was* there, and my baby was on my lap as plain as day.

MRS. GIBBS. Yes, of course you can.

EMILY. I can go back there and live all those days over again . . . why not?

MRS. GIBBS. All I can say is, Emily, don't.

EMILY (*She appeals urgently to the* STAGE MANAGER). But it's true, isn't it? I can go and live. . . . back there . . . again.

STAGE MANAGER. Yes, some have tried—but they soon come back here.

MRS. GIBBS. Don't do it, Emily.

MRS. SOAMES. Emily, don't. It's not what you think it'd be.

EMILY. But I won't live over a sad day. I'll choose a happy one—I'll choose the day I first knew that I loved George. Why should that be painful?

(*They are silent. Her question turns to the* STAGE MANAGER.)

STAGE MANAGER. You not only live it; but you watch yourself living it.

EMILY. Yes?

STAGE MANAGER. And as you watch it, you see the thing that they—down there—never know. You see the future. You know what's going to happen afterwards.

EMILY. But is that—painful? Why?

MRS. GIBBS. That's not the only reason why you shouldn't do it, Emily. When you've been here longer you'll see that our life here is to forget all that, and think only of what's ahead, and be ready for what's ahead. When you've been here longer, you'll understand.

EMILY (*softly*). But, Mother Gibbs, how can I *ever* forget that life? It's all I know. It's all I had.

MRS. SOAMES. Oh, Emily. It isn't wise. Really, it isn't.

EMILY. But it's a thing I must know for myself. I'll choose a happy day, anyway.

MRS. GIBBS. *No!*—At least, choose an unimportant day. Choose the least important day in your life. It will be important enough.

EMILY (*to herself*). Then it can't be since I was married; or since the baby was born. (*To the* STAGE MANAGER, *eagerly.*) I can choose a birthday at least, can't I?—I choose my twelfth birthday.

STAGE MANAGER. All right. February 11th, 1899. A Tuesday.—Do you want any special time of day?

EMILY. Oh, I want the whole day.

STAGE MANAGER. We'll begin at dawn. You remember it had been snowing for several days; but it had stopped the night before, and they had begun clearing the roads. The sun's coming up.

EMILY (*with a cry; rising*). There's Main Street . . . why, that's Mr. Morgan's drugstore before he changed it! . . . And there's the livery stable.

(*The stage at no time in this act has been very dark; but now the left half of the stage gradually becomes very bright—the brightness of a crisp winter morning.* EMILY *walks toward Main Street.*)

STAGE MANAGER. Yes, it's 1899. This is fourteen years ago.

EMILY. Oh, that's the town I knew as a little girl. And, *look*, there's the old white fence that used to be around our house. Oh, I'd forgotten that! Oh, I love it so! Are they inside?

STAGE MANAGER. Yes, your mother'll be coming downstairs in a minute to make breakfast.

EMILY (*softly*). Will she?

STAGE MANAGER. And you remember: your father had been away for several days; he came back on the early-morning train.

EMILY. No . . . ?

STAGE MANAGER. He'd been back to his college

to make a speech—in western New York, at Clinton.

EMILY. Look! There's Howie Newsome. There's our policeman. But he's *dead;* he *died.*

(*The voices of* HOWIE NEWSOME, CONSTABLE WARREN *and* JOE CROWELL, JR., *are heard at the left of the stage.* EMILY *listens in delight.*)

HOWIE NEWSOME. Whoa, Bessie!—Bessie! 'Morning, Bill.

CONSTABLE WARREN. Morning, Howie.

HOWIE NEWSOME. You're up early.

CONSTABLE WARREN. Been rescuin' a party; darn near froze to death, down by Polish Town thar. Got drunk and lay out in the snowdrifts. Thought he was in bed when I shook'm.

EMILY. Why, there's Joe Crowell. . . .

JOE CROWELL, JR. Good morning, Mr. Warren. 'Morning, Howie.

(MRS. WEBB *has appeared in her kitchen, but* EMILY *does not see her until she calls.*)

MRS. WEBB. Chil-*dren!* Wally! Emily! . . . Time to get up.

EMILY. Mama, I'm here! Oh! how young Mama looks! I didn't know Mama was ever that young.

MRS. WEBB. You can come and dress by the kitchen fire, if you like; but hurry.

(HOWIE NEWSOME *has entered along Main Street and brings the milk to* MRS. WEBB'S *door.*)

Good morning, Mr. Newsome. Whhh—it's cold.

HOWIE NEWSOME. Ten below by my barn, Mrs. Webb.

MRS. WEBB. Think of it! Keep yourself wrapped up. (*She takes her bottles in, shuddering.*)

EMILY (*with an effort*). Mama, I can't find my blue hair ribbon anywhere.

MRS. WEBB. Just open your eyes, dear, that's all. I laid it out for you special—on the dresser,

there. If it were a snake it would bite you.

EMILY. Yes, yes . . .

(*She puts her hand on her heart.* MR. WEBB *comes along Main Street, where he meets* CONSTABLE WARREN. *Their movements and voices are increasingly lively in the sharp air.*)

MR. WEBB. Good morning, Bill.

CONSTABLE WARREN. Good morning, Mr. Webb. You're up early.

MR. WEBB. Yes, just been back to my old college in New York State. Been any trouble here?

CONSTABLE WARREN. Well, I was called up this mornin' to rescue a Polish fella—darn near froze to death he was.

MR. WEBB. We must get it in the paper.

CONSTABLE WARREN. 'Twan't much.

EMILY (*whispers*). Papa.

(MR. WEBB *shakes the snow off his feet and enters his house.* CONSTABLE WARREN *goes off, right.*)

MR. WEBB. Good morning, Mother.

MRS. WEBB. How did it go, Charles?

MR. WEBB. Oh, fine, I guess. I told'm a few things.—Everything all right here?

MRS. WEBB. Yes—can't think of anything that's happened, special. Been right cold. Howie Newsome says it's ten below over to his barn.

MR. WEBB. Yes, well, it's colder than that at Hamilton College. Students' ears are falling off. It ain't Christian.—Paper have any mistakes in it?

MRS. WEBB. None that I noticed. Coffee's ready when you want it. (*He starts upstairs.*) Charles! Don't forget; it's Emily's birthday. Did you remember to get her something?

MR. WEBB (*patting his pocket*). Yes, I've got something here. (*Calling up the stairs*) Where's my girl? Where's my birthday girl? (*He goes off left.*)

MRS. WEBB. Don't interrupt her now, Charles. You can see her at breakfast. She's slow enough as it is. Hurry up, children! It's seven o'clock. Now, I don't want to call you again.

EMILY (*softly, more in wonder than in grief*). I can't bear it. They're so young and beautiful. Why did they ever have to get old? Mama, I'm here. I'm grown up. I love you all, everything.—I can't look at everything hard enough.

(*She looks questioningly at the* STAGE MANAGER, *saying or suggesting: "Can I go in?" He nods briefly. She crosses to the inner door to the kitchen, left of her mother, and as though entering the room, says, suggesting the voice of a girl of twelve.*)

Good morning, Mama.

MRS. WEBB (*crossing to embrace and kiss her; in her characteristic matter-of-fact manner*). Well, now, dear, a very happy birthday to my girl and many happy returns. There are some surprises waiting for you on the kitchen table.

EMILY. Oh, Mama, you *shouldn't* have. (*She throws an anguished glance at the* STAGE MANAGER.) I can't—I can't.

MRS. WEBB (*facing the audience, over her stove*). But birthday or no birthday, I want you to eat your breakfast good and slow. I want you to grow up and be a good strong girl.

That in the blue paper is from your Aunt Carrie; and I reckon you can guess who brought the postcard album. I found it on the doorstep when I brought in the milk— George Gibbs . . . must have come over in the cold pretty early . . . right nice of him.

EMILY (*to herself*). Oh, George! I'd forgotten that. . . .

MRS. WEBB. Chew that bacon good and slow. It'll help keep you warm on a cold day.

EMILY (*with mounting urgency*). Oh, Mama, just look at me one minute as though you really saw me. Mama, fourteen years have gone by. I'm dead. You're a grandmother, Mama. I married George Gibbs, Mama.

Wally's dead, too. Mama, his appendix burst on a camping trip to North Conway. We felt just terrible about it—don't you remember? But, just for a moment now we're all together. Mama, just for a moment we're happy. *Let's look at one another.*

MRS. WEBB. That in the yellow paper is something I found in the attic among your grandmother's things. You're old enough to wear it now, and I thought you'd like it.

EMILY. And this is from you. Why, Mama, it's just lovely and it's just what I wanted. It's beautiful!

(*She flings her arms around her mother's neck. Her* MOTHER *goes on with her cooking, but is pleased.*)

MRS. WEBB. Well, I hoped you'd like it. Hunted all over. Your Aunt Norah couldn't find one in Concord, so I had to send all the way to Boston. (*Laughing*) Wally has something for you, too. He made it at manual-training class and he's very proud of it. Be sure you make a big fuss about it.—Your father had a surprise for you, too; don't know what it is myself. Sh—here he comes.

MR. WEBB (*off stage*). Where's my girl? Where's my birthday girl?

EMILY (*in a loud voice to the* STAGE MANAGER.) I can't. I can't go on. It goes so fast. We don't have time to look at one another.

(*She breaks down sobbing.*

The lights dim on the left half of the stage. MRS. WEBB *disappears.*)

I didn't realize. So all that was going on and we never noticed. Take me back—up the hill—to my grave. But first: Wait! One more look. Goodbye. Goodbye, world. Goodbye, Grover's Corners . . . Mama and Papa. Goodbye to clocks ticking . . . and Mama's sunflowers. And food and coffee. And new-ironed dresses and hot baths . . . and sleeping and waking up. Oh, earth, you're too wonderful for anybody to realize you. (*She looks toward the* STAGE MANAGER *and asks abruptly, through her tears:*) Do any human beings ever realize life while they live it?—every, every minute?

STAGE MANAGER. No. (*Pause*) The saints and poets, maybe—they do some.

EMILY. I'm ready to go back. (*She returns to her chair beside* MRS. GIBBS. *Pause.*)

MRS. GIBBS. Were you happy?

EMILY. No . . . I should have listened to you. That's all human beings are! Just blind people.

MRS. GIBBS. Look, it's clearing up. The stars are coming out.

EMILY. Oh, Mr. Stimson, I should have listened to them.

SIMON STIMSON (*with mounting violence; bitingly*). Yes, now you know. Now you know! That's what it was to be alive. To move about in a cloud of ignorance; to go up and down trampling on the feelings of those . . . of those about you. To spend and waste time as though you had a million years. To be always at the mercy of one self-centered passion, or another. Now you know—that's the happy existence you wanted to go back to. Ignorance and blindness.

MRS. GIBBS (*spiritedly*). Simon Stimson, that ain't the whole truth and you know it. Emily, look at that star. I forget its name.

A MAN AMONG THE DEAD. My boy Joel was a sailor—knew 'em all. He'd set on the porch evenings and tell 'em all by name. Yes, sir, wonderful!

ANOTHER MAN AMONG THE DEAD. A star's mighty good company.

A WOMAN AMONG THE DEAD. Yes. Yes, 'tis.

SIMON STIMSON. Here's one of *them* coming.

THE DEAD. That's funny. 'Tain't no time for one of them to be here.—Goodness sakes.

EMILY. Mother Gibbs, it's George.

MRS. GIBBS. Sh, dear. Just rest yourself.

EMILY. It's George.

(GEORGE *enters from the left, and slowly comes toward them.*)

A MAN FROM AMONG THE DEAD. And my boy, Joel, who knew the stars—he used to say it took millions of years for that speck o' light to git to the earth. Don't seem like a body could believe it, but that's what he used to say—millions of years.

(GEORGE *sinks to his knees, then falls full length at* EMILY'S *feet.*)

A WOMAN AMONG THE DEAD. Goodness! That ain't no way to behave!

MRS. SOAMES. He ought to be home.

EMILY. Mother Gibbs?

MRS. GIBBS. Yes, Emily?

EMILY. They don't understand, do they?

MRS. GIBBS. No, dear. They don't understand.

(*The* STAGE MANAGER *appears at the right, one hand on a dark curtain which he slowly draws across the scene.*

In the distance a clock is heard striking the hour very faintly.)

STAGE MANAGER. Most everybody's asleep in Grover's Corners. There are a few lights on: Shorty Hawkins, down at the depot, has just watched the Albany train go by. And at the livery stable somebody's setting up late and talking.—Yes, it's clearing up. There are the stars—doing their old, old crisscross journeys in the sky. Scholars haven't settled the matter yet, but they seem to think there are no living beings up there. Just chalk . . . or fire. Only this one is straining away, straining away all the time to make something of itself. The strain's so bad that every sixteen hours everybody lies down and gets a rest. (*He winds his watch.*)

Hm. . . . Eleven o'clock in Grover's Corners.—You get a good rest, too. Good night.

Act Three

Getting at Meaning

1. Reread the Stage Manager's opening monologue in Act One. What details prepare the audience for the events of the final act?

2. The playwright does not reveal immediately the name of the person whose funeral is being held. What effect does he achieve? Why is the death of Emily so shocking? Would the death of another character have the same effect on an audience? Explain.

3. As he looks at the graveyard, what observations does the Stage Manager make about grief? about eternity?

4. Unlike Emily, the rest of the dead do not seem particularly interested in life. Why? What have they learned?

5. Emily is warned not to revisit her life, but she ignores the warning and returns to a seemingly unimportant day. What does she discover? What makes the experience so bittersweet, so filled with both pain and pleasure?

6. What does Emily mean when she says that human beings are "blind people"? What is Wilder saying about life as most people live it?

7. Even in death, Simon Stimson is true to character. How did he die? What is his judgment about life? How do Mrs. Soames and Mrs. Gibbs present a more balanced view of life?

8. In *Walden,* Henry David Thoreau writes, ". . . reality is fabulous. If men would steadily observe realities only, and not allow themselves to be deluded, life, to compare it with such things as we know, would be like a fairy tale and the Arabian Nights Entertainment." Do any statements in Act Three of *Our Town* express the same sentiment voiced by Thoreau almost a century earlier?

Developing Skills in Reading Literature

1. **Mood.** The events of Act Three easily could be treated in a melodramatic or maudlin manner. Through his skillful management of the elements of drama, however, Wilder maintains the same under-stated, natural feeling characteristic of the first two acts. In what specific ways does he accomplish this consistency of mood in Act Three? Do any parts of Act Three come close to melodrama through an excessive appeal to the emotions of the audience? Explain your answer.

2. **Thematic Unity.** Thematic unity is achieved when an idea presented in one part of a literary work is further developed later in the work. Consider the Stage Manager's closing lines about the planet Earth: "Only this one is straining away, straining away all the time to make something of itself." What optimistic idea is the Stage Manager suggesting? What similar idea does he express in Act Two when he mentions the "real hero" of the wedding? At the beginning of Act One, how is this same idea apparent in Dr. Gibbs's reason for working all night? If there were a fourth act to *Our Town,* what do you think would be its subject?

In Act Three, George has no speaking lines, but the audience sees him and hears about him from other characters. How does the view of George presented in this act show the truth of Mrs. Gibbs's statement in Act Two that George truly has become a man?

Developing Vocabulary

1. **Inferring Word Meaning.** From the context of the sentence, try to determine the meaning of each italicized word. Then use the dictionary to verify your definitions.

"He chose his own epy-taph (*epitaph*). You can see it there. It ain't a verse exactly."

"Don't you remember, Mother Gibbs—the *legacy* you left us? Why it was over three hundred and fifty dollars."

". . . Shorty Hawkins, down at the *depot,* has just watched the Albany train go by."

2. **Descriptive Language.** Use the dictionary to find the definitions of the following words from the play.

hovered
listlessness
bereaved

lugubrious
wan
anguished

Write a one-paragraph description of a scene or a person, using all of these words to evoke a single mood, or feeling.

Developing Writing Skills

1. **Developing an Argument.** The death of Emily and the scene in the graveyard are consistent with the purpose of *Our Town,* as expressed by the Stage Manager at the beginning of the play. In the 1940 movie version of the play, however, Emily does not die; she merely dreams the graveyard sequence. In a composition discuss whether the death of Emily makes the play ultimately depressing or whether the more positive aspects of the play overcome the effect of Emily's death. Consider the Stage Manager's observa-

tions, the quality of life portrayed in Grover's Corners, the nature of other characters and incidents, and the mood and tone of the play.

2. **Using Comparisons.** After re-living her twelfth birthday, Emily, bursting with emotion, says: "I didn't realize. So all that was going on and we never noticed. . . . Goodbye to clocks ticking . . . and Mama's sunflowers. And food and coffee. And new-ironed dresses and hot baths . . . and sleeping and waking up. Oh, earth, you're too wonderful for anybody to realize you. . . . Do any human beings ever realize life while they live it?—every, every minute?"

The Stage Manager responds, "No. . . . The saints and poets, maybe—they do some."

From the poems that you have studied in this book, select three or four that reveal the poets' special sensitivity and receptivity to life. Summarize the meaning of each poem, and explain how each poet affirms the wonder of life and living.

Unit Review *Drama*

Understanding the Unit

1. Thornton Wilder's tone, or attitude, toward his characters is clearly sympathetic and understanding. Even Simon Stimson is treated gently. Does Eugene O'Neill indicate any sympathy for Captain Keeney? What is his tone toward this character? Explain your conclusion.

2. If you were to describe the American character using these two plays as representative sources, what qualities would you infer from the characters portrayed by O'Neill and Wilder? Are elements of the Puritan heritage apparent in the characters of each play? Explain your answer.

3. Neither play depends upon the kind of sensationalism and gadgetry evident in some contemporary plays. There are no daring chases, no graphically intimate scenes, no spectacular choreography, no computers or robots, no blood spilling. What, then, makes these dramas appealing? Why do they appeal to your interest and to your emotions? If either one were to be presented today, what changes would you suggest to enhance their interest to a present-day audience?

Writing

1. Although considerably different in plot, characters, and style, both "Ile" and *Our Town* include characters who are dedicated to the typical American quest for self-fulfillment. This quest, although it assumes quite different forms, always involves sacrifices, the setting of priorities, and the single-minded pursuit of a goal.

Compare the two plays as they demonstrate the quest for self-fulfillment. Consider the following questions: Why is the oil so important to Captain Keeney? What sacrifices does he make to pursue his goal? What is George's and Emily's quest? What is the nature of the quest shared by most of the people in Grover's Corners? What sacrifices do they make?

Begin your composition with a paragraph that explains the specific nature of the quest in each play. Write fully developed paragraphs that describe the goals, efforts, and sacrifices of the characters. In your concluding paragraph, try to judge the relative success of the characters.

2. At the core of every play is some kind of conflict, or struggle between opposing forces. Conflict may exist between the main character and an antagonist, which may be nature, chance or fate, society, or another character or between contending forces within the main character. In great drama, the opposing forces usually represent two conflicting ideas. The resolution of the conflict serves to clarify the theme of the play.

What is the major conflict in "Ile" and in *Our Town*? In each play, what ideas do the opposing forces represent? How is the conflict resolved? How does the resolution of the conflict relate to the theme of the play?

Present your analysis in a well developed composition in which you make use of evidence from the plays to support your conclusions.

3. Much of American literature is concerned with the effects of isolation and association on the individual. What happens to the person who is isolated from family and from community? Is being an integral part of a community a necessary basis for happiness and for full growth as a human being? What does a community do for an individual? What is the individual able to accomplish as part of a community?

What do the two plays in this unit show about the effects of isolation and association on the individual? In a five-paragraph composition, compare several characters, some of whom are isolated from a community, some of whom are associated or connected with a community. What conclusion do you draw about the needs of human beings?

Handbook of Literary Terms

Allegory. An allegory is a narrative in which the characters often stand for abstract concepts. An allegory generally teaches a lesson by means of an interesting story. One example of an allegory is "The Devil and Tom Walker," in which the devil, a character who represents evil, tempts Tom Walker, who comes to stand for greed.

Alliteration. Alliteration is the repetition of initial consonant sounds. An alliterative pattern sometimes is reinforced by the repetition of the same consonant sounds within and at the ends of words. Alliteration occurs in both prose and poetry, as well as in everyday speech. Poets use alliteration to emphasize words, to create mood, to unify lines, to reinforce meaning, and to impart a musical quality to their poems. Notice the alliteration of the *s* sound in the following lines; observe the way that the alliterative pattern is reinforced.

In Salem seasick spindrift drifts or skips
To the canvas flapping on the seaward panes
Until the knitting sailor stabs at ships
Nosing like sheep of Morpheus through his brain's
Asylum. . . .

ROBERT LOWELL
"Salem"

See *Consonance.*

Allusion. An allusion is a reference to an historical or literary person, place, or event with which the reader is assumed to be familiar. Many works of both prose and poetry contain allusions to the Bible or to classical mythology.

In *The Bluest Eye*, for example, the narrator alludes to Vulcan, the Roman god of fire and metalworking, when describing her father's tending the winter fire:

A Vulcan guarding the flames, he gives us instructions about which doors to keep closed or opened for proper distribution of heat, lays kindling by, discusses qualities of coal, and teaches us how to rake, feed, and bank the fire.

TONI MORRISON

Analogy. An analogy is a point by point comparison between two dissimilar things for the purpose of clarifying the less familiar of the two things. In purpose and structure, an analogy is different from the figures of speech that are also comparisons: simile, metaphor, and personification. In the selection from *Life on the Mississippi*, which appears in Unit 4, Mark Twain draws an analogy between the Mississippi River and a book. The analogy describes the challenges and complexities of the river for the reader unschooled in river lore.

Anaphora. In rhetoric, anaphora is the repetition of words, phrases, or sentences, often at the beginnings of successive sentences, clauses, or paragraphs. A kind of repetition, anaphora is used by speakers and writers to heighten the impact of their ideas. For example, to stress his disillusionment with government promises, Chief Joseph uses anaphora in this passage from "Nez Percé Surrender and Outcome":

Good words do not last long unless they amount to something. Words do not pay for my dead people. They do not pay for my country, now overrun by white men. They do not protect my father's grave. They do not pay for all my horses and cattle. Good words will not give me back my children. Good words will not make good the promise of your War Chief General Miles. Good words will not give my people good health and stop them from dying. Good words will not get my people a home where they can live in peace and take care of themselves.

Antagonist. The antagonist of a novel, drama, or short story is the character or force against which the protagonist is pitted. An antagonist may be another character, as it is for the boy in "Barn Burning." The antagonist also may be society, nature, or one side of a character that battles another side in an internal conflict.

Aphorism. An aphorism is a brief statement that expresses a truth about life. Usually one sentence long, the aphorism is often humorous and pointed.

Poor Richard's Almanack by Benjamin Franklin is a collection of aphorisms, or proverbs; for example, "Three may keep a secret, if two of them are dead." The style of Ralph Waldo Emerson and Henry David Thoreau is marked by aphorisms. One succinct truth written by Emerson is, "Trust thyself: every heart vibrates to that iron string."

Aside. See *Drama*.

Assonance. Assonance is the repetition of a vowel sound within words. Writers of both poetry and prose use assonance to give their work a musical quality and to unify stanzas and passages.

Notice how the following lines from "We Real Cool" repeat the long *e* and long *a* sounds.

> We real cool. We
> Left school. We
> Lurk late. We
> Strike straight . . .
>   GWENDOLYN BROOKS

See *Consonance*.

Autobiography. An autobiography is the story of a person's life written by that person. Autobiographies can be episodic, impressionistic narratives or connected, chronological accounts, as is the *Autobiography* by Benjamin Franklin. Unit 6 of this text includes several excerpts from autobiographies written in the twentieth century. They exemplify the kind of introspective analysis typical of contemporary autobiographical narratives.

Ballad. A ballad is a narrative poem that was originally meant to be sung. Ballads are generally about ordinary people who have unusual adventures, with a single tragic incident as the central focus. They usually begin abruptly, contain dialogue and repetition, and imply more than they actually tell. Traditional ballads are written in four-line stanzas with regular rhythm and rhyme.

The first two stanzas from a modern ballad by W. H. Auden illustrate the characteristics of this verse form.

> O what is that sound which so thrills the ear
>   Down in the valley drumming, drumming?
> Only the scarlet soldiers, dear,
>   The soldiers coming.

> O what is that light I see flashing so clear
>   Over the distance brightly, brightly?
> Only the sun on their weapons, dear,
>   As they step lightly.
>   "O What Is That Sound"

See *Narrative Poem, Refrain*.

Blank Verse. Blank verse is unrhymed poetry written in iambic pentameter. Each line has five metrical feet, and each foot has an unstressed syllable followed by a stressed syllable.

Blank verse has been popular with some twentieth-century American poets, such as Robert Frost. See Frost's poem "The Death of the Hired Man" and Richard Wilbur's "Digging for China," both in Unit 7, for examples of blank verse.

See *Meter*.

Character. Characters are the people and sometimes the animals who participate in the action of a literary work. A character may be main or minor, depending on his or her role in the short story, novel, play, or narrative poem. While some characters are two-dimensional, with one or two dominant traits, a fully developed character has a unique complex of traits. In longer works of fiction, main characters often change as the plot unfolds. Such characters are called dynamic, the opposite of static characters, who remain the same. Successful characters are not only individuals but also in some way examples of the universal human condition.

See *Antagonist, Characterization, Foil, Protagonist, Stereotype*.

Characterization. Characterization refers to the techniques employed by writers to develop characters. There are five basic methods of characterization.

1. The writer may use physical description. In "Bartleby, the Scrivener," for example, Herman Melville describes Bartleby as "a motionless young man" and "pallidly neat."

2. Dialogue spoken by the character and by other characters is another means of characterization. For example, Melville characterizes Bartleby's passive resistance through the scrivener's repeated response, "I prefer not to."

3. A character's actions may be a means of characterization. For example, John Oakhurst in "The Outcasts of Poker Flat" is shown to be kind and fair when he returns the fortune that he won from the innocent Tom Simson.

4. The reactions of another character may also be revealing. Oakhurst's essential nobility is emphasized, for instance, when Tom Simson reacts as a "devoted slave."

5. A character's thoughts and feelings may also be a means of characterization. Dexter's musings, for example, in "Winter Dreams" help to show that he is ambitious and idealistic.

See *Character*.

Climax. In dramatic or narrative literature, the climax is the turning point of action, the moment when interest and intensity reach their peak. The climax of *The Wizard of Oz*, for example, occurs when Dorothy and the Wizard leave Oz on their return flight to Kansas. All the events in the story lead up to this dramatic, emotional scene when it is clear that Dorothy finally is about to achieve her elusive goal.

See *Conflict, Plot, Surprise Ending*.

Conceit. See *Extended Metaphor*.

Concrete Poem. A concrete poem presents something important about the poem's meaning. In concrete poetry, a direct and often obvious relationship exists between form and meaning. The following clever poem illustrates this relationship.

```
a     a     a     a     a

   c     c     c     c

 r     r     r     r     r

   o     o     o     o

 b     b     b     b     b

   a     a     a     a

 t     t     t     t     t

   s     s     s     s

 t     t     t     t     t
```

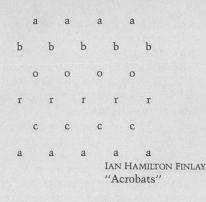

```
 a     a     a     a

b     b     b     b     b

   o     o     o     o

 r     r     r     r     r

   c     c     c     c

a     a     a     a     a
```
IAN HAMILTON FINLAY
"Acrobats"

Conflict. Conflict is the struggle between opposing forces that is the basis of plot in dramatic and narrative literature. The conflict provides the interest or suspense in a short story, drama, novel, narrative poem, or nonfiction narrative. Conflict may be one of five kinds:

1. A character may struggle against nature, as in "The Outcasts of Poker Flat" in which the characters try to survive a snowstorm with few provisions.

2. One character may struggle against another. The boy in "Barn Burning" for example, opposes his father in order to stop the barn burnings.

3. A conflict may occur between a person and the forces of society, as in "Flight," in which Pepé tries to escape society's punishment by eluding a posse.

4. A character may be pitted against supernatural forces, as in Greek and Roman myths.

5. A conflict also may occur within a character, between opposing tendencies in the individual's makeup. An example is Aunt Georgiana in "A Wagner Matinee," who undergoes a struggle between her loyalty to her family and her reverence for music.

The first four conflicts are external; that is, they occur between a character and an outside force. The fifth conflict is internal, as it occurs within one character.

Many plots involve two or more kinds of conflicts. In "Flight," for instance, Pepé struggles against society and also against nature to survive and with himself to prove his manhood.

See *Antagonist, Climax, Plot*.

Connotation. The emotional response evoked by a word is its connotation. *House* and *home*, for example, often are considered synonyms. However, *home* carries stronger connotations of warmth and security. The connotation of a word often involves personal associations, unlike its denotation, which is the objective dictionary definition of the word.

See *Diction*.

Consonance. Consonance is the repetition of consonant sounds within and at the ends of words. Consonance often is used in conjunction with alliteration, the repetition of initial consonant sounds. Consonance, like alliteration and assonance, gives writing a musical quality and may be used to unify poems and passages of prose writing. Notice the repetition of the *r* sound in these lines.

The heavy bear who goes with me,
A manifold honey to smear his face,
Clumsy and lumbering here and there,
The central ton of every place,
The hungry beating brutish one
In love with candy, anger, and sleep,
crazy factotum, . . .
                    DELMORE SCHWARTZ
                    "The Heavy Bear Who Goes with
                    Me"

See *Alliteration, Assonance*.

Contrast. Contrast is a stylistic device in which one element is put into opposition with another. The opposing elements might be contrasting structures, such as sentences of varying lengths or stanzas of different configurations, or they might be contrasting ideas or images juxtaposed within phrases, sentences, paragraphs, stanzas, or sections of a longer work of literature. Writers use contrast to clarify ideas and to elicit emotional responses from the reader.

Couplet. A couplet is two consecutive lines of poetry that rhyme. A simple couplet may be written in any rhythmic pattern.

See *Heroic Couplet, Stanza*.

Denotation. See *Connotation*.

Dénouement. The dénouement is the final unraveling or outcome of the plot in drama or fiction during which the complications of the plot are resolved, any mysteries are solved, and any secrets are explained. The dénouement of "The Devil and Tom Walker," for instance, explains what becomes of Tom's ill-gained wealth after his death and describes what New Englanders learn from his experience.

See *Plot*.

Description. Description is writing that appeals to the senses. Effective description enables a reader to see, hear, smell, taste, and/or feel the subject that is described. Precise adverbs, adjectives, nouns, and verbs, figures of speech, as well as carefully selected detail, create successful description.

Description can stand alone, as in a descriptive essay, or it may be combined with other types of writing, as in a short story.

Dialect. A dialect is the particular variety of language spoken in one place by a distinct group of people. Dialects exhibit regional pronunciations, vocabulary, colloquial expressions, and grammatical constructions. Writers use dialect to establish or emphasize a setting and to develop characters.

The following excerpt is written in a frontier dialect of the nineteenth century:

So he flew off and fetched another acorn and dropped it in, and tried to flirt his eye to the hole quick enough to see what become of it, but he was too late. He held his eye there as much as a minute; then he raised up and sighed and says, "Confound it, I don't seem to understand this thing no way, . . ."
                    MARK TWAIN
                    "What Stumped the Bluejays"

See *Local Color*.

Dialogue. Dialogue is written conversation between two or more characters. Although dialogue is generally associated with drama and fiction, it is used in most forms of prose writing, as well as in narrative poems. Realistic, well paced dialogue advances the action in a narrative and reveals the traits of the characters.

See *Characterization, Drama*.

Diction. Diction is a writer's choice of words, a significant component of his or her style. The diction of a poem or passage of prose involves both the denotative and the connotative meanings of the words. Diction may be formal or informal, abstract or concrete, technical or common, literal or figurative.

See *Connotation, Style.*

Drama. Drama is literature that develops plot and character through dialogue and action; in other words, drama is literature in play form. Dramas are intended to be performed by actors and actresses who appear on a stage or before cameras or microphones.

According to Aristotle's definition, drama is an imitation of life. However, because the imitation cannot be a true representation of reality, the audience must accept certain devices, called dramatic conventions. The audience must accept the actors, for example, as representations of the characters and the stage as the representational setting for the action.

Other conventions are monologues, or soliloquies, which are lengthy speeches generally delivered when a character is alone, and asides, which are remarks made directly to the audience. To accept such stage conventions as real, the reader or spectator must bring to a drama what Samuel Taylor Coleridge called "the willing suspension of disbelief."

Most plays are divided into acts, with each act having a climax. Sometimes the acts of a play are subdivided into scenes, with each scene limited to a particular time and place. While Shakespeare's plays have five acts, modern dramas usually have two or three acts. Some plays, like "Ile," have only one act.

The script for a play contains stage directions, instructions that help the reader to visualize the stage setting and the characters' movements and to "hear" the dialogue as it might be spoken. Stage directions may also provide suggestions for staging, lighting, music, and sound effects.

See *Dialogue.*

Dramatic Irony. See *Irony.*

Dramatic Lyric. A lyric is any short poem in which one speaker expresses thoughts and feelings. Poet Ezra Pound used the term *dramatic lyric* to refer to a lyric poem in which the speaker is an imagined character rather than the poet. His poem "The River Merchant's Wife: A Letter," found in Unit 7, is a dramatic lyric. The individual poems of Edgar Lee Masters's *Spoon River Anthology*, five of which appear in Unit 7, also fit Pound's definition of the dramatic lyric. In each of the Masters poems, a dead speaker reflects on his or her life.

See *Lyric.*

Elegy. An elegy is a poem written in tribute to a person, usually someone who has died recently. The tone of an elegy is usually formal and dignified. "O Captain! My Captain!" found in Unit 4, is Walt Whitman's elegy for Abraham Lincoln.

Elizabethan Sonnet. See *Sonnet.*

End Rhyme. See *Rhyme, Rhyme Scheme.*

English (Shakespearean) Sonnet. See *Sonnet.*

Epic. See *Mock Epic.*

Epigraph. In literature, an epigraph is a motto or quotation that appears at the beginning of a book, play, chapter, or poem. Occasionally, an epigraph shows the source for the title of a work. Because the epigraph usually relates to the theme of a piece of literature, it can give the reader insight into the work. "The Love Song of J. Alfred Prufrock," for example, is preceded by an epigraph in Italian from Dante's *Inferno.*

Epistle. An epistle, or literary letter, is a formal composition generally addressed to one person but intended for a wide audience. An epistle may concern politics, philosophy, or religion. Michel-Guillaume Jean de Crèvecoeur's *Letters from an American Farmer*, excerpts from which are found in Unit 2, is a series of epistles. Addressed to his European contemporaries, these formal letters contain astute observations of colonial America.

Epitaph. An epitaph is the inscription on a tombstone or monument in memory of the person or people buried there. *Epitaph* also refers to a brief literary piece that sums up the life of a dead person.

Following is an epitaph for poet Paul Laurence Dunbar.

Born of the sorrowful of heart
Mirth was a crown upon his head;
Pride kept his twisted lips apart
In jest, to hide a heart that bled.
COUNTEE CULLEN
"Three Epitaphs"

Epithet. An epithet is an apt phrase used to identify a person or thing. Usually an epithet is memorable because of its original and appropriate way of pointing out some trait. The epithet for Tom Simson in "The Outcasts of Poker Flat," for instance, is "The Innocent."

Essay. The essay is a brief, nonfiction composition that offers an opinion on a subject. The purpose of an essay may be to persuade or to inform, as in "The Unimagined America" by Archibald MacLeish, which argues for reevaluating and re-creating American society. The purpose of an essay may be to entertain while making a wry comment on a contemporary issue. "Walden" by E. B. White is this kind of essay. An essay also may aim to explain or analyze. One such essay is "We Aren't Superstitious," in which Stephen Vincent Benét tells his purpose for describing the Salem witch trials: "That story is worth retelling as a very typical example of what wild belief and crowd hysteria can do to an average community."

A distinction can be made between the formal essay and the informal essay. While the formal essay tends to deal objectively with ideas, the informal essay is more personal. The formal essay is more tightly structured than the informal essay, which may be rambling or innovative in form. While the tone of the formal essay is dignified, the informal essay may be light and humorous.

Essays also can be classified as descriptive, narrative, or explanatory. Most essays, however, combine all three types of writing. "Self-Reliance," for example, is primarily expository, for it explains Emerson's philosophical belief in the individual. The essay also relates incidents, which are narrative elements, and describes both society and the individual with vivid figurative language.

Eulogy. A eulogy is a public speech or written tribute praising the virtues or achievements of a person, especially one who has died recently. Adlai Stevenson's "Her Journeys Are Over," a eulogy for Eleanor Roosevelt, exemplifies the dignified, serious tone characteristic of a eulogy. In highly laudatory terms, Stevenson recalls Mrs. Roosevelt's courage, compassion, and wisdom.

Exaggeration. See *Hyperbole.*

Exposition. Exposition is a detailed explanation, often at the beginning of a work of literature, that lays the groundwork for the narration and that provides pertinent background information. In a short story the exposition usually appears in the opening paragraphs; in a novel the exposition is usually part of the first chapter. However, exposition may be interspersed throughout a narrative through the use of flashbacks.

Plays, too, employ exposition. In "Ile" the opening dialogue between Ben and the steward explains the tense situation on board the *Atlantic Queen,* thus preparing the reader or audience for the action that follows.

Extended Metaphor. In an extended metaphor, two unlike things are compared at some length and in several ways. Sometimes the comparison is carried throughout a paragraph, a stanza, or an entire selection.

Like an extended metaphor, a conceit compares two apparently dissimilar things in several ways. The word *conceit* usually implies a more elaborate, formal, and ingeniously clever comparison than the extended metaphor. "Huswifery," a poem by Edward Taylor that appears in Unit 1, illustrates the use of a conceit.

See *Analogy, Figurative Language, Metaphor.*

External Conflict. See *Conflict.*

Fable. A fable is a brief tale told to illustrate a moral. The characters in a fable are usually animals, but sometimes they are humans. The most famous fables are those of Aesop, a Greek slave who lived about 600 B.C. Traditionally, the fable is handed down from generation to generation as oral literature. However, any writer may create a new fable to illustrate a point, as Rachel Carson does in "A Fable for Tomorrow."

Falling Action. See *Climax, Conflict, Plot.*

Fiction. Fiction refers to imaginative works of prose, including the novel and the short story. While fiction is sometimes based on actual events and real people, it primarily comes from the imagination of the writer. Fiction aims to entertain, but it also can enlighten by providing a deeper understanding of the human condition.

The basic elements of fiction are plot, character, setting, and theme. Subtypes of fiction include science fiction, fantasy, and the folk tale.

See *Allegory, Character, Fable, Folk Tale, Gothic Literature, Nonfiction, Parable, Plot, Science Fiction, Setting, Short Story, Tall Tale, Theme.*

Figurative Language. Language that communicates ideas beyond the ordinary, everyday meaning of the words is called figurative language. Instead of communicating literal truth, figurative language creates fresh, or vivid impressions. For example, "A War God's Horse Song" includes the comparison "My horse's body is like an eagle-feathered arrow." While the horse does not literally look like an arrow, the figurative language conveys the image of the horse's leanness and swiftness in a striking, original way. Likewise, in "For Poets" Al Young writes, "Don't forget to fly." The literal meaning is absurd, for humans cannot fly. Clearly, Young intends a figurative meaning that emphasizes the poet's need for unrestrained imagination.

Figurative language is used in both prose and poetry, as well as in oral expression. The most common figures of speech are simile, metaphor, personification, and hyperbole.

See *Hyperbole, Metaphor, Personification, Simile.*

First-Person Narration. See *Point of View.*

Flashback. A flashback is a conversation, a scene, or an incident that happened before the beginning of a story, or at an earlier point in the narrative. A flashback is a way of advancing a plot in a dramatic way and is sometimes presented as a character's recollection. In "A Wagner Matinee," for example, Clark recalls experiences with his Aunt Georgiana thirty years earlier. In "I Stand Here Ironing," the narrator's recollections about her daughter's life help characterize both Emily and the narrator.

Foil. A foil is a character who provides a striking contrast to another character. A writer may use a foil to call attention to certain traits possessed by a main character or simply to set off or enhance the character through contrast. For example, in "The Outcasts of Poker Flat" Tom Simson, innocent and naive, is a foil for John Oakhurst, a notoriously shrewd gambler.

Folk Tale. A folk tale is a short story that exhibits an atmosphere of fairy-tale unreality, often suggested by phrases such as "once upon a time" and "according to old stories." Folk tales often are set at unspecified moments in the past and sometimes involve supernatural elements. A folk tale usually reveals something about the culture in which it has originated. Washington Irving's story "The Devil and Tom Walker" in Unit 3 is a folk tale.

Foreshadowing. Foreshadowing is a writer's use of hints or clues to indicate events that will occur later in the narrative. In "Dr. Heidegger's Experiment," for example, the transformation of a withered rose to a bright bloom when it is immersed in the potion foreshadows its effect on the doctor's friends.

A writer uses foreshadowing to create interest or suspense. Foreshadowing also may make a plot resolution more believable. In "The Story of an Hour," for instance, hints about Louise Mallard's heart condition prepare the reader for her heart attack.

Free Verse. Poetry written without regular patterns of rhyme and meter is known as free verse. Like most poetry, free verse is usually more rhythmic than ordinary language. Much of the poetry written in the twentieth century is free verse.

Walt Whitman is credited with originating free verse in *Leaves of Grass*. The excerpts from Whitman's "Song of Myself" in Unit 4 demonstrate his early use of this unstructured form. Many of the twentieth-century poems in Unit 7, such as Carl Sandburg's "Chicago," illustrate how natural and appropriate free verse is for poets of the modern age.

Gothic Literature. Gothic literature is fiction in which strange, gloomy settings and mysterious, violent, often supernatural events create suspense and terror. Horrors abound in these stories, which emphasize setting and plot rather than characterization. "The Pit and the Pendulum" by Edgar Allan Poe uses devices of early Gothic novels. Its gloomy setting is a dungeon teeming with rats, and the tension and terror build as the narrator faces descent into a pit or mutilation by a razor-edged pendulum.

Haiku. Haiku is a Japanese poetry form. When written in Japanese, the haiku has seventeen syllables arranged in three lines. The first line has five syllables, the second line has seven, and the third line has five. When haiku are translated from Japanese into other languages, however, it is difficult, if not impossible, to maintain the syllable count while conveying the appropriate meaning. Translators therefore concentrate on capturing the mood and imagery of the original. Poets writing haiku in languages other than Japanese tend to emphasize content rather than syllable count.

Haiku communicate meaning through imagery. The form is highly condensed, causing poets to rely heavily on connotation. Haiku focus on human emotions and on the way in which nature reflects these emotions.

The Imagist poets of the early twentieth century demonstrated a keen interest in haiku and other Oriental verse forms. The following poem by Ezra Pound meets all the qualifications of haiku. Notice that Pound, writing haiku in English, is more concerned with content than with syllable count.

> Green arsenic smeared on an egg-white cloth,
> Crushed strawberries! Come, let us feast our eyes.
> "L'Art," 1910

Heroic Couplet. A heroic couplet is two consecutive lines of poetry that rhyme and that are written in iambic pentameter. A line of iambic pentameter consists of five metrical feet; each foot is made up of an unstressed syllable followed by a stressed syllable. Heroic couplets can function alone as units of meaning or can be combined into longer poems. In Unit 2, the poem "To the Right Honourable William, Earl of Dartmouth" by Phillis Wheatley consists of heroic couplets.

Humor. See *Hyperbole, Irony, Tone.*

Hyperbole. Hyperbole is a figure of speech in which the truth is exaggerated for emphasis or for a humorous effect. For example, in "Mannahatta" Whitman exaggerates the size and vigor of the city in phrases such as "Numberless crowded streets . . ." and "the countless masts . . ." He emphasizes the qualities of its citizens in these lines:

> A million people—manners free and superb—open voices—hospitality—the most courageous and friendly young men,

Iambic Pentameter. See *Blank Verse, Heroic Couplet, Meter, Sonnet.*

Imagery. The term *imagery* refers to words and phrases that create vivid sensory experiences for the reader. Because sight is the most highly developed sense, the majority of images are visual. Imagery also may appeal to the senses of smell, hearing, taste, and touch. Good writers, both in prose and in poetry, often use images that appeal to several senses at the same time. Notice the appeal to various senses in this stanza:

> A land of leaning ice
> Hugged by plaster-grey arches of sky,
> Flings itself silently
> Into eternity:
> > HART CRANE
> > "North Labrador"

The term *synesthesia* refers to imagery that appeals to one sense when another is being stimulated; for example, description of sounds in terms of colors, as in "red wail," or description of colors in terms of feeling, as in "hot pink."

The following passage illustrates the skillful use of imagery in prose.

> Winter tightened our heads with a band of cold and melted our eyes. We put pepper in the feet of our stockings, Vaseline on our faces, and stared through dark icebox mornings at four stewed prunes, slippery lumps of oatmeal, and cocoa with a roof of skin.
> > TONI MORRISON
> > *The Bluest Eye*

Imagist. See *Haiku, Style.*

Internal Conflict. See *Conflict.*

Internal Rhyme. See *Rhyme*.

Irony. Irony is a contrast between appearance and actuality. The three main types of irony are irony of situation, verbal irony, and dramatic irony.

An ironic situation occurs when something happens that is entirely different from what is expected. For example, in the poem "Richard Cory" a gentlemen who is admired and envied commits suicide.

In verbal irony a writer says one thing but means something entirely different. The title "Do Not Weep, Maiden, for War Is Kind" is ironic since the poem shows just the opposite.

Dramatic irony occurs when the reader knows information that the characters do not. The final act of *Our Town* turns on dramatic irony, for the reader, aware that Emily has died, witnesses her reliving a birthday.

See *Understatement*.

Italian (Petrarchan) Sonnet. See *Sonnet*.

Literal and Figurative Meaning. See *Figurative Language*.

Literary Letter. See *Epistle*.

Local Color. Local-color writing, popular in the late 1800's, exploits the speech, dress, mannerisms, customs, character types, and landscape of a certain region. Setting is significant in local-color writing, with dialect being used to create a sense of place. Early local-color stories tend to be sentimental or humorous in plot and characterization. Later writers broadened the realism of setting typical of local-color stories to the other elements of their stories. The introduction to Unit 4 describes the characteristics of local-color writing and identifies the prominent writers associated with this type of fiction.

See *Realism*.

Lyric. In ancient Greece, the lyre was a musical instrument, and the lyric became the name for a song accompanied by music. In common speech, the words of songs still are called lyrics.

In literature, a lyric is any short poem that presents a single speaker who expresses thoughts and feelings. In a love lyric, a speaker expresses romantic love. In other lyrics, a speaker may meditate on nature or seek to resolve an emotional crisis. Ralph Waldo Emerson's poem "The Rhodora" in Unit 3 is a lyric poem. So is Robinson Jeffers's "Evening Ebb" in Unit 7.

See *Dramatic Lyric, Sonnet*.

Metaphor. A metaphor is a figure of speech that makes a comparison between two unlike things that have something in common. While similes use the words *like* or *as*, metaphors either make comparisons directly or imply them.

The following lines present a metaphorical description of an emotional state.

But her eyes had no reflection,
They swam in a grey smoke,
The smoke of smoldering ashes,
The smoke of her cindered heart.
AMY LOWELL
"The Dinner-Party"

Metaphors are used in prose as well as in poetry, as evidenced by the following passage, which describes two fighters just before their match.

Sandel . . . had everything to win by it—money and glory and career, and Tom King was the grizzled old chopping block that guarded the highway to fame and fortune.
JACK LONDON
"A Piece of Steak"

See *Extended Metaphor, Figurative Language, Simile*.

Meter. Meter is the repetition of a regular rhythmic unit in a line of poetry. The meter of a poem emphasizes the musical quality of the language and often relates directly to the subject matter of the poem.

Each unit of meter is known as a foot, with each foot having one stressed and one or two unstressed syllables. The four basic types of metrical feet are the iamb, an unstressed syllable followed by a stressed syllable (˘ ´); the trochee, a stressed syllable followed by an unstressed syllable (´ ˘); the anapest, two unstressed syllables followed by a stressed syllable (˘ ˘ ´); and the dactyl, a stressed syllable followed by two unstressed syllables (´ ˘ ˘).

Two words are used to describe the meter of a

line. The first word describes the type of metrical foot; the second word describes the number of feet in the line: dimeter (two feet), trimeter (three feet), tetrameter (four feet), pentameter (five feet), hexameter (six feet), and so forth. Thus, the meter of a poem might be anapestic trimeter or trochaic hexameter.

The following excerpt is an example of iambic pentameter, the most common form of meter in English poetry.

Ăh, Dóug|lăss, wĕ | hăve fall'n | ŏn é|vĭl dáys,

Sŭch dáys | ăs thóu, | nŏt é|vĕn thóu | dĭdst knów,

Whĕn thĕe, | thĕ eýes | ŏf thát | hăsh lóng | ăgó

Săw, sá|lĭĕnt, ắt | thĕ cróss | ŏf dé|vĭoŭs wáys,

PAUL LAURENCE DUNBAR
"Douglass"

Most poems are not written in exact meters but in a combination of meters. An iambic line may end with an anapestic foot, for example, or lines of iambic tetrameter may alternate with lines of iambic trimeter. Such variations are conscious choices made by the poets to achieve desired effects.

See *Rhythm*.

Mock Epic. An epic is a long narrative on a serious subject, presented in an elevated style, and concerned with a heroic character or characters whose actions speak for a particular group of people, such as a nation or a race. The first epics were *The Iliad* and *The Odyssey*, Homer's famous tales about the ancient Greeks.

A mock epic is a form of satire that mocks low characters and insignificant events by using the literary traditions of the epic. Such characters and events are made ridiculous or humorous by their incongruous presentation with the elevated style of the epic. In the passages from *Walden* in Unit 3, for example, Henry David Thoreau describes a battle among ants with the grandiose epic style that Homer employs to glorify human warriors in *The Iliad*.

Monologue. See *Drama*.

Mood. Mood is the feeling, or atmosphere, that a writer creates for the reader. Connotative words,

sensory images, and figurative language contribute to the mood of a selection, as do the sound and rhythm of the language.

Notice how the writer of this paragraph creates a feeling of luxurious contentment.

> October is the richest of the seasons. The fields are cut, the granaries are full, the bins are loaded to the brim with fatness, and from the cider press the rich-brown oozings of the York Imperials run. The bee bores to the belly of the yellowed grape. The fly gets old and fat and blue; he buzzes loud, crawls slow, creeps heavily to death on sill and ceiling. The sun goes down in blood and pollen across the bronzed and mown fields of old October.
>
> THOMAS WOLFE

Motivation. Motivation is the stated or implied reason behind a character's behavior. The grounds for a character's action may not be obvious, but they should be comprehensible and consistent, in keeping with the character as developed by the writer. Characters sometimes do sudden, unexpected things, as people do in real life. In John Steinbeck's story "Flight" from Unit 5, Pepé abruptly kills a man. The reader feels that the action is in character, however, because Steinbeck has provided an understandable motivation for such an act.

See *Character*.

Narration. See *Narrator, Point of View*.

Narrative Poem. A narrative poem tells a story. John Greenleaf Whittier's poem "Snowbound," sections of which appear in Unit 3, is a famous narrative poem of some length. Randall Jarrell's "The Death of the Ball Turret Gunner," found in Unit 7, may well be the shortest narrative poem ever written. The ballad is a special type of narrative poem, usually intended to be sung.

See *Ballad*.

Narrator. The narrator is the person from whose point of view events are related. The narrator may be a main or minor character in a story, an external witness to the action created by the writer, or the writer presenting events from his or her own point of view.

See *Point of View*.

Naturalism. An extreme form of realism, naturalism in fiction presents life objectively and precisely, without idealizing. Like the realist, the naturalist accurately portrays the world. However, the naturalist creates characters who are victims of environmental forces and internal drives.

Naturalism as a style of fiction arose during the late nineteenth century. Two great American naturalists are Theodore Dreiser and Jack London. In "A Mystery of Heroism," Stephen Crane, also a naturalist, portrays his main character as a victim of war and physical needs, both forces beyond his control. Like most naturalistic writing, the story shows its main character as an uncomprehending cog in the machinery of a cruel world

See *Realism.*

Nonfiction. Nonfiction is prose writing about real people, places, and events. Unlike fiction, nonfiction is largely concerned with factual information, although the writer shapes the information according to his or her purpose and may exhibit bias in the selection and presentation of facts. Forms of nonfiction include biographies, autobiographies, letters, essays, journals, speeches, and news articles.

See *Autobiography, Epistle, Essay, Eulogy, Fiction.*

Onomatopoeia. The word *onomatopoeia* literally means "name-making." It is the process of creating or using words that imitate sounds. The *hiss* of a snake and the *bang* of a gun are onomatopoetic words.

Onomatopoeia as a literary technique goes beyond the use of simple echoic words. Writers, particularly poets, choose words whose sounds suggest their denotative and connotative meanings. Notice the musical effects that are created in these lines, each of which is the final line of a stanza from "The Bells."

From the jingling and the tingling of the bells.
To the rhyming and the chiming of the bells!
In the clamor and the clangor of the bells!
To the moaning and the groaning of the bells.
EDGAR ALLAN POE

Oral Literature. Literature that is passed from one generation to another by performance or word-of-mouth is called oral literature. Folk tales, fables, myths, chants, and legends are part of the oral tradition of cultures throughout the world. The Native American poems in Units 1, 3, and 4 originate in the oral literature of tribal groups. The poems once were performed for a certain purpose, perhaps accompanied by music and dancing.

Oxymoron. See *Paradox.*

Parable. A parable is a short tale that teaches a lesson or illustrates a moral truth. A parable differs from an allegory in that its characters often do not represent abstract qualities. Instead, the characters in a parable are developed as individuals. "The Minister's Black Veil" by Nathaniel Hawthorne is a parable. The Reverend Mr. Hooper, the main character in the parable, wears a black veil to symbolize secret sin. The parable's moral truth is expressed by the minister's final words, "I look around me, and lo! on every visage a Black Veil!"

Paradox. A paradox is a statement that seems to be contradictory or ridiculous but is actually quite true. Henry David Thoreau uses a paradox in *Walden* when he writes, "In proportion as he [the human being] simplifies his life, the laws of the universe will appear less complex, and solitude will not be solitude, nor poverty poverty, nor weakness weakness." The truth behind this seemingly contradictory statement is that the simple life can make any problem seem less worrisome.

A special kind of paradox is the oxymoron, which brings together two contradictory terms. Two examples appear in these lines from "Let Us Move Evenly Together":

O my gentle village fierce
O my powerful people weak

Parallelism. When a speaker, poet, or other writer expresses ideas of equal worth with the same grammatical form, the technique is called parallelism, or parallel construction. Attention to parallelism generally makes both spoken and written expression more concise, clear, and powerful. In the *Declaration of Independence*, which appears in Unit 2, Thomas Jefferson describes the offenses of King George III of England in a series of parallel clauses that begin, "He has refused," "He has dissolved," "He has obstructed," and so forth.

Parody. A parody is an imitation of a serious work of literature for the purpose of criticism or humorous effect or for flattering tribute. Like the caricature in art, the parody in literature mimics a subject or a style. In *The Adventures of Huckleberry Finn*, the poem "Ode to Stephen Dowling Bots, Dec'd" parodies certain romantic poetry popular during Mark Twain's time. E. B. White's essay "Walden" parodies Henry David Thoreau's work of the same title.

See *Satire*.

Personification. Personification is a figure of speech in which human qualities are attributed to an object, an animal, or an idea. Like the simile and the metaphor, personification helps writers to communicate feelings and sensory images to the reader, as evidenced in the following couplet.

> We dance round in a ring and suppose,
> But the Secret sits in the middle and knows.
> ROBERT FROST
"The Secret Sits"

Persuasion. Persuasion is a technique used by speakers and writers to convince an audience to adopt a particular opinion, perform an action, or both. The effectiveness of persuasion is based on rhetorical devices that make the ideas presented both intellectually and emotionally appealing. Advertisements, newspaper and television editorials, and political speeches exemplify the use of persuasive techniques.

Unit 2, which focuses on the literature of the American Revolution, contains several famous pieces of political persuasion. Thomas Paine's essay from the "Crisis" papers is one example.

Petrarchan (Italian) Sonnet. See *Sonnet*.

Plain Style. See *Style*.

Plot. Plot refers to the planned series of interrelated actions and events that take place in a dramatic or narrative work. The action of the plot progresses because of a conflict, or struggle of opposing forces. The conflict usually builds to the emotional peak of a climax, and a dénouement follows.

The events that occur before the climax, or turning point, are referred to as the rising action, while the events that take place after the climax are called the falling action.

Long pieces of literature frequently have subplots, which are minor plots subordinate to the overall story. The main plot in *Our Town*, for example, centers on the lives of Emily Webb and George Gibbs; a subplot is the story of Simon Stimson, the church organist.

See *Climax, Conflict, Dénouement*.

Poetry. Poetry is an arrangement of lines in which form and content fuse to suggest meanings beyond the literal meanings of the words. The language of poetry is compressed, without extraneous words. The language also is musical, enhancing meaning through the sounds of words and phrases and through the sound patterns of lines and stanzas.

Poetry is inherently emotional. William Wordsworth defined it as "the imaginative expression of strong feeling, usually rhythmical." Characteristic of poetry is the use of imagery, or language that appeals to the senses. Poetry is also rich in connotative words and figurative language, with some poems depending more heavily on imaginative language than others.

Some poets conform to traditional patterns of rhythm, rhyme, meter, and stanza length while others experiment with flexible or unconventional forms. Such experimentation is more typical of twentieth-century poets than of poets of earlier periods.

Point of View. Point of view refers to the narrative method used in a short story, novel, or nonfiction selection. The three most common points of view are first-person, third-person omniscient, and third-person limited.

In first-person point of view, the narrator is a character in the story, narrating the action as he or she understands it. First-person point of view is indicated by the pronoun *I*. *The Adventures of Huckleberry Finn* is told in the first person by the main character. The narrator may be a character other than the main character, as in "Bartleby, the Scrivener," which is narrated by Bartleby's employer. Nearly all autobiographies employ the first-person point of view.

Third-person narration is indicated by the pronouns *he, she,* and *they*. A third-person narrator is not a participant in the action and thus maintains a certain distance from the characters. In the third-person omniscient point of view, the narrator is all-knowing about the thoughts and feelings of the characters. With this point of view, the writer can reveal the emotional responses of all the characters and can comment at will on the events taking place. In "Sophistication," for example, the narrator sees into the minds of both George Willard and Helen White, giving the story a depth of psychological insight that would not be possible through another point of view.

Sometimes a writer tells a story in the third person but presents events as experienced by only one character. In that case, the point of view is said to be limited. The third-person limited point of view is used in "The Stone Boy," told from Arnold's viewpoint.

Protagonist. The central character in a short story, play, or novel is called the protagonist. The protagonist always is involved in the central conflict of the story and often changes after the climax. If the conflict is between the protagonist and another character, that character is his or her antagonist. The narrator may be the protagonist of a story if, as in *The Adventures of Huckleberry Finn*, the story is told in the first person by the main character.

See *Antagonist, Character.*

Psalm. A psalm is a sacred song or hymn. With a capital *p*, the word refers to any of the sacred songs or hymns collected in the Old Testament *Book of Psalms.*

Quatrain. See *Sonnet, Stanza.*

Realism. As a way of handling material in fiction, realism is the truthful imitation of actual life. The realist tends to use clear, direct prose to present the ordinary, everyday events of a particular milieu.

Realism became an important literary movement in the latter half of the nineteenth century, developed by writers such as Mark Twain, Edith Wharton, and Henry James. In part, realism arose as a reaction against the sentimentality of most Romantic fiction. Nearly all of the major short story writers of the twentieth century incorporate aspects of realism into their writing.

See *Local Color, Naturalism.*

Refrain. In poetry, a refrain is part of a stanza, consisting of one or more lines that are repeated regularly, sometimes with changes, often at the ends of succeeding stanzas. Most ballads contain some kind of refrain.

The following two stanzas from a poem by Vachel Lindsay illustrate the use of a refrain.

A little colt—broncho, loaned to the farm
To be broken in time without fury or harm,
Yet black crows flew past you, shouting alarm,
Calling "Beware," with lugubrious singing . . .
The butterflies there in the bush were romancing,
The smell of the grass caught your soul in a trance,
So why be a–fearing the spurs and the traces,
O broncho that would not be broken of dancing?

You were born with the pride of the lords great and
    olden
Who danced, through the ages, in corridors golden.
In all the wide farm-place the person most human.
You spoke out so plainly with squealing and
    capering,
With whinnying, snorting, contorting and prancing,
As you dodged your pursuers, looking askance,
With Greek-footed figures, and Parthenon paces,
O broncho that would not be broken of dancing.
              "The Broncho That Would Not Be Broken"

See *Ballad, Repetend.*

Regionalism. See *Dialect, Local Color.*

Repetend. Repetend refers to a word or phrase that is repeated in part or all of a poem to produce a special effect. Notice the repetition of the phrases "the czar" and "eight million" in the lines that follow.

"The czar has eight million men with guns and
    bayonets.
"Nothing can happen to the czar.
"The czar is the voice of God and shall live forever.
"Turn and look at the forest of steel and cannon
"Where the czar is guarded by eight million soldiers.
"Nothing can happen to the czar."
              CARL SANDBURG
              "The People, Yes"

Repetition. Repetition is a literary technique in which a sound, word, phrase, line, or grammatical construction is repeated for emphasis. Repetition is a general term that includes specific skills associated with both prose and poetry.

See *Alliteration, Anaphora, Assonance, Consonance, Parallelism, Refrain, Repetend.*

Rhetorical Question. A question that is intended to produce an effect, usually emotional, and not an answer is called a rhetorical question. In his "Inaugural Address" John F. Kennedy poses the rhetorical question, "Can we forge against these enemies a grand and global alliance, North and South, East and West, that can assure a more fruitful life for all mankind? Will you join in that historic effort?" Kennedy does not expect answers but rather hopes to arouse feelings of passion and patriotism. In the poem "Stanzas on Freedom" James Russell Lowell challenges the reader to make a commitment to freedom, using this rhetorical question:

If there breathe on earth a slave,
Are ye truly free and brave?

Rhyme. Rhyme is the similarity of sound between two words. Words rhyme when the sound of their accented vowels, and all succeeding sounds, are identical. For true rhyme, the consonants that precede the vowels must be different.

When rhyme comes at the end of a line of poetry, it is called end rhyme, as in this example:

An ant on the table cloth
Ran into a dormant moth
Of many times his size.
He showed not the least surprise.
ROBERT FROST
"Departmental"

Rhyme that occurs within a single line, as in the following example, is called internal rhyme.

The vanished gods to me appear;
And one to me are shame and fame.
RALPH WALDO EMERSON
"Brahma"

End rhymes that are not exact but approximate are called imperfect rhymes, near rhymes, or off-rhymes. Sometimes they are also called slant rhymes. Many twentieth-century poets favor off-rhyme. Lines 1 and 3 of the following stanza illustrate off-rhyme.

And here face down beneath the sun
And here upon earth's noonward height
To feel the always coming on
The always rising of the night:
ARCHIBALD MACLEISH
"You, Andrew Marvell"

See *Rhyme Scheme.*

Rhyme Scheme. A rhyme scheme is the pattern of end rhyme in a poem. The pattern is charted by assigning a letter of the alphabet, beginning with the letter *a*, to each line. Lines that rhyme are given the same letter. The rhyme scheme for the following poem is identified to the right of the poem.

He is that fallen lance that lies as hurled,	a
That lies unlifted now, come dew, come rust,	b
But still lies pointed as it plowed the dust.	b
If we who sight along it round the world	a
See nothing worthy to have been its mark,	c
It is because like men we look too near,	d
Forgetting that as fitted to the sphere,	d
Our missiles always make too short an arc.	c
They fall, they rip the grass, they intersect	e
The curve of earth, and striking, break their own;	f
They make us cringe for metal-point on stone.	f
But this we know, the obstacle that checked	e
And tripped the body, shot the spirit on	g
Further than target ever showed or shone.	f

ROBERT FROST
"A Soldier"

See *Rhyme.*

Rhythm. Rhythm refers to the cadence of a poem, often denoting the regular, patterned recurrence of strong and weak elements. A poem without a standard meter may have a strong rhythm, for poetic devices such as rhyme, alliteration, consonance, assonance, and other forms of repetition often create a musical flow in poetry. Poets use rhythm to heighten the power of the language, to emphasize ideas, to create mood, and to reinforce content.

See *Meter.*

Rising Action. See *Climax, Conflict, Plot.*

Romanticism. Romanticism is a movement in the arts that flourished in Europe and America throughout much of the nineteenth century. Romantic writers glorified nature, idealized the past, and celebrated human experience. Their treatment of subject was emotional rather than reasonable, intuitive rather than analytical. The transcendentalists, one group of American Romantics, believed fervently in the innate goodness and limitless potential of the human being. Among other Romantics, the focus on the human being was manifested in a fascination with the eerie and exotic and with the effects of guilt, evil, isolation, and terror on the human psyche. The introduction to Unit 3 discusses in detail the Romantic period and identifies many of the significant Romantic writers.

Sarcasm. Sarcasm, a type of verbal irony, refers to a critical, contemptuous remark expressed in a statement in which literal meaning is the opposite of actual meaning.

See *Irony*.

Satire. Satire is a literary technique in which foolish ideas or customs are ridiculed for the purpose of improving society. Satire may be gently witty, mildly abusive, or bitterly critical. Short stories, poems, novels, essays, and plays all may be vehicles for satire. In *The Adventures of Huckleberry Finn* Mark Twain satirizes false sentimentality in literature by parodying such excesses in the poetry of Emmeline Grangerford, which is written only about dead people. Huck comments sarcastically, "I reckoned that with her disposition she was having a better time in the graveyard."

See *Irony, Mock Epic, Parody, Sarcasm*.

Science Fiction. Science fiction is prose writing that presents the possibilities of the past or the future, using known scientific data and theories as well as the creative imagination of the writer. Most science fiction comments on present-day society through the writer's fictional conception of a past or future society. For instance, "Harrison Bergeron," a short story in Unit 5, presents a frightening society in which equality is carried to an extreme and the possession of talent is penalized.

Setting. Setting is the time and place of the action of a story. *Our Town*, for example, is set in the fictitious town of Grover's Corners, New Hampshire, beginning in 1901. Setting also includes the social and moral environment that form the background for the action of a short story, novel, play, or nonfiction narrative. As such, the setting of *Our Town* is the friendly milieu of a small town with its traditional religious values and social customs.

While setting is important in some works of literature, sometimes being a prime source of conflict, it is incidental and only vaguely defined in others. Fiction written primarily to convey the flavor of a locality is often called local-color writing. "The Outcasts of Poker Flat" and "What Stumped the Bluejays" are two local-color stories set on the Western frontier in the late nineteenth century.

See *Gothic Literature, Local Color*.

Shakespearean (English) Sonnet. See *Sonnet*.

Short Story. A short story is a work of fiction that can be read at one sitting. Usually it develops one primary conflict and produces a single effect. The four basic elements of a short story are its plot, characters, setting, and theme. The plot is the story that unfolds as the result of a struggle between opposing forces. The characters are the people or animals who take part in the action. The setting is the time and place in which the action occurs. An outgrowth of these three, the theme is the central idea or message conveyed by the writer.

See *Fiction*.

Simile. A simile is a stated comparison between two things that are actually unlike, but that have something in common. Like metaphors, similes are figures of speech. While a metaphor implies a comparison or states it directly, a simile expresses the comparison by the use of the words *like* or *as*.

Writers, both of poetry and of prose, use similes to give readers a fresh look at familiar things, as in the following famous examples.

Our dried voices, when
We whisper together
Are quiet and meaningless
As wind in dry grass
Or rats' feet over broken glass
In our dry cellar
                    T. S. ELIOT
                    "The Hollow Men"

On every side it [the fog] sat like a lid on the mountains and made of the great valley a closed pot. On the broad, level land floor the gang plows bit deep and left the black earth shining like metal where the shares had cut.

JOHN STEINBECK
"The Chrysanthemums"

See *Figurative Language, Metaphor.*

Sonnet. A sonnet is a lyric poem consisting of fourteen lines of rhymed iambic pentameter. For centuries the sonnet has been a popular form, for it is long enough to permit the complex development of an idea, but short and structured enough to present a significant challenge to any poet's artistic skills. Sonnets written in the English language generally follow one of two forms.

The Petrarchan, or Italian, sonnet takes its name from Petrarch, an Italian poet of the fourteenth century. This sonnet consists of two parts, an octave and a sestet. The octave, the first eight lines of the sonnet, usually has the rhyme scheme a b b a a b b a. This part of the sonnet poses a question or states a problem. The sestet, the final six lines of the sonnet, can have a variable rhyme scheme, such as c d e c d e, or c c d d e e. The sestet usually resolves or comments on the problem presented in the octave. "Embassy" by W. H. Auden, in Unit 7, is an example of the Petrarchan sonnet.

The Shakespearean, or English, sonnet is sometimes called the Elizabethan sonnet. It consists of three quatrains, rhyming a b a b c d c d e f e f, and a couplet, g g. The couplet usually answers or somehow comments on the important issue developed in the three quatrains. "On Hearing a Symphony of Beethoven" by Edna St. Vincent Millay and "The Sonnet-Ballad" by Gwendolyn Brooks, both in Unit 7, are examples of the Shakespearean sonnet.

See *Lyric.*

Speaker. The speaker in a poem is the voice that "talks" to the reader, analogous to the narrator in a work of fiction. Speaker and poet are not necessarily synonymous. Often, a poet creates a speaker with a distinct identity in order to achieve a particular effect. For example, in each of the poems by Edgar Lee Masters in Unit 7, the speaker is a dead person who summarizes his or her life. In Edward Taylor's poem "Huswifery" in Unit 1, the speaker is a housewife, not the poet.

Stage Directions. See *Drama.*

Stanza. A stanza is a group of lines that form a unit of poetry. The stanza is roughly comparable to the paragraph in prose. In traditional poems, the stanzas usually have the same number of lines and often have the same rhyme and meter as well. Twentieth-century poets have experimented more freely with stanza forms than did earlier poets, sometimes writing poems that have no stanza breaks at all.

The quatrain, or four-line stanza, is common in English poetry. A three-line stanza is called a tercet. A couplet set off by itself functions as a two-line stanza.

In Unit 7, "Anecdote of the Jar" by Wallace Stevens consists of three quatrains. "Acquainted with the Night" by Robert Frost consists of four tercets and a couplet. "The Love Song of J. Alfred Prufrock" by T. S. Eliot contains stanzas of varying lengths, from couplets to stanzas of ten or more lines.

See *Couplet.*

Stereotype. In everyday speech and in literature the term *stereotype* refers to something that conforms to a fixed or general pattern, without individual distinguishing marks or qualities. Often a stereotype is a standardized mental picture, held in common by members of a group, which represents an over-simplified opinion, such as of a race or national group. Sweeping generalizations about "all Italians" or "every Southerner" are stereotypes.

Simplified, or stock characters in literature are often called stereotypes. Such characters do not usually demonstrate the complexities of real people. A familiar stereotype from popular literature is the absent-minded professor.

Stream of Consciousness. The technique of presenting the flow of thoughts, responses, and sensations of one or more characters is called stream of consciousness. A stream-of-consciousness narrative is not structured into a coherent, logical presentation of ideas. The connections between ideas are associative, with one idea suggesting another, as in T. S. Eliot's "The Love Song of J. Alfred Prufrock," found in Unit 7.

Often, the psychological workings of a character are integrated into a more traditional narrative approach, as in "Barn Burning" by William Faulkner. This passage from the story illustrates Faulkner's use of the technique.

> He could not see the table where the Justice sat and before which his father and his father's enemy (*our enemy* he thought in that despair; *ourn! mine and hisn both! He's my father*) stood, but he could hear them . . .

Structure. Structure is the way in which a work of literature is put together. In poetry, structure refers to the arrangement of words and lines to produce a desired effect. A common structural unit in poetry is the stanza.

In prose, structure is the arrangement of larger units or parts of a selection. Paragraphs, for example, are a basic unit in prose, as are chapters in novels and scenes and acts in plays. A prose selection can be structured by idea or incident, as are most essays, short stories, and one-act plays.

The structure of a poem, short story, novel, play, or nonfiction selection usually emphasizes certain important aspects of content. For example, in "Barn Burning," a short story in Unit 5, the way in which the story is structured, with a courtroom scene at the beginning and flashbacks throughout, dramatically increases the tension in the story. The structure also is a means through which the writer adds layers of psychological complexity to the characters.

Style. Style is the way in which a piece of literature is written. Style refers not to what is said, but to how it is said. Many elements contribute to style, such as diction, syntax, figurative language, imagery, tone, point of view, irony, and techniques of characterization. A literary style might be described as formal, conversational, objective, wordy, home-spun, or flowery. Every writer has a way of expressing ideas that constitutes a personal style. The styles of some writers are so consistent and recognizable that their names have become associated with the general characteristics of their styles; for example, William Faulkner's name is associated with the stream-of-consciousness technique.

A group of writers might exemplify common stylistic characteristics; for example, the Puritans who wrote in the plain style, a simple direct way of expressing ideas, or the Imagists whose poems are marked by compression and rich sensory images.

Surprise Ending. A surprise ending is an unexpected twist in plot at the conclusion of a story or drama. The revelation of Peyton Farquhar's actual situation, for example, at the end of "An Occurrence at Owl Creek Bridge," a story in Unit 4, constitutes a surprise ending for the reader.

See *Climax, Plot.*

Suspense. Suspense is the tension or excitement felt by the reader as he or she becomes involved in a narrative and eager to know either the outcome of a conflict or how the outcome occurred. In "The Pit and the Pendulum," for instance, suspense builds as the reader gradually realizes the narrator's predicament, reaching a peak just as a plunge into the pit seems inevitable.

Symbol. A symbol is a person, place, or object that represents something beyond itself. Symbols can succinctly communicate abstract, complex ideas. For example, in Sherwood Anderson's short story "Sophistication" the maturing corn is a symbol of George Willard and Helen White and of the way in which they are maturing. In Thomas Wolfe's story "The Far and the Near" the woman who smiles and waves at the passing train symbolizes for the engineer "something beautiful and enduring, something beyond all change and ruin."

Synesthesia. See *Imagery.*

Tall Tale. A tall tale is a kind of humorous story that uses ordinary speech to tell extravagantly impossible happenings. Usually the events occur because of a character's superhuman powers. Stories about Paul Bunyan and Mike Fink, for example, are popular American tall tales.

Tercet. See *Stanza.*

Thematic Unity. See *Unity.*

Theme. A theme is the main idea or message in a work of literature. It is a writer's perception about life or humanity shared with a reader. Some pieces of literature are intended for entertainment only, and as such have no underlying messages. Most serious writing, however, comments on life or the human condition. Themes seldom are stated directly and may reveal themselves only through careful reading and thought.

In William Faulkner's "Barn Burning," located in Unit 5, a major theme is the difficulty of escaping from one's past and one's family heritage. Another message is that the repressive social structure of the Old South often led to acts of physical and psychological violence.

Third-Person Narration. See *Point of View.*

Title. The distinguishing name attached to any piece of writing is its title. A writer can use the title of a piece of literature to highlight its theme. Often, a poet provides in the title significant information necessary for understanding a poem. For example, a reader of Sylvia Plath's poem "Mirror," in Unit 7, might not recognize the subject matter without the clue in the title.

Tone. Tone is the attitude a writer takes toward a subject. All of the elements in a work of literature together create its tone, which might be humorous, serious, bitter, angry, or detached, among other possibilities. Tone is different from mood, which refers to the way a reader responds to a selection. For example, in Ray Bradbury's short story "A Sound of Thunder," included in Unit 5, the mood is tense and eerie. Bradbury's tone, however, is somewhat playful and ironic.

Transcendentalism. See *Romanticism.*

Understatement. Understatement is the technique of creating emphasis by saying less than is actually or literally true. As such, it is the opposite of hyperbole, or exaggeration. An example of understatement in "Bells for John Whiteside's Daughter" is the remark "we are vexed," when speaking of the child's death.

A form of irony, understatement can be used for humorous effect, as when Emily Dickinson refers to God as "a noted Clergyman." Understatement also may be used to create biting satire or to achieve a restrained tone.

Unity. Unity is the harmonious blend of elements in a work of literature. Almost any technique used in fiction, nonfiction, and poetry can function as a unifying device. Consistency of tone, mood, and characterization, for example, contribute to unity, as does foreshadowing, balanced structure, and parallelism. In poetry, rhythm, meter, rhyme, sound devices such as alliteration, assonance, and consonance, along with repetition in the form of repetend and refrain all create and reinforce unity. Thematic unity, which is characteristic of longer works of fiction and drama, occurs when an idea presented in one part of a literary work is further developed later in the work.

Verbal Irony. See *Irony.*

Glossary

The glossary is an alphabetical listing of words from the selections, along with their meanings. If you are not familiar with a word as you read, look it up in the glossary.

The glossary gives the following information:

1. **The pronunciation of each word.** For example, **turbulent** (tur′ byələnt). If there is more than one way to pronounce a word, the most common pronunciation is listed first. For example, **status** (stā′ təs, stat′ əs).

    A primary accent ′ is placed after the syllable that is stressed the most when the word is spoken. A **secondary accent** ′ is placed after a syllable that has a lighter stress. For example, **imitation** (im′ə tā′shən). The Pronunciation Key below shows the symbols for the sounds of letters, and key words that contain those sounds. Also, there is a short pronunciation key at the bottom of each right-hand page in the glossary.

2. **The part of speech of the word.** The following abbreviations are used:
    adj. adjective *conj.* conjunction *pro.* pronoun *prep.* preposition
    adv. adverb *n.* noun *v.* verb *interj.* interjection

3. **The meaning of the word.** The definitions listed in the glossary are the ones that apply to the way a word is used in these selections.

4. **Related forms.** Words with suffixes such as *-ing*, *-ed*, *-ness*, and *-ly* are listed under the base word. For example, **decisive** *adj.* . . . **decisively** *adv.*, **decisiveness** *n.*

Pronunciation Key

Symbol	Key Words	Symbol	Key Words	Symbol	Key Words	Symbol	Key Words
a	ask, fat, parrot	oi	oil, point, toy	b	bed, fable, dub	t	top, cattle, hat
ā	ape, date, play	ou	out, crowd, plow	d	dip, beadle, had	v	vat, hovel, have
ä	ah, car, father	u	up, cut, color	f	fall, after, off	w	will, always, swear
e	elf, ten, berry	ur	urn, fur, deter	g	get, haggle, dog	y	yet, onion, yard
ē	even, meet, money			h	he, ahead, hotel	z	zebra, dazzle, haze
i	is, hit, mirror	ə	a in ago	j	joy, agile, badge		
ī	ice, bite, high		e in agent	k	kill, tackle, bake	ch	chin, catcher, arch
			i in sanity	l	let, yellow, ball	sh	she, cushion, dash
ō	open, tone, go		o in comply	m	met, camel, trim	th	thin, nothing, truth
ô	all, horn, law		u focus	n	not, flannel, ton	*th*	then, father, lathe
ōō	ooze, tool, crew			p	put, apple, tap	zh	azure, leisure
oo	look, pull, moor	ər	perhaps, murder	r	red, port, dear	ŋ	ring, anger, drink
yōō	use, cute, few			s	sell, castle, pass	′	able (ā′b′l)
yoo	united, cure, globule						

This pronunciation key is from *Webster's New World Dictionary, Students Edition.* Copyright © 1981, 1976 by Simon & Schuster. Used by permission.

abandonment (ə ban′ dən ment) *n.* Unrestrained freedom of actions or emotions. —*also* ABANDON

abash (ə bash′) *v.* To make ashamed and embarrassed.

abate (ə bāt′) *v.* To make less.

abbot (ab′ ət) *n.* A man who is head of an abbey of monks.

abdicate (ab′ də kāt′) *v.* To give up or surrender.

aberration (ab′ ər ā′ shən) *n.* A deviation from the normal; mental lapse.

abeyance (ə bā′ əns) *n.* Temporary suspension.

abide (ə bīd′) *v.* To stay, remain.

abject (ab′ jekt) *adj.* Miserable, wretched, of the lowest degree.—**abjectly** *adv.*

abolition (ab′ ə lish′ ən) *n.* An abolishing or doing away with something.

abolitionist (ab′ ə lish′ ən ist) *n.* Anyone who favored the abolishing of slavery in the U.S.

abrasion (ə brā′ zhən) *n.* A scraping or rubbing off, as of skin.

abridge (ə brij′) *v.* To reduce or lessen.

abrogation (ab′ rə gā′ shən) *n.* Cancellation, abolishment.

absolutism (ab′ sə loo′ tiz′m) *n.* The quality of being absolute or positive.

absolve (ab zälv′) *v.* To pronounce free from guilt or blame.

abstraction (ab strak′ shən) *n.* Preoccupation or absent-mindedness.

abusive (ə byoos′ iv) *adj.* Coarse and insulting.

abyss (ə bis′) *n.* A bottomless gulf.

accentuation (ak sen′ choo wā′ shən) *n.* A pronouncing or emphasis.

acquiesce (ak′ wē es′) *v.* To consent quietly without protest, but without enthusiasm.—**acquiescent** *adj.*

acrid (ak′ rid) *adj.* Sharp, bitter, stinging.

actuality (ak′ choo wal′ ə tē) *n.* A fact or actual condition.

actuate (ak′ choo wāt′) *v.* To cause to take action.

adhere (əd hir′) *v.* To stick or stay attached.

adieu (ə dyoo′) *interj.* Goodbye, farewell.

admonition (ad′ mə nish′ ən) *n.* Warning to correct some fault.—**admonish** *v.*

adroit (ə droit′) *adj.* Skillful, clever, expert.

advent (ad′ vent) *n.* A coming or arrival.

adversity (ad vur′ sə tē) *n.* A state of wretchedness, misfortune, or trouble.

affection (ə fek′ shən) *n.* A mental or emotional state or tendency.

affinity (ə fin′ ə tē) *n.* A natural liking or sympathy.

afflictive (ə flik′ tiv) *adj.* Causing pain or misery.

affluence (af′ loo wəns) *n.* Wealth, abundance of riches.

affront (ə frunt′) *n.* An open insult or slight to one's dignity.

agate (ag′ ət) *n.* A hard, semiprecious stone.

agrarian (ə grer′ ē ən) *adj.* Of agriculture or farming.

ague (ā′ gyoo) *n.* A fit of shivering.

alacrity (ə lak′ rə tē) *n.* Eager willingness or readiness.

alburnum (al bur′ nəm) *n.* The soft wood between the bark of a tree and the heartwood.

allay (ə lā) *v.* To relieve, lessen.

alleviate (ə lē′ vē āt′) *v.* To make less hard to bear.

allure (ə loor′) *v.* To tempt, attract.

allurement (ə loor′ mənt) *n.* Attraction, fascination.

alluvion (ə loo′ vē ən) *n.* Sand, clay, etc. gradually deposited by moving water.

alms (ämz) *n.* Money, food, or clothes given to poor people.

almshouse (ämz hous′) *n.* A home for people too poor to support themselves.

aloe (al′ ō) *n.* A plant of the lily family.

aloof (ə loof′) *adv.* At a distance but in view.—**aloofness** *n.*

altercation (ôl′ tər kā′ shən) *n.* An angry argument.

amber (am′ bər) *n.* A yellow fossil resin used in jewelry.

ambiguity (am′ bə gyoo′ ə tē) *n.* Vagueness, uncertainty.

ambivalence (am biv′ ə lens) *n.* Having simultaneous conflicting feelings toward a person or thing.

amble (am′ b'l) *n.* A leisurely walking pace. *v.* To move at a smooth, easy gait.

amiability (ā′ mē ə bil′ ə tē) *n.* Friendliness, likeability, pleasantness.

amicable (am′ i kə b'l) *adj.* Friendly, showing good will.

ammoniac (ə mō′ nē ak′) *n.* A pungent gum resin used in perfumes and cements.

amphitheater (am′ fə thē′ ə tər) *n.* A level place surrounded by rising ground.

amulet (am′ yə lit) *n.* Something worn because of its supposed magic powers; a charm.

anaemia (ə nē′ mē ə) *n.* Lack of vigor or vitality; lifelessness.

anarchy (an′ ər kē) *n.* Political disorder and violence; lack of government.

andiron (an′ dī′ ərn) *n.* Either of a pair of metal supports used to hold wood in a fireplace.

angler (aŋ′ glər) *n.* A fisherman who uses hook and line.

animalism (an′ ə m'l iz′m) *n.* The activity, appetites or nature of animals.

animation (an′ ə mā′ shən) *n.* A bringing to life; a brisk, lively quality.—**animated** *adj.*

annex (ə neks′) *v.* To add on or attach.

annihilation (ə nī′ ə lā′ shən) *n.* Complete destruction.—**annihilate** *v.*

anoint (ə noint′) *v.* To put oil on in a ceremony of making sacred.

anonymity (an′ ə nim′ ə tē) *n.* The condition of not being easily distinguished from others because of a lack of individual character.

anthropological (an′ thrə pə läj′ i k'l) *adj.* Of the study of humans, especially their culture, customs, and social relationships.

antipathy (an tip′ ə thē) *n.* A strong dislike.

apace (ə pās′) *adv.* With speed; swiftly.

aperture (ap′ ər chər) *n.* An opening or gap.

apocryphal (ə pä′ krə f'l) *adj.* Not genuine; counterfeit.

apparition (ap′ ə rish′ ən) *n.* **1.** The act of appearing or becoming visible. **2.** A strange figure appearing suddenly.

append (ə pend′) *v.* To attach or affix.

apprehend (ap′ rə hend′) *v.* To perceive or understand.

apprehensive (ap′ rə hen′ siv) *adj.* Uneasy, anxious.—**apprehension** *n.* **apprehensively** *adv.*

apprise (ə prīz′) *v.* To inform or notify.

approbation (ap′ rə bā′ shən) *n.* Official approval.

arbitrary (är' bə trer' ē) *adj.* Capricious; based on whim or preference; not fixed by rules.

arcana (är kā' nə) *n.* Mysteries or hidden knowledge.

ardently (är' d'nt lē) *adv.* Enthusiastically, passionately. —**ardent** *adj.*

arduous (är' jōō wəs) *adj.* Difficult, laborious.

array (ə rā') *n.* An orderly grouping or arrangement, especially of troops. *v.* **1.** To place in order. **2.** To dress in fine clothing.

arrestingly (ə rest' iŋ lē) *adv.* In a way that attracts attention; strikingly.

arsenal (är' s'n əl) *n.* A place for storing weapons.

articulate (är tik' yə lit) *adj.* **1.** Clearly presented. **2.** Expressing oneself clearly and easily.

artifact (är' tə fakt') *n.* Any object made by human work, especially a primitive or simple one.

ascendancy (ə send' ən sē) *n.* Supremacy; position of power.

ascertain (as' ər tān') *v.* To find out with certainty.— **ascertainable** *adj.*

ascetic (ə' set' ik) *n.* A person who leads a life of contemplation and self-denial for religious purposes.

ascribe (ə skrīb') *v.* To assign, attribute.

askance (ə skans') *adv.* With suspicion or disapproval.

aspect (as' pekt) *n.* Looks, appearance.

aspirant (as' pər ənt) *n.* A person who yearns or seeks, as after honors, high position, etc.

aspirated (as' pə rāt' id) *adj.* Preceded or followed by the speech sound represented by the letter *h.*

assail (ə sāl') *v.* To begin working on or have a forceful effect upon.

assent (ə sent') *n.* Consent or agreement. *v.* To agree.

assiduously (ə sij' ōō wəs lē) *adv.* With consent and careful attention.

assignable (ə sīn' ə b'l) *adj.* Able to be transferred to another.

assuage (ə swāj') *v.* To lessen or relieve.

astride (ə strīd') *adv.* Extending across.

asunder (ə sun' dər) *adv.* Into parts or pieces.

athwart (ə thwôrt') *prep.* Across.

atrocity (ə träs' ə tē) *n.* A brutal, cruel act.

attenuate (ə ten' yōō wāt') *v.* To make slender or thin.

audacity (ô das' ə tē) *n.* Bold courage; daring.

audibility (ô' də bil' ə tē) *n.* Ability to be heard.

auditor (ô' də tər) *n.* A listener.

aught (ôt) *n.* Anything whatever.

augment (ôg ment') *v.* To increase or become greater.

auroral (ô rôr' əl) *adj.* Of the dawn.—**aurora** *n.*

austere (ô stir') *adj.* Severe, stern; self-disciplined.

authoritative (ə thôr' ə tāt' iv) *adj.* Having or showing authority; official.

autocrat (ôt' ə krat') *n.* A dictator; a domineering, self-willed person.

avarice (av' ər is) *n.* Greed for riches.

aversation (av' ər sā' shən) *n.* An act of turning away.

aversion (ə vur' zhən) *n.* An intense dislike.

avert (ə vurt') *v.* **1.** To prevent, keep from happening. **2.** To turn away.

avidity (ə vid' ə tē) *n.* Eagerness, enthusiasm.

avocation (av' ə kā' shən) *n.* Something one does in addition to his regular work.

avow (ə vou') *v.* To declare openly.

awestricken (ô' strik' ən) *adj.* Filled with profound respect or wonder.

azure (azh' ər) *n.* Sky blue.

B

badger (baj' ər) *v.* To torment or nag at.

ballpeen (bäl' pēn) *n.* The hemispherical head of a hammer.

balm (bäm) *n.* Anything healing or soothing.

banal (bā' n'l) *adj.* Dull or stale because of overuse.

bandy (ban' dē) *v.* To pass about freely and carelessly.

banishment (ban' ish mənt) *n.* A sending into exile.

barbarous (bär' bər əs) *adj.* Primitive, crude, coarse.

bark (bärk) *n.* A sailing boat.

barnacle (bär' nə k'l) *n.* A saltwater shellfish that attaches itself to rocks, ship bottoms, etc.

baroque (bə rōk') *adj.* Of the period in which much ornamentation in architecture flourished.

base (bās) *adj.* Showing little or no honor, courage, or decency; ignoble.

bastard (bas' tərd) *n.* Anything false, inferior, or varying from standard.

beachhead (bēch hed') *n.* A position gained as a secure starting point for any action; foothold.

bedeck (bi dek') *v.* To cover with decorations.

bedraggled (bi drag' 'ld) *adj.* Wet, limp, and dirty.

begrudge (bi gruj') *v.* To give with ill will or reluctance.

beguile (bi gīl') *v.* **1.** To pass the time pleasantly; while away the hours. **2.** To charm or delight.

belabor (bi lā' bər) *v.* To criticize or attack with words.

beleaguer (bi lē' gər) *v.* To besiege, as with an army.

bellicose (bel' ə kōs') *adj.* Eager to fight; warlike.

bemuse (bi myōōz') *v.* To muddle, stupefy, or preoccupy.

benediction (ben' ə dik' shən) *n.* A blessing.

benefactor (ben' ə fak' tər) *n.* A person who has given help.

benevolently (bə nev' ə lənt lē) *adv.* Kindly.—**benevolent** *adj.*

benign (bi nīn') *adj.* Kindly, good-natured.

bequeath (bi kwēth') *v.* To hand down or pass on.

bereavement (bi rēv' mənt) *n.* A sad or lonely state, caused by loss or death.

beseech (bi sēch') *v.* To beg or ask for earnestly.

besiege (bi sēj') *v.* To hem in with armed forces and keep under attack so as to force a surrender.

bestir (bi stur') *v.* To exert or busy (oneself).

bestride (bi strīd') *v.* To sit on or straddle.

betoken (bi tō' k'n) *v.* To indicate or show.

bevel (bev' 'l) *v.* To slant or cut to an angle.

bewail (bi wāl') *v.* To mourn or complain about.

billet (bil' it) *v.* To be assigned to a post.

billow (bil' ō) *n.* A large wave.

bisect (bī sekt') *v.* To cut in two.

---

fat, āpe, cär; ten, ēven; is, bīte; gō, hôrn, tōōl, look; oil, out; up, fur; get; joy; yet; chin; she; thin, *th*en; zh, leisure; ŋ, ring; ə for *a* in *ago, e* in *agent, i* in *sanity, o* in *comply, u* in *focus;* ' as in *able* (ā'b'l)

bittern (bit' ərn) n. Any of various wading birds of the heron family.

blackguard (blag' ərd) adj. Vulgar, low.

blanch (blanch) v. To whiten, turn pale.

blazonry (blā' z'n rē) n. Any brilliant display.

blight (blīt) n. Anything that destroys or prevents growth.

blousy (blou' sē) var. of BLOWSY adj. Untidy, having a sloppy, uncared-for appearance.

blunder (blun' dər) n. A foolish or stupid mistake.

bobbed (bäb'd) adj. Cut short.

bobolink (bäb' ə liŋk) n. A migratory songbird.

bodice (bäd' is) n. A kind of vest worn over a dress or blouse; the upper part of a dress.

boding (bō' diŋ) adj. foreboding; of an omen.

bole (bōl) n. A tree trunk.

bondage (bän' dij) n. Slavery or subjection to some force.

boot (bo͞ot) v. To profit, benefit.

bootless (bo͞ot' lis) adj. Without benefit; useless.

booty (bo͞ot' ē) n. Loot taken from the enemy; anything valuable seized by force.

bovine (bō' vīn) adj. Oxlike; slow, dull, stupid.

brandish (bran' dish) v. To wave or flourish in a threatening exultant way.

bravado (brə vä' dō) n. Pretended courage or defiant confidence where really there is none.

brazen (brā' z'n) adj. Of brass.

breaker (brāk' ər) n. A wave that breaks into foam against a shore.

bric-a-brac (brik' ə brak') n. Knickknacks or small decorative objects.

brimful (brim' fo͞ol') adj. Full to the brim.

bristle (bris' 'l) v. To become stiff and erect, like bristles.

broider (broi' dər) v. To embroider.

brook (bro͝ok) v. To put up with.

browbeat (brou bēt) v. To bully or intimidate.

bruit (bro͞ot) v. To rumor, repeat, spread news of.

buckle (buk' 'l) v. To bend, warp, or crumple, as under pressure or intense heat.

bullion (bo͝ol' yon) n. Gold and silver as raw material.

bullock (bo͝ol' ək) n. A steer or bull.

buoyancy (boi' ən sē) n. The ability to float.

burgeon (bʉr'jən) v. To expand or grow rapidly.

burlesque (bər lesk') adj. Comically imitating, parodying.

burnish (bʉr' nish) v. To polish or make shiny.

bustle (bus' 'l) n. Hurrying busily and noisily with much fuss and bother.

buttery (but' ər ē) n. A pantry.

C

cadaverous (kə dav' ər əs) adj. Like a dead body, especially pale, gaunt, and ghastly.—**cadaverously** adv.

cadence (kād' 'ns) n. Measured movement, as in dancing or marching.

callow (kal' ō) adj. Immature, unsophisticated.

camaraderie (käm' ə räd' ər ē) n. Loyalty and warm friendly feeling among comrades.

cancerous (kan' sər əs) adj. Like a tumor or malignant new growth anywhere in the body.

cannel (kan' 'l) n. A variety of tough coal that burns with a bright flame.

cannonade (kan' ə nād') n. A continuous firing of artillery.

cannoneer (kan' ə nir') n. A gunner.

cañon (kan' yən) n. A canyon.

canonize (kan' ə nīz') v. To declare a saint in a formal church procedure.

capacious (kə pā' shəs) adj. Spacious, roomy.

capital (kap' ə t'l) adj. First-rate, excellent.

carbuncle (kär' buŋ k'l) n. A certain deep-red gem.

careen (kə rēn') v. To lurch from side to side, especially while moving rapidly.

career (kə rir') v. To rush wildly or move at full speed.

caricature (kar' ə kə chər) n. A likeness or imitation that is so distorted as to seem ridiculous.

carnage (kär' nij) n. Bloody and extensive slaughter.

carouse (kə rouz') n. A noisy, merry drinking party.

carp (kärp) v. To complain or find fault in a petty or nagging way.

casement (kās' mənt) n. A window frame that opens on hinges along the side.

caste (kast) n. Social position; any distinct social class.

catapult (kat' ə pult') v. To leap, move quickly, or be hurled.

causey (kô' zē) n. A raised path or road.

cavernous (kav' ər nəs) adj. Like a cave; deep, hollow.

celestial (sə les' chəl) adj. Of heaven; divine.

celibacy (sel' ə bə sē) n. The state of being unmarried.

censer (sen' sər) n. An ornamented container in which incense is burned.

censurer (sen' shər ər) n. One who condemns or expresses disapproval.

cerebral (ser' ə brəl) adj. Intellectual; of the brain.

ceremonial (ser' ə mō' nē əl) adj. Ritual, formal, polite. n. A rite or ceremony.

cessation (se sā' shən) n. A ceasing or stopping.

chafe (chāf) v. **1.** To rub, so as to make warm. **2.** To become irritated or impatient. n. An injury or irritation caused by rubbing.

chalice (chal' is) n. A cup-shaped flower.

chasm (kaz' 'm) n. A break, crack, or gap.

chasten (chās' 'n) v. To punish in order to make better.

chide (chīd) v. To scold.

chimera (ki mir' ə) n. Any impossible or foolish fancy or imagining.

cholera (käl' ər ə) n. Any of several intestinal diseases.

choleric (käl' ər ik) adj. Showing a quick temper.

chorister (kôr' is tər) n. A member of a choir.

chuckle-headed (chuk' 'l hed' id) adj. Empty-headed, characteristic of a stupid person.

circuitous (sər kyo͞o' ə təs) adj. Roundabout, indirect.

circumstantial (sʉr' kəm stan' shəl) adj. Depending on circumstances or accompanying events.

cistern (sis' tərn) n. A large underground tank for storing water.

civility (sə vil' ə tē) n. Politeness.

clamber (klam' bər) v. To climb with effort or clumsily.

clammy (klam' ē) adj. Unpleasantly moist, cold, and sticky.

clangor (klaŋ' ər) n. A loud, harsh cry.

cleave (klēv) v. To cling or be faithful (to).

cleaver (klēv' ər) n. A tool for cutting or splitting.

cleft (kleft) *n.* A crack or hollow between two parts.

clime (klīm) *n.* A region or realm, especially with reference to its climate.

cloche (klōsh) *n.* A close-fitting bell-shaped hat for women.

clod (kläd) *n.* Earth, soil.

cloister (klois' tər) *n.* Any place where one may lead a secluded life, especially a religious one.

clout (klout) *n.* A blow, as with the hand.

cloven (klō' v'n) *adj.* Divided, split.

cognizance (käg' nə zens) *n.* Knowledge.

coherence (kō hir' əns) *n.* The quality of being logically integrated, consistent, and intelligible.—**coherent** *adj.* **coherently** *adv.*

collective (ko lek' tiv) *adj.* Of all individuals in a group working together.

colloquial (kə lō' kwē əl) *adj.* Conversational.

colonnade (käl' ə nād') *n.* A series of columns, set at regular intervals, usually supporting a roof.

combatant (käm' bə tənt) *n.* A fighter.

combativeness (kom bat' iv nis) *n.* Fondness for fighting; readiness to fight.

comeliness (kum' lē nəs) *n.* Beauty, attractiveness.

commensurate (kə men' shər it) *adj.* Equal in measure or size.

commingle (kə miŋ' g'l) *v.* To intermix or blend.

commiseration (kə miz' ə rā' shən) *n.* Sorrow, pity, or sympathy.

commissary (käm' ə ser' ē) *n.* A store where food and supplies can be obtained.

commode (kə mōd') *n.* A chest of drawers.

commodious (kə mō' dē əs) *adj.* Spacious, roomy.

commonwealth (käm' ən welth) *n.* A nation or state in which there is self-government.

commune (kə myōōn') *v.* To be in close rapport.

communion (kə myōōn' yən) *n.* The act of sharing.

compass (kum' pəs) *v.* To surround completely.

compassionate (kəm pash' ən āt') *v.* To pity.

compatriot (kəm pā' trē ət) *n.* A colleague.

complacency (kəm plās' 'n sē) *n.* Self-satisfaction or smugness.—**complacent** *adj.*

complainant (kəm plān' ənt) *n.* A person who files a charge or makes the complaint in court.

complaisant (kəm plā' z'nt) *adj.* Agreeable, willing to please.

complement (käm' plə mənt) *v.* To make complete.

compliance (kəm plī' əns) *n.* A giving in.

complicity (kəm plis' ə tē) *n.* Partnership in wrongdoing.

comport (kəm pōrt') *v.* To agree (with).

compulsively (kəm pul' siv lē) *adj.* Resulting from an irresistible driving force.

compunction (kəm puŋk' shən) *n.* A sharp feeling of uneasiness brought on by a sense of guilt.

concentric (kən sen' trik) *adj.* Having a center in common.

conciliate (kən sil' ē āt') *v.* To win over or soothe the anger of.

confederate (kən fed' ər it) *n.* An ally or associate.—**confederation** *n.*

conflagration (kän' flə grā' shən) *n.* A big, destructive fire.

confound (kən found') *v.* To confuse, bewilder.

congeniality (kən jēn' ē al' ə tē) *n.* Friendliness, sympathy, agreeableness.

conjecture (kən jek' chər) *n.* Theorizing or guesswork. *v.* To guess.

conjoin (kən join') *v.* To unite, combine.

conjugation (kän' jə gā' shən) *n.* Arrangement of verbs to show changes in tense, number, person, etc.

conjure (kän' jər) *v.* To call upon or appeal to.

conjurer (kän' jər ər) *n.* A magician.

connive (kə nīv') *v.* To scheme or cooperate secretly.

consanguinity (kän' saŋ gwin' ə tē) *n.* Relationship by descent from the same ancestor.

consecrate (kän' sə krāt') *v.* To make sacred or holy; dedicate.

consolation (kän' sə lā' shən) *n.* A comforting.—**console** *v.* **consolingly** *adv.*

consort (kən sôrt') *v.* To keep company.

consternation (kän' stər nā' shən) *n.* Great shock that makes one feel bewildered.

constrain (kən strān) *v.* To force or oblige.

consul (kän' s'l) *n.* A person appointed by his government to live in a foreign city and serve his country's citizens and business interests there.

consumptive (kən sump' tiv) *adj.* Destructive, wasteful, tending to consume.

contemporaneous (kən tem' pə rā' nē əs) *adj.* Happening in the same period of time.

continent (känt' 'n ənt) *adj.* Of a mainland or large land area.

convalescent (kän' və les' 'nt) *n.* A person who is gradually recovering health after an illness. *adj.* Having to do with recovery after illness.

conventicle (kən ven' ti k'l) *n.* An assembly, especially a secret religious assembly.

converge (kən vurj') *v.* To come together or move toward the same place.

conveyance (kən vā' əns) *n.* A means of carrying.

convolution (kän' və lōō' shən) *n.* A twisting, coiling, or winding together.

convoy (kän' voi) *v.* To escort.

convulsion (kən vul' shən) *n.* Any violent disturbance.—**convulsive** *adj.* **convulse** *v.*

coolie (kōō' lē) *n.* An unskilled native laborer, especially formerly in India or China.

coquetry (kōk' ə trē) *n.* Flirting.

coquettish (kō ket' ish) *adj.* Behaving like a woman who flirts and tries to get men's attention.

cornice (kôr' nis) *n.* A horizontal molding projecting along the top of a wall or building.

coronet (kôr' ə net') *n.* A small crown, an ornamental band worn around the head.

cosmical (käz' mik əl) *adj.* Relating to the universe as an orderly whole.

---

fat, āpe, cär; ten, ēven; is, bīte; gō, hôrn, tōōl, look; oil, out; up, fur; get; joy; yet; chin; she; thin, then; zh, leisure; ŋ, ring; ə for *a* in *ago, e* in *agent, i* in *sanity, o* in *comply, u* in *focus;* ' as in *able* (ā'b'l)

cosmopolitan (käz′ mə päl′ ə t'n) *adj.* At home in all countries or places, not bound by local habits or prejudices.

cosmos (käz′ məs) *n.* Any complete and orderly system.

countenance (koun′ tə nəns) *n.* The face. *v.* To support, approve, or tolerate.

coupé (k͞oo pā′) *n.* A closed, two-door automobile with a body smaller than that of a sedan.

courser (kôr′ sər) *n.* A graceful, spirited, or swift horse.

courtier (kôr′ tē ər) *n.* An attendant at a royal court.

covet (kuv′ it) *v.* To long for with envy.

cow (kou) *v.* To make timid by filling with fear or awe.

cower (kou′ ər) *v.* To cringe or shrink and tremble, as from someone's anger or threats.

coy (koi) *adj.* Affecting innocence or shyness, especially in a playful manner.—**coyly** *adv.*

crabbed (krab′ id) *adj.* Ill-tempered, cross, peevish.

crag (krag) *n.* A steep rock that rises above all others.

craven (krā′ vən) *n.* A thorough coward.

credibility (kred′ ə bil′ ə tē) *n.* The quality of being believable or reliable.

creosote (krē′ ə sōt′) *n.* An oily liquid with a pungent odor, used as a preservative for wood.

crestfallen (krest′ fôl′ ən) *adj.* Dejected, disheartened, or humbled.

crotchety (kräch′ it ē) *adj.* Full of peculiar whims or stubborn notions; eccentric.

crypt (kript) *n.* An underground chamber or vault.

cryptic (krip′ tik) *adj.* Mysterious; having hidden meaning.

cumber (kum′ bər) *v.* To hinder or burden.

cur (kur) *n.* A mongrel; dog of mixed breed.

curlew (kur′ l͞oo) *n.* A large, brownish wading bird.

cynicism (sin′ ə siz'm) *n.* The attitude that people are insincere or motivated in their actions only by selfishness.—**cynical** *adj.*

D

dally (dal′ ē) *v.* To trifle, toy, or deal lightly with.

dappled (dap′ 'ld) *adj.* Marked with spots.

dastardly (das′ tərd lē) *adj.* Mean, sneaky, and cowardly.

daunt (dônt) *v.* To make afraid or discouraged.

dauntless (dônt′ lis) *adj.* Fearless.

debar (dē bär′) *v.* To prohibit or exclude.

decadence (dek′ ə dəns) *n.* A condition of decline, decay, or deterioration.

declension (di klen′ shən) *n.* Arrangement of nouns or pronouns to show changes in case or person.

decorously (dek′ ər əs lē) *adv.* Properly and in good taste.—**decorous** *adj.*

decorum (di kôr′ əm) *n.* Fitness, propriety, and good taste in behavior, speech, etc.

decoy (di koi′) *v.* To lure or be lured into a trap.

decrepit (di krep′ it) *adj.* Broken down or worn out by old age.

decrepitude (di krep′ ə t͞ood′) *n.* Feebleness.

defection (di fek′ shən) *n.* Desertion; becoming disloyal and then deserting what one had been supporting.

deferential (def′ ə ren′ shəl) *adj.* Very respectful.—**deference** *n.* **deferentially** *adv.*

defunct (di fuŋkt′) *adj.* No longer living.

degenerate (di jen′ ər it) *adj.* Having sunk below a former or normal condition; deteriorated.

degradation (deg′ rə dā′ shən) *n.* A bringing into dishonor or contempt.

deity (dē′ ə tē) *n.* God.

delirium (di lir′ ē əm) *n.* **1.** A temporary state of extreme mental excitement, marked by restlessness, confused speech, and hallucinations. **2.** Uncontrollably wild excitement.—**delirious** *adj.*

deliverance (di liv′ ər əns) *n.* A rescue or release.

delude (di l͞ood′) *v.* To fool, mislead, or trick.

deluge (del′ yo͞oj) *n.* An overwhelming, floodlike rush of anything. *v.* To flood or overwhelm.

delusive (di l͞oos′ iv) *adj.* Misleading; unreal.—**delusion** *n.*

demigod (dem ē gäd′) *n.* In mythology, an offspring of a human and a god.

demur (di mur′) *v.* To object.

denizen (den′ i zən) *n.* An inhabitant.

denominate (di näm′ ə nāt) *v.* To call or give a specified name to.

denouement (dā n͞oo′ män) *n.* Any final outcome.

denunciation (di nun′ sē ā′ shən) *n.* The act of condemning or accusing.

deploy (dē ploi′) *v.* To station or place (forces, etc.) in accordance with a plan.

depose (di pōz′) *v.* To state or testify under oath.—**deposition** *n.*

deputation (dep′ yo͞o tā′ shən) *n.* A group of people appointed to represent others.

derange (di rānj′) *v.* To make insane.

deride (di rīd′) *v.* To ridicule, make fun of.

derisive (di rī′ siv) *adj.* Showing ridicule or contempt.—**derisively** *adv.* **derision** *n.*

derivative (də riv′ ə tiv) *adj.* Not original; taken from other sources.

designedly (di zī′ nid lē) *adv.* Purposely.

desolate (des′ ə lit) *adj.* Forlorn, wretched, lonely.

desolation (des′ ə lā′ shən) *n.* A laying waste.

despatch (dis pach′) *v.* To put an end to; kill.

despondency (di spän′ dən sē) *n.* Loss of courage or hope.

despotic (de spät′ ik) *adj.* Autocratic, tyrannical.—**despotism** *n.*

destitute (des′ tə t͞oot′) *adj.* Living in complete poverty.

devastate (dev′ ə stāt′) *v.* To make helpless; overwhelm.

devious (dē′ vē əs) *adj.* Going astray; deviating from the proper course.

diabolical (dī ə bäl′ i k'l) *adj.* Very wicked or cruel.

dictum (dik′ təm) *n.* A statement.

diffusion (di fyo͞os′ zhən) *n.* A dissemination or spreading.—**diffuse** *v.*

dignitary (dig nə ter′ ē) *n.* A person holding a high office.

digress (dī gres′) *v.* To turn aside, ramble.

din (din) *n.* A loud, continuous noise.

dirge (durj) *n.* A slow, sad song, poem, or musical piece expressing grief.

disarm (dis ärm′) *v.* To make friendly.

disavow (dis′ ə vou′) *v.* To disclaim or deny approval of.

discernment (di surn′ mənt) *n.* Keen judgment; insight.—**discerning** *adj.*

disconcert (dis kən surt′) *v.* To confuse or upset the composure of.

disconsolate (dis kän′ sə lit) *adj.* So unhappy that nothing will comfort.—**disconsolately** *adv.*

discordant (dis kôr′ d'nt) *adj.* Not in harmony; clashing.—**discord** *n.* **discordantly** *adv.*

discretion (dis kresh′ ən) *n.* The quality of being careful about what one does and says.

disdain (dis dān′) *n.* Aloof contempt or scorn. *v.* To regard as unworthy.

disembowel (dis′ im bou′ əl) *v.* To take out the bowels, or guts, of.

dishabille (dis′ ə bēl′) *n.* The state of being dressed only partially or in night clothes.—*also* DESHABILLE

disheveled (di shev′ 'ld) *adj.* Untidy, rumpled.

disillusion (dis′ i loo͞′ zhən) *n.* The fact of being freed from false ideas; disenchantment.

dismantle (dis man′ t'l) *v.* To strip of covering.

dismission (dis mish′ ən) *n.* A dismissing or discharging from employment.

disparate (dis′ pər it) *adj.* Distinct or different in kind.

dispassionate (dis pash′ ən it) *adj.* Calm, impartial.

dispel (dis pel′) *v.* To scatter and drive away, cause to vanish.

dispersion (dis pur′ zhən) *n.* A being scattered or spread about.

disposition (dis′ pə zish′ ən) *n.* **1.** A putting in order; arrangement. **2.** A getting rid of something.

dispraise (dis prāz′) *n.* Blame, criticism.

disquieting (dis kwī′ ət iŋ) *adj.* Disturbing; causing anxious or uneasy feelings.

dissension (di sen′ shən) *n.* Disagreement, especially violent quarreling.

dissever (di sev′ ər) *v.* To separate.

dissipation (dis′ ə pā′ shən) *n.* Indulgence in pleasure.

dissolution (dis′ ə loo͞′ shən) *n.* A dissolving or breaking up into parts.

dissuade (di swād′) *v.* To turn (a person) aside by persuasion.

distillation (dis′ tə lā′ shən) *n.* The product of the process of separating a mixture to make purer substances.—**distill** *v.*

divergence (də vur′ jəns) *n.* A becoming different in form or kind; separating or branching off.—**diverge** *v.*

divers (dī′ vərz) *adj.* Several, various.

diverting (də vurt′ iŋ) *adj.* Amusing, entertaining.

divest (də vest′) *v.* To deprive, rid, or strip.

divine (də vīn′) *v.* To guess or prophesy.

docilely (däs′ 'l lē) *adv.* Obediently, in an easily managed way.

doggedly (dôg′ id lē) *adv.* Stubbornly, persistently.—**dogged** *adj.*

doleful (dōl′ fəl) *adj.* Sad, sorrowful, mournful.—**dolefully** *adv.*

domicile (däm′ ə sīl) *v.* To house permanently.

dominion (də min′ yən) *n.* Rule or power to rule.

dormant (dôr′ mənt) *adj.* As if asleep; quiet, still.

dotage (dōt′ ij) *n.* Feeble and childish state due to old age.

dour (door) *adj.* Stern, severe, gloomy.

dowry (dou′ rē) *n.* The property that a woman brings to her husband at marriage.

draggle (drag′ 'l) *v.* To make wet and dirty by dragging in mud.

draught (draft) *n.* The amount taken at one drink.

drone (drōn) *n.* A male bee, which has no sting and does no work.

drought (drout) *n.* A prolonged or serious shortage or dryness.—*also* DROUTH

dun (dun) *n.* A person who demands payment of a debt.

dunderhead (dun′ dər hed′) *n.* A stupid person.

dyspeptic (dis pep′ tik) *adj.* Of or having indigestion.

E

earnestly (ur′ nist lē) *adv.* Seriously, intensely, sincerely.—**earnestness** *n.* **earnest** *adj.*

earthwork (urth wurk′) *n.* An embankment made by piling up earth, especially as a fortification.

eccentricity (ik′ sen tris′ ə tē) *n.* Deviation from what is customary; oddity, unconventionality.

éclat (ā′ klä) *n.* Brilliant or conspicuous success.

eclipse (i klips′) *n.* A dimming or extinction, as of fame, glory, etc.

eddy (ed′ ē) *v.* To move with a circular movement. *n.* A whirlpool.

edification (ed′ ə fi kā′ shən) *n.* Instruction or improvement.

edifice (ed′ ə fis) *n.* A building, especially one that is large or looks important.

efface (i fās′) *v.* To wipe out.

effectual (ə fek′ choo wəl) *adj.* Producing the desired effect; effective.—**effectually** *adv.*

effervescent (ef′ ər ves′ 'nt) *adj.* Bubbling up; foaming—**effervesce** *v.*

efficacy (ef′ i kə sē) *n.* Power to produce intended results.

effrontery (e frun′ tər ē) *n.* Unashamed boldness.

ejaculation (i jak′ yə lā′ shən) *n.* A sudden exclamation.

elude (i loo͞d′) *v.* To avoid or escape.

elusive (i loo͞′ siv) *adj.* Hard to grasp; baffling.

emanate (em′ ə nāt′) *v.* To come forth, issue.

emancipate (i man′ sə pāt′) *v.* To set free.—**emancipation** *n.*

embolden (im bōl′ d'n) *v.* To give courage to.

embroil (im broil′) *v.* To draw into a conflict.

emigrant (em′ ə grənt) *n.* A person who leaves one country to settle in another.—**emigration** *n.* **emigrate** *v.*

eminence (em′ ə nəns) *n.* A high place.

eminent (em′ ə nənt) *adj.* Famous, distinguished.—**eminently** *adv.*

emphatically (im fat′ ik ə lē) *adv.* Forcefully, definitely, with emphasis.

emphysema (em′ fə sē′ mə) *n.* An abnormal swelling and wasting away of lung tissue, accompanied by impairment of breathing.

emulous (em′ yə ləs) *adj.* Desirous of equaling or surpassing.

encumber (in kum′ bər) *v.* To hold back the motion of, as with a burden.

---

fat, āpe, cär; ten, ēven; is, bīte; gō, hôrn, to͞ol, lo͝ok; oil, out; up, fur; get; joy; yet; chin; she; thin, *th*en; zh, leisure; ŋ, ring; ə for *a* in *ago*, *e* in *agent*, *i* in *sanity*, *o* in *comply*, *u* in *focus*; ′ as in *able* (ā′b'l)

enfranchise (in fran′ chīz) v. To free from slavery.

enigmatic (en′ ig mat′ ik) adj. Perplexing, baffling.

enshrine (in shrīn′) v. To hold as sacred; cherish.

ensign (en′ sīn) n. A flag.

entreaty (in trēt′ ē) n. An earnest request.—**entreat** v.

entrenchment (in trench′ mənt) n. Any defense or protection.

entrepreneur (än′ trə prə nʉr′) n. A person who organizes and manages a business undertaking.

environs (in vī′ rənz) n. The surrounding area.

ephemeral (i fem′ ər əl) adj. Short-lived.

epigram (ep′ ə gram) n. Any short, witty, pointed statement.

equanimity (ek′ wə nim′ ə tē) n. Calmness, evenness of temper.

equilibrium (ē′ kwə lib′ rē əm) n. A state of balance or equality between opposing forces.

equity (ek′ wət ē) n. Fairness, impartiality, justice.

eradicate (i rad′ ə kāt′) v. To tear out by the roots.

espouse (i spouz′) v. To support or advocate.

espy (ə spī′) v. To catch sight of.

essay (e sā′) v. To try, attempt.

esteem (ə stēm′) v. To value highly. n. High regard, respect.

ethereal (i thir′ ē əl) adj. Not earthly; heavenly.

evangelist (i van′ jə list) n. A traveling preacher.

evasive (i vā′ siv) adj. Not straightforward; tricky.

evince (i vins′) v. To show plainly.

evitable (ev′ ə tə b′l) adj. Avoidable.

exalt (ig zôlt′) v. To lift up or elevate.

excruciatingly (iks krōō′ shē āt iŋ lē) adv. With great mental suffering.

execrable (ek′ si krə b′l) adj. Very inferior; abominable.

exemplary (ig zem′ plə rē) adj. Worth imitating; serving as a model.

exhort (ig zôrt′) v. To urge strongly.

expatriate (eks pā′ trē it′) n. A person who is withdrawn from his or her native land.

expatriated (eks pā′ trē āt′d) adj. Driven out of one's native land; banished.

expedient (ik spē′ dē ənt) adj. Useful for getting a desired result; convenient. n. A means to an end.

expendable (ik spen′ də b′l) adj. That can be replaced or used up.

extemporize (ik stem′ pə rīz′) v. To furnish (things) in a makeshift way to meet a pressing need.

extenuate (ik sten′ yōō wāt′) v. To lessen the seriousness of.

extort (ik stôrt′) v. To get from someone by violence or threats.

exuberant (ig zōō′ bər ənt) adj. Growing profusely; luxuriant.

exude (ig zōōd′) v. To pass out in drops; ooze.

F

faction (fak′ shən) n. Partisan conflict within a country.

fain (fān) adv. Gladly, with eagerness.

fallible (fal′ ə b′l) adj. Liable to be mistaken or deceived.

fallowness (fal′ ō nis) n. The state of remaining uncultivated and unused.

falsetto (fôl set′ ō) adj. Of an artificial way of speaking in which the voice is much higher than natural.

famish (fam′ ish) v. To become weak from hunger.

fanaticism (fə nat′ ə siz′m) n. Excessive and unreasonable zeal.

fanciful (fan′ si fəl) adj. Imaginative.

fantasia (fan tā′ zhə) n. A musical composition of no fixed form.

fastidious (fas tid′ ē əs) adj. Dainty or refined.

fastness (fast′ nis) n. A stronghold or secure place.

fatalistic (fāt′ ′l is′ tik) adj. Accepting every event as inevitable.

feint (fānt) v. To deliver a pretended blow to take the opponent off his guard.

felonious (fə lō′ nē əs) adj. Traitorous, intending to commit a grave crime.

fervid (fʉr′ vəd) adj. Impassioned, fervent.

festoon (fes tōōn′) n. Material hanging in a loop or curve.

fetlock (fet′ läk′) n. A tuft of hair on the back of the leg of a horse.

fetter (fet′ ər) n. A chain, or any restraint.

fictionmonger (fik′ shən muŋ′ gər) n. A dealer in made-up stories.

fidelity (fə del′ ə tē) n. Faithful devotion, loyalty.

filament (fil′ ə mənt) n. A very slender thread or fiber.

fillet (fil′ it) n. A narrow band worn around the head.

finesse (fi nes′) n. Skillfulness and delicacy of performance.

firebrand (fīr brand′) n. A person who stirs up others to revolt or strife.

firmament (fʉr′ mə mənt) n. The sky.

fissure (fish′ ər) n. A long, narrow crack.

fixity (fik′ sə tē) n. Steadiness.

flagrant (flā′ grənt) adj. Glaringly bad; outrageous.

flak (flak) n. The fire of antiaircraft guns.

floe (flō) n. An extensive area of floating sea ice.

fluent (flōō′ ənt) adj. Flowing or moving smoothly and easily.

fluky (flōō′ kē) adj. Constantly changing, fitful.

fodder (fäd′ ər) n. Coarse food for cattle, horses, sheep, etc., as cornstalks, hay, and straw. v. To feed with fodder.

folio (fō′ lē ō′) adj. Of the largest regular size for a book.

foray (fôr′ ā) n. A sudden attack or raid in order to seize things.

forbear (fôr ber′) v. To refrain from or avoid.

forbearance (fôr ber′ əns) n. Patient restraint.

forenoon (fôr′ nōōn′) n. Morning.

foretime (fôr′ tīm′) n. The past.

formidable (fôr′ mə də b′l) adj. Hard to overcome; strikingly impressive.

forsake (fər sāk′) v. To leave, abandon.

forsaken (fər sā′ kən) adj. Abandoned, lonely, forlorn.

fortitude (fôr′ tə tōōd) n. The strength to bear misfortune.

fortuitous (fôr tōō′ ə təs) adj. Accidental, fortunate, happening by good luck.

fraternal (frə tʉr′ n′l) adj. Brotherly.

freebooter (frē bōōt′ ər) n. A pirate.

freshet (fresh′ it) n. A stream of fresh water flowing into the sea.

frigidly (frij′ id lē) adv. Coldly, stiffly, or formally.

frivolity (fri väl' ə tē) *n.* The quality of being trivial, not serious, or silly.
frolicsome (fräl' ik səm) *adj.* Full of gaiety and high spirits.—**frolicsomeness** *n.*
frugally (froo' gə lē) *adv.* Thriftily, economically; not wastefully.
functionary (funk' shən er' ē) *n.* An official who performs a certain function.
furred (furd) *adj.* Coated with diseased or waste matter.
furrow (fur' ō) *n.* A narrow groove made in the ground by a plow.
furtively (fur' tiv lē) *adv.* In a sneaky, secret manner.—**furtive** *adj.*

G

gainsay (gān' sā') *v.* To deny or contradict.
galling (gôl' iŋ) *adj.* Irritating, annoying.
galvanic (gal van' ik) *adj.* Producing an electric current.
gambol (gam' b'l) *v.* To jump and skip about in play.
gape (gāp) *v.* 1. To open wide. 2. To stare with the mouth open.
garner (gär' nər) *v.* To get, earn, or gather.
garret (gar' it) *n.* An attic.
garrison (gar' ə s'n) *n.* A military post or fort.
gasconade (gas' kə nād') *v.* To boast or bluster.
gauche (gōsh) *adj.* Awkward, lacking social grace.
gaunt (gônt) *adj.* 1. Thin, bony, hollow-eyed, and haggard. 2. Looking grim or forbidding.
gawky (gô' kē) *adj.* Awkward, clumsy.
genealogist (jē' nē äl' ə jist) *n.* One who studies family descent or ancestry.
generic (jə ner' ik) *adj.* Referring to a whole kind, class, or group.
gentry (jen' trē) *n.* People of high social standing.
genuflect (jen' yə flekt') *v.* To act in a submissive or servile way.
gesticulate (jes tik' yə lāt') *v.* To make or use gestures.
glib (glib) *adj.* Done in a smooth, offhand fashion.—**glibness** *n.*
gluttony (glut' 'n ē) *n.* The habit of eating too much.
gnash (nash) *v.* To grind or strike (the teeth) together, as in anger or pain.
gondola (gän' də lə) *n.* A car suspended from and moved along a cable, for holding passengers.
gossamer (gäs' ə mər) *adj.* Light, thin, and filmy.
gouty (gout' ē) *adj.* Having gout, a disease that causes swelling and severe pain, notably in the big toe.
grackle (grak' 'l) *n.* A blackbird.
grandiose (gran' dē ōs') *adj.* Impressive; seeming or trying to seem important.
grandsire (gran' sīr') *n.* A grandfather, male ancestor.
granular (gran' yə lər) *adj.* Consisting of grains or tiny particles.
green-sick (grēn sik') *adj.* Having chlorosis, a kind of anemia sometimes affecting girls at puberty.
grimace (gri mās') *n.* A twisting or distortion of the face.
grizzled (griz' 'ld) *adj.* Having gray hair.
grotesquerie (grō tesk' ər ē) *n.* The quality of being bizarre, strange, or fantastic.
guffaw (gə fô') *v.* To laugh in a loud, coarse way.
guile (gīl) *n.* Slyness and craftiness in dealing with others.

guileless (gīl' lis) *adj.* Frank, candid.
guttural (gut' ər əl) *n.* A sound produced in the throat.
gyration (jī rā' shən) *n.* Circular or spiral motion.

H

habitation (hab' ə tā' shən) *n.* The act of dwelling.
habituate (hə bich' oo wāt) *v.* To accustom or make used (to).
habitude (hab' ə tood') *n.* The habitual or characteristic condition of mind or body.
hallow (hal' ō) *v.* To make holy or sacred.
hallucination (hə loo' sə nā' shən) *n.* The apparent perception of sights, sounds, etc. that are not actually present.
hamlet (ham' lit) *n.* A very small village.
handsel (han' s'l) *v.* To use for the first time.
hapless (hap' lis) *adj.* Unfortunate, unlucky.
haply (hap' lē) *adv.* Perhaps; by chance.
harass (hə ras') *v.* To trouble or torment.
harpy (här' pē) *n.* A relentless, greedy, or grasping person.
harrow (har' ō) *v.* To torment or cause mental distress. *n.* A heavy frame with spikes or sharp disks, used for breaking up and leveling plowed ground.
harry (har' ē) *v.* To force or push along.
haughtiness (hôt' ē nis) *n.* Great pride and contempt or scorn for others.—**haughty** *adj.*
headwaters (hed wôt' ərz) *n.* The small streams that are the sources of a river.
heather (heth' ər) *n.* A plant with stalks of small purplish flowers.
hector (hek' tər) *v.* To bully.
heft (heft) *n.* Weight, heaviness.
helve (helv) *n.* The handle of a tool.
hemp (hemp) *n.* A fiber used to make rope.
heresy (her' ə sē) *n.* A religious belief opposed to the established doctrines of a church.
hermitage (hur' mit ij) *n.* A secluded retreat; the place where a hermit lives.
heyday (hā' dā') *n.* The time of greatest health, vigor, success, etc.
hiatus (hī āt' əs) *n.* A gap or opening.
hillock (hil' ək) *n.* A small mound.
hoary (hôr' ē) *adj.* 1. Very old, ancient. 2. White.
hobgoblin (häb' gäb' lin) *n.* An elf; frightening apparition.
homage (häm' ij) *n.* Anything done to show reverence, honor, or respect.
hostler (häs' lər) *n.* A person who takes care of horses at an inn or stable.
hovel (huv' 'l) *n.* Any small, miserable dwelling; hut.
howitzer (hou' it sər) *n.* A kind of short cannon.
huswifery (hus wif' ər ē) *n.* Housekeeping.
hypocritic (hip' ə krit' ik) *adj.* Pretending to be something without really being so.

---

fat, āpe, cär; ten, ēven; is, bīte; gō, hôrn, tool, look; oil, out; up, fur; get; joy; yet; chin; she; thin, *th*en; zh, leisure; **ŋ**, ring; ə for *a* in *ago, e* in *agent, i* in *sanity, o* in *comply, u* in *focus;* ' as in *able* (ā'b'l)

hysteric (his ter′ ik) *adj.* Emotionally uncontrolled and wild.

I

iambic (ī am′ bik) *n.* A verse made up of metrical feet of two syllables, the first unaccented and the other accented.

idealize (ī dē′ ə līz′) *v.* To regard or show as perfect or more nearly perfect than is true.

idyll (ī′ d′l) *n.* A peaceful scene of rural, pastoral, or domestic life.

ignominiously (ig′ nə min′ ē əs lē) *adv.* Shamefully, dishonorably.

illiberal (i lib′ ər əl) *adj.* Not generous; intolerant.

illuminate (i lōō′ mə nāt′) *v.* To enlighten, inform, instruct.—**illumination** *n.*

illumine (i lōō′ min) *v.* To light up.

illusion (i lōō′ zhən) *n.* A false idea or conception.

illustrious (i lus′ trē əs) *adj.* Very distinguished, outstanding, famous.

imbibe (im bīb′) *v.* To drink in or absorb.

imbue (im byōō′) *v.* To permeate.

immemorial (im′ ə môr′ ē əl) *adj.* Extending back beyond memory; ancient.

imminent (im′ ə nənt) *adj.* Likely to happen without delay.

impassiveness (im pas′ iv nis) *n.* Calmness; not showing emotion.

impediment (im ped′ ə mənt) *n.* An obstacle; anything that obstructs or delays.

impend (im pend′) *v.* To be about to happen.

imperative (im per′ ə tiv) *adj.* Absolutely necessary.

imperceptible (im′ pər sep′ tə b′l) *adj.* So slight or subtle as not to be easily perceived.

imperialist (im pir′ ē ə list) *n.* One who believes in the practice of seeking to dominate weaker countries.

imperially (im pir′ ē ə lē) *adv.* Majestically, magnificently.

imperious (im pir′ ē əs) *adj.* **1.** Urgent. **2.** Proud and domineering.—**imperiously** *adv.*

impertinent (im pʉr′ t′n ənt) *adj.* Not showing proper respect or manners.—**impertinence** *n.*

imperturbable (im′ pər tʉr′ bə b′l) *adj.* That cannot be disturbed or excited; calm.—**imperturbably** *adv.*

impervious (im pʉr′ vē əs) *adj.* Incapable of being passed through or penetrated.

impetuous (im pech′ ōō wəs) *adj.* Rushing; moving with great force or violence.

impious (im′ pē əs) *adj.* Lacking reverence for God.

implacable (im plak′ ə b′l) *adj.* That cannot be appeased or pacified; inflexible.

implore (im plôr′) *v.* To ask or beg earnestly.—**imploringly** *adv.*

importune (im′ pôr tōōn′) *v.* To trouble with requests or demands.—**importunity** *n.*

impound (im pound′) *v.* To gather and enclose (water).

imprecation (im′ prə kā′ shən) *n.* A curse.

imprecision (im′ pri sizh′ ən) *n.* Vagueness; the quality of not being exact or definite.

impregnable (im preg′ nə b′l) *adj.* Not capable of being captured or entered by force.

impressionist (im presh′ ən ist) *n.* A painter whose aim is to capture a momentary glimpse of a subject, applying paint in short strokes of pure color, as exemplified by Monet, Pisarro, Sisley, etc.

imprimis (im prī′ mis) *adv.* In the first place.

impropriety (im′ pro prī′ ə tē) *n.* Improper action or behavior.

imprudently (im prōōd′ ′nt lē) *adv.* Rashly; without thought of the consequences.

impudent (im′ pyōō dənt) *adj.* Shamelessly bold.

impute (im pyōōt′) *v.* To attribute, ascribe.

inaccessible (in′ ək ses′ ə b′l) *adj.* Impossible to reach.

inadvertence (in′ əd vʉr′ təns) *n.* An oversight or mistake. —**inadvertently** *adv.*

inanimate (in an′ ə mit) *adj.* Not alive; dead.

inanition (in′ ə nish′ ən) *n.* Exhaustion from lack of food.

inarticulate (in′ är tik′ yə lit) *adj.* Produced without the normal sounds of understandable speech.

inattention (in′ ə ten′ shən) *n.* Failure to pay attention.

inauspicious (in′ ô spish′ əs) *adj.* Unlucky; not boding well for the future.

incantation (in′ kan tā′ shən) *n.* The chanting of magical words that are supposed to cast a spell.

incarnate (in kär′ nit) *adj.* Personified, in human form.—**incarnation** *n.*

incessantly (in ses′ ′nt lē) *adv.* Constantly; without stopping.—**incessant** *adj.*

incipient (in sip′ ē ənt) *adj.* In the first stage of existence.

incoherence (in′ kō hir′ əns) *n.* Lack of logic; state of being rambling or disjointed.

incontinently (in känt′ ′n ənt lē) *adv.* Without self-restraint.

incorrigible (in kôr′ i jə b′l) *adj.* That cannot be improved or reformed, especially because firmly established.

incredulous (in krej′ ōō ləs) *adj.* Showing doubt or disbelief.

increment (in′ krə mənt) *n.* Increase, gain, growth.

incubus (iŋ′ kyə bəs) *n.* A burden; anything oppressive.

indecipherable (in′ di sī′ fər ə b′l) *adj.* Illegible.

indecorous (in dek′ ər əs) *adj.* Not in good taste.

indeterminate (in′ di tʉr′ mi nit) *adj.* Vague, indefinite.—**indeterminately** *adv.*

indignity (in dig′ nə tē) *n.* Something that humiliates, insults, or injures self-respect.

indiscretion (in′ dis kresh′ ən) *n.* A lack of good judgment; an unwise act.

indispensable (in′ dis pen′ sə b′l) *adj.* Absolutely necessary or required.

indolent (in′ də lənt) *adj.* Lazy.

indubitably (in dōō′ bi tə blē) *adv.* Unquestionably, without doubt.

ineffable (in ef′ ə b′l) *adj.* Too overwhelming to be expressed in words.

ineffectually (in′ i fek′ chōō wə lē) *adv.* Not effectively.—**ineffectual** *adj.*

ineradicable (in i rad′ ə kə b′l) *adj.* Not able to be removed or gotten rid of.

inert (in ʉrt′) *adj.* Tending to be inactive, dull, slow.

inertia (in ʉr′ shə) *n.* A tendency to remain in a fixed condition without change.

inestimable (in es′ tə mə b′l) *adj.* Too valuable to be measured.

infallible (in fal' ə b'l) *adj.* Dependable, sure.

infamy (in' fə mē) *n.* Disgrace, dishonor; very bad reputation.—**infamous** *adj.*

infatuation (in fach' ōo wā' shən) *n.* Foolish or shallow love or affection.

infidel (in' fə d'l) *n.* A person who holds no religious beliefs.

infinitesimal (in' fin ə tes' ə məl) *adj.* Too small to be measured.

infirmity (in fur' mə tē) *n.* An instance of weakness, either physical or moral.

inflection (in flek' shən) *n.* Any change in tone or pitch.

ingenuous (in jen' yōo wəs) *adj.* Frank, simple, naive.

inglorious (in glôr' ē əs) *adj.* Shameful, disgraceful.

inherent (in hir' ənt) *adj.* Innate, basic, inborn.

iniquity (in ik' wə tē) *n.* Wickedness.

injunction (in juŋk' shən) *n.* A command or order.

inquisitorial (in kwiz' ə tôr' ē əl) *adj.* Of an official whose work is examining or investigating.

insatiable (in sā' shə b'l) *adj.* Constantly wanting more; very greedy.

inscrutable (in skrōōt' ə b'l) *adj.* Mysterious; that cannot be easily understood.

insensibility (in sen' sə bil' ə tē) *n.* Unconsciousness.—insensible *adj.*

insidious (in sid' ē əs) *adj.* Sly, crafty, treacherous.

insinuate (in sin' yōo wāt') *v.* To suggest indirectly.

insolent (in' sə lənt) *adj.* Boldly disrespectful.—**insolence** *n.*

inspirit (in spir' it) *v.* To give life or courage to; cheer.

insubstantial (in' səb stan' shəl) *adj.* Weak; not solid or firm.

insular (in' sə lər) *adj.* Like an island; detached, isolated.

insulate (in' sə lāt) *v.* To set apart, isolate.

insuperable (in sōō' pər ə b'l) *adj.* That cannot be overcome.

insurgence (in sur' jəns) *n.* A rising in revolt.

insurrection (in' sə rek' shən) *n.* Rebellion, revolt.

integral (in' tə grəl) *adj.* Essential, necessary for completeness.

intercession (in' tər sesh' ən) *n.* The act of intervening to produce agreement; mediation.

interloper (in' tər lō' pər) *n.* A person who meddles in others' affairs.

interment (in tur' mənt) *n.* Burial.

interminableness (in tur' mi nə b'l nis) *n.* Endlessness; the quality of seeming to last forever.—**interminable** *adj.* **interminably** *adv.*

intermittent (in' tər mit' 'nt) *adj.* Stopping and starting again at intervals.—**intermittently** *adv.*

internecine (in' tər nē' sin) *adj.* Deadly or harmful to both sides involved in a conflict.

interpose (in' tər pōz') *v.* To place or put between.

intimate (in' tə māt') *v.* To hint or make known indirectly.

intonation (in' tə nā' shən) *n.* The act of chanting or uttering in a singing tone.

intrigue (in trēg') *n.* Secret or underhanded plotting.

intuition (in' tōo wish' ən) *n.* The direct knowing of something without the use of reasoning.—**intuitive** *adj.*

invective (in vek' tiv) *n.* A violent verbal attack; strong criticism.

inveigle (in vē' g'l) *v.* To lead on or trick into doing something.

inveteracy (in vet' ər ə sē) *n.* Habit, practice.—**inveterate** *adj.*

invincible (in vin' sə b'l) *adj.* That cannot be overcome.—**invincibleness** *n.*

inviolable (in vī' ə lə b'l) *adj.* Not to be violated; sacred.

inviolate (in vī' ə lit) *adj.* Kept sacred or unbroken.

invocation (in' və kā' shən) *n.* The act of praying or calling on a god for help.—**invoke** *v.*

invulnerable (in vul' nər ə b'l) *adj.* That cannot be wounded or injured.

irascible (i ras' ə b'l) *adj.* Irritable, quick-tempered.

irksome (urk' səm) *adj.* Annoying, irritating, tiresome.

irresolution (i rez' ə lōō' shən) *n.* The condition of wavering in purpose; indecisiveness.

irreverence (i rev' ər əns) *n.* An act or statement showing disrespect.

irrevocably (i rev' ə kə blē) *adv.* Unalterably; without the ability to be undone.

irruption (i rup' shən) *n.* The act of bursting suddenly or violently.

J

jerk (jurk) *v.* To preserve (meat) by slicing it and drying strips in the sun.—**jerky** *n.*

jocular (jäk' yə lər) *adj.* Joking, witty, full of fun.—**jocularity** *n.*

jubilant (jōō' b'l ənt) *adj.* Joyful, triumphant, rejoicing.

K

kindred (kin' drid) *n.* Relatives or family. *adj.* Similar.

kinetic (ki net' ik) *adj.* Of or resulting from motion.

knotty (nät' ē) *adj.* Wiry, tough, rugged.

L

lacerate (las' ə rāt') *v.* **1.** To mangle or tear jaggedly. **2.** To wound, hurt, or distress.—**laceration** *n.*

laconic (lə kän' ik) *adj.* Concise; using few words.

laden (lād' 'n) *adj.* Loaded.

lamentably (lam' ən tə blē) *adv.* Deplorably, distressingly.

languish (laŋ' gwish) *v.* To become weak, lose vigor.

lanthorn (lan' tərn) *n.* Lantern.

latent (lāt' 'nt) *adj.* Present but inactive.

leaden (led' 'n) *adj.* Of a dull gray.

lee (lē) *n.* Shelter, protection.

legion (lē' jon) *n.* A large number.

lethargy (leth' ər jē) *n.* A condition of dullness and sluggishness.—**lethargic** *adj.*

lettered (let' ərd) *adj.* Well educated; literate.

levy (lev' ē) *n.* An imposing and collecting of a tax.

---

fat, āpe, cär; ten, ēven; is, bīte; gō, hôrn, tōol, look, oil, out; up, fur; get; joy; yet; chin; she; thin, then; zh, leisure; ŋ, ring; ə for a in ago, e in agent, i in sanity, o in comply, u in focus; ' as in able (ā'b'l)

liaison (lē' ə zän') *n.* A linking up or connecting parts of a whole.

libation (lī bā' shən) *n.* The ritual of pouring out wine or oil upon the ground as a sacrifice to a god.

lightsome (līt' səm) *adj.* Lighthearted, gay.

limber (lim' bər) *adj.* Flexible, easily bent.

limbo (lim' bō) *n.* An indeterminate state midway between two others.

list (list) *v.* To tilt to one side.

literalist (lit' ər əl ist) *n.* One who believes in realism in art.

lithe (līth) *adj.* Limber, flexible, bending easily.

livery (liv' ər ē) *n.* A stable where horses and carriages can be had for hire.

loath (lōth) *adj.* Unwilling, reluctant.

loathsome (lōth' səm) *adj.* Disgusting, detestable.— **loathsomely** *adv.*

locution (lō kyoo' shən) *n.* A particular style of speech.

logger-head (lôg' ər hed') *n.* An upright piece of timber.

lope (lōp) *n.* A long, easy, swinging stride.

lordly (lôrd' lē) *adj.* Noble, grand, suitable for a lord.

lozenge (läz' 'nj) *n.* A diamond.

lucid (loo' sid) *adj.* **1.** Bright, shining. **2.** Clear, readily understood.

ludicrous (loo di krəs) *adj.* Laughably absurd.

lugubriousness (loo goo' brē əs nis) *n.* Sadness or mournfulness, especially in an exaggerated way.

lumbago (lum bā' gō) *n.* Backache, especially in the lower back.

lumber (lum' bər) *v.* To move heavily and clumsily.

luminary (loo' mə nər' ē) *n.* A body that gives off light, such as the sun or moon.

luminous (loo' mə nəs) *adj.* Shining, bright.

lustily (lus' tə lē) *adv.* Heartily, vigorously, strongly.— **lusty** *adj.*

lyceum (lī sē' əm) *n.* An organization presenting public lectures.

lynch (linch) *v.* To murder by mob action and without a lawful trial, as by hanging.

lyrical (lir' i k'l) *adj.* Expressing great enthusiasm or joy.

M

macabre (mə käb' rə) *adj.* Gruesome, grim, and horrible.

mackinaw (mak' ə nô') *n.* A short, double-breasted coat made of heavy woolen cloth.

magistrate (maj' is trāt) *n.* A minor official with limited judicial powers.

magnanimity (mag' nə nim' ə tē) *n.* The quality or state of being noble, generous.

magnitude (mag' nə tood') *n.* Greatness of importance or influence.

main (mān) *n.* Poetic term for the open sea.

malady (mal' ə dē) *n.* A disease or sickness.

malediction (mal' ə dik' shən) *n.* A curse.

malevolent (mə lev' ə lənt) *adj.* Wishing evil or harm.

malinger (mə liŋ' gər) *v.* To pretend to be ill in order to escape duty or work.

manifestation (man' ə fes tā' shən) *n.* A making clear or evident.

manifesto (man' ə fes' tō) *n.* A public declaration of motives and intentions.

manifold (man' ə fōld') *adj.* Many and varied.

mansard (man' särd) *n.* A roof with two slopes on each of the four sides, the lower steeper than the upper.

mantle (man' t'l) *n.* Anything that covers or conceals.

marge (märj) *n.* A border, edge.

marmot (mär' mət) *n.* Any of a group of thick-bodied, burrowing rodents, as the woodchuck.

martial (mär' shəl) *adj.* Of or suitable for war.

martyrdom (mär' tər dəm) *n.* The death or sufferings of a person who chooses to suffer or die rather than give up his principles.

mashie (mash' ē) *n.* A golf club for making medium shots.

maudlin (môd' lin) *adj.* Foolishly and tearfully sentimental.

maxim (mak' sim) *n.* A statement of a general truth.

mead (mēd) *n.* Meadow.

mean (mēn) *adj.* Poor, inferior, shabby.— **meanly** *adv.* **meanness** *n.*

meddlesome (med' 'l səm) *adj.* Interfering.

mediaeval (mē' dē ē' v'l) *adj.* Of the Middle Ages.

meditative (med' ə tāt' iv) *adj.* Indicating deep, continued thought.

melancholy (mel' ən käl' ē) *adj.* Sad, gloomy.

menace (men' is) *n.* A threat. *v.* To threaten or be a danger.— **menacingly** *adv.*

mendicant (men' di kənt) *n.* A beggar.

mercenary (mur' sə ner' ē) *n.* A professional soldier hired to serve in a foreign army.

meridian (mə rid' ē ən) *n.* **1.** Noon **2.** Prime or highest point. *adj.* Of or at noon.

mesmerize (mez' mər īz') *v.* To hypnotize, spellbind, or fascinate.

meteorological (mēt' ē ər ə läj' i k'l) *adj.* Of weather or climate.

metered (mēt' ər'd) *adj.* Having a specific rhythmic pattern in verse.

metro (met' rō) *n.* A subway or underground railway, as in European cities.

mettlesome (met' 'l səm) *adj.* Spirited.

mien (mēn) *n.* Appearance; manner.

militarist (mil' ə tər ist) *n.* A person who believes in having the military dominate government.

mince (mins) *n.* Walking with short steps or in an affected, dainty manner.

minion (min' yən) *n.* A subordinate official.

mirth (murth) *n.* Joyfulness, merriment, gladness.

mitigate (mit' ə gāt') *v.* To make milder or less severe.

mogul (mō' g'l) *n.* A bump or ridge of closely packed snow.

moiety (moi' ə tē) *n.* A half.

molder (mōl' dər) *v.* To crumble into dust; decay.

mollify (mäl' ə fī') *v.* To make less intense; soothe or appease.

moonstruck (moon struk') *adj.* Affected mentally in some way, supposedly by the influence of the moon.

moor (moor) *n.* A tract of open, rolling wasteland, usually covered with heather.

morass (mə ras') *n.* A marsh or swamp.

morbidly (môr' bid lē) *adv.* Horribly, gloomily.

morose (mə rōs') *adj.* Gloomy, ill-tempered, sad.

mortal (môr' t'l) *adj.* Extreme, very great.— **mortally** *adv.*

mortified (môr' tə fīd') *adj.* **1.** Decayed or gangrenous. **2.** Shamed or humiliated.

mosaic (mō zā' ik) *adj.* Resembling a design made by inlaying small bits of colored stone or glass in mortar.

mosque (mäsk) *n.* A Moslem temple or place of worship.

mottle (mät' 'l) *v.* To mark with blotches, streaks, and spots of colors.

moult (mōlt) *v.* To shed feathers or outer skin at certain intervals. *also* MOLT

mulish (myōōl' ish) *adj.* Stubborn.

multiplicity (mul' tə plis' ə tē) *n.* A great number.

multitudinous (mul' tə tōōd 'n əs) *adj.* Very numerous, many.

mundane (mun dān') *adj.* Commonplace, ordinary, practical.

munificent (myoo nif' ə s'nt) *adj.* Very generous in giving.

murky (mur' kē) *adj.* Dark, gloomy.

musk (musk) *n.* An odor that resembles a substance with a strong, penetrating odor obtained from the male musk deer and is used in perfumes.

musketry (mus' kə trē) *n.* Firearms.

myriad (mir' ē əd) *adj.* Of an indefinitely large number.

mystical (mis' ti k'l) *adj.* Mysterious; of obscure meaning; spiritually significant.

mystified (mis' tə fīd') *adj.* Puzzling, mysterious.

mythical (mith' i k'l) *adj.* Imaginary, fictitious.

N

nary (ner' ē) *adj.* Not any.

naturalist (nach' ər əl ist) *n.* A person who studies nature, especially by direct observation.

naturalization (nach' ər ə li zā' shən) *n.* The act of conferring the rights of citizenship upon.

negation (ni gā' shən) *n.* The lack or opposite of some positive quality.

nemesis (nem' ə sis) *n.* Anything by which, it seems, one must inevitably be defeated.

nettle (net' 'l) *v.* To irritate, annoy.

neurotic (noo rät' ik) *adj.* Of a mental disorder marked by anxiety, phobias, depression, etc.

niggard (nig' ərd) *adj.* Stingy, miserly.

nocturnal (näk tur' n'l) *adj.* Happening in the night.

noisome (noi' səm) *adj.* Having a bad odor.

nomadic (nō mad' ik) *adj.* Characteristic of people who have no home but move about constantly.

nonchalance (nän' shə läns') *n.* The quality of being cool and calmly indifferent.

noncommittal (nän' kə mit' 'l) *adj.* Not committing oneself to any point of view.

nostalgic (näs tal' jik) *adj.* Longing for something far away or long ago.

notoriety (not' ə rī ə tē) *n.* The state of being well-known, usually unfavorably.—**notorious** *adj.* **notoriously** *adv.*

noxious (näk' shəs) *adj.* Harmful, corrupting, unwholesome.

O

obeisance (ō bā' s'ns) *n.* A gesture of respect or reverence.

obliquely (ə blēk' lē) *adv.* At a slant, usually somewhat diagonally.

obliterate (ə blit' ə rāt') *v.* To erase or blot out.—**obliteration** *n.*

oblivion (ə bliv' ē ən) *n.* The condition of being forgotten.

obscurity (əb skyoor' ə tē) *n.* **1.** The quality of being dark, dim, or indistinct. **2.** The condition of being not well-known.—**obscurely** *adv.* **obscure** *v.*

obsession (əb sesh' ən) *n.* The state of being preoccupied with a persistent idea, desire, or feeling.

obstinate (äb' stə nit) *adj.* Stubborn.—**obstinacy** *n.*

obstreperous (əb strep' ər əs) *adj.* Noisy or unruly, especially in resisting.

obtrude (əb trood') *v.* To offer or force upon others unasked.

obtuse (äb toos') *adj.* Dull, slow to understand.

occult (ə kult') *adj.* Designating certain mystic or mysterious arts, such as magic or astrology.

office (ôf' is) *n.* Something performed for another.

ominous (äm' ə nəs) *adj.* Threatening, sinister.—**ominously** *adv.*

omnipotent (äm nip' ə tənt) *adj.* All-powerful.

onslaught (än' slôt') *n.* A violent, intense attack.

opiate (ō' pē it) *n.* Anything tending to quiet, soothe, or deaden.

opportunistic (äp' ər toon is' tik) *adj.* Adapting one's actions to circumstances as in politics, in order to further one's immediate interests, without regard for basic principles.

oppress (ə pres') *v.* **1.** To worry, trouble. **2.** To rule harshly or keep down by cruel use.—**oppression** *n.*

opulence (äp' yə ləns) *n.* Wealth, richness, abundance.

oracle (ôr' ə k'l) *n.* Any person of great knowledge or in communication with a deity.

oration (ō rā' shən) *n.* A formal public speech.

oratorically (ôr' ə tôr' i kə lē) *adv.* In the manner of a skilled public speaker.

orbicular (ôr bik' yoo lər) *adj.* Spherical, circular.

ordinance (ôr' d'n əns) *n.* That which is held to be a decree of a deity.

organdy (ôr' gən dē) *n.* A very sheer, crisp cotton fabric.

organic (ôr gan' ik) *adj.* Involving the basic makeup of a thing.

orthodox (ôr' thə däks') *adj.* Approved, conventional, conforming to established doctrines.

oscillation (äs' ə lā' shən) *n.* A swinging back and forth.—**oscillate** *v.*

ostentation (äs' tən tā' shən) *n.* Showy display; pretentiousness.—**ostentatious** *adj.* **ostentatiously** *adv.*

outcrop (out' kräp') *n.* A breaking forth of mineral from the earth. *v.* To emerge in this way.

outgeneral (out jen' ər əl) *v.* To surpass in leadership or management.

outpoint (out point') *v.* To score more points than.

overprepossessing (ō' vər prē' pə zes' iŋ) *adj.* Excessively pleasing or attractive.

---

fat, āpe, cär; ten, ēven; is, bīte; gō, hôrn, tool, look; oil, out; up, fur; get; joy; yet; chin; she; thin, *th*en; zh, leisure; ŋ, ring; ə for *a* in *ago, e* in *agent, i* in *sanity, o* in *comply, u* in *focus*; ' as in *able* (ā'b'l)

overture (ō' vər chər) *n.* A musical introduction to a large musical work.

P

pacifism (pas' ə fiz'm) *n.* Opposition to the use of force under any circumstances.

palatial (pə lā' shəl) *adj.* Like a palace; large and ornate, magnificent.

pall (pôl) *n.* A dark or gloomy covering.

pallet (pal' it) *n.* A small, inferior bed or a pad filled as with straw and used directly on the floor.

pallid (pal' id) *adj.* Pale, faint in color.—**pallidly** *adv.*

palm (päm) *n.* Victory, triumph.

palmy (päm' ē) *adj.* Flourishing, prosperous.

palpitation (pal' pə tā' shən) *n.* A throbbing or rapid beating.

palsy (pôl' zē) *n.* Paralysis of a muscle as a result of a nervous system disorder, sometimes accompanied by tremors.

paltry (pôl' trē) *adj.* Practically worthless; insignificant.

pamphleteer (pam' flə tir') *n.* One who writes pamphlets arguing a political or social issue.

pandemonium (pan' də mō' nē əm) *n.* Any place or scene of wild disorder, noise, or confusion.

paradox (par' ə däks') *n.* A situation that seems to have contradictory or inconsistent qualities.

paragon (par' ə gän') *n.* A clothing and upholstery fabric of the 17th and 18th centuries.

parenthesis (pə ren' thə sis) *n.* An episode, often an irrelevant one.

parley (pär' lē) *n.* A talk or conference for the purpose of settling a dispute.

paroxysm (par' ək siz'm) *n.* A fit or sudden outburst.

parsimony (pär' sə mō' nē) *n.* Stinginess, unreasonable economy—**parsimonious** *adj.*

parsonage (pär' s'n ij) *n.* The dwelling provided by a church for the use of its parson.

partisan (pärt' ə z'n) *adj.* Of a person who strongly and emotionally supports one side.

pastoral (pas' tər əl) *adj.* **1.** Characteristic of rural life, idealized as peaceful, simple, and natural. **2.** Of a pastor or his duties.

pastorate (pas' tər it) *n.* The position or duties of a clergyman.

pathological (path' ə läj' i k'l) *adj.* Governed by an irresistible, irrational impulse; compulsive.

pathos (pā' thäs) *n.* The feeling of pity, sympathy, or sorrow.

patriarch (pā' trē ärk') *n.* The father and ruler of a family or tribe.—**patriarchal** *adj.*

patronage (pā' trən ij) *n.* Support, encouragement, sponsorship.

patronize (pā' trə nīz') *v.* **1.** To be a regular customer of. **2.** To treat in a condescending manner.

pedantic (pi dan' tik) *adj.* Laying unnecessary stress on minor points of learning; displaying a scholarship lacking in judgment.

pendent (pen' dənt) *adj.* Hanging, suspended.—*also* PENDANT

penury (pen' yə rē) *n.* Extreme poverty.

perceptible (pər sep' tə b'l) *adj.* Able to be observed.

perfidy (pur' fə dē) *n.* The deliberate breaking of faith; betrayal of trust.

perforce (pər fôrs') *adv.* By necessity.

pernicious (pər nish' əs) *adj.* Deadly or causing ruin.

perpetuate (pər pech' oo wāt') *v.* To cause to be remembered.

perquisite (pur' kwə zit) *n.* A privilege or benefit to which a person is entitled by virtue of position or status.

persevere (pur' sə vir') *v.* To continue in some effort; persist.

pertinacity (pur' tə nas' ə tē) *n.* Stubborn persistence.

pertinence (pur' t'n əns) *n.* The quality of being appropriate; relevance.

perturbation (pur' tər bā' shən) *n.* Disturbance, alarm, agitation.

peruse (pə rooz') *v.* To read carefully.—**perusal** *n.*

pervade (pər vād') *v.* To spread throughout.

perverseness (pər vurs' nis) *n.* Stubborn contrariness, wickedness.

perversion (pər vur' zhən) *n.* A distortion or bringing into a worse condition.

pestilence (pes' t'l əns) *n.* Any fatal contagious disease.

petition (pə tish' ən) *n.* A solemn, earnest request. *v.* To make a request.

pettishness (pet' ish nis) *n.* Crossness, irritableness.

petulance (pech' oo ləns) *n.* Irritation or petty annoyance.—**petulantly** *adv.*

philosophic (fil ə säf' ik) *adj.* Sensibly composed or calm.

picket (pik' it) *n.* A group of soldiers or a single soldier stationed, usually at an outpost, to guard a body of troops from surprise attack.

piety (pī' ə tē) *n.* Devotion to religious duties.

pilfer (pil' fər) *v.* To steal.

pilgrimage (pil' grəm ij) *n.* A long journey, especially to a holy place.

pillage (pil' ij) *n.* The act of ravaging, robbing, or spoiling.

pinnacle (pin' ə k'l) *n.* The peak or highest point.

pique (pēk) *v.* To offend or arouse resentment in. *n.* Resentment at having been slighted.

plaintive (plān' tiv) *adj.* Mournful, sad, expressing sorrow.

plash (plash) *n.* A splash.

pleach (plēch) *v.* To cause to intertwine or interlace.

plucky (pluk' ē) *adj.* Brave, spirited, courageous.—**pluck** *n.*

plummet (plum' it) *n.* A plunge or drop downward.

plunder (plund' dər) *v.* To rob or take by force.—**plunderer** *n.*

poignant (poin' yənt) *adj.* Sharp, keen, pointed, or penetrating.—**poignancy** *n.*

politic (päl' ə tik) *adj.* Having practical wisdom; shrewd, diplomatic.

polytone (päl' i tōn) *n.* In music, the simultaneous use of two or more keys.

pommel (pum' 'l) *n.* The rounded, upward-projecting front part of a saddle. *v.* To beat or hit with repeated blows.

pomp (pämp) *n.* Stately display, splendor, magnificence.

ponderous (pän' dər əs) *adj.* Very heavy, bulky.

portal (pôr' t'l) *n.* A doorway, gate, or entrance.

portend (pôr tend') *v.* To be an omen or warning of.

portent (pôr' tent) *n.* Something that warns of an event about to occur.

portico (pôr' tə kō') *n.* A porch or covered walk, consisting of a roof supported by columns, often at the entrance of a building.

posterity (päs ter' ə tē) *n.* All succeeding generations.

posthumously (päs' choo məs lē) *adv.* After the author's death.

potation (pō tā' shən) *n.* A drink.

poultice (pōl' tis) *n.* A hot, soft, moist mass, as of flour or herbs, applied to a sore part of the body.

prattle (prat' 'l) *v.* To talk much and foolishly, chatter.

precarious (pri ker' ē əs) *adj.* Risky, insecure—**precariously** *adv.*

precept (prē' sept) *n.* A rule of moral conduct.

precipice (pres' ə pis) *n.* A steep cliff.

precipitate (pri sip' ə tāt') *v.* **1.** To bring on, hasten, cause to happen before expected. **2.** To throw headlong.

precipitately (pri sip' ə tit lē) *adv.* Suddenly, abruptly.—**precipitate** *adj.*

precipitous (pri sip' ə təs) *adj.* Steep, almost vertical.

precocious (pri kō' shəs) *adj.* Matured or developed to a point beyond that which is normal for the age.

preconception (prē' kən sep' shən) *n.* An idea or opinion formed beforehand.

predisposing (prē' dis pōz' iŋ) *adj.* Making receptive beforehand.

preeminence (prē em' ə nəns) *n.* Superiority, prominence, dominance.

prefabricate (prē fab' rə kāt') *v.* To make up beforehand.

pregnant (preg' nənt) *adj.* Inventive, productive of results, fruitful.

prelude (prel' yood) *v.* To serve as an introduction (to). *n.* Anything serving as an introduction to a principal event.

preposterous (pri päs' tər əs) *adj.* Absurd, ridiculous.

presentiment (pri zen' tə mənt) *n.* A feeling that something, especially of an evil nature, is about to take place.

presume (pri zoom') *v.* **1.** To rely too much (on). **2.** To take something for granted, make suppositions.

presumption (pri zump' shən) *n.* The act of taking something for granted.

pretension (pri ten' shən) *n.* A cover-up or false claim.

preternatural (prēt' ər nach' ər əl) *adj.* Abnormal.

prevail (pri vāl') *v.* To triumph, succeed, be effective.

priggish (prig' ish) *adj.* Excessively precise, proper, and smug, to the annoyance of others.

primal (prī' m'l) *adj.* First in time; original.

primeval (prī mē' v'l) *adj.* Of the earliest age.

prithee (prith' ē) *interj.* Please.

privy (priv' ē) *n.* A toilet, especially an outhouse.

probity (prō' bə tē) *n.* Uprightness, honesty, integrity.

prodigal (präd' i gəl) *adj.* Extremely generous, lavish, wasteful.—**prodigally** *adv.*

prodigy (präd' ə jē) *n.* Something so extraordinary as to inspire wonder.

profane (prə fān') *v.* To treat with irreverence or contempt.

proficiently (prə fish' ənt lē) *adv.* Expertly, skillfully, competently.

profusion (prə fyoo' zhən) *n.* Abundance; rich or lavish supply.

proletarian (prō lə ter' ē ən) *adj.* Of the working class.

promontory (präm' ən tôr' ē) *n.* A peak of high land that juts out into a body of water.

propensity (prə pen' sə tē) *n.* A natural tendency.

propitiate (prə pish' ē āt') *v.* To win or regain the good will of.—**propitiatory** *adj.*

propitious (prə pish' əs) *adj.* Favorable, advantageous.

propriety (prə prī' ə tē) *n.* Conformity with what is proper or fitting.

prostrate (präs' trāt) *v.* To lie flat on the ground in demonstration of great humility. *adj.* Lying flat.

proverbially (prə vur' bē ə lē) *adv.* Of a well-known nature because commonly referred to.

providence (präv' ə dəns) *n.* **1.** The care or kindly guidance of God. **2.** [P-] God, as the guiding power of the universe.

provocative (prə väk' ə tiv) *adj.* Provoking, as to thought, action or feeling; stimulating, erotic.

prowess (prou' is) *n.* Superior ability or skill.

prudence (prood' 'ns) *n.* Sound judgment or careful management—**prudential** *adj.* **prudent** *adj.*

psyche (sī' kē) *n.* The mind.

pueblo (pweb' lō) *n.* A type of village built by certain American Indians, consisting of flat-roofed structures arranged in terraces.

pugilistic (pyoo jə lis' tik) *adj.* Of boxing.—**pugilist** *n.*

pullet (pool' it) *n.* A young hen.

pulverize (pul' və rīz') *v.* To crush or break down completely.

purge (purj) *v.* To cleanse, rid, or clear.

pursy (pur' sē) *adj.* Obese, fat.

purveyor (pər vā' ər) *n.* A supplier.

putrid (pyoo' trid) *adj.* Rotten and foul-smelling.

Q

quaff (kwäf) *v.* To drink deeply.

quagmire (kwag' mīr') *n.* Wet, boggy ground, yielding under the feet.

quail (kwāl) *v.* To lose courage or draw back in fear.

quarry (kwôr' ē) *n.* A place where stone is excavated.

querulous (kwer' ə ləs) *adj.* Complaining.—**querulously** *adv.*

quiescent (kwī es' 'nt) *adj.* Quiet, still.

quoth (kwōth) *v.* Said.

R

rabble (rab' 'l) *n.* A mob or noisy, disorderly crowd.

rack (rak) *v.* To move with a gait in which the horse's legs move in lateral pairs.

---

fat, āpe, cär; ten, ēven; is, bīte; gō, hôrn, tool, look; oil, out; up, fur; get; joy; yet; chin; she; thin, then; zh, leisure; ŋ, ring; ə for a in ago, e in agent, i in sanity, o in comply, u in focus; ' as in able (ā'b'l)

rail (rāl) v. To speak bitterly or complain violently.

rakishly (rā' kish lē) adv. In a trim, neat way, suggesting speed: said of a boat.

rampart (ram' pärt) n. Any defense or protection.

ramrod (ram' räd') n. A rod used for ramming down the charge in a gun that is loaded through the muzzle.

rangy (rān' jē) adj. Long-limbed and slender.

rankle (raŋ' k'l) v. To fester or cause to have long-lasting anger or resentment.

rapt (rapt) adj. Completely absorbed or engrossed.

rapturous (rap' chər is) adj. Extremely joyful, ecstatic.

rasp (rasp) n. A rough, grating sound.

ravage (rav' ij) v. To ruin, destroy violently.

ravening (rav' 'n iŋ) adj. Greedily searching for prey.

ravenous (rav' ə nəs) adj. Greedily or wildly hungry.

ravine (rə vēn') n. A long, deep hollow or gorge in the earth's surface.

rebuff (ri buf') v. To check, snub, or refuse bluntly. n. An abrupt, blunt refusal.

rebuke (ri byook') n. A sharp scolding.

reckon (rek' ən) v. 1. To judge, consider, estimate. 2. To depend, rely.

recompense (rek' əm pens') n. Something given or done in return for something else; repayment.

recondite (rek' ən dīt') adj. Dealing with difficult subjects.

reconnoiter (rē' kə noit' ər) v. To explore or examine, as in seeking out enemy positions.

rectify (rek' tə fī') v. To put right; correct.

rectitude (rek' tə tood') n. Conduct according to moral principles.

recumbent (ri kum' bənt) adj. Lying down; reclining.

redemptive (ri demp' tiv) adj. Serving to restore or make amends.

red herring (red her' iŋ) n. Something used to divert attention from the basic issue.

redolent (red' 'l ənt) adj. Sweet-smelling, fragrant.

redress (rē' dres) n. Compensation or satisfaction, as for a wrong done.

refectory (ri fek' tər ē) n. A dining hall.

regale (ri gāl') v. To delight with something pleasing or amusing.

regenerate (ri jen' ə rāt') v. To cause to be renewed, reborn, or restored.

reiterate (rē it' ə rāt') n. To repeat.

rejoin (ri join') v. To answer.

rejuvenescent (ri joo' və nes' ənt) adj. Renewing youthfulness.

relent (ri lent') v. To yield, soften, or become less stubborn or severe.

relentless (ri lent' lis) adj. Harsh, pitiless.—**relentlessly** adv.

relinquish (ri liŋ' kwish) v. To give up or abandon.

remand (ri mand') v. To send back.

remembrancer (ri mem' brən sər) n. A reminder, memento.

remonstrate (ri män' strāt) v. To object or plead in protest.—**remonstrance** n.

remunerative (ri myoo' nə rāt' iv) adj. Profitable.

rend (rend) v. To tear or pull apart with violence.

render (ren' dər) v. To give, hand over, or present.

renegade (ren' ə gād') n. A person who abandons a movement and goes over to the other side; traitor.

reparation (rep' ə rā' shən) n. A making up for a wrong.

repercuss (re' pər kus') v. To reverberate or rebound.

repine (ri pīn') v. To complain.

repose (ri pōz') n. Resting v. To rest.

repression (ri presh' ən) n. The process by which ideas or impulses are forced into the unconscious and kept from becoming conscious.

reprisal (ri prī' z'l) n. Retaliation or injury done in return for injury.

reproach (ri prōch') n. Shame, disgrace, discredit.

reproachful (ri prōch' fəl) adj. Full of blame.

reprove (ri proov') v. To express disapproval of (something done or said).

reptilian (rep til' ē ən) adj. Of the reptiles.

republican (ri pub' li kən) adj. A person who favors a government in which supreme power rests in all the citizens entitled to vote.

requiem (rek' wē əm) n. Any musical service or hymn for the repose of the dead.

resilient (ri zil' yənt) adj. Bouncing back into shape after being stretched or compressed.—**resiliency** n.

resonance (rez' ə nəns) n. The quality of increasing the intensity of sounds by sympathetic vibration.—**resonate** v.

respite (res' pit) n. An interval of rest or relief.

restiveness (res' tiv nəs) n. Balkiness, unruliness, restlessness.—**restive** adj.

retaliatory (ri tal' ē ə tôr' ē) adj. Paying back evil for evil.

retinue (ret' 'n oo') n. A body of assistants, followers, or servants attending a person of importance.

retribution (ret' rə byoo' shən) n. Deserved punishment for evil done.

retrospectively (ret' rə spek' tiv lē) adv. Looking back on.

revel (rev' 'l) n. Merrymaking, celebration.

revelation (rev' ə lā' shən) n. A striking disclosure.

reverie (rev' ər ē) n. A daydream or dreamy thinking.

revile (ri vīl') v. To call bad names.

revulsion (ri vul' shən) n. Extreme disgust or shock.

rhetoric (ret' ər ik) n. The art of using words effectively in speaking or writing.

riband (rib' ənd) n. Ribbon.

rift (rift) v. To split, crack, or burst open. n. A crack or opening.

righteousness (rī' chəs nəs) n. Moral rightness; fairness and justice.—**righteous** adj.

rill (ril) n. A little brook.

riotous (rī' ət əs) adj. Disorderly without restraint.

rivulet (riv' yoo lit) n. A little stream.

rockaway (räk' ə wā') n. A light horse-drawn carriage.

roguishly (rō' gish lē) adv. Playfully, mischievously.

roseate (rō' zē it) adj. Rose-colored.

rout (rout) n. An overwhelming defeat.

ruddy (rud' ē) adj. Red or reddish.

rude (rood) adj. Crude or rough in form.—**rudely** adv.

rudiment (roo' də mənt) n. A first slight beginning of something.

rue (roo) v. To regret.

ruminate (roo' mə nāt') v. To ponder or turn something over in the mind.

S

sable (sā' b'l) *adj.* Black, dark.

sacked (sak'd) *adj.* Looted or plundered.

sacrament (sak' rə mənt) *n.* In Christianity, any of certain rites ordained by Jesus and regarded as a means of grace.—**sacramental** *adj.*

sadistic (sə dis' tik) *adj.* Getting pleasure from inflicting pain on another.

sagacious (sə gā' shəs) *adj.* Having keen perception and sound judgment.

sallow (sal' ō) *adj.* Of a sickly, pale-yellow color.

salutary (sal' yoo ter' ē) *adj.* Healthful, beneficial.

salutation (sal' yoo tā' shən) *n.* The act of greeting or addressing by gestures or words.

sanctity (saŋk' tə tē) *n.* The fact of being sacred or not to be violated.

sanguine (saŋ' gwin) *adj.* Cheerful, passionate.

sapless (sap' lis) *adj.* Without vigor or energy.

sardonic (sär dän' ik) *adj.* Bitterly sneering or sarcastic.

scandalize (skan' də līz') *v.* To shock or offend by improper conduct.

scenario (si ner' ē ō) *n.* An outline or script of a motion picture.

scholasticism (skə las' tə siz'm) *n.* Close adherence to traditional teaching methods prescribed by schools.

scimitar (sim' ə ter) *n.* A short, curved sword.

scintilla (sin til' ə) *n.* A particle; the least trace.

scoff (skôf) *v.* To show mocking contempt or scorn.

scoria (skôr' ē ə) *n.* The waste matter left after metal has been separated from ore.

scourge (skʉrj) *v.* To punish harshly.

scow (skou) *n.* A large, flat-bottomed boat with square ends.

scrabble (skrab' 'l) *v.* To struggle.

scruple (skroo' p'l) *v.* To be unwilling because of one's conscience.

scud (skud) *n.* The spray, rain, or snow driven by the wind.

scullion (skul' yən) *n.* A servant doing the rough, dirty work in a kitchen.

secession (si sesh' ən) *n.* The withdrawal of the Southern States from the Federal Union.

secessionist (si sesh' ən ist) *n.* One who favors secession.

seclusion (si kloo' zhən) *n.* Isolation; being shut off from others.

secular (sek' yə lər) *adj.* Relating to worldly things as opposed to things relating to church and religion.

sedulous (sej' oo ləs) *adj.* Working hard and with care.

seine (sān) *n.* A kind of large fishing net.

self-righteous (self rī' chəs) *adj.* Filled with one's own conviction of being morally superior.

semblance (sem' bləns) *n.* Outward form or appearance.

sentinel (sen' ti n'l) *n.* A person posted to guard a group.

sepulcher (sep' 'l kər) *n.* A grave or tomb.

seraph (ser' əf) *n.* Any of the highest order of angels.

servile (sur' v'l) *adj.* Like a slave; humbly yielding or submissive.

servitor (sur' və tər) *n.* A servant or attendant.

servitude (sur' və tood') *n.* Subjection to a master.

sexton (seks' tən) *n.* A church official in charge of the maintenance of church property.

sheepishly (shēp' ish lē) *adv.* In an embarrassed, shy, or timid way.

shiftless (shift' lis) *adj.* Lacking the will or ability to accomplish; lazy.—**shiftlessness** *n.*

shoat (shōt) *n.* A young hog of between 100 and 180 pounds.

shovelboard (shuv' 'l bôrd) *n.* Shuffleboard, a game in which large disks are pushed to land in numbered squares.

shrew (shroo) *n.* A small, slender mouselike mammal.

sideboard (sīd bôrd') *n.* A piece of dining-room furniture for holding linen, silver, and china.

sinewy (sin' yoo wē) *adj.* Tough, strong; having good muscular development.

sinuous (sin' yoo wəs) *adj.* Wavy, winding, or curving in and out.

sire (sīr) *n.* A father.

siren (sī' rən) *n.* In mythology, any of several sea nymphs who lured sailors to their death by seductive singing.

skeptical (skep' ti k'l) *adj.* Doubting, questioning; not easily convinced.

skulk (skulk) *v.* To move or lurk about in a sneaky, secret way.

slattern (slat' ərn) *n.* A woman who is careless and sloppy in her habits.

slaver (slav' ər) *v.* To slobber or drool on.

sloe-eyed (slō' īd') *adj.* Having large, dark eyes.

slough (slou) *n.* A place full of soft, deep mud.

slovenly (sluv' ən lē) *adj.* Untidy, careless in appearance.

slumberous (slum' bər əs) *adj.* Sleepy, drowsy.

smite (smīt) *v.* To bring to a specified condition by a blow.

snaggled (snag' əld) *adj.* Markedly uneven; irregularly projecting.

snigger (snig' ər) *n.* A sly or scornful, partly stifled laugh.

snivel (sniv' 'l) *v.* To cry and sniff.

sojourn (sō' jʉrn) *v.* To live somewhere temporarily. *n.* A visit or brief stay.

solace (säl' is) *n.* An easing of grief or loneliness; comfort. *v.* To comfort, console.

solar plexus (sō' lər plek' səs) *n.* The area of the belly just below the breastbone.

solicitation (sə lis' ə tā' shən) *n.* A request or earnest appeal.

solicitous (sə lis' ə təs) *adj.* Showing care, attention, or concern.—**solicitude** *n.*

soluble (säl' yoo b'l) *adj.* That can be dissolved.

somnambulant (säm nam' byoo lənt') *adj.* Moving about while asleep; sleepwalking.—**somnambulistic** *adj.*

somnolence (säm' nə ləns) *n.* Drowsiness, sleepiness.—**somnolent** *adj.*

sorcery (sôr' sər ē) *n.* Seemingly magical power or charm.

sordid (sôr' did) *adj.* Depressingly ignoble, wretched, and base.

sorrel (sôr' əl) *adj.* Light reddish-brown.

---

fat, āpe, cär; ten, ēven; is, bīte; gō, hôrn, tool, look; oil, out; up, fʉr; get; joy; yet; chin; she; thin, then; zh, leisure; ŋ, ring; ə for a in ago, e in agent, i in sanity, o in comply, u in focus; ' as in able (ā'b'l)

sound (sound) v. To measure the depth of water.

sovereign (säv' rən) adj. **1.** Independent of all others. **2.** Supreme, excellent.—**sovereignty** n.

spar (spär) n. **1.** A boxing match. **2.** Any pole supporting a sail of a ship.

spasmodic (spaz mäd' ik) adj. Sudden, violent, and temporary.—**spasmodically** adv.

specter (spek' tər) n. A ghost.—also SPECTRE

speculation (spek' yə lā' shən) n. The act of buying and selling stocks or taking part in any risky venture on the chance of making huge profits.

speculative (spek' yə lāt' iv) adj. Theoretical, guessing.—**speculation** n. **speculatist** n.

sporadic (spô rad' ik) adj. Not constant or regular; widely scattered or separated.

spur (spur) n. A range or ridge projecting from the main mass of a mountain.

spurn (spurn) n. Scornful treatment or rejection.

squalor (skwäl' ər) n. Filth, wretchedness, and misery.

staccato (stə kät' ō) adj. Made up of abrupt, distinct elements.

staid (stād) adj. Quiet, dignified, and serious.

stalwart (stôl' wərt) adj. Sturdy, brave, or firm.

stammer (stam' ər) v. To stutter or say with involuntary pauses.

staunch (stônch) adj. Strong, solidly made.

stealthily (stelth ə lē) adv. Secretly, slyly.

steward (stoo' ərd) n. A person put in charge of the affairs of a large household.

stigma (stig' mə) n. Mark of disgrace.

stipend (stī' pend) n. A regular or fixed payment.

stockade (stä kād') n. A barrier of stakes driven into the ground side by side.

stolid (stäl' id) adj. Showing little or no emotion.—**stolidly** adv.

stonily (stō' nə lē) adv. Coldly, unfeelingly.

stoop (stoop) n. A small porch or platform with steps at the door of a house.

stratagem (strat' ə jəm) n. A trick or scheme.

striation (strī ā' shən) n. Any of a number of parallel lines, stripes, or bands.

strife (strīf) n. Conflict, struggle.

stupefaction (stoo' pə fak' shən) n. Stunned amazement or utter bewilderment.—**stupefy** v.

subjective (səb jek' tiv) adj. Of a particular state of mind; not objective.

subjugation (sub' jə gā' shən) n. Control, conquest.

sublime (sə blīm') adj. Noble, exalted, majestic.—**sublimity** n.

subliminal (sub lim' ə n'l) adj. Below the threshold of consciousness.

submission (səb mish' ən) n. Obedience, meekness.

subordinate (sə bôr' də nit) adj. Lower in rank or power.

subsist (səb sist') v. To continue to be or exist.

subsistence (səb sis'təns) n. Means of support or livelihood.

subtlety (sut' 'l tē) n. Something delicately suggestive, indirect, or sly.

subversion (səb vur' zhən) n. Ruin, overthrow.

succor (suk' ər) n. Aid, help, relief.

succorless (suk' ər lis) adj. Helpless, without aid.

sufferance (suf' ər əns) n. The capacity to endure pain or distress.

suffice (sə fīs') v. To be enough, be adequate.

suffrage (suf' rij) n. A vote.

suffusion (sə fyoo' zhən) n. A glow or filling with color.—**suffuse** v.

suggestibility (səg jes' tə bil ə tē) n. Ready influence by suggestion.

sullenly (sul' ən lē) adv. Glumly, gloomily, sadly.—**sullen** adj.

sully (sul' ē) v. To soil or stain, especially by disgracing.

sultry (sul' trē) adj. Sweltering, extremely hot and moist.

summary (sum' ə rē) adj. Hasty and arbitrary.—**summarily** adv.

sundry (sun' drē) adj. Various.

superfluity (soo' pər floo' ə tē) n. Something not needed.

superfluous (soo pur' floo wəs) adj. Unnecessary, being more than is needed.

supernal (soo pur' n'l) adj. Heavenly, divine.

supernumerary (soo' pər noo' mə rer ē) adj. Extra.

supervene (soo' pər vēn') v. To come or happen.

supinely (soo pīn' lē) adv. Lying on the back, face upward.

supplication (sup' lə kā' shən) n. The act of humbly requesting or praying. **supplicate** v. **supplicatingly** adv.

surcease (sur sēs') n. An end.

surfeit (sur' fit) n. Overindulgence, especially in food and drink.

surmise (sər mīz') n. A guess. v. To guess.

surreptitiously (sur' əp tish' əs lē) adv. Secretly.—**surreptitious** adj.

suspiration (sus' pī rā' shən) n. The taking of a long, deep breath; sighing.

suture (soo' chər) n. The line along which a joining is made, as in sewing.

swaddle (swäd' 'l) v. To wrap, as in bandages.

swarthy (swôr' thē) adj. Having a dark complexion.

swath (swäth) n. The space covered with one cut of a scythe or other mowing device.

swathe (swāth) v. To wrap.

synchronize (siŋ' krə nīz') v. To cause to agree in rate or speed.

syntax (sin' taks) n. Organization or arrangement of word groups.

syringa (sə riŋ' gə) n. A hardy shrub or tree of the olive family with clusters of tiny, fragrant flowers.

T

tacit (tas' it) adj. Unspoken, not expressed.

taciturn (tas' ə turn') adj. Almost always silent.—**taciturnity** n.

tallness (tôl' nis) n. [Obs.] Handsomeness or braveness.

tallow (tal' ō) n. Animal fat.

taloned (tal' ənd) adj. Having a claw.

tamp (tamp) v. To pack firmly by a series of blows or taps.

tarn (tärn) n. A small mountain lake.

tarry (tar' ē) v. To delay, linger, wait.

tawdry (tô' drē) adj. Cheap and showy, sleazy.

temper (tem' pər) v. To become moderate or reduced in intensity.

temperance (tem' pər əns) n. Self-restraint or moderation, especially in drinking alcohol.—**temperate** adj.

tempest (tem′ pist) *n.* A violent outburst.

temporal (tem′ pər əl) *adj.* Of this world.

tenacious (tə nā′ shəs) *adj.* Holding firmly; persistent.

tenancy (ten′ ən sē) *n.* Possession or occupation of property.

tender (ten′ dər) *v.* To offer.

tendril (ten′ drəl) *n.* A threadlike part of a climbing plant, often in a spiral form.

tenuous (ten′ yoo wəs) *adj.* Slight, flimsy, not substantial.

tenure (ten′ yor) *n.* The right of holding office.

tepid (tep′ id) *adj.* Barely warm, lukewarm.

termagant (tur′ mə gənt) *n.* A quarrelsome, scolding woman.

terrestrial (tə res′ tre əl) *adj.* Earthly, of this world.

terse (turs) *adj.* Concise in a smooth, polished way.

testy (tes′ tē) *adj.* Irritable, touchy.—**testiness** *n.*

tether (teth′ ər) *v.* To tie with a rope to keep within certain limits.

theologian (thē′ ə lō′ jən) *n.* A specialist in the study of religious doctrines and matters of divinity.

thewed (thyood) *adj.* Muscled, powered.

throttle (thrät′ ′l) *v.* To choke or suffocate.

timorous (tim′ ər əs) *adj.* Timid, full of fear.

titular (tich′ ə lər) *adj.* Existing only in title.

torpor (tôr′ pər) *n.* A state of being inactive.

tourniquet (toor′ nə kit) *n.* Any device for compressing a blood vessel to stop bleeding.

tractable (trak′ tə b′l) *adj.* Easily managed.

transcend (tran send′) *v.* To go beyond the limits of; surpass.—**transcendent** *adj.*

transcendentalist (tran′ sen den′ t′l ist) *n.* One who, like Ralph Waldo Emerson and some other 19th-century New Englanders, believes in searching for reality through spiritual insight.—**transcendental** *adj.*

transfigure (trans fig′ yər) *v.* To transform or change the outward appearance of.

transfusion (trans fyoo′ zhən) *n.* An instance of transferring.

transient (tran′ shənt) *adj.* Passing quickly; fleeting.

translucently (trans loo′ s′nt lē) *adv.* In a way that lets light pass while diffusing it so that objects on the other side cannot be clearly distinguished.

transpire (tran spīr′) *v.* **1.** To happen, come to pass. **2.** To be given off.

transplantation (trans′ plan tā′ shən) *n.* A digging up from one place and planting in another.

travail (trav′ āl) *n.* Intense pain, agony.

traverse (tra vurs′) *v.* To cross.

treachery (trech′ ər ē) *n.* Betrayal of trust; disloyalty, treason.

tremulous (trem′ yoo ləs) *adj.* Trembling, quivering.—**tremulously** *adv.*

trepidation (trep′ ə dā′ shən) *n.* Fearful uncertainty or worry.

tribulation (trib′ yə lā′ shən) *n.* Great misery or distress.

trifle (trī′ f′l) *v.* To act or talk in a joking way.—**trifler** *n.*

trifling (trī′ fliŋ) *adj.* Having little value; trivial.

trippingly (trip′ iŋ lē) *adv.* Lightly and quickly.

troubadour (troo′ bə dôr′) *n.* A minstrel or poet-musician.

tulle (tool) *n.* A thin, fine netting used for veils, scarfs.

tumultuous (too mul′ choo wəs) *adj.* Wild, uproarious, agitated.—**tumultuously** *adv.* **tumult** *n.*

turbulent (tur′ byə lənt) *adj.* Unruly, boisterous; full of commotion or disorder.—**turbulence** *n.*

turnkey (turn′ kē) *n.* A person in charge of the keys of a prison.

turret (tur′ it) *n.* A small dome-like structure for a gun and gunner, as on a bomber.

twiddle (twid′ ′l) *v.* To twirl or play with idly.

U

unabiding (un ə hīd′ iŋ) *adj.* Not lasting or enduring.

unaffectedly (un ə fek′ tid lē) *adv.* Simply, sincerely, naturally.

unalienable (un āl yən ə b′l) *adj.* Not capable of being withdrawn or transferred.

unalloyed (un ə loid′) *adj.* Pure, not mixed with anything else.

uncanny (un kan′ ē) *adj.* Eerie, weird, mysterious.

unceremoniously (un′ ser ə mō′ nē əs lē) *adv.* Informally; so abruptly as to be discourteous.—**unceremonious** *adj.*

uncouth (un kooth′) *adj.* Strange; crude.

uncovenanted (un kuv′ ə nən tid) *adj.* Not bound by a promise.

undaunted (un dôn′ tid) *adj.* Not discouraged.

undecipherable (un di sī′ fər ə b′l) *adj.* Unable to make out the meaning of; not understandable.

undulation (un′ joo lā′ shən) *n.* Waves or waving motion.—**undulate** *v.*

unengaging (un in gāj′ iŋ) *adj.* Unattractive, unpleasant.

unerringly (un ur′ iŋ lē) *adv.* Surely, certainly, without fail.

unexampled (un ig zam′ p′ld) *adj.* Having no parallel or precedent.

unfaltering (un fôl′ tər iŋ) *adj.* Not wavering or losing strength.

unfathomed (un fath′ əm′d) *adj.* Not understood thoroughly.

unflagging (un flag′ iŋ) *adj.* Not losing strength.

ungainly (un gān′ lē) *adj.* Coarse and unattractive.

ungodliness (un gäd′ lē nis) *n.* Sinfulness, wickedness.

unhallow (un hal′ ō) *v.* To take away the sacredness of.

uninquisitive (un in kwiz′ ə tiv) *adj.* Not curious or eager to learn.

unintelligible (un in tel′ ij ə b′l) *adj.* That cannot be understood.

universality (yoo nə vər sal′ ə tē) *n.* The state of being present or occurring everywhere.

unnerve (un nurv′) *v.* To cause to lose one's courage or confidence.

unobliged (un ə blī j′d′) *adj.* Not compelled by moral, legal, or physical force.

---

fat, āpe, cär; ten, ēven; is, bīte; gō, hôrn, tool, look; oil, out; up, fur; get; joy; yet; chin; she; thin, then; zh, leisure; ŋ, ring; ə for *a* in *ago*, *e* in *agent*, *i* in *sanity*, *o* in *comply*, *u* in *focus*; ′ as in *able* (ā′b′l)

unobstrusively (un əb trōō' siv lē) *adv.* In a way that does not call attention to itself.

unpalatable (un pal' it ə b'l) *adj.* Not fit to be eaten; unpleasant to the taste.

unquenchable (un kwench' ə b'l) *adj.* Unable to be overcome or subdued.

unredressed (un ri dres'd') *adj.* Not set right, unremedied.

unrequited (un ri kwīt' id) *adj.* Not returned.

unsalable (un sāl' ə b'l) *adj.* Not marketable or able to be sold.

unseemly (un sēm' lē) *adj.* Not decent or proper.

unsheathe (un shē*th*) *v.* To remove from a case.

unsolicited (un sə lis' it id) *adj.* Unsought, not asked for.

unsurmised (un sər mīz"d) *adj.* Unimagined.

untempered (un tem' pərd) *adj.* Not reduced in intensity.

unutterably (un ut' ər ə blē) *adv.* In a way that cannot be described or expressed.

unwarrantable (un wôr' ənt ə b'l) *adj.* Not justifiable.

unwary (un wer' ē) *adj.* Not watchful, cautious, or alert to possible danger.

unwieldiness (un wēl' dē nəs) *n.* Difficulty in managing, as because of large size or weight.

unwonted (un wun' tid) *adj.* Unusual, rare.

upbraid (up brād') *v.* To scold sharply.

uppercut (up' ər kut') *v.* To hit with a short, swinging blow directed upward.

usurer (yōō' zhoo rər) *n.* A person who lends money at interest.—**usurious** *adj.*

usurpation (yōō' sər pā' shən) *n.* The act of taking, as of power, and holding by force or without right.—**usurp** *v.*

utilitarian (yoo til' ə ter' ē ən) *adj.* Stressing usefulness or practical matters.

utopia (yoo tō' pē ə) *n.* Any idealized place, state or situation of perfection.—**utopian** *adj.*

V

vagary (və ger' ē) *n.* An odd or unexpected action or bit of conduct.

vagrant (vā grənt) *n.* A person who wanders from place to place or leads a wandering life.

vainglory (vān' glôr' ē) *n.* Extreme self-pride and vanity.

valise (və lēs') *n.* A piece of hand luggage.

vanquish (van' kwish) *v.* To conquer or defeat.

vaunt (vônt) *v.* To boast, brag.

venerable (ven' ər ə b'l) *adj.* Worthy of respect by reason of age and dignity.

venery (ven' ər ē) *n.* The indulgence of sexual desire.

vengeance (ven' jəns) *n.* Revenge.

venomous (ven' əm əs) *adj.* Poisonous.

venturous (ven' chər əs) *adj.* Bold, inclined to take chances.

veracious (və rā' shəs) *adj.* Honest, habitually truthful.

veriest (ver' ē ist) *adj.* Being such to the highest degree.

verity (ver' ə tē) *n.* A truth; a principle taken to be fundamentally and permanently true.

vermin (vur' min) *n.* Any of various insects of small animals regarded as objectionable because destructive or disease carrying.

vernacular (vər nak' yə lər) *n.* The everyday language of ordinary people in a particular place.

vestige (ves' tij) *n.* A trace or sign of something that once existed but has passed away.

vexation (vek sā' shən) *n.* Annoyance, distress.—**vex** *v.*

viand (vī' ənd) *n.* An article of food.

viburnum (vī bur' nəm) *n.* A shrub or small tree of the honeysuckle family, with white flowers.

victual (vit' 'l) *n.* Food or other provisions.—*also* VITTLE

vigilant (vij' ə lənt) *adj.* Staying watchful and alert to danger.—**vigilance** *n.*

vintner (vint' nər) *n.* A person who sells wine.

visage (viz' ij) *n.* **1.** The face. **2.** Appearance.

visitant (viz' it ənt) *n.* A visitor, especially one from a strange place.

vituperative (vī tōō' pə rə' tiv) *adj.* Scolding or talking about in an extremely harsh way.

vociferation (vō sif' ə rā' shən) *n.* A crying out or shouting with great feeling.

voodoo (vōō' dōō) *n.* A primitive religion based on a belief in sorcery and the power of charms, etc.

voracity (vô ras' ə tē) *n.* Greediness, eagerness.—**voracious** *adj.* **voraciously** *adv.*

vortex (vôr' teks) *n.* A whirlpool or whirling mass of water.

vouchsafe (vouch sāf') *v.* To be gracious enough to give.

vulnerable (vul' nər ə b'l) *adj.* Easily hurt.

W

waggery (wag' ər ē) *n.* A joke or jest.

wan (wän) *adj.* Sickly pale.—**wanly** *adv.*

wanton (wän' t'n) *adj.* **1.** Senseless, unprovoked, unjustifiable; **2.** Unrestrained.—**wantonness** *n.*

wary (wer' ē) *adj.* Cautious, on one's guard.—**warily** *adv.*

wean (wēn) *v.* To withdraw (a person) by degrees, as by substituting some other interest.

whelk (hwelk) *n.* A pimple.

whorl (hwôrl) *n.* Anything with a coiled or spiral appearance.

wight (wīt) *n.* A living being.

wince (wins) *v.* To shrink or draw back slightly, usually with a grimace, as in pain or embarrassment.

wistful (wist' fəl) *adj.* Showing vague yearnings; longing pensively.

wont (wōnt) *adj.* Accustomed.

worst (wurst) *v.* To get the better of; defeat.

worsted (woos' tid) *n.* Fabric made from a smooth, hard-twisted thread or yarn.

writ (rit) *n.* A formal legal document ordering some action.

writhe (rī*th*) *v.* To make twisting or turning movements, contort the body.

wry (rī) *adj.* Perverse, ironic.—**wryly** *adv.*

Y

yaw (yô) *v.* To turn or deviate unintentionally from the planned course.

yawp (yôp) *n.* Noisy and stupid talk.

Index of Titles and Authors

Index of Fine Art

796   *The Blind Botanist.* Ben Shahn.
826   *New York Movie.* Edward Hopper.
841   *Northern Seascape, off the Banks.* Marsden Hartley.
844   Costume design for *Our Town.* Patricia Zipprodt.

Whitney Museum of American Art

Noontide in Late May. 1917. Charles Burchfield.
Watercolor and gouache, 21⅝ × 17½ inches.

Ice Glare, 1933. Charles Burchfield.
Watercolor, 30¾ × 24¾ inches.

Tombstones, 1942. Jacob Lawrence.
Gouache, 28¾ × 20½ inches.

Fear, 1949. Yves Tanguy.
Oil on canvas, 60 × 40 inches.

Song of Esther, 1958. Abraham Rattner.
Oil on composition board, 60 × 48 inches.

Cobb's Barns, South Truro, 1931. Edward Hopper.
Oil on canvas, 34 × 50 inches.

Saw and Sawed, 1969. Neil Jenny.
Acrylic on canvas, 58½ × 70⅜ inches.

Sunset, 1914. John Marin.
Watercolor, 16½ × 19¼ (overall).

Autumn, 1941. Thomas Hart Benton.
Oil and tempera on composition board, 22½ × 28½ inches.

The White Flower, 1931. Georgia O'Keeffe.
Oil on canvas, 30 × 36 inches.

Early Sunday Morning, 1930. Edward Hopper.
Oil on canvas, 35 × 60 inches.

The Museum of Modern Art

New York Movie, 1939. Edward Hopper.
Oil on Canvas, 32¼ × 40⅛".

American Landscape, 1930. Charles Sheeler.
Oil on canvas, 24 × 31" (61 × 78.8 cm).

Train at Night in the Desert, 1916. Georgia O'Keeffe.
Watercolor, 12 × 8⅞".

Index of Skills

Reading and Literary Skills

Act 842, 874
Allegory 132, 149
Alliteration 189, 193, 201, 204, 213, 228, 299, 315, 322, 461, 612, 620, 652, 663, 665, 667, 690, 719, 727, 740, 741, 764, 765, 794, 812
Allusion 30, 85, 122, 174, 194, 204, 251, 346, 627, 647, 662, 732, 743, 758, 790, 860
Analogy 88, 204, 215, 265, 272, 313, 332, 380, 578
Anapestic Meter 32–33, 299, 724
Anaphora 85, 186, 627
Anthropomorphism 11
Aphorism 81, 88, 237, 251, 617
Assonance 228, 461, 556, 612, 648, 719, 737, 765, 812
Audience 46
Autobiography 43, 265, 612
Ballad 189, 267, 781
Blank Verse 198, 673, 677, 788
Character 64, 142, 174, 284, 292, 297, 346, 380, 414, 418, 425, 438, 446, 461, 470, 477, 481, 490, 499, 510, 518, 526, 532, 651, 683, 696, 700, 732, 737, 777, 780, 797, 842, 860
　Foil, 346
　Main and Minor Characters, 414, 425
　Motivation, 64, 438, 446, 461
　Protagonist, 425
　Steroetype, 131, 265, 308, 414, 470
Characterization 368, 446, 460, 518, 532, 612, 683, 732, 860
　Through Actions, 368, 446, 518, 532, 612
　Through Dialogue, 446, 460, 518, 532, 860
　Through Physical Description, 518
　Through Reactions and Comments of Other Characters, 368, 518, 532, 683
　Through Reactions and Thoughts, 368, 518, 612
Climax 297, 425, 541
Comparison. See Analogy.
Conceit 40
Concrete Poem 698, 785, 794
Conflict 297, 346, 425, 499, 541
　Conflict with Nature, 346, 425
　Conflict with a Person, 425, 541
　Conflict with Society, 346, 425
　Internal Conflict, 346, 425, 541
Connotation 11, 27, 46, 64, 308, 322, 572, 612, 623, 645, 657, 661, 671, 690, 692, 694, 700, 750, 780
Consonance 228, 648

Contrast 198, 222, 333, 346, 354, 368, 572, 578, 620, 652, 661, 709, 751, 760, 799, 842
　Foil, 346
Couplet 30, 33, 38, 98, 215, 222, 231
　Heroic Couplet, 33, 38, 98
Dactylic Meter 32–33
Dénouement 346
Description 19, 284, 292, 415, 438, 526
Dialect 346, 354, 460
Dialogue 418, 683, 781, 842
Diction 12, 142, 149, 175, 232, 332, 333, 470, 649, 657, 661, 665, 690, 700, 719, 739, 750, 756, 765, 780
Drama 841, 842, 874
　Act, 842, 874
　Extended Definition, 829, 841
　Scene, 841
　Stage Directions, 842, 874
　See study questions in Unit 8, Drama
Dramatic Irony 345
Dramatic Lyric 695
Echoic Words. See Onomatopoeia.
Elegy 299, 797
Epic 251
Epigraph 732
Epistle 74, 95
Epitaph 645
Epithet 313
Essay 53, 63–64, 237, 581, 588, 633
　Descriptive, 63–64, 237
　Expository, 64, 237, 588
　Formal, 237, 633
　Informal, 237, 633
　Narrative, 63–64, 237, 588
Eulogy 12, 72, 299, 578
Exaggeration 354, 562, 636
Exposition 842
Extended Metaphor 7, 35, 40, 46, 74, 213, 299, 572, 704, 713
Fable 636
Fiction 131
　Allegory, 132, 149
　Extended Definition, 131
　Fable, 636
　Folk Tale, 131
　Parable, 142
　Science Fiction, 546, 562

Vocabulary and Language Skills

Writing Skills

Art Credits

Acknowledgments   Continued from copyright page

Isaac Asimov, from *American Way*, inflight magazine of American Airlines; copyright 1977 by American Airlines. Beacon Press: For "Autobiographical Notes," from *Notes of a Native Son* by James Baldwin; copyright © 1955 by James Baldwin. Brandt & Brandt Literary Agents, Inc.: For "We Aren't Superstitious" by Stephen Vincent Benét; copyright 1937 by Esquire, Inc., copyright © renewed 1965 by Thomas C. Benét, Rachel Benét Lewis and Stephanie Benét Mahin. Don Congdon Associates, Inc.: For "A Sound of Thunder" by Ray Bradbury, published in *Collier's*; copyright 1952, renewed 1980 by Ray Bradbury. Delacorte Press/Seymour Lawrence: For "Harrison Bergeron," excerpted from *Welcome to the Monkey House* by Kurt Vonnegut, Jr.; Copyright © 1961 by Kurt Vonnegut, Jr., originally published in *Fantasy and Science Fiction*. For "I Stand Here Ironing" by Tillie Olsen, excerpted from *Tell Me a Riddle* by Tillie Olsen; copyright © 1956, 1957, 1960, 1961 by Tillie Olsen. Dodd, Mead & Company, Inc.: For "Life's Tragedy," "Douglass," and "We Wear the Mask" by Paul Laurence Dunbar, from *The Complete Poems of Paul Laurence Dunbar*. Elizabeth H. Dos Passos: For "Tin Lizzie," from *U.S.A.* by John Dos Passos; copyright by Elizabeth H. Dos Passos. Doubleday & Company, Inc.: For "Old Florist" by Theodore Roethke, copyright 1946 by Harper & Bros.; "The Pike" by Theodore Roethke, copyright © 1963 by the Administratrix to the Estate of Theodore Roethke, from *The Collected Poems* of Theodore Roethke. For "In the Pocket" by James Dickey, from *The Eye-Beaters, Blood, Victory, Madness, Buckhead and Mercy*; copyright © 1970 by James Dickey. For an excerpt from "The House Nigger" by James Baldwin, from *Tell Me How Long the Train's Been Gone*; copyright © 1968 by James Baldwin, a Dial Press book. E. P. Dutton, Inc.: For "The Flower-Fed Buffaloes" by Vachel Lindsay, from *Going-to-the-Stars*; copyright 1926 by D. Appleton & Co., copyright renewal 1954 by Elizabeth C. Lindsay. Farrar, Straus & Giroux, Inc.: For "The Ball Poem," from *Short Poems* by John Berryman; copyright 1948 by John Berryman, copyright renewed © 1976 by Kate Berryman. For "House Guest," from *The Complete Poems* by Elizabeth Bishop, copyright © 1969 by Elizabeth Bishop. For "Death of the Ball Turret Gunner," from *The Complete Poems* by Randall Jarrell; copyright 1945, 1969 by Mrs. Randall Jarrell; copyright renewed © 1973 by Mrs. Randall Jarrell. For "A Lullaby," from *The Complete Poems* by Randall Jarrell; copyright 1944 by Mrs. Randall Jarrell, copyright renewed © 1971 by Mrs. Randall Jarrell. For "Water," from *For the Union Dead* by Robert Lowell; copyright © 1956, 1960, 1961, 1962, 1963, 1964 by Robert Lowell. For "A Summer's Reading," from *The Magic Barrel* by Bernard Malamud; originally appeared in *The New Yorker*. David R. Godine Publisher: For "The Achievement of Desire," from *Hunger of Memory* by Richard Rodriguez; Copyright © 1981 by Richard Rodriguez, reprinted by permission of David R. Godine, Publisher, Boston. Harcourt Brace Jovanovich, Inc.: For an excerpt from "The Kitchen," from *A Walker in the City* by Alfred Kazin; copyright © 1951, 1979 by Alfred Kazin. For "The Angry Winter," from *The Unexpected Universe* by Loren Eiseley; copyright © 1968 by Loren Eiseley. For "Boy at the Window," from *Things of This World* by Richard Wilbur; copyright 1952 by The New Yorker Magazine, Inc., renewed 1980 by Richard Wilbur. For "Digging for China," from *Things of This World*; copyright © 1956 by Richard Wilbur. For "A Worn Path," from *A Curtain of Green and Other Stories* by Eudora Welty; copyright 1941, 1969 by Eudora Welty. For "He," from *Flowering Judas and Other Stories* by Katherine Anne Porter; copyright 1930, 1958 by Katherine Anne Porter. For "Sandhill" and "Jazz Fantasia," from *Smoke and Steel* by Carl Sandburg; copyright 1920 by Harcourt Brace Jovanovich, Inc., renewed 1948 by Carl Sandburg. For "The Harbor" and "Chicago," from *Chicago Poems* by Carl Sandburg; copyright 1916 by Holt, Rinehart and Winston, Inc., copyright 1944 by Carl Sandburg. For "Grass" and "Prayers of Steel," from *Cornhuskers* by Carl Sandburg; copyright 1918 by Holt, Rinehart and Winston, Inc., copyright 1946 by Carl Sandburg. For "Preludes" and "The Love Song of J. Alfred Prufrock," from *Collected Poems 1909-1962* by T. S. Eliot; copyright 1936, by Harcourt Brace Jovanovich, Inc.; copyright © 1963, 1964, by T. S. Eliot. For "Expect Nothing," from *Revolutionary Petunias & Other Poems* by Alice Walker; copyright © 1973 by Alice Walker. For "The Life You Save May Be Your Own," from *A Good Man Is Hard To Find and Other Stories* by Flannery O'Connor; copyright 1953 by Flannery O'Connor; renewed 1981 by Mrs. Regina O'Connor. For "Gus, the Theatre Cat," from *Old Possum's Book of Practical Cats* by T. S. Eliot; copyright 1939 by T. S. Eliot, renewed 1967 by Esme Valerie Eliot. Harper & Row, Publishers, Inc.: For "Baker's Bluejay Yarn," from *A Tramp Abroad*, Vol. 1 by Mark Twain. For "The Grangerfords Take Me In," from *The Adventures of Huckleberry Finn* by Mark Twain. For "Traveling Through the Dark," from *Stories That Could Be True: New and Collected Poems* by William Stafford; copyright © 1960 by William Stafford. For "The Arrival of the Bee Box" and "Mirror," from *The Collected Poems of Sylvia Plath*, edited by Ted Hughes; copyright © 1963 by Ted Hughes, originally appeared in *The New Yorker*, For "Any Human to Another," from *On These I Stand* by Countee Cullen; copyright 1927 by Harper & Row, Publishers, Inc.; renewed 1955 by Ida M. Cullen. For "From the Dark Tower," from *On These I Stand* by Countee Cullen; copyright 1935 by Harper & Row, Publishers, Inc.; renewed 1963 by Ida M. Cullen. For "The Sonnet-Ballad," "The Explorer," and "Life for My Child Is Simple," from *The World of Gwendolyn Brooks* by Gwendolyn Brooks; copyright 1949 by Gwendolyn Brooks Blakely. For a selection abridged from Chapter 1 in *American Hunger* by Richard Wright; copyright 1944 by Richard Wright; copyright © 1977 by Ellen Wright. For "Walden" by E. B. White, from *One Man's Meat*; copyright 1939 by E. B. White. For *Our Town: A Play in Three Acts* by Thornton Wilder; copyright 1938, © 1957 by Thornton Wilder. *Caution! Our Town* is the sole property of the author and is fully protected by copyright. It may not be acted without formal permission and the payment of a royalty. All rights, including professional, amateur, stock, radio and television broadcasting, motion picture, recitation, lecturing, public reading, and the rights of translation into foreign languages are reserved. All professional inquiries should be addressed to the author's agent: Brandt & Brandt Literary Agents, Inc., 1501 Broadway, New York, New York 10036. All requests for amateur rights should be addressed to Samuel French, Inc., 25 West 43rd Street, New York, New York 10036. Harvard University Press: For "To My Dear and Loving Husband" and "Upon the Burning of Our House" by Anne Bradstreet, from *The Works of Anne Bradstreet*, edited by Jeannine Hensley, Cambridge, Mass.; The Belknap Press of Harvard University Press, copyright © 1967 by the President and Fellows of Harvard College. For "Letter to Her Husband" by Abigail Adams, from *The Book of Abigail and John*, edited with an introduction by S. H. Butterfield, Cambridge, Mass.; The Belknap Press of Harvard University Press, copyright © 1975 by the Massachusetts Historical Society. For thirteen poems from *The Poems of Emily Dickinson*, edited by Thomas H. Johnson, Cambridge, Mass.; copyright 1951, © 1955, 1979 by The President and Fellows of Harvard College. David Freeman Hawke: For "What Happened Till the First Supply," from *Captain John Smith's History of Virginia*, by permission of the author. Holt, Rinehart & Winston, Publishers: For "Poets" by Al Young, from *The Song Turning Back Into Itself*; Copyright

Death to Morning; copyright 1935 International Magazine Co., Inc., renewed 1963 by Paul Gitlin. For "Richard Cory" by Edwin Arlington Robinson, from *The Children of the Night,* 1897. For "Miniver Cheevy," from *The Town Down the River* by Edwin Arlington Robinson; copyright 1910 by Charles Scribner's Sons and renewed 1938 by Ruth Nevison. For "Winter Dreams," by F. Scott Fitzgerald; copyright 1922 by Charles Scribner's Sons; copyright renewed 1950, from *All the Sad Young Men.* For Ernest Hemingway's "Old Man at the Bridge" in *The Short Stories of Ernest Hemingway;* copyright 1938 Ernest Hemingway; Copyright renewed 1966 Mary Hemingway. Américo Paredes: For "Guitarreros," from *Southwest Review,* Autumn, 1964; permission given by the author. Sunstone Press: For "Song of the Sky Loom," from *Songs of the Tewa* (The Winged Serpent), edited by Herbert Spinden. Mrs. James Thurber: For "The Catbird Seat," from *The Thurber Carnival* by James Thurber; copyright © 1945 James Thurber, copyright © 1973 Helen W. Thurber and Rosemary T. Sauers, published by Harper & Row. Twayne Publishers (G. K. Hall & Co.): For "The Tropics in New York," from *The Selected Poems of Claude McKay* by Claude McKay; copyright 1953 by Twayne Publishers, Inc. Viking Penguin, Inc.: For "Sophistication," from *Winesburg, Ohio* by Sherwood Anderson; copyright 1919 by B. W. Heubsch, copyright renewed 1947 by Eleanor Copenhaver Anderson. For "The Little House," from *Come Along with Me* by Shirley Jackson; copyright © 1962, 1968 by Stanley Edgar Hyman. For "Flight," from *The Long Valley* by John Steinbeck; copyright © 1938 by John Steinbeck, copyright © renewed 1966 by John Steinbeck. A. Watkins, Inc.: For "The Soldier Ran Away" by Kay Boyle, originally appeared in *The Saturday Evening Post;* copyright 1953 by Kay Boyle. Wesleyan University Press: For "Mutterings Over the Crib of a Deaf Child" by James Wright, from *Collected Poems;* copyright © 1957 by James Wright, first appeared in *Green Wall* published by Yale University Press. For "The Heaven of Animals" by James Dickey, from *Drowning with Others;* copyright © 1961 by James Dickey, first appeared in *The New Yorker.* The H. W. Wilson Company: For "Her Journeys Are Over" by Adlai E. Stevenson, from *Representative American Speeches: 1963-1964,* edited by Lester Thonssen, copyright © 1964 by The H. W. Wilson Company. Nancy Wood: For "I Went To Kill the Deer," "I Have Killed the Deer," and "Let Us Move Evenly Together," from *Hollering Sun* by Nancy Wood; copyright © 1972. Ian Hamilton Finlay-The Wild Hawthorn Press, Scotland: For pages 93 and 96, from *Poems from My Windmill,* 1964. Holt, Rinehart and Winston, Inc.: For "A Soldier," from *The Poetry of Robert Frost,* edited by Edward Connery Lathem; copyright 1923, 1928, 1934, © 1969 by Holt, Rinehart and Winston, Inc., copyright 1936, 1942, 1951, © 1956, 1962 by Robert Frost, copyright © 1964, 1970 by Lesley Frost Ballantine. For "The Secret Sits" by Robert Frost, from *Complete Poems of Robert Frost;* copyright 1930, 1949. New Directions Publishing Corporation: For "Haiku" by Ezra Pound, from *Personae;* copyright 1926 by Ezra Pound. Sterling Lord Agency: For "Preface to a Twenty Volume Suicide Note" by Amiri Baraka (LeRoi Jones); copyright © 1961 by LeRoi Jones (Amiri Baraka). The authors and editors have made every effort to trace the ownership of all copyrighted selections found in this book and to make full acknowledgment for their use.

Handbook:

How To Write
About Literature

Yellow Level

McDougal, Littell & Company

Contents

ISBN: 0-88343-449-0

Copyright © 1985 by McDougal, Littell & Company
Box 1667, Evanston, Illinois 60204

Introduction

As an art form, literature elicits a variety of responses, which may be expressed in many different ways. Essay questions and writing assignments provide opportunities for students to respond both creatively and analytically to literary selections. In this book, most of the writing assignments in **Developing Writing Skills** and in the **Unit Reviews** assign paragraphs and compositions that are one or a combination of three basic kinds of writing: narration, description, and exposition. Essay questions, too, require the same kinds of writing, although the emphasis generally is on exposition.

Narration. Narrative writing requires well developed storytelling skills and familiarity with the basic narrative elements: character, setting, plot, point of view, and theme. The following kinds of assignments require a narrative response:

Extend a story
Retell a story from a different point of view
Narrate an autobiographical incident
Re-create a meaningful experience
Write a fable
Write a folk tale
Write a tall tale
Write a short story

Description. Descriptive writing requires a keen sense of observation and the ability to select and arrange details to create a desired effect. Description often is woven into writing that is primarily narrative or expository. Questions and assignments requiring descriptive writing include those that direct you to:

Describe a character
Describe a person
Describe a place

Create a mood
Select specific details
Use the senses

Exposition. Expository writing requires a careful, logical development of ideas, with specific details drawn from literary selections and other written material or from your own experiences and those of others. Expository writing is the kind of writing that you do when asked to analyze a literary element, such as plot, symbol, style, or theme.

Other kinds of questions and assignments requiring expository writing are those that direct you to:

Explain an idea
Support an opinion
Develop an argument
Compare and contrast two selections
Define a concept
Write a report

Creative and analytical writing, fiction and nonfiction, prose and poetry: these may seem to have little in common. However, the characteristics of good writing and the skills needed to communicate effectively remain the same. No matter what the assignment, the writer needs to understand and apply the literary techniques available to all writers through the basic process of writing.

How To Write About Literature teaches an approach to essay questions and to writing assignments related to the four literary genres represented in this book: short story, poetry, nonfiction, and drama. The guidelines presented in this handbook also provide a sound basis for answering examination questions and for dealing with the writing assignments included in college entrance exams.

LESSON 1 Pre-Writing: Establishing a Clear Direction

The process of writing is composed of three sequential stages: **pre-writing, writing the first draft,** and **revising**. Pre-writing involves a series of decisions and planning steps that will help you to clarify your ideas about literature and to communicate these ideas effectively in the writing and revising stages.

As you study the process of writing, try to apply the process to a specific essay question or **Developing Writing Skills** or **Unit Review** assignment. If you have not yet been assigned a writing exercise, review the process, focusing on the samples and on the assignments based on the samples. You can refer to the process again, when you need help answering a question or completing an assignment.

Analyzing Writing Assignments

Sometimes you will be able to choose your own topic related to a literary selection. In doing so, you will need to be sure that your topic can be covered in the assigned length. A subject such as a short story, for example, may need to be narrowed to the characters in the story, and possibly to one character or even to one aspect of that character, depending on whether you must write a paragraph, a brief composition, or a lengthier composition.

Often, you will be writing in response to a specific assignment or essay question. When this is the case, spend time analyzing the directions carefully. Look for key words, such as:

discuss	contrast	select	show
evaluate	describe	explain	cite
compare	analyze	define	quote
demonstrate	identify	support	

Other key words include *how, why, attitude, effect,* and *significance;* and literary terms such as *tone, theme, imagery, character, symbol,* and *irony.* Also note the length specified or implied, and clarify the meanings of key words, using a dictionary and the Handbook of Literary Terms as necessary.

Understanding directions will enable you to do a thorough job of completing an assignment without going beyond its limits. It will help you to formulate a clear purpose for writing and to organize ideas to accomplish that purpose.

Determining Purpose

Your purpose when answering an essay question or completing a writing assignment might be to inform or to persuade your audience about your ideas and conclusions regarding a work of literature. You might write to define, to describe, to analyze, or to explain. Often, an assignment will have both a main purpose and subordinate purposes. For instance, you might be directed to write a paragraph discussing the interrelationship of imagery and tone in a poem. In developing this topic, you might need to describe the prevailing tone, identify key images, and explain how these images create tone.

A simple statement of purpose can serve as a useful guide when writing longer compositions, especially if you tend to lose sight of your main idea when you write. Such a statement can begin: "The purpose of this composition is to _____ ." It should be written at the top of the sheet of paper on which you will record your other pre-writing notes.

Considering Audience and Tone

Audience. In writing about literature, you generally can assume that your readers are familiar with your subject. The work of literature is the "common ground" that you share with your audience. As a rule, this assumption makes plot summaries unnecessary. However, shared familiarity with a work does not lessen the need to develop ideas with adequate detail, particularly when a question asks you for an opinion or an assignment directs you to analyze an aspect of a selection.

Keeping your audience in mind is equally important when drawing from personal experience or from your imagination. For example, if you are attempting to re-create a mood, you need to anticipate your reader's responses to connotative words and phrases.

Tone. Tone is the attitude that you assume toward your subject. Your tone will depend on the kind of assignment that you are completing. When you are recounting an experience or writing a poem, for example, your tone will reflect your subjective responses. When analyzing literary elements, on the other hand, you should maintain an objective tone, with ideas presented in a straightforward fashion. You should state opinions and conclusions clearly and support them with reasons and evidence from the selection.

the writings of Edwards and of <u>William Bradford</u>, <u>Anne Bradstreet</u>, and <u>Edward Taylor</u> as well. <u>Refer</u> to specific <u>passages</u> in each writer's work to <u>support</u> your <u>analysis</u>. Devote one <u>body paragraph</u> to each writer, <u>framing</u> those four paragraphs with an <u>introduction</u> and a <u>conclusion</u> that <u>link</u> the four writers.

EXERCISES   Applying the Process: Pre-Writing

1. Study the sample writing assignment, making sure that you understand the meanings of all key words. What is the purpose of the assignment? What length is specified? What other guidelines are provided? Write a possible statement of purpose for the assignment.

Read (or reread) the poems by Anne Bradstreet on pages 32 and 34. These poems are the subject of the sample pre-writing notes and the sample paragraph developed in the next three lessons.

2. Now analyze the **Developing Writing Skills** or **Unit Review** assignment on which you are currently working. What are the key words? Do you understand their meanings? What length is specified or implied? Are any other guidelines provided? Determine your purpose and think about your audience and the tone that you wish to maintain. Be sure, of course, that you are thoroughly familiar with the literature upon which the assignment is based.

Sample Writing Assignment

The following writing assignment is from the **Unit Review** on page 65. The key words are underlined.

<u>Jonathan Edwards</u> wrote in his personal narrative, "I made <u>seeking</u> my <u>salvation</u> the main business of my life." Such was the duty of all good Puritans.

Write a <u>composition</u> of <u>six paragraphs</u> in which you <u>show how</u> this goal is <u>apparent</u> in

LESSON 2 Pre-Writing: Generating and Organizing Ideas

Supporting details can come from a variety of sources: from your own experiences and ideas, from the experiences of others, from literary selections, and from other printed materials. For essay questions and writing assignments that focus on literary elements, the appropriate sources are the literary selections that are the subjects for analysis.

Many of the writing assignments in this book include questions or suggestions to guide you in generating ideas. When you are dealing with a question or an assignment without specific directions, it is helpful to jot down a series of questions about the topic in your pre-writing notes. These questions should include the key words that you identified in your analysis of the directions and should focus on the *who, what, how, where,* and *when* of the topic. Consider, for example, the following assignment:

> Choose one important character from a short story in this unit, and discuss the methods of characterization used to develop that character.

Questions related to this topic might include these: Who are the important characters? Which character will I write about? What are the common methods of characterization? The answers to this last question might suggest additional questions, such as these: What does the character look like? What does the character say and do? Why? What do the words and actions show about the character? How do the other characters react to the character? What does this reveal about him or her?

Gathering Details

Once you know the kinds of details required, go to your source or sources to gather information. If you are writing about a short story, an essay, a nonfiction excerpt, or a poem, it may be possible to reread the entire selection. However, for full-length novels and plays, you probably will choose to reread or examine closely only those portions that relate to your topic.

Whether you draw your details from the selection or from other sources, it is important to take precise notes. Answer the questions related to your topic, accurately copy material you wish to quote, and summarize specific examples that illustrate your points. When paraphrasing, restating passages in your own words, be sure to retain the sense of the original material.

Organizing Details

Many of the writing assignments in this book suggest ways to structure ideas. For example, the sample writing assignment in Lesson 1 tells you what to discuss in the introductory paragraph, in the body paragraphs, and in the conclusion. When it is up to you to do the organizing, keep in mind that for most of your paragraphs and compositions you should follow a general to specific approach. State the main idea, then support that idea with specific details presented in an order that suits the material. Five common methods of organization are listed here.

Five Methods of Organizing Details

Chronological Order. In this method, you present details in the order in which they occur. This method is useful in analyzing development of character, plot, and symbols and in writing original stories and narrative poems.

Spatial Order. In this method, details are organized in the order in which a viewer might notice them. This method generally is used in describing setting and the physical appearance of characters or of people in real life.

Order of Importance. This method can be applied in two ways: arranging details from least to most important or from most to least important. The first approach allows you to build to a strong conclusion. For example, if you are discussing the significance of a quotation, you might first discuss its importance in its immediate context, next as it relates to another part of the story or to a character, and finally, its significance to the central conflict or to the theme of the selection.

In analyzing the style of a poem, you would probably take the opposite approach, giving the dominant stylistic characteristics first, then pointing out others that are less significant or that appear only in parts of the poem.

Most to Least Familiar Idea. Using this method, you would present ideas that are familiar to your readers before introducing new concepts. This method is useful when discussing the relationship of a selection to its historical period.

Comparison and Contrast. In this type of writing, supporting ideas are balanced, with statements about one selection or literary element countered with statements about the other. The way these statements are interwoven depends on your material.

You will be assessing and refining ideas throughout the writing process. Do not hesitate to add or to delete details as your writing takes shape, always keeping in mind the purpose of the assignment.

Sample Pre-Writing Notes

The following pre-writing notes are a response to the sample writing assignment. The notes relate only to one writer, Anne Bradstreet, and to one poem, "Upon the Burning of Our House, July 10th, 1666."

Where is salvation mentioned?

lines 43-44:
Thou hast an house on high erect,
Framed by that mighty Architect,

lines 51-54:
There's wealth enough, I need no more,
Farewell, my pelf, farewell my store.
The world no longer let me love,
My hope and treasure lies above.

What literary technique conveys her feelings?

Extended metaphor comparing the afterlife to a richly furnished house designed by God

What are her feelings about salvation?

Feelings of loss and despair over the destruction of her things
Recalls that God's house is "permanent"
Accepts loss as God's will—salvation is the main business of life
Values earthly life but the afterlife is better

EXERCISES Applying the Process: Pre-Writing

1. The sample pre-writing notes show questions and answers related to one of Anne Bradstreet's poems. Complete the notes for "To My Dear and Loving Husband." Then determine an appropriate order for presenting all the details on Bradstreet's poems.

2. Generate ideas for the **Developing Writing Skills** or **Unit Review** assignment on which you are currently working. Use the guidance provided in the assignment and additional questions, if necessary. Prepare pre-writing notes that show these details numbered in the order in which they will appear.

LESSON 3 Writing the First Draft

A first draft is the intermediate stage in the process of writing, an important developmental link between pre-writing and revising. While your pre-writing notes are a form of self-communication that make perfect sense to you, they are not an appropriate format for communicating your ideas to an audience. Your first draft expands your pre-writing notes into sentences and paragraphs and gives you an opportunity to determine whether your ideas will work together to fulfill the requirements of the assignment.

At this stage, simply write to get your ideas down on paper. Do not hesitate to add new details or to delete and rearrange details as you write. Do not be concerned with grammar and mechanics. Your energy should be focused on the development of your ideas.

As you write, keep the following guides in mind.

Guidelines for Writing a First Draft

Maintain Your Purpose. As one of the pre-writing steps, you determined your purpose for writing. As you write your first draft, keep this purpose in mind. Refer to your statement of purpose, if you included one in your pre-writing notes. Avoid retelling the plot, and mention plot details only to support your points.

Paraphrase Accurately. When you took your pre-writing notes, you were careful to retain the sense of the original material. Exercise the same care when translating the notes into a first draft.

Document Quotations. When you use a quotation, you should provide enough information so that your readers can locate it for themselves. For direct quotations, a page reference or a line number provided in parentheses or within the sentence introducing the quotation is sufficient.

Integrate Quotations. A quotation should strengthen rather than interrupt your flow of ideas. Therefore, it is important to incorporate quotations smoothly within your writing.

Avoid Unsupported Generalities. Although you must summarize, avoid using sweeping, unsupported statements. If you make a generalization, back it up with specific detail.

Include Adequate Explanations. Often, your pre-writing notes will include a phrase suggesting an idea and a quotation or example that supports the idea. You know what originally prompted you to link the idea and the detail. Be sure to make the connection clear for the reader.

Sample First Draft

The following first draft is the beginning of a paragraph based on the sample pre-writing notes.

In both poems Anne Bradstreet shows that she likes earthly life but that she thinks that salvation is more important. In "Upon the Burning of Our House, July 10, 1666" she uses the loss of her house to show the central importance of salvation in her life. She tells about the destruction of her house by fire. She has feelings of loss and despair over the destruction of her things, but she accepts the fire and her loss as God's will, and she is ultimately reconciled to her loss and realizes that the loss of her house is no big deal. The final two stanzas of the poem has an extended metaphor. She compares the afterlife to a richly furnished house designed by God, "Thou hast a house on high erect, Framed by that mighty Architect." (lines 43 and 44) She reminds herself that this house is permanent and indestructible unlike her earthly house, which was not. This is a nice metaphor because it gives the poet a new house. She comforts herself with the realization that the most important thing in life is eternal salvation. "The world no longer let me love, My hope and treasure lies above."

EXERCISES   **Applying the Process: Writing the First Draft**

1. Study the way that the sample pre-writing notes have been incorporated into the sample first draft. Then complete this first draft, using your pre-writing notes on "To My Dear and Loving Husband."

2. Study your pre-writing notes on Jonathan Edwards, William Bradford, or Edward Taylor. Then write the first draft of a paragraph based on these notes.

3. Write the first draft of the Developing Writing Skills or Unit Review assignment on which you are currently working.

LESSON 4   Revising

Revision is the last stage of the writing process. While revising, you may still find yourself adding, deleting, and rearranging details as your paragraph or composition assumes its final shape. You also will pay close attention to the technical aspects and subtle elements of writing that contribute to effective communication.

Guidelines for Revising

Begin revising by reading your first draft several times. With each reading, check a few elements and make any necessary changes. Make sure that you have done the following:

- Answered the question or fulfilled the requirements of the assignment
- Written for a specific audience
- Maintained a consistent, appropriate tone
- Paraphrased accurately
- Documented quotations
- Integrated quotations smoothly

In addition, check your writing for the following.

Unity. Unified writing is tightly structured, with each sentence within a paragraph and each paragraph within a composition developing one main idea.

Coherence. Coherent writing results from logical relationships among sentences and paragraphs.

Emphasis. Proper emphasis means that all ideas are related to one central idea and that the most space is devoted to the most important supporting ideas.

After you have revised your first draft for content, proofread your writing for errors in grammar and usage, spelling, punctuation, and capitalization. Refer to a dictionary or an English text and to the Checklist for Proofreading Titles and Quotations on page 955 for help in making corrections. Then make a final, neat copy of your paragraph or composition, using correct manuscript form.

Revised Sample Paragraph

"Upon the Burning of Our House, July 10th, 1666"
and "To My Dear and Loving Husband,"

In ~~both poems~~ Anne Bradstreet shows that

while
she ~~likes~~ *values* earthly life ~~but that~~ she ~~thinks~~ *believes* that

salvation is more important. In "Upon the

Burning of Our House~~,~~" ~~July 10, 1666~~" she

skillfully juxtaposes earthly loss with spiritual
~~uses the loss of her house to show the cen-~~
wealth.
~~tral importance of salvation in her life. She~~

~~tells about the destruction of her house by~~
mourns
~~fire.~~ She ~~has feelings of loss and despair over~~

possessions
the destruction of her ~~things,~~ but she ac-

cepts the fire ~~and her loss~~ as God's will/ and

e
~~she is~~ ultimatly ~~reconciled to her loss and~~

her true wealth is not earthly.
realizes that ~~the loss of her house is no big~~

develop
~~deal.~~ The final two stanzas ~~of the poem has~~

in which
an extended metaphor~~,~~ ~~She compares~~ the af-

is compared
terlife to a richly furnished house designed

by God, ~~"Thou hast~~ a house ~~on high~~ erect,

"Framed by that mighty Architect." (lines 43

~~and~~ 44) She reminds herself that this *"heavenly* house"

is permanent and indestructible ~~unlike her~~

~~earthly house, which was not. This is a nice~~

~~metaphor because it gives the poet a new~~

~~house.~~ *In the last two lines* She ~~comforts herself with the realiza-~~

~~tion that the most important thing in life is~~
focuses clearly on *saying*
eternal salvation, "The world no longer let

me love,/My hope and treasure lies above."

EXERCISES   Applying the Process: Revising

1. Study the sample revised paragraph to be sure that you understand each change. Then revise the sentences that you added, which discuss "To My Dear and Loving Husband." Use the revision questions in Guidelines: The Process of Writing and the Checklist for Proofreading Titles and Quotations on page 955. Make a final copy of the entire paragraph.

2. Revise the first draft of the Developing Writing Skills or Unit Review assignment on which you are currently working, and make a final copy.

Guidelines: The Process of Writing

Pre-Writing

1. Analyze the essay question or writing assignment.
2. Determine a purpose for writing.
3. Think about your audience and the tone that you wish to maintain.
4. Gather and list details. Follow the suggestions within the assignment, or formulate and answer questions based on the assignment.
5. Organize the details. Use a general to specific order, possibly in combination with one of the following:

Chronological Order
Spatial Order
Order of Importance (most to least, least to most,)
Most to Least Familiar Idea
Comparison and Contrast

6. Add or delete details as necessary.

Writing the First Draft

1. Using your pre-writing notes, put your ideas into sentence and paragraph form. Add, delete, and rearrange details if necessary.
2. Keep the following in mind:

Maintain your purpose
Paraphrase accurately
Document quotations
Integrate quotations smoothly
Avoid unsupported generalities
Include adequate explanations

Revising

Read what you have written. Answer the following questions:

1. Have you answered the question or fulfilled the requirements of the assignment?
2. Have you kept your audience in mind?
3. Have you maintained a consistent, appropriate tone?
4. Have you paraphrased accurately?
5. Have you documented quotations and integrated them smoothly into the text?
6. Do all your sentences and paragraphs develop a main idea?
7. Are your ideas presented logically?
8. Do you devote the most space to the most important supporting ideas?

Revise as necessary, then proofread your work to check grammar and usage, spelling, punctuation, and capitalization.

Checklist for Proofreading Titles and Quotations

1. Have you capitalized the first word and every important word in the titles of books, short stories, essays, articles, plays, and poems?
2. Have you used quotation marks to enclose the titles of chapters and other parts of books? The titles of short stories, poems, essays, and articles?
3. Have you underlined the titles of books and full-length plays?
4. Have you used quotation marks to enclose the exact words of a writer?
5. Have you indented and set off quotations of four or more lines?
6. Have you used a slash mark (/) to indicate the end of a line when quoting two or three lines of poetry?
7. Have you indicated missing words from a quotation with an ellipsis (. . .)?

LESSON 5 The Topic Sentence

The topic sentence of a paragraph or composition is a general statement that introduces the idea to be developed in the supporting sentences or paragraphs. The topic sentence controls the content and limits the scope of a piece of writing, for all details must develop the main idea expressed in that sentence. Although exceptions are possible, and sometimes desirable, most paragraphs and compositions should include a topic sentence. This is especially true of expository writing, the kind of writing that you do when you analyze literature.

A good topic sentence is an invaluable resource during the process of writing. At the pre-writing stage, this sentence can help to crystallize ideas about a topic. In writing a first draft, the topic sentence is a guide in expressing ideas. Finally, during the revision stage, the topic sentence serves as a point of reference when checking for unity and emphasis.

Paragraphs and Compositions

In a one-paragraph response to an essay question or writing assignment, the topic sentence serves as an introduction by presenting both the topic and the writer's conclusions about it.

Sample Topic Sentence

In the excerpt from "Sinners in the Hands of an Angry God," striking figures of speech intensify the dramatic impact of the sermon.

The sample topic sentence introduces a paragraph dealing with the figurative language in "Sinners in the Hands of an Angry God." The

writer's conclusion is that figurative language adds to the dramatic impact of the sermon.

In a multi-paragraph composition the entire first paragraph serves as an introduction. The topic sentence of the introductory paragraph states the main idea both of that paragraph and of the entire composition.

Sample Introductory Paragraph

Although "The Pit and the Pendulum" is a short story and "Annabel Lee" and "The Raven" are poems, certain characteristics mark these selections as the work of the same writer. Noteworthy are the sound devices, which are based on various kinds of repetition. Also significant are the words and phrases that create a subtle similarity of mood among the selections. A fascination with the supernatural, too, is apparent in the story and the two poems.

The sample introductory paragraph introduces a composition on the similarities among three selections by Edgar Allan Poe, which are included in Unit 3. This idea is presented in the topic sentence, the first sentence in the paragraph, and expanded in the rest of the sentences. The three succeeding paragraphs each will focus on one of the characteristics named in the introductory paragraph; each paragraph will begin with a general statement about the one characteristic to be discussed in that paragraph.

Writing a Topic Sentence

After an initial analysis of an essay question or a writing assignment, you might have a good idea about what you want to say. If so, try writing a topic sentence immediately, with the understanding that it can be modified or changed completely as your ideas develop. In most cases, however, your topic sentence will evolve gradually as your ideas take shape. You can then follow this approach:

Steps in Writing a Topic Sentence

1. Complete your pre-writing notes.
2. Study your notes carefully.
3. Draw conclusions and formulate opinions based on your notes.
4. Incorporate your ideas into a topic sentence, as the first step in writing a rough draft.

Occasionally, you might be faced with an open-ended essay question, such as this:

In what ways does the American literature of the nineteenth century reflect the period in which it was written?

This topic is so broad that complete coverage probably would fill a book. For such a question, the quality of your analysis depends not only on your understanding of the material but also on your ability to discriminate. To avoid writing a series of sweeping generalizations, you would need to select a few major characteristics and representative literary works and to write a topic sentence that pulls together those specific characteristics.

No matter what kind of writing you are doing and what circumstances prompt the writing, your topic sentences should exhibit certain basic qualities.

A Good Topic Sentence

• Is general enough so that you can support your idea adequately in a well developed paragraph or series of paragraphs.
• Is limited enough so that you can develop your idea within the limits of a paragraph or composition.

• Is interesting enough to catch your reader's attention. In expository writing, specific statements and thoughtful opinions create interest in a topic and in your ideas about it.

Sample Writing Assignment

The following writing assignment is from the **Unit Review** on page 65. The key words have been underlined.

Compare and contrast the attitude toward nature that pervades the Native American selections with the attitude that Captain John Smith and William Bradford project. How do you explain the similarities? How do you account for the differences?

Sample Topic Sentence

As reflected in their writings, the Native Americans and the English colonists had distinctly different attitudes toward nature; but, in their struggle for survival, the colonists modified their view somewhat so that their attitude became closer to that of the Native Americans.

Studying the Samples

Notice that the topic sentence repeats the key phrase "attitude toward nature," which is the topic to be discussed, and includes the words *different* and *closer*, which pick up the idea of comparison and contrast. Notice, too, that "distinctly different," "modified their view," and "closer to that of the Native Americans" summarize the writer's conclusions. These conclusions were formed on the basis of pre-writing notes (not shown here) that describe the attitudes of both groups and that include references to colonial and Native American literature. The notes also answer the two questions posed in the assignment.

To develop adequately the idea in the sample topic sentence, the writer will:

• Identify the Native American attitude toward nature

• Provide at least one example from the literature to illustrate the Native American view

• Identify the colonists' attitude toward nature

• Provide at least one example from the literature to illustrate the colonists' view

• Explain why the attitudes of the two groups are different

• Indicate how the colonists' attitude drew closer to the Native American view

• Provide an example from the literature to illustrate the change

EXERCISES   Writing Topic Sentences

1. Read (or reread) the Native American selections and the writings of Captain John Smith and William Bradford in Unit 1. Prepare pre-writing notes that follow the plan presented in Studying the Samples.

2. Prepare pre-writing notes and write a topic sentence for the following assignment:

Choose one poem, short story, or brief example of nonfiction writing, either from this book or from another source. In a well developed paragraph, discuss the theme of the selection, supporting your points with specific references to lines, passages, incidents, or ideas within the selection.

3. Write a topic sentence for the Developing Writing Skills or Unit Review assignment on which you are currently working. If you are in the process of revising a piece of writing, pay particular attention to the topic sentence.

LESSON 6 Developing a Paragraph or Composition

Whether you write a paragraph, a brief composition, or a lengthier essay depends on the topic, on the directions given, and sometimes on the available time. In a testing situation, time most likely will limit your discussion of a topic. It is important to make a realistic estimate about how much you can write during the test period and to write a topic sentence that can be developed adequately within the allotted time.

Most of the assignments in this book prescribe a length, such as a paragraph or a five-paragraph composition. Most essay questions, however, do not mention length. For these kinds of questions, the amount of information in your pre-writing notes can be a guide for determining how much to write. A list of six or eight closely related ideas, for example,

probably could be woven into one paragraph. Numerous specific ideas that answer three or four general questions might require a five-paragraph or a six-paragraph composition: an introduction followed by three or four supporting paragraphs and a conclusion.

Occasionally, the wording of an assignment implies length. When you are directed to follow a model, for example, you can assume that your writing will be approximately the same length.

Writing a Composition

A composition has three main parts: an introduction, body paragraphs, and a conclusion. You already have studied the function and structure of an introductory paragraph.

Besides stating the main idea of the composition, this paragraph can be used to provide necessary background information, to identify the selections and writers to be discussed, to define literary terms, and to explain more fully the ideas in the topic sentence.

When writing the paragraphs of a composition, you will want to use transitional devices to establish relationships among ideas and to smooth the flow from one idea to the next. Transitional devices are words and phrases that tie together sentences and paragraphs by referring both to the idea that precedes and to the idea that follows.

Transitional Devices

Indications of Time:

first	finally	afterwards	until
next	before	today	later
then	after	meanwhile	since

These words are especially important when discussing narrative writing and when ordering ideas chronologically.

Indications of Relationships:

and	because	besides	similarly
also	therefore	moreover	unless

Many of these words are particularly useful for explanations that must be clear and exact.

Indications of Opposites:

but	while	on the other hand
however	although	in contrast

These transitions are crucial to developing effective comparisons and contrasts.

Repetitions of Words and Phrases. This device can give you practice in using literary terms. Repetitions also can reinforce important concepts.

Synonyms and Definitions. When you need to recall the meanings of literary terms, you can accomplish this smoothly through the use of this device.

Pronouns. When discussing a literary selection, be especially careful that the referent for each pronoun is absolutely clear.

Concluding a Composition

As the final paragraph in a composition, the conclusion has a special relationship to the topic sentence. The conclusion can do one or more of the following:

Restate the idea in the topic sentence.
Summarize the supporting ideas.
Offer a final comment on the main idea.

Sample Conclusion

The following paragraph concludes the composition that begins with the sample introductory paragraph on page 956.

The three selections demonstrate a basic consistency of subject and style. The sounds of the lines combine with richly connotative language to create a haunting mood. This mood is appropriate to the eerie, melancholy subjects identified with Edgar Allan Poe.

Compare this conclusion with the introductory paragraph, noting the way that the ideas in the introduction are restated and extended in the final paragraph.

EXERCISES   Expressing Ideas in Paragraphs and Compositions

For the following assignments, use the process of writing, which is summarized on pages 955.

1. Using your pre-writing notes and the sample topic sentence, write a paragraph comparing and contrasting the attitudes toward nature evident in the Native American selections and in the writings of Captain John Smith and William Bradford.

2. Complete the paragraph on the theme of a short story, poem, or nonfiction selection, using your pre-writing notes. Be certain that each sentence relates directly to the idea in your topic sentence.

3. Complete the **Developing Writing Skills** or **Unit Review** assignment on which you are currently working. During revision, pay special attention to transitional devices and to the way that each sentence relates to the topic sentence.

LESSON 7 Writing About Poetry

Poetry is defined as "an arrangement of lines in which form and content fuse to suggest meanings beyond the literal meanings of the words." The language of poetry is suggestive, the sounds musical, the structure compact. The poet shapes ordinary words into poetic language, which includes imagery, allusion, symbol, and figurative language: metaphor, simile, hyperbole, and personification. To create musical effects, the poet uses sound devices such as meter, rhyme, assonance, consonance, alliteration, and onomatopoeia. Together, all of these techniques convey the tone, the mood, and ultimately the theme, or main idea, of a poem. (See the Handbook of Literary Terms for definitions of poetry terms.)

When thinking about a poem, you might use the following questions as a guide.

What kind of poem is it?

What seems to be the poet's intent?

What kind of rhythm is evident? Is it consistent throughout the poem? How is it created?

What sounds dominate the poem? Do these sounds form patterns? Do they reinforce key ideas?

What words and phrases are particularly striking or suggestive?

What kinds of poetic language does the poet employ?

What tone and mood are conveyed? Are the tone and the mood similar?

What theme emerges from the poem?

Considering the Assignment

An essay question or writing assignment may ask you to analyze one aspect of a poem: to explain the meaning of a symbol, to analyze the imagery, or to discuss the theme or a quotation that summarizes the theme. An assignment may focus on several poems, asking you to discuss treatment of a common theme or to contrast elements such as tone and mood. An assignment may ask you to examine the relationship between form and meaning: to explain how a poem's form suits its content, or to discuss how poetic techniques are used to establish a poem's message.

Completing a Writing Assignment

When writing about a poem, you should complete each step in the process of writing: pre-writing, writing the first draft, and revising. The process is explained on pages 950-954 and is summarized on page 955. As you work through the steps in the process, keep the following in mind.

Pre-Writing

Literary terms often are incorporated within a writing assignment for poetry. Be sure that you have more than a "general understanding" of these terms. Check definitions in the Handbook of Literary Terms or in a dictionary or other reference book, if necessary.

Although a poem generally is short and thus quickly reread, as many as three readings may be necessary to penetrate the layers of meaning. For the first reading, be open to the impression created by the sounds and images. For the second, think about the literal and figurative meanings of words and phrases, and for the third, concentrate on the poet's message.

You may find it helpful to generate questions in two stages. For instance, if a writing assignment contains a broad term such as *figurative language*, *form*, or *technique*, you may want to ask a general question, such as "What types of figurative language are used in the poem?" You then could use the answer to this question to generate a second series of more specific questions, which might include "What effect is created by the similes in the poem?"

A symbol, an image, a theme, or another major element often is developed throughout a poem. A paragraph or composition that analyzes such an element usually can be structured in chronological order.

Writing the First Draft

Pay close attention to your topic sentences. Avoid making generalities that are not supported by the details in the poem. Also avoid statements that are too broad to be supported adequately within the limits of a paragraph or brief composition.

Revising

Consider your audience's familiarity with literary terms and with the selection. Include definitions and specific references and quotations to aid reader understanding.

Sample Writing Assignment

This writing assignment relates to the poem that precedes Unit 1. The key words have been underlined.

In "The Gift Outright" Robert Frost uses several techniques to establish the theme of the poem. Identify these techniques, and in a five-paragraph composition, discuss the way that they contribute to the development of the poet's message.

Pre-Writing

Below are partially completed pre-writing notes, based on questions formulated from the assignment.

What is the theme of the poem?

land didn't really belong to Americans when they were still colonists; Americans committed themselves completely when they fought England; great potential of land opened up

What poetic techniques does Frost use?

repetition lines 1-7
alliteration lines 8-11
metaphor lines 12-16

How do these techniques contribute to the development of the poet's message?
How does repetition function?
How does alliteration function?

alliteration in middle section: highlights shift of idea; unifying device
emphasizes "we were withholding" (idea presented in first section)
emphasizes "land of living," "forthwith found," and "salvation in surrender" (ideas in third section)

How does metaphor function?

Writing the First Draft and Revising

Below is a revised draft of one of the paragraphs written for the sample assignment.

Alliteration unifies the middle section of
(lines 8-11)
the poem and highlights the shift in idea
ʌ

that occurs in these lines. In the eighth line,
"Something we were withholding made us weak," ʌ
the poet repeats the w sound to emphasize
ʌ *initial*

the idea described more fully in the first seven lines. The eighth and ninth lines describe an important discovery: "Until we found out that it was ourselves/We were withholding from our land of living." "We were withholding" reinforces once again the idea in the first section of the poem, while "land of living" suggests a new vitality, emphasized by the repetition of the l sound. *,"And forthwith found salvation in surrender,"* The final line of this middle section announces an end to the withholding, an idea elaborated upon in the third section. Alliteration of the f and s sounds gives the phrases in this line additional impact.

Studying the Sample

Notice that the answer to the question "How do these techniques contribute to the development of the poet's message?" led to the more specific questions: "How does repetition function?" "How does alliteration function?" "How does metaphor function?"

Although Frost's poem is not divided into stanzas, it is structured in three parts, with one poetic technique predominating in each part. The structure of the assigned composition should parallel the structure of the poem. Alliteration is important in the middle section of the poem and therefore should be discussed in the middle of the composition, after the discussion of repetition. Within the

sample paragraph, the organization is similar, with detail presented in chronological order.

In this final revision, the writer added a page reference, two direct quotations, and the word *initial*, which recalls the meaning of *alliteration*. These changes make it easier for the reader to follow the development of idea. They also expand the detail that supports the generalization in the topic sentence.

EXERCISES **Writing About Poems**

For the following assignments, use the process of writing and the guidance provided in this lesson and in the lessons on writing paragraphs and compositions.

1. Complete the writing assignment for "The Gift Outright." Add five paragraphs to the sample paragraph: an introduction, paragraphs discussing repetition and metaphor, and a conclusion.

2. Complete your current writing assignment dealing with poetry.

LESSON 8 Writing About Nonfiction

The forms of nonfiction cover a wide spectrum: speeches, journals, diaries, letters, essays, biographies, and autobiographies. Regardless of the form, however, an analysis of a nonfiction selection always involves a concern for both what is said (content) and how it is said (style).

When thinking about a nonfiction selection, begin by identifying its form. Then focus on the specific elements of that form, using the questions given here as a guide.

Essay and Speech. An essay is a brief composition that offers an opinion on a subject. A speech, too, often presents an opinion, although a speech is primarily an oral form. Questions to consider when thinking about an essay or a speech include the following:

Is the writer's overall purpose to persuade? To inform? To entertain? To analyze?

What is the writer's theme, or message about life?

What specific ideas does the writer present? In what order?

Does the writer use examples, facts, statistics, description, or anecdotes?

Is the appeal emotional, intellectual, or both? (See **Rhetorical Question** in the Handbook of Literary Terms.)

What sound devices are used? (See **Repetition** in the Handbook of Literary Terms.)

Biography. A biography is an account of a person's life written by someone other than the subject. When thinking about a biography, ask yourself questions such as these:

What is the writer's attitude toward the subject? The writer's purpose?

Is the treatment balanced and unbiased?

Does the writer use description? Dialogue? Commentary?

What picture of the subject emerges?

Autobiography. An autobiography is the story of a person's life written by that person. Autobiographical writing includes journals, letters, and diaries as well as longer, more formal autobiographies. These questions can guide you in thinking about autobiographical writing:

Who is the intended audience?

What is the writer's purpose?

What actions and reactions are described?

What comments does the writer make?

Is the tone personal, objective, or a combination?

What qualities does the writer possess?

What kind of society is depicted?

Considering the Assignment

An essay question or writing assignment concerning nonfiction may direct you to discuss the theme of a work. An assignment may focus on style, asking you to analyze the elements of a writer's style or to explain how style reinforces theme. An assignment may require you to identify a writer's purpose and the means by which he or she achieves that purpose. Often, an assignment will present a quotation from a literary selection and then ask you to discuss the way that the quotation embodies the theme or typifies the style of the entire selection.

Completing a Writing Assignment

When writing about nonfiction, you should complete each step in the process of writing: pre-writing, writing the first draft, and revising. The process is explained on pages 950-954 and summarized on page 955. As you work through the steps in the process, keep the following in mind.

Pre-Writing

An assignment may imply literary terminology without using the exact terms. For example: "Identify the writer's attitude toward the subject" actually is asking for a description of tone; "Explain how the writer achieves a humorous effect" is asking for an analysis of style in relation to mood.

When gathering details for a discussion of a quotation, first locate the quotation within context. If guidance is not provided within the assignment, formulate questions to use in clarifying the relationship between the quotation and other ideas in the selection.

Writing the First Draft

Use your pre-writing notes as a guide and a point of reference, but continue to modify, add, and delete ideas as you write.

Often, pre-writing notes consist of a phrase suggesting an idea and examples and quotations that support the idea. Be sure that you make clear the connection between the idea and the details.

Revising

Your focus must remain clear throughout your paragraph or composition. Even insightful ideas may have to be deleted for the sake of unity.

Sample Writing Assignment

This assignment relates to the selection that begins on page 55. The key words in the assignment have been underlined.

In the concluding paragraph of "We Aren't Superstitious," Stephen Vincent Benét states, "We have no reason to hold Salem up to obloquy." Why might this strike the reader as an unusual thing to say? How does this statement relate to the message developed throughout the essay? In a well developed paragraph, discuss the significance of the statement within the context of the essay.

Pre-Writing

These notes include a definition and answers to the two questions within the assignment.

obloquy: "widespread censure or verbal abuse"
points out irrationality and hysteria surrounding the Salem events; implies that those people deserve criticism.
ironic tone (see title)
message: Salem is not unique; we are superstitious, prejudiced, intolerant, too; we shouldn't censure Salem as if we would never do such things.
"The pot shouldn't call the kettle black."

Writing the First Draft and Revising

After getting ideas down on paper and revising the paragraph, the writer made a fresh copy. She then marked one final change, which is shown here.

Stephen Vincent Benét's assertion "We have no reason to hold Salem up to obloquy" reinforces the message that he develops throughout the essay. At first, this statement may seem unusual, for Benét carefully documents the irrational, hysterical nature of the Salem events. On one level, however, the statement is consistent with the ironic tone of the essay. Even the title "We Aren't Superstitious" is ironic because the message is that we are superstitious, that twentieth-century Americans are not immune to superstition, prejudice, and intolerance. When Benét writes, "We have no reason to hold Salem up to obloquy," he is not suggesting that the people of Salem were blameless but rather that we are not blameless either. His

> point is that we should not censure Salem
> as if we were incapable of the same actions.
> ~~Benét would agree with that old saying,~~
> ~~"The pot shouldn't call the kettle black."~~

Studying the Sample

Obloquy is the only unusual word within the writing assignment. The writer clarified its meaning before taking the rest of her pre-writing notes. Although the terms *tone* and *theme* are not used, the wording of the assignment implies that the writer must be concerned with these two elements.

Notice that the writer establishes logical relationships among the ideas generated in her paragraph. For example, she notes the ironic tone of the essay as a way of explaining the apparent irony of the statement. From the discussion of the irony in the title comes the discussion of theme and then of the statement as it relates to the theme.

During revision, the writer deleted the final sentence. Although it states the important idea of common guilt, this point already has been made. Also, including a reference from outside the literary selection detracts from the unity of the paragraph, which focuses entirely on the essay.

EXERCISES Writing About Nonfiction

For the following assignments, use the process of writing and the guidance provided in this lesson and in the lessons on writing paragraphs and compositions.

1. Complete your current writing assignment dealing with a nonfiction selection.

2. Choose a nonfiction selection either from this book or from another source. Then do the following:

a. Identify a statement that relates in some way to the theme of the selection. Discuss the significance of the quotation in a well developed paragraph.

b. Write a composition that answers this question: What is the writer's purpose, and how does he or she accomplish this purpose?

LESSON 9 Writing About a Short Story

Every short story writer begins with the same basic elements of fiction: character, setting, plot, and point of view. The unique development of each of these elements and their interplay in conveying theme constitute the writer's art.

Before writing about a story, it is often helpful to think about its five elements.

Character. Characters are the people or animals who take part in the action. Questions to consider when thinking about characters include these: Who are the main and minor characters? Does the main character change during the story? If so, how? How do you learn about the characters? (See **Characterization** in the Handbook of Literary Terms.)

Setting. Setting is the time and place of the action. When thinking about setting, ask yourself questions such as these: Where and when does the story take place? What kind of society is depicted? What atmosphere is conveyed by the setting? Does the setting determine the action in any way? Would the story be considerably different if set in another time and place?

Plot. The plot is the structure of events, which result from a conflict. (See **Conflict** in the Handbook of Literary Terms.) These questions can guide you in thinking about plot: What happens during the course of the story? At what point is excitement at a peak? How does the writer signal the turning point of the action? Are all the loose ends tied up at the end?

Point of View. Point of view refers to the narrative method used in a short story. (See **Point of View** in the Handbook of Literary Terms.) When thinking about point of view, ask yourself: Who tells the story? What does the unique point of view add to the story? How would the story change if it were told from a different point of view?

Theme. Theme is the writer's message about human nature or the human condition. After considering character, setting, plot, and point of view, ask yourself: What is the writer attempting to say? What elements seem to be the most important in conveying theme? What fresh insight or new understanding did you gain from the story?

Considering the Assignment

An essay question or writing assignment may focus on a single story element. For instance, it may ask you to write about character: to describe the qualities of a character, to explain a character's actions, to analyze a character's role in the story, or to discuss the relationship between two characters. An assignment may ask you to describe the characteristics of a region, to cite the details that evoke a sense of time and place, to trace the development of a conflict, or to evaluate a writer's views as optimistic or pessimistic. A writing assignment may be limited to a specific technique, asking you to analyze the meaning of a symbol or to describe how irony is used to achieve an effect. Finally, an assignment may focus on several elements or techniques in relation to each other. Such an assignment may ask you to discuss the characteristics of a writer's style or to explain how setting, plot, and character interact to reveal theme.

Completing a Writing Assignment

When writing about a short story, you should complete each step in the process of writing: pre-writing, writing the first draft, and revising. The process is explained on pages 950-954 and is summarized on page 955. As you work through the steps in the process, keep the following in mind.

Pre-Writing

When the choice of a story to write about is up to you, it is not always wise to select your favorite story. Choose instead a story in which the element to be analyzed or all the major elements are developed fully.

The source for ideas is the short story itself. All opinions and conclusions should be inferred from and supported by evidence from the story. ·

Assignments that contain words such as *cite* and *quote* require text references and direct quotations to support ideas. Be both specific and accurate in recording incidents and actions and in quoting dialogue.

Writing the First Draft

For each direct quotation, either give a page number in parentheses directly after the quotation or place the quotation in context by noting the action that prompted the comment or the point in plot development to which the quotation relates.

Revising

The appropriate tone for analytical writing is objective. Delete loaded words that indicate personal feelings and judgments.

Sample Writing Assignment

This assignment relates to a story that begins on page 143. The key words in the assignment have been underlined.

The characters in "Dr. Heidegger's Experiment" are more representative of ideas and abstractions than of real human beings. What does each character represent? What evidence from the story supports your conclusions? Present your ideas in a well developed composition in which a paragraph is devoted to each character.

Pre-Writing

Below are pre-writing notes on one of the characters.

Widow Wycherly: waste of beauty

"she was a great beauty in her day; but . . . she had lived in deep seclusion, on account of certain scandalous stories which had prejudiced the gentry of the town against her." (p. 143)

"she stood before the mirror curtsying and simpering to her own image and greeting it as the friend whom she loved better than all the world beside," (p. 146) (shows self-admiration)

she "neither granted nor quite withheld her favors." (p. 148) (flirtation, toying with people's feelings)

Writing the First Draft and Revising

After getting ideas down on paper and revising the composition, the writer made a final copy. Below is one of the revised paragraphs.

The Widow Wycherly represents the waste of beauty. She has squandered her major asset without gaining any return. At the beginning of the story, the narrator says, " . . . she was a great beauty in her day." However, this beauty has evidently not brought the Widow happiness, for she has lived for a long time "in deep seclusion, on account of certain scandalous stories." (page 143) As the story unfolds, Hawthorne provides an additional insight into how the Widow misused her asset. After drinking the

Doctor's elixir, she not only regains her beauty but also reverts to her former behavior. She rushes immediately to a mirror, where she stands "curtsying and simpering to her own image and greeting it as the friend whom she loved better than all the world beside." (page 146) She flirts and teases, toying with her admirers' feelings, as one "who neither granted nor quite withheld her favors." (page 148) The Widow demonstrates that, for her, beauty is a source of self-admiration and self-love, corrupting rather than enhancing her life and the lives of others.

Studying the Sample

The sample writing assignment states a conclusion that is the basis for an introductory paragraph. No specific direction is given for organization. Of the five characters, only Dr. Heidegger seems to stand apart. Therefore, the order of discussion for the other four characters is interchangeable, but the analysis of Dr. Heidegger should be placed either first or last to highlight his importance. Within the sample paragraph, the organization is general to specific, with supporting evidence presented in chronological order.

Notice the way that the quotations are identified. The first is placed "at the beginning of the story"; the others are identified by page number. Notice also that the writer maintains an objective tone throughout, even though the paragraph presents opinions.

EXERCISES   Writing About Short Stories

For the following assignments, use the process of writing and the guidance provided in this lesson and in the lessons on writing paragraphs and compositions.

1. Complete your current writing assignment dealing with a short story.

2. Choose a story that you have read, and write a one-paragraph analysis of an important element. You may describe the main character, discuss the importance of setting, analyze the plot structure, or discuss the point of view.

3. Choose a story that you have read, and in a five-paragraph or six-paragraph composition, analyze the way that each major element contributes to theme.

LESSON 10 Writing About Drama

Defined as "literature that develops plot and character through dialogue and action," drama has basic elements in common with narrative writing. These elements include character, setting, plot, and theme. What sets drama apart is the manner in which the elements are developed and the fact that drama is written to be performed on a stage or before cameras or microphones.

When thinking about drama, begin with the guide questions on character, setting, plot and theme, which are given in **Writing About a Short Story,** pages 966-968. Then focus on the characteristics that are unique to drama and to written scripts, using the following questions as a guide.

How is the play structured? How many acts does it have? Are the acts divided into scenes?

What happens in each act?

In which act does the turning point take place?

What dramatic conventions are used? What information is given in the stage directions? (See **Drama** in the Handbook of Literary Terms.)

Is the play entertaining? Thought-provoking? Chilling?

Considering the Assignment

An essay question or writing assignment concerning drama may ask you to analyze character, setting, plot, or theme; to discuss the tone or mood of a play; or to comment on its ironies or dramatic conventions. An assignment may present a passage of dialogue and ask you to discuss its significance in relation to character, plot, or theme. Because drama often contains symbols, you probably will be asked at some time to discuss the abstract concept represented by a character, setting, or object.

Completing the Assignment

When writing about drama, you should complete each step in the process of writing: pre-writing, writing the first draft, and revising. The process is explained on pages 950-954 and is summarized on page 955. As you work through the steps in the process, keep the following in mind.

Pre-Writing

As you read a play, visualize the setting and the movements of the characters and imagine the sound effects and the way that the dialogue would be spoken. This kind of preparation helps in interpreting the meaning of a play.

Consider assignment directions carefully, being alert for clues to organizing details. The word *trace*, for example, indicates that an explanation should be presented chronologically; *assess* suggests order of importance.

Most plays are well developed, multi-act literary works. Being aware of the length specifications in an assignment will help you to determine the amount of detail to include in your pre-writing notes.

As you study the development of an element throughout a play, try to identify emerging patterns. For example, a setting might consistently evoke a certain mood, or a symbol might be associated with one character.

Writing the First Draft

Keep the purpose of your discussion clearly in mind. If your purpose is to establish the significance of a symbol, for example, this should be the main focus of your writing, with incidents from the plot included only as supporting evidence.

Although the dialogue in a play is not enclosed in quotation marks, use quotation marks and speech tags when quoting lines of dialogue within a paragraph or composition.

Revising

For your readers to accept and fully understand your points, you must provide enough evidence from the selection. Add examples to illustrate your ideas, if necessary.

Sample Writing Assignment

This assignment relates to the play that begins on page 831. The key words in the assignment have been underlined.

The ice, the organ, and the oil are all important symbols in "Ile." In a five-paragraph composition, discuss these symbols, devoting a separate paragraph to each. Your composition should answer these questions: What are the associations between each symbol and the characters in the play? What abstract idea does each symbol represent? What is the role of each symbol within the play?

Pre-Writing

Below are pre-writing notes on one symbol. They answer the three questions posed in the writing assignment.

Captain: "I done my best to make it [the ship] as cozy and comfortable as could be. I even sent to the city for that organ for ye, thinkin' it might be soothin' to ye to be playin' it times when they was calms and things was dull like." (P. 837)

organ is attempt to meet his wife's needs; later, refuses to meet her need to return home

Annie: "I hate the organ. It puts me in mind of home." (p. 834)

after Captain breaks his promise, she doesn't

speak again; plays instead "wildly," "softly," and as curtain falls "wildly and discordantly";

means of expression for Annie—organ almost becomes extension of herself

Symbolism: organ represents refinement, civilization, home; underscores theme of isolation; Captain has cut himself off from refinement, civilization, and human society and feelings

Writing the First Draft and Revising

The writer of this paragraph revised carefully, yet he failed to correct two major problems. See if you can detect them.

associated with both Captain Keeney and his wife Annie.

The organ is a significant symbol in "Ile." As the play opens, the organ is described as part of the setting. The organ also is mentioned in the first conversation between *the* ∧ Captain ~~Keeney~~ and ~~his wife~~ Annie, which reveals that all is not well between them. Annie declares that she hates the organ because it puts her "in mind of home." In their next discussion, Captain Keeney reveals his reason for buying the organ, saying, "I done my best to make it [the ship] as cozy and comfortable as could be. I even sent to the city for that organ for ye, thinkin' it might be soothin' to ye to be playin' it times when they was calms and things was dull like." (page 837) After this scene, ~~things~~ *the situation* go*es* from bad to worse~~, aboard ship~~. The Captain promises Annie that they will head for home immediately, but then he reverses his decision. This betrayal drives Annie into madness. She never speaks again, but instead alternates between playing the organ "wildly" and "softly." As the curtain falls, she is playing "wildly and discordantly." All of these examples prove that the organ represents refinement, civilization, and *possibly* ~~in the end~~ Annie Keeney herself.

Studying the Sample

The writing assignment specifies both the length and the overall structure of the composition. Of the three symbols named, the oil is the most important and the organ is the least important. It seems logical, then, to discuss the organ first, followed by the ice and the oil, thus ending with the strongest point. Within each body paragraph, details may be presented chronologically, as they appear in the play.

One major problem in the sample paragraph is that the writer retells the story without relating the events to symbolism. Another problem is that he does not make clear the role of the symbol within the play, even though he included this idea in his prewriting notes. (You will have an opportunity to correct these problems in Exercise 1, which follows.)

EXERCISES   Writing About Drama

For the following assignments, use the process of writing and the guidance provided in this lesson and in the lessons on writing paragraphs and compositions.

1. Revise the sample paragraph to correct the two major problems. Use the same incidents and quotations, but make sure that they underscore conclusions about what the organ represents. Add a sentence summarizing the role of the symbol in relation to theme. Also expand the topic sentence to include this idea.

2. Complete your current writing assignment dealing with drama.

3. Choose a play that you have read or have seen performed recently. Then respond to two of the following questions and assignments, writing a well developed paragraph or composition for each.

a. Who is the main character, and how does he or she develop and change throughout the play?

b. Identify one character, object, or aspect of setting that you would consider a symbol. Explain the meaning of this symbol in the context of the play.

c. Choose one statement or passage of dialogue that seems especially notable or meaningful. Discuss the way that it relates to the characters, setting, or theme of the play.

d. What is the mood of the play, and how is it created? Consider subject, characters, dialogue, pace, setting, and theme before drawing your conclusions.

LESSON 11 Writing a Comparison/Contrast

The process of comparing and contrasting, of identifying similarities and differences, is one way of organizing data and of making sense of the world. Applying this process to literature enhances your ability to read critically and your understanding of selections.

Before writing a comparison or contrast, it is important to become thoroughly familiar with the short stories, poems, plays, or non-fiction selections that you will be discussing. Read the selections carefully, then think about them, using the questions provided in **Writing About Poetry**, **Writing About Nonfiction**, **Writing About a Short Story**, or **Writing About Drama** (pages 960-971). For selections in this book, the questions in **Getting at Meaning** and **Developing Skills in Reading Literature** help you in analysis and interpretation.

Considering the Assignment

An essay question or writing assignment may ask you to identify similarities, to find differences, or to discuss both similarities and differences. An assignment can deal with any kind of literature and with any aspect of that literature. One assignment may direct you to contrast the tone and mood of two poems, another to contrast the attitudes toward society expressed in two essays. An assignment may ask you to compare the themes of two plays or the main characters within a short story or to compare and contrast the experiences of two autobiographers. The questions and assignments that require comparison and contrast are many and varied; they deal with what writers say and how they say it.

Completing a Writing Assignment

When writing comparisons and contrasts, you should complete each step in the process of writing: pre-writing, writing the first draft, and revising. The process, explained on pages 950-954, is summarized on page 955.

Pre-Writing

Often, assignments incorporate key words such as *compare* and *contrast*, *similarity* and *difference*, or *alike* and *vary*. Other assignments imply the act of comparison and contrast. For example, an assignment may ask you to discuss the ways a poet deviates from the traditional poetry of the time. To do so, you must identify the characteristics both of traditional poetry and of the poet's work, then compare and contrast these characteristics.

Most essay questions and writing assignments include specific points of comparison and contrast. Occasionally, however, you might be faced with an assignment such as this: Compare and contrast two poems, short stories, or autobiographical narratives. You would need to narrow your focus to a few important elements and techniques.

Even if you use questions to generate supporting details, you may find it helpful to compile your data in chart form. Generally, a chart is set up to show the titles of the selections and the elements being compared, with space for pre-writing notes.

Among your choices of methods for organizing details are the following: (1) discuss one selection completely with regard to each point of comparison or contrast, then do the same for the other selection(s), noting similarities and differences; (2) discuss one point of comparison or contrast as it relates to selections, then do the same for the other points; and (3) discuss each selection separately before pointing out the specific similarities and/or differences. If you are both comparing and contrasting, you might choose to discuss all the similarities and then all the differences.

Writing the First Draft

In your topic sentence be sure to name the selections, to indicate whether they are being compared, contrasted, or both, and to identify the aspects of the selections that are the focus of the paragraph or composition.

Avoid prefacing quotations with statements such as "A quotation that proves this is . . . " or "This idea is proven by. . . ." Instead, link ideas and supporting quotations in a smooth flow from point to point.

Revising

Be sure you have used transitional words and phrases to clarify organization and to help readers make associations among your ideas.

Sample Writing Assignment

This assignment relates to the first three selections in Unit 1. The key words in the assignment have been underlined.

"Song of the Sky Loom," "Calendar Fragments," and "Sun, My Relative," convey concepts of nature that are similar but that also differ in some subtle ways. Think about each selection, using the following questions: Is nature portrayed as cyclical? If so, how? Does nature possess human qualities? Is nature wild and untamed? Gentle and nurturing? In a well developed paragraph, compare and contrast the ways that nature is portrayed in the three selections.

Pre-Writing

SELECTIONS   POINTS OF COMPARISON AND CONTRAST

	cyclical	wild/gentle	human qualities
"Song of the Sky Loom"	no	nurturing, protective clothes humans in "a garment of brightness" (l. 9) nature in domestic terms	weaving Mother Earth Father Sky (ll. 1, 12)
"Calendar Fragments"	cycle of seasons begins and ends with renewal April: "the grass is sprouting" (l. 2) February: "the season of sprouting" (l. 19)	wild, untamed spiders, butterflies, grasshoppers, eagles, bear, whale, deer, snakes, frogs	bear says "I am fat" (l. 15) frogs sing (l. 20)
"Sun, My Relative	refers to sun's cycle	powerful, control over humans "Make good things for us men./ Make me always the same as I am now." (ll. 12, 13)	sun = "my relative" petitions sun to "be good"

Writing the First Draft

The writer began her first draft with this topic sentence.

"Song of the Sky Loom," "Calendar Fragments," and "Sun, My Relative" share a sense of harmony with nature, although the concept of nature varies among the three selections.

Studying the Sample

The questions in the writing assignment direct the writer to consider specific points of comparison and contrast. These points are written across the top of the pre-writing chart, under "Points of Comparison and Contrast." The titles of the three selections are written along the left side of the chart, under "Selections."

The creator of the pre-writing chart considered all four methods of organizing details. She narrowed these options to two: (1) discuss the first point of comparison and contrast with regard to all three selections, then do the same for the other two points, or (2) discuss the first selection with regard to all points of comparison and contrast, then do the same for the other two selections. The first option would require many shifts in focus and several repetitions of titles. The second would allow the writer to discuss the concepts of one selection completely before moving on to the next. This seems to be the better option.

Notice that the topic sentence names the three selections, indicates that the paragraph will deal with both similarities and differences, and introduces the "concept of nature" idea that is the topic of the paragraph.

EXERCISES Writing Comparisons and Contrasts

For the following assignments, use the process of writing and the guidance provided in this lesson and in the lessons on writing paragraphs and compositions.

1. Study the sample pre-writing chart, and read or reread the three Native American selections. Then write a series of statements on the similarities and differences among the selections. Make only one comparison or contrast in each statement, and follow the organization identified as the "better option" in Studying the Sample. After you are sure that you understand clearly the relationships among the selections, weave your sentences into a unified, coherent paragraph. Use the sample topic sentence, or revise the sentence if you wish.

2. Complete your current writing assignment calling for comparison and contrast.

LESSON 12 Writing About Literature in Its Historical Context

Before writing about a literary selection in its historical context, it is essential to be familiar with the short story, poem, play, or nonfiction selection that you will be discussing. Read the selection carefully, then think about it, using the questions provided in **Writing About Poetry**, **Writing About Nonfiction**, **Writing About a Short Story**, or **Writing About Drama** (pages 960-971). For selections in this book, the study questions in **Getting at Meaning** and **Developing Skills in Reading Literature** provide a basis for analysis.

Also, consider the period's historical characteristics, using these questions as a quide:

What is the approximate time frame of the period? What major events took place?

Who were the social and political leaders?

What problems faced the nation? How was the country changing?

What characterized the spirit of the age?

How did most people earn their livings?

What were the living conditions of most families?

What was the role of women? Of children?

Who were the major minority groups? What was their role in society?

Did any major movements emerge?

What was the prevailing attitude toward nature? Human beings? The deity?

Considering the Assignment

An essay question or writing assignment may present several characteristics of an historical period and ask you to discuss how a selection reflects these characteristics. An assignment may ask you to explain how a particular selection or writer either exemplifies or breaks with the literary traditions of an age. An assignment may ask you to identify certain historical forces that are evident in a writer's work or the characteristics shared by various writers within a movement.

Completing a Writing Assignment

When writing about a literary selection in its historical context, you should complete each step in the process of writing: prewriting, writing the first draft, and revising. The process is explained on pages 950-954 and summarized on page 955.

Pre-Writing

When writing about literature, the literary work is generally your source for details. However, when writing about literature in its historical context, you may find it necessary to review the unit introductions in this book and to consult reference materials such as encyclopedia articles and history texts.

Writing the First Draft

When you paraphrase a writer's ideas, you must maintain the integrity of the original writing. Guard against oversimplification and taking ideas out of context. If a writer qualifies a statement, do not neglect that qualification in your paraphrase.

Revising

While rereading, check for coherence and for logical relationships among sentences and paragraphs. Attention to organization and to transitional words and phrases will make your ideas easy to follow, which is crucial when simultaneously discussing history and literature.

Sample Writing Assignment

This writing assignment relates to the selection that begins on page 77. The key words have been underlined.

The Autobiography of Benjamin Franklin reflects the optimistic spirit and the emphasis on reason and order that characterized the eighteenth century. In one paragraph, explain how the excerpt "Moral Perfection" embodies these characteristics.

Writing the First Draft and Revising

Following is the writer's final version.

"Moral Perfection," an excerpt from *The Autobiography* of Benjamin Franklin, reflects the optimistic spirit and the emphasis on reason and order that characterized the eighteenth century. The title "Moral Perfection" suggests Franklin's optimistic goal. He believed that ~~everyone could be perfect.~~ *human perfectability is possible and that it is attainable through a conscious decision "to live without committing any fault at any time."* Consequently, he resolved to do right and avoid wrong. When this resolve did not lead to the desired perfection, Franklin the optimist did not give up his quest for a "steady, uniform rectitude of conduct." Instead, he set up another, more calculated plan. *First* He clarified his goal through a list of virtues defined by specific precepts. *Then,* Having learned from his first failure, he ~~decided to~~ concentrated on perfecting one virtue at a time rather than attempting all at once. ~~Franklin~~ *Furthermore, he* ordered the thirteen virtues hierarchically, to facilitate their acquisition. He again demonstrated his systematic nature by maintaining a carefully ruled little book and by scrutinizing his moral progress daily, a practice that he continued "for some time."

Studying the Sample

Franklin's optimism is demonstrated by his goal of moral perfection. The way that he attempted to achieve this goal is reasoned and orderly. It was natural, then, for the writer to focus on optimism first and then on order and reason. This organization also reflects the way that "Moral Perfection" is developed.

Notice that the writer corrected an overgeneralized, misleading paraphrase in the third sentence. He also reversed the order of two sentences and added the transitions *first*, *furthermore*, and *then*, changes that help to distinguish the two phases of Franklin's plan.

EXERCISES   Writing About Selections in Their Historical Contexts

1. Complete your current writing assignment dealing with literature in its historical context.

2. Choose an historical period that interests you, and identify two or three major characteristics of the period. Then select a representative work of literature, and in a well developed paragraph discuss the way that the literature reflects these characteristics.